Interior Design & Decoration

Stanley Abercrombie

Sherrill Whiton

Michael Moran Photography, Inc.

PEARSON

Prentice
Hall

Upper Saddle River, New Jersey 07458

Library of Congress Cataloging-in-Publication Data

Abercrombie, Stanley.
  Interior design & decoration/Stanley Abercrombie.—6th ed.
    p. cm.
  Rev. ed. of: Interior design & decoration/Sherrill Whiton, Stanley
Abercrombie. c2002.
  Includes bibliographical references and index.
  ISBN 0–13–194404–5
  1. Interior decoration.   2. Decoration and ornament.   I. Whiton,
Augustus Sherrill, 1887–1961. Interior design & decoration.   II. Title.
III. Title: Interior design and decoration.
NK2110.W55 2006
747—dc22

2006019572

Editor-in Chief: Sarah Touborg
Editorial Assistant: Jacqueline Zea
Director of Marketing: Brandy Dawson
Marketing Managers: Marissa Feliberty/Andrea Messineo
Developmental Editor: Clare Payton
VP, Director of Production and Manufacturing: Barbara Kittle
Senior Managing Editor, Production: Lisa Iarkowski
Production Liaison: Harriet Tellem
Manufacturing Manager: Nick Sklitsis
Manufacturing Buyer: Sherry Lewis
Creative Design Director: Leslie Osher
Art Director: Amy Rosen
Interior Design: Kenny Beck
Line Art Coordinator: Maria Piper
Layout Artists: Amy Rosen, Gail Cocker-Bogusz
Cover Design: Laura Gardner

Cover Illustration/Photo: Frank Gehry's cafeteria design for the headquarters of Condé Nast, New York. Michael Moran Photography, Inc.
Imaging Specialists: Corin Skidds, Ron Walko
Director Image Resource Center: Melinda Patelli
Photo Researcher: Julie Tesser
Manager, Visual Research: Beth Brenzel
Manager, Rights and Permissions: Zina Arabia
Image Permission Coordinators: Debbie Latronica, Carolyn Gauntt
Manager, Cover Visual Research and Permissions: Karen Sanatar
Cover Image Coordinator: Cathy Mazzucca
Copyeditor: Stephen Hopkins
Composition: Techbooks
Full-Service Project Management: Shelley L. Creager
Cover Printer: Lehigh Press
Printer/Binder: RR Donnelley-Willard

Credits and acknowledgments borrowed from other sources and reproduced, with permission, in this textbook appear on appropriate page within text.

Pearson Education LTD.
Pearson Education Australia PTY, Limited
Pearson Education Singapore, Pte. Ltd
Pearson Education North Asia Ltd
Pearson Education, Canada, Ltd
Pearson Educación de Mexico, S.A. de C.V.
Pearson Education—Japan
Pearson Education Malaysia, Pte. Ltd

10 9 8 7 6 5 4 3 2 1
ISBN 0-13-224142-0

Brief Contents

Contents

PART 3 THE MIDDLE AGES

Preface

Through many thousands of years, interior design has played an important role in the efficiency and pleasure of human activity. Every aspect of our lives is affected by the character of the space in which it takes place. Knowledge of interiors from people in other times and places helps us to evaluate and improve our own environments. Such knowledge is fundamental to civilization, dealing with a whole range of interrelated design disciplines from architecture and its interiors, to furniture design, to the decorative arts that make our spaces useful and attractive. This book seeks to make its readers conversant with that whole spectrum of artistic activity.

The book's coverage begins before recorded history, continues to the present, and touches on the design of every continent. It examines tools and techniques used in working with materials as common as mud brick and as rarefied as gilt bronze. It records principles of composition—indeed, it outlines the principles of symmetry and axiality in its very first chapter. It introduces key design figures, landmark accomplishments, and a vocabulary of terms worthy of a professional in the field. Yet, there are obvious limitations. Condensing all interior design history into a single volume necessitates that some fine designers and designs have to go unmentioned. There are limitations as well in explaining three-dimensional designs on two-dimensional pages, a problem that recurs daily in the practice of interior design, and thus, a number of different methods of two-dimensional presentations are shown: photographs, line drawings, computer drawings, floor plans, sections, and diagrams and details of many kinds.

The History of Interior Design & Decoration

It has been said that the modern profession of interior design was established by Edith Wharton and Elsie de Wolfe. It might also be said that the modern discipline of interior design was established by Frank Alvah Parsons, for whom the Parsons School of Design was named, and by Augustus Sherrill Whiton, the author of the original text upon which the present book is based.

Sherrill Whiton (1887–1961) was the founder of what would become the New York School of Interior Design in 1916. He was born in New York in 1887, the son of Louis Claude Whiton, a lawyer, and the former Harriet Bell. He earned a degree in architecture at Columbia University, then went to Paris for study at the Ecôle des Beaux-Arts, which was a part of every architecture student's goal at the time. While in Paris, he married Claire Henriette Bouché, whose family was French. However, the family moved to New York in the 1870s, and Claire's father, Henri Bouché, was a designer employed by Tiffany & Co.

Whiton returned with Claire to New York and, finding the field of architecture in a slow period, conceived and wrote a series of Home Study Catalogues in the Decorative Arts. The first catalogue was published in 1916 and was followed by several others, leading naturally to classes based on the catalogues, held at Whiton's office on East 40th Street. In 1924, Whiton moved his operations to the southwest corner of Madison Avenue and 57th Street, where a 43-story office tower by architect Edward Larrabee Barnes now stands. His school was then called the New York School of Interior Decoration, and Whiton's title was President. In 1924, the year of the move, the school was chartered by the New York State Board of Regents, perhaps the first interior design school to be so recognized.

The Home Study Catalogues were assembled in book form and published by Lippincott in 1937 as *Elements of Interior Decoration.* New editions followed in 1951, 1957, and 1963, then retitled *Elements of Interior Design and Decoration,* the last of these being published after Whiton's death in 1961. Whiton's son, Sherrill ("Pete") Whiton, Jr., succeeded him both as president of the school and as reviser of the textbook. After Whiton's early and sudden death in 1972, his work on the revision was published with the simpler title *Interior Design and Decoration.*

Pedagogical Features

In many schools of interior design, Sherrill Whiton's book has been known for generations as "the bible" from which many professionals learned their trade. In order to meet the needs of today's students embarking on careers in the design fields, a number of pedagogical features have been developed to guide them:

Determinants of Design sections open every chapter to ground students in each cultural period, by hallmarking a set of determinants that shaped the culture's aesthetics and design history.

In *Geography and Natural Resources*, discussion begins with how the land and its natural resources have greatly affected aspects of architectural design as well as the types and uses of materials and, ultimately, their design ends.

There follows *History* (and, whenever applicable, *Political and Military Factors*), which briefly explores those historical factors that have shaped a society's design expressions, whether in design created to celebrate triumph and prosperity or design created to simplify living.

Next, *Religion* discussions offer special attention, whenever appropriate, to the religious beliefs of a culture, offering analysis of how religious ideals are manifested in design characteristics.

By the nineteenth and twentieth centuries, new determinants emerge in *Media* and *Technology*, and those are explored as primary and forceful disseminators of design models, knowledge, and a wide variety of end products newly available to the masses.

Summary of Design sections close every chapter with material intended to engage students in larger design concerns.

Looking for Character discerns the underlying characteristics within the design periods, asking, for example, which characteristics seem to be common to all Greek vases and which seem specific to a single vase. Such explorations enable students to identify and evaluate the characteristics that past designers upheld as they shaped and developed their works. Since we know that an important factor in becoming a successful designer is the development of the trained eye, these discussions serve to help students develop that visual acuity.

In *Looking for Quality*, questions are asked and assessments are made to stimulate the student's ability to recognize the quality and sophistication of certain design elements from each period and culture. Since another important factor of the designer's eye is informed judgment, this material asks students to exercise that judgment while looking at particular examples.

In *Making Comparisons*, discussion moves to comparing specific designs from diverse times and places. For example, in assessing the differences in design expression between a Gothic ceiling and a Gothic Revival ceiling, students learn to better articulate the design aesthetics of both periods, thus strengthening their adeptness for further study.

Maps and timelines, corresponding to every chapter, provide visual aids for students to contextualize their study of design history in a place and time on earth. The maps have been revised for better accuracy and improved visual appeal, and they are now placed in an appendix, found at the back of the book for easy student access throughout the semester. The chapter timelines continue to offer students the sweep of a culture's history in one chart.

A **glossary,** located at the end of the book, identifies all key figures and terms, which are outlined in boldface type within the text. This glossary has been updated to house over 3,000 entries, offering the most comprehensive glossary available in any design history textbook.

Extensive **bibliographies** date back to the 1974 edition but have been faithfully updated for each subsequent edition, including this one. New texts have been added to keep the lists updated with current scholarship. Knowing that students will use this course as a springboard to further study, entries have been divided into topics for further research study, and additionally, there is now a general bibliography of key texts relevant to interior design history as a whole.

New to this Edition

Evolving perceptions about past and present design demand evolving means of presentation, and this edition appropriately introduces several new features.

Revised Content and Organization

In this revision, special attention was given to strengthening the overall organization of each chapter, making more obvious—both visually and textually—the chronological progression of a culture's design. Thus, images are better ordered to illustrate the development of design over time, and textual material, in turn, has been revised to connect design developments in a chronological order. Some chapters have also received a parallel formatting of time periods; in particular, the chapters on Italy, Spain, France, and England, have been organized similarly, to cover the same approximate time periods and styles, while still heralding the distinctive qualities of design in each country. Strengthening the organization not only allows both instructors and students to follow a recognizable course through the field of study but also gives students the connections necessary for building a contextual history of design.

In addition, every chapter of the text now follows a standard order of presentation moving from large-scale to small-scale design: *Architecture and Interiors*, *Ornament*, *Furniture*, and *Decorative Arts*, so that students and instructors alike can attune themselves to the book's inherent rhythm.

Within the *Architecture and Interiors* section, improvements have been made in pairing exteriors with interiors more often and, subsequently, pairing those exteriors with their accompanying ornament, furniture, and decorative arts. Such treatment clarifies for students how designers create interior spaces and other design effects within existing exteriors, and this further enhances students' contextual awareness.

New Chapter on Africa

As design interests have extended to cultures around the globe, an eager call has come from many instructors to introduce today's students to the design history of non-Western cultures. Such attention prepares designers of the future to work globally, with a broad knowledge of the styles and techniques of many different times, locations, and civilizations. In the last edition, whole chapters were added on China, Japan, India, the Islamic world, and pre-Columbian America. In this edition, a brand-new chapter has been written to cover Africa. However vast the continent, there have been some commonalities in African design in certain aspects of the aesthetics and the materials, and the chapter material strives to earmark those commonalities even as it lauds the unique design characteristics from a number of African cultures and time periods. By no means thorough or comprehensive, this chapter still offers a solid introduction to the spirit of African design and its importance to its people and to the world.

New Boxed Features Program

Many instructors, during a review phase of our text, wrote of the challenges facing them in teaching a sweeping survey of design history. Some of these pedagogical needs had the potential to be solved in a new boxed feature program. The chief challenges were how to help students learn the artisanship behind the design expressions of various periods and how to help students gain an awareness of the master design professionals and their perspectives on the historical arenas. We created new boxed features to aid in this instruction:

1. Tools & Techniques. This boxed feature focuses on a particular craft or technology, outlining the basic methods used to achieve the design effects: the tools used, the materials used, and the new techniques developed to master the art. Examples of coverage include explaining the tools and techniques for fresco painting, developing windows with window glass, weaving rugs, and upholstering furniture.

2. Viewpoints. This boxed feature serves to bring the voices of master professionals into your classroom. Here, famous designers comment on the design of other eras, noting the important legacies left behind from earlier designers and thus speaking to a shared collective wisdom in the professional arena. Voices include Sir John Soane, Ludwig Mies van der Rohe, Marcel Breuer, and Andrée Putman, among many others.

3. Tables. Emphasizing diagrams over text, new tables present visual aids for learning basic design vocabulary. The varied subjects include types of wood joints, characteristics of period chair legs, and styles of arches.

Improved Art Program

Special care was taken in the revision to select a number of new images for this edition, in response to instructor feedback. The goal has been to further emphasize the myriad relationships between the various design elements of a period, which, in successful design, merge to a coherent whole. To that end, images were selected to pair many exteriors with interiors in an effort to reflect the relationship between the architectural exterior and setting of a building and its interior design expression. In addition, a greater emphasis has been placed, whenever possible, on the original settings for the furniture, with more room interiors shown. Studying with this improved art program, students learn to recognize how designers work most often (and best) in the context of a pairing between exterior and interior spaces.

Further replacements of images were done to improve the art program. With now over 100 new images in color—and an enlarged sizing of many images—students can now better appreciate the beauty and craftsmanship of design through the ages. In addition, improvements have been made to overall picture quality, by gathering the latest museum reproductions available.

A mention must be made about the meticulous line drawings by Gilbert Werlé, each a composite of many representative images and therefore a compact conveyor of much visual information. Werlé was a key faculty member of Sherrill Whiton's school. All of his illustrations from the first edition have been reinstated in this edition and restored to Werlé's original and skillfully tight compositions.

New Text Design

Our text design for the sixth edition better complements the designs of the many periods presented in this book, with larger images for better viewing and a more sophisticated palette for harmony with design across the ages.

Acknowledgments

No one writes or revises a book of this scope alone, and I have been blessed with talented associates. First, I thank the late architect and author Paul Heyer, who, while President of the New York School of Interior Design, suggested that I become the author for the fifth edition published in 2002. I also thank Inge Heckel, Paul's able and energetic successor, who has supported my editorship of this sixth edition. I am also grateful to Barbara Whiton and other members of the Whiton family for their gracious acceptance of my revisions.

Among the many scholars on whose ideas I have depended are Dr. David G. De Long, Founding Director of the Historic Preservation Program at the University of Pennsylvania, who suggested improvements in many chapters, and Prof. Jody Brotherston, former Interior Design Chair at Louisiana Tech University, who was my chief guide for expanded coverage of the interior design of Spain.

A number of instructors took the time to review this text and offer sharp and relevant advice in preparation for this edition. Their ideas were instrumental in shaping the editorial decisions of this edition. They are: Joyce Butts at the Florida Community College at Jacksonville, Joyce M. Davis at Valdosta State University, Susan Tate, AIA, at the University of Florida, and Crystal Weaver at the Savannah College of Art and Design.

At Prentice Hall, I thank Sarah Touborg, the editor-in-chief of the arts and humanities, for her original enthusiasm for a new edition and for her always gracious but nevertheless firm guidance. Next, I thank my development editor, Clare Payton, for setting a high standard of breadth, consistency, and logic for this edition and for being properly demanding about its being accomplished. Other great assets to this edition are the book design by Kenny Beck and page layouts by Amy Rosen, who have brought clarity, elegance, and order to what must have seemed a bewildering variety of ingredients. In addition, a wonderful team of editorial and production staff were at hand to assist in the making of this book. They include: senior managing editor, Lisa Iarkowski, and editorial assistant, Jacqueline Zea, who together have kept a long process skillfully on track; senior production editor Harriet Tellem, who has been a conscientious and patient caretaker of a million details; Julie Tesser, who has been an admirably resourceful photo researcher; Shelley Creager of Techbooks; Stephen Hopkins for sensitive and skillful copy editing; and Brandy Dawson for her marketing expertise.

Finally, of course, thanks to Sherrill Whiton for initiating a project that remains vital and relevant as it nears a century of continued growth and change.

Stanley Abercrombie

Design Before History

Before 3400 B.C.

"The human species is forever in a state of change, forever becoming."

— Simone de Beauvoir (1908–86), French writer and philosopher

In the earliest traces of human life that we have found, there is evidence of two human inclinations. One is the nesting instinct, or the desire for a permanent and personal home. The other is the urge to impose visual organization and create visual significance in our environments. These two inclinations remain today, as in prehistoric times, the basis of interior design.

What is interior design? Interior design is the composition and adornment of interior spaces on a habitable scale. It is an art that usually occurs within the art of architecture, but not always. The artworks found in the cave dwellings (fig. 1–1) in this chapter are exceptions to the usual relationship of interior design to architecture. Because interior design does usually occur within architecture, however, these two arts must find some means of relating to one another in order that the total result will have a pleasing

◄ 1–1 *Hall of Bulls*, Lascaux caves, Dordogne, France, c. 15,000–13,000 B.C. Paint on limestone, length of the largest aurochs (bull) 18 ft. (5.5 m).
Sisse Brimberg/National Geographic Image Collection

coherence. These two arts, then, share some of the same materials, techniques, and forms.

Whether architecture or interior design should be conceived first in the design of a building and which should dominate the collaboration are questions to be decided on the basis of specific circumstances and talents. Because the interior design of prehistory seems to have begun within naturally existing caves before any long-lasting freestanding structures were erected, we could say that interior design is older than architecture. Indeed, cave culture endured for more than 20,000 years, nearly twice as long as the time that has passed since it ended.

It is worth noting that the great twentieth-century architect Le Corbusier, in his 1923 book *Towards a New Architecture*, wrote: "A plan proceeds from within to without. A building is like a soap bubble. This bubble is perfect and harmonious if the breath has been evenly distributed and regulated from the inside. The exterior is the result of the interior."

In any case, both architecture and interior design arose from the human need for appropriate shelter. Shelter, whether found or constructed, answered this basic urge by

Approximate Date	Human Developments	Developments in Art
35,000 years ago	Old Stone Age begins	
30,000 years ago		Paintings in Chauvet caves
25,000 years ago		Fertility figures
16,000 years ago		Paintings in Lascaux caves
10,000 years ago (8000 B.C.)	Origins of food cultivation; New Stone Age begins	Paintings in Altamira caves
6,000 years ago		Houses and shrines at Çatal Hüyük
5,000 years ago	Origins of metallurgy	
3,400 years ago	Origins of literacy in Sumeria	
3,000 years ago		Houses and furniture at Skara Brae

providing protection against climate and preying animals. Later, it may have been recognized as satisfying a more subtle need—for a bit of territory that was personal and private. Primitive humans must have made progress in their long evolution by providing themselves with acknowledged addresses, and a personalized environment must have supported the development of human personality.

Determinants of Prehistoric Design

The terms *prehistoric art* and *primitive art* have very different meanings. Prehistoric art may not be primitive, and primitive art may not be prehistoric. *Prehistoric art* is a term relating to art in a specific time period, specifically to the period before the invention of writing c. 3400 B.C. by the Sumerians (in what is now Iraq). The earliest roots of interior design were in this preliterate time, but we know little about the humans who might be called our first interior designers.

On the other hand, the term *primitive art* relates to character, specifically to a simple, crude, or untrained character in the art. Some of the earliest artworks we know, such as the exquisitely realistic animal murals in prehistoric French and Spanish cave dwellings, are prehistoric but hardly primitive. Some later art of the New Stone Age, however, which regresses to a hasty shorthand of abstract strokes, could fairly

be said to have become primitive. So-called primitive art continues to be produced today in small villages and even in the hearts of great cities throughout the world.

We must be careful not to misuse the term *primitive*. Many observers, outside the tradition in which a particular art is produced, may assume that art to be primitive, whereas those peoples within the tradition, aware of the art's significance and subtleties, recognize it to be quite sophisticated. We must also be careful not to think of primitive art as being negligible or unworthy. It can be moving, and it can be powerful. Artists of the early modern period found valuable inspiration in primitive art. Today, accustomed as we are to interpreting abstractions of every kind, much primitive art is meaningful to us to a degree previously unknown to those outside the culture in which it was made. Although few of us would be comfortable in a thoroughly primitive interior, elements from primitive cultures can make arresting and stimulating contributions to interior design.

Stone Age Design

The earliest art we know dates from the Stone Ages. The Old Stone Age, called the Paleolithic period (c. 35,000–8000 B.C.), is sometimes called the age of chipped stone, because in that era tools were made by chipping stone until sharp edges were produced. The New Stone Age, called the Neolithic period (beginning c. 8000 B.C.), is sometimes called the age of polished stone, for its stone tools came to be more skillfully finished. The New Stone Age ended at different times in different locations with the invention of writing and the development of ways of working with metals.

The Old Stone Age and Its Design

During the Old Stone Age people lived in caves or in the shelter of stone outcroppings, and they gathered food in the form of fruit, nuts, berries, and edible roots. Gradually they began to hunt for meat as well, adding protein to their diets. Their art was surprisingly skillful and realistic.

▲ 1–2 Clay relief of two bisons from a cave at Le Tuc d'Audoubert, France, c. 13,000 B.C., 25 in. (64 cm) long.
Yvonne Vertut

The earliest examples found so far date back to 28,000 B.C. and are small sculptures composed of found objects such as stones and animal bones, depicting animal or human figures. Some of these depict nude pregnant women and may have served as fertility charms. Later sculptures found in Africa, Europe, and Asia were shaped by chipping stones or shaping clay, such as this relief of bisons (fig. 1–2) discovered in a cave in southern France and dated to c. 12,000 B.C.

The most striking manifestations of Old Stone Age art—and the oldest evidence of anything we might call interior design—are the paintings on walls and ceilings of caves found in Spain and France. The Altamira painted caves in northern Spain are dated to between 9,000 and 11,000 years ago. The Lascaux painted caves in southern France (fig. 1–1) are dated to between 15,000 and 17,000

years ago. The Chauvet painted caves, also in southern France, are dated to roughly 30,000 years ago. Important groups of ancient cave paintings have also been found in Lesotho, Africa; near Bhopal, India; in Wollemi National Park, Australia; and in Algeria, Argentina, Brazil, China, and Siberia.

In most cases, the paintings occur in remote underground chambers difficult to reach. These painted chambers are not, therefore, thought to have been living quarters but secretive shrines. In these dark recesses, lit only by torches in ritual ceremonies, the painted images exercised their magic to increase the number of edible animals, to guide the hunters to their locations, and to help the hunters triumph over their prey. A few of the painted animals are shown with weapons striking them, and occasionally human figures are also shown. Most of these paintings cannot be considered domestic décor, although cave dwellers must have done something to improve their living quarters. Undoubtedly, animal skins were hung at the cave entrances to keep out wind, rain, and animals, and they were used to create comfortable sleeping areas. But only the wall paintings remain, and many of them are remarkably well preserved. As examples, we will look at the oldest ones known, those in the Chauvet caves.

Cave Paintings at Chauvet In 1994, Jean-Marie Chauvet and two other explorers in southeastern France uncovered a long-hidden entrance to a complex of underground caverns. Inside, they found footprints, the remains of ancient fires, and the skeletons of bears. Most astonishingly, they found more than 300 vivid wall paintings, dating to the beginning of the Old Stone Age, and preserved from sunlight and the changing conditions of the earth's surface.

The paintings are of two types: pictures of animals and pictures of geometric signs. Sometimes the two are combined,

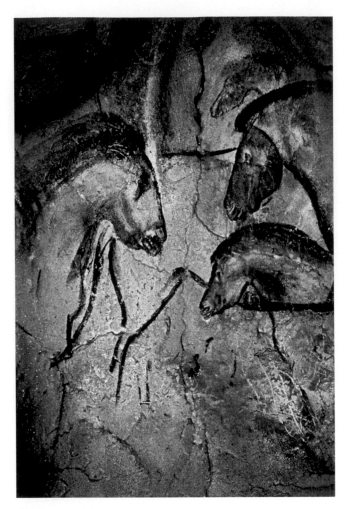

▲ **1–3** Cave paintings, Chauvet cave, Vallon-Pont-d'Arc, Ardèche gorge, France, c. 28,000 B.C.
Corbis/Sygma

as in five red stripes on the neck of a lion, or two red dots and a stripe on the muzzle of a horse. The animals depicted include bison, reindeer, mammoths, lions, panthers, bears, rhinoceroses, and horses (fig. 1–3). Animals of the same species are often shown in groups (such as a row of four horses) and often in action (stalking lions, running deer). There are no complete images of human figures at Chauvet, but there are a few segments of human figures and one curious composite creature, with a bison upper half and a human lower half.

Cave painters primarily used red and black, but there are also traces of yellow. The red was made from the rusted veins of iron ore found in stone, the black from soot and charred wood, and the yellow from pollen or other plant sources. Color-stained tubes of hollow bone found in the caves indicate that pigment was blown on rather than

painted. Black outlines too precise to have been blown on may have been wiped on with bits of moss or animal skin. There is no evidence that brushes were used.

Perspective effects were produced by overlapping, showing some animals in front of others. Sometimes an animal was shown full-face, staring directly out at the spectator, while its body was shown in profile. Shading was also employed, with paint spread in gentle gradations to suggest rounded forms. By almost any present-day standards of artistry and realism, these earliest known works of art are remarkably skillful.

But no attention was given to overall compositions on these cave walls and ceilings. The focus is on individual images of animals or groups of animals, not on the surface as a whole. This does not mean that the painters were incapable of composition; it simply means that their intention was different.

Interestingly, the impulse behind the cave paintings and the impulse behind the stained-glass windows of Chartres Cathedral (see fig. 8–21) are not entirely different. Both make their appeal to the supernatural rather than the natural world. Their subjects are realistic, but their intended function is to lift our thoughts to a higher reality or to improve our fortunes.

Other Pictorial Forms   Other images found in Old Stone Age paintings reflect the early humans' fascination with their own bodies: They are simply outlines of the human hand (fig. 1–4). These were probably unrelated to hunting and may have originated simply in prehistoric humans' desires to record their own presence.

Other artistic expressions in abstraction and geometric forms have been discovered. On decorated bones and tools, tangles of accidental scratches were translated into neat series of parallel stripes. *Symmetry*, a design quality of balanced arrangement, was probably first observed by humans in their own bodies. In the Old Stone Age it was introduced by mirroring the stripes and creating V shapes or chevrons. Symmetry was applied in another direction, and the V became an X. Shapes were alternated with other shapes, and rhythm was introduced: two chevrons, a circle, another two chevrons, another circle. The paintings and patterns of the Old Stone Age were the foundation for the bolder artistic accomplishments that would follow.

The New Stone Age and Its Design

In the New Stone Age, which began c. 8000 B.C., cave paintings continued to be produced, but rather than hiding them deep in the caves as before, painters placed them near the cave entrances. They were meant to be seen. Had the painters become conscious of the artistic value of their work? We'll never know.

Subject matter changed as hunters began to settle down, raise animals, and grow crops. The depiction of animals was partly replaced by the depiction of human figures, with exaggerated gestures and proportions, shown as they tended crops, hunted, fought, and danced. Runners were shown with impossibly long legs, and strong warriors were shown with many arms. These exaggerations led to the use of suggestive strokes that represented actions without clearly showing the figure. The realism of the Old Stone Age was thus replaced by the symbolism of the New Stone Age.

There were new crafts as well. The weaving of straw and cloth was begun in this period, and baskets were made for food gathering. Later, pottery, sometimes richly decorated, began to replace some stone utensils. It also aided in cooking. There are few known examples of this, but in general, they reflect an art and ornament less realistic and more abstract.

The Beginnings of the City

When humans learned to feed themselves more efficiently by domesticating animals and cultivating crops, these new activities required that they stay in the same places for long periods. This new stability led to the growth of villages of built—rather than found—dwellings. Most of these were

▼ 1–4 Stencils of human hands at Cueva de las Manos, Argentina, perhaps c. 7300 B.C. More rarely at this location are seen stencils of human feet and of the three-toed feet of large flightless South American birds called rhea.

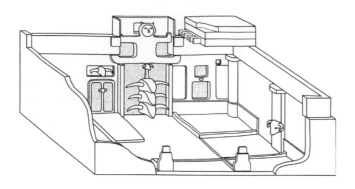

▲ **1–5** Composite reconstruction drawing of a shrine room at Çatal Hüyük.
Ralph Solecki, Columbia University

constructed of wicker or thatch, but some more permanent dwellings were made of wood, stone, and mud brick. Living in small groups led, in turn, to the need for greater social organization. Rudimentary cities were born, rulers and administrators were named, human activities became specialized, and technology advanced. Most of these early settlements have perished, but a few that were built partly of masonry have left visible ruins. We shall look briefly at two of them.

Çatal Hüyük Çatal Hüyük was a settlement occupied from c. 6500 to c. 5700 B.C. in Anatolia, in what is now Turkey. It is an area with very little native stone, so stone construction was not possible. At the height of its prosperity, Çatal Hüyük covered 32 acres. It was a prosperous town, controlling the trade of obsidian, a black volcanic glass that was prized for its use in making both tools and ornaments.

The town was constructed of rectangular buildings of wood and mud brick built one against another. This gave them greater structural stability than if they had been freestanding. Scholars debate whether there were passages between some of the houses; if not, they must all have been entered, for security reasons, not through doors but by ladders from openings in their roofs.

Within the wood framing, the walls were filled in with sun-dried rectangular mud bricks, well formed in wooden molds and joined with mortar. Typically, two stout main wooden beams and numerous small beams supported the roof, which was made of bundles of reeds covered with a thick layer of mud. Although all Çatal Hüyük's buildings shared the same construction technique and were not greatly different in size, their interiors suggest

that about a fourth of them were shrines (fig. 1–5) and the rest were houses.

Inside all the buildings, the wood framing divided the wall surfaces horizontally and vertically into panels. Usually, the framing was visually emphasized with red paint. Red also sometimes accented doorways, niches, and platforms. In houses, the lower panels, no more than 3 feet (1 m) high, were decorated in a number of ways: Most numerous were plain panels in various shades of red, but there were also geometric patterns and images of hands and feet. One house had panels with a pattern of stars and concentric circles, and another had pictures of birds, but such naturalistic subjects were generally found not in houses, but in shrines. The red pigment was derived from minerals—iron oxide for a rust red, mercury oxide for a deep red—mixed with fat. Black was obtained from soot, blue from the mineral azurite, and green from the mineral malachite. These colored paints were applied with brushes on backgrounds of white, cream, or pale pink.

A house's single room was divided by use: about a third of the space devoted to a hearth and oven, the remainder to other uses. Each house had a fixed wooden ladder leading to a hole in the roof, which also served as a chimney for smoke from the hearth, oven, and lamps. From the main room, small secondary rooms used for storage were entered through open doorways no more than 2 or 3 feet high.

In the two-thirds of the house not devoted to cooking, raised mud-brick platforms, carefully plastered, were arranged around the walls. These, we know from paintings of the interiors, were often covered with reed or rush matting on which cushions and bedding were placed. The padded platforms were designed for sitting, working, and sleeping. They also served a funerary purpose, former occupants of the houses being buried within the mud-brick platforms. Their skeletons suggest that a small, square platform in one corner belonged to the chief male of the household, and one or more longer platforms belonged to the females and children. Platforms also occur in buildings identified as shrines, with the bodies of priests and their families within. The shrines are slightly larger than the houses and are distinguished by elaborate wall paintings that seem to have ritual significance. There are also plaster reliefs of gods, goddesses, and animals. Human skulls and bull's skulls and horns (some real, some plaster) adorn the built-in benches and platforms.

Other animals represented are stags, leopards, vultures, and foxes.

Traces of finely woven textiles, probably made of wool, have been found at Çatal Hüyük. These are the oldest textiles discovered so far. Three different types of weave have been identified, and some of the geometric patterns painted on the walls are thought to represent the patterns of **kilims**, flat-weave textiles without pile that are used for carpets. This may indicate that carpet weaving was practiced in Stone Age times.

These ruins of ancient buildings (fig. 1-6) have also yielded a number of artifacts, some of them quite luxurious in character: hand mirrors of polished obsidian, wooden vessels, metal trinkets, baskets, ceramics, and tools of obsidian, flintstone, copper, and lead. Weapons buried with the men include obsidian spearheads and flint daggers with bone handles and leather sheaths. Jewelry buried with the women and children includes necklaces, bracelets, anklets, and arm bands made of stone, shell, chalk, clay, copper, and mother-of-pearl.

Skara Brae At Skara Brae on Pomona, the largest of the Orkney Islands off the northern coast of Scotland, a cluster of houses was built c. 3000 B.C. Because the climate here can be fierce with heavy winds, and because there is an ample amount of stone, construction was sturdy. Even interior furnishings were built of stone.

At least seven dwelling units have been discovered so far, built closely together in what might be called a small village or an early example of multiple housing. They were built in the form of squares with rounded corners. Their stone walls, built of layers of stone without mortar, were 6 feet (2 m) thick at the base and thinner at the top, not only tapering but also curving slightly inward as they rose. Now roofless, they may have originally been roofed with whalebones covered with animal skins or turf. The largest rooms are about 21 feet (6.4 m) wide. As in the houses of Çatal Hüyük, the main rooms were supplemented with small storage spaces; at Skara Brae, these were hollowed out of the thick stone walls.

In a typical main room (fig. 1–7), the central focus is a large rectangular hearth edged with stone. An opening in the roof directly above it would have allowed smoke to escape and daylight to enter the windowless room. At the end of the hearth opposite the entrance, a square stone seat may have been a seat of honor for the head of the household, with the other family members seated on the floor or stone benches. On either side of the hearth, against the wall, were two beds, stone-sided containers that were filled with leaves, reeds, or mosses, and covered with animal furs. Beyond the hearth against the wall is an impressive piece of built-in furniture, a sort of cabinet that is a predecessor of a dresser or sideboard, its vertical supports and its two horizontal shelves all made of stone. This symmetrical, carefully

▲ 1–7 House interior at Skara Brae, off the coast of Scotland, c. 3000 B.C. The hearth is in the center of the room; a stone seat and two-tiered cabinet on axis beyond it.
Mick Sharp Photography

built two-tiered stone cabinet, prominently placed on axis with the door and the hearth, must have been used to display the family's prized possessions, such as pottery bowls with incised decoration, some remnants of which have been found at Skara Brae. The cabinet itself is clearly the result of attention to aesthetics as well as to function. Some of the stone furnishings seem to have been decorated with incised lines and dots, although much of this decoration has worn away.

In addition to pottery, many other artifacts made of ivory, bone, and stone have been found at Skara Brae. A whalebone dish containing red pigment was found in one house and a finely carved stone ball in another. Some of the pottery displays spiral designs.

From Prehistory to History

We have seen, in the transition from Old Stone Age to New, the partial replacement of realism by abstraction. The new interest in abstraction led to geometric decoration. Pictographs that represented objects in simplified forms eventually led to alphabets and writing. Increasingly complex interactions among humans in increasingly large settlements led to the need for setting down laws and keeping records. Writing became both possible and necessary.

In addition to the development of writing, humans at the end of the New Stone Age developed the ability to extract metals from the rocks around them. These metals were blended and formed into objects. The earliest metal artifacts discovered so far are copper pieces from southern Turkey and dated c. 7000 B.C. They had been not only hammered into shape but also **annealed**, heated in a fire to make them malleable rather than brittle. Gradually, stone tools and weapons were replaced by much more efficient metal ones. At different times in different locations, the Stone Ages yielded to the Bronze Age and then to the Iron Age.

With writing and metal tools, the stage was set for the development of the earliest of the historical civilizations. Of these, the most accomplished was that of Egypt, the subject of our next chapter.

Summary: Prehistoric Design

As will be the case in all the chapters of this book, we will close with an attempt to analyze and summarize the nature of the period or culture's art and interior design. Typically, we will look briefly for the distinguishing common characteristics and for demonstrations of quality. We will then compare examples within the period. We will also compare some examples with those from other times and places, to see how one period or style relates to others.

Looking for Character

No single style can be identified as prehistoric. Different tribes in different places, facing different climates and finding different materials to work with, naturally produced different effects. What they produced was likely more varied, more surprising, and more remarkable than we can imagine today, for we have discovered only a minute fraction of what was produced.

We know of skillfully realistic cave paintings, of ambitious stone monuments, and of interiors where attention has been given to both use and appearance. This evidence tells us clearly that the instincts and abilities that are at the root of interior design and all aesthetic endeavor have been with us a very long time. For almost as long as we have been humans, we have been artists and interior designers.

Looking for Quality

A great principle that becomes obvious when looking at the design of many different cultures is that each one has its own determining network of traditions, goals, and expectations. Yet a sympathetic spectator in one culture can detect and appreciate quality in another. We may know very little about the lives and thoughts of prehistoric humans, but we can still admire their works.

The paintings of the prehistoric caves impress us with their execution. These animal representations seem to have been produced exactly as their artists intended, with nothing essential missing and nothing extraneous added, and they stand as evidence of artistic mastery among some of the earliest members of the human family.

Making Comparisons

One comparison we might make reveals a surprising likeness between prehistoric and later art. If we imagine ourselves entering the Skara Brae dwelling, we would be struck by the orderliness of the scene before us. The great stone hearth pit, the stone seat, and the stone cabinet directly align with our view from the door. The two beds match in balanced symmetry. Symmetry is a design principle that will be used to powerful effect throughout history: in the temples of Greece, in the Roman baths, in the Gothic cathedrals, in the French chateaux, and in many more buildings and interiors. The little room at Skara Brae demonstrates how old this principle must be.

Egypt

4500 B.C.–A.D. 30

2

"For anyone who sees Egypt, without having heard a word about it before, must perceive, if he has only common powers of observation, that Egypt . . . is an acquired country, the gift of the Nile."

— Herodotus (c. 485–425 B.C.), Greek historian

At the beginning of recorded time we find Egypt, a vigorous, fully developed civilization that evolved from the prehistoric era. Its art, monumental and majestic but designed and erected according to fastidious standards, was an immense achievement.

In Egypt, power and faith combined to support the rule of a series of monarchs believed also to be gods. The absolute authority of these monarchs, called *pharaohs* (fig. 2–1), enabled them to command the construction of some of the world's most enormous and most elegantly finished monuments, but the arts of Egypt were also, to a rare degree, determined by the country's unique geography, climate, and natural resources.

Determinants of Egyptian Design

Among all the civilizations of the world, only China surpasses Egypt in the length of its history, and none surpasses Egypt in its constancy. Although enduring for almost 5,000

◀ **2–1** King Tutankhamun funerary mask, made of gold inlaid with semiprecious stones, c. 1330 B.C., 21 in. (54 cm) high.
The Egyptian Museum

years, the culture of Egypt and its art maintained a strikingly unchanging identity, an outcome of its geography and natural resources, the religious beliefs of the Egyptians, and the political structures of their society.

Geography and Natural Resources

Africa's Nile is the world's longest river. In an entrenched valley seldom more than 10 miles (16 km) wide and often only a little wider than the river itself, Egypt was made arable every year when spring rains and melting snow from the highlands far to the south flooded the area and left deposits of rich sediment. Controlling the river's floods and distributing the water required the building of dikes, reservoirs, and canals, and in their construction the Egyptians became early masters at engineering.

Beyond the green, irrigated valley, lush with date palms and figs, pomegranates, and papyrus, the desert stretched impenetrably on either side. It was Egypt's protection against invasion, immigration, or even visits from outsiders. Thus isolated, Egypt was allowed a freedom from foreign interference rare in human history, ensuring for the Egyptians a continuing and unadulterated

Approximate Date	Period	Dynasties	Rulers	Location of Capital	Chief Products and Events
2686–2134 B.C.	Old Kingdom	Dynasties 3–8	Hetepheres, Khufu, Khafre, Menkaure	Memphis	Age of Pyramids: Great Pyramids of Giza
2065–1783 B.C.	Middle Kingdom	End of 11th dynasty to dynasties 12–13	Series of kings named Mentuhotep, Amenemhat, and Sesostris	Thebes, then Memphis	Funerary temple of Deir el Bahari; development of portraiture
1550–1070 B.C.	New Kingdom	Dynasties 18–20	Hatshepsut, Tutankhamun, Akhenaten, Nefertiti	Thebes, then Tel-al-Amarna, then back to Thebes	Funerary temple of Hatshepsut; temples of Luxor and Karnak
332–31 B.C.	Ptolemaic Period		Alexander the Great, Ptolemy I–XV, Cleopatra, Julius Caesar	Alexandria	In 332 B.C. Alexander occupies all Egypt; in 48 B.C. Julius Caesar lands to defend Cleopatra
31 B.C.– A.D. 642	Roman Period		Roman rule		New Roman temples constructed to Egyptian gods

development. Its relative isolation from other cultures, however, contributed to a repetition of established art forms throughout its long history, and this stable (though not, as we shall see, entirely unchanging) character is one of the most pronounced features of Egyptian art. The forms and details of Egypt's architecture, its interior embellishment, and its furniture remained largely the same for more than 4,000 years.

Egypt's river valley offered not only fertile soil but also large quantities of hard and durable building stones, such as granite, basalt, and diorite—stones without which the pyramids and other great monuments of Egyptian architecture could not have been built. Limestone and sandstone, softer and more easily cut materials, were available for use in protected places. Wood, however, was in limited supply. Where wood was needed for structural purposes, the palm tree, the papyrus reed, the acacia, and the sycamore were used, with some heavier lumber imported from Syria. The leaves and branches of these trees and the wildflowers from the banks of the Nile became principal inspiration for Egyptian ornamental design.

Religion

The dependable cycle of the Nile's annual flooding set the rhythm of agricultural work and was fundamental to the Egyptian experience. The Egyptians divided their year into three seasons: Flood Time, Seed Time, and Harvest Time. The cycles of the Nile were echoed in the cycles of the sky: The sense of endless repetition was reinforced by the similarly dependable course of the sun through generally cloudless skies. Their environment of apparent constancy is thought to have been the source of the Egyptians' firm belief in continued life after death. This belief was in turn the source of their astonishing architecture, for the Egyptians built for eternity. When the Greeks invaded Egypt in 332 B.C., they found what seemed to them to be a tremendously old and changeless culture. Indeed it was; by then the pyramids were almost 2,000 years old.

Kingdoms, Dynasties, and Pharaohs

Egypt became a cohesive country c. 3100 B.C., when Upper Egypt, the narrow strip following the Nile northward from the highlands, was unified under strong rulers with Lower Egypt, the land of the Nile Delta, the fan-shaped area where the river enters the Mediterranean Sea. Even in a civilization as steady and unchanging as that of Egypt, there were ups and downs. Despite the regularity of the Nile flood, there were droughts. Despite the protection of the desert, there were invasions. In the course of a history that endured for 4,000 years, there are three periods that seem to us now to have been times of extraordinary achievement. These are known today as the Old Kingdom (2686–2134 B.C.), the Middle Kingdom (2065–1783 B.C.), and the New Kingdom (1550–1070 B.C.). Each kingdom is further divided into dynasties, with successions of rulers from the same family. Individual rulers were called *pharaohs*, meaning "great house," though this term did not come into use until the New Kingdom. The first dynasty came to power at the time of unification, c. 3100 B.C., five centuries before the beginning of the Old Kingdom. The last dynasty, the thirty-first, ended in 332 B.C., when the great Macedonian military leader Alexander the Great conquered Egypt and established a new series of rulers known as the Ptolemies. Roman rule began in 31 B.C., and Arab rule followed in A.D. 642.

Egyptian Architecture and Interiors

The Egyptians' reverence for their gods and for their god-related rulers fostered one of history's most ambitious building programs, including the construction of pyramids, sphinxes, obelisks, and temples, some of which were stupendous in scale.

Pyramids and Monuments

Pyramids   The most famous of Egypt's artistic and engineering triumphs, the Great Pyramids of Giza (fig. 2–2), were built not in the culmination of Egypt's long history but relatively early, during the Old Kingdom. It was during that time that the rulers came to be identified as living gods and thus were able to command the wealth and energy of all their people for the construction of any project they imagined, and it was for three of these pharaohs that the great trio of pyramids at Giza was built. The pyramid, although it had symbolic uses as well, was primarily a protective shield built to encase the mummy (the eviscerated, embalmed, and carefully wrapped corpse) of a member of the Egyptian royalty.

▼ **2–2** The Great Pyramids of Giza. The most distant is the pyramid of Khufu, largest of the three, 460 ft. (140 m) high. At center is the pyramid of Khafre, and in the foreground is the pyramid of Menkaure. Even nearer are three subsidiary pyramids for the wives of Menkaure.

Famed twentieth-century architect and furniture designer Marcel Breuer (see figs. 21–9, 21–10, 21–56, 21–57, and 21–58) greatly admired the Egyptian pyramids. In his introduction to Jean-Louis de Cenival's 1964 book *Egypt*, he wrote: "The Pharaonic builder employed his material with an authority, a force and a sophistication that has never been surpassed; no-one has better learned the language of gravity, of weight and of the stone cube. Nowhere else, and at no other time, has the stone mound been transformed so basically into geometry. . . . What other period of the past had the courage to tilt a triangle 700 feet long against another of equal length?"

The three Great Pyramids were built as parts of religious precincts. At Giza on the western edge of the Nile floodplain, the ruling pharaohs had three adjacent valley temples built for the ritual purification of their bodies and, next to the central temple, the lion-bodied statue of the Great Sphinx. From these temples, causeways for water transport of the royal bodies terminated at the three enormous granite pyramids: from north to south, and from largest to smallest, the pyramids of Khufu, his son Khafre, and Khafre's successor, Menkaure (in Greek: Cheops, Chephren, and Mycerinus).

These structures impress first with their sheer mass. The pyramid of Khufu, 460 feet (140 m) tall, is built of 6 million short tons (5.4 million t) of stone, each casing block weighing 2 short tons (1.8 t) or more. But there is more to wonder at, for these stones are fit together with joints of only $1/50$ inch (0.5 mm): a mountain erected with a jeweler's precision. Beyond both mass and precision, their elegance and austerity still inspire awe.

The pyramid was a potent symbol of Khufu's power and assumed immortality. It was also a solid four-sided shield for his burial chamber, but it was in no way an expression of interior space. The burial chamber at the heart of the pyramid is, in fact, tiny (fig. 2–3). Inside the structure, measuring 755 feet (245 m) for each side of its base, the chamber occupies only about 17 by 34 feet (5.5 × 11 m). Passages leading to it, however, as well as false passages leading deceptively away from it to thwart robbers, display impressive constructional ingenuity. For example, the walls of the Great Gallery, a 150-foot-long (49 m) corridor sloping upward toward the burial chamber (fig. 2–4), has 26-foot-high (8.5 m) walls that are **corbeled**, each of their layers of stone projecting slightly beyond the one beneath.

This monumental structure—and smaller ones like it—functioned not only as tributes to the dead rulers but also as protection for them in the afterlife. "You have not gone away dead, you have gone away alive," begins a ritual from the ancient Egyptian Pyramid Texts inscribed in pyramid burial chambers. These chambers were rich treasuries of objects the mummified ruler might desire. Though some of the objects were symbolic (dishes and pitchers represented food and drink; a model of a house represented a house), many were real pieces of furniture (fig. 2–5), statuary, jewelry, and even games (fig. 2–6). Though most ancient burial chambers have been robbed by thieves, those objects that have been discovered have been wonderfully informative about Egyptian life. These have been supplemented by paintings and carvings on the chambers' walls and by writings on scrolls of papyrus (fig. 2–7), a paperlike material made from the plant of the same name.

▼ **2–3** Section through the pyramid of Khufu. After Edwards

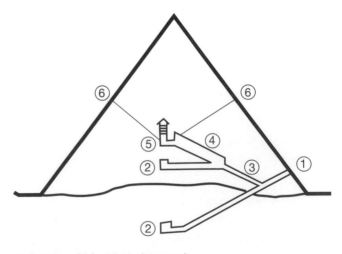

1. Entrance, 55 ft. (17 m) above grade
2. Unfinished chambers
3. Ascending corridor
4. Great Gallery
5. King's chamber
6. Ventilation shafts

▲ **2–4** The Great Gallery in the pyramid of Khufu leads upward to the king's burial chamber.
Herve Champollion/AKG-Images

Sphinxes A **sphinx** is a mythical monster with the body of a lion and the head of another animal, a deity, or a human. In the largest and most famous example, the Great Sphinx of Giza, the head is that of the Pharaoh Khufu, wearing the royal headdress (fig. 2–8) or, in the opinion of some, Horus, the god of the rising sun. Perhaps it is both Khufu *and* Horus, for the Egyptians were not troubled by multiple meanings. In the long row of sphinxes that links the temple of Luxor with the temple of Karnak, the heads are those of rams. In the many later examples used as carved or painted decoration or as furniture legs during the Renaissance, Adam, Empire, and Regency periods, the heads and busts are those of women.

▲ **2–5** King Tutankhamun's chest. The cabinet was fastened with a cord wrapped around the knob on the top and the one on the front. The austere plainness of the straight legs gives them a modern look.
Robert Harding Picture Library, London

The Great Sphinx is thought to date from the reign of Khufu and to have been repaired by his son Khafre. It is adjacent to the valley temple of Khafre and therefore lies at the foot of the three Great Pyramids, facing the Nile. The body of the Great Sphinx is 150 feet (46 m) long, and between its paws is a large flat slab that may have been a sacrificial altar. Its beard was found buried in the sand nearby.

▲ **2–6** A senet game from Egypt's sixteenth dynasty, c. 1600 B.C. The box, the top of which is a playing board, is of ebony inlaid with ivory, and the blue playing pieces are of Egyptian faience. Found in the tomb of Akhor at Thebes. 10¾ in. (4.25 cm) long.
Werner Forman/Art Resource, NY

Obelisks Like the pyramid, the Egyptian obelisk is a form imbued with a natural authority that we continue to recognize. An obelisk is a tall, slender, four-sided tapering shaft of stone (generally of granite, quarried from a single piece) that tapers upward to a pyramidal tip (fig. 2–9). It is most often square in plan, but occasionally rectangular. Like the pyramid, its tip may have at times been gilded, and its four faces were carved with dedicatory inscriptions in hieroglyphics, the most frequent dedication being to the sun god Ra.

Written records of obelisks date back to the Age of Pyramids in the Old Kingdom, but none quite that old has been discovered. In all, at least a hundred large obelisks were erected in Egypt—perhaps many more. Some were over 100 feet (30 m) high, and their raising was a remarkable engineering feat. The Romans, who ruled Egypt for almost seven centuries, adopted a cylindrical version of the obelisk, a freestanding column (fig. 5–11) that, like the obelisk, was faced with commemorative text.

Temples Awesome as are the pyramids and striking as are the obelisks, these two structures offer only exterior views. It is in the Egyptian temples that both a manipulation of enclosed volume and a sense of movement through space were skillfully developed.

Temples had always been part of the sacred areas adjacent to pyramids, but increasingly they came to be built independently of pyramids. Large temples generally conformed to the same **axial** plan, by which pairs of elements were symmetrically arrayed around a center line. Typical elements of the temple plan (fig. 2–10) included an avenue

▼ **2–7** In this detail from a painting on papyrus, a gazelle sitting on a folding stool and a lion sitting on a rigid stool play a board game, probably senet. From Thebes, c. 1100 B.C., 6 in. (15.5 cm) high.
Heritage Images © The Trustees of the British Museum

▲ **2–8** The Great Sphinx, Giza, c. 2551—2528 B.C., 65 ft. (20 m) high.
Petera A. Clayton

of sphinxes or other statues leading to the entrance; sometimes a pair of obelisks before the entrance; tall entrance pylons with battered faces; an open courtyard with colonnaded sides; an inner **hypostyle** hall (a large hall with a roof supported by many columns); and, finally, an inner sanctuary with an image of the deceased ruler, sometimes surrounded by storerooms and living quarters for priests. The whole plan was ordered to accommodate a procession, the spaces becoming increasingly sacred and private, increasingly small in scale, and increasingly dark.

The largest and most impressive of the temples built to this general plan include the hypostyle hall at the Temple of Karnak (fig. 2–11), which has densely spaced columns rising 70 feet (22 m) and bearing stone **architraves** (horizontal members spanning between columns) weighing 60 tons (54 t) each.

As robbery became an evident problem, many Egyptian burial chambers ceased to be housed in freestanding structures and were built into rock cliffs. Though never meant to be publicly seen, these chambers were often enriched with elaborate painting and sculpture (fig. 2–12).

Egyptian Houses

Our impressions of Egyptian design are dominated by the magnificence of its major monuments, which were built for the glorification of gods, the commemoration of great rulers, or the protection of royal mummies. None of this monumental architecture was meant to shelter the living (except for a few priests). Where, then, did the Egyptians

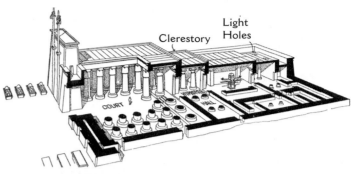

▼ **2–10** Cutaway perspective view of the Temple of Khons at Karnak, c. 1200 B.C. In a typical Egyptian temple plan, rows of sphinxes lead to the frontal pylons. Inside, there is a series of increasingly private and sacred spaces. The object shown near the back is the sacred boat of the god Khons.
Sir Banister Fletcher, "A History of Architecture on the Comparative Method," (London: B. T. Batsford, 1954, 16th ed.) Reprinted by permission.

▲ **2–11** The Great Hypostyle Hall of the Temple of Karnak, built in the thirteenth century B.C. The shape of the column capitals is an abstraction of the lotus bud, and carvings near the base of the columns spell out "Ramesses II is adored by all the people."
Dagli Orti/Picture Desk, Inc./Kobal Collection

▶ **2–9** The hieroglyphics-covered tip of one of the two obelisks of Hatshepsut at Karnak. Carved from a single block of rose granite. 97 ft. (30 m) high.

▼ **2–12** The Temple of Ramesses II at Abu Simbel is cut into a rock cliff. The vestibule is flanked by statues of Ramesses II as the god Osiris. Each figure is 33 ft. (10 m) high. In the sanctuary beyond are seated figures of Ramesses II and three Egyptian Gods.
© Fridmar Damm/zefa/CORBIS All Rights Reserved

▲ **2–13** Wooden model of the garden and portico of an eleventh-dynasty Egyptian house, c. 2000 B.C., found in the tomb of Mekutra at Thebes. The columns of the portico have papyrus bud columns.
Model of House and Garden, from the Tomb of Mekutra (mekat-Re), Thebes, Dynasty 11, ca. 2009–1998 B.C. Wood, painted and gessoed. Pool: copper lined. H 15½ in. (39.5 cm). The Metropolitan Museum of Art, Rogers Fund and Edward S. Harkness Gift, 1920 (20.3.13). Photograph © 1992 The Metropolitan Museum of Art.

live? The Egyptians built their houses, even the palaces of the great, with less permanence in mind than for their pyramids, obelisks, and temples. They used rubblestone or mud brick, which was fired for the homes of the wealthy and unfired for the poor (monuments were made from **ashlar**, a precisely cut, straight-sided stone). Such materials have vanished with few physical traces, but even so, foundations still indicate where Egyptian houses were built, and drawings, paintings, and models (fig. 2–13) provide records of what they were like.

The earliest Egyptian house, and the simplest one in all periods of Egyptian history, was nothing more than a single rectangular room with an entrance door on one of the shorter sides and, on the opposite side, a small open window for ventilation. The door, and sometimes the window, too, was topped by a wooden **lintel**, a member spanning the opening and carrying the weight of the wall above it.

More affluent Egyptians had houses of several rooms and on several levels, the lowest level used for food preparation, storage, and utility, and perhaps a workshop, and the upper levels used for living quarters. Those even more prosperous had elaborate layouts with porticoes, colonnades, and enclosed gardens. In almost every house type, however, an important feature was at least one flat roof area used for living and sleeping in hot weather; if possible, it was screened from the neighbors' view with trelliswork, and, for much of the year, it was the center of family activity.

Residences of rulers, priests, and nobles, along with the necessary satellite structures, were often built adjacent to great temples as parts of royal precincts. In the teeming cities, however, Egyptian town planning apparently lacked the great order and discipline we associate with Egyptian architecture: The houses of noblemen might be next to the houses of workmen, and residential buildings might be scattered among bazaars, workshops, storehouses, shrines, wells, and parks, all packed closely together.

Egyptian Furniture

Just as some of the most powerful architecture ever built dates back to Egypt, so do some of the most elegant and elaborate pieces of furniture ever made. Two important groups of that furniture, dating roughly a thousand years apart but discovered within three years of one another, are the furniture belonging to Queen Hetepheres, entombed c. 2300 B.C. and unearthed in 1925, forty-two centuries

▲ 2–14 Furniture of Queen Hetepheres was built of wood encased in gold. Seen here are a chair, a sloping bed with "pillow" and footrest, and around the whole group, a frame for fabric hangings.
Remains of furniture found in Giza, Egypt, tomb of Hetep–heres I. Pharaonic, 4th dynasty, ca. 2613–2494 B.C. The Egyptian Museum, Cairo/Werner Forman Archive/Art Resource, N.Y.

▲ 2–15 The ceremonial chair found in Tutankhamun's tomb. Made of ebony that is gold-leafed and inlaid with ivory, colored glass, Egyptian faience, and precious stones. 44 in. (112 cm) high.
Rainbird: Robert Harding Picture Library Limited

later, and the furniture belonging to King Tutankhamun, buried c. 1300 B.C. and uncovered in 1922.

The Furniture of Queen Hetepheres

Queen Hetepheres was the mother of the Pharaoh Khufu. A complete suite of her furniture was discovered at the bottom of a deep shaft close to her son Khufu's pyramid. It is the oldest Egyptian furniture that has so far been found. Even though it was built of wood that had been destroyed by rot or insects, the wood members had been encased in heavy gold plates that are still intact; now encasing new supports, they form a dazzling display in the Cairo Museum (fig. 2–14).

The furniture includes an armchair, a bed, a headrest, a great framework for netting or draperies that could be hung to enclose the bed, and a box for jewelry, all finished in the most perfect technique. The armchair is low, with a wide, deep seat, animal legs, and open arms filled with representations of papyrus flowers.

The Furniture of King Tutankhamun

Eighteenth-dynasty King Tutankhamun, who after the discovery of his tomb in 1922 came to be popularly called "King Tut," died when he was only about 18 years old. His burial chamber, like those of most Egyptian royalty, was filled with treasures to accompany him through eternity; unlike all the others that are known, it remained hidden and unplundered until modern times. King Tutankhamun's furniture was more abundant, more varied, and more elaborately decorated than that of Queen Hetepheres, although the similarities reflect a good measure of Egyptian conservatism. The opening of the tomb in 1922 revealed some sensational riches, and jumbled among them were about fifty pieces of royal furniture. They included armchairs, armless chairs, a number of stools—some fixed, some folding, many four-legged, some three-legged—several beds with one of them folding for travel and thirty chests of different size and design with interiors carefully fitted to hold specific contents.

The two most impressive pieces of furniture found were a ceremonial chair and a gold throne. The ceremonial chair (fig. 2–15) has a curiously shaped wood seat on a base obviously meant to represent a folding stool, although it was not built to actually fold. The seat is primarily made of ebony inset with ivory in a pattern resembling leopard's skin, with strips that imitate the skins of other animals. Under the seat, remnants of red leather are visible. The base still displays, between the front legs, part of a gold grillwork of entwined lotus plants, symbolizing the unification of Upper and Lower Egypt. The ceremonial chair was accompanied

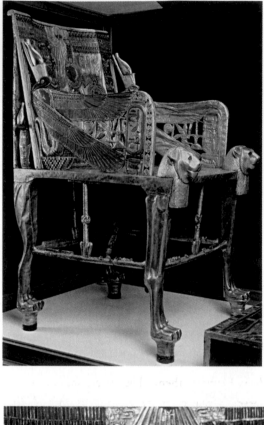

▲ **2–17** Detail of the backrest of the gold throne (fig. 2–16). At left, the young king Tutankhamun sits on an upholstered chair with animal legs, his feet on an upholstered stool. The rays of the sun god Aten shine on him and his wife.

by a low footstool. A simple rectangular box in shape, it was inlaid with pictures of a row of bound prisoners, placed so that the young pharaoh could rest his feet on the subjugated enemy.

The gold throne from Tutankhamun's tomb is a far more fanciful concoction (fig. 2–16). Encased almost entirely in gold, it incorporates inlaid details of silver, lapis lazuli, translucent crystal, Egyptian faience, and colored glass. The chair legs are in the form of a lion's, and the front legs are topped by lion's heads. The side panels are formed primarily by a pair of glass-eyed cobras with the sweeping wings of vultures. The double crowns of Upper and Lower Egypt, which the cobras are wearing, tilt backward and rest against the chair back. On the back itself (fig. 2–17), the sun disk shines above a domestic scene of the young king and his slender wife, wearing silver robes.

Even more dazzling than Tutankhamun's furniture was his sarcophagus, carved from the hard gray stone called quartzite. Opening it, archaeologists found a coffin of gilded wood; inside that, a second, more elaborately gilded coffin; and inside that, a third coffin of pure polished gold with inlays of colored glass and a face with eyebrows and ceremonial beard made of lapis lazuli (fig. 2–18). This inner coffin weighed 250 pounds (114 kg). When it was opened, a further discovery was made: Inside was the young king's gold face mask (fig. 2–1), inlaid with lapis lazuli, carnelian, feldspar, turquoise, and Egyptian faience.

Other Furniture

Furniture for commoners, on the other hand, was less admirable in both materials and workmanship than furniture for royalty, but the basic designs of Egyptian pieces differed little throughout the social scale. Paintings and carvings suggest well-furnished interiors, but these depictions are probably representative of only wealthier households. The poorest Egyptians probably had no movable furniture, for the shortage of appropriate trees in Egypt must have made freestanding wood furniture expensive.

Some Egyptian furniture was built as an integral part of the mud-brick house. For example, there was often a **dais**, or platform, built and plastered and whitewashed or edged with limestone, which could serve as a dining area, and also a **mastaba**, or seating bench. For storage, open cupboards were carved out of the masonry walls. But within the house,

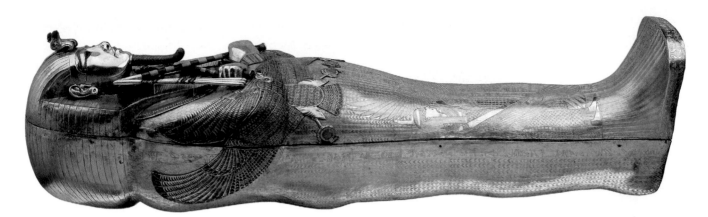

▲ **2–18** Inner coffin of Tutankhamun's sarcophagus. Tomb of Tutankhamun, Valley of the Kings, near Deir el-Bahri, eighteenth dynasty, c. 1336–1327 B.C. Glass, semiprecious stones, inlaid gold. 6 ft. ⅞ in. (1.85 m). The Egyptian Museum, Cairo.
Araldo de Luca Studio/Index Ricerca Iconografica

the Egyptians also enjoyed a highly developed assortment of movable furniture.

Seating   The chair was an important piece of furniture in Egypt, though not as common as the stool. Ordinary chairs were similar to royal ones, but, naturally, had less extravagant ornamentation. Some, by today's standards, seem unusually low, perhaps due to the fact that they were first made for people accustomed to sitting on the earth. Chair seats were often of woven rush. Many chairs were given animal legs, the hind legs of the animal in the rear and the forelegs in front, all facing the same direction as in nature (fig. 2–19). The feet, carved like paws, rested on small blocks of wood that probably disappeared into the straw matting that usually covered the floors.

Stools were more common than chairs, many of them quite humble. Some—like the portable stools of army commanders—carried the prestige of rank; some were used by pharaohs themselves. Some stools folded; some did not; and some were in the form of folding ones but did not actually fold.

Beds   Beds were rarer than chairs in Egypt. Those who lacked wood-framed beds slept on reed mats or on mud-brick platforms. The simplest wooden bed frames had rails at each edge, supported by a leg at each corner. The center was spanned with plaited rope or leather thongs. Even the simplest versions, however, often had legs carved as animal legs and side rails carved in a curve that the Egyptians apparently found comfortable. Some Egyptian beds not only curved but sloped, with the head end raised slightly

above the foot, as was the bed of Queen Hetepheres (fig. 2–14). Footboards added to such sloping beds could be elaborately carved and decorated. One of the seven beds or couches found in Tutankhamun's tomb (fig. 2–20) is unusually high above the floor (4 feet) and is in the form of two elongated cows. On the cow heads are pairs of horns with solar disks between them. The wood frames are covered with **gesso** (a plaster made from gypsum and chalk or

▼ **2–19** Painted relief on the limestone Stela of Wep-Em-Nefret. 4th Dynasty. Reign of Khufu, c. 2551–2528 B.C. Like most Egyptian figure drawings, this one combines profile and frontal views. The stool has legs carved in the shape of animal legs. 18 in. (45.7 cm) high.
Phoebe Hearst Museum of Anthropology, University of California at Berkeley

▼ **2–20** A funerary bed from Tutankhamun's tomb, carved in the form of two elongated cows. 81 in. (208 cm) long.
Giraudon/Art Resource, NY

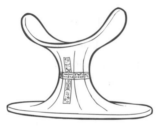

▶ **2–21** From the eighteenth dynasty, a "pillow" or headrest made of turquoise-colored glass.
Abercrombie, after Hall

▲ **2–22** A jewel chest and its rounded lid from the eighteenth-dynasty tomb of Yuya and Tuyu, c. 1360 B.C. The legs are inlaid with rectangles of Egyptian faience and pink-painted ivory separated by bars of ivory and ebony. The sides and lid have hieroglyphic markings in gilded wood. The curved molding at the top of the chest imitates the cavetto cornice of a temple. 16 in (41 cm) high.
Scala/Art Resource, NY

animal glue) and gold leaf and painted with leopardlike black spots.

Used in conjunction with such beds were Egyptian "pillows" or headrests. A gold one belonging to Queen Hetepheres is in place on the head of her bed. They were most commonly made of wood, but could also be made of ivory or even of colored glass (fig. 2–21). The Egyptians generally slept on them with their heads turned, cradling the sides of their heads in the support, and the headrest was often wrapped in linen for greater comfort. Such headrests are still made in West Africa, and similar ones are also seen in other cultures; it has been speculated that they were popular in those societies where elaborate hair arrangements were considered important, or in hot climates, where lifting the head slightly above the bed allowed greater air circulation.

Tables Tables existed from at least as early as the Old Kingdom. Some have been found from the time of the pyramids that are small, round, and made of alabaster; it is assumed that they were used for some kind of sacrifice or other ritual. There were also round wooden tables at a convenient height for use with chairs. And, from the sixth dynasty on, there were also small tables with square tops.

Other Furnishings There were many wooden pieces for storage, from small jewel chests (fig. 2–22) to larger chests. One from Tutankhamun's tomb (fig. 2–23) is topped by a carved figure of a jackal, representing the god Anubis, one of whose titles was "Supervisor of the Secrets." Both this chest and the jewel chest are topped with a **cavetto** (a curved

▲ **2–23** Chest of gilded wood with a reclining jackal on its lid, eighteenth dynasty, c. 1330 B.C., 46 in. (118 cm) high.
Egyptian National Museum, Cairo, Egypt/The Bridgeman Art Library International

molding, such as might be seen at the top of a temple or other important building).

Loose cushions covered in cotton, painted leather, or even metallic cloth added comfort and further color to Egyptian seating. Though none has survived, they can be clearly seen in wall paintings and carvings. In addition to storage niches in the walls, wooden boxes and baskets also held household goods, including clothing and bedding. For lighting, there were oil lamps, the most common made of pottery, the finest made of bronze. For eating, the affluent Egyptians used tableware made of pottery, alabaster, bronze, gold, and silver.

Egyptian Decorative Arts

The character of any body of art is dependent not only on general and pervasive factors such as geography, government, and religion, but also on the minute details of the specific tools and techniques employed to create the art. We will not fully understand any art without understanding something of how it has been made. The construction methods used in building the pyramids and erecting the obelisks and temples are well covered in other texts; what concerns us for the study of interior design are the Egyptians' methods of painting, carving, and working with materials like ceramics, glass, wood, and textiles.

For the Egyptians, almost all decoration in all these mediums conveyed distinct meanings. Many of those meanings were related to the complex religious beliefs of the Egyptians, so that decoration was often, for them, a form of worship.

Wall Painting

Most of the surfaces of the great monuments, both outside and inside, were covered with paintings and low relief carvings. For the paintings, outlines were first sketched with charcoal; then a shallow groove was chiseled around the outline of each shape. The grooved surface was then covered with a thin layer of **plaster** (a paste usually made of cement, lime, or gypsum that, when mixed with sand and water, forms a hard surface when dried). Colored pigment—often in brilliant colors—was then applied to the plaster. The Egyptians obtained their pigments from minerals, which contributed to their permanence. Iron oxides, for example, were used to create red and yellow, and carbonate of copper was used to create blue. Large areas of pigment were applied

with coarse brushes made of palm fibers, and fine outlines and details were applied with thin brushes made of reeds. Generally, each colored area was flat and uniform, no attempt being made to suggest gradations, shadings, shadows, or highlights.

The subject matter of these mural decorations included the daily life of individuals, religious and allegorical events, flowers and birds, boats and barges on the Nile, wild animals being hunted in the desert, warriors and workers, musicians and dancers, tragedy and humor. Around and between these scenes, the wall surface was frequently filled with hieroglyphic writing, further explaining the figures and events. The pictures and hieroglyphics together have given historians detailed knowledge of Egyptian life. An extensive example of Egyptian wall painting, discovered near Thebes in 1904 (but not fully restored until 1992), is in the tomb of Queen Nefertari, the most favored of the many wives of the great pharaoh Ramesses II (fig. 2–24).

The character of this art had no use for the convention of perspective that is a familiar part of most Western art. Instead, the Egyptians suggested depth by the placement of one object above another. Size, in the Egyptian convention, was used to indicate importance, a ruler being drawn larger than a slave or an enemy, for example. In early periods, women were drawn smaller than men; in the New Kingdom, they were the same size.

The representation of the human figure was strictly conventionalized, represented in poses only a contortionist could hold: The legs and feet were in full profile with the insides of both feet facing outward, the upper torso in a three-quarter view, with the profiles of hip and breast visible, the shoulders in a fully frontal view, and the head again in profile but with the single visible eye drawn as if from the front. To the Egyptian eye, this composite view (as we saw in fig. 2–19) gave a good two-dimensional representation of a three-dimensional figure.

To represent the features of a specific individual was a goal at some stages of Egyptian art, while in others, a more generic figure was accepted. At no time, however, was the personality of an individual artist expressed; indeed, most murals and sculptures were collaborations of a number of painters or carvers. In any case, the goal was almost always to conform to an existing artistic ideal, not to explore new territory. If what we today think of as the creative artist is missing from Egyptian art, so also, in many cases, is what we think of as the spectator, for much of the finest Egyptian

▲ **2–24** Wall paintings in the tomb of Nefertari in the Valley of the Queens, Thebes, c. 1270 B.C. Nefertari was the Great Royal Wife of Ramesses II, and the paintings on thick plaster over rock show her being presented to various Egyptian gods. The ceiling is painted to represent a starry night sky.
Giraudon/Art Resource, NY

art was created to be sealed in the interiors of tombs, never to be seen by the living.

Sculpture

The Egyptians excelled in sculpture, not only in the raised **reliefs** that often covered wall surfaces or the sides of obelisks, but also in freestanding sculpture (sculpture made to be viewed from all sides). Because of the hardness of the stone from which it was carved, much of the sculpture was extremely simple in form. The surfaces were smooth, and a strong, dignified effect was obtained through clear, vigorous massing.

Wall paintings and raised reliefs (reliefs made with the backgrounds cut away from the figures) were generally found in temple interiors, and sunken reliefs (reliefs made with the figures cut into the surface and casting stronger shadows) were more often found on exterior surfaces. Both types of relief were usually gently plastered and then painted.

▲ **2–25** Painted limestone bust of Queen Nefertiti, wife of Akhenaten, c. 1360 B.C., 19 in. (50 cm) high.
Art Resource/Bildarchiv Preussischer Kulturbesitz

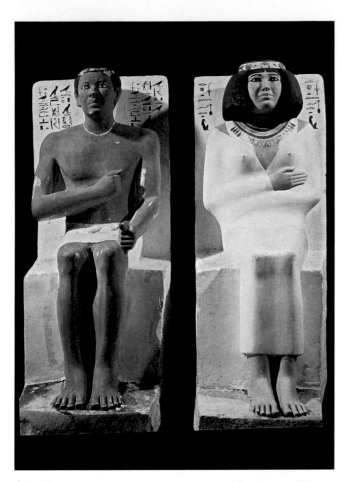

▲ **2–26** Painted limestone funerary statues of Rahotep and his wife Nofret, members of the royal circle during the fourth-dynasty reign of Sneferu (2575—2551 B.C.). The difference in skin tones is an Egyptian artistic convention: pale and creamy for females, dark and ruddy for males. The eyes are inlaid with quartz and rock crystal. 47 in. (121 cm) high.
Egyptian Museum, Cairo/Picture Desk, Inc./Kobal Collection

orated. At certain times and locations, the pottery was decorated with light lines on dark grounds; at others, with red lines on buff-colored grounds. Geometric ornament prevailed, but there were also stylized representations of animals, birds, plants, and humans. In eighteenth-century England, the famous potter Josiah Wedgwood would base some of his designs on Egyptian sphinxes, lions, candlesticks, cameos, and **canopic** vases (jars for the viscera of mummies).

Ivory and Alabaster

Ivory, a material technically known as dentine, is found most commonly in the tusks of elephants, and Egyptians employed it along with the ivory from hippopotamuses. Ivory's close grain makes it an ideal medium for carving. Because elephant tusks are seldom more than 7 inches (18 cm) across, however, the size of an ivory carving is limited. Many of the Egyptian objects we have seen have been decorated with ivory inlays, and another frequent use of ivory was for the feet of wooden furniture legs. One finely carved example (fig. 2–27) shows the details of veins and tendons. The holes at the top are for attaching it to the wood leg.

Alabaster is another attractive, easily carved material favored by the Egyptians. They used it for vessels (fig. 2–28), and sometimes for the linings of sarcophagi and for the ceilings and walls of tombs. It is white or pale brown and

The elegant bust of Queen Nefertiti (fig. 2–25), wife of the pharaoh Akhenaten, was made of painted limestone c. 1360 B.C. and discovered by German archaeologists in 1912 in the workshop of its sculptor. The Egyptians also sculpted funerary statues of minor royalty and even of nonroyal Egyptians. The painted limestone figures of Rahotep and his wife Nofret (fig. 2–26) depict a pair who were part of the royal circle, though not themselves of royal blood, and their likenesses were the work of court artists. Writing on the back of Rahotep's chair lists his duties as priest and superintendent of works and of expeditions, signifying his importance to court.

Ceramics

As early as predynastic times, the Egyptians were producing pottery, primarily utilitarian pieces, though interestingly dec-

▶ **2–27** Ivory furniture leg in the shape of a bull's foot. Elephant ivory, Thinite period, 3100—2700 B.C. The holes at the top are for attaching it to the wood frame.
Leg from a Piece of Furniture in the form of a Bull's Foot, Elephant Ivory, Egyptian, Thinite Period, 3100–2700 B.C. Louvre, Paris, France/Bridgeman Art Library.

▶ **2–28** Alabaster jar made for an upper-class burial, mid-fourth to mid-fifth dynasty, 13 in. (33 cm) high.
Egyptian Stonework Vessels, 21.2.8, Jar, Dynasty 6, ca. 2323–2150 B.C. Egyptian alabaster, H. 33 cm; The Metropolitan Museum of Art. Photograph © 1994 The Metropolitan Museum of Art

powdered quartz (another silicate) and a binding agent such as a solution of sodium carbonate, a salt found in nature. By 3000 B.C., Egyptian faience was being used not only for beds and amulets, but also for small statuettes. Later it was also used for decorating wall tiles and, in the Middle Kingdom, for many delightful small animal figures, such as the hedgehog (a desert symbol) and the hippopotamus (a Nile symbol sometimes decorated with lotus flowers). Egyptian faience was also a popular material for the fashioning of the *ankh* sign (fig. 2–29), which is the hieroglyph meaning "life." The ankh was a frequent element of royal funerary equipment.

Of course, the Egyptians also produced glass. Glass, like Egyptian faience, is largely a product of firing crushed quartz or sand. Following its use as glazing for other

◀ **2–29** Ankh amulet of Egyptian faience from the tomb of Thutmose IV in the Valley of the Kings, eighteenth dynasty, 9¼ in. (9.3 cm) high.
Model ankh amulet, Egyptian Faience. Photograph © 2007 Museum of Fine Arts, Boston.

slightly translucent. The alabaster used by the Egyptians was of a type sometimes called *Oriental alabaster* or *onyx marble*, which is a calcium carbonate, whereas today what we call alabaster is a kind of *gypsum*, a calcium sulphate.

Egyptian Faience and Glass

Glasslike substances first appeared in Egypt around 4000 B.C. as glazes for decorative beads. Soon after, the glazes were refined into **Egyptian faience**, a nonclay ceramic made of

Tools & Techniques | EGYPTIAN FAIENCE

The paste of Egyptian faience could be modeled or turned on a potter's wheel, then hardened by firing. The product was naturally white but could be painted with powdered minerals before firing, giving it both color and a fine, smooth finish. Different minerals produced different colors, but by far the most popular colors for the Egyptians were blue and green, possibly because of their resemblance to some of the most costly materials known to them: lapis lazuli, malachite, and turquoise. Ever conscious of symbolism, the Egyptians may also have seen in these colors a reference to the life-giving Nile.

The glasslike material described here is best called by the complete name *Egyptian faience,* because later we will see the general name *faience* as a term originating in sixteenth-century France (and derived from the Italian town of Faenza). The French term will commonly be used to describe a very different kind of product, an opaque-glazed earthenware such as English delftware and Italian majolica.

materials, it came to be used independently. The earliest Egyptian glass products were flawed with small bubbles, the result of firing temperatures lower than ideal. But by the eighteenth dynasty, good, clear glass was being made. With additives, the Egyptians developed glass in blue, green, red, gold, black, and opaque white.

In the New Kingdom, purple and lemon yellow were added to the palette of colors. New Kingdom glassware was generally delicate and ornamented, and was most often made by **core forming**, in which ropes of soft glass were wound around a core of dung or clay. An alternate method was to dip such a core in molten glass. After the vessel was **annealed**, or heated and then slowly cooled, the core material was broken up and extracted through its mouth.

Other techniques used by the Egyptians were **cold cutting**, in which crude glass forms were refined by chipping at them with flint or quartz instruments, and molding, in which molten glass was poured into a mold. An elaborate type of molding process was the **lost wax** or *cire perdue* (a French term pronounced "seer pehr-dyoo") method, in which the desired shape was made of wax and encased in clay but with an opening left in the clay. The object was then heated until the wax melted and could be poured out. The result was a clay form into which molten glass could then be poured. After the object had cooled, the clay was removed and the hardened glass shape revealed.

Wood

Of the few native woods available for furniture, acacia was the most frequently used, the others being willow, sycamore, and tamarisk. Better quality wood was imported: cedar from Lebanon, which was used for the furniture found in Tutankhamun's tomb; ebony from Ethiopia, which, although hard to work, was a favorite of the Egyptians and found in Tutankhamun's bed frames; yew from Syria; and oak from Turkey.

Because of the rarity and consequent value of good native hardwood in Egypt, it was used with appropriate economy. And understanding that the valued wood could warp, twist, split, and shrink, the Egyptian craftsmen

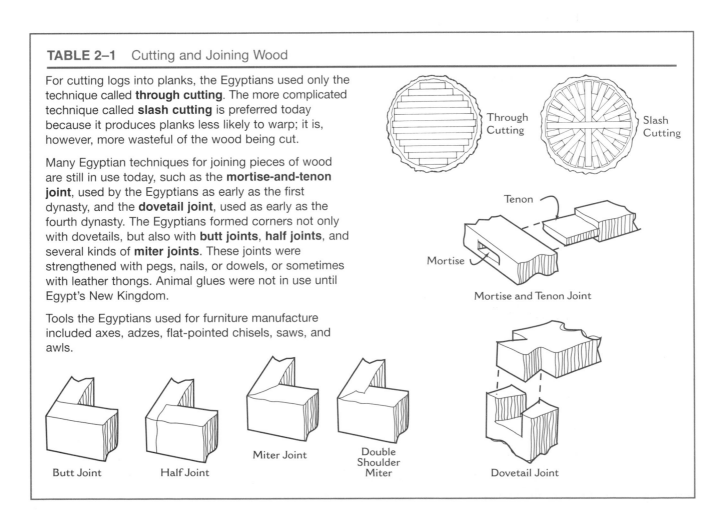

TABLE 2–1   Cutting and Joining Wood

For cutting logs into planks, the Egyptians used only the technique called **through cutting**. The more complicated technique called **slash cutting** is preferred today because it produces planks less likely to warp; it is, however, more wasteful of the wood being cut.

Many Egyptian techniques for joining pieces of wood are still in use today, such as the **mortise-and-tenon joint**, used by the Egyptians as early as the first dynasty, and the **dovetail joint**, used as early as the fourth dynasty. The Egyptians formed corners not only with dovetails, but also with **butt joints**, **half joints**, and several kinds of **miter joints**. These joints were strengthened with pegs, nails, or dowels, or sometimes with leather thongs. Animal glues were not in use until Egypt's New Kingdom.

Tools the Egyptians used for furniture manufacture included axes, adzes, flat-pointed chisels, saws, and awls.

Through Cutting

Slash Cutting

Tenon

Mortise

Mortise and Tenon Joint

Butt Joint   Half Joint   Miter Joint   Double Shoulder Miter   Dovetail Joint

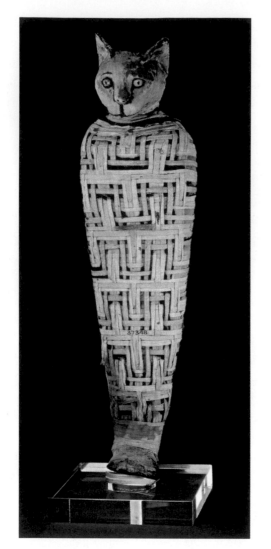

▲ **2–30** Mummy of a cat, probably a royal pet, wrapped in an elaborate pattern of linen strips.
Copyright The British Museum

developed sophisticated techniques for the design and construction of wood furniture. Many of their techniques were duplicated in unrelated cultures; many are in use today (table 2–1).

When only poor quality wood was available for important pieces, it was finished with veneers made from **flitches** (thin sheets of veneer) of cedar or ebony, these held in place with tiny pegs of wood or ivory. Decorative **inlays** (shaped pieces of one substance embedded in another) in lighter woods were also made of ebony, as well as of ivory and Egyptian faience. An early version of **plywood** (a structural material now made by gluing sheets of veneer together) was even manufactured by the Egyptians by laminating thin sheets together, with the grain of one sheet at right angles to that of the next, the sheets held together with wooden pegs. Ivory pegs were also used for joining wood. Decorative

treatments of wood furniture, in addition to inlays, included paint, plaster, **varnish** (a protective coating made of resin dissolved in alcohol or oil), **gesso** (a pore-filling ground made of glue and whiting), **gilding** (thin gold leaf over gesso), and thicker sheets of gold or silver.

Textiles

While modern Egyptians are admired for their production of a strong, lustrous, long-staple cotton, ancient Egyptians began weaving less extravagantly, using such home-grown materials as the country's plentiful reeds and rushes, which were used to make baskets and even wickerwork tables and stools. But the cultivation of the flax plant, a winter crop, and its use in weaving **linen** was already a sophisticated industry in predynastic times. Different harvesting times yielded different products, the young green stems being appropriate for very fine thread, the tougher ripe stems for ropes and matting. Cleaning and combing processes also affected quality. The final results varied from a coarse canvaslike linen pale brown in color, to a fine gauze, bleached white and with as many as 200 threads per inch, reserved for royal use, including the wrapping of royal mummies (fig. 2–30). It was described in Egyptian writings as being so fine as to be translucent, sometimes even transparent.

Wool, shorn from both sheep and goats, was also produced for curtains and wall hangings, as well as for blankets and clothing.

Egyptian weaving was highly skilled, with very few weaving errors found among surviving textiles. The royal harem instructed and trained textile weavers, important private estates employed their own weavers, and all temple complexes included weaving studios that produced textiles not only for funerary garments and other ritual use, but also for sale or barter.

Summary: Egyptian Design

It is natural that the Egyptians, surrounded by a vast, empty desert, gave little thought to the creation of spacious interiors. They concentrated instead on an impressive provision of monumentality achieved through weight and mass. The most obvious example is the Egyptian pyramid, a giant casing protecting one or two small rooms. In the Egyptian temple, as well, the interior volumes are overwhelmed by their stone columns, great in number, close in spacing, and gigantic in size.

▲ **2–31** Detail of a bracelet found on the mummy of a twenty-second-dynasty pharaoh. It is made of gold, Egyptian faience, lapis lazuli, and carnelian. The eye-shaped motif is called an *udjat*; it was thought to be a powerful protection for its wearer.
Henri Stierlin

Looking for Character

Egyptian architecture and its interiors give us the earliest and most thorough demonstration of the psychological effects that can be created through sheer amounts of construction. This monumentality was reinforced by the use of symmetry and axial movement. With the exception of the pyramid, the sphinx, and the obelisk, virtually every element in Egyptian monumental design is mirrored by an equal element. In the vast temple complexes, symmetry and repetition abound, surrounding visitors with a sense of the vast, perfectly ordered, and timeless universe of Egypt, a universe combining both the natural and the supernatural. Even in the small personal objects of daily life, such as a bracelet (fig. 2–31), supernatural forces were called upon for good fortune or protection.

Looking for Quality

A remarkable number of the techniques used by the Egyptians to produce their art and their crafts—in wood-working, weaving, and glassmaking, among other skills—are still in use today, reminding us that the study, care, and energy that the Egyptian artisans poured into their artwork heightened not only the quality of their art but also ensured a longevity to their art forms for centuries to come.

Making Comparisons

Egyptian art is remarkable not only for its scope and its detail, but also for its persistence, not just through Egypt's own long history, but also afterward. The political, religious, and social institutions that fostered the distinctive style of Egyptian architecture and design vanished long ago, of course, yet the Egyptian style has not vanished. Egyptian art directly influenced the Greek and Roman art that would follow and that would in turn influence all subsequent Western art. Centuries later, traces of the Egyptian heritage can be found in art as different as the work of Baroque goldsmiths, a clock by Percier and Fontaine, a mausoleum in Buckinghamshire, and the ornament of the Art Deco period. A particular resurgence of interest in Egyptian art followed Napoleon's North African campaign at the end of the eighteenth century and the flood of drawings and information it produced. Another resurgence followed the sensational news of the twentieth-century discovery of the tomb of Tutankhamun.

Even in our own time, in a phenomenon we shall see repeated with other highly developed styles, the distinctive character of what the Egyptians produced endures as an established part of our artistic vocabulary. It may be absurd to build a Las Vegas hotel in the shape of a pyramid and to name it the Luxor, but such absurdity shows that the works of Egypt still have a place in the popular imagination. Similar reminders of Egypt are the pyramid on the U.S. dollar bill and the one that appears when we log on to America Online. In more serious design, Egyptian motifs abound in Regency and Empire furniture that we still appreciate and sometimes reproduce.

The Ancient Near East

2800–636 A.D.

"The antique Persians taught three useful things,
To draw the bow, to ride, and speak the truth."

— Lord Byron (1788–1824), English poet

As the Egyptian civilization developed along the Nile, other civilizations were forming along the Tigris and Euphrates rivers, in what is now Iraq. Some spread their control and influence over much of Asia and Africa into what are now the nations of Israel, Jordan, Syria, Lebanon, Turkey, and Iran. Collectively, these civilizations constitute what we call the Ancient Near East. The Ancient Near East can be divided geographically into three main areas: Anatolia, Mesopotamia, and Persia.

Anatolia, roughly equivalent in area to the modern state of Turkey, was the northwestern part of the Ancient Near East. As we saw in Chapter 1, it was the site of Çatal Hüyük, a settlement that flourished 3,000 years earlier than the Old Kingdom of Egypt. Some of the decorative motifs of the town's wall paintings persisted in the area for many centuries.

The heart of the Ancient Near East was in Mesopotamia. The name Mesopotamia, meaning "between the rivers," is

derived from two Greek words, *mesos* (meaning "middle") and *potamos* (meaning "rivers"). The two rivers are the Tigris and the Euphrates, and so rich was the soil they deposited that the area has been called the Fertile Crescent. So rich has been its history that it has also been called "the cradle of civilization."

East of Mesopotamia was ancient Persia (now Iran), with the Caspian Sea on its north and the Persian Gulf on its south. Southwest of Mesopotamia were the politically fragmented lands of the Ancient Near East sometimes collectively called Syria-Palestine and occupied today, from north to south, by Syria, Lebanon, Jordan, and Israel. In ancient times, Syria-Palestine was ruled by a succession of people from the north: first the Assyrians, then the Babylonians, and then the Persians. Then, with its conquest by Alexander the Great in the third century B.C. it became part of the Greek world (and later it was a Roman province).

Our knowledge of the historically diverse Ancient Near East is relatively recent and probably far from complete. Archaeological findings there have not been as spectacular as in Egypt, at least in part because Ancient Near Eastern architecture and design are not as well preserved. Unlike

◄ **3–1** Detail from a Sumerian mosaic panel called "The Royal Standard of Ur," depicting a military victory, c. 2600 B.C., 8 in. (20 cm) high.
© Copyright The British Museum

31

Egypt, these lands were not protected by desert from foreign invaders, nor did they have Egypt's dry climate to help preserve their art. Lacking Egypt's plentiful supply of fine building stone, some parts of the Ancient Near East also built with more perishable materials. However, from the remains that have been discovered, we can discern a distinctive character. Just as the Egyptians had discovered the artistic effectiveness of mass combined with elegance and had used that combination to great advantage, the artists of the Ancient Near East discovered the potency of stylization, repetition, rhythm, and energy. This artistic character made interesting contributions to the later Islamic art of the same region.

Determinants of Ancient Near Eastern Design

Though the history of the Ancient Near East is diverse and complex, we can see that the region's geography, natural resources, and religion had definite effects on how the people of its various societies lived and how they designed.

Geography and Natural Resources

The Ancient Near East had a topography that left it more exposed than Egypt. It could be easily invaded from every side—which it was—and thus its history is consequently complex. Unlike the Nile, the Tigris and the Euphrates are turbulent rivers for much of their length, making communications between areas difficult, another deterrent to unity. As it turned out, the areas of the Near East suffered a succession of raids and battles, triumphs and collapses, and the rise and fall of various rulers, capitals, and gods. These upheavals meant that a long period of peace, as in Egypt, was impossible. Unity was partial and temporary, and the upheavals meant that a large part of the area's wealth and energy was necessarily spent on arms and battles rather than on the arts.

Although much of the Near East deserves the name Fertile Crescent, some parts of the region are mountainous, some marshy, and some desert. Still, an enormous natural asset of the ancient Near East was its rich soil, variable climate, and fresh water from the two rivers. Together, they combined to produce conditions extremely well suited for the cultivation of crops and the development of agriculture as a major way of life.

Because Mesopotamia lacked building stone as well as timber, its chief building material was mud brick, made of wet clay and chopped straw. Most mud brick was simply dried in the sun, but some was baked in kilns, which made it slightly more durable. Thick walls of mud were spanned by roof constructions of palm tree trunks, virtually the only wood available except for expensive cedar imported from Lebanon. Roofs also were made with vaults constructed of mud brick. Such construction dictated that the dimensions of the spans be kept short, although the numbers of spanning members could be multiplied as needed. Therefore, Mesopotamian architecture of all types, as we shall see, was characterized by a series of long, narrow rooms, generally clustered around interior courtyards.

The land also lacked large amounts of metals. Silver was found only in the areas now occupied by Turkey and Syria. Copper may have been imported from India, and gold may have come from the Caucasus Mountains that separate Asia from Europe. The intensely blue stone called lapis lazuli, which forms the background of the "Royal Standard of Ur" (fig. 3–1), was imported from Afghanistan. For their imports, the peoples of the Ancient Near East traded crops, crafts, and textiles.

Religion

The religions of the Ancient Near East were as diverse as its governments, but gradually there was a development among them toward belief in one supreme god (at some times and places, a mother goddess). This development became the basis for three of the world's great religions—Judaism, Christianity, and Islam.

Religious leadership in the ancient Near East seems often to have taken a practical course, with local temple leaders organizing their dependent societies into efficient workforces. The temple collected and distributed food for the community and directed the construction not only of palaces and temples but also oversaw the impressive systems of dikes, ditches, and canals for flood control and improved irrigation. These organized enterprises demanded record keeping and management, and so an unprecedented number of legal codes were made. Written language was invented here—almost, it seems, by necessity—earlier than anywhere else we know. Common among the findings from excavations in the Near East are clay tablets inscribed with lists of accounts and laws used to govern the area.

Approximate Date	Dominant Cultures	Artistic Achievements
2800–2003 B.C.	Sumerians	Ziggurat at Ur
2003–1171 B.C.	Babylonians	
884–612 B.C.	Assyrians	Sargon's Palace
612–538 B.C.	Neo-Babylonians	Hanging Gardens Walls of Babylon Ishtar Gate Tower of Babel
538–331 B.C.	Persians	Persepolis
A.D. 224–636	Sasanians	Ktesiphon

Five Peoples of the Ancient Near East and Their Architecture

As the Ancient Near East varies from place to place, it varies, too, from time to time. A whole parade of people with different origins and different goals arrived and departed through its early history. We shall concentrate on five of these peoples, and some of the architecture that they produced. In every culture there were three main building types: the house, the palace, and the temple.

The Sumerians (c. 2800–c. 2003 B.C.)

The Sumerians were a settled people of Mesopotamia, raising livestock and cultivating crops. They joined together in cooperative projects for the clearing of the two rivers, the control of floods, and the irrigation of the surrounding fields. Their various communities prospered and developed into a number of city-states, each composed of an important town and the surrounding territory that the town dominated. The most important of these city-states was Ur, the seat of the earliest Sumerian government. Also important was the city-state of Nippur, which seems to have been a prominent religious center. Other Sumerian city-states were Umma, Kish, and Lagash.

An artifact found at Ur is the "Royal Standard of Ur" (fig. 3–1), a double-faced mosaic panel on wood; its chips of shell and red limestone against a background of lapis lazuli depict a Sumerian king during a victory celebration, standing before his horse-drawn chariot, his troops, his prisoners, and his followers.

It is the Sumerians who are thought to have been the first inventors of written language. Literacy was widespread in the society (though far from universal), and Sumerian literature included *The Epic of Gilgamesh*, considered the world's first great poem and still read today. The Sumerians may also have produced the earliest versions of the potter's wheel, which aided them in their development of ceramics. In addition, the Sumerians may have invented the plow as well as some advanced techniques of boat building.

The most impressive buildings of the Sumerians are their **ziggurats**, artificial mountains of sun-dried mud brick faced with dried brick. Their vigorous, animated, and dramatic design, full of movement and excitement, was later adopted by both the Babylonians and the Assyrians. The ziggurats are in the form of truncated pyramids, usually in several tiers accessed by one or more staircases. The upper tiers, which have vanished, probably supported temples. The ziggurat at Ur (fig. 3–2) was built c. 2100 B.C. and covers an area of 28,000 square feet (2,600 sq. m.); this is one-twentieth the area covered by the pyramid of Khufu in Egypt.

On the other extreme is a typical Sumerian dwelling—usually a one-story house of mud brick, not very wide, due to the limited spans of the mud brick vaults that covered them. Rooms opened to a central courtyard. For most inhabitants, furnishings were probably limited to floor mats, rugs, and cushions. Typically, a stair led to a flat roof, where people could gather in the cooler night air.

The supremacy of Sumer was interrupted c. 2340 B.C. by the Akkadians, a dynasty founded by King Sargon. From the city of Akkad in Babylonia, the dynasty ruled a large territory stretching from the Mediterranean to the Persian Gulf, but their power declined and ended two centuries later, c. 2150 B.C. Ur regained a measure of its previous importance between 2135 and 2027 B.C., and some monumental architecture was built there, including a great palace for the Akkadian, King

▼ 3–2 Reconstruction drawing of the assumed appearance of the ziggurat at Ur.
© Dean Conger/CORBIS All Rights Reserved

Sargon. A few decades later, however, Ur and all of Sumer were overcome by invasions of tribes from beyond the valley: the Elamites, the Amorites, and the Semites.

The Babylonians (c. 2003–c. 1171 B.C.; 612–331 B.C.)

Near the beginning of the third millennium B.C., the city of Babylon became the chief center of all Mesopotamia, and the Babylonian king Hammurabi became the chief power. He ruled from 1792 until 1750 B.C., conquering Sumer and commanding a unified state that also included what is now northern Syria. Under Hammurabi, Mesopotamia reached a golden age. Agriculture, finance, and commerce all flourished. The Babylonian of this period is perhaps the first character on the human stage who can properly be described as a businessman.

Hammurabi is most often remembered, however, for his code of laws. There had been a number of earlier legal codes in Mesopotamia, now lost, but the Code of Hammurabi summarized, systematized, and modernized them. The code of Hammurabi suggests some restrictive conventions of the Ancient Near East, conventions that demanded individual conformity to group standards. Such pressure to conform must surely have been felt throughout society, including in

the realms of architecture and design, though the code itself does not address artistic matters. In addition, the code tells us much about Babylonian social organization; professions mentioned include those of shoemaker, metalsmith, sculptor, and master builder (or architect).

The wealth of Babylonia tempted invaders from many directions, and finally, the dynasty established by Hammurabi was overtaken by the Assyrians in 1171 B.C. However, after the death of the last great Assyrian ruler, King Assurbanipal, the Assyrians lost control of Babylonia, and it again flourished as an independent state, with its King Nebuchadnezzar taking the country and capital to even greater levels of accomplishment than before. This revival of Babylonian prominence, during the years 612 B.C.–538 B.C., is sometimes called the Neo-Babylonian period.

The capital city of Babylon, 50 miles (80 km) south of modern Baghdad, was famous for its brilliant color and luxury. Covering more than 2,100 acres and surrounded by fortification walls, its main streets ran roughly parallel to—or at right angles to—the Euphrates and terminated at the walls in bronze gates. The most famous of streets was the Processional Way that led from the massive Ishtar Gate to the heart of the city. The walls along the Processional Way and the gate itself (fig. 3–3) were decorated in colorful

◀ **3–3** In a modern reconstruction, rows of identical lions parade along Babylon's Processional Way.

▲ **3–4** Facsimile of a wall painting on mud plaster from the palace at Mari showing the investiture of King Zimri-Lim, who ruled from 1779 to 1757 B.C., 65 in. (1.7 m) high.
Musée du Louvre, Paris / The Bridgeman Art Library International

glazed brick with shallow reliefs of highly stylized palm trees, bulls, lions, and fantastic dragons. Lions were the symbol of Ishtar, a widely worshipped fertility goddess.

Royal palaces in Babylon included the Summer Palace, the Northern Palace, and the Southern Palace, the last consisting of over 200 rooms and apartments clustered around five great courtyards. A ziggurat in Babylon was said to have had eight tiers and reached a height of 300 feet (92 m); it appears in the biblical Book of Genesis as the Tower of Babel. Also famous—but also now completely vanished, their very nature the subject of speculation, were the Hanging Gardens of Babylon, praised by the Greek historian Herodotos and considered, along with the walls of Babylon, one of the Seven Wonders of the Ancient World. The Hanging Gardens are thought by some to have been given their name because they rose in several terraces; they may even have been planted on the upper levels of the ziggurat. Also on the Euphrates but 250 miles (400 km) north of Babylon was the prosperous commercial center of Mari,

controlled by people who, in the Old Testament of the Bible, are called the Amorites. Here at Mari was the temple of Ishtar and the great palace of King Zimri-Lim, a contemporary and onetime ally of Hammurabi. His palace covered 15 acres and was rich in its art (fig. 3–4) and its archive of 20,000 clay documents. Hammurabi turned against Zimri-Lim c. 1757 B.C. and had Mari largely destroyed.

In 538 B.C. Babylon and its dominions were captured by the Persian leader Cyrus the Great, and Mesopotamia fell under rule of the Persian Empire.

The Assyrians (884–612 B.C.)

The Assyrian people from the northern part of Mesopotamia had previously been held in subjection to other Mesopotamians, but they came to power themselves during the last two centuries of the first millennium B.C. Their capital was first at Assur, then at Nimrud, and finally at Nineveh. Their chief rulers were Assurnasirpal (884–859),

▲ **3–5** One of a pair of winged bulls with human heads (and five legs) flanking the palace entrance at Dur Sharrukin, Assyria, c. 720 B.C., limestone, 13 ft. 10 in. (4.2 m) high.
Scala/Art Resource, NY

Sargon II (722–705), Sennacherib (705–681), and Assurbanipal (668–626). These rulers commanded impressive armies, and their empire extended beyond Mesopotamia to Syria, Palestine, Cyprus, and even parts of Egypt.

In the fifth year of his reign, Sargon II built a great palace for himself at Dur Sharrukin (now modern Khorsabad). It straddled the city wall on a raised terrace 1,000 feet (300 m) long and 25 feet (8 m) high. The royal apartments and reception rooms were decorated with wall paintings and reliefs, and the entrance to the throne room was flanked by a giant pair of exotic winged bulls with human heads (fig. 3–5) carved from imported limestone.

The last great Assyrian capital city was Nineveh, which King Assurbanipal embellished with a splendid palace of its own and a library holding a valuable collection of inscribed tablets. Like Babylonia, Assyria was eventually captured by the Persian leader Cyrus the Great and became part of the Persian Empire, a few years after Assurbanipal's death in 626 B.C.

The Persians (538–331 B.C.)

Like Mesopotamia to its west, Persia was early to develop agriculture and settled communities. Unlike much of Mesopotamia, it enjoyed a good supply of building stone. The dynasty founded there by Cyrus the Great was named in honor of a mythical king, Achaemenes, from whom Cyrus claimed to be descended. The period dominated by that dynasty is therefore sometimes called Achaemenid Persian. After Cyrus's army of Persians captured Babylon in 538 B.C., it conquered Egypt in 525, and by 480 B.C. the Persian Empire had become the largest that the world had ever known. It stretched from the Danube River in what is now Germany to the Indus River in what is now Pakistan.

The capital of this empire moved from place to place, but the great royal complex remained at Persepolis, (now Takht-I-Jamshı̄-d), at the foot of the mountains near the Persian Gulf. Today ruins of Persepolis constitute the empire's principal relic. Its construction took almost sixty years, having been begun about 518 B.C. by one of Cyrus's successors, King Darius, and completed in 460 B.C. by Darius's son and heir, King Xerxes.

The vast royal complex was a citadel with ceremonial and administrative elements for state occasions. It was raised on a series of platforms from 20 to 50 feet (6–15 m) above the surrounding plain, and down below was a sprawling group of palaces for lesser royalty. The platforms

---

Viewpoints | AN ART THEORIST LOOKS AT A BULL STATUE

Noted twentieth-century art theorist and psychologist Rudolf Arnheim wrote in his book *Art and Visual Perception* (1954) that there is a type of sculpture in which " . . . the variety of aspects is reduced to the four that are the perceptually simplest: the symmetrical views of front and back and the two profiles." He stated that "the independence of the four views is most strikingly illustrated by the winged bulls

. . . that served as gatekeepers of Assyrian palaces. Viewed from the front, such an animal shows two symmetrical front legs standing still. The side view has four legs walking. This means that from an oblique point of observation we count five legs. But such adding up of unrelated elements violates the intended concept. The important thing for the Assyrians was the completeness of each view in itself."

covered an area roughly 900 feet wide by 1,400 feet long (about 300 × 450 m). Beneath the platforms was a great system of drainage tunnels, and climbing the platforms from the west was a monumental stairway (fig. 3–6) with generous treads, gentle risers, and handsomely carved stone parapets. These carvings depicted a seemingly endless parade of warriors, each identical to the next, all obviously fiercely loyal to the Persian Empire. This anonymous but innumerable force must have impressed all who saw it with the invulnerability of Persia. As a design it employed the power of repetition on a scale never before imagined. With building stone available, the ancient Persians were able to construct a columnar architecture that would have been impossible with the mud bricks of the Mesopotamians. One example of such columnar architecture is the Chehil Minar or Audience Hall in the royal complex. It is 250 feet (76 m) square, and it originally held thirty-six columns 64 feet (20 m) tall. The dozen columns that remain show them to have been more slender than their counterparts in either Egypt or Greece. The column shafts were finely carved into **flutes**, parallel vertical semicircular grooves or channels, such as had begun to be used in Greece, leading some to speculate that the stone carvers may have been Greek. The columns must have supported a wooden roof, because their small size and wide spacing would not have carried beams of stone. The room's brick walls were faced with tiles, their brightly enameled surfaces depicting animals and flowers. Beyond the Audience Hall, similarly columned antechambers adjoined it on three sides.

Another major space is the Throne Hall or Hall of the Hundred Columns. In this room, it is said, King Xerxes sat on a golden throne under a golden canopy. Its columns are more closely spaced than in the Audience Hall, and they did, in fact, number a hundred. Their **capitals**, the upper parts of their shafts, are topped with curious pairs of bulls' heads and forequarters. A depression between these bulls' heads formed an unusual sort of "cradle" that held a wooden beam (fig. 3–7). There is no known precedent for this column design. Similar columns elsewhere in the palace were in the shape of pairs of bulls' heads with the forequarters of lions, or unicorns (mythical horselike beasts with single horns in the middle of their foreheads), or eagles (or perhaps griffins, mythical animals with eagles' heads and lions' bodies).

In 331 B.C. Alexander the Great of Greece defeated Darius III, conquered Persia, ended its empire, and sacked Persepolis—perhaps in revenge for Persian raids on the Athenian Acropolis 150 years earlier. The stones of

▼ **3–6** At the great ceremonial center of Persepolis, carved reliefs on the balustrade of the great stair, 518–460 B.C.
© Werner Forman/CORBIS All Rights Reserved

▲ **3–7** A column capital in the shape of a pair of bulls' heads. Now in the Louvre, Paris, the capital was from the Hall of the Hundred Columns, Persepolis.
Two bulls' heads. Capital and pillar. Grey limestone. From Susa, Iran. Musée du Louvre/RMN Reunion des Musées Nationaux, France. Erich Lessing/Art Resource, NY

Persepolis that remain, however, still make a profound impression.

The Sasanians (A.D. 224–636)

After Alexander's capture and sack of Persepolis, the story of the Ancient Near East becomes part of the stories of Greece and Rome. An exception, however, was the Sasanian (or "New Persian") dynasty that was founded in A.D. 224, when the Sasanian ruler Ataxerxes conquered the Parthians. The Sasanians traced their history to a (perhaps legendary) figure named Sasan. Lasting four centuries, the Sasanian Empire was ruled by an efficient bureaucracy, and its chief rulers, invested with symbolic power by the state religion, were given such names as Artaxerxes and Shapur. The empire's capital cities included Susa and Ktesiphon, on the Tigris River south of Baghdad.

Only a small part of the palace at Ktesiphon remains (fig. 3–8), but it includes a great royal reception room in the form of an **iwan** (a vaulted hall open at one end), an element that will later be often used by Islamic builders in the Near East and India. The parabolic vault covering the hall was 114 feet (35 m) high. Built of brick without **centering** (a temporary structure to support the construction until it becomes self-supporting), it was the largest of its type in the world. The opening of the iwan was flanked by an extensive façade in which engaged columns and niches form a pattern of **blind arcades** (decorative arcades without actual openings) in six levels.

The Sasanians were driven from their lands by Arabs in A.D. 636. That was four years after the death of the prophet Muhammad, founder of the worldwide religion of Islam, which would come to dominate this region's politics and culture—and its art and architecture.

▲ 3–8 The vaulted royal reception room of the Sasanian palace at Ktesiphon, built in the mid-sixth century A.D. The right half of the part shown here collapsed in 1888.
Royal Geographical Society, London, UK/The Bridgeman Art Library International

Furniture of the Ancient Near East

The furniture of Mesopotamia and Persia has not survived, and what we know of it is based almost wholly on depictions, which were carved in sculpture, in relief panels and plaques, or on **cylinder seals**, small embossed cylinders that could be rolled through wax, moist clay, or ink to leave an image or inscription. Some cylinder seals were no larger than a little finger, but they have left us much valuable information.

The peasant of the Ancient Near East probably had no furniture other than a few cushions. Most middle-class seating seems to have been made of wood (a costly material) and woven reeds. Some storage pieces, which we might today call sideboards, appear to have been made of wood lattice. For the royal furniture of Babylonia and Assyria, more precious materials were also employed: bronze, gold, silver, and inlays of ebony and ivory.

Surviving images indicate a taste for elaborate ornamentation. Chair legs and their **stretchers**, the bracing members that connect the legs and strengthen the construction, were often elaborately **turned**, rotated on a lathe and shaped with cutting tools into a series of swellings, concavities, and disklike shapes. The legs sometimes terminate in carvings imitating animal paws. Some chair legs rest on inverted cones, resembling small, upside-down ziggurats. Chair backs are often elaborately scrolled. A good example can be seen in the carving at Persepolis, which shows Darius the Great seated on his throne (fig. 3–9).

▲ 3–9 A relief carving at Persepolis shows King Darius's throne and footstool with turned legs and stringers.
Courtesy of the Oriental Institute of the University of Chicago

There were stools as well as chairs, and the folding stool is depicted as early as 2300 B.C., suggesting that its appearance in the Near East may have been earlier than in Egypt. Squarish four-legged stools that did not fold are also depicted.

Decorative Arts of the Ancient Near East

We saw in prehistoric art the tendency toward realistic representation, later joined by symbolic abstraction. Both realism and abstraction were present in the art of the Ancient Near East, as they were in Egypt. In the abstract realm, there were patterns that were purely geometric—squares, rectangles, circles—and some that were geometricized versions of plant forms.

Some Ancient Near Eastern decoration has already been mentioned—processions of carved figures, reliefs of lions, bull-headed column capitals, turnings on chair legs. Altogether, this decorative art was highly stylized, brightly colored, and often exotic in subject matter.

Characteristic of Ancient Near Eastern art are animalistic decorations that are realistic yet strange. At about the same time that the Egyptians were carving the human-headed lion we call the Sphinx, the artists of the Near East were painting, carving, or inlaying figures that were also fantastic hybrids. In addition to the Assyrian bulls with wings and human heads that we saw in figure 3–6, the people of the Ancient Near East imagined female human figures with the heads of a lioness, scorpions with men's heads, and other bizarre composite creatures. Their exact meaning is a mystery not yet solved.

Wall Treatments

In addition to the carved reliefs, walls were sometimes faced with tile or brick with a glazed enamel surface. One unusual

▲ **3–10** Babylonian decoration formed by colored clay cones hammered into a mud wall.
© Bildarchiv Preussischer Kulturbesitz/Art Resource, NY

sort of **mosaic** (a decorative panel composed of small pieces) frequently used by the Babylonians was in the form of pointed clay cones, their circular flat surfaces brightly colored. The cones, after being painted or glazed, were hammered into the walls, with only the colored circles left exposed (fig. 3–10).

Walls were also painted with frescoes, only a few remnants of which have survived. On a base of white lime, these were painted in flat tones without the use of shading or perspective. The pigments were of mineral origin, such as calcite for white, azurite for blue, malachite for green, and various soils for reds, browns, and yellows. The few remaining fragments show that subject matter included religious figures, winged lions and other mythical beasts, and fancifully stylized trees and plants.

Tools & Techniques | THE POTTER'S WHEEL

Although the development of the potter's wheel is credited to the Ancient Near East, it may have been developed simultaneously and quite independently in China and ancient Greece. It is simply a flat disk that can be rotated on a central shaft, propelled either by hand or by kicking (or, in modern times, of course, by electric power), and it aids the forming of clay by using centrifugal force. Such wheels are still in use today, and the act of forming ceramic shapes on a wheel is called "throwing."

Metalwork

Because the Near East had limited mineral resources, it is remarkable how early metalworking began there (c. 6000 B.C., long before any of the ruling dynasties mentioned here) and how sophisticated it became. The **lost-wax** technique used in Egypt was also used in the Ancient Near East. The Sumerians made objects of gold, silver, and **bronze** (an alloy of copper and tin), and the Akkadians produced quality objects of copper. The Assyrians also worked with lead and used **cloisonné** and **filigree**, techniques we shall consider later when their use becomes more widespread. The Persians designed **rhytons**, ceremonial drinking vessels, of gold and silver, some terminating in animal heads. One example (fig. 3–11) was found among the Oxus Treasure, a hoard of precious objects and jewelry dating from the sixth to the fourth centuries B.C. and discovered in 1877.

Ceramics

Ancient Near Eastern ceramics also have a long history, a painted beaker from Susa, near Persepolis, having been dated to 4000 or 5000 B.C. Pottery was at first largely plain, utilitarian, and buff in color. White inlay was added later, then painted and incised ornamentation, often in red and black. The red-slipped ewer (fig. 3–12) from Anatolia (now Turkey), is undecorated, but its bowed handle and beak-shaped spout are spirited and sophisticated in form. Glazed terra-cotta was also used for making large figures of guard animals.

Textiles

As we saw in Chapter 1, textiles were being produced in Anatolia at least as early as the settlement at Çatal Hüyük. Basketry, weaving, sewing, and mat making probably were well developed here even before metalworking and ceramics, but fragile textiles are difficult to preserve, and little evidence remains of early examples. The chief plant fibers in use were probably flax, hemp, reed, rush, and palm, and animal fibers used were probably those from sheep, goats, deer, horses, and camels. Written texts indicate the domestication of sheep and goats and the exporting of wool before 2000 B.C. Sophisticated looms for weaving were in use in Persia by the third century A.D., if not earlier. A Sasanian woven silk (fig. 3–13), dating from the last years of the Ancient Near East, is the product of such a loom.

◀ **3–13** A Sasanian silk textile woven with a lion motif. SCALA/Art Resource, N.Y.

The Near East has long been famous for its rugs, and since ancient times there were carpets for the floors and hangings for the walls, all sumptuously colored to brighten important interiors. Although these early textiles have vanished, they are mentioned in written accounts, and some of them were imitated in more permanent colored paving stones or carved marble in areas of heavy traffic. When the weaving tradition of the Ancient Near East came into the hands of the later Persians, they would continue to produce rugs that came to be the envy of all Europe.

Summary: Ancient Near Eastern Design

The varied styles of the Ancient Near East shared some strong common characteristics. They were rhythmic and energetic. They possessed a high degree of stylization. In many examples—a man clasping a pair of lions, a tree flanked by a pair of winged men—they displayed a heraldic symmetry. In others, axes were bent and processional routes were repeatedly turned, adding a sense of mystery and anticipation, while sacrificing the nobility of a more axial approach.

Looking for Quality

The subject matter of Ancient Near Eastern art and decoration seems to our eyes full of strangeness. We see animals performing actions that, in reality, we have never observed. We also see composite beasts never encountered except in myths and dreams. It was an art apparently intended to amaze or even terrify, not to ingratiate or comfort, and its exotic display will be glimpsed again in the mysterious art of the Byzantine Empire and in the later Islamic art of Syria and Palestine.

Looking for Character

It was also an art determined to impress. Perhaps its most striking single characteristic is its use of repetition. The repetition of columns at Persepolis is one of many possible examples. The Ancient Near Eastern artists apparently never worried that regimentation would bore their audience and dull the mind. They knew that instead the multiple images would inspire awe, respect, and perhaps even fear at the power of the rulers who could command such numbers.

Making Comparisons

The Ancient Near East failed, as almost all subsequent cultures have failed, to match the controlled grace and elegant polish of Egyptian art. The Ancient Near East also lacked, as do all other cultures, the harmony, balance, and humanism we shall see in the architecture of Greece, an art that was beginning to develop at the same time. But Ancient Near Eastern art had a robust vitality and an insistence on reinforcing the strengths of the cultures' military powers in ways that, in the end, cannot be ignored. It was an art that achieved its goals.

Greece

2000–30 B.C.

"The great decorators . . . were ever governed, in the use of ornamental detail,
by . . . the 'wise moderation' of the Greeks."

— Edith Wharton (1862–1937), American writer and interior designer

The ancient Greeks reached unprecedented heights of accomplishment in philosophy, ethics, politics, and the fine arts, reflecting a respect for nature and humanity. Even their gods were given human appearances and traits (fig. 4–1). The Greeks also showed predilection toward restraint, an attitude we still respect. For all their accomplishments, however, the frequent creation of outstanding interiors was not among them, yet so sublime was their architecture that its elements are still in use, not only on the exteriors of our buildings, but also in our interiors, and frequently in our furniture. The elements of Greek architecture are still an important part of our design vocabulary. Whether or not today's designers ever work in the classical idiom, they still learn the basic elements of Greek architecture (table 4–1, page 56), and an understanding of the relationships among those elements is an essential part of design literacy.

◄ **4–1** From the east frieze of the Parthenon, Athens, the gods Poseidon (left) and Apollo converse on stools (diphroi) with turned legs. c. 440 B.C., 42 in. (106 cm) high.
Erich Lessing/Art Resource, NY

The Beginnings of the Classical World

The early Greek artists were undoubtedly influenced by Egyptian art. This is seen in their continued use of the column and lintel form of construction that the Egyptians had used extensively. The Greeks refined the Egyptian column, made it a less literal copy of natural forms (such as bundled reeds), made it more slender and more graceful, allowed it more space, and used more moldings for its enrichment. In place of the convex tubes of Egyptian columns, Greek columns were faced with concave grooves called **flutings**. Influence from the Ancient Near East in general and from Persia in particular was most notable in Greece in the seventh century B.C.: The century has come to be called Greece's Orientalizing period. Relationships between Greece and Persia were not always friendly. Expansion of the Persian Empire led to the Persian Wars, which lasted for fifty years beginning in 499 B.C. From these, however, Greece emerged victorious and with a greater degree of unity than it had previously enjoyed. A later conflict came in 331 B.C., when Alexander the Great, the mighty warrior from Macedon in northern Greece, conquered Persia and burned Persepolis.

Date	Period	Political and Cultural Events	Artistic Accomplishments
1000–700 B.C.	Geometric	Olympic Games instituted, 776 B.C.	Vases and ornament with geometric designs
700–600 B.C.	Orientalizing	Alexander the Great conquers Egypt, 332 B.C.	Influences from the Near East, including curvilinear designs
600–480 B.C.	Archaic	Greek victory in the Persian Wars, 480 B.C.	Vase painting; early Doric temples; proto-Ionic columns
480–404 B.C.	Classical	Greek drama, poetry, history, philosophy; Pericles, 495–429 B.C.; Sparta defeats Athens, 404 B.C.	Perfection of the Doric and Ionic orders; buildings on the Acropolis, including the Parthenon
404–323 B.C.	"Fourth Century"	Death of Alexander, 323 B.C.	Introduction of Corinthian order
323–146 B.C.	Hellenistic	Roman conquest, 146 B.C.	Venus de Milo; Altar at Pergamon

There were other factors as well that shaped Greece, among them the examples of earlier cultures. The most remarkable of those cultures—according to our present knowledge—were on the island of Crete and at Mycenae, on the mainland of Greece.

Crete

Crete, 60 miles (97 km) from the Greek mainland, is a narrow strip of an island, 170 miles (275 km) long. An agricultural society may have existed there from c. 6000 B.C., joined c. 3000 B.C. by emigrants from Asia Minor who brought with them new metalworking skills for making tools and weapons. The Cretans enjoyed extensive trade routes to central Europe, from which they imported tin and copper. They built important cities, centered on impressive compounds of reigning priest-kings, but the largest, most sumptuous palace compound was at Knossos, near the center of the northern coast. It was the palace of King Minos, a ruler whose name has been taken for the entire culture—the Minoans.

Although the Minoan influence on classical Greece (either directly or indirectly through the Mycenaeans) is difficult to trace, Minoan influence on the contemporaneous cultures of Egypt and the Ancient Near East is clearer. Minoan artifacts have been found in both places, indicating the existence of trade and, to some degree, an admiration for their culture.

There was much to admire, not least the prevalence of a lighthearted, fanciful character. In many cultures and periods we will survey, religion dominated the architecture and design; in others, the need for military security was paramount. What we know of Crete, however, suggests that most of its art was created for the pleasure of living.

Unfortunately, the history of Crete was punctuated by disasters. Around 1700 B.C. a major earthquake destroyed most of the structures on the island, including the first palaces. Around 1470 B.C. a catastrophic volcanic eruption sent tremors, tidal waves, and volcanic ash over Crete. A final disaster, probably an invasion by the Mycenaeans from the Greek mainland, occurred around 1380 B.C., causing the abandonment of most of the palace centers.

Minoan Architecture   The city of Knossos is thought to have had a population of about 100,000, including those in the great palace compound. The palace complex (fig. 4–2) is roughly rectangular, some 320 feet (98 m) from north to south and almost 500 feet (154 m) from east to west. Its rectangular central court is its most immediately striking element. The side walls of the court are diverse in function and appearance, many freely disposed elements being given monumental façades and porticoes.

▼ **4–2** Drawing of the palace complex at Knossos, Crete.
c. 1990–1375 B.C.
Courtesy McRae Books, Florence

▲ **4–3** Reconstruction of a room in the queen's quarters of the palace at Knossos. The portico looks into one of the palace's many light shafts.
Corbis/Bettman

▲ **4–4** The brightly frescoed throne room of the palace at Knossos. The king's throne is surrounded by benches for his council.
Giraudon/The Bridgeman Art Library International

This diversity pervades the complex that surrounds the court. The impression of a chaotic lack of design belies a skilled arrangement of some of the parts: Many rooms open to loggias or terraces (fig. 4–3) with carefully framed views of the landscape or the central court. The palace's **circulation pattern**—a traffic system dictated by the layout of doors, corridors, and stairs—is a free and open one, with long corridors leading from one part to another. There are also many exits and entrances between rooms, rather than rooms entered only from the corridors. The palace's most splendid and significant room is the throne room (fig. 4–4), which contains a stone throne built for the ruler and a row of stone benches at each side for his council. Its walls are covered with frescoes of mythical beasts and foliage. A stately and commodious staircase (fig. 4–5) connects three floors of the palace, wrapped around a large light well. It is lined by a procession of fourteen distinctively tapered columns, which, quite unlike earlier Egyptian columns and later Greek ones, flare outward so that they are larger at their tops than at their bases.

According to myth, the legendary craftsman and inventor Daedalus, who had fled from Greece to Crete, was ordered by King Minos to build a labyrinth near the palace that was used to conceal the Minotaur (a creature half human and half bull), but no evidence of the labyrinth (or the creature) has been found.

Minoan Pottery   The ceramic arts in Minoan Crete developed with ever increasing skill and exuberance and show an artistic excellence that may have influenced the Greeks. As will be true of later Greek wares, Minoan pottery was varied in its number of shapes but limited in its colors (most often buff, gray, and red). Some examples were left plain, some marked with incisions, some decorated with spirals, curvaceous floral motifs, or marine creatures (fig. 4–6). Handles and spouts were often integral parts of the ornamental patterns. Early Minoan pottery was made by hand, but the potter's wheel was introduced in the twentieth century B.C. Fine examples of painted pottery have been dated to the twelfth century B.C. and even earlier, both on mainland Greece and in the Aegean islands.

Murals of Akrotiri   In the Cyclades, which is a cluster of islands north of Crete and south of the Greek mainland, is the island of Thera (now called Santorini). About 1600 B.C. a violent volcanic eruption changed the shape of the island

▼ **4–5** The staircase of the Knossos palace, its columned flights wrapping around a light well open to the sky.
Roger Wood/Corbis/Bettman

▼ **4–6** Minoan jar wth the figure of an octopus, 11 in. (27 cm).
SCALA/Art Resource, NY

▲ **4–7** "Spring Fresco" mural from a house at Akrotiri on the Cycladic island of Thera, near Crete, c. 1650 B.C.
Studio Kontos Photostock

and buried many towns in ash. One of these towns was Akrotiri, where archaeologists have found houses (not palaces as on Crete) with murals that were remarkably well preserved in the ash. One example (fig. 4–7), has been called the "Spring Fresco." Devoid of human figures, it is a romantic landscape of colorful rocks, swaying plants, and flying swallows, full of the same sinuous movement and carefree spirit often seen in Minoan pottery.

Mycenae

Mycenaean culture lasted slightly longer than Minoan. The Mycenaeans occupied the entire southern part of mainland Greece; their language was an early form of Greek, and they also left the Greeks technical skills in pottery making, metallurgy, and architecture.

The culture was centered in the city of Mycenae, from which it took its name, but other important Mycenaean cities were Tiryns and Pylos. The Mycenaeans are thought to have entered Greece from the north c. 2000 or 1900 B.C., gaining supremacy in the Aegean after the violent destruction of Knossos c.1380 B.C.—perhaps because of their own invasion of Crete—and ruling until c. 1200 B.C. Like the Minoans, the Mycenaeans erected large palaces and decorated them with bas-reliefs and brightly colored frescoes. They also made pottery and metalwork painted with both geometric and naturalistic designs.

The Palace and Megaron Palaces and towns in Mycenae were sited on hilltops or other easily protected locations and were strongly walled. Some of the walls were built thick enough to contain a network of corridors and storage rooms for arms and food. Massive fortified walls surrounding the Mycenaean palace were interrupted by only two gates, one of them—the Lion Gate—topped by sculptured figures of two lionesses, now headless.

▲ **4–8** Reconstruction of the possible appearance of the megaron of Pylos.
Piet de Jong, The Throne Room of the Megaron. Reproduced by permission of the Department of Classics, University of Cincinnati.

Related to this concern for protection, the Mycenaean palaces were not centered, like the Minoan ones, on large open courtyards, but on spacious interior halls called **megara**, meaning "great rooms." At Pylos, the megaron (fig. 4–8) measured 34 by 39 feet (11 × 12.5 m). The megaron was often placed at the north side of a courtyard, which it faced with a **portico** or porch that had a roof supported by columns. Beyond the portico was an entrance vestibule, and beyond the vestibule was the megaron itself, usually the largest room in the palace, centrally located and rectangular. At the center of the megaron was a fixed circular hearth, where religious rituals involving fire may have been performed. Four columns were symmetrically placed around the hearth; they supported a raised portion of roof, allowing smoke to escape and providing indirect light to enter from above. The megaron and its hearth had symbolic

Tools & Techniques | FRESCO PAINTING

Fresco is the Italian word for "fresh." When pigment is applied to freshly laid lime plaster while the plaster is still wet, it soaks into the plaster, crystallizing as it dries, and becomes an integral and long-lasting part of the surface. One difficulty is that the plaster remains wet enough to absorb the pigment for only a few hours, so large frescoes have to be painted in stages, and one day's wet pigment has to be matched to the dry pigment of the previous day's work.

▲ 4–9 Gold cup found in a tomb at Mycenae, second millennium B.C. The decoration of intertwining spirals was taken from Minoan art.

Giovanni Dagli Orti/National Archaeological Museum

significance, and some believe its use was restricted to the men of the palace.

The circulation pattern of the Mycenaean palace sites the megaron in isolation, so that it is reached only through a single door from its vestibule. Often the megaron is surrounded by a corridor, so that it does not even share a wall with any other room. Unlike the linked rooms of the Minoan palace, the principal rooms of the Mycenaean palace open onto corridors or courtyards that provide the rooms' only access. This type of circulation pattern was to be seen later in the Greek house and, after it, in the Roman house.

Mycenaean Burial Structures   Other Mycenaean structures were related to burial rituals, including a shaft grave and a round, beehive-shaped burial chamber called a **tholos**. The tholos was built of stone, and, except for narrow entrance passageways, the tholoi were generally buried in earth. Their distinctive shape was engineered to resist the earth's weight. Among the treasures found in tholoi are works by Mycenaean goldsmiths: gold funeral masks, gold drinking cups (fig. 4–9), gold signet rings, and gold weapons with figurative black inlay. The Greeks would later adapt the circular plan of the tholos for places of assembly or ritual; their interiors would sometimes be ringed with a circular bench and their exteriors sometimes ringed with columns.

Determinants of Greek Design

Although the natural setting, religion, and history of the Greek people cannot fully explain the brilliance of their accomplishments, they can at least partly explain the development of Greek character.

Geography and Natural Resources

As in Egypt and the Ancient Near East, geography was again an influence on the civilization that occupied it. While the geography of Egypt, ringed by desert, had imposed centuries of isolation on the Egyptian culture, the more exposed geography of Greece encouraged interaction with other lands and peoples.

Greece comprises a large peninsula extending south toward the Mediterranean Sea, and many islands in the Ionian Sea to its west and in the Aegean Sea to its east. The climate and geography of this country are different from those of Egypt and produced different effects on those who lived there. The long, ragged Greek coastline with many bays and inlets bounds a fertile land of sunshine and rain. Tall mountains tower above it.

An important contributing factor to the character and detail of Greek architecture and decoration was the ready availability in those mountains of a perfect building material: marble. Harder than alabaster but softer than granite, this magnificent white stone had a fine grain and texture and could be cut easily into shapes having minute details with crisp edges. It was found on the Greek peninsula as well as on the adjacent islands, the most prized being the Parian marble from Paros, one of the islands called the Cyclades, and the Pentelic marble from the Pentelikon mountain of central Greece, northeast of Athens.

This mountainous topography of the land tended to isolate neighboring communities, which resulted in misunderstandings, jealousies, and a lack of amity. Strife between isolated city-states was constant and political cohesion unattainable. Ancient Greece remained a loose federation of communities, led by the most advanced and accomplished of them: Athens.

The geographical character of peninsula and islands produced a race of seafaring people, and the search for metals and other materials and for new trade opportunities impelled the Greeks to adventurous sea travel. Far from home, they encountered foreign and often subversive ideas.

With foreign ideas to consider, and with local character a matter of rivalry and pride, independence of thought developed, making the Greeks the great individualists of antiquity. They were adamant in their desire for freedom to act, speak, and think as they wished. They considered as barbarians all those who lived under despots, accepted rule blindly, or lived without liberty, which included most of the then-known world. They regarded wisdom as the greatest of human attributes, and to attain it, they thought it essential to be curious and inquisitive, to doubt and to question all things until they were proved. To know truth and to understand were the Greeks' passions.

Religion

The dramatic geography of Greece and her islands also influenced Greek religion, which was founded on the worship of nature. Special gods and goddesses were thought to embody the spirits of places. Mountains, valleys, islands, and harbors were protected by their own guardian divinities. Each god was also associated by the Greeks with one of the fundamental forces of nature.

The greatest three of these gods were Zeus, Athena, and Apollo. Zeus, the supreme god, was associated with earth and heaven and was responsible for storms and darkness; he was supposed to favor the locations of Olympia and Dodona. Athena, queen of the air, was especially linked with the city of Athens. And Apollo, the sun god, had as his favorite sites Delos and Delphi.

Greek divinities were peculiarly human. For the Greeks, humanity was the focus of attention and admiration, and the Greek gods were not the divine, supernatural, mysterious beings we find in most religions. They were slightly larger-than-life but still quite recognizable men and women. They were credited with powers that humans are denied, but their ambitions, problems, weaknesses, and passions were very human indeed.

The Greeks honored these near-human deities with shrines and temples that were appropriately scaled—not as modest as Greek domestic architecture, but far less grandiose than the monuments of Giza, Luxor, Babylon, or Persepolis. Greek religious art is fully comprehensible to a human observer, and gods and goddesses, heroes and heroines, men and women were all considered joint participants in a remarkably balanced life. The Greek religion focused on life, not on an afterlife. Emotional satisfactions attained full scope in religious festivals and processions, athletic games, and every phase of private life. Idealism was maintained in all the best creative efforts.

Political and Military Factors

The population of Greece itself was composed of many diverse groups. One of these was the Dorian people, originally barbarians from the northwestern mountains. Between 1100 and 950 B.C., they swept down into the Greek mainland, possibly bringing iron tools with them, and settled largely in Crete and Sparta. It is for them that the **Doric order** is named, the simpler and sturdier of the two main Greek **orders**, or building styles.

As the Dorians penetrated the Greek peninsula, several groups already living there fled elsewhere. Some settled in Ionia, a strip of land along the coast of what is now Turkey, which therefore became part of the Greek world. Others settled on some of the islands in the Aegean. It is for them that the **Ionic order** is named, the more delicate of the two main Greek orders.

As a nation, the Greeks were essentially proud and convinced, not without reason, that they were superior to all others as warriors, artists, philosophers, mathematicians, and writers. The first duty of every Greek citizen was service to the state, which included its glorification and the promotion of its cultural development. Its city-states, the semi-autonomous cities with their surrounding, dependent lands, were small enough that every individual could be known.

The isolation of Greek city-states from one another also brought a regrettable amount of warfare. Throughout Greek history, one city-state quarreled with another. The most famous quarrel was that between Athens and Sparta, the city-state settled by Dorians and nestled in a mountain-ringed valley. The Spartans were courageous, self-disciplined, and warlike, but lacked Athens's impressive numbers of philosophers, historians, or artists. Sparta defeated Athens in 404 B.C., but Athens's idealism and achievements proved to be immortal.

By the standards of all the cultures that had preceded it, Greece was a marvel of democracy—for men. Only men had the rights of citizenships; women and slaves were not citizens. For male citizens both freedom and equality were enjoyed. Extremes of wealth and poverty were little tolerated, and wealth was seldom displayed.

The happy result of the Greek spirit of service to the state and the Greek version of democracy was that the greatest amount of available funds, effort, and artistry was spent not on glorifying individual citizens, political leaders, or military figures, but on glorifying the locality's resident gods and goddesses. For most of their history, the Greeks themselves lived modestly while enshrining their deities in some of the most perfect structures ever built.

The Chronology of Greek Art

In Greek art, we see a development toward increasingly naturalistic representation of the known world. And throughout this development we see an equally striking desire to find order in (or to superimpose order on) our bewildering human experience. The advancement of Greek art and architecture was remarkably steady. Even so, scholars divide the development into three formative periods—the Geometric, the Orientalizing, and the Archaic—followed by three mature periods—the Classical, the "Fourth Century" (or Late Classical), and the Hellenistic. All, of course, had been preceded by prehistoric phases—a Stone Age, which occurred in Greece around 4000 B.C., and a Bronze Age, occurring around 2800 B.C.—but little evidence has been discovered that could tell us what those times were like.

Three Formative Periods

Three early phases—the Geometric, Orientalizing, and Archaic periods—established the foundation for the great flowering of Greek art that would immediately follow.

Geometric Period (1000–700 B.C.) The earliest stage of truly Greek art, considered to have begun about 1000 B.C., is termed the Geometric period. In contrast to the naturalistic and fluid style of Crete, its decoration was highly

▲ **4–10** An amphora from the Geometric period, late ninth century B.C., 20 in. (51 cm) high.

abstract and angular, more akin to the style of Mycenae. Limited in type and formal in character, we find pottery vases, for example (fig. 4–10), displayed with elaborate panels and horizontal bands of linear, geometric patterns—circles, triangles, squares, diamonds, and zigzag shapes. Even when human and animal forms were finally reintroduced, they were at first highly schematic, reduced to a series of geometric shapes.

The Olympic Games were initiated near the end of this period, in 776 B.C. to honor Zeus, the supreme god. Because the games, held every four years, represented an unusual expression of national unity and cooperation, the Greeks themselves considered this date the true beginning of their civilization.

Orientalizing Period (700–600 B.C.)

The seventh century B.C. is often called the Orientalizing period of Greek art, as influences from the Ancient Near East brought more lifelike representations as well as the introduction of arabesques and floral decoration. New subject matter appeared, such as stylized plants, animals, birds, and mythical beasts, which better expressed actual Greek life and thought. A pitcher found on the Cycladic island of Paros (fig. 4–11) has its spout in the head of a griffin, a beast that was half eagle and half lion. Other influences from the Ancient Near East came from trading for luxury goods—spices, perfumes, textiles, and objects made of ivory and precious metals. Imported to Greece as well were the alphabet, astronomy, and mythology. Other new ideas came from Egypt, which had been visited by Greek seafarers. Egypt would remain a source of inspiration for the Greeks for a long time. (Alexander the Great would found his city Alexandria there in 331 B.C.)

Archaic Period (600–480 B.C.) During the time of the Persian Wars, the Archaic period saw the flourishing of vase painting, and sculpture became a major form of Greek artistic expression. Statues of sphinxes, adapted from Egyptian

▲ **4–12** A marble sphinx from Delphi, c. 560 B.C., 91 in. (230 cm) high. It sits on an early version of an Ionic column.

precedents, were also produced. An example (fig. 4–12) found at Delphi, the site favored by Apollo and the home of the famous Delphic oracle, is perched on an early version of an Ionic column, the volutes of its capital spread more widely from the column shaft than would be the case in later versions.

Greek architecture, too, was becoming a recognizably powerful artistic form around the beginning of the Archaic period. Large limestone and stucco temples were built by the Dorians, both in Greece and in the Greek colonies in Sicily, southern Italy, and elsewhere. The Dorians, originally barbarians from the northwestern mountains, had swept down into the Greek mainland between 1100 and 950 B.C., perhaps, as we have said, with iron tools, and settled largely in Crete and Sparta. The Dorians built temples that were massive, and their design was dominated by rows of columns on the outside of the buildings. One of the earliest examples of a recognizable Doric style is seen in the great cluster of temples at Paestum in southern Italy, which demonstrate robust early versions of the Doric order (fig. 4–13). The columns are thick with exaggerated swelling, and they are topped with wide and sturdy capitals. At Paestum the subtle refinements of the finished Doric

order have not yet been worked out, but the Doric temple has already begun to express itself with authority and strength.

Three Mature Periods

Even in the transition from its formative to its mature phases, Greek art showed a remarkable consistency in artistic vocabulary. There are no abrupt changes, no swings of fashion, no shifting of goals, no abandonment of ideals. Once an agreed-upon standard was reached in the formative periods, it was repeated in the mature periods with only minor changes. The pinnacle of Greek art, therefore, is generally thought to be in its first mature period, when many of the standards were first set.

Classical Period (480–404 B.C.) The Classical period marks the time of greatest artistic achievement in ancient

◀ **4–13** Inside the ruins of an early Doric temple dedicated to Athena at Paestum, southern Italy, built c. 510 B.C. Abercrombie

Greece. It came between Greece's victory in the Persian Wars with the Battle of Marathon in 480 B.C. and Athens's defeat by Sparta in the Peloponnesian War in 404 B.C. This time is variously called the Classical period, the Golden Age, or the Age of Pericles, the Athenian statesman who lived c. 495–429 B.C. and led the country to an unprecedentedly democratic form of government. In the fifth century the city of Athens was at the height of its artistic and intellectual glory. This was the age of the Greek dramatists Aeschylus, Sophocles, Euripides, and Aristophanes, the poet Pindar, the historians Herodotus and Thucydides, and the master of philosophers, Socrates. The harmonic proportions of the Doric and Ionic orders were perfected in this period, with a number of great Doric monuments built in Athens, including the Hephaestum in 465 B.C., the Parthenon (c. 447–432 B.C.), and the Propylaea (437–432 B.C.). The most magnificent of the Ionic temples were built at Miletus, but the Ionic order was also employed for the Erechtheum on the Athenian Acropolis (421–405 B.C.) and for the interior of the nearby Propylaea.

The Fourth Century (404–323 B.C.)   The "Fourth Century" is a term loosely applied to the period from the defeat of Athens (404 B.C.) to the death of Alexander the Great at Babylon (323 B.C.), although the term *Late Classical* is also used. Although Athens had been defeated, Greek civilization expanded. This was the time of the orator Demosthenes, the philosophers Plato and Aristotle, and the "father of medicine," Hippocrates. Greek art continued to be increasingly realistic, but the ideal forms of the Classical period were replaced by more emotional forms, as seen in the works of gifted sculptor Praxiteles. In architecture, the Corinthian order began to be used, although it never rivaled the Doric and Ionic orders in popularity with the Greeks.

Hellenistic Period (323–146 B.C.)   The effects of Alexander's conquests spread Greek culture over the Near East and far into Asia, with important new centers at Pergamon, Rhodes, and Alexandria. Advances were made in mathematics and science, but, compared with their earlier achievements, Greek literature became relatively ponderous, Greek architecture relatively complicated, and Greek art relatively sentimental. Even so, many familiar Greek masterpieces date from Hellenistic times, such as the sculpture of the *Venus de Milo*, her name a distortion of the Aegean island of Melos where, in her armless state, she was found. Other Hellenistic triumphs include the citadel at Pergamon and its Great Altar and remarkable friezes.

Greek Architecture and Interiors

Greek architecture is basically functional, with every feature having a practical purpose. Columns were used solely for support, never for decoration. Although structural surfaces were enriched, the ornament was never applied to a degree that would reduce the structure to secondary importance in the design.

The prehistoric inhabitants of Greece undoubtedly built their houses of wood cut from the ample forests that covered the hills and valleys of the peninsula. There is much evidence in the early stone architecture of the Greeks to indicate that details and ornament were cut in stone to imitate original wooden features, as the early Egyptian builders had also done. However, Greek architecture remains famous for its achievements in stone. The Greeks lavished most of their great architectural skills on their public buildings, and craftsmanship was carried to a supreme degree of perfection. Walls of the great temples were in solid marble throughout, with stones so accurately cut that it was not necessary to use mortar in the joints (although metal clamps were often used to tie blocks of marble together). Careful attention was given to the ratios between all the parts of the building, even to the placement of joints between stones and to the relationship of the rhythms of the stone joints and of the roof tiles above them.

Although Greek architecture now appears in the natural white of its marble (and many later imitations would be built with light-colored stone), evidence remains that the Greek buildings were originally brightly painted. Like the Egyptians, the Greeks chose colors for their symbolism and based on traditional use. Relief carvings, for example, were customarily painted in blue, green, and two shades of red, with their backgrounds painted in blue. For the relief figures of the Parthenon frieze, the background was a brilliant scarlet.

The Temples of the Gods

The Greek gods and goddesses and their innumerable offspring were first worshipped at altars open to the sky, then under increasingly elaborate shelters, these temples developing—as did the Greek house—from rounded to rectangular in plan. These last were entered at the center of one of the short sides, often between pairs of columns that formed a roofed porch. Roofs were originally of **thatch**, a covering of straw, or of **wattle and daub** (thin wood strips plastered with clay or mud). Later, roofs were made of terracotta tile.

As these temples increased in size, internal columns were also needed to support the roof. Growing still larger, the temples required two interior **colonnades**, or two rows of supporting columns. These formed a central section with side aisles and focused visitor attention on the statue, at the rear of the sanctuary, of the honored god or goddess. It was customary for these cult statues to be placed facing eastward, where they would be lighted by the morning sun, thus establishing an east–west axis that would be applied to many later temples and churches.

These early temples were composed of two elements, the sanctuary, called the **cella**, or **naos**, and the porch, called the **pronaos**, and sometimes a third element, the **adytum**, a second inner room considered more sacred than the first. Exterior walls were of mud brick, an unsatisfactory material to leave exposed to the weather, so that soon the front porch was extended to the sides and rear of the building as protection for these walls. The basic character of the Greek temple was thus established early in Greece's formative period.

Also protecting the building from weather was the slightly pitched roof ending in **pediments**, triangular portions of wall carrying the pitched roof. Cicero, in his handbook on oratory, noted that the temple pediment was first devised simply to make roofs shed their rainwater; but, having become a familiar and respected design element, the pediment would be repeated "even if one were erecting a citadel in heaven, where no rain could fall."

These basic elements—a sanctuary wrapped by a colonnade and topped with a pedimented roof—constitute the Greek temple form. It was a simple formula for a building, but one that was capable of infinite variation and the most subtle refinement. As an example, the Parthenon on the Acropolis of Athens stands as a masterpiece that, according to architectural historian A. W. Lawrence, "is the one building in the world which may be assessed as absolutely right."

The Acropolis and the Parthenon

An *acropolis*, meaning "the high point of a city," was an elevated section in a Greek town. Some of them were fortified and used for defensive purposes, like their Mycenaean predecessors, although the most famous one (spelled with a

▲ **4–14** Model of the Acropolis, Athens, as it looked c. 400 B.C.
With permission of the Royal Ontario Museum © ROM

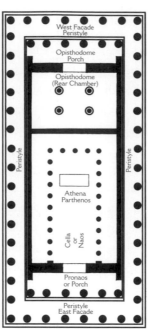
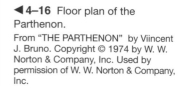

◄ **4–16** Floor plan of the Parthenon.
From "THE PARTHENON" by Viincent J. Bruno. Copyright © 1974 by W. W. Norton & Company, Inc. Used by permission of W. W. Norton & Company, Inc.

▲ **4–15** The east front of the Parthenon and its eight Doric columns.
John G. Ross/Photo Researchers, Inc.

capital A), the Acropolis at Athens (fig. 4–14), was devoted solely to religious purposes. The buildings were erected under Pericles in the latter half of the fifth century B.C., a time of wealth, security, and confidence following Athens' victories in the Persian Wars.

The Parthenon (fig. 4–15) was designed by architects Ictinus and Callicrates; Phidias was its master sculptor. Constructed from fine white Pentelic marble, it measured roughly 101 by 228 feet (31 × 69 m), for a proportion of about 4 to 9. It was **peripteral**, or surrounded with columns, with eight columns at each short end and seventeen on each long side. It stood on a **crepidoma**, a stepped platform, the upper step of which is called the **stylobate**. Within its surrounding **ambulatory**, or covered walkway, the body of the building consisted of two rooms (fig. 4–16). The smaller

Viewpoints | A MODERN DESIGNER LOOKS AT THE ACROPOLIS

Max Bill (1908–94), the Swiss architect, designer, and educator, a student at the Bauhaus and later founder of the Hochschule für Gestaltung in Ulm, Germany, wrote: "In 1935 I came to Paris. . . . Everywhere the formal canon of Greek architecture was applied—to every house and every balcony. In 1926 I arrived in Rome. . . . Everything was rooted in the Greek heritage. . . . Finally, in 1927, I came to Berlin. The flood of . . . Greek con-

tinued there. . . . In 1965 I scaled the Acropolis for the first time. . . . Amid the buildings surmounting the Acropolis there is great spatial and rhythmic unity. They stand apart, but in another sense: the buildings of the present lie as far below. Up above there continues an important lesson in aesthetics situated outside time and based on order, proportion, and space."

room was entered from the building's western porch and may have served as a treasury. The larger room, the **cella**, was entered from the eastern porch, the **pronaos**, and featured two rows of Doric columns, connected—perhaps for the first time in Greek architecture—across the back of the space. Within these columns, near the back, was placed Phidias's 40-foot-high (12 m) statue, *Athena Parthenos* (fig. 4–17). Done in gold and ivory with precious jewels for the eyes, the virgin goddess has been recreated to show how the statue may have looked in its famed setting. There are written descriptions of another sculpture by Phidias, the statue of Zeus at Olympia. Both these colossal figures were made of a composite material called **chryselephantine**, a combination of ivory veneers from Elephantine in Egypt, which was used to represent skin, and beaten gold, which was used to represent the gods' garments. In both the Parthenon and the Temple of Zeus, it is thought that shallow pools between the entrances and the statues reflected light from the exterior onto the figures of the gods. The upper part of the Parthenon's cella walls and the vertical surfaces above the porticoes constituted a 525-foot-long (170 m) frieze in shallow relief, showing the Panathenaic ("all Athens") procession, a ritual undertaken every fourth year in honor of the goddess. Masterful sculpture filled the pediments at each end of the building, the group on the eastern end representing the birth of Athena and the grouping on the western end showing the contest between Athena and Poseidon. Brilliant color was applied to parts of the stonework.

Although the harmony of the basic form of this building is impressive and the sculpture exquisite, the Parthenon was further enhanced by a number of subtle refinements. Probably never in history has greater thought been devoted to the design of one building.

The stylobate, for example, was not perfectly flat but was curved slightly upward in the center of each side, giving the whole floor a carefully calculated compound curvature. Columns near the corners of the building tilt slightly inward. Corner columns are given an added thickness of diameter and are placed slightly closer to their neighbors than typical. All columns are given a slight convex bulge or **entasis**. And inscriptions were carved with slightly larger lettering on the top lines. These refinements have been much studied but—except for the entasis, which appears on almost all columns—they have been seldom imitated.

These refinements, all deviating slightly from the expected rectangularity, repetition, and even spacing, must have

▲ **4–17** Nineteenth-Century restoration of a section through the Parthenon. Edouard Lovit, 1881.

Athena Parthenos (Athena in Cella). With permission of the Royal Ontario Museum © ROM

added a great deal of difficulty to the construction process. Not all spacings are equal; not a major line is straight; not a major surface is level. We naturally wonder why the Greeks felt these refinements were worth the effort. The most frequent speculation has been that they were calculated to correct optical illusions that, without them, would have occurred. For example, if the corner columns, which are sometimes seen in outline against the sky, were not thicker than those seen against the temple wall, they might appear to be thinner than the others. Or, if the stylobate did not rise slightly in the center, it might seem to sink; if the lettering were not adjusted, the letters would not appear from below to be of equal size. But, although the refinements are subtle, they are not invisible. They were clearly meant to be seen, and compensating for possible illusions does not seem to fully explain them. Nor does their possible functional value: The inward tilt of its columns may somehow have added to the temple's structural stability, and the curving of its stylobate may have speeded the drainage of rainwater, but these seem minor advantages for such difficult adjustments.

Undoubtedly, a heightened aesthetic experience was their goal. Perhaps the convergence, at an imaginary point roughly a mile overhead, of the centerlines of all the columns gives the composition a unity and coherence it would otherwise lack. And certainly the curving of the stylobate and the bulging of the column shafts, and the variations in their spacing, give the building a sense of movement and organicism—of being similar to the form of a living organism—that a more static building could not have achieved.

The Greek Orders

When the term *order* was first introduced earlier in this chapter, it was defined simply as a building style. It is that, but it is more. A classical order, either Greek or Roman, specifies the style of a column, the style of the **entablature** (the beamlike member that the column supports), the details of that column and entablature, and the relationships between the component parts of the whole assemblage. Such a system of specifications was not a matter of individual inspiration or originality; it developed only through years of study, trial and error, and constant refinement. In all the history of Greek architecture, there were only two principal orders, the **Doric** and the **Ionic** (Table 4–1), and one subsidiary order, the **Corinthian**.

The Doric and Ionic orders developed on opposite shores of the Aegean Sea—the Doric on the west, the Ionic on the east—though both have common elements inherited from Mycenae and Egypt. The Doric order had achieved a definite, recognizable form by the seventh century B.C., the Ionic by the sixth, and both were perfected in the fifth.

All three Greek orders are ruled by detailed guidelines about which parts best complement other parts to achieve desired results. In addition to these guidelines, however, there were other considerations for the Greek builders. Their attention was applied to the ratios between all parts, to the placement of joints between stones, and to the relationships of entablatures to the roof tiles above them. Thus, the guidelines were not precise formulas; within and beyond them, individual architects and sculptors could create individual effects, and no two Greek temples are exactly alike.

Doric Order   The earliest, most severe, and most popular of the Greek orders is called Doric because it was the most frequent style in those western areas inhabited by the Dorian Greeks. We have seen an early version at Paestum (fig. 4–13), but more mature versions were used not only for the Parthenon but also for the temple of Apollo at Delos, for the temple at Segesta, Sicily, for the temple of Zeus at Stratos, and for countless other structures.

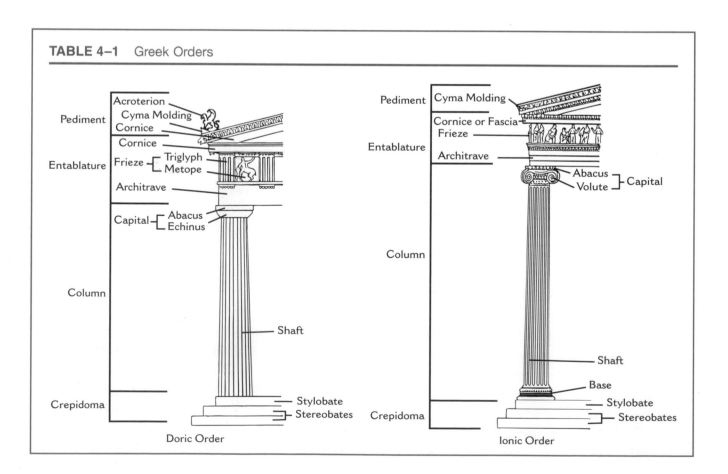

TABLE 4–1 Greek Orders

Doric Order

Ionic Order

The Roman architect and theorist Marcus Vitruvius Pollio, called Vitruvius, wrote his ten-volume *De Architectura* in the late first century B.C. The only major work on architecture to survive from classical times, it was much used as a guide in the Renaissance period. Vitruvius, in a manner some today would consider woefully sexist, characterized the two chief Greek orders as male and female: "The Doric column . . . began to exhibit the proportion, strength, and beauty of the body of a man." The Ionic column, he thought, expressed "the slenderness of women" and the Ionic volute their "graceful, curling hair." Thus for the Doric and Ionic orders, the Greeks "borrowed manly beauty, naked and unadorned, for the one, and for the other the delicacy, adornment and proportions characteristic of women."

Ionic Order   The Ionic order, which originated in the eastern part of Greece, is less architecturally limiting than the Doric, allowing more decorative features and more variety. It appears less frequently than the Doric, but it was used for some of the largest and some of the most beautiful Greek buildings ever erected.

▼ **4–18** Top and bottom parts of an Ionic column from the temple of Artemis at Sardis, third to second century B.C. The central drums of its shaft are missing.
Portion of a Column with Ionic Capital, from the Temple of Artemis at Sardis, ca. 300 B.C. Marble, H. (as exhibited) 142⅛ in. the (361 cm). The Metropolitan Museum of Art, Gift of the American Society for the Excavation of Sardis, 1926 (25.59.1), Photograph by Schecter Lee. Photograph © 1986 The Metropolitan Museum of Art.

A section of an Ionic column from the Temple of Artemis at Sardis, now part of Turkey (fig. 4–18), is a fine example of the order. Only the capital, the base, and parts of the shaft survive; the intervening drums have been destroyed. If still whole, the column would rise an impressive 56 feet (17 m) high. A comparison between this mature version of the Ionic order and the earlier version seen in figure 4–12 gives a clear indication of how the Greeks refined their designs until an ideal form was realized.

Corinthian Order   The Corinthian order is more decorative than the Doric or the Ionic, and it is believed to have been first introduced in the Greek city of Corinth. Considered by many to be an ornate version of the Ionic, the Corinthian order appeared relatively late and was used for relatively few Greek buildings. It was used for some important ones, however. A single Corinthian column, a recent invention at the time, appeared in the interior of the fifth-century Temple of Apollo at Bassae. It was more extensively used in the Temple of Zeus Olympius (also called the Olympieion) at Athens (fig. 4–19), in the Temple of Zeus at Euromus, and in the temple at Knidos, in Turkey, which may have housed Praxiteles's famous statue of Aphrodite. Later, the Corinthian order would become a favorite of the Romans.

The Corinthian column shaft has a smaller diameter than either the Doric or the Ionic, but the order's chief distinction is its capital (fig. 4–20). In addition to pairs of spiral volutes like those of the Ionic capital, the Corinthian capital, in the shape of an upside-down bell, bristles with a multitude of leaf shapes modeled on the prickly foliage of the acanthus plant. Other differences occur chiefly in the entablature. The frieze is sometimes omitted, and even when it is present, the Corinthian entablature is the lightest of any order, for it is carried by the most slender columns.

▼ **4–19** Corinthian columns and a remnant of a stepped architrave from the Olympieion, Athens, c. 170 B.C.
Dagli Orti/The Art Archive

▲ **4–20** Corinthian capital from the temple of Asklepios at Epidauros, fourth century B.C., 26 in. (66 cm) high.
Vanni/Art Resource, NY

Caryatids   A **caryatid** is a sculptured female figure used in place of a column. Not an order, but a dramatic exception to the three orders mentioned above, such figures occur often in Greek furniture designs, forming chair and table legs, but they also made occasional appearances in Greek architecture. Perhaps the earliest caryatids were a pair at the entrance to the Siphnian Treasury (a storehouse for the men of Siphnios) in the sanctuary of Apollo at Delphi; it dates from around 520 B.C. But the most prominent use of caryatids is on the south porch of the Erechtheum on the Acropolis of Athens

(fig. 4–21), built between 421 and 405 B.C. Six figures stand erect, facing the Parthenon, their heads supporting abaci and the entablature above, the pleats of their gowns simulating column flutes. Their arms were probably extended, holding cups as offerings to passing processions.

These striking exceptions to the vocabulary of the orders may have had their inspiration in Egypt, where colossal statues of the god Osiris were sometimes used in place of columns. A Greek variation on the caryatid is a similar figure carrying a replica of a basket on her head, rather than an abacus; she is called a *canephora*. The Romans would later produce a male version called a *telamon*, even later Renaissance architecture would produce partial figures called *herms* and *terms*, and the German Baroque would revive the telamon and call it an *atlas*.

Greek Houses

The average Greek house was a simple affair. There were many variations, as would be expected in a democracy of such varied city-states and such individualistic citizens. Made of impermanent materials, added to and remodeled many times over the ages, most of them have been destroyed, but some examples have been unearthed, as in Olynthus, a

▼ **4–21** On the Acropolis, caryatids (sculptured female figures) support the roof of the south porch of the Erechtheum, 421–405 B.C.
Corbis/Bettman

town invaded from the north in 348 B.C. (fig. 4–22). Based on this town's ruins and other evidence, we can make some generalizations about a typical Greek house.

Windowless to the outside, the rooms of the Greek house opened to a central courtyard or a series of courtyards. Its floors were commonly of hardened earth, sometimes paved with stone, sometimes covered with reed mats. Its walls of sun-dried mud brick, sitting on foundations of stone, would, in early Greece, have been simply plastered and whitewashed. The fifth-century statesman and general Alcibiades, in fact, created a scandal among his fellow Athenians when he painted the walls of his house. Within a few years, however, as in so many aspects of Greek life, simple traditions gave way to more elaborate ones. By the end of the fifth century, house walls were being covered with real or imitation marble, mosaics, murals, and tapestries.

Even a house built for an affluent Greek probably followed a standard plan composed of standard elements; more humble houses followed the model as best they could. A general planning principle in Greece designed rooms accessed from the interior courtyards, as seen at Mycenae. Following this planning principle, the humble Greek house was organized around a single open courtyard, and a more prosperous Greek house around two of them. From the street, a narrow entrance hall led to the first (or only) courtyard, the *andronitis*, which served as the chief living room where the master of the house would receive guests and where many household chores might be done.

This courtyard opened to a central covered space, the *andron*, which was used for dining (for the men) and where there was an altar to the household gods. The andron was the most honored room in the house, and the one most likely to be adorned with mosaic designs on the floor. It varied in size, but the most conventional size accommodated seven couches (**klini**) placed around the walls for reclining diners. Sometimes a vestibule was placed between the courtyard and the andron, and it, too, was likely to boast a mosaic floor. Occasionally the andron in turn opened to a rear courtyard, but this rear courtyard was sometimes omitted. Both courtyards were surrounded by colonnades and, beyond those, by a series of small rooms. These rooms were generally without windows, lighted only by their single doorways, but extant examples show that, in the bright sunlight of Greece, this degree of lighting was adequate. The rooms surrounding the outer courtyard were men's bedrooms, and those surrounding the inner courtyard were women's bedrooms and a

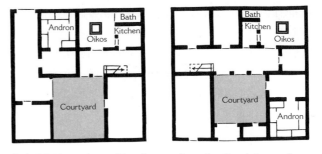

▲ **4–22** Floor plans of two houses from the Greek town of Olynthus show individual variations using the same basic elements. Each is inward facing, with a courtyard open to the sky. From Boardman, Ed., *The Oxford History of Classical Art*. Oxford: Oxford University Press, 1993. By permission of Oxford University Press

kitchen. Heating, when needed, was obtained from portable charcoal braziers made of terra-cotta or bronze. Behind the house was a small private garden.

Other Greek Building Types

The temple and the house were both private buildings—the temple entered only by a few priests, the house only by family and guests—but there were also Greek structures for public gatherings. Only a few of them had enclosed interiors. One example was the council house, or *ekklesiasterion*, a roofed assembly hall. The one at the town of Priene, built c. 200 B.C., could seat six or seven hundred on tiers of backless stone seats, virtually the whole population of the town at the time. Its stone walls and stone piers supported a wooden roof. Similar council houses were built at Miletus and Athens.

Related to the council house is the *bouleuterion*, a small rectangular or semicircular theater building. There were splendid open-air theaters built into the hillsides of many Greek cities, some of them exhibiting impressive acoustics. Stadiums and gymnasiums were built, too, as largely unroofed structures for athletic games and exercise.

The Stoa Other types of public gatherings took place in the Greek **stoa**, much like our present-day shopping mall. The stoa often had multiple uses. It served as a place for shops, offices, law courts, votive sculpture, and commemorative art, and it was a popular Greek building form from the seventh century through the first century B.C. In its simplest form, the stoa was a long, narrow building with a columned portico along one of its long sides. More complex versions had two colonnades and a wall. And the most elaborate had a row of enclosed shops at the back, rather than a simple wall. The Stoa of Attalos at Athens (fig. 4–23), built in the mid-second century B.C., was even grander with two floors, each having two rows of columns and a row of shops. On the lower floor, the outer colonnade was of the Doric order, and the inner was Ionic. On the upper floor, the outer colonnade was Ionic, and the inner a simplified version of Corinthian. Its total depth was 66 feet (20 m), and its length was an impressive 377 feet (115 m).

The Tholos Another building type is the circular **tholos**, which was started by the Mycenaeans and transformed by the Greeks into a highly finished and elegant building form. The Greeks generally built tholoi as memorials to the dead but sometimes gave them other uses (a fifth-century one at Athens seems to have served as a sort of dining club for the Athenian senators). Sometimes tholoi were surrounded by colonnades, sometimes not. In the fourth-century example at Epidauros (fig. 4–24), there were colonnades both inside and out. In this case, the twenty-six exterior columns were of the Doric order, the fourteen interior ones Corinthian, and there was also a striking pavement pattern of alternating diamonds of black and white stone.

The Mausoleum One last category of Greek architecture includes those buildings constructed as tombs and funerary structures. The largest and most legendary of these was built for a provincial governor in the east, Mausolus of Halicarnassus (now Bodrum, Turkey). The building gave its name to a whole genre of building—the mausoleum—a building used for entombment. It was built c. 352 B.C. and was considered one of the Seven Wonders of the Ancient World, but nothing remains of the building except fragments of its sculpture.

Greek Furniture

Lacking the preservation aid of Egypt's dry climate, Greek furniture has not generally survived, except for rare items made of bronze or stone. However, because furniture was frequently pictured on Greek vases and sculpture (and described in Greek literature), we have a good idea of its appearance.

Evidence suggests that the furnishings of Greek buildings and houses were spare indeed by present standards. This is certainly consistent with our knowledge of Greek restraint and moderation. "Nothing in excess" was a maxim of the Delphic oracle.

Wood was the dominant material for Greek furniture, and there was a plentiful supply of beech, citrus, maple, oak, and willow. Marble and bronze were sometimes used, and the finest of the wood pieces had inlays of ivory, ebony, and precious stones. The feet of tables and chairs were sometimes encased in silver.

▼ **4–24** Plan of the circular tholos at Epidauros, showing exterior and interior rings of columns and the paving pattern. The outside diameter is 66 ft. (22 m).
From "Greek Architecture" by A. W. Lawrence, Harmondsworth, Penguin, 3rd Ed., 1973, © Yale University Press.

▼ **4–23** Stoa of Attalos, Athens, the lower portico, built 160–138 B.C., now restored.

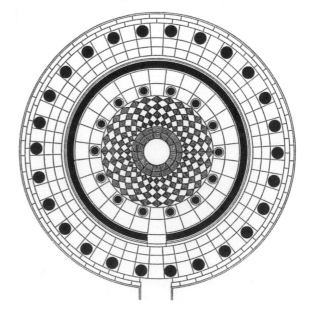

Greek furniture, like Greek architecture, was characterized by elegance, not by opulence, and never by extravagance. Later, in the Neoclassical period of the eighteenth century, we'll see a great revival of interest in Greek and Roman design, with furniture made to resemble Greek temple architecture and elaborate systems of miniature orders decoratively applied to cabinets, bookcases, tables, and clocks. While such applications were not unknown in ancient Greece (the Ionic order may have appeared in furniture before architecture), in general, such decoration was not typical. Greek furniture design was derived from its own function.

The Greeks used all the woodworking tools known to have been used by the Egyptians and, in addition, the plane, and, after the seventh century B.C., the wood-turning lathe. Joints were made with mortise and tenon, nails, and glue. A passage in Homer claims that Greek carpenters were "welcomed the world over."

The vocabulary of Greek furniture was small. Pieces were limited to a handful of types—beds, chairs, stools, tables, and chests—and each type was limited to a small number of conventional forms, persisting from century to century. But within those limitations, there was opportunity for infinite variation.

Seating and Beds

In the cultures we have studied so far, beds and chairs that approach today's standards of comfort seem to have been used only by royalty or religious leaders. In Greece, more democratic than any civilization before it, such furniture finally became widespread.

The Thronos The **thronos** was a formal chair of honor. Unlike most Greek furniture, it was often highly decorated, and there are many literary references that describe thronoi as "shining," "golden," "silver-studded," "ivory-inlaid," "many-colored," or "beauteous." The geographer and writer Pausanius reported that Phidias's celebrated statue of Zeus at Olympia was seated on a thronos "adorned with gold and precious stones, also with ebony and ivory, and with painted figures and wrought images." These ceremonial seats were not limited to shrines and sanctuaries, however; they also appeared in private houses, at least in the most prosperous ones. Even there, their use was reserved for the most important person present at any gathering. Stone versions of thronoi also appeared as seats of honor in Greek theaters.

The thronos took several forms. Its back was often low. It could have arms, sometimes supported by sphinxes, or it could be armless. Legs in the Archaic period were carved like birds or ended in animal feet. In the fifth and fourth centuries legs were rectangular or turned. In Hellenistic times, thronoi had solid sides, sometimes with their whole front edges in the forms of animal legs. Cushions and fabrics were sometimes used to add comfort and color; the *Odyssey*, for example, describes a thronos "strewn with purple coverlets."

The Klismos The most graceful, the most characteristic, and the most influential piece of Greek furniture was the **klismos**, or wood side chair (fig. 4–25). It seems to have been a purely Greek invention, without Egyptian, Assyrian, or Aegean precedent, but it was a design that would last. Echoes of the klismos appear centuries later in chairs of the Directoire, Empire, Regency, Duncan Phyfe, and even modern styles. Unlike the thronos, it was generally left undecorated, its beauty deriving solely from its form.

Like the Greek temple, the klismos took some time to evolve into its perfected state. Early versions in the formative periods had parts that were not so harmoniously related to one another as in later versions. And Archaic klismoi sometimes had decorative elements—such as

▶ **4–25** Painting on a white-ground lekythos (oil jug), c. 440 B.C. shows a woman seated on a *klismos.*
"The Achilles Painter". Oil Flask (iekythos). Greek, Classical Period, about 440 B.C. Place of Mfg: Greece, Attica, Athens. Ceramic, White Ground. H: 34.7 cm (13¹¹⁄₁₆ inches). Francis Bartlett Donation of 1912. 13.187. Photograph © 2007 Museum of Fine Arts, Boston.

backs terminating in swans' heads or finials—that were later eliminated.

In its perfected form, the klismos featured a curved backboard and curved legs. The curved backboard was generally supported by a broad central **splat**, or wooden panel, with a narrow **stile**, or vertical wood strip, on either side, and these side stiles were made from the same piece of wood as the rear legs, forming one continuous sweeping curve. The front legs, curving in the opposite direction, were broad at the top, tapering to a smaller end that projected beyond the chair frame. The frames of the seats were mortised into the legs with tenons or dowels (see table 2–1), and sometimes, as an expression of the construction, these bits of joinery were shown protruding through the sides of the legs. The seat within the frame was made of plaited leather thongs, their edges visible as black lines against the brown chair frame (fig. 4–26). Sometimes a cushion or animal skin was added for comfort.

In addition to their beauty, klismoi had many practical uses. They were lightweight and easily portable. Their depictions on vases show them being carried about and being used by craftsmen and workers, as well as by noblemen and -women. The women usually dined seated on klismoi while the men reclined on klini.

The Diphros The **diphros** was a stool without arms or back. It was of two types, one with fixed legs and the other with folding legs. The fixed legs generally were perpendicular to the seat, cylindrical, and turned on a lathe (see fig. 4–1). Sometimes there were stretchers between the legs, sometimes not. Diphroi were made of many kinds of wood, but the nicest ones were made of ebony or other costly woods and had their legs tipped with silver feet. Leather slings or interlacings of leather thongs were suspended within the wood frames to form the seats.

This popular furniture design remained in vogue throughout the fifth and fourth centuries B.C. Later, in Hellenistic times, some modifications were made, the lower part of the legs becoming taller and more spindly, and more elaborate turnings being introduced. A quite different leg design was also seen on some diphroi, divided into two sections, both slightly concave, with the upper section thicker than the lower one.

The hinged, folding version of the Greek stool was called a *diphros okladias*. Like the Egyptian model on which

▲ **4–26** Modern reconstruction, based on vase paintings, of a *klismos* chair. This version, executed by T. H. Robsjohn-Gibbings, has a frame of walnut and a seat of leather thongs.
Gretchen Bellinger Inc.

it was probably based, its two pairs of legs crossed in an X shape and were joined, below the crossing, by stretchers. They sometimes had straight legs and sometimes curving legs that ended in animal hooves or claws. They were used indoors and out. Paintings on Greek vases show that a privileged Greek would sometimes be followed through the streets by a slave carrying his master's stool, ready to unfold it whenever it was wanted.

The Kline The **kline** (fig. 4–27) was a bed but also functioned like our modern sofa and even served as seating for dining. It was in many ways similar in use to the modern **chaise longue** or "long chair," used for sleeping, napping, eating, drinking, lounging, and conversing.

The kline was usually made of wood; maple and olive are specifically mentioned in Homer's *Odyssey*. Wood klini were sometimes finished with silver or ivory feet. They were also made of iron or bronze, as our example shows (fig. 4–28).

Klini had sweeping curved headboards, which also acted as headrests for those who were reclining while dining. In some cases, they also had footboards, which were generally lower than the headboards. The legs were of three types: rectangular in section and curving away from the frame;

▼ 4–27 A fifth-century B.C. vase painting shows a young man carrying furniture. On his back is a *kline*, similar to a *chaise longue*, and on it, upside down, a small table.
Ashmolean Museum, Oxford, England, U.K.

round in section and vertical, with **turnings**—swellings, disks, and other shapes produced by the lathe—and sometimes carved with little sphinxes; or in the shape of animal legs, probably borrowed from the Egyptians. The frames formed open rectangles, within which were strung interlacings of cords or leather thongs. These interlacings supported mattresses stuffed with wool or feathers, mattress covers, pillows, and sometimes animal skins and fleeces. Linen or wool bedclothes, sometimes perfumed, were added for sleeping, and embroidered mattresses and cushions might be added for dining.

Tables

By our own standards, the Greeks used few tables. With fewer possessions, and with less inclination to display them, the Greeks used tables primarily for serving and eating meals. They were often brought out before a meal, placed by the sides of the gentlemen's klini, one for each person, and then taken away. Many were low enough to be pushed under the klini when not in use. The general name for a Greek table is **trapeza**. They were most frequently made of wood, but there were more luxurious versions in bronze, marble, or carved ivory. Sometimes wood tops were supported on bronze legs.

The most commonplace Greek table was probably the three-legged trapeza (fig. 4–29). Greek house interiors were often roughly finished, and a three-legged table stands more securely on an uneven surface than a four-legged table, which might rock. The table usually had a rectangular top, with the three legs fastened into it with tenons or dowels. The top projected beyond the pair of legs at one end, but was fairly flush with the single leg at the other. These legs were sometimes, but not always, connected by a T-shaped stretcher.

There were at least four variant table designs used by the Greeks: a rectangular table with four legs; a rectangular

▲ 4–28 Bronze version of a *kline*, Staatliche Museen zu Berlin-Preussischer Kulturbesitz, Museum fur Islamische Kunst.
Photo by Ernst Herzfeld, Bildarchiv Preussischer Kulturbesitz, Berlin 2002.

▲ **4–29** Detail from a red-figure vase. A vase painter is seated on a *klismos* and working on a large *kylix*. Beside him, holding his bowls of paint, is a trapeza.
Canali Photobank

▲ **4–30** Gold funerary chest from a royal tomb at Vergina, near Thessaloniki, 330 B.C., 8 in. (20 cm) high.
Archaeological Museum, Thessaloniki, Greece/The Bridgeman Art Library International

table on two transverse solid supports, usually being made of stone; a round table on three legs, usually given animal form; and a round table on a single central pedestal above spreading feet.

Storage Furniture

The Greeks devised pieces of storage furniture to put away clothing, jewelry, tools, and other objects. Chests, boxes, and caskets were often used. Greek clothing for both men and women consisted primarily of simple rectangles of cloth that were draped around the body in various ways and could be easily folded. There has also been no reference to any sort of tall Greek cupboard or armoire; the Greeks instead put mirrors, drinking cups, and other household objects on open shelves or hung them on the wall from pegs. Oil lamps were usually freestanding.

The **kibotos** was a wooden chest used for storage; its hinged lid could be used as a seat. The four-sided kibotos could have flat, gabled, or curved covers, and it stood on four short legs extending from its corner posts. In some cases, the legs terminated in lion's-paw feet. Typically, its top was not secured with a lock, but by winding a string or thong around two knobs, one on the hinged lid and one on the chest. Its sides could be plain or decorated with any number of the characteristic Greek ornaments, executed in ivory or polychrome inlays.

More elaborate storage pieces served royal or ritual uses, such as a gold chest (fig. 4–30) made to hold the cremated remains of King Philip II. It was discovered in his tomb near Thessaloniki, and it is decorated with a sixteen-point star on its top and rosettes and anthemion patterns on its sides.

Greek Decorative Arts

On a smaller scale than architecture, sculpture, and furniture, the Greek artistic genius was evident in a number of other fields—in weaponry and armor; in vessels and figurines of bronze; in jewelry of bronze, silver, and gold; in molded terra-cotta objects and figures; and in finely made silver coins stamped with animals and portraits. The techniques of Egyptian faience were admired by the Greeks and duplicated by them in the late seventh century B.C. In particular, they excelled at designing wall and floor decoration, at creating moldings and patterns for ornament, and at advancing pottery to great achievement.

Wall and Floor Decoration

Painted decoration was at first entirely subordinate to Greek architecture; later it became an independent art. Many of the walls of Greek buildings were covered with paint or glazed color both inside and out. Brick and stone were often covered with cement stucco that was polished so highly it reflected like a mirror. Scenic decoration and conventional ornament were used to enrich marble, wood, and plaster.

We have seen the paving pattern of colored stone from the circular tholos at Epidauros (see fig. 4–24). The Greeks also decorated floors with mosaics made from smaller pieces pressed into wet plaster. There were two general types of Greek floor mosaic. The earlier type, called pebble mosaic, was made with pebbles of varying color, left in their natural shapes (fig. 4–31). Pebble mosaics reached a high degree of sophistication by the fourth century B.C., with pebble sizes carefully graded and the smaller sizes used for fine detail. Generally, pebble mosaic floors had a dark ground with a design in lighter colors.

The later, more elaborate mosaic type, popular in the Hellenistic period, was made with **tesserae**, small pieces of cut stone with squared edges; made from pebbles, stones, lead, or terracotta. A greater variety of colors was possible with tesserae, and some began to be made with darker figures against a light ground, although a dark ground was still more common.

Mosaic floors were used in public buildings such as temples and stoas, but also, as already mentioned, in the *andrones* and the courtyards of private houses. For home-owners unable to commission their own mosaic designs, there were lead templates and patterns available.

Moldings

As masters of harmonic structure, the Greeks embraced ornament sympathetic to such harmonic structure, rarely using overall patterns that might obscure architectural forms but developing instead graceful linear patterns that would accentuate them. The Greek vocabulary of architectural ornament (table 4–2) was small, with a few devices thoroughly studied and refined and with such devices adapted for furniture, vases, and other decorative objects. The Greeks also developed a distinct difference in character between the ornament intended for the earnest, sober structures of the Doric order and those meant for the more elaborate Ionic and Corinthian orders.

Greek moldings, later adopted by the Romans and thus known now by their Latin names, were designed to accentuate edges or junctions or to divide large surfaces into smaller areas. Their shapes were derived from the geometric curves known as the ellipse, the parabola, and the hyperbola, and were carefully calculated to produce the desired highlights and shadows.

Patterns

Whereas the simplest of the Greek moldings—the fillet, fascia, scotia, and cavetto—were usually left plain, the others were often inscribed with various enriching patterns that made their shape more apparent.

The Greek ornamental patterns are often used in combination. In the Ionic capital in figure 4–19, we can see egg-and-dart, anthemion, and bead-and-reed patterns.

In addition to these repeating or "linear" patterns, there were a large number of motifs that appeared singly in Greek decoration. Many single motifs were geometric, such as the spiral or the **swastika**, a cross composed of equal L-shaped arms. Some were derived from plant forms, such as rosettes and garlands, or from animals, such as horses, lions, oxen, birds, and fishes, and some came from ornaments themselves, like festoons and ribbons.

The Greek Vase

The painted Greek vase was a utilitarian object, intended for practical use, not for museum display, yet, at its best, it

▼ **4–31** A pebble mosaic from the floor of a house in northern Greece shows Bellerophon riding the winged horse Pegasus and killing the Chimera (a combination lion/goat/dragon). Fourth century B.C., 4 ft. (1.25 m) wide.
Neil Setchfield/Alamy Images

TABLE 4–2 Greek Moldings and Patterns

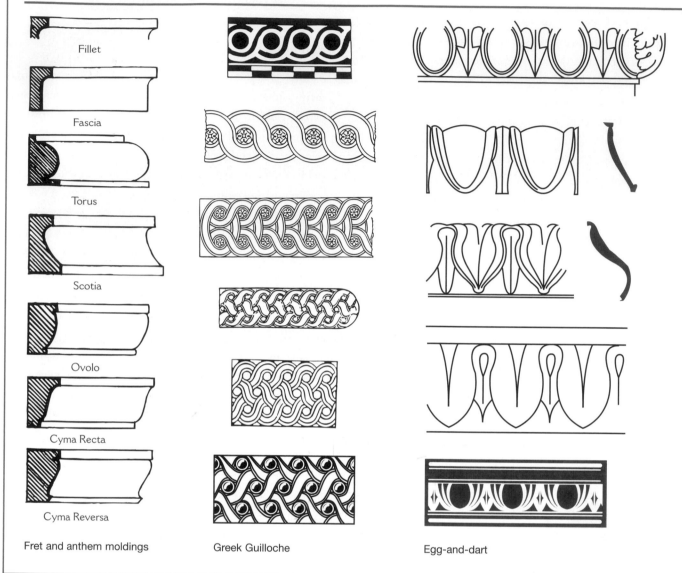

Fillet

Fascia

Torus

Scotia

Ovolo

Cyma Recta

Cyma Reversa

Fret and anthem moldings

Greek Guilloche

Egg-and-dart

was one of the supreme achievements of all the history of the decorative arts. As we have seen, the Cretans and Mycenaeans were practiced potters, but their Greek successors carried the craft to a new level, adopting the pottery wheel at least as early as 1800 B.C.

The Greeks sought to display perfection using highly conventionalized forms, with certain shapes designed for certain uses. And each **krater** vase, for example, was to emulate the ideal krater shape known to every Greek potter, just as every Doric column emulated the ideal Doric column. The vase was also to display perfection in surface decoration, though each was highly individual, with scenes different from all others and with no detail wasted

or lacking in character. The shape and decoration displayed perfection in the relationship of decoration to form, with the pictorial element enlivening but never violating the shape beneath. To this end, no perspective effects, no casting of shadows, no shadings or excessive modelings were allowed to create any illusion of three-dimensional form that would contradict the flat surface of the vase.

Vase Shapes and Their Uses Greek vases were made for use, not for display. However beautiful and admirable we may find them today, our present notion of a vase as a decorative object would seem quite strange to an ancient

Bead-and-reel molding   Greek fret   Anthemion patterns

Greek. However, the Greeks valued fine painted pottery—both aesthetically and monetarily—more highly than their plain unpainted wares.

By the eighth century B.C., most of the basic forms of Greek vases, suited to their uses, had been established, and these basic forms (table 4–3) continued to be used unvaryingly for four or five hundred years. Some vases were uses in dedications to the gods, some became part of burial rituals, and many were for more mundane uses, such as carrying and holding water and wine or storing grains and oils.

Some miniature vases were meant to be children's toys, and some—the Panathenaic amphorae—were prizes given to champion athletes, one side painted with a figure of the goddess Athena carrying a shield, the other with scenes of athletic games.

Vase Types: Black-Figure and Red-Figure The earliest examples of Greek vases we know, from the formative periods, are made with a buff-colored ground, on which geometric designs—and, later, animal and human figures—were sketched in black paint. To this, gradually, were added details in red and purple paint. Occasionally, in some city-states, yellow and blue paints were used, but as Greek art entered its Classical period, the colors of the Greek vase were simplified and standardized. Some vase shapes came to

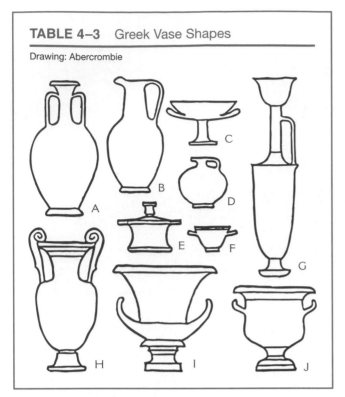

TABLE 4–3 Greek Vase Shapes

Drawing: Abercrombie

Types of Greek vases: a, amphora, used for wine storage; b, oinochoë, a wine jug; c, kylix, a drinking cup; d, aryballos, a container for olive oil, used by the Greeks as soap; e, pyxis, a container for toiletries; f, skyphos, another drinking cup; g, lekythos, an oil jug; h, volute krater; i, kylix krater; j, bell krater. All three types of krater were used for mixing wine and water.

▼ **4–32** Signed by the vase painter Exekias, a black-figure amphora, c. 530 B.C. Two heroes of the Trojan War, Ajax and Achilles, are seen playing a board game.
Exekias (6th BCE), "Achilles and Ajax playing dice." Black-figured amphora, Attic. Museo Gregoriano Etrusco, Vatican Museums, Vatican State. Scala/Art Resource, NY

be traditionally made in the **black-figure** style (fig. 4–32), some were usually in the **red-figure** style (fig. 4–33), and some could be either.

The switch from black-figure to red-figure styles came in the years c. 530 or 525 B.C., and, in the context of Greek artistic conservatism and gradual development, it seems a radical change of fashion. Not only that, the change was accompanied by a new degree of pictorial invention. Figures that had previously been shown only in profile or in full frontal view were now seen in three-quarter view or even, in rear view.

Both black-figure and red-figure types were produced from the last quarter of the sixth century B.C. to the first quarter of the fifth. In addition to the two basic colors of red and black, some small amounts of white, gold, and red-purple paints were sometimes used to pick out details. And, adding to the exceptions, some vases, such as the tall, slender-necked **lekythoi**, were produced with a white ground and painted in red or black, or in browns shading from gold to almost black. By the fourth century B.C., other colors—blue, green, and pink—came to be sanctioned for some vase shapes.

▲ **4–33** A red-figure kylix krater for mixing wine and water, c. 510 B.C., attributed to the vase painter Euphronios. The scene shows the body of the warrior Sarpedon being carried from the battlefield at Troy, while the god Hermes (at center) watches. Above and below the scene are rows of anthemion ornament.
The Metropolitan Museum of Art, Purchase, Bequest of Joseph H. Durkee, Gift of Darius Ogden Mills and Gift of C. Ruxton Love, by exchange, 1972. (1972.11.10, Side A)

In the most famous examples from Greece's mature periods, the surfaces of vases contain only areas of glowing red-orange and areas of glossy black. The red-orange was derived from clay from the area of Cape Kolias that had been treated with red ochre. The areas of black were derived from varnish brushed onto the fired clay that is then fired again. As first developed in Corinth, in Chalcis, and then in Athens in the early sixth century B.C., the scenes, figures, and decorations were painted in black on the red clay; the results are called **black-figure vases** (fig. 4–32). In the most refined examples, the painted areas are not solid black, but have thin lines incised through them with a metal tool; these lines indicate facial features, the shapes of muscles, or the folds of drapery and clothing.

A few decades later in Athens, a new style brought a reverse practice: painting the background black and leaving the pictorial elements in the red-orange clay color. The results are called **red-figure vases** (fig. 4–33). As incised lines add detail to the black painted areas, now thin black brush strokes add detail to the unpainted areas.

Vase Subject Matter   The subjects of the designs painted or outlined on Greek vases were as varied as life itself and included the actions of gods, heroes, and common folk. We see Achilles bandaging the wound of his friend Patroclus, Herakles slaying his children, the contest of Hercules and Apollo, the rape of Europa, the judgment of Paris. We see dogs and horses, jars and ewers, stools and chairs. We see athletes and warriors, farmers and bathers, lovers and satyrs. And, naturally, we see potters and vase painters picturing themselves (fig. 4–29), possibly with no suspicion of how greatly admired their work would be more than 2,000 years later.

Textiles

Greek fabrics have largely vanished, but a fragment of fifth-century B.C. linen with gold threads in a diaper pattern survives. Others fabrics are depicted on vases (and described in Greek literature), suggesting that striped patterns were popular. There were many sheep, so wool was plentiful, but linen, silk, and cotton were all imported.

Wool-making was the work of women. They washed and beat the wool in the courtyards of their houses, then took it inside where, sitting on chairs with the wool across their knees, they divided it into hanks. For this work, they protected their legs with special shields, of which some decorated terra-cotta examples survive. The hanks were dyed with a variety of mineral and vegetable dyes, and a popular purple dye was extracted from a Mediterranean shellfish. The wool was then spun into fine yarn and woven on upright wooden looms.

Summary: Ancient Greek Design

No nation or race of people has had more cultural influence on Western civilization than ancient Greece. Its architecture, decoration, literature, and sculpture have rarely been equaled and have stood as models for centuries. How can those Greek achievements be characterized, and in what ways did the Greeks excel at design?

Looking for Character

Greek art is intellectual. Its beauty arises from exquisite proportions, graceful lines, and simplicity. While color and surface ornament are often integrated parts, the emotions they arouse are never allowed to obscure the intellectual satisfaction provided by the perfection of the underlying form.

Greek art is serious. There are, to be sure, elements of slapstick in the comedies of Aristophanes and elements of ribaldry in Greek vase painting, but, for the most part, the Greeks were almost modern in their anxiety about life.

Greek art does not reflect a concern for novelty, innovation, or originality. Its development was a necessarily gradual approach to an imagined ideal, almost never reflecting a change of taste. The Greeks were as disinterested in the impressions made by giant scale or enormous mass as they were in the shock of new fashions. They sought clarity and a comprehensible relationship to the human condition.

To achieve these ideals, the Greeks developed a well-ordered system, in which all parts were interdependent and mutually attuned. In Plato's words, "Measure and commensurability are everywhere identified with beauty and excellence." The language of Greek architecture and its components, interiors, and ornaments obeyed rules of composition at least as strict as those of music and written language. So consistently logical and perfectly composed was that language system that still today, 2,500 years later, it continues to be understood and admired.

In all Greek art—temples, orders, sculpture, vases—there are rules. The success of these rules—and the reason for our continued respect for them—is that they are not absolute. They encourage continuity but allow change. They impose ideals but admit individuality. They supply formulas but can be infinitely varied.

An important lesson of Greek architecture and its interiors is the sense of strength imparted by the clear expression of logical structure. The Greek structural vocabulary, repeated in example after example, is simple and basic: Vertical supports (columns) carry horizontal members (entablatures).

Even more important is the sensitive relationship of details to wholes. In the Greek temple, the structure is embellished in ways that explain and refine the basic statement, never obscure it. In the Greek vase, similarly, the vase form is painted with designs that enhance, never contradict it.

Most important, Greek architecture demonstrates the value of a dominant system of proportions that rules over all constituent parts. If a single dimension of a Greek temple is changed, all other dimensions must be adjusted accordingly. This internal interdependence of elements, Greek examples show, can impart a sense of repose, rightness, and harmony of design.

Looking for Quality

Much has been said about the quality of the Greek temple and the Greek vase, but perhaps not enough has been said about the wide extent of such quality. It is not that just one painted Greek vase or one rare Greek temple is excellent; it is that almost every painted Greek vase and almost every Greek temple are superb. One reason seems to be the power in Greek art of established types and established relationships. Once a successful form had been reached, it was repeated with only minor attempts at further refinements. With little experimentation and search for novelty and no apparent urge to be original, the Greeks instead focused on the attainment of perfection in their ideals.

Yet, in the field with which we are most concerned here—interior design—the highest quality was still to come. Classical Greece was a land largely without palaces or mansions, largely without buildings for public worship or government. It was, therefore, largely a land without interiors. Greek temple architecture had some admirable interiors, to be sure, but they were rare, accessible to very few, and of secondary importance to the magnificence of the exterior shell. Greek stoas and theaters were open-air architecture, without significant interior spaces. And most Greek houses were simple affairs, plainly built of plain materials. Where it existed, as in architecture, Greek quality was of the highest level and contributed greatly to subsequent interior design, but Greek interiors themselves were not a chief focus of the Greek genius.

Making Comparisons

One way to compare the design of two cultures is to compare their most outstanding achievements. The Great Pyramid of Giza is still an astonishing sight: No more powerful structure has ever been conceived in 4,000 years. It must have been even more astonishing to see when it still had its outer casing of dressed stone so that its enormous triangular faces reflected the sun with crisp edges.

In size, the Parthenon is puny by comparison. It astonishes as well, but not at first glance. Like the pyramid, it is a wonder of mathematical calculation and precise construction, but its effects are quieter. It is a complex composition of many parts, and our appreciation of its beauty arises slowly from our contemplation of the relationships between those parts. The pyramid has a boldness and scale appropriate for the launching of the spirit of a great pharaoh into the heavens, and, as we view it, we marvel at the power of the mighty Khufu and the mysteries of eternity. The Parthenon honors a goddess and commemorates a procession of her admirers, but, as we view it, we marvel at the creativity of its architects and sculptors and at the civilization that supported them. The pyramid operates in the realm of the superhuman, the Parthenon in the human.

Another way to compare two bodies of art is to compare more mundane objects, such as chairs. Egyptian furniture achieved great elegance. Of the surviving examples, perhaps the most beautiful are the pieces made for Queen Hetepheres, found in 1925. The obvious Greek parallel is the thronos, similarly meant to convey honor or express importance. But the most beautiful Greek seating is the more popular klismos, its curves cohering in a perfect composition that needs no embellishment. In this case, the Egyptian chair would be diminished without its rich casing of precious metal, and the Greek klismos would be diminished if ornament were added.

We have seen in the art and design of Mesopotamia, Assyria, Babylon, and Persia a dramatic striving for size, power, and spectacle. If we consider the Persian palace at Persepolis to be an example standing for the whole of the Ancient Near East, we see that the architects in the Ancient Near East meant to amaze and humble the visitor, in this case with a grand hall densely packed with colossal columns. Then, if we consider the Parthenon to be a Greek parallel, we see a building with roughly half the number of columns that is meant to engage and delight the visitor with the gracefulness and subtle perfection of the columns and their placement. Persepolis demonstrates the effect of physical might; the Parthenon demonstrates intelligence.

Details of the two buildings offer a similar contrast. In the carved reliefs of Persepolis, the figure of a warrior is repeated endlessly, impressing us with the inexhaustible vastness of the military force of which the figure is an element. We lose count of the repetitions. In the Parthenon frieze, we are also impressed by the numbers of marchers in the procession, but here each is a different individual. Persepolis deadens our senses with superhuman innumerability; the Parthenon intrigues us with human variety.

Similar comparisons could be made between the two cultures' use of color and materials. The Persians knew the bewitching effects of brilliant color and the dazzling reflections of gold and brass. The Greeks enjoyed bright color, too, but used it in ways that identified and clarified their architecture and sculpture, never allowing it to blur contours or destroy the sense of form. Persian color overrides the senses and fills the spectator with awe; Greek color appeals to the senses and offers clarification.

Persian design is typical of all design meant to induce a sense of mystery; Greek design is the epitome of all design meant to establish understanding. In the fourth century A.D., we shall see these two very different attitudes combine when Persian and Greek influences meet in the art of Byzantium.

Rome

753 B.C.–A.D. 550

"By virtue of its plastic unity Roman architecture achieves spatial unity. Organic structures . . . become preeminently hollow forms, containers of highly complex functions organized according to the principles of clarity and hierarchic ordinances."

— Paolo Portoghesi (1931 –), Italian architect and architectural historian

The Romans took the architectural vocabulary that the Greeks had perfected and added construction techniques the Greeks had seldom used. With the Romans' virtuoso use of the vault, the arch, and the dome, and with their employment of massive piers and walls in addition to column supports, the simplicity and restraint of Greek architecture were lost. Instead, the Romans built a dazzling variety of impressive interior spaces, unprecedented in size, openness, structural daring, and complexity of form.

While Greece had been a civilization anchored in constancy, with an art aimed at a fixed ideal, Rome was a civilization interested in the new, curious about the exotic, and highly conscious of changing fashion. The Romans readily adopted fashionable trends in diet, clothing, social duties, language, and—of course—in interior design and decorative arts (fig. 5–1). They eagerly followed the taste of the emperor or other statesmen; they watched with curiosity the importation of foreign objects and materials from the outskirts of

their vast empire; they reveled in experiment, change, luxury, and sensation. They were, in other words, much like us.

Determinants of Roman Design

Rome, at its greatest extent, had an impressive reach. The edges of its empire were in outposts as remote as Africa, Britain, and Syria (see fig. 5–2). The customs of Roman society and the new design techniques in art and architecture prevailed at long distances, and had to cope with variations in geography, natural resources, and religions, and with the influences of other cultures.

Geography and Natural Resources

We have seen that the deserts of Egypt enforced a long isolation on the Egyptian people and that the long, rocky coastline of Greece encouraged seafaring and exploration. The Italian peninsula and the land around Rome were less dramatic—gentle, rolling hills and an agreeable shore— and its climate mild and pleasant. The peninsula's commanding location in the center of the Mediterranean made

◀ **5–1** Detail, wall painting from the Villa of Livia on the Palatine Hill, Rome. Late first century B.C.
Canali Photobank

Date	Period	Political and Cultural Events	Artistic Accomplishments
753–386 B.C.	Early Rome	Foundation of the city of Rome; Etruscan rule; Gauls sack Rome	Etruscan temples and tombs; the Cloaca Maxima
386–44 B.C.	Republican Rome	Roman conquest of northern Italy; Roman conquest of Greece; Julius Caesar	Construction of Appian aqueduct; Vitruvius's *De architectura*
44 B.C.–A.D. 50	Early Empire	Egypt declared a Roman province; emperor given supreme power	Ara Pacis
A.D. 50–250	High Empire	Fire destroys most of Rome; volcano destroys Pompeii; expansion of empire	Domus Aurea; Colosseum; Pantheon; Hadrian's Villa; Forum of Trajan; Baths of Caracalla
A.D. 250–550	Late Empire or the Decline of Rome	Founding of Constantinople; last reign of a Roman emperor in the West	Baths of Diocletian; Villa at Piazza Armerina; Basilica of Maxentius

▲ 5–2 This portrait of the Roman official Helioporus is from the ceiling of the House of Scribes in Dura, Syria, a Roman frontier town on the Euphrates River. Second or third century A.D.
Yale University Art Gallery

it a natural place from which to export its culture, art, and architecture to the surrounding lands. At its height, the Roman Empire stretched over a vast area, encompassing every extreme of geography and climate, yet Roman culture remained remarkably uniform throughout the empire, little influenced by local conditions. The Greeks' chief building material had been marble. The Romans had marble as well, notably a distinctively fissured type called **travertine**, but they also had clay for producing terra cotta and brick. Most fortunately, they had a kind of volcanic sand, **pozzolana**, which, when mixed with lime and water, produced a remarkable building material: concrete.

Religion

The contemplative life of the Greek philosophers did not appeal to the Romans, but the Romans appropriated gods from the Greek pantheon and gave them new names and, to some extent, new attributes. Zeus, the leader of the Greek gods, became Jupiter in the Roman Empire. Jupiter's influence was now allied to the state and the political and military needs of a growing empire. Political and military leaders used religion to advance the state and themselves, while the personal religion of the individual became less important. Greek idealism was subordinated to Roman realism. Realism also governed the laws and customs that made such a large, complicated society workable. Greek simplicity was subordinated to Roman complexity, and Greek modesty to Roman pomp.

The Roman combination of realism, force, and complexity was highly successful, particularly after Rome's conquest of the eastern Mediterranean. Wealth poured into Rome, both for the state and for private citizens, making possible an ostentatious display of embellishment of both public and domestic interiors.

The Etruscan Heritage

The Romans owed many aspects of their culture to the Greeks, but they were also inheritors of the Etruscan civilization. Etruscan kings (the Tarquins) ruled the city of Rome for much of the sixth century B.C., and during their reign the Cloaca Maxima (the city's great sewer) was

▲ **5–3** A frieze of painted figures on a terra-cotta slab from the Etruscan city of Caere (now present-day Cerveteri). c. 530 B.C. 4 ft. 5½ in. (137 cm) high.
Herve Lewandowski/Art Resource/Réunion des Musées Nationaux

constructed, the city was walled, and the first temples were built in the Forum.

The Etruscans were perhaps immigrants to Italy from Asia Minor who, in turn, had been influenced by both Greece and the Near East. They developed a prosperous and accomplished culture between the eighth and fourth centuries B.C. Their tombs are virtually all that remains of their buildings, but the frescoes, stucco reliefs, and terra-cotta slabs (fig. 5–3) found in those tombs show elegant domestic interiors.

Etruscan temples were also impressive, generally with wide spacings between unfluted columns (so that wooden beams, not stone, were required to span them), with deep porches and wide eaves (to protect the walls of mud brick), and with entrances centered at each end. The temples were enlivened with painted pediments and terra-cotta ornament: The Etruscan temple had steps, but only at the front entrance, not surrounding the building like the Greek temple (the Romans would follow the Etruscan example). The Etruscans also built corbelled **ashlar** (stone "dressed" to have squared edges) masonry tombs in circular form (**tholoi**), as

▲ **5–4** Etruscan throne of bronze with relief carvings. Seventh century, B.C.
Herve Lewandowski, courtesy Réunion des Musées Nationaux/Art Resource, NY

was seen at Mycenae. Although much of Etruscan construction was crude, the mud-brick structures were sometimes faced with sheets of bronze, as were some chariots and fine pieces of furniture (fig. 5–4). The Etruscans also excelled in working with gold. All in all, the Etruscan style was robust, vivacious, and exuberant, and they reinforced the influence of Greece on the Romans, for the Etruscans—long before the Romans—were great admirers of Greek accomplishments, which had been discovered through trade. Many painted Greek vases have been unearthed in Etruscan tombs, suggesting a great esteem for their quality. It would never have occurred to the Greeks themselves to be buried with their vases.

The History of the Roman Empire

Rome was, of course, a great city before it gave its name to a great empire. According to legend, the city was founded by orphaned twins, Romulus and Remus, in 753 B.C. In those earliest days, to be a Roman meant to be an inhabitant of that city. By the founding of the empire in the first century B.C. (and for three and a half centuries more), Roman citizenship was also bestowed on worthy allies and brave soldiers from England in the north to Egypt in the south, from the Iberian Peninsula on the west to Mesopotamia on the east. The history of these Romans, who commanded the largest and most powerful political unit ever assembled, can be divided into several stages.

Early Rome

The earliest Romans, contemporary with the Etruscans and the Geometric period of the Greeks, were a rude lot, erecting huts of wattle and daub, the ruins of which have been found at Villanova, near the present-day city of Bologna, and on Rome's Palatine Hill. These tiny hamlets were amalgamated by the Etruscans into a single city-state in the eighth century B.C. The Romans overthrew their Etruscan rulers c. 500 B.C. and, while keeping many aspects of Etruscan art and architecture, they established the Roman Republic, which would last for four centuries. In the Republic (never a true democracy), the patrician class controlled the government, and the *plebians*, the general body of Roman citizens, were given increasingly large amounts of power.

In the fourth century B.C., Rome exerted its influence over the surrounding areas and came into full contact with the Greek culture. At this time, the top of the Capitoline Hill in Rome was cleared for the building of three great temples, dedicated to Jupiter, Juno, and Minerva.

The Republic and Early Empire

In Roman settlements throughout Italy and far beyond, the typical city plan was distinguished by a strict grid of right-angled streets. In Rome, Julius Caesar (102–44 B.C.), the great political and military leader, initiated some ambitious building programs, most notably the forum that bears his name. His tumultuous career was a turning point in Roman history, and—after his assassination in 44 B.C.—the republic ended, a state of anarchy ensued, and foundations were laid for the empire.

Caesar's nephew and heir, Octavian, restored order, was given the title Augustus, and is considered the first Roman emperor. He presided over an age of stability, expansion, and prosperity, and the two hundred years of peace that followed is known as the Pax Romana. As Octavian boasted, he "found Rome a city of brick and left it a city of marble."

The High Empire

Around A.D. 50, Rome entered its most successful and productive period, the High Empire. The city of Rome grew to over a million residents and boasted many public amenities, including baths, sports arenas, stadiums, bridges, and aqueducts. There were an excellent water supply and an elaborate sewerage system. It would not be until the eighteenth century that any other European city would match the efficiency and luxury of ancient Rome.

Abroad, the power of the empire stretched to the Danube, the Rhine, the Irish Sea, the Red Sea, the Black Sea, and the Arabian Desert. The great public construction projects of the High Empire included the Colosseum, the Pantheon, the Forum of Trajan, and the Baths of Caracalla; private building efforts included Nero's Domus Aurea and Hadrian's Villa.

Most consider the end of the Roman Empire to have come c. A.D. 550 because of a number of factors, including the deception of the Caesars, the unpopularity of military despotism, the rise of Christianity, and the invasions of barbarians from Germany and other northern countries. Other causes may have been pestilence, lowered moral standards, the exhaustion of natural resources, and the burdens of heavy taxation.

Roman Architecture and Interiors

The buildings of the Roman Empire are as distinguished for their diversity as those of Greece were for their uniformity. The range of building types, the vocabulary of building forms, the expression of individual tastes, the influences of unusual elements from afar—all these contributed to an architecture of great variety and richness.

The architecture of Rome was also an important propaganda tool for the empire. This was nothing new; pyramids and ziggurats had proclaimed the power of the rulers in Egypt and the Ancient Near East, and the Parthenon had heralded the glories of Athens, but Rome was the most dominant civilization yet known. It seems appropriate that a large number of her buildings are powerful, magnificent, and even, at times, ostentatious. Contributing to the grandeur and boldness of the empire's public buildings was the Romans' development of concrete, a remarkably flexible building material that would make possible dramatic new building forms.

Public or domestic, Roman architecture was more than just a pretty face. To a degree unprecedented in history, the design of the interior came to be as well considered as that of the exterior. So important are the size, shape, and character of some Roman interiors that many Roman buildings can truly be said to have been designed "from the inside out."

The Development of Concrete

The use of concrete completely differentiates Roman architecture from earlier styles. An inexpensive and strong material, **concrete** was made by a mixture of small stones, the volcanic sand called *pozzolana* (already mentioned), lime, and water. This mixture was poured into temporary wooden forms, becoming a solid, monolithic mass as it dried and hardened (**cured**). As concrete was considered unsuitable for finished effects, its surface was covered with slabs of marble, alabaster, brick, or stucco, and these **veneers** (facings or overlays of different materials) served to protect as well as dress the concrete beneath.

The Roman development of concrete occurred not in a single leap but in a gradual evolution, using mixtures that cured increasingly slowly, which allowed them to become increasingly stronger. Using ever more regular placements

Tools & Techniques | CONCRETE CONSTRUCTION

Concrete was used mainly where downward pressure was the principal force, such as in walls, arches, and domes. There is no evidence that Roman engineers knew the principles of modern methods of reinforcing concrete with iron rods; the material was therefore never used for beams that were subjected to a bending stress. Instead, the Romans developed a composite construction technique of pouring concrete between walls of the soft stone called **tufa**, then facing the visible parts with stone ashlar (see fig.).

The types of concrete and methods listed below span the ages but give a clear indication of how useful and pervasive this type of construction is in our world, from the Romans onward.

- **adobe** Traditional masonry technique using sun-dried mud brick.
- **aggregate** Sand or gravel particles in a concrete mix.
- **cement** Binding agent in a concrete mix.
- **cement mortar** Concrete mix with high lime content, used for joining masonry materials or for surfacing.
- **cement plaster** Exterior grade of plaster containing Portland cement.
- **concrete** Substance formed by the mixture of cement, aggregate, and water.
- **ferrocement** Sand-aggregate concrete mix forced into several layers of wire mesh.
- **ferroconcrete** Steel-reinforced concrete, including ferrocement.
- **grout** Thin mortar that can be poured or injected into narrow joints.
- **lime** Powder used in many cement mixes, made by burning crushed limestone.
- **masonry** Structure built of substances used by masons, including stone, brick, and concrete.
- **mortar** Mixture of a cementlike material (such as cement, plaster, or lime) with sand and water.

- **plaster** Hard-surfaced material composed of cement, lime, or gypsum with sand and water.
- **plaster of paris** Quick-setting plaster composed of calcined gypsum and water.
- **Portland cement** Cement most commonly used in recent years. (Discovered in 1824, it resembles the limestone quarried on the English isle of Portland.)
- **reinforced concrete** Composite building material composed of concrete and (usually) steel reinforcement.
- **slurry** Mixture of cement and water without aggregate, sometimes used as a finish material.
- **stucco** Nonstructural exterior masonry coating made of lime, cement, sand, and water, usually roughly textured; also, a plaster used for decorative effects on interior walls.
- **terra-cotta** Hard, glazed earthenware, used as tile or as decorative elements.
- **terrazzo** Concrete incorporating irregular pieces of stone, most often used for flooring.

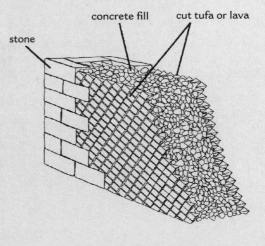

Composite Construction

of stone or brick insertions, the crafstmen made more and more use of particular volcanic sands that, mixed with lime, produced a mortar of great strength. At the same time, in the quarries at Carrara, marble became abundantly available as a facing material.

The Arch, the Vault, and the Dome

The Roman builders adopted the principles of Greek construction in using the column, lintel, and truss. In addition, with the new possibilities afforded by the use of concrete, they also began to span space with the structurally curved forms of the arch, vault, and dome (table 5–1).

With concrete, an **arch** could be constructed as a whole element poured in one piece. The arch became an intrinsic part of Roman architecture and greatly affected both exterior and interior design. It was also used for decorative purposes in doorways, windows, arcades, and niches. Its use served to introduce a variety of shapes in Roman design that did not exist in earlier styles.

TABLE 5–1   The Arch, the Barrel Vault, and the Groin Vault

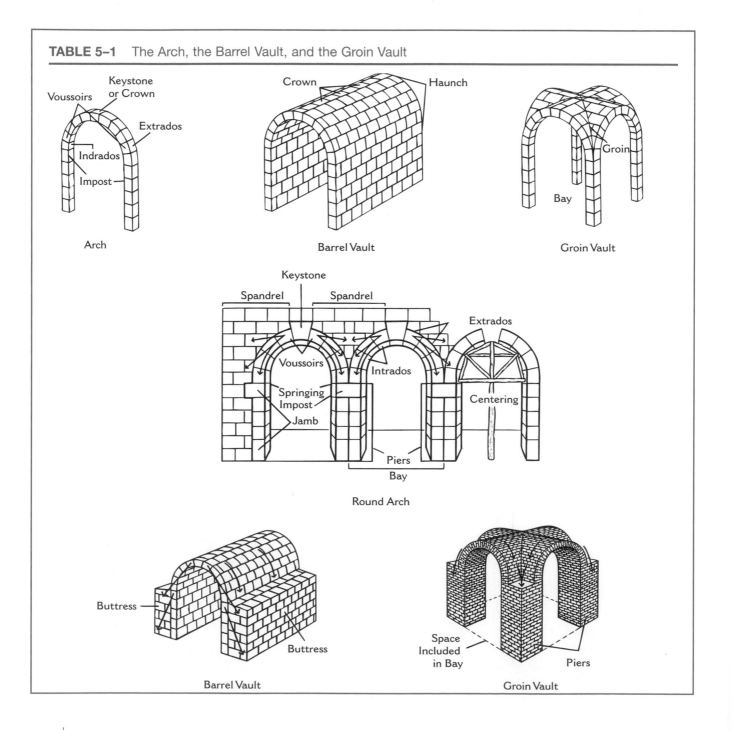

Extending the principle of the arch over a larger area, the Romans evolved the **barrel vault**, or curved ceiling. Semicircular in cross section, it was supported by parallel walls, arcades, or buttresses. Where two barrel vaults met at right angles, a **groin vault** might be formed. Rotating the principle of the arch around a central point produced a **dome**. These forms had been invented before, of course, but never before had they been built so easily and on so large a scale. The new methods also brought a freedom from the previous dependence on the **column** and the **architrave**, a freedom that would eventually relegate those elements to mere decorative appliqué.

Roman Variations on the Greek Orders

With the advent of the arch, vault, and dome, buildings were no longer dependent on the principle of columns supporting entablatures, but the Greek architectural orders remained a fundamental element in Roman design. But, as with so many other parts of their inheritance from Greece, the Romans made changes.

The three orders of Greek architecture were increased to five (table 5–2). The Romans altered slightly the Doric and Ionic orders to their tastes, and developed a variant of the Doric order called the **Tuscan order**, derived from Etruscan models. The Romans' favorite order, however, was the **Corinthian order**, with this order's capacity for elaborate decorative treatment, particularly in the capitals with their ornament based on acanthus leaves. And, further indulging their taste for richness, the Romans also devised a new order called the **Composite order** (fig. 5–5), its capitals combining the volutes of the Ionic with the acanthus leaves of the Corinthian. The Composite is the most elaborate, most slender, and most decorative of all five Roman orders.

During the reign of Augustus, the first-century Roman architect Vitruvius wrote a treatise called *De architectura*, in which he codified the proportions of the orders. This code greatly facilitated the building of the various administrative buildings needed throughout the Roman colonies, work that often had to be undertaken by local builders and stone-cutters who lacked training and aesthetic judgment. The codes of Vitruvius would be rediscovered and translated by Italian architects in the fifteenth century, and they would influence all the Renaissance styles of Western Europe.

Important additions made by the Romans to the Greek classical language of architecture include the *pilaster* and the *pedestal*. **Pilasters** are shallow piers that are sometimes half-round, sometimes rectangular versions of actual columns

---

TABLE 5–2 The Five Roman Orders

The Greek Doric order has been added for comparison, even though it was not used by the Romans.

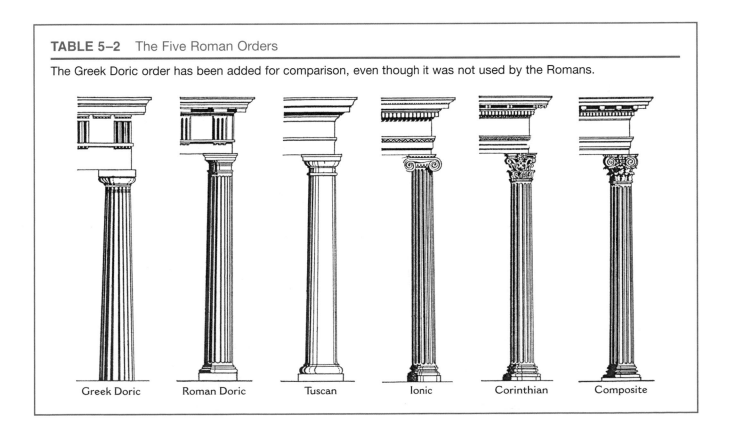

| Greek Doric | Roman Doric | Tuscan | Ionic | Corinthian | Composite |

▲ **5–5** An early example of the capital of the Composite order, carved c. 30 B.C., and later reused in the church of Santa Costanza, Rome.
Febermeyer/German Institute of Archaeology, Rome, Italy

that appear on wall surfaces as decoration. When rectangular, their projection from the wall was never more than half their width, and usually only one-fourth. Their capitals and bases were often identical with those of the columns they represented.

The **pedestal** under the base of a column was a Roman invention to enhance the loftiness of the orders. About a fourth or a third the height of the column, it was square in plan, featured its own cornice and base, and can be thought of as a Roman substitute for the Greek *crepidoma*. Used first on the exteriors of buildings, it later became an important feature of interior design; it was the prototype for the **dado** (or **chair rail**) of many later interior wall treatments. The dado molding stands about waist height and divides an interior wall into upper and lower sections.

Temples

The most impressive architectural achievement of the Greeks had been the Greek temple. Naturally, the admiring Romans would want to imitate it and, if possible, to make it bigger and better. For the Romans, as for so many of the world's builders (the Greeks being the notable exception), bigger *was* better. The Romans also felt a functional need for a larger temple interior (the **cella**), for the Roman temple became a depository of the spoils of war. Shields, trophies, and enemy weapons were often brought into the temple as tributes to a god or goddess thought to have guided the Romans to military victory.

Another dramatic change from the Greeks was the increased variety in Roman temples, not just in the number and shapes of the orders employed but also in the shape and configuration of the temple form itself. One of the most impressive Roman temples, the Pantheon in Rome, was circular in plan and topped by a dome, a structure not built by the Greeks.

The Pantheon   The Pantheon (from the Greek, *pan*, meaning "all," and *theos*, meaning "god") was a temple devoted to all the Roman gods of classical mythology. Although there were earlier versions on the same site, what we now see is almost entirely the work of the emperor Hadrian, probably built between A.D. 120 and 124.

The composition of the building is in two parts, their conjunction into a single composition being an example of Roman ingenuity without Greek precedent (fig. 5–6). The

▼ **5–6** Plan of the Pantheon, Rome, with the entrance portico at the bottom of the drawing.
Georges Ed. Berthoud

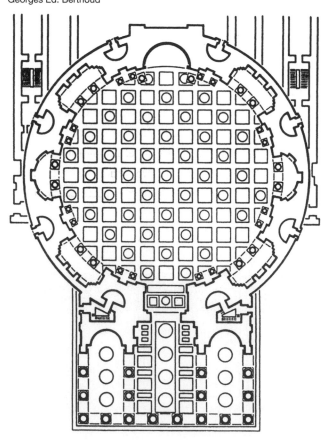

▲ 5–7 Looking into the Pantheon's great rotunda from the entrance portico.
American Academy in Rome

front part of the building, which may have been all that was clearly visible when it was first constructed in the heart of Rome, is a classical pedimented portico. It is in a giant Corinthian order, and it was originally several steps higher above ground level than it appears today. Its columns divide the façade into three aisles, two leading to apses set into the wall, the central one leading to a large entrance door.

Beyond this is the second part of the building, and entering it is a powerful experience (fig. 5–7). Inside is a vast **rotunda** (a building or interior round in plan and cylindrical in shape), 142 feet (44 m) in diameter, and measuring the same 142 feet from its floor to the top of its dome. These identical dimensions mean that the interior could hold within it a perfect sphere. Though such a sphere is not seen, it is implied, and the proportions of the space give it a harmony and repose that few other spaces can approach.

Lacking conventional window openings, the rotunda admits light through an **oculus** (a circular opening) overhead, an opening to the sky. The inside of this great masonry drum is visually lightened by the insertion of eight symmetrically placed round-headed niches, and its floor and walls are richly patterned with multicolored marbles. The **coffers** (sunken panels) of the dome interior emphasize the dome's curvature and thickness; this is ornamentation with perfect rightness of purpose.

In this building, the rectangularity of the Greeks was supplanted by a curved form, their post-and-beam method of construction replaced by a daringly domed one, and their persistence in the exteriority of their buildings given over to a new focus on interior volume.

Other Roman Temples   The Pantheon was not typical; most Roman temples followed the Etruscan model of a rectangular structure with a columned portico fronting a cella. A significant alteration from the Greek temple, as we have noted, was that the Roman cella and portico were raised on a relatively high base and approached by a tall flight of stairs. The portico itself was often deeper than was usual in Greece, creating a dramatic depth of shadow at the entrance. Proportions, too, were changed, for the Romans preferred taller, slenderer shapes, not just for columns but for the buildings themselves.

Public Buildings

The Roman temples were public in the sense that they reminded the entire population of their religious duties, but they were not meant to be entered except by a few priests and priestesses. The Romans did, however, construct magnificent buildings for the public.

Viewpoints | A HISTORIAN LOOKS AT THE PANTHEON

Architectural historian J. B. Ward-Perkins, in his definitive *Roman Imperial Architecture*, wrote that the Pantheon was "Perhaps the first great public monument—it is certainly the first on anything like this scale that has come down to us—to have been designed purely as an interior. . . . With the building of the Pantheon the revolution was an accomplished fact. Architectural thinking had been turned inside out; and henceforth the concept of interior space as a dominant factor in architectural design was to be an accepted part of the artistic establishment of the capital."

Baths Among the most impressive examples of Roman public architecture were the great **thermae**, or baths, which were rich in decoration and spatial variety. Based on the Greek gymnasia, the Roman thermae far surpassed them in both size and complexity. By the first century B.C., the Romans had developed hypocaust heating (with underground furnaces and tile flues), and used it for their baths. Layouts varied but generally included a changing room, a warm room without a bath, a hot room with a hot plunge bath, and a cold room with a cold plunge bath. Natural light, which had hardly penetrated Greek interiors, was a powerful and enlivening presence in many of these rooms, entering their upper reaches through great window areas. Bath complexes sometimes also included an outdoor swimming pool, a porticoed enclosure for wrestling and boxing, an indoor or outdoor space for other athletics (*gymnasium*), and, often, generous garden areas and even lecture halls and libraries. Two of the grandest of the thermae were those built in Rome by the emperors Diocletian and Caracalla. The complex built by Caracalla in the early third century, covered 50 acres, providing gardens, libraries, auditoriums, dressing rooms, and exercise grounds in addition to the central building housing the baths, which itself covered 5 acres (fig. 5–8). Our photograph of the baths' ruins (fig. 5–9) was taken before the space of the circular *caldarium* (hot bath) was converted into a giant stage for open-air opera.

Sometimes associated with the thermae were public lavatories (fig. 5–10), with unpartitioned lines of wooden or stone seats set over a sewer flushed with waste water from the baths. Thus, from the Romans comes the genesis of the modern toilet.

Forums The public architecture of the Romans included several innovations in building types for public assembly and entertainment, many of them grouped in civic centers called **forums**. The two greatest of these were the Forum Romanum, a collection of many buildings constructed over a long period, and the Forum of Trajan, a majestic compo-

▼ **5–9** Aerial view: Ruins of the principal building of the Baths of Caracalla.
Alinari/Art Resource, NY

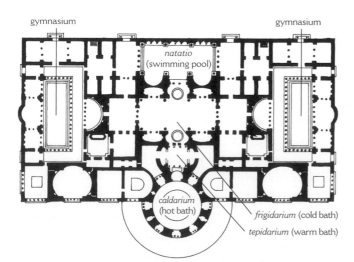

▲ **5–8** Plan of the principal building of the Baths of Caracalla, Rome, third century A.D. The length of the building is more than 600 ft. (185 m).

▲ **5–10** A communal lavatory at a Roman bath complex at Leptis Magna, North Africa, c. A.D. 127.
Ali Meyer/The Bridgeman Art Library International

▲ 5–11 Restored perspective view of the central hall, Basilica Ulpia, in the Forum of Trajan, Rome. A.D. 113. A section of the Column of Trajan is visible at right through the arcade. Drawn by Gilbert Gorski. Courtesy Dr. James E. Packer

sition conceived all at once (fig. 5–11). Within the forums were great **basilicas** (or halls with interior colonnades), which have been likened to Greek temples turned inside out, and which later formed the model for the earliest Christian churches. The Basilica Ulpia, just one part of the immense Forum of Trajan complex, was used as a place for commercial exchange.

Theaters and Amphitheaters The Romans built open theaters on Greek models but also invented a small, roofed theater, the **odeum**, and an enormous new building type, the *amphitheater*. The earliest known amphitheater was built in Pompeii c. 80 B.C.; Rome's first permanent one was built in 29 B.C. They were round or oval structures with sloping tiers of seating focusing on an open space, the *arena*, where gladiatorial events and shows of wild beasts took place. In some cases, voluminous fabric awnings could be unfurled to protect the spectators, and, in the largest examples, trapdoors in the arena floor could be opened to corridors and chambers below.

The largest and most remarkable was the Flavian amphitheater in Rome, commonly called the Colosseum (fig. 5–12). It was begun by the emperor Vespasian in A.D. 70 and completed ten years later, shortly after his death. Measuring 510 by 615 feet (156 × 188 m), it was built of a combination of concrete, the porous rock called tufa, and travertine (a type of marble, which is itself a type of limestone). It accommodated between 45,000 and 55,000 spectators, channeled to their seats through an elaborate system of barrel-vaulted corridors, radiating stairs, and ramps. Its three tiers of exterior arches were embellished with purely decorative half-round columns, ascending from the ground in Tuscan, then Ionic, and finally Corinthian orders, and, above these, an attic story carried tall Composite pilasters.

Other Roman Building Types Other nondomestic Roman building types included the *circus* for chariot races, the *stadium* (a building type taken from the Greeks) for other athletic events, the imperial reception hall, great aqueducts for water supply, city walls and gates, and warehouses and granaries. Most characteristically Roman of all were the

▲ **5–12** Colosseum, Rome. The orders applied in the form of half-round columns and pilasters are decorative, not structural.
Canali Photobank, Milan

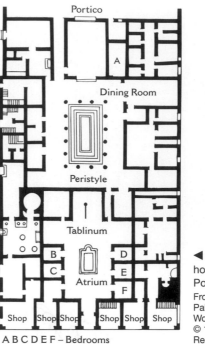

◄ **5–13** Floor plan, the house of Pansa, Pompeii.
From "Houses, Villas, and Palaces in the Roman World" by A. G. McKay, © 1973 Thames & Hudson. Reprinted by permission.

A B C D E F – Bedrooms

memorial columns and triumphal arches that marked city entrances or important spaces and that celebrated important figures and events.

Roman Houses

Unlike the Greeks, whose domestic architecture did not match their public architecture, the Romans' living quarters were as highly developed as personal finances would allow. Roman citizens lived in town houses, apartments, and country villas, and Roman emperors lived in incredibly elaborate versions of the Roman house or villa.

The Domus The Roman town house or **domus** was most commonly a single-family house. It was generally on a single level, but there was frequently a cellar below grade, including a water cistern. Some remains of second stories have been found, but it is generally thought that these were built later, added as city conditions became crowded. The domus was usually constructed of stone or stucco-faced brick, and the interior surfaces were highly decorated.

While the Greek house had been a private enclave, used only by the family and occasionally by a few male dinner guests, the Roman house was much more public, serving as a place for impressing visitors with a family's importance, affluence, and taste, and for meeting business and political

associates. (The master of a Roman household did not go to an office; he worked at home.)

Although it might have a couple of small windows facing the street, the domus focused inward (fig. 5–13). Its major rooms clustered around an **atrium**, or central hall (fig. 5–14), usually lit from above by a central opening in the roof called a **compluvium**. Through this opening, rainwater was directed into a catch basin, the **impluvium,** in the floor. The atrium served as a reception hall and circulation space. Recesses at the sides of the atrium, called **alae** (meaning "wings"), could be used as waiting rooms.

A narrow passage led from the street to the atrium. It was called the **fauces**, literally meaning "jaws" or "throat." The fauces was sometimes flanked by small shops or food stalls called **tabernae**, the source of our word "tavern." The tabernae opened to the street but not into the house itself. The exterior doors that opened into the fauces were wooden and generally double. Doors themselves were of hardwood, mortised to a cylindrical hardwood projection that rotated in sockets above and below the opening. Often the frame around these doors was elaborated with pilasters made of stone or stucco-covered brick, supporting an entablature, an assemblage sometimes called an **aedicule**, although the term more properly applies to a small temple so framed. If the entablature extended beyond the pilasters, as it often did in Roman houses, the

▲ **5–14** Looking from the atrium into the peristyle in the House of Pansa, Pompeii.
Alinari/Art Resource, NY

frame type is called an **aedicule with ears**. This type was popular again in the Renaissance and in the Neoclassical period.

Centered on the atrium at its far end, opposite the fauces, was a large room called the **tablinum**. This important space housed the family records and the images of its ancestors. It also served as a chief reception area for important visitors and for formal functions. Suitably, the tablinum's entrance from the atrium was often treated with pilasters supporting a cornice, and for privacy this entrance could be shielded with curtains or folding screens. The three adjacent spaces of fauces, atrium, and tablinum—usually arranged on an axis with their openings in an aligned procession called an **enfilade**—combined to make an impressive architectural statement for the most public part of the domus.

Also important was the dining room, called the **triclinium** because it was traditionally furnished with three banqueting couches called **klinia**. The three klinia, much larger than the Greek klini, were placed around three sides of the dining room, at right angles to each other, and the male family members and guests reclined on the klinia while eating. Women sat on chairs. The most typical number of diners at a Roman banquet was nine, with three to each couch. A very elaborate domus might have more than one dining room. The domus also contained a number of bedrooms, called **cubicula** (fig. 5–15). The typical bedroom was sometimes divided by curtains into three parts, one being a section for the attendant, the second for dressing, and the third—furnished only with a bed, called a **lectus**—for sleeping. The term *cubiculum* was sometimes extended to describe other small, private rooms in the domus; it is the source of our word *cubicle*.

Other rooms of a domus might include a daytime resting room, another room for entertaining guests, a shrine that honored the household gods, a kitchen and lavatory, placed near the kitchen to minimize the carrying of water; and sometimes a rear garden. A scholar's house would also contain a library, a **bibliotheca**.

The domus grew larger and more elaborate as the Roman Empire grew wealthier. By the time of the High Empire, the traditional atrium-centered spaces near the street were being used only for formal purposes, while most family activity centered on a generously sized **peristyle**, a

▲ **5–15** Bedroom from the house of Publius Fannius Synistor, Boscoreale, near Pompeii, late first century A.D.

Reconstruction of a cubiculum (bedroom) from the Villa of P. Fannius Synistor at Boscoreale, ca. 40–30 B.C.; Late Republican, Roman. Room: 8 ft. 8½ in. × 10 ft. 11½ in. × 19 ft. 7⅛ in. (265.4 × 334 × 583.9 cm). Rogers Fund, 1903 (03.14.13a–g). The Metropolitan Museum of Art, NY. Photograph © 2006 The Metropolitan Museum of Art, NY

rear garden courtyard that opened to the sky and was surrounded by a colonnade. Many of the houses had roof gardens. Terrariums, aquariums, and flower boxes were frequently featured. Cool water was carried by lead pipes to elaborate baths, ornamental pools, and drinking taps. Heat was obtained from portable charcoal-burning braziers or, in the houses of the most affluent, from central heating systems. By any preceding standards—and by most that would follow—the Roman domus was a dwelling of rare elegance.

Many rooms in Roman houses, as well as many shops and many inner precincts of temples, were windowless. However, in finer houses windows did appear, and a few of those were filled with window glass, an invention of the Romans (see the section on "Glass" on page 96). Those that were not filled with glass were sometimes filled with parchment, prepared from untanned animal skins. They could also have been filled with thin sheets of *mica*, a crystalline mineral substance that easily separates into thin, translucent sheets,

or with grilles of fine metal mesh. Roman windows of all kinds were also frequently covered, as were doorways and cupboards, with fabrics hung from bronze or wooden rings.

Ceilings were generally high, however, by today's standards, and doorways were also tall. Whenever possible, floors were paved with mosaics of marble tesserae, sometimes with black-and-white patterns, sometimes with colored designs. Ceilings were painted in geometrical patterns of intertwining floral and leaf designs, often accented with perched or flying birds, or gilded beams or panels, but the richest decorative effects were saved for the walls of Roman rooms.

The Insula   By the end of the first century, overpopulation and scarcity of land in Rome and other large towns dictated that only a few could afford the luxury of the domus, and so a majority of people began living in relatively cramped urban apartment houses called **insulae**.

The Roman insula was an apartment building four or five floors high, the upper apartments reached by communal stairs (fig. 5–16). Insulae were of varying size, but typically were built six or eight to a block. On the ground floor were shops or warehouses with large windows facing the street. Living above these shops without access to private gardens and with less interior space, the occupants of an insula were obviously less fortunate than the occupants of a domus, but the insula came to greatly outnumber the domus. Actual fourth-century records cite 46,000 insulae in the city of Rome, each with six to ten apartment units or sometimes more, and less than 1,800 examples of the domus.

Constructed at first of wood and mud brick (but later, at least partly, of concrete), the insulae were notoriously subject to collapse and fire (not surprisingly, as heating and cooking in the apartments were done by brazier). The apartments were often clustered around an open courtyard, as was the domus, but because the insulae were so tall, the courts were relatively dark, and their air relatively stale. Communal latrines were generally found only on the ground floors of these apartment blocks. Generally, a family owned its own domus, but apartment dwellers rented from a landlord, usually one who lived elsewhere. After a terrible fire in Rome in A.D. 64, Emperor Augustus instated reforms to legislate better housing conditions, and he imposed a maximum building height of 60 Roman feet or about 58 feet (17.75 m), or five stories. Such building regulations

▲ 5–16 Ground floor of an apartment block (*insula*), Ostia. First–second century A.D.
Araldo de Luca/Index, Ricerea Iconografica

were inconsistently enforced, and, in many ways, very little—except indoor plumbing—has changed in apartment-dwelling conditions or in the existence of housing-regulation headaches from Roman times until now.

The Villa   While the masses were living in apartments, the most affluent Romans embraced a new fashion: to leave the restrictions and noise of the city for life in the surrounding countryside. Collectively called **villas**, the suburban houses that they built and their surrounding lands were of several types and sizes, both by the sea or in the hills. For senators and other prominent citizens, direct connection to privately owned land was considered a source of status, so even when they were not working farms but only weekend retreats for city dwellers, they contained some agricultural component.

The villa, which might also be called a farmhouse, could take many forms. The atrium and peristyle of the urban domus were frequently present, but there were elements necessary to the working farm as well: workrooms, store-rooms, threshing floors, water cisterns, olive presses, and animal quarters. In addition to this practical element, the villa also served the loftier purpose of accommodating relaxed living and entertainment. Baths, libraries, colonnades, dining rooms, and gardens with fruit trees and fountains provided pleasant retreats for the Roman gentry. Inside, some rooms might be furnished with central heating, and many would boast painted walls and mosaic floors.

In addition to these three characteristic types of Roman housing—domus, insula, and villa—two very uncharacteristic houses, built for their own pleasure by two remarkable emperors, should be noted. Although one bears the name *domus* and the other the name *villa*, both must be classed as palaces. They are Nero's Domus Aurea and Hadrian's Villa.

The Domus Aurea   The emperor Nero's Domus Aurea (meaning "golden house") was built beginning in A.D. 64, when a disastrous fire (which some believed Nero had set himself) swept the city, clearing a vast area that Nero then claimed for his building site. The result was a palace of many levels, making full use of recently developed concrete building techniques, and richly decorated.

One of the house's spectacular rooms, described in literature, was a circular dining room in which the dinner guests were seated on a revolving platform. Another, the ruins of which are still visible, was a domed octagonal room centered

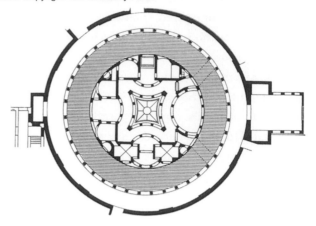

▼ **5–18** Floor plan of the island villa, one small part of Hadrian's Villa. The diameter of the outer wall is 135 ft. (44 m).

J. B. Ward-Perkins, "Roman Imperial Architecture, Harmondsworth: Penguin, 1981. Copyright Yale University Press.

▲ **5–17** A model of the vast complex of Hadrian's Villa at Tivoli, built between A.D. 118 and 134.
German Institute of Archaeology, Rome, Italy

on a fountain. Parts of the exterior walls are thought to have been faced with gold, and some interior walls were inlaid with gems and mother-of-pearl. Through openings in fretted ivory ceilings, flowers were dropped on the guests below, and through other openings, jets of rose water and other scents were sprayed. "Now at last," Nero is reported to have said upon the completion of the Domus Aurea, "I am beginning to be housed like a human being."

Today, little remains but the concrete shells of some original spaces now stripped of their finished surfaces.

Hadrian's Villa Emperor Hadrian oversaw the building of the Pantheon, but nothing could be more different from the Pantheon than the country villa he had built near the suburb of Tibur (now Tivoli). The Pantheon is a model of order, unity, centrality, and geometric discipline; the villa's fanciful elements are dispersed in a free, sprawling, picturesque composition (fig. 5–17) that, in its present ruined state, shows that it surpassed any of its predecessors.

Hadrian began his villa in A.D. 118, and construction continued for twenty years. Scattered over many acres, the elements of the villa included various porticoes and pavilions, banqueting halls, guest quarters, large and small baths,

▲ **5–19** The island villa as it appears today.
American Academy in Rome

a temple, an exercise ground, a stadium, a theater, a library, and a number of ornamental pools and water courts, many of them formally distinguished by compound curves and complex geometry.

One of these elements, the island "villa" (also called the island enclosure, or the Teatro Marittimo), can serve to demonstrate the ingenuity and originality typical of the whole complex (fig. 5–18). Within a vaulted ring supported by a colonnade of forty unfluted Ionic columns, a moat open to the sky surrounds an island retreat reached by two bridges (fig. 5–19). The island is divided by curving walls into four groups of domed and vaulted rooms: on the north, a semicircular entrance vestibule; to the east, a small bedroom suite with two bedrooms and two latrines; to the south, a dining room with antechambers; to the west, a small bath complex with hot and cold plunges. Surprising vistas into unusual spaces, dramatic effects of light and shade, and the reflectivity of the sunlit water must all have contributed to a rare experience.

Roman Ornament

We have seen how the Romans developed concrete and used it as the basis for a whole new vocabulary of building forms. They were equally inventive in ornamenting these forms. In the hands of the Greeks, the classical orders had always been structural; with their new vaulted spaces, the Romans no longer needed to rely on columns for structure, but began to apply them ornamentally. They also had a more enthusiastic taste for ornament of all sorts, including wall painting. Whenever possible, Roman interior surfaces—no matter what the building type—were ornamented.

Wall Treatments

Wall surfaces of Roman rooms were treated with fine marble veneers, painted murals, or carved stone reliefs. When such luxury was not possible, relief panels might be made of stucco, or masonry walls might be coated with plaster that was then ruled to imitate stone coursing. The most common interior wall treatment, however, was painting.

Often the paintings represented architecture or materials that were not present, in techniques that today would be called **trompe l'oeil** (French for "fool the eye"). The walls were divided into a lower section treated as a pedestal or a dado and a high upper section reserved for more decorative paintings. The panels in the pedestal or dado often imitated marble slabs or a balcony **balustrade** (a series of short vertical posts or miniature columns).

Often the high upper section was divided into vertical panels by painted columns or pilasters, crowned with entablatures realistically represented in perspective. The painted architectural features were often reduced to the most delicate and slender proportions, showing that Roman painters understood the possibilities of their medium, which was not subject to real-life structural limitations.

Since these imaginary constructions did not need to support themselves, their painters felt no need to observe the Vitruvian rules for the proportions of the orders.

The panel centers within these frameworks were treated in one of several ways: They could be painted a plain color framed with painted moldings, or they could enclose an ornamental arabesque or a scenic pattern. The most interesting of the Roman mural decorations were those showing scenic effects in which the subject matter was drawn from an infinite number of sources. Mythology, allegory, history, landscape, still life, humor, city streets, portraiture, and animals were charmingly depicted. Playful nymphs and satyrs were shown in woodland settings. The draperies of a dancing girl would so accurately indicate the movement of her body that one could almost feel the rhythm of the dance. A forest grove would transport a city dweller to a verdant retreat, as in the wall paintings (see fig. 5–1) from the house of Livia (mother of the emperor Tiberius), built on the Palatine Hill in the first century B.C.

In many murals, the colors were comparatively brilliant, as was necessary in rooms having only a dim light. The medium was true fresco, the pigments being applied to and absorbed by the wet plaster. When dried, the surface was waxed and polished for protective purposes. Backgrounds were most commonly in black, white, or red, but other colors were also used, including saffron yellow, vermilion, and a bright green obtained from malachite.

Based on the discoveries at Pompeii and Herculaneum, scholars have determined a series of four distinct painting styles, in use from the second century B.C. until the eruption of Mt. Vesuvius in A.D. 79. These four styles are thought to have also been in general use in the areas around Naples and Rome at the same time.

- The **First Style**, or Incrustation Style, used in the second century B.C., employed a *faux marbre* technique to imitate inlaid marble slabs ("crustae"). Even when succeeded by other styles, the marble representations of the First Style continued to be used along the dadoes or bottom portions of walls.

- The **Second Style**, or Architectural Style, employed painting to resemble a building or a colonnade, usually seen from within with open countryside visible beyond. An example is the panorama on a wall of the cubiculum seen in figure 5–15.

▲ **5–20** Painted wall decoration of the Third Style in the villa of Agrippa Postumus at Boscotrecase, c. 20 B.C.
National Museum of Naples, Italy/Gemeinnutzige Stiftung Leonard von Matt, Buochs, Switzerland

▲ **5–21** Fourth Style wall painting in the House of the Prince of Naples, Pompeii.
Canali Photobank

- The **Third Style**, also known as the Ornate Style, still included architectural forms, but in a more ornamental way, among figures and landscapes. Delicate bands divided the panels, some of which were painted in solid colors. An example from Boscotrecase, near Pompeii, is predominantly red (fig. 5–20).

- The **Fourth Style**, or Intricate Style, employed fantastic structures in grotesque and sometimes impossible arrangements. An example is seen in Pompeii's House of the Prince of Naples (fig. 5–21).

Details of stylistic differences in wall painting and stucco are important only to designers, perhaps, but the fact that such differences did exist and were so widely followed gives us unmistakable proof of the importance of changing fashion to the Roman artist and connoisseur.

Variations on Greek Patterns, Moldings, and Motifs

In general, Roman ornament was more elaborate than Greek and was applied more lavishly, but the craftsmanship was sometimes less refined than found in Greek work, partly because the limestone and cast stucco often used by the Romans allowed less precision than the Greek marble.

The Greek fret was frequently used by the Romans, as in a mosaic floor from Pompeii (fig. 5–22). More abstract, less representational ornament was patterned after Greek motifs, such as the fret, swastika, key, spiral, egg-and-dart, and dentil patterns. The acanthus leaf appeared not only on the Corinthian and Composite capitals but was also carved in festoons and scrolls, as in a marble pilaster from the Hellenistic period (fig. 5–23). The honeysuckle and anthemion also made an appearance, as did other foliage. Human figures, divinities, and small cupids—also called **putti**—were frequently employed, as were serpents, swans, eagles, lions, and oxen. Fantastic figures such as sphinxes, satyrs, griffins, and genii were used in "grotesque" ornament.

Roman moldings were taken directly from Greek models, but most underwent slight modifications (fig. 5–24). In general, the Greek precedents were based on complex geometrical figures such as the parabola and the ellipse; their curvatures were subtle and varied. Their Roman counterparts were based on simpler geometrical figures such as the circle; they were bolder and more obvious. But the Roman moldings were appropriate for the forceful character of most Roman architecture, and they had the great advantage of being simple to lay out and simple to carve.

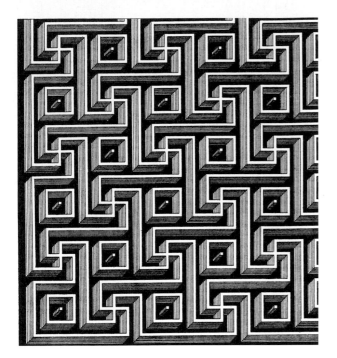

▲ 5–22 From a mosaic found at Pompeii, a Roman pattern based on the Greek fret.

W. & G. Audsley, "Designs and Patterns from Historic Ornament," Dover Publications, Inc., New York, 1968, Plate 2, Fret Ornament, fig. 1. From "Outlines or Ornament in the Leading Styles," Scribner and Welford, 1882.

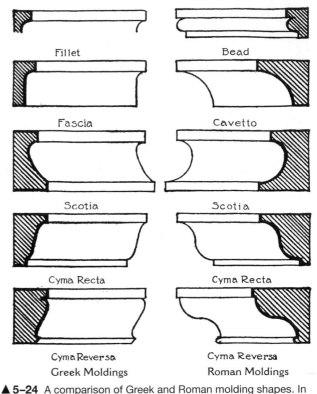

Fillet   Bead

Fascia   Cavetto

Scotia   Scotia

Cyma Recta   Cyma Recta

Cyma Reversa   Cyma Reversa
Greek Moldings   Roman Moldings

▲ 5–24 A comparison of Greek and Roman molding shapes. In general, the Romans regularized the more subtly curved Greek models.

Gilbert Werlé/New York School of Interior Design

▲ 5–23 Detail, carved marble pilaster of scrolling acanthus leaves.

Section of a Pilaster with Acanthus Scrolls, Julio–Claudian period, first half 1st Century A.D. Marble, H. 43½ in. (110.5 cm). The Metropolitan Museum of Art, Rogers Fund, 1910 (10.210.38). Photograph © 2000 The Metropolitan Museum of Art.

Roman Furniture

How the interiors were finished and furnished was of great concern to the Romans. What evidence we have suggests that the Romans were more restrained in matters of furnishings than in some other areas. Rooms seem to have been sparely furnished with a small number of objects, but often much care and expense was lavished on those few so that the furnishings of the Roman house grew to be as elegant as the house itself. By the time of the emperor Cato (234–149 B.C.), couches were inlaid with decorations of ivory, bone, antler, silver, and gold. Tables and chairs were inlaid with metals and precious stones. Beds were made of wood or metal, their slender legs often ending in animal feet. Elegant bronze tripods served as end tables, and highly polished bronze plates served as mirrors. Bronze **braziers** (a container for burning coals) warmed the rooms (fig. 5–25). Bronze oil lamps lighted the rooms. Elaborate library cabinets were built with pigeonholes for rolled manuscripts. Rich furnishings were more widespread than ever before in history.

▼ **5–25** Roman brazier on a folding tripod base, bronze, first century A.D. The legs have animal heads and feet.
Réunion des Musées Nationaux/Art Resource, NY

Seating and Beds

More than the people of any other culture we have considered, the Romans enjoyed being seated. Like the Greeks, they reclined while dining. Their dining and sleeping beds, their thrones, chairs, and stools all had Greek origins but were given Roman interpretations.

The Lectus   The Roman couch or **lectus** was a highly valued piece of Roman household furniture. It was single, double, or even triple in width and was used either for sleeping or dining. The Etruscan and Roman versions were in some cases somewhat lower to the floor than the Greek couch, and the Roman version usually had turned legs decorated with moldings (fig. 5–26). It had a headboard, and often a footboard, both elaborately shaped and carved. Sometimes it also had a back, so that it resembled a modern sofa. Ropes or metal strips within the rectangular frame supported a straw or wool mattress, which might be covered with silk cushions or costly textiles imported from the East.

When used for dining, the usual arrangement was to place a couch at each of three sides of the room, with a square table in the center. Two or three reclining diners

▲ **5–26** Bronze and wood lectus found at Boscoreale, the wood parts seen here having been restored. Note the similarities with the Greek kline (Figure 4–28)
Scala/Art Resource, NY

might share a single lectus. In this arrangement, one lectus might have only a headboard, the one opposite only a footboard, and the central one neither headboard nor footboard, so that the diners might have more flexibility in placing themselves. A lectus in a dining room was called a **klinium**, a descendent of the Greek **kline**.

The Solium One passage in Roman literature describes the **solium** as a chair so important it was reserved for emperors and gods; another describes it as a chair for patrons only. In either case, it was a seat of honor used in formal receptions. Closely based on the Greek thronos, there were also Etruscan precedents made of bronze (see fig. 5–4) or of white marble. In the domus, the solium might be rendered in stone and prominently displayed in the atrium. Like the thronos, it might have had several forms, but the most favored had a rounded or rectangular back and solid sides, the fronts of which might be carved in the forms of animals or monsters.

The Cathedra More often used was the *cathedra*, but even this chair was sometimes reserved for dignitaries and women of noble families. It was based on the Greek klismos (see figs. 4–26 and 4–27) having a rounded back supported on vertical stiles, curving legs, and (usually) no arms. Though based on the Hellenistic klismos, it lacked the gracefulness of the Greek version, judging from carved and painted representations. It was also used as a litter for conveying wealthy Roman women about town. Later, the cathedra would give its name to the cathedral, the "seat" of a bishop.

Stools and Benches The most common Roman seating was the wooden stool, and one popular version, based on the Greek dipthros, had a sturdy seat on four perpendicular legs that were ornamented with turnings. Some stools were made of bronze with concave seats, on which cushions were placed (fig. 5–27). Even more popular was the folding stool, or **sella** (fig. 5–28). Also modeled on the diphros, it was made of wood, bronze, or iron. Its crossed legs were sometimes straight and sometimes curved, sometimes plain and sometimes terminated in animal feet.

The most illustrious version, which came to be associated with political power, was the *sella curulis* or **curule**. This was a stool on an X-shaped base with multiple parallel legs in two interlocking sets, as seen in a carving on a grave stele (fig. 5–29). It came to be a symbol of the authority of the

▲ **5–27** Bronze stool. First century A.D. A cushion would have been used on the concave seat.
© The Trustees of the British Museum

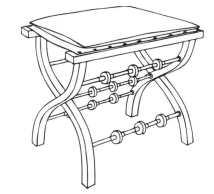

▲ **5–28** The Roman *sella* or folding stool. Examples were made in both wood and metal.

◄ **5–29** The *sella curulis* of a Roman magistrate. It is carved here on a first century A.D. grave stele, indicating that the deceased had been a government official.
Musée Calvet, Avignon, France. Photo by Andre Guerrand.

Sometimes an ancient tragedy is the cause of preservation for the future. Such was the case with two Roman towns near the Gulf of Naples, Pompeii and Herculaneum. In A.D. 79 they were buried under the sudden fallout of ash from the nearby volcano Vesuvius, which had erupted violently. What Vesuvius buried for centuries to depths of up to 60 feet (18 m) were settlements of considerable elegance, with interior decor more elaborate and more refined than other, more badly weathered Roman houses had ever revealed. Most remarkable of all is the series of wall murals that the volcano preserved for us to see.

In 1711 a chance discovery during the digging of a well unearthed the first stone and concrete fragments from Herculaneum. Further digging produced three statues of women; dubbed "Vestal Virgins," they were taken to Vienna for exhibition. In 1748 the first human body was found. Discovery of the larger and even richer site of Pompeii came a decade later. Excavations were aided by the fact that the cities were found under open fields, not beneath newer construction, and by their being buried—to a large extent—under light volcanic ash. Findings of the excavations reached a wide audience, thanks to a series of publications that began with eight volumes of drawings ordered by Charles III, King of the Two Sicilies; they became a wonderful resource for scholars and designers.

Roman magistrate, and eventually its use was limited to high public officials. Some officials had sellae made of ivory, and Julius Caesar is said to have had one made of gold. Roman literature mentions the sella curulis as an adaptation of an Etruscan stool and describes it as an emblem of dignity, along with the purple robe, the signet ring, and the gilded laurel wreath. Later, the Roman Catholic Church would appropriate the sella curulis as the special seat of a bishop, which was also called a *cathedra*.

Tables

The Greeks had used tables primarily during meals and then put them away. The Romans, having greater numbers of possessions and greater pride in showing them, needed tables as permanent display platforms. The great orator Cicero (100–43 B.C.) was reported to have paid an enormous sum for a table made of citrus wood, while tables of cypress were even more highly prized, and the finest were made of marble, bronze, silver, or gold.

The dining table, called a **mensa**, sat low among the klinia for diners. The Romans also used smaller, taller tables for holding flowers or candles or other objects. The Greek trapeza with its round top and three animal-shaped legs became very popular with the Romans. They also popularized a type rarely used by Greeks—a table with a round or square top on a single central support, here seen in a marble top version, edged with bronze on a marble and bronze pedestal (fig. 5–30).

The **cartibulum** was a ceremonial marriage table made of marble, which might have had a place of honor in the atrium of a domus, and on which might have been a display of fine utensils and serving ware (fig. 5–31). Marble was also used for the decorated slab supports of a table popular for outdoor use (fig. 5–32); its rectangular top was sometimes made also of marble, sometimes of wood. It became a favorite again during the Italian Renaissance, when copies were made entirely of wood.

▼ **5–30** Table on a single pedestal. Its square marble top is edged in bronze. Such tables were also made with circular tops.
Table of variegated marble, with bronze rim decorated with design in silver and niello; reconstructed from a number of fragments; Roman, 1st century A.D., Boscoreale, Italy. The Metropolitan Museum of Art, Rogers Fund, 1906. (06.1021.301)

The ceremonial table called a *cartibulum*, shown here beside the *impluvium* (water basin) of the *atrium* of a house in Herculaneum. The table top is 4 ft. (1.3 m) long.
Alinari/Art Resource, NY

▲ 5–32 Carved marble support of a table found at Pompeii.
Alinari/Art Resource, NY

Storage Furniture

Storage furniture in Rome was rare by today's standards. In modest houses, clothing and other family possessions were hung on hooks or nails. The Romans were probably the first to develop the open cupboard or sideboard on which family treasures of glass, silver, or gold could be displayed; it was called an **armarium**. A typical example might have had an upper part, with statuettes of the household gods, the Lares and Penates, made in the form of a miniature temple, flanked by small Corinthian columns; this may have served as a shrine. The lower part might be a cupboard with shelves, where were found glassware, vases of bronze and terra-cotta, and a number of small ornamental objects.

On a smaller scale, there were chests, some of them elaborately finished. Boxes and containers of many shapes and sizes, generally called *arca*, were small and round or rectangular for jewelry and for toilet articles. In a society without bank vaults or safety deposit boxes, there were, of course, strongboxes for the keeping of valuables.

Lighting

Roman lamps held wicks floating in oil. Made of pottery, iron, carved stone, or bronze, they were all decoratively embellished. Some were designed to sit on tables or stands; some were on tall pedestals, usually with a tripod base; and others were designed to be hung from the ceiling on chains. An example found at Pompeii (fig. 5–33), executed in bronze, has a base on which a satyr is riding a panther. Above, four oil lamps hang from branches that curve outward from the elaborate (and unidentifiable) capital of a square column.

Candles and candleholders were also used, whether table, stand, or floor versions. From Hadrian's Villa, examples remain of floor **candelabra**–branched, highly ornamental candle–holders—that are more than 6 feet (2 m) tall (fig. 5–34).

◄ 5–33 From the Villa of Diomedes at Pompeii, an ornate lampstand made of bronze, holding four oil lamps.
Alinari/Art Resource, NY

▶ **5–34** From Hadrian's Villa, one of a pair of carved marble candelabra, more than 6 ft. (2 m) high.
Alinari/Art Resource, NY

Roman Decorative Arts

The Romans enjoyed a great appetite for decorative objects brought from the far reaches of their empire, as well as for those they made at home. Their ceramics never reached the level of excellence we saw in the Greek vase, but their accomplishments in glass and mosaic work were outstanding.

Ceramics

The Greek painted vase is so highly praised that it is natural to ask if the Romans did not inherit some of the great artistry of the Greek vase. Romans did indeed manufacture and export large amounts of pottery (tableware, figurines, candleholders, lamps, and storage vessels), but much of this pottery was crude. The best, called **terra sigillata**, was finely made, though seldom with decoration of Greek excellence. *Terra sigillata* means "clay stamped with a seal" (a *sigillum*) identifying the maker. It was usually red in color and made from fine red clay, and unglazed, but some black and even some marbled examples have been found.

Glass

Glass was invented somewhere in the Eastern Mediterranean area; some think the process of glassblowing began in Syria in the first century B.C. We have already noted the glass beads and pendants of Crete, and the casting and molding

of solid glass objects in Egypt. By the middle of the first century A.D., sophisticated glassmaking was well established in Rome and well adapted to Roman taste. In quality, quantity, and variety, the Romans produced glass as no earlier civilization had done.

Roman glass included extraordinary showpieces for the delectation of the aristocracy. It also included mass-produced items for common use. It served utilitarian purposes, as vessels for holding either perfumes or pungent sauces made from preserved fish. It also served as propaganda, displaying images of emperors and gods. Because much of the distribution was done by Phoenician merchants, however, it has sometimes been called Phoenician glass.

Window Glass The Roman use of glass in window openings had a huge impact on the character of interior space. Both shattered glass and strips of leading, used between glass panes, have been found at Pompeii. Though such use was not widespread and occurred only in very small openings, its future potential was enormous.

Within the Roman interior, there were many examples of glass objects displaying unprecedented techniques and ingenuity.

Flashed Glass and Cased Glass A category of free-blown glass is **flashed glass**, which involves coating the outer surface of a glass object with a thin coating of glass in another color. The coating can then be partly carved away to produce a desired design, and repetition of the process can produce multilayered, multicolored effects. Another name for the flashing technique is dip-overlay, and in France such glass is known as **verre doublé**.

Roman glass ceased to be considered an imitation of silver or ceramics and came to be appreciated for its own qualities. Even so, the most spectacular examples of early Roman free-blown glass were the **glass cameos**, carved by glasscutters in imitation of onyx and other fine layered stones. Many glass cameos were found at Pompeii.

An opposite technique to flashed glass, which became popular in the nineteenth century, involves coating the *inner* surface of one glass with another; it is called **cased glass** (or **cup-overlay**).

Cage Cups A type of glasscutting at which the Romans excelled was the creation of some astonishing pieces called **diatreta** (fig. 5–35), after the Roman term for glasscutter,

▲ **5–35** A Roman cage cup of almost colorless glass. c. A.D. 300. 4¾ in. (12 cm) in diameter.
Roman cage cup of almost colorless glass. Collection of The Corning Museum of Glass, Corning, New York. Gift, funds from Arthur Rubloff Residuary Trust (87.1.1)

▲ **5–36** Painted glass bottle from the eastern part of the Roman Empire. Late third century. 6 in. (15 cm) high.
Painted glass bottle from the eastern part of the Roman Empire, late 3rd century. Collection of The Corning Museum of Glass, Corning, New York. Museum Endowment Fund purchase (78.1.1)

diatretarius. Today they are often called **cage cups**. In these vessels, thick glass was cut into deep relief, and the relief then undercut, leaving it attached to the solid vessel by a structurally minimal number of glass bridges. The process was laborious, requiring much time and great skill, and the results were extremely fragile; obviously these were luxury items.

Painted Glass Painting on glass, developed in the first century A.D., occurred before the vessels were fired so that the paint would be fused to the glass (fig. 5–36). Subjects included plant and animal forms as well as mythological and domestic scenes. Painting was sometimes combined with gilding, for the Romans also produced vessels and portrait medallions in which gold leaf was sandwiched between disks of colored and clear glass. This gold-between-glass technique became popular again in Germany beginning in the eighteenth century and is known as **zwischengoldglas.**

Other Roman Glass Techniques Other glassmaking techniques used by the Romans included mosaic glass (fig. 5–37), made by fusing together monochrome or polychrome elements cut from colored canes (thin glass rods or bundles of such rods) to create patterns sometimes brilliant

▲ **5–37** Bowl of mosaic glass from central Italy. Second century B.C. 5 in. (13 cm) in diameter.
© The Trustees of the British Museum

in color; a variation of mosaic glass is called *millefiore* (Italian for "thousand flowers"). A more subtle accomplishment was the fragile opalescent ware known as **murrhine**, used for wine cups, vases, and other ornamental vessels. The name *murrhine* is sometimes used today for a product imitating the Roman ware, in which a transparent body holds embedded pieces of colored glass. All three of these complex, multicolor processes were perhaps attempts to imitate the great virtuosity being displayed in mosaic work.

Materials said to be **vitreous** (glasslike) can be divided into four chief categories: *Egyptian faience*, which we have already seen; *glaze*, a surfacing on such material as earthenware; *enamel*, a surface generally fused onto metal; and glass itself. All four are made by firing together some form of silica (such as sand) and an alkali (such as soda or potash), although Egyptian faience contains less alkali than the others. Lime is usually added as a stabilizer, and other additives can produce special effects (lead, for example, making the glass heavier and more brilliant).

Glass results from work with a material that must be formed while it is too hot to touch with the hands. Special tools are needed. The earliest tool for gathering molten glass from a furnace and for beginning to form it was a solid metal rod called a **pontil** or punty. It is still used as an auxiliary tool, but the chief tool—which some think was invented in Syria in the first century B.C.—is the hollow blowpipe, at the end of which a mass of molten glass can be inflated. Before the introduction of the blowpipe, all Roman glass had been cast, formed in molds. Molds were made from pottery or, for finer pieces, metal. Because glass does not shrink slightly as it cools (as clay does), the molds were made in two or more pieces for easy removal.

When the blowpipe was introduced in the second half of the first century B.C., Romans at first employed **free-blown** techniques, in which the glass bubble is shaped in the open by gravity, by swinging the blowpipe, or by using special tools such as pincers and pliers. Around A.D. 25, Romans began inserting the blowpipe into molds and blowing the glass to fill them. With this mold-blown method, a predetermined and complex shape could be repeatedly achieved, and glass objects became less expensive and more widely used than ever. Whether cast, free-blown, or mold-blown, Roman glass was given a wide variety of shapes and decorative treatments.

Mosaics

The technique of facing surfaces with a layer of small, closely spaced pieces of near-uniform size is known as **mosaic** work, and the pieces themselves are known as **tesserae**. Mosaics are older than Roman civilization; the Greeks had made frequent use of them. In Rome, however, they became an important art form for the first time, and the mosaic techniques spread to many parts of the empire: Britain, France, Spain, North Africa, and elsewhere.

While Greek tesserae had generally been pebbles, usually white or pale tan ones, creating designs against black or dark blue backgrounds, Roman tesserae were made of a wide range of materials, mostly small cubes of marble, or other natural stone, but also shells, terra-cotta, mother-of-pearl, colored glass, and, in later years, glass with applied or embedded pieces of tin, silver, or gold. Generally, the sparkling glass mosaics were used for wall panels, pools, or niches holding statuary or fountains, and the sturdier stone mosaics were used for floors that received foot traffic.

Most Roman mosaics were assembled on site, but some incorporated *emblemata*, small decorative panels of unusually fine work that could be prepared in an artisan's studio on a tray of slate or terra-cotta, and then brought to a building site and set into a larger composition. The emblemata were clearly luxury items with limited use.

A type of Roman mosaic called *opus vermiculatum* (fig. 5–38) is composed of tightly spaced tesserae in undulating rows that might be described as wormlike (or vermicular) in appearance. Floor and wall mosaics used the same decorative patterns inherited from the Greeks, including elaborate

▼ **5–38** An example of *opus vermiculatum*, made of tiny tesserae in wavy rows.
Scala/Art Resource, NY

▲ **5–40** "Beware of the Dog" was as frequent a warning in Roman cities as in our own, often symbolized in mosaic at the threshold of a house.
Scala/Art Resource, NY

vigorously embraced naturalistic motifs, placing them wherever they liked, with subjects including groupings of masks, heads, garlands, and wreaths. Pigeons drink from a bowl, parrots strut, ducks waddle. Some of the floors at Piazza Armerina show chariot races, children hunting, cupids fishing, couples dancing and kissing, an elephant and a rhinoceros, and bikini-clad girls performing some sort of exercises with dumbbells. A mosaic of a barking dog on a vestibule floor expresses the message *Cave Canem*, or "Beware of the Dog" (fig. 5–40). If we assume that the Roman makers of mosaic, millefiori, and murrhine glassware were, to some extent, imitating the mosaicist, we may also assume that the Roman mosaicist was imitating the painter and sculptor, applying tesserae in such a way as to make the result as convincingly realistic as possible.

Textiles

It is clear from painted, carved, and written descriptions that fabric hangings and fabric-wrapped cushions and mattresses were important features of the Roman interior. Because these goods are extremely perishable, however, our knowledge about how they looked is speculative. We do know that materials used included wool, linen, silk, and leather, and we know that fabrics were not only woven but also embroidered and sometimes painted.

In the Roman domus, doorways of the cubicula and other rooms were often closed with curtains hung on bronze rings, rather than with pivoting wood doors. Curtains also substituted for doors in some cupboards.

While what we today call upholstery—padding fixed to a chair or sofa frame—would not be developed until the

rinceaux, arabesques, and geometric devices. There were combinations of geometry and stylized plant forms, such as those unearthed at a Roman villa (fig. 5–39) near the town of Piazza Armerina in Sicily. The villa, built in the fourth century A.D., contained roughly forty-five rooms. Almost all the rooms—a total of 38,000 square feet—were paved with mosaics!

The Romans also used highly realistic scenes for both walls and floors; today such scenes would be considered appropriate for walls, but seldom for floors. The Romans

seventeenth century, it was commonplace for Romans to soften a seat with a cushion, elaborated with fringes and tassels.

It seems from painted evidence that there were also decorative curtains, wall hangings, canopies, and the Roman equivalent of what we call **valances**—pieces of fabric that finish the tops of curtains or that hang over the frame of a bed or couch. And there were, of course, mattresses and bed pillows. For floors, a kind of rush matting was woven.

Painted evidence indicates that most of these soft goods were highly decorative (striped cushion covers are seen in a Pompeii wall painting). Probably many of them were brilliantly colored. The evidence has mostly vanished, but all we know of Roman taste and temperament suggests that these furnishings would not have been left unadorned.

Summary: Ancient Roman Design

The Romans were responsible for disseminating the ideas and achievements of Greek art and architecture throughout a vast empire, for which we owe them a great debt. But Rome was no mere conduit. The Romans left behind a culture of distinct personality.

Looking for Character

One remarkable characteristic of Roman design was its uniformity. Despite Rome's widespread dominion across miles, climates, peoples, and cultural traditions, Rome's design aesthetic remained dominant and identifiable. Even as the Romans assimilated many of those traditions from the lands they conquered, there was a distinct Roman city plan, whether laid out in Britain or North Africa, and there were recognizable cultural artifacts: temples, houses, tables, lamps, and wall paintings—just about everything they produced.

Another remarkable characteristic of Roman design was its emphasis on decorative effects. The Romans, like no other culture before them, had a flair for elaboration and embellishment, and this flair was not confined to special precincts for the gods or the special possessions of rulers. The Romans brought decorative art into their homes, and to the greatest extent possible, Roman citizens lived richly and luxuriously among their products of design.

But how were these two characteristics of widespread uniformity and decorative expressiveness reconciled? The

fact was that design had to be interpreted and reproduced by a great variety of artisans (local and foreign) with different training and different abilities, so some simplification and standardization of Roman art was necessary. We saw an example of this in the Roman variations on Greek moldings. The Greek curves were, perhaps, more subtle and more intriguing, at least to the trained eye; but the more regular Roman curves were more easily understood, more easily drawn, and more easily carved. This regularization of design was not a faltering of principles but a brilliant recognition of the realities of efficiently conveying design ideas.

Looking for Quality

We most often look for quality in small things, and in Roman art we can find many examples of wonderful quality: in the delicacy of a cage cup, the intricate details of a mosaic floor, the fine brushwork of a wall mural. But Roman art displays quality in the large and robust, and perhaps the supreme achievements of Roman art are its most expansive: the great sweep of an arena, the exhilarating span of a huge dome, the power of a great vault, the magnificence of a long enfilade of aligned doorways. However exquisitely faced or finished these architectural forms may be, their intrinsic drama is in their basic construction, and it is a drama best appreciated in interior spaces.

Making Comparisons

Much of this chapter has been concerned with comparing the civilizations of Greece and Rome, but in the end, Greek art and Roman art were different largely because the Greeks and Romans had different ideas, different ideals, and different aims.

Many of these differences are obvious if we compare the Greeks' finest building, the Parthenon, to the Romans' finest building, the Pantheon. Both were major temples, both important to their cities, their religions, and their native populations. The Greek Parthenon excelled in its subtle refinements and acute optical adjustments to an orderly scheme. The Roman Pantheon excelled in the resonance of a perfect geometric harmony. We cannot say that one of these great buildings is superior to the other, however, because each succeeds inimitably well in expressing its culture's goals. In buildings less perfect than the Pantheon,

Roman architects achieved a size and complexity that Greek architects never approached (and perhaps never wanted to).

In the field of furniture, though, we can say that the Romans were productive and creative, but that nothing they designed seems to have had the splendid grace of the Greek klismos chair. In pottery, as well, the painted Greek vase was on a level superior to its Roman counterparts. If we turn to the fields of glass and mosaic, however, the Romans surpassed the Greeks in both technical skill and inventive design, and if we consider interior design, the Roman genius clearly outshines the Greek genius. In the quality and quantity of Roman interior design, a new art was born.

Early Christian and Byzantine Design

6

A.D. 1–800 and 330–1453

"Roman statecraft, Greek culture, and Christian belief are the three wellheads of Byzantine development. If any of these three had been missing, Byzantium as we know it could not have existed."

—George Ostrogorsky (1902–76), art historian

Christianity originated in ancient Judea (now Palestine), an eastern outpost of the Roman Empire, but its important first years and early growth occurred in Rome itself. The Romans had enjoyed unprecedented power and influence, and their architects and designers had relied heavily on the genius of Greek models. But for the Early Christian architects and designers, no such models existed. Theirs was a new religion, and it demanded new forms of expression. Adapting existing elements of building and decoration and transforming them into a physical embodiment of the Christian spirit involved trial and error, success and disappointment, invention and inspiration. The result would progress beyond the Early Christian and Byzantine styles into the Romanesque and eventually culminate in Europe's great Gothic cathedrals.

The term "Byzantine" art is used to indicate the art of imperial Constantinople, the city founded on the site of Byzantium. It was long-lived and broad-based, lasting from the establishment of the city by the emperor Constantine in A.D. 330, until the Turkish conquest of the city in 1453, at which time it was renamed Istanbul. Its influence extended to the Italian cities of Ravenna and Venice, to Syria, to Greece, and to Russia. Although it has been called the culmination of the Early Christian style, the Byzantine (fig. 6-1) departed from both Early Christian and classical precedents.

Determinants of Early Christian and Byzantine Design

We can generalize that Early Christian was a style of Western Europe, its chief example being Old St. Peter's (A.D. 330) in Rome, and that Byzantine was a style of Eastern Europe, its chief example being Hagia Sophia (A.D. 537) in Constantinople, but in Ravenna and some other places, the two styles were built side by side. It is important to consider the striking geography of Byzantium as a factor affecting later Christian design. Religious and political factors were even more influential.

◄ **6-1** Detail of the mosaic portrait of the Empress Theodora in the church of S. Vitale, Ravenna, Italy, c. 547.
Scala/Art Resource, NY

Timeline | EARLY CHRISTIAN AND BYZANTINE DESIGN

Date	Political and Cultural Events	Events in Early Christian Design	Events in Byzantine Design
c. A.D. 30	Crucifixion of Christ; persecution of Christians	Decoration of catacombs	
4th century	Edict of Milan, 313; toleration of Christianity, capital of empire moved to Byzantium, 330	Old St. Peter's erected, 330; S. Costanza, Rome, 350; St. Paul's Outside the Walls, 386	
5th century	Visigoths invade Italy; last Roman emperor abdicates	S. Maria Maggiore, Rome, 440	Mausoleum of Galla Placidia, Ravenna, 420; Baptistery of the Orthodox, Ravenna, 452
6th century		S. Apollinare Nuovo, Ravenna, 525; S. Apollinare in Classe, Ravenna, 549	Hagia Sophia, Constantinople, 537; S. Vitale, Ravenna, 547
Later centuries	Charlemagne crowned Holy Roman Emperor, 800; Turks capture Constantinople and end Byzantine Empire, 1453	Transition to Romanesque	St. Mark's, Venice, 1085; St. Basil's, Moscow, 1560

Geography and Natural Resources

The Early Christian design styles emerged from Rome, the seat of the Roman Empire. But, by the time the building of Old St. Peter's was completed, the Roman emperor Constantine had become attracted to the physical beauty and military advantage of the ancient Thracian city of Byzantium. Sited on a peninsula beside a crescent-shaped inlet, it was a meeting point between Europe and Asia. In A.D. 330, he officially declared it the capital of the empire, changing its name to New Rome (because it replaced Rome as the capital of the Roman Empire), but later he acquiesced to calling it Constantinople.

Constantinople rests in one of the world's most spectacular sites, where Europe and Asia are divided only by the narrow strip of water known as the Golden Horn. From here, the emperor could control important trade routes on both land and sea. This was a splendid location, not only from which to rule an empire, but also from which to forge a sophisticated design vocabulary. Design influences were imported here from many quarters of the world, and from here they were widely exported.

Byzantium itself lacked fine building stone, but such was the vitality of trade with other regions that whatever was needed was brought. The Romans also brought here their own building forms and techniques, of course, but modified them to fit the local customs that included Near Eastern buildings with domes and living areas on flat roofs.

Religion

As the Roman Empire had been maintained by the power of the state, personified in the Caesars, so, too, the ages of the Early Christian era and the Byzantine Empire were unified by the power of the church and personified by the popes.

The earliest Christian meeting places were literally underground, for the new sect needed the protection of secrecy. Its fate changed dramatically in A.D. 313, when Constantine, himself a recent convert, decreed that Christianity would be tolerated throughout the Roman Empire. Thereafter, all of Europe joined in focus on the Christian religion, and all that had come before, including most of the great accomplishments of Rome and all those of Greece, were considered pagan and were therefore condemned.

As Constantine established Christianity in the new Constantinople, design began to change. Byzantine design was original, powerful, and lavish. It departed from both Early Christian and classical precedents. The scale, grace, and balance of early Greek art—though it had been enlarged and complicated in Hellenistic times and then enlarged and complicated further in Rome—remained rooted in the natural world. From the Eastern element in Byzantium and from the emotional element in Christianity came another artistic vision entirely, one that disdained both nature and the niceties of composition and sought instead a raw religious emotion. The Greek god Apollo had been depicted with cool restraint; Christ, the sufferer, the martyr, the redeemer, needed to be depicted with passion.

Political and Military Factors

The Roman Empire, which had once seemed invincible, began to decline in the first centuries of the Christian era. As vast and powerful as it had been, the empire had its geographic limits, and beyond these were hostile un-Romanized groups. The Roman legions, at the fringes of their realm, suffered defeats that weakened the confidence of Rome, as did internal problems—insurrections, civil wars, economic decline, and the murder of emperors. The last Roman emperor abdicated in A.D. 476.

Into the disintegrating fabric of the old society came more violent interruptions from German invaders such as the Goths and the Vandals. But the Middle Ages between the fourth and fifteenth centuries, between classical antiquity and the Renaissance, was not only a time of relative barbarism—it was a time of the invaders' contact with the remnants of Roman civilization and their consequent process of learning and assimilation. Although overshadowed by what came before and after, these twelve hundred years had a glory of their own.

The zenith of the Byzantine Empire lasted for centuries. Although it suffered many invasions, the Byzantine Empire did not end until 1453, when Constantinople was captured and pillaged by Sultan Muhammad II and, renamed Istanbul, became the capital of the Ottoman Empire.

Early Christian and Byzantine Architecture and Interiors

Early Christian and Byzantine art and architecture were dominated by work for the church, though there was, obviously, some secular building. Around the oldest part of Constantinople, for example, a great fifth-century double wall, studded with towers, still partly stands. The emperor Justinian himself was responsible for the Senate House, for a monumental column crowned by his own equestrian statue, and for the reconstruction of most of the imperial palace. Yet little is known about Byzantine domestic architecture, and therefore most attention is paid to ecclesiastical architecture.

During its first three hundred years, the new faith did not build churches. As historian Richard Krautheimer has noted, the religion's "early believers had neither the means, the organization, nor the slightest interest in evolving an ecclesiastical architecture. They met in whatever place suited the occasion." As time went on, the early Christian societies developed architectural plans that suited their liturgical purposes and expressed their religious attitudes. Later, Byzantine architects would respond to changes in both liturgy and attitudes. The two styles of Early Christian and Byzantine are strikingly different in their responses to the same religious beliefs, the first architecturally simple, though subject to a great degree of interior ornamentation, the second architecturally complex and subject to even greater elaboration.

Early Christian Architecture

The early Christians were faced with the problem of finding an architecture appropriate for a religion that had not existed before, but their more immediate problem was to find meeting places for a religion that was not yet legally sanctioned.

Catacombs Among the Christians' earliest meeting places were the **catacombs**, underground burial galleries beneath the streets and buildings of Rome and cut into the soft tufa rock outside the city. They were crude spaces, and the meetings and entombments held there were furtive. They were decorated, if at all, in a style adapted from the domestic buildings of the time. On the ceiling of the catacomb of SS. Pietro e Marcellino in Rome, for example, we see a painting (fig. 6–2) that at first glance might seem close to the spare, attenuated style—with isolated figures floating within spidery lines—that was popular at the same time above ground. But here in the catacomb the early Christian painter has begun to employ forms and images of religious significance: The great circle represents the dome of heaven, the five smaller forms within it are arranged in a cross pattern, and the **medallion** (or central circle), shows a shepherd with one of his sheep on his shoulders, a popular and symbolic way of depicting Christ tending his flock. In the

▲ **6–2** Details of a ceiling painting in the catacomb of SS. Pietro e Marcellino, Rome, fourth century A.D.
Canali Photobank, Caprarola, Italy

lunettes (or semicircular areas), we find images from the Old Testament's story of Jonah and the whale.

Christianity would not remain an underground religion, however, and it was Constantine who changed the course of Christianity. For the first time in the young religion's history, a ruler demanded the building of Christian architecture and interior design. But what would such design look like?

The earliest Christian structures simply resembled pagan temples. As the wave of religious enthusiasm encouraged building activity, no stone quarries were more convenient than the ruined temples of the old Roman gods. These classical "spare parts" of marble columns and decorative panels were the building blocks from which the new churches were constructed, with little regard to established orders or other traditional architectural relationships. At the same time, the newly liberated church was developing more elaborate rituals of worship and growing in both size and wealth. In 324, Constantine authorized the building of a large church in Rome that would house the shrine of St. Peter and would accommodate thousands of pilgrims. It would be the most important building of the Early Christian style.

Old St. Peter's, Rome For his model, Constantine turned to the ancient **basilica**, a building type that had been in continual use since the second or third century B.C. A basilica is a large meeting hall that was conceived by the Romans as a simple, aisleless hall, subdivided by structural elements as necessary, and roofed with wooden trusses. In the Early Christian era (and on into the Byzantine and Romanesque eras), the basilica was more often a building with a high,

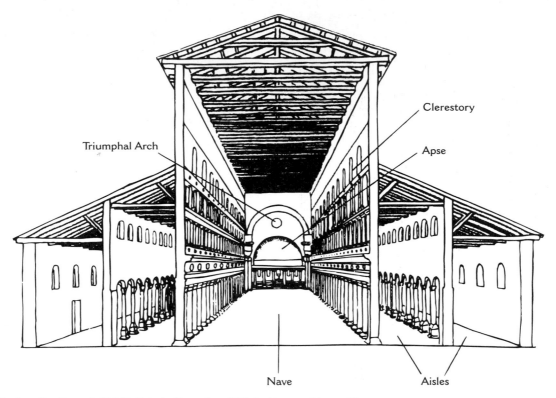

Triumphal Arch
Clerestory
Apse
Nave
Aisles

▲ **6–3** Vertical section through Old St. Peter's, Rome (A.D. 300), looking west toward the apse.
After Conant

wide, central nave flanked by two or more lower, narrower, side aisles.

With its long, narrow form and central aisle, it was well suited for ritual processions, with the congregation using one or more pairs of side aisles to watch. The masonry walls of the central space were straight and tall and sometimes lifted on **arcades** (a series of adjoining arches with supporting columns or piers). The walls were then pierced with windows at the top and supported a wood roof. The basilica of Old St. Peter's, once completed in 330, stood as the chief monument of Christianity. Simply put, the building was enormous, with five parallel aisles, the large central one rising 120 feet (37 m) and terminating in an apse (fig. 6–3). The main body of the church was fronted by a **narthex** (an antechamber or vestibule at the entrance) and by an **atrium** (a forecourt open to the sky), architectural enhancements that would be standard in many churches to come. The church's nave was as high as those of many of the Gothic cathedrals that would follow, and its total length of 700 feet (213 m) was almost as long as the new St. Peter's that would replace it in the Renaissance.

Typical of the Early Christian basilicas, the exterior of Old St. Peter's was severely plain, but, in compensation, its interior was overlaid with the lavish application of precious materials: murals, mosaics, giant bronze peacocks and pinecones, columns of porphyry, green serpentine, and yellow *giallo antico*, topped with capitals of Corinthian or Composite order, and with the space further adorned with hangings and altar cloths of purple and gold. Nothing of all this remains.

Other Early Basilicas Slightly later than St. Peter's, but similar in scale and still standing, is the five-aisled St. Paul's Outside the Walls (in Italian, S. Paolo fuori le Mura), built at what was then the edge of the city of Rome. Its enormous nave is lined with eighty great granite columns, and above them are mosaic medallions with portraits of the early popes. The building was begun in 386 by the emperor Theodosius; the mosaics in its apse were added in the thirteenth century. The church's **ciborium** (an open-sided canopy over an altar) and **apse** (semicircular extension at the east end) (fig. 6–4) display a wealth of mosaics on the vault of the apse. They were commissioned by the Empress Galla Placidia, an important patroness of the arts (who later had a church named in her honor).

Two other important Early Christian basilicas were built in Ravenna, a town in northern Italy with an adjacent

▲ **6-4** Looking toward the altar, St. Paul's Outside the Walls, Rome, begun in 386.
Scala/Art Resource, NY

by a barrel-vaulted ambulatory (fig. 6–7). An example of the mosaics decorating its vaults (fig. 6–8) demonstrates the new religious uses for the classical decorative motifs of Greece and Rome.

The Byzantine Church

Under the emperor Justinian, who ascended to the throne in Constantinople in 527, the Christian liturgy changed. The celebration of Mass, not the procession of clergy down the nave, became the central event. This change of use required a change of design, and the centralized plan now seemed more appropriate than the basilica plan. Unlike the model of Sta. Costanza, however, which had been a dome over a circular plan, the new Byzantine model combined the dome of the East with the classical temple of the West. The new ideal—a dome above a square plan—presented an inherent problem: How to fit the circular base of the dome on the walls of the square?

Two solutions were devised, and both were used extensively. The earlier and cruder method was to place a **squinch** (or diagonal element) across the top of each corner, turning the top of the square into an octagon, closer to the shape of the dome. The second, more sophisticated method was to

port (Classe) on the Adriatic. These were S. Apollinare Nuovo, built between 493 and 525, and S. Apollinare in Classe, built between 534 and 549. Both these buildings are magnificently clear and simple in plan (fig. 6–5), with arcades adorned with remarkable mosaic murals (fig. 6–6). Both naves end in semicircular apses, and both had interior surfaces enriched with marble **revetments** (facings over less attractive or less durable materials) and mosaics. Adjoining S. Apollinare in Classe on its north side is a cylindrical *campanile* (bell tower), one of the first built.

Buildings with Centralized Plans   Not all Early Christian church buildings had a basilica plan. A number of Early Christian buildings had centralized plans, either round, polygonal, or cruciform (cross-shaped). These were used as baptisteries, as mausoleums, or as *martyria*, memorial shrines to martyrs or saints. One of these, Sta. Costanza, was built in 350 as a mausoleum for Constantine's daughter. It features a domed central cylinder lighted by clerestory windows, that central space ringed by an arcade of twelve pairs of Composite columns, and that arcade in turn ringed

▼ **6-5** S. Apollinare in Classe, Ravenna, built 530–49.
Scala/Art Resource, NY

▼ **6–6** A mosaic mural in S. Apollinare Nuovo, Ravenna, 493–525, shows Theoderic's Palace with tied curtains hanging in its arcade.
Scala/Art Resource, NY

▲ **6–7** Interior, Sta. Costanza, Rome, C. A.D. 350.
Nicolas Sapieha/CORBIS, NY

▲ **6–8** Detail of a vault mosaic, Sta. Costanza, Rome. Within a variant of the Greek guilloche we see cupids, human figures, birds, and animals.
Scala/Art Resource, NY

TABLE 6–1 Dome Supports

In the left diagram can be seen the constructed **squinches**, which are diagonal members supported on the arches. In the right diagram are shown **pendentives**, or concave triangular surfaces. Pendentives start at a point on the corner of a pier, rise, and spread out to the two upper points of the triangle, creating a concave-curved fanlike shape until they approach the horizontals and meet the circle at the lowest part of the dome.

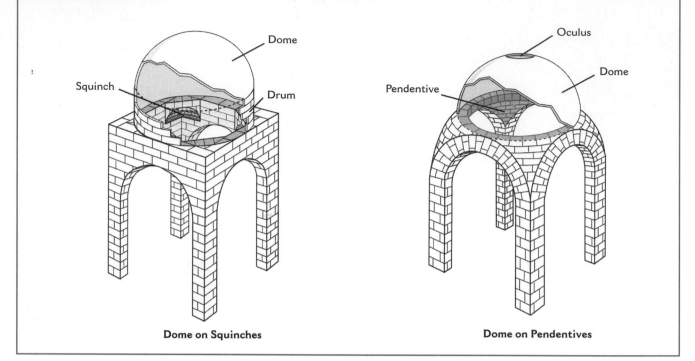

Dome on Squinches

Dome on Pendentives

add a **pendentive** (or a concave curved element) to each corner (see table 6–1). The visual effect is that of a dome resting on the tops of four arches, the spaces between the arches and the ring of the dome filled with triangular segments of a sphere. Pendentives were employed not only in important Byzantine churches, but also in some Romanesque ones, and later in some churches of the Renaissance. In some designs a **drum**, circular in plan but with vertical sides, was inserted between the supporting square and the dome, and sometimes the drum was punctured with windows.

Hagia Sophia, Constantinople Justinian is reputed to have built more than thirty churches (all now destroyed) in Constantinople alone on the new model described previously—a model that would prevail for the next thousand years, but the greatest was the church of Hagia Sophia (Holy Wisdom) in Constantinople.

Built at the site of a previous basilica church, which had burned, the Hagia Sophia was unprecedented in structural daring, in decorative splendor, and in size, boasting for centuries the largest enclosed space in the world. The two

architects Justinian chose to design Hagia Sophia were Anthemius of Tralles and Isidore of Miletus, both geometricians. Anthemius is credited with a specialized definition of architecture: the application of geometry to solid matter. To him, presumably, is owed the clarity of the building's basic structure. Within a rectangular plan 230 by 250 feet (71 × 77 m), four immense piers inscribe a central square. Seventy feet (21 m) above it, four great arches are joined by pendentives, each rising 60 feet (18.5 m) and curving forward 25 feet (8 m). Above the tops of the arches and pendentives rises the great dome, 100 feet (31 m) in diameter, "floating" above an unprecedented number of windows ringing its base, and the astonishing volume beneath it is supplemented by half domes at each end (fig. 6–9).

The result is a combination of the classically rational and the mysterious, the church's well-lighted central space and main structure clearly intelligible, but its subsidiary

▶ **6–9** Under the great dome of Hagia Sophia, looking toward one of the adjacent half domes.
Walter B. Denny

spaces—beyond screened aisles, galleries, and hangings—dark, complex, and obscure. The sense of enigmatic immateriality is furthered by decorative treatments that emphasize surfaces, not mass: multicolored mosaics of marbles and porphyry, carnelian and onyx; mother-of-pearl and ivory inlays; silver in the chancel screen; gold in the hanging lamps; colored glass in the window openings; and column capitals, spandrels, and ornamental metalwork overrun with **rinceaux** (scroll-like patterns based on vegetation).

In this building we see a characteristic that will pervade much of Byzantine construction: the concentration of decorative art in the interior, resulting in an architecture of plain exterior surfaces (if not always simple exterior forms) enclosing spaces of fantastically opulent ornament. After the Turkish conquest of 1453, minarets were added at each corner of the church, mausolea were added to the sides, whitewash was painted over the mosaics, and huge shields with verses from the Koran were hung in the interior.

Mausoleum of Galla Placidia, Ravenna In A.D. 420, after the Roman Empire had been divided into Eastern and Western parts, a small mausoleum was built in Ravenna for the Empress Galla Placidia. Small in size, its longest interior dimension only 39 feet (12 m), it was cruciform in shape—it may even have been the *first* cruciform building. While unassuming on the exterior, its rich interior contained walls lined with marble slabs, and vaults and a dome faced with striking mosaic work (fig. 6–10). The arms of the cross plan hold massive stone sarcophagi. Especially notable is the central dome, which is constructed so that the dome and its supporting pendentives are all parts of the same hemisphere; there are no seams. Its mosaics are unusual, too, with their abstract pattern of gold stars against the deep

▲ **6–10** In the Mausoleum of Galla Placidia, Ravenna, mosaics in the dome over the crossing show the cross against a night sky with rings of golden stars.
Scala/Art Resource, NY

blue ground of night sky; and the circular geometry of the star pattern perfectly complementing the geometry of the dome. In each corner, we find one of the Four Evangelists (fig. 6–11).

S. Vitale, Ravenna Begun in A.D. 526 by the Emperor Justinian I, S. Vitale is another central plan church, but one with a complex geometry of interlocking volumes. Outside and inside (fig. 6–12), the graded relationships of stacked volumes make the building a worthy successor to the earlier and much larger Hagia Sophia.

Viewpoints | A HISTORIAN ON CENTRALIZED-PLAN CHURCHES

William MacDonald, an architectural historian, has written extensively on the Early Christian centralized plan churches: "These enveloping, seamless vaulted forms . . . traced revolving imitations of the cosmos with expanses of modeled surfaces so fluidly interconnected as to conjure away their material reality. They stated direct lines of force and connection from centered, hallowed ceremonial spots below to . . . heavens above. . . . [T]hey did not

describe adequate ceremonial spaces and lacked processional axes," yet "their symbolic significance and their memorial associations were so important that ways were sought to combine them with congregational and processional buildings, and in Early Christian architecture a number of attempts were made to marry the horizontal shed with the verticalized pavilion. . . . [U]ltimately, the problem was solved in Hagia Sophia."

▼ **6–11** Beneath the dome of the Mausoleum of Galla Placidia, Ravenna. Sarcophagi are visible in the cruciform building's short arms.
Canali Photobank, Milan

▲ **6–12** S. Vitale, Ravenna, finished A.D. 547. View from the apse showing the small church's complex massing.
Canali Photobank, Milan

A tall, domed inner octagon, 55 feet (17 m) across, is enclosed by a lower outer octagon, 115 feet (35 m) across. One of the inner octagon's eight sides opens toward an altar, and the other seven open to semicircular arcades that project into the surrounding ambulatory and carry an upper-level gallery. The pendentives supporting the dome are formed of small arches, giving the lower part of the dome an unusual scalloped appearance.

Like the adjacent Mausoleum of Galla Placidia, S. Vitale has a plain brick exterior that gives no hint of the riches within it. The building's interior details include some fine marbles and quite famous mosaics, some depicting the emperor, Justinian, and his wife, Theodora, in gift-bearing processions (see fig. 6–1). Delicate stone carvings on the capitals of the columns (fig. 6–13) are in the form of truncated upside-down pyramids, flaring outward as they rise. Known as **impost capitals**, the term originates from **impost**, meaning a member (such as a bracket projecting from a wall) on which an arch rests. Between the impost capital and the arch above is an additional, similarly shaped block called a **dosseret** or, sometimes, a super-abacus. The dosseret, frequently used in Byzantine design, also appears in Romanesque design.

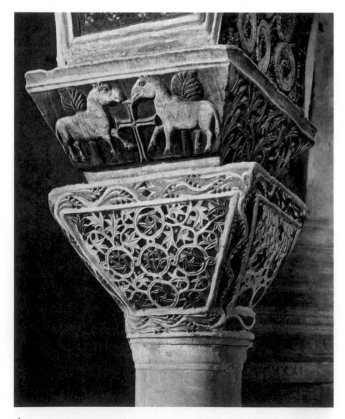

▲ **6–13** Impost capital and dosseret atop a column in S. Vitale, Ravenna.
Alinari/Art Resource, NY

St. Mark's, Venice

The most sumptuously decorated of all Byzantine buildings is St. Mark's (fig. 6–14), guarding the entrance from the Grand Canal to Venice's famous Piazza San Marco. A basilican church had been built on this prominent site in 864 to hold the body of St. Mark, which had just been abducted by the Venetians from its previous location in Alexandria. Construction of the present church was begun in 1063 and was basically finished in 1085.

Decoration and additions continued for centuries, however. The interior colonnades were finished in the eleventh and early twelfth century, the marble revetments on the piers and inside walls were applied in the twelfth century, and most of the mosaics were laid in the twelfth and thirteenth centuries. The façade's Gothic gables, the **ogee** arches (arches with S-shaped sides; see table 7–1) above them, and the **crocketed** (edged with a series of projecting ornaments) pinnacles rising between them were all added in the fifteenth century.

Its plan is a **Greek cross** (a cross with four arms of equal length) inscribed in a square, and its great central dome, 42 feet (13 m) in diameter, is supplemented by a smaller dome over each arm of the cross. The piers that carry the dome are massive, 21 by 28 feet (6.5 × 8.5 m), but they are lightened with passages through them on both the ground and gallery levels. The domes on pendentives and the half dome above the apse are ringed with windows so that the brilliantly colored mosaics in the upper reaches of the church are softly lighted.

St. Basil's, Moscow

Even after the empire's fall in 1453, Byzantine design persisted. Russia's Ivan the Terrible (Ivan IV, 1530–84), who was descended from the last of the Byzantine emperors, assumed the title of czar in 1547 and established the Byzantine style in buildings at Kiev, Novgorod, and Moscow.

Adjacent to the Kremlin, which is Moscow's 90-acre administrative center built within fifteenth-century walls, is St. Basil's Cathedral (Vasily Blazheny). Its construction was begun in 1555 and finished five years later.

Here, a decorative quality, which is fantastic to the point of playfulness, replaces the austerity and mystery of other Byzantine works. The domes are onion shaped, each with its own pattern—stripes, spiral, or chevron—of

▶ **6–14** Interior of St. Mark's Venice, A.D. 1063–85
Canali Photobank, Milan

TABLE 6–2   Types of Crosses

The cross is the chief symbol of Christianity because of the belief that Christ was executed by crucifixion, an event described in all four Gospels. The shape of the cross was not specified by any of the Four Evangelists, however, and it has taken many forms, some shown here. In practice, crosses can be two- or three-dimensional, monumental and fixed, portable, or pectoral (worn around the neck on a chain or ribbon).

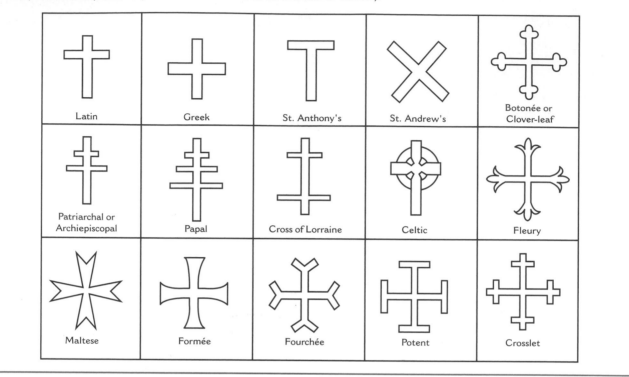

Latin	Greek	St. Anthony's	St. Andrew's	Botonée or Clover-leaf
Patriarchal or Archiepiscopal	Papal	Cross of Lorraine	Celtic	Fleury
Maltese	Formée	Fourchée	Potent	Crosslet

▲ **6–15** Detail of a chapel, St. Basil's, Moscow, with a small corridor leading to another chapel.
© 1991 John Freeman

brightly colored tile. The interior space (fig. 6–15) is as complex as the exterior, the church's large central space ringed by eight other chapels, each topped by its own dome, and all nine spaces linked by narrow passages. Despite the impressiveness of the building's exterior, its overall plan makes it impractical for congregational use.

Early Christian and Byzantine Ornament

As we saw in Egypt, Greece, Rome, and the Ancient Near East, and as we shall see in several later cultures, ornament is often designed to convey messages about the prevailing religion. In the young Christian religion, there was the added incentive to spread knowledge about a body of faith that was not yet widely understood. There were secular images as well, of course, pertaining to the rulers and the aristocracy—to successes on the battlefield and in the arena, to palaces and gardens, hunting parties, and many aspects of daily life. But the richest imagery of the times was that of the church.

Contemporary with the mainstrean developments of Early Christian ornament (see table 6-3) based in Rome and with Byzantine ornament based in Constantinople, there were two relatively minor stylistic offshoots that we should mention: Coptic ornament in Egypt and Celtic ornament in the British Isles.

Christian Symbols

This period saw the inception of a proliferation of Christian symbolism. Some symbols, such as the peacock representing eternal life and the fish representing Christianity in general, were adapted from earlier pagan symbols. The Good Shepherd as an allegory for a caring Christian was also an adaptation of a pagan figure bringing an offering to an altar. One new symbol, in use since the time of Constantine, was the "monogram of Christ" combining the first two Greek letters in the name of Christ; these letters are *chi* and *rho*, resembling our *X* and *P*, and the symbol, superimposing one on the other, is called a *chi-rho*. Human figures seen from the earliest Christian times include the Four Evangelists (Matthew, Mark, Luke, and John (see table 6-3). In early Christian art (see figs. 6–11 and 6–16) they were shown with wings; in later times, they

would lose their wings. They were also given different guises: Matthew depicted as a man, Mark as a lion, Luke as an ox, and John as an eagle. Other Christian symbols in early use were taken from the Bible. From the Old Testament came the Temptation of Adam and Eve, Jonah in the Whale, and Noah's Ark. From the New Testament came the Nativity, the Baptism, the Last Supper, the Crucifixion, and the Trinity.

Coptic Design

Coptic design refers to the design of Christianized Egypt. It came to full maturity in the late fifth century and flourished until the Arab conquest of Egypt in 640, after which Islamic forms dominated Egyptian art (except for a Coptic revival in the thirteenth-century). Coptic design is characterized by highly stylized, flat forms, pure and simple in outline. It found expression in sculpture, bronze, glass, ivory, woodwork, wall paintings, and manuscripts, which, because they were decorated in gold, silver, and/or brilliant colors, were said to be **illuminated**. Coptic textiles, some with striking geometric ornamentation in decorative panels and bands

---

TABLE 6–3 Christian Symbols

In all periods of Christianity, ornament and decorative art have been rich with symbolism. Some of the chief symbols, other than the cross, are shown here. In many cases, the symbols have been shared with pagan imagery or with other religions.

The Dove

The Fish

Matthew

Mark

Monograms

The Lamb

Luke

John

The Four Evangelists

▲ **6–16** Fragment of a Coptic textile of linen and wool (fifth century), showing an angel.
Panel: tapestry woven wool on linen: Flying Angel with Wreath & Cross; Egyptian (Coptic); 400–599.
Victoria & Albert Museum, London/Art Resource, NY

(fig. 6–16), achieved a high level of skill and appeared in cathedral treasuries across Europe. White limestone was a common material for important buildings, and frescoes and other decorative elements were often in red, yellow ocher, and other bold colors on white grounds.

Celtic Design

The art and artifacts of the Celts can be defined as the art and artifacts of those who spoke the Celtic language, and they include the people of Ireland but also the people of Wales, parts of Scotland, the Isle of Man, the English county of Cornwall, and the French province of Brittany. Its origins are pagan, and it was devised to accompany the worship of a complex pantheon of nature gods—worship led by Druid priests. After the conversion of Ireland and northern England to Christianity, the same artistic style was applied to the new faith, so that in medieval times it was a Christian style. It flourished in the seventh and eighth centuries and influenced the European monasteries established by Irish missionaries. It did not recover from the Viking invasions that began in the A.D. 800's.

It is a complex style. Plant forms, mythological beasts, and even human figures appear in it, but it is highly abstract, not an art of realism or naturalism. Perhaps its most characteristic manifestation is **knot work**, decorative motifs in which tangles of linear elements are intricately interwoven (fig. 6–17). It is also represented by tall stone crosses of a distinctive design that we call the Celtic cross (see table 6–2), by pottery, by metal artifacts such as chariot fittings, helmets, shields, spearheads, and scabbards, and by illuminated manuscripts.

Icons and Iconoclasm

In the Early Byzantine era, **icons**, or art depicting images of religious figures, were widely available for use by the devout. Some were small enough to be carried around, but many were housed in the Byzantine churches in the **iconostasis**, the tall screen used to separate the sanctuary and the clergy from the congregation. Most often, icons were painted in tempera on wooden boards, but there were icons of mosaic and fine metals as well.

▲ 6–17 An example of a Celtic knot-work pattern.
Aidan J. Meehan, "Celtic Patterns Painting Book," Copyright Aidan Meehan 1997

Certain characteristics were developed to distinguish the new icons from the idols of pagan worship. Icons, for instance, exhibited flatness and lack of shadows, and used symbolic color and unrealistic proportions, even while showing the recognizable images of holy figures (fig. 6–18).

▲ 6–18 Central portion of an icon depicting the Archangel Michael, silver gilt with enamel, c. A.D. 1100, 9½ in. (24 cm) high.
Carrieri Fotografo, Treasury of the Cathedral of St. Mark, Venice

Yet in the year A.D. 726, the Byzantine Emperor Leo III ordered that the icon of Christ over the door of the Imperial Palace be destroyed. He had by no means lost his faith. In fact, he had joined a particularly pious group that considered Christ too holy to be pictured. This rejection of religious imagery, called iconoclasm ("image breaking") lasted for over a century, instating a ban on the production of icons and violent punishment to any icon-makers. At times, the prohibition of images was extended to all living things, including birds, trees, and flowers.

Early Christian and Byzantine Decorative Arts

Early Christian and Byzantine decorative arts were unusually lavish, even in buildings with plain exteriors. They were also unusually important elements in the interiors, making clear the building's purpose and its dedication to a body of beliefs.

Lighting

Other ornamental features of this period's interiors were the often impressive fixtures with which they were lighted. Many church services in Hagia Sophia and other Byzantine churches took place in the early morning and in the evening, so lighting was needed. Candles and oil lamps were placed in a variety of fixtures. With their flickering light in the gilt, polished stones, and glass mosaics, the interiors came alive with shimmering reflections. One type of lighting fixture was called a **polykandelon** (in Greek, "many lights)." The polykandela were often made of thick sheets of hammered silver and were rectangular, cruciform, or circular in shape (fig. 6–19). They hung from chains so that their flat shapes were parallel to the floor; their circular cutouts held small glass oil lamps. Other, more delicate fixtures were called **choros**; they were made from networks of thin metal strips and rods, also suspended on chains. They often held both candles and oil lamps. Both types of fixtures were hung very low, just over the heads of worshippers.

Ivories

An unusual Byzantine art form was ivory carving. **Ivory**, technically known as dentine, is most commonly found in

▲ **6–19** A silver *polykandelon* decorated with dolphins, made in Constantinople, sixth century, 2 ft. (56 cm) in diameter. The sixteen circular openings held glass cups filled with oil.
Dumbarton Oaks, Byzantine Photograph and Fieldwork Archives, Washington, DC

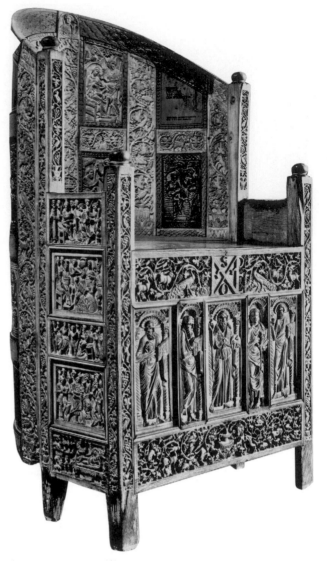

▲ **6–20** The sixth-century ivory throne of the Byzantine archbishop of Ravenna, Maximian.
Alinari/Art Resource, NY

elephant tusks, although other substances—all chemically identical—have been used: tusks of the walrus, pig, and boar, and teeth of the whale and hippopotamus. A substitute for ivory is sometimes taken from the beak of a bird called the helmeted hornbill, and synthetic substitutes have been produced since 1865. Ivory jewelry and figurines date back to around 20,000 B.C. Ivory objects were found in the tomb of Tutankhamun, and used in parts of the great statue of Athena in the Parthenon. Ivory carving was also practiced in the Ancient Near East, on Crete, and by North American Indians. Carving of ivory from rhinoceros horn was practiced in China until the end of the nineteenth century.

Byzantine ivory came from elephant tusks, imported from either Africa or India. It must have been an expensive medium because the tusks are seldom more than 7 inches (18 cm) in diameter. Ivory ware was limited to small objects or objects made of several pieces fastened together. It was carved into religious symbols and figures of saints, which were often gilded and painted.

An impressive example of ivory work—and one of the few pieces of furniture still extant from the early Middle Ages—is a sixth-century bishop's throne or *cathedra* made for Maximian, the Archbishop of Ravenna (fig. 6–20). The ivory plaques that covered its whole visible surface were

probably once supported by a wooden substructure that has rotted away, but the external appearance of the throne is still as it was originally. Every square inch is intricately carved with foliage, birds, animals, and biblical scenes. The front panels beneath the seat show John the Baptist and the Four Evangelists, and above and below these figures are panels of rinceaux.

Less extravagant wood pieces were often given decorative ivory inlays. And some ivory panels—whether a two-panel **diptych** or a three-panel **triptych**—give us information about the more humble furniture forms that have vanished. A ninth-century plaque, for example (fig. 6–21), shows us not only a monk at his studies but also some wooden furniture and curtains hung from a rod.

Mosaics

Though traditions of wall painting continued through the Early Christian and Byzantine eras, it was the art of mosaic that reached new heights of splendor and importance in the buildings of the Byzantine era. These mosaics, spread over entire areas from wall to arch, from pendentive to dome, were capable of dissolving interior structures into dazzling, shimmering surfaces, seemingly without substance.

Subject matter for many mosaics was religious, but perhaps even more famous among Byzantine examples are the highly stylized secular portraits at S. Vitale of the emperor Justinian and his empress Theodora (see fig. 6–1), shown carrying offerings to the altar, with their attendant retinues. These portraits began a long series of depictions of rulers upholding the Church.

Decorative patterns in Byzantine mosaics are based on a variety of symbols—the monogram of Christ, the endless knot symbolizing eternity, and the peacock symbolizing eternal life. Other decorative bands flatly simulate the three dimensions of projecting moldings. Among religious subjects, perhaps the quintessential Byzantine images are those of Christ as *Pantocrator* ("ruler of all"). A representative example dates from c. 1020 in the formerly fortified monastic church at Daphni, near Athens (fig. 6–22). As in other such depictions, Christ looks sternly down from this mosaic set in the dome above. This placement gives Christ a powerful hold on the Christians below, reminding them that the Kingdom of God is entered through a devout life.

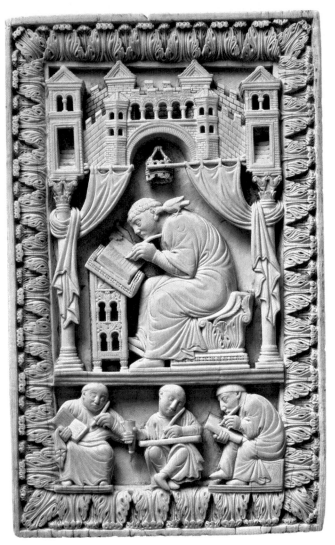

▲ **6–21** A ninth-century ivory carving shows a monk at his studies. This work also provides a record of some of his furniture. Carolingian, Franco-German School, c. 850–75.
St. Gregory writing with scribes, Carolingian, Franco–German School, c 850–875 (ivory). Kunsthistorisches Museum, Vienna, Austria/Bridgeman Art Library.

Tools & Techniques | BYZANTINE MOSAICS

Byzantine mosaics are distinguished from their predecessors by the size of their **tesserae**, being generally smaller than the ½-inch-square (13 mm) pieces used by the Romans and much smaller than some of the stone pieces used in Early Christian work. They are also distinguished by their glitter, their backgrounds often having been made of reflective glass squares bonded with gold leaf. Silver and mother-of-pearl were also sometimes used.

In Byzantine mosaic work, the tesserae were applied directly on floor, wall, vault, or dome surfaces that had first been prepared with one, two, or three layers of plaster and with the sketching of preliminary designs (sinopia) on the plaster. The finest, most closely spaced work, using the most delicate tesserae, was used for showing hands and faces. As the skills of the Byzantine mosaicists developed, clearly defined monochrome areas were abandoned in favor of subtle shadings and gradual transitions.

Byzantine mosaic artists were respected master craftsmen and were commissioned to execute important works in Rome (a chapel in Old St. Peter's), in France (the apse of Germigny-des-Prés), in Jerusalem (the Dome of the Rock), and in Spain (the Great Mosque, Córdoba; see figs. 14–2 and 14–3).

▲ **6–22** Dome with mosaic of Christ the Pantocrator in the eleventh-century church at Daphni, Greece. Beneath the dome, one of the four supporting squinches can be seen.
Dagli Orti/The Art Archive

At their best, the mosaics did not simply embellish the architecture but cooperated with it, producing a total effect that would involve, impress, and move the observer. The mosaics indicate a relationship with Christianity that is certainly more intimate than it would be for later Western medieval art. In Byzantium, beholders were not kept at a distance from the image; they entered within its aura of sanctity, and the image, in turn, partook of the space in which they moved. They were not so much "beholders" as "participants."

Ceramics, Glass, and Metalwork

The Byzantine Empire relied on Roman pottery, imported from production centers in Italy and North Africa, until Arab invasions in the early seventh century interrupted the trade routes. When Byzantine pottery developed to replace

it, different clay and different techniques created pottery at first heavy and thick-walled compared to its Roman models, and with limited decorative colors. But by the end of the ninth century, new sources of fine clay had been found, and in the tenth century new glazes were developed. The ceramics, called polychrome ware, raised the standards for ceramics by employing for the first time metals such as manganese and copper to stabilize clear blacks and whites and vivid primary colors.

Glass was widely used in the Byzantine Empire for mosaic tesserae, most obviously, and also for vessels, beads, window panes (even painted-glass panes for church windows), and lamps for the polykandela and choros (see fig. 6–19).

Gold, silver, and bronze were used for a variety of ecclesiastical objects–chalices, censers, crosses, reliquaries, patens (circular dishes for communion bread), lighting, and icons, such as the one seen in fig. 6–18. Often metalwork was decorated with skillful **enamel**, a technique that will reach its zenith in China.

Summary: Early Christian and Byzantine Design

Early Christian and Byzantine design have been covered in a single chapter because for much of their time, the two coexisted and, at times, merged. For example, Ravenna's S. Apollinare Nuovo is a clear example of an Early Christian basilica, yet its striking mosaics show elements of exoticism that are related to Byzantine style. It must be admitted, therefore, that the distinctions between the styles are oversimplifications of a complex situation. Perhaps the Christian design of the centuries following A.D. 330 can most accurately be thought of as a continuum, with Early Christian examples at one extreme, Byzantine examples at another, and a wide range of expressions between.

Looking for Character

In Early Christian design we recognize signs of the heritage of the classical world; in Byzantine design, we see the more exotic influence of the Near East. Not even Early Christian design, however, sought either a continuation or a revival of Roman design principles. Both Early Christian and Byzantine design styles shared the single goal of all art through the Middle Ages: to herald the triumph of Christianity and to manifest the spirit of a supreme being and order in the universe. Compared to the confident daring that the Gothic would eventually bring to this task, the early attempts of Early Christian and Byzantine work will seem tentative and only partly successful. But inherent in these designs is the sincere attempt to give a new religion appropriate material form, and this attempt will serve as the foundation for the Gothic.

Looking for Quality

Because Early Christian and Byzantine styles differ, we must look at them in different ways. Early Christian design offers simpler, more basic satisfactions of logical plans—both the basilica and the centralized plan—built with conviction and sometimes built at impressive scale. The spiritual world is evoked in them through the power of their ordered exteriors and ornate interiors, though the direct strength of these buildings was diminished as their decoration increased and their simple organization was obscured.

In the Byzantine style, obscurity—expressed as a sense of mystery—is a chief goal, and that sense is further enhanced as ornamentation proliferates. The spiritual world is evoked in them through astonishment. We find the highest quality of this style, therefore, in the ornament itself—the colors of the murals, the minute and dazzling tesserae of the mosaics, and the carvings in wood, ivory, and stone.

Making Comparisons

The Early Christian and Byzantine styles—along with the Romanesque, Gothic, and Islamic styles—surfaced between the classical world and the Renaissance. Both of those eras are distinguished by beauty achieved through the exercise of logic and the exalting of human accomplishment (i.e., celebrating the things of this world). In the Middle Ages humans looked beyond this ordered and rational world to the spiritual realm. Their ideal became not worldly harmony, composure, and comprehension but the apprehension and exaltation of an otherworldly divine spirit.

Romanesque

c. 800–c. 1200

"Light and shade are the heralds of this architecture of truth, calm, and strength. There can be nothing else to add."

— Le Corbusier (1887–1965), architect

The term *Romanesque* means "in the manner of the Romans." It was coined by nineteenth-century art historians because the round-headed arches and vaults characteristic of the style were similar to forms that had been used in ancient Rome. The term is applied to the style of art that arose in Italy and southern France around 800 and continued until it evolved in the twelfth century into Gothic. In this chapter the term Romanesque will stand for both Romanesque and Norman design.

Determinants of Romanesque Design

All phases of Christian design in the Middle Ages, beginning with Early Christian and culminating in Gothic, shared a single chief determinant: the search for the most appropriate and effective representation of the religion. Within that search, however, other factors caused a variety of results. Romanesque design was strikingly different from what preceded it and what would follow.

Geography and Natural Resources

Romanesque design (fig. 7–1) flourished in many different places. It came to its earliest maturity in central and southwestern France, northern Italy, and along the Rhine. In 1066 the style was carried by William the Conqueror from Normandy in France to England, where it was called *Norman* design. By the end of the eleventh century, the Normans had captured Sicily from the Arabs, and Sicily became a home to Norman architecture. The basic differences between the Romanesque and the Norman are political rather than stylistic, although there are variations. In Sicilian Norman buildings, for example, the characteristic round-headed arch is sometimes replaced by the pointed arch inherited from the conquered Arabs.

Some of the early Romanesque churches in Italy, like Early Christian ones before them, were constructed in part from the ruins of ancient Roman buildings, but in western

◄ **7–1** Reliquary statue of Saint Foy from the Abbey Church of Conques, France, late ninth century, silver gilt with gemstones, 33 in. (85 cm) high.
Gemeinnutzige Stiftung Leonard von Matt, Buochs, Switzerland

Date	Cultural and Military Events	Design Achievements
9th century	Charlemagne crowned first Holy Roman Emperor, 800; Arabs sack Rome, 846	Mosaics in church of St. Germain-des-Prés, Paris, 803
10th century	Benedictine Abbey founded at Cluny, 910	Monastery church at Cluny, 980
11th century	The second millennium, 1000; Norman Conquest of England, 1066; Norman Conquest of Sicily, 1072; First Crusade, 1095	Winchester Cathedral begun, 1050; Bayeux Tapestry, c. 1080; Pisa Cathedral begun, 1063; Ste.-Madeleine, Vézelay begun, 1089; Durham Cathedral begun, 1093
12th century	Second Crusade, 1145; Third Crusade, 1189	Fontenay Abbey, Burgundy, France, begun 1132

Europe, and particularly southern France, there was an insufficient number of these ruins to fulfill the demand for materials. The stone that was required for the new structures often had to be transported from distant quarries, and the character of the arched construction necessitated that such materials be cut into small sizes. The Christians did not have the slave and military labor that had been available to the Romans, but many devout believers contributed their services.

Religion

The period during which Romanesque style flourished was a comparatively tranquil one that settled upon Europe after the barbarian invasions. Peace and security were offered by the rulers, who now carried a cross as well as a sword, promised religious salvation through the church, and proposed a practical system of daily life. The response, impelled by loyalty and necessity, resulted in the construction of churches throughout Europe that were to serve not only as places of worship but also as strongholds, schools, libraries, town halls, museums, and centers of social life. The monks, although amateur architects, were the great organizers. They taught craftsmen elementary masonry, carpentry, and ironworking. Untrained as designers, the builders necessarily used the only models that were at hand. Thus, their designs expressed their own crude conception of Roman architecture adapted to Christian requirements.

Some churches (including Rocamadour in France, Canterbury in England, and Santiago de Compostela in Spain) were singled out as destinations for pilgrimage. The pilgrimage routes became trade routes as well, and the travelers, all subjects of the Pope in Rome, passed easily from one kingdom or principality to the next. In the eleventh century, European Christians began a series of Crusades to recover the Holy Land of Jerusalem from Islam, and these wars would bring more long-distance travel. Europe, in Romanesque times, enjoyed a rare international character.

The Coming of the Millennium

A unique determinant increasing the spread of Romanesque design was the coming of the millennium, in 1000. Enormously superstitious, the people put great trust in signs and symbols. It seemed to them certain that the world would end when the thousandth year of the Christian era arrived, but when the year came and passed safely, there was widespread relief, joy, thanksgiving, and optimism about the future.

These feelings gave rise to a new wave of religious construction. Led by the monks, the people donated their time, energy, and worldly goods to the promotion of a Christian civilization and its external evidences. As Raoul Glaber, a historian of the time, wrote in 1003, "especially in Italy and in Gaul [the Roman name for France], [there was] a great renewal of church buildings.... It was as if the world had shaken itself, and, casting off its old garments, had dressed itself again in every part in a white robe of churches."

TABLE 7–1 Types of Arches

Romanesque design was characterized by the use of the round or round-headed arch. Gothic design (Chapter 8) used the pointed arch. Here, for comparison, are a number of other arch shapes and their names.

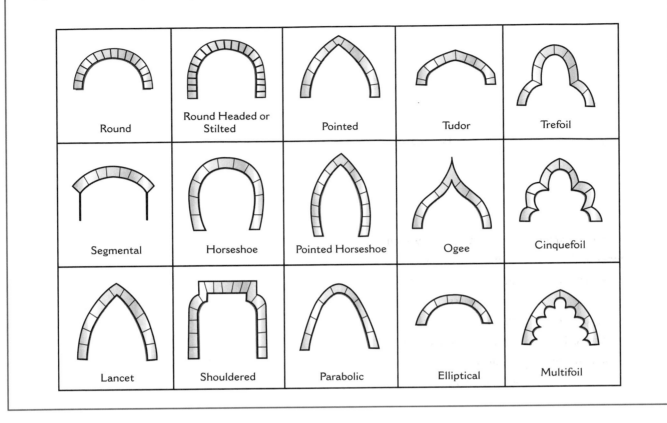

Round	Round Headed or Stilted	Pointed	Tudor	Trefoil
Segmental	Horseshoe	Pointed Horseshoe	Ogee	Cinquefoil
Lancet	Shouldered	Parabolic	Elliptical	Multifoil

Romanesque Architecture and Interiors

Construction of architecture during the Romanesque era was limited by the materials, craftsmanship, and tools that were available. The buildings that resulted were massive and strong, simple in surface enrichment, and often forbidding in appearance, but they faultlessly expressed the spirit of a simple but devout population and the vigor of early Christianity.

Church Buildings

Beginning in Early Christian times, the steady growth of monastic orders had demanded a growth of accommodations for the monks, their prayers, and their processions; lay worshippers, too, needed appropriate space. In many cases, the church became the central building for living quarters and services of an entire village. Romanesque church complexes exist in France at Vézelay, Fontenay, Caen, Cluny, and Conques, and in Germany at Speyer and Hildesheim. Norman examples are in England at Durham, Winchester, Lincoln, Gloucester, and Peterborough, and in Sicily at Monreale, Palermo, and Cefalu.

Romanesque builders depended entirely upon the stone arch (table 7–1). In addition, not only was the Roman semicircular arched vault used in the construction of the roof, but this arch form was eventually to become the shape of all doors, windows, and other openings, and finally it was used for purely ornamental purposes. Because all round-headed arches, of whatever size, share the same proportion (their spans exactly twice their height), their use can give a building a rare sense of congruence. (The pointed arch, in contrast, can have a wide variety of proportions.)

The basilica plan, perhaps for reasons of symbolism, gave way to one in the form of a **Latin cross** (see table 6–2), having a horizontal member shorter than the vertical member. This change was effected by the introduction of the **transept** (the horizontal member).

The nave of the church was separated from the side aisles by a row of heavy columns proportioned without regard to Vitruvian standards, which had been forgotten. A semicircular arch rose directly from the capital of each column, and spanned to an adjoining column. This row of arches supported a wall pierced with **clerestory** windows (windows high in a nave wall, above the roof of an adjacent aisle). In later Romanesque churches, the arched ceiling was supported by the ribs that crossed the nave both at right angles and diagonally.

Ste.-Madeleine, Vézelay, France Atop a prominent hill in the village of Vézelay in the Burgundy region of France is the abbey church dedicated to Ste.-Madeleine (Mary Magdalen). A nunnery had been established on the site in 860, but the present building was begun at the end of the eleventh century. A disastrous fire in 1120 damaged the church and killed many pilgrims, but the rebuilding was completed in 1146, with the nave designed in the new Gothic style. On Easter Sunday of that year, the preacher at Vézelay was Bernard of Clairvaux (later St. Bernard), and his sermon spurred the second Crusade to Jerusalem.

Beyond the portals, the nave (fig. 7–2) is roofed with groined vaults in each bay. Transverse arches between the vaults carry much of the thrust from these vaults to the piers, thus allowing windows to be cut in the upper of the nave's two stories. The arches are picked out in alternating light and dark stone colors, a treatment that will become particularly popular in Italy.

Durham Cathedral, Durham, England In Durham, near the city of Newcastle in the North of England, is the chief monument of English Norman architecture. Construction was begun in 1093 and finished forty years later. Later additions, particularly on the east end, are in the Gothic style.

Foursquare and solid, the three-storied nave (fig. 7–3) is supported by two rhythmically alternating types of support: thick cylindrical columns and piers of compound shape with many thin half-columns applied. The cylindrical columns also alternate in their treatment, some fluted, some incised with zigzag patterns, some with diagonal checkerboards. The ceiling is an early—possibly, even, the first—

▼ **7–2** The Romanesque nave of Ste.-Madeleine, Vézelay, France. The apse beyond is in the later Gothic style.
Caisse National des Monuments Historique et des Sites

▲ **7–3** Nave (looking east), Durham Cathedral, England 1093–1130.
A. F. Kersting

▲ **7–4** The chapter house of the Cistercian Monastery of Fontenay in the Burgundy section of France, c. 1150.
Erich Lessing/Art Resource, NY

example designed with ribbed vaults, a device standard in the Gothic cathedrals.

Fontenay Abbey, Burgundy, France   St. Bernard established a monastery at Fontenay in 1118, but the present complex of limestone structures dates from 1132. In addition to its religious role, it was an economic force, producing goods of both wool and iron. The church is austere, even by Romanesque standards, with no clerestory but only blank walls above the

slightly pointed nave arcades. Other elements of the complex include a gate-house, a **sacristy** (a room storing sacred utensils and vestments), a cloister, a chapter house (fig. 7–4), a dormitory with a day-room below, a kitchen, and a forge.

Cathedral Complex, Pisa, Italy   Prosperous from their trade with the East, the people of Pisa began an ambitious building program in 1063. Dedicated in 1118 and completed in 1172, the famous composition on a large open site (fig. 7–5)

▲ **7–5** The Pisa baptistery, cathedral, and campanile as viewed from the west, 1053–1272.
Scala/Art Resource, NY

▲ **7–6** Inside the Cathedral of Pisa, looking down the nave toward the apse.
Edward Chauffourier/Art Resource, NY

includes a walled cemetery and three free-standing buildings: the cross-shaped cathedral, the cylindrical baptistery, and the tall campanile, or "Leaning Tower," now famous for having settled unevenly. All three components make use of the nearby marble quarries that are still operating today, and all are faced with delicate marble arcades of round-headed arches.

Inside the cathedral (fig. 7–6), the nave is edged with double sets of side aisles. The nave ends in a great apse, and the two transepts end in smaller apses. An ellipsoidal dome covers the crossing, and the rest of the nave is covered with a flat coffered ceiling. The chief decorative effects of the interior are produced with stripes of colored marble, not by elaborate or emotion-charged carvings. An important religious site, alterations were made in the twelfth and thirteenth centuries, and Gothic touches were added to the baptistery in the fourteenth.

Secular Buildings

Few secular Romanesque and Norman buildings still exist, because they were considered temporary structures. However, some stone house-barns can still be seen in northwestern Spain, their design dating to Celtic times. They are mortarless stone structures with rounded corners and thatched roofs, which originally had interior partitions separating the human and animal quarters (the humans on the uphill side). There is, too, a surviving shell of a town house in the French town of Cluny; it has an elegant stone face and space for a shop on the ground floor. It dates from before 1150, and its fine carvings were probably by the artisans who

came to work on the town's great monastery. Castlelike Romanesque structures had narrow window slits in deep recesses within their thick walls, winding staircases, closets (*garderobes*), private chapels (*oratories*), and even small sleeping chambers.

Romanesque Ornament

Even as examples of Romanesque architecture display the clarity and rationality of their structure, some of their ornament expresses both mystery and irrationality. These dual aspects coexisted throughout the Romanesque era. The strength and logic of Romanesque churches may appeal directly to our modern sensibilities, but we misunderstand the Romanesque spirit if we neglect the dark and sometimes grotesque imagery of its ornament.

The interior of the abbey church at Vézelay, for example, is crowded with the carvings of panels and capitals riddled with saints, monsters, and other figures. Not only are its capitals full, but on each **tympanum** (a semicircular panel above a portal) are displayed many figures, as would be typical of tympana throughout Romanesque churches (and later, Gothic). The tympanum of the central portal, almost 20 feet (6 m) in diameter, is both the largest and the most emotionally charged of the carvings (fig. 7–7); it shows Christ, in swirls of draped clothing, surrounded by people from many lands to whom the Gospel had been preached.

To instruct and rule an illiterate people, the ornament that enriches the interiors of Romanesque churches depicts many things: scriptural subjects, such as allegorical scenes

▲ 7–7 Looking towards the apse through the entrance portal at Vézelay with its semicircular carved stone *tympanum*. The carved center support under the tympanum is called a *trumeau*.

Scala/Art Resource, NY

▼ **7–8** An imaginary winged beast, possibly a sphinx, is seen in two joined profile views at the corner of a column capital in the church of St.-Pierre de Chauvigny, Chauvigny, France. The animal is devouring an unfortunate sinner.
Sonia Halliday Photographs

indicating the rewards of virtue or the terrifying punishment of vice (fig. 7–8), seasonal occupations, historical events, and fantastic animals. Capitals of columns might show the foliage of classic Corinthian capitals intertwined with figures of biblical personages. Some decorative columns were *Solomonic* (carved in a spiral, as had been done in a first century A.D. structure in Jerusalem, thought to have been the Temple of Solomon). In addition, patterns were included, such as the checkerboard, the **chevron** (or zigzag), rosettes, embattlements resembling the fret, and swirls of vegetation recalling Greek rinceaux (fig. 7–9). Other compositions were directional: Church floors contained patterns that gave directions for religious services, leading along a central axis through the chancel of the nave and up to the altar.

Ruined architecture from the Romans was still used as building material, but Roman columns and panels were often reused in new ways. Ancient columns of verde antique,

▲ **7–9** Three stone piers carved with Norman decoration, Lincoln Cathedral, England, 1185–1280.
James Kellaway Colling, "Medieval Decorative Ornament," Dover, Mineola, NY, 1995.

▼ 7–10 Cosmati work at Westminster Abbey, London: The "Great Pavement" in front of the High Altar, made in 1268 of marbles and onyx set in Purbeck marble, 28 ft. (8.6 m) square.
Copyright Dean and Chapter of Westminster/Robert Harding World Imagery, London

▲ 7–11 Rondels of chip carving in three patterns decorate a thirteenth-century English chest.
Victoria and Albert Museum, London/Art Resource, NY

porphyry, and other stones, for example, were sawn into thin slices. These provided decorative stone disks for floor or wall patterns or for liturgical furniture. The most famous of such decorative stonework was called **Cosmati** work (fig. 7–10), named for a family of Roman marbleworkers.

Romanesque Furniture

Romanesque furniture was made of various kinds of native woods, chiefly oak and walnut in England and northern Europe, beech and fir in southern Germany, and cypress in Italy. A rough sort of lumber called "riven timber" was often used. Made by splitting logs radially, that is, from their outside bark to their centers (similar to the slash cutting technique shown in table 2–1), it produced planks that were admirably strong but often quite rough in appearance.

The roughness was often mitigated with carving, the most commonplace being the type called **chip carving**, in which chips of the wood surface were gouged or chiseled away to form patterns. The patterns were usually contained within a circular or oval shape called a **rondel**. Crude as it was, such carving could create interesting effects (fig. 7–11).

Turning, or *turnery*, was also frequently used. It was popular throughout the Middle Ages and remains popular today. In this process of shaping wood (or other materials), the turner spins the piece of wood on a lathe and, while it is spinning, presses it against a knife edge or some other cutting or abrading tool. It is a particularly appropriate type of ornament for long, thin furniture members such as legs, arms, and stretchers. Later, it would also become a popular treatment for spindles and balusters.

Tools & Techniques | COSMATI WORK

Cosmati stonework is different from mosaic stonework. Mosaic is pieced together from small square or rectangular tesserae, each piece virtually the same in size as its neighbor, whereas Cosmati work is composed of pieces different in shape and size, some of them quite large. These were set in lime mortar. Cosmati work is richly colored and generally geometric, not representational. In its design, interwoven bands (which might incorporate pieces of glass and gold tesserae) often outline or encircle large pieces of decorative stone. Though generated from one family, it was practiced by many workers and was exported far from its origin, even to the pavement of Westminster Abbey in London (fig. 7–10).

Seating

The most common seat, through all the Middle Ages, was probably a floor cushion, yet there were a few pieces of seating furniture. Finely carved chairs with backs or half backs existed for grand people and occasions. More often, seating was on benches or on folding stools, similar to those that had been used by the Romans, the Greeks, and even the Egyptians.

An illustration from the Canterbury Psalter (fig. 7–12) shows "the scribe Eadwine" seated in an elaborate chair working (with both hands) at a manuscript. The vertical posts at the corners of his chair have been transformed by turning into cylinders with bulbous projections, not unlike the bead-and-reel ornament of classical architec-

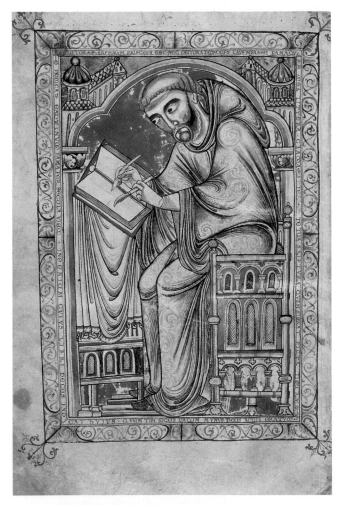

▲ **7–12** "The scribe Eadwine" from the Canterbury Psalter, seated on a chair with architectural motifs, c. 1150.
Monk Eadwine at work on the manuscript, c. 1150. Eadwine Psalter, c. 1150. Trinity College, Cambridge, U.K./Bridgeman Art Library.

ture (see table 4–2). Eadwine's chair and writing desk (draped with a fabric cover) also display another sort of ornament popular in Romanesque furniture: its treatment as a piece of miniature architecture. The side of his chair has a base in imitation of an arcade, and the bands above represent two successive stories of round-headed windows. Even small diamond-shaped panes of glass are shown.

Beds

The English word *bed* and the French word *lit* may have originally meant only the collection of what we today call bed linens. Beds had become familiar by medieval times but without the connotations of privacy they now possess. Family members of several generations were accustomed to sharing a bed, and, when traveling, so were complete strangers. Medieval beds were therefore, by our own standards, enormous. In the most stately homes, beds were surrounded by fabric canopies, generally hung from frames separate from the structure of the bed. Still, some beds, called **trussing beds**, were small, portable ones that could be folded and wrapped up (trussed) for carrying. A small daybed called a **couchette** could also be folded; it sometimes was on wheels so that it could be moved from room to room.

Tables

Like much of the other furniture of the Middle Ages, most tables were designed to be collapsed when not in use, the tops being tilted or taken off, and the whole assembly stored against a wall. The term *table* referred only to the top, with the base of legs and rails called the *frame*, and the whole assembly called a *table and frame*. Our expression "set the table" originally referred to the act of assembling a table in preparation for a meal, not in covering it with dishes and utensils.

However, there were tables with tops permanently attached to their bases and meant not to be moved. They were called *tables dormant*. Semicircular **console tables** were designed to be placed against a wall, as in Roman times, and their wall-facing sides were left unfinished; unlike the console tables that became very popular in the eighteenth century, they were not actually attached to the wall.

Casegoods

Common to most households were chests and cupboards, constructed of heavy wooden planks hewn with axes rather than cut with saws. Smaller wooden caskets held valuables (see fig. 7–11), with the more expensive ones made of ivory or silver. These, and even the larger, heavier chests were inevitably carried along when travels were made, but beginning in the fifteenth century, a distinction was made between the smaller chests meant to travel and the larger chests (*great standing chests*) meant to stay at home. Corner legs (*standards*) were also developed for the stay-at-homes, in order to lift storage compartments above the damp floors. There were also cupboards (literally "cup boards"), wardrobes, and washstands. Many of these received the mock-architectural treatment mentioned previously in seating, a treatment that will have a long life in furniture design.

Romanesque Decorative Arts

Stone carvings—sometimes of the most fantastic nature—were an integral part of many Romanesque churches as were the stonework of the Cosmati. In the decorative arts, Romanesque artisans inherited and continued the Byzantine art of ivory carving; they pushed Roman glass methods towards stained glass; and they heightened the sophistication of metalwork and textiles.

From the tenth to the twelfth centuries, exquisite enamelware, brass utensils, and textiles were made, many for royal or liturgical use being elaborately patterned and made of expensive materials, such as heavy silk. Monks spent their lives working on richly illuminated manuscripts (fig. 7–12). The expenditure of effort and labor was of no consideration so long as it resulted in a perfect object of lasting beauty that would contribute to the glory of the church.

Metalwork

In the late years of the Romanesque style there was a wave of skilled work in metal. Much of the wooden furniture, particularly chests and cupboards, was strengthened with metalwork, which protected it against wear and decoratively embellished it with metal straps, hinges, bolts, and bindings of various sorts.

▲ **7–13** Grille in Winchester Cathedral, England.
Dover Publications, Inc.

Bronze doors for cathedral fronts began to replace carved wooden ones in the eleventh century. Some were cast in a single piece, others in separate small plates that were then nailed to wood boards. Generally they were sculptured in low reliefs showing biblical scenes, kings, prophets, saints, and animals, both real and imagined. The bronze was sometimes gilded. Inside the churches, metals were used in many ways, iron for grilles of various designs (fig. 7–13) and more precious metals for liturgical pieces.

The statue of Saint Foy (see fig. 7–1) at the Abbey Church of Conques, France, is a silver-gilt casing that covers the skull of the child martyr. It was made in the late ninth century and is embellished with gems, cameos, and crystal spheres. Romanesque relics of saints were frequently given such splendid treatment.

▲ **7–14** A section from the textile known as the *Bayeux Tapestry*, c. 1066–82, linen and wool, 20 in. (51 cm) long. This section depicts the preparation and blessing of a feast.
Erich Lessing/Art Resource, NY

Textiles

Few textiles remain, of course, from the Romanesque period, but even with few artifacts, we know from writings, carvings, and paintings that the Romanesque age was a time in which textiles in interiors were both more abundant and more prestigious than furniture.

Rich textiles, such as silk wall hangings and altar cloths, were common in church interiors, but fine textiles were also used in important houses. For example, to block drafts, the beds were surrounded by fabric hangings (or recessed in alcoves closed by fabric hangings), which were given the most artful attention. Other hangings covered wall surfaces; carpets covered floors; fabric was draped over benches or seatbacks; and hung on walls behind benches. Tables, often crudely made, were covered with tablecloths before being used.

One of the few remaining Romanesque textiles is the Bayeux Tapestry (fig. 7–14), a strip of linen with wool embroidery (strictly speaking, not a tapestry at all) showing scenes from the Norman Conquest of 1066. It is thought to have been woven before the end of the eleventh century, pos-sibly in Canterbury or Winchester, England, although tradition attributes it to Queen Matilda, the wife of William the Conqueror, and her handmaidens. Now in a museum in Bayeux, France, its surviving section of 238 feet (68 m) long and 20 inches (50 cm) high, offers a parade of scenes that have provided much information about English history and many aspects of daily life in early medieval Europe.

Summary: Romanesque Design

The great virtue of the Romanesque—and its great design lesson for those working in any style—is its consistency and its consequent harmony. Yet, within its harmonious shell, Romanesque ornament could be grotesque and macabre.

Looking for Character

Unlike Early Christian models, the Romanesque builders employed powerful, thick walls, relieving and often emphasizing their thickness with a variety of articulations—projections, niches, piers, half columns, blind arcades, and openings.

Unlike Byzantine models, they offered an architecture of clarity, not one of mystery. Simple basilica plans were given three-dimensional expressiveness by using round vaults, hemispherical domes, and groin vaults intersecting over the central squares (where the naves and transepts meet). Ornament in stone, brick, metal, and wood was often rich and geometrically complex but also sympathetic to (and never obscuring) the construction beneath it.

Looking for Quality

As we have seen, the Romanesque architectural vocabulary was a relatively small one. For example, the round-headed arch was employed almost exclusively (with a few exceptions in Burgundy and Sicily). Surprisingly, the insistent repetition of this single element seldom produced a boring result; rather, it almost always produced a pleasingly coherent one. Intentionally limiting themselves to one consistent shape (which has, in its own proportions, an inner consistency), Romanesque builders created an earthly replica of their vision of God's harmonious Kingdom.

Making Comparisons

The Romanesque church is a strong, well-built edifice. It deserves the implicit comparison with Roman construction (and even with Greek), but its characteristics are primarily its own, not imitative. While the design displayed in Romanesque vaults, domes, and round-headed arches all came originally from Rome, the Romanesque was not a "rebirth" of classical principles, such as we will see with the Renaissance style.

Compared with the Early Christian and Byzantine styles that immediately preceded it and to the Gothic that immediately followed, the Romanesque employed forms more similar to those of the Romans, but the Romanesque designers adopted relatively little of the order (or the orders), the discipline, and the sense of proportion and composition that the Romans, following the Greeks, had mastered. In the end, the Romanesque is not a continuation of classical design principles, but instead a new invention of handsome strengths, moving simplicity, and clear dedication.

The Gothic

1132–c. 1500

8

"Great buildings, like great mountains, are the work of centuries. . . . Time is the architect; the nation is the mason."

— Victor Hugo (1802–50), French writer

The end of the period dominated by Romanesque design was marked not by a political, military, or social event, but by a series of architectural inventions: the pointed arch (fig. 8–1), the flying buttress, and the ribbed reinforcements in stone vaulting. These three became part of a new architectural vocabulary that we call the Gothic. The Romanesque style gradually phased out as it became possible to build something more dramatic.

Gothic was a pejorative term coined later, in Italy in the fifteenth century, when the people of the Renaissance began to honor classical design. They were referring to the "barbarian" Goths, who had come from the North and during conquests had wrecked many of the great classical monuments. Only such barbarians, Renaissance thinkers assumed, could have preferred the emotional extremism of the Gothic to the decorous principles of ancient Greece and Rome. Today, Gothic designates a style that first appeared in France before the middle of the twelfth century, reached its height

in thirteenth-century France and England, and endured to the beginning of the fifteenth century in central Italy (and even later in Spain and northern Europe). In this period, Christian fervor led to the conception and building of the many cathedrals that stand as supreme architectural achievements of human history.

Determinants of Gothic Design

Gothic design was formed by conventions, emotions, and beliefs, as well as by natural and historical factors. Its most impressive monuments transcended worldly considerations in order to express otherworldly aspirations and beliefs, and Gothic designers ignored the "rules" of classical harmony and proportion in an effort to express the infinite. Yet these monuments were made by humans obeying human conditions. Their accomplishments, by any standards, were remarkable.

Geography and Natural Resources

Gothic design was the architectural expression of almost the whole of Europe, but local variations were caused by local conditions. Natural resources varied with the regions; Italy is

◀ **8–1** Detail of nave wall, Chartres Cathedral, France, c. 1194-1260. The splashes of color are from the stained glass windows (see fig. 8–21).
Jean Bernard, Aix-en-Provence, France/Bordas Publication

Timeline | GOTHIC CULTURE

Date	Cultural Figures and Events	Secular Buildings
12th century	St. Bernard; Abbot Suger; second and third Crusades	
13th century	Later Crusades; Magna Carta; St. Thomas Aquinas	Palazzo Pubblico, Siena
14th century	Giotto; Petrarch; Dante; Boccaccio; Chaucer; the Black Death; beginning of the Hundred Years' War	Doge's Palace, Venice; Penshurst Place, Kent

rich in white marble and colored stone, but France and England have an abundance of coarser, grayer stone. Climate played a role as well. Outside light was more welcome under the gray skies of the north than in the sunny south, although the spiritual qualities of colored light were appreciated in all countries. So, too, areas of heavy snowfall needed more steeply pitched roofs.

Religion

Religious expression was at the heart of Gothic design, but beyond that, historical changes occurred in church organization and in the forms of worship. The popes came to have immense power in Gothic times, and the clergy became all-important figures in temporal as well as spiritual matters, bringing much wealth and power to the church. Their numbers swelled as the size of congregations increased, requiring larger interior spaces for services and processions. Increasingly, the honoring of the church's wealthy patrons and saints gave further impetus to the building of chapels and other accompanying buildings.

In the early days of the Christian church, great reverence was given the relics of the saints. *Reliquaries* were made in gold and enamel and inlaid with precious jewels to hold sacred fragments of all kinds. By the tenth century a large commerce had developed in these objects, which sold for enormous prices and were often later proved to be spurious. The church authorities, realizing a change in the practice was necessary, began to substitute images of the Virgin for

adoration. Christ was considered too sublime, too regal, for this purpose, his divinity placing him aloof. But not even the frailest or most sinful would fear to approach or revere one whose attributes were infinite humility, love, pity, and forgiveness, and so attention was focused on the mother of Christ. Cathedrals built in dedication to Notre Dame (Our Lady) and "Lady Chapels" in other churches reflected the new importance of the Madonna (the virgin mother of Christ) in Christian liturgy and devotions. The Madonna, as an ideal of artists in every medium, has been used in every art period of the Christian world. Only the style of representing her has changed.

History

While during the Romanesque period Western Europe enjoyed a rare degree of internationalism, in the Gothic period it was marked by an increased building of new rival city-states and nations. Competition among these was a great spur to cathedral construction. Social institutions such as knighthood and chivalry and social organizations such as guilds of artisans and tradesmen combined elements of church and state, producing an environment that stressed collective behavior and supported the vast joint enterprise of cathedral construction.

Historical backgrounds were also a factor. English cathedrals showed their area's Norman backgrounds. Italian examples adhered to Romanesque proportions and avoided the French Gothic heights. Spanish churches reflected Moorish influence and were richly ornamented. Across Europe, however, churches for the sober new orders of Dominicans and Franciscans moved toward more restrained ornament.

Finally, the economic crises of fourteenth-century Europe and the devastating plague called the Black Death (which in the year 1349 alone killed a third of the population of England and in the years 1347–51 killed a total of 75 million people) brought many of the ambitious building programs of the Gothic period to a close.

Gothic Architecture and Interiors

There is no question that the highest level of Gothic ingenuity, effort, dedication, and sacrifice was spent on the Christian cathedral, and on the characteristics that distinguished it. However, as city-states formed and wealth increased for the

Date	French Cathedrals	English Cathedrals	German Cathedrals	Italian Cathedrals
12th century	St. Denis; Notre Dame, Paris; Chartres	Lincoln; Ely		
13th century	Rheims; Amiens; Beauvais; Ste.-Chapelle, Paris	Wells; Salisbury; Westminster; Abbey; York	Strasbourg; Cologne	Siena; Florence
14th century		Gloucester	Ulm	Milan

ruling landowners, there was an increase in the sophistication of secular and domestic buildings and interiors as well.

The great Gothic cathedrals were the culmination of the Christian Middle Ages and are among the most surprising achievements in architecture. In their high-reaching spires, they still convey how intense their builders' faith and dedication must have been. Generations of male citizens spent their lives helping to build them.

The Gothic style was not a fixed style but changed as it developed chronologically and spread geographically. Chronologically, scholars divide it into the Early Gothic (replacing the Romanesque about 1160 in France, about 1175 in England and Germany, about 1200 in Italy, and later in other countries), the High Gothic (from about 1240 to 1350), and the Late Gothic (from about 1350 to 1420). In France, where the style first developed, the three phases of Gothic are sometimes called the *lancette* (spearlike), the *rayonnant* (radiant), and the *flamboyant* (flamelike). In England, they are called Early English, Decorated, and Perpendicular.

Architectural Components

Intentionally, the Gothic cathedral was an architecture of excess. Unlike the classical architecture that came before it and the Renaissance architecture that would follow, both of which were concerned with carefully reasoned harmonies among building elements, Gothic cathedrals strove for extreme dimensions and proportions. They were concrete expressions of strongly felt emotion, not expressions of logic or rationality.

Not that logic was absent. An elaborate and highly rational system of construction had to be devised to erect such magnificent structures. That technology was at the heart of the nineteenth century's admiration for Gothic architecture, and it is widely admired still. But Gothic architecture did not value an organic unity between the exterior and interior or between the structure and space. Its structural system upheld—but was largely unexpressed in—its great interior spaces. What the visitor to these spaces saw were walls so towering and transparent that their mere existence seemed impossible. Indeed, without the support of structural buttresses invisible from within, they *would* have been impossible. Inside, the vertical lines of piers and the arching lines of ribs all pointed heavenward, emphasizing height and contributing to the otherworldly effect. Surfaces glistened with mosaics or glowed with stained glass, further helping to dematerialize the building when seen from inside.

A related preference was for weightlessness, which was further emphasized by constructing tall walls with as little visible support as possible. Contributing to the desired effect was the practice of piercing the walls as much as possible and filling the openings with a new art form: stained glass. The total effect transcended earthly experience and approached the miraculous.

The plans of Gothic churches generally follow the basilica plan we have seen before. They are usually in the form of a **Latin cross**, which has a horizontal member shorter than the vertical member (see table 6–2). The long vertical member corresponds to the **nave**, the main body of the church extending from the entrance, which is usually at the west end of the building, to the liturgical focus (the choir, chancel, altar, or apse—or a combination of these) usually at the east end. The short horizontal member corresponds to the **transept**, the transverse part of the church that runs from north to south, crossing the nave at right angles. The nave is usually supplemented by one or more pairs of parallel side aisles lower than the nave, and these in turn are sometimes flanked by small chapels dedicated to saints. In some plans, the side aisles continue to form a semicircular passageway

▼ **8–2** Floor plan of the cathedral at Amiens, France, begun in 1220.
Sir Banister Fletcher, "A History of Architecture on the Comparative Method," (London: B. T. Batsford, 1954, 16th ed.)
Reprinted by permission.

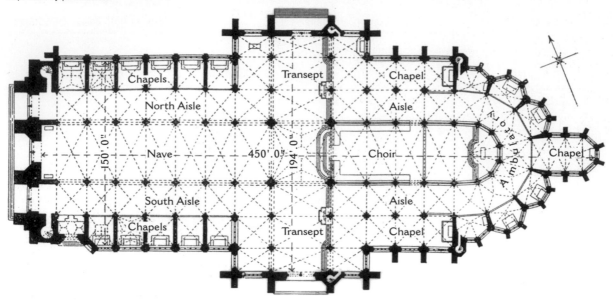

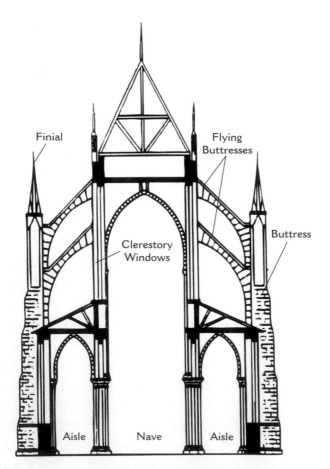

▲ **8–3** Typical vertical section through a Gothic church or cathedral. The two levels of flying buttresses counter the thrust of the arch above the nave. Clerestory windows light the nave from above the side aisles.
Gilbert Werlé/New York School of Interior Design

called an **ambulatory** behind the choir, and the ambulatory may also be flanked by chapels. The plan of Amiens Cathedral (fig. 8–2) is an example, although its transepts are shorter than typical. In some other examples, however, such as the cathedrals of Bourges and Albi, the transepts are omitted altogether, and at Albi the side aisles are omitted as well.

The vertical sections of Gothic cathedrals (fig. 8–3) are dominated by the central nave, their tallest feature. The height of the nave is generally divided into several levels, the lowest being called the **arcade**, the next highest (usually in the form of a narrow gallery) being called the **triforium** or tribune, typically opening to the nave through arcades of three arches in each bay. In a few cases, there are two intermediate levels, the lower being called the tribune and the upper the triforium. The highest portion of the nave walls, rising clear above the structures of the side aisles, are pierced with windows called **clerestories**.

There were three construction innovations that made the Gothic cathedral possible: the pointed arch, the flying buttress, and the ribbed vault. All three had been in use before the Gothic era, but Gothic architects combined them in the service of a wholly new vision.

The Pointed Arch   The most easily recognized characteristic of Gothic design is the **pointed arch**, visible in the interiors of the cathedrals at Chartres (see fig. 8–1), Amiens (see fig. 8–10), and Wells (see fig. 8–11). It replaced the round arch

▲ 8–4 Flying buttresses supporting the nave walls of Chartres Cathedral, France.
© Dean Conger/CORBIS All Rights Reserved

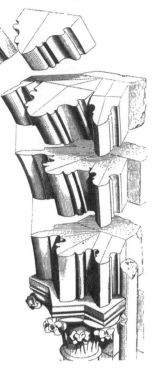

◄ 8–5 Stone courses near the spring line of a ribbed arch. The top course is seen dividing into separate ribs.
From "Dictionnaire raisonne de l'architecture Francaise du XIe au XVIe siecle" by E. Viollet-le-Duc, Paris 1858–68. Thames & Hudson. Reprinted by permission.

of the Romanesque style. The pointed form had been used in ancient times but never to the extent to which it was applied in the Gothic period. The shape probably developed from the necessity for having arches of the same height starting at the same level but having different widths of span. The arch across the nave was often 50 feet (15 m) wide, whereas the arch from pier to pier along the length of the nave averaged 20 feet (6 m), yet the design called for near similarity in height. As the height of a round arch is always only half its width, similar heights could not be attained from the same **spring line** (the level at which the supporting piers stop and above which the actual arch begins). The pointed arch fulfilled this requirement by allowing different widths to be paired with identical heights.

Much has been written about the fact that such an arch points toward heaven and symbolizes aspiration. This is undoubtedly true, but it is also true that the pointed arch, more flexible in its proportions than a round arch, was a practical solution to the problems of Gothic church design.

The Flying Buttress　The elimination of the supporting wall through the repeated use of arches often placed too great a weight upon the piers, a problem that was solved by making the pier thicker in depth by the introduction of a **buttress** on the outside. This buttress was not originally exposed, but was concealed beneath the roofs of the side aisles. By the end of the twelfth century, it had become acceptable to expose these supports, and once support was divorced from the visible

walls of the interior, the nave design could be entirely rethought, and the amount of glass dramatically increased.

Where a single buttress was still insufficient in weight, another buttress was built a short distance beyond, which was connected to the pier buttress by an arch. This construction, supporting the church wall but standing some distance from it, was called a **flying buttress** (fig. 8–4). Buttresses were also given greater stability by crowning them with a weighty **finial**, or **pinnacle**, and these were generally given elaborately ornamental shapes.

The Ribbed Vault　Gothic ceiling vaults were not built monolithically, as Roman vaults had been. Instead, they were built by first constructing heavy, arched stone **ribs** connecting opposite piers. Other ribs starting from each support ran in a diagonal direction to the adjoining opposite piers. When the construction of the rib cage was completed, the space between the ribs was filled in with masonry supported by the ribs. As the ribs were visible and projected below the infilling masonry, the pattern formed by the rib intersections produced a gossamer effect. Ribbed construction was one of the most characteristic features of Gothic design. Even when the ribs were not structurally necessary (and often the vaults could stand without them), they served as a valuable visual diagram: As they carry our eyes upward, they clarify and dramatize the construction.

The diagram in figure 8–5 was drawn by Eugène Viollet-le-Duc, a nineteenth-century architect and archaeologist who

▲ 8–6 Ribs springing from the central column of the Chapter House at Wells Cathedral, England.
© Angelo Hornak/CORBIS All Rights Reserved

▲ 8–7 Fan vaulting in King's College Chapel, Cambridge, England.
A. F. Kersting

restored the cathedrals of Notre Dame in Paris and Amiens; it shows stone courses forming a rib that springs from the top of a pier and then divides into smaller ribs. Ribbed vaulting reached its most extravagant expression in some English Gothic cathedrals and chapels. An example is the Chapter House at Wells Cathedral (fig. 8–6), so-called because a chapter of scripture was traditionally read there daily to the assembled monks. Octagonal in plan, it has a central column from which thirty-two ribs soar upward and outward to support the roof.

A later, grander example, also English, is the ribbed vaulting of King's College Chapel in Cambridge, built between 1446 and 1515 and credited to architect John Wastell and master mason Reginald Ely. Here (fig. 8–7), in what is called **fan vaulting**, the ribs flare out in the shape of inverted cones. The edges of the cones or fans meet at the top of the vault, and the diamond-shaped areas between the fans have been given projecting ornaments called **pendant bosses**. In the view shown, the choir screen topped by an organ and trumpeting angels is a later addition (see fig. 16-4).

Gothic Cathedrals

Great rivalry developed between towns and villages to outdo each other in the beauty, size, and grandeur of their cathedrals. This resulted in a trend toward larger and higher buildings.

Date Begun	Cathedral	Nave Height	Width-to-Height Ratio
1132	St.-Denis	88 ft. (27 m)	1 to 2.2
1163	Notre Dame, Paris	105 ft. (32 m)	1 to 2.6
1194	Chartres	120 ft. (37 m)	1 to 2.5
1211	Rheims	124 ft. (38 m)	1 to 3
1220	Amiens	138 ft. (42 m)	1 to 3.4
1225	Beauvais	156 ft. (48 m)	1 to 3.5

Considered the earliest Gothic cathedral, the 1132 Abbey Church of St.-Denis near Paris had a nave height of 88 feet (27 m), but forty years later Notre Dame in Paris would rise to 105 feet (32 m), then Chartres, also near Paris, to 120 feet (37 m), and thirteenth-century Amiens to 138 feet (42 m). There was a progression of proportions as well as dimensions: St.-Denis's nave was slightly more than twice as high as it was wide; Amiens's nave height was almost 3½ times its width.

As these buildings were designed without modern engineering calculations or building codes, however, some construction projects proved overly ambitious. Beauvais Cathedral, for example, intended to be the highest in the world with a vault height of 156 feet (48 m), stood for only a few decades before collapsing in a high wind in 1284. For all their emphasis on height, however, the Gothic "hero-architects" did not attempt world height records, as would the twentieth century's skyscraper builders. (Ancient Egypt's Great Pyramid of Khufu, for example, was three times the height of Beauvais

Cathedral.) What interested the cathedral builders more was the emotional reaction of the buildings' visitors. The intention was not to demonstrate the builders' power but their subservience to—and aspirations toward—the divine.

Geographically, Gothic spread from its origins near Paris in the north of France throughout most of Europe. There were Gothic buildings and interiors in Belgium, the Netherlands, and Austria. Some of the Gothic design of Spain will be considered in Chapter 14. Most of the great cathedrals outside of France, however, were built in England, Germany, and Italy.

Chartres Cathedral The Cathedral of Notre Dame at Chartres (fig. 8–8), on the outskirts of Paris, is one of the world's most famous buildings. Its construction was begun in 1194 and substantially completed in 1260, and it is considered to have ushered in the High Gothic period. Its fame comes largely from the opinion that its 180 stained glass windows are so glorious (see fig. 8–21) and on the fact that so

Viewpoints | HENRY ADAMS ON CHARTRES

American historian and scholar Henry Adams (1838–1918) wrote *Mont-Saint-Michel and Chartres* in 1904, a book in which he contrasted the Romanesque church of Mont-St.-Michel with the Gothic cathedral of Chartres. Here is one of his observations: "If you are to get the full enjoyment of Chartres, you must . . . try first to rid your mind of the traditional idea that the Gothic is an intentional expression of religious gloom. The necessity for light was the motive of the Gothic architects. They

needed light and always more light, until they sacrificed safety and common sense in trying to get it. They converted their walls into windows, raised their vaults, diminished their piers, until their churches could no longer stand. You will see the limits at Beauvais; at Chartres we have not got so far, but even here, in places where the Virgin wanted it—as above the high altar—the architect has taken all the light there is to take."

▲ 8–8 West front, Chartres Cathedral, France.
© Achim Bednorz, Koln

▲ 8–9 The labyrinth in the nave floor pavement, Chartres.
Foto Marburg/Art Resource, NY

many of them are still in place. Chartres is also admired for its west front (see fig. 8–8) with two distinct towers, the south one (on the right as one enters) being earlier, shorter, simpler, and the one more praised by connoisseurs. Between the towers are three portals with three tall windows above, all of them very subtly pointed. The central portal, called the Porte Royale, recessed in a niche covered with relief sculpture, was a model for many church entrances that would follow. The elongated figures on the **jambs** (sides) of the door, standing on small, highly decorative columns, are seen in figure 8–18. Above the portals and windows is a large rose window.

An innovation at Chartres is that such a composition of portals and windows occurs not only on the west front but also on the north and south ends of the transept, and there are smaller rose windows at the top of each bay of the nave. The most important advance over earlier cathedrals is the enlargement of the clerestory window area. This offered not only an unprecedented amount of stained glass; it also demanded an unprecedented amount of exterior buttressing, supplied in multiple tiers (see fig. 8–4).

The nave walls, as is typical of Gothic cathedrals, consist of three parts: the lowest part an arcade open to side aisles par-

allel to the nave; the central part, a triforium (a smaller-scaled arcade) with a gallery behind; and the top part, the largely glazed clerestory above the roof of the side aisle. We have seen a detail of the triforium of Chartres in figure 8–1.

A feature of the stone pavement of the nave at Chartres is one of many medieval labyrinths (fig. 8–9). The labyrinth was a symbol of a pilgrim's spiritual journey toward Christ, and walking it was thought to be an aid to meditation. It was also the master builders' reference to a legendary predecessor, Daedalus, builder of the great labyrinth of King Minos on Crete. The example at Chartres was designed with the same size and shape as the rose window above it, covering the whole width of the nave floor, and it terminates at a central six-foiled ornament (see table 8–1, p. 155).

Amiens Cathedral Called "the Bible of Amiens," because of its instructive carvings and windows, the Cathedral of Notre Dame at Amiens (fig. 8–10) is in the province of Picardy in the far north of France. Along with the cathedrals at Chartres and Rheims, it is considered one of the three masterpieces of the French High Gothic. Of the three, architect/restorer Viollet-le-Duc (who drew fig. 8–5) preferred Amiens because of its structural consistency and precise order. It was built between 1220 and 1270 of chalk-white limestone

▶ 8–10 The nave, Amiens Cathedral, France
© Angelo Hornak/CORBIS All Rights Reserved

from nearby quarries. Compared to other cathedrals, its transepts project only slightly from the body of the church (see the plan, fig. 8–2). Its eastern end, the last major part of the cathedral to be built, terminates in a splendid **chevet**, a semicircular combination of choir (where the carved wood choir stalls are much admired), ambulatory, and seven radiating chapels, six of which are also semicircular.

But the most remarkable aspects of Amiens are the size and slenderness of its interior. The nave is 40 feet (12 m) wide, an impressive 470 feet (145 m) long, and an even more impressive 140 feet (43 m) high, more than twice the height of Wells and as tall as a modern fourteen-story office building. With the exception of unfinished Beauvais, it is the highest of all Gothic cathedrals, although the cathedrals at Milan and Seville (see fig. 14–8) both exceed it in volume. The nave has the usual tripartite elevation of arcade, triforium, and clerestory, but in this case the arcade is unusually tall, almost as high as the triforium and clerestory together, and its clustered pillars correspondingly tall and slender. In the eastern arm of the church the triforium is pierced through to the exterior and glazed.

The west front follows the general model of Chartres, except that the towers are much shorter, hardly taller than the nave roof, and the southern one was never completed. The portals, however, are imposing, presenting a collection of fifty-two saints in sculptured relief.

Like Chartres, Amiens had a labyrinth in the pavement of its nave, laid in 1288 and inscribed with the names of the cathedral's three consecutive master builders. The first of these, Robert de Luzarches, began his work in 1220 (for an unknown length of time) and is thought to be responsible for the cathedral's plan and for the construction of its remarkable nave. His successors as master builders were Thomas de Cormont, probably responsible for the lowest levels of the transept and choir, and his son Regnault de Cormant, probably responsible for the upper levels.

Wells Cathedral   By the end of the twelfth century, great Gothic cathedrals were beginning to be built in England. The English cathedrals were not as likely as the French ones to be found at the heart of a town. Set somewhat aside in a clearing, on a hill, or along a riverbank, they are spectacular elements in the English countryside. Their naves generally lack the extreme height and narrowness of the French naves, but they are often extreme in another dimension: their length.

A typical French nave might have a length four times its width, but an English nave's length might be six times its width. English ground plans are also more complex: in French cathedrals, the transepts project only slightly, but in English ones they project much more boldly, and sometimes (as at Salisbury) there is even a second pair of transepts smaller than the first. The English cathedral is also more likely to be complicated by other adjoining elements, such as sacristies, chapter houses (monastic assembly halls), cloisters, and walled enclosures with gatehouses. Apses at the east ends of cathedrals are generally semicircular in France and generally square in England. The interiors of the English cathedrals, while less tall than the French, are sometimes even more ornate. While less rational, they are sometimes even more decorative and picturesque.

Wells Cathedral (fig. 8–11) is in Somerset, a county of southwestern England. It was built of local limestone in two phases, c. 1185–1240 and c. 1275–1350. It is a thick-walled structure with its clerestory windows deeply recessed and hardly visible from the nave floor. The rib-vaulted nave, if one includes the choir, the altar, and the Lady Chapel in the eastern arm, is 380 feet (117 m) long and 67 feet (21 m) high. The stone tower above the crossing of nave and transept was added between 1315 and 1322 and originally had a tall spire of lead-sheathed wood that burned down in the following century. The weight of the new tower was seen to cause some stress in the structure below, however, and about 1350 this was remedied by the radical insertion of strainer arches, arches built between piers to hold them apart, acting more as buttresses than as spanning devices. In the case of Wells, these are actually pairs of arches, the upper ones inverted to form enormous X-shapes. With multiple moldings sweeping around them, these forms provide great visual drama as well as structural strength.

We have already seen in figure 8–6 the distinctive ribbed vaults of the Chapter House added in the early fourteenth century. The west towers flanking the entrance were added in 1370 and 1410, and the Renaissance pulpit was added in 1547.

The Cathedral of Siena   As we noted at the beginning of this chapter, Italy was more resistant to France's Gothic ideas than was the rest of Europe. The number of Italian Gothic monuments is therefore relatively small. Even within this relatively small group, the Italian enthusiasm for the Gothic may seem lukewarm: The naves are tall and narrow, but—by

▲ 8–11 "Strainer arches" at the crossing of nave and transept, Wells Cathedral, England.
Florian Monhiem/Bildarchiv Monhiem/AGE Fotostock America, Inc.

▲ 8–12 A view into the domed crossing of the Siena Cathedral, begun in 1245. The stripes in the colored marble are horizontal, contrary to the lines of most Gothic interiors.
Scala/Art Resource, NY

French standards—not *very* tall and narrow; the arches are pointed, but not *very* pointed.

Even so, the Cathedral of Siena (fig. 8–12), erected between 1245 and 1380 in Tuscany, constitutes one of the greatest building programs of the Gothic era. Its present nave is 320 feet (98 m) long, but the astonishing intent at one time was that this element would eventually be only the finished church's transept and that a much longer nave—never completed—would be added to the southeast. Construction

actually began on this ambitious project, but it was halted by a famine in 1326 and the Black Death in 1348.

The cathedral is built completely of colored marble; green from Prato, white from Carrara (in the twenty-first century still an important source), and a deep rose with purple and black veining from Siena itself. Its exterior departs from the cathedrals of France and England: Here we see no buttresses, but instead at the center of the building we see a dome. Covered with copper in 1263, it is popularly called the *mela* ("apple"), and, inside, the dome's twelve-sided arcaded drum is carried on squinches above an octagonal floor plan. Most striking is that, both outside and in, the Gothic penchant for repeated verticals is here replaced with strong horizontal stripes (see fig. 8–12). The design of the Siena Cathedral is attributed to Nicola Pisano (c. 1220–c. 1284), who later designed the pulpit in the baptistery at Pisa (see fig. 8–22). His son Giovanni Pisano (c. 1245–c. 1319) continued his father's work and designed the pulpit in Siena.

Secular Buildings

The social and political conditions of the Middle Ages permitted little comfort or luxury in domestic living, except in the feudal fortress castles of the nobles. This was as true of the early Gothic period as it had been for all of the Early Christian, Byzantine, and Romanesque periods. The mass of the population lived in log or stone houses roofed with thatch. It was not until the thirteenth century that the medieval castle began to look less like a fortress and to have a few conveniences and comforts.

One reason for the change was an advance in weapons technology. Rather than fostering a demand for more fortifications, they made the old fortified castles obsolete. The power of government also advanced, and with the increasing power and efficiency of the laws, it was no longer necessary to consider strength before comfort in residential design. Instead of seeking a hilltop or other easily defensible position, people began to choose sites that were simply agreeable or beautiful, where they might be protected from the inclemency of the weather, and where gardens and orchards could be planted.

Living conditions were still far from ideal. In northern Europe the winter was chill, dark, and damp. Glass for windows did not become common in dwellings until the fifteenth century. Before that period the windows had wooden shutters, pierced with small holes that were filled with translucent materials such as mica, waxed cloth, or horn to admit a small amount of light.

In the houses of the common people, the stone walls were often bare or covered with rough plaster. After 1400, tapestries were extensively used in the princely castles of both France and England to cover walls, to hang over windows and doors, to enclose beds, or to partition large rooms for privacy. When actual tapestries were not available, the interior walls of the castles were sometimes painted in imitation of hung textiles or with mural decorations of historical and religious scenes or legends of chivalry.

The ceilings of the rooms usually showed the exposed beams or trusses of the roof construction, frequently enriched with colorful painted ornament. On plaster ceilings gold star patterns on a blue or green ground were often painted. When flat-beamed ceilings were used, the ends of the beams were supported by projecting ornamental brackets, variously shaped or carved into figures.

As examples of some of these practices, we shall see, in chronological order, a room in a municipal building in Siena, a room in an English country house, and a palazzo in Venice.

Palazzo Pubblico, Siena   Begun in the 1280s, the Palazzo Pubblico dominates Siena's central square, called the Campo, and was built to hold the customs offices, the mint, and the mayor's residence. A few blocks away from the Cathedral of Siena, it is not a religious building but it is a severe and grave one, as befits its civic duties. Faced with brick above a stone-faced ground floor, the building's exterior has windows under pointed arches and battlements along its parapet.

Its chief interior spaces include the Sala del Mappamondo (Hall of the World Map, named for a large rotating map that was affixed to the wall in the fourteenth century) and a room (fig. 8–13) originally called the Sala dei Nove (Hall of the Nine, named for a nine-man governing council); after the overthrow of the Nine, it was renamed the Sala della Pace (Hall of Peace, after one of a pair of murals painted by Ambrogio Lorenzetti). The murals, painted in 1338–40, depict civic figures rather than biblical ones. We see symbolic representations of Peace, Winter, the Common Good, Providence, Temperance, Justice, and, lastly, Faith, Hope, and Charity (Christian attributes, admittedly). There are also depictions of the throngs of Sienese citizens among the buildings of their city, some of the architecture overtly Gothic, some not. Above and below the murals are decorative painted bands featuring quatrefoils (see table 8–1). The ceiling is flat, not vaulted, with painted beams supported on brackets.

This interior is a reminder that, however devout the Gothic age was, there was attention to municipal as well as religious affairs; to some extent, it is a foretaste of the more worldly Renaissance that was soon to follow.

Penshurst Place, Kent   Penshurst Place, Kent, England, was built c. 1340 for the wealthy London merchant Sir John Pulteney. A lightly fortified country house, it was built around a series of courtyards, its chief room being its Great Hall. This room was not only the center of an important house but also the center of an entire community, accommodating banquets, entertainments, trials, and other uses. As a gathering place for the landowner's tenants, it also served as a symbol of feudal authority.

▲ 8–13 The Sala della Pace of the Palazzo Pubblico, Siena, Italy, with frescoes of Siena street life added by Ambrogio Lorenzetti.
Canali Photobank

Spanning the room is a fine example of timber roof construction (fig. 8–14), thought to have been the work of carpenter Thomas Hurley. It is natural that in an age devoted to stone construction there should also be skill in wood construction, for the stone vaults were often constructed on timber scaffolding (called **centering**), which was then removed (or *struck*) after the stones were in place and self-supporting. The Great Hall at Penshurst is bridged by a series of parallel **trusses**, combinations of wood members working together. The longest members of a truss are called its *chords* and the shorter ones joining them constitute its **web**. The vertical members at the top of Penshurst's trusses directly beneath the roof ridge (members not present in all trusses) are called *crown posts*.

Below the timber trusswork, two side walls of stone, 64 feet (20 m) long, have tall windows opening to courtyards. Built before the widespread use of window glass, these windows may have at first been filled with oiled parchment. At

▲ 8–14 Above two suits of medieval armor, the trussed timber roof structure over the Great Hall at Penshurst Place, Kent, England.
Fred J. Maroon

one end of the room (fig. 8–15) there was a screen of paneled oak that shielded doorways into the kitchen and service areas, and above the screened passage was a "minstrel gallery" for musicians. At the opposite end there was a **dais** (raised platform) on which the lord and lady of the house sat on canopied thrones. A fire was laid on an octagonal hearth in the center of the tiled floor, its smoke escaping through louvers in the ceiling. During the fourteenth century, such a central fire would be replaced in fashion by a fireplace in a side wall with a projecting hood built over it to direct the smoke out through either a wall hole or a chimney. The projecting hood was frequently ornamented with architectural forms or a carved coat of arms. Chairs or benches and a small rug were frequently placed before the fire. It was at this time that the fireplace and hearth became the symbols of the home.

Around Penshurst's central hearth, the rest of the floor was probably scattered with straw and leaves, including those of sweet-scented shrubs and herbs, chosen for their aroma—or for their ability to disguise other aromas. Near Eastern carpets (see Chapter 9) were first imported into England in the thirteenth century, but they were rare for many years. Furniture for the Great Hall was sparse, benches and trestle tables being brought in as the occasion required, then dismantled. The walls may have originally been hung with embroidered linen panels, replaced in the late fourteenth century by richer tapestries. Newer additions to Penshurst Place are Tudor, Jacobean, and Renaissance in style.

▼ **8–15** The Great Hall, Penshurst Place. At the far end is a screens passage with a minstrel gallery above. A fire is laid in the center of the stone floor, and simple tables and benches are placed along the walls. A. F. Kersting/AKG-Images

The Ca d'Oro, Venice An exception to the relatively tepid Italian response to the Gothic influence was in the northeastern Italian city of Venice, then busily engaged in trade with northern Europe and enthusiastic about northern fashions. There were a large number of ecclesiastical and secular buildings in Venice in the Gothic style, and these included the Doge's Palace and the Ca d'Oro.

The Doge's Palace, built between the basilica of St. Mark's and the lagoon, is a key part of an ambitious urban design scheme. The present façades date from 1309–1424 and feature open arcades on two lower levels topped by walls of white and rose-colored marble pierced by Gothic windows. The notable features of the interior are all of a later period, postdating a disastrous fire of 1577.

The Ca d'Oro (House of Gold) is one of Venice's great private palaces (fig. 8–16), built for Marin Contarini, a member of one of Venice's oldest and most distinguished families and a procurator of St. Mark's. The house owes its name to the fact that the finials of the parapet, the cusps of the stone tracery, the lions on the corner capitals, and many pieces of stone molding were all once faced with gold leaf, an extravagant treatment that must have been difficult to maintain in the city's humid atmosphere.

Built along the Grand Canal between 1421 and 1436, its façade has one area of almost solid masonry but a much larger area that is remarkably open. The notion of an almost completely porous exterior wall made of tiers of arcades, each more delicate than the one beneath, comes close to the glass-walled cathedral in structural daring. And the interior effect also rivals stained glass: dazzling views of the Grand Canal through the filigree of stone tracery (fig. 8–17). Such tracery is akin to the Islamic and Indian wood lattices for shading windows from the hot sun (see Chapters 9 and 10). Other interior spaces are disposed around a pair of interior courtyards. Some details of the palazzo (the entrance door, the courtyard arcade and window, and the open staircase climbing around two sides of a courtyard) were the work of sculptor Matteo Raverti, who also worked on the Gothic ornament of the Milan Cathedral, but all these elements were lost during nineteenth-century renovations, when the palazzo was owned by a famous ballerina, Maria Taglioni. Since 1927 the Ca d'Oro has been owned by the municipality of Venice, and it is now a museum for the collections of its last private owner, Baron Giorgio Franchetti, which include works by the Renaissance painters Andrea Mantegna and Giovanni Bellini.

▼ **8–16** The Ca d'Oro, Venice, Italy, seen from the Grand Canal.
Scala/Art Resource, NY

▲ **8–17** View of the Grand Canal through the loggia tracery of the Ca d'Oro.
Richard J. Goy

Gothic Ornament

Many of the Gothic structural features already mentioned—pointed arches, flying buttresses, and ribbed vaults—were in themselves quite ornamental. Even at its simplest, the Gothic style was a more decorative one than the earlier Romanesque.

Gothic design accentuated the vertical dimension, producing churches with extraordinarily tall naves. In addition, verticality was heightened on the interior in most cases by the striping of piers and ribs, and on the exterior by the addition of towers, spires, and pinnacles. Many of the horizontal moldings and cornices associated with classical temples were discarded. The spirit of the time preferred the vertical, seeing it as a symbol of the aspirations of the faithful, soaring above the problems of the earthbound and pointing toward their future home in heaven.

This preference was expressed not only in the proportions of naves and the repetitions of shafts and ribs, but also in the sculptured figures carved into the stone. The figures at the portals on the west front of Chartres (fig. 8–18) are so tall, thin, and attenuated as to seem hardly human. They stand erect, with arms close to their bodies and clothing in minute vertical folds. Not only does their elongation reflect the architecture, but these figures are themselves integral parts of the architecture, designed to fit particular places among the building's shafts and ribs.

As would be expected, many of these statues were of saints, prophets, and other religious personages, or portraits of royalty, or less holy and less dignified figures, such as dwarfs, grinning goblins, devils, monkeys, donkeys, and fantastic animals. Gutter ends and waterspouts were carved into **gargoyles** of grotesque animal forms. Figures of those who labored on the buildings were also used as decoration: the architect in a quandary, the mason straining to lift a stone, the carpenter raising his hammer, or the painter with his brush and palette. Many of the sculptured representations had a Christian historical or symbolic association, such as St. Peter with his key, St. George and the Dragon, the Creation of Man, Jonah and the Whale, the Wise and Foolish Virgins, and the Last Supper. To the medieval mind nearly everything was symbolic, and the ornament of the church was an encyclopedia in stone.

More abstract ornament was found at the top of the windows in the arched mullions, which were often treated with **foiled** ornament (Table 8-1).

The finials crowning vertical forms were enriched with **crockets**, or projections cut in the form of stylized buds or

▲ **8–18** Carved stone figures at the Porte Royale of Chartres repeat the upward elongation of the cathedral.
Art Resource, NY

leaves. Niches were formed with pointed tops to frame the important statuary, or projecting canopies were placed above free-standing statues. Geometrical forms such as frets, dogteeth, chevrons, zigzags, battlements, and crenellations often formed running ornament. Family crests, monograms, coiling stems with foliage, and the oak branch and leaf were the most common forms of ornamental motifs.

Wood Paneling

Oak paneling was built in both ecclesiastical and domestic interiors to give greater warmth and finish to a room. The panels of the Gothic period were of small dimensions of waxed

TABLE 8–1 Gothic Foiled Ornament

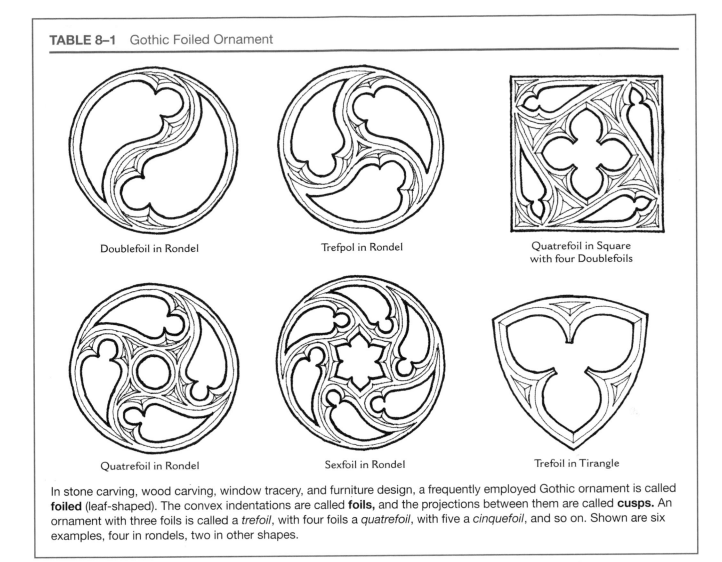

Doublefoil in Rondel

Trefpol in Rondel

Quatrefoil in Square with four Doublefoils

Quatrefoil in Rondel

Sexfoil in Rondel

Trefoil in Tirangle

In stone carving, wood carving, window tracery, and furniture design, a frequently employed Gothic ornament is called **foiled** (leaf-shaped). The convex indentations are called **foils,** and the projections between them are called **cusps.** An ornament with three foils is called a *trefoil*, with four foils a *quatrefoil*, with five a *cinquefoil*, and so on. Shown are six examples, four in rondels, two in other shapes.

wood, usually placed vertically, and were called **wainscoting**. The panel field was sometimes left plain, but was more often carved with a **linenfold** pattern (fig. 8–19), a pattern imitating fabric in soft vertical folds. Other patterns imitated Gothic window tracery and nature: oak branches, leaves, and acorns.

The framework holding the panels was rectangular and composed of vertical **stiles** and horizontal **rails** with molded edges on only three sides of each panel frame. The top rail and the two stiles of each frame were treated with a simple curved molding; the lower rail was plain and **splayed** (slanted downward). The woodworker's method mimicked the method of the stoneworker, who placed a trim molding on three sides of a window with a slanting sill at the bottom to carry off rainwater.

A few moldings ran along the top of the wainscot or **dado** (the top molding of which is called a **dado cap** or **chair rail** because it protects the plaster wall from being hit by chair backs),

and the cresting was often treated with a carved tracery design and finial motifs. The average dimension for a Gothic panel was

▼ **8–19** Wood paneling carved in a linenfold pattern.
Victoria & Albert Museum, London/Art Resource, NY

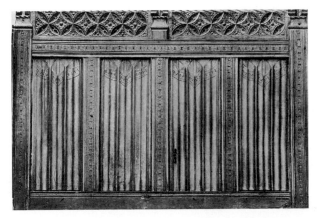

about 9 inches (23 cm) wide—never wider than a single plank of oak—and was sometimes 2 or 3 feet (60 or 90 cm) high.

Stained Glass

Stained-glass windows not only transmitted light but provided architectural ornament in the ways previously done by murals and mosaics. They also provided instruction for the masses by depicting saints and scenes from the Scriptures.

Romanesque stained glass had been limited to relatively small openings in relatively large wall surfaces. With the shift from the Romanesque to the Gothic, the solid wall was minimized and the window area, now devoted to stained glass, was increased enormously. Some of the finest Gothic stained glass ever produced was also some of the earliest, including the choir windows ordered by Abbot Suger for the abbey church of St.-Denis. Soon after, a larger amount of stained glass was made for the Gothic rebuilding of Chartres Cathedral, providing the "miraculous light" praised by Suger.

The colored glass, being translucent but not transparent, eliminates all exterior views, isolating the sacred interior from the secular world outside. The windows, sometimes seeming not to be transmitting outside light but to be luminous themselves, can be so brilliant that their varicolored light obscures—rather than clarifies—the structure around it, but

Tools & Techniques | STAINED GLASS

From "Rose Windows" by Painton Cowen, Thames & Hudson Ltd., London. Reprinted by permission

The techniques for making stained-glass windows originated in the Romanesque period. Pieces of colored glass, necessarily small because of the limits of manufacturing techniques, were assembled to create pictorial images. To join these pieces together, grooved strips of lead, collectively called **leading**, were used to hold together the glass. The leading was produced in geometric patterns so that, in the most artful windows, it was part of the design.

In the largest windows, the areas of glass and leading were held in place by slender stone divisions called **mullions**. The overall mullion pattern is called **tracery**. The earliest tracery, called *plate tracery*, simply pierced the **spandrel** (in an arcade, the roughly triangular area between arches; later, in multistory buildings, the word will refer to flat panels between the window of one floor and the window of the next) with a circle, quatrefoil, or other opening that was then glazed. Later, tracery first introduced at Rheims became known as *bar tracery*, and consisted of vertical mullions crowned with simple pointed arches. In the thirteenth century, *rayonnant tracery* in a radiating wheel-like pattern was used for the circular "Rose" windows at Rheims, Bourges, Amiens, and elsewhere. In the fourteenth and fifteenth centuries, tracery members became **ogive** in type, each side following an S-curve, as seen in Ste.-Chapelle (see diagram).

Within the tracery and the leading, each piece of glass was typically a solid color. As in mosaic work, multicolored pictorial effects were achieved by juxtaposing these pieces. The colors have often been described as "jewel-like" and were dominated by deep blues and reds. Some red and yellow glass was made by the multi-layered **flashed glass** technique that had been developed by the Romans (see page 96). Most famous of all, perhaps, was a sapphire blue or *bleu de ceil* used at both Chartres and York. An exception to the brilliant colors of Gothic glass was in the Cistercian structures, where colorless (or very softly colored) *grisaille* panels were used. And in the last century of the Gothic period, the deep colors were replaced in most new construction by paler, subtler hues.

In addition, details were added by painting in black or gray on the inside surfaces of some of the panes. At first, this was limited to such items as eyes, mouths, and folds of drapery. By the middle of the fourteenth century, however, a taste for increased naturalism had resulted in more widespread painting. What had been the art of the glazier had become a collaboration between glazier and painter. Modeling in terms of light and shade was achieved in different ways, the most common being to paint shadows on the glass.

▲ 8–20 The upper chapel of the Sainte-Chapelle, Paris. Its walls are almost completely glazed.
Jean Bernard, Aix-en-Provence, France/Bordas Publication

the cathedral builders valued a sense of mystery more highly than clarity. The culminating masterpiece of Gothic stained-glass design was the Ste.-Chapelle, begun in 1242 and located near Notre Dame in Paris (fig. 8–20). It was built as part of the royal palace and has chapels on upper and lower floors. The upper one is a structure in which the walls have virtually disappeared, replaced by an astonishing quantity of windows bathing the interior in colored light.

The windows of the Late Gothic period were marked by the ultimate dominance of the painter, who usurped the premier position of the glazier. Larger sections of glass were used as surfaces and completely painted over with biblical illustrations. The effect of these late windows moved away from the spirituality of the earlier Gothic style and anticipated the realism of the oil painting of the Renaissance. For this reason, some of the earliest of Gothic stained glass is considered the finest, for example the glass of Chartres (fig. 8–21), among others.

▲ 8–21 The stained glass window of *Notre Dame de la Belle Verrière*, Chartres, after 1200, approx. 14 ft. (4.3 m) high.
Photo Josse

Gothic Furniture

In the Gothic period, furniture continued the tradition, prominent during the Romanesque, of imitating architectural details. Naturally, therefore, the rounded Romanesque arches on furniture gave way to pointed Gothic ones, and plain surfaces became more elaborately ornamented. The ornamental forms consisted almost entirely of small-scale carved architectural details such as the pointed arches but also tracery, rose windows, buttresses, finials, and crockets were used.

Local woods were necessarily used, but there was a taste for natural-finished oak whenever it could be obtained. Occasionally walnut was used. Thrones and seats of honor were elaborately carved and sometimes gilded. Mostly rectangular in design, the pieces were heavy in proportion and dimension. The parts were assembled with wooden dowels rather than screws or nails, and with **dovetail** and

▼ **8–22** Nicola Pisano's marble pulpit for the Baptistery, Pisa, Italy, 1269. The six outer columns with Corinthian capitals rest on the backs of lions.
Canali Photobank, Milan

▲ **8–23** A round fourteenth-century table from the Chapter House of Salisbury Cathedral. Its top has been replaced.
English Heritage/National Monuments Record

mortise-and-tenon wood joints, two types of joinery that we saw used by the Egyptian woodworkers (see table 2–1). Furniture panels were usually enriched with carved linenfold motifs, just as wall paneling was. Tracery motifs and coats of arms were abundant, and, as in the wainscoting, moldings were placed only on the top and two sides of the panel, the lower stile having a splayed edge.

The hardware on doors and Gothic case furniture was in hammered wrought iron and was always placed on the surface of the woodwork, rather than being countersunk (or "let") into the surface. Hinges, locks, and bolts with scroll and foliage designs were used.

Among liturgical furniture designed for the cathedrals, churches, and chapter houses were some elaborately carved pulpits, such as one designed by Siena Cathedral architect Nicola Pisano for the Baptistery at Pisa (fig. 8–22), in which six outer columns of marble in various colors rest on the backs of small lions. Pews, stalls, pulpits, thrones, screens, and tables (fig. 8–23) were also carved.

Seating and Beds

The Gothic chair was frequently in the form of a small chest with arms and a high back (fig. 8–24), and was reserved for the use of important persons. The panel in the back was usually decorated with a carved pattern and often crowned with a wooden canopy. The dominant lines of the design of chairs

► 8–24 A walnut chair from fifteenth-century France. It is carved with linenfold paneling and a band of tracery across the top. The hinged seat covers a storage chest.

Courtesy Metropolitan Museum of Art, "Chair, High Backed". Walnut. 3/4 view front. The Metropolitan Museum of Art, The Cloisters Collection. 1947 (47.145). Photograph, all rights reserved, the Metropolitan Museum of Art.

were straight; the seat was square and covered with a loose cushion for comfort.

Gothic beds were gorgeously carved and were sheltered with a canopy and curtains hung from the ceiling or supported by corner posts. Sometimes the canopy was made larger than the bed, to enclose a chair within the drawn curtains (fig. 8–25). In this painting, you can see Christine de Pisan presenting a book to Isabel of Bavaria, the wife of Charles VI ("Charles the Mad"), who reigned from 1380 to 1422, indicating how "public" the bed really was during this time.

A **hutch** or chest containing the family valuables was placed at the foot of the bed where it could be watched by its owners. An oil lamp hung within the canopy, and a stool or step was placed beside the bed. Beds were covered with mattresses, finely woven linen sheets, and many pillows. Servants

▼ 8–25 Painting of a canopied Gothic bed in a royal bedchamber.

Christine de Pisan presents her book to Isabelle of Bavaria. Miniature from the "Works" by Christine de Pisan (1364– c. 1430). London, England, c. 1413. Harley 4431 T.1 fol.3. Art Resource, NY

OAK CHEST WITH TRACERY CARVING

LATE TYPE OF CAPITAL

EARLY ROSE WINDOW

WINDOW SHOWING STONE TRACERY

FINIAL MOTIF SHOWING CROCKETS

CLUSTERED COLUMNS

LINENFOLD MOTIF

CREDENCE

CHAIR SHOWING LINENFOLD, TRACERY AND BUTTRESSES

▲ 8–26 Details of Gothic architecture and design.
Gilbert Werlé/New York School of Interior Design

or children frequently slept on a low *truckle*, or **trundle bed**, that was stored under the large bed and pulled out at night.

Casegoods

The chest (see the upper left in fig. 8–26) was the most important piece of residential furniture because it could be easily transported, a necessary advantage during unsettled political conditions. The cupboard was a chest on legs. The **credence**, or serving table (see the lower right in fig. 8–26) originally derived its name from the Latin word *credere*, meaning "to believe," because food placed upon it was tested by a servant before it was offered to the master of the house, who lived in dread of poisioned potions. Today, the Italian word for "credence," *credenza*, is used to indicate a variety of chests and cupboards.

Gothic Decorative Arts

Although tapestry was the decorative art that absorbed the most time and care in Gothic times and that will receive most of our attention here, there were other mediums in which Gothic designers excelled.

Metalwork

Gothic objects produced in fine metals such as gold and silver were largely liturgical: crosses, chalices, and patens (dishes on which bread is offered during the celebration of Mass). Pewter (an alloy of tin and lead) was also sometimes used for such work. Brass (an alloy of copper and zinc) and bronze (an alloy of copper and tin) were used for door-knockers, ewers, bells, and censers (incense burners). Iron was used for hinges, handles, and other hardware on doors and furniture, for screens and grilles, and for lighting fixtures.

Enamels

Enamel work, which we shall consider in more detail later, involves fusing a vitreous (glasslike) substance, usually brightly colored, to a metal backing, often into grooves in the metal surface. It was often used for Gothic liturgical pieces such as tabernacles and reliquaries. From the twelfth century on, a great center for such work was the town of Limoges, France, which would later become noted for its production in the related field of porcelain. Gothic enamel work was also done in Paris and in Austria, Spain, England, and elsewhere.

Tapestries

Tapestries, one of the highlights of the Gothic decorative arts, were not only decorative and colorful but soft. Their use could transform the bare and damp interiors of churches, castles, and citadels into spaces with a degree of warmth and beauty. They were also eminently movable, a characteristic well suited to the peripatetic lives of medieval nobles and their families.

The oldest surviving examples of medieval tapestry date from the end of the eleventh century and are attributed to Germany. By the middle of the fifteenth century, tapestries had become widely popular with the nobility of Germany, France, Italy, Spain, and England. By the sixteenth century—

Tools & Techniques | TAPESTRY WEAVING

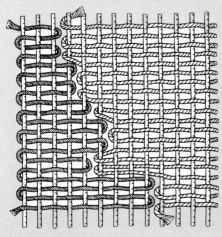

"Oriental Carpets, A Complete Guide" by Murray L. Eiland, Jr. and Murray Eiland III (London, Lawrence King Publishing, 1998).

The weaving of tapestries differs from the weaving of most cloth. In almost all weaving, there are two sets of threads. One set, called the **warp**, consists of parallel threads running the length of the loom. The other set, called the **weft** (or the *woof* or the *filler*) consists of parallel threads running crosswise on the loom. The weft threads are woven in and out of the warp threads, usually by means of a shuttle or bobbin.

In tapestry work (and in many other types of weaving), the weft threads are then compacted with some sort of comb so that they completely conceal the warp threads. The weft threads in tapestry work are not generally sent the full width of the loom but are kept within the areas where their color is wanted so that each section of color is built up independently (see diagram). This peculiarity means that, between areas of different colors, there is a discontinuity or split, which, if small, can be left open, or, if extensive, can be tied together with other threads. One tapestry technique modifies these boundaries between color areas by giving them a sawtooth or comblike edge rather than a straight one.

The simple tapestry weaving technique can be enriched and complicated by many variations. The weaving can be coarse, employing approximately eight warp threads per inch, or it can be much finer, employing twenty-four threads per inch. The weaving can also be patterned. Gold and silver threads, sometimes following the outlines of a design, sometimes not, can add a rich brocaded effect. Wool tapestries can be given vitality and sheen by introducing silk for certain highlights, or embroidery can be added for such details as the faces of figures.

a time of change from Gothic to Renaissance taste—Flanders was established as the most important center for production, with Flemish tapestries considered the finest.

As a rule, Gothic tapestries are of the **millefleurs** (thousand flowers) design. In such a design, the background or other parts of the tapestry are covered with images of numerous small animals and bushes, plants, flowers, and leaves, as seen, for example in the background of figure 8–27. Tapestries done in the **millefleurs** design contain special characteristics. The laws of perspective were considered unadaptable to the tapestry medium, so pictorial depth was not shown. Consequently, in Gothic tapestries objects behind other objects are not reduced in size, nor do they become fainter in tonal value to indicate atmospheric depth. Shadows are absent or only vaguely suggested; horizon lines are close to the top of the

▼ **8–27** "The Hunt of the Unicorn, VII: The Unicorn in Captivity," a tapestry woven of silk, wool, silver and silver-gilt threads, Franco-Flemish, c. 1500, approx. 12 ft. (3.7 m) high. It shows a penned unicorn against a *millefleurs* background.

"The Unicorn in Captivity," From: "The Hunt of the Unicorn. One of six hangings and two fragments from two or more sets of tapestries. Silk, wool, silver and silver–gilt threads. H.: 145 in. W. 99 in. (368 × 251.5 cm.). The Metropolitan Museum of Art, Gift of John D. Rockefeller, Jr., The Cloisters Collection, 1937. (37.80.6) Photograph © 1993 The Metropolitan Museum of Art.

composition; and the design as a whole contains little or no gradations in the coloring or rounding of forms. The general effect is stiff and conventional, though beautiful and dignified. Just as the best vase painting avoids effects that negate the shape of the vase, the best tapestry work avoids effects, such as dramatic perspective, that negate the flatness of the wall surface on which it hangs.

Gothic tapestries can also be identified by subject matter. Religious subjects were paramount. Biblical, allegorical, and ecclesiastical personages were often pictured in a setting of Gothic architectural forms. Scenes of pastoral, agricultural, and courtly life were often represented. Many Gothic tapestries were made showing animals chased by hounds and hunters or caged in a pen. The Unicorn tapestries (fig. 8–27) are a suite of seven tapestry panels by the same artist (name unknown), probably woven in Brussels c. 1500, which show the various stages in hunting and capturing a unicorn. A unicorn is a mythical beast with a horse's body, a goat's beard, a lion's tail, and a single long horn in the middle of its forehead. It was a symbol of purity and strength not only in medieval Europe but also in ancient Egypt and the Ancient Near East.

The great beauty of Gothic tapestries lies in the qualities in which they are unlike paintings, and not in the qualities in which they resemble them. They are distinctly textile patterns and never attempt to compete with painted decoration. It is the design interest, not the pictorial interest that makes them superior to the later weaves that followed.

Summary: Gothic Design

The accomplishments of the Gothic style still astonish us, and the daring of those Gothic builders still impresses us. For many, the towering spaces of the Gothic cathedrals inspire worship as much today as when they were built. While less astonishing, examples of secular design are also quite distinct from the Romanesque that preceded them and the Renaissance that would follow. The Gothic style demanded extraordinary dedication and effort from its builders, most of whom led difficult, impoverished lives. The Gothic style could not be sustained without an extraordinary faith.

Looking for Character

The supreme symbol of Gothic design and the most succinct embodiment of its character is the pointed arch. It is ubiquitous, serving as structural support, window frame, door frame, niche outline, furniture detail, and decorative carving. It appears in stone, wood, glass, metalwork, and tapestry. Like so much of Gothic architecture, the pointed arch served as both an economical solution to a constructional problem and—in its reach heavenward—a potent sign of spirituality.

Looking for Quality

The highest quality in Gothic design is naturally found where the greatest amount of effort, energy, imagination, ingenuity, and funds were directed: in the great cathedrals. This is true not only for the exterior and interior shells of the buildings but also for all the myriad components that constituted the finished church: the stained glass, the tapestries, the carvings, and the furnishings. But in both religious and secular design, when we look for design quality, we must be careful to look through the lens of the Gothic era. It was in many ways a period of mystery, magic, faith, and passion; it cannot be fairly judged by classical standards of reason or by our own modern tastes. We may know that unicorns do not exist, but we should remember that people of Gothic times knew that they did.

Making Comparisons

We have already mentioned the differences between the sturdy masses of the Romanesque style and the airy dematerializations of the Gothic. We have made some comparisons between the Gothic cathedrals of France and those of England and Italy.

Comparing the Romanesque and the Gothic style, we can say that the two share some characteristics, such as the basilica form with its central nave rising above the side aisles and pierced with windows so that the central part of the building is given outside light. Yet the Romanesque church and the Gothic cathedral have quite different aims: the first to display the solidity and strength of its massive construction, the second to amaze us with its apparently impossible absence of mass.

Nor is there a natural transition to Gothic from either Early Christian or Byzantine construction. There is a geographic difference as well, for the areas in which the most characteristic Romanesque structures were built—central and southwestern France, northern Italy, and along the Rhine—were not the areas of the great Gothic cathedrals. These had their birth in northern France, in the provinces near Paris. We must, therefore, see the Gothic cathedral as a new invention, quite distinct from its Romanesque precedents.

One of the most striking contrasts in the history of design is that between the Gothic period and the Renaissance that would directly supersede it. Because of this striking revolution in culture and design, we shall—after our look at Islamic design—take this occasion to break with our generally chronological survey and look at what has been happening in the ancient civilizations of the Eastern Hemisphere. As the spiritual focus of the Middle Ages gave way to the humanistic focus of the Renaissance era and as religious fervor waned, the Gothic style would be replaced with a new architecture. When we return to Europe in the Renaissance period, we shall witness the birth of a new attitude that will have to be expressed in new design.

The Islamic World

A.D. 622 to the Present

9

"Islamic art is . . . a reflection of the heavenly realities on earth, a reflection with the help of which the Muslim makes the journey . . . to the Reality which is the Origin and End of Art itself."

— Jacob Burckhardt (1818–97), Swiss art historian

slamic design is a term that does not denote a specific period of *time*, as, for example, the term Romanesque design does—for Islamic design has existed from the seventh century when the religion of Islam was formed. Neither does Islamic design denote the design of a specific *location*, as, for example, Egyptian design does, because Islam's influence is seen in many parts of the world. And, although its branches certainly share some stylistic characteristics, Islamic design does not denote a *style* as strictly as, for example, Gothic design does; any art form that stretches around the globe and extends for thirteen centuries must undergo many changes. And, finally, it does not denote a *religion* as strictly as, for example, Buddhist and Christian design do, because Islamic design covers all aspects of life, including buildings, interiors, and decorative elements designed for secular use. Islamic design, therefore must be defined carefully: design that is the product of cultural groups that, in general or in the majority, profess the Islamic faith.

◀ **9–1** A Safavid dynasty Iranian tent panel of silk and metallic thread, c. 1600. It depicts a hunting scene.
The Metropolitan Museum of Art, Fletcher Fund, 1972. (1972.189).
Photograph © 1994. The Metropolitan Museum of Art.

Determinants of Islamic Design

The factors that unified Islamic design were, as with most design styles: cultural, geographic, religious, political and temporal.

Some of its characteristics—generally geometric but sometimes representational ornament (fig. 9–1)—can be said to have been based on the Christian art of Byzantium, heir to the pagan civilizations of Greece and Rome, of which the earliest Islamic design was itself an inheritor. The Persian Empire, with a foothold in southwestern Arabia, was also a factor.

Geography and Natural Resources

With the conquest of Constantinople (formerly ancient Byzantium), the Turks controlled the junction of Europe and Asia at this spectacular site, now called Istanbul. Islamic culture spread far beyond Istanbul, taking root not only in the Middle East, but also in North Africa, Europe, and Asia. We shall consider some outstanding examples of Islamic interiors in our later chapters on India and Spain.

Early Islamic design built upon the traditions, the climates, the materials, and the methods of the various lands

165

Period	Date	Politics, Culture, and Religion	Achievements in Art and Design
Early Islamic	622–c. 900	Migration of Muhammad, 622; his death, 632; rule of the caliphs; great territorial expansion; Umayyad dynasty rules in Syria, late 7th century; Baghdad founded by Abbasids, 762	Umayyad hunting lodges and mosaics; Dome of the Rock, Jerusalem, 691–92; Great Mosque, Samarra, Iraq, 848–52
Medieval	c. 900–c. 1250	Fatimid dynasty begins, 909; Marrakesh founded by Almoravids, 1062; Berber empires, 11th and 12th centuries; Mongol invasions led by Genghis Khan end Seljuk rule	Rock crystal carving in Cairo, 11th century; jade carving in India; ivory carving in Spain
Late Medieval	c. 1250–c. 1500	Baghdad sacked by Mongols; Mamluk regime; Osman founds Ottoman Empire; Timur creates Timurid empire; Sa'di dynasty in Morocco; Sufism	Rise of artists as independent personalities; establishment of carpet factories; expansion of Isfahan; construction of Topkapi Palace, Istanbul, begins, 1473
Early Modern	c. 1500–c. 1800	Safavid dynasty in Iran, 1501–1732; Suleyman the Magnificent, Sultan, 1520–66; Shah' Abbas, 1588–1629; Napoleon invades Egypt, 1798	Iznik pottery; Ardabil carpet; architecture of Sinan: Suleymaniye Mosque, Istanbul, 1552–59, Ali Qapu Palace, Isfahan, 1597

where it was found. These local conditions were determinants of the national variations within Islamic design. Often a vegetative or agricultural motif can be found in Islamic art, for in the Islamic lands of the Near East, olive trees, date palms, cereals, indigo, fruits, and vegetables grew plentifully, as did the sugar cane of Egypt and Morocco.

In addition, an unusual combination of factors caused the central Islamic lands to be called the Rug Belt. These conditions were both cultural and geographic: ties to a nomadic past in which personal belongings had to be portable and durable, providing a weaving tradition of hand knotting; and terrain and climate suitable for sheep grazing, which provided a fine supply of wool.

Not only was there suitable terrain for sheep grazing but also good land for the cultivation of flax, which is used to make linen. Cotton was introduced from India, probably before the birth of Muhammad, and silk from China not long after, all contributing to an illustrious textile tradition.

Religion

Islam means "submission to God." Like Judaism and Christianity, it is a monotheistic religion and, like those faiths also, it has a basis in prophecy. Its prophet was Muhammad, a native of the city of Mecca in what is now Saudi Arabia. The Prophet Muhammad founded Islam in the year A.D. 622 when he established himself as the head of the (then small) Muslim community. That year in the Christian calendar is the first year of the Muslim calendar, and one definite thing we can say about Islamic design is that it cannot have existed earlier than that date.

Opposition to Muhammad's preaching led to his emigration 200 miles (320 km) north to the city of Medina in A.D. 622, where he continued to preach and began to organize the first Muslim state. After Muhammad's death, in 632, there was an impressively rapid territorial expansion of Islamic influence, with military forces carrying the new religion into Egypt, Syria, Iran, and Iraq, and eventually into North Africa and Spain and the steppes of Central Asia. With the new religion came the design that had been devised to reveal Islam on earth, just as the Gothic style had striven to reveal Christianity on earth.

Muhammad's teachings are collected in the Koran, the sacred book of Islam. For the faithful, the teachings specify five obligations: the profession of faith; charity to the poor; daytime fasting during the annual period of Ramadan; a pilgrimage to Mecca at least once during a lifetime; and, five times a day, a ritual prayer performed, if possible, in a

▲ 9–2 Ruins of the Great Mosque at Samarra, Iraq, ninth century. Before it, the spiral *minaret* still stands.
Simmons Aerofilms, Limited

mosque, a building for public worship. These were built in many sizes and forms, the largest in the Islamic world having been the ninth-century Great Mosque at Samarra (fig. 9–2), north of Baghdad. It was 1440 feet (444 m) long, and its minaret, still standing on axis with the mosque entrance, is 163 feet (50 m) high.

There are two major sects in Islam: the Sunni and the Shia (or Shiite). The division occurred during a seventh-century dispute over the proper succession to Muhammad. The Sunni were orthodox Muslims who held that, after Muhammad's death, leadership of the Islamic community was elective. The Shia held that Islamic leadership could only be hereditary—that is, only direct descendents of Muhammad could rule.

Sufism, prominent in Persia and India, should also be mentioned; it is a mystical and ascetic order that emerged from the Shia sect in the last years of the tenth century and later became integrated into some Sunni sects. Its name derives from the fact that Muslim mystics often dressed in cloaks made of coarse wool (*suf*). The Sufis maintained craft guilds, considered artistic beauty a reflection of inner beauty, and were firm believers in a saying attributed to Muhammad: "God is beautiful and loves beauty." The Sufis were not only inclined to value the arts, but also to value art of a specific kind: ecstatic, allegorical, metaphorical, and rich with layers of religious reference not immediately obvious.

History

Following Islam's military conquests between the seventh and fourteenth centuries, great Middle Eastern cities were built that became seats of Islamic learning, many of them responsible for preserving the records of antiquity while Western Europe was in chaos. Mecca was the center of the faith; Kufa and Basra were the seats of Arabian theology. Damascus boasted of her poetry, science, and industry. Baghdad, built on the ruins of ancient Babylon, was one of the proudest cities in the world. The mere mention of Tabriz, Isfahan, and Samarkand recalls the romance of the *Thousand and One Nights*. Delhi, Agra, and Lahore, in India, and Cordova, Seville, and Granada, in Spain, were centers of luxury and splendor whose beauties still remain.

There were also temporal variations, of course. Various dynasties and their rulers had differing tastes and differing priorities, and in all Islamic lands the structures and decorations of prosperous times differed from those of political and economic decline. Such differences included, in good times, the use of stone rather than mud brick, a higher degree and quality of ornamentation, and the preservation of older structures rather than their destruction in order to reuse their materials. Similarly, decorative objects in precious and semiprecious metals were preserved in prosperous times but melted down in other times.

The spread of Islam and Islamic design was not steady or continuous; in A.D. 1000, for example, Islamic art was being produced in Spain but not in Turkey, yet in 1500 it was being produced in Turkey but not in Spain.

Islamic Architecture and Interiors

The most important types of Islamic architecture are religious buildings such as the mosque, the shrine, the convent, the mausoleum, and the religious school called a **madrasa** (fig. 9–3), and secular buildings such as the palace, the citadel, the bazaar, the hospital, and the inn for traveling caravans (*caravanserai*). Secondary constructions include such structures as bridges and fountains, and the **minaret**, a slender tower attached to—or near—a mosque from which the faithful can be called to prayer. Some minarets are cylindrical; some are square in plan for their whole height; some have a square base, an octagonal central section, and a cylindrical top; perhaps the most beautiful are the spiral minarets, as seen in figure 9–2.

part of the mosque interior. The steep minbar is usually adjacent to the mihrab and is most commonly built of wood, although there are examples in stone and brick; the minbar also is richly decorated with panels and carvings, and it generally carries an inscription honoring the sultan in whose reign it was built.

These simple requirements were joined, naturally, by more elaborate architectural conventions such as arcades, portals, and supplemental prayer halls. These were not strictly necessary for the performance of the required ritual, but became customary nevertheless. And the structure of the mosque, though basically simple, came to be dazzlingly ornamented.

The Islamic people who came to rule Constantinople and all of Turkey naturally found the church of Hagia Sophia to

The Islamic ritual of worship within the mosque was strictly codified and invariable throughout the Muslim world, demanding interiors with a few essential elements. First, there was a central area, either opened or covered, where the faithful could pray. Next, a prayer niche or **mihrab** (fig. 9–4) served to indicate the direction of Mecca, which the faithful faced during their prayers. And finally, a pulpit or **minbar** (fig. 9–5) stood adjacent to the prayer niche; and a water basin was nearby where the faithful performed a ritual washing before their prayers. The mihrab niche may have been derived from the apse of the Roman throne room and is traditionally the most highly decorated

▶ **9–4** A *mihrab* from the Madrasa Mimami, Isfahan, Iraq, c. 1354, faced with a mosaic of glazed tiles, 11 ft. (3.4 m) high. The calligraphy of the inner panel reads, "The mosque is the house of every pious person."

Mihrab, Iranian, 14th Cencury, c. 1354. Composite bidy, glazed, sawed to shape and assembled in mosaic, H. 11 ft. 3 in. (342.9 cm). The Metropolitan Museum of Art, Harris Brisbane Dick Fund, 1939 (39.20). Photograph © 1982 The Metropolitan Museum of Art.

▲ 9–5 A *minbar* in a mosque in Istanbul, Turkey. From its top, the sermon is preached during Friday prayers.
SuperStock, Inc.

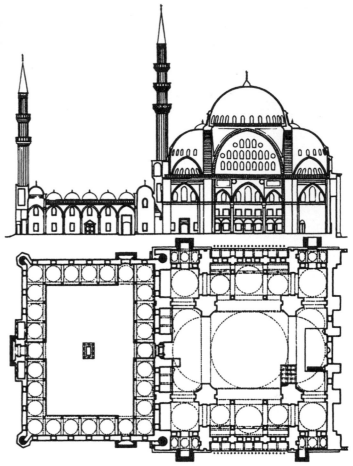

▲ 9–6 Longitudinal section and plan, Sulimaniye Mosque, Istanbul. The height of the tallest minarets is 272 ft. (83 m).
Georges Ed. Berthoud

be one of the great buildings of the city of Constantinople that they inherited from the early Christians through conquest. Just as the early Christians did not hesitate to adopt the temples and basilicas of pagan classicism for Christian purposes, the Muhammadans did not hesitate to adopt this Christian monument for Islamic use. The architectural achievements of the Hagia Sophia are echoed in many of the finest mosques of the Islamic world, such as the Suleymaniye Mosque in Istanbul.

The Suleymaniye Mosque

The Suleymaniye Mosque (fig. 9–6) was built by the great architect Sinan (c. 1490–1588). Sinan was fifty years old before designing his first building, but he is credited with 136 mosques and more than 300 other buildings. He was chief architect for a series of powerful sultans (Suleyman the

Magnificent and two of his successors) during the most glorious period of the Ottoman Empire. Sinan's earlier work was as a mechanic and engineer, so he came to architecture with an extremely practical knowledge of construction. His many experiments with the possible forms of monumental domed structures were all guided by his sense of construction logic, not by theories of geometric combinations and formal harmony—as was the case with Italian Renaissance architects Bramante and Leonardo da Vinci. Sinan was, in the fullest sense, a master builder.

Sinan designed this great mosque for his chief patron, Sultan Suleyman, also known as Suleyman the Magnificent. The mosque sits on an Istanbul hilltop overlooking the Golden Horn, the arm of the Bosporus in Turkey that forms the harbor. The building's great dome (fig. 9–7) has a diameter of 87 feet (26.6 m) that is half its height, and it rests on four massive piers. Unlike the shadowed mystery of

▲ **9–7** Sinan's dome and two adjacent half domes form the ceiling of the Sulimaniye Mosque.
Henri Stierlin, Geneva

the Hagia Sophia, the Suleymaniye Mosque is flooded with light, and the structural system supporting the dome is made obvious. The entirety of the huge building can be perceived at a glance.

The Corinthian columns of the interior were taken from an earlier—probably Byzantine—structure. Interior surfaces are enriched with great quantities of tiles, constituting the first large commission given to the tile makers of Iznik. Also specially commissioned for the mosque were carved wood shutters and doors (see fig. 9–16), stained glass, carpets, mosque lamps, and Koran manuscripts and stands to hold them. In all, more than 3,500 craftsmen are said to have worked on the mosque. For all its ornament, however, it has an air of austerity, perhaps because its two chief materials,

ivory-colored stone for the exterior and dark gray lead for its roofing, are so simple.

The arches of the Suleymaniye Mosque (see fig. 9–6) are almost round, but there is a slight point to them. In other structures, such as the madrasa in figure 9–3, a more definitely pointed arch is seen. Most characteristic of Islamic architecture is the **horseshoe arch**, a semicircular shape above straight piers that narrows further below its **spring line** (the imaginary horizontal line above which the arch begins to curve). Horseshoe arches could have round or pointed tops, and some were **foliate** or **cusped**, with small arcs or scallops cut into their intrados. In the Kutubiya Mosque in Morocco, a colonnade of such arches can be seen (fig. 9–8).

▲ 9–9 Rooftop views of the domes and chimneys of the Topkapi Palace, Istanbul, with the Bosporus beyond.
Rainer Hackenberg/AKG-Images

▲ 9–8 A series of horseshoe arches, the outer one *foliate* or *cusped,* forms a colonnade at the Kutubiya Mosque, Marrakech, Morocco, built in 1147.
Roland and Sabrina Michaud/Hachette Photos Presse

The Topkapi Palace

Near the Suleymaniye Mosque in Istanbul, on a point of land overlooking the Bosporus strait and the Golden Horn, is the Topkapi Palace, home to the Ottoman sultans (including Suleyman) from the mid-fifteenth century to the mid-nineteenth century. The labyrinthine palace (fig. 9–9) occupies the site of an earlier structure, the great palace of the Byzantine emperors. Begun in 1459, the construction of Topkapi continued over several centuries, and some additions in the sixteenth century were designed by the great Sinan, including the gigantic kitchen complex that remains the complex's largest single structure.

The overall effect of Topkapi is that of the accretion of many different ideas and styles. It lacks a powerful unified image, but it does possess a clear organization: The plan is of scattered pavilions, kiosks, halls, harems, libraries, and service buildings, but these all find their proper places within three consecutive courtyards. These three are arranged in the order

of increasing privacy, with only the sultan, his family, his most honored guests, and their attendants allowed into the innermost courtyard and the royal audience hall.

A relatively late but unusually agreeable interior in Topkapi is the Kiosk of Mustafa Pasha within the innermost courtyard (fig. 9–10). It is simple and open, but with an elaborately molded, paneled, and painted ceiling. Its slightly raised seating platform, called a *tazar*, enjoys views through generous expanses of window.

The Private House

Although much wealth was controlled by royalty and lavished on their palaces, there were also important houses belonging to the nonroyal upper and middle classes. These might be unassuming from the street, presenting a blank wall with windows only on the upper floor, but the interiors would be built around as many as four courtyards filled with fountains, flowers, and fruit trees. Chief rooms opening from these courtyards might have marble floors and high decorative ceilings. One such room, built in Damascus, Syria, in 1707, but now reconstructed from its original elements in the Metropolitan Museum of Art, New York, is seen in figure 9–11. As was typical, it is entered on a level even with the courtyard, with an entrance area featuring a low marble fountain. Beyond this is a raised *tazar* for the host and important guests. Seating within the *tazar* was governed strictly by rank, the most honored guest seated closest to the host and raised (on cushions) highest above the floor.

9–10 The Kiosk of Mustafa Pasha in the Topkapi Palace. Its large windows overlook the sea. Most of its seating consists of low cushions on a slightly raised platform.
From "Ottoman Turkey", Henry Stierlin, Ed. © Benedikt Taschen Verlag GmbH, Cologne, Germany.
Photo by: Eduard Widmen.

The Tent

In addition to the great cities already mentioned as centers of Islamic culture, there was also an Islamic tradition of nomadic life, served not by permanent structures, but by tents. Some nomads' tents were simple indeed, hardly more than sunscreens and windbreaks, but some royal tents were very elaborate. One of the tents of the fourteenth-century ruler Timur (also called Tamerlane), pitched on a plain near Samarkand, was said to be large enough to hold 10,000 people, but visible evidence of this structive has vanished. Another of Timur's tents was described as having gates, an upper gallery level, battlements, and turrets, and its interior was said to have been richly furnished with carpets, tapestries, and silk cushions. A miniature painting shows Timur in a much smaller tent receiving a deputation. Under his

9–11 Reception room from an early-18th-century house in Damascus, Syria, looking towards the raised *tazar*. The ceiling height is 22 ft. (7 m).
The Nur al-Din Room. Reception room from a house in Damascus. View #2: overall looking toward the elevated section, the "tazar". Wood, marble stucco, glass, mother-of pearl, ceramics, tile, stone, iron, colors, gold, H. 22 feet ½ in., W.16 feet 8 ½ in., L. 26 feet 4 ¾ in. The metropolitan Museum of Art, Gift of the Hagop Kevorkian Fund, 1970 (1970.170). Photograph © 1995 The Metropolitan Museum of Art.

▲ 9–12 The Mongol conqueror Timur receiving a delegation under a tent with a floral pattern, as painted c. 1600.
HIP/Art Resource, NY

throne is a carpet (fig. 9–12). A surviving fragment of an Iranian tent panel is seen in fig. 9–1.

Some audiences, banquets, and religious services were held outside without even a tent, and these also employed carpets and fabrics. The famous Ardabil carpet (fig. 9–28), at 36 feet (11 m) long, is too long to have fit in any room of the Ardabil shrine and must therefore have been used outside.

The study of the interiors of nomadic tents is limited, of course, by their impermanence. Today we can only imagine what some great tented spaces must have been like, with their richly colored fabric flowing between exposed structural elements and billowing in the wind, and with the earth beneath covered with fine carpets.

Islamic Ornament

Much has been written about what Islamic ornament is *not*. Because of religious constraints, we often read, it is not representational of living things, and is consequently reliant on geometric design. This is partially true, but an oversimplification. Indeed, a characteristic of much Islamic art is the representation of luxuriant plant life, although it does tend to be highly stylized. Animal forms appear less often, human forms scarcely at all, and almighty Allah never. For a Muhammadan, the depiction of God as an old man with a beard (as in the work of Michelangelo in the Italian Renaissance) would seem both blasphemous and ridiculous.

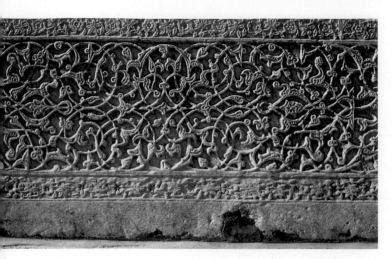

▲ **9–13** An arabesque carved in stone at the mausoleum of Timur in Samarkand, Uzbekistan, early fifteenth century.
Josephine Powell

Geometry was a natural alternative to the depictions of humans and animals. In the development of geometric patterns, the most complicated interlacings of lines occur, as seen in the carpet detail (see fig. 9–1) and the mihrab (see fig. 9–4). Squares, rectangles, hexagons, octagons, stars, and an infinite variety of irregular and overlapping forms are seen. In ceramic and textile design, rosettes, pearls, dots, hatchings, diamonds, circles, stars, vase forms, and many other motifs were employed. **Diaper** patterns—checkerboards of lozenge shapes—were often subdivided into panels formed by lines or bands arranged in an ogival, circular, or scalloped manner.

Prominent among Islamic ornament is a composition based on plant life that is aptly called the **arabesque** (fig. 9–13). The term was invented in the Italian Renaissance and was (curiously) applied to some classical ornament, such as the **rinceau**. The arabesque is fanciful, with interlacing vines, foliage, and tendrils, sometimes combined with spirals, knots, or medallions.

In discussing Islam as a determinant of ornament, it is necessary to distinguish between the beliefs of two major sects: the Sunni and the Shia (or Shiite). The Sunni, prominent in Turkey, Arabia, and Spain, were strictly opposed to the representation of living things in art, on the basis that they were idolatrous. The Shia held more liberal artistic views and allowed floral, animal, and human subject matter in their designs. In Shia designs, real and imaginary animals play a prominent part; the ibex was a royal symbol, and the lion represented power. Equestrian subjects were common. Human

beings, birds, leaves, flowers, ivies, and trees were often beautifully combined in patterns or arabesques. Pine cones were considered a symbol of good luck. After the Mongol invasion, patterns often also showed the use of Chinese motifs such as clouds, butterflies, rose and peony blossoms, and plants growing out of rocks.

No matter what the sect of the artist, however, some general principles apply to all Islamic design. All patterns are relatively small in scale, and much conventionalization is used. Even when the representation of living things is allowed, the emphasis is always placed on the decorative quality rather than the representational.

Wall Treatments

Islamic interiors were furnished very sparsely by our own standards, but ornamented very lavishly. We have already seen some characteristic motifs such as the arabesque and more geometric patterns, but there was a large vocabulary of ways the Islamic designer could apply them—for example, in plaster and stucco, woodwork, and tile.

Plaster and Stucco   **Plaster** is a composition of soft material that hardens after being spread in place; while soft, it can receive fine carving and decoration. It is usually composed of lime, gypsum, sand, and water, and hair is sometimes added.

Stucco is a term used as a synonym for any plasterwork, but sometimes it refers only to a slow-setting kind of plaster. It can be molded while damp or allowed to harden and then carved like wood. Because it is relatively cheap and can be applied relatively quickly, it was extremely popular. Ornamental effects vary from simple cross-hatching to elaborate geometricized vegetal forms.

Such materials were used in many cultures, including the Minoan, the Mycenean, and the Roman, as the basis for wall paintings. And they were popular in Islamic design. One example is the interior wall decoration that can be seen in the ruins of a house in Samarra, Iraq, dating from the ninth century (fig. 9–14).

A specialized use of plasterwork in Islamic ornament is the **muqarna**, also called *honeycomb work*. Muqarnas consist of superimposed tiers of concave shapes, like a great network of adjacent pendentives. One example is in the Music Room of the Ali Qapu Palace (fig. 9–15), one of the structures edging the Royal Maidan, the great open space of Isfahan, Iraq. The Music Room's stucco work is pierced in shapes

▼ **9–14** Carved plaster wall decoration of the ruins of a house at Samarra, Iraq, ninth century.
Prof. Alastair Northedge, Paris

◀ **9–15** Muqarnas of the Music Room, Ali Qapu Palace, Isfahan, Iran, begun in the late sixteenth century.
Paul Almasy/Corbis/Bettmann

► **9–16** Detail of wood door carving, Suleymaniye Mosque, Istanbul.
F. Godfrey Goodwin/Thames & Hudson International, Ltd.

that resemble Chinese porcelains and musical instruments; the actual building structure is beyond and unseen in our figure.

Woodwork   Ornamental woodwork was an important part of Islamic buildings and interiors, although wood was in scarce supply in some Islamic lands. When available, it was used for a number of architectural elements—door panels (fig. 9–16), wall panels, tie beams—and it was used as well for smaller objects—furniture, chests, Koran covers. Exuberant floral motifs are common in varying degrees of geometricization, their exuberance often held in check by surrounding geometric frameworks—rectangles, ovals, lozenge shapes. Within the carved wood pieces, there were often inlays of ivory, bone, and mother-of-pearl.

A particular glory of Islamic woodwork is the open grille of turned-wood members, sometimes used within a mosque to separate a princely sanctum from the rest of the congregation. And a particularly interesting and prevalent use of turned-wood grillwork is the **mashrabiya** or window grille (fig. 9–17). Found throughout the Islamic world, its chief use is as a privacy screen for the women's quarters of a residence or palace, allowing the women inside to observe the street life outside, while preventing them from

being seen. Not incidentally, the *mashrabiya* effectively screens an interior from fierce sunlight and gives it a touch of mystery.

Tile   Islamic design is hardly imaginable without the profuse and virtuoso use of glazed ceramic tile. Like mosaics, these were used outside and in, on both vertical and horizontal surfaces. Samples of the brilliant, decorative effects of tiled surfaces have been seen in a mihrab niche (see fig. 9–4) and the dome of the Suleymaniye Mosque (see fig. 9–7), which made the first major use of polychrome underglaze-painted tile from Iznik, Turkey, a town that would become famous for its ceramics.

Production techniques for tile are related, of course, to those for other ceramic work, to be discussed shortly. Here we need only note that the range of sizes of Islamic tiles was enormous, from a few inches to 3 feet (8–100 mm) high, and the quality often displayed an impressive technical command.

Designs with tile can be divided into two basic types: those in which the design is made by the outlines of the tiles

► **9–17** A latticed window and its many-patterned shadows in the Palace of Bashtak, Cairo, 1334-39.
Henri Stierlin, Geneva

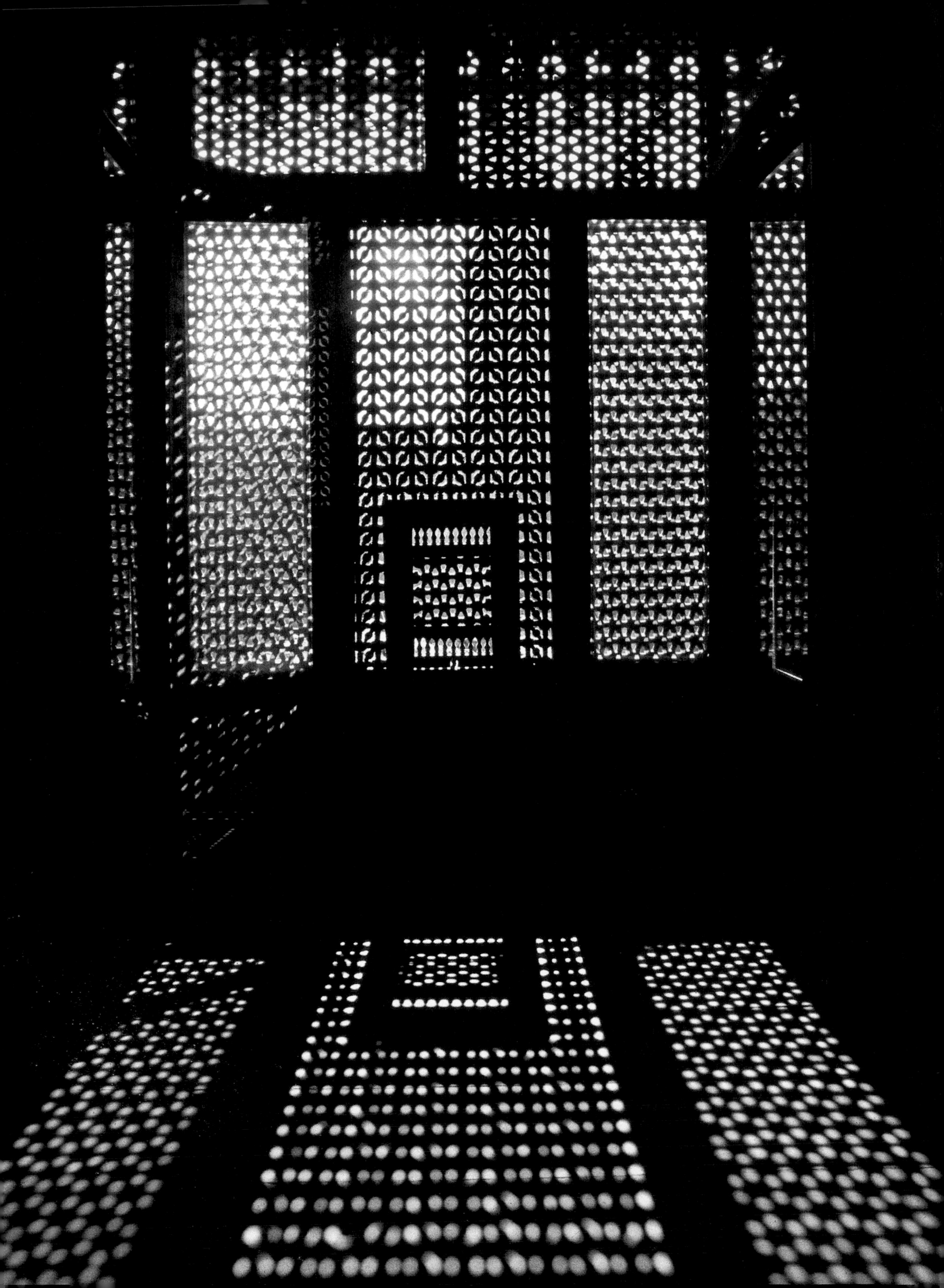

▲ **9–18** Shaped and decorated tiles from Iran, late thirteenth or fourteenth century.
Ashmolean Museum, University of Oxford UK/The Bridgeman Art Library International

▲ **9–19** Panel of 28 Iznik-ware tiles. Although the tiles are all square, the overall image is of a Tree of Life growing from a Vase of Immortality, Turkish, 1650-1700.
Victoria & Albert Museum, London/Art Resource, NY

themselves (fig. 9–18), and those in which the design extends across numbers of tile (fig. 9–19). In the first type of design, the tiles are plain but eccentrically shaped, and the design is derived from the interlocking of those shapes. In the second type, the tiles are simple in shape but covered with complex patterns that are unrelated to those shapes.

Mosaics as well as tile designs were also used on both building exteriors and on the interiors, in flooring as well as wall decoration. When used as flooring, mosaic work sometimes was designed in imitation of rugs or carpets; at other times, it was gloriously abstract and endlessly inventive. In the grandest of mosques and palaces, gold-glass mosaic was used. Even the most ordinary mosaic work, however, was relatively difficult and expensive. Ornamental and pictorial effects were more readily available with tile work.

Islamic Furniture

It has been said that Islamic interiors are rooms without furniture. This is an exaggeration, but certainly the amount of furniture was minimal compared with that of most other cultures, luxurious carpets and cushions being preferred to seats and benches. One factor may have been that wood was scarce in many Islamic lands, yet there are a few examples of wood furniture.

For seating, there were long, low benches, some of them upholstered in luxurious fabrics. The Arabic word for such a long seating element was *suffa*, obviously the source of the English word sofa. Examples are visible in the Topkapi Palace interior (see fig. 9–10) and the reception room from Damascus (see fig. 9–11). More often, people sat on the carpets and used small mats called *pushti* (meaning "back"),

▲ **9–20** Side view when folded of a thirteenth-century carved wooden stand for reading the Koran. It is decorated with calligraphy and floral motifs.
Georg Niedermeiser/Art Resource/Bildarchiv Preussischer Kulturbesitz

Thrones existed for the use of rulers and people of authority, and one is visible at the left side of figure 9–10; secondary officials might be seated near the ruler on folding stools. In lieu of beds, it was customary to sleep on the *suffa*, on cushions, or on carpeted floors. For meals, diners traditionally sat in a circle with the food in the center, either on a mat at floor level or on a low wood or metal table.

In domestic interiors there were low tables and storage chests, used for domestic wares. The Music Room in Isfahan (see fig. 9–15) had shaped cavities in the walls that could be used for storage, and some libraries had bookcases with hinged wooden doors that could be locked.

In mosques, there were the pulpits called *minbars*, screened enclosures called *maqsuras*, reading stands for the Koran (fig. 9–20), and bookcases. In both mosques and houses there were elaborately carved wooden chests for storing manuscripts of the Koran.

Islamic Decorative Arts

Almost without exception, Islamic interior design is richly decorative. Even when a mosque, house, or other building shows a severely plain exterior to the street, its interior can be bursting with imaginative detail and creative energy. This detail and energy take many forms, in work of many materials—wood, metal, ivory, mosaics and tile, painting and lacquer, glass and rock crystal, and in the *calligraphy* ("beautiful writing") with which so many Islamic wares are adorned. The three most celebrated of Islamic decorative arts are ceramics, metalwork, and textiles.

Ceramics

Islamic ceramics are of many types and reached respected pinnacles of excellence. Many grades of ceramics were made, ranging from humble earthenware to the harder and more delicate wares with elements fused by heat. Lacking the proper clay, traditional Islamic potters were never quite able to duplicate the brilliant whiteness and exquisite translucency of Chinese porcelains. Yet some of their ceramics demonstrate a remarkable mastery of decoration and a fertile inventiveness of technique.

Among the many types of Islamic ceramics are found the simple **earthenware** pieces mentioned above (and in our chapters on Egypt and Rome). Sometimes these were left a coarse tan color, but at other times they were coated with a

which were traditionally used to cover cushions placed against a wall for support. They are only about 2 by 3 feet (60 × 90 cm). There were also pillow covers called *balisht* (meaning "cushion" or "bolster") woven in the same manner as carpets. These pillows were sometimes used directly on the floor, sometimes on the *suffa*, and often with a low table nearby.

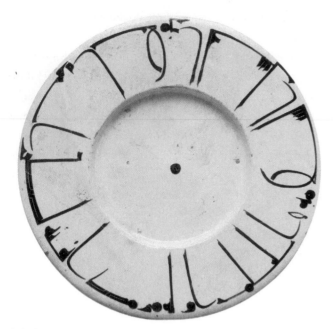

▲ **9–21** Earthenware bowl with a lead glaze, decorated with calligraphy from Samarkand in what is now Uzbekistan, 9th–10th century, 14½ in. (37 cm) diameter.
Thierry Ollivier/Art Resource/Reunion des Musees Nationaux

▲ **9–23** Lajvardina bowl with overglaze painting from Iran, early fourteenth century, 8 in. (21 cm) diameter.
Herve Lewandowski/Reunion des Musees Nationaux/Art Resource, NY

glossy white slip and painted with calligraphy (fig. 9–21). The slip-coated earthenware could also be incised with decorative patterns, then glazed in green, yellow, or brown, with the glaze collecting in the incisions.

Fritware is a white ceramic (fig. 9–22) made from white clay, crushed quartz, and glass *frit*. (Frit is a powder made by firing the ingredients of glass, then grinding the results; frit can also be used as a glaze.) It was developed in the eleventh century as an imitation of Chinese porcelain, and it is similar in composition, though not in appearance, to Egyptian faience (see figs. 2–29 and 2–31).

Mina'i ("enamel") ware refers to wares that were once called *haft rang*, which means "seven-color." As the names

suggest, such wares have the bright gloss of enamel and are multicolored. In making them, some colors are applied to the clay, glazed over and fired, and then more colors are applied and fired. **Lajvardina** ware is a similar product made with a similar technique. In general, *lajvardina* ware (fig. 9–23) employed more somber colors and more abstract designs than did *mina'i* ware. But sometimes gold, hammered into strips and then cut into small pieces, was applied to the surfaces of *lajvardina*. Both were luxury items, meant for display rather than practical use.

Iznik ware is the most famous of all types of Islamic ceramics. Iznik was an important trading stop in Western Anatolia (present-day Turkey) on the ancient Silk Road linking Europe and Asia. Highly valued Chinese blue-and-white porcelains were frequently traded there, and in the late fifteenth century the Iznik potters began making their own blue-and-white wares. By the early sixteenth century, production was at a high level of quality and quantity, and Sinan used enormous quantities of Iznik underglaze tiles to face the walls of his Suleymaniye Mosque. Iznik techniques were also used for candlesticks and a variety of dishes and implements for both the mosque and the domestic table. The backgrounds of the Iznik wares were invariably a white glaze, and the patterns on them most often blue, but not always, sometimes being sage green, turquoise, lilac, manganese purple, or tomato red. In addition to the basic color scheme, the Iznik

▼ **9–22** Fritware bowl with blue underglaze painting from Iran, fifteenth century.
Victoria & Albert Museum, London/Art Resource, NY

▲ 9–24 Late fifteenth-century Iznik ware basin in the typical blue and white coloring, 16½ in. (42 cm) diameter.
Victoria & Albert Museum, London/Art Resource, NY

potters also adopted some Chinese designs—clouds, waves, clusters of grapes, and trios of balls—and added some of their own—arabesques, scrolls, chevrons, and other geometric and vegetal motifs (fig. 9–24). They added some roughly realistic representations as well—ships, rabbits, and tulips (native to Turkey before they were introduced to the Netherlands). They also emulated the dazzling luster of the Chinese wares, developing a formula that was 90 percent silica (glass) and 10 percent clay.

Metalwork

Because washing before prayer is part of the Muslim ritual, metal ewers and basins for that purpose were beautifully crafted, and metals have also been used for chests, lamps, candlesticks, censers, hand warmers, ornaments, furniture, and jewelry. They were worked by casting, by hammering, by embossing, by filigree, or by the lost wax (*cire perdue*) technique that we saw used by the Egyptians for molding glass (see Egyptian Faience and Glass in Chapter 2).

The most extraordinary metalwork, not surprisingly, was done with the most precious metals, gold and silver, and such pieces were often signed by their artists, indicating general recognition of individual talents. The most pious of the Muslims, however, came to feel that it was distastefully ostentatious or even sacrilegious to drink or eat from precious metal. More humble metals therefore became popular, such as iron, steel, bronze, and brass.

A happy compromise that seemed to please both the pious and the impious was to enrich the appearance of these base metals with relatively small additions of precious ones. One technique for such enrichment was known as **damascening** (from Damascus, the ancient capital of Syria and, for a time, the capital of the whole Islamic world). Damascening is a form of decorating by inlaying, a process of beating thin gold or silver wires into tiny grooves that have been cut into the surface of the base metal. The grooves form decorative patterns that thus become highlighted (fig. 9–25). Damascening is most often applied to steel objects, but it can also be applied to iron, copper, or brass. The inlays, in addition to gold and silver, can also be of *niello*, a silver compound with a lustrous black appearance.

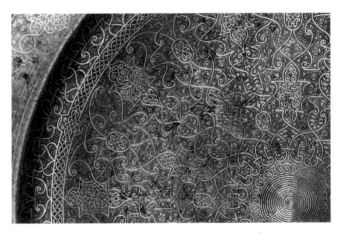

▲ 9–25 Detail of a damascened brass dish, Saracenic, early sixteenth century. Arabesques surround a central maze.
Victoria & Albert Museum, London/Art Resource, NY

Textiles

The Islamic world inherited a long weaving tradition from the Ancient Near East, and most Islamic societies were weaving cultures. Women were trained as young girls to spin and weave, while men took charge of dyeing and marketing. Through the Silk Road, exporting textiles became an important part of the Islamic economy.

Silks were the luxury products of the Islamic textile trade. The silks and silk velvets woven at Bursa and elsewhere served as covers for the sofas and low divans of Turkish palaces and fine houses and for window coverings. In interiors that were furnished with a minimum of hard furniture, soft furnishings such as cushions, quilts, window coverings, and carpets

provided color, warmth, and comfort for seating and sleeping. And many varieties of Islamic storage bags are made with at least one side faced with carpetlike pile; they can also be used as pillow covers.

The variety and quality of Islamic textiles is suggested by their influence on Western Europe. Many English terms come from the Arabic: alpaca, blouse, chiffon, cotton, damask, mohair, muslin, and satin.

There was a wide range of textile quality, from humble cloth for basic needs to rich silks of complex design for religious and royal use. One rich example is a quilt cover from the Topkapi Palace (fig. 9–26), made of forty-nine pieces of silk sewn together, each 6 inches (15 cm) square. The pattern against a white ground is also found in Iznik ceramics.

Carpets

The signature product of Islamic design was the carpet. With an abundant supply of wool and a cultural heritage of weaving, production of carpets increased rapidly, and the fashion for carpets spread throughout the Islamic world to places that lacked these supportive conditions, and beyond the Islamic world to Europe and America. So-called Oriental carpets outgrew their origins and became popular in many parts of the world.

There are three basic types of traditionally woven carpet: Persian, Turkish, and Chinese (see Chapter 11). The first Eastern carpets that came on the Western market were bought from Turkish merchants in Istanbul; thus, whatever their origins, they were referred to as Turkish, and European and American imitations were called "Turkey work." Later, it became known that many of the carpets had originated in Persia, present-day Iran, and had been brought to Istanbul by caravan. So romantic were the connotations of the term *Persian* that it was then for a while applied to all such carpets.

Today these names are understood to indicate the country of origin. Turkish carpets were more strictly obedient than many Persian ones to Islamic edicts against the representation of living things and were therefore more stylized and geometric. The Turkish technique was also slightly less refined, though some carpets were still dazzling.

Persia is generally considered the center of fine carpet weaving, and its highest level of achievement is thought to have been in the Safavid dynasty, from 1505 to 1722. There are many types of Persian carpet, each with its special

▲ **9–26** Detail of a silk quilt cover from the Topkapi Palace, made from squares of seven different small-scale patterns, early sixteenth century.
Topkapi Sarayi Muzesi Mudurlugu

The appeal of Persian and Turkish carpets extends to the highest level of modernism. Their comfortable cut pile and beguiling colors can add softness and richness to interiors that might otherwise seem cold, yet the abstraction of their patterns does not jar against other artworks as would more literal or representational designs; traditional as they are, they do not seem dated. Photographs of Mies van der Rohe's pioneering 1930 Tugendhat house in Brno, Czechoslavakia (for which Mies was concerned with every detail of furnishing) show Persian carpets in the living room under the piano and in the library. Stephen Calloway has written in *Twentieth-Century Design* that "In [the house's] free-flowing spaces a new richness of materials contributed to the total effect, and elsewhere in the house Persian carpets added a note of more luxurious pattern and vibrant color."

characteristics (table 9–1). Most of them are named for their places of origin, some for the tribes that wove them, some for the places where they were frequently traded.

Carpet Production Traditionally, Islamic carpets were knotted by hand. Today, hand-knotting techniques are still practiced in some countries where there is cheap labor, but in other places people have been replaced by machines, which have even introduced new types of carpet weaves (see Chapters 20 and 21). Before the machines, there were four basic types of carpet, distinguished by the ways in which they were made: *embroidered and needleworked, flat-woven,*

TABLE 9–1 Characteristics of Islamic Carpets

Name	Knot Type	Knots Per sq. in.	Fiber Content	Typical Appearance
Bijar (or Bidjar)	Symmetrical	100–160	Wool	Medallions and scrolls; rich reds and blues
Feraghan (Farahan)	Asymmetrical	60–160	Wool pile on a cotton foundation	Fish bordered with vines; blue or green
Hamadan	Asymmetrical	40–100	Wool with camel hair on cotton	Central medallion; red and blue floral design on yellow or brown ground
Herez (Heriz, Heris)	Asymmetrical	30–80	Wool on cotton	Lobed medallion with straight outline; floral patterns in red and blue with lighter borders
Isfahan	Asymmetrical	As many as 750	Mohair or silk	Floral medallions, animals, or palmettes; rich red, sometimes with gold or silver threads
Kashan	Asymmetrical	200	Merino wool or silk with velvetlike pile	Center medallion, floral surrounds
Saraband (Sereband)	Older knots asymmetrical; newer ones symmetrical	Varies	Usually wool on cotton	Rows of *botehs,* bordered with narrow bands; dark reds and blues
Tabriz	Symmetrical	40 to over 400	Wool, but sometimes silk	Large center medallions surrounded by smaller ones
Teheran (Tehran)	Asymmetrical	130 to 325	Wool on cotton	Floral designs and pine tree patterns
Ushak (Oushak)	Symmetrical	Varies	Wool	Medallions, stars, or white ground

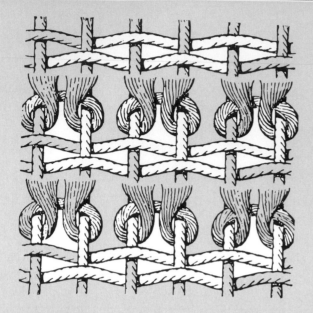

▲ **A** Symmetrical
"Oriental Carpets, A Complete Guide" by Murray L. Eiland, Jr. and
Murray Eiland III (London, Lawrence King Publishing, 1998).

▲ **B** Asymmetrical
"Oriental Carpets, A Complete Guide" by Murray L. Eiland, Jr. and
Murray Eiland III (London, Lawrence King Publishing, 1998).

As in most weaving, pile carpet is composed of **warp** and **weft** threads, which run at right angles to one another. The weft threads, running across the face of the loom, are woven in and out of the warp threads, running the length of the loom. Additionally, short pieces of cut yarn are knotted around one or more warp threads and held in place by one or more weft threads. The projecting ends of these short lengths produce the pile.

Important distinctions are made among carpets on the basis of the kinds of knot used. In Islamic carpets, there are only two basic knot types, but each of them has four names.

- The first type wraps its short lengths of yarn around two adjacent warp threads, then pulls them under and out (fig. A). This is called the *Turkish knot*, the *Ghiordes knot* (for the ancient Turkish town of Ghiordes), the *closed knot*, or, most descriptively, the *symmetrical knot*.
- The second type wraps the yarn under one warp thread, over the adjacent warp thread, then pulls it back between the two warp threads and out (fig. B). This is called the *Persian knot*, the *Senna knot* (for the city of Sinneh in western Persia), the *open knot*, or the *asymmetrical knot*. The asymmetrical knot results in a projection of pile in every space between the warp threads, and therefore can produce a denser and more even pile than can the symmetrical knot.

Some of these names can be misleading: Persian knots are not restricted to Persian carpets, nor Turkish knots to Turkish carpets, and carpets made in the city of Sinneh do not use the Senna knot that is named for it.

For each of these two basic knot types, which here we shall call *symmetrical* and *asymmetrical*, there is a variant called the *jufti knot* or *double knot*, which stretches the short length of yarn over three or more warp threads rather than the usual two, but ties it in the same way. The double knot is often used in solid-color areas of carpets, but seldom in patterned areas or outlines. Whatever knot is used, the face of the carpet has to be sheared to give an equal length to the pile.

When the finished carpet is cut from the loom that has held it taut, the ends of the warp threads projecting from the top and bottom edges form the fringe, either knotted or plaited. The two long sides of the carpet, without projecting fringe, have edges that are formed when the warp threads reverse direction; they are often reinforced with rows of additional weft and warp threads (called *overcasting*) that are not part of the rug design. These edges, not only in Islamic carpets but also in most textile products, were originally called *self-edges*, then *selvedges*, and are now called **selvages**.

tapestry-woven, and *pile*. The carpets of the Islamic world are *cut-pile* carpets—that is, their surfaces are textured with the cut ends of pieces of yarn projecting upward from the surface.

Materials used for these carpets are most often wool and silk for the visible pile and wool or cotton for the underlying foundation. Therefore all wool and all-silk carpets exist. Goat or camel hair is sometimes added to wool for the pile, and jute is sometimes substituted for cotton on the foundation.

Carpet Quality

Carpet quality is generally based not on the type of knots used but on their density. The lowest density in any respectable Islamic carpet is around 25 knots per square inch (4 per cm²), but 100 knots per square inch (16 per cm²) is commonplace, and fine examples can have several times that number and can be old or new. A Mughal carpet in the Metropolitan Museum of Art, New York, has a knot count of 2,500 knots per square inch (390 per cm²), and an all-silk prayer rug woven in the western Turkish town of Hereke, made around 1970, is said to have an astonishing 4,360 knots per square inch (676 per cm²). Since an experienced weaver can tie only twenty knots per minute, weavers can take months or years to finish the finer carpets. The designer considering buying a carpet can usually count from the back of the carpet the number of knots in a horizontal inch (2.54 cm) and the number in a vertical inch, multiplying them together to give the density.

Although high knot density is generally an asset, some relatively coarse tribal rugs can be more beautiful and more valuable than their refined city cousins. An inherent irregularity of color (called *abrash*), the result of an uneven absorption of dye by the yarn, is considered an attractive feature (unless it is so pronounced that it has obviously been planned). The mellowing effects of slight fading with age are also admired. And even a certain amount of visible wear is often considered an aesthetic asset, if it stops before the fabric is actually threadbare.

Carpet Shapes and Sizes

Many carpet types have characteristic shapes, even though they may come in a variety of sizes. Shapes are sometimes defined by a **shape ratio** that expresses the length of the carpet divided by the width. The shape ratio of a carpet 12 by 9 feet (360 × 270 cm), for example, would be 1.33.

Carpet sizes are extremely variable, limited only by the sizes of available looms. Those larger than 14 by 24 feet (430 × 730 cm) are generally called "palace carpets." Traditional village carpets, made to fit long, narrow rooms, were most commonly 60 by 108 inches (150 × 365 cm), a size called a *keleh*. There are also long, narrow rugs called "runners" (*kenarehs*) useful for hallways and stairs. Those examples smaller than 4 by 6 feet (120 × 180 cm) are sometimes called "scatter rugs," as are any flooring textiles of small size; if used as a cover for a bed or for furniture, they may be called "throw rugs."

Carpet sizes are related to carpet placement. The common placement today is in the center of a room, but the common placement in a traditional Islamic room would have been around the edges, with a *keleh* at the head of the room, where the hosts might be seated, and two *kenarehs* at right angles to the *keleh*, along the side walls where guests might be seated. Since the middle of the nineteenth century, sizes have been adapted to suit the squarer rooms of western Europe and America, two common sizes now being 79 by 118 inches (200 × 300 cm) and 108 by 144 inches (275 × 370 cm).

A specialized type of small rug is the *prayer rug* (fig. 9–27), more often made of silk than of wool. It is an important feature of Islamic life, used in mosques to provide a clean, soft area on which to kneel. It is unlike its larger counterparts not only in being small, sized to accommodate a single person, but also in being asymmetrical in design, one end of it woven with a design, usually in the shape of a mihrab, that indicates the direction of Mecca.

Carpet Designs

Designs on Islamic carpets can be geometric or curvilinear or an infinite number of combinations of those extremes. Tribal carpets, with their coarser weaving, which makes curves difficult to execute, are more likely to be geometric; city-woven carpets, with more refined techniques and greater density, tend to be more curvilinear.

The patterns of these carpets are not invented by individual weavers, but taken from traditional vocabularies, some now unknown to the modern user and even to the modern weaver. Some carpets have bold central figures surrounded by smaller, supplementary ones. Some have all-over patterns of small figures. Some are compartmentalized, with figures within each compartment. In every case, there are borders around the edges. And in every case, also, standardized motifs are used and reused.

Many carpets feature important central design elements. The famous Ardabil carpet (fig. 9–28), mentioned in the

A Types of Gul
Dowlatshaht, "Persian Designs and Motifs, Dover, 1979

B Boteh Motifs
Dowlatshaht, "Persian Designs and
Motiffs, Dover," 1979.

C Tree of Life Motifs
Peter F. Stone, "The Oriental Rug Lexicon," Seattle, University
of Washington Press, 1997, pp. 17, 45, 48, 222 and 223

D Herati
Peter F. Stone, "The Oriental Rug Lexicon,"
Seattle, University of Washington Press,
1997, pp. 17, 45, 48, 222 and 223

A few of the very many Islamic carpet motifs are described below.

- The **gul** or *gol* is a geometric emblem. Its name is the Persian word for "'flower" or "rose," so it may have been floral in origin, but it has evolved into octagonal, hexagonal, diamond, or serrated shapes. Many nomadic tribes have their own "signature" guls that are traditionally woven into carpet designs (fig. A).
- The **boteh** is the motif familiar from the Paisley pattern. It probably originated in Kashmir, but it is named for the town of Paisley, Scotland, where, in the nineteenth century, the pattern was duplicated in the manufacture of shawls. It is sometimes called a "pear" because of its shape, although it has also been said to resemble a leaf, a pinecone, an almond, or a flame. It can appear singly on a carpet, but it is usually seen repeated in an overall pattern (fig. B).
- The **tree-of-life** motif symbolizes the life force in the form of a tree, sometimes with fruits and birds in the branches. It is seen in many cultures and in many variations. In Islamic carpet design it is often highly geometricized (fig. C).

- Similar in significance and appearance to the tree of life is the **vase of immortality**, a motif showing similar foliage sprouting from a vase rather than from the ground. The vase has been a favorite motif in all classical and neoclassical styles. In the Islamic world, many parts of which are hot and dry, the vase carries special intimations of a supply of life-giving water.
- The **herati** is a floral representation within curving or diamond-shaped figures. A linear series of such motifs is called a *herati border* (fig. D).
- The **hands-of-Fatima** motif is named for the daughter of Muhammad and refers to the outlines of a pair of hands found near the tops of some prayer rugs. They indicate where the worshipper's hands might be placed when kneeling, and the thumb and outstretched fingers are reminders of the Five Pillars of Islam.
- The **mihrab** shape, rectangular with an arched top, represents, as we know, the prayer niche of a mosque. In carpets, as in mosques, these can take a variety of shapes.
- The **palmette** is a floral motif based on the lotus. It is depicted in profile, with a stem end at the bottom and spreading petals above. As with many of the other motifs listed here, it is found on fabrics as well as on carpets.

▲ **9–27** A prayer rug from Bursa, Turkey, woven of silk, wool, and cotton, late sixteenth century, 66 in. (168 cm) high. The design shows a mosque arcade with a mosque lamp hanging in the central bay.

Turkish. Textiles-Carpets. Bursa, probably. Ottoman period, late 16th Century. Prayer Rug. Silk, wool and cotton. 66 × 50 in (167.6 × 127 cm) The Metropolitan Museum of Art, The James F. Ballard Collection, Gift of James F. Ballard 1922. (22.100.51)

▲ **9–28** Detail of the Ardabil carpet, perhaps the most famous of all Persian carpets. It was signed by Maqsud Kashani and completed in 1530 in northwest Iran. Silk and wool, 36 ft. (11 m) long.

Victoria & Albert Museum, London/Art Resource, NY

section on tents because of its likely use outside, has a central-lobed medallion surrounded by sixteen ovoid shapes. Within and around them swirl myriad arabesques. Ushak carpets from Anatolia, the Asiatic part of Turkey, come in three designs: the "Star Ushak" (see fig. 9–1) has an eight-pointed star at its center; the "Medallion Ushak" has a medallion in the center; and the "White Ushak" has an overall pattern against a white or beige ground. (Ushak is sometimes spelled Oushak, derived from a city in Uzbekistan that is now spelled Uşak; such variations in terminology are typical.)

Summary: Islamic Design

Even the grandest of mosques, which may make a splendid exterior effect with their domes and minarets, reserve most of their ornament for their interiors. Interior embellishment is paramount in Islamic design, but this embellishment is rarely of the type that emphasizes or explains the building's structure. It may even obscure and negate the structure, creating a sense of weightlessness and insubstantiality. This sense is one it shares with the Gothic, although we would never mistake a Gothic interior for an Islamic one. Both styles, we may say, are spiritual in purpose, not elucidating a physical form or force, but expressing a metaphysical one.

Looking for Character

Islamic design is most strongly characterized by a prevailing sense of order. Islamic arts exhibit obedience to traditions that existed before and beyond the works at hand and also obedience to an inner organization that assigns every detail to its proper place. This high degree of order is related to one important Islamic belief: As everything in existence has been willed by Allah and has its place in Allah's divine scheme, it would be unseemly and false to represent any part of that scheme as unruly, wild, or chaotic. Thus, in Islamic design nature is never seen in random extravagance, but always in orderly patterns, systematically imposed. And the genius of Islamic art, of course, is that such a worldview is at least partly self-fulfilling. A filigreed lamp, a tiled wall, or a carpet pattern in which every element has a well-considered relationship with every other element can lead us to a trancelike contemplation of those relationships. Hypnotized by interlocking angles and swirling arabesques, we can come nearly to believe that the universe is as ordered as the art we see.

Looking for Quality

Perhaps it is this unaccustomed mathematical perfection of Islamic patterns that makes the foreign observer treasure the occasional flaw—the faded area, the worn spot, the discontinuity that occurred when the loom was moved. But such charming incidents are unrelated to the main point of Islamic design: the mastery of an intricately balanced sense of order and the mastery, too, of impressive techniques for presenting that sense of order. Islamic design takes unapologetic pleasure in displays of virtuosity and in high levels of manipulation and polish. Expressions can be bold and vigorous or they can be subtle and refined, and equal excellence can be found in both extremes. Both extremes of Islamic design also obey tradition, and the highest quality in Islamic design obeys tradition most reverently. This is not an art in which originality is a measure of success.

Nor is the achievement of realistic effects highly valued. Islamic design's strengths are in its very artificiality, its wondrous decoration, its transformation of natural forms into supernaturally composed patterns. Islamic design does not record nature or humanity; it suggests divinity in its miraculously complex organization.

Making Comparisons

Within the realm of Islamic design, comparisons can be made between the work of the nomadic tribespeople and that of the city dwellers, between old hand techniques and new machine ones, between native inclinations and foreign impulses (or native impulses to please a foreign market), or between straight lines and curves.

Between Islamic design and the Christian styles with which it shares the period of the Middle Ages, there are great differences, just as there are great differences between Islamic and Christian society. While both were strongly focused on their own religions, Islamic society was often superior in literacy and in the pursuit of art, science, and philosophy. We might even say that the Islamic world during the Middle Ages exhibited much of the sophistication of the Renaissance that would follow in Christian Europe. Paradoxically, just as that Renaissance was reaching its highest level, Islamic accomplishments began to decline. This, some have suggested, may have occurred because Islamic society, passionately enamored of richly handcrafted manuscripts, virtually ignored a development that transformed European society: the invention of printing. In any case, Islamic design has at times been in advance of—and at other times behind—other styles. Throughout its history, its ideals and accomplishments, its conventions and character, have been distinctly its own.

Another comparison may be provoked by this chapter's placement in the book: preceding it, the styles of the rest of the Middle Ages; and following it, the styles of the Far East: Indian, Chinese, and Japanese. Islamic design stands between these two great bodies of culture and art, conspicuously separate from both of them.

Most of all, the Islamic respect for virtuosity, abstraction, and richness is thoroughly opposed to those styles (including some Japanese design, Shaker design, late-nineteenth-century Arts and Crafts design, or the design of twentieth-century modernism) that respect simplicity, naturalism, and even roughness.

Of all the design styles previously considered, Islamic style shares the most geography and history with the design of the ancient Near East. Of all the design styles to come, it overlaps the most with the Mughal phase of Indian design. And its exoticism and penchant for detail certainly show the influence of Byzantium. The products of Islamic design—most famously, its carpets—can be handsomely and effectively combined with French armchairs or English paneling or a Mies van der Rohe daybed, but they retain their own character. Islamic design is to a rare degree a world of its own, self-sufficient, self-referential, and self-perpetuating.

Finally, Islamic design, compared to other design styles is strictly traditional. David Talbot Rice concludes in the last sentence of his *Islamic Art* that it demonstrates "that the great concern with self and self-expression which so much obsesses the artists of today in the West is not necessarily to be regarded as an essential in the production of good art." Islamic art and design was generally unconcerned with originality and personal vision. In this regard, it stands close to much of the art and design of the Far East, the subject of our next section.

10

India

2500 B.C. to the Nineteenth Century

"Behind all forms lies hidden the music of the divine lute."

—Rabindranath Tagore (1861–1941), Indian poet

ndia, along with most Eastern cultures, was long considered remote and mysterious by most Westerners. Until the development in the second century B.C. of the Silk Road, the network of roads traveled by traders between China and Eastern Europe, the wonders of the East were unknown in Europe. Not until the wide-ranging travels of the Venice-born merchant Marco Polo (1254–1324) did these wonders come to be popularly known. Since then, possibly as a result of their long unfamiliarity, Eastern and Western cultures have demonstrated a deep curiosity about one another.

Determinants of Indian Design

No less than its Western counterparts, the design of India was affected by the country's geography, religion, and political developments.

◀ **10–1** Detail of the *pietra dura* inlay on the walls of the Taj Mahal, Agra.
Francesco Venturi/CORBIS, NY

Geography and Natural Resources

The subcontinent of India, an irregular diamond in shape, juts into the Indian ocean from the continent of Asia, from which it is separated by the Himalayas and other mountain chains. This separation has given India some cultural and artistic unity, but little religious or political unity. Stretching more than 1,500 miles (2,500 km) from north to south, the country is predictably varied, the deserts of the north giving way to the jungles of the south. There are great plains as well, and mighty river systems such as the Ganges, a river sacred to the Hindus. Dry winds and monsoons bring periods of drought and flooding.

There is excellent building stone, including the fine marble used in the buildings of Delhi and Agra (fig. 10–1). The low plains near Calcutta, however, offer little stone, and there the soil is made into mud bricks. Teak is the country's chief timber, but there are also ebony, bamboo, and palm.

Religion

India's religions, especially Hinduism and Islam, were major determinants of the country's arts, including its architecture. Other religions indigenous to the country are Jainism, Buddhism, and Sikhism. Religions brought into India from the

Date	Cultural Developments	Artistic Developments
2500–1500 B.C.	Height of the Indus civilization	City of Mohenjo-Daro
800–400 B.C.	Vedas in written form; life of Buddha, 563–483	
400–100 B.C.	Maurya period, 322–185; spread of Buddhism and Jainism	Edict pillars of Asoka; stupa at Sanchi; first cave decorations at Ajanta
100 B.C.–A.D. 300	Composition of the Bhagavad-Gita	
A.D. 300–800	Gupta period; 300–540	Cave temples at Ajanta, Ellora, and Elephanta
800–1100		Carved temples at Khajuraho
1100–1400	Muslim conquest of Northern India, 1192; sack of Delhi by Timur, 1398	Qutb-Minar at Delhi
1400–1500		Artistic renaissance in Rajputana
1500–1600	Founding of Mughal dynasty by Babur; reign of Akbar	Humayun's tomb, Delhi; building of Fatehpur Sikri
1600–1650	Reign of Jahangir; reign of Shah Jahan	Shalimar gardens, Kashmir; Delhi and Agra forts; Taj Mahal
1650–1700	Founding of Calcutta	Rajasthani miniature painting
1700–1750	Death of Aurangzeb	Last Mughal mosques; founding of Jaipur; palaces at Udaipur
1750–1800	British East India Company rules India	Palaces at Jodhpur
1800–1850		Golden Temple, Amritsar
1850–1900	British Crown appoints Viceroy to India; Queen Victoria named Empress of India	British neoclassical architecture in Bombay and Calcutta
1900–1950	Independence for India and Pakistan, 1947	Building of new capital at New Delhi, 1913–31
Since 1950	First general elections in India, 1952	Le Corbusier buildings in Chandigarh; Crafts Museum established in New Delhi; National Institute of Design established in Ahmedabad

Near East, or from Western Asia, are Islam, Christianity, and Zoroastrianism. In certain eras, these religions have coexisted; in other eras, the domination of particular faiths was reinforced by political power, such as the Islamic invasion of India c. A.D. 1000 and the conquest of India by Portugal and England in the late eighteenth and nineteenth centuries.

Even as India is a land of many beliefs—each with its own artistic expression—Indians and their designers adhere to rules that govern the relationship of the real and the spiritual. There are rules, therefore, that govern the design of real buildings, spaces, or objects meant to invoke the spiritual. Indian design is often the product of tradition and religious dictates. Always underlying the design is some organizing

pattern. It may also be the result of inspiration or of skill, but it is never the result of chance or whim. So while, at least to an outsider, Indian religions seem primarily transcendent, otherworldly, and spiritual, more concerned with higher states of being than with the here and now, Indian design, perhaps necessarily, seems palpably present, appealing directly to our human senses.

Political Developments

As with any culture, India has a rich and varied history in which peoples lived in peace or were overthrown by other groups. Greatly simplifying the complex history of India, we can divide it into four broad phases to help us with our study of design:

The prehistoric civilization (c. 2500–1500 B.C.) of India centered around the Indus River in northwestern India. Most of its cities have yet to be excavated, but it is thought that there were settlements making objects of pottery, bronze, copper, and terra-cotta even earlier than 2500 B.C. We know as little about this civilization's origin as we do about its decline, but there may have been some connection with the Sumerian culture of the Ancient Near East.

In the next era (c. 250 B.C.–A.D. 1000), the foundations of Indian philosophy were established and the three most significant Indian religions—Hinduism and its offshoots of Jainism and Buddhism–began to coexist. Some of the cultural achievements during this time included advances in mathematics, astronomy, and language. Design achievements included the perfection of the religious monument called the *stupa*, the first rock-cut tombs, and the earliest temples.

During an Indo-Islamic period (c. A.D. 1000–1750), Muslims from the Ancient Near East brought Islamic culture and design to India and established its chief sultanate at Delhi. The Muslim influence can be seen in the building of mosques and tombs.

After the 1750 domination of the country by the British East India Company, India went through enormous social and political changes, taking it from a country of provincial viceroys and turning it into a country unified under foreign control. Design reflected not only the taste of the princes of India, but also of the British royalty and government officials. India, along with Pakistan, declared independence in 1947, and the first Indian elections were held in 1952.

Indian Architecture and Interiors

Indian architecture is chiefly an architecture of monuments, some glorifying religious figures, some earthly rulers. Both types could be imposing and dazzlingly ornamented, but both were also well grounded in reason.

Religious Monuments and Temples

The most rational of all planning devices—the grid—is often the basis of sacred Indian construction, for the grid—especially a grid of multiple squares—was endowed with spiritual significance. Such a composition of squares is the basis of many Indian buildings and building complexes, including the Hindu temple, and the Islamic mosque and mausoleum. Each square was thought to be occupied by a god, and the location of a square within the plan was related to the importance of the god. In a typical temple plan the square at the very center of the plan was thought to be the abode of Brahma, who (with Krishna and Siva) was one of the three chief Hindu gods.

Even though the buildings were based on simple squares and circles, they were rarely simple in appearance but overlaid with ornament. Columns were complex in form, with bell-shaped bases, octagonal shafts, and capitals in the shape of a lotus blossom or a honeycomb. The square is also found in numerous decorative motifs in the temple interiors, such as ceiling designs. Circles, octagons, equilateral triangles, and other geometric forms also played symbolic roles. The **mandala** (Sanskrit for "circle") is, for Buddhists and Hindus, both a graphic symbol of the universe and an aid to concentration and meditation. Not surprisingly, the circle was the basis for one of the earliest manifestations of Indian religious architecture, the *stupa*.

The Stupa   Adopted by both the Jain and Buddhist religions, the **stupa** was a hemispherical mound, containing religious relics (fig. 10–2). The mound was often topped with a multitiered ornamental umbrella called a **chattra**, and often surrounded with a path, a circular railing, or a fence with gates at the four points of the compass. The chattra-topped stupa of India is the likely the predecessor to other similar

▲ **10–2** The Buddhist stupa at Sanchi in central India, first century A.D. It is of brickwork, 106 ft. (33 m) in diameter.
Edifice © CORBIS All Rights Reserved

structures: the pagoda of China and Japan, the dagoba of Ceylon, the chorten of Nepal and Tibet, and the stepped square platforms at Borobudur, Java.

The Cave Temple   Between c. 250 B.C. until c. A.D. 700, a large number of temples, many of them for Buddhist worship, were cut into the face of stone cliffs. Some took the basilica form that we have seen in Roman and Early Christian architecture—that is, the long, vaulted, central spaces for processions paralleled by side aisles, and the aisles separated by rows of columns from the "nave." In the Indian cave temples (fig. 10–3), these central spaces might end with a stupalike form topped by a version of the chattra. Others might have giant sculptures of seated or reclining Buddhas. Many were noted for their colorful murals and their elaborate carvings on columns and lintels. The most extensive groups of such cave temples are at Ajanta, where twenty-eight were built between 200 B.C. and A.D. 200, and at Ellora, where thirty-four were built between A.D. 575 and 900.

The Northern Temple   In addition to the temples carved into rock cliffs, there were, of course, many Indian temples, shrines, mosques, and monasteries built above ground. They differ according to religion, time, location, and local custom, but they are generally divided into two chief types: northern and southern temples. Like the temples of Egypt—but quite unlike the churches and cathedrals of Christianity and the mosques of Islam—the Indian temples were built for the use of small groups of priests or monks, not for large congregations.

The temple of northern India is characteristically a tall, tapering form built of stone. Often elaborately carved in ways that do not interfere with the basic form, it contains space for all the rituals of worship. So massively thick is the temple's outer construction that its interior space is less vast than the exterior would lead us to expect. Large examples of the northern temple have an interior hall surrounded by an ambulatory and entered through a vestibule. Some temples also have entrance porches and are set on large platforms. An outstanding group is at Khajuraho (fig. 10–4). These buildings date from the ninth through the twelfth centuries and include both Jain and Hindu temples. It is thought that there may have been eighty-five temples at Khajuraho, but only twenty-five are now in a good state of restoration. Many of the stone carvings are erotic in nature, showing groups of writhing figures; others are elaborate exercises in the geometry so fundamental to Indian design (fig. 10–5).

▲ **10–3** A rock-cut cave temple with richly ornamented ceiling and columns, Ajanta, India, c. 100 B.C.
Jean-Louis Nou/AKG-Images

▲ **10–4** Temples at Khajuraho, their exteriors covered with carvings.
Abercrombie

The Southern Temple The temple of southern India is a simpler, more rectangular form (or a stack of forms), capped by a miniature cupola (fig. 10–6). It had a series of interior rooms, richly carved and aligned in a series of increasing ceiling heights. At Pattadakal, there is a single Jain temple and a number of Hindu ones, all built between A.D. 700 and 900. Some are in typical southern style; others combine northern and southern characteristics. Sites in the deep south of India

▼ **10–5** Stone ceiling carving at Khajuraho.
Abercrombie

include Mahabalipuram, where The Seven Pagodas once included both temples and cave temples dating from the seventh century. At the sacred city of Kanchipuram, a vital center for more than 2,000 years, Buddhist, Jain, and Hindu faiths are all represented.

The Fort, the Palace, and the House

Some of the most impressive examples of nonreligious Indian architecture are the large complexes known as forts, such as the Fort at Agra, the Red Fort in Delhi, and the Amber Fort near Jaipur. Their finest interiors, surprisingly, are indistinguishable from palace interiors, for they served as the residences of royalty.

Palace architecture, along with the palace quarters of forts, was composed of many distinct elements such as audience halls, throne rooms, men's quarters, and women's quarters. The design of each element was often symmetrical, modular, and strictly ordered, although the overall composition, accrued incrementally over a long period, was often less orderly.

The chief building material for palaces was stone, sometimes reddish sandstone, as at Fatehpur Sikri (near Agra c. 1600), and sometimes white marble, as at the *diwan-i-am* (public audience hall) and the *diwan-i-khas* (private

▲ **10–6** A southern Hindu temple complex, the Kesava Temple in Somnathpur, Mysore, India, thirteenth century.
© Sheldan Collins/CORBIS, NY

audience hall), both built within the Red Fort at Delhi. In Jaisalmer and other locations, mansions (*haveli*) for wealthy merchants were built of amber- or ochre-hued sandstone, centered around interior courtyards and rising several floors high. Houses for the middle class might be made of fired brick and tile, more modest houses of sun-baked mud brick.

Water was often a delightful accompaniment to palace architecture. Water gardens, symmetrically laid out, incorporated plantings, terraces, fountains, and water channels (fig. 10–7). Both palaces and large houses were centered around interior courtyards, often rising several floors high. House plans often included verandas and planted courtyards, and, as in Egypt and the Near East, roof terraces were much enjoyed.

Architectural ornament appeared in window openings, which were often covered with pierced screens carved from stone. Doors and other interior woodwork were also elaborately carved whenever the owner's budget allowed. In addition, palace and house walls, inside and out, were frequently elaborately frescoed. An example is a reception room in the sprawling City Palace complex of the city of Jaipur (fig. 10–8). The complex is composed of a city, laid out on a strict grid pattern, and a palace, begun by Maharajah Jai Singh in 1727. The palace's reception room, in a restrained palette of blue and white, is enveloped in frescoed floral designs. But these flowers, stalks, and tendrils are not in natural disarray. Instead, among straight lines with right angles, and in circles within circles, they obey a pervasive geometry.

We should also note the room's scalloped arches and slightly bell-shaped columns with lotus-blossom capitals. Unlike the stupas and temples we saw earlier, this room was created after the Islamic conquest of India, and with Islamic rule came these Islamic design features. The particular dynasty in power when Jaipur was built was the Mughal dynasty, founded in the sixteenth century by Babur, a descendent of Genghis Khan. The Mughal reign had great impact on the development of architecture, interior design, and other arts. We shall look now at its best-known monument, the Taj Mahal.

The Taj Mahal

The Taj Mahal (a name meaning "Crown of the Palace") was built by the Mughal Emperor Shah Jahan as a mausoleum for his wife, Mumtaz Mahal ("Exalted One of the Palace"), who died in childbirth in 1631. The building was completed in 1648 amid spacious gardens graced with fountains, waterways, plantings, and marble paths (fig. 10–9). Rather than being centered in the garden, however, as would have been typical for such a royal mausoleum, it was placed near the end of the garden on a bluff overlooking a river.

The Taj Mahal is the epitome of balanced architectural composition (fig. 10–10, page 200). It is also a masterpiece of finish, demonstrating the key importance in Mughal architecture—and in Indian architecture in general—of decorative detail. The building itself is faced with white marble decorated with precious and semiprecious stones in patterns of floral sprays, arabesques, and Islamic calligraphy. The use of white marble, striking in the intense Indian

▲ **10–7** Water channels in the terrace of the Itimad-ud Daulah mausoleum, Agra.
Abercrombie

▲ 10−8 Painted with blue-and-white floral designs, a reception room in the City Palace, Jaipur. Construction began in 1727.
© Antonio Martinelli, 2004

▲ **10–9** One of the most famous sights in the world, the Taj Mahal, Agra, completed in 1648.
Abercrombie

sunlight, had a precedent in the Itimad-ud Daulah, the mausoleum Shah Jahan's father had built in Agra for his empress's parents (see details in fig.10-14).

The center of the Taj Mahal is topped—and the entire composition is dominated—by a slightly swelling 200-foot-high (66 m) onion dome, another Indian architectural feature with Islamic heritage. Close around it, near the corners of the main structure, are four **chattri**. At each corner of the building's marble platform stands a 133-foot-tall (44 m) **minaret**, a slender tower usually associated with a mosque.

▶**10–10** Vertical section, the Taj Mahal, Agra. The construction is so heavy that the interior spaces are small, compared to the exterior.
Abercrombie

These minarets are divided into sections by narrow balconies from which the faithful can be called to prayer, and the balconies align with the floor levels of the main structure, helping to tie the composition into a whole. On the left of the main building, when viewed from the gardens, is a small mosque; balancing it on the right is an identical building that has been called a guest house, although its only purpose may have been symmetry.

The building's interior is no less impressive. Although square in plan and symmetrical in both directions, the building is entered through the great portal on its south side. The interior is subdivided into a composition of nine squares, and the first space one encounters is one of the ring of eight interconnected spaces circling the central one. A second ring of another eight rooms is on the floor above, overlooking the central space through pierced marble screens. The central octagonal space rises to a dome 80 feet (26 m) tall, high but considerably more human in scale than the great dome visible outside. The chief material here is white marble, again inlaid with **pietra dura** work (again, see fig. 10–1). While the stone mosaic at the Itimad-ud Daulah had been chiefly geometric, the pietra dura at the Taj Mahal was chiefly floral and gently lyrical. For all its richness and movement, the decoration of the Taj Mahal is spare, embellishing but never dominating the building's forms.

Within the central space is an octagonal screen of pierced marble 6 feet (2 m) high. Centrally placed within the screen is Mumtaz Mahal's **cenotaph**, a monument honoring a person whose body is elsewhere (in this case, a crypt directly below the space). Next to her is Shah Jahan's own cenotaph, his body also in the crypt below. Both monuments are covered with white marble inlaid with colored stones, the pietra dura work here surpassing in quality that found anywhere else in the building and perhaps equaling that found anywhere in the world. Shah Jahan's cenotaph features a flaming halo and highly geometricized plant forms; his wife's features similar plant forms and Islamic calligraphy.

Viewpoints | A MODERN TAJ MAHAL

In the February 1991 issue of *Interior Design,* architect and critic Peter Blake once compared the Taj Mahal with Donald Trump's "Trump Taj Mahal" in Atlantic City, New Jersey. He quoted Frank Dumont, Trump's designer for the "TTM," as saying, "We're striving for authenticity, and have spent years researching . . . the period, down to the most minute detail." The Atlantic City version was to have "over forty colorful minarets" and "penthouse suites named for, and in the styles of, the Kubla Khan, Leonardo da Vinci, Cleopatra" as well as restaurants named Safari Steak House, the Casbah, and the New Delhi Deli. "I have seen both the TM and the TTM," Blake wrote, "and the former may be divine, but it hasn't got a deli."

Indian Furniture

Traditional Indian interiors, both institutional and domestic, were spare in their use of furnishings. Seating was generally on the floor, softened by cashmere or cotton rugs or, in simpler circumstances, grass matting. The most common article of domestic furniture was the **char-pai**, or rope cot, its four-legged frame laced with rope that would support bedding. In wealthy houses, the feet of the bed might be gold and the rope might be replaced with boards of wood or even strips of ivory, but the basic form of the char-pai remained.

Chairs were not in common use, but thrones were made for important personages. Gold thrones were mentioned in Indian religious texts such as the Vedas, the Ramayana, and the Mahabharata. Wood thrones (more frequent than gold) were often inlaid with gold, silver, copper, and crystal. Carvings represented lions, horses, elephants, conch shells, the bull, the peacock, or the lotus. In addition, thrones were draped in plain or brocaded silks.

The most famous single piece of Indian furniture belonged to the Mughal Emperor Shah Jahan, the builder of the Taj Mahal. Called the Peacock Throne, it was canopied and made of jewel-embellished gold and depicted the favored peacock in its center. A watercolor of c. 1635 (fig. 10–11) shows it with a maroon and gold bolster and resting on a Mughal carpet. The Peacock Throne was captured during the looting of Delhi in 1739, taken to Teheran, and dismantled.

In the sixteenth through the eighteenth centuries much furniture was exported from India to the West in both Indian and European styles. Among the Indian furniture techniques welcomed in Europe were lacquering and ivory inlay for chests and cabinets (fig. 10–12), and cane chair seats and backs. Cane is the common term for the outer skin of the rattan palm; the stiffer inner stem is called **wicker**.

Indian Decorative Arts

The pietra dura of the Taj Mahal was a luxury item, of course, but similar decorative treatments were fashioned for more humble interiors. One technique used for interior wall

▼ **10–12** Writing cabinet on table, wood inlaid with ivory, with handles and hinges of chased silver, eighteenth century, total height 61 in. (156 cm).

Cabinet and stand; rosewood inlaid with ivory; Indian (Vizagapatam); Mid 18th century. Victoria & Albert Museum, London/Art Resource, NY

▼ **10–11** A miniature painting of Emperor Shah Jahan on his Peacock Throne, c. 1635. Watercolor and gold on paper, 6½ in. (16.5 cm) high.

Attributed to Govardhan, "Shah Jahan on the Peacock Throne," South Asia, India, ca. 1634–1635. Opaque watercolor and gold on paper, 16.5 cm × 12.4 cm. Courtesy of the Arthur M. Sackler Museum, Harvard University Art Museums, Private Collection, 651.1983. Photographic Services © President and Fellows of Harvard College

Pietra dura is the Italian term for "hard stone," although—because the work it refers to usually involves a variety of stones—some prefer the plural form, *pietre dure*. The term can be applied to any decorative use of hard gemstones, particularly richly colored ones like malachite (bright green), jasper (dark green), carnelian (red), lapis lazuli (azure blue), or bloodstone (green with red flecks). The hardness of these stones allows them to be given a high polish. More specifically, the term refers to a type of inlay in which the colored stones are set into recesses chiseled into the surface of a plainer stone. In India the stones were often set into sheets of white marble, although in some early work of the Indo-Islamic period the white marble was used as inlay in grounds of red sandstone. Because the Italian city of Florence became famous for pietra dura in the Renaissance, such work is sometimes called "Florentine mosaic."

surfacing involved the fitting together of small, regularly shaped (often hexagonal) pieces of painted wood. Sometimes these wood compositions included many small mirrored pieces and were called mirror mosaics (*shish*). Ivory inlay was also popular, particularly in the Punjab region.

Indian carvings, both in wood and stone, were frequently used and highly developed. Pierced window screens or lattices of marble or sandstone called *jalis* (fig. 10–13), were fashioned in complex geometric patterns to filter India's strong

▲ **10–13** In the interior of Humayun's mausoleum, Delhi, built c. 1565, light is filtered through a pierced marble screen.
Abercrombie

sunlight but still admit the breeze. While the material and texture of these screens is different from those of the wood lattices of Islamic design (see fig. 9–17), the interior effect is similar.

The stone mosaic on the walls of the Itimad-ud Daulah mausoleum, built in Agra by Shah Jahan's father, has a variety of patterns, accomplished and impressive. Even using a narrow family of colors and using a limited vocabulary of simple shapes, the many patterns are all different, yet not one seems jarring or unrelated (fig. 10–14).

Wood carvings were used lavishly and expressively throughout Indian interiors, appearing on columns, door panels, door and window frames, roof brackets, balcony parapets, ceiling panels, low headpieces of beds, and elsewhere. The character of the carving was naturally affected by the wood being used, and the artisans used each type expertly. As two early twentieth-century writers on Indian crafts, Watt and Brown, noted, there were the "deep under-cutting and sculpture that is possible with teak, redwood and walnut, the low relief of *shisham* and *deodar,* the incised designs of ebony, the intricate and minute details of sandal, and the barbaric boldness of *rohira, sal,* and *babul* (*kikar*) and other coarse grained and hard woods."

Indian interiors also had their complement of accessories and small objects: small wooden containers in the shape of stupas, with chattras as their handles; carved ivory Buddhas and chessmen; cups of crystal; bowls of jade; and more. There were Indian carvings of ivory, and Indian literary references as early as the fifth century A.D. to building interiors with ivory portals. Ivory was also used for the facing of columns and as inlay on wooden doors, small wooden tables, and musical instruments. Carved ivory was also seen in the form of

▲ **10–14** Three patterns in stone mosaic at the Itimad-ud Daulah mausoleum, Agra.
Abercrombie

Buddhas, chessmen, small puppets, combs, and boxes. In the Mughal period, there were sumptuous cups and bowls of carved crystal and jade. There were also, particularly in the northern state of Kashmir, Indian objects of painted **papier-mâché**, a material made of pulped paper and glue that became popular in seventeenth-century France.

Textiles

Whether in use as clothing or as a feature of interior design, Indian textiles have long constituted a highly significant vocabulary of techniques, designs, and colors. The cultivation of cotton and the weaving of textiles have been important parts of India's culture since prehistoric times. Evidence for this has been found in what is now Pakistan at a grave site dated to c. 5000 B.C. In the Vedas, the Hindu religious texts compiled c. 1500 B.C., there are references to fabrics made of cotton, wool, and silk, both woven and embroidered, and the universe itself is described as a fabric woven by the gods. Actual fragments of cotton cloth, along with a needle made of bronze and spindles made of terra-cotta, survive from the ruins of Mohenjo-Daro, the city that flourished during the Indus Valley civilization. One of the fragments found was

dyed with *red madder*, a plant-derived dye also sometimes called "turkey red," showing that India long ago mastered the use of **mordants**, catalysts necessary for cotton's absorption of almost all dyes. The early perfection of this technique gave Indian weavers a great advantage, and the virtuoso use of brilliantly colored dyes became a major feature of Indian textile art.

Foreigners were impressed. When European visitors first saw cotton plants in India, they described them as wool-growing trees. Both the plants themselves and the fabrics woven from them were exported to Egypt and Rome in ancient times, and, in Nero's reign, Indian **muslin** (a plain-woven white cotton named for Mosul, where it was first made) was all the rage in Rome. This delicate, soft, translucent cotton was sometimes given the full name *Indian muslin*. Within India, the nearly invisible material was given such poetically descriptive names as "running water," "evening dew," and "woven air." Such material was infinitely finer than what we today call muslin: a stout, plain cotton cloth used for shirting and bedsheets. Some of the original Indian exported muslin was embroidered with gold or silver threads.

India had imported its first silk from China, where its manufacturing process had been discovered, but India also made its own silk. The lustrous fabric's affinity for absorbing dye and the Indians' affinity for color were a natural pairing. The silk moth cultivated in China is not native to India, but wild moths in India produced a distinctively nubby silk called **tussah**. It is strong but coarse. Two popular fabrics made from tussah silk are **pongee**, a soft, medium-weight weave with obvious nubs and irregularities, and **shantung**, also roughly textured and named for the Chinese province of Shandong, where it was made.

Indian textiles began to be distributed by the British East India Company in the early seventeenth century. In the following two centuries, India became the largest textile producer and exporter the world had ever known. All Europe was hungry for Indian textiles, and England especially so. In the seventeenth and eighteenth centuries there was great English demand for wall hangings, tablecloths, bedclothes, and yard goods from India. The **palampore** was a particular favorite: a hand-painted cotton bedcover with a central medallion and related corner patterns, similar to some Persian carpet designs. Many Indian fabrics are familiar to us today, and their names (of Hindi origin) are familiar as well; among these are **calico**, a cotton heavier than muslin, from *Calicut* (the Hindu word for "India"); **chintz** ("spotted"); seersucker (literally "silk and sugar," suggesting a mix of textures), and **khaki** ("dust-colored").

In India, **embroidery** (an embellishment of needlework designs applied to any cloth) has often been applied by women. The types of stitching—with such names as satin stitch, chain stitch, and cross-stitch—as well as designs and colors reflect regional tastes. Although hand embroidery is still practiced, it has now been largely replaced by machine embroidery.

Designs Painting and block printing were two techniques Indians used for applying design motifs to textiles, the latter depending on a design cut into a wooden block (fig. 10–15), then stamped onto the cloth.

Like so much else in Indian art and life, Indian textile design is largely a matter of tradition and symbolism. Perhaps the most basic traditional Indian design motifis is called a boota and is clearly related to the *boteh*, or Paisley motif that we saw in Islamic carpet design. It is a series of small floating shapes, most usually based on flowers, singly or on sprigs or sprays, and appearing against a plain background. Handwoven cotton fabric employing such motifs is called *boota muslin.*

Tools & Techniques | INDIAN DYEING METHODS

Animal fibers such as wool and silk take dye readily but not vegetable fibers such as cotton or *flax*, the plant from which linen is made. But a long-lasting bridge can be built between fiber and dye with a substance called a **mordant**. A mordant is a metallic salt with which the resistant fibers can be saturated; the dye solution then reacts chemically with the mordant and forms an insoluble colored compound called a **lake**. Before the eighteenth century, the most commonly used mordant was *alum*, an aluminum sulfate, but today mordant substances contain iron, tin, aluminum, chrome, or tannic acid. Practice is needed in the use of mordants, for variations in the amounts applied can alter the hue and intensity of the resultant color.

The Indian application of mordants and dyes was accomplished in many ways, each technique producing its own special effect. The complex techniques used in India are the following:

- **Resist-dyeing** involves treating parts of the cloth with a substance that resists dye. The entire cloth is then dyed, leaving a pattern of natural and colored areas
- **Tie-dyeing**, sometimes called *tie-and-dye*, sometimes called *bandanna work*, is a technique done by hand and not dependent on chemical reaction. Small sections are gathered and tied tightly together with thread or waxed string. The whole cloth is then submerged in the dye, which is unable to penetrate the tightly bound sections. The result is a pattern of undyed areas against a dyed background.
- **Ikat** is a technique similar to tie-dyeing in which the yarn is treated or tied to resist dyeing before the cloth is woven. If this is done in a carefully measured manner, a planned pattern then emerges as the weaving proceeds. The edges of the woven patterns cannot be exactly predetermined, however, so they appear with a slightly blurred outline.

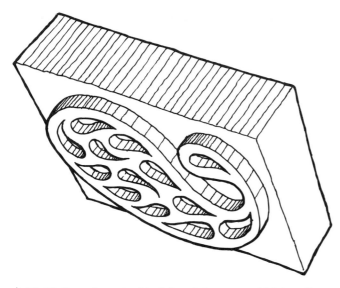

▲ **10–15** Carved wooden block for printing a repeat fabric pattern.
Abercrombie

▲ **10–16** A printed cotton from South India in a Paisley pattern.
Victoria & Albert Museum, London/Art Resource, NY

Other frequently seen design motifs are based on native animals, birds, or plants, such as the parrot, the goose, and the lotus, each being symbolic of a particular god or attribute. The *peacock,* now India's national bird, symbolizes a wide variety of attributes, including love, courtship, fertility, and immortality, and as a motif it is found in ancient Indus Valley burial pots, in Buddhist sculpture, and in Mughal miniature paintings, as well as in textiles. There are also hunting scenes with obvious references to vigor and physical activity, with depictions of horsemen pursuing elephants, tigers, rabbits, deer, and other animals, all seen in forest or jungle settings.

By far the most famous design motif of Indian textiles, however, is the **Paisley**, (fig. 10–16). It is less venerable than many other Indian motifs (introduced less than 300 years ago), but it is now immensely popular. Its origins are probably Persian, "derived, almost certainly, from the Persian wind-blown cypress," according to art historian Ananda Coomaraswamy. By the Mughal period in the seventeenth century, the motif had evolved into floral and tree-of-life designs. By the late eighteenth century, it had been codified into today's familiar leaf-shaped form with rounded base and curving, pointed top (sometimes also compared to an amoeba). The Paisley motif appeared frequently on the famously sheer wool shawls woven in Kashmir. Popular items for foreign export, Paisley textiles eventually became popular items for foreign imitation. The most famous imitations were those made in the Scottish town of Paisley (hence the name), where a weaving factory had been established in 1759.

Colors   In textiles of all kinds, the Indian taste has generally been for a generous variety of vibrant colors: the Paisley shawls of India were made in more than 300 colors. Indian dyes were traditionally made from natural substances. Reds came from *madder root, lac root,* and *al root* (Indian mulberry), or *cochineal,* a substance made from the dried bodies of a particular insect. Yellows came from turmeric, now used as a condiment. Greens came from pomegranate rind. Blacks came from a mixture of iron shavings and vinegar. Blues, the most potent dyes of all (so strong they could be applied without a mordant), came from the indigo plant, *indigofera tinctoria.* It produced a deep purplish blue color popular in India and throughout Southeast Asia.

Colors in Indian textiles traditionally had their own symbolism. Some colors represented particular gods—white being the color of Shiva, blue the color of Vishnu or Krishna. In earlier times, colors represented castes or social divisions—red or white being the color of the Brahman class, green the color of merchants and traders, yellow the color of the religious and ascetic, blue the color of the low caste. For Indians, colors have also held subjective meanings—white the color of purity and mourning, saffron yellow the color of spring and youth, red the color of early marriage and love.

▼ **10–17** Mughal carpet made in Lahore (now in Pakistan) c. 1650, 14 ft. (4.3 m) long. Clumps of stylized flowers on a plain background were a popular design during the reign of Shah Jahan.
Indian. Textiles-Carpets. Mughal, Period of Shah Jahan (1628–1658). Early 17th Century. Floral Rug. Cotton and wool. 14 feet × 6 feet 7 in. The Metropolitan Museum of Arts, Purchase, Bequest of Florance Waterbury and Rogers Fund, 1970. The Metropolitan Museum of Art. (1970.321)

Carpets and Floor Treatments

Like their Persian models, early Indian carpets were patterned in brilliant colors with flowers, leaves, and vines (fig. 10–17), sometimes with a few animals added among the foliage. In the earlier carpets, few of which remain, the weavers drew the flowers with great care, as if they were botanical specimens.

Indian carpet-weaving skill and originality grew steadily. The Lahore carpets came to be particularly fine, their pile often made of **pashmina**, Kashmir goat's hair, known to us as *cashmere*, rather than the coarser sheep's wool. The Lahore carpets were extremely well made, their weaves ranging from about 400 knots per square inch (62 knots per cm²) to—it is said—more than 2,000 (300 per cm²)! For good reason, these carpets are generally known as *Indian fine-weave carpets.*

Important rooms boasted a carpet, with the carpet corners held down by carpet weights (fig. 10–18) of gold, bronze, marble, or alabaster, which were sometimes inlaid in patterns reminiscent of the Taj Mahal's pietra dura.

In addition to carpets, Indian floors were painted for special events and celebrations, in a ritual called *alpana*. The painted

▼ **10–18** An alabaster rug weight with gemstone inlay, c. 1700, 4 in. (10 cm) square. Such weights were placed on the corners of rugs to keep them flat.
Weight for floor covering, North India, probably Agra, ca. 18th century. Calcite alabaster with glass, carnelian agate, lapis lazuli inlay. 3¾ in. high × 3⅜ in. W × 3⅜ in. D. Virginia Museum of Fine Arts, Richmond. Gift of Paul Mellon, The Nasli and Alice Heeramaneck Collection. Photo: Katherine Wetzel © Virginia Museum of Fine Arts.

▲ **10–19** Indian women decorate a floor with rice flour paste and colored pigment in preparation for a wedding ceremony.
Robert Frerck/Odyssey Productions, Inc.

designs, done with a white paste made from rice flour or from chalk (fig. 10–19), show a great sense of geometric structure.

Summary: Indian Design

It is difficult to summarize India's design, for like its geography, its religions, and its history, it is extremely varied. There are, however, some shared characteristics.

Looking for Character

Most Indian design is created in service to Indian religion. It does this primarily through ornament. At every scale, the ornament is elaborate, detailed, complex, and intricate. It is also often highly repetitive: a row of identical Paisley motifs, a row of identical pointed arches. As we saw in the Ancient Near East, such repetition can have powerful, hypnotic effects. An insistently repeated design element acting on the consciousness like an insistently repeated chant can achieve a degree of transcendence that matches its spiritual subject matter. In the West, we have come to equate serenity in de-

sign with plainness or emptiness; the design of India achieves it through multiplicity, never random nor disordered.

Looking for Quality

The traditional interiors and furniture of India do not always meet our current standards of comfort and function, and they certainly do not satisfy the modernist taste for simple forms and unadorned surfaces. The major concessions to comfort are in the area of soft goods—carpets, fabric hangings, and large, soft cushions. Yet these are far from minimally decorated. When circumstances allow, walls, floors, and ceilings are embellished with intricate designs, well conceived and expertly executed. Remarkable, too, is the relationship of this decoration to the architectural form beneath. The form is generally a strong one, and the decorator of form respects it.

Making Comparisons

We have noted that Indian design enjoys the hypnotic effects of multiplicity. But this use of a hundred scrolling plant tendrils or a thousand writhing figures never has the purpose of overwhelming the structure beneath. On the contrary, this very repetition turns the decoration into a surface pattern spreading rather evenly over a form. A multitude of small decorative effects distracts us much less from the form beneath than would a small number of large ones.

Indian decoration is similar in one respect to Greek vase painting. Both are admirable in themselves, but doubly admirable in their deference to the shapes they embellish. Neither is so bold that it blinds us to that underlying shape, and neither uses illusionistic three-dimensional effects that would visually distort that shape. They lie flat, so that we can see both the Greek battle scene and the *krater* on which it is painted, both the Indian stone inlay and the building to which it is applied. And as the Indian stone inlay enhances the building form beneath it, that form in turn is based on a foundation of geometry, and that geometry in turn is only a symbol of the gods and their attributes. The design of India is richly layered.

China

4000 B.C.–A.D. 1912

"The reality of the building consisted not in the four walls and the roof, but in the space within."

— Lao-tzu, born c. 600 B.C., the founder of Chinese Taoism

With almost a quarter of the world's people, China is immense in size and influence, venerable in age, and enduringly stable in its customs and its arts. Yet within this powerful tradition, we shall find a variety of expressions and a rich vocabulary of decorative techniques. Some of them, such as the manufacture of porcelain (fig. 11–1) and silk, are truly Chinese inventions.

Determinants of Chinese Design

The strength of Chinese tradition comes in part from a single written language common to the whole country. While dialects vary greatly from area to area, all educated Chinese use the same script. A sense of tradition also comes, as we shall see, from a shared philosophy. Beyond these unifying factors, design determinants have included, as they so often do, geography and natural resources, religion, and history.

◀ **11–1** Ming dynasty porcelain flask with blue underglaze decoration, c. 1430.
Victoria & Albert Museum, London/Art Resource, NY

Geography and Natural Resources

Because of its size—larger than all of Europe—China naturally has a varied geography: mountains in the west, steppes and deserts in the north, the sea in the south, and several great river systems, most notably the Yellow and the Yangxi. A chain of oases in the north made possible the trade routes collectively known as the Silk Road, so important to the distribution of China's famous silk. An abundance of minerals, including iron and copper, made China a rich country.

For temple and house construction, there were great forests of pine and bamboo, and heavy rains (and even monsoons) encouraged the development of building forms with widely overhanging roofs to handle the runoff. Pine and bamboo were also used for furniture, but the most frequently used furniture woods were varieties of rosewood. The most highly prized rosewood is *huang-hua-li*, a fragrant wood that can acquire a soft, seemingly translucent luster.

There was the mud needed for brick making, the clay needed for terra-cotta, and the white clay and "chinastone" (a finely grained rock) needed for porcelain. All in all, China was a land of natural wealth, which the Chinese would exploit artistically to great acclaim.

Date	Dynasty or Period	Key Rulers and Figures	Religious and Political Events	Technical and Artistic Highlights
2205–1766 B.C.	Hsia			
1766–1123 B.C.	Shang			Beginning of poetry tradition; bronze ceremonial vessels; jade ornaments
1122–255 B.C.	Chou	Lao-tze, Confucius	Origins of Taoism and Confucianism	Use of iron; gold and silver ornament
	Period of warring states			
255–206 B.C.	Ch'in	"First Emperor" Shih Huang-ti and counselor Li Ssu	Conquest and unification of China	Terra-cotta tomb figures; Great Wall begun
206 B.C.– A.D. 221	Han		Peace, expansion, the arrival of Buddhism	Manufacture of paper; establishment of Silk Road
221–581	Minor dynasties	Painter Ku K'ai-chih	Warfare	Oldest extant pagoda
581–618	Sui		Building of Chang-an; beginning of golden age	Great age of Buddhist sculpture
618–905	T'ang	Painters Li Ssu-hsün, Wang Wei, and Wu Tao-tze	Establishment of examination system for civil service employment	Invention of porcelain; oldest extant woodblock prints; oldest extant printed book
907–960	5 dynasties and 10 independent states		Chaotic times	Paper money; block printing of Chinese classics
960–1127	Northern Sung	Painter Li Lung-mien		First novel; first great Chinese encyclopedia
1127–1279	Southern Sung	Genghis Khan	Invasion of China	Conventional painting
1260–1368	Yüan	Kublai Khan	Mongol rule	Islamic influence
1368–1644	Ming	Ch'eng Tsu	Portuguese settlement of Macao	Earliest known cloisonné; monochromatic porcelain; fine furniture; the Forbidden City begun
1644–1911	Ch'ing	Emperors K'ang Hsi and Ch'ien Lung	Manchu rule; abolition of examination system; Canton opened to foreign trade; Boxer Rebellion; revolution, 1911	Elaborately patterned porcelain
1911–49	Republic of China	Sun Yat-sen first president; Chiang Kai-shek	Emperor abdicates	
1949 to the present	People's Republic of China	Mao Tse-tung		

Religion and Philosophy

Two chief Chinese religions have been Confucianism, based on the ethical teachings of Confucius (551–479 B.C.), and Buddhism, introduced from India c. A.D. 90. But older than either of these was a philosophical system called Taoism, its founding attributed to the philosopher Lao-tzu, born about 600 B.C. Early Taoists practiced various forms of meditation, including some *yoga*-like practices.

Important, too, have been the three Confucian fundamentals of Chinese morality: reverence (for one's parents in particular and one's ancestors in general), responsibility, and humanity. The Chinese cosmological principle of *yin* and *yang* is represented by a circle divided into white and black sections by an S-shape, which symbolizes the coexistence in all things of opposing qualities. *Yin* stands for the male, for the dark, for things at rest, for even numbers, and for the tiger. *Yang* stands for the female, for light, for things in action, for odd numbers, and for the dragon.

Related to *yin* and *yang* is *feng shui* (pronounced "fung shway"), meaning "wind and water." It is not a religion and, although it has been called "the art of placement," it is not an art, though its application can affect the orientation of buildings, building elements, and furniture. It is a complex system in which some principles have a firm footing in common sense (for example, the fact that living quarters should be exposed to the sun in winter and sheltered from it in summer), but other principles have an origin now forgotten.

History

At the time of the building of the Great Pyramids in Egypt, but before any of the great accomplishments of Greece or Rome, China was already using the potter's wheel, making bronzelike alloys of copper and lead, and building large meeting houses of timber with thatched roofs. With different techniques and philosophies, China was well underway to creating a culture of significant sophistication and renown.

Chinese history, like Egyptian history, is measured in dynasties of related rulers, the earliest generally thought to have been the Hsia, which began in 2205 B.C. Beautiful objects were produced in all periods, but most of the Chinese art we see today was made during the last two dynasties, the Ming (1368–1644) and the Ch'ing (1644–1911).

Chinese Architecture and Interiors

Chinese architecture is rigorously conventional, its basic forms repeated for centuries. Although other building traditions feature tall structures and daring engineering as expressions of unprecedented achievement, Chinese architecture expresses instead the qualities more highly regarded by its builders: repose and adherence to precedence.

The buildings are generally **modular**, based on repeated identical units, generally built in wood, and generally horizontal. The module in early buildings was often a bay roughly 10 by 20 feet (3 × 6 m), but from the tenth century on very important structures might have bays as large as 15 by 30 feet (5 × 10 m). Larger bays than that were precluded by the wooden construction, the beams being incapable of longer spans. Most commonly, a building had an odd number of bays, the central one being considered the chief one, and sometimes this central bay was slightly larger than the others.

A complex was typically composed of a large number of such simple structures, although they were often clustered around courtyards and joined by covered walkways or verandas. These modular building elements were generally arranged in an **axial** plan, one arranged symmetrically around an axis or center line. Just as the central bay was the most important space within a building, the central building—on the main axis or at the intersection of two perpendicular axes—was the most important building in a complex. Adhering whenever possible to *feng shui* ideals, the Chinese placed this most important building at the northern part of the site, facing south, and its back wall might be solid, or built of earth rammed into wooden forms, or fired into brick.

The most distinguishing part of a Chinese building is its roof. The roof was larger than the building beneath it, extending

Viewpoints | CAROLYN IU ON CHINESE DESIGN

Carolyn Iu is a founding partner of the New York firm Iu + Bibliowicz Architects and a member of the *Interior Design* Hall of Fame. She grew up in Hong Kong, and thus is very familiar with Chinese culture. "Here in the West," she says, "we can look at a room or a chair and say 'That's eighteenth century' or 'That's 1950s,' but in China design evolved much more slowly so that dating styles is much less easy. Our own design is modern, of course, because it has to accommodate modern functions and modern attitudes. But I often like to include something from a different time or place so that an interior isn't so predictably of the moment. Something China can teach us, I think, is that timelessness is sometimes preferable to timeliness."

▲ **11–2** Sectional perspective of a typical temple construction, c. 1000, showing the complex brackets between columns and roof.
Oxford University Press

to form wide, sheltering eaves, and these eaves were supported on wooden brackets projecting from the tops of the supporting columns. These brackets were sometimes elaborated into constructions of dazzling complexity (fig. 11–2). Another striking feature of the roof is the fact that it curves gracefully upward as it extends outward, giving an admirable sense of lightness and movement to a building form that is basically a rectangular box.

The building characteristics outlined above were applied to a wide range of building types—temples, palaces, government buildings, and all but the most humble residences. We shall look first at examples of Chinese civic and religious architecture, and then at architecture on the domestic scale.

Temples and Pagodas

Two distinctive types of Chinese religious buildings are the temple and the *pagoda*, a towerlike building that is often part of a temple complex. We have seen temples in many cultures and in many forms; the pagoda we shall see only in the East.

Temples   The Chinese temple is just one example of the modular, axial assemblage of bays into a distinctly skeletal form of construction, with regularly spaced columns providing support for the roof. Walls between these columns, thus deprived of structural necessity, can be thin screens. Most traditional temple structures are a single story high, although their roofs might be built with more than a single tier. Most are built of wood, often of an aromatic Persian cedar.

The temple is distinguished from other Chinese architecture by the splendor of its decoration. The roofs were often faced with glazed tile, sometimes in brilliant colors (although yellow roof tiles were reserved for use only by the emperor), and the roof-supporting brackets carved and painted. It is primarily the degree of this ornamentation, growing richer over time, that dates a Chinese temple, for its form remained basically unchanged for centuries.

A temple complex was surrounded by an exterior wall providing privacy and protection and was entered through a

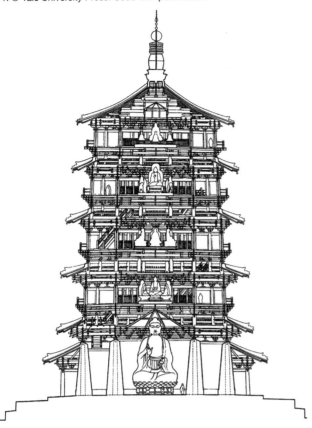

▼**11–3** Section through a wooden pagoda with a large Buddha on the lowest level and smaller figures on four higher levels, 11th century. Cross-section of the Fogong–si in Ying–xian, Shanxi. The large Sakyamuni image is on the ground floor. Above rise four storeys, each with grouped images. After HDACA. Percival David Foundation of Chinese Art. Yale University Press, 2000, William Watson, "The Arts of China 900–1620," p. 71. © Yale University Press. Used with permission.

central gate (and often through a second, "spirit" gate). For privacy the first gate was sometimes placed off center, opening only to a small forecourt, with a passage to a more impressive axial gate. More public areas were closer to the gate, more private ones (such as residential units for royalty or the priesthood) farther removed, and even within rooms such hierarchy was observed, the places of greatest honor being those farthest from the entrance.

Pagodas It is possible that the chattra-topped stupa of India may have led to the pagoda of China. The pagoda can also be seen as a combination of the stupa with the watchtowers of the Han dynasty, or as a vertical stacking of small temple forms, each with its own overhanging roof on brackets. Pagodas were built of wood, stone, or brick with the roof elements faced with tile. While some early ones were without interiors, serving only a symbolic use, later pagodas featured interior spaces housing figures of Buddha (fig. 11–3) or *bodhisattvas*, earthly beings close to enlightenment.

The Forbidden City

The greatest Chinese temple complex of all is the one called the Forbidden City (fig. 11–4). Under the reign of the Ming emperor Ch'eng Tsu (1403–25), a great burst of building activity produced an enormous ensemble of royal buildings

▲ **11–4** Near the entrance to the Forbidden City, the so-called River of Golden Water and the Gate of Supreme Harmony.
Dean Conger/National Geographic Image Collection

at the heart of Beijing. The ensemble is called the Forbidden City, for it was originally forbidden to all but members of the imperial household and their servants and guests. It is entered through the Gate of Heavenly Peace (*Tian-an Men*), actually a complex structure of five vaulted gateways topped by a pavilion. Beyond the vast Square of Heavenly Peace is another gate, the Meridian Gate, and, beyond that, an immense courtyard with a waterway crossed by five bridges, and then still another gate, the Gate of Supreme Harmony. The Forbidden City beyond contains almost a thousand structures linked by marble terraces edged with marble balustrades and interspersed with courtyards, waterways, bridges, and additional walls and gates. For almost five hundred years, China was ruled from this complex, and it was both headquarters and home for fourteen emperors of the Ming dynasty and ten of the Ch'ing.

The buildings and areas can be divided symbolically by their correspondence with *yin* or *yang*. An inner courtyard embodies *yin*, while the outermost courtyard embodies *yang* (having, for example, three halls and five gates, both odd numbers). The buildings can be divided by size into the larger ones nearer the entrance, used primarily for ceremonies,

banquets, lectures, sacrifices, and receptions of visiting dignitaries, and the smaller ones farther from the entrance, used as the emperor's residence. Largest of all is the Hall of Supreme Harmony (fig. 11–5) on the important central axis shared by the entrance gates. It is 197 feet (60 m) wide and 108 feet (33 m) long; its roof height is the same as its length. Its hipped-roof construction is of the double-eaved type. It is the largest of all the traditional wood-framed halls of China, and the most elaborately ornamented. Inside, in its central bay, is an elevated platform (fig. 11–6), approached by three short flights of stairs and carved with dragons, clouds, and stylized lotus petals. On the platform is the imperial dragon throne of carved gilt lacquer, behind it is a screen of the same material, and beside it are bronze incense burners in the shape of elephants. Around the platform are six gold-faced columns with images of dragons wrapping around them. The panels of the coffered ceiling above display more dragons, and everywhere—including on door and window frames—is the sparkle of gold.

The smaller, more private buildings, within their own wall, repeat the plan of the first cluster at smaller scale: They are the Palace of Heavenly Purity, where the emperor held

▼ **11–5** The Hall of Supreme Harmony, the main throne hall in the Forbidden City, Beijing, c. 1406.

▲ 11–6 Inside the Hall of Supreme Harmony, stairs lead to the ceremonial throne.
Alfred Ko/CORBIS, NY

private audiences; the Hall of Union, where the imperial seals were kept; and the Palace of Earthly Tranquility, which was the domain of the empress. The interiors of these somewhat smaller pavilions are less stupendous in their effect than those of the public ones, but they are by no means simple or plain, and some of their furnishings are quite extraordinary.

All the buildings of the Forbidden City are elaborately decorated. Their tile roofs are brilliantly colored, and the intricate wooden brackets supporting them are brightly painted. Virtually every surface of every interior is embellished, the chief colors throughout being red, blue, green, and—the color with imperial associations—yellow. Yet, despite its size, variety, and vivid colors, the Forbidden City appears cohesive. Its vocabulary of building forms is a small one, its elements are symmetrically disposed, and its organization is orderly and readily understood.

Chinese Houses

Houses of all sizes were generally composed around a central courtyard, or sometimes a progression of courtyards. In the grander houses, these were carefully landscaped, planted with weeping willows, quivering ginkgos, bamboo, and flowering shrubs, and also furnished with paths, pools, moss-covered rocks, footbridges, and pavilions. Flowers—lotus, peony, azalea, chrysanthemum—were chosen not only for their appearance and the time of their blooming, but also for their symbolic meaning. And hanging from archways and beams to light the gardens were colorful lanterns.

Within this natural context, the living quarters of a large house were disposed in a number of related but unconnected units (fig. 11–7). These units were graduated in size and importance, expressing the Chinese tradition of the patriarchal family, with several generations living in the same domestic compound, and the younger members subordinate to their elders.

The windows of the houses were traditionally infilled with strong white paper rather than glass. Whatever their thermal shortcomings, they were important decorative features, both inside and out, being also filled with narrow strips of wood in geometric latticework patterns. Sunlight through these during the day cast an interesting play of shadows on the interior; at night, lighted from within, they cast a similar shadow play on the surrounding garden walls.

The Chinese house and its garden courtyards were interwoven, inextricable parts of a whole composition. The design of the house, symmetrical, regular, and axially disposed,

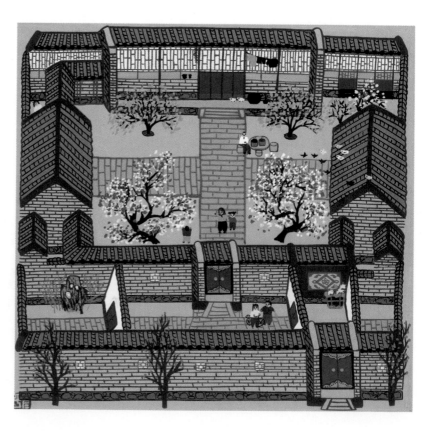

▶ **11–7** Perspective drawing of a typical Chinese courtyard house. Except for the entrance, elements are symmetrically disposed around a central axis.
The Mukashi Collection/SuperStock, Inc.

▲ **11–8** A scholar's study named the Studio of Gratifying Discourse, 1797.
"The Studio of Gratifying Discourse," 1797, Ch'ing dynasty, Lake Tai, Jiangsu Province, China. Wood, ceramic tile, stone lacquer and rocks, 216 × 226 × 528 in. The Minneapolis Institute of Arts, Gift of Ruth and Bruce Dayton 98.61.2

may be said to conform to Confucian ideals of discipline and hierarchy, of man in harmony with orderly society. The design of the garden, however, more irregular, more animated, and with more surprises, was in accordance with the Taoist notions of man in harmony with unpredictable nature. The total composition of buildings and gardens demonstrates the assimilation of divergent forces, the *yin* and *yang*, typical of Chinese life and design.

Inside the house in both China and Korea, men's and women's quarters were separated and given furniture and décor of different character. The eighteenth-century scholar's study that has been reconstructed at the Minneapolis Institute of Arts, for example (see fig. 11–8), is clearly masculine in character. The windows open to a garden through a variety of wood lattice patterns, and furnishings, appropriately, are restrained and simple, saved from severity only by a few

graceful curves. An inscription on a ceiling beam describes the room as "the studio of gratifying discourse."

For comparison, a wood-block print from around 1600 shows an interior of quite different character (fig. 11–9). We are in the women's quarters here. The furniture is more curvaceous and more ornate, and the openings are covered not merely by lattice but also by quantities of flowing fabric. The table in the lower left corner of the print is the type traditionally used for burning incense.

Placement of furniture within houses was strictly ordered and related to the status of its users. Within the major reception room of a house or palace, the place of honor was farthest from the entrance and facing directly toward it. Less important chairs for less important people were placed in pairs, sharing a small table between them, around the walls of the room, all perfectly parallel to the walls behind them.

The Chinese characters on the illustration, reading vertically:

玉臺窺簡

四奉新詩四句喑藏乘夜中情

發來假怒一塲明掩思春外跡

▲ **11–9** A scene in the women's quarters, wood-block illustration from the drama *The West Chamber,* Nanjing edition, Ming dynasty, Wanli period (1573–1620).
After Fu Xihua, fig 77; From: "Lost Interiors: Woodblock Prints and the Evidence for Chinese Furniture" by Craig Clunas in *Orientations*, January 1991, volume 22, number 1, p. 84, fig. 5.

The notion of an informal furniture grouping in the center of a room would be anathema to traditional Chinese taste.

Chinese Ornament

The brackets supporting the Chinese roof were, as we have seen, both structural and ornamental, and roof ridges were often emphasized with fish and other figures in glazed terra cotta. In the Hall of Supreme Harmony we saw ornamented columns and ceiling coffers (see fig. 11–6). Ornamental lattices covered house windows. Glazed tiles were also an important part of Chinese architectural ornament, used both on walls and roofs, and the up-tilting roof eaves are also delightfully ornamental.

Color is an integral part of Chinese architecture and a reference to social organization. Yellow being the color for the emperor, red for the mandarin class just beneath him, and blue, green, and purple for people of lesser rank.

For the Chinese, peonies were symbols of wealth and rank, and figures called "endless knots" (see fig. 11–16) were symbols of long life. But the single most representative Chinese ornamental motif is the dragon. We have seen that it represented the *yang* of *yin* and *yang.* It also represented the spring solstice, perhaps because of a hibernating type of crocodile that reappeared each spring. It is also a celestial symbol and, despite its apparent fierceness, considered mysterious but benign. The dragon robe was a staple of formal apparel in the Ming and Ch'ing dynasties, and its design strictly regulated: The number of dragons depicted on a robe represented the wearer's status, not even the emperor being permitted more than nine, and five-clawed dragons indicated higher rank than four-clawed ones. A stylized four-clawed dragon can be seen in blue against the white ground of figure 11–1.

Later we shall see the dragon and other Chinese motifs repeated in the *chinoiserie* popular in eighteenth-century Europe.

Chinese Furniture

Inside the Chinese house, even inside the most important of Chinese houses, furniture was scarce by today's standards. But the furniture and décor that existed were often of the highest quality. And, on festive occasions, the rooms were brightened and softened with fabrics: carpets, brocade runners draped on chairs, and ornamental frontal pieces tied to tables. As with Chinese architecture, Chinese furniture types remained constant for centuries.

Wood elements in Chinese furniture were assembled without dowels or nails (except in later repairs and for attaching metal hardware). Glue was rarely used in China, and the mortise and tenon (see table 2–1) was the mainstay of furniture construction because it allows the wood greater movement than any other sort of connection, an important factor in a country where temperatures can change radically from hot to cold during the course of one day and night. The wood finishes of Chinese furniture were impeccable, as flawless as their makers could manage.

Seating

Throughout most of the East, life was traditionally lived on or near the floor, sometimes with nothing more than a mat separating people and earth. The Chinese were exceptional in

▲ 11–10 Rosewood chair topped with a slightly projecting crest rail, Ming dynasty, 16th–17th century.
Chair, rosewood. Chinese, Ming dynasty, 16th–17th century. Victoria & Albert Museum, London/Art Resource, NY

having developed the custom of sitting in chairs. The origin of this custom has been the subject of much speculation, but it may be that, in the fourth century, the chair and the folding stool were both brought to China from India (where they may have been brought from Europe by the forces of Alexander the Great). In any case, chairs were in general use in affluent Chinese households by the ninth century. There were both armchairs and armless versions, and often the seats of Chinese chairs were unusually high, as they were designed to lift the occupants' feet above the cold floor. Their **stretchers** (the horizontal members connecting and stabilizing the legs) were characteristically close to the floor.

One version of Chinese chair has a **crest rail** (a horizontal member or **slat** across the top of its back) projecting slightly beyond the vertical members that support it (fig. 11–10). The **splat** (or central vertical member at the back) might often be a plain, wide plank, but subtly and very beautifully curved. Such chairs were originally intended for emperors or high officials, and the projections were originally of gold or brass, decorated with dragons' heads. Another elegant type of Chinese chair also has a plain central splat, but

it rises to join a slat that is in a horseshoe shape, continuing down to form an arm and continuing even further to become the front leg (fig. 11–11). In the example shown, the **apron** just under the seat and perpendicular to it is made of a slightly curved horizontal stretcher joined to the bottom of the seat with short vertical members.

Some thrones for emperors and top civil servants, rather than having seats high above the floor, had low, wide seats (fig. 11–12) to accommodate a cross-legged posture with one

▼ 11–11 Rosewood chair with a horseshoe back continuous with the front legs, Ming dynasty, 17th century.
Armchair. China, Ming dynasty, 17th century. Rosewood, 85.4 × 58.4 × 63.6 cm. © The Cleveland Museum of Art, The Norweb Collection, 1955.40.1.2.

▲ 11–12 A red lacquered throne from a royal hunting lodge near Beijing, Qing dynasty, 18th century.
The Imperial Throne of Emperor Ch'ien Lung (1736–96): red carved lacquer on wood; on a stand; front view; Chinese (Qing Dynasty); c.1775–80. Victoria & Albert Museum, London/Art Resource, NY

▲ **11–13** A sixteenth-century k'ang bed frame with six vertical posts supporting a tester. It is primarily of *huang-hua-li* wood with some pieces of red pine, 77¼ inches high, 81½ inches wide, 47½ inches deep.
Philadelphia Museum of Art: Purchased

leg tucked under the body. This was the posture seen in Shah Jahan on his Peacock Throne (see fig. 10–11), and it is the one accommodated by one of China's most distinctive pieces of furniture, the **k'ang**.

The K'ang

The **k'ang** was a large, low platform for sleeping. In the cold north, the k'ang was often placed along an interior wall and built of brick with a system of flues beneath it for heating, using the warm air from a nearby cooking stove. In the warmer south, the k'ang was usually freestanding and built of wood (fig. 11–13). Even in the north, it eventually evolved into a wooden platform, and, for privacy and comfort, it often had uprights supporting an overhead **tester** (pronounced "tee-ster" from the French *testière* meaning "headpiece"). The tester is sometimes of solid wood; sometimes only a wood frame for the support of a fabric covering. In either case, side panels of fabric could be hung vertically from the tester, and the k'ang could also be supplemented with screens, rush mats, and silk-covered cushions. Sometimes backrests were added, and sometimes also side rails, turning the platform into a kind of sofa with low enclosures on three sides.

Tables

Eventually, the k'ang platform, without its tester, was adopted for a low table. A characteristic detail, in both bed and table form, was the corner leg that curved gracefully inward as it descended, recalling the lilt of the Chinese roof gable (see figs. 11–4 and 11–5). Early in the Ming dynasty, these legs began to be terminated by the form of a horse's hoof, and in the eighteenth century a scroll form replaced the horse's hoof.

For formal banquets, the custom was to provide each guest with a small private table. For daily dining, however, there were rectangular and square tables. Because, as we have seen, Chinese chair seats were high by our present standards, so were tabletops. There were small side tables with six curving legs that, because of their shape, were called melon tables. There were long, narrow tables meant to be centered against a wall (fig. 11–14), and there were also tables for writing, tables for painting, game tables, altar tables, nested tables, and lute tables, these last designed to hold a Chinese zither.

▶ **11–14** A Ming dynasty k'ang table of huang-hua-li wood, its curved legs ending in a small ball toe. The height is 1 foot (30.5 cm) and the rectangular top is 23 inches by 3 feet (92.4 cm).
Chinese K'ang Table, 15th century, Ming Dynasty (1368–1644). Carved huanghuali wood, 11⅞ × 36¾ × 24³⁄₁₆ in. (30.2 × 93.4 × 61.5 cm). The Nelson–Atkins Museum of Art, Kansas City, Missouri (Bequest of Laurence Sickman) F88–40/51.

▲ **11–15** A Ming dynasty coffer of *huang-hua-li* wood, height 35 in. (90 cm), c. 1550–1600.
Coffer; Huali wood; Chinese; c. 1550–1560, Ming Dynasty. Height: 35 inches. Victoria & Albert Museum, London/Art Resource, NY

Storage Furniture

Storage furniture was very highly developed in China, there being no closets built into the thin-walled houses. Chests were built for storing books and manuscripts, and there were pairs of chests, chests on chests, and cupboards with open shelves. Tall, rectangular cupboards for clothing (or wardrobes) were commonplace and were made with various numbers of doors, although the most typical had a single pair of doors, sometimes with a single compartment beneath. Sometimes such **casegoods** (today's commonly used term for storage furniture) had a single door and sometimes removable lids. Many casegoods had handles at their sides for easy transportation, and many were fitted with carefully designed hinges, mounts, pulls, and escutcheons of nickel silver, brass, and other metals, these often being *countersunk* so that their surfaces were flush with the wood or lacquer. A Ming dynasty coffer (fig. 11–15) displays two details that remained characteristic for 200 years: the upcurving flanges at the ends of the top surface, recalling the curve of roof eaves, and the simply decorated apron under the storage compartment.

Specialized storage units not originally built as furniture (although sometimes used today as coffee tables or end tables) are Chinese wedding boxes. They were traditionally paraded through the streets before wedding ceremonies, their number and beauty indicating the worth and prestige of the bride's family. After the ceremony, they were used for clothing storage. Made of wood, the boxes were covered with pigskin, the leather serving as a hinge for the lid. The leather was typically painted with a wedding scene or other decoration.

Chinese Decorative Arts

Chinese artisans were adept at sculptural form, as well as at ways to decorate form. We shall look first at ceramics, a field in which China (and Korea) excelled.

Ceramics

In Chinese design, no accomplishment is more revered than the creation of fine ceramics. That accomplishment came in both technical skills, as in the invention of porcelain and glazes, and in aesthetic finesse, as in the abstract pattern made by the distribution of white and colored areas as seen in figure 11–1. It is entirely appropriate that the common term today for any vitrified (glasslike) ceramic is *china*. The range of character of decoration on Chinese ceramics is also large, encompassing elaborate, multicolored scenes and floral patterns as well as some wares that, emphasizing pure form and color, dispense with decoration altogether. These plain, monochrome porcelains, more appreciated in China than in the export market, are thought by many to be the highest artistic achievement of the Chinese culture. By the end of the Sung period, the fine cracks called **crazing** that may appear in a glaze during firing came to be admired as decorative and were deliberately sought as a ceramic finish.

Terra-cotta   The term **terra-cotta** literally means "cooked earth." The product of a type of natural plastic clay that hardens when fired, terra-cotta is most often associated with a rich reddish brown color, which is the result of iron oxide in the clay. The presence of other impurities and variations in firing techniques can give the material other colors, however, and the terra-cottas of China are often a warm gray in color.

Terra-cotta was used in China as molds for casting bronze objects at least as early as the third century B.C. Being more fragile, however, few of the earliest terra-cotta artifacts have survived. Those we know were made for uses both functional and ritual, as would be expected. Terra-cotta was also sometimes used for the molds in which bronze vessels were made (see the "Bronzes" in this chapter). Other Chinese uses for terra-cotta were for roofing tiles, small burial figurines, life-size effigies, tomb construction, and, to be placed in the tombs, models of houses, palaces, pagodas, and scenes from daily life.

Earthenware and Stoneware   Made not only in China but all over the world from the earliest times, **earthenware** is an opaque, nonvitreous ware that is fired at a relatively low temperature; it is porous unless glazed. It is sometimes called "pottery," though that term is also used as a synonym for all ceramics. Most clays are appropriate for making earthenware, and it can be formed into many shapes. Because of its low firing temperature, it requires no sophisticated kilns.

The earliest Chinese ceramics, dated approximately 6,000 years ago, were red pottery funeral vessels. Meant to be seen from above, in graves surrounding the dead, their tops were decorated with fertility symbols and other painted designs. By 2000 B.C., other types of pottery were being produced, including hard, lustrous, jet-black pottery and gray pottery decorated with cord and basket markings. In the Shang period, stylized animals appeared on glazed pottery, and in Chou times the Shang style was continued but with the more flowing curved forms that would characterize Chinese vases ever afterward.

Stoneware, which developed later, is a hard, dense, relatively nonporous ware that must be fired at a high temperature. It is composed of clay and stone containing *feldspar*, a crystalline mineral; in firing, the stone is vitrified, but the clay is not. As we shall see, stoneware was used as a body for the famous celadon glazes of Korea.

Porcelain   The Chinese invention of **porcelain** in the sixth century A.D. was a milestone in the decorative arts, although its perfection took centuries more. By the Ming dynasty (1368–1644), Chinese potters had achieved an absolute whiteness and an exquisite thinness in a material translucent when held to the light, sonorous when tapped, nonporous even if left unglazed, and so hard that it cannot be scratched with a steel knife, as earthenware and stoneware can.

Chinese porcelain was not always left white, of course. The so-called Ting ware, an imperial favorite during Sung times, was given an ivory glaze and occasionally a protective rim of copper. The fourteenth and fifteenth centuries saw underglazes of coppery red. There were also glazes of rich browns, black, powder blue, celadon, and a deep red known in Europe as **sang de boeuf** (bull's blood) or, when the red glaze had a streaky effect, as *flambé*. Other subtle colors were given romantic names in the West, such as peach bloom (peach dappled with green), ashes of roses (rosy gray), and clair de lune (silvery blue). In the Ming dynasty three-color and five-color wares were popular. In the Ch'ing dynasty, monochrome porcelains in a soft golden yellow were limited to use by the imperial family, although the most favored concubines were granted use of wares that were yellow outside and white inside. Export porcelains and porcelains later made in Europe were named for "families" of color: *famille*

Tools & Techniques | THE SECRET OF PORCELAIN

The Chinese kept their porcelain manufacturing technique a national secret as long as possible, and the subsequent history of ceramics is crowded with attempts—some successful, some not—at reproducing it. Chinese porcelain is a type of ceramic with specific requirements, made of two essential ingredients, both native to China. The first is a white clay called *kaolin,* or *china clay*. The second is *chinastone*, which is a fusible crystalline mineral derived from decomposed granite and prepared in the form of small white blocks. Kaolin and chinastone are sometimes called the "bones" and "flesh" of porcelain. The combination, when fired at the very high temperature of 2,335 degrees Fahrenheit (1,280 Celsius) yields the vitrified material just described. It is sometimes called **hard paste porcelain** or by the French term *paté dure*.

Soft-paste porcelain, or *pâte tendre*, was produced in the West as a porcelain imitation before the true formula for porcelain manufacture was known there. It can be made of many combinations of materials, one being white clay and ground glass. It is fired at a much lower temperature than porcelain, and its wares are much less durable. Because of its very vulnerability, some soft-paste ware has become rarer and more valuable than the genuine article.

Wares described as **porcelaneous** generally contain kaolin but not chinastone. They are fired at slightly lower temperatures, and may or may not achieve a translucent, vitrified character. An unusually strong type of porcelaneous ware, which would be patented in Staffordshire, England, in 1813, is **ironstone**, its toughness coming from the inclusion of glassy iron slag.

Somewhere between hard-paste and soft-paste porcelain is **bone china**, softer than the former, but both harder and less expensive to produce than the latter. First patented in Bow, England, in 1748, it is basically a soft-paste porcelain to which bone ash has been added. Agreeably white and translucent, it became the standard for English ceramic wares of the nineteenth century.

▲ **11–16** A pair of Ch'ing dynasty porcelain bowls in the *famille rose* style. Among the painted symbols are peonies and (at the center of the bowl on the left) an "endless knot."
Pair of bowls. Cincinnati Art Museum, Bequest of Katherine J. Appleton. 1949.123.124

verte with a brilliant apple green background; *famille jaune* with a yellow ground; *famille rose* using a soft pink color (fig. 11–16); and—popular in the nineteenth century—*famille noire* made with a brown-black pigment. And, finally, white porcelain products, from the seventeenth century onward, were shipped to Europe, where they were called **blanc de chine**.

The most famous of all Chinese porcelains, however, is **blue-and-white**, which featured designs in a deep cobalt underglaze against a white ground (see fig. 11–1). These designs were originally all hand-painted, but later some came to be applied by transfer printing. Designs included overall patterns of scrolls, flowers, and aquatic birds, but others were more extensive scenes of landscapes and figures, sometimes wrapping around vessels with little apparent regard for their shape. The famous **willow pattern**, depicting a story of eloping lovers, originated in England, not China. It became so popular in the eighteenth century, however, being imitated by over a hundred English sources, that it was eventually copied also in China.

Blue-and-white was admired and emulated in Japan (in some Imari ware), Persia, Indochina, England (Lowestoft), and the Netherlands (Delft). Sets of blue-and-white vases in groups of three and later in groups of five or more (but always an odd

▲ **11–17** Korean vase of porcelaneous stoneware with a celadon glaze over an incised design of dragons and clouds.
Vase (maebyong) 11th–12th century. Glazed stoneware with incised decoration of dragons. H: 35.3 cm (13⅞ in.); D: 23.1 cm (9⅛ in.) Special Korean Pottery Fund. © 2000 Museum of Fine Arts, Boston. All Rights Reserved.

number), alternating in shape, were popular on the European market and were frequently displayed with pride on seventeenth- to nineteenth-century parlor mantelpieces or over doorways. They were called **garniture de cheminée**. It is, indeed, because of serious European attention to Chinese porcelain in the nineteenth century (such as Jacquemart and Blant's study, *Histoire de la Porcelaine*, published in Paris in 1862) that many of the terms used today to describe porcelain and its substitutes are French.

Korean Celadon The term **celadon** refers to a soft gray-green glaze but the term is also applied to any ceramic vessel using such a glaze, it being most often applied either to stoneware or porcelain. Although it probably originated in China and came to be made throughout the East, it is most closely associated with Korea, where—with the availability of perfect iron-rich clay and the development of exactingly controlled glazes—it came to represent the pinnacle of Korean ceramic achievement. Some Korean celadon of the Koryo dynasty has been said to evoke "the blue of the sky after the rain" and "the radiance of jade and the crystal clarity of water." The Chinese themselves proclaimed it "first under heaven" (fig. 11–17).

Celadon depends on the use of iron oxide for its distinctive coloring, which can vary from soft olive to greenish-blue. (Copper oxide can produce a very different kind of green glaze.) It is fired only once, but at a high temperature. It is said that at the peak of celadon artistry, only one of ten pieces met the strict color standards of the Korean potter, and that those pieces that failed to achieve the desired color were destroyed.

Celadon was used for many wares: bowls, cups, dishes, wine pots, and oil bottles for the table; water bottles for the desk; water sprinklers for Buddhist rituals; tall, small-mouthed vases for holding plum blossoms; incense burners; roof tiles; toilet cases; and even (as in Egypt) ceramic pillows.

There were two general types of Koryo celadon: painted and inlaid. Painted celadon, the type adapted from Chinese precedents, was made by painting a design on the unfired, unglazed clay with an iron solution (or sometimes a copper oxide solution), then glazing and firing it. Inlaid celadon, unique to Korea, was made by incising a design into the raw clay (the incised designs being called *sonhwa*), filling the incisions with white or red slip, then biscuit-firing it (a preglazing firing at relatively low temperature). After being given the celadon glaze, it was fired again at higher temperature. Frequent subjects for the painted or incised designs were the peony, the lotus, stylized clouds, flying cranes, and dragons.

Metalwork

The chief Chinese accomplishments in metal were the use of bronze and the development of a number of decorative treatments of metal surfaces.

Bronzes   The oldest artifacts from China that we know are bronzes. China made mirrors of bronze as early as 500 B.C., and there were also bronze bells and gongs. The practice of bronze casting may have begun as early as 1500 B.C., and soon it acquired an astonishing level of skill and sophistication. Chinese bronzes can be divided into the functional and the ritual. Functional bronzes included cooking vessels, food servers, water containers, wine jars, and wine goblets. Ritual bronzes were intended for important ceremonies, and, because those ceremonies involved the ritual offerings of food and drink to deceased ancestors, their shapes were patterned after those of the functional bronzes (fig. 11–18). The shapes of both types of vessel were as highly specific, conventionalized, and repetitive as those of Greek vases. The ritual bronzes were, however, more carefully made and more richly decorated than their functional counterparts. Decorative motifs included dragons, birds, oxen, sheep, and goats. Inscriptions were made of the names of ancestors and inlaid with gold, silver, copper, and turquoise. The vase in figure 11–18 was inlaid with silver. To inlay gold or silver into harder metals by means of cutting grooves and hammering gold or silver wire into the grooves is called **damascening**.

Enamel and Cloisonné   Techniques for embellishing metals are enamel, cloisonné, and variations on cloisonné. **Enamel** is a term with several meanings. It can refer to a thin coating of material that, when fired, gives a durable, glossy surface to another material, such as pottery or porcelain; in these cases, it is synonymous with glaze. As commonly used today, it refers to a paint that imitates such a glaze. In the decorative arts of China and Japan, among others, enamel refers to a paste—thicker than a surface finish—that vitrifies when fired, becoming hard and glassy; as this process occurs, it fuses with

Tools & Techniques | THE CASTING AND CARVING OF BRONZE

Bronze is an excellent medium for the reproduction of decorative motifs in fine detail. It can be molded or carved, being able in its molten state to flow into every crevice of a mold and also highly susceptible to the graver's tool. It is an alloy of copper and tin (other alloys frequently used in the decorative arts being **brass**, composed of copper and zinc, and **pewter**, composed of lead and tin). In ancient Chinese bronzes, the percentage of tin varied from 5 percent to 20 percent. The addition of a small amount of lead made the material flow better, lowered the alloy's melting point, and improved the finished surface. Alloys were heated in earthenware crucibles, then poured into clay molds or forms made by the **lost wax** method, in which plaster or clay is formed around a wax model that, when melted, provides a cavity in which a replica alloy form can be cast. The techniques of Chinese bronze casting were dependent on the techniques of the potter, which were even older (just as the potter was preceded by the basket maker). Bronzes, in turn, influenced later pottery, with the shapes of the metal containers translated into less expensive ceramic versions.

There are a number of variations in the techniques of cloisonné. One technique used by the Romans is **champlevé**, in which the small cells are formed not by attaching wires but by carving or etching hollows in the base metal. In **repoussé** work, the metal surface (usually silver or copper) is beaten or hammered into low relief; this term is applied even to metal relief work that is not enameled. In **basse-taille** (French for "shallow cut"), the surface (usually silver or gold) is similarly beaten or hammered, but then immersed completely in a translucent enamel, so that the entire surface is coated, but with the color of the enamel strongest where the relief is more deeply indented. Fourteenth-century basse-taille pieces made in France were called **Paris enamels** and contemporary pieces from Italy were called *basso relievo*. In **plique-a-jour** (French for "against the light"), translucent enamel is spread over a thin metal filigree so that light can shine through it.

▲ **11–18** Inlaid bronze ceremonial vase with cover, from the Warring States period, 6 inches (15 cm) high.
Ting, China, 4th–3rd century B.C. Bronze with inlaid silver decoration. The Minneapolis Institute of Arts. Bequest of Alfred F. Pillsbury. 50.46.76a,b.

▲ **11–19** Cloisonné enameled basin with a lobed rim, c. 1600, 20 in. (50 cm) in diameter.
© The Trustees of the British Museum

its metal backing or metal container. It would be relatively simple to create such a surface in a single color, but a challenge to create multicolored designs. To prevent areas of one color from bleeding into areas of another, techniques were devised in the East for containing the prefiring pastes within small cells. The best-known of these techniques is **cloisonné**, in which the cells are created by gluing or soldering thin metal ribbons or wires to a metal plate, forming thin partitions (in French, *cloisons*) within which the paste could be held. The cloisonné technique was perfected in China c. 1430 and used for basins (fig. 11–19), dishes, jars, ice chests, incense burners, and more.

Lacquer and Shellac

Lacquer is a durable, glossy, tough material that can be brilliantly colored and expressively carved. Its production requires time, skill, and patience. It is made from the sap of the *lac* tree, a variety of sumac indigenous to China and Korea and later introduced into Japan. When the raw lac is gathered

▲ **11–20** A Ming dynasty lacquer dish reproducing a 4th-century party scene, 19 in. (49 cm) in diameter.
© The Trustees of the British Museum

and purified, it is a shiny, translucent gray syrup that, on exposure to the air, **polymerizes**, its small molecules combining to form larger ones. This process causes the syrup to harden into a tough, durable material. The syrup, therefore, must be stored in airtight jars until the hardening is wanted.

Lacquerwork is a technique of multiple layering, letting each layer dry before applying the next. Most commonly, the layers coat a core of wood or woven bamboo, but some lighter, thinner, more delicate examples are made by alternating layers of cloth and lacquer, or by lacquering onto a foundation of cloth, which is later removed.

Color is not natural to the lac but is created by adding mineral pigments, such as iron to produce black or mercury to produce red, the two most traditional colors. The brownish red called *cinnabar*, made with mercuric sulphide, was a particular favorite. Multicolored and sculptural effects are also possible. Different layers can be of different colors, and the outer layer then incised to reveal the color beneath. Lacquerwork objects include dishes (fig. 11–20), bowls, jars, toilet boxes, trays, cabinets, low tables, and folding screens.

In the eighteenth century, there was a great demand in the West for the import of Chinese lacquerwork, particularly large screens in low relief (while similar but smaller screens were being made for the Chinese home market). So many of these were shipped to Europe, Russia, Mecca, and elsewhere by way of the Coromandel Coast of southeast India, where the East India Company had a trading post, that the popular term in England for this kind of lacquerwork was **Coromandel ware**.

Because true lacquerwork was expensive to produce and difficult to access out of China, imitations such as shell-lac, seed-lac, and gum-lac were developed. The most successful of these was shell-lac, or **shellac**, obtained by boiling an insect larva until it secretes a liquid, or by taking the liquid from tree branches where the insect has deposited it. The liquid hardens when spread in thin sheets, and the sheets can later be dissolved in an alcohol medium, then used as a transparent paint to produce a lacquerlike appearance. It is not, however, as durable or waterproof as true lacquer.

Shellac was not used in China, but it was used extensively in the European eighteenth-century imitation lacquerwork called *japanning*. Japanning reached its highest level of accomplishment in France with developments made by Guillaume Martin (died 1749) and his three brothers; their products, and later imitations of them, were called **vernis Martin**. (The term *japanning* is also used for some kinds of painting on metal, such as toleware, which will be considered in a later chapter.)

Textiles

Textiles of many kinds were important to the economic and cultural development of China. Here we shall concentrate on the two most important examples, Chinese silk and Chinese carpets.

Silk   To the ancient Romans, China was *Seres*, the Land of Silk. The process of making silk was discovered, according to the *Odes* of Confucius, when the Princess Hsi-Ling (c. 2700 B.C.) was drinking tea under a mulberry tree from which a cocoon fell, unraveling its lustrous thread in her teacup. The actual history of silk may have been less poetic, but the raising of silkworms for the production of silk in China was well established by c. 1750 B.C.

Silk is the world's most beautiful textile fiber, wonderfully supple and possessing an unmatched natural luster. Having also a natural affinity for dye, it can be produced in brilliant colors. Its filaments are extremely long, with

Silk production begins with the growing of white mulberry trees, then proceeds to the selective breeding and raising of the grayish silkworms that are the larvae of the moth *Bombyx mori*. These caterpillars, said to be so delicate that loud noises or strong smells may kill them, feed on the young mulberry leaves, freshly gathered and finely chopped for them daily, and then, from glands in their heads, spin their cocoons. If the chrysalis within a cocoon is allowed to mature, it will eat its way out, severing the long filaments. The cocoon must therefore be heated to kill the chrysalis. Unwinding the filament is the next painstaking chore, traditionally done with the cocoons floating in a bowl of boiling water, the strands from six or eight of them unraveled at once and spun together on a reel. Dyeing, weaving, and finishing processes can then begin.

There are many types of silk, and many grades. The two most fundamental categories are the **true silk** from the *Bombyx mori*, described above, and so-called **wild silk** produced by other species of silkworms. Among true silk, the finest is that made from the longest filaments, such as the types called *thrown silk*. In their production, an important step between reeling and weaving is the "throwing"

or twisting together of filaments, a greater number of twists per inch producing a yarn with greater contraction. Types of thrown silk include **tram** and **organzine**, both rather loosely twisted, and **crêpe**, tightly twisted, some strands to the left, some to the right, and placed alternately. **Crêpe de chine** is a type of construction with crêpe yarn made from **raw silk**, which is silk not cleansed of the natural gummy protein that binds it together in the cocoon. The retention of the gum results in an uneven absorption of dye, and this unevenness is considered attractive for many uses. Another construction made from crêpe yarn, of a transparent fineness, grainy texture, and soft sheen, is **silk chiffon**. Filaments too short to be twisted into thrown silk are twisted more crudely into *spun silk*, considered of lesser quality. A silk made of even rougher, more uneven filaments is known as *bourette*.

Best known among the types of wild silk is the *tussah* of India that was mentioned in the last chapter. The species of silkworm that produce wild silk feed on oak leaves, cherry leaves, fig leaves, or the poorer varieties of mulberry, and the results derived from these species vary greatly.

600 yards (550 m) being typical. Compare this to cotton, with filaments of 1 to 2 inches (25–50 mm) or wool, with filaments 1 to 18 inches (25–450 mm). Silk, being extremely thin yet extremely strong, is surpassed in strength only by nylon.

Silk has some disadvantages, however. Because of their very thinness, many silk filaments must be spun together to make a thread the size of a human hair, and the contents of 2,500 cocoons are needed to produce 1 pound (454 g) of silk yarn. Strong natural light, over a period of years, can cause silk not only to discolor, but to actually disintegrate. In humid conditions, the fibers are subject to mildew and rot. They swell when damp and shrink when dry, creating a condition called *hiking*. Silk fibers will burn (slowly), and they will abrade (roughen when rubbed), particularly in textiles that blend them with other fibers of high tensile strength. Another disadvantage, although one that lends silk some of its charm, is the curious process of producing it, a process that was a closely guarded secret of the Chinese for centuries and one that is largely immune to modern efforts at industrialization.

Silk fabric is sometimes classified as plain, figured, or embroidered. *Plain silk* is woven with no integral decora-

tion or pattern; *figured silk* does have such an integral pattern woven into it; and *embroidered silk* has a pattern applied to its surface by needlework (fig. 11–21). One type of figured silk is **brocade**, in which a raised pattern is created by interwoven threads of silver or gold. There are also a number of fabric types that were created to be made from silk fibers. These include **satin**, woven with its face smooth and lustrous, its back dull, and **taffeta**, a crisp weave with both sides glossy. Both are still made from silk, but now also from a number of other materials, such as rayon.

Silk production has, since its introduction, been an important part of Chinese life and lore (fig. 11–22). The Chinese monopoly on the process continued well into the Middle Ages when, c. 550, two Christian missionaries are said to have smuggled a few of the silkworm larvae from China to Constantinople.

Carpets   The finest Chinese carpets were woven of silk, and, for imperial use, metal threads were sometimes added to the silk. Wool was also used. Although some Chinese

◀ **11–21** Detail of a wall hanging with embroidery of colored silk floss and gold-wrapped thread on dark blue silk satin, Ming dynasty.
"Bodhisattva of Wisdom (Manjusri)," 1368–1644. Silk with silk and gold wrap threads. 17⅜ × 17⅝ in. Indianapolis Museum of Art, Martha Delzell Memorial Fund. 1992.66

carpets were designed in imitation of Persian examples, many were of designs original to China. These designs could be symbolic (employing Buddhist, Confucian, or Taoist symbols) or floral, or both at once. Some Chinese carpets, beginning in the nineteenth century, were pictorial, showing realistic figures or landscape scenes. Many designs have round or octagonal central medallions in a field that may be plain or diaper patterned. Corners may repeat segments of the central medallions, and borders between them are generally narrow.

No Chinese carpets earlier than the fifteenth century survive, but there are a number of examples from the early Ch'ing dynasty. Large-scale carpet production was not introduced in China until the late nineteenth century, however. Chinese carpets primarily use the **asymmetrical** or **Persian knot** (see Table 9–1: Characteristics of Islamic Carpets), with the **symmetrical** or **Turkish knot** (see "Tools & Techniques: Carpet Weaving" on page 184) sometimes used at the edges. In general, Chinese carpets are not finely knotted, having between 30 and 120 knots per square inch (5–20 knots per cm²).

The most popular colors in Chinese carpets were yellow, tan, blue, and white. Reds were sometimes used as well—never bright primary reds, but soft apricot or peach shades, or a deep persimmon color. The surface of the pile was often cut down around flowers, figures, or symbols, so that these stood out in relief.

An unusual Chinese use for carpets was to wrap them around cylindrical columns. Such carpets are narrow and long, with patterns—frequently depicting dragons—that align when their sides are joined. Generally called **pillar rugs**, (fig. 11–23) they were used in Buddhist

▲ **11–22** Detail from *Ladies Beating and Preparing Silk,* a painting attributed to the Sung dynasty emperor Hui Tsung.

Court Ladies Preparing Newly Woven Silk, detail. Photograph © 2007 Museum of Fine Arts, Boston.

temples in northern China, Mongolia, and Tibet. Another Chinese use for carpets is as chair covers (fig. 11–24). These were made in two pieces, one for the seat and one for the back, and the back cover was often stepped or scalloped to fit the form of the chair. Rectangular pile carpets were also used as k'ang covers.

Summary: Chinese Design

In the history of all the countries of the Far East, the culture of China has at every stage been both the oldest and the most advanced. It has also had the power to absorb and transform most outside influences, never losing its own well-established character. Despite invasions by Mongols and Tartars, despite intercourse with border nations such as India, Persia, and Scythia, and despite later contact with the West after the

◄ **11–23** Detail of a pillar rug with a dragon motif. When the rug is wrapped around a column, the two halves of the dragon align.

The Textile Museum, Washington, D.C., RR51.2.1 Acquired by George Hewitt Myers in 1927.

▲ **11–24** Chair seat and back of knotted wool pile, nineteenth century. The loose weave in the middle would have been cut and stitched back to make two separate peices. It has forty-nine knots per square inch.

Cover for seat and chair back; hand–knotted woollen pile; Chinese; c. 19th century. Victoria & Albert Museum, London/Art Resource, NY

opening of the silk trade routes, Chinese design maintained its own dignified, independent, and highly accomplished course for thousands of years.

Independent as China remained from foreign influences, its own influence abroad was enormous, especially on its neighbors to the east—Korea and Japan. Less pervasive, but perhaps even more remarkable, has been China's influence in Europe and America. Chinese enamels and porcelains were brought to Europe by non-Chinese travelers. Throughout the seventeenth and eighteenth centuries, the East India trading companies imported large numbers of porcelains and silks, firing a European passion for duplicating their closely guarded methods of production. By the middle of the eighteenth century, Chinese taste affected European furniture design, interior design, and every branch of the decorative arts. In France, Chinese style was thought to blend particularly well with the Rococo style of Louis XV, and, at the chateau of Chantilly and elsewhere, entire rooms were painted in the modified Chinese style that the French called **chinoiserie**. In England, Thomas Chippendale was an enthusiast of Chinese taste, using it to create a new hybrid furniture style that was widely imitated. In the American colonies, wallpapers in Chinese style covered important rooms in Williamsburg and Philadelphia.

Looking for Character

Chinese beauty is quiet beauty. Its essence is a small, finely wrought, perfectly formed object and a serene, uncluttered space in which to enjoy it. Chinese art also shares with other art of the East a character—conventional, symbolic, and highly stylized—that is immediately recognizable as being outside the Western tradition. The occasional and understanding introduction of such serenity, simplicity, quality, and character into today's Western interiors can be a valuable element in the interior designer's vocabulary. We also see in Chinese design a tendency toward the use of curving and circular forms: vases swell, roof eaves curve, table legs turn, painted landscapes are caught up in a rhythmic swirl. Related to this tendency, there is also an apparent preference for continuity, whenever possible. When rosettes or stars or other small motifs are repeated, they are generally not isolated but are bound together with connecting elements such as scrolls or ribbons or branches.

The world is a coherent whole, the Chinese designer seems to be saying, and it is a coherent whole alive with movement.

Looking for Quality

Even in the smallest of details—or, more accurately, *especially* in the smallest of details—the Chinese artist was a perfectionist. We see this demonstrated in many arts and crafts, but we see it most clearly in finely made, subtly shaped furniture, in lustrous silks, and in exquisite porcelain. We shall see in the next chapter that Japanese designers admired and cultivated a degree of roughness and informality in some of their work. So did some Korean designers, but we see none of this tendency in Chinese designers. All Chinese artists and craftsmen kept before them the ideal of a faultless product; a surprisingly large number of them had the techniques to achieve it.

Making Comparisons

Chinese design is the chief embodiment of the qualities that distinguish Eastern design from Western. The distinctions are perhaps most strikingly shown when we compare Chinese design in its native home with Chinese design intended for export to the West and conforming (the Chinese thought) to Western taste. We may also compare real Chinese design with the Western *chinoiserie* that was a foreign imitation of it, conforming (the Europeans thought) to Chinese taste. The export versions and the imitations, by themselves, would give us an impression that Chinese design was often overwrought and overly ornate, and that the Chinese designer was often a sentimental clown. This is a false impression. Chinese design for a Chinese audience was impressively mature, serious, sophisticated, and sober. In the fields where it focused its attention, it was masterful.

Japan

A.D. 593–1867

"Wood is universally beautiful. . . . And yet, among higher civilizations, the Japanese understood it best. . . . The simple Japanese dwelling with its fences and utensils is the *revelation* of wood."

— Frank Lloyd Wright (1867–1959), architect

China profoundly influenced Japanese design, but Korea, Europe, and Polynesia also affected Japan. In most cases the Japanese imbued the foreign styles and forms with Japan's own character. In place of Chinese formality and axiality, for example, the Japanese liked things impromptu and off center; in place of the Chinese admiration for age, lineage, and permanence, the Japanese valued serendipity and change; and in place of the Chinese ideal of perfection, the Japanese, like the Koreans, at times treasured variation, even imperfection.

Determinants of Japanese Design

Japanese design has a distinctive character of plainness, naturalness, and attention to minute detail (fig. 12–1). And this attention to detail extends to some endeavors other cultures take for granted: the preparation of tea, the display of flowers, the arrangement of stones in a garden, the writing of characters. For the Japanese, these all have subtle relationships to religion and to design as well.

Geography

Japan is a group of islands off the east coast of Asia. There are four chief islands, the largest being Honshu, where the old capitals of Nara and Kyoto and the present capital of Tokyo are all located. There are almost 4,000 small islands. To Japan's south and east is the Pacific Ocean; to its north and west, the Sea of Japan. Mountains, many of them volcanic, crowd the main islands, which are intensively cultivated and densely populated. In Japan few places lack a view of the mountains or are far from the sea.

Plentiful forests have encouraged building in wood and bamboo, a practice further encouraged by Japan's frequent earthquakes, in which wooden structures are safer than heavy masonry ones. However, granites and volcanic rocks are often used for platforms and foundations.

Religion

From India, through China, came Buddhism, and directly from China came Confucianism, both of which became

◀ **12–1** Detail of a panel in a pair of two-panel folding screens by Sakai Hoitsu in ink, gold, and silver on paper, c. 1821, 6 ft. (182 cm) high.
Sakai Hoitsu, "Flowering Plants of Summer and Autumn." Tokyo National Museum, TNM Image Archives Source: http://TnmArchives.jp

233

Date	Period	Cultural Events	Artistic Events
A.D. 593–644	Asuka	Capital at Asuka; Buddhism introduced from Korea; emulation of China	Buddhist temple at Hōryū-ji
645–710	Early Nara	Capital at Ōtsu and elsewhere	Hōryū-ji burned and rebuilt
710–784	Nara	Capital at Nara	Shoso-in Imperial Repository established
784–1185	Heian	Capital at Kyoto; high court culture; esoteric Buddhist sects	Hand scroll painting; calligraphy; Hōōdō; *Tale of Genji*
1185–1334	Kamakura	Capital at Kamakura; Zen Buddhism adopted; military dictatorship	Painting; lacquerwork
1334–1573	Muromachi	Capital at Kyoto; Zen dominant; rule by warlords	Ink landscapes; Noh drama
1573–1614	Momoyama	Capitals at Momoyama and Azuchi; first Westerners arrive	Warlords' castles; gold screens; Shinto shrines; Zen temples; raku ware
1615–1867	Edo	Capital at Tokyo; Japan closed to foreigners; ceramic artists brought from Korea; peace and prosperity	Wood-block prints; Katsura villa; "scholarly decorators"; lacquerware
1868–1912	Meiji restoration	Japan open to foreigners; industrialization	Traditional and Western arts coexist

major religions (or ethical systems) in Japan. But there was also Shinto (or "the way of those above"), an ancient religion native to Japan. In Shinto belief, "those above" are supernatural deities with power over important human activities and fortunes, such as the fertility of crops.

The Shinto deities were not generally worshiped with icons and images. Shinto art is therefore an art of a limited variety of artifacts, such as vessels and relics. But a distinctive Shinto architecture of simple, unpainted wooden shrines did develop, usually placed in quiet, serene settings. In contrast, Buddhist temples are plentiful and often built in the hearts of cities. Sometimes a Shinto shrine is part of a Buddhist complex, representing local natural forces among the universal values of Buddhism.

Through many centuries, Buddhism, Confucianism, and Shintoism have affected Japanese thought and design. Japanese Buddhism, for example, split into individualistic sects, such as Zen, which fostered its own style of worship and of art. Zen Buddhism focuses on an individual's "inner" Buddha. It arose in China (where it was called *Ch'an*) and was introduced to Japan in the twelfth century. It emphasizes simplicity and self-discipline and promotes a daily routine of meditation and manual labor. Naturally, it appealed to the caste of professional warriors called *Samurai* who were fiercely proud of their indifference to hardship.

Although not a technique for producing artifacts but spiritual enlightenment, Zen affected both interior design and landscape design. Gardens were important to Zen Buddhists, with chores such as weeding and raking gravel seen as likely paths to enlightenment. In garden design, Zen influence favored nonflowering plants and grasses and naturalistic effects: arbors, irregular stepping stones, and low water basins for hand washing. In the Muromachi period (1338–1573), Zen gave rise to the tea ceremony, which, as we shall see, demanded a distinctive etiquette, a distinctive set of artifacts, and a distinctive interior. This demand was, in turn, a great stimulation to Japanese ceramic arts. For design in general, the Zen taste was for irregularity, asymmetry (although Zen temples were usually symmetrical, surrounded by asymmetrical gardens), and accidental or unexpected effects (such as the blue and white checkerboard wall in the Katsura Palace, as seen in fig. 12–5).

History

In the first centuries A.D., Japan was ruled by competing clans, with the Yamato clan gradually becoming stronger than others, laying the foundation of national unity and the rule of emperors. Contacts with Korea, less than a day's boat trip away, were always close, and from the sixth through the eighth centuries there was strong influence from the T'ang dynasty in China. Other families came to power and there were years of civil warfare until, in the twelfth century, the country came under the rule of military dictators called Shoguns. The Shoguns ruled Japan for the next seven centuries.

The first Japanese contact with Europe was the arrival of Portuguese ships in 1542, and a small amount of trading with the West developed. In 1638, however, Japanese ports were closed to all foreign vessels, and for roughly 200 years Japan existed in splendid isolation, cut off from other cultures and strengthening its own tastes and traditions without outside influence. In 1854 American ships under Admiral Perry forced the opening of trade with the West. In 1867 the Shogun resigned. The next year imperial rule was restored and the capital moved from Kyoto to Tokyo, formerly called Edo. Since then Japan has become one of the most industrialized countries in the world.

Japanese Architecture and Interiors

As in Chinese architecture, wood is the chief material of Japanese architecture. Rows of columns—infilled with thin, often movable, panels of woodwork, plaster, or rice paper—became the chief structure. As in Chinese and Greek architecture, framing is essentially **orthogonal** (vertical and horizontal). Graceful curves are introduced, however, in column outlines, rafters, roof brackets, and the great overhanging roofs they support.

Because this sort of wood construction is incapable of long spans, Japanese buildings are basically repetitions of bays, although bays at the center of an important structure may be twice the size of the typical bays. Structures may be three, five, seven, or some other odd number of bays long. Almost all traditional Japanese structures, sacred and secular alike, reflect certain similar characteristics. There are fixed

relationships between elements, and as one dimension is increased, others are increased proportionally.

Between the structural posts around a Japanese building's perimeter, the infill is much thinner than Western custom (or Japan's sometimes severe winters) would lead us to expect. A chief element of the exterior wall is the *shoji*, a sliding panel made of a light wood lattice with panels of translucent paper, functioning either as a door or window. This was often covered by a sturdier sliding wood shutter, the *amado*.

Interior areas among the various modular bays and around the columns that demarcate them are often divided quite freely. The spatial divisions are often made by *fusuma*, movable screens or panels sliding in floor tracks. They can be easily reconfigured (fig. 12–2). Like the shoji of the exterior wall, the fusuma was often made of paper, but sometimes silk was used, and sometimes it was decoratively painted. Above these sliding panels, which were generally about 6 feet (2 m) high, there were partially open areas that could be filled with rice paper or wooden grilles.

In addition to the modular repetition of identically sized bays in a typical Japanese structure, the sizes and shapes of rooms are traditionally based on a floor mat called the **tatami**

▼ **12–2** Movable screens, or *fusuma,* slide apart to reveal a reception room in the Old Shoin of the Katsura villa. Above them are panels of rice paper or open wood lattice. In the background at left is a slightly raised display niche called a *tokonoma.*
Photograph copyright © Yasuhiro Ishimoto. Courtesy of Photo Gallery International, Tokyo.

TABLE 12–1   Room Plans Based on Tatami Mats

Symmetrical arrangements, like the one at left, were used only for shrines or royal quarters. All other plans avoid four intersecting lines. The drawings show a variety of sizes, from the small four-and-a-half mat room, which would be appropriate for a small teahouse (the half mat for the fire pit) to an eighteen-mat room.

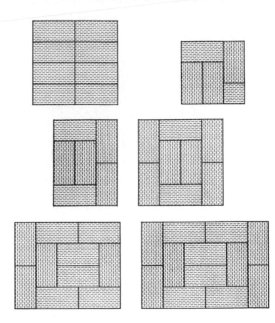

After Drekler

(see table 12–1), placed over floors of wood planks. The tatami is made from rice straw (although in modern times it has been reproduced in vinyl), its edges bound with black tape. It is about 2 inches (5 cm) thick and slightly larger than 3 by 6 feet (1 × 2 m). As shoes are not worn inside a Japanese house, the tatami remained clean enough to sit or lie on.

Some tatami used in a modern American context are seen in figure 21–65.

An interesting way of creating hierarchy within a room was for the rooms to have elevated areas where some emperors and Shoguns received their honored guests. Though also seated on the tatami-matted floor, their floor area was often raised one step above the rest.

In Japanese exteriors and interiors, the decorative elements are subordinate to the construction so that they embellish it without obscuring it. For an interior example, the **tokonoma** or display niche for flower arrangements, scrolls, or other art works, graces important rooms in Japanese houses without overpowering the uncluttered space of the interior. Figure 12–2 shows how the tokonoma (located near the rear entryway) is set off, with its floor raised slightly above the floor of the room, and partially enclosed to express its dis-

tinction. It becomes a natural yet understated focus, as the fireplace is the natural focus of many rooms today.

Lighting within the typical Japanese structure is diffuse, partly because the interior is shielded by deeply overhanging eaves, partly because the major spaces are often at the center of the structure, without direct illumination, and partly because openings are often screened with wooden shutters or paper partitions that softly filter the light.

Finally, the well-designed Japanese building presents its users with a consciousness of its surroundings. *Engawas*, or surrounding verandas, are transitional spaces between indoors and outdoors. Exterior walls have many operable elements that fold out or swing upward to afford views, and these views are often carefully calculated to include a distant mountain or an interestingly planted garden area. Whenever possible, such views are integral parts of room designs. They often are partial views (of a path or a stream, for example), leaving the rest to the observer's imagination. And in addition to gardens featuring plant material, there are Zen-inspired gardens of stones, pebbles, and sand (see fig. 12–24).

Japanese building types include Buddhist temples, Shinto shrines, pagodas (generally square in plan but sometimes octagonal and often attached to temples), palaces, houses, inns, and teahouses. As examples, we shall look at a temple, a house, and a teahouse.

A Buddhist Temple Precinct

After Buddhism was introduced to Japan in the sixth century A.D., buildings were needed for its observance. These were naturally based on Chinese examples, but with more attention to the provision of picturesque approaches and settings. A fine early example is the great late seventh-century Buddhist monastery complex of Ho-ryu-ji (pronounced "ho-ree-oo-gee"), near the ancient capital of Nara.

The 22-acre (9 hectare) complex houses the oldest Buddhist buildings in Japan. They include a series of gateways, a central lecture hall, a five-story pagoda, and a surrounding engawa. The original buildings are thought to have been built by Korean artisans in the late sixth century, but they were destroyed by fire in 670 and rebuilt. Added in the eighth century were a new outer gateway and an octagonal tile-roofed structure called the Yume-dono, or "Hall of Dreams" (fig. 12–3). The roof is supported on an elaborate system of brackets, adapted from Chinese precedents, and the interior houses a gilt-wood statue of the complex's founding Buddhist priest, which is kept in strict secrecy.

A Country Villa

Built by a member of the Japanese royal family, the Katsura Detached Palace is an imperial country retreat built near Kyoto. Construction began early in the seventeenth century

▲ **12–3** Interior of the octagonal Hall of Dreams at the Horyu-ji temple complex. In the foreground is a statue of the Buddhist priest who established the shrine.
From "Architecture of the World": Japan, Henri Stierlin, ED. Lausanne: Benedikt Taschen Verlag GmbH, Cologne, Germany. Photo by Yokio Futagawa.

Viewpoints | CHRISTOPHER DRESSER ON THE JAPANESE HOUSE

British designer Christopher Dresser (1834–1904) was a pioneer of modernism (see fig. 20–59) and has been called the first independent industrial designer. In 1862 he first saw Japanese objects at the London Exhibition, and in 1876 he was the first European designer to visit Japan. In 1882 he wrote one of the first European books on Japanese design, *Japan: Its Architecture, Art, and Art Manufactures.* This was his impression of the Japanese house: "[T]he Japanese may be said almost to live an out-of-door life, the house being rather a floor raised above the ground with a substantial roof than a series of rooms . . . enclosed by substantial side walls. . . . The windows consist of light frames filled in with a delicate and beautiful wood latticework covered with thin paper. . . . The floor is covered with matting; the ceiling, like the window-sashes, is entirely of unpainted wood, and altogether the room has an air of cleanness and beauty which is most pleasing. . . . [A]ll Japanese kneel upon the floor when collected together for any entertainment; indeed, there is neither chair, table, nor anything that we can regard as furniture in any native Japanese room."

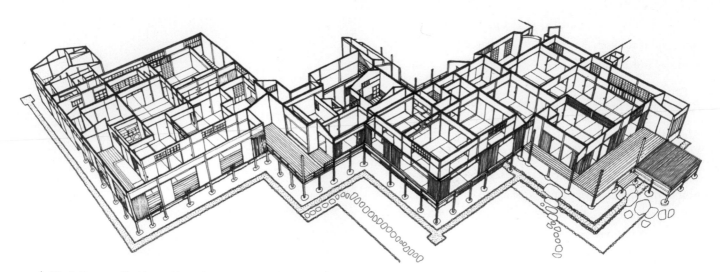

▲ **12–4** Perspective view with roof removed, Katsura Imperial Palace. From left to right, the new Shoin, the Middle Shoin, and the Old Shoin with its projecting moon-viewing platform.
Kazuo Nishi and Kazuo Hozumi, "What is Japanese Architecture?," New York, Tokyo and San Francisco: Kodansha, Reprinted by permission of Kodansha America, Inc.

and was completed in 1658. The complex of main house, teahouses, and Buddhist chapel is arranged around the shores of an irregularly shaped pond.

The main house is in three linked sections (Old Shoin, Middle Shoin, and New Shoin) in a zigzag plan, called in Japanese a "flying geese" plan (fig. 12–4), a break from the earlier Chinese model of rectangular structures. Its construction is wooden post-and-beam with a roof shingled with cypress bark and deep eaves. Main living spaces face the pond, and behind them are kitchens, service areas, and servants' quarters. While the rooms of the New Shoin are more elaborately decorated than those of the two earlier wings, all three sections contain rooms that are simple and plain by most standards—and certainly by most imperial standards (fig. 12–5). Rooms are based on tatami mat patterns, giving the rambling composition a pleasant cohesiveness.

The spaces open freely to each other through sliding partitions. And they not only open to each other, but also to the exterior. Many spaces—platforms, covered verandas, entrance foyers—are intermediaries between the outside and the inside (fig. 12–6). This relationship between inside and outside may be the villa's most admirable feature. While the arrangement of the rooms and the landscaping of the gardens both display an apparent casualness, both of them—and the relationships between them—have been designed with great attention to detail.

A Teahouse

Accommodations for the highly ritualized ceremony of brewing and serving tea are varied. Sometimes they consist of only a small alcove within a building that serves other purposes. Ideally, they are separate, small buildings dedicated only to tea, and built in picturesque garden settings.

On the grounds of the Katsura villa, there were at one time five teahouses, four of which are still extant. These are even more rustic than the main house. We shall look at one of them, the Shokin-tei or "Pine-Lute Pavilion" (fig. 12–7). It is unusually large in size, having two rooms: an irregularly shaped room with eleven mats and a hearth, and a rectangular room with six mats. There are some subsidiary spaces in addition to the tearoom.

It is also exemplary in other ways. On a promontory extending into the pond, the teahouse can be approached by a boat mooring or by a stone slab bridge. The path from the stone bridge passes a spot at the edge of the pond where visitors can wash their hands in running water, and other

▶ **12–5** Interiors of the Katsura Imperial Villa, near Kyoto, 17th century: above, a checkerboard wall behind the *tokonoma* of the First Room of the Shokin-tei teahouse; below left, the entrance to the Shoiken Pavilion; below right, the Second Room of the Shokin-tei looking into the First Room.
Tibor Bognar/Alamy Images

▼ 12–6 Entrance porch to Katsura's Old Shoin mediates between exterior and interior.
Abercrombie

▲ 12–7 In the Katsura Villa's Shokin-tei teahouse, an artfully composed backdrop for the tea ceremony.
Photograph copyright © Yasuhiro Ishimoto. Courtesy Photo Gallery International, Tokyo.

nearby garden features include areas called the Beach Garden and the Outside Resting Place. This exemplifies the Japanese theory that the ideal setting for a teahouse is in a garden, with a path leading through it that is indirect and circuitous. It may follow the edge of a small stream, then cross it with an arched bridge, as here at Katsura Villa. Along the way may be flowering shrubs and trees, stone lanterns, and a view of a distant mountain. Finally reaching the teahouse, the tea master and his or her guests stoop to enter, for the door (a "creeping-in door") is too small and low to enter standing up.

Once inside, even the conversation of the guests is prescribed, proper subjects including paintings, poetry, and the arrangement of flowers. As Dr. Rand Castile, Founding Director of the Japan Society in New York and later the Director of the Asian Art Museum in San Francisco, wrote in his 1971 book *The Way of Tea*: "Basically, drinking tea is an ordinary experience, but in the tea ceremony the experience is so concentrated that one finds [oneself] encouraged to look within, to discover not a new self but the natural self so often covered up by successive layers of civilization."

Within the Sho-kin-tei, a carefully considered asymmetrical composition of elements is the backdrop for the tea ceremony. Lines are straight and surfaces rectangular, except for the wall plane bounded by a structural support formed from a slightly bent tree trunk. It rises from one corner of a shallow pit where the fire will be made for boiling the tea. Beyond the tree-supported wall plane, a pair of shelves is held in place by a bamboo pole hung from the ceiling, providing a place for some of the tea utensils.

Japanese Ornament

As in China, building roofs were given graceful upward tilts with elaborate overhanging eaves supported on brackets. Beam ends were protected from the weather with ornamental metal caps. Doors of temples and other important buildings were given huge hinges and studded with ornamental nails, some with nailheads as large as three inches in diameter (fig. 12–8). Other ornamental metal fittings included locks, latches, escutcheons around keyholes, pulls, hinges, handles, rings through which carrying poles could be threaded, and finger holes for sliding panels. These fittings were made of iron, brass, copper, silver, or silver-nickel, although iron was by far the most widely used.

Motifs in Japanese ornament are taken from nature. A popular one is the image of Mount Fujiyama, its top crowned

▼ **12–8** Christopher Dresser's drawing of ornamental nailheads from Japanese doors.
Christopher Dresser, "Traditional Arts and Crafts of Japan." Dover Publications, Inc., New York, 1994, p. 114.

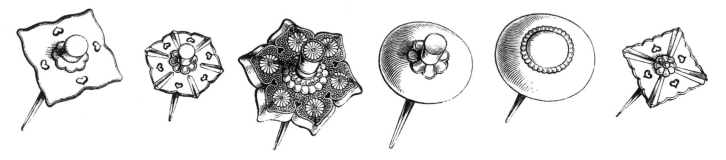

with snow, its base ringed with Shinto shrines; it is as prominent in art and decoration as it is in the landscape. Other motifs include the chrysanthemum (an emblem of imperial rule), the crane (representing both national eminence and personal prosperity), the tortoise (longevity), and the bamboo (youth and strength). Prominent among Buddhist symbols is the "Wheel of Life," emblematic of the faith. There are also themes taken from classical literary works such as the twelfth-century *Tale of Genji*, and every important Japanese family has its hereditary crest.

Japanese Furniture

In a traditional Japanese interior, the center of gravity is low, and the focus is on the floor. Within the flexible spaces, furniture is minimal and movable, so that by simply putting away a low table and bringing out a rolled pad, a room can be transformed from a dining room into a bedroom.

Seating and Beds

The most popular Japanese furniture woods included magnolia (in Japanese *ho-no-ki*), paulownia (*kiri*), zelkova (*kikeya*), white mulberry (*kuwa*), and chestnut (*kuri*). Chairs, until recently, have had only brief periods of popularity in Japanese interiors. Usually, the Japanese sat directly on the tatami mat, or they used one of two types of cushion. The first is an **enza**, or "round seat". About 20 or 22 inches (50 or 55 cm) in diameter, it is made of rice straw (like the *tatami*), rush, or some other plaited grass (fig.12–9). The enza were used in a wide variety of building types until the beginning of the seventeenth century; since then, they have been used primarily in temples and shrines. More popular now is a square padded cushion called a **zabuton**. Roughly 2 feet (60 cm) square, it is covered with cotton,

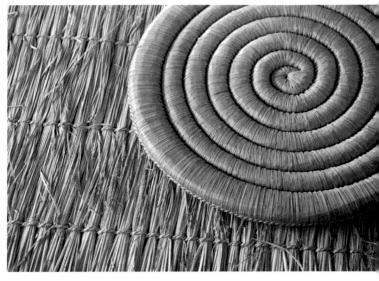

▲ **12–9** A rice straw cushion woven in a spiral, sitting on a straw mat.
Photo Japan/Alamy Images

linen, silk, or sometimes even leather, and is often embellished with *sashiko*, decorative stitching in geometric patterns. It is eminently easy to store, carry, or stack as desired. Adding to the comfort of sitting on the floor were wood armrests.

Beds traditionally played a minor part in the Japanese interior, as places for sleeping are generally **futon**, thin mattresses of padded cotton, which are rolled up and put away when not in use. Supplementing the futon are pillows and quilted coverlets.

Tables

Small tables were natural accompaniments to the floor-focused life, as were trays. Some of these small tables were on central pedestals (fig. 12–10), some were on broad

▲ 12–10 Footed tray table finished in lacquer. The height is 8 in. (20 cm) and the top is 12 in. (30 cm) square.
From "Traditional Japanese Furniture" by Kazuko Koizumi. Tokyo and New York: Kodansha International. 1986 and 1995. Reprinted by permission.

▲ 12–11 Lacquered broad-pedestal tray table, 16th century, 7 in. (18 cm) high.
From "Japanese Antique Furniture", Tokyo and New York: Weatherhill, 1983. Fifth printing 1996. Reprinted by Permission. Photo by Rosy Clarke.

▲ 12–12 Lacquered reading desk for religious tracts, early 17th century, 8 in. (20 cm) high.
From "Traditional Japanese Furniture" by Kazuko Koizumi. Tokyo and New York: Kodansha International. 1986 and 1995. Reprinted by permission.

pedestals with decorative cutouts (fig. 12–11), and some were on corner legs.

There were small desks or writing tables as well, often used at special gatherings for the writing of verses or the reading of holy scriptures, and other scholarly pursuits. Emblematic of aesthetic, scholarly, or pious pursuits, they were often more elaborately carved or decorated than was usual in Japanese furniture (fig. 12–12). Emphasis on the accoutrements of writing may be related to the high regard given the art of calligraphy (see fig. 12–22), valued as artistic expression as well as communication.

Storage Furniture

The most popular piece of Japanese furniture is the storage chest called the **tansu**, considered so characteristic that the term is sometimes used for the whole field of Japanese cabinetwork. The plural is called *dansu*. The *tansu* is similar to the Chinese and Korean chests we have already seen, but the Japanese versions are more varied, often more complex, with more elaborate interior fittings, and more determinedly characterful and asymmetric. The most frequently seen are the merchant's chests, or *cho-dansu* (fig. 12–13), and the clothing chests, or *isho-dansu*, but perhaps the most striking are the staircase chests or *kaidan-dansu*, which doubled as storage and as stairs leading from the main floor of a house to its sleeping loft (fig. 12–14).

▲ 12–13 Merchant's chest of burl *zelkova* wood with iron hardware. The wood has been polished with rice bran to accentuate its grain. 19th century, 34 in. (87 cm) high.
Jay Dotson Photography

▼ **12–14** Staircase chest of cryptomeria wood, 19th century, 70 in. (177 cm) high.

Screens

Moveable screens were important parts of Japanese domestic interiors. A one-panel screen, standing about waist high on bracket feet, was often placed opposite the entrance to a house (fig. 12–15). More important were the folding screens, which could be moved about the house as needed, and used for breaking the line of vision in the open interiors, for blocking the wind, for shielding a veranda from the sun, and for marking off special areas of space, such as a sleeping area for a guest. When they had highly reflective gold backgrounds, they were useful in reflecting light into dim corners.

Folding screens were made of wood or of wood-framed canvas, paper, or silk. They might have any even number of panels, from two to ten. There were small versions, less than 2 feet (60 cm) high, called *pillow screens*; there were screens used around braziers during the tea ceremony; and there were screened clothes racks. The most classic examples, however, were those with six tall panels. A detail of a screen painting is shown in fig. 12–1, and a six-panel screen is seen in

▲ **12–15** A plate from a book printed in 1788 shows a standing screen on bracket feet. To its left, we see part of a folding screen. In the foreground is a performance by musicians and a trained monkey.
© The Trustees of the British Museum

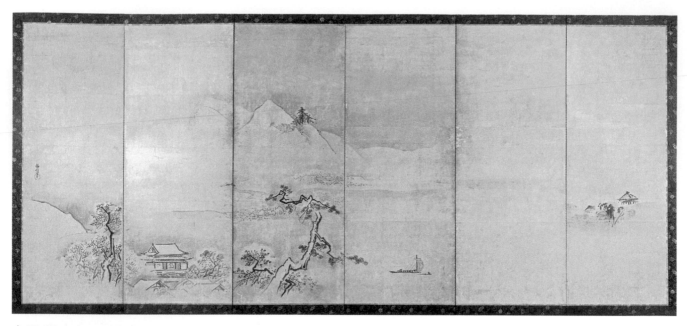

▲ **12–16** A six-panel screen titled "Winter Landscape" by Kanō Tōun Masunobu, ink and gold on paper, second half of the 17th century, 11 ft. 6 in. (351 cm) wide. The bold highlights and evocative empty areas are in the style of the artist's master, Kanō Tanyū.
Victoria & Albert Museum, London/Art Resource, NY

figure 12–16. Today, we consider Japanese screens works of art; to their original owners, they were pieces of practical furniture that happened to be decorative.

Lighting and Accessories

Minimal as Japanese furnishings were, they included a number of items for increasing comfort or usefulness. There were lighting devices, often incorporating the translucent papers that were so important to the Japanese interior during daylight hours (fig. 12–17). For those bravely enduring the Japanese tradition of unheated interiors, there were charcoal braziers or *hibachi*. These were never intended to heat a room in any substantial way, but merely to warm the hands of those seated nearby.

But perhaps the most important accessories in any home were those used in the Japanese tea ceremony. The process requires the use of a number of objects, each one of which may be a work of art (fig. 12–18). From the seventeenth and eighteenth centuries, these traditional implements for the Japanese tea ceremony include (left to right in fig. 12–18): a bamboo tea whisk made from a single section of a bamboo stalk; a cane holder for the tea whisk; a porcelain napkin ring; a black lacquer container for teabowls; an earthenware tea-caddy with a round ivory lid; and an earthenware teabowl.

▼ **12–17** An 18th-century painting on paper shows a lady grinding an ink stick on an ink stone. Behind her is a folding screen, and in front of her a paper lantern, similar to its modern interpretation by sculptor Isamu Noguchi.
Detail of painting by Nishikawa Sukenobu (1671–1751). Courtesy of the Freer Gallery of Art, Smithsonian Institution, Washington, D.C. F1899.19.

Other implements might include a wide-mouthed water jar, a bamboo dipper for taking water from the jar, an iron kettle for warming the water, a circular mat on which the hot kettle can be placed, a bronze rest for the lid of the kettle, a

▲ **12–18** Tools and containers for use in the Japanese tea ceremony, seventeenth and eighteenth centuries.

shallow basket for charcoal, a pair of bronze tongs for handling the charcoal, a feather brush for dusting away cinders or ash, a box for incense that can be added to the fire, a square of silk for wiping the teabowl after it has been washed, and—finally—the cups from which the tea will be drunk.

Japanese Decorative Arts

In Japan, more than anywhere else, it is difficult to make distinctions among arts, crafts, techniques, and rituals. Some pursuits, such as **ikebana**, the art of arranging flowers, are raised to high art in Japan, and some, such as making and serving tea, are central to the most refined rituals in Japan.

Ikebana

The art of arranging cut flowers has achieved a degree of excellence in Japan as it has nowhere else and is an important display in the designed interior. Called *ikebana*, or "living flowers," it has an intense aesthetic sensibility and an ancient lineage, the earliest school of flower arranging having been founded 1,300 years ago by a member of the royal court who sought to devise appropriate floral offerings to Buddha. Now there are more than 300 distinct schools of flower arranging

in Japan, each with its own philosophy and style, but all share the general precept that flowers and plant materials are to be presented in ways that suggest how they naturally grow. This goal of representing natural form, however, is accompanied by the goal of adhering to strict and quite man-made rules about the numbers (always an odd number) of major branches in the arrangement, and the lengths and shapes of those branches. Ikebana presents another example of the curious practice in Japanese art of the application of artificial rules to achieve natural appearance. The *tokonoma* (fig. 12–19) is the alcove in homes used for the display of ikebana and other artistic treasures.

Ceramics

It is probably due to the long popularity of the tea ceremony that ceramics have a place of special importance in Japanese culture. The earliest Japanese ceramics—and these may date from as long ago as 10,000 B.C. and are possibly the oldest ceramics in the world—were formed by coiling cords around the moist clay, leaving the finished pots with impressions of the cords. The potter's wheel may have been introduced in the fifth century A.D., and at about the same time, itinerant potters from Korea produced Japan's first stoneware. Fired at a

◀ **12–19** A *tokonoma* alcove in the Ryogen-in Temple, Kyoto, displays an *ikebana* flower arrangement in a bronze vase and a scroll of dramatic calligraphy.
Ken Straiton Photography

and *Imari ware* are used for that area's porcelains, and the term *Hizen ware* for any of its ceramics. Imari ware, in particular, was shipped to Europe in great quantities in the eighteenth century and much imitated in the eighteenth and nineteenth centuries by European porcelain factories, such as Derby and Spode in England, Sèvres in France, and Meissen in Germany. In the Zwinger Palace, Dresden, near the Meissen factory, there are some Imari-style vases and covered jars of monumental size. Imari designs (fig. 12–20) were very showy by Japanese standards, usually based on a blue underglaze partly covered by brightly colored enamels, especially a deep red, and sometimes with gilt added.

Tea Ceremony Wares   Very different from Japan's fine porcelains were the wares meant for use in the tea ceremony. For this use a natural appearance was wanted, and the most highly prized pieces were intentionally rough and irregular. These may be made of **raku**, or "enjoyment," ware (fig. 12–21), which is a molded (not thrown) earthenware that originated in Kyoto. It is a rough-textured, low-fired pottery with black, white, brown, or pink glaze, usually formed without a handle. For the tea ceremony's evocation of nature, the *raku* cup is considered perfect in its deliberate imperfection. Its insulating property keeps the tea hot and makes the cup comfortable to hold; black or dark brown raku ware, in particular, was thought to complement the color of the frothy green tea. Production methods were often passed from generation to generation in families of potters, and the vessels themselves were passed from tea-master to tea-master, gaining in value as their pedigree grew.

high temperature, the stoneware was, unlike the earthenware produced earlier, waterproof.

In the sixteenth century, Korean potters also established potteries in the Japanese province of Satsuma. Satsuma wares were of two distinct types: simple earthenware vessels made for Japanese consumption, and elaborately decorated tin-glazed wares made for export to the West.

Porcelain   By the seventeenth century deposits of China clay had been found in Japan, and the Japanese began imitating the fine porcelain wares of China and Korea. An important early center of porcelain production was at Arita in the province of Hizen, and its wares were shipped from the port of Imari. Today the terms **Arita ware**

▲ **12–20** An *imari* ware plate in a typical palette of enamel colors over underglaze blue. Made at Arita, late 19th century.
Bryan Sentance from: "Ceramics: A World Guide to Traditional Techniques," Thames & Hudson, London & New York

▲ **12–21** A *raku* ware tea bowl, early 17th century, 5 in. (13 cm) in diameter.

Tea bowl, named "Tamamushi (Golden Beetle)," Japanese, Edo period, early 17th century. Black Raku ware, earthenware with black lead glaze. H. 3⅜ in., Diam. 5 in., Bottom 2 in. Seattle Art Museum, Gift of Dr. Masatoshi Okochi, Tokyo. Photo: Paul Macapia

Lacquer

The previous chapter traced the development of lacquer in China and mentioned that European imitations of Eastern lacquer wares were called "japanning." Many terms for lacquer styles and techniques are, in fact, Japanese. That is natural, for after lacquering techniques were introduced into Japan from China, the Japanese became unequaled, even by the Chinese, in their use. An example of Japanese lacquer, and also another example of the Japanese reverence for all things related to writing, is a small container for writing implements (fig. 12–22); it also demonstrates how the Japanese use artistry to raise a simple daily chore almost to the level of religious ritual.

Textiles

Textiles were important parts of Japanese interiors, used for screens, scrolls, cushion covers, and protective bags for treasured tea ceremony utensils. Textiles were also important parts of religious rituals in temples and shrines. The earliest Japanese textiles were made from *bast*, a woody fiber taken from plants such as hemp, wisteria, mulberry, and *ramie* (a member of the nettle family). Silk was introduced from China in the second century A.D., and eighth-century Japanese poems suggest that by then silk had become the preferred luxury cloth, though bast continued to be used by commoners. Cotton may have been brought from Portugal in the fifteenth century, and soon after it was being cultivated in Japan for use in clothing, curtains, towels, cushion covers, and bedding.

Gradually, a Japanese taste for woven textile decoration was supplanted by a taste for surface decoration. Japanese surface treatments include painting, wood-block printing, wax-resist printing, and bound-resist dyeing (also called

---

Tools & Techniques | JAPANESE LACQUER

Japanese lacquer is sometimes called "true lacquer." Like Chinese lacquer, but unlike many imitations, it uses the sap of the lac tree, called *urushi* in Japan. Historically, Japanese lacquer was made in many variations. It was almost always applied to a wood base, but sometimes it was applied to leather (as in the case of *samurai* uniforms), and to metal, ivory, and porcelain. The number of layers was also variable, the finest wares going through as many as sixty stages of lacquer application and sanding, with one to five days of drying after each one. As in China, layers could be of several different colors, and designs could be incised in the surface to reveal the colors below. The Japanese also developed lacquer techniques with only a single layer, some of them transparent to reveal the wood grain beneath. In some versions, the wood is first colored with a tint, often yellow. Other techniques involve repeatedly brushing clear lacquer on the wood or rubbing it on with a cloth, then wiping off the excess, preventing a buildup on the surface, but allowing the liquid to penetrate deeply into the wood.

There are also dozens of variations in the techniques and materials used, each with its own name. A large category called *maki-e* is prepared by sprinkling ground gold and silver powders on a wet surface; within the category are many subcategories for different colors, different particle sizes, and different types of sanding. The teabowl container seen in the center of figure 12–18 is of *maki-e*, as is the writing box in figure 12–22. *Raden* is lacquer with mother-of-pearl inlay. Other lacquers have inlays of ivory, pewter, eggshell, glass, or ceramics. Some are decorated with small pieces of gold or silver foil. Some wares used in Buddhist ceremonies have black lower layers with a few red layers on top; the red layers are then sanded so that some black is exposed, imitating the effects of age and wear.

▲ **12–22** Interior of a lacquered wood writing box with an oval iron water dropper, a rectangular ink stone, and compartments for ink sticks and brushes. 17th century, 8 in. (21 cm) wide.

Interior of a writing box. Design of gosho–guruma (nobleman's cart) in maki–e lacquer. Tokyo National Museum, TNM Archives Source: http://TnmArchives.jp

▲ **12–23** A 17th-century weft-patterned silk brocade with a design of clouds and embroidered dragons.
Werner Forman/Art Resource, NY

tie-dyeing). Dyeing was initially limited to simple dyes like indigo that needed no mordant for setting; more sophisticated dyes followed. Even today—with plentiful chemical dyes—natural dyes are preferred in Japan for fine fabrics. Stencils were popular, and a Japanese variation (also developed quite independently in Nigeria) applied starch through stencils to form patterns resistant to dyeing. In another variation, adhesive was applied through stencils, and then gold powder, gold leaf, or silver leaf was pressed onto the adhesive. Embroidery (fig. 12–23) was used as early as the sixth century, and seventeenth-century illustrations show the large wooden frames on which long, narrow strips of cloth were dyed and then embroidered. A technique that seems particularly suited to the refined Japanese sensibility is one in which silk is stretched over carved wooden blocks and then stained by rubbing it with flower petals.

Summary: Japanese Design

The design of Japan is distinctive among the cultures of the East, but that distinction is not easily defined. The Japanese have a term for their artistic ideal: *shibui*. That ideal is generally defined by sets of contrasting qualities: an object with

shibui is quiet, but not inert; simple, but not superficial; beautiful, but not ostentatious; original, but not foreign; sober, but not dull. The Japanese ideal, therefore, is an artistic expression that strikes a careful balance and avoids extremes. The Greek ideal of "nothing in excess" might apply here, but the serene classical composure of Greek art is a world away from the character of Japanese art and design.

Looking for Character

Japanese design displays a respect for the idiosyncrasies as well as the harmonies of nature. It often eschews the axiality and alignment favored by Chinese design, preferring instead asymmetry and a dash of eccentricity. The Japanese artist shows us that imperfection—if presented with taste and restraint—can sometimes be more interesting than perfection.

Looking for Quality

If the Japanese artist values imperfection, then it would be strange for us to look for perfection. There is much immaculate craftsmanship in Japanese design, but we find the essence of Japanese taste elsewhere, when we look for the subtle exceptions to expected rules: the little bubble in the glaze of the teabowl, the tiny young bamboo sprout growing from the side of the bamboo vase, the irregular grain in the wood. To be more specific, the wood post in the Katsura teahouse (see fig. 12–7) is clearly natural and clearly not exactly vertical, yet it is not exaggeratedly picturesque or so eccentric that the room becomes undignified. This ability to find the correct balance between freedom and discipline is the mark of quality in Japanese design. It is the ability, for another example, to make an artistic statement in the placement of fifteen stones in a field of sand (fig. 12–24). No other culture would think to pose this problem; no other culture would solve it so beautifully.

Making Comparisons

The obvious comparisons for Japanese design are with the Chinese and Korean precedents that influenced it so profoundly, and there are many times when those precedents were followed slavishly.

The telling comparisons, of course, are those between Chinese art and that part of Japanese art that seeks to assert its own independent nature. Such a telling comparison can be made with bowls. The Chinese bowl may be a masterpiece of porcelain technique, a masterpiece of subtly curving form, and a masterpiece of glazing. It is an unquestionably admirable object. But the Japanese artist, like his Korean counterpart, does not always seek to emulate such an object, preferring at times to offer us a rougher form in cruder material and with apparently hastily applied glazing. The Chinese bowl is sublime in its quiet perfection; the Japanese bowl is sublime in its naturalness and its ingratiating character. Luckily for us, we can appreciate both models.

▲ **12–24** In the 17th-century garden of the Ryoan-ji Temple, Kyoto, 15 stones are artfully placed in a bed of raked sand.
Abercrombie

Italy: Renaissance to Neoclassical

Fifteenth to Eighteenth Centuries

13

"Gazing on beautiful things acts on my soul."

— Michelangelo Buonarroti (1475–1564), architect and artist

The word *Renaissance* means "rebirth." It identifies the renewed appreciation of the achievements of ancient Greece and Rome that began in the Italian town of Florence in the fourteenth century and eventually spread throughout Europe. Although a return to the art and knowledge of more than a thousand years before may not seem progressive, there was a feeling in Renaissance Italy that the achievements and attitudes of the ancient past were more applicable to new design needs than were those of the immediate past, the Middle Ages. And although this movement began with the imitation of past design it grew to include artistic productions of brilliant originality (fig. 13–1).

Determinants of Italian Design

The Italian Renaissance was a revolutionary, not an evolutionary, development in the history of design. Its great blossoming of creativity seems almost due to a profound change

◀ **13–1** Detail of the stair in Michelangelo's Laurentian Library, Florence, 1519.
Dagli Orti/The Art Archive

in human nature, so it is difficult to fully understand what brought it about. Nevertheless, we can identify some contributing factors.

Geography and Natural Resources

In the north the mountain chain called the Alps divides Italy from France, Switzerland, and Austria. In the northeast Italy shares a border with Yugoslavia. Except for these boundaries, the country is a long boot-shaped peninsula between branches of the Mediterranean Sea (the eastern branch is called the Adriatic, the western branch the Tyrrhenian.

At the time of the Renaissance, the country was not yet unified but divided into different city-states, each with its own customs, dialect, and resources. The three most important ones for the development of Renaissance design, and the ones most often mentioned here, were Florence, Rome, and Venice.

Florence is located slightly north of the center of the country, and under its economic and political influence were Genoa, Milan, and Pisa. Marble quarries in the nearby mountains offered an endless supply of beautiful marble with which to build. In Florence (and even more so in Rome) bright sun discouraged large windows and encouraged shady courtyards and colonnades, and throughout Italy the lack of snow made steep roofs unnecessary. The warm climate also suggested high ceilings and cool floors of tile, brick, or marble.

For Rome, the chief quarries were its own ancient monuments that lay all about, more plentiful and complete then than now. The Pantheon, the Colosseum, the forums and the baths were all mined for their travertine and other marbles, and for their columns, pilasters, and decorative carvings.

Venice was an island city offering almost no resources for building, but the Republic of Venice's seapower could bring quantities of stone, brick, and wood from many other locations. Because the shortage of land made gardens rare luxuries and because the summer heat was mitigated by sea breezes, balconies and belvederes were popular features. Cold winters made heating desirable, so the Venice skyline has a greater number of chimneys than other parts of the country.

Religion

In the Middle Ages, the Roman Catholic church, with its head in Rome, had become very powerful in Italy. But with great power had come the corruption and misconduct of church authorities. Even though Rome was the administrative center of the Roman Catholic church, Italians began to rebel against church strictures, their rebellion fueled by excessive taxation by church authorities, by corrupt church practices, and by the beginnings of scientific discoveries that eroded faith in church doctrine.

Reforms within the church were attempted by the Dominican monk Savonarola, who was burned at the stake for heresy in Florence in 1498, and by the German priest Martin Luther, who was excommunicated by the pope in 1520. These activities led to the Reformation and the Counter-Reformation, and out of these struggles emerged Protestantism. Although the Roman church retained some of its former power—and some of the greatest design of the Renaissance would be in service to the church—its domination was no longer absolute. Power was shifting. Secular interests were given new respect.

History and Patronage

Italians, in the Middle Ages, had come with some justification to consider themselves more civilized and more intelligent than the "barbarians" of northern Europe. The Italian poet Dante in his fourteenth century *The Divine Comedy* (a work revolutionary in being written in Italian rather than

Latin, the language of scholars) had given the country a vision of individuals as their own masters, not meant to be intellectual slaves of either church or state. Dante, as well as the poets Petrarch and Boccaccio, were all parts of a movement called Humanism. The Humanists were scornful of superstition, respectful of classical knowledge as well as of modern science, and concerned with the human condition and the arts. Their thinking revived a long-dormant appreciation of the pleasures of nature, the beauty of design, the joy of living, and the worth of the individual.

Joining the poets and intellectuals among the Humanists was Lorenzo de' Medici, a member of the now-famous family from Florence—a family that rose from obscurity to wealth through their work as merchants and bankers. Eventually, among the Medici family members would be three popes, several cardinals, two queens of France, and countless dukes. But they are most noted, as we shall see in this chapter, for their patronage of the arts.

The Medici were not alone in patronizing Renaissance arts and artists. Other artistically enlightened families included the Pitti and the Strozzi of Florence, the Sforza and Visconti of Milan, the Borgia and Borghese of Rome, and the Foscari and Vendramini of Venice. Rivalries developed among them, each wanting to outshine the others in the magnificence and excellence of their palaces and furnishings. Rivalries developed among cities as well. Both families and cities jealously protected their finest artists and craftsmen, generous benefactors furnishing them with studios and workshops.

Interest in art was not limited to the rich and powerful, however; it was also commonplace. It has been said that in the Italian Renaissance every farmer and clerk was a judge of art. The whole of Italy was obsessed with an enthusiasm for beauty.

Italian Architecture and Interiors

In a number of previous chapters we have focused on religious architecture and interiors. There continues to be outstanding examples of religious architecture in the Italian Renaissance, but there also begins ambitious residential design arising from the wealth and prosperity of the patrons from the upper class. Their palaces (*palazzi*) and villas are among the finest achievements of the Italian Renaissance.

Because the use of gunpowder by the armies of Europe greatly increased during the fifteenth century, the medieval fortified castle with its moat, drawbridge, and portcullis

Period & Date	Political & Cultural Events	Major Artistic Figures	Major Artistic Works
Early Renaissance, 1300–1500	The Black Death, 1348; Boccaccio's *Decameron*, 1353; Medici family gains power, by 1450; Lorenzo the Magnificent prominent in Florence, 1469–92	Giotto (1266–1337); Brunelleschi (1377–1446); Luca della Robbia (1399–1482)	Palazzo Davanzati, Florence, c. 1390; Brunelleschi's dome for the Florence Cathedral, 1420–36; Brunelleschi's Old Sacristy, San Lorenzo, Florence, 1421–29
High Renaissance and Mannerism, 1500–1600	Martin Luther spurs the Protestant Reformation, 1517; Vasari's *Lives of the Artists*, 1550	Leonbattista Alberti (1404–72); Donato Bramante (1444–1514); Leonardo (1452–1519); Michelangelo (1475–1564); Andrea Palladio (1518–80); Tintoretto (1518–94)	St. Peter's, Rome, begun 1506; Michelangelo's Sistine Chapel, Rome, 1508–41; Raphael's *stanze* and *loggie* in the Vatican, Rome, 1508–19; PalazzoFarnese, Rome, 1517–50; Michelangelo at San Lorenzo, Florence, 1519–62; Palladio's Villa Capra, Vicenza, 1565
Baroque, 1600–1720	Italian opera is born, early 17th century; Galileo uses a telescope to look at stars, 1610; his findings banned by the church, 1633	Gianlorenzo Bernini (1598–1680)	St. Peter's, Rome, completed in 1626; Bernini's work at St. Peter's, 1624–67
Rococo and Neoclassicism, 1720–1800	Last Medici ruler dies, 1737; excavations begun at Herculaneum, 1738	Filippo Juvarra (1678–1736); Giovanni Battista Tiepolo (1696–1770); Giambattista Piranesi (1720–78)	Tiepolo frescoes; Juvarra's hunting lodge at Stupenigi, 1729–35; Piranesi's S. Maria del Priorata, Rome, 1764.

became of little value for defensive purposes. As the forts were removed to more strategic outlying districts, construction of more luxurious city dwellings and suburban villas began to appear outside the ancient city walls. The Italians were the earliest designers of domestic architecture in which comfort, convenience, and beauty were the important considerations, rather than safety, strength, and protection. Consequently, most scholars agree that the maturing of the art of interior design began with this domestic architecture.

Early Renaissance Style

Scholars have divided the artistic wonders of Italian architecture in different ways. In this book we shall divide our discussion into four period styles: the Early Renaissance, the Renaissance and Mannerism, the Baroque, and the Rococo and Neoclassical.

Some historians date the beginning of the Early Renaissance to the early fourteenth century when Giotto, the Florentine painter, worked to observe nature closely and represent it truthfully in painting. This period can be said to

have lasted until the end of the fifteenth century, when it was replaced by the High Renaissance. Yet the Early Renaissance, as dramatically different from the preceding period as it was, cannot be said to have been fully born in a single moment or with a single artist's work. In all the fourteenth-century art forms, a transition from the lingering Gothic style is visible. An example is the Davanzati Palace, built in Florence a half century after Giotto's death.

Palazzo Davanzati, Florence   The façade of the late fourteenth-century Palazzo Davanzati has three wide-arched openings on the ground floor, in a departure from the small iron-grilled openings of earlier times. The two side openings are thought to have led to ground-floor shops selling wool, but the center arched opening leads to an interior courtyard surrounded by a loggia at all four levels, where the living quarters are located. This living-over-the-store arrangement recalls the ancient Roman *insula*.

Interiors combine old and new elements (fig. 13–2). The painted wood ceiling beams could be mistaken for medieval designs. The hooded fireplace in the corner is also a relic of

▲ **13–2** Painted walls of a bedroom in the Palazzo Davanzati, Florence, late 14th century.
Erich Lessing/Art Resource, NY

older times; it would be replaced in later buildings by designs similar to that in the upper right of figure 13–3, with a less prominent hood and a more prominent fireplace surround. The walls of the tall room, however, have been divided into geometric bands, and the band nearest the ceiling has been frescoed (see p. 265) with a pleasant arcade of vaults on pairs of Corinthian columns, the vaults being round, not Gothic points. A fresco in another room shows a parade of parrots, and still another depicts peacocks. On other walls, hooks are imbedded for the hanging of tapestries. Conveniences modern for their time include built-in cupboards and an enclosed dumbwaiter that could lift water or other supplies to all the upper floors.

Old Sacristy, San Lorenzo, Florence   In 1418, only about two dozen years after the Palazzo Davanzati was built and just a few blocks from it, Florentine architect Filippo Brunelleschi was invited by the Medici to design a new building for their parish church, San Lorenzo. In his work there we see no trace of the medieval past, but instead a vocabulary of forms wholly adapted from ancient Rome.

Brunelleschi (1377–1446) was born in Florence, the son of a minor government official, and after six years of apprenticeship was named a master goldsmith. After losing (to Lorenzo Ghiberti) a 1401 competition for the design of the now-famous doors of the Baptistery of Santa Maria del Fiore, Brunelleschi went to Rome to study ancient

▼ 13–3 Italian Renaissance architectural forms and furniture.
Gilbert Werlé/New York School of Interior Design

Credenza
About 1550

Table with baluster legs
16ᵗʰ Century

15ᵗʰ Cent. Hooded Mantel

Marble Mantel Late 15ᵗʰ Cent.

Florentine Arches

▲ 13–4 Brunelleschi's Old Sacristy in the church of San Lorenzo, Florence, 1418–29.
Scala/Art Resource, NY

architecture firsthand. In 1404, he joined an advisory commission on San Lorenzo, then under construction, beginning his long involvement, which would culminate in his design for the cathedral's dome, a technical and aesthetic triumph completed in 1434. Other famous designs by Brunelleschi, who must be considered the outstanding architect of the Early Renaissance, include the 1419 Ospedale degli Innocenti, a hospital for orphans, also in Florence. Its arcades of round-headed arches were ornamented with terra-cotta rondels designed by Luca della Robbia (see fig. 13–22).

At San Lorenzo, which replaced a Romanesque church from the fourth century, Brunelleschi's role in the design of the main church is uncertain, but his design of the Old Sacristy is undisputed. Begun in 1421, the Old Sacristy was the first part of the new church to be completed and now stands in the northwest corner of the complex. Its interior (fig. 13–4) is a perfect cube of space (from which dome-supporting pendentives in each corner are removed) topped by a hemispherical twelve-lobed melon dome. A smaller chapel with a lower ceiling is centered in the wall opposite the entrance, topped by its own smaller hemispherical dome. Sacristy and chapel share an entablature that runs around the whole perimeter and is articulated with fluted Corinthian pilasters. Circular ornaments fill the centers of the pendentives, taking the form of shells in the chapel, and each lobe of the main dome has a circular window. In the center of the sacristy are the sarcophagi of Brunelleschi's Medici patron and his wife, for this little building served as a mortuary as well. Materials and colors are minimal. The structural and important ornamental elements—the dome ribs, the pendentive outlines, the entablature and pilasters—are emphasized in gray sandstone, but all other surfaces are unadorned white plaster. The Old Sacristy was the first of Brunelleschi's buildings to be finished, and it established at once a high standard for the Renaissance: a thoughtfully composed, coherent space, its parts and their interrelationships artfully articulated.

High Renaissance Style and Mannerism

Brunelleschi led the way to the great artistic riches of the High Renaissance, which lasted from the beginning until the end of the sixteenth century. But along the way Michelangelo led some designers toward a less rational type of design called **Mannerism**, which still used a vocabulary of classical elements but in less conventional ways.

Other important High Renaissance figures include architect and theoretician Leonbattista Alberti (1401–72), who was from a Florentine family but moved to Rome in 1430 to study classical design. Alberti is best known for the church of Sant' Andrea in Mantua, begun in 1470, its façade based on Rome's Arch of Constantine. Donato Bramante (1444–1514) was born near Urbino in central Italy two years before Brunelleschi died; he designed the tiny but much admired "Tempietto" in 1502 for Rome's church of S. Pietro in Montorio. Antonio da Sangallo (1485–1546) was born in Florence, where both his uncles were also architects; he worked with Michelangelo on the design of the Palazzo Farnese in Rome, begun in 1517, now the French Embassy. All three of these architects worked on the design of the most monumental project of all, St. Peter's, which we shall see in our section on the Baroque.

Palazzo Medici-Riccardi, Florence It is said that Cosimo de' Medici, the elder son of the patron for the Old Sacristy, commissioned Brunelleschi to design his palace in Florence, but rejected the design as too grandiose for the family's attempt to appear as ordinary citizens. Brunelleschi was replaced by Michelozzo di Bartolommeo (1396–1472). The palace is now known as the Palazzo Medici-Riccardi, because the Riccardi family bought it in the late seventeenth century and added several new but identical bays to its already considerable size.

Its three floors rise to a massive cornice (fig. 13–5), similar to that of a Roman temple but 70 feet (21 m) above the street, and, as they rise, their stonework becomes more smoothly textured at each level. The round-headed windows of the upper floors are separated by delicate colonnettes with Corinthian capitals. Window areas are small on the street, but are more generous in size when opening to the private courtyard. The pedimented windows in the ground floor arches originally opened to a loggia leading to an interior courtyard surrounded by an arcade (fig. 13–6). These windows were added by Michelangelo in the sixteenth century. Austere and fortresslike, the Palazzo Medici-Riccardi set the pattern for Florentine and Roman *palazzi* for the rest of the century and beyond.

The floor plans for the arrangement of rooms in all these *palazzi* used three guiding principles. First, there was the principle of symmetry, urged by all the architectural writers of the Renaissance. In the interest of order and clarity, this ideal mandated a central entrance, often with a vestibule leading straight to a central courtyard, with identical arrays of

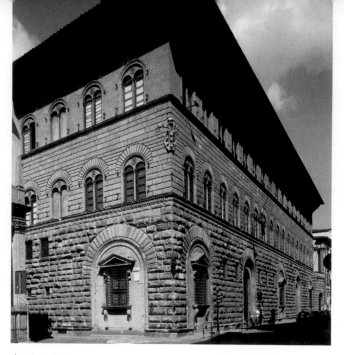

▲ **13–5** Palazzo Medici-Riccardi, Florence, by Michelozzo, begun 1446.
Scala/Art Resource, NY

rooms on either side. This ideal could not always be observed because in old cities there were many irregular pieces of land that prevented such construction.

Second, there was the principle espoused by Leon Battista Alberti and other writers that the most public rooms were those most immediately accessible from the main entrance, and that the deeper one penetrated into a house the more private the spaces became. This is so natural a principle that its use is commonplace in many cultures (in China, for one example).

Third, somewhat less obvious than the first two, was the principle of dividing large houses or *palazzi* into apartments, each a group of contiguous rooms that constituted the private realm of a single person (or married couple, although it seems to have been more common for a couple to have two linked apartments). This principle has remained a historically significant rationale for the floor plans of interiors. Within principle three, principle two was often at work: Within an apartment a linear sequence of rooms, whether in a straight line or in some other configuration, led from the most public rooms to the most private ones. Somewhere in the middle of the series would be the *camera*, or bedchamber, preceded by spaces where the occupant might receive guests, and followed by closets, studio, and toilet, perhaps terminating with a back stairway that could offer a private exit.

Care was also given to the vertical distribution of rooms. The most important and the most well-embellished spaces

▲ **13–6** The courtyard of the Palazzo Medici-Riccardi, with round-headed arches above Corinthian columns.
Cantarelli/Index Ricerca Iconografica

were one level above the street on the *piano nobile* (pronounced "pee-ah-no noh-bee-lay"). The ground floor of a palazzo might have only a few finely finished spaces—an entrance vestibule, of course, and perhaps a summer bedroom for the owner, the thick walls of the lowest floor helping to keep it cool. Other residence-related spaces on the ground floor might include a kitchen, toilets for the staff, and storage rooms. Also on the ground floor of most palazzi—at least until the mid–sixteenth century—were shops that opened to the street but not into any other interior spaces. The floor or floors above the piano nobile were, just as they would be today, devoted to less important family quarters.

Vatican Loggie, Rome The Vatican Palace is a vast, irregular complex of buildings stretching 1,500 feet (460 m) long. It is the residence of the pope, but also contains offices, a library, and a museum of religious and secular treasures. It incorporates the work of many of the Renaissance's greatest artists and designers. Among them are Bramante, responsible for the courtyard known as the Cortile del Belvedere;

Bernini, who designed the Scala Regia or Royal Stair; Michelangelo, who painted the frescoes in the Sistine Chapel; and Raphael, responsible for the *stanze* and *loggie*.

Raffaello Sanzio (1483–1520), called Raphael (and often with an epithet such as "the gentle" or "the divine"), was born in Urbino and became admired for both painting and design. In 1508, impressed by some Madonnas that Raphael had painted in Florence, the pope invited him to decorate the Vatican's Stanza della Segnatura (Room of the Signature). He did so with masterful frescoes on the walls, the ceiling, and in the lunettes (crescent-shaped areas) over the windows. Pleased, Pope Julius II asked Raphael to decorate two adjacent *stanze* as well. After the death in 1514 of Bramante, who had been chief architect of the new St. Peter's, Leo X, who had become pope the year before, gave the job to Raphael. Raphael's plan for the great church was an important factor in the final design, though he died before his plan could be completed.

For the Vatican Palace Raphael also designed some of the *loggie* ("loggias," or rooms with open arcades or colonnades along

▲ **13–7** The Vatican Loggie decorated by Raphael and his assistants, 1514–16.
Scala/Art Resource, NY

▲ **13–8** In the New Sacristy of San Lorenzo, Michelangelo's tomb of Giuliano de' Medici.
Scala/Art Resource, NY

one side). The work was done between 1514 and 1519, and the striking decorations of the pilasters (fig. 13–7) are in the style of decorative motifs found in the underground chambers (grottoes) of ancient Rome. Called **grotesques**, these motifs would be enormously influential in future decoration (see, for example, the late eighteenth-century French wallpaper in fig. 15–41).

New Sacristy, San Lorenzo The great Michelangelo's first major architectural commission was for the façade of the church of S. Lorenzo in Florence, considered by the Medici family as their parish church. Michelangelo Buonarroti (1475–1564) was a towering figure of many talents, excelling in architecture, interior design, painting, sculpture, and poetry. He was a man of ferocious energy, independence, and restlessness in both his life and his art. He moved from his birthplace,

Caprese, to Rome, then to Florence, then back to Rome, and in his art he moved away from the serene order of the High Renaissance to the dynamic distortions of Mannerism.

The façade for S. Lorenzo was never built, but Michelangelo did carry out two major works of interior design within the church complex. The first, begun in 1519, was the New Sacristy, also called the Medici Chapel. It was meant to be a balancing element for the Old Sacristy that Brunelleschi had designed a century earlier. The New Sacristy, like the Old Sacristy, was meant to serve as a tomb for members of the Medici family. The room's high windows have been tapered, their sides converging slightly as they rise. The two major sculptural groups—one dedicated to Giuliano de' Medici (fig. 13–8) and incorporating symbolic figures representing Night and Day, and the other dedicated to Lorenzo de'

Medici ("Lorenzo the Magnificent"), with figures of Evening and Dawn, seem to be deliberately squeezed between the gray stone pilasters that frame them. Work on the New Sacristy continued until 1534, when Michelangelo moved from Florence back to Rome.

Laurentian Library, San Lorenzo In 1523, Michelangelo was also asked to design a library at S. Lorenzo to house the books of Lorenzo de' Medici, uncle of the newly elected pope. It is called the Biblioteca Laurenziana (Laurentian Library), and work on it continued until 1562, two years before Michelangelo's death. Open to all scholars, it has been called the first public library in Europe.

There are two chief elements: a tall vestibule with a monumental stair and, at the top of the stair, a reading room. The library's vestibule is the more eccentric (fig. 13–9). Its pairs of Tuscan columns, rather than forming an arcade in front of the walls or supporting an entablature, are recessed into niches, and they rest on volute-shaped brackets. Also recessed in the walls are empty **aedicules**, shaped like miniature temples and also resting on brackets. The stair that almost fills the vestibule begins on the lower level with three parallel flights, the center one with curved steps, the outer ones with straight ones. All three merge into one at an intermediate landing. The center flight is divided eccentrically into flights of three, seven, and five steps, their ends spiraling into cushionlike forms (see fig. 13–1).

The reading room (fig. 13–10) is long and rectangular and entered through one of the short ends. Its walls are rigorously organized with a regular pattern of dark stone pilasters against white walls, and the three-part division of Michelangelo's ceiling design is paired with the division of the end walls into wide central bays between narrow outer bays.

Both the New Sacristy and Biblioteca Laurenziana were once described by Giorgio Vasari (1511–74), architect and chief biographer of Renaissance artists, as breaking with both ancient and modern tradition. In these rooms Michelangelo produced effects never seen in any treatise, and his highly individual, dynamic, emotional compositions have come to be considered the essence of Mannerism.

Villa Capra (La Rotonda), Near Vicenza Resting atop a gentle hill near Vicenza, the Villa Capra was begun in 1565 and finished four years later. It was designed by Andrea Palladio (1508–1580) and was a built expression of his architectural principles, which he published in a famous treatise, *The Four*

▼**13–9** Vestibule and stair, Laurentian Library
Canali Photobank

▲ **13–10** Reading room of Michelangelo's Laurentian Library, at the top of the stairs, Florence, 1523–71.
Scala/Art Resource, NY

▼ 13-11 The Villa Capra, near Vicenza, designed by Andrea Palladio, 1557–83. Its four identical porticoes enjoy sweeping views over the countryside.
© Achim Bednorz, Koln

Books of Architecture, in 1570. It is a centralized structure, bilaterally symmetrical, showing on its exterior four identical porticoed façades (fig. 13–11), the sort of structure often conceived by Renaissance architects but seldom actually built. Inside, the arrangement of rooms is as orderly and as repetitive as the exterior implies (fig. 13–12), and at their center, under a shallow dome, is a cylindrical sala, the obvious heart of the house (fig. 13–13). Four vestibules lead from the four porticoes

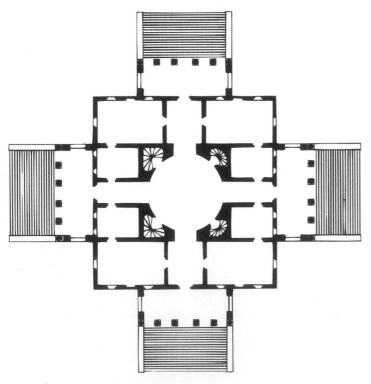

▲ 13-12 Plan of Palladio's Villa Capra.
From "Palladio" by James S. Ackerman, "Villa Rotonda Plan," Figure 32 (p. 77), Baltimore: Penguin, 1966. Copyright James S. Ackerman, 1966. Reproduced by permission of Penguin Books Ltd.

▲ 13-13 The domed central room of the Villa Capra.
Pino Guidolotti

to the central space, but, allowing himself some degree of variation, Palladio has not made the vestibules of equal width. Every relationship of house to site, of room to room, and of width to length to height within each room has been carefully considered, and the result is a remarkably cohesive realization of an ideal country villa. La Rotonda, as it is sometimes called, is one of those few accomplishments in the history of art and design that seem to deserve the adjective *perfect*.

Palladio became one of the most influential architects in Western history. Those he influenced included Ange-Jacques Gabriel in France (see fig. 15–16), Inigo Jones in England (see fig. 16–9), and Thomas Jefferson in America (see fig. 19–9). Ironically, his name is identified by many with a motif he used but did not invent, the so-called Palladian window of a central arched opening with a smaller rectangular opening

▲ 13–14 "Palladian" window forms in Palladio's 1546–49 remodeling of the Gothic basilica in Vicenza.
Pino Guidolotto

at either side (fig. 13–14). This motif is also sometimes called a *Serliana* because it was shown in Sebastiano Serlio's architectural treatise *L'Architettura*, published in installments between 1537 and 1575. But, more commonly, it is called a Venetian window.

What Palladio is more properly remembered for is his application to design of systematic intellectual order and his dramatic use of classical form; he was the first to apply a classical temple front to a villa. Yet, all his proportional systems and classical forms were fused with practical function. Among his other buildings are three churches, a theater, some municipal buildings, and many fine villas, clustered in and around Venice and Vicenza.

Baroque Style

If we think of the rectangle as having been the dominant form of Ancient Greek design and the circle as the dominant form of Roman design, then the ellipse is the dominant form of the **Baroque**. Not as simple a form as the others, the ellipse is a complex movement around two points. Baroque wall surfaces, inside and out, were given surprising concavities and convexities expressing the ellipse, and designs were dominated by vivacity, optical illusion, and florid ornament. While still using the classical orders, the Baroque spirit was far removed from classical simplicity and was instead full of motion and emotion. It dominated Italian design from the beginning of the seventeenth century into the first quarter of the eighteenth.

Michelangelo's work on the Palazzo Farnese in Rome is Baroque, as is the work of Guarino Guarini (1624–83) in Turin. Baroque design is also seen in the church of S. Maria della Salute in Venice by Baldassare Longhena (1598–1682), its dome buttressed by a ring of giant scrolls. But the great epitome of Baroque design is St. Peter's.

St. Peter's, Rome   St. Peter's (fig. 13–15) has been called the pinnacle architectural achievement of the Italian Renaissance. Occupying the same site as the Old St. Peter's, which was the most important of Early Christian structures (see fig. 6–3), the new St. Peter's was built on such a colossal scale that it is almost impossible to visually gauge its dimensions. The measurements are astonishing: the building is 710 feet (216 m) long and covers 227,000 square feet (21,000 m²). Its

Viewpoints | HANS SCHAROUN ON THE BAROQUE STYLE

Modern German architect Hans Scharoun (1893–1972) was the designer of Berlin's Philharmonic Hall. His work has generally been called Expressionist, but writing in 1964, he expressed his debt to Baroque design: "In the Middle Ages, planning and building were subordinated by the requirements of religious symbolism; the Baroque approach relates man directly to interior space. . . . Nowadays, artistic development is no longer left to individual intuition, as with the Baroque. Humanity has a new task. Yet we could never perceive it in its entirety without knowledge of what has preceded it. It is therefore extremely important that we should concern ourselves with the work of the Baroque which still influences our world today."

▶ **13–15** The Basilica of St. Peter's, with Bernini's colonnaded piazza before it. The buildings at the right in the photo are parts of the Vatican palace, and the whole ensemble is called Vatican City. At the center of the piazza is an obelisk from Egypt.
IKONA

dome is 450 feet (137 m) high; the nave is 84 feet (26 m) wide, roofed by a great barrel vault 150 feet (46 m) high, and the supporting Corinthian pilasters are 84 feet (26 m) from base to capital. The statues of the saints in their niches are 16 feet (5 m) tall, and the "little" cherubs are 7 feet (2 m). Without seeing it in person, it is hard to fathom, but St. Peter's expresses the classical orders on a scale never equaled before or since.

Work on St. Peter's was begun in 1506, in the first years of the High Renaissance period, and it was not finished until 120 years later, well into the Baroque period. Those who worked on its design constitute a roster of Renaissance talent. The first plans were produced by Alberti in 1454 and called for a huge basilica in the shape of a Latin cross. In 1506 Bramante replaced Alberti's scheme with one for a Greek cross and a great central dome, but alterations to the Bramante plan were made by Raphael, who responded to the new pope's demands for a larger, grander building. Michelangelo was appointed chief architect in 1546. By then, six architects had worked for a total of forty years under the direction of five popes on the enormous project. A further complication was that both design and construction (which had been proceeding simultaneously) were interrupted by the Sack of Rome in 1527; an imperial army of German and Spanish troops invaded the city, thousands were killed, the pope was imprisoned, and soldiers set up their headquarters in the Vatican *loggie,* stabling their horses inside the recently frescoed Sistine Chapel. It was not until 1534 that work could resume.

In his remaining eighteen years Michelangelo would succeed, as Vasari wrote, in "uniting into a whole the great body of that machine." Michelangelo proposed a return to Bramante's Greek cross plan, which he thought to be "clear, comprehensive, and luminous." For both Bramante and Michelangelo, the centralized plan suggested the universality of God. However, after Michelangelo's death the nave was extended by Carlo Maderno, returning to the Latin cross plan of the Old St. Peter's. Maderno also added the travertine façade and its giant Corinthian order (see fig. 13–15). An imposing colonnade (also shown in fig. 13–15) was begun in 1656 by sculptor, painter, and architect Gianlorenzo Bernini (1598–1680). It grips the façade like a great pair of tongs and encloses the Piazza di San Pietro and its ancient Egyptian obelisk.

Within the Michelangelo/Maderno shell, the interior of St. Peter's is a vast display of arches, columns, pilasters, and other classical architectural details in colored marbles, frescoes, mosaics, sculpture, grilles, candelabra, paintings, organ pipes, gilded plaster ornament, and inlay work. Alabaster altars and chapels are ornamented with gold, rock crystal, and enamel. But the generous dimensions of the interior easily accommodate the wealth of decoration.

Bernini, who was named architect of St. Peter's in 1629, is responsible for the remarkable Baldacchino (fig. 13–16), the four-columned canopy at the crossing of the church's

▶ **13–16** Bernini's gilded bronze *Baldacchino* at the crossing of St. Peter's, added 1624–33. The *Gloria* is visible beyond.
Scala/Art Resource, NY

nave and transept. It stands a hundred feet high over the high altar and over the tomb of St. Peter, a floor below. Its gilded bronze columns are twisted ("Solomonic"), fluted, and entwined with vines; they support massive entablatures, an angel at each corner, and four brackets that outline an open top, crowned by an orb and cross centered under the great dome.

Later Bernini would add the composition *The Glory* (fig. 13–17) in the apse of St. Peter's, covering the wall farthest from the entrance. Created between 1647 and 1653, it is a dramatic sunburst of golden rays, surrounded by angels and clouds of gilded stucco and centered on a radiant oval window, its stained glass representing the Dove of the Holy Spirit. Lower on the same wall and added the following decade is

▼ **13–17** On the apse wall of St. Peter's, Bernini's sunburst *Gloria* and, beneath it, his *Cathedra Petri*.
Scala/Art Resource, NY

the *Cathedra Petri* or Throne of Peter. What Bernini designed, however, is nothing like the humble wooden stool that was the actual relic of the saint's life. He has given us instead an opulent and gigantically scaled throne rendered in bronze, marble, and stucco, held aloft by figures of the Four Doctors of the church. The back of the throne bears a relief illustrating Christ's charge to Peter, "Feed my Sheep," and just above it two *amorini* hold the papal keys and tiara. At the foot of the composition, gilt bronze statues of two Greek and two Latin Fathers of the church stand on a colossal base of red jasper and black marble.

Rococo and Neoclassical Styles

In Italy, as in much of Europe, the Baroque style was succeeded in the eighteenth century by the **Rococo**, which brought new levels of novelty and lyricism. Design became lighter and more graceful, with the curved line preferred to the straight, the pale color to the strong, and the small salon and boudoir more fashionable than the grand *salone*. A representative architect of the Italian Rococo is Filippo Juvarra (1678–1736), who followed Guarini as the outstanding architect of Turin. Juvarra's work in Turin included the monastery of La Superga (1727–31) and the royal hunting palace of Stupinigi (1729–35). Other buildings representative of the Rococo are Rome's Spanish Steps of 1723–6 and the nearby cluster of apartment blocks with undulating walls at the Piazza di San Ignazio of 1727–35. In painting, the Rococo master was Tiepolo, some of whose murals appear in the villas of Palladio.

Unlike other periods of the Italian Renaissance style, which were prevalent all over the country, the Rococo was taken up most enthusiastically in Venice. A fine example is a bedroom of the Palazzo Sagredo (fig. 13–18) on Venice's Grand Canal, next-door neighbor to the Venetian Gothic Ca' d'Oro (see figs. 8–16 and 8–17). The Sagredo palace is of mid–fourteenth-century origins, but its interiors were entirely redone in the Rococo style when bought by the Sagredo family c. 1718. Above a bed alcove we see winged children of painted and gilded stucco holding up a fringed and tasseled canopy.

In the last half of the eighteenth century, design was heavily influenced by the excavation of Italy's ancient cities, and consequently there was a passion for the antique as well as a reaction against the frivolity of the Rococo. Curved lines were straightened; excess was banished. This **Neoclassical** style was

▲ **13–19** Piranesi's Neoclassical façade for the church of Santa Maria del Priorato, Rome, 1764–5.
Abercrombie

practiced by Giovanni Battista Piranesi (1720–78) and others, anticipating the revival styles of the nineteenth century. Piranesi is best known today as an engraver, but he was also at times an etcher, architect, interior designer, furniture designer, archaeologist, and theorist. His only building, however (and it was a remodeling of an older structure), was the small church of Santa Maria del Priorata (fig. 13–19), designed in 1764 for the Knights of Malta atop Rome's Aventine hill. One of his last portfolios of engravings, the *Diverse maniere d'adornare . . .*, published in 1769, showed over a hundred pieces of furniture and sixty-one fireplaces, eleven of them in Egyptian style, most in a rather sumptuous version of the Neoclassical style.

Italian Ornament

The Italian Renaissance was noted not only for its architecture and interiors, but also for the wealth of ornament that enriched them. Brunelleschi's Old Sacristy (see fig. 13–4) expresses Early Renaissance architectural form delineated by ornamental stone outlining. Bernini's Baldacchino (see fig. 13–16), his Gloria, and his Cathedra Petri (see fig. 13–17) for St. Peter's offer an indication of Baroque ornamental flourishes; and the Sagredo bedroom from Venice (see fig. 13–18) provides a glimpse of the ornate taste of the Rococo. These and other styles of Renaissance interiors were unusually rich in ornamental effects, and interesting techniques for decorating walls developed in Italy during the fourteenth through eighteenth centuries.

Frescoes

The words *mural* and **fresco** are sometimes used interchangeably to refer to large wall or ceiling paintings. More strict usage, however, considers all such paintings as murals but only those prepared in a special way as frescoes. True fresco painting—or, in Italian, *buon fresco*—is a demanding art, requiring long preparation and swift execution.

Famous frescoes of the Italian Renaissance include Raphael's work in the *stanze* of the Vatican, Giulio Romano's *Fall of the Giants* in his Mannerist Palazzo del Tè in Mantua, and, of course, Michelangelo's frescoes in the Vatican's Sistine Chapel—the ceiling painted between 1508 and 1512, and the terrifying end wall depicting *The Last Judgment* between 1536 and 1544. In Annibale Carracci's ceiling for the

Fresco painting is always on plaster that has been applied first to a wall of brick or stone. It must be executed before the plaster has dried so that it becomes not another layer on a hard surface but an integral part of the plaster surface. **Plaster** is a compound containing slaked lime and water. Plaster remains wet enough for good results for only about six hours, so large frescoes must be painted in stages. Several rough undercoats may be applied to the entire surface and left to dry, but the final, smooth coat is added only to the area to be painted immediately. Earth or mineral pigments mixed with water (some insist that only distilled water be used) are then applied to the fresh plaster. As the painted plaster dries, it absorbs carbon dioxide from the air, which crystallizes as calcium carbonate, binding the materials together into a hard, durable, and beautifully reflective substance. Fresco work requires no protective finish like varnish; indeed, such a finish might react destructively with the natural glassy surface of calcium carbonate.

Not only must fresco painters be quick and accurate, but they must have at their command considerable knowledge about their materials, as many pigments applied to wet plaster undergo a chemical change and an alteration of color in the process. Because of its demands as well as because of its beauty, true fresco work is a highly regarded art form.

Grand Gallery of the Palazzo Farnese, Rome (fig. 13–20) there is a dramatic representation of classical themes. Titled *Loves of the Gods*, the series of frescoes celebrates sensuality as a compulsion from which even the Greek gods were not exempt. Carracci (1560–1609) came from a family of noted painters in Bologna, and his ceiling within Michelangelo's architectural framework combined classical references with naturalistic portraiture, a combination of reverence for the past and honesty about the present that was intrinsic to Renaissance design.

Far less durable than true fresco work is **tempera** painting, which is a type of watercolor combined with a binding substance such as egg, milk, or gum. Other substitutes for true fresco are called *fresco secco* and *distemper*. All these are types of painting on *dry* plaster. Leonardo da Vinci experimented with a mixture of tempera and oil paint on dry plaster for *The Last Supper* in Milan; and predictably, despite its artistic merit, preservation problems for this work have been notoriously hard to solve.

Intarsia Work

Intarsia is the technique of creating decorative patterns or representational scenes with small, thin pieces of wood or wood veneer. A type of intarsia had been practiced by the ancient Romans, called *tarsia certosina*, which consisted of hollowing out small cavities in pieces of solid wood and filling the cavities with precisely sized pieces of veneer. This sort of work is what is today called **inlay**. The practice fell into disuse in the Middle Ages, but it was revived during the Italian Renaissance, and another type of intarsia was added, *tarsia geometrica*, which consisted of entirely covering a surface with an assemblage of small pieces of veneer. No cavities were needed.

The earliest intarsias of the Italian Renaissance were confined to geometric patterns formed from pieces of veneer with straight sides. Later, representational scenes with appropriate perspective effects were added, and the pieces of veneer were more irregularly shaped. In the fifteenth century, intarsia artists (*intarsiatori*) began tinting pieces of wood by boiling them in water with penetrating dyes, adding a further touch of realism. The illusion of shadows was also created by singeing pieces of wood over fire. And in addition to wood, inlays were sometimes made of lapis lazuli, onyx, amber, ivory, and crystal.

A virtuoso example of intarsia work lines the walls of the *studiolo* (a small study, often windowless) of Federico II da Montefeltro in the Palazzo Ducale, Urbino (fig. 13–21), finished in 1476. The tiny pieces of veneer form a realistic picture of cabinetwork: Some of the imaginary cabinet doors open to reveal books, statues, and musical and scientific instruments. One intarsia panel depicts a rural landscape seen through a classical arcade. Woods used include walnut, oak, poplar, and several fruit woods. The intarsia is sometimes attributed to two Florentine brothers, Giuliano da Maiano

◀ **13–20** Annibale Carracci's ceiling fresco for the Gallery of the Palazzo Farnese, Rome.
Canali Photobank

▲ **13–21** The *studiolo* in the Palazzo Ducale at Gubbio. The intarsia work portrays cabinets filled with books, a caged parrot, and musical and scientific instruments.
Scala/Art Resource, NY

(1432–90) and Benedetto da Maiano (1442–97), who were both also noted as architects and sculptors.

In the next chapter, we shall see how French artisans developed Italian intarsia work into brilliant displays of **marquetry**. The techniques differ only in that marquetry involves cutting through two or more sheets of differently colored veneers to produce pieces for intricately interlocking patterns. The marquetry technique was also very popular in the Netherlands and, later, in England.

Della Robbia Work

An important ceramic product in the Italian Renaissance was the ornamental plaque or panel designed to be built into a wall surface, either exterior or interior. The most famous of these were produced by members

▲ **13–22** Luca della Robbia's tin-glazed terra-cotta rondel of *Madonna and Child with Lilies,* Florence, c. 1455, 6 ft. (1.8 m) in diameter.
Luca della Robbia, the Elder (c. 1400–1482). "Madonna and Child". Medaillon of the Guild of Doctors and Apothecaries. Glazed terracotta. Orsanmichele, Florence, Italy. © SCALA/ Art Resource, NY

of one Florentine family, the della Robbias. The founder of the family workshop was Luca della Robbia (c. 1399–1482), who is credited with inventing the tin-glazed terra-cotta sculpture for which the family was famous. Most of his work was executed in a chaste color scheme of white figures in high relief against a light blue ground. Luca's nephew Andrea della Robbia (1435–1525) inherited the workshop and introduced more complex compositions and additional colors. Coming later to the workshop at various times were Andrea's five sons, and in the sixteenth century two of them carried the della Robbia artistry to France, where they worked for the royal court. The della Robbias' typical subject matter was religious, and the most frequent subject of all was the Madonna and Child (fig. 13–22). These were most often displayed in circular forms or **rondels**, ringed with simple frames or wreaths of leaves, flowers, and citrus fruit.

Italian Furniture

In the Early Renaissance, furniture was sparingly used, and what existed was consistent in scale with the large dimensions of the rooms. Much of the furniture was monumental, and its logical position was against the wall, forming a dominant note in the wall composition, along with decorative wall plaques, portrait busts on brackets, heavily framed paintings, or panels of relief sculpture. By the middle of the fifteenth century, there was a more general demand for improved richness and comfort in the movable furnishings of the house, and, because great thought was given to entertaining, the general design and arrangement of furniture was made with this activity in view. By the sixteenth century, the Italians had developed a variety of furniture forms (fig. 13–23).

FLORENTINE TABLE

DANTE CHAIR

SAVONAROLA CHAIR

SGABELLO →

← CANDLELABRUM

CASSONE

ARMCHAIR

CASSAPANCA

▲ **13–23** Italian Renaissance furniture types.
Gilbert Werlé/New York School of Interior Design

The **sedia**, or chair, came in several varieties, which were not comfortable by today's standards but were an improvement over medieval standards. The armchair was rectangular in its main lines, with square, straight legs. The legs were connected with **stretchers**, which were sometimes placed so as to rest on the floor, as in the example at lower left in figure 13–23. A characteristic feature was the upward extension of the rear legs to form the back uprights, which were terminated with a finial motif intended to represent an acanthus leaf bracket. The arm support was usually turned in the form of a **baluster**, an architectural detail never used by the Romans, but extremely popular in the Renaissance. Upholstery of back and seat consisted of velvet, damask, or ornamental leather, trimmed with silk fringe. In the Baroque period, as would be expected, the armchair became more ornate, its arms and legs carved into exaggerated sculptural forms.

The smaller side chair was built on the same general lines as the armchair, but often was made entirely of wood and enriched with simple turnings. Seats were made of rush, wood, or textiles. Ornamental nailheads were used with leather upholstery.

Other chairs were of the folding or X-shaped type, of which there were three varieties. The **Savonarola** type (see center left in fig. 13–23) was composed of interlacing curved slats and usually had a carved wooden back and arms. The **Dante** type (see upper right in fig. 13–23) had heavy curved arms and legs, and usually had a leather or cloth back and seat. The monastery type was smaller and was built of interlacing straight splats. Folding chairs were also made of wrought iron with brass trimmings and cushion seats.

The **sgabello** (see center right in fig. 13–23) was a light wooden chair used for dining and other purposes. The early types had three legs, small octagonal seats, and stiff backs. The later examples show two trestles or splat supports, and when carving was introduced, both the trestles and backs were elaborately treated. An *sgabello* in figure 13–24 is from sixteenth-century Florence and is one of the more elaborately carved examples of the type. The *sgabello* was also made without a back, forming a low bench.

The **letto**, or bed, was often a massive structure with paneled headboard and footboard, sometimes raised on a platform above the drafty floor. We have seen an early Renaissance bed in the Palazzo Davanzati (see fig. 13–2) and a late one in the Palazzo Sagredo (see fig. 13–18). Other beds

◀**13–24** A *sgabello* chair from the mid-sixteenth century, Florence.
Sotheby's Picture Library/ London

were of the four-poster variety: a *letto a baldacchino*. This bed was likely to have a fabric tester (*cortinaggio*) above. Such hangings were commonplace, useful for both warmth and privacy. Many beds were treated with richly carved, painted, or intarsia ornament. Cradles were made in the form of miniature beds or hollowed-out half cylinders that could be easily rocked.

Tables

Tables were made in all sizes. Large rectangular **refectory** tables often had tops made of single planks of walnut. The supports were elaborately carved trestles, dwarf Doric columns, or turned baluster forms (fig. 13–25). Both plain and carved stretchers were used. Small tables often had hexagonal and octagonal tops, and were supported by carved central pedestals; an example is the Renaissance style table at top left in figure 13–23. The edges of the tabletops were usually treated with ornamented moldings.

In the Early Renaissance, when prosperous families often moved from one residence to another, tables (as well as some chairs) were designed to be easily folded or taken apart. In the High Renaissance more permanent living arrangements allowed less portable furniture and—especially in Florence— tabletops came to be impressively inlaid with colored stones

▲ **13–25** A 16th-century walnut table on four richly carved cylindrical columns and three baluster-turned columns. Victoria & Albert Museum, London/Art Resource, NY

(see fig. 13–30). Wood intarsia was also used. Tables in the seventeenth-century Baroque style grew more monumental, with tops of marble or of *scagliola*, an imitation marble described in the next section. Baroque table bases were often of gilded bronze, although console tables, meant to stand against walls, often had bases of carved and gilded wood. Rococo tables were more curvaceous in shape and were frequently lacquered. And in the Neoclassical style of the late eighteenth century, marble tabletops and bases recalled examples of Roman furniture (as in fig. 5–31).

Casegoods

Storage furniture in Renaissance times included storage chests, sideboards, drop-leaf writing cabinets, wardrobes and armoires, bookcases, double-deck storage cabinets, and—after c. 1600—chests of drawers.

The **cassone** was a chest or box of any kind, from the small jewel casket to the enormous and immovable wedding or dowry chest that was the most important piece of furniture in the Italian room. The cassone was also used as traveling baggage. The lid was hinged at the top, and when the piece was closed, it could be used as a seat or a table. The cassone served the purposes of the modern closet. It could also be highly decorative, its long front panel richly carved or painted. A carved wood one is shown in figure 13–23, and in figure 13–26 we see a gilt one with a panel painted by Francesco di Giorgio (1439–1501), an architect and scholar from Siena.

▲ **13–26** A gilt *cassone* with a panel painted by Francesco di Giorgio. Victoria & Albert Museum, London/Art Resource, NY

▲ **13–27** Detail from a 1485 painting, *Herod's Feast,* shows dinner guests seated against a fabric hanging called a *spalliera.* Above it is a row of candle pickets.
Art Resource, NY

Lighting

After sunset, interiors were dark except for the light from fireplaces, candles, and lanterns. There were many sizes and grades of candles, the finest perhaps being beeswax candles produced in Venice. And there were many types and qualities among candleholders. Some of these were given the names *candelieri* and *candelabre,* words that are obviously the origins of our terms chandeliers and candelabra.

The most common candleholder was of the picket type, a flat base with an affixed spike onto which the candle was pressed. Sometimes they were small, for tabletop or mantel use; sometimes they were taller, standing on the floor; and sometimes they were attached to the walls (fig. 13–27). They were often of brass or silver, either of which nicely reflected the candlelight, but also of bronze, iron, or wood. Candleholders were also made—as they are today—with cylindrical cups into which the candles are fitted.

Lanterns featured shields of sheet metal around the candles, which protected the flame from drafts, and were punctured with holes to let the light through. They were particularly useful for moving about the house after dark. There were also lamps that burned oil.

Italian Decorative Arts

As would be expected, Italian achievements during the Renaissance in architecture, interiors, ornament, and furniture were fully matched and complimented by their accomplishments in the decorative arts. A love of beauty so penetrated the Italian mind that even the most insignificant article of household use was designed with care and thought.

The **cassapanca** (see bottom right in fig. 13–23) was a large cassone with a back and arms added to it to form a settee or sofa. It was thus both seating and (beneath the seat) storage. The cassapanca was particularly popular in Florence. Loose cushions were used for comfort.

The medieval *credence* (see bottom right in fig. 8–26) developed into the Renaissance **credenza** (see top left in fig. 13–3), a cabinet-sideboard with doors and drawers intended for the storage of linen, dishes, and silverware. It was made in various sizes, and the smallest type was known as a *credenzetta.* The credenza often had an ornamental wooden back rising from its shelf.

A small counterpart to those larger pieces was the *cofanetto,* a storage casket for personal treasures. It was most often made of walnut, cypress, ivory, or amber, and was often decorated with ornaments in *pastiglia,* gesso relief that was painted or gilded or both.

Ceramics

In the late fourteenth and early fifteenth centuries, with Gothic notions still lingering, Italy produced some delightfully plain ceramics with simple designs in green, yellow, or dark blue painted on cream-colored grounds. Later ceramics, however, reveled in decoration. During the height of the Renaissance, ceramics became a familiar part of Italian life and an important feature of Italian interiors, as seen in the della Robbia work used to decorate wall surfaces of buildings.

Majolica   The name *majolica* (pronounced "muh-*jah*-lih-kuh) is one of those terms—like China plate, Oriental carpet, and Turkish knot—that have their basis in a misconception. Majolica is derived from the island of Majorca, off the coast of Spain at the western end of the Mediterranean. When first imported to Italy in the fifteenth century, the wares given that name were supposed to have been made on that island, though probably

▲ **13–28** A globe-shaped majolica jar from Venice, c. 1545. The decoration shows fruit hanging from curves of leafy vines.
One of a pair of caffagiola jars. Italian, 16th century. Ceramic, 13 in. (33 cm) high × 13 in. (33 cm) in diameter. Virginia Museum of Fine Arts, Richmond. Gift of Mrs. E.A. Rennolds in Memory of Mr. and Mrs. John Kerr Branch. © Virginia Museum of Fine Arts. 53.18.85/86.

they had been made on the Spanish mainland and brought to Italy by Majorcan traders. By the sixteenth century, the Italian potters had surpassed their Spanish inspiration, but the name had stuck: All wares of that type, including those known not to have a Spanish origin, were called Majolica, even in languages other than Italian, and even to the present time.

As in the other arts, the decoration of Italian ceramics came to be dominated by classical themes. Majolica of the sixteenth century often were copies of engravings of classical scenes, which were copies from paintings or murals by Michelangelo or Raphael (Raphael, himself, is said to have painted majolica in his youth). Animals, flowers, and fruits were popular (fig. 13–28), along with cherubs and dolphins and not-so-simple garlands, arabesques, and grotesques. Other subjects were portrait busts

Tools & Techniques | MAJOLICA

Majolica is a type of earthenware, originally treated with an opaque white glaze to resemble highly prized porcelain from China. The more common transparent glazes are made with lead or silicon; the opaque white glaze with tin. The tin glaze was found to be an excellent ground for colored decoration, not only because of its solid whiteness, but also because it was stable when fired and pigments painted over it did not "run" or blur in the kiln. In fact, during firing the pigments actually fused into the glaze so that their brilliance became permanent. A disadvantage of the technique, however, is that a brush stoke of pigment on the unfired white glaze is irrevocable; there is no chance for erasure or correction. The decoration of majolica therefore often appears more spontaneous and fresh, even at times more naive and accidental, than the decoration on porcelain, which can be retouched as needed.

For the painting, a limited range of pigments was developed that would not fade in firing. These were chiefly made from the metallic oxides. Ones frequently used for the outlines of the decoration were a deep manganese purple and, later, a cobalt blue, and, by the middle of the sixteenth century, a brownish black. Other colors included a green made from copper, a yellow from antimony, and an orange from iron rust. A rich cherry red was the secret of some potteries. Luster colors with iridescent effects, known in Renaissance Italy from earlier Islamic and Spanish wares, were also sometimes used, though these required an additional firing. Another sort of decoration, in direct imitation of Chinese blue-and-white porcelains, was limited to those two colors. Such blue-and-white wares were called *alla porcellana*.

A variant of majolica is called *sgraffiata* ware, a term that literally means "scratched." Rather than applied with a paintbrush, the decoration is made with a sharp wood or metal tool that cuts through the white glaze to reveal the dark red or buff-colored earthenware beneath. If the earthenware is painted before the glaze is applied, those colors are revealed.

and the shields and arms of noble families. On flat plates, such subjects were sometimes painted within decorative circular borders; at other times they occupied the entire surface. As the Renaissance progressed, the decoration came to be increasingly important and the utility of the plate or vessel less so. Platters, urns, bowls, pitchers, vases, and apothecary jars continued to be made for everyday use, but the "show dish"—the *piatta del pompa*—intended only for display was born. Such frankly ornamental wares were an important decorative element in Italian Renaissance interiors, as they were again later in Victorian homes. Beginning in the sixteenth century, there were even some examples of majolica floors, as in the 1510 Cappella dell' Annunziata in S. Sabastiano, Venice.

Porcelain The first attempt to make porcelain in Europe was in Venice in the the fifteenth century. In the early sixteenth century, the Medici family supported these efforts, and finally there was a translucent soft-paste ware resembling opaque glass. It was called "counterfeit porcelain" but is now known as *Medici porcelain*. It was used to make dishes, platters, ewers, and flasks (fig. 13–29) in colored patterns taken from both Renaissance and Eastern sources. This Medici porcelain was produced only between the years 1575 and 1587, and only about five dozen pieces are known to survive today. For all its rarity and curiosity, it is thought that Medici porcelain served as an inspiration for the important soft-paste porcelain in France. The first hard-paste porcelain was produced in the Vezzi ceramics factory, founded in 1719 in Venice.

The oldest factory still producing ceramics today is the one founded at Doccia in 1737 by the Marchese Carlo Ginori. It produced hard-paste porcelain. The early paste was dull and slightly gray, but was brightened and whitened by various experiments later in the eighteenth century. The wares featured pierced decoration and figures in relief. In 1896, it merged with Milan's Società Ceramica Richard and became Richard-Ginori.

A final important factory was begun at Capodimonte in 1743 by Charles VII, king of Naples. It produced a clear, white, soft-paste porcelain. Its decoration included *chinoiserie*, battle scenes, peasant figures, and characters from the *commedia dell' arte*, a form of comic theater using masked figures that was popular in Italy from the sixteenth through the eighteenth centuries. Useful tableware was made at Capodimonte, as were snuff boxes and figurines. A celebrated commission executed by the factory was for the painted and relief tiles lining the Salottino di Porcellano (Small Porcelain Salon) of the Palazzo Reale in Pórtici. The room was designed by Giovanni Natali, and the tiles were made between 1757 and 1759. When Charles VII, patron of the factory, became Charles III, king of Spain, in 1759, the factory was closed and reopened in Madrid; we shall see some of its products in Chapter 14 on Spain.

Stonework and Imitation Stonework

Mosaic work, so important in the Italy of Roman and Byzantine times, continued to be done, although by the fourteenth century its role was largely taken over by fresco painting, which was quicker, less expensive, and more realistic. The quality of mosaic work suffered a decline as it came increasingly to imitate painting and as its production was divided between those who designed it and those who executed the designs. Still, famous artists designed glorious mosaics: Giotto for St. Peter's, Raphael for the Chigi Chapel of S. Maria del Popolo in Rome, and Titian and Tintoretto, for San Marco in Venice.

There was a great enthusiasm for **pietra dura** (see fig. 10–1 and Tools & Techniques: Pietra Dura in Chapter 10). During the Renaissance it was used often for the tops of important

▼ **13–29** A flask of Medici porcelain made in Florence c. 1580. It is 10 in. (26 cm) tall.
The J. Paul Getty Museum, Los Angeles, Medici Factory, Pilgrim Flask (Fiasca da Pellegrino), about 1575–1587, H: 10⅛ in.; Maximum W: 7⅜ in. (H: 26.4 cm; diameter (lip): 4 cm; Maximum W: 20 cm)

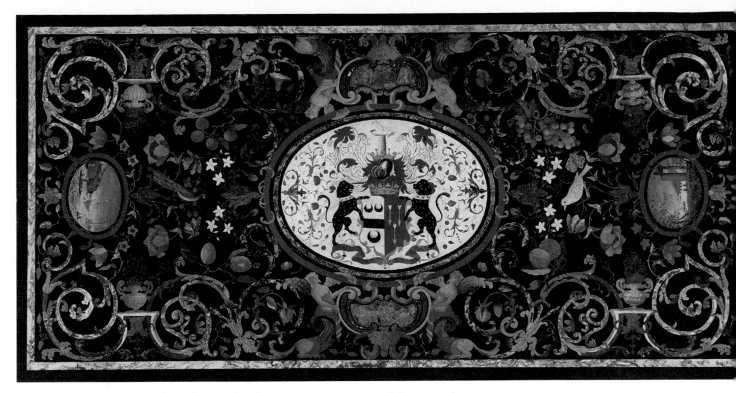

▲ **13–30** Side table with an intarsia top of colored marbles, made in Livorno, Italy, c. 1776 for England's Earl of Litchfield.
Victoria & Albert Museum, London/Art Resource, NY

tables (fig. 13–30) and also for plaques and cabinet panels. Later these two-dimensional applications were joined by large vases, ewers, bowls, and statuary set into gold and enamel mounts. The stones were generally of fanciful color and often of great value, popular types being onyx, malachite, carnelian, and polished quartz. The main center for the art of *pietra dura* was Florence, where in 1588 the Grand Duke Ferdinando de' Medici established a factory in the Uffizi. It was called the Opificio delle Pietra Dura, and its products were sometimes called *Florentine mosaics*. The factory is still in operation. Similar workshops were formed in other parts of Italy, however, as well as in other European countries. There were some geographical differences of taste: In the north of Italy, around Florence, the most popular effects were highly naturalistic, imitating birds, flowers, animals, and landscapes. In Rome and the south, there was a fashion for choosing stones of extraordinary color and veining and then leaving them in their natural state.

Scagliola is a technique for imitating marble developed in Italy in the seventeenth century. It has been used for columns, pilasters, moldings, tabletops, and fireplace surrounds. Later, it was much employed in England in the eighteenth century and is still sometimes used today. It consists mainly of plaster into which are embedded fine chips of marble and other minerals, especially a crystalline form of gypsum called *selenite*. Coloring can also be added, and the result is generally given a high polish.

Glass and Mirrors

From medieval times, the center of Italy's glass industry was Venice, more specifically, Murano, an island in the Venetian lagoon (chosen because of the risk of fire), where fine glassware is still made. During the Renaissance and thereafter, Venice was renowned for the high quality of its glassware, both ornamental and practical.

Most Venetian glass was produced with the blow-pipe. Because of its thinness, it was never cut but modeled, sometimes into extraordinary shapes. Many types of Venetian glass were developed and made into goblets, vases, plates, beakers, and bowls. They were variously colored—most often in turquoise, emerald green, dark blue, and amethyst—and decorated with enameling and gilding in forms resembling dolphins, flowers, wings, stems, leaves, or abstract patterns. Other surface finishes included net, crackled, marbled, lace, and spiraled effects. Specific Venetian glass types included *millefiori* (meaning "thousand flowers" and incorporating multicolored blossoms), *filigrana* (striped), *calcedonio* (resembling the pale blue or gray precious stone chalcedony), *aventurino* (flecked with sparkling particles like the mineral aventurine), *ghiaccio* (resembling ice), and *lattimo* (resembling milk).

Lattimo glass was probably the invention of Angelo Barovier (c. 1400–1460), a member of a family of glassmakers that had been working in Murano as early as 1324. In 1450 Barovier perfected his greatest invention, a glass type called *cristallo*—the first **crystal**. The astonishing quality of Barovier's new glass—though it may be difficult today to appreciate its novelty—was that it was absolutely transparent. No previous glass had been so clear. To make cristallo involved taking ash imported from Islamic lands and cleansing it and the other ingredients through repeated boiling. The Italians did not leave cristallo ware plain and transparent. Perhaps, as expensive luxury ware, it was thought to need appropriately opulent decoration, or perhaps it was thought that its transparency was best displayed by a contrast with opaque areas (fig. 13–31).

Mirrors were made throughout medieval times from highly polished metal, but the process of mirroring glass with an amalgam of tin and mercury (quicksilver) was first used in Venice in 1317. So costly and valued were early mirrors that they were usually covered by a silk curtain or by a wooden door or panel, with great attention paid to their frames. In the sixteenth century, mirrors increased in size, and the convex mirror increased in popularity. In that century also, small bits of mirror were sometimes incorporated into patterns of wood wall paneling, providing unexpected glitter in the often-dark interiors.

Another Italian Renaissance glass technique was *eglomisé*, its name derived from eighteenth-century French artist Jean-Baptiste Glomi, who made picture frames using this technique. Eglomisé had been known to the Romans and practiced in both Christian and Islamic lands, but it became popular in Italy much later. The technique involved painting on the back of glass and then protecting the paint with a thin sheet of metal foil (such as gold leaf), a coat of varnish, or another sheet of glass.

Metalwork

The Italians developed extraordinary ability as workers in both precious and base metals. In the thirteenth and fourteenth centuries, Siena was a center for the production of bronze and wrought iron objects—oil lamps, andirons, and decorative hardware. In the sixteenth century, excellent, high-quality brass objects—plates, cups, incense burners, and candleholders—were produced in Venice. In other times and places, extensive work was done in copper, bronze, and pewter. After the sixteenth-century Counter-Reformation, there was great demand for metal liturgical objects such as candelabra and cruicfixes; among these were the ones in gilt bronze that Bernini designed for St. Peter's.

Prominent among the artistsans was the Italian Mannerist goldsmith and sculptor Benvenuto Cellini (1500–1571), who worked in several places: in his native Florence for the Medici, in Rome for several successive popes, and in France for King Francis I. One of his small but exquisite works for Francis I was a gold and enamel saltcellar (fig. 13–32); it is topped by figures of Neptune and Earth, and the base is decorated with smaller figures of Morning, Day, Evening, and Night. Another famous Cellini work, on a larger scale, is the statue *Perseus with the Head of Medusa* in the Loggia dei Lanzi at Florence, outside the Palazzo Vecchio. Cellini wrote a *Treatise on Goldsmithing and Sculpture*, in which he named Michelangelo among the leading goldsmiths of his time.

Of particular importance in embellishing the domestic interior of the Italian Renaissance were small bronzes. The production of bronze statuettes by the **cire perdue** or lost wax process was a flourishing decorative art used to enrich

▼ **13–31** Venetian goblet of Renaissance *cristallo* glass, made between 1475 and 1525.
Victoria & Albert Museum, London/Art Resource, NY

mantels, shelves, and tables. Even as important large statues were cast in this sensuous material for public display, miniature bronze objects and statuettes were done for cultured aristocrats to display in their homes. Such objects included medals, vases, mirrors, lamps, reliefs, and plaques.

In the eighteenth century, Italian metalwork was influenced by French work as well as by the Rococo fashion. There were two important eighteenth-century workshops run by two Roman families, the Guarnieri family of silversmiths and the Valadier

▲ **13–32** Benvenuto Cellini's gold and enamel *Saltcellar of Francis I*, c. 1543, 13 in. (33 cm) wide.
Kunsthistorisches Museum, Vienna, Austria

family, the latter headed by Giuseppe Valadier (1762–1839), son of the founder. Valadier was not only a goldsmith but also an important Neoclassical architect in Rome and the draftsman of fine archaeological drawings of ancient Roman monuments. The Valadier family was noted for pendulum clocks, tableware, sanctuary lamps, and reliquaries in the Neoclassical style, and they continued working until the middle of the nineteenth century.

Textiles

The people of the Italian Renaissance had great enthusiasm for fine fabrics and the skill required in producing them. The making of fine laces, for example, was a specialty in Venice beginning in the middle of the sixteenth century and lasting until the early eighteenth century. Lavish embroideries were another specialty of the Italian Renaissance, used in secular interiors as borders on linen drapery and upholstery. After the invention of the printing press, pattern books were published for the designs of both lace and embroidery.

Italian Renaissance wall hangings were of at least two types: the *capoletto* and the *spalliera*. The *capoletto* originated as a type of bed canopy, hanging suspended from the wall at the head of a bed (*capo* meaning "head" and *letto* "bed"), but the name came later to be used for other hangings as well, such as canopies over dining tables. The *spalliera* (see fig. 13–27) was originally a long horizontal hanging against a wall behind a dining room bench, so that diners could lean

their shoulders (*spalle*) on something softer and warmer than the wall itself. In addition to these wall hangings and bed hangings, there were hangings in front of doorways to eliminate drafts, these being called **portiere**. The portiere (from *porta*, meaning "door") were generally of the same design as adjacent wall hangings, but sometimes a contrast was provided.

Carpets imported from the East were also used in many interiors for table covers as well as for floor coverings.

An important advance in the upholstery of seating furniture came in sixteenth-century Italy. This was not only an aesthetic advance, with matched fabrics giving visual unity to a room, but also a technical advance, with new techniques such as quilting (stitching in grids of parallel lines) for securing the padding in place, thereby retaining its shape.

Tapestries The tapestry production of the Middle Ages continued without interruption into Renaissance times, becoming increasingly democratized and affordable by more households. Through the fourteenth century, tapestry making continued to be based in northern France and Flanders, although the tapestry designs often had Italian origins: Leonardo da Vinci and Raphael were among the Italian artists who drew tapestry cartoons sent north to be woven. Raphael designed ten tapestries for the Vatican's Sistine Chapel; they were never woven, but seven of his designs are in the Victoria & Albert Museum in London. Giulio Romano, architect of Mantua's Palazzo del Tè, was the designer of a set of fourteen tapestries begun for the Duke of Mantua and, after his death, continued for his brother Cardinal Ercole Gonzaga. Called the *Puttini* tapestries, because of their many small, winged angels, they were woven with weft threads wrapped in silver and gold metal.

By the early fifteenth century some Italian courts were employing northern-trained tapestry weavers. Perhaps they were hired originally to maintain the courts' existing inventory, but soon there were weavers at work on new tapestries in Ferrara, Milan, Urbino, Naples, and in the papal court in Rome. Itinerant weaver-merchants from the north also settled in Venice and Milan. An Italian word for tapestry is *arazzi*, derived from the town of Arras in northern France, even though such textiles were made in many locations.

Silks   Italian Renaissance textiles used for draperies and upholstery were usually of silk, and during this period Italy became a dominant force in silk manufacture. But Italian silk expertise had begun in medieval times. Silks had been imported to Venice from the Byzantine Empire since the eighth century. Silk weaving had also been introduced into Sicily by its Islamic rulers in the years before the eleventh-century Norman Conquest. After a political upheaval in Sicily in 1266, many of the Sicilian silk workers moved to Lucca in northern Italy. Lucca became a great center of both *sericulture* (the raising of silkworms) and silk weaving, with over 3,000 active looms. After the Mughal conquest of India in the thirteenth century and the opening of trade between Europe and the East, Italian silk design was stimulated by exposure to Islamic and Eastern ideas: exotic creatures such as the dragon and the phoenix were introduced, and the stately rows of roundels were replaced by diagonal arrangements and more animated compositions. To the plain silk velvets of the thirteenth century, the fourteenth-century silk weavers added stripes and floral patterns, including Chinese varieties like the lotus and peony. The pomegranate, a popular motif in Persian design, was also adopted by the Italians and transformed into an artichoke, which came to be one of the dominant motifs of the Renaissance. Among more classical motifs, the ogee curve (composed of both concave and convex parts, as in the *cyma recta* and *cyma reversa* moldings of fig. 5–24) was developed into an elongated S-shaped scroll.

By the last quarter of the fourteenth century, as the Early Renaissance was dawning, Lucca was producing three-color velvets in two pile heights. The combination of cut and uncut piles, with the cut pile higher than the uncut, became popular and was known as *ciselé* velvet. *Ciselé* is a French term for chiseled, carved or cut, and velvet is a fabric (not necessarily of silk) with a rich, soft texture. A *ciselé* velvet with a cut pile of multicolored silk above an uncut ground of gold silk is seen in figure 13–33; it reflects the Baroque style of the first half of the seventeenth century and was probably woven in Genoa, although it is now in use as an altar cloth in a church in Stockholm. In other examples, details, such as the heads and feet of exotic beasts, were often picked out in gold against grounds of other colors.

▲ **13–33** Detail of a silk *ciselé* velvet with raised silk ornament above a gold ground, Genoa, 1600–1650.
National Heritage Board/Riksantikvarieambetet

But Venice came to outshine Lucca in the fifteenth century with over 10,000 looms. Venetian gold brocades employed gold thread against a silk ground, and even more extravagant was the Venetian "cloth of gold" (*drap d'or*) with a silk pattern against a gold ground.

The fourth great Italian silk city—along with Lucca, Florence, and Venice—was Genoa, prominent in silk making from the fifteenth century. By the end of the High Renaissance, in the sixteenth century, Genoa was producing more silks than any other Italian city. Remarkable among them, beginning in the sixteenth century, was a polychrome velvet of scrolled or floral design with the plain linen or hemp weft left visible between parts of the design; these were often given a wax finish. From the middle of the eighteenth century, these silks were imitated at Versailles, France, where they were given the name *velours de Gêne* (velvets of Genoa). Another

Genoese silk specialty was called *ferronerie* because its patterns of delicate tracery resembled work in wrought iron (*ferro*).

By the end of the seventeenth century, when French silks had become more fashionable than Italian ones, silk weavers left Italy to work in France, enriching the industry there with their expertise.

Summary: Italian Design

In almost every field of human endeavor—certainly in every field of art and design that was undertaken—the Italian Renaissance was a time of remarkable achievements. The influence of those achievements was felt throughout Europe and beyond. We can feel them still today.

Looking for Character

In Italian Renaissance design, the heaven-focused extremities of the Gothic have been humanized. Spirituality has been replaced by rationality, mystery by understanding. There is a resumption of the classical vocabulary of columns, bases, entablatures, pediments, and ornaments, all harmoniously interrelated, and a resumption of the classical system of proportions. There is systematic coherence among parts and between exterior and interior. And this new logic, clarity, and cohesion is found in the hyperactive Baroque examples and the florid Rococo ones almost as obviously as it is in the serene examples of the Early Renaissance.

Looking for Quality

It is obvious that certain aspects of the Italian Renaissance are remarkable for their quality: the quiet simplicity of Brunelleschi's Old Sacristy, the muscular cascade of Michelangelo's stairs for the Laurentian Library, the balanced perfection of Palladio's Villa Capra. But there is a broader sort of quality that pervades the accomplishments of this period. The goal of the Italian Renaissance may have been the resurrection of classical antiquity—and that it accomplished imperfectly—but it accomplished something else that has proved even more valuable: the formulation of new ways of looking at buildings and interiors and furniture and ornament, and the formulation of new ways to unite those elements into well-composed wholes. Whether or not the Italian Renaissance can properly be considered a rebirth of classical design, we must acknowledge that in the Italian Renaissance our own knowledge of how to design was born.

Making Comparisons

Comparisons beg to be noticed between the Italian Renaissance and contemporaneous developments in other countries. When, in the early sixteenth century, the High Renaissance period was at its peak in Italy, the rest of Europe was still repeating the formula of Gothic style. And when, a century later, Italy moved beyond the High Renaissance into the Baroque, the rest of Europe was finally beginning to understand the fundamentals of Renaissance design.

In design, it seems, locations have their times. France, as we have seen, was supreme in the last glorious days of Gothic cathedral building, and France, as we shall see, would be supreme again in the refinements of the eighteenth century. But in the centuries between, it was Italy that, remembering the glories of her ancient past, brought to the modern world a rebirth that still inspires, ennobles, and warms us.

Spain: Hispano-Moorish to Neoclassical

Eighth to Eighteenth Centuries

"Life was never easy for the inhabitants of Spain ... whose climate is 'mingled of fire-and-ice.' It is only natural that the hardy Spanish race preferred the depiction of keen character to that of suave beauty."

— Oskar Hagen (1888–1957), art historian, in *Patterns and Principles of Spanish Art* (1948)

Spanish design is distinctive but varied. It can be lavishly ornamental, as in figure 14–1, or severely plain. In either case, it is design of unusual formality, dignity, strength, and vigor.

Determinants of Spanish Design

Spanish design was influenced not only by the varied characters of Spain's own regions but also by foreign design, particularly that of the Italians, the French, and the Moors, who came to Spain from North Africa.

Geography and Natural Resources

The Iberian Peninsula, which Spain shares with the smaller country of Portugal, is the westernmost part of the continent of Europe. In its northeast corner it is divided from France

◀ **14–1** Detail of ceiling with inlaid woodwork in the Alcazar Palace, Seville, fourteenth century.
Robert Frerck/Odyssey Productions, Inc.

by the Pyrenees Mountains. In its south it is divided from Africa only by the narrow Straits of Gibraltar; and elsewhere, it is completely surrounded by bodies of water.

Much of Spain is mountainous, rocky, and arid. The weather is hot and dry for much of the year. Severe conditions demanded strength, endurance, and stoicism in its people and in the buildings and artifacts they produced. The mountains hindered transportation and slowed the exchange of ideas, dividing the land into distinct areas and cultures. Strong sunshine and heat suggested construction with thick walls and small windows.

Spain has few forests but many stone deposits, so masonry construction is the norm. Red sandstone comes from the Pyrenees and from Andalusia in the south; limestone also comes from the south; and granite comes from the north. Marbles are found in many areas. Clay has been made into brick at least since the country's occupation by the ancient Romans, and Roman engineering genius, as seen in the triumphal arch and amphitheater at Mérida and the aqueduct at Segovia, must have served as examples of stone construction. Iron, copper,

Date	Period	Cultural and Political Events	Developments in Design
8th–15th centuries	Moorish Spain	Religious wars; *Chansons de Roland*	Palaces, mosques, *artesonado*, tiles; La Mezquita, Córdoba; Alhambra, Granada
12th–16th centuries	Middle Ages	Discoveries of West Indies, North and South America; expulsion of Jews; Christian reconquest of southern Spain; Spanish Inquisition	Cathedrals of Burgos, Toledo, Seville, and Gerona; Gothic and Plateresco styles;
16th–17th centuries	Spanish Renaissance	Hapsburg rule; Spanish Armada defeated; *Don Quixote*	Desornamentado style; El Escorial; Churrigueresco style: Cathedral of Valencia
18th century	French and Italian influences	Bourbon rule	Palácio Nacional, Mafra; Palácio Real, Madrid; Transparente, Toledo

zinc, and coal are mined from Spanish lands and used in many ways.

History

Intimate with the sea, Spain and Portugal produced some of the world's most famous explorers. They established colonies in Africa and parts of Asia, and after Spain's backing of Columbus's voyage in 1492, her reign extended to the New World as well. But Spain and Portugal were themselves often invaded and conquered. The Romans and, in turn, the Visigoths occupied the land for centuries. There is hardly a major power of antiquity that did not establish some settlement on the Iberian Peninsula.

The most dramatic and most lasting foreign influence came from the Moors, Islamic people from North Africa who crossed the Straits of Gibraltar and overwhelmed the weak and disorganized Christian feudal states of Iberia in A.D. 711 and who maintained a degree of control there until 1492. In 1085 Alfonso, king of the Spanish regions of Aragon and Navarre, bordering France, captured the city of Toledo from the Moors and began the long struggle to push them out of Spain. In 1492 the last Moorish stronghold in Spain, the kingdom of Granada, fell to the Christians. Foreign influence also came from two royal families: the Hapsburgs from Austria, who ruled in Spain from 1516 to 1700, and the Bourbons from France, who ruled there from 1700 to the twentieth century.

Within the peninsula, cultural life was also influenced by differences between Spain and Portugal. Portugal had freed herself of Moorish control in 1140, three and a half centuries before Spain, and Portugal's contacts abroad included India and China, whereas Spain's were largely in the Netherlands and the Americas. The Moorish influence is thus less strong in Portugal than in Spain, while the Eastern influence is far stronger in Portugal. Officially, Spain was unified for centuries under a single king's rule, but politically it long remained a collection of small states within the wrinkles of its topography.

Religion

Two of the world's great religions—Islam and Christianity—have dominated the history of Spain, and much Spanish history is the record of the violent struggles between them. Spanish design combines both influences. Christianity in Spain was long dominated by Roman Catholicism. The Roman church's penchant for ceremony and ritual has been amply satisfied by the richness of Spanish church architecture, interiors, and decoration. In fact, the medieval church of Santiago da Compostela, built in the eleventh century, was an important pilgrimage site for all of Europe.

The Islamic faith encouraged rich design in another way. At times forbidding the use of the human figure and other natural forms in decoration, it encouraged intricate geometry and the multiplicity of small motifs in flat patterns. But some Islamic design in Spain was monumental: The greatest of the Spanish mosques, the one at Córdoba (see figs. 14–2 and 14–3) is larger than any Christian church ever built, even St. Peter's in Rome.

Spanish Architecture and Interiors

Spanish design roughly followed the same progression of styles as that of Italy and other parts of Europe, but at later dates and with many differences. For example, we have just seen Italian Renaissance design progress from early essays in the revival of classic design to more sophisticated efforts, then to the complexities of the Baroque, and then to a renewed and more academic Neoclassicism. The Spanish parallel is more complex, at times moving back and forth between very ornate and very plain styles. For easy comparison, we have given the phases of Spanish design the same time-period names as we used in discussing Italy but we have also used Spanish names, where appropriate, for these styles.

Hispano-Moorish Style

Though influenced by their Spanish setting, the Moors' Islamic architecture and interiors where they settled in southern Spain shared many of the characteristics found in their architecture in northwest Africa. In Spain there appear the same characteristic arches of Moorish buildings—the horseshoe, the pointed horseshoe, and the ogee (see table 7–1)—as in Africa. Another arch, called the **multifoil** arch (see table 7–1 and fig. 9–8), is also found scalloped, foliated, or cusped (see fig. 14–4). The multiple concave ceiling constructions called **muqarnas**, corbelled one over another (see fig. 9–15), appear in many buildings of Spain (see fig. 14–4). Two indispensable features of the Islamic mosque, the niche called a **mihrab** (see fig. 9–4) and the tall pulpit called a **minbar** (fig. 9–5) also appear abundantly.

The focus of Hispano-Moorish buildings was invariably on the interior. Exterior surfaces are blank, plain, and unadorned, leaving the first-time visitor without anticipation of the richly decorated wonders they enclose. Some scholars have viewed this "plain brown wrapper" approach as a form of security for the Moors, hiding their interior treasures from the view of potential thieves. Others have seen it as part of a tradition dating from the desert tents of the nomadic Arabs, who lived in canvas tents with blank exteriors exposed to the sun, sand, and wind but with interiors filled with luxurious hangings, beautiful rugs, and colorful cushions.

Structurally, the villas of the Moors were simple, with plain exterior walls and few windows. They were built around a landscaped patio off which the rooms were placed. Elaborate arrangements were made for reception rooms, master's quarters, and baths, and an isolated section with a private garden was devoted to the use of women and children. The Moors were adept at formal gardening and used this art to its fullest extent as a contribution to the enjoyment of life. Their gardens, closely related to the composition of the house, were terraced and trellised, and pools and fountains were welcome relief from the heat.

The interior walls were treated with plain plaster, colored tile in geometric patterns, brickwork, colored plaster ornament in relief, ornamental leather, or a combination of these materials. Woodwork was limited to the doors and ceiling. The floors were in tile, brick, or stone, and were covered with rugs of both tapestry and pile weave in Muhammadan patterns (see fig. 14–31). Heavy earthenware pottery was arranged in compositions on shelves and walls. Colors used for tilework, plaster ornament, painted woodwork, and in the rich wool textiles were the brilliant primary hues inherited from nomadic forebears.

The Mezquita, or Great Mosque, Córdoba The Mezquita (pronounced "meth-*kee*-tah"), or Great Mosque, of Córdoba, is one of those buildings that, on the exterior, appears to be extensive but thoroughly ordinary and dull. The approach to the building through a walled patio of orange trees is pleasant, but nothing outside the mosque prepares us for its interior.

The first part to be built, about a third of the present structure, was finished in the year 785. It replaced a Christian church formerly occupying the site, and it incorporated stone pillars from that church, some of which had already been recycled from even older Roman buildings in the area. Other stone pillars came from other buildings in Spain; some were shipped from Carthage in North Africa, and some from Constantinople. They are naturally of different heights, with varying bases to compensate for the differences. The capitals were all of carved and gilded marble, but most have been replaced by concrete replicas.

Three additions were made during the next two centuries, bringing the mosque to its present enormous size of 390 by 600 feet (120 × 185 m). There is a seeming infinity of marble pillars supporting arches made of alternating bands of red brick and pale yellow limestone. These arches are the most striking feature of the interior (fig. 14–2). To achieve the desired ceiling height of about 40 feet (13 m) with the much shorter existing column shafts, an unusual double-arch design was devised. The lower arches spring freely through the air at the tops of the columns, obviously supporting nothing, but

▲ **14–2** The two-tiered arches of the great Mosque, Cordoba.
© Achim Bednorz, Koln

▲ **14–3** In the Great Mosque of Cordoba, the dome in front of the *mihrab*.
Werner Forman/Art Resource, NY

acting as stiffening braces for the taller arches above them which actually carry the roof. The striking visual effect of this multiplicity of similar elements is thereby doubled.

The *mihrab* of the Mezquita is more than a mere niche, for it is approached under a series of three domes. The central and largest dome (fig. 14–3) features intersecting arches that form an eight-pointed star, with surfaces faced in gold mosaics.

Viewpoints | AN ITALIAN WRITER IN THE MOSQUE AT CÓRDOBA

The Italian writer Edmondo de Amicis (1846–1908) wrote about his visits to Spain in *La Spagna* (1873). This is his description of the Mezquita: "Imagine a forest, and imagine that you are in the depths of this forest, and that you can see nothing but the trunks of the trees. Thus, no matter on what side of the mosque you look, the eye sees nothing but columns. It is a limitless forest of marble. . . .

Nineteen naves extend before the visitor; they are intersected by thirty-three other naves, and the whole building is supported by more than nine hundred columns of porphyry, jasper, *breccia*, and marbles of every color. . . . It is like the sudden revelation of an unknown religion, nature, and life, which carries your imagination to . . . Paradise."

The Alhambra, Granada The Alhambra in Granada, begun in 1309 and finished in 1354, was the last of the Spanish palaces constructed by the Moors before their expulsion, and it remains today the supreme achievement of Moorish architecture and decoration. The Alhambra is planned around numerous arcaded courtyards, agreeably blending architecture—though the exterior is exceedingly plain—with gardens, fountains, and reflecting pools. In this complex a visitor seldom loses the sound of splashing waters or the perfume of jasmine and orange. Its enclosing walls maintain the desired seclusion, while arched openings offer vistas overlooking distant snowy peaks. One of the Alhambra's two principal courtyards is the Patio de la Albérca, or Court of the Pool, sometimes also called the Court of the Myrtles for the plantings that edge its 113-foot-long (35 m) reflecting pool. The other principal courtyard is the Patio de los Leónes, or Court of the Lions (fig. 14–4), named for a central fountain supported by twelve figures of lions, exceptions to the Islamic proscription against natural representations. The lions support a polygonal fountain basin, a source of water for the shallow troughs that extend from it in four directions.

The interior walls of the surrounding rooms are covered with fantastic and minutely colored ornamental details scaled to be subordinate to the effect of the whole. Private apartments overlook the more public courtyards through the interstices of decorative wooden grilles. Tiled niches accommodate beds. Elaborate baths contain taps from which once spouted cold, hot, and perfumed water. The majority of the rooms are treated with tiled wainscoting in colorful geometric patterns to a height of about 4 feet (120 cm), above which there is a wall surface covered with the delicately tinted all-over plaster ornament called **yesería** (see fig. 14–17). Near the ceiling the walls are often treated with friezes, most often enriched by decorative cursive inscriptions stating that "There is no God but Allah."

Gothic Styles: Mudéjar and Christian Gothic

The Gothic period arrived in Spain when the country was still torn between Islamic and Christian factions. The Moors were no longer the powerful rulers they had been, but they had not yet been expelled. Two groups, the **Mudéjars** and the **Mozarabs**, shared characteristics of both cultures. The Mudéjars were Moors who had converted to Christianity; in changing their religion, however, they did not necessarily change their taste in design, and the Mudéjar style of

architecture and interiors incorporates Islamic decorative details and workmanship. The Mozarabs were Christians living in areas still under Arab rule. Both groups produced designs that blended Islamic elements with Christian elements, first with Romanesque and later with Gothic details.

There was much that was beautiful in the Moorish decorative materials and patterns, and those that were suitably free from Muhammadan religious significance were eagerly adopted by Christian builders of the Gothic period. Many of

▲ 14–4 The Court of the Lions in the Alhambra, Granada.

the interiors in the fused styles of Mudéjar and Mozarabic Spain exhibit Islamic and Gothic influences together, as in a room reconstructed at the Decorative Arts Museum, Madrid (fig. 14–5).

While the Moors in southern Spain were building their elegant palaces and impressive mosques, the Christians in northern Spain were building in a style closely related to the Gothic work we have seen north of the Pyrenees. Two major expressions of the Christian Gothic style were castles and cathedrals, while the communal bath became popular with the Moors.

Baths Communal baths, which were first built in Spain under Moorish domination, were modeled not on the monumental Roman complexes, though the Romans had built some baths in Spain, but on the Islamic *hammam*. These were sometimes privately operated for profit and sometimes part of religious complexes, but always they served the Moslem emphasis on ritual ablutions and cleanliness. Unlike the Roman baths, there were no adjacent courtyards for physical exercise nor were there any *frigidaria* for cold plunges. Essential elements were simply an entrance hall,

▶ **14–5** A reconstruction of a sixteenth-century Mudéjar interior with *artesonado* ceiling treatment, a hooded fireplace, and a carpet with arabesque medallions.
National Museum of Decorative Arts, Madrid, Spain

often domed (the dome often pierced with small glazed windows), and a hot room with pool. The entrance of a twelfth century bath in Gerona is seen in figure 14–6.

Castles Beginning in the eighth and nineth centuries, noble Christian families embarked on a program of castle building, particularly in the province that—because of the number of such castles—came to be called Castile. There were probably more of these fortified castles in Spain than in any other European country, many of them built in the years of the gradual Christian reconquest of Spain from the Moors. An example is La Mota Castle (fig. 14–7), which was built in the north central province of Valladolid in the twelfth century but was later altered in the fifteenth century. It has an outer crenellated wall with round turrets, an inner wall with rectangular towers, an interior courtyard three floors high, and a tall square corner tower or *keep,* which contained the owners' living quarters. Spanish castles were mostly built on precipitous heights and were not only of formidable defensive strength but also

▲ **14–7** Aerial view, La Mota Castle, Medina del Campo, fifteenth century.
Robert Harding Picture Library Ltd. Alamy Images

elaborately treated in Gothic detail in their residential sections.

Cathedrals   The Gothic arts practiced in Italy, France, and northern Europe were introduced into Spain chiefly by the Cistercian monks of Cluny. Churches with sculptured portals and adjacent cloisters, famous for their carved columns and capitals, rose along the roads that were used by the pilgrims to visit Santiago de Compostela. The thirteenth- and fourteenth-century Gothic cathedrals of Burgos, Toledo, León, Salamanca, and Seville appear at a later date than their counterparts in France, yet they reflect all the splendor and power of the Gothic movement.

These and other cathedrals with their almost incredible wealth of altarpieces, sculptured alabaster, polychromed woodwork, gilded wrought-iron grills, and marble tombs are treasure-houses of decorative detail. The Spanish Gothic churches usually have smaller **fenestration** (the overall design and arrangement of windows) than those in northern climates, coming from the necessity of tempering the glare and heat of the southern sun. The large wall areas produce a marked austerity, but these large surfaces are extensively ornamented with geometric patterns in the Moorish manner. The horseshoe arch is often used, as is the Gothic pointed arch. The somberness of the interiors accentuates the brilliance of the color on the walls and pavements revealed by the diagonal rays of the sun through the stained-glass windows. In the darker corners there is an impressive use of candlelight.

In Portugal, an impressive Gothic example is the Monastery of Santa Maria of Victory in Aljubarrota. Completed in 1433, it commemorates the 1385 battle there that secured Portuguese independence from Spain.

Cathedral of Seville   Judged on the basis of floor area, the cathedral of Seville is the third largest in the world, the only larger ones being St. Peter's in Rome (see fig. 13–15) and St. Paul's in London (see fig. 16-11). However, so high are its ceilings that, on the basis of enclosed volume, the cathedral of Seville is the world's largest. It is 406 feet long, 268 feet wide, and 99 feet high (126 × 83 × 30 m), the vault over the nave rising still farther to 130 feet (40 m). Some French Gothic cathedrals, as we have seen in Chapter 8, rose to greater heights at their tallest points, but they did not maintain those heights over such a large area. Commissioned in

▲ **14–8** Gothic vaulting in the cathedral of Seville, almost 100 ft. (30.5 m) above the floor.
Abercrombie

1401, Seville Cathedral took more than a century to build and was consecrated in 1519.

The interior of the cathedral is divided into a nave and double aisles by thirty-two immense, clustered piers. In addition, there are numerous side chapels and a *parroquia*, or parish church. Stained glass is amply used and bold in color. Within the lofty ceiling vaults (fig. 14–8), the ribs are arranged in a pattern more decorative than structurally logical, and between the ribs there are fields textured with projecting **bosses**, or pendant ornaments, typically used at the intersections of ribs. The *rejas* (pronounced "*ray*-hass"), or iron grilles, are highly decorative, and the **retablos** (pronounced "ray-*tah*-blohss"), or altar screens, are among the richest specimens of medieval woodworking to be found anywhere.

Adjacent to the cathedral are two remnants of the mosque that previously occupied the site. One is the forecourt, planted with orange trees, through which the building is entered. The other is the Giralda Tower. The original tower, standing 197 feet (60 m) high, was built in the twelfth century as the mosque's minaret. To this simple square structure was added a more elaborate cathedral bell tower, bringing the total height to 320 feet (98 m), including a rotating iron weather vane or *giraldillo* that gave the tower its name.

Renaissance Styles: Plateresco and Desornamentado

In the late fifteenth century, the discoveries and foreign conquests of both Spain and Portugal were powerful influences on design. In both countries, a taste developed for covering wide surfaces with rich, small-scale ornament. This taste seems to have come from two origins: the myriad details of Moorish decoration (though not always applied with Moorish delicacy), and the wealth of riches and exotic goods flooding into the peninsula. In Spain, this phase of superabundant ornament was called *Isabellina* after Queen Isabella I, who reigned from 1474 to 1504. The Portuguese equivalent of Isabellina originated during the reign of king Dom Manuel I (1495–1521) and was called *Manuelino*. It differed from the Spanish style by being more hybrid in origin and expression. The Manuelino included reminiscences of Roman construction, Gothic arches, architectural features from Arabia and India, and marine ornaments that seemed to symbolize the seafaring destiny of Portugal. But the more important styles to emerge during the Renaissance were the styles called **Plateresco** and **Desornomentado**.

Plateresco   As quantities of gold and silver continued to flow to Spain from the new colonies in America, there was ample opportunity for displays of virtuosity by the Spanish silversmith, the *platero*. The fine detail and elaborate ornament of such metalwork lent its name to the **Plateresco** style, which is distinguished from the Isabellina only in being later, not in being basically different. Its source is not solely the work of the silversmith, of course, but also that of the architect. Underneath its profusion of ornament, the Plateresco structure can be either Gothic or Renaissance in its construction and volume, but it is the ornament itself that defines the style. One example (fig. 14–9) is the sacristy doors and adjacent pilasters seen in the Toledo Cathedral, carved in 1549. The ornament included heraldic shields, portrait medallions, and elaborations on Italian motifs such as the rinceau, the acanthus, and the anthemion (see table 4–2).

The Plateresco style was primarily used for exterior architectural treatments, patios, formal rooms in churches and public buildings, and for furniture and accessory design. It was not extensively used as a style for the interior walls of houses, but domestic interiors of this period begin to reflect the greater richness of detail, an increase in types of furniture,

▲ **14–9** Sacristy doors and adjacent pilasters in an anteroom of the chapter house of the Cathedral of Toledo, carved in the *Plateresco* style by Gregorio Pardo in 1549.
Instituto Amatller de Arte Hispanico, Barcelona, Spain

and improvements in comfort and conveniences that were seen in contemporary Italian rooms. In the middle of the sixteenth century, after treatises on the classical orders by the Italian architect and theorist Sebastiano Serlio were first published in Spain, the Plateresco passion for ornament began to abate somewhat, easing the transition to the very different style that would follow, the Desornamentado.

Desornamentado   Noted for its severity, **Desornamentado** (pronounced "day-sor-nah-men-*tah*-do"), meaning "unornamented," was a powerful style characterized by austerity. The style was limited to court, ecclesiastical, and public buildings and was never considered fully suitable for domestic use. Plain surfaces appeared with carefully refined proportions. Its great monument, El Escorial, was built by the Hapsburg ruler Philip II. The Hapsburgs were the ruling house of Austria, who had gained control of the Spanish throne by means of well-planned marriages and through conquest by the Hapsburg Holy Roman Emperor, Charles V, Philip's father. Philip II (1527–98) also inherited Portugal and the Italian provinces of Naples and Sicily. He presided over the beginning of a so-called golden age of Spanish art and literature, and both his power and his personality were critical elements in the formation of the severe new style.

El Escorial, Near Madrid   El Escorial, 30 miles (48 km) northwest of Madrid, is one of the great archetypes of architectural history, a gigantic structure hardly matched for its sobriety, plainness, and simplicity. Built of solid gray granite quarried from the neighboring mountains, it measures 570 by 740 feet (175 × 228 m), not including the altar wing that is the sole projection beyond the plan's basic 8-acre rectangle. Within the rectangle, a grid plan divides the complex into square and rectangular courtyards surrounded by building masses that contain a royal palace, a large church, a monastery, an infirmary, and a mausoleum for a large number of Spanish monarchs (fig. 14–10). The building mass is enlivened only by corner towers and by the 300-foot-high (92 m) church dome rising above the rest. Its endlessly repetitive windows are evenly spaced and in unadorned frames. Outside and in, detailing is spare and restrained. When a classical order is applied, it is, in most cases, the simple, sturdy Tuscan. Planning for El Escorial was begun in 1559, when the Italian-trained Juan Bautista de Toledo (c. 1515–1567) was brought from Naples by Philip II and appointed architect. Bautista was succeeded by his former assistant Juan de Herrera (1530–97), an architect, mathematician, and Humanist, who continued Bautista's work until the building was finished in 1584.

Nothing like it had existed before. We may see four factors in its original style: first, an expression of the rational, pious, and grave personality of its patron, Philip; second, a reaction against the sometimes frivolous complexities of the ornate Plateresco style that had prevailed before it; third, an expression of faith; and, fourth, an admiring knowledge by both Bautista and Herrera of recent accomplishments in Renaissance Italy. Bautista, indeed, was reported to have

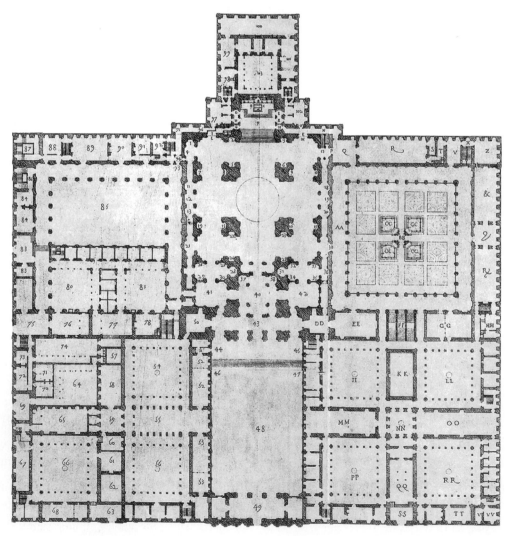

▶ **14–10** Plan of the ground floor of the Escorial. The church is at top center, and the king's private apartments in the wing projecting beyond it. The library is space "MM" in the lower right quadrant.
After Kubler, *Building The Escorial,*
© 1982 Princeton University Press

▲ **14–11** Library of the monastery of the Escorial, 1584. Ceiling frescoes represent the seven liberal arts.
Tourist Office of Spain

▲ **14–12** Looking into the tiny private bedroom of King Felipe II in the Escorial. The door seen just beyond the bed opens to the altar of the church.
Album/Joseph Martin/The Art Archive

worked on St. Peter's under the leadership of Michelangelo. Only the most insignificant and utilitarian buildings of the Italian Renaissance would have been as plain as Philip's palace, but what St. Peter's and El Escorial share is a ruling sense of proportion and a profound respect for reason.

In El Escorial, Philip saw the new austerity as an ideological declaration. Purged of unnecessary ornament, the building manifested the severe discipline of Catholic orthodoxy at the time. It was conceived as a highly moral building, truly a "sermon in stone." In this sense, it may seem odd that the least severe part of the huge complex is the church itself, but the message must have been that spiritual matters are worthy of glorification, but worldly matters are not.

El Escorial's austerity was a moral declaration. The building's only richly embellished spaces are the church and the library, demonstrating that religion and religious learning are to be celebrated, unlike more mundane things. The library's

great vault (fig. 14–11), soaring above bookcases of ebony and walnut designed by Herrera and containing rare Greek, Latin, and Arabic manuscripts, is punctuated with **lunettes**, half-round framed openings, and is painted with allegorical frescoes.

But the most characteristic of all the many rooms of El Escorial are the private apartments of Philip II in the projecting east wing. They are poignantly simple. Their door and window openings are framed in pale gray marble, their floors are of clay tile, and their walls are whitewashed above a wainscot of glazed Talavera tile. A tiny sleeping alcove (fig. 14–12) opens directly onto the church's high altar, so that the king—even when bedridden in his painful last years—could hear the Mass. A small canopied bed virtually fills the room. Next to it is another small alcove that served as the king's study. It is modestly furnished with a straight-backed armchair, a second chair on which he could rest his infected leg, a book stand, and a writing desk.

Baroque Style: Churrigueresco

The architecture and decoration of the Iberian Peninsula came into its own in the century between 1650 and 1750. During this period a style emerged that had never been—and probably never could have been—created elsewhere: **Churrigueresco**. It was a style steeped in a riotous enrichment that seemed to express the Spanish character at its most passionate.

Churrigueresco With the death of Herrera in 1597, a reaction against the severity of the Desornamentado quickly developed. To replace the Desornamentado, popular taste returned enthusiastically to the lavish use of ornamentation. Feeling a need to reassert the vigor of the Roman church after the Reformation movement and sensing the new style's emotional effect on the masses, the Jesuits promoted it strongly.

The new architectural conceptions were promoted by a remarkable family of sculptors, wood carvers, and architects named Churriguera. The founder of the family tradition was José Simón de Churriguera, "the elder," who died in 1679. Joining him in the family profession were his five sons and three of his grandsons. The Baroque Churrigueresco style they fostered was primarily a style of surface decoration, rather than one of structural changes. Its most characteristic features were applied to exterior entrance doorways, to the interior decoration of palaces, and to church **retables** (decorative screens or panels behind altars). In a considerably subdued form it reached the houses of the people, where it was seen more in the furniture and accessories than in the decorative treatment of the walls.

The new style was not just a revival of the Plateresco. Its scale was larger and its effects more three-dimensional. Natural objects used for the new ornamental motifs were in bold relief and frequently heroic in size. In the design of public buildings, the classical orders were used in free and unconventional ways. Columns were often Solomonic, with spiral shafts; at other times, they were disguised with heavy rustication. Entablatures and moldings bulged upward or outward; broken and scroll pediments ended in squirming volutes; Doric capitals sprouted Corinthian acanthus leaves; brackets were nonsupporting; and pyramidal forms stood on their apexes. Stucco decoration was modeled to imitate rock formations, waterfalls, and drapery swags. Nude figures cringed under heavy loads; cherubim and seraphim emerged from plaster clouds, and religious symbols were profuse; optical illusions bewildered their observers; and transparent alabaster carvings glowed with the light from dozens of candles. Silver, tortoiseshell, and ivory inlay enriched the remaining wall surfaces. Fantasy ruled.

Other prominent Churrigueresco designers included Antonio Tomé and his two sons, Narciso and Diego, who were responsible for the façade of the University of Valladolid. Narciso Tomé is credited with the Transparente in the Cathedral of Toledo.

The Transparente, Toledo The Cathedral of Toledo, an example of Spanish Gothic architecture, was built in the thirteenth century and finished before the Cathedral of Seville was begun. Narciso Tomé added the retable called the Transparente to its ambulatory in the years 1721–32. It is perhaps the most extreme example of the Churrigueresco style (fig. 14–13). Between stacked pairs of columns with angel's heads along their shafts and around their capitals, a great conflation of bronze sunbeams and marble figures sweeps upward towards a large window in the cathedral's vault, its opening ringed with more angels. There are elements of fresco work as well. Like Bernini's Baldacchino at St. Peter's, designed a century earlier, it is difficult to know whether to call it architecture or sculpture. Tomé's work is undeniably effective in imparting a sense of drama and high energy.

Rococo and Neoclassical Styles

As we saw in Italy (and as we shall see in France), following the Baroque but preceding the Neoclassical was the **Rococo** style. It was lighter than the Baroque in both weight and color. Its profuse ornament was often asymmetrical and dominated by C-shaped and S-shaped (ogee) curves.

In earlier Spanish design we have noted that the extensive but quiet patterns of Moorish ornament combined well with Spanish taste. We have seen that the harmonic proportions of the Italian Renaissance, as in El Escorial, also complemented the sober Spanish temperament. Imports from Italy during the Rococo period were far less restrained and seem more foreign to the Spanish tradition. In fact, they *were* foreign. The clients for these interiors were the Bourbons who had arrived from France in 1700 to rule Spain, and most of the artists and artisans they hired were from other parts of Europe, chiefly from Italy and Sicily. Still, the Rococo seen

◄ 14–13 The Transparente retable of the Cathedral of Toledo, designed by Narciso Tomé and his family and finished in 1732.
Scala/Art Resource, NY

here is not the Rococo of Italy (nor the Rococo of France). Less delicate than either of those, it has a truly Spanish vigor, as expressed in the Palácio Real in Madrid.

In the last half of the eighteenth century, Spanish taste turned to a more strictly classical style, the **Neoclassical**, which was considered a truer expression of the classical principles of antiquity than the earlier Renaissance style had been.

In 1752 the Real Academia de Bellas Artes de San Fernando (Royal Academy of Fine Arts of San Fernando) was founded and began sending six artists every year to Rome to study the ancient monuments. Ventura Rodríguez (1717–85), who had apprenticed under Juvarra and worked under Juvarra's successor Sacchetti, began as a Baroque architect and ended as a Neoclassical one. However, Juan de Villaneuva (1739–1811)

▲ **14–14** The Porcelain Room in Madrid's Palacio Real, surfaced with Rococo porcelain plaques.
Patrimonio Nacional, Madrid

was more closely identified with the new style, and his major achievement is the Prado Museum in Madrid.

Palácio Real, Madrid   Spain's great Rococo palace, the Palácio Real, was built on the Madrid riverfront site where both a Moorish castle and later the Alcazar Palace had stood. The new building was begun by Felipe V just after the Alcazar burned in 1734, and it would be the residence of Spanish royalty and the seat of Spanish power until the Republic was proclaimed in 1931. For its design Felipe chose Filippo Juvarra (1678–1736), an Italian Rococo architect from Turin. But Juvarra died in 1736, and the king replaced him with his disciple Giovanni Battista Sacchetti (1690–1764), also from Turin. In 1760 the new king Charles III replaced

Sacchetti with the architect Francesco Sabbatini (1721–97), who was from Naples, and who completed the palace four years later. Together, Juvarra, Sacchetti, and Sabatini produced a design reflecting the current Italian taste, with a nicely articulated mass of pale gray stone built around a square courtyard roughly 165 feet (51 m) to a side. Its exterior impresses by its extent and rectitude, but it hardly prepares one for the rich exuberance within. While the overall architecture of the Palácio Real is too reserved and too classical to be considered Rococo, that term seems appropriate for the interiors. A whole series of workshops—the Talleres Reales—were set up to produce the wanted components of marble, bronze, textiles, plasterwork, porcelain, cabinetry, and upholstery, thus institutionalizing these trades in Spain. Staffing the workshops were Italian, French, German, and Flemish artisans, with a few native Spaniards.

Italy's great Rococo painter Gaimbattista Tiepolo, who painted murals in some of Palladio's villas, lived the last eight years of his life in Spain and contributed three ceiling frescoes to the palace. Major spaces include an impressive pair of stair halls flanking the Hall of the Halberdiers (site of one of the Tiepolo frescoes) and, adjacent to that hall, a throne room with walls faced with red velvet in gilt frames. Sharing the central axis with this suite of rooms, but across the courtyard, is the Royal Chapel. Two of the most interesting interiors, however, are the Porcelain Room and the Gasparini Room.

The Palácio Real's Porcelain Room (fig. 14–14) is a relatively small room that was used as the king's boudoir. Its walls, except for some inset mirrors, are completely surfaced with porcelain plaques screwed into a hidden wood framework, presenting surfaces of unfading color and unusual sheen. The effect is somewhat similar to that of a room faced with ceramic tile, but it is not the same: The porcelain plaques are more varied in size, many of them larger than tile; the joints between them are mostly hidden; and they are far more three-dimensional than tile, some porcelain representations of medallions, urns, cupids, garlands, and drapery swags extending several inches beyond the wall plane. The rich modulation and sheen of the wall surface are tempered by a restrained color palette, the background color of the plaques being cream and the ornament being limited to green and gold.

This was not the only porcelain finished room in existence. A possible inspiration for such a room is one in the Santos Palace at Lisbon, Portugal, dating from the middle of the seventeenth century, which has a ceiling virtually covered with Chinese blue-and-white porcelain plates held within a

▲ **14–15** The Gasparini room in the Palacio Real, designed by Matteo Gasparini and begun in 1761. Patrimonio Nacional, Madrid

wood frame. Contemporary with the Porcelain Room at the Palácio Real is another in the palace at Aranjuez, Spain, depicting scenes such as the mythical Andromeda chained to a rock, Chinese figures dancing and swinging from trees, and a man in a turban climbing a tree to escape a leopard. In Italy, a porcelain-lined room was constructed at Naples, but later dismantled and reassembled at Capodimonte. Behind all such rooms, of course, was the European fascination with things Chinese: The Porcelain Pagoda in Nanking, for example, completely faced with porcelain tile, had become famous in Europe after publication of its design in 1665.

The most impressive, the most florid, and generally the most successful rooms in the Palácio Real are those designed by Mattia Gasparini (died 1774), and the most spectacular is the one named for him, the Gasparini Room (fig. 14–15). It was designed to be the king's dressing room, but in times

when the king's dressing was not a private matter but a court ceremony. The room can fairly be called a Rococo fantasy or, better, a *fantasia*, a word shared by both Italian and Spanish languages, because it is evident that its influences are Italian, but evident as well that the room is Spanish.

The most striking feature is the floor, an ebullient swirl of inlaid marbles in rust, olive, pale blue-gray, beige, and gold. Its ceiling, equally exuberant, displays life-size Chinese figures at each corner and, between them, ornate jungles of vegetation on a cream-colored ground. A high glaze gives these ceiling decorations the sheen of porcelain, but they are in fact stucco. From the center of the ceiling hangs an enormous chandelier (of later date) with a gilded bronze lion (symbolic of a king) lying among its crystal pendants. The whole room is saved from careening into madness by its walls. These most visible surfaces mediate between the great dramas of the floor and ceiling with quieter, more delicately detailed designs of silk embroidery in pale shades of gold and silvery green. This fabric participates fully in the room's Rococo spirit, but its *relative* simplicity and *relatively* small scale skillfully moderate the bolder gestures above and below. The wall's wainscoting, cornice, and door and window surrounds are of beige marble, and these are quite plain—in this context, even rather severe—in form. Together, the wall fabric and the marble trim, through all the room's torrent of movement, maintain a crisp distinction of planes; we are never disoriented here, for walls, floor, and ceiling all read clearly as separate elements. Throughout the room, colors are often strong but carefully chosen and limited in number.

The Prado, Madrid   Villaneuva's supreme Neoclassical building began as the Academia de Ciencias (Academy of Sciences); designed in 1787, it was later named in 1819, by mandate of King Ferdinand VII, the Prado Museum. It is a symmetrical structure of stone and brick with an impressive Doric entrance portico or *propylaeum* (fig. 14–16), modeled closely—including the larger opening between the center columns—on the Propylaia of the Athenian Acropolis (see fig. 4–15). On either side, the ground floor alternates arches and niches, the niches filled with classical urns and statues of the Arts by Valeriano Salvatierra, who had studied in Rome as a member of the Royal Academy. The floor above is faced with a long Ionic colonnade, and the great bas-relief panel over the entrance depicts Ferdinand VII as protector of the Arts. Two perpendicular axes dominate the interior; its second floor, originally planned to house a museum of natural history, is a long continuous sweep of wide connecting galleries and has a separate entrance at one end of the building.

Spanish Ornament

We have said that Spanish design can be plain or ornamented. When it was ornamented, the ornament could reach great heights of richness and complexity, whether its forms were natural or geometric. As we have seen in Chapter 9, some Islamic sects forbade the copying of natural forms. Therefore, the Moors, who were excellent mathematicians, resorted to geometry for pattern inspiration, and they developed an extraordinary originality in the design of surface ornament. The most intricate arrangements of interlacing straight and curved lines were devised. Squares and rectangles were usually avoided, but stars, crescents, crosses, hexagons, octagons, and many other forms were used. As in the Middle East, the **arabesque** and other plantlike ornaments were also used.

In the Moorish period geometric ornament was adapted to wood, plaster, tile, and textile designs, and was accentuated by gorgeous coloring in red, blue, green, white, silver, and gold. The

▲ **14–16** Façade detail, Prado Museum, Madrid, designed 1787 by Juan de Villanueva.
Hidekazu Nishibata/SuperStock, Inc.

somewhat resembling red pine. In dwellings, the wood-paneled ceilings and doors were usually left in natural finish; in public buildings, gilding or color was sometimes used.

Doors

Ornamental door panels and door surrounds were important features of Spanish design throughout its many periods. These began, as would be expected, in Moorish times with carved geometric effects and arabesques.

Long after the Moorish period ended, Spanish doors continued to be carved in the artesonado style, similar in design to the ceilings described above. In the Plateresco phase of the Renaissance, ornamental work was produced in wood and other materials. We have seen the pair of sacristy doors in the Cathedral of Toledo (see fig. 14–9), which demonstrate the style, and were added roughly 180 years before Tomé's Transparente.

In the severely plain audience chamber of El Escorial, adjoining Philip II's private alcoves, the only touch of ornamental luxury is in five pairs of finely detailed marquetry doors made as a gift for the building by German artist Bartolomé Weisshaupt. A more simply paneled door from Philip's bedroom to the altar is visible in figure 14–12, and another example is seen near the center of figure 14–19. A single square panel, which might be repeated all over a door surface, is seen at the left in figure 14–22.

A special decorative feature popular in the Moorish house was the ornamental wall niche. Recessed for a distance of about 18 inches (46 cm), it started at the top of the wainscot and normally carried two hinged doors similar to modern window shutters. Sometimes the doors were pierced with silhouettes or painted with bright patterns on both sides. The rear and sides of the niches were treated with colored tiles or painted in brilliant colors, forming a strong point of contrast with the neutral plaster walls. The niches were furnished with shelving that supported useful and ornamental accessories.

Spanish Furniture

Before the Renaissance, rooms in Spain, as elsewhere in Europe, were sparsely furnished. Paintings and inventories of those times indicate the few types of furniture that were used. There were stools, benches, folding seats, chairs of honor, canopied beds, simple desks, occasional sideboards, and cab-

inets with drawers. Dining tables were assembled from loose planks set on trestles and were often covered with a rug of Middle Eastern or Far Eastern design.

Moorish houses in Spain contained benches that were built in and attached to the wall. Cushions and straw mattresses were placed on the floor, a custom continued from the times of the nomads. Rugs were used in profusion on floors, benches, and as wall hangings. Leather and wood chests were used for the storage of clothes. Pottery, bronze, and copper were the materials for cooking and eating utensils. Elaborate embroideries, laces, and loom-made textiles added color and pattern interests. Bottles, flasks, and perfume containers were made of iridescent glassware of great beauty.

Much Spanish Gothic furniture was painted in bright colors and gold. Detail was taken from Christian Gothic architectural elements, but many pieces show Mudéjar influence in the use of geometrically patterned inlays. Heavy proportions and sound construction were the rule and were considered more important than lightness or elegance. Pieces were well joined and were often braced with wrought iron.

With the advent of the Renaissance, luxury was introduced to Spanish interiors from Italian precedents, and with it many new forms of furniture and decorative details (fig. 14–19). Almost all Spanish furniture from 1500 to 1650 was of Italian inspiration. Although local conditions and traditions affected designs, little was produced that was wholly indigenous. Some of the finest furniture was created for the church, and its ornament was naturally sacred in character, including such symbols as the pope's miter and the keys to heaven.

The woods most commonly used for Spanish Renaissance furniture construction were walnut (a great favorite), chestnut, cedar, oak, pine, pear, box, and orange, with inlays of ebony, ivory, and tortoiseshell. Beginning about 1550, the Spaniards were the first Europeans to use mahogany as a cabinet wood, importing it from their colonies in the West Indies. Often it was recycled: Because of the enormous size of the mahogany trees, the wood had first been used in the construction of Spanish galleons; when these ships were wrecked or taken out of service, the wood was then salvaged for smaller structures and for furniture. Such wood was sometimes called *Spanish mahogany*.

By 1725 the nobility and the upper classes of both Spain and Portugal began to decorate and furnish rooms in the French manner. Rooms became smaller, and furniture was reduced in scale. The Spanish versions of French forms were bolder, heavier, richer, and more masculine, and they were

Vargueno

Spiral Shaft

Table with Trestle Support

Chair

Nailhead Patterns

Leather Upholstered Chair

Wood Panelled Door

Geometrical Tile Pattern

Shell Motif

Torch Stand

Window Grille

Moorish Arch Form

◄14–19 Spanish furniture and details
Gilbert Werlé/New York School of Interior Design

often exaggerated in form, color, and ornament. There was a general tendency to finish furniture in white lacquer and gold or in pastel tints. Mirrors played a prominent part in interior design and were inserted in the wall panels or placed in elaborately carved frames and hung on the wall. Many new types of furniture were introduced, such as card tables, consoles, varieties of sofas and settees, clocks, and commodes. Comfortable upholstery was introduced. The Spaniards con-

tinued their traditional use of leather upholstery and often applied it to French furniture framework.

From the beginning of the eighteenth century the English also shipped a great deal of furniture to both Spain and Portugal. The style of Queen Anne became popular and was extensively copied by local craftsmen. The chair backs, however, were usually much higher than in the English examples. Later in the century, Chippendale forms were adopted.

England made special furniture for export, and many of the English pieces were finished in red lacquer, to appeal to the Spanish taste. With this finish, cheaper woods could be used in construction, with the result that both tables and chairs often required the use of stretchers. Many of the chairs had caned seats and backs. In much of the furniture made in Spain, both English and French elements were combined in the same piece. In the Mediterranean regions of Spain—Valencia, Catalonia, and the Balearic Islands of Majorca and Minorca—there was also influence from Venice.

In the eighteenth century, the influence of Venice was strong in southern Spain. This accounts for the fine lacquered furniture, at first imported and later copied locally, found in these regions. Chairs, console and corner tables, and handsome secretary cabinets were generally lacquered in red, yellow, green, and sometimes in blue. The surface decoration, consisting of **Chinoiseries**, or stylized eighteenth-century motifs, was applied in different shades of gold, reinforced with black lines.

Toward the end of the eighteenth century, both interiors and furniture began to be influenced by the Adam brothers of England, who had studied the ruins of Pompeii and other cities of antiquity. English Hepplewhite and Sheraton furniture in satinwood and painted finishes was also much in demand. Antique classical, rather than Renaissance forms, also came through French designers who were creating the Baroque style named for Louis XVI, who ruled France from 1774 to 1794. The straight line was substituted for the curved or rococo forms; the cabriole leg was eliminated; and all the sentimental elements of design associated with Louis XVI and Marie Antoinette became fashionable.

All the types of furniture used in Spain were seen in Portugal, but in Portuguese examples, the size and complexity of the turnings that were used for chair and table supports and for the headboards of beds were likely to be more exaggerated. Spiral and bulbous shapes were also more common. In addition, it is claimed that furniture caning and the cabriole leg were first used in Europe by the Portuguese, who brought them from China. Lacquered furniture was also brought from the Far East, and Oriental woven and printed textiles were first imported into Western Europe by the Portuguese traders. During the Manuelino period (1495–1521), in such places as Batalha and Tomar, the East Indian influence was very strong and expressed itself in extravagantly rich detail that seemed to be inspired by crustacean and tropical vegetation forms. This was the first Far Eastern influence on Western art.

▲ **14–20** A seventeenth–century Spanish *frailero* with embroidered and fringed upholstery.
National Museum of Decorative Arts, Madrid, Spain

Seating

The Spanish term for a side chair is *silla*; for an armchair, *sillón*. There are many categories of each, of course. *Sillas del Renacimiento* means simply chairs of the Renaissance. The *sillón de cadero* was a chair with an X-shaped frame, modeled on Italy's so-called **Dante chair** or *Dantesca* (see top right in fig. 13–23). It was a favorite in early sixteenth-century Spain and was frequently upholstered in crimson velvet edged with fringe. It is sometimes called a *scissors chair* or a *hip chair*. The best known of Spain's chairs, however, was the *sillón de frailero*, commonly referred to simply as a *frailero*. This "monk's chair" was introduced late in the sixteenth century (fig. 14–20) and given its name because it was so frequently used in monasteries. It had a wooden frame of square or rectangular members, sometimes with turnings, and a straight

Wood Door Panel | Clavated and Column Forms | Table with Splayed Legs – Metal Stretcher

▲ **14–22** Spanish furniture legs and carvings.
Gilbert Werlé/New York School of Interior Design

back separate from the seat, and both back and seat were most frequently upholstered in leather. The leather was commonly fastened to the chair frame with a double row of nails with ornamental heads. Sometimes the stretchers between the legs were removable, so that the chair could be folded. Its arms sometimes ended in rather Baroque volutes. The Portuguese version was slightly different, with a higher back, more elaborately turned legs, and ball-and-claw feet (fig. 14–21).

Short **clavated** (club-shaped) turnings were popular for use on furniture legs and on stretchers between legs, and a clavated leg is illustrated in the center of figure 14–22. The use of splayed or slanting legs was also popular. At the ends of furniture legs, several types of feet were used, but the most characteristic is called the **Spanish foot** (see table 19–3). It is shaped like a hoof or paw, its surface cut in narrow grooves. It projects outward from the leg, then curves inward slightly at the floor. Much used in Spain and Portugal beginning in the seventeenth century, it was also used on English and American furniture of the eighteenth century.

The florid Rococo style of the Palacio Real's Gasparini Room (see fig. 14–15) is matched by the furniture designed by Gasparini and built by Spanish cabinetmaker José Canops (flourished c. 1759, died 1814). The tulipwood

▲ **14-24** A seventeenth-century Spanish bed with spiral posts and an elaborately carved headboard.
Instituto Amatller de Arte Hispanico, Barcelona, Spain

▲ **14-25** A collapsible table braced with iron *fiadores*, late seventeenth century. The lacquer decoration shows a Chinese influence.
Victoria & Albert Museum, London/Art Resource, NY

sofas and the chairs (fig. 14–23) for the room are larger in scale than their French models and have arms supported by extraordinary serpentine curves that reverse their direction not once, but twice. (The chair known as the *Spanish chair*, a low, armless, upholstered piece with the seat and back joined in a continuous curve, was not in fact Spanish at all, but an English chair of the Victorian period.)

Beds

Beds were made both with and without corner posts. Spiral (Solomonic) posts were often used, frequently with the addition of fabric valances (fig. 14–24). Headboards (*olatinas*) were some-

times separate from the bed, fastened to the wall, and they could be elaborately painted, designed as an architectural pediment, or carved with a pattern of intricate scrolls. Beds were often draped with silk damask enriched by fringes and tassels. The small but damask-hung bed of Philip II is seen in figure 14–12.

Tables and Mirrors

Spanish tables were sometimes supported on four legs, sometimes on a pair of *trestles* (wooden supports, oftentimes X-shaped; see upper right, fig. 14–19). In rare cases, the tables were so long that intermediate pairs of legs or trestles were also needed. The legs represented straight or spiral classical columns or balusters. The trestle supports were much simpler than those found in Italy; they were usually pierced and silhouetted in a series of contrasting curves, often taking the approximate shape of a lyre. Both table legs and trestles were often splayed and braced by a diagonal wooden or curved iron piece that started at the center point of the underside of the tabletop and ended at the stretcher connecting the end legs, near the floor. Such curved iron bars were known as *fiadores* (see upper right in fig. 14–19). A folding version with lacquered surfaces is seen in figure 14–25. Tabletops frequently had a long overhang, with plain, square-cut edges.

Following Italian taste, the console table, designed to be placed against a wall, became very popular in Spain. In 1739, for example, forty console tables designed by Juvarra, the original designer of the Palácio Real, were bought for the palace of La Granja, then nearing completion outside Segovia. And popular on the walls above console tables were mirrors.

Mirrors of all shapes and sizes were so popular that in 1736 Felipe V had established a royal mirror factory near La Granja. Some of its products were the largest mirrors that had ever been produced, and one example, with its frame, was said to weigh 9 short tons (8.2 t). Toward the end of the eighteen century, one particular type of mirror design, featuring gilt-wood moldings over strips of marble veneer and, at the top, a small painting within an oval medallion came to be known as a *Bilbao mirror,* named for the northern Spanish city of its origin. Because Bilbao was a frequent port for American ships on their way to or from France, many Bilbao mirrors were brought to America.

Casegoods

Throughout Spanish history, the most common piece of furniture, used in almost every room, was a storage chest with a

▲ 14–26 A *vargueño* on a trestle stand, sixteenth or seventeenth century. The metal pulls and hardware are mounted on small panels of velvet. Behind the fall-front desk are many small storage compartments.

Cooper-Hewitt, National Design Museum, Smithsonian Institution

hinged lid. It served as storage for the elaborate clothes worn at special occasions—banquets, fiestas, jousting tournaments, and bullfights—but it also was used as a seat, a table, or a writing desk. It was made in all sizes and in many different woods and was often covered with embossed leather, decorated with metal ornaments, and fitted with complicated locks.

Many other sorts of casegoods were also popular in Spain. Drawer pulls for these various case goods were of two chief types: turned wood knobs and iron drop handles. These included the large chest called the *arcaza* or *arcón* with a flat top surface that could serve as a seat and, when covered with a straw mattress, as a bed. There were also the simple box or *arca,* the trunk or *baúl,* the sideboard or *credencia,* the clothing armoire or *armario,* the writing desk or *vargueño,* and the writing cabinet or *papalera.*

The Vargueño Beginning in the Plateresco period of the sixteenth century, no Spanish domestic interior was considered complete without the writing desk known as the **vargueño** (fig. 14–26). The earliest examples were simple unadorned boxes, with a hinged lid at both the top and the front, both furnished with strong locks (see upper left, fig. 14–19). Handles were always placed at each end, so that the *vargueño* could be easily transported. The interior was subdivided into many drawers and compartments for papers, writing equipment, and valuables, some of the compartments with secret sections, and the front of each subdivision came to be elaborately decorated with metal hinges and ornaments or with inlaid patterns made of ivory, mother-of-pearl, and wood. Beginning in the seventeenth century, miniature classical architectural motifs were also applied.

Runners were pulled out from the case to support the drop front, which then served as a writing surface. The body of the vargueño rested on a variety of supports—on simple trestles, on turned legs braced by wrought-iron fiadores, on tables, or on chests. In every case the vargueño was separate from the support below.

The vargueño was usually made of walnut, but in the early years of the seventeenth century, mahogany was sometimes used. In the later examples, the front of the drop lid became highly decorated with inlay or lacelike pierced metal mounts, gilded and applied to small squares of crimson velvet that were distributed in a pattern over the woodwork. The locks, corner braces, keyholes, bolts, and handles were both numerous and decorative and were often supplemented with ornamental nailheads arranged in patterns such as

▲ **14–27** A *tabernaculo* made by silversmith Doménico Montini in 1619 of silver, gilt bronze, and gemstones, 70 in. (176 cm) high. It is now in the Palacio Real, Madrid.
Patrimonio Nacional, Madrid

religious uses, such as reliquaries and tabernacles, and Spain was unusually rich in them. The veneration of relics and their encasement in elaborate reliquaries reached a peak in sixteenth- and seventeenth-century Spain, although the practice was also popular in France, Italy, and Spanish America. When the body of St. Teresa of Ávila was discovered in 1583, her arms and heart were enshrined in golden reliquaries on the altar of the Carmelite convent at Alba de Tormes, Spain. Many reliquaries and tabernacles took the form of miniature architecture, lavished with rich materials (fig. 14–27).

Spanish Decorative Arts

The vigorous Spanish spirit was expressed in every sort of decorative art and craft. Here, however, we shall focus on a few techniques and materials that seemed most particularly to catch the Spanish imagination. The most obvious of these, already seen in many of this chapter's illustrations, is tile.

Tile and Other Ceramics

The tile of Spain and Portugal has an outstanding place in the history of ceramics. Once again, we see a Moorish inheritance behind the Iberian accomplishment. While pottery was certainly made in Spain before the arrival of the Moors, the Moors in Spain greatly expanded the use of ceramic material for decorative and practical purposes and added refinements such as lead and tin glazes and the **luster** technique (see Tools & Techniques: Making Multicolored Tile).

The Moors furnished Spain not only with new ceramic techniques but also with new motifs. Patterns, both stamped and painted on Hispano-Moresque ware, consisted of geometric and abstract forms, coats of arms, figures, and conventionalized floral forms. One of these last, somewhat resembling an acanthus leaf caught in a pinwheel current, is called the *florón arabesco* motif (fig. 14–28). After the Reconquest and the Christian subjection of the Moors, human and animal figures and Christian symbols were more commonly represented in the tile patterns.

Architectural Uses The floors of Spanish rooms were frequently covered with small quarry or baked clay tile of a dull red color. Color accents were often introduced by insertions of glazed tile in contrasting tones. Black-and-white

swags, circles, and geometric shapes. The vargueño can be considered the ancestor of the French *secrétaire à abattant*, a drop-lid desk.

Similar to the vargueño, but often smaller and always without the drop front/writing surface, is the cabinet called a **papelera**. It featured a variety of storage compartments, the faces of which were also often elaborately decorated and which were visible, given the absence of the drop front. The *papelera* stood on feet, sometimes pear-shaped ones.

Liturgical Pieces Not strictly furniture but crafted as carefully as any furniture are the many objects designed for

checkerboard effects were popular. Brick floors were usually laid in square or herringbone patterns.

Tile was also used for dadoes carried up the walls to a height of 3 or 4 feet (90–120 cm), as seen in Philip's Escorial bedroom (see fig. 14–12). These were invariably in polychrome effects and in geometric patterns. A band course at the top of the wainscot, often consisting of a repeating conventionalized pine tree motif, varied the pattern of the field. Door and window facings, window jambs and seats, risers of steps, and linings of niches were also made of ceramic material.

The wall tile was most often about 5 or 6 inches square (12–15 cm²) and was known in both Spain and Portugal as **azulejos**. Some say the term is derived from the Arabic *al zulaich,* meaning "little stones"; others say it derives from the Arabic *az-zulaca,* meaning "brilliant surface." It was first used by the Moors of North Africa to describe the mosaic pavements they found in the ruins of Roman cities there, such as Volubilis in Morocco or Leptis Magna in Libya. The Moors

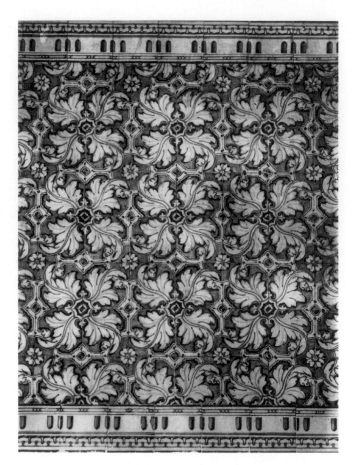

▶ **14–28** Blue and white tile in a *florón arabesco* pattern made for the Escorial about 1570. Each tile is about 4 in. (10 cm) square. Instituto Amatller de Arte Hispanico, Barcelona, Spain

Tools & Techniques | MAKING MULTICOLORED TILE

Making multicolored tile is complicated by the fact that adjacent areas of different color glazes tend to "run" into one another during firing, producing muddy effects. The Spanish tile factories developed two related techniques to deal with the problem: *cuerda seca* and *cuenca.* A final technique, *lusterware,* added an iridescent sheen to the tile from Spain.

Cuerda seca, which means "dry cord," was much used in Spain during the fifteenth and sixteenth centuries. It involves drawing lines around each colored area with a mixture of dark ceramic pigments and some sort of grease that will repel the water-based glazes. The lines keep each area distinct until, during firing, the grease burns away, leaving a slightly recessed unglazed line between the glazed areas. Similar results can be obtained by imprinting a design in the soft clay with a mold and, after a first firing, filling the sunken lines incised by the mold with a greasy substance. Tile of the *cuerda seca* type were exported from Spain to Italy, and examples exist in the Borgia apartments of the Vatican.

Cuenca, which means "bowl" or "valley," is a later technique employing individual molds for each color area. Imprinting them in the soft clay leaves thin ridges around each area. The hollows inside the ridges are then filled with the colored glazes. Obviously, tile made with either the *cuerda seca* or the *cuenca* method need to be kept horizontal during firing to keep the glazes within their boundaries.

Lusterware adds a second glaze to already glazed tile or pottery. The second glaze, using pigments made from metallic oxides, is fired at a relatively low temperature (about 800 degrees Celsius). A thick glaze can produce the effect of burnished metal, and a thin glaze, allowing the color beneath to show, can produce unusual iridescent effects. Luster glazing seems to have been practiced in Egypt in the seventh or eighth century A.D., and in Baghdad in the ninth. It was brought to Spain by the Moors, where it was used at least as early as the thirteenth century chiefly in Málaga (where it is still used).

▲ **14–29** Hispano-Moresque ware dish with a luster finish, probably made in Valencia in the fifteenth century.
D. Arnaudet/Reunion des Musees Nationaux/Art Resource, NY

and other arrangements, often producing a dazzling appearance. These products were considered of such high quality that in 1455 the Venetian senate decreed that "the majolica of Valencia should be admitted duty-free (to Venice) for such is their quality that local kilns cannot compete with them."

Metalwork

We have seen several examples of metalwork in Spain: the iron weather vane atop the Giralda Tower of the Cathedral of Seville; the iron fiadores bracing the legs of Spanish tables; the brass escutcheons around the locks of *varguenos*; and the decorative nailheads along the seats and backs of Spanish chairs. Other uses included braces and brackets supporting balconies and other architectural elements, candelabra, torch holders, door knockers, braziers, locks, bosses, and hasps (fasteners consisting of hinged plates that fit over projecting pins or staples). Door hardware in Spain was developed to a degree never imagined elsewhere. In Mudéjar interiors, the doors themselves and pulpits were beaten from sheets of iron.

The most impressive and virtuosic metalwork of Spain, however, appears in the grilles or gratings known as *reja* (pronounced "*ray*-hah"), the metalwork involved being called *rejería* (pronounced "ray-hah-*ree*-ah"). When these grilles were used to protect window openings, as they often were, they were called *reja de ventana*. The most elaborate *rejería* was reserved for the large screens that enclosed the altars of churches and cathedrals, protecting their treasures. These *rejas* were not mere expanses of grillwork, but were laden with religious symbolism and ornament. Although made of basic wrought iron, they were enriched with silver and gold. An elaborate example (fig. 14–30) is the *reja* of the Cathedral of Granada. Beyond the gilded wrought-iron *reja*, the Capilla Real (Royal Chapel) holds the Renaissance tombs of Ferdinand and Isabella and other Spanish rulers.

The silver and gold were sometimes in the form of **filigree**, delicate openwork decorations made of slender metal threads and tiny metal balls. Filigree was used not only for *rejas* but also for jewelry, small decorative caskets, handles of flatware, reliquaries (vessels made to hold the relics of saints), imperial crowns, miniature pieces of furniture, and other uses. Spain was famous for such work until late in the eighteenth century—as were Venice and Genoa. In Italy, some filigree work is still produced but chiefly as tourist souvenirs.

later used these Roman mosaic pavements for their own tile production.

These azulejos, though Moorish in origin, were readily adapted for Christian as well as secular uses. There was apparently never a prejudice in Spain that Moorish materials or motifs might be inappropriate for places of Christian worship. In 1503, for example, the **retablo** or altarpiece of the chapel of the Alcázar in Seville was completely faced with azulejos in a design by Niculoso of Pisa.

Nonarchitectural Uses   In addition to the production of the architectural and ornamental wall tile, vast quantities of heavy earthenware plates, jugs, ewers, vases, fountains, washbasins, and pitchers were made. These objects, produced from the thirteenth century in southern Spain, particularly in Málaga and Paterna, and also produced from the fifteenth century in Valencia and Seville, are given the name **Hispano-Moresque ware** (fig. 14–29). They constitute the finest ceramics produced in Europe since the classical era, and they were a direct and important inspiration for Italian majolica (see fig. 13–28).

While not attached to floors or walls, these wares were nevertheless important elements in the interior design of their time. Pitchers and vases were scattered profusely on shelves, and plates of all sizes were hung on the walls in circles, curves,

Iron, discovered in prehistoric times, is the fourth most abundant of all the elements. It is a common ingredient of the earth's crust, but usually is found in combination with other elements, from which it can be separated under intense heat. Even after separation, what is called iron is almost always an alloy of iron with traces of carbon and other elements. In early times, molten iron was cast into rough depressions in beds of sand; the resultant crude castings were called *pigs* and such unrefined iron is called **pig iron**. If pig iron is remelted and poured into more precise forms or molds, the result is called **cast iron**. Cast iron has been much used, particularly in the nineteenth century, in producing columns and other architectural elements, machinery, radiators, stoves, and other equipment, but cast iron is a material of limited malleability, which can be neither hammered nor welded. In China, cast iron was used for making molds in which bronze castings were made.

If pig iron is remelted and purified in a second furnace and then pressed between rollers, the result is called **wrought iron**. It is purer and more malleable than cast iron; it also can be welded and is thus appropriate for producing a wide variety of ornamental forms. Wrought iron was used extensively in many types of household furniture. Chairs, beds, chests, tables, washbasins, candlestands, and other objects were often made entirely of wrought iron, and it was also used in combination with wood, such as in chairbacks and in the gracefully curved braces between table legs.

When iron is refined to remove undesirable alloying elements and to add desirable ones, the result is **steel**, a material so hardened that it strikes sparks from a flint. The steel produced in Toledo, Spain, was particularly admired for its quality. When a large percentage of chromium is added to purified iron, the result is **stainless steel**, a rustproof, stainproof, and lustrous material in extensive use today.

There are three basic methods of forming metals into decorative and functional shapes. The first, called **casting**, is to pour molten metal into forms. The second is to shape sheet metal by hammering it by hand or stamping it by machine. The third, once performed by hand and now by machine, is to draw thin metal rods through progressively smaller openings to form wires that can then be fashioned into screens.

There are many treatments, such as etching and polishing, for enriching the surfaces of metals. Other metalworking techniques popular in Spain were damascening and repoussé. **Damascening**, also used in Islamic design (see fig. 9–25) and in India, is a process of beating thin wires of gold or silver into grooves cut in the surface of a less precious metal such as steel, iron, or brass. **Repoussé** decoration is obtained by hammering the backs of metal sheets so that a desired pattern projects on the front. As damascening can be described as a kind of inlaying, repoussé can be described as a kind of embossing. Repoussé was one of the earliest methods of metal decoration to be developed—as early as 1600 B.C. in Crete.

▶ **14–30** Detail of the great *reja* of the sixteenth-century Capilla Real in the Cathedral of Granada.
Bartolome Ordonez/Instituto Amatller de Arte Hispanico, Barcelona, Spain

After silver began to be mined in the colonies of the West Indies, silver began to be used quite generously in Spanish furniture design, some wood pieces being entirely surfaced with silver, and a few other pieces being made of solid silver.

Nailheads of both iron and brass were used with great enthusiasm by Spanish and Portuguese furniture makers. Large and elaborate, they were used not only to secure upholstery materials to wood frames but also by themselves to decorate plain surfaces. Three decorative nailhead patterns are seen in the center of figure 14–19. Also used for enrichment were metal ornaments of iron or silver in the form of rosettes, scallop shells, or stars, or in the form of sheets with patterns of pierced openings.

Leatherwork

The term *leather* is used for any preserved animal hide or skin. Both hides (from large animals like horses or cows) and skins (from small animals like goats or lizards) are organic tissues composed of water and proteins; without being preserved, they naturally decay. Creating leather is a venerable process, having been practiced in prehistoric times: the Egyptians used leather for bags, clothing, and sandals before 5000 B.C.

There are three traditional methods of preserving leather, and all are known as *tanning*. The most often used—and the one that has given the process its name—steeps the leather in solutions containing *tannin*, a substance that can be obtained from soaking tree bark, leaves, or nuts. This process is called *vegetable tanning*. Less frequently used are *oil tanning* or *chamoising* (pronounced "sham-ee-zing"), which involves soaking the leather in animal or fish oils to soften it, and *mineral tanning* or *tawing*, which involves soaking it in solutions of mineral salts such as alum. Since the nineteenth century, all three of these traditional methods have been replaced by *chemical tanning* processes. The new chemical processes are more easily controlled and produce leather that can accept brighter dyes than before, but the vegetable tanning process had produced leather that was both thicker and more natural-looking than modern leather. The older method also produced very sturdy products: Roman soldiers, for example, fought with battle shields made of vegetable-tanned leather.

More than any other people, the Spanish were fond of using leather in their interiors. They used it not only for chair upholstery and cushion covers, but also for making large hangings and covering whole walls and even floors. Chests for clothing were often traditionally clad in leather (while chests for household silver were traditionally clad in velvet). As fabric seat coverings can be stitched into desired shapes, leather ones can be shaped with metal studs or decorative nailheads, as in the bench. Especially in Andalusia, leather chests and boxes decorated with brass studs and escutcheons were very popular.

The Spanish did not leave much of their leather unadorned. Their methods of decorating it included piercing, scoring, punching, carving, dyeing, painting, gilding, embossing, scorching, and molding (see Tools & Techniques: Decorating Leather).

As early as the tenth century, the Spanish city of Córdoba was famous for producing a soft leather called *guademeci* or *guademecil*. It was characterized by raised patterns and brilliant coloring, with gold or silver sometimes added. Its name was derived from the town of Ghadames in Libya, where a similar leather was produced. So admired was the leather of Córdoba that in 1502 Queen Isabella ruled that no leather produced elsewhere could use that city's name for their product. In 1570 Catherine de Médici ordered four sets of Córdoban guademeciles for the decoration of the Louvre. The city of Córdoba lent its name to our term *cordovan* (which is a soft, fine-grained, colored leather), but fine leathers were also produced in Valencia, Granada, Seville, and other Spanish cities.

Cork

Cork shares with leather a soft cushioned texture, but it is a different material from a far different source: trees rather than animals. An abundance of cork trees (an evergreen species of oak) in Portugal meant that Portuguese interiors featured the use of **cork**, the spongy bark of those trees. (There is a layer of cork in all trees, but in these particular oaks it is unusually thick.) Cork is resilient, light, chemically inert, water and sound absorbent, and has excellent insulating properties against extremes of heat or cold. It has long been used for bottle stoppers and fishing floats, and at least since the Middle Ages, it has also been used for interior wall surfacing, flooring, tabletops, and seat covers.

Portugal remains a major source of cork. Today, cork for interior use is most often seen in tile form, and sometimes in thin sheets. Some of it is still the natural material, which—for all its virtues—is easily dented and stained. Most of the cork commercially produced now is therefore made more

There are a number of techniques that can be employed to decorate leather for interior and personal use. Stamping and tooling are techniques using metal implements to decorate bookbindings and small articles. More important for decorating furniture covers and wallcovering are gilding, embossing, scorching, and molding.

- To **gild** leather, a design is pressed or carved into the leather surface with hot tools. An adhesive, such as beaten egg whites called *glair*, can then be applied, and sheets of gold leaf laid over it. The gold leaf will adhere to the uncarved surfaces, and when the excess is brushed away, the design is revealed. So popular was this technique in Spain that gilt leather is sometimes called **Spanish leather**. In a less expensive variation, silver or tin foil is used and then painted with yellow varnish to simulate gold.

- To **emboss** leather, designs are etched into metal plates or cut into wood blocks that are forced onto the leather surface in a screw press or roller press. Sometimes a countermold with the design in reverse is simultaneously pressed into the rear

surface. Alternately, a small tool called a *spade* can be used to flatten some areas of the surface, leaving others raised. Today, embossed leather is called by the French term **gauffrage** by design professionals.

- To **scorch** leather, light tan sheepskin is brought into brief contact with heated metal that leaves decorative patterns of brown scorch marks. Some old inventories list items said to be made of "leather damask," and these are thought to have probably been scorched leather.

- To **mold** leather, a technique in use since Neolithic times, the first step is to soak the leather in very hot water (which led to the French term *cuir bouilli*, "boiled leather"). The second step is to mold the wet leather around a form of wood, stone, or metal to produce the desired shape. This technique was often used to produce leather cups, jugs, or flasks, for which a lining of wax or resin was often added. The formed leather could then be decoratively treated in any of the above methods.

durable by being laminated with vinyl or impregnated with vinyl resins.

Textiles

Like other Spanish and Portuguese decorative arts, the textiles of Iberia were often strikingly patterned and brilliantly colored. The Islamic influence was obvious in the Middle Ages. Later, the walls in the royal palaces and mansions of the nobles were often hung with tapestries from Flanders, a part of the Netherlands under Spanish rule from the fifteenth to eighteenth centuries. During the Renaissance, Italian influence was also felt, with many of the textiles used for draperies, cushions, and upholstery either imported from Italy or woven in Spain to Italian designs. In the eighteenth century Portuguese cotton prints were also in favor in Spain.

Among the specialized Iberian textile techniques were embroidery, tapestry weaving, carpet weaving, and needlepoint.

Embroideries Spanish embroidery was at first inspired by the fine pre-Columbian embroideries imported from Peru, discovered during the explorations of Pizarro in 1532. In turn, the Spanish artisans then influenced the rest of Europe. and their so-called "Spanish work" became highly popular. It is thought that Katharine of Aragon, the daughter of Spain's Ferdinand and Isabella, introduced the art to England in the early sixteenth century when she became the first wife of Henry VIII. Spanish work was made with black outlines on a white ground and, later, in all black. Gold and silver threads were also sometimes added. Within Spain, rich embroideries were used for ecclesiastical work, and sometimes to reproduce paintings by Murillo and other popular artists. In Portugal, embroidery showed more influence from the East, and flowers, birds, butterflies, and dragons became popular motifs. The upholstery of the *frailero* in figure 14–20 shows the fineness of Spanish embroidery, as do the silk wallcoverings of the Gasparini Room in figure 14–15.

Carpets At least since the fifteenth century, the weaving of carpets (*alfombras*) has been an important industry in Spain. The earliest Spanish carpets were long and narrow and were often woven with Spanish coats of arms and other heraldic devices, set as central features on backgrounds of **diaper** patterns (checkerboards of diamond shapes). Colors were limited to a small but intense palette of blue, red, green, and yellow. Other early carpet designs reproduce Eastern or Moorish patterns, some of them recalling tile work.

Two important Spanish centers of carpet weaving were Alcaraz and Cuenca. The Alcaraz factory, operating from the late fifteenth to the mid-seventeenth century, produced carpets with wool pile on undyed wool foundations. The dominant color of Alcaraz carpets was red, and the chief design motifs were geometric. The Cuenca weavers, continuously active since the fifteenth century, produced carpets with wool pile on foundations of goats' hair. The early models for Cuenca designs were Turkish carpets, but later designs imitated Aubusson and Savonnerie carpets. The soft coloring of the carpet in figure 14–31 is characteristic of Cuenca carpets. Note the delicate balance of the blue and ivory on a ground of pale yellow.

Many Spanish carpets are woven with a distinctive knot that loops once (or sometimes twice) around only a single warp thread. Although such knots have been found in rugs from other places (such as Chinese Turkestan and Coptic Egypt), this knot is generally known as a **Spanish knot**. It is distinct from the **symmetrical** (or **Turkish knot**) and the **asymmetrical** (or **Persian knot**), both of which are attached to two warp threads (see Chapter 9). In its most common version (fig. 14–32), the Spanish knot is tied to alternate threads in one row and to the other threads in the row above, producing a weave with smooth diagonals but with slightly serrated vertical and horizontal lines. The knot was used at both the Alcaraz and Cuenca factories, although at Cuenca it was replaced by the symmetrical knot in the late seventeenth century.

In Portugal, needlepoint rugs named for the small town of Arraiolos, near Lisbon, have been made as early as the seventeenth century. The *Arraiolos* rugs were originally pile-less needlework rugs stitched with wool on a linen ground, and later on linen, jute, or hemp canvas. In design, they imitated Persian carpets, for which they were an economical substitute, and at times they were laid over the more expensive Persian imports to preserve them for special

▼ **14–31** A carpet from Cuenca, probably seventeenth century or earlier, with an arabesque design.
The Textile Museum, Washington, DC R44.3.3. Acquired by George Hewitt Myers in 1940.

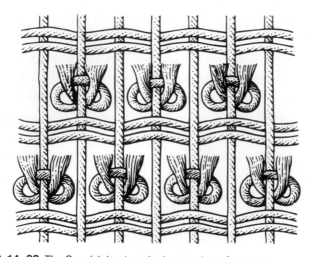

▲ **14–32** The Spanish knot or single-warp knot for carpet weaving, each knot wrapping around a single strand.
"Oriental Carpets, A Complete Guide" by Murray L. Eiland, Jr. and Murray Eiland III (London, Lawrence King Publishing, 1998).

occasions. During the nineteenth century there was a decline in the production of *Arraiolos*, and by the end of the century the art was almost forgotten.

Summary: Spanish Design

The design of Spain and Portugal is obviously an important part of the story of European design, but Spain has been overshadowed by Italy and France, despite the fact that Spain's own design history is larger and deeper. It began earlier, for example, with the Moorish wonders of southern Spain, which surpassed in sheer delight anything then being produced in the rest of Europe. And its influence penetrated farther: As we shall see in Chapter 18, virtually the whole of Central America and South America and a large part of the West Indies were under Spanish or Portuguese control and were influenced by Iberian design. The character of Spanish design is therefore one of the most important elements of the entire world picture of design.

Looking for Character

Art historian Oskar Hagen has suggested that the character of the Spanish people and their design can best be expressed with two Spanish terms, *grandeza* and *sosiego*. *Grandeza* can be translated as "greatness or nobility," and *sosiego* as "calm or composure." Together, they give us a picture of a national spirit that is formal, dignified, quiet, self-assured, sober, and strong.

There are grand gestures and violent passions in Spanish art, but these are generally kept in check by an inherent restraint. Spain, in its national character and in its design, seeks to demonstrate its exercise of control over the emotional forces it obviously feels. Such a demonstration can at times be melancholy or melodramatic, but at other times it can be genuinely dramatic and powerfully moving.

The character of Spanish taste was expressed not only in Moorish decoration, but also in the florid Spanish Gothic, in the Plateresco of the Renaissance, and in the Churrigueresco of the Baroque period, with interior planes completely overspread with intricate pattern. But not only was the Spanish spirit receptive to the overall planar ornament of Moorish décor, it was also receptive to the fact that such décor is generally subservient to the planes it ornaments. Moorish and Spanish décor are remarkably extensive in scope, seeming to encompass everything within reach, but remarkably reticent in detail.

Looking for Quality

Much of the Spanish architecture, interior design, and furniture that we have seen is a local translation of foreign influences. In many cases, perhaps most clearly in Spanish versions of French and Italian Renaissance furniture, some of the originals' fineness of detail, subtlety of curve, or elegance of finish seems to have been lost. But there are impressive compensations. The Spanish versions almost always express the same tendencies with greater vigor. Proportions are more masculine, scale is larger, members are heavier and stronger, gestures tend to be more angular, expressions are bolder. One quality we find in Spanish design to an exceptional degree is forcefulness of expression.

Yet there is fineness and delicacy, too. Solid interiors and sturdy pieces of furniture can be given surface treatments of fascinating intricacy. A curving chair arm can reverse its direction a surprising number of times. Metalwork can be wondrously filigreed or richly inlaid. Leather can be decoratively treated in ways unimagined elsewhere. And there is a wonderland of small-scaled geometric tile patterns.

Making Comparisons

The most obvious comparisons are between Spanish design and the Italian and French design. At times Italian and French design so strongly influenced Spanish culture that it was deliberately imitated. Italian design of the Renaissance constituted one of the great artistic achievements of history, particularly in architecture and painting. French design also reached great heights of accomplishment, particularly in furniture design and the decorative arts. These both set very high standards against which to judge any other work. Even so, we see in Spanish design a unique combination of vigor, strength, and pride. At its best, Spanish design possesses a nobility beside which Italian design can seem frivolous and French effete. In all the centuries between the classical period of Greece and Rome and the modern period that began in the eighteenth century, Italian and French design may surpass all other European efforts in their perfected refinement, but Spanish design reminds us that refinement is not the only quality worth valuing.

Another obvious comparison is between Spain and Portugal, a neighbor with which its history is inextricably bound. As already suggested, the differences between these two bodies of art can be traced to Spain's longer exposure to the design of the Moors and to Portugal's greater exposure to the design of the East. The two countries, of course, were well aware of each other's artistic activity, so that Spain was not immune to influences from Portugal's Far Eastern colonies; nor was Portugal removed from Moorish influences from Spain.

Finally, comparisons demand to be made *within* the Spanish vocabulary. We have seen Spanish ornament at its most dense—and at times there seems to have been no room for one more tile or one more tendril—yet even then, there is a reticence and a regularity that respects the integrity of the *plane* (not plain) surface and that keeps every element in its place. Even at its most profuse, there is a stillness at the heart of Spanish ornament. Spanish design may be effusive, but it is seldom disorganized. It may be emotional, but it is seldom sentimental. It may at times lack humor and charm, but never nobility and strength.

France: Renaissance to Neoclassical

Sixteenth to Eighteenth Centuries

15

"Deprive France, and especially its capital, of luxury, and you will kill the greatest part of its trade; I say more, you will have deprived it of much of its supremacy in Europe."

— The Baronne d'Oberkirch, 1759–1803, Alsatian nobleman and memoirist at the court of Louis XVI

In France, the Gothic style had been employed with passion in building the greatest of the Gothic cathedrals, and consequently, France was slower than Italy in moving beyond the Gothic vocabulary. When the French Renaissance finally appeared, however, it developed with extraordinary skill and grace, producing some of history's most beautiful rooms, most elegant furniture (fig. 15–1), and most lavish decorative arts.

Determinants of French Design

In many times and places we have seen interior design influenced by the religious and political history of the eras, led by the rule of pharaohs, kings, sultans, and popes, but in no case has a ruler's influence been as pervasive as in Renaissance France. We shall see that of all factors affecting design in the sixteenth to eighteenth centuries—in any of the European countries—"royal taste" was the chief determinant.

◄ **15–1** Detail of the corner of a Rococo console table attributed to Nicolas Pineau, c. 1725. The whole piece is seen in 15–30. Boulle, Andre Charles (1642–1732), "Mazarine" commode. Tortoiseshell and copper marquetry on ebony, engraved and gilded bronze, top of marble griotte. Executed c. 1708–1709 for the bedroom of Louis XIV in the Grand Trianon, Salon de Mercure. V 901; VMB 14279 1. Chateaux de Versailles et de Trianon, Versailles, France. Blot/Lewandowski/Réunion des Musées Nationaux/Art Resource, NY.

Geography and Natural Resources

The country of France enjoys a privileged position in Europe, open to the waters of the English Channel on the north, the Atlantic on the west, and the Mediterranean on the south. Its natural land boundaries are the Alps separating it from Italy, the Jura Mountains from Switzerland, the Pyrenees from Spain, and the Rhine River from Germany. It has a moderate climate and soil conducive to agriculture, including the winemaking at which it excels.

History

France has been part of much of the history we have already studied. It was part of the Roman Empire for more than five centuries. Normandy, in the north of France, was home to the Normans, who conquered England in 1066. France was central to the Romanesque style. In the Gothic period, it gave birth to more masterpieces than any other country. Between Gothic and Renaissance glories, however, France suffered difficult times: The Black Death struck France in the middle of the fourteenth century, and about the same time France

315

and Germany embarked on the Hundred Years' War, from 1337 to 1453. By its end, the fighting had virtually destroyed France's feudal nobility, and all of France looked to King Louis XI (reigned 1461–83) to effect a new national unity under strong royal authority.

Royal Taste

Along with the new absolute power of France's monarchy came renewed national prosperity and international prestige. The strength of Louis XIII (who reigned from 1610 to 1643) was observed with awe throughout Europe, and the strength and pomp of the long reign of his son Louis XIV (1643–1715) was even more impressive. It is fitting that the styles of French interior design, furniture, and decorative arts are traditionally identified by the names of French rulers, for they engaged in the development of signature styles throughout their reigns. Fortunately, the extraordinary power and wealth of the French monarchs was accompanied by extraordinary discernment in using the wealth to achieve highly artistic effects. Lavish spending, even on objects of artistic excellence, can have its critics, however, and centuries later the people of France rose up in revolution in 1789 and effected a change of government to alter the distribution of power and wealth. Despite such efforts, France still recovered its reputation for luxurious design and living for the upper classes.

Despite such imperial power during the Renaissance and beyond, France's great Renaissance writers and philosophers—Rabelais, Montaigne, Descartes—are in the background of our design story, for they were the intellectual forefathers of modern tolerance and democracy. With the rise of the *bourgeoisie*, or French middle class, came design styles that were affordable and well suited to their lifestyles.

The Rise of the Decorator

Designing a luxurious room that was consistent and harmonious and then implementing the design became a complex task. A knowledgeable supervisor was needed. This role had at times been taken by a building's architect, at other times by a *tapissier* (a tapestry maker or upholsterer). In Renaissance France, a new profession was born that would affect the process of much future interior design: the *ornemaniste* or decorator.

Among the skills of the *ornemanistes* was a talent for engraving—they could conceive the design of an interior and, through the medium of engraving, explain the design to a client. Both clients and artisans were then better able to choose and design appropriate furniture, fabric, carpet, wall paneling, chandeliers, sconces, clocks, and other decorative details. And many of these engravings directly influenced furniture designs by furniture and cabinetmakers, the *menuisiers* and *ébénistes*, whose duties intertwined with those of the decorators (see the section entitled "French Furniture"). The *ornemaniste* Abbé Jaubert, wrote in his 1773 *Dictionnaire . . . des arts et métiers* (*Dictionary of Arts and Crafts*): "The decorator is the only person who knows how to use the talent of each artist to best advantage, to arrange the most elaborate pieces of furniture, to position them to best effect. . . . To excel in this art, which has been born before our eyes, it is necessary to have a good eye, to have a good knowledge of design, to understand perfectly the merits of each piece of furniture, to show them in their true light, and to create an ensemble that will give a pleasing impression."

One of the members of this new category of designers was Nicolas Pineau (1684–1754), who also worked as a sculptor and architect. In addition to his work in France (see fig. 15–35), Pineau designed for Tsar Peter the Great in Russia, among others. Other notable *ornemanistes* include Juste-Aurèle Meissonnier (1695–1750), both an architect and a goldsmith, and Jean-Charles Delafosse (1734–89), who in a 1768 publication of his work described himself as an "architect, decorator, and teacher of design."

French Architecture and Interiors

Although the king's taste was a dominant design determinant, national tastes did not change overnight when one reign succeeded another. There are in fact some noticeable discrepancies between the dates of French rulers and the dates of the styles named for them. For one example, Louis XV was overseen by a regency from age 5 to age 13, but what we now call the Régence (Regency) style is considered to have begun earlier and lasted longer. And what we call the Louis XVI style began fourteen years before Louis XVI was crowned. Perhaps, therefore, a better policy is to pair the traditional monarch-related terms with the period terms used in other chapters: Renaissance, Baroque, Rococo, and Neoclassical. Thus, the dates given are the generally accepted dates for French styles, not the dates of actual reigns.

The Renaissance and Baroque (Louis XIV) Styles

French Renaissance stylistic details (fig. 15–2) include work from several reigns, including those of François I (1515–47), his son Henry II (1547–49), and, from another lineage, Louis XIII (1610–43). Through all the period following the bubonic plague and Hundred Years' War up until the reign of Louis XIV (immediately after that of his father, Louis XIII), design moved from the structural and decorative perpendicularity of the outgoing Gothic style toward the regularity and harmony of the incoming Italian Renaissance style. Spanish, Dutch, and Flemish influences were added at the end of the period (see upper right, fig. 15–2). Throughout the period, the keynote was formality.

Chambord Among the period's royal constructions was the chateau of Chambord (fig. 15–3), a royal hunting lodge in the Loire Valley. Not merely a hunting lodge but also a semifortress,

Louis XIII Cabinet

Salamander Motif

Louis XIII Cabinet Flemish Influence

Henri II Caquetoire

Henri II Cabinet

Francis I Chair
Henri II Wood Panel

▶ **15–2** French Renaissance furniture and details.
Gilbert Werlé / New York School of Interior Design

▲ **15–3** The Château of Chambord, begun 1519.
Topham/The Image Works

▲ **15–4** The dousble spiral stair of the Château of Chambord, 26 ft. (8 m) in diameter.

it combined massive construction on its lower floors with high-pitched roofs and an array of fanciful dormers, chimneys, and rooftop ornaments. It was begun by François I in 1519 and completed by his son Henri II in 1550. It is distinguished by its size, its façade being more than 500 feet (150 m) long, and by its eight enormous cylindrical towers housing mostly rectangular rooms. Within the enclosed courtyard is a smaller, bilaterally symmetrical element 143 feet (44 m) square with a hall in the shape of a Greek cross (see table 6–2). At the crossing is a double spiral stair, one run above the other, interlocking so that those ascending one stair never meet those descending the other (fig. 15–4).

The top of this central stair culminates in a lantern adorned with a giant **fleur-de-lys** (see table 15–1), the lily that has been the emblem of the French kings since the twelfth century. Around the lantern is a fantastic rooftop landscape of chimneys, turrets, pinnacles, and dormer windows, medieval in character, but the pure geometry and symmetry of the floors below are clearly derived from the Italian Renaissance. Its plan (and particularly its ingenious stair) may have in fact been partly based on drawings by Leonardo da Vinci, who had been asked by François I to design a chateau for another site, but Leonardo died the year construction began. Chambord became a favorite property of Louis XIV, who would succeed to the throne almost a century after construction was finished.

Louis XIV, popularly called *Le roi soleil* ("The Sun King"), used his seventy-two–year-long reign to affect many changes in the French state (transforming it into an absolute monarchy), the French court (endorsing an elaborate ceremonial etiquette), French design (emphasizing lavish display), and other French arts (supporting the music of Couperin and Lully, the plays of Racine and Molière, and the paintings of Lorraine and Poussin). The style (fig. 15–5) named for Louis XIV is considered to have lasted from the beginning of his rule in 1643 until the end of that century, even though he would rule for another fifteen years; it is also called France's Baroque period.

Louis XIV style continued the formality of the Early Renaissance but adds more flourishes, more sculptural effects, and more theatricality. It was ornamented with bulbous shapes at times, with elaborate moldings at others. Symmetry still reigned, but surfaces were often richly embellished. The court of Louis XIV was characterized by unprecedented pomp, ceremony, and rules of etiquette, and these enrichments and complexities were fully reflected in the period's architecture, interiors, ornament, furniture, and decorative arts.

Versailles   The history of Louis XIV style is embedded in the history of Versailles. Louis XIV's father, Louis XIII, had chosen Versailles, a dozen miles (about 20 km) southwest of Paris, as the site for another hunting lodge. Louis XIV's decision around 1660 to develop it as a monument to royal

Showing Ormolu Mounts and
Tortoise Shell and Pewter Marquetry
Boulle Cabinet

Walnut Stool
Showing Flemish
Influence

Chair
About 1675

Ornament for
Panel Corner

Carved Wood
Panel

Wood Carving
Detail of Chapel Door, Versailles

**Mantelpiece,
Versailles**

▲ **15–5** Baroque furniture and interior details.
Gilbert Werlé/New York School of Interior Design

power was a surprise to all. He found his designers at Vaux-le-Vicomte, a chateau that had been built by his superintendent of finance, Nicolas Fouquet. Attending a party there in his honor, Louis XIV was aroused to a great fit of jealousy by the magnificence of the event and of the house (fig. 15–6), which featured a domed oval salon, ornamented with elaborate stucco work, and was hung with 143 tapestries. He had Fouquet arrested and imprisoned for life, had some of his garden's finest trees and statues moved to Versailles, and appropriated Fouquet's designers and craftsmen for his own use. Chief among them were architect Louis Le Vau (c. 1612–70), interior painter Charles Le Brun (1619–90), and garden designer André Le Nôtre (1613–1700).

His father's brick and stone lodge was too small and dated for Louis XIV's ambitious plans, but tearing it down, he feared, might seem disrespectful. Le Vau produced the happy solution called the *enveloppe*, which retained the old lodge but wrapped it almost completely in new construction. Faced all in white stone ashlar, the *enveloppe* had a rather solid ground floor as its base, a tall *premier étage* ("second floor" in American usage, "first floor" in English, "*piano nobile*" in Italian), and a short top floor for subsidiary rooms. A giant order of Ionic pilasters marched along the exterior of the *premier étage*. Inside that chief floor, the Grand Appartement of the king was in the north wing and consisted of a *chambre* or bedchamber, an *antichambre* or waiting room, a *garde-robe* or dressing room, and three *cabinets* or offices. The south wing held the apartments of the queen, her children, and the king's brother. On the long west side facing the gardens, a marble terrace on the *premier étage* linked the quarters of the king and queen. Interiors that survive from this earliest stage of new construction show the clear influence of the Italian Baroque: a lavish use of marble wall paneling in geometric patterns, illusionistic murals by Le Brun and his staff on walls and ceilings, and a profusion of gilding and statuary.

In 1678 a new phase of work began at Versailles under the direction of Jules Hardouin-Mansart (1646–1708), who was appointed first architect of the king in 1681 and who was a great nephew of the architect François Mansart, for whom the double-pitched **mansard** roof was named. Hardouin-Mansart had already designed the Hôtel des Invalides, the enormous Paris building for wounded and retired soldiers.

Hardouin-Mansart transformed Versailles into a great residential complex unprecedented in scale. He added three important elements: the Grand Trianon, the Galerie des Glaces (Hall of Mirrors), and the chapel. The one-story Grand Trianon was faced with white stone and pink marble, refined and austere. Louis XIV occupied a suite there between 1691 and 1703. Its interior decorations featured a series of twenty-one views of Versailles and its gardens, painted by Jean Cotelle (1642–1708), which are still *in situ*.

▲ 15–6 Charles Le Brun's richly ornamented dining room in the Château of Vaux-le-Vicomte, 1660.
Erich Lessing/Art Resource, NY

▲ **15–7** The Galerie des Glaces (Hall of Mirrors) at Versailles, by Jules Hardouin-Mansart and Charles Le Brun, begun 1678.
Artedia

Hardouin-Mansart's Galerie des Glaces is the most spectacular room at Versailles and one of the most spectacular in the history of interior design, filling in the space once occupied by a marble terrace. A vaulted room 237 feet (73 m) long, it is a dazzling parade of seventeen tall windows reflected in a matching series of seventeen mirrors (fig. 15–7), both windows and mirrors alternating with Corinthian pilasters of green marble. The semicircular ceiling vault, which springs from a richly treated entablature, is painted by Le Brun. The Gallerie des Glaces terminates at one end with the Salon de la Paix (Hall of Peace) and at the other with the Salon de la Guerre (Hall of War), both by Hardouin-Mansart and Le Brun, with the aid of sculptor Antoine Coyzevox (1640–1720). The oval stucco relief by Coyzevox in the Salon de la Guerre (fig. 15–8) shows the king on horseback wearing classical armor and trampling an enemy. Together, these three rooms stretch the whole length of Versailles's central wing.

▲ **15–8** The Salon de la Guerre at one end of the Galerie des Glaces, Versailles.
Giraudon/Art Resource, NY

The last element added by Louis XIV was the chapel (fig. 15–9), begun in 1699 from designs prepared a decade before by Hardouin-Mansart. It was finished in 1710 under the direction of architect Robert de Cotte (c. 1656–1735). Two stories tall, its lower level was meant for the courtiers and the public; its more important upper level was for the king, and it was entered directly from his private *appartement*, and ringed by Corinthian columns supporting an entablature from which the painted vault springs.

Régence and Rococo (Louis XV) Styles

When Louis XIV died in 1715, the crown passed to his great-grandson Louis XV, then a child of 5. A regent governed until the king was of age, and the court was temporarily moved from Versailles to Paris. The style of the **Régence** period was one of transition from the exuberant but sometimes ponderous Baroque to the more delicate Rococo. A new lightness of touch was evident. In Régence style, symmetry was still preserved, but the rigidity of the Baroque style was softened with new serpentine forms as demonstrated by the changes in chair legs (fig. 15–10). Colors and materials were simplified, a spare palette of white and gold being very popular. Seating moved away from the walls and was placed more informally in the center of the room. The Régence period is considered to have lasted from about 1710 to about 1730. Some scholars have classified the chapel at Versailles (see fig. 15–9), finished in 1710, as Régence, but it displays little of the simplicity and curvaceousness that was to come.

Typical Rococo details are shown in the furniture drawings of figure 15–11. Note the organic curves and asymmetry of the wood panel at center left in the drawing, the graceful outline of the commode shown just below it, and the pure whimsy of the ornament at lower center.

Salon de la Princesse Those Rococo qualities are fully evident in the *hôtel particulier* (see page 328) in the Marais district of Paris called the Hôtel de Soubise. It had been designed in 1705 for Prince and Princesse de Soubise by architect Pierre-Alexis Delamair (c. 1676–1745) in a conservative style with rooms *en enfilade* and a colonnaded *cour d'honneur*. Needing an addition and wanting something in the latest fashion, the prince turned in 1732 to architect Germain Boffrand (1667–1754), who provided a new two-story pavilion with several oval salons. Its Salon de la Princesse (fig. 15–12) is the epitome of Rococo lightness, delicacy, and

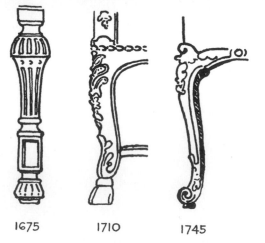

▲ **15–10** Changes in chair leg profiles reflect the progression of French styles. From left to right: Baroque, Régence, and Rococo legs.
Gilbert Werlé/New York School of Interior Design

1675   1710   1745

Console Table

Bergère

Side Chair

Marble Mantel

Wood Panel

Chair Leg
Showing Cabriole Form

Commode with Ormolu Mounts

• Painting showing 'Singerie'
• and 'Chinoiserie' Motifs

Wood Panel

▲ **15–11** Rococo furniture and ornament.
Gilbert Werlé/New York School of Interior Design

▼ **15–12** In the Hôtel de Soubise, Paris, a salon designed by Germain Boffrand in 1736 for the Princesse de Soubise. All the relief work here is gilded, and the spandrels filled with paintings.
Wim Swaan/The Getty Research Institute for the History of Art and the Humanities

▲ **15–13** Detail of François Boucher's portrait of his wife, *Madame Boucher*, oil on canvas, 1743.
Copyright The Frick Collection, New York

movement, its sinuously framed spandrel panels between mirrored recesses filled with paintings by Charles-Joseph Natoire. Other painters engaged for work in the new pavilion were Pierre-Charles Trémolières and François Boucher, one of whose works we see in figure 15–13. The Hôtel de Soubise now houses the Archives Nationale.

Another skilled designer in the Rococo style was Nicolas Pineau, who was mentioned earlier as an *ornemaniste*. An example of his work is a gilt mirror surround (see fig. 15–35), the shape of which we might characterize as playful, an adjective we could never have used for Louis XIV style.

Period and Date	Chief Reigns and Dates	Architects, Designers, and Artisans	Artistic Milestones
Early Renaissance, 1484–1547	François I, 1515–1547	Lescot	Chambord, from 1519; Fontainebleau, from 1530; remodeling of Louvre, from 1546
Middle Renaissance, 1547–89	Henri I, 1547–59	De l'Orme; du Cerceau	Work continues at Louvre
Late Renaissance, 1589–1643	Henri IV, 1589–1610; Louis XIII, 1610–43	Mansart	Hunting lodge at Versailles, 1623; Hotel Lambert, 1640
Baroque, 1643–1700	Louis XIV, 1643–1715	Le Vau; Le Brun; Le Notre; Hardouin-Mansart; Le Pautre; Boulle; Berain; Perrault	Vaux-le-Vicomte, 1653–61; Versailles enlarged, Grand Trianon at Versailles; Louvre enlargement finished
Régence, 1700–1730	Louis XV king, but Philippe II d'Orleans acting as regent, 1715–23	de Cotte; Cressent; Delamair	Chapel at Versailles, 1699–1710; Hôtel de Rohan, 1705
Rococo, 1730–60	Louis XV, 1723–74	Boffrand; Oeben; Pineau; Verberckt; Meissonnier	Reconstruction of royal apartments at Versailles; Hôtel de Soubise, c. 1740
Neoclassical, 1760–89	Louis XVI, 1774–93	Gabriel; Ledoux; Boullée; P. Garnier; de Lalonde; Riesener; Carlin; Roentgen; Delafosse; Dugourc	Petit Trianon, 1768; the Ópera added to Versailles, 1748–70; Hôtel de Salm, 1783
Revolution and Directoire, 1789–1800	The Directorate, 1795–99; The Consulate, 1799	Weisweiler; Jacob; Molitor	Production revived at the Sèvres and Savonnerie factories

Louis XV did not move to Versailles until 1722. Beginning in 1738, the young king made extensive interior changes there, creating many smaller, more intimate rooms, some faced with magnificent white and gold paneling by *ornemaniste* Jacques Verberckt (1704–71) and architect Ange-Jacques Gabriel (1698–1782). In 1748–70, Gabriel would also add an opera house to Versailles, which would be the setting for the future Louis XVI's marriage to Marie-Antoinette.

French Provincial The Rococo style, for all its elegance, was not limited to the royalty of Versailles and the nobility of Paris. Although the style seems economical compared with the Baroque, with smaller rooms and lighter furniture, it was simplified even more for use in the countryside and small towns where there were smaller budgets for interior embellishment and fewer skilled craftsmen to produce it. The result has come to be known as French Provincial (or sometimes as Country French).

Wood paneling was in fashion in rural France, as it was in the great houses of the cities, but the chief rooms of humbler dwellings often had only a single wall of paneling, with the others painted, covered with wallpaper, or stenciled to imitate wallpaper. Native woods were used for both paneling and furniture: pale, honey-colored walnut, beech, chestnut, cherry, or apple.

The motif of a fireplace topped with a mirror was popular throughout France, but in the provinces the mirror was likely to be composed of smaller panes than their cosmopolitan counterparts. Woodwork was generally painted in the soft colors of the period, with simple moldings picked out in contrasting colors. Bookshelves were built in, and sleeping rooms contained alcoves for the beds.

In François Boucher's 1743 portrait of his wife (fig. 15–13), the wall cabinet, the bedside table, and the nearby stool might be called French Provincial because of their plainness, even though the Bouchers lived in Paris. And some other French Provincial furniture pieces (fig. 15–14)

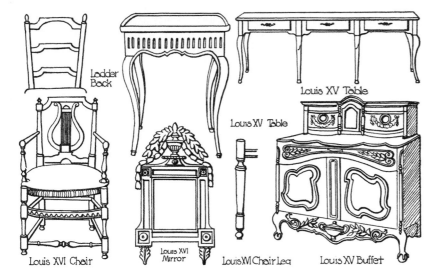

◀ **15–14** French Provincial furniture.
Gilbert Werlé/New York School
of Interior Design

Ladder
Back

Louis XV Table

Louis XV Table

Louis XVI Chair

Louis XVI
Mirror

Louis XVI Chair Leg

Louis XV Buffet

suggest the nature of the style: Rococo in out-line, but with a minimum of Rococo detail. Some later Neoclassical (Louis XVI) furniture was also susceptible to provincial treatment (see the lower left in fig. 15–14), but it was not as widespread as the Rococo versions. Accompanying such furniture would have been attractive but simple fabrics, such as the *toile de Jouy* we shall see later (see fig. 15–40).

At its most debased, the Rococo style was sentimental and trivial; at its best, it was pure delight. It was perhaps the most original and characteristically French of all the French styles, and for thirty years it enjoyed popularity at all levels of society.

Neoclassical (Louis XVI) and Directoire Styles

By 1760, guided by the taste of Louis XV's influential mistress Mme. de Pompadour, the country was ready for a more restrained expression. They found it in **Neoclassicism**, which is a style that returns to the symmetry, formality, and classical order of the Renaissance, Régence, and Baroque styles while retaining some of the lightness and grace of the Rococo. It is a serious style, but not a pretentious one. Examples of French Neoclassical furniture and ornamental details are seen in figure 15–15.

Side Chair

Rosettes

Console Table

Urn Motif

Commode

Arabesque

Detail of
Chair Leg

Over-door Motif – Medallion, garland, ribbon

Arm Chair

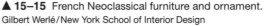

▲ **15–15** French Neoclassical furniture and ornament.
Gilbert Werlé/New York School of Interior Design

Juan Pablo Molyneux, born in 1946 in Chile, has his own design practice in New York with a satellite office in Paris. A monograph of his work *Molyneux* was published by Rizzoli in 1997. He has written of Gabriel's "exquisite, perfectly proportioned" Petit Trianon that it is "one of the great small buildings of all time." He adds that "There is a wonderful sentence about Gabriel's work in the old *Encyclopedia*

Britannica. It says that his architecture was esteemed for its elegance 'in an age that regarded elegance as commonplace.' That in itself is a very Gabriel-like encapsulation, because his work is very much like that: a little more elegant than everyone else's, with gestures that retain their impact today. . . . In the vast context of Versailles, he understood the need to change the rhythm, to seek out intimacy."

The Petit Trianon In 1761, Louis XV, as requested by Mme. de Pompadour, asked Ange-Jacques Gabriel to design a small pavilion on the grounds of Versailles. The Petit Trianon was built between 1762 and 1768, a perfect little white stone palace (fig. 15–16). It embodied a reaction to the Rococo style that preceded it: Its rooms were square or rectangular, with no rounded corners; its ceilings were flat, with no coves; and its restrained ornamental details were the classical ones of acanthus, guilloche, garland, and wreath; gilding and lacquering were avoided; and most rooms were painted a soft off-white or pastel (fig. 15–17). The designer of some of the restrained wall paneling was Antoine Rousseau.

The Petit Trianon is designed on three floors, but the lowest, with only a few round windows, is virtually invisible from the garden front. The Petit Trianon's largest room, in the center of the main floor, opens to a balustraded terrace and the gardens beyond. Typical of the concern for privacy and quiet as a relief from the bustling activity of Versailles was the design of a dining table (never built) that could be raised from the basement so the royal couple and their guests could dine without the presence of servants.

By the time of the little building's completion, Mme. de Pompadour had died and the Petit Trianon was first used by the king's new mistress, Mme. du Barry, who often gave supper parties there for the king and his intimate friends. After Louis XV's own death in 1774, his grandson was crowned Louis XVI, and the new king gave the Petit Trianon to his queen, Marie-Antoinette. The French Revolution began in

▼ **15–16** The Petit Trianon at Versailles, designed by Ange-Jacques Gabriel and built 1762–8.
Caisse Nationale des Monuments Hitoriques et des Sites

▲ **15–17** Marie-Antoinette's private sitting room in the Petit Trianon. The Neoclassical chairs were designed by Georges Jacob.
Dagli Orti/Picture Desk Inc./Kobal Collection

1789, and King Louis XVI and Marie-Antoinette (as well as Mme. du Barry) were guillotined in 1783.

Directoire　Political unrest brought a temporary suspension of design activity. The abolition of artisans' and craftsmen's guilds allowed more freedom, but ended the enforcement of high standards for craftsmanship. In 1795 a new governing body called the Directorate was established, lasting only until 1799, and the style that prevailed during its rule is called **Directoire**. As might be expected, the style retreated from the sumptuousness of the previous French styles. Furniture became more severe and angular, though it was still classical in form. Large surfaces of plain waxed wood and painted wood replaced elaborate marquetry, and gilt bronze enrichments were curtailed. Imagined parallels between democratic Greece and revolutionary France brought a popular revival of Greek furniture forms. A brief transitional style, the Directoire continued the forms of the Neoclassical style with even more austerity, a notable exception being an increased elaboration in the use of fabric (fig. 15–18), a trait we shall see continued in the Empire style that follows in the next century.

▼ **15–18** A window treatment in a Directoire interior.
Yale University Press

The Hôtel Particulier

The private town house known as a *hôtel particulier* was an important part of French urban life for almost the whole period this chapter covers. At first the term was restricted to city residences of the nobility, crowded together on small plots of land in order to be close to the royal palaces; later, with distinctions between the more ordinary *maison* (house) and the *hôtel* fading, the latter term came to be used as well for city houses of the rising middle class. Thousands of such houses were built, and dozens of manuals were published giving examples that might be followed, starting with a publication by architect and designer Jacques Androuet du Cerceau (1515–85), in 1559.

Two chief characteristics distinguished the *hôtel particulier* from the town house of other capitals: open space at both its front and back, and the carefully contrived appearance of symmetry. Although in London and elsewhere, town houses of all sorts were built flush with the property line at the street, the French version whenever possible had a forecourt in front and a garden in back. This layout was literally called the *hôtel-entre-cour-et-jardin*, and the principal building block in the center was called the *corps de logis*. Narrow service wings might extend along the sides of the forecourt, and small service courts, shielded from the view of visitors, might be placed at the sides.

In the design of the *hôtel particulier*, care was taken that every visible element—the entrance wall, the façade seen from the forecourt, the façade seen from the back garden—be perfectly symmetrical. Often, however, because of irregularly shaped sites, ingenious planning devices were employed to create impressions of an overall order that was not fully present (fig. 15–19).

Inside the fashionable *hôtel*, there were public reception rooms, such as the entrance vestibule and a salon for social gatherings, and there were several private *appartements*, one for each important member of the family, including separate *appartements* for the master and mistress of the house. Each of the private suites consisted of a *chambre*, one or more *antichambres*, one or more *cabinets*, and a *garde-robe*. The most elaborate hôtels might also have a *galérie*, a *bibliothèque*, a *salle de compagnie* for entertaining, games, and music, and—for dining—a specially designated *salle à manger*. The rooms within an *appartement* were often arranged **en enfilade**—that is, in a row, with doorways aligned so that long vistas through series of spaces were created. In figure

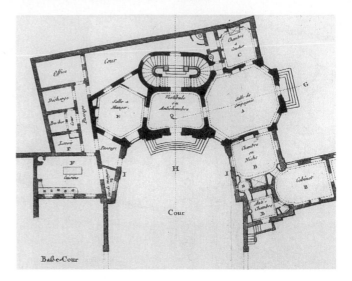

▼ **15–19** Jacques-François Blondel's 1773 plan for an abbot's *hotel particulier*. Although on an irregularly shaped site, its chief façades give an impression of symmetry.
RIBA Library, Photographs Collection, London.

15–19, for example, the entrance door, the door to the stair hall, and the window beyond are *en enfilade*, and on the cross axis at right angles to that one, the two doors from the vestibule and the fireplace in the *salle à manger* at the left are aligned (though, because of the irregular site, the axis has been bent for the room on the right). For this and other planning compositions, architects and theorists used the general term *distribution*, a matter given unprecedented attention from the Rococo period on.

Although the progress of French interior design was often, as we have noted, dictated by the king himself, the *hôtel particulier* was often the source of new design directions. The Marquise de Rambouillet in the second quarter of the seventeenth century, for example, is credited in her *hôtel* (now replaced by the Ministry of Finance) with the introduction of the tall floor-to-ceiling windows that became so important to both the exteriors and interiors of French architecture.

The Marquise de Rambouillet may have also established the practice of giving the homes a monochromatic—or at least closely harmonizing—color scheme, which gave unity to the rooms arranged *en enfilade*. The Chambre Bleu of the Hôtel de Rambouillet, where the marquise entertained, featured blue walls, blue woodwork, and blue furnishings. Similarly, it was the fashion to coordinate all the textiles within a room: Wall coverings, draperies, table covers, chair covers, and bed hangings might all be made from the same fabric.

Wood parquetry was the flooring of choice (see fig. 15–20), except for vestibules and corridors, where stone or tile was the rule. Oriental carpets or products of the Savonnerie or Aubusson factories (see "Carpets" on page 344) were used over the wood floors. Tapestries also continued to appear as wall coverings. Silk or cotton curtains over windows and portieres over doorways were generally hung straight from metal rings over metal rods, with the fabric split into two halves, each drawn to the side. Between these draperies and the window glass, sheer white muslin curtains cut the glare of outside light.

French Ornament

France, from the Renaissance through Neoclassicism, produced the most impressive ornament the world has ever known. It is impressive not only in its quantity, but also in the lavish quality of its materials. Until the French Revolution and the Directoire period that followed, French design was inseparable from—and unthinkable without—its ornament.

Motifs and Symbols

We have mentioned the long-lived *fleur de lys* (table 15–1), which had been part of the coats of arms of the kings of France since the twelfth century and which remained an important part of the French design vocabulary until, in the populist spirit of post-Revolutionary France, it was temporarily outlawed.

In the early Renaissance, a lighter, more fanciful touch to the linenfold and tracery motifs inherited from Gothic times was added by **grotesque** ornament (from the word *grotto* because such ornament was found in underground Roman ruins, and meaning a fantastic composition of figures, foliage, people, and real and mythical beasts—similar to *arabesque* ornament but including human figures). In the first half of the sixteenth century some further changes took place: Gothic pilaster decoration was replaced by classically proper fluting with capitals and bases. As an example of grotesque ornamentation, the salamander, a mythical lizard able to endure fire without harm (center left in fig. 15–2), was a symbol of the Renaissance king François I, who reigned from 1515 to 1547.

The Baroque period naturally brought ornament referring to the Sun King himself, such as intertwined L's and flaming sun faces with spreading rays (see table 15–1). Walls of the Galerie des Glaces (see fig. 15–7) were festooned with gilded imitations of fabric, and the Salon de la Guerre (see fig. 15–8) featured shields, swords, armor, trophies, bound slaves, and angels playing trumpets. Other Baroque ornament included lyres, cornucopias, and the heads of rams and lions.

In the Régence and Rococo periods, formal classical motifs were replaced with more whimsical ones: ribbons, garlands, and **putti** (see table 15–1), which are wingless cherubs or cupids (the singular is **putto**). They were also popular in Italy, where they were called *amorini*, "little loves." Also popular in Rococo interiors were Eastern motifs such as *chinoiseries*, imaginary Chinese landscapes or domestic

TABLE 15–1 French Ornament

A few examples of ornament from seventeenth and eighteenth century France: left to right, an *espagnolette*, a *fleur-de-lys*, a *fasces*, a putto, and a sun face.

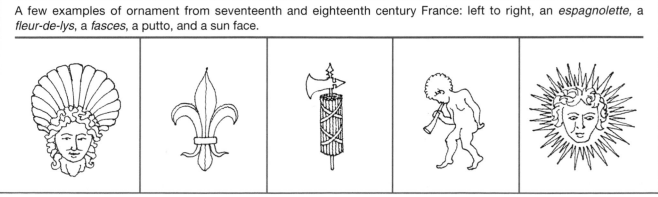

Drawing: Abercrombie

Parquetry and marquetry are done today with extremely-thin sheets of veneer—about $\frac{1}{100}$ inch (0.25 mm) in the case of marquetry—but in the seventeenth century, when such work was first being perfected in France, thicknesses were sometimes ten times as much. A wide variety of native woods was employed, including box, cedar, hawthorn, lime, oak, olive, sycamore, and walnut. To these were added in the seventeenth and eighteenth centuries more exotic woods imported from the tropics, such as amboyna, amaranth, ebony, rosewood, and tulipwood. By the end of the eighteenth century, the vocabulary of woods used in France reached almost a hundred varieties. Scorching the woods in trays of heated sand produced additional variations in appearance, as did scoring and engraving.

Usually several layers of veneer, often in contrasting colors, are cut at once, producing a number of identical pieces. A special type of treadle-operated sawhorse called the fretcutter's donkey was developed in the eighteenth century to hold the layers in place during cutting. After cutting, two methods are used to secure the veneers to the supporting surface. One still in use involves putting the just-glued veneers under a heavy heated press, the press plates usually faced with zinc or brass. Hand veneering without a press was done by layering the support with glue, dampening the veneer and placing it onto the glue, passing a warm iron over the veneer, then hammering it into place.

Before the twentieth century, the adhesives for such work were made of animal glues. They were neither waterproof nor heatproof, but allowed a bit of flexibility of movement if the wood expanded or contracted because of temperature or humidity changes. For that reason, some artisans today still prefer to use the animal glues.

---

scenes, and **singeries** (see lower center in fig. 15–11), scenes of monkeys (*singerie* being French for monkey trick) often dressed as humans and playing music or gaming with playing cards. Such motifs were not only painted on walls but also used in the design of porcelain, marquetry, and textiles. Other ornamental devices were scrolls in C-shapes and S-shapes and *espagnolettes* (see table 15–1) or female heads surrounded by large lace collars, such as might have been worn in Spain.

The Neoclassical period regarded the Rococo as frivolous, frowning on **chinoiseries** and **singeries** and preferring instead plant forms (palm fronds, bouquets, rosettes), animal images, **arabesques** (see the upper right in fig. 15–15), and **medallions** (see the lower left in fig. 15–15). The discoveries of the Roman ruins at Herculaneum in 1738 and Pompeii a decade later led to the publication, beginning in the 1750s, of several collections of engravings that had broad influence on ornament. The acanthus leaf of the Corinthian capital made a reappearance. Symmetry returned, and whatever fanciful devices remained from the Rococo were subdued within rectangular frames. Walls were often articulated with pilasters (not for the first time, of course), and ornament was put to the service of architecture, emphasizing room boundaries and openings.

During the Directoire period, ornament began to include symbols of the Revolution, such as the **fasces** (see table 15–1), which is a bound bundle of rods with an axe in the middle (a device borrowed from ancient Rome, where the rods had represented the different classes of Roman society and the axe stood for the government's absolute authority). Other Directoire ornaments included spears, drums, and the cap of Liberty, and the colors of the new Republican flag—white, with small areas of blue and scarlet—began to appear on trimmings, edgings, and small moldings. In general, however, Directoire design brought a dramatic diminution to the amount of ornament used in rooms and on furniture; this was probably due not only to a change of taste accompanying the replacement of a monarch by a Republic, but also by economic necessity. Almost bankrupted by revolution and war, France for a while would have to forego its former luxuries.

Parquetry and Marquetry

Parquetry and **marquetry** are techniques for covering surfaces with compositions of shaped pieces of wood or wood veneer. Some use the term parquetry for geometric designs such as stripes, diamonds, or herringbones and the term marquetry for more representational designs imitating flowers, foliage, or birds. The distinction more often made, however, is that parquetry is a technique applied to flooring and marquetry a very similar technique applied to furniture. In practice, these definitions usually coincide, for the geometric patterns are more popular for flooring (fig. 15–20) and the representational ones for furniture (fig. 15–21).

Both parquetry and marquetry correspond to the *tarsia geometrica* of Italy (see Chapter 13), but both are different from *tarsia certosina* or **inlay**, in which isolated pieces of veneer are sunk into surfaces of solid wood. The term **intarsia** is often used to cover both techniques, although some reserve that term for work that combines wood with contrasting materials such as brass, pewter, ivory, and mother-of-pearl. Such combinations of wood with other materials are also called **Boulle work** in honor of the great furniture maker André-Charles Boulle (1642–1732), who was an innovative master of the technique (see fig. 15–1 and fig. 15–30).

Examples of parquetry can be seen in the floors of the Galerie des Glaces (see fig. 15–7) and the Salon de la Guerre (see fig. 15–8) at Versailles. Examples of marquetry are the commode made by Boulle for Louis XIV (see fig. 15–1 and fig. 15–30) and the roll-top desk made by Jean-François Oeben (1721–65) and Jean-Henri Riesener (1734–1806) for Louis XV (see fig. 15–31).

▲ **15–20** A room in the Château de Blois, where Louis XII was born in 1462. The heavy ceiling beam is original, but the room—including its wallpaper, fabric portieres, and parquet flooring—has been redesigned in the Louis XIV style of two centuries later.

Dagli Orti/Picture Desk Inc./Kobal Collection

◄ **15–21** Detail of marquetry on a desk designed by Jean-François Oeben, c. 1760.

Daniel Arnaudet/Hervee Lewandowski/Art Resource/Reunion des Musees Nationaux

French Furniture

The French, particularly in the seventeenth and eighteenth centuries, produced some of the most elegant pieces of furniture the world has known. They also produced a remarkable number of new furniture types, their subtle differentiations of shape and character matched to almost every activity and nuance of sophisticated society. The finest examples were impeccably made, luxuriously finished, and comfortable—beyond any that had come before. When Mlle. Victoire, a daughter of Louis XV, was asked if she were going to enter a convent as her sister had, she replied that she was "too fond of the comforts of life," and, pointing to her comfortable **bergère**, she said, "An armchair like that is my undoing."

The Division of Occupations

The French produced an elaborate system of furniture making, with guilds of artisans who were specialists of various crafts. The guilds held high standards, with strict entrance requirements and carefully defined duties. These artisans were employed in addition to the *ornemanistes* in charge of a room's overall design. We shall look first at these guilds of workers and then at some of the furniture they produced.

At some time in the Middle Ages, the artisans who produced wood crafts (*métiers du bois*), including wood furniture, had broken free of the guild of carpenters and formed a separate group with its own guild, called the **menuisiers**. Within this general group there were several specialties, such as those who joined solid wood furniture and those who applied veneers and marquetry. In 1743, this latter group began to call itself *menuisiers en ébène* or, more simply, **ébénistes** (the name suggesting how frequently ebony was the wood of choice), and the guild was officially renamed that of the *menuisiers-ébénistes*.

Distinctions between the *menuisiers* and the *ébénistes* were formally established in a 1745 revision of the guild's statutes: The first group produced chairs, beds, and tables of solid wood but were prohibited from adding extensive ornamental carvings; the second group produced case pieces embellished with marquetry and gilt-bronze mounts. In practice there were exceptions and overlapping. Georges Jacob (1739–1814), who produced furniture for Marie-Antoinette (see fig. 15–17), is the rare artisan who excelled both as a *menuisier* and as an *ébéniste*.

The *ébénistes* considered most highly skilled were singled out for a special honor: They were appointed *maître-ébénistes* or master cabinetmakers. Once named *maître-ébénistes*, artisans were required to have the quality of their work examined several times a year and to use personal stamps to identify most of their output. The stamping was generally out of sight—under the seats of chairs or under the tops of tables—but it has greatly aided the identification of eighteenth-century furniture and is still in use today. (It has also led to the idea in today's antiques market that a stamped piece is more valuable than an unstamped one, though the finest pieces, commissioned directly by the royal household, were often unstamped.)

Over 1,000 artisans were named *maître-ébénistes* during the eighteenth century. André-Charles Boulle, Jean-François Oeben, and Jean-Henri Riesener were already mentioned. These three and a few other *maître-ébénistes* went on to become *ébénistes du roi*, an honor that brought them direct patronage from the king and a freedom from guild restrictions, such as the prohibition against working in more than one occupation.

Also important in the division of work were the *vernisseurs* (lacquerers), the *tabletiers* (makers of small intricate objects such as toiletry cases), and the *tapissiers* (upholsterers, some of whom also designed and made draperies, and some of whom sold the furniture they had upholstered).

Seating and Beds

During the Early Renaissance reign of François I, chairs were still medieval in character: massive square objects with storage compartments sometimes under their hinged seats. When his son Henri II came to the throne with Catherine de' Medici from Italy as his queen, the storage function was abandoned and the whole chair was lightened, an opening made beneath the chair arms and another between the seat and the back, and the legs joined by a stretcher near the floor. Other chairs did away with the arms altogether in order to accommodate the current fashion of women in hoopskirts. A lighter chair among these relatively heavy Early Renaissance types is the **caquetoire**, a movable little piece that could be pulled up for "cackling" or gossiping (fig. 15–22). It was similar to the Italian **sgabello** (see fig. 13–24) that Catherine had known at home. The hardness of the seats was mitigated by *carreaux*, flat square cushions with big tassels by which they could be easily picked up; they were used on the floor as well.

▲ **15–23** Walnut armchair from the late seventeenth century. Its cabriole legs are braced by an X-shaped stretcher.
Woodwork, Furniture-French-End of XVII c., Louis XIV period. Arm Chair. Walnut, wax polished. The Metropolitan Museum of Art, Gift of J. Pierpont Morgan, 1907. (07.225.500)

By the time of Louis XIII in the seventeenth century, as the Renaissance era was ending, new standards of comfort called for upholstery rather than cushions. The upholstery was secured to the seat and back with rows of decorative metal nails, and the chairs were still boxy in form. For Louis XIV these chairs developed into armchairs of generous size, at once more imposing and more pleasing than their predecessors—in keeping with the new Baroque love of grand effects and strong impressions. Their tall upholstered backs were suitable backdrops for the elaborate hairstyles of both women and men. The earlier H-shaped stretchers bracing the legs were replaced by the more graceful X-shaped ones (fig. 15–23). The arms ended in curves or volutes. Of most importance for the future of furniture design, the legs assumed the shape of a languorous S curve, a **cabriole**.

With the addition of an upholstered pad on the arm, this became a **fauteuil**, a furniture type popular through many succeeding styles. In the Renaissance era, the *fauteuil* was not usually upholstered, but beginning in the Baroque period it was. The Baroque *fauteuil* also had its arms placed directly over its front legs, but beginning in the Régence period the arms were moved farther back and the legs became shorter, lowering the seat. As the chairs became lower and lighter, the structural need for stretchers between the legs diminished. Examples of Neoclassical style *fauteuils* are seen in Marie-Antoinette's room in the Petit Trianon (see fig. 15–17). In recent years, the word *fauteuil* has come to mean any upholstered armchair, including a theater seat, but strictly used the term refers only to a chair with an open side between arm and seat.

When that opening is filled in with upholstery, the armchair is called a **bergère**, which dates from the late Régence period. The Neoclassical version of a *bergère* seen in figure 15–24 is of carved and gilt beech upholstered in *petit point* (small-stitch needlepoint); it was designed c. 1780 by Jean-Baptiste Claude Sené (1748–1803), another *maître-ébéniste*. It is seen on a Savonnerie carpet made c. 1740.

There were useful stools as well as chairs, a popular type being the **tabouret**, originally with a circular seat (see the upper right in fig. 15–5), but from the early eighteenth century with a rectangular upholstered seat and straight legs. At the court of Louis XIV it was considered an honor to be allowed to sit on a *tabouret*. Other stools were the *placet*, slightly taller than the *tabouret*, and the *ployant*, a folding stool with crossed legs.

▲ 15–25 A Rococo *marquise* (loveseat) with a gilded wood frame, designed by Louis Delanois, mid-eighteenth-century.
Louis Delanois (1731–1792), ìWingchair or Bergere en Cabriolet (from a pair) î. ca. 1765. Stamped L. Delanois. OA6548. Musee du Louvre, Paris, France Rèunion des Musées Nationaux/SCALA/Art Resource, NY

French furniture makers applied great ingenuity to devising sofas and daybeds of unprecedented comfort. The **marquise**, which can be thought of simply as a wide *bergère*, is just large enough for two people in intimate conversation. It was introduced in the Rococo period. The Rococo example in figure 15–25 is the design of *maître-ébéniste* Louis Delanois (1731–92), who supplied furniture for Mme. du Barry's rooms at Versailles. A *marquise* is also sometimes called a *tête-à-tête* or *confident*. If it had a back so tall and enveloping that it gave a great deal of privacy to the seated pair, it was called a *bergère en confessional*. A *canapé* was wider than a *marquise* but still intended for only two people; its name is derived from the fact that in the seventeenth century it was covered with a canopy, which later disappeared.

The **méridienne**, popular in the Neoclassical period and also called a **veilleuse**, was a sofa with an asymmetrical back, one side higher than the other. But here, because the user could stretch out with his or her head supported by the higher end, we have entered the realm of the daybed or **chaise longue** (long chair). Mme. Boucher in figure 15–13 seems to be comfortable on hers. If the daybed were in two sections, like an armchair with a large stool, the combination was called a **duchesse brisée**.

▼ **15–27** A *lit d'alcôve* (alcove bed), c. 1770, among carved wood and fabric décor. The small carpet is Aubusson, c. 1780.
Jean-Pierre Legiewski/Art Resource/Reunion des Musees Nationaux

Variations included the *lit à l'impériale*, which had a canopy shaped like a dome, and the *lit d'alcôve*, which was placed with its long side against a wall and could be used as a sofa during the day. The head, base, and wall side of the *lit d'alcôve* were of the same height, and it was sometimes covered with a small canopy attached to the wall. The Neoclassical example seen in figure 15–27 in a curtained alcove is of gray-painted beech with red damask and dates from c. 1770.

Tables

The medieval table of boards laid on trestles and covered with fabric continued to be used in Renaissance France, though it could hardly be considered fashionable. It was gradually replaced by tables with round, square, or octagonal tops on central supports. Some tops could fold out to larger sizes. These tables were often heavy and ornate, but beginning with the Baroque style they became lighter, with their legs often braced by X-shaped stretchers. As with all other furniture types, the Rococo period brought graceful cabriole legs, and the Neoclassical period a newly restrained classicism. The large round table seen in figure 15–28, attributed to *ébéniste du roi* Jean-Henri Riesener, was made for Louis XVI's study at Versailles; its top remarkably, was made from a single piece of mahogany.

Beds in the Renaissance, in Louis XIII's time, had come to be draped in a great deal of fabric, no longer hung from the ceiling as it had been in Gothic times, but hung as a **tester** from four wood pillars, one at each corner of the bed. Because of these columnar posts, such a bed was called a *lit à colonnes*, but it was also known as a *lit à la française*.

For the Baroque court of Louis XIV and its imitators, the bedroom was not the intimate chamber it has since become, but was a very public space in which visitors were received with great ceremony: a *chambre de parade*. The bed itself, the *lit de parade*, was ceremonial, too, an object of great splendor. Louis XIV's own bed (fig. 15–26), near the exact center of Versailles, was on a slightly raised platform isolated from the rest of the room (where courtiers could gather) by a balustrade. It was hung with crimson silk velvet embroidered with gold and silver thread and topped with four ostrich plumes.

▼ **15–28** A round Neoclassical table from Louis XVI's study at Versailles. Its top, almost 7 ft. (2.15 m) in diameter, is made of a single piece of mahogany.
Réunion des Musées Nationaux/Art Resource, NY

There were various sorts of game tables (*tables à jeux*), as specialized as the games played. Square-topped ones meant for four players were by far the most frequently seen design, but others had triangular tops for three or pentagonal ones for five; others had hinged tops that could be unfolded to form larger playing surfaces. Almost all were surfaced with fabric. Some of them had circular depressions at the corners for holding candlesticks, and when they did not they were often accompanied by small table-height candlestands, also called **torchères**, which probably originated in the sixteenth century and were used until electric lighting made them obsolete.

A **console** table, fixed to the wall and supported by only two legs, was used beneath mirrors, and a small French Provincial table with a single drawer is at Mme. Boucher's side in figure 15–13. A small pedestal table or candlestand called a **gueridon**, modeled on an ancient Roman design, is seen in figure 15–29. Of chased and gilt bronze with a marble top, it is from the Directoire period and attributed to Pierre-Philippe Thomire (1751–1843), a noted sculptor and bronze-worker (*bronzier*); he designed a candelabrum for Versailles commemorating the American Declaration of Independence and, during the French Revolution, is said to have offered his foundry for the production of armaments.

Casegoods

André-Charles Boulle was the first great *maître-ébéniste* and the head cabinetmaker to Louis XIV. The designer for whom **Boulle work** was named, Boulle displayed that technique

▼ **15–30** A commode by André-Charles Boulle in ebony marquetry with ormolu mounts, one of a pair made for Louis XIV. Note that Boulle has supported it on eight legs. See also fig. 15–1.

"Mazarine" commode. Tortoiseshell and copper marquetry on ebony, engraved and gilded bronze, top of marble griotte. Executed c. 1708–1709 for the bedroom of Louis XIV in the Grand Trianon, Salon de Mercure. Reunion des Musees Nationaux/Art Resource, NY

▲ **15–29** A *guéridon* table of chased and gilt bronze attributed to Pierre-Philippe Thomire, end of the seventeenth century, 31 in. (.8 m) high. The screen behind it has Savonnerie panels, c. 1735–40. The rug is Savonnerie, 1678.

Michele Bellot/Art Resource/Reunion des Musees Nationaux

▲ **15–31** The *bureau à cylinder* (roll-top desk) of Louis XV by Jean-François Oeben and Jean-Henri Riesener, finished in 1769, nine years after its design. It has marquetry of holly, box, and other woods.

D. Arnaudet/Réunion des Musées Nationaux/Art Resource, NY

with virtuosity on a pair of Baroque **commodes** (fig. 15–30) he designed for Louis XIV's bedroom at the Grand Trianon, one of the subsidiary buildings on the grounds of Versailles. The commode, a low two-drawer or three-drawer chest, was a smaller, lighter version of the Italian **cassone** (see fig. 13–26), which had begun to be popular around 1690. Some commodes, in which the rounded drawer fronts recalled the shape of a sarcophagus, were called *commodes en tombeau*. Boulle's commode, however, rather than being wholly convex, became concave directly beneath its marble top, then prominently convex, then concave again at the bottom. Such an undulating form is called **bombé**, and it would be popular in the Régence and Rococo periods that followed. A curiosity of Boulle's design is that he has supported it on eight feet.

Over time, one type of table made especially for writing, the **bureau** (the forerunner of our desk) became so sophisticated through the use of cabinetry above or below the writing surface that it became part of the category of casegoods. The name *bureau* comes from *bure*, a coarse wool fabric that was used as a cover for a writing surface. The simplest version, the **bureau plat**, had four legs and no drawers. Many other versions had small drawers and storage compartments. A storage element with a grid of pigeonholes for papers was called a *cartonnier* and could be used on one end of the top of a *bureau plat*.

One of the most ingenious and elaborate versions of the *bureau* was the **bureau à cylindre**, or cylinder-front desk. When closed, its writing surface was covered by a partial cylinder of wood veneer. (A nineteenth-century version, with the cover made of a tambour of wood slats, would be called a roll-top desk.) When this cover was rolled back, an inner mechanism pushed the writing surface forward. The earliest example, and a superb piece of Rococo furniture (fig. 15–31), was begun for Louis XV by Jean-François Oeben in 1760 and finished after Oeben's death by Jean-Henri Riesener in 1769; in this case, it is unnecessary to roll back the cover, for an ingenious system of springs opens it automatically when a button is pressed.

Made by Riesener for Marie-Antoinette around 1770 was a Neoclassical desk (fig. 15–32) in a simpler drop-front style (in French, a **secrétaire à abattant**). Under a marble top, the exterior of the desk is veneered with ebony and faced with seventeenth-century panels of black-and-white Japanese lacquer and gilt-bronze ornament, made by Riesener himself. In the gilt-bronze frieze across the top, the queen's initials (MA) appear three times. When the writing surface is lowered, it re-

▲ **15–32** A Neoclassical *secrétaire à abattant* (drop-front desk) designed by Jean-Henri Riesener for Marie-Antoinette and faced with Japanese lacquer panels, c. 1770. The paneling behind it is edged with egg-and-dart molding.
The Metropolitan Museum of Art, Gift of Mrs. Herbert N. Straus, 1942. (42.203.1). Photograph © 1995 The Metropolitan Museum of Art.

veals an interior veneered in bands of purplewood and tulipwood and including a strongbox and a secret compartment for the queen's use.

French Decorative Arts

The French interior was noted for the complete integration of a design vision. The interiors had furniture that fully complemented the rooms, and accompanying them were a range of decorative arts, each element contributing to the total ensemble.

Pottery

French ceramics during early medieval times had been limited chiefly to paving tiles for churches. Useful wares such as pots, bowls, and jugs were being produced in the twelfth century, and the 1399 inventory of Charles VI mentions "a pottery beaker from Beauvais mounted in silver." By the end of the fifteenth century France was producing earthenware stoves, fountains, statues, and other religious wares, and also a large variety of tableware, including such specialized items as paté dishes.

In the sixteenth century, candlesticks and bowls were made from fine clay inlaid with brown and black slips and covered in a transparent lead glaze. Decorations included new Renaissance fashions brought from Italy, such as grotesques, arabesques, and Vitruvian scrolls. Within this un-remarkable context, a late sixteenth-century artist of idiosy-cratic vision produced some remarkably original work.

▲ 15–33 A lead-glazed earthenware platter by Bernard Palissy with reliefs of a snake, a perch, a crayfish, and other sea creatures, second half of the sixteenth century, 19½ in. (49 cm) wide.
Large Oval Dish, French, Bernard Palissy or a follower, late XVI century. By kind permission of the Trustees of the Wallace Collection.

Palissy   Bernard Palissy (1519–90) traveled throughout France in his younger days working as a *peintre-vitrier*, a worker in stained glass. By the middle of the sixteenth century Palissy had developed a mixture of glazes that could make ceramics resemble jasper and other exotic stones then coming into fashion. The wares were called *terre jaspées*. The French Renaissance queen, Catherine de' Medici named him *inventeur des rustiques figulines du roi*. His *rustiques figulines* were most typically oval platters covered in representations of ferns, mosses, and shells against which squirmed three-dimensional snakes, lizards, lobsters, frogs, insects, and other assorted creatures (fig. 15–33). For Catherine, Palissy used the same marine-reptilian vocabulary in a grotto for the Tuileries garden in Paris. His work was highly influential, and many later French ceramics were produced in the Palissy style, even as late as the nineteenth century.

Faience and Creamware   The celebrated **faience** of Italy and Moorish Spain was introduced to France in the fourteenth century. Potters from Faenza and other Italian centers were active in France in the sixteenth century. In 1603, Henri IV granted a thirty-year monopoly for the production of faience to the three Conrade brothers in Nevers, whose production included some work in the style of the della Robbias. Italian styles continued in popularity for a long time, although they were joined by a more native style based on the paintings (admittedly Italianate) of Poussin, and after 1670 by Eastern influences, such as blue-and-white ware and, later, *famille verte*. In the late seventeenth and early eighteenth centuries, the Potera family established an important faience pottery at Rouen, producing pale blue monochrome wares with decorations picked out in reddish brown (*style rayonnant*).

By the end of the eighteenth century, however, the popular taste had turned from faience to English **creamware**, a cream-colored type of earthenware that was less expensive and thought to be more suitable for the new Neoclassical designs. In 1772 the Pont-aux-Choux factory in Paris declared itself the "Royal Manufacturer of French earthenware in the imitation of that of England." Potters came from the famous English factory at Staffordshire to open new factories in France, and by 1786 creamware was being made at Lunéville and Chantilly. It was called *faïence fine*.

Porcelain

As we would expect from the luxuriousness of much of what we have seen, that most admired ceramic product, porcelain, was an important presence in these interiors. Soft-paste (*pâte tendre*) porcelain (see Tools & Techniques: The Secret of Porcelain in Chapter 11) was made as early as 1672 at the factory of St.-Cloud near Paris, established under royal patronage. Its products included blue-and-white ware and all-white ware made in imitation of Chinese *blanc de chine*, and some of the St.-Cloud tiles and vases were made for Versailles.

A more important factory was established in 1740 at Vincennes, its success greatly aided by a series of royal privileges and licenses. Its first director had discovered a method of making a soft-paste porcelain of unusual whiteness, and an important part of its early production was small porcelain blossoms that could be mounted on gilt-bronze stems and placed in vases and in wall sconces and chandeliers—early and charming versions of artificial flowers. Dinner services were also made, at first on yellow grounds and later on pale greens and blues, including a turquoise hue called *bleu céleste*. Early customers were royalty and nobility, including Louis XV and Mme. de Pompadour, but around 1751 a shop was opened in Paris selling Vincennes wares to affluent members of the public. In 1756 the factory was moved to Sèvres, lending the name **Sèvres** to this extremely high quality French porcelain.

At Sèvres, the factory's reputation and technical skills both flourished, although there was no access to kaolin (china clay) until 1769, which meant that the manufacture of true hard-paste porcelain was not yet possible. (The German factory at Meissen had already been making hard-paste porcelain.) By the end of the eighteenth century, Sèvres offered hard-paste porcelain exclusively.

Sèvres was noted for figures, figurines, and porcelain plaques for furniture, but it was perhaps best known for its vases. These took many forms,

▼ **15–34** A Sèvres vase in Neoclassical style with gilding.
Victoria & Albert Museum, London/Art Resource, NY

including Neoclassical ones such as that shown in figure 15–34, as well as Rococo fantasies, *chinoiseries*, and some novelties in the shape of elephants' heads.

Glass

French glassware was strongly influenced by the glass of Venice. Much Venetian glass was imported to France until the end of the seventeenth century, and many who made glass in France had moved there from Italy. Renaissance glassworks at St.-Germain-en-Laye were supported by Henri II and his wife Catherine de' Medici, and Baroque glassworks at Orléans were patronized by the Duc d'Orléans, the brother of Louis XIV. There, Bernard Perrot, a native Italian, created techniques for making *porcelaine en verre* (an opaque white glass resembling porcelain), *rouge des anciens* (a transparent red glass imagined to be similar to ancient products), and, of most importance, cast (rather than blown) panels of flat glass (although Perrot was not the inventor of flat glass, small panes having been produced by the ancient Romans).

Flat glass and mirrors were important ingredients of French interior design, and mirrors, of course, performed the valuable function of reflecting light, an important service in an age dependent on candlelight. Producing them, rather than importing them at great cost, was the goal of Louis XIV who founded a plate-glass factory employing Italian workers in 1665 in the Paris suburb of St.-Antoine. It was the St.-Antoine factory that, between 1678 and 1683, provided the glass and mirrors for the Galerie des Glaces at Versailles. Another royal glass factory was established in 1693 at St.-Gobain, and in 1695 the two factories were merged to form the Manufacture Royale des Glaces de France.

Nicolas Pineau, whom we met as an *ornemaniste*, also designed a Rococo gilt mirror surround for the 1731 Hôtel de Villars, Paris (fig. 15–35). It has now been moved to Waddesdon Manor, the Rothschild family estate near London.

▲ **15–35** A Rococo gilt mirror surround designed by Nicolas Pineau in 1731 for the Hôtel de Villars, Paris, now moved to England. There was originally a console table beneath it.

Francois-Nicolas Pineau, "Mirror Frame surmounted by a painting representing a Sibyl, after Guido Reni" circa 1731 (Hotel de Vilars). Acc 3634.1. Waddesdon Manor (The National Trust), Photo: Eost and Macdonald, 1977.

In smaller blown-glass wares such as vases and cups, the late seventeenth and early eighteenth-century fashion was for cut and faceted pieces. "English crystal" or lead glass, containing a large amount of lead oxide, was developed in England in 1676 and was thought to be particularly appropriate for such treatment. During the next century, many French glass factories turned to the production of lead glass, including the famous Baccarat factory, which had been founded in 1764, and the St.-Louis factory, founded in 1767.

Lacquer

Beginning in the seventeenth century but reaching its height in the Rococo period, the French fashion for Chinese decoration included an interest in Chinese lacquer. It was both imported and imitated, and panels, drawer fronts, and other furniture parts were sent from France to China to be lacquered. It was not until the eighteenth century that a really convincing French technique of imitating Chinese lacquer was invented by two brothers, Guillaume and Etienne-Simon Martin, in 1730, and in 1744 they were granted a monopoly on such work for twenty years. It was then produced by two generations of Martins. Most of the Martins were granted the title *vernisseur du roi*, and the company was called the Manufacture Royale des Vernis Martin.

The Martins' lacquer was produced in the typical Chinese colors of black and scarlet, and also in a deep blue, and in the pale tints of yellow, green, and lilac that were so popular in Rococo France. The Martins produced lacquer not only as furniture but also as pieces as large as carriages and sedan chairs and as small as fans and snuffboxes. The term **vernis Martin** (Martin varnish) was used for their lacquerwork and, later, for their furniture designs, and, still later, after their monopoly expired, for the work of their many imitators. An example is the Neoclassical green and gold *vernis Martin* inkstand (fig. 15–36) made by René Dubois (1737–99), best known as a furniture designer. *Vernis Martin* was of sufficient quality to be found in some apartments of Versailles and to have been ordered by the great connoisseur of things Chinese, Mme. de Pompadour.

Gilding and Ormolu

The glitter of gold is an enlivening ingredient of many French interiors. **Gilding** is the application of a gold-colored finish to a variety of materials—wood, plaster, metal, ceramics, glass, textiles, leather, or even paper. **Ormolu**, from the French *or moulu* (ground gold), is the creation of an amalgam of gold and mercury from which the mercury evaporates under heat (see Tools & Techniques: Gold Leaf and Ormolu, below). It is applied to metal objects, which can serve as door hardware, furniture mounts, andirons, firescreen supports, and many other uses. The same terms and techniques generally apply also to silver-colored finishes and substances, so the terms apply more to the crafts than to the ingredients.

Gilding has traditionally been accomplished in two basic ways. The first method is with gold leaf, paper-thin sheets of real gold, a technique first used by the an-

cient Egyptians as early as 1500 B.C. The second gilding method, which was considered inferior, is with gold liquid, made by dissolving gold powder in either paint or lacquer. In common practice, "gold" paint is often made with brass or bronze powders and "silver" paint with aluminum, and the quality of the appearance in these substitutes falls short of the real thing.

Ormolu is often decorative metalwork made of fire-gilt bronze. Much of the brilliance we associate with fine French furniture from all the periods covered in this chapter is due to the application of ormolu to furniture mounts (hardware such as handles, hinges, escutcheons,

▼ **15–36** A Neoclassical inkstand designed by René Dubois, lacquered with green and gold *vernis Martin*.
Neoclassical inkstand designed by René Dubois. Wallace Collection, London, UK/Bridgeman Art Library

---

Tools & Techniques | GOLD LEAF AND ORMOLU

Gold Leaf

Gilding in gold leaf is done either with water or with oil.

With water, the surface is first covered with several coats of **gesso**, a paste made of a white substance such as chalk or gypsum mixed with glue that fills any uneven areas in the surface and can be ground to become a very smooth foundation. More glue may be applied over that. The gesso is dried, and then water is brushed onto it. The gold leaf, already cut to the required size and shape, is then picked up with a brush and placed on the wet surface, to which it adheres.

With oil, the surface is sealed and then painted with several coats of oil paint, often red or yellow. A mixture of oil and glue is then painted on and allowed to dry for a day, the gilder watching carefully for the right balance of moisture and dryness to be achieved. When that occurs, the leaf is picked up with a brush and applied. Oil gilding requires more skill but is more durable than water gilding.

After the leaf has adhered to the surface, either kind of gilding can be pressed with a soft material or stippled with bristles to reduce the visibility of joints between pieces of leaf.

Ormolu

The fire-gilding process of true ormolu depends on the ability of heated mercury to unite with gold, forming an amalgam. In the French Renaissance and later periods, it was accomplished in two ways.

In the first, a bronze (or, quite often, brass) surface was coated with mercury, and then thin sheets of gold were applied to the surface and forcefully burnished. In the second method, gold filings were added to heated mercury, the result stirred with an iron rod until it was the consistency of butter, then brushed onto the surface. In both methods, a final step applied heat to evaporate the residual mercury. If wanted, chemicals could then be used to alter the color or texture of the result. The technique, using either method, was fraught with difficulties and serious health hazards. It has been replaced by electrogilding, a type of electroplating.

The finest ormolu is distinguished not just by the quality of the material and the overall design outline, but also by details of treatment, such as **chasing**, a method of decorating metal surfaces by embossing or incising them with tools such as punches, small hammers, or the pointed blades called burins. The finest work may also make subtle distinctions between matt and burnished areas, giving different degrees of reflectivity.

▲ **15–37** Rococo ormolu mounts by Jacques Caffiéri on two drawer fronts of a commode by Antoine Gaudreau for the *chamber* of Louis XV at Versailles, 1739.

Antoine-Robert Gaudreaus, "Chest-of-drawers (commode)", French, 1739, detail of the central cartouche. © The Trustees of the Wallace Collection, London. By kind permission of the Trustees of the Wallace Collection.

and drawer pulls, as well as ornamental medallions and moldings). Ormolu is also known as *bronze doré* or, in English, *gilt bronze,* and the French themselves refer to it as *les bronzes d'ameublement* or simply *les bronzes.*

True ormolu should not be confused with the inferior effects of imitation ormolu, which is made by dipping metal objects in acid and then painting them with gold-tinted lacquer. This less expensive alternative to fire gilding was used on many furniture mounts until the end of the Louis XV period, and is called *bronze verni* (bronze varnish). In later centuries the term *ormolu* would come to be used also for materials—alloys of copper and zinc, for example, sometimes with the addition of tin—that only approximated the appearance of real gold.

During the Rococo period, members of the Caffiéri family were prominent artisans of ormolu work, particularly Jacques Caffiéri (1678–1755), a detail of whose work is seen in figure 15–37, and his son Philippe Caffiéri II (1714–74). Prominent in the late Rococo and Neoclassical period were Etienne Forestier (1712–68), who supplied bronze mounts for André-Charles Boulle and Jean-François Oeben. Pierre Gouthière (1732–c. 1813) was credited with the invention

of the matte-finish ormolu work popular in his day. Another prominent worker in ormolu during the eighteenth century was Pierre-Philippe Thomire, whose table is seen in figure 15–29, and who was also employed as a designer at the Sèvres porcelain factory, where many ornamental porcelain objects were mounted in ormolu and others were gilded (see fig. 15–34). As the *ancien régime* of the French monarchy came to an end, so did the most brilliant period of ormolu work.

Tapestry

In the Renaissance, from the middle of the fourteenth century to the middle of the fifteenth, the most important French center of tapestry production was the northern town of Arras, which has given its name to a wall hanging or screen. In the 1600s François I established a royal tapestry workshop at Fontainebleau, and later Henri IV established one in the Galeries du Louvre.

The prestige of three chief centers of French tapestry production—Gobelins, Beauvais, and Aubusson—varied through time, but in general we can say that the works of the Gobelins were designed for the king, those of Beauvais for the nobility, and those of Aubusson for the prosperous middle class. After the French Revolution, tapestry production would continue on a greatly diminished scale.

The Gobelins   Tapestries had been woven since 1607 in a Paris town house called the Hôtel des Gobelins (goblins). In 1658 Nicolas Fouquet, Louis XIV's superintendent of finance, established his own workshop solely for the production of tapestries for his grand château of Vaux-le-Vicomte, then under construction. When Louis arrested Fouquet three years later, he confiscated the tapestry workshop along with the château. Colbert, the king's chief minister, established in Gobelins in 1663 a factory to supply a wide variety of luxury goods—including tapestries—for the royal households. It was formally known as the Manufacture Royale des Meubles de la Couronne, but informally known all over the world as the Gobelins, a name that—like Arras—has come to be almost synonymous with tapestry.

The painter Charles Le Brun was artistic director of the entire enterprise, and under him more than 300 workers and apprentices staffed the tapestry studio. Le Brun approved every tapestry's subject matter and quality, both of which were intended to enhance the image of Louis XIV as the Sun King. Some designs were made by Le Brun himself, including a cycle called *Story of the King*, woven between 1665 and 1678. One panel of the cycle (fig. 15–38) depicted the king visiting the Gobelins and inspecting a wide variety of rich goods, all probably intended for Versailles, as was the tapestry cycle itself.

The expenses of war depressed the activity of the Gobelins in the last decade of the seventeenth century, but a revival was effected in 1699 by architect Jules Hardouin-Mansart, the crown's new Superintendent of Buildings. To suit the Rococo taste for smaller, more intimate rooms, the products of the Gobelins became smaller and their appearance more delicate. Historical scenes were still popular, but so were more lighthearted genre scenes depicting everyday life. An eighteenth-century innovation was the portrait tapestry; the first was of Louis XV. The last half of the century, of course, brought Neoclassicism to the Gobelins as it did elsewhere.

▼ **15–38** A Gobelins tapestry, *Louis XIV Visiting the Gobelins*, designed by Charles Le Brun and woven c. 1667.
Studio of Leblond (after Charles Le Brun): Visit of Louis XIV to the Gobelins Workshop, October 15, 1667. Gobelins tapestry, from the series of the History of the King. Reunion des Musees Nationaux (RMN)/Art Resource, NY

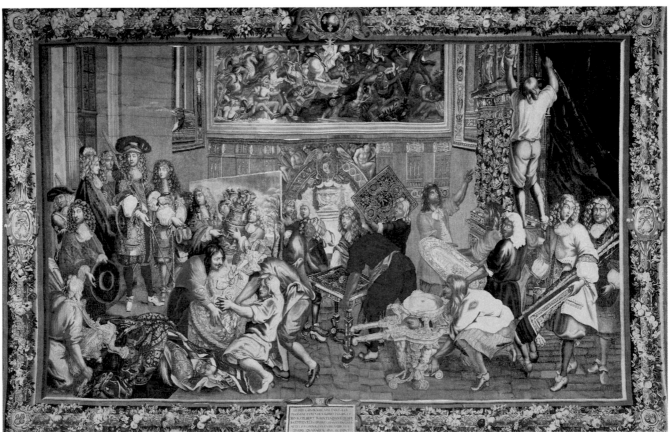

Beauvais   In 1664, the year after establishing the Gobelins, Colbert also founded a tapestry workshop at Beauvais, the cathedral town northwest of Paris. Beauvais struggled for success in its first sixty years, but after François Boucher (see fig. 15–13) was invited to Beauvais as its chief painter in 1736, the factory's success was assured. Beauvais subjects included *verdures* (representations of leafy plants), *chinoiseries*, masked figures from the Italian *commedia dell'arte*, and pastoral and mythological scenes. In addition to tapestries, Beauvais produced woven furniture covers, usually designed to match the wall hangings. Louis XV supported Beauvais with funds and honored it by purchasing its tapestries for diplomatic gifts.

Aubusson   The towns of Aubusson and Felletin in south central France had been centers of tapestry production beginning in the sixteenth century. Royal support in the early seventeenth century eliminated customs on tapestries sent from Aubusson to Paris, and by 1637 two thousand workers were employed at Aubusson, working out of their homes rather than (as at the Gobelins) in a central factory. During the next century, quality was improved as well, and Boucher began to design for Aubusson as well as Beauvais. A tapestry woven at Aubusson is seen in figure 15–39; it was based on a design by Charles Le Brun, who had painted the interiors of Vaux-le-Vicomte and Versailles.

Carpets

Copies of carpets imported from the Near East had been made in France as early as the fifteenth century, and pile carpets made in France were listed in the inventories of François I in the sixteenth century. The French carpet factories that would become world famous, however, Savonnerie and Aubusson, were not established until the early seventeenth century.

Savonnerie Carpets   By 1608, under the patronage of Renaissance king Henri IV, a workshop was set up in space beneath the Grande Galerie of the Louvre, the great palace in the heart of Paris, for the manufacture of carpets in the Turkish fashion. In 1627, the workshop expanded into additional quarters just outside Paris that had previously been occupied by a *savonnerie* (a soap factory), which gave its name to the workshop's later production.

Using cheap labor from a nearby orphanage, the Savonnerie factory flourished. Together with the factory at the Louvre, it was granted a monopoly on carpet manufacture for eighteen years along with a prohibition on imports. The name *Savonnerie* came to be applied to the Louvre products as well, and in 1663 Jean-Baptiste Colbert placed all carpet production within the jurisdiction of the Gobelins.

By this time, Renaissance imitations of Islamic designs had been superseded by designs in the French Baroque style, and the Gobelins' director Charles Le Brun mandated that the carpet designs be coordinated with current furniture designs—largely ebony pieces inlaid with floral motifs and arabesques. The typical result was a wool carpet of floral and vegetal motifs, often with a scenic panel at each end and a central medallion which always referred to Louis XIV, by depicting him in a sunburst or as the head of Apollo. Details of such carpets can be seen in figure 15–24, figure 15–25, and figure 15–29. Le Brun ordered more than a hundred carpets of this type for rooms at the Palais du Louvre and the Palais des Tuileries, and some think them the finest carpets ever made in Europe. They were woven on upright looms with a **symmetrical** (or *Turkish* or *Ghiordes*) **knot** (see Tools & Techniques: Carpet Weaving in Chapter 9),

▼ **15–39** An Aubusson tapestry with a design by Charles Le Brun depicting "The Triumph of Alexander, the Battle of Arbelles," 17th century.

Charles Le Brun (1619–1690), "The Triumph of Alexander, the Battle of Arbelles". Aubusson tapestry after design by Charles Le Brun, 17th c. Musee de Vulliod Saint-Germain, Pezenas, France. GIraudon/Art Resource, NY.

and they have 90 knots to the square inch (14 per cm²). In addition to carpets, the Savonnerie workshops produced wall hangings, door hangings, bed canopies, and covers for chairs and sofas.

In the early nineteenth century Napoleon declared Savonnerie an imperial factory and allowed it to produce fine works in the Neoclassical Empire style. In 1825 the Savonnerie workshop would be absorbed by the Gobelins; by then, however, its prominence had been eclipsed by that of Aubusson.

Aubusson Carpets   We have identified the town of Aubusson as an important center of tapestry production. In a 1743 reorganization of the Aubusson factory, carpet manufacture was added to tapestry work, and for three years the new venture had the financial support of the king. At the time, the total output of the Savonnerie factory was earmarked for royal use, but Aubusson found a ready market among the nobility and middle classes. Samples of Turkish carpets were sent to Aubusson to be copied, but by 1750, reflecting the new Rococo taste, Savonnerie carpets were being sent to Aubusson instead. The Aubusson versions, however, were generally simpler than their Savonnerie originals. The Aubusson factory produced both tapestry-weave carpets woven on horizontal looms and pile carpets woven on vertical ones. Colors were generally soft and pale: rose, dove gray, buff, light brown, and light yellow. Examples were obtained for some of the smaller rooms at Versailles, and there were Aubusson exports to northern Europe and even to the United States. A small Aubusson carpet is seen in the foreground of figure 15–27.

Other Textiles

In addition to tapestries and carpets, the French Renaissance produced interesting lace (used primarily for clothing), embroidery (used for bedcovers and wall hangings as well as for clothing), silk, and printed cotton.

Silks   Early Renaissance attempts at establishing a native French silk industry were dependent on royal patronage, but French silks were still plain and dull compared to the richly figured silks and velvets from Italy. A talented weaver was brought from Milan to Lyon in 1604 to teach the French new techniques and to adjust their looms for more elaborate effects; in 1665 Louis XIV's minister Colbert set new stan-

dards for silk production, including a mandate for the production of new designs every year; and in 1667 there was a ban on imports.

By the eighteenth century France's leadership in all phases of fashion made French silks highly desirable. Lyon became the most important silk city of Europe. In Paris, the related craft of silk ribbon weaving flourished. At the beginning of the Régence period in the early years of the century, silk designs were dominated by dense floral patterns, from the 1720s by geometric bands and diaper patterns, in the next decade by naturalistic effects. In the 1740s the Rococo style had emerged, with its asymmetrical sprays of plant forms. Later in the century, the paintings of Boucher were influential, as was the general Rococo craze for *chinoiserie*. One of Lyon's weavers, Philippe de Lasalle (1723–1804), achieved an international reputation: Some of his silk brocades were commissioned by Russia's Catherine the Great for her palaces and some by Marie-Antoinette (though she never lived to see them).

Toile de Jouy   The word *toile* can be translated as "linen" or "canvas." **Toile de Jouy**, however, identifies printed cotton of the type originally made in the French village of Jouy-en-Josas, near Versailles. Indian chintzes and other cottons had been imported into France in the late sixteenth century, and France had experimented in the Baroque seventeenth century with duplicating Indian techniques. Both the Indian originals and the French copies became so popular that they threatened the carefully nurtured silk industry and the wool industry as well, leading to legal prohibitions against the cottons beginning in 1686. It is said to have been the Rococo king Louis XV's manipulative and fashion-conscious mistress Mme. de Pompadour who persuaded the king to lift the ban in 1759.

Taking full advantage of the new law, Christophe-Philippe Oberkampf opened his Jouy-en-Josas factory in 1760. Soon he abandoned wood block printing for a new technique using large copper plates, invented by Irish textile artist Francis Nixon. Oberkampf's operation would be a very fashionable success through the end of the century, and it would continue after his death in 1815, not closing until the 1840s. Contributing to Oberkampf's success was his insistence on quality material, fast dyes, fine craftsmen, expert engraving, and the use of the most modern techniques, introducing France's first copper-roller printing machine in 1797.

The most prominent of his artists was Jean-Baptiste Huet (1745–1811). His charmingly provincial *toile de Jouy*

▲ 15–40 A pastoral *toile de Jouy* designed by Jean-Baptiste Huet, c. 1797.
Design Library

designs included pastoral scenes (fig. 15–40), as well as mythological, historical, and allegorical ones. Some actually depicted the manufacture of *toile de Jouy*. They were designed in fine lines meant to be printed in a single color—blue, red, green, sepia, eggplant, or black—against a pale cream-colored ground. The results were popular for upholstery, curtains, and wallcoverings, and Huet's designs are still imitated today, although his printing technique has been replaced by roller printing.

Wallpaper

The earliest record of painted or printed papers for use on walls comes from a French château in the late fifteenth century. Early wallpapers were printed in single colors from wood blocks on small sheets of paper. In the Baroque seventeenth century color was applied to paper through stencils, and the paper was used not only on walls and ceilings but as linings for drawers. Customers for such papers were members of the recently emerging middle class. They were acutely aware of—but unable to afford—the fashion among royalty and nobility for luxurious wall coverings such as stuccowork, frescoes, tapestries, and paneling in wood, marble, and leather. Decorative papers that imitated these rich treatments offered a very welcome solution. Then in the Rococo period, when scenic papers were being imported from China at great expense, the French papermakers learned to imitate them as well.

The Papillons   Jean-Michel Papillon (1698–1776) finished the first history of wallpaper in the last year of his life,

his *Traité historique et pratique de la gravure sur bois*. Regarding his father, Jean Papillon II, he wrote that "we owe the invention of *papiers de tapisserie* [papers imitating tapestries], for which he started a fashion in 1688." What Jean-Michel's father may have done is to make repeating patterns on large carved wood blocks that would match on all sides when separate printed images were joined. The wood blocks were covered with pigments and then pressed against the paper, and, by using separate blocks for each color, Papillon could print his repeating patterns in any number of colors.

Jean-Michel Papillon's text included practical information about hanging papers, even in such difficult places as circular rooms and around stairways, and it gave an idea of the variety of papers that had already been developed in the Régence and Rococo styles: flocked paper, imitation wood paneling, imitation cut velvet, floral designs, landscapes, borders, friezes, and rosettes for ceilings.

Réveillon   The Papillon family's accomplishments were overshadowed later in the eighteenth century by those of Jean-Baptiste Réveillon (1725–1811) who established his business in 1752, after Jean-Michel Papillon had left the wallpaper business to concentrate on wood engravings. Réveillon's techniques were similar to those developed by the Papillons, but he practiced them on a much larger scale, eventually employing over 300 workers. He bought his own paper factory so that he could control paper quality, and he was equally meticulous about the pigments used. Rather than attempt to design everything himself, he assembled a staff of designers, some of them previously employed at the Gobelins tapestry factory.

The designs produced by the Réveillon factory were dominated by the *grotesques* (fig. 15–41) that Raphael had adapted from Roman models for his *loggie* at the Vatican two and a half centuries earlier (see fig. 13–7) and by the similar but more natural *arabesques* taken from Islamic art. Réveillon's great contribution to interior design was his arrangement of these motifs into elements that could be adapted to rooms of varying shapes and sizes. There were large paper panels for large wall surfaces, smaller panels for overdoor use, narrow vertical panels that could be extended to any height like pilasters, and narrower strips that could be used as borders and frames. These parts could be assembled to give any room not only decoration in the latest taste, but a sense of architectural order it may have lacked.

▲ **15–41** Wide and narrow panels of Réveillon wallpapers with *grotesque* patterns set within wood moldings at the château of Frucourt, near Amiens, c. 1780.
From: "The Papered Wall" edited by Lesley Hoskins, new and expanded edition. © Thames & Hudson, London and New York. Private Collection. Reprinted by permission.

Louis XVI made Réveillon a royal warrant holder in 1784, and from then until the Revolution of 1789 his wallpapers were stamped "Manufacture Royale." His factory, which he had worked to make symbolic of aristocratic taste, was one of the early casualties of the Revolution. Despite the destruction of Réveillon's factory, some of his original wood blocks are still in existence and are used today for making copies of his designs.

Summary: French Design

In Renaissance France, interior design became institutionalized as never before: Style became a part of government policy; opulence became an advertisement for the state; the products and techniques contributory to design became a part of the national economy; the state determined who was qualified for different design tasks; and almost every level of French society became a participant in the pleasures of beautiful rooms and fine furniture design. Louis XIV left as a heritage the ultimate of all the arts: He had taught his people the art of living.

Looking for Character

We have seen a variety of artistic expressions in French design: the formality of the Renaissance style, the pomp and power of the Baroque, the delicacy of the Régence, the verve of the Rococo, the restraint of the Neoclassical, and the austerity of the Directoire. Fundamental to all these styles are three char-

acteristics of French thinking: a love of romance, a love of order, and a remarkable openness to intellectual freedom. Although the French were Gothic leaders in the race for the tallest and most structurally unlikely cathedrals (exercising their love of romance), from the Renaissance on they have been noteworthy for their candid acknowledgment of human instincts that the Middle Ages had preferred to screen. As noted earlier, French thinking and writing laid the foundation for modern ideas of democracy, and the dominant influence of an aristocracy was balanced by a passion for equality and freedom. Congruent with this tradition has been the French production of interiors remarkable not only for their high style and artistic unity, but also for their unprecedented comfort.

Looking for Quality

We have said that French Rococo design could be a pure delight or something lesser. Such variations in quality are found to some degree in the design of all times and places. In no case, however, is lack of quality in any French style due to lack of attention to detail. Fine materials, fine finishes, and meticulous workmanship characterize all French design, even the provincial. In the rare cases that may be judged unsuccessful, the fault is likely to be a surfeit, rather than a lack, of attention to detail. It is in their overabundance that some French styles may be perceived today as less than ideal. Even though these styles are not our current styles and French taste not necessarily our own taste, we can see that, at their best, French interiors, furniture, and decorative arts from the sixteenth through the eighteenth centuries reached levels of quality that have never been surpassed.

Making Comparisons

Comparisons among the French styles have already been noted: the Rococo lighter, more lyrical than the Baroque; the Neoclassical more restrained than any other. Comparisons between French styles and the Italian and Spanish styles that inspired them are clear: The French design with less passion and less movement than the Italians, yet with less solemnity and less severity than the Spanish. In Chapters 16 and 19, dealing with England and Early America, we shall see how French taste was tempered to fit into other cultures.

Beyond any comparison, however, is the enduring position of France in general and of Paris in particular as outstanding arbiters of taste and civilization. For centuries the world has turned to French culture—and not least to French interior design—for artistic nourishment.

England: Renaissance to Neoclassical

16

Fifteenth to Eighteenth Centuries

"This royal throne of kings, this scepter'd isle, . . . This blessed plot, this earth, this realm, this England . . ."

— William Shakespeare (1564–1616), poet and playwright

Despite a long English devotion to Gothic form and ornament, the Renaissance spirit inevitably crossed the English Channel from the continent of Europe to the British Isles. We shall see that, after a tentative beginning, the spirit of "re-birth" would produce in England interiors of great distinction (such as those of Robert Adam, whose ceiling design we see in fig. 16–1) and some of the most famous furniture designers of all time.

Determinants of English Design

Design is affected by many events, some of them seemingly unrelated. The increased use of gunpowder in Renaissance times, for example, not only changed the nature of warfare, but also the appearance of country houses by making heavy fortification useless: The castle was replaced by the manor house, then by the stately mansion. And the advent of printing and the influence of fifteenth-century English printer and typographer William Caxton led to a proliferation of printed and illustrated books that were key to the spread of knowledge about classical design.

◀ **16–1** Detail of a Neoclassical ceiling design by Robert Adam for a house at 5 Royal Terrace, Adelphi, London, in 1771. The house belonged to actor, playwright, and theater manager David Garrick. Victoria & Albert Museum, London/Art Resource, NY

Geography and Natural Resources

England, largest of the several lands that comprise the United Kingdom, is an island nation. Its isolation by sea has encouraged both a vigorous shipping trade with other countries and the development of a strong and independent national character. In design, the former has brought the importation of many foreign influences; the latter has transformed those influences into a native taste and tradition. England's relative distance from Italy may explain why Renaissance thought and design came later to England than to some other countries.

Naturally available building materials include plentiful stone. Famous examples are Portland stone, a limestone from the Isle of Portland used by architects Inigo Jones and Sir Christopher Wren; Doulting limestone, which built the Gothic Cathedral of Wells (see figs. 8–6 and 8–11); sandstones of Yorkshire and the West Midlands; granites of Devonshire and Cornwall; and marble from the Isle of Purbeck. Fine forests in Sussex, Lancashire, and other counties provided oak, but the use of wood in construction diminished as the danger of fire became apparent (particularly in the Great Fire of London in 1666) and as forests were cleared for the cultivation of crops. Clay from the river valleys

349

was used for brickmaking as early as Roman times, and terra-cotta was brought to England by Italian artisans in the sixteenth century.

The climate of England is temperate but wet, with some snow and much wind and rain, calling for steeply pitched roofs, protective porches, and fireplaces in most major rooms. The limited supply of strong sunlight promoted large windows.

Religion

Christianity was brought to England during its occupation by the ancient Romans and remains the chief religion there. Yet, despite that, there have been many struggles between the church and the monarchy and, within the church, many controversies between the Roman Catholic and Protestant branches of the faith. Even within Protestantism, there have been disputes among the Calvinists, Lutherans, Evangelicals, Puritans, and other branches.

One religious dispute with discernible effects on design was the Protestant Reformation of the 1530s, in which the English king Henry VIII rejected the rule of the popes and established the Church of England with himself as its head. The Roman Catholic monasteries were closed, their lands were confiscated and sold, and many of their buildings were replaced by—or incorporated into—large new private houses for the nobility and a growing number of wealthy merchants. Religious properties were also transformed into secular ones. Of more consequence is that this break with the Church of Rome also temporarily interrupted England's contact with Italy as a direct source of classical design ideas. For a while those ideas came to England filtered through the tastes of Holland, Germany, and particularly Flanders, one of the Low Countries ruled for a time by France and then by Spain (Flanders is now divided between Belgium and France). And the Dutch influence can also be seen in a good deal of English design.

History

Henry VIII was a member of the Tudor family that ruled England for more than a century, from 1485 to 1603. Under its rule, there was not only the new identification of church with state, but also new economic prosperity, a strengthening of England's naval power, and a flourishing of scholarship and literature: It was the beginning of the age of Shakespeare. In architecture and design, the term **Tudor** refers specifically to works and design created during the first half of the six-teenth century, during the reigns of Henry VIII, his father (Henry VII), and two of his children (Edward VI and Mary I). His third child, Elizabeth I, ruled from 1558 to 1603 and for her the **Elizabethan** style is named; in her reign England defeated the Spanish Armada, furthering English independence, and adventurers such as Sir Francis Drake and Sir Walter Raleigh made great discoveries in the New World.

The rule of the Tudors was followed by the rule of the Stuarts, which also lasted more than a century, from 1603 to 1714. In design, the Stuart king James I lent his name to the **Jacobean** style of the first half of the seventeenth century, with its great interest in work of the Italian Renaissance. James I was a patron of the rigorously classical architect Inigo Jones, but this style continued after Jones, through the reign of James's son Charles I, which lasted until 1649. During Charles I's reign the first great English collections of European art were assembled.

This cosmopolitanism was interrupted, however, by a Civil War in 1642–9 and a following Commonwealth period, 1649–60. Charles I was beheaded and the monarchy overthrown, the army placing the Puritan leader Oliver Cromwell in control as Lord Protector. During the social upheaval of the Commonwealth most artistic activity was suspended. Cromwell died in 1658, and the English experiment with republican government could not be sustained.

The monarchy was reestablished in the **Restoration** period of 1660–88 and the new Stuart king was Charles II, who had lived at the French court of Louis XIV and brought his knowledge of French design to England. (The Restoration period is less frequently called the *Carolean period*, a name derived from Charles, and sometimes it is called the *Stuart period*, after the royal family, but *Restoration* is the most widely used term.) Court life resumed in the Restoration, as did an interest in architecture, design, and the arts in general.

The **William and Mary** style, 1689–1702, is named for the Stuart rulers William III and Mary II. William III, a grandson of England's Charles I and the husband of the English princess Mary, was summoned from the Netherlands in 1689 and accepted the English throne jointly with his wife. Upon the death of the childless couple (Mary in 1694 and William in 1702), the throne passed to Mary's sister Anne and the **Queen Anne** period began. When Anne died without any surviving children, the Stuart reign was at an end.

The crown passed to the House of Hanover, a German royal family related to James I, who had ruled England a century before. The Hanovers ruled then from 1714 into the nineteenth century. The **Georgian** period, the great culmination of the English Renaissance, dates from soon after the accession to the throne of the first Hanover king, George I, and continued through the reigns of George II and George III until the end of the eighteenth century.

English Architecture and Interiors

The history of English design is usually told through the above eight stylistic periods, most of them named for the monarchs ruling at the time. We can simplify this list, however, and consolidate the periods into four that roughly—but only roughly—correspond to the divisions used for our discussions of Italy, Spain, and France: **Early Renaissance**, **High Renaissance**, **Baroque**, and **Neoclassical**. In this manner, we can see similarities and differences in how design was shaped by various cultures during these major time periods.

Within these four main divisions, stylistic variations occur during the briefer periods identified with the monarchs above. For example, the Early Renaissance begins with the Tudor phase, which is followed by the Elizabethan phase. The High Renaissance comprises the Jacobean phase and the monarchless Commonwealth phase. The Baroque period begins with the Restoration of the monarchy and continues with the William and Mary and Queen Anne phases. Finally, in the eighteenth century, we shall come to an undivided period: The Neoclassical period is identified wholly with the Georgian monarchs.

It is true that some historians would add an English Rococo period in the middle decades of the eighteenth century, but the Rococo was a minor phase of English design; there is no English building we can call Rococo, though the style did appear in some interior details, such as plasterwork, furniture (some of Thomas Chippendale's designs, for example), and decorative pieces such as picture frames and candlestands. **Chinoiserie**, though considered a style by some scholars, appeared at many times in English design and usually in combination with other elements, so we cannot clearly distinguish a chinoiserie period.

Early Renaissance Styles: Tudor and Elizabethan

The Early Renaissance saw a transition from the last phase of English Gothic to more classical design, and at the same time the fortified character of earlier houses was replaced by increased privacy and domestic comfort. Early Renaissance is a suitable heading for most English design of the sixteenth century and a bit earlier and later, including the Tudor style of 1485–1558 and the Elizabethan style of 1558–1603.

Timeline | THE ENGLISH RENAISSANCE & LATER DEVELOPMENTS

Period & Dates	Rulers	Principal Designers	Design Milestones
Early Renaissance 1485–1603	Henry VII, Henry VIII, Edward VI, Mary I, Elizabeth I	Robert Smythson	Compton Wynyates, 1520; Choir screen, King's College Chapel, Cambridge, 1533: Hardwick Hall, 1590–96
High Renaissance 1603–49	James I, Charles I	Inigo Jones	Stairway, Knole, Kent, after 1605; Banqueting Hall, Whitehall, 1619–22; Wilton House, 1630–50
Baroque 1649–1714	Oliver Cromwell, Charles II, James II, William and Mary (William III and Mary II), Anne	Christopher Wren, John Vanbrugh	Wren's London churches, 1670–1711; St. Paul's Cathedral, London, 1675–1711; Blenheim Palace, 1705–16
Neoclassical, 1714–1800	George I, George II, George III	Lord Burlington, William Kent, Thomas Chippendale, George Hepplewhite, Robert Adam, Thomas Sheraton	Chiswick House, London, 1725–30; Syon House, London, 1760–70

▲ **16–2** Exterior of the Tudor country house Compton Wynyates in Warwickshire, completed c. 1520.
English Heritage/National Monuments Record

The **Tudor** style is a transitional phase combining elements inherited from the Gothic—such as Great Halls and small-paned windows—with Renaissance ones—such as details from the classical orders. Tudor exteriors at first employed tall **gables** (triangular-shaped pieces of wall closing the ends of pitched roofs) topped with pinnacles. The walls below were sometimes of brickwork, sometimes of **half-timbered** construction, which was built partly of heavy timber members that were visible on both the exterior and the interior. These members were spaced roughly 2 feet (60 cm) apart with occasional diagonal members connecting them for bracing. The spaces between them were filled with plaster or masonry or, in more rustic cases, **wattle-and-daub**, which is a mixture of woven twigs, clay, and mud. Buildings were often irregular in shape, and either fully or partially enclosing courtyards. Leaded windows were standard, as were trussed timber roofs (see fig. 8–14) and the Tudor arch (see table 7–1), which was pointed like the Gothic arch but lower and more gently curved. It was used over windows, doors, and fireplaces. Tudor examples include parts of Henry VIII's country palace, Hampton Court, a chapel built by the same king, and several of the colleges at Cambridge and Oxford universities.

Compton Wynyates, Warwickshire   Portions of a moat remain that once surrounded a thirteenth-century house on the site, but the present structure was completed in 1520. It was built for Sir William Compton, who had served as a page to the young prince who would become Henry VIII, and there is a bedroom in the house where the king stayed when he visited. The exterior of Compton Wynyates (fig. 16–2) is a picturesque Tudor country house, a jumble of pink brick with roofs of local stone, topped with chimneys and battlements. None of the elevations has been made symmetrical, nor is the entrance centered in the composition; clearly, the building's form and door and window placement have been determined solely by interior function. The Big Hall (fig. 16–3), with its minstrel gallery above a screen of wood linenfold paneling, continues the tradition of the Great Hall at Penshurst Place (see fig. 8–15), built almost two hundred years earlier. The house's half-timbered construction is visible in the end wall of the Big Hall and in two exterior gables.

▲ **16–3** The Big Hall of Compton Wynyates. Its end wall is of half-timber construction above a screen of linenfold wood paneling.
Country Life Picture Library London, England

▲ **16–4** John Lee's arcaded wood Tudor choir screen added to the Gothic chapel of King's College, Cambridge, in 1533.
English Heritage/National Monuments Record

Most of the windows are square-headed, but the Tudor arch is used over the entrance door (see fig. 16–2) and over the Big Hall's windows (at left in fig. 16–3).

King's College Chapel, Cambridge
Cambridge University is one of England's most venerable educational institutions, founded in the early twelfth century. It is divided into several residential colleges, each built around its own quadrangle on the general model of a Medieval manor house. One of these, King's College, was established in the fifteenth century, and its sixteenth-century chapel (see fig. 8–7) is pure Late Gothic in its overall style with fan vaulting above large stained glass windows. However, in 1533 an important element was built that expresses the new interest in classical design. That is the great oak choir screen (fig. 16–4). Its design is by English architect John Lee (1507–33). Spanning across the chapel, supporting a great pipe organ, the screen has an arcaded lower section with a two-bay-wide central opening leading to the choir. Above the arcade is a curved soffit supporting the upper part of the screen, and both lower and upper sections are richly carved with Renaissance ornament and round-headed

arches, which were replacing Tudor arches (just as Tudor arches had replaced Gothic ones). The urns and garlands on the pilasters between the arches recall Raphael's décor for the Vatican *loggie* (see fig. 13–7), and other details have been compared with designs by the Italian Renaissance architect and theorist Sebastiano Serlio.

The later **Elizabethan** style retained less of the Gothic and added more of the Renaissance than the Tudor style had. Large glass areas with straight rather than arched lintels were typical. Chimneys were composed of clusters of classical orders. Columns and pilasters appeared. Symmetry replaced asymmetry in floor plans and façades. Large houses might still be built around courtyards, but more common were E-shaped or H-shaped plans. Walls of Elizabethan rooms were frequently paneled as in earlier times, at least in their lower sections, but ceilings were given plasterwork as a replacement for the exposed wood trusses of earlier houses. The great hall of the larger medieval houses remained a major feature for a while, but its importance was lessened during this time period by the addition of new and separate rooms, such as dining rooms, parlors, studies, galleries, important stair halls in place of narrow stairways between walls, and multiple bedrooms. Eventually the great hall lost its focus as a chief gathering place and became a double-height entrance hall.

Flooring on the ground levels of sixteenth-century English houses was usually of flagstone or slate. The flooring of upper levels was of random-width oak planks, generally the full size of the logs from which they were cut. Through the end of the century, however, even some of the grandest houses continued the medieval custom of strewing rushes and grasses over the floor. More up-to-date was an important private house of the Elizabethan phase of the Early Renaissance, Hardwick Hall.

Hardwick Hall, Derbyshire
Elizabeth Talbot, known as Bess of Hardwick, was renowned for her ambition, shrewdness, and temper. She left four marriages with ample financial settlements and undertook a number of building projects, including her largest project, Hardwick Hall, which she began in 1590 when in her seventies. It adjoined a small manor house where she had been born and which she had later enlarged and then partly demolished. What remained of it would house servants and guests, allowing the new Hardwick Hall (fig. 16–5) to provide only rooms for the family and public entertaining. Hardwick Hall was designed by a native Englishman, architect Robert Smythson (c. 1534–1614), whose other houses include Longleat in Wiltshire, also in the Elizabethan style.

"Hardwick Hall, more glass than wall" was a popular jingle of the day, and the stone house did have an extraordinarily large window area, its sandstone walls reduced to hardly more than window frames. It must have been an astonishing sight at a time when window glass was still very expensive. The floor plan is a simple rectangle with six attached towers. Important rooms include Bess's own chambers on the second floor and the Great High Chamber on the third floor. Also significant is the 160-foot (49-m) Long Gallery lighted by twenty tall windows (fig. 16–6). The gallery was used for grand entertainments, being large enough to accommodate even visiting royalty with their retinues of attendants, and, on rainy days, it was used for long walks by the owner. The long galleries of manor houses have been compared with the cloisters of monasteries: Both are sheltered spaces for exercise in inclement weather.

The furnishings of Hardwick Hall include two magnificent sets of tapestries from Brussels illustrating *The Story of Ulysses*. Bess had bought them before construction began, and the high great chamber and adjacent long gallery were designed with wall space on which to hang them. A decorating curiosity—infuriating to textile enthusiasts but giving an impression of profligate richness—is that a large collection of family and royal portraits has been hung directly over the valuable tapestries. The tapestries in the Great High Chamber (fig. 16–7) cover only the lower half of the wall, and above them is a mural of painted plaster depicting a woodland scene with life-size figures, in which, for realism, actual trunks of small trees were embedded in the plaster. The room's monumental fireplace surround is of alabaster inset with blackstone. The plaited and stitched rush matting on the floor of the Great High Chamber is of a weave that has been copied elsewhere under the name *Hardwick matting*.

High Renaissance Style: Jacobean

The High Renaissance moved in the seventeenth century into a period of more confident design. The classical elements that had begun to be used earlier were now used more generously and with greater care for their placement, proportions, and roles in classical composition. This phase of the Renaissance in England included the Jacobean era of 1603–1649, and the Commonwealth era of 1649–60, which was a period of unrest and actually an interruption of design activity.

The **Jacobean** style builds on the classicism of the Early Renaissance but adds influences from the Netherlands and Flanders to that from Italy. Trade was established with the East during this period, adding another design flavor. There is a new three-dimensional fullness and decorative richness in carvings and moldings. Colors become brighter. Unlike the smooth flat planes of the ceilings of Hardwick Hall, Jacobean ceilings begin to be decorated with plaster reliefs.

Knole, Kent
The country house of Knole in Kent is an ancient one, its original sections built in the fifteenth century. It was added to over several centuries, its various wings and estimated 365 rooms surrounding seven courtyards, so that its exterior now resembles a small village. Knole was the home of five successive archbishops of Canterbury (heads of the Church of England) and was then acquired by Henry VIII in 1535. In 1566, Elizabeth I gave it to her cousin Thomas Sackville. Above its gables, pinnacles are carved in the shapes of leopards, symbols of the Sackville family.

◀ **16–5** The glass-filled façade of Robert Smythson's Hardwick Hall, Derbyshire, completed 1596 in the Elizabethan phase of the Early Renaissance. The towers are capped with the initials of the owner, Elizabeth Shrewsbury.

▲ **16–6** The long gallery at Hardwick Hall. Its height and length were designed to accommodate tapestries, some of which have been covered with paintings.

Andreas Von Einsiedel/The National Trust Photographic Library, London, England.

▲ **16–7** The Great High Chamber at Hardwick Hall. The top half of the wall is a painted plaster frieze incorporating real tree trunks; the lower half is hung with tapestries. The floor is covered with rush matting.

John Bethell/The National Trust Photographic Library, London, England.

▶ **16–8** The stair hall of Knole in Kent, as redesigned in the early Jacobean phase of the High Renaissance. The arches are round, and the spandrels between them are ornamented with strapwork.
Andreas Von Einsiedel/The National Trust Photographic Library

The Great Staircase, which we see in figure 16–8, is part of additions and alterations by Sackville that were begun in 1605, the third year of the reign of the Stuart king James I, and finished five years later. The staircase may be the first example of one rising in straight runs around the sides of a square, leaving the center of the square open. Tudor arches have been abandoned here for more classical round-headed ones. Doric columns support the lower floor, Ionic columns the second floor, and above them, between the arches, are Corinthian pilasters. The ceiling covers the whole structure with a plane of plaster with a raised pattern of interlocking circles, and the painted *grisaille* wall decoration is adapted from Flemish prints. Standing on a newel post of the stair, the carved Sackville leopard, which originally held a lantern, faces a mirror image of itself painted on the opposite wall.

Inigo Jones   Inigo Jones (1573–1652), though most celebrated today as an architect, seems to have been best known in his own time as a designer of entertainments for the Stuart courts of James I and Charles I. His knowledge of both stagecraft and architecture was gained in an extensive and

fortuitous trip to Europe: From 1598 to 1603 he studied in Venice and other Italian centers, where he bought a copy of Palladio's *Quattro Libri dell'Architettura*. Equipped with Palladio's examples, Jones carried the English High Renaissance to new levels of correctness and consistency. Although all his mature work and most of his adult life was in the Jacobean era, his design is by no means typical of that era. Jones's work was curtailed by the English Civil War, which broke out a decade before his death, but he would still have a great influence on England's Neoclassical eighteenth-century style. Jones's architectural masterpiece was the Banqueting House in his native London, and his hand is seen in another fine work of the time, Wilton House.

The Banqueting House, London   Inigo Jones's Banqueting House (fig. 16–9) was built between 1619 and 1622 as part of the vast Whitehall Palace on the banks of the Thames in London. Begun in the 1530s and added to in many stages, Whitehall grew to an area greater than that of Versailles. When the old palace was destroyed by fire in 1698, Jones's 76-year-old Banqueting House was the only major element to be saved.

▲ **16–9** The double-height interior of Inigo Jones's High Renaissance Banqueting House, London, 1630–35. The ceiling painting is by Rubens.

Inigo Jones/Historic Royal Palaces Enterprises Ltd.

Jones's building was meant to accommodate royal entertainments and masques, allegorical performances in which the actors wear masks. The seven-bay façade of Portland stone, a creamy white limestone, is designed in two stories with superimposed orders, Corinthian above Ionic, over a rusticated base. These are impeccably proportioned, and the column shafts are given a classical *entasis* (swelling). The interior (see fig. 16–9), proportioned as a double cube (its length twice its height and width) repeats the Corinthian and Ionic orders of the exterior. The room is ringed by a colonnaded balcony supported on brackets and is spanned by a flat ceiling. The ceiling's paintings, within plaster moldings, were executed by the great Flemish painter Peter Paul Rubens and installed in 1635. So admired were they that they virtually ended the building's original use for masques because smoke from those torchlit performances would have damaged the art on the ceiling. In later years the Banqueting House was used as a royal chapel and then as a military museum. In its time, the Banqueting House was the finest demonstration yet built in England of the principles of Greek and Roman design as interpreted by Palladio.

Wilton House, Wiltshire   Inigo Jones is also often credited with the design of Wilton House in the 1630s, a major addition to an older group of buildings known as Wilton Abbey, but it is now thought that Jones's role may have been only supervisory, with the actual design executed by Isaac de Caus, a French architect working in England.

However the responsibilities were divided, the collaboration produced a celebrated new south front 420 feet (130 m) long with a stately pavilion at each end. De Caus is also credited with the original layout of the garden that the new front faces. After a disastrous fire in 1647 gutted the new south wing, its interiors were re-created by Inigo Jones's pupil John Webb.

The interior of Wilton is distinguished by a number of finely proportioned state rooms, notably the Single Cube Room and, twice as long, the white and gold Double Cube Room (fig. 16–10). Handsome as these two rooms are, their geometry is not quite as easily grasped as that of the Banqueting House because in Wilton deeply curving ceiling **coves** (concave surfaces connecting the ceiling and walls) protrude into the cubic volumes. The ceiling panels within elaborately carved frames are richly painted by Giuseppe Cesari, Edward Pierce, and others, the oval central panel depicting

▲ **16–10** The Double Cube Room at Wilton. The original shape of the room is by Isaac de Caus under the supervision of Inigo Jones; the chimneypiece is by John Webb; the furniture by William Kent.
A. F. Kersting

an imaginary dome. The white-painted, pine-paneled walls are adorned with carved and gilded garlands and swags. Portraits of family members and royalty by Anthony Van Dyck hang in both rooms. The furniture designed later in Baroque style for the Double Cube Room was by eighteenth–century architect and furniture designer William Kent (see fig. 16–24).

The Jacobean era was followed by the Commonwealth era, an important period in England's history but not in its design. It was a pause in the centuries-long progress of English design, the momentum of which would soon be regained.

Baroque Styles: Restoration, William and Mary, and Queen Anne

The Baroque phase of English design history was characterized by design with more weight, more drama, and more dynamic movement than earlier phases, although it remained somewhat more sedate than the Baroque of Italy and Spain. The English Baroque began in the Restoration period (1660–88) and matured during the reigns of William and Mary (1689–1702) and Queen Anne (1702–14).

The **Restoration** period that followed the Commonwealth in 1660 saw not only the restoration of the monarchy, but also the restoration of a taste for opulence in English art and design. The Puritanism and military control of the Commonwealth was replaced by a new sense of freedom. During his exile in France, the newly crowned Charles II had acquired a knowledge of the latest European designs, and so he brought his knowledge, as well as some French artisans, back to England. Also, Royalists who favored the monarchy had sought refuge in the Netherlands, and they returned with knowledge of the latest Dutch design.

In addition, the **William and Mary** period, which brought William III from the Netherlands to England, naturally brought his own knowledge of Dutch design. But there was great influence from France as well, as that country's 1685 law denying equality of citizenship to Protestants had brought a flood of refugees from France to England, and there were many designers and artisans among them. Even without their presence, Louis XIV's Versailles, begun in 1661, had become an international model for royal pomp and display. There was also a new degree of interest in the design of China and other Eastern countries. These all contributed to the rich mixture that was English Baroque.

Queen Anne, who succeeded William and Mary, was the last of the Stuart rulers at a time of declining royal power. The **Queen Anne** design that characterized her reign, while within the Baroque style, was simpler and less ornate than that of William and Mary. A Queen Anne chair, for example (see fig. 16–31) has a back splat effusively Baroque in outline, but within that outline it is an unadorned plane. Both the William and Mary and Queen Anne styles were more clearly evident in their furniture and decorative arts than in their architecture and interiors, however, so that for those categories of design we can simply use the inclusive term Baroque.

Sir Christopher Wren   The greatest designer of Baroque England and the most famous architect in English history was Sir Christopher Wren (1632–1723). Wren liked to design, he said, "in a good Roman manner." From his father, a rural clergyman, he acquired an interest in mathematics, mechanics, and structure, and as a young man he was a professor of astronomy. In 1660, he was a founder of the Royal Society of London for Improving Natural Knowledge, which still exists. In 1663 he designed his first building, a simple chapel with a classical temple front for Pembroke College, Cambridge, and in 1665 he visited France for nine months, seeing Versailles under construction and making a careful analysis of current French Renaissance design. When the Great Fire swept London in 1666, six years after the restoration of the monarchy, he was ready to take a leading role in rebuilding the city. His master city plan of broad, straight avenues was not executed, but between 1670 and 1711 he designed fifty-two London churches, each of remarkable individuality and most of them still standing. But his greatest achievement was a new St. Paul's.

St. Paul's Cathedral, London   The site of the great Baroque cathedral of St. Paul's, according to tradition, was once the location of a Roman temple, and the first church dedicated to St. Paul was built there in the seventh century. Many successive buildings followed, and it was a fourteenth-century structure (remodeled by Inigo Jones in 1628) that the Great Fire destroyed.

In 1673 Wren produced a model of his design for the new cathedral, built in wood and almost 18 feet (5.5 m) long; it can still be seen in the church itself. Actual construction began in 1675 and was substantially completed in 1710, by which time Wren had made many changes. A great dome, one of the world's most impressive, dominates the final design.

The exterior of St. Paul's (fig. 16–11) is fronted with two levels of paired Corinthian columns with a pediment above. At either side are towers with round openings (*oculi*) in their bases and topped with many-columned pavilions. Far from flat, this façade is remarkable for its deep penetrations, its complexity and sense of depth identifying it strongly with the Baroque style. The interior (fig. 16–12) has a three-aisled nave extending west from the central crossing under the dome and a choir of equal size extending east. Colored marbles surface the ceiling vaults, and the church's ornate choir stalls,

▼ **16–11** Façade of Wren's St. Paul's, with the great dome in the distance.

▼ **16–12** Beneath the great dome of Wren's St. Paul's.

A. F. Kersting

▲ **16–13** Aerial view of John Vanbrugh's Baroque palace of Blenheim, Oxfordshire, built around several courtyards, 1705–20.

Aerofilms

organ screen, and bishop's chair were carved from wood by Grinling Gibbons (see "English Ornament" in this chapter).

Blenheim Palace, Oxfordshire Blenheim, begun in 1705, has been called "England's biggest house for England's biggest man." The "biggest man" was John Churchill, the first Duke of Marlborough, and the house was a royal gift to him in gratitude for his 1704 military victory over the French at the Bavarian village of Blindheim. Queen Anne invited the duke to choose his own architect, and his choice was Sir John Vanbrugh, then forty-one, a playwright, a noted wit, the comptroller (under Sir Christopher Wren) of the Queen's Works, and a genius. Vanbrugh chose as his assistant the more experienced Nicholas Hawksmoor, also a distinctive talent.

Blenheim (fig. 16–13) is built around a vast entrance courtyard and two smaller kitchen and stable courtyards, the three elements linked by colonnades. The palace is said to have 187 rooms, and several of them are enormous. It is entered through a clerestoried great arcaded hall 67 feet (20.5 m) tall, from which one can turn left or right to monumental stairs and, beyond them, to symmetrical suites of State Apartments, suites of rooms set aside for the use of visiting royalty, each with bedchamber, antechamber, and drawing room. Straight ahead from the entrance is a south-facing saloon in the center of the garden front. This 30-foot-high (9 m) room was (and still is) used for dining on important state occasions (fig. 16–14), even though it is more than 1,000 feet (0.4 km) from the kitchen wing. The family's own quarters, on a slightly more domestic scale, are along the east side of the main block. Another important interior is Blenheim's Long Gallery, which stretches 180 feet (55 m) along the whole west end of the main block. Like the soaring entrance hall, the Long Gallery has an excessive dimension that ignores classical proportion in favor of Baroque drama. Originally built as a picture gallery, where works by Titian, Rubens, and Raphael were hung, it was furnished as a comfortable library shortly after construction.

Mural painters at Blenheim included Sir James Thornhill and Louis Laguerre, and the chief carver at Blenheim was Grinling Gibbons, here working chiefly in stone rather than his more customary wood. The state apartments were hung with Brussels tapestries. Blenheim's formal gardens, originally laid out by Vanbrugh and Henry Wise, and were later redesigned by English landscape architect Lancelot "Capability" Brown in his more natural style in the 1760s and 1770s. Some of the palace's interiors were redesigned by

▼ **16–14** The saloon, Blenheim. From the murals by Lou Laguerre, figures representing the four continents peer d[o] assembled diners. Doors and fireplaces are framed in ma[r] A. F. Kersting

William Chambers in the same years. Sir Winston Churchill, grandson of the seventh Duke of Marlborough and prime minister of England during World War II, was born at Blenheim in 1874.

Neoclassical Style: Georgian

In 1714, the royal house of Hanover began providing the English throne with a succession of kings named George. The newly powerful Whig political party, upholders of the power of Parliament against the power of the king, rejected the Baroque style as one reflecting the absolute power of the monarchy. They sought an expression of a more democratic state. Greece and Republican Rome were seen as models. The **Georgian** period, after the drama of the Baroque, returned to a more proper, respectful, and sedate classicism. The Palladianism of Inigo Jones, with his Banqueting House as its finest expression, had been cut short by the Civil War and the Commonwealth; it was now revived and was joined by new attention to Palladianism's own source, the design of ancient Greece and Rome. At the time, those practicing it referred to it as "the antique manner," but today we term it the **Neoclassical** style. Neoclassical England was, above all, dignified, and it was also confident about what constituted correct design, which came in part from the publication of two books: *Vitruvius Britannicus* (1715), by Scottish architect Colen Campbell, and Palladio's own *Quattro Libri*, which was translated into English in 1715.

For freestanding houses, the E-shaped and H-shaped floor plans were largely replaced by simpler square and rectangular blocks, perhaps with a central bay projecting very slightly from the general mass. These simple shapes were repeated in the rooms inside. For city dwellings, there were rows of adjoined and matched townhouses, usually in straight blocks but sometimes in sweeping crescents. Window and door openings were largely rectangular, with occasional exceptions being so-called **Palladian** windows of central arched openings between two rectangular ones (see fig. 13–14). Arched openings and arcades became rare, except that important doorways were often topped with semicircular windows, known as fanlights. Windows were fitted with double-hung sashes. Columns and pilasters were plentiful. Ceilings were given decorative

reliefs in plaster, but reliefs were low and the designs were decorous.

Chiswick House, London

Richard Boyle, the third Earl of Burlington, who owned Chiswick House and who designed it in collaboration with architect and designer William Kent (1685–1748), see figure 6–24, was one of the great art patrons of his day. He was among the first of the many English nobles who completed their education with a grand tour of European cities and ancient monuments, and upon his return to England he supported a number of painters and sculptors, the architecture of Kent and Colen Campbell, the music of Handel, the philosophy of Bishop Berkeley, the satirical writing of Jonathan Swift, and the poetry of Alexander Pope.

In design, Lord Burlington's taste was for the Palladian, and it was epitomized by Chiswick House, begun in 1725, which he and Kent based on Palladio's Villa Capra (see figs. 13–11 and 13–12). The exterior of the house (fig. 16–15), which was chiefly the work of Burlington, presents us with four symmetrical elevations but not four identical ones, as Palladio had designed. Rising above them is a central dome on an octagonal drum punctuated by "thermal" windows (that is, semicircular windows with round tops and straight sills, such as those found in ancient Roman baths or *thermae*). The rest of the roof is very gently sloped, despite England's substantial rainfall. Near the corners of Chiswick's roof are four chimneys, shaped like obelisks. On the house's exterior, the classical orders are used only in a structural way, not as decoration, and many of the wall surfaces are severely plain.

The interior (fig. 16–16), chiefly the work of Kent, is more ornamented and Baroque, though the order, proportions, and geometric clarity of the basic layout remain strongly legible. Kent's work shows his knowledge of the precedent set by Inigo Jones. The ground floor of the house held Lord Burlington's library; the main floor was intended for entertaining and for displaying Burlington's painting collection, its layout encouraging circulation through a series of interconnected spaces. The rooms of Chiswick are small but stately nevertheless, meant to impress us with their perfection rather than with their size. The Domed Saloon or "Tribunal" at the center of the house is a tall octagonal space with pedimented doorways in four of its sides and, between the doors, classical busts on brackets. Across the garden front, opposite the entrance, is a suite of three connecting rooms

▼ **16–15** The east front of Chiswick House, London, a Neoclassical house begun in 1725.
© Achim Bednorz, Koln

For all Adam's accomplishments and influence, in just twenty years after his death, he was temporarily out of fashion. Seeking to revive his reputation, Sir John Soane (1753–1837), himself a brilliant designer of the nineteenth century (see fig. 20–8), spoke of Adam in several lectures to the Royal Academy, which Wren had helped form. In 1815 Soane said to the Academy: "[W]hen the higher excellencies of art are felt by an enlightened public, taste and elegance will become generally diffused. The light and elegant ornaments, the varied compartments in the ceilings of Mr. Adam, imitated from the ancient works in the baths and villas of the Romans, were soon applied in designs for chairs, tables, carpets, and in every other species of furniture. To Mr. Adam's taste in the ornaments of his buildings and furniture, we stand indebted, . . . [admiring] the electric power of this revolution in art."

used as a gallery, the central one a rectangle with **apsidal** ends (concave, as in the apse of a church; see fig. 16–16), the others circular and octagonal. Smaller but more richly decorated are the surrounding rooms called the Red Velvet, Blue Velvet, and Green Velvet rooms; these were named for their original wall coverings, which have now been replaced with flocked papers. In geometry and in color the rooms show great variety, yet all share the same general character of Palladian classicism. A lavish touch occurs throughout in Kent's generous use of gilding on wainscoting and moldings and

▼ **16–16** The Gallery, Chiswick House, London.
A. F. Kersting/AKG-Images

on the furniture, which he designed specifically for the house.

Outside, the gardens designed by Kent are credited with beginning a trend away from the geometric formalism for which the house is noted and toward the more natural landscaping that would be popularized by "Capability" Brown in his work at Blenheim and elsewhere. Chiswick, set in its own small park, is a perfect gem.

Robert and James Adam   The last decades of the eighteenth century brought a new seriousness to the revival of classicism in England. Architects and designers studied the Greek and Roman antiquities themselves and worked to replicate the original models to exact specifications, and prominent among these was Robert Adam (1728–92). Adam was born into a prominent Scottish family of architects and designers. His father, William (1689–1748), was Scotland's leading architect in the second quarter of the eighteenth century. Robert's older brother John (1721–92) took over the father's business, taking Robert into the firm with him and later practicing alone in Edinburgh. Robert's younger brother James (1732–94) also joined his brothers in the Scottish practice and later joined Robert in a London partnership. James traveled in Italy as Robert had, and most of his work was done in England within the partnership with Robert, but after Robert's death he spent his last two years doing independent work in Scotland.

Robert was the chief designer of the firm he shared with James. It was Robert's study of classical precedent and the writing based on his study that was a chief instrument leading to classicism's dominance of English design; and it was Robert's own design (fig. 16–17), beginning even before the publication of a book in 1773, that served as the chief glory of that dominance. Jones, Burlington and Kent, and others had brought to England Palladio's vision of classicism with its carefully proportioned cubes and rectangles. Robert Adam brought to England a virtuoso vocabulary of complex interior forms that had not been used since the buildings of Rome, and with these forms he brought an equally rich vocabulary of ornament (see fig. 16–1).

It was not Roman antiquity alone that formed Adam's style, however. The Palladianism introduced to England by Inigo Jones was a significant influence, as were French planning principles such as the use of **enfilades**, which are alignments of doorways in suites of rooms to give long vistas through them. The Italian Neoclassical architect and designer Piranesi (see fig. 13–19), whom Adam had met in Italy, was also influential; Adam wrote of him that his "amazing and ingenious fancies . . . are the greatest fund for inspiring and instilling invention in any lover of architecture that can be imagined," and he returned to London with two Piranesi drawings.

In 1773, having mastered a synthesis of all these elements, Adam and his younger brother began to publish their own work: *The Works in Architecture of Robert and James Adam*, which appeared in three volumes. Spurred by the brothers' example, classical precedent became the concern of every social level that could afford choices about lifestyle, and it affected those choices at every scale, from architecture to the smallest article of household furnishing. A major benefit of this obsession was a rare degree of unity in room design, and it was best demonstrated by Robert Adam himself, who, having designed the building and the volume and proportions of each room, considered the room's wall and ceiling surfaces, and then proceeded to design practically everything in it, including door and window frames, chimneypieces, furniture, carpets, lighting fixtures, textiles, silver, pottery, and metalwork. His carpet designs often reflected the designs of the ceilings above them.

Syon House, London

In 1760 Adam began working on Syon House to make it a fashionable residence of the eighteenth century. Syon House was originally a Tudor nunnery; its exterior, with battlements across the top and towers at each corner, could not be changed. Its interior, however, was transformed into what some consider Adam's masterwork, a suite of spatially varied rooms wrapping around a central quadrangle. Adam proposed that an enormous rotunda be built within the quadrangle but the rotunda proved too expensive even for Adam's wealthy client, the Duke of Northumberland.

Even without this climactic focus, Syon House offers plenty of visual drama. One enters a great hall (fig. 16–18), finished with stucco decoration by Joseph Rose (one of Adam's favorite artisans), with a coffered apse at one end and a screened recess at the other, both ends framing classical sculpture and both accommodating stairs to the adjacent rooms, for the old structure's floor levels were uneven. Adam capitalized on this flaw. In his own words, "The inequality of the levels has been managed in such a manner as to increase the scenery and add to the movement." The Doric order, Adam's frequent choice for entrance halls, was used, and colors here were limited to white, cream, and (in the marble floor paving) black.

▼ **16–17** Examples of Robert Adam's Neoclassical details and ornament.
Gilbert Werlé/New York School of Interior Design

Corner of Door Trim

Mantel

Paterae

Frieze Ornament

Vase Motif

Sconce

Architectural Wall and Doorway

Pedestal and Urn

▲ **16–18** View through a pair of Doric columns into the Neoclassical entrance hall of Robert Adam's Syon House, London. The bronze of *The Dying Gaul* in the foreground is a copy of a Hellenistic Greek original.
A. F. Kersting

▲ **16–19** The south anteroom, Syon House, adjacent to the entrance hall.
Richard Bryant/Arcaid

The adjacent rooms up a few steps from the hall are both anterooms, the one on the north (left of the entrance) leading to the private family dining room, the one on the south leading to the larger state dining room. The south anteroom (fig. 16–19), originally 36 by 30 feet (11 × 9 m) and 21 feet (6.5 m) high, has been given correction of proportions by means of a screen of columns held away from the wall on one side, within which the area seems a perfect square. The dozen *verde antico* columns were shipped from Italy, and the wall panels between them bear gilt representations of military trophies, a motif Adam borrowed from Piranesi. The gilt anthemion frieze near the ceiling is on a blue background; the ceiling, echoing the geometric pattern of the floor, is gold on cream; and the floor is brilliantly colored **scagliola**, the imitation marble invented in seventeenth-century Italy (see page 275).

Adam and his brothers, as royal architects, had many commissions requiring monumental treatment and an extensive use of the classical orders. In only a few instances were columns or pilasters entirely omitted from an interior wall treatment, and even in those cases classical architectural effects were obtained with entablatures, arches, domes, vaults, and ornamented panels. The semicircular arched wall niche, an innovation from the first years of the eighteenth century, was adopted by Adam and became a very common feature of his design, used to frame a plaster cast or marble reproduction of an antique statue or urn. Many of the Adam rooms had semicircular, segmental, or octagonal end walls embellished with architectural orders, a treatment copied from ancient Roman prototypes.

English Ornament

The progress of English ornament from the fifteenth through the eighteenth centuries, like that of architecture and interiors, moves beyond the Gothic toward the classic—at first the classicism of the Renaissance, and later that of Greece and Rome. Some interiors, such as Inigo Jones's Banqueting House (see fig. 16–9), have been rather chastely ornamented, while others, such as the Double Cube Room at Wilton (see fig. 16–10), supervised by the same designer, have been lavishly ornamented.

We shall look first at ornamental strapwork, which was particularly popular in England's Early Renaissance, and then at the two materials that were of chief importance for ornament throughout the whole period: wood and plaster.

Strapwork

Strapwork is a type of ornament that gives the false impression of having been cut from a flat material such as leather or sheet metal and then intricately interlaced. Whether rendered in plaster, wood, or silver, strapwork (like linenfold wood paneling before it), always seems to be imitating some more flexible material. In England, it was popular in the Elizabethan period that closed the Early Renaissance and in the Jacobean period that began the High Renaissance, and some see it as a source for the ribbonlike bands on the splats of Chippendale's eighteenth-century chairs. Strapwork is visible in the spandrels above the arches in the Knole stairhall (see fig. 16–8), where it is made of plaster. Another example is a panel of carved and painted oak (fig. 16–20) by Flemish designer, painter, and architect Hans Vredeman de Vries (1527–1606), whose etchings of architecture and ornament were widely published in book form in many languages. And there is a strapwork frieze above the tapestries of Hardwick

▲ **16–20** From the Jacobean phase of the High Renaissance (c. 1600), an oak panel carved and painted with strapwork ornament by Flemish designer Jan Vredeman de Vries.
Victoria & Albert Museum, London/Art Resource, NY

Hall's Long Gallery (see fig. 16–6). Precedents for such English and Flemish examples include the interlacing bands of Arabesque ornament introduced into Venice from the Near East around 1500 (see fig. 9–13) and parts of Raphael's slightly later decoration of the Vatican *loggie* (see fig. 13–7).

Woodwork

In England, unlike in France and other countries, forests of high quality wood were readily available, and thus England produced highly skilled woodworkers to carve wood paneling and other ornamental features as well as beautiful wood furniture. Their achievements are among the glories of the country's interiors.

Wood Paneling   **Linenfold** paneling within small framed panels and flush unframed boards survived from Gothic times (see fig. 8–19) and continued to be used in England's Early Renaissance paneling (see fig. 16–3), but it was gradually replaced by a more classical vocabulary of motifs. In the Baroque period the walls of the majority of rooms continued to be treated with wood paneling, although the panels themselves were enlarged to run the full height of the room from the dado cap molding to the wooden cornice, after the manner of the new designs introduced at Versailles for Louis XIV. The panels were rectangular, framed with a heavy **bolection** molding (a molding projecting beyond the adjacent surfaces). An example can be seen in the ones surrounding the rectangular panels at Wilton (see fig. 16–10).

Door openings were formally treated with wood architectural trim and complete entablature, including architrave, frieze, and pedimented cornice. Occasionally, both door and window openings were framed in a heavy projecting bolection molding in marble or wood.

The wood, usually oak or walnut, was often left in a natural waxed finish, although poppy oil and linseed oil were

also used. Sometimes the wood was reddened with the root of the henna shrub, and the richest effects were produced by painting the woodwork to imitate marble. Where cheaper woods, such as fir and **deal** (pine), were used for the paneling, the wood was frequently grained to imitate walnut or olive. Moldings and ornament were sometimes gilded. Where wood paneling was not employed, the plaster walls were covered with stretched velvet or damask.

The marquetry used in the William and Mary phase of the Baroque period frequently took the form of elaborate floral patterns (see fig. 15-21). Colored woods and natural and stained ivory veneers added to the richness of effect. One type of marquetry design that reached its height of popularity in the William and Mary and Queen Anne periods is known as **seaweed marquetry** (fig. 16–21). It uses two woods of contrasting appearance in intricate arabesque design of tiny leaves and scrolling, seaweedlike tendrils. Seaweed marquetry—as well as metal inlay—seems to have been introduced in England by Gerrit Jensen (died 1715), a cabinetmaker who worked for William and Mary and some of whose furniture is in Kensington Palace.

In addition to marquetry, the imitation lacquerwork called **japanning** (see the section of lacquer in Chapter 12) was a popular decorative treatment for wood furniture and other wood objects, especially in the late seventeenth century, and sometimes whole walls were covered with japanned boards. Another very popular English treatment of wood furniture and objects was **parcel gilt**, which is simply the practice of gilding parts, rather than whole surfaces.

In the Queen Anne period, *crossbanding* became popular in the veneering of frames and panel borders. **Crossbanding** is the placing of the grain of the veneer at right angles to the frame or panel border; in other words, the wood grain crosses the band. (Today the term has an additional meaning applied to plywood manufacture: placing a veneer with its grain at right angles to that of the core in order to resist shrinkage.) But the great glory of English Renaissance woodwork was the low relief—and the sometimes astonishingly high relief—of wood carvings.

Grinling Gibbons   Born in Rotterdam, Grinling Gibbons (1648–1721) became the most famous carver of his time and one of the chief creators of the English Baroque decorative style of the late seventeenth century. Diarist John Evelyn claims to have discovered Gibbons in London carving a wooden copy of a *Crucifixion* painted by Tintoretto and to

▼ **16–21** Seaweed marquetry on the case of an English longcase clock, 17th century.
The Bridgeman Art Library International

have introduced the young carver to Charles II. Evelyn may also have introduced him to Sir Christopher Wren, for whom he worked, and a carved relief portrait of Wren is attributed to Gibbons.

Gibbons is best known for his wood carving—mostly in lime-wood and oak, but also in box and pine—but he also worked in bronze and in marble and other stones. His work was fanciful, rich, and realistically detailed, in high relief and with deep undercuttings. Its subject matter included fruits, vegetables, flowers, trophies, musical instruments, animals, birds, fish, and dead game in panels, swags, garlands, and wreaths. It appeared on chimneypieces, overmantels, door-frames, overdoors, picture frames, organ screens, choir stalls, and funerary monuments. His many royal commissions

▼ **16–22** Grinling Gibbons's carving of the overmantel in the King's Eating Room, Windsor Castle, Berkshire, 1677–78. The portrait by Jacob Huysman is of Charles II's queen, Catherine of Braganza.

Windsor Castle, The King's Dining/Drawing Room. The Royal Collection © 2001, Her Majesty Queen Elizabeth II. Photo by John Freeman

included work at Windsor Castle (fig. 16–22), where he worked from 1677 to about 1682, Hampton Court, St. James's Palace, Whitehall, and Kensington Palace. A celebrated piece signed by Gibbons is a lime-wood relief, *The Attributes of the Arts*, which was given by Charles II to Cosimo de' Medici III, Grand Duke of Tuscany, in 1682. Gibbons's chief rivals among English carvers were his contemporary Edward Pierce, whose father's paintings we saw in the Double Cube Room at Wilton (see fig. 16–10), and the later Neoclassical carver Thomas Johnson.

Plasterwork

In the early Renaissance and through Elizabethan times, floors were made of hard plaster (for example, in some ground-floor rooms of Hardwick Hall), but by the middle of the sixteenth century, as the Tudor phase of the Early Renaissance was ending, plaster began to be used for ceilings and for walls. The heavy roof beams and elaborate trusses that had survived from medieval times were covered over with plasterwork. At first the plaster imitated the appearance of the old beams, and then on the walls, the plaster repeated the rectangular shapes used for wall paneling. Soon, however, plasterwork began to develop a freer decorative style of its own.

An early, relatively simple example was the ceiling of interlocking circles we saw in the Knole stairhall (see fig. 16–8), and a later, far richer example was the detail of a Robert Adam ceiling seen in figure 16–1. Even Adam's plasterwork vocabulary was largely limited to geometric shapes, but at Kedleston Hall, Derbyshire, begun in 1760, he revived the Italian manner of hanging paintings in fixed locations and surrounding them with plaster ornament. More virtuoso work included fruits, flowers, garlands, urns, scrolls, ribbons, and *putti*, even though these might be within geometrical compartments. From the early seventeenth century plasterwork also represented classical myths and biblical stories.

Such fanciful decoration was associated with Italy, and many noted Italian plasterers were brought to England to execute it. One well-known Italian plasterer was Giuseppe Artari (died 1769), who did stucco work for architects John Vanbrugh, James Gibbs, and Colen Campbell. But England developed its own skilled plasterers as well. Charles Williams, who had studied his trade in Italy, was hired to cover the

Ancient Egyptians, Minoans, Mycenaeans, Etruscans, Romans, Indians, and Chinese—all these cultures have used forms of plaster to provide smooth surfaces, insulation, and weatherproofing to exterior and interior walls. In all cases, the plaster must be applied to a surface roughly textured enough to grip the plaster until it dries. In the early sixteenth century, wood **lath** (closely spaced, narrow, parallel strips of wood) was developed for such use. The plaster itself is usually applied in several successive layers. Each coat is allowed to dry before the next is applied, but ornamental effects must be carved (or troweling must be done for a smooth surface) while the outer coat is still damp.

Plaster consists chiefly of sand, lime, and water, but a number of other substances may be added. A binding agent of fiber or hair may be added to the innermost coat to help hold it to the lath until dry. More water may be added to slow the drying process, or gypsum may be added to accelerate it, and Henry VIII imported large quantities of gypsum from France for use in the plasterwork of his palaces. Almond oil or glue may be added for greater pliancy, and marble dust may be added to the outer coat for finish. Some mixtures were so unique that they were patented.

Stucco is an ambiguous term sometimes used for any sort of plasterwork, sometimes only for plasterwork molded into ornamental relief or of heavy texture, and sometimes for exterior finishes. When used for interior work, stucco usually means a type of plaster, described previously, and is distinguished from other plaster only because it is rougher in texture. When used for exterior work, stucco usually means a finish made of lime, sand, and water but also containing brick dust, stone dust, or lumps of burnt clay to give the desired texture. *Stucco lustro* is an imitation marble, in which pigment is scattered across the wet plaster and then brushed to resemble marble veining. **Pargeting** is plaster that has been given an incised texture with a wooden tool or comb.

Forming the plaster or stucco into decorative shapes can be done in several ways. Repetitive motifs are sometimes created by press-molding—that is, by pressing pieces of wood, cut to the desired shapes, into the moist plaster. Plaster can also be cast into wood or metal molds (the molds being first lined with marble dust or petroleum jelly to make removal easy), and the cast pieces, when dry, attached to walls or ceilings with a thin layer of wet plaster. Continuous moldings can be made by running wood or metal templates along wet plaster surfaces. Single decorative figures in high relief can be modeled by hand with the fingers or with wooden spatulas. Today, however, intricate plaster decorations are often imitated in polyurethane.

---

timber ceilings of the great house of Chatsworth in Derbyshire with plaster. Noted late seventeenth-century plasterers included John Grove and his son (also named John), who were responsible for the interiors of Wren's London churches. Also from the Baroque period are some plaster ceiling ornaments at Ham House, Surrey (see fig. 16–47).

An interruption in the use of plaster ornament came in the relatively modest days of Queen Anne's reign, when flat, unadorned ceilings such as those of Hardwick Hall (see fig. 16–7) were popular again. And, near the end of the eighteenth century ceiling plasterwork lost much of its popularity to a renewed fashion for allegorical ceiling and wall painting, as had been used on the ceilings of Inigo Jones's Banqueting House (see fig. 16–9) and at Wilton (see fig. 16–10).

English Furniture

The history of English furniture from Gothic times to the end of the eighteenth century is a remarkable progression from some of the heaviest furniture ever made to some of the lightest. In the very beginning of the Early Renaissance, furniture was strongly built and massive in appearance, the various parts held together by wooden dowels and pins or wrought-iron nails.

Early Renaissance furniture supports during the Elizabethan period were often of the bulbous form, resembling a large melon and occupying all but the extreme top and bottom of the support or leg. The melon portion was usually carved at the top with a **gadroon**, a band of parallel egg-shapes or ovoids, and at the bottom with an acanthus leaf; the top of the support crudely imitated a Doric or Ionic capital. The bulbous legs on the tables seen in Hardwick Hall (see fig. 16–7) are typical of the time. During the Jacobean period, the bulbous form of support gradually gave way to dwarf columns of straight or spiral shape or to the twisted rope form. An early inventory of Hardwick Hall's furnishings mentions a "sea-dog" table, supported on thick legs shaped like mythical sea creatures.

In the Early Renaissance, the structure of the case and cabinet furniture was similar to that of the wainscots. The stiles and rails, however, were often enriched by simple surface grooving, by a narrow strip of inlay in contrasting wood, by a checker effect, or by a crudely carved pattern in low relief, inspired by the classical *rinceau*, *arabesque*, or *guilloche* (see table 4–2). The field of the panel was usually carved with a linenfold motif, as seen at Compton Wynyard (see fig. 16–3), or a coat of arms. As the Italian influence increased, the panels were enriched by a carved or inlaid arabesque pattern or medallion, or by a dwarf arch, the latter type being called an **arcaded panel** (see fig. 16–4). During Jacobean times the panels became larger, were treated with moldings on four sides, often had plain fields, and sometimes were shaped as diamonds, crosses, hexagons, double rectangles, and other geometric forms.

▼ **16–23** Furniture and details from the Baroque and Neoclassical periods.
Gilbert Werlé/New York School of Interior Design

Charles II Chair

Trumpet Spiral Bell Turning Composite
William and Mary Supports

Wm. and Mary Marquetry Table

Wm. and Mary Walnut Highboy

Queen Anne Lacquered Corner Cabinet

Lion Mask Cabriole Leg

Claw and Ball Cabriole with Shell Motif

Two Queen Anne Mirrors

1708   1715   1735

Queen Anne Chairs   Early Georgian Chair

By the end of the fifteenth century in Tudor times, thin panels were being dropped into frames with mortise-and-tenon joints (see table 2–1), this construction being lighter and less subject to warping; the joiner gradually replaced the carpenter as chief furniture maker. The turner was also at work, and a company of turners was incorporated in London around 1605. (For various types of wood turning, see table 19–2.) A company of "upholders," or upholsterers, had been incorporated even earlier, and Henry VIII's inventory of 1547 mentions upholstered furniture. In decorative detail, it was the middle of the sixteenth century before Renaissance ideas wholly supplanted Gothic ones.

In addition to the simple inlay work and crude low relief and strapwork carving, furniture was sometimes enriched by an ornament known as the **split spindle**. The split spindle consisted of a short, turned piece of wood, often ebony, that was split into two parts and applied to the surface of the stiles of an oak cabinet or chest, a miniature version of a half-column or pilaster applied to a wall. Drawer pulls and knobs at the top of chairbacks were sometimes carved in a caricature of a human head. Carved Italian grotesques, face profiles, and the upper part of the human body, rising from a group of scrolls and leaves, were also used for furniture enrichment.

The Restoration of 1660 ushered in the Baroque period and brought a new wave of prosperity and sophistication. The English no longer needed to look abroad for stylish furniture. In London, skilled cabinetmakers supplied a variety of goods and services for furnishing houses, including fashionable walnut furniture, while in the country craftsmen still provided sturdy oak pieces. Examples of furniture and furniture details from the Baroque and Neoclassical periods are seen in figure 16–23.

Baroque furniture was strongly influenced by both France and Flanders. Furniture design began to show greater consideration for the comfort of the individual, as well as increased richness of form and ornament. The low relief carving of the earlier type continued to be used. The spiral turnings for legs and stretchers became much more frequent and the most characteristic feature was the Flemish S- or C-shaped curve, sometimes known as the **Flemish scroll**. Legs and stretchers, arm uprights, backs, aprons, and crestings were created with Flemish scroll arrangements.

In the early years of Neoclassical style, the lion mask appeared, coming into fashion about 1725, and that motif was placed on the knee of cabriole legs (center, fig. 16–23), or frequently used as a central motif on the apron of tables, consoles, and other pieces of furniture. At the same time, the claw foot gave way to the lion's paw grasping a ball. Variations were seen in the use of satyr and human mask motifs as furniture feet. Neoclassical furniture was lighter and adhered to classical proportions and aesthetics.

The Eastern element in furniture structure and finish became less common c. 1725, and lacquerwork disappeared, though Chippendale later revived Chinese forms for a brief period.

Furniture Woods

The wood used in English furniture is of such great distinctive beauty that the woods themselves used during certain eras shaped the characteristics of the design, and so these four great ages should be mentioned.

The Age of Oak (1500–1660)   Oak had been the great wood of Gothic Europe. In France it had been largely replaced in the early sixteenth century by walnut, a more finely grained wood that allowed more delicate moldings and more minutely carved ornament, but walnut was scarce in England. The English planted many walnut trees beginning in the middle of the sixteenth century, but oak would keep its popularity for another century.

The Age of Walnut (1660–1720)   A good supply of English walnut was ready to be carved as the Baroque period was beginning, and walnut became the wood of choice for furniture throughout the period. Walnut, however, never replaced oak completely, and because it was particularly subject to worm damage, its use was discontinued when mahogany became available early in the eighteenth century.

The Age of Mahogany (1720–70)   Mahogany was imported from the Caribbean, and the dark, rich red variety from Santo Domingo was considered the finest. Its use grew to such an extent that all native woods were eliminated for cabinet-making, except in the provincial districts. Mahogany trees grew to a very large size, and the wide boards made from them eliminated the necessity for veneered surfaces. Mahogany was both less susceptible to worm attack and stronger than walnut, allowing structural portions of furniture, such as the legs, to be made in more slender proportions,

and it could be richly carved with greater ease, because it is a slightly softer wood.

The Age of Satinwood (1770–1820)   During the last decades of the eighteenth century and the first part of the nineteenth, there was great admiration for an exotic wood called **satinwood**, popularized by furniture designer George Hepplewhite. Light blond with a satiny finish and a handsome figure, satinwood was cut from various species of trees that grow in India, Florida, and the West Indies. The variety from India—hard, aromatic, and a warm yellow—was thought to be the finest. Satinwood was only used for finishing the finest work, particularly inlay and marquetry. It was frequently used in combination with other exotic species: zebrawood, tulipwood, kingwood, "harewood" (sycamore dyed gray), and amboyna. Also adding to the colorful mixture were veneers of beech or pear that were stained green with the use of copper oxide.

Furniture Designers

The five towering figures of eighteenth-century English furniture were William Kent, Thomas Chippendale, Robert Adam, George Hepplewhite, and Thomas Sheraton. Together they constitute a continuous chain of talent lasting more than a century, and their influence was enormous—not only on one another but also on the general public, due in part to unprecedented publicity. Each of the five had his designs published in one or several books available to the public. Through widespread imitation their popularity was secure.

William Kent   William Kent (1685–1748) was one of the first English architects to be equally concerned with interior design and furniture design, and perhaps the very first to view a building, its interiors, and its furniture as a single aesthetic whole. In these respects his career was a model for that of Robert Adam. First, Kent studied painting in Italy during the decade 1709–19, and while there he met Richard Boyle, the Earl of Burlington, who would be his lifelong patron. A commission for the decoration of state rooms for George I at Kensington Palace followed the Earl's introduction. As furniture designer, Kent's work included a gilt console table, its design based on a Corinthian capital (fig. 16–24), and thus it exhibited the same reverence for classical design as the house itself. Later, Kent designed an elaborate suite of furniture for the Double Cube Room at Wilton (see fig. 16–10), which followed the overall aesthetic of the architecture and interior ornament.

Kent also designed interiors and furniture for Houghton Hall in Norfolk, a Baroque house belonging to English statesman Sir Robert Walpole, with a design begun by James Gibbs and completed by Colen Campbell. Kent's furniture there was large, rich, heavy, and flamboyant, as the house called for. Compared with the much simpler designs of the day, such furniture must have seemed a sensational departure, but it set a new fashion for a time and led to Kent's appointment as master carpenter in the Office of Works.

Thomas Chippendale One of the best-known names in the history of furniture design is that of Thomas Chippendale (1718–79). His design was in the Neoclassical style but a highly eclectic version of it; he called some of his designs Rococo, for example, some of them French, and some of them Chinese. After apprenticeship to his father, who was a joiner, Chippendale moved to London in his twenties and settled his cabinetmaking business in St. Martin's Lane in 1753.

In the next year, he published the first edition of his book *The Gentleman and Cabinet-Maker's Director,* which brought Chippendale many admirers and many imitators. It was an age when plagiarism was rampant (indeed, plagiarism from the ancients was the highest ideal), and Chippendale encouraged it by providing clear drawings, dimensions, and instructions for making his furniture.

Chippendale's design is seen most characteristically in his chairs, and they were designed in a variety of styles. The **ribband-back** design (seen in figs. 16–25 and 16–32) bears some resemble to the strapwork ornament of an earlier time (see fig. 16–20). He also designed many other types of furniture, from insignificant washstands to magnificent bookcases, desks, sofas, clocks, organ cases, four-poster beds,

▲ **16–24** Neoclassical pedestal table designed by William Kent for Chiswick House, London. It incorporates the acanthus leaves of the Corinthian capital.

Console Table. Probably Made by John Boson (fl. 1720–43) for Richard Boyle, Earl of Burlington, for Chiswick House. c. 1730. 88.9 × 68.6 × 44.5 cm. Victoria & Albert Museum, London/Art Resource, NY

piecrust and gallery-top tables, benches, consoles, mirrors, and dining and serving tables (see fig. 16–25). In Chippendale's earliest work, which shows some affinity with Queen Anne design, the chair, stool, and chairback sofa displayed the cabriole leg with carved foot that was a staple of that earlier style. In his later work, he preferred to use the straight leg and the block-footed straight leg known as the **Marlborough leg** (fig. 16–26), and with them Chippendale reintroduced stretchers between them for greater strength. Intricate backs imitating Gothic tracery were introduced, as were backs featuring Chinese latticework, bamboolike forms, ribbons, and ladder slats with gracefully curved lines.

Chippendale's principal ornaments were Greek and Chinese foliage, fretwork, flutings, husks, cartouches, and **paterae**, round or oval medallions with sprays of leaves (see upper right corner of fig.16–17). His designs were taken from many sources: Classical, Louis XV, Gothic, and Chinese forms and ornament were combined in extraordinary harmony. Chippendale worked almost exclusively in mahogany, although after 1765 he made a few pieces in satinwood, rosewood, and other species, and there are in existence a few painted, gilded, lacquered, and japanned pieces attributed to him. In general, Chippendale's designs are sturdy in structure and robust in proportion, which accounts for their durability. A Chippendale room is seen in fig. 16–48.

Robert Adam Robert Adam, like William Kent before him, was as adept at furniture design as at architecture and interiors (see fig. 16–17). He was particularly noted for his designs for commodes, side tables, consoles, cabinets, and bookcases, but Adam also designed mirrors, candelabra, silverware (see fig. 16–44), inkwells, sedan chairs, fireplace

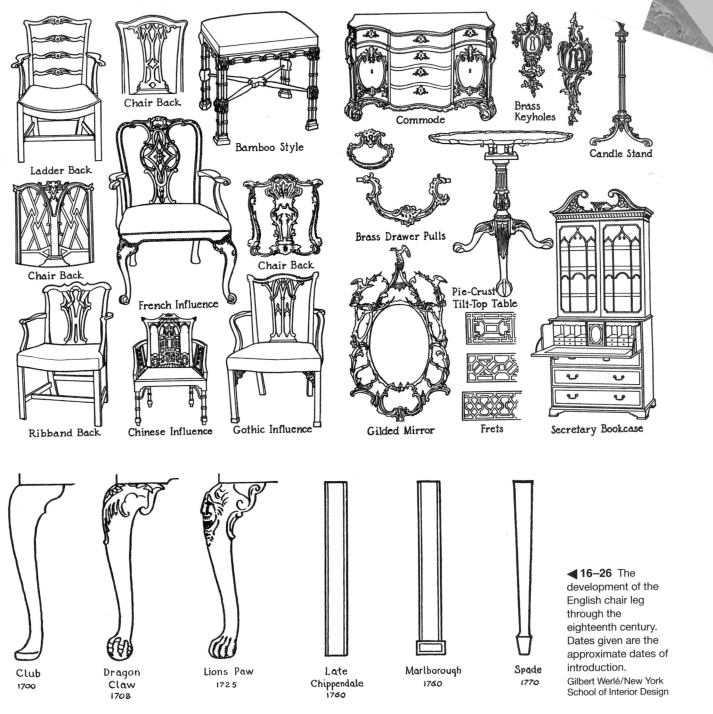

▼ **16–25** Chippendale furniture, furniture details, and furniture hardware.
Gilbert Werlé/New York School of Interior Design

Chair Back

Bamboo Style

Commode

Brass Keyholes

Candle Stand

Ladder Back

Chair Back

French Influence

Chair Back

Brass Drawer Pulls

Pie-Crust Tilt-Top Table

Ribband Back

Chinese Influence

Gothic Influence

Gilded Mirror

Frets

Secretary Bookcase

Club
1700

Dragon Claw
1708

Lions Paw
1725

Late Chippendale
1760

Marlborough
1760

Spade
1770

◄ **16–26** The development of the English chair leg through the eighteenth century. Dates given are the approximate dates of introduction.
Gilbert Werlé/New York School of Interior Design

furnishings, door hardware, and window treatments. Adam is credited with the invention of the sideboard, a wide table with drawers, meant to be placed against a dining room wall for use in serving (fig. 16–27). More rarely he designed chairs, settees, and beds. The first two volumes of Adam's famous book *The Works in Architecture* include many of his furniture designs.

The most characteristic furniture decorations popularized by Adam were the Grecian honeysuckle and fret, the fluted frieze or apron, the patera, the rosette, the urn, and the husk. Husks were arranged in swags or drop ornaments and were frequently tied with ribbons. All Adam's designs were delicate and finely detailed (*overly* detailed, his critics complained); all his reliefs were low and flattened, all the results elegant.

▲ **16–27** A gilded sideboard flanked by a pair of pedestals with urns, all designed in Neoclassical style by Robert Adam for the dining room of Osterley Park House, Middlesex, 1750–75.
© The Art Archive/ Victoria & Albert Museum, London/Dagli Orti–Ref AA367235

George Hepplewhite   Considering the familiarity of his name, surprisingly little is known about George Hepplewhite, not even the year of his birth. He made furniture in London as early as 1760 and was a leader in the Neoclassical taste for delicacy of line and fine proportion in furniture. He died in 1786, but his pattern book, the *Cabinet-maker and Upholsterer's Guide,* was published two years later.

The chair was the most typical example of Hepplewhite's designs, and the forms and ornament used in that piece were seen in nearly all his other pieces. He specified the use of both mahogany and satinwood. His leg designs were always straight and slender, either round or square in section, tapered toward the foot, and sometimes ending in what is known as a **spade** (see table 19–3). He used five different shapes for chairbacks: shield, camel, oval, heart, and wheel (fig. 16–28). All of them employed curves in one form or another. The tops, pediments, and aprons of Hepplewhite's tables and casegoods

were also often designed with curves, as were the testers of his beds.

His carved furniture decoration was sparsely applied, and consisted of wheat blossoms, paterae, ribbons, fluting, reeding, vases, and festoons. Ornamental figures—humans, nymphs, and *putti*—were carved on chairbacks and **pier glasses** (see fig. 16–48), which are mirrors hung on piers (or wall areas between pairs of windows). Painted decorations showed the three-ostrich-feather crest of the Prince of Wales, natural flowers, and classical figures. Marquetry was frequently seen in tulip, sycamore, yew, holly, pear, ebony, rose, cherry, and kingwood.

Hepplewhite is credited with three features of English furniture design: the popularizing of satinwood after 1765, the use of painted motifs as a means of surface enrichment, and the movement toward greater delicacy of line. Hepplewhite's designs were, in some cases, structurally fragile, partly because of their slender proportions and

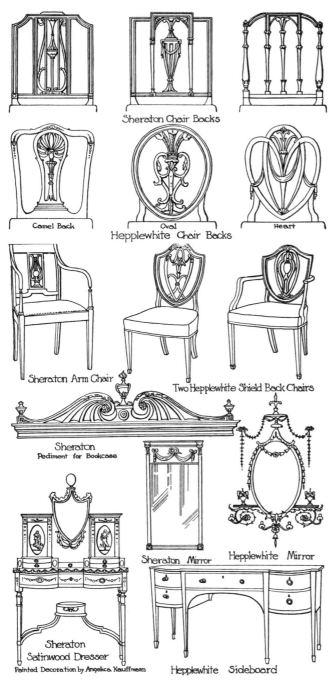

▲ **16–28** Hepplewhite and Sheraton furniture designs.
Gilbert Werlé/New York School of Interior Design

crisp, and light, reflecting the Neoclassical taste of the eighteenth century. He replaced the serpentine lines of Hepplewhite (by whom he was nevertheless greatly influenced) with segmental curves and straight lines, just as the style of Louis XVI had straightened the curves of Louis XV. Sheraton's designs, in fact, were quite popular in France, where the new Regency taste was in fashion. Hepplewhite and Sheraton are often mentioned together, and indeed their designs share the qualities of rationality and elegance (see fig. 16–28); both took the Neoclassicism of Robert Adam and adapted it for use in small domestic interiors, as in the Sheraton chair of figure 16–33.

Sheraton specified mahogany and satinwood for many of his furniture designs, noting that the former was a "masculine" species appropriate for dining rooms and libraries, the latter a "feminine" species right for ladies' withdrawing rooms and dressing rooms. He also specified exotic woods—tulipwood, zebrawood, kingwood—for many of his furniture designs, and he ornamented wood with delicate marquetry and paintings of flowers, feathers, acanthus leaves, and classical urns. He was the first in England to propose attaching ornamental porcelain plaques to furniture, helping to make Wedgwood plaques as fashionable in England as Sèvres medallions had been in France.

Sheraton's chair legs were similar to Hepplewhite's. His chairbacks, however, were more rectangular in shape (see the top row of fig. 16–28). The rear legs of the chair usually continued upward to form the side braces of the back (third row of fig. 16–28). A horizontal rail was placed near the seat, between the two back uprights, and an ornamental rail was placed at the top. The space between the rails was filled with one or more ornamental splats, the center one sometimes having the form of an elongated vase. Many of Sheraton's designs were for dining room furniture and for very small pieces of furniture suitable to the dressing room and boudoir.

Seating

The characteristic chairs of the Early Renaissance and of the Jacobean phase that began the High Renaissance were those known as **wainscot chairs** or panel chairs, because their backs, often carved or inlaid, resembled the panels of a wainscot wall. These heavily proportioned chairs were usually made with a high rectangular seat (so that they required a footstool), turned or column legs, and slightly curved arms.

partly because they were veneered on softwood carcasses. What the furniture lacked in strength, however, it gained in gracefulness, beauty of color and enrichment, and charm.

Thomas Sheraton   It is probable that Thomas Sheraton (c. 1751–1806) never had a furniture shop of his own, but he published *The Cabinet-maker and Upholsterer's Drawing-book* (1793) and several other books. Sheraton's style was elegant,

▼ **16–29** A turned oak chair with triangular seat from the Jacobean phase of the High Renaissance, first half of the seventeenth century.

Victoria and Albert Museum, Art Resource, NY

▲ **16–30** Walnut stool in the William and Mary style, c. 1690, with C-scroll and S-scroll legs and stretchers. Its slip seat is upholstered with tapestry.

Cooper-Hewitt National Design Museum/Smithsonian Institution

Other Jacobean designs, called **turned chairs** (fig. 16–29), had triangular seats with arms, back, and legs entirely composed of short, thick turnings. During Jacobean times, chairs were improved in comfort by the addition of upholstered seats and backs nailed to a rectangular framework.

In the Baroque period, chairs underwent a definite change. Chair seats and backs were made with caning and covered by loose cushions, and the front legs were joined by an S- or U-shaped scroll called a **Flemish scroll** or by an elaborately carved **stretcher**. Lavish upholstery textiles and leather, both plain and patterned, with heavy handmade silk fringes, were also used. Some woodwork was gilded. The backs of large chairs were slanted for comfort. The **wing back** was introduced, so-called because of the "wings" or projecting panels on either side of the back to shield the sitter from drafts. Stools and benches were also important pieces of furniture during early Baroque times, and they were made quite as elaborate as chairs.

The William and Mary phase of the Baroque period is illustrated by the beech-and-cane side chair in figure 16–30, dating from about 1690. The legs of chairs and tables have returned to the straight form. Some were square and tapered, after the French fashion of the Baroque Louis XIV style. Most of them were turned with large mushroom, bell, and inverted-cup turnings. Flat-shaped stretchers were usually used, and feet were made to imitate spherical balls, called **ball feet**, or flattened balls called **bun feet** (see table 19–3 Furniture Feet). If either of these were carved into lobes, it was called a **melon foot**. The bun foot was on axis with the leg above it, but if the flattened sphere was off center, projecting to the side like the head of a golf club, it was called a **club foot**. If it rested on a small flat disk it was called a **pad foot**, as in the later Queen Anne chair (see fig. 16–23). The **barley twist**, resembling a twisted rope, was seen in a variety of patterns—for example, in the William and Mary chair of figure 16–30. The **trumpet leg** (see table 19–2), with a flared end resembling the bell of a trumpet, was also popular. During the William and Mary period, settees designed with two, three, and four chairbacks in a row were introduced.

The Queen Anne style saw more development in furniture design than in other aspects of interiors. The products of the joiner and cabinetmaker were of great purity and beauty, and the principal characteristics were the introduction of the curved line as a dominating motif in furniture design, the first use of mahogany as a cabinet wood, the use of the **cabriole leg**, and the great development of the use of lacquer as a finishing material. A fine example (though it employs no lacquer) is the armchair seen in figure 16–31. In its curvaceous but unornamented back splat and its graceful S-shaped arms and cabriole legs, it reflects the conventionalized knee-and-ankle form, coming down to a pad foot. In the adjustable book rest attached to one arm and the candle holder attached to the other, there is something of the period's attention to comfort and convenience.

After 1725, the splat of the splat-back chair was elaborated to an extreme degree by mean of piercing and carving. The tops of some chairbacks assumed what is known as the **yoke** form of two S-shaped curves, thought to resemble an ox yoke, not unlike the "horseshoe" back of the Chinese chair in figure 11–11. Variations of the classical acanthus leaf and other types of foliage were substituted for the shell motif of the earlier part of the century. Wing armchairs and other forms of upholstered seats, stools, benches, and sofas became much more popular.

The early years of the Georgian period, beginning around 1720, may be considered the flowering of Neoclassical furniture, which abandoned the plainness of some aspects of Queen Anne design for richer expressions. From the middle of the century is a Chippendale ribbon-back (spelled "ribband-back" at the time) sidechair (fig. 16–32), taken from a design in the 1754 *Director*, which illustrates the new spirit. The cabriole leg we saw in the Queen Anne example (see fig. 16–31) is here still but is now encrusted with embellishments. The back splat is retained as well, but its solidity dissolved into a delicate tangle of ribbons. Like linenfold and strapwork, here is another example of wood pretending to be some much more fragile material.

A later design is a Sheraton style chair (fig. 16–33) of painted West Indian satinwood with elements of beech and birch and with silk taffeta upholstery. Designed in the last decade of the Neoclassical eighteenth century, it is more strictly Neoclassical than the Chippendale example. While not a slavish reference to any Greek, Roman, or Renaissance example, it has a rectitude, poise, and restraint we naturally associate with classicism. It is not lacking in decoration, but it exhibits, to use a Greek expression of praise, "nothing in excess."

One piece of English seating was so distinctive and so popular that it deserves special attention. It was originally called the stick chair for obvious reasons but is now known as the **Windsor chair** (fig. 16–34). Its first appearance seems to have been in the early eighteenth century, and by the middle of the century it was already much in use. Seats of

▼ **16–31** A Queen Anne library armchair, c. 1715. Its cabriole legs end in pad feet.
Queen Ann Library Armchair, Circa 1715. With permission of the Royal Ontario Museum © ROM

▲ **16–32** A carved mahogany "ribband-back" chair based on a design in Chippendale's 1754 *Director*.
Victoria and Albert Musuem/Art Resource, NY

▼ 16–33 A painted satinwood chair based on a design in Sheraton's *Drawing Book, 1791–1793.*
Woodwork–Furniture. English. 18th Century, 1795. Side Chairs (2). Sheraton style. West Indian satinwood, beech, birch, with painted decoration. Modern silk taffeta upholstery. H. 34½ in. W. 19½ in. D. 17¼ in. The Metropolitan Museum of Art, Fletcher Fund, 1929. (29.119.3–4)

▲ 16–34 A comb-back Windsor chair of painted wood that belonged to the playwright Oliver Goldsmith (1728–74). The top rail curves upward at its ends into "ears."
Victoria and Albert Museum, London/Art Resource, NY

Windsors are generally solid and gently scooped to a slightly concave shape for comfort. The seat is supported by straight turned legs set at a slight splay. In all true Windsors, the back legs are inserted into the bottom of the seat rather than continuing upward to form the back. Many Windsors have stretchers between their legs, most commonly in an H shape and more rarely in an X shape. The arms generally continue in a curve through the back of the chair, with the spindles passing through.

There are many variations of the Windsor chair. In the **comb-back** Windsor, spindles of equal length rise to meet a straight top rail. But, there is also the bow-back Windsor, with spindles of differing length connecting to a curved back member, and a shawl-back Windsor, which is a comb-back that rises to a top rail curved to hold a draped shawl.

Beds

The beds used in the homes of the nobility were often of great size by today's standards and were the chief pieces of furniture in most households. Beds were designed with four carved corner posts or with two posts at the foot and a paneled headboard. The posts were often enriched by a bulbous ornament and an architectural capital that supported a wooden tester, modeled as a simplified entablature. Long velvet draperies hanging from the tester were drawn at night for warmth and privacy. These draperies became increasingly elaborate until they were principal decorative features of the bed, as in figure 16–35. This bed, with its tester fashioned as the roof of a pagoda, demonstrates the *chinoiserie* fashion of the mid-eighteenth century.

The four-sided wood frame at the bottom of a bed was drilled with holes through which ropes were strung, and on the ropes rested the mattress, filled—according to budget—with rushes, wool, or feathers and down. Beds with fabric canopies but without wood testers began to be popular in the eighteenth century, and a bed with a canopy suspended from the wall or ceiling was called an **angel bed**.

Tables

Although collapsible trestle tables continued to be used during the sixteenth century, the permanent table was also a feature of the furnishings. Large refectory tables were built with solid oak tops, some of which were of the extension type, and used for the elaborate banquets of the time. Both

◄ 16–35 A carved and japanned pine bed of the Neoclassical period attributed to William Linnell, c. 1755. It is in the Chinese Bedroom at Badminton House, Gloucestershire. Victoria and Albert Museum, London/Art Resource, NY

Japanese lacquer ornament and marquetry (see fig. 16–21) were applied to tabletops (see fig. 16–23), and such enrichment would increase until it reached a peak in the Baroque late seventeenth century.

Drop-leaf tables with hinged leaves that hung vertically when not in use were often found in smaller houses because of their variable size. One popular type was the **gateleg**, which supported the raised leaves on swinging gatelike structures. A two-gate version was the most common, but single-gate versions were made. A large gateleg table with four gates (fig. 16–36) displays the William and Mary phase of the Baroque; its richly turned legs and gates make an interesting contrast with the plain surfaces of the leaves. In later Neoclassical times, the gateleg was replaced in popularity by a smaller, visually simpler drop-leaf design called a **Pembroke** table (fig. 16–37), its leaves are supported on brackets hinged to the table's frieze, which may enclose a pair of small drawers.

Round tables and smaller tables were popular in the Baroque era, beginning with the convivial Restoration period, when coffee, tea, and chocolate became popular. One popular small table in the Baroque era was the **tilt-top** (see fig. 16–25), usually on a three-legged base with a hinged top that could be tilted into a vertical position, saving space and displaying the decorative features of the tabletop. Round tables

▶ **16–36** A gate-leg table of carved and turned elm from the William and Mary phase of the Baroque period, c. 1700.

English furniture, Mid–XVII Century. Table, gate–leg. H. 31, Diams.: 84 and 88", W. center section 30¾ in. The Metropolitan Museum of Art, Gift of Mrs. George Whitney, 1960 (60.25).

▲ **16–37** A Pembroke drop-leaf table of satinwood inlaid with ebony from the Neoclassical period, c. 1800.

Woodwork – English – XVIII, 1775–1800. Table, Pembroke, sheraton style. Sycamore on mahogany. The Metropolitan Museum of Art, Gift of Mrs. Russell Sage, 1909. (10.125.165)

▲ **16–38** A Sheraton two-tier mahogany dumbwaiter, Neoclassical period, late eighteenth century, with a gallery top of pierced brass.

Sheraton two-tier mahogany dumb waiter, Mallett & Son Antiques Ltd., London/Bridgeman Art, Library Int'l Ltd, London/New York.

with a scalloped wood rim were called **piecrust tables** (also fig. 16–25). Serving tables with a raised edge of wood or metal filigree to prevent small objects from falling off were called **gallery-top** (see fig. 16–38). **Dumbwaiters** (fig. 16–38) were tiered tables, often on a three-legged base, that were two or three tiers high, with each circular surface projecting from a central support and with the surfaces sometimes designed to rotate around the support for serving.

Console tables are, as we saw in our chapter on France, meant to stand with one of their long sides against a wall.

At times they were attached to a wall, with only their front legs freestanding, and more rarely they were legless, supported only on decorative brackets. We saw a Neoclassical console on a pedestal base by William Kent in figure 16–24.

Casegoods

The heavy wooden cupboards and chests reflecting a medieval origin had persisted through the Early Renaissance period and even into the High Renaissance. After the Restoration opened the Baroque era, however, such casegoods were joined and eventually supplanted by many new types of cabinets, clocks, writing desks, dressing tables, and bureau mirrors. The most important introduction of the Restoration period was the highboy, or tallboy. A William and Mary example with trumpet legs is at upper right in figure 16–23. When the upper section is built separately from the lower and can be lifted off, the ensemble is called a chest-on-stand, and when the lower section is used independently as a dressing table, it is called a lowboy. By the subsequent Queen Anne phase, such a cabinet would be standing on cabriole legs with a carved apron between them and would have gained an impressive pediment and finials on top. A tallboy became a secretary (fig. 16–39 and the lower right in fig. 16–25) when it incorporated a writing surface with a fall front (vertical when closed) or slant front (angled when closed) and when bookshelves behind solid or glass doors replaced its upper drawers. (The English version does not exactly correspond to the French **secrétaire**, which lacked the upper chest.)

Sideboards and cabinets were made throughout the stylistic eras to display the collections of imported ware. We have seen one of Robert Adam's sideboards in figure 16–27. From the Queen Anne period onward, case furniture, such as china cabinets, bookcases, and secretary desks, had double doors with single panels that were designed with broken curves at the top. The edges of the glass were *beveled*, as they had been in the time of William and Mary.

In the Neoclassical period, consoles, wardrobes, chests with drawers, wall tables, sideboards, dressing tables, and commodes (see top center, fig. 16–25) were even more abundantly in use. A small, masculine desk with storage drawers and a slanted writing surface, called a **davenport**, became popular. The **canterbury** was a storage unit on a stand, used beside a piano to hold music or by a dining table to hold plates and cutlery, and somewhat resembling today's magazine rack.

▲ **16–39** A secretary from the Queen Anne phase of the Baroque period, c. 1705–15. Its broken pediment top with finials is characteristic. It is decorated with Chinese scenes in red and gold japanning.
Secretary: Black and gold lacquered. ca. 1700–1715. The Metropolitan Museum of Art, Bequest of Annie .c. Kane, 1926. (26.260.15)

English Decorative Arts

The interiors and furniture of England during this time were amply decorated. Marble worker and plasterer, wood-carver, textile designer, and painter turned to classical mythology and represented the gods, the demigods, the mythological beasts, and the Muses. The work of Italian painters covered the walls, the overdoors, overmantels, and furniture of this period with paintings of draped figures, Italian landscapes, and the ruined temples of Greece and Rome. The overall use of decorative accessories greatly increased during the Neoclassical eighteenth century. New items included mirrors, clocks, statues, busts in marble and bronze, and a variety of objects collected from foreign travels for the wealthy and cultivated classes to display.

Ceramics

In medieval times, English ceramics had been sturdy and utilitarian. They included bowls, mugs, jugs, pitchers, pots, chamber pots, candlesticks, and cisterns for brewing beer. The custom of drinking from cups instead of bowls was not widespread until the end of the fifteenth century. In the sixteenth century other new forms were also introduced: **porringers** (small one-handled bowls), **tygs** (large mugs with several handles or with two handles close together), **posset pots** (to hold drinks of milk and ale or milk and wine), sweetmeat dishes (to hold candied fruit), and chafing dishes (to warm food in dining rooms). For the finest tables, stoneware was imported from Germany and faience from Italy.

When William and Mary left Holland to take the throne of England at the end of the seventeenth century with ornate tastes that would usher in England's Baroque period, they brought with them their collection of Delft and Chinese ceramics, strengthening the English passion for such wares. They also brought to London the designer Daniel Marot (1661–1752), who was mentioned as a designer in Régence France and who had been working for William and Mary in Holland. In designing the interiors of Hampton Court for the royal couple, Marot decided their plates should not be limited to table use; he arranged them on walls, placed them in rows along cornices and mantels, and displayed them in cabinets, beginning a fashion that still continues.

In addition to these imports, the production of the native ceramics factories was pushed to the highest level of perfection. It has been said, relative to the importance of ceramics in the later Baroque period of Queen Anne, that everyone in England had become "a judge of teapots and dragons." By the end of the seventeenth century, Delftware imitations were being made in factories at Lambeth, while factories all over England, some using imported clays and improved firing techniques, were

struggling to imitate Chinese porcelains. These attempts continued into the eighteenth century, joined by English copies of Meissen wares from Germany and of Sèvres wares from France. This experience led, by the middle of the Neoclassical eighteenth century, to the establishment of a large English ceramics industry, successful commercially, technically, and artistically. The wares of this industry were most often identified by the towns or areas where they were made, such as Bristol, Derby, Worcester, Lowestoft, and Coalport, Bow, Chelsea, and Staffordshire. But the most famous artisan was known by his own name: Wedgwood.

Bow The Bow ceramics factory, which was founded in the East End of London, made the earliest known soft-paste products, appearing in 1748. Bow's white wares and figures were influenced by Chinese **blanc de chine**, the European term for the white porcelain products imported from China (see Chapter 11 and fig. 11–16). Painted china, in both underglaze and overglaze enamels, was also produced. The subjects of Bow decoration included Chinese domestic scenes (fig. 16–40), bamboo and plum branches, partridges, grotesque animals, and sportive boys with small red flowers. The early tableware was frequently edged in brown. The glaze of Bow wares has altered over the years and now often appears iridescent and discolored. Bow ware was mainly of useful form and rough decoration; more ornamental forms with finer decoration came from the factory at Chelsea.

Chelsea The fanciful wares from Chelsea, like those from Bow, aspired to the imitation of *blanc de chine* and produced undecorated wares in a creamy paste with a satin texture. Other Chelsea products showed the influence of French wares from Vincennes and Sèvres, with rich ground colors such as dark blue and claret, and panels painted with pastoral scenes, bouquets, and exotic birds.

▲ **16–40** From the Bow factory, a soft-paste porcelain dish, transfer-printed in brown and painted in enamels, Neoclassical period, c. 1765.
Victoria & Albert Museum, London/Art Resource, NY

An early (and perhaps the first) manager of the Chelsea factory was Nicolas Sprimont, a silversmith by training, and many of its product designs were based on metalwork.

In 1769 the Chelsea factory was sold to some Derby potters, whose work was mostly in the Japanese taste with paintings of flower sprays, insects, and other old Japanese patterns. Thereafter, the whimsical Chelsea forms (fig. 16–41) gave way to the simpler effects of the classical revival, while in their decoration lapis lazuli, gold stripes, medallions, and biscuit reliefs made their appearance.

Staffordshire The county of Staffordshire in west central England has been an important producer of earthenware for centuries. Its prominence is due to the quality, variety, and color of the local clays, the plentiful supply of coal for kilns, and the easy river access to the sea for distribution. In the late seventeenth century, the area's factories were noted for their slip ware (pottery decorated with colored slip, a thin mixture of clay and water) and for their stoneware. The early eighteenth century saw the production of salt-glazed ware, and the factories devised a rich finish of enamel glazes over salt glazes. Noted Staffordshire potters Thomas Minton and Josiah Spode, both of whom operated factories in Stoke-on-Trent, became well known there for their imitations of Chinese wares. Then, in the late eighteenth century, the production of porcelain began.

Wedgwood Josiah Wedgwood (1730–95) was born into a family of Staffordshire potters. He founded Wedgwood pottery when he was 29, expanding it soon after and eventually taking his sons and nephews into his business. He contributed a number of technical innovations to the

▼ **16–41** From the Chelsea factory, a soft-paste porcelain vase painted in enamels with gilding, 1760–5. Victoria & Albert Musuem, London/Art Resource, NY

business of making ceramics, such as finding an accurate method for determining the heat inside a kiln, and for these he was made a Fellow of the Royal Society in 1783. Famous Wedgwood products include cream-colored earthenware in Neoclassical shapes (known as **Queen's Ware** because of royal patronage), a large dinner service finished in 1774 for Catherine the Great of Russia, black basalt ware that copied ancient Greek urns, red stoneware called *Rosso Antico*, and a white stoneware called *Terracotta*. The factory's most celebrated product, however, was called **Jasperware**.

Jasperware, the result of more than 5,000 recorded experiments, was a dense, finely textured white biscuit ware that could be colored integrally or with a surface wash. A soft cobalt blue was the most popular color, but it was also made in olive green, sage, yellow, lilac, brown, gray, and black. On the colored ground were mounted (or **sprigged**) white ornaments, plaques, medallions, and figures in low relief. Frequent subjects for the ornaments were Greek motifs, children at play, and classical figures in graceful robes. An example (fig. 16–42) shows the legend of *The Apotheosis of Homer*, and its decoration in white relief was adapted from a plaque by Neoclassical sculptor John Flaxman, noted for his church monuments and his delicate outline illustrations of texts by Homer and Dante. Other artists employed by Wedgwood included Lady Diana Beauclerk, the daughter of the Duke of Marlborough, and George Stubbs, famous for his paintings of horses and other animals.

In addition to a variety of tabletop items and some jewelry, Jasperware included a large number of items for use in interior design: busts, clocks, candelabra, tiles, medallions for furniture and pianos, plaques for insertion in plaster wall treatments, medallions for chimneypieces, and even entire

▲ **16–42** A Jasperware vase by Josiah Wedgwood with white relief on a blue-dipped body, Neoclassical period, 1786, 18 in. (46 cm) high. The relief is adapted from a plaque by John Flaxman.
Image by courtesy of the Wedgwood Museum Trust Limited, Barlaston, Staffordshire, England.

▲ **16–43** A Neoclassical cut-glass chandelier of lead crystal probably made in London c. 1765 for a church in Ireland, 4 ft. 6 in. (1.4 m) high.
Victoria & Albert Museum, London/Art Resource, NY

chimneypieces. They were perfect complements to the Neoclassical style then being popularized by Robert Adam and others.

Glass

The person often called the father of English glass was a Venetian, Jacob (originally Jacopo) Verzelini, who in 1575 was granted a patent and a temporary monopoly on glass making by Queen Elizabeth I. The first important glass industry in England that was of purely English origin was founded in 1673 in London by George Ravenscroft (1632–81). In 1676 Ravenscroft perfected lead crystal, a glass containing lead oxide. Lead crystal is brilliant, clear, and highly refractive, giving a lively play of light, but it was thicker and heavier than the

Venetian *cristallo*, imported from Venice. Lead crystal put England at the top of the world's glass market, and within two decades there were more than a hundred English glasshouses producing it.

A major part of glass design is accomplished by glassblowers while their material is still hot and ductile. However, from the sixteenth through the eighteenth centuries, the English developed two methods of decorating cooled glass (already being done in Germany): **engraving** and cutting. Both are accomplished with rotating wheels that distribute waterborne abrasives. Engraving (which was used by Verzelini for decorating most of his Elizabethan glass) could produce inscriptions, coats-of-arms, and chinoiserie scenes, among other effects. Cutting could produce scallops, diamond patterns, serrations, flutings, grooves, and facets.

The weight of lead crystal made it perfect for the new cutting techniques. Faceted glass made its most dramatic appearance in glass chandeliers, their prisms reflecting and multiplying the candlelight in England's most important rooms. A Neoclassical chandelier, with almost every surface faceted, is seen in figure 16–43. Its six branches surround a series of spheres and vase shapes. It is thought to have been made in London for a parish chapel in County Kilkenny, Ireland.

Metalwork

In the fifteenth through the seventeenth centuries, gold and silver were used lavishly by royalty, sparingly by others, although most noble households had a cupboard with a display of **plate**—a term referring not specifically to plates or to plated metals but to any objects of silver or gold. Royal dinner tables sparkled with silver *chargers* (dishes on which meat was cut), *trenchers* (dishes on which cut meat was served), *standing salts* (elaborate saltcellars that were placed to identify the seat of the host), dishes, bowls, drinking vessels, spoons, and knives. Forks began to be used—at first only for desserts—in the seventeenth century. For Knole (fig. 16–8), a Flemish cabinet maker is said to have made furniture in silver, and Knole is known to have boasted silver andirons.

By the Neoclassical eighteenth century, great importance had come to be attached to the ceremony of dining, even in middle-class homes. Pewter utensils were replaced by silver ones whenever possible, and fashionable tables and sideboards were laden with silver tureens, sauceboats, candelabra, and *epergnes* (ornamental stands for the center of the table, usually with central dishes and branching arms holding several smaller dishes). A sauceboat, one of a set of eight, designed by Robert Adam is an example of how elegant late eighteenth-century English tableware could be (fig. 16–44). It was made to Adam's design by silversmiths Matthew Boulton and John Fothergill. Dining rooms and other fine rooms might also employ silver for chandeliers or for sconces and **girandoles**, which are multibranched candelabras, often incorporating cut-glass pendants and sometimes incorporating mirrors.

Baser metals, such as brass, had an important place in English interiors, too. Brass was particularly popular for lighting

---

Tools & Techniques | MAKING SILVER PIECES

The metallic element silver is capable of being easily formed and highly polished. It is regarded second only to gold as a valuable material for decorative arts. The earliest known silver objects were found in the Near East and date from c. 2500 B.C. Although silver occurs uncombined in nature, it occurs more often as compound ores from which it must be extracted by a process called smelting that uses heat to separate the compound's elements. When pure silver is obtained, however, it is too soft for most uses and is usually alloyed with copper, which gives it hardness. Silver coins are generally 90 percent silver, 10 percent copper, and what we call **sterling silver** is 92.5 percent silver, 7.5 percent copper.

A technical innovation of 1743 made silver more affordable. Thomas Boulsover of Sheffield invented a way to apply a thin plating of silver to a base of copper; the result was called **Sheffield plate**, based on Boulsover's accidental discovery that, when sheets of silver and copper are heated together almost to their melting point, their contact surfaces will fuse. The process was improved by Matthew Boulton, who began in 1765 to make candlesticks, bowls, teapots, coffeepots, and other wares of Sheffield plate in his factory at Birmingham. One of Boulton's improvements was the addition of solid silver wires along those edges and rims that receive the most wear. By 1770 plated wares were popular all over England. In the middle of the nineteenth century, the cheaper and safer **electroplating** process would supersede the Sheffield process; since then, most

silver plating has been done on a base of nickel. Silver sheets can be formed into holloware, which are containers or pieces other than flatware, (eating utensils) by hammering or—in modern times—by die-stamping.

Three basic treatments for decorating silver pieces are etching, *repoussé*, and inlay. **Etching**, first widely used in medieval times to decorate armor, employs an acid and a **resist**, a substance like wax, resin, or tar that is impervious to acid. The silver surface is coated with the resist, which is then cut away to reveal the area to be etched, and the object is immersed in acid, which eats into the exposed surface.

Repoussé, already described in our sections on Chinese enamel and Spanish silver, shapes the metal surface with hammers and other implements. **Embossing** is a type of *repoussé* that beats the metal chiefly from the back to produce raised areas (or **bosses**), and **chasing** is a type of *repoussé* that beats the metal with smaller instruments and chiefly from the front to add final details. The effect of chasing can resemble that of engraving, but without actually removing any of the silver surface.

Inlay inserts another material into the surface, and a type of inlay popular for decorating silver is **niello**, which adds decorative black markings to the bright base metal. The black substance was traditionally silver sulphide, but it is now a compound of silver, sulphur, copper, and lead. Finally, cast silver ornaments and handles of various shapes can be soldered onto the silver body.

▲ **16–44** One of a set of silver Neoclassical sauceboats designed by Robert Adam, 1776–77, 10 in. (25 cm) long.
Victoria & Albert Museum, London/Art Resource, NY

and for hardware and trim on doors and windows, and some of these fittings received elaborate decorative treatment. Brass substituted for silver tableware in less prosperous dining rooms, and it was also used for candlesticks, chandeliers, sconces, tobacco boxes, snuff boxes, clocks, nutcrackers, and trivets. Pewter was now less popular than in medieval times, but it continued to be made, and because it was manufactured by casting in reusable molds, its style remained surprisingly constant. Copper and copper alloys were used for large sturdy wares such as basins, buckets, kettles, and pans. Iron and steel appeared in architectural elements such as gates, fire grates, grilles, and balustrades.

Textiles

The textile industry in England was greatly enlarged and improved by the arrival of Huguenot (Calvinist Protestant) immigrants from France who fled persecution after 1685, just when the High Renaissance period was developing into the Baroque. Textile colors became particularly brilliant. Velvets, brocades, damasks, crewel embroideries, and needlepoint were used. The latter years of the seventeenth century saw the introduction of chintz, as a decorative fabric for interiors.

Chintz   Both **chintz**, a painted cotton cloth that originated in India, and **palampores**, Indian bedcovers made of chintz (see Chapter 10), began to be imported into England, the Netherlands, and France (where it was called **indienne**) in the last half of the seventeenth century. In all three countries, local imitations were made. In England in 1676, William Sherwin obtained a patent for printing and coloring cotton based on Indian techniques. English-made versions of chintz, for the most part, repeated the intricate floral designs of their

Indian models (fig. 16–45). Chintz was popular then for table covers, seating upholstery, bed hangings, wall hangings, and window draperies, and it continues to be used in both England and America.

The chintz of India was admired in Europe because the cotton yarn of India was finely spun and because India was a leader in the use of **mordants**, metal salts used to set dyes (see Chapter 10). Brilliant colors could be used without fear of fading. In addition, chintz was given an appealing body and finish by being **glazed** with an application of starch or wax or (in more industrial times and places) by being **calendered**, pressed between heated hollow metal cylinders to achieve a shiny finish. When chintz is not glazed or calendered, it is called **cretonne**. Because both the native chintz of India and its European imitations were characterized by bold, colorful patterns, usually floral, the word has come to be loosely used for any such patterned fabric.

Printed Fabrics   Block-printed cottons and linens were made in factories in the London area beginning in the late seventeenth century. In the middle of the eighteenth century, the Drumcondra printworks near Dublin may have been the first source of copperplate printing on fabric, soon followed by a factory at Merton, Surrey. Copperplate was a method of printing fabrics by means of an engraved flat plate of copper with incised areas filled with colored pigment; the plate and the fabric come in contact under great pressure. A later development passed the fabric over engraved copper cylinders. Some copperplate printing was able to print as many as sixteen colors simultaneously, and the speed and efficiency of the process revolutionized the industry.

Many English textiles were exported to America in the eighteenth century, including some **blue resist** patterns, in which the parts of their grounds meant to remain white were coated with a resist of wax before being dipped in blue dye.

Embroideries   Embroidery has a venerable history in England. As we saw in the Romanesque period, the famous eleventh-century Bayeux Tapestry was not actually woven tapestry but embroidery of linen and wool. For centuries, the ability to embroider remained a skill expected of women of almost every background. In the English Renaissance and beyond, embroidery was used for wall hangings, bed hangings, table covers, and cushion covers, as well as for clothing.

Embroidered motifs developed from sprigs of flowers (mid-sixteenth century) to classical and biblical scenes (early

▼ **16–45** An English bed curtain of cotton and linen embroidered with wool from the Baroque period, 1690–1710. It is inspired by printed textiles from India, and its floral pattern is typical of those used on glazed cotton chintz.

Victoria & Albert Museum, London/Art Resource, NY

seventeenth century) to highly stylized scrolling foliage (late seventeenth century). An example of this last type is the wool-on-silk embroidery used as upholstery on the settee in figure 16–46, which is characteristic of its Baroque period, but the later Neoclassical period employed more restrained motifs. By the end of the eighteenth century, embroidery was largely replaced by patterned silks.

Wall, Bed, and Window Treatments

In the Early Renaissance and even in the Jacobean period of the High Renaissance, English furniture was still sparse, and the chief color and interest of the interiors came from fabrics on the walls, either figurative tapestries or embroidered hangings. Though now faded, remnants of such fabric wall treatments at both Hardwick Hall (see fig. 16–7) and Knole (see fig. 16–8) are testimony to the role of fabrics in interiors of the Elizabethan and Jacobean periods.

By the end of the High Renaissance almost a century later, walls were being covered with textile hangings other than

▲ **16–46** Silk upholstery with wool embroidery on a settee made for Hampton Court, Hertfordshire in the William and Mary phase of the Baroque period, c. 1695. The legs are walnut.

Victoria & Albert Museum, London/Art Resource, NY

indeed have been cartoons for tapestries.

The elaborate fabric treatments around beds (as in fig. 16–35) may seem strange to us today, but we must remember the severe lack of heat in most English bedrooms of the time. Fabric was a necessary protection against drafts. A custom of the time was that important persons received visitors in the morning while still in bed, and extravagant hangings were considered appropriate symbols of status. These were generally on all four sides of the bed, hung by rings from the tester frame that, in the most imposing cases, might be a dozen feet or more above

tapestries or embroideries. In the State Bedroom of Osterley Park House, London, for example, Robert Adam covered the walls from dado to cornice with shirred silk. Some rooms had different wall hangings for summer and winter, and some used combinations of two or more fabrics in contrasting textures and colors. An example of fabric used as both wall panels and draperies in the same room is the Green Closet Ham House, Surrey (fig. 16–47), which was designed in the Restoration phase of the Baroque period. It was once used as a "cabinet of curiosities" or small personal museum. Above its damask panels, coves and ceilings are painted with tempera on paper by Franz Cleyn, the artistic director of the nearby Mortlake tapestry works. The paintings may

the floor. Above and in front of these curtains, which could be usefully drawn shut, were other fabric draperies added solely to make a visual impression of grandeur. Tassels might be hung from the draped fabric as a further flourish, and in the grandest examples the composition was topped with an ostrich plume at each corner.

The treatment of windows was similarly complex and set a standard that still persists today in our most traditional interiors. By the beginning of the Baroque period, symmetrically divided draw curtains had become popular for windows as well as for beds.

Thomas Chippendale, though much better known as a furniture designer, seems—from records of business transactions—

to have been responsible for the overall decor of the State Bedchamber of Nostell Priory, Wakefield, West Yorkshire, including the room's graceful and decorous draperies over both bed and windows (fig. 16–48). The green and gold hangings and wallcoverings have a Chinoiserie motif, a Chippendale favorite, and the general spirit of the room is Neoclassical.

As the eighteenth century progressed, window treatments grew in importance and complexity. Some treatments used three sets of curtains. First, the one nearest the glass was always thin and translucent, if not partially transparent, and usually was hung straight; this came to be called a **glass curtain**. Second came a curtain of medium-weight, opaque material

▲ **16–48** Thomas Chippendale's fabric-enriched design for the State Bedchamber of Nostell Priory, West Yorkshire, mid-17th-century.

◀16—49 A "summer bed," a 1793 Thomas Sheraton design for twin beds with corner posts, separated by a space between them but joined by a drapery-hung cornice.
Stapleton Collection, UK/The Bridgeman Art Library International

Holbein the Younger, we can see Turkish carpets (which were therefore sometimes called "Holbeins") on floors and tables. Carpets were also used as coverings for chests, chairs, and settees. About the same time, knotted carpets began to be made in England of wool pile on a hemp warp; their designs were imitations of Near Eastern and Middle Eastern ones, though some also incorporated the coats of arms of the English families for whom they were made. This so-called **Turkey work** (see Chapter 9) was costly, and it was used not only for carpets but also for more modestly sized objects, such as upholstery panels and cushion covers. It remained popular until the late seventeenth century, when there was increased importation of carpets from Turkey and Persia.

With the importation of carpets from the Near and Middle East, the English production of knotted carpets virtually stopped until 1750, when it was revived by two weavers from the French Savonnerie factory, Louis Théau and Pierre Poiré. They founded short-lived weaving workshops at Fulham and Exeter and later a new workshop at Moorfields. Given a royal warrant in 1763, Moorfields produced carpets for the Prince of Wales (later George IV) and other royalty. Moorfields also worked on carpets for Robert Adam's Syon House (see figs. 16–18 and 16–19) and for Osterley Park House, also in London, for which Adam had the factory design carpets to match his ceiling designs overhead.

Contemporary with the Moorfields workshop, Thomas Whitty, a Devonshire weaver, began producing Turkish-type

hung on a rod so that it could be drawn closed; this was called the **draw curtain**. And, third, in front of those two, came the overdraperies, as lavish as the budget allowed, fixed in place and festooned in any of a thousand different manners. A large number of drapery designs for both windows and beds appear in Neoclassical furniture designer Thomas Sheraton's 1793 *Director* (fig. 16–49).

Carpets and Floorcloths The first pile carpets in England were imported from the Near East and Spain, and these imports probably began in Early Renaissance times. By the middle of the sixteenth century, Henry VIII was reported to have amassed a collection of 800 pieces of fabric, and in several portraits of Henry VIII by the German painter Hans

carpets at Axminster using a vertical loom, which proved more suitable than the horizontal ones previously used. As Moorfields wove carpets to the designs of Adam, Axminster wove them to designs by Chippendale.

Other English developments sought less expensive alternatives to hand-knotted carpets. One of these was a strong flat-weave worsted wool floor covering made from the late sixteenth century by individual weavers in Kidderminster. In 1735 a factory was established there, and the product **Kidderminster**, or Scotch carpet, was made in a limited color range but in long lengths.

Also in long lengths and more durable than Kidderminster was so-called **Brussels** carpet, patented in 1741. Brussels carpets, woven in strips, could be cut and sewn to fit any floor area, and they were considered so useful they were imported by France, where they were called *moquettes.* A later variation in which the loops of the Brussels carpet were cut to form a velvetlike pile was known as **Wilton** carpet. Both techniques were imitated by the Kidderminster workshop, so that Wilton and Kidderminster became direct competitors during the last half of the eighteenth century.

Where budgets were modest, substitutions for carpets or other expensive flooring were made from painted canvas. These were called **floorcloths**, and were inevitably patterned to imitate carpet designs, tile work, marble patterns, or parquet flooring. Before the eighteenth century, such patterns were painted by hand, but after c. 1700 they were most often produced by stencils, and in 1755 Smith and Baber of London began printing floorcloths with wood blocks. One early source of patterns was the book *Various Kinds of Floor Decoration . . . Being Useful Designs . . . Whether of Stone or Marble, or with Painted Floor Cloths* (1739). Many floorcloths were exported from England to the American colonies (see fig. 19–36), and they were popular in both countries until replaced by flooring of linoleum and vinyl.

Tapestries   Tapestries were the most expensive fabrics of their time. This made them inaccessible to many, but it also gave them prestige, and they continued to be a symbol of luxury through the end of the eighteenth century. The first known tapestry factory in England was in Barcheston, Warwickshire, with a second one at Bordesley, Worcestershire, both established c. 1560 by William Sheldon. Sheldon's factories wove some large pieces, but most of their products were small cushions and seat covers. The pieces were woven of silk and wool, and perhaps their most interesting designs were maps of English counties. The Netherlands and Flanders continued a near monopoly in the English tapestry market until 1619, when James I and his son (later Charles I) founded a workshop at Mortlake on the River Thames, near London. Charles brought dozens of Flemish weavers to work at Mortlake, and he bought Raphael's cartoons for the *Acts of the Apostles,* from which several sets of tapestries were woven.

William and Mary and Queen Anne continued to import Flemish tapestries, but a number of workshops were operating by then in the Soho district of London, their products called **Soho tapestries**. The most important of these was the workshop of John Vanderbank the Elder, who had been named Royal Arras Maker in 1689. Vanderbank's work included copies of Brussels and Gobelins designs and some *chinoiserie* designs for Kensington Palace, London. His workshop was noted for bringing celebrated tapestry design to England and making it available at relatively affordable prices. By the end of the eighteenth century, however, the venerable respect for tapestry hangings had begun to be eclipsed by a growing taste for paint and wallpaper.

Wallpaper

The earliest English wallpaper that has been identified dates from the first decade of the sixteenth century and was used on the ceiling of the Master's Lodge at Christ's College, Cambridge. Most wallpaper in England, however, was imported from France until the end of the seventeenth century. The Great Fire of London in 1666 and the consequent need for quick and extensive rebuilding boosted the wallpaper trade (as it did many others). The great breakthrough in prestige for English wallpaper came c. 1720 when architect William Kent, decorating the Great Drawing Room at Kensington Palace for George I, chose to cover the walls with printed paper rather than velvet hangings. Royal use conveyed instant respectability.

Among the general eighteenth-century popularity of English wallpapers, two particular fashions were important. The first was for **flock paper** that imitated the texture of velvets by means of dusting finely sieved shearings of wool over surfaces where glue had been applied in desired patterns (the French made similar papers). A variant of flock paper was spangled paper, which was dusted with powdered *isinglass* (the mineral crystal we now call mica) to give the effect of velvet embroidered with silver threads. Improvements for the manufacture of flock paper have continued to the present time, even as its popularity has declined. (When flock paper is made today, its applied particles are of synthetic material and they are held to the paper electrostatically.)

The second eighteenth-century fashion was for pictorial and scenic papers imported from China and, when that was too costly, for the English imitation of Chinese papers. This fashion was wholly consistent with similar fashions in architecture, furniture, and decorative arts of all sorts.

In the last decades of the eighteenth century there were more than seventy wallpaper establishments (popularly called paper stainers) active in London alone and many others elsewhere in England. Among all these, the most important figure was John Baptist Jackson (c. 1701–c. 1780). Some of his papers reproduced paintings by the Venetian masters Titian and Tintoretto, and the subjects of others included landscapes in the manner of Piranesi, statues, trophies, and stucco representations of foliage. Some were series of small round or oval scenes framed in branches or garlands. Even in these, and particularly in the larger scenic papers (fig. 16–50), the scale and sweep of his work were in striking contrast to the delicate detail of the Chinese papers then in vogue. Jackson was also technically innovative, creating his large decorative panels by fastening several sheets of paper together before printing them. His use of oil paints produced paper surfaces that could be wiped clean when necessary.

Another technical innovation, credited to Edward Deighton in 1753, was that of printing papers on a cylinder press using a metal plate engraved with the design, then brushing the colors on by hand. This hand-coloring process is still available today from very high-end manufacturers.

▲ **16–50** Neoclassical wallpaper by John Baptist Jackson with an Italianate landscape of architectural ruins.
Victoria & Albert Museum, London/Art Resource, NY

But Jackson's chief competitors and most important successors were the Crace family, English wallpaper makers who also offered complete interior design services, much as some French upholsterers were to do. Edward Crace, the son of a coach maker, became a coach decorator, setting up shop in the Covent Garden area of London in 1752. By 1768 he had progressed to the decoration of houses, and two years later he received an important commission for the interiors of James Wyatt's Pantheon in London, now destroyed. For the Pantheon he provided **grisaille** panels, **scagliola** columns, and gilt furniture. In the decades that followed, Edward Crace's son and grandsons would carry the firm to greater size (a hundred employees) and greater prominence (papers and decorations for the Opera House at Covent Garden, Windsor Castle, and the Royal Pavilion, Brighton).

Summary: English Design

English design between the Gothic period and the nineteenth century reached remarkable levels of achievement and individuality, displaying both great character and great quality.

Looking for Character

The character of English design in this period was deliberately based, as we have seen, on styles of the past—classical, primarily, but with some attention to the Gothic. Yet the English results are an excellent demonstration of how variously and individually the past can be interpreted. The classical style as interpreted by Palladio and reinterpreted by Inigo Jones or William Kent yields one result; the classical style as interpreted more directly by Robert Adam yields another. And reactions to these variations demonstrate very well the changeability of taste over time, suggesting that no single expression, however fine, satisfies forever.

Yet all these versions share to some extent a single character that is English, distinct from any French, Spanish, or German interpretation: a courtly sturdiness that can be likened to the manners of an English country gentleman—robust and sporting, yet cultured and artistically aware. There is much in English design that is refined and elegant, but nothing that could be considered prissy or effete. The great glassy walls of Smythson's Hardwick Hall and the huge dome

of Wren's St. Paul's embody the spirit of England in their boldness.

Looking for Quality

The English country house and the English city palace set a standard for gracious interiors that has never been surpassed. If it were not for the English carelessness about heating, most of us would be happy to live in such rooms today. English furniture, especially that of the Queen Anne and Neoclassical periods, reached a level of excellence that ranks it, along with the French furniture of the Louis XV and Louis XVI styles, as some of the most assured, consistent, and graceful pieces ever made. And individual artists—some now famous, some anonymous—rose at times above the general level to even finer achievements: the spatial and decorative inventiveness of an Adam floor plan, the impeccable composition of curves in a Queen Anne chair, the virtuosity of a Gibbons carving.

Making Comparisons

Chief among many parallels between French and English design is the fact that both built upon Italian accomplishments, taking the revolutionary ideas of the Italian Renaissance in new directions. One difference is that in France artistic standards were set—and artistic fashions established—in Paris and in neighboring Versailles, while in England love of the countryside and love of the outdoor life prevented London, as great a city as it was, from playing a similarly dominant role. Another difference is that the decorative arts were never made a national industry in England as they were in France, nor given the same degree of royal patronage. And perhaps the greatest difference is that English conservatism and respect for tradition prevented the whole notion of artistic fashion from assuming the importance it held in France. The English welcomed stylistic change in a slower and more measured way.

Yet it may be this less enthusiastic view of current fashion that has encouraged some English designers in their individuality, sometimes even in their eccentricity, a trait more readily accepted in England then in most countries. The great figures in English design—Jones, Chippendale, Gibbons, Wedgwood—followed their personal visions to a remarkable degree, establishing new standards we still admire.

Africa

Prehistory to the Present

"My artwork is the knowledge I carry in my mind from my previous life."

— Katala Flai Shipipa, born 1954, painter from Longa, Angola

The chair in figure 17–1 is undoubtedly one of the most arresting pieces of furniture in our text, and it has much to tell us about its origins. It is imposing in scale, designed to convey the importance of its user. It has been carved from a single large piece of wood, suggesting the nearby existence of old-growth forest. Considerable ingenuity is displayed in its making (for example, in the complex joints between seat and legs), suggesting a tradition of furniture craftsmanship. There are only three legs, a strategy used by designers when making furniture for use on uneven floors or outdoors (as the Greeks did with their *trapeza*, seen in fig. 4–29).

The most striking thing about the chair is the figure carved on its back. It is not a realistic depiction of a human; its body is long and thin, as is its neck, and its hands are unnaturally large. The head on the long neck is observant and watchful, the big hovering hands are protective; it is a *guardian spirit* for the chair's user. The culture of this chair's origin is one in which spirits are highly respected: Tanzania on the eastern coast of Africa. Such respect for the spiritual world is evident in the design of much of the African continent.

◀ **17–1** Back and front views of the throne of the Sultan of Buruku, Tanzania, carved in the late nineteenth century, 42 in. (107 cm) high.
Heini Schneebeli/Bildarchiv Preussischer Kulturbesitz/Art Resource/Bildarchiv Preussischer Kulturbesitz

Determinants of African Design

Up until the mid-twentieth century, the population density of Africa was low, and the relative isolation among settlements led to many different cultures with many different design traditions. With increased mobility, technology, and urbanization (a quarter of all Africans have lived in cities since 1970, but about half of all Africans are expected to live in cities by 2025), the continent is experiencing an unprecedented growth in population and economy, thus drastically altering what was, for many centuries, a rural way of life.

Geography and Natural Resources

The continent of Africa, completely surrounded by water, comprises one fifth of the world's land area. In fact, the whole of the contiguous United States would fit within Africa's Sahara Desert without touching its borders. The distinctive geography of Egypt in North Africa created a society in harmony with the flooding of the Nile River, but the African continent's very size means that there are many peoples living in many types of geography and climate: desert, mountains, tropical rainforest, grasslands, and savanna woodlands.

The fundamental resources of plentiful water supply and fertile soil determined patterns of settlement, of course. For building materials, Zambia and Zimbabwe offer granite. Softer stones are found in Sierra Leone, Guinea, and the lower Congo River valley. Hardwood is plentiful in the forests, and softer, lighter woods in the open parklands. For tying timbers together and for making mats, baskets, ropes, and fish traps, there are a variety of canes, creepers, palms, reeds, rushes, and papyrus. Hides are used to make tents, sacks, clothing, and thongs. Elephant tusks provide ivory. Iron ore is found at Nok in northern Nigeria. Bronze and brass casting have been practiced by the coastal tribes of Guinea. All in all, the richness of the natural resources of the African continent has allowed humans to live and thrive there for a very long time.

Religion

Two of the world's great religions, Islam and Christianity, are well represented in Africa, Islam coming with the invasion of the Arabs in the seventh century and Christianity with the invasion of the Portuguese in the fifteenth century. But native African religions take many forms and influence many types of design, and, overall, there is an intense focus on individuals of uncommon spiritual power. Sometimes these individuals are dead ancestors or tribal chiefs, sometimes living people. These spirits often retain human form (although a degree of abstraction is obviously allowed); sometimes they take the form of animals. Whatever form of expression, religion is a dominant presence in African design. Truly, African design is seldom without a spiritual component; much of it is made for use in social, tribal, or mystical rites or decorated with an awareness of the needs and tastes of spiritual beings.

History

Egypt in northern Africa, as we know, was one of the world's earliest advanced civilizations. Before that, there were prehistoric painted caves in the African country of Lesotho, but design activity in Africa is even older than those examples. In fact, the oldest example of human design yet discovered is a piece of red ocher with multiple diagonal scratches forming a diamond pattern. Found in the Blombos Cave near the southern tip of Africa, this rock has been dated to at least 65,000 years ago, twice as old as the painted caves, and it is considered the oldest trace of intentional graphic activity in the world.

Many other civilizations we have studied made incursions into the African continent and left their influences: the Minoans in the second millennium B.C., the Assyrians in the seventh century B.C., the Romans in the first century B.C. to the fourth century A.D., and the Arabs in the seventh through the eleventh centuries. Portuguese explorers rounded the Cape of Good Hope in the fifteenth century, and Portugal established coastal stations in Africa for trading, including the trading of slaves. A Dutch colony followed in the Cape area (now the Republic of South Africa), an English colony in Sierra Leone, and French colonies in western and northern Africa. The discovery of rich deposits of diamonds in 1865 and gold in 1886 attracted new prospectors from Europe. By 1912 the whole continent was ruled by Europeans with the exception of Ethiopia and Liberia, but in the 1950s a great surge of nationalism began. Today there are fifty-five independent African nations. For most of its history, however, even in the years of the most extensive colonization, African people continued many of their social patterns and design traditions regardless of external interference.

Conservation

What we can learn about African design is limited by how much design remains for us to see. Many antique artifacts made of wood have, unfortunately, been victims of heat and humidity and insect pests. We assume that much recent design seen in this chapter follows long tradition, but in some cases this is only speculation. Nor does preservation seem to have been a major concern of older Africans. If an object, however significant, decayed or was devoured by white ants, it was reproduced and a dedication ceremony conducted to invest the new version with the same spirits that had imbued the older one. We shall see the same attitude in building construction, some of which was effectively rebuilt annually.

African Architecture and Interiors

Some African people, such as the Bushmen of southern Africa and the Pygmies of the Congo River valley, have traditionally migrated in search of game or fresh pastures for their sheep or cattle. Many others, however, lived in agrarian societies and developed permanent settlements. These included mud buildings, stone buildings, mud buildings with stone foundations, and wood-frame buildings with their walls covered with painted mud or with woven mats.

Period	Cultural And Artistic Events
65,000 years ago	Graphic designs in the Blombos Cave
30,000 years ago	Painted caves of Lesotho
4500 B.C.–A.D. 30	The civilization of ancient Egypt
3rd century B.C.	Ethiopia established
1st century B.C.	Northern Africa is a Roman province
7th century A.D.	Invasion of Arabs; Beginning of Islamicization of Africa; Coptic Christian art
8th century	Walled city of Kano in Nigeria
11th century	Royal stone buildings in Ghana
12th century	Silk weaving in Tunsia and Morocco
13th century	Cliff top palace at Kilwa
15th century	Invasion of Portuguese; Beginning of Christianization of Africa
18th century	Chinese silk made in Ethiopia
19th century	Emir's Palace, Kano, Nigeria
20th century	Great Friday Mosque; Djennè, Mali, Nankani Compound, Ghana; Kente cloth

Although designs differ, there is a general pattern of settlement that prevails in most of Africa: Living units are based on extended families. Several generations with a shared lineage often live together under the guidance of a respected family elder, with a shared kitchen and courtyard. Interior doors often connect more private spaces hierarchically, with the elder's family quarters the innermost and least accessible, the youngest family's quarters the most accessible.

We shall look at such a settlement, then at a large religious building, and then at a palace.

Nankani Compound, Ghana

The town of Sirigu in northern Ghana has one of many examples of African communal living. The Nankani living there are an extended family. Their traditional religion worships ancestors, and elders are the governors and chief decision makers of their village. The elders are assisted by landowners who regulate the distribution of land for the building of new units.

Construction (fig. 17–2) is of sun-dried earthen brick and mud mortar, used for the building of two distinct dwelling types: those circular in plan, which are the homes of the women of the family; and those rectangular in plan, which are the homes of men. Both types have flat roofs of mud over supporting wood members. Every adult has his or her own room, and if the head of a family has more than one wife, his senior wife has the central room of the women's compound, with other wives in adjoining circular rooms. An outdoor kitchen area (in the foreground of fig. 17–2) is also considered the women's province. There are also areas for farm animals (cattle, goats, and poultry) and conical buildings with straw roofs that are used as granaries.

Men are charged with the basic construction of the buildings, and women with the decoration of the walls, both inside and outside. The women's murals are typically in three colors (black, white, and red), obtained from natural materials such as white earth, leaves, tree bark, and cow dung (although the introduction of commercial paints is altering this tradition). Patterns may be geometric, as in the repeated triangles of figure 17–2, or may incorporate stylized animals such as cows (symbols of prosperity), pythons (symbols of protection), or crocodiles (symbols of the clan). Some walls are given incised or low relief sculptures as well.

▲ **17–2** Residential compound for an extended Nankani family at Sirigu in northern Ghana, twentieth century.
© Margaret Courtney-Clarke/Corbis All Rights Reserved

The Sirigu women are also skilled at pottery, mat-sewing, and basketweaving, a characteristic basket being roughly conical in shape with a square base and a round opening at the top. As with Greek vases in this respect, the pots are either red with black designs or black with red ones.

Mosque at Djenné, Mali

The town of Djenné in Mali was established at least as early as the eleventh century. The Friday Mosque dates from the fourteenth century, although it was considerably rebuilt in 1906–7 under the direction of architect Ismaila Traoré, then head of the town's guild of masons. The results of that rebuilding are what we see today (fig. 17–3). Built on a platform almost 250 feet (75 m) square, it rises above the rest of the town and is visible for miles. It is the largest mud building south of the Sahara Desert. Its eastern façade (at the left of the photo) features three towerlike minarets, and a staircase inside one of them leads to the flat roof. On the top of each of these spires, in a modern gesture, is an electric

Pablo Picasso first discovered African art in the Trocadero Museum, Paris, in 1907, when he was 25 years old. It had a profound effect on him and his own art. Here is his description of his reaction: "Men had made those masks and other objects for a sacred purpose, as a kind of mediation between themselves and the . . . forces that surrounded them. . . . At that moment I realized that this was what painting was all about. Painting isn't an aesthetic operation; it's a form of magic designed as mediation between this strange, hostile world and us, a way of seizing power by giving form to our terrors as well as our desires. When I came to that realization, I knew I had found my way."

▲ 17–3 Northeast corner of the Friday Mosque, Djenne, Mali, as rebuilt in 1907 in the style of the fourteenth-century original. A tented market is in the foreground.
Getty Images Inc.—Image Bank

light, powered from a nearby generator, and, in a more traditional gesture, a pair of ostrich eggs, symbols of purity. The wooden beams projecting from the walls not only provide a decorative pattern of shadows but also support the scaffolding erected annually for the replastering of the walls.

Inside the mosque there are nine rows of adobe brick columns with eleven columns per row, which support a flat 33-foot-high ceiling of palm logs. The floor is of cool sand, where the men walk barefoot and kneel for prayer. Behind the mosque is a walled courtyard, almost as big as the mosque itself, where the women pray.

Emir's Palace, Kano, Nigeria

Palaces play an important role in African architecture and history. Chiefs' palaces in Ethiopia since the fifth century have been round in plan and built of dry stone walls. In eleventh-century Ghana there was a royal cluster of stone buildings with wood roofs. At Great Zimbabwe, the so-called

Elliptical Building, which is now in ruins, was probably a palace; its interior furnishings of finely molded and painted clay included sleeping platforms, benches, and hearths. The Swahili of East Africa built a clifftop palace at Kilwa overlooking the Indian Ocean with a great central corridor roofed with a series of domes. When it was built in the thirteenth century, it was the largest building south of the Sahara.

Newer and still in use today is the Emir's Palace (Gidan Sarki) in Kano, Nigeria. This is the territory of the Hausa people who number more than 15 million. One million of them live in the walled city of Kano, founded about A.D. 900 and long famous for textiles and leatherwork. In the early 1840s, the emir at the time employed Babban Gwani ("Great Builder") to construct his palace. It eventually grew to cover 33 acres including some grazing fields. It is surrounded by a wall almost 30 feet high, and it houses an extended family with their servants and guards, totaling roughly a thousand people. Its main entrance faces a large public space (the *dendal*) where, today, the whole city sometimes congregates to show their loyalty to the emir, and where every Friday he leads a procession from the palace to the nearby mosque.

The outer reception hall of the Emir's Palace (fig. 17–4) remains in its original earthen construction, one of the few parts of the complex not rebuilt in more permanent materials. The tall ceiling of the rectangular room is supported on intersecting arches built of corbelled mud blocks plastered over with mud to hide the **corbels** (steps of blocks projecting beyond the ones below) to create the effect of a continuous curve. There are decorative brass plates where the arches intersect. The vividly painted decoration covers the arches, walls, and ceilings and dates back to the 1930s. Some parts of the painted designs seem purely geometric, others show abstract representations of swords, spears, rifles, and other weapons representing the emir's power.

African Ornament

As we have noted, much African design is meant to promote beneficial events or prevent harmful ones through symbolic ornament. Ornament is richly present in African sculpture, masks, headdresses, and costumes, areas of design that—striking as they often are—are only tangential to our concerns here. Here, the focus is on ornament that relates directly to architecture and its interiors.

On a grand scale, sometimes entire villages, such as those of the Dogon in Mali, are planned to symbolize the human

▲ **17–4** Reception hall, Emir's Palace, Kano, Nigeria, begun c. 1840.
© James Morris 1999/2000

body, with both male and female organs represented in their centers. On a smaller scale, many symbols are used. Some are simply exaggerated portraits of important kings, chiefs, or ancestors. Others depict figures with deformities or abnormalities (one leg, two heads), referring to antisocial behavior or unnatural powers.

Animal images are generally metaphorical, and their meaning may vary from one tribe to another. However, elephants and leopards represent authority and leadership throughout Africa. A fragment of a carved wood panel from a palace in Edo, Nigeria (fig. 17–5), combines an image of the king and two of his attendants with the image of a crocodile eating its own tail, symbol of death and regeneration and of the cyclical nature of time. Between them is a more abstract pattern, resembling basketry or weaving.

Ornament of Earth

The chief focus of architectural ornament is the wall, and the chief material of the wall is mud—the earth. Such sophisticated use of common materials is typical of African architecture and design. We have seen an example of wall painting in the Nankani compound in Ghana (see fig. 17–2). Other kinds of wall ornamentation can indicate social standing. In Benin, a country that won its independence from France only in 1960 but that occupies the land where the kingdom of Dahomey existed since the fifteenth century, the Palace of the King of Dahomey was built, like other houses, of courses of mud. But the King's walls were not only built thicker and taller than the others; they also enjoyed an ornamental treatment. This treatment is a repeated convex fluting running

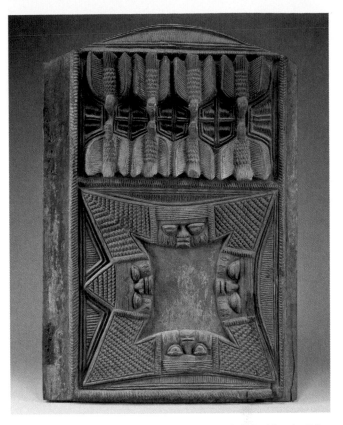

▲ **17–5** Carved wooden panel from a palace in Edo, Nigeria, 5 ft. (140 cm) long.
Franko Kyory/National Museum of African Art/Smithsonian Institution

horizontally around the walls. Chief's houses were also allowed fluting on the exterior, but only high-ranking chiefs were allowed interior fluting as well, and commoners were allowed no fluting at all. Because of the king's wall thickness, his walls also had sunken cavities that could be used for storage or display between sections of fluting.

Tools & Techniques | EARTHEN MASONRY

Molded bricks are made of grass, water, and mud with a large component of clay. In older times, rice or chaff (seed coverings from grain) was used instead of grass; sheep or goat feces has also been used. These bricks, when in place, were plastered inside and out with a similar substance, but one with a content of less clay and more sand, giving a smoother, less cracked surface. To this surface decorative washes of clay and water were then added, often applied in color gradations from deep gray at the floor to almost white at the ceiling.

All exposed and unfired mud construction is temporary, unless there is continued maintenance, ideally given annually. At the Djenné mosque, for example, thousands of people from the community convene on two consecutive weekends each year before the spring rains to help resurface the revered structure. Although gathering materials and preparing the mud is a citywide effort, the actual application of the mud is done only by masons. In many places in Africa, masons have been organized into guildlike groups divided into levels by skill and seniority.

▲ **17–6** In a house in Agouni Guerhane, Algeria, a raised platform and clay vessels are painted blue and walls have symbolic decoration.
Margaret Courtney-Clarke/CORBIS/Bettmann

In another example, a house built of mud in Agouni Guerhane, Algeria, wall bases, a raised platform, and other architectural details—as well as some large clay storage pots—have been painted blue. More inventively, wall panels around the room, some featuring niches for storage and display, have been covered with decorative motifs representing plants, animals, and insects (fig. 17–6).

The construction of the wall itself, as well as its maintenance, could also be ornamental as well as structural, and this construction was most often some form of earthen masonry. Africa has a centuries-long tradition of such building, and the compound at Sirigu, the mosque at Djenné, and the house in Algeria were all, in different ways, made of mud.

In Nigeria, bricks shaped by hand or in wooden molds and sun-dried but not fired have been use to build two- and even three-story houses. Wherever used, thick earthen walls effectively slow heat transmission so that rooms retain heat at night but are relatively cool during the day.

Ornament of Wood

In a continent where, in many areas, there was plentiful wood, wood objects (such as the chair in fig. 17–1) were carved from single pieces of wood. The chief tools, even after the modern introduction of saws and drills, are knives and adzes (axelike tools with the handle and blade at right angles to one another), both of which come in many sizes. Sometimes the adze blade can be taken out of its handle and used as a chisel. The adze, cutting deeply into the wood, is used for initial shaping of an object; the knife for finer details. Before modern sanding techniques, final finishing was done with sand itself or with rough leaves.

For wood objects that will serve some ritual purpose, appropriate rites must be performed at several stages of production, beginning before the tree is cut down. Carving is primarily a male activity, although some women of Kenya are admired for their elegant work.

The products of wood carving include impressive ceremonial objects and elements of important buildings, such as the doors of the palace of the King of Ikere in southwest Nigeria (fig. 17–7). These were made by a famous carver, Olowe of Ise, one of the Yoruba people. Its figures in high relief show a visit to the king by a British official; at the upper right he is shown being carried to the king in a litter. Wood carvings also include simple utilitarian objects, of course, such as bowls, mortars, hoe handles, milk pails, headrests, snuff containers, drums, and much more. Even the simplest of these, such as the spoon in figure 17–8, can be imbued with resonant life.

African Furniture

African interiors, for the most part, are sparsely furnished. Chairs and stools are the most frequent pieces of native African furniture; stools are more common than chairs. Many wood stools (fig. 17–9) are supported by figures of women (a fewer number by men). The female supports are called **caryatids**, although in attitude they have little in common with the demurely robed maidens supporting the Erechtheum on the Greek Acropolis (see fig. 4–21). The example pictured is from the Hemba people of Zaire, and the coiffures and belly tattoos of the back-to-back figures show them to be from the upper class of society, possibly ancestors of the chief for whom it was carved.

A rarer form of stool is one from Cameroon (fig. 17–10). The base is covered with beadwork and the seat with cowrie shells. The supporting figures in this case are not proud ancestors but respectful servants. Their faces are covered with thin plates of hammered copper and they wear beaded hoods.

▼ **17–7** Pair of wood doors from the palace in Ikere-Ekiti, Nigeria, carved c. 1906, 7 ft. 6 in. (2.3 m) high.
Werner Forman/Art Resource, NY

▼ **17–9** A caryatid stool by the Hemba from Zaire, 21 in. (53 cm) high.
© Sandro Bocala and the Vitra Design Museum

Still another type (fig. 17–11), from the Asante people of Ghana, is of wood completely covered with brass. Along with it came a footstool. In some societies, such as Ghana, footstools (shown in fig. 17–11 in the form of a crocodile) are also made for chiefs so that their feet would not touch the ground, which would signify pollution and might bring bad fortune to the whole community. As in Japan, those who sit on the floor rather than on chairs or stools often use portable backrests; these are particularly popular in Zaire.

Although stools were used more often than chairs, there are African chairs. Some were quite close to the ground, such as the wood chair (fig. 17-12) made by the Dan people of the

◀ **17–8** Wooden spoon made by the Dan in the Ivory Coast, 19 in. (49 cm) high.
© abm—archives barbier-mueller-studio Ferrazzini-Bouchet, Geneve

▼ 17–10 A king's stool of the Bamun from Cameroon, covered with beadwork, 22 in. (57 cm) high.
© Sandro Bocala and The Vitra Design Museum

▲ 17–11 A stool and footrest made by the Asante of Ghana, wood faced with brass. The stool is 26 in. (46 cm) wide.
Heini Schhneebeli/© Sandro Bocala and the Vitra Design Museum

Ivory Coast and Liberia. Its seat is a simple plane, and its back a single graceful curve.

Beds are generally mats that may be placed on built-in platforms or, in the case of nomadic people, directly on the ground.

▶ 17–12 A low wood chair of the Dan people, Ivory Coast or Liberia, 13 in. (33 cm) high.
Aldo Tutino/Art Resource, NY

These are often accompanied with headrests carved in wood, a necessity for societies in which elaborate hairdos are the rule. Chiefs may have bedsteads, however, carved from wood or constructed from bamboo and overlaid with mattresses.

Tables are uncommon except in Northern Africa, where small tables (or trays on stands) derive from Arab tradition. Storage is often in wall niches (as in fig. 17–6) or in hanging nets, and some household items are stored by hanging them on wall hooks or sticking them into the roof thatch. Some chests appear, and a nineteenth-century example from Benin City, Nigeria, now in the British Museum, London, has been carved to imitate woven basketry, suggesting that it may have had basketwork predecessors.

African Decorative Arts

African design displays a passion for decoration, which is applied to buildings, furniture, utensils, ceramics, metalwork, woodwork, and textiles, as well as being frequently applied to the Africans' own bodies. In addition to woods and metals, ivory was used for musical instruments, bracelets, even hairpins. Basketwork had many uses, and brightly colored ceramic beads, glass beads, pearls, cowrie shells, feathers, and vegetable fibers were popular for many decorative treatments.

Ceramics

Clay used for earthenware varies in composition from region to region, some of it gray, some pink, much—but not all—coarse-grained. As elsewhere, vessels are formed either by modeling lumps of clay or by coiling ribbons of clay. Often the vessel will be preheated before firing—sometimes by inverting it over a fire, sometimes by filling it with straw and burning the straw—to dry it out so that the firing can be relatively brief and at low temperature.

Methods of decorating earthenware vessels include the application of colored slips (vessel colors, like wall colors, most frequently being black, white, and red) or by using implements such as sticks or small picks to incise grooved patterns in the surface. Some earthenware is varnished for a final finish, some blackened with graphite. In most African societies, pottery making is considered proper work only for women.

The pottery vessel shown in figure 17–13 is for palm wine, from which it would have been sipped through straws.

▼ **17–13** Pottery wine vessel of the Mangbetu from the Democratic Republic of the Congo, 2½ in. (32 cm) high. Erik Hesmerg/Bildarchiv Preussischer Kulturbesitz/Art Resource

It was made by the Mangbetu people of the Democratic Republic of the Congo, probably in the early twentieth century, and its top shows a fanlike hairdo then worn by the royal women of the Mangbetu.

Metalwork

Metalwork has a long history in Africa and one tinged with mystery. Because the process of making metal objects involves the transformation of material under intense heat, there is something inherently otherworldly about it. The metalsmith therefore became involved in the rites of burial, circumcision, and ritual sacrifice. He (always a man) was both respected and feared.

The most plentiful African metals were iron, copper, and gold, with lesser amounts of tin, lead, and silver, and manufactured alloys of brass and bronze. Copper was used in the stool in figure 17–11, completely sheathing it in thin plates of brass. Brass was also made into weights for weighing gold, and the whole range of metals was used in jewelry and ritual objects. The use of smelting furnaces for extracting metal from ore seems to have been widespread in Africa by A.D. 1000. Steel was also produced, but cast iron only rarely. Lost-wax casting was used in West Africa, open-mold casting in Central Africa. The people of Benin have been known for 500 years as virtuoso metal casters, creating freestanding figures, decorative plaques in high relief, and iron altars.

Textiles

Some Chinese silk from the mulberry-feeding *bombyx mori* silkworm was imported to Africa by Arabian traders following the seventh-century Arab invasion of Africa. It was used for textiles for the Muslim ruling class. More common in Africa, however, is a type of wild silk, called **African silk**. It is a product of moths that feed on fig trees and construct large nests with clusters of cocoons. Another moth, native to Nigeria, feeds chiefly on tamarind trees and produces a coarse, dull yarn. By the twelfth century, silk-weaving centers and silk-weaving guilds were established in Tunis, Tunisia, and Fez, Morocco. After the fall of Granada in 1492 to Christian rule, Jews were expelled from Spain, and many of them came to Africa with more sophisticated weaving skills.

In some parts of the continent (such as Zaire and East Africa) weaving is traditionally considered a male activity; in

▲ **17–15** A kente cloth by the Asante of Ghana, twentieth century, 10 ft. 5 in. (3.2 m) wide.

a few others (such as Madagascar and North Africa) it is a female activity. Rarely is it practiced by both men and women, and if so, they use different kinds of loom. (For example, Hausa men in Nigeria use horizontal looms making narrow strips of cloth, yet Hausa women use vertical ones making wider cloth.) But in almost all this activity, weaving is generally the work of men, while embroidery is considered women's work.

An example of Chinese silk woven in Ethiopia (fig. 17–14) is this eighteenth-century hanging panel, originally one of three, intended for use in a church. The woven figures represent a funeral procession for a king.

The narrow-band loom, capable of producing strips of cloth (whether silk, cotton, linen, or wool) that are only four to eight inches wide but many feet long, has long been popular in Africa, and such looms have been found in Mali that date back to the eleventh century. If the narrow strips have colored stripes running their whole length they are said to be **warp**-faced because the long warp threads are dominant; if the colored stripes run across the narrow width of the strips, they are said to be **weft**-faced. These strips are often woven together or cut and sewn together selvage to selvage to create patterns of dazzling complexity. Examples are the ceremonial **kente** cloths (fig. 17–15) made by the Ashanti people of Ghana.

Quilting is a textile technique known throughout Muslim Africa, and quilted bedcoverings have been made there since the fourteenth century. Appliqué is used as well, notably by the Kuba people of Zaire, who sew small geometric shapes cut from raffia cloth (made from the fibers of the raffia palm) onto base cloths of the same material. Embroidery is also part of the textile vocabulary, particularly skillful in the hands of the Hausa, who use it not only for their spectacular robes, but also for cushion covers.

Summary: African Design

We have said that Africa is an enormous continent with a long history and multiple cultures. Nevertheless, there are some shared design characteristics.

Looking for Character

The character of traditional African design is religious, but it is not solemn, dour, or overly pious. It is direct, vibrant, and joyously in touch with its society's ancestors and heroes and their continuing presence. It evinces a vitality few other design vocabularies can match.

Looking for Quality

Quality in African design, for its makers and users, has little to do with the provision of beauty (though that certainly may be present), but instead with the ability to placate spirits. This improved relationship with the spirit world will then have real-world effects: curing illness, cursing enemies, fostering prosperity or fertility, insuring the health of crops or cattle, or (as in the case of the chair in fig. 17–1) protecting the user of the design. In addition, the splendor of the mosque at Djenné, the animated painting of the reception hall at Kano, the vigor of a carved stool, and the vivid color combinations of textiles are significant design accomplishments by any standards. We cannot often reconstruct the ceremonies, music, rhythm, ritual, and states of mind that contributed to the awe in which these objects were once held; even so, they convey an impressive artistic energy.

Making Comparisons

The mosque we saw in Djenné is different in character from a mosque in the Ancient Near East, the caryatid supporting a Zaire stool is different from one supporting a Greek temple, and the Chinese silk from Ethiopia is different from a Chinese silk from China. These comparisons make clear that African design is a true creation with clear identity, far from being indebted to outside influences.

Thus, African design, as with many other design expressions we have seen, is highly individual and independent. It has a purpose—to please the ruling spirits—and a strength of design focused on satisfying that purpose. For its creators, it was superbly potent and functional. For us, it is superbly dynamic and stimulating. Long-lived and traditional as African design is, it was seen in the twentieth century to have an affinity with the modern movement in art and with jazz in music. It invigorated painting and sculpture and then, through those arts, architecture and interiors. Worldwide design today would be paler, duller, and weaker without its energizing transfusion of African influence.

Pre-Columbian America

18

Before the Sixteenth Century

"When a baby girl is born to your tribe, you shall go and find a spider's web . . . and rub it on the baby's hand and arm. Then when she grows up she will weave, and her fingers and arms will not tire from the weaving."

— Spider Man in Navajo legend

Beginning in 1492, the explorations of Christopher Columbus and others changed humanity's perception of itself. Two important groups of cultures, previously unaware of each other, met for the first time, and in everyone's consciousness the world was permanently enlarged. The continents of North and South America and the isthmus connecting them had been the scene of a series of fascinating cultures (fig. 18–1) that had flourished for centuries before their first contact with their European counterparts.

Because the geographic scope of this chapter is so large, and because the cultures of these lands are so numerous and varied, this chapter will take a look briefly at some of the key cultures and what is known of their design. There are many questions about their history and the meaning of their artifacts, but we can study their cultural designs with fascination and admiration for the sophistication of their art forms and their intelligent use of local materials.

◀ **18–1** A Mayan ceramic censer depicting a ruler of Copán in what is now Honduras, a center of Mayan astronomical learning, 7th century, 41 in. (105 cm) high.
Erich Lessing/Art Resource, NY

Central and South America

It is believed that the first settlers of the Americas came across the Bering Straits from northeast Asia into what is now Alaska near the end of the last Ice Age, using a strip of land that, after the melting of the ice, fell below sea level. They therefore probably settled North America first, some continuing their travels to Central and then to South America. Though the southern areas may have been the last settled, these cultures were the first discovered by European explorers.

Determinants of Central and South American Design

Central and South America's geography, stretching from Mexico to Chile's Cape Horn, reflects wide diversity in rainfall, vegetation, and topology—both cool, dry highlands and steamy, wet lowlands. The equator crosses the South American countries of Ecuador, Colombia, and Brazil, but elsewhere there are snowcapped mountains. Like other areas of the world, natural resources play a part in types and styles of design. Here, metals include copper, gold, silver, and tin, and minerals include iron ores, slate, onyx, obsidian, jade, and turquoise. The

Date	South America	Central America	North America
Before 500 B.C.	Chavin de Huantar culture in the Andes 1200–400 B.C.	Maya precursors 1500–500 B.C.; Olmec culture at La Venta, Olmec jade carvings, 1200–400 B.C.	Basket Maker culture
500–1 B.C.	Pre-Inca Nazca and Chimú cultures in Peru	Monte Albán founded in Mexico by Zapotecs; ball game invented by Olmecs; Pyramid of the Sun at Teotihuacán	Precursors of the Pueblos
A.D. 1–500	Moche pottery in Peru; painted fabrics on Peru's Paracas Peninsula	Mayan ceremonial Centers; Monte Albán rebuilt; Mayan cities of Chichen Itzá, Tikal, and Palenque built	Mound Builders in central North America
500–1000	Monumental carvings at Tiahuanaco; painted underground tombs in Colombia; pre-Inca culture in valley of Cuzco	Mayan city of Uxmal built; Mixtecs capture Monte Albán and build Mitla	Pueblo culture begins in Utah, Colorado, and Arizona; Mimbres pottery
1000–1500	City of Cuzco founded; growth of Inca culture; Chimu and Mochica cultures in Peru	Aztecs found Tenochtitlán; Mayan frescoes at Tulum and Bonampak; many Mayan cities abandoned	Cliff Dweller culture in Colorado; Great Kiva at Aztec, New Mexico

principle textile resources are cotton and the wool of the llama, vicūna, and alpaca, but in dry areas the agave plant also provides fibers for coarser textiles, rope, and twine.

Religion, as we have seen elsewhere, exerts a strong influence on architectural design. Before the sixteenth-century European invaders imposed their own faith of Christianity on the inhabitants, Central and South Americans practiced a variety of religions. Some beliefs (like those of the Incas of Peru) focused on the power of the society's own rulers; some (in areas with undependable water supplies) worshiped rain gods; and others deified snakes, jaguars, or other creatures. Some religious practices involved hallucinogenic drugs, and some included human sacrifice. Whatever the nature of these beliefs, the size and complexity of the monuments built to honor them, and the effort and care with which they were built, testify to their great power over the believers.

The Olmecs (2000 B.C.–300 B.C.)

The earliest of the important Central American civilizations to reach maturity was the Olmec (a name meaning "people of the rubber country"). They reached a height of accomplishment in the humid tropical lowlands and foothills along the southernmost Gulf Coast of what is now Mexico,

between 1000 and c. 400 B.C., when they seem to have come to a sudden, violent, and unknown end.

The Olmecs have been called the great founders of Mesoamerican culture; they have also been called the Jaguar People because that animal, a rain symbol, was their chief deity. They devised a calendar but not a written language. Without inventing the wheel, they still managed to carry huge stones great distances; without a potter's wheel, they still excelled at pottery. They built great ceremonial centers of Olmec settlements in the Mexican states of Tabasco and Veracruz, the most evocative of which is La Venta.

La Venta   Built on an island less than 1 mile (1.6 km) long in the Tonalá River amidst great mangrove swamps, La Venta is the first example we know of the temple-focused city type that was to flourish throughout Central America. Its ceremonial center, more than 1,000 feet (308 m) long, was dominated by a great pyramid of beaten earth. Exactly a double square in plan at its base, its sides sloped upward to a height of over 100 feet (30 m), where it was topped by a square platform.

Other elements of the center were disposed symmetrically around the long axis of the pyramid. Immediately to the north was a ball court, roughly the size of a modern football field and the earliest known among the many ball courts found in Mesoamerica, supporting the notion that the Olmecs were the inventors of the basketball-like game using a hard rubber ball that was both a sport and a ceremony and was popular in many pre-Columbian cultures. There are also smaller pyramids, burial mounds, great colonnaded courtyards and plazas, and—as if guarding the island's sacred precinct—giant stone heads as much as 9 feet (2.8 m) high (fig. 18–2). Each was carved to depict the wearing of a close-fitting helmet, such as may have been worn in the ceremonial ball games that were popular in many Central and South American cultures. Thus protected, La Venta was an environment for assembly, procession, and elaborate ritual.

Other monumental stoneworks of the Olmecs include the stelae, carved with calendric glyphs in low relief, presumably commemorating astronomical events. Large monolithic altars were also produced, their carvings showing the jaguar god, priests in elaborate collars and headdresses, and what appears to be the sacrifice of young children. Sandstone sarcophagi have also been found.

At a very different scale, the Olmecs also carved delicate miniatures of jade, rock crystal, and less valuable stones. Some of these were in the form of ax heads; some were masks; some were purely decorative objects. The techniques involved seem to have included all those developed later: abrasion, chiseling, drilling, crumbling, and (using finely powdered stones) polishing. Subject matter included the jaguar god, jaguar teeth, figures part jaguar and part human, deer jaws, stingray tails, clamshells, bats, and parts of the human body—hands, toes, and ears. Small flat stones were also arranged in mosaic patterns and used for flooring. The finest Olmec work, however, was of jade.

▲ **18–2** An Olmec stone head, c. 1200 B.C., 9 ft. (2.85 m) high.

Jade   We have mentioned that the Chinese made jade disks symbolizing the heavens; jade was also a favorite of the Olmecs. **Jade** is cool to the touch, lustrous, sometimes translucent, and can be given a high, oily polish. It is also exceptionally hard, impossible even to scratch with steel, and the consequent difficulty of mining and carving it only adds to the value of finished pieces. An example with assumed religious significance is a standing figure, now missing a leg (fig. 18–3); the figure he is holding may represent the supernatural or may be a masked baby about to be sacrificed.

Tools & Techniques | JADE CARVING

The term **jade** is used for two minerals, nephrite and jadeite. Both are silicate minerals, slightly different in composition, but similar in appearance and nature. Pieces of jade were sawed by drawing cords repeatedly back and forth across the surface until grooves were formed, then continuing to make the grooves deeper while using a solution of hard stone particles in water to create greater friction. Drills of bone and even of hardwood were employed, again using finely crushed stone and water as the actual cutting agent. So hard is jade, however, that a single straight cut through a cubic foot of it with these methods would take several weeks of work. The amounts of patience and skill needed were remarkable, but amply supplied by Olmec artisans. Prominent among their subject matter was the all-important jaguar and a number of supernatural figures, and objects in these forms were used as pendants and in religious rituals. In South America, jade carving was practiced not only by the Olmecs, but also by the Maya and the Aztecs. Elsewhere, jade carvers included the Chinese, the Ottoman Turks, and the Maori in New Zealand. Sources of jade other than South America and China include Myanmar, Siberia, and Alaska.

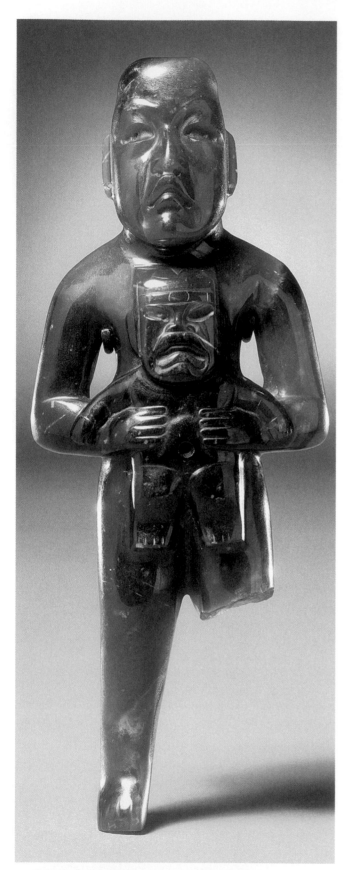

Other Olmec Arts Other decorative arts practiced by the Olmecs were mural paintings, traces of which have been found in caves, and pottery decorated with lizardlike figures with hands rather than claws. None of the pre-Columbian Americans cultivated the *Bombyx mori* that produced such lustrous silk for China, but another kind of silkworm in the Oaxaca area of Mexico, feeding on the ailanthus tree, produced a crêpe fabric (one with tightly twisted filaments) that was often dyed bright magenta. It is called **American silk**.

Teotihuacán (250 B.C.–A.D. 900)

Teotihuacán is not the name of a group of people but the name of a city that existed northeast of the central lake in the great plain of the Valley of Mexico, near the present capital city. *Teotihuacán* is an Aztec term for "Place of the Gods." But the city had been abruptly deserted before A.D. 750, long before it was found by the Aztecs, a group that came to dominance only about 1400. Unlike some other Central American sites that were ceremonial centers without dwellings, Teotihuacán was a true city (fig. 18–4). In the sixth century it may have had 200,000 inhabitants, making it the most populous city in the Americas and the sixth most populous in the world

The city's most remarkable feature was its great ceremonial center, almost 2 miles (3.2 km) in length, disposed about a 130-foot-wide (40 m) central spine, the "Road of the Dead." Along this spine—the scene, undoubtedly, of many impressive processions—were hundreds of stone platforms and groups of chambered buildings. And dominating all were three powerful structures: at the spine's southern end, the Temple of Quetzal-coatl (the "Plumed Serpent"); near its midpoint, the so-called Pyramid of the Sun; and serving as its northern terminus, the Pyramid of the Moon. The structures were faced with fine stone carvings and finished with layers of white and red stucco.

A distinctive architectural feature common throughout the ceremonial complex was a framed masonry panel (*tablero*), its surface long but vertical, cantilevered from the sloping sides of the pyramids (fig. 18–5). The repetition of such panels gave the composition of buildings a remarkable cohesion. The framed surfaces of these panels was generally used for decoration, usually in the form of painted frescoes, and in the case of the temple, that decoration was especially elaborate, not painted but sculptured in stone reliefs. For the most part, these reliefs pictured the heads of two gods: the Plumed Serpent himself, shown as a sharp-fanged, fire-breathing, feathered dragon; and Tlaloc, the rain god, shown as a geometrically stylized mask

▲ **18–3** Olmec jade figure holding a supernatural figure or offering, carved 800–500 B.C., 8½ in. (22 cm) high.
"Standing Figure Holding a Masked Baby," Mexico, Olmec, 800–500 B.C. Jade, 8⅝ × 3³/₁₆ × 1⅝ in. From the collection of Robin B. Martin on loan to the Brooklyn Museum. L47.6

▲ **18–5** Carved *tableros* projecting from the Temple of the Feathered Serpent, Teotihuacán, Mexico.
Dagli Orti/The Art Archive

with ringed eyes. In the background of the panels are nautical motifs (such as shells and sea creatures) and meander patterns representing the Plumed Serpent. More stone heads of Quetzalcoatl lined the ramps that climbed the pyramid.

Teotihuacán was laid out on a regular grid, and beyond the center were the houses of the ruling elite on raised platforms around square or rectangular courtyards; beyond these were houses of artisans and peasants. The city lacked surrounding walls or fortifications, evidence of a society so powerful that it was virtually without enemies.

A variety of decorative and utilitarian pottery was found at Teotihuacán, including bowls, effigy pots in the form of human figures, and censers (vessels for burning incense). Decorative motifs on the pottery included birds, butterflies, flowers, and abstract signs, possibly calendar-related. The earliest examples were hand-modeled, but the pottery mold came into use about 350 years before the city's mysterious end.

The Zapotecs (500 B.C.–A.D. 800)

More than 200 miles (321 km) southeast of Teotihuacán's plateau, the geography becomes mountainous. The early civilization here was known as Zapotec. Here, 1 mile (1.6 km)

▼ **18–6** The central plaza ball court at Monte Albán, edged with rows of temple/tombs.
Abercrombie

above sea level, is the present-day city of Oaxaca, and, 1,300 feet (400 m) higher still, was the ancient city of Monte Albán (White Mountain), sacred capital of the Zapotecs.

Leveled by years of labor, the mountaintop acropolis was protected against invasion by steep cliffs falling away on all sides, and on this man-made plateau a great complex of temples was built. Unlike Teotihuacán, Monte Albán seems not to have been a real city with a resident population, but a city of the gods and of the dead, visited by pilgrims from afar.

On a north-south axis, its central plaza is 850 feet (260 m) wide and slightly less than 1 mile (1.6 km) long. In its center and ringing its edges are disposed a dozen impressive pyramidal temple-tombs (fig. 18–6), and among and below these are hundreds of smaller tomb chambers, many of them still unexcavated. There is also an impressive ball court for the ceremonial games mentioned earlier.

Like the ancient Egyptians, the people of Monte Albán seem to have lavished their finest design on spaces for the dead, and some of these tomb interiors were vibrant with frescoes of deities and priests mysterious to us today. Exterior building surfaces were faced with polychrome stucco, which, in the clear atmosphere and bright Mexican sun, must have given a dazzling effect, and even some tomb exteriors meant to be buried in the earth were elaborately carved.

The Mayas (300 B.C.–A.D. 1521)

The Mayan civilization flourished for more than 1,800 years until it was destroyed in the Spanish Conquest of 1519–21. The Mayans occupied both lowlands and highlands in Central America, and among its earliest great cities was Palenque in southern Mexico, less than 100 miles (160 km) from the territory of the Olmecs. Palenque was inhabited as early as 300 B.C., with the height of its importance coming

▲ **18–7** One of the four stairways climbing the Castillo, Chichén Itzá. Inside the visible structure is buried an older, smaller one.
Cosmo Condina/Getty Images Inc.-Stone Allstock

c. A.D. 600–900, and it was in Palenque that the ceramic censer shown in figure 18–1 was found. Other important cities and ceremonial sites were Uaxactun and Tikal in what is now Guatemala, Copán in what is now Honduras, Bonampak in what is now southern Mexico, and Uxmal and Chichén Itzá on what is now Mexico's Yucatan Peninsula.

Chichén Itzá   The great Mayan ceremonial site of Chichén Itzá (fig. 18–7) flourished from about A.D. 900 until the Spanish invasion. Its name means "mouth of the well of the Itzá" and it refers to the city's sacred *cenote,* a deep pool used for sacrificial offerings, in which have been found articles of jade, gold, wood, textiles, and ceramics. The city's ballcourt (fig. 18–8) is 475 feet (146 m) long, the largest built in Central America, and has sculptured relief panels showing a victorious team holding the severed heads of their opponents.

▲ **18–9** A limestone sacrificial altar called a *chacmool*, 5 ft. (1.5 m) long.

Players of the game, using only their upper arms and thighs, had to throw a hard rubber ball through the stone rings projecting from the side walls. Among the city's other structures are a three-sided building called (perhaps erroneously) the Nunnery and a circular tower called the Caracol ("snail") with a spiral staircase leading to an observation chamber, its windows focused on the movements of the planet Venus.

The heart of Chichén Itzá is the four-sided pyramid called the Castillo. It is 78 feet (24 m) high with a staircase on each side guarded by serpent heads. The temple chamber at the top is 20 feet (6 m) wide with a door in each side. Archaeologists discovered that the pyramid was built around an earlier, smaller one that remains intact, even including the temple on its top, and inside the antechamber of the temple was found a **chacmool**, a characteristic piece of ritual furniture, in the form of a reclining human figure and usually carved of stone (fig. 18–9). It was placed before an altar or a priest's throne, with its face turned toward the audience of worshippers, its knees raised, and holding on its stomach a container for offerings (such as the viscera of human sacrifices).

Beyond the antechamber, in the buried temple's inner chamber, was found a piece of furniture for the exclusive use of the ruler. Known as the Jaguar Throne (fig. 18–10), it is carved from limestone, painted with vermilion cinnabar, and

has teeth made of white flint, eyes of jade spheres, and on its body dozens of spots of jade disks.

Frescoes at Bonampak Bonampak is a Mayan word meaning "painted walls." Bonampak was a ceremonial center built in the tropical rain forest near Palenque. A three-room building there has pyramid-shaped interiors, their walls covered with murals. Because of water damage to the original paint, careful reconstructions have been made at the Museo Nacional de Antropologia, Mexico City, and the University of Florida Museum of Natural History, Gainesville (fig. 18–11). The paintings depict two events in the years A.D. 790 and 791: the first, the presentation of a child of the royal family to a group of nobles; the second, a celebration with music, dance, and costumes. The painting was applied to damp stucco. Primary colors dominate but have been joined by browns, pinks, and other hues. Black outlines and white highlights were added after the main color areas. Each room was entered by a single exterior door and benches were continuous around the rest of the walls to accommodate assemblies of nobles or priests.

Mayan Furniture The carvings and paintings of the Mayans, like those of other pre-Columbian cultures, show little furniture except for royalty. We have seen the Jaguar Throne, and there were similar thrones with jaguar heads at each end, and some with no heads. There were also some stools and slablike altar tables. Special attention was paid, however, to the design of stone threshing and food-grinding tables, perhaps because food preparation was a respected ritual. Some of these tables were three-legged (more stable than four on uneven floors, as the Greeks and Africans knew). One found at Mercedes in what is now Costa Rica (fig. 18–12) is carved in the shape of a jaguar with monkeys between his legs. Others depicted serpents, double-headed crocodiles, and other monsters.

The Moche (A.D. 100–750)

The Moche culture evolved in the dry deserts of the north coast of what is now Peru as early as A.D. 100, flourished c. A.D. 500, and endured for two centuries more. The Moche people built pyramids and palaces of plastered walls covered with polychrome murals, but they are perhaps best known today for their expressive pottery. Moche wares represent fruits and vegetables, animals, deer hunts, warriors in combat, and human sacrifices. Some portrait vessels (fig. 18–13) are topped with distinctive stirrup-shaped spouts that are unknown outside Central and South America. The Moche also practiced the casting of copper, silver, and gold and the alloying of metals, and they used looms to weave cotton and wool. By A.D. 1200, however, the Moche and other early cultures of the area had all been consolidated under the rule of a new group, the Incas.

The Incas (A.D. 1000–1476)

The Incas occupied parts of the modern South American nations of Peru, Ecuador, Bolivia, and Chile, with settlements along the Pacific coast and high in the Andes mountain range. The area's varied ecology—ranging from a warm, dry coast to cool highlands to hot, humid inland slopes—demanded a variety of building types, as did the availability of building materials. Adobe was much used on the coast, stone in the highlands, and wood on the eastern slopes. For

---

Viewpoints | FRANK LLOYD WRIGHT ON MAYAN STONEWORK

Frank Lloyd Wright often employed pre-Columbian American reliefs in his buildings, including the 1917 Barnsdall house and the 1923 Ennis house, both in Los Angeles. In a 1928 article published in *Architectural Record,* he wrote: "[M]ost building stone [is] like a sheet of beautiful paper, on which it is appropriate to cut images . . . to sink or raise traces of the imagination like a kind of human writing. . . . The Mayas used stone most sympathetically with its nature and the character of their environment. Their decoration was mostly *stone-built.* And when they carved it the effect resembled naturally enriched stone surfaces such as are often seen in the landscape."

important public buildings everywhere, however, the Incas used stone, and their skill with that material is famous.

Machu Picchu   The Inca capital was Cuzco, the home of the ruler of the Inca Empire (called the Inca), and it is still a thriving Peruvian city. There, the Incas built a Temple of the Sun decorated with gold ornaments. Their most dramatic building achievement, however, was the mountaintop citadel of Machu Picchu (fig. 18–14), built, between 1450 and 1530 A.D., almost 9,000 feet (2,800 m) above sea level. It was untouched by the Spaniards and lay undisturbed and unknown until discovered in 1911 by a young American historian (and later senator and governor of Connecticut), Hiram Bingham.

Surrounded by terraced platforms used for agriculture, the settlement is centered on an oblong plaza, the only level area. There are burial caves, storehouses, shrines in niches, and a number of buildings thought to have been used for religious rituals, including the Temple of the Sun and the Temple of the Three Windows (fig. 18–15). In the ruins of this last building we can see some of the remarkable Incan stonework. The

▼ **18–14** The ruined Incan citadel of Machu Picchu: temples and housing compounds on a terraced mountaintop; 1450–1530, Peru.

▲ **18–15** Remains of the interior of Machu Picchu's Temple of the Three Windows.
Mireille Vautier

granite blocks, quarried on the site, are often massive in size, with dimensions of more than 20 feet (6 m). Sometimes irregular in shape, these blocks have been ground to be so smooth that they fit together without mortar, their joints so tight that not even a knife blade can be inserted between them. There are some refinements to these walls not immediately noticed: They batter (tilt) inward at an angle of only about 5 degrees, their stones generally diminish in size as the wall rises, and they display a slight entasis (swelling), such as we saw in the columns of Greek temples. All these refinements add subtly to the impression of strength and height. The Incans also used stone for roads and drainage systems and for smaller objects such as bowls.

About sixty of Machu Picchu's buildings are thought to have been residences. The plan of the Incan house was generally rectangular, enclosing a single room with a roof of thatch, porous for the escape of smoke from heating or cooking. When, in other settlements, the walls were of adobe, carved niches within them held household wares. Hides or mats covered floors of beaten earth, and other mats covered doorways.

Textiles   Before the Incas, the Moche culture, the Chancay culture of Peru's central coast, and the Paracas culture of the Central Andes were all adept at textile design and production.

The Incas had no silk or flax (the fiber from which linen is made); they had cotton and an abundance of good wool (for their cool climate) from the llama and of much finer wool from the alpaca and the vicuña. So fine, indeed, was this wool, and so skillful its weaving, that the first Spanish invaders mistook it for silk. The cotton and wool varied in color—white, tan, yellow, brown—and for richer colorations animal and plant dyes were used—indigo for blue, mollusks for purple, and insect-derived cochineal for red (fig. 18–16). Finished textiles were also sometimes painted.

▲ **18–16** Detail of an Incan tapestry-woven wool fabric in natural and dyed colors.
Mereille Vautier

Not only was Inca weaving remarkably skilled, employing extremely fine threads and yarns, but it was also remarkably varied, including almost every kind of preindustrial weaving technique known anywhere: plain weaves, pattern weaves, tapestries, plaiting and braiding, twill, tie-dye, double cloth, gauze, reps, pile knots, embroidery, and brocade. The loom generally used was of the backstrap type, with the frame tied to a tree branch or other support. The weaver (usually, but not invariably, a woman) could then adjust the tension in the loom by leaning slightly forward or backward.

The woven products used in interiors included a thick and heavy baizelike woolen textile for bed and floor coverings. Perhaps the most unusual fabrics were those in which the colorful feathers of jungle birds were inserted quill first into the warp of the cloth being woven. Gold particles were also incorporated in Inca fabrics, as were gold bangles and tiny bells. The finest fabrics of all, however, woven only by specially trained "chosen women," were for the succession of elegant vicuña wool tunics for the Inca rulers, who wore each of them only once.

The Mixtecs (A.D. 1200–1521)

The Mixtec people, around A.D. 1000, conquered the Zapotec city at Mitla and made it a royal burial site. The ruined palace complex we see there today was built around 1400. Mitla lacks the dramatic site of Monte Albán or Machu Picchu, but here are thoughtful compositions, well-proportioned public squares, interesting interior spaces, and unsurpassed decorative panels. There are five groups of buildings at Mitla, all with long rectangular elements (concealing cruciform burial chambers beneath them) surrounding central plazas. The best preserved group, called the Column Group, consists of buildings on low pyramidal mounds arranged orthogonally around two plazas, their axes parallel but offset. Unlike those of the other groups, these two plazas are open at the corners as well as along one side. The central building facing the northern of the two plazas was entered through a room (fig. 18–17) that still displays the six cylindrical columns of monolithic volcanic stone that have given the group its modern name. These columns originally supported a flat wooden roof.

▲ **18–17** The Hall of Columns in the palace complex called the Column Group, Mitla, 14th century. The six columns, each a single piece of stone, supported a wooden roof that has disappeared.
Super Stock, Inc.

▲ **18–18** Three patterns of decorative frieze carved in stone, Column Group, Mitla; 14th century.
Adalberto Rios Getty Images, Inc.-Photodisc

The façades and courtyard walls of buildings in this group are decorated with horizontal friezes, each slightly overhanging the one below it (fig. 18–18). The repeated motifs of the friezes may remind us of Greece, being recognizable as key frets, spiral frets, rinceaux, and meanders, but here they have been treated in a resolutely geometric manner, most curved forms replaced by angular ones. Their construction is of two types, some carved into large stone panels, some assembled mosaiclike from small stones set into clay.

North America

Contact with Europeans was not as immediately destructive to the native cultures of North America as it had been in some parts of Central and South America. It did, however, often bring disruption and change. The sixteenth-century introduction of horses and firearms and the extermination of buffalo herds, for example, revolutionized the life of some tribes.

Determinants of North American Design

The cultural map of North America is even more complex that that of Central and South America. It is divided first into nine areas (such as Southwest, Plains, Plateau, and Arctic), each with its own geography, climate, and raw materials. These areas are further divided into twenty-two language groups (such as Algonquian, Muskogean, Eskimo-Aleut, and Siouan). Then there are finer divisions into more than 180 tribes (such as Cherokee, Acoma, Hopi, and Zuni). The tribes' mythology and religious ceremonies were similarly diverse, but many shared a common *animisim*, a belief that the visible world is pervaded by invisible spirits, and a related *shamanism*, a belief that in each tribe a *shaman*, or "medicine man," could achieve mystical communion with those spirits.

North American Architecture and Interiors

North American tribal architecture was of three chief types—defensive, ceremonial, and domestic—with some funerary and storage buildings in addition. For defense against rivals, tribes built ramparts of earth and palisades of vertical timbers. Similar enclosures were built around some ceremonial centers. For domestic use, nomadic tribes developed portable structures like the tepee, and more settled tribes constructed permanent buildings of wood, stone, and adobe.

Pueblos and Kivas   One type of communal settlement has been common to many tribes: the *pueblo*. In addition, one type of ceremonial chamber, the **kiva**, has also had widespread use. The Spanish gave the name *Pueblo* to some of the native peoples of the Southwest. Spelled with a lower case *p,* the word is also used for a tribal community and for a communal dwelling for the community. Developed in the ninth to fourteenth centuries, the pueblo is a large, terraced, multiroomed community house accommodating many uses. The Cliff Palace pueblo in Mesa Verde National Park, Colorado, is an example (fig. 18–19). This is the heartland of the Anasazi tribe, and the earliest dwellings here were pit houses entered through their roofs. When these were replaced by surface structures, some pit houses were kept for use as kivas. The society being matriarchal, these houses were owned and inherited by women. About A.D. 1150 more defensible locations were sought on the canyon shelves beneath overhanging cliffs, and the Mesa Verde village, built of stone, contained 220 one-room dwellings and 23 kivas. As this was a high percentage of kivas to dwellings, Mesa Verde may have served as a ceremonial center for several villages. It is thought to have been abandoned c. 1350, perhaps because of crop failure or invasion by other tribes. Other pueblos in more accessible locations were multilevel "apartment houses" with shared walls of stone or adobe, and with roof terraces that were used as the chief living areas (fig. 18–20); the entrance to each unit was by ladder.

▼ 18–19 Detail of the communal dwelling called the Cliff Palace at Mesa Verde, Colorado, c. 1150. The circular forms, now roofless, are underground *kivas*.

▲ 18–20 The Zuni Pueblo in western New Mexico, photographed in 1899.

National Anthropological Archives

▲ **18–21** Inside a circular kiva we see: at the bottom of the picture, the fire pit; behind it, a rectangular wall to deflect drafts; behind that, an opening to the ventilation shaft; and, encircling everything, raised seating platforms.

▲ **18–22** A pair of *tepee* occupied by people of the Crow tribe. The one at left may have had its cover partly removed to catch the breeze.
National Anthropological Archives

We have mentioned the ceremonial chambers, often built within the community house complex, called **kivas**. They were used not only for rituals but also for storytelling, weaving, and instructing children. The kiva was usually underground, entered by a ladder through its roof, and usually, but not always, circular. The circular kiva walls (now roofless) can be seen in the ruins of the Mesa Verde pueblo (see fig. 18–19).

The kiva interior is lined with stone blocks or adobe brick and typically contains some standard features (fig. 18–21). At its central and lowest point there is a small sand-filled pit, called a *sipapu*, which symbolizes the prehistoric emergence of the Pueblo people from the underworld. Near it is a larger pit in which fires are maintained during the ceremonies, representing the legendary fire with which life began. A ventilation shaft to the outside has an opening near the fire pit to clear the interior of smoke (although the roof hole for the ladder is also left open), and a slab of stone or adobe rises between the fire pit and the ventilator opening in order to block drafts. Graduated tiers of seating circle these central elements, the priests being seated closest to the center on the lowest level (symbolizing their humility), novices on a higher level, and uninitiated spectators on the highest level of all.

Dwellings The largest of the North American dwellings were the *longhouses* built by the Iroquoi and Huron tribes of the Northeast cultural area as early as the fourteenth century. Built of wood frames (basically bent saplings) covered with sheets of bark, these could be more than 100 feet long, and traces of one more than 300 feet long have been found near Syracuse, New York. They were essentially barracks with rows of sleeping bunks along each side and central aisles for cooking and other chores. They were occupied year-round by extended families and could be lengthened to accommodate newly married couples.

More typically, the peoples of North America lived in single-room, single-family houses, augmented by community facilities such as the kiva. There are many types of houses, but among the most distinctive are the tepee and the wigwam.

The *tepee*, also spelled *tipi*, was popular with tribes such as the Crow, the Blackfeet, and the Sioux in the Plains area. It was a conical tent of wooden poles covered with buffalo hides (fig. 18–22). It usually had an opening at the top to allow smoke from a central fire to escape. It was easily movable, which suited the seminomadic lives of these tribes.

The *wigwam* was a house type used by such Midwest tribes as the Chippewa and Winnebago. It was usually round in plan and dome-shaped (fig. 18–23), made of saplings arched over, tied together, and covered with reed mats, bark, or thatch. They varied in diameter from about 7 to about

▲ **18–23** A *wigwam* of the Winnebago tribe, covered with reed mats.
Nebraska State Historical Society

their household goods, the lower one for the men and their tools. The snow shell was often lined with animal skins, held by cords drawn through the dome and tied to outside toggles.

North American Decorative Arts

The skills of the Native American artists and craftsmen are evident in many media. They excelled at ceramics, the carving of turquoise, basketry, and textiles. Their other talents included wood carving, rock painting, sand painting, wall painting inside and out, and the production of spoons made of horn, pipes made of pewter, tools made both of iron and antlers (bone), beadwork, and leatherwork.

20 feet. A gap between mats was often fireproofed with baked clay and served as a smoke hole. Sleeping mats surrounded a central fire, and other furnishings might include earthenware pots, bark buckets, maple bowls, and a hardwood mortar and pestle. When moving on to another campsite, their owners might leave the naked wigwam frames in place and carry only their household goods and rolled-up mats.

Other house types include the *chickee*, popular in the Southeast, an open-sided hut with a broad-eaved thatched roof and a living platform raised above the ground, and the conical *hogan* of the Navajo, sometimes built of stone and sometimes of logs.

In the arctic the *igloo*, or *iglu*, was a dome built of blocks of snow stacked in an ascending spiral. It was entered through a low vaulted passage, its openings at either end blocked by hanging skins. Inside a large igloo, the floor was generally stepped into two levels, the upper one for the women and

▲ **18–24** The hole in the bottom of this Mimbres bowl shows that it has been "killed."
Mimbres Bowl #4278. Courtesy of Dr. Steven A. LeBlanc, University of California, Los Angeles/The Mimbres Foundation/Peabody Museum of Archaeology.

Ceramics   For most tribes—certainly those in the Southwest and in the eastern half of North America—ceramics (specifically earthenware, since the materials for porcelain were not available) were an important part of daily life, ceremony, and trade. Major pottery traditions include those of the ancient Hohokam and Mogollon people of the prehistoric Southwest and the later Anasazi people of the same area. Related to those and most celebrated of all are the Mimbres wares of southwestern New Mexico. The first Mimbres pottery vessels (fig. 18–24) seem to have been made about A.D. 200, the last ones about 1100, and between those dates they progressed from plain brown wares to burnished red ones and, about 650, when large ceremonial structures were being built, to the painted bowls that are so admired today. Among the painted bowls there was a progression from geometric patterns to abstracted representation. Many of the bowl paintings depict animals and birds, and some show men (perhaps priests) dressed in bat costumes or with antlers on their heads. In every case, the images are simple but intense.

We do not fully understand the significance of these bowls

to the Mimbres. Bowls were placed upside down over the faces of the dead, who were buried beneath the floors of their families' houses. We also know that the potters who made them felt that when they completed a bowl, they breathed life into it. When it had outlived its usefulness or when its owner died, a hole was broken in its center, "killing" the bowl. Some Mimbres patterns are still in use today by the potters of the Acoma and Laguna pueblos.

Turquoise   Turquoise (fig. 18–25) is a semiprecious gemstone, its name derived from the French term for Turkish, because the stone was imported from Persia to Europe by way of Turkey. Just as many Central and South American people, especially the Olmecs, admired jade work, many North Americans, particularly the Navajo and Hopi in the southwest, admired turquoise work. Both considered it a defense against evil spirits. The stone is found in what are now the states of New Mexico, Nevada, Arizona, Utah, and

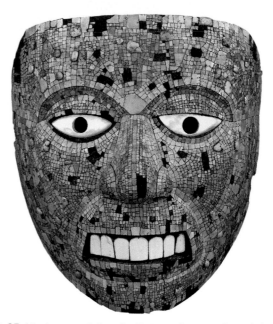

▲ **18–25** Mexican mask faced with turquoise mosaic and shell, fifteenth century, 6½ in. (17 cm) high.
© The Trustees of the British Museum

Tools & Techniques | BASKET WEAVING

Basketry is one of the world's oldest crafts. Egyptian baskets for grain storage have been unearthed and dated to 5000 B.C. Traditionally, baskets are made of plant material: roots, grasses, twigs, straw, or osiers (willow). There are two basic basketry techniques, weaving and coiling. In the first there are two groups of elements (as in weaving textiles), the warp and the woof, held together by interlacing. In the second there is a single element that is coiled in a spiral and held together by sewing. These two techniques have myriad variations, of course. In *lattice* weaving, a network of strips crossing at right angles is fixed by wrapping the intersections with cord. In *imbricated* coiling, a strip of soft material is folded back and forth over the stitched coils. With multicolored material, there are also myriad variations in design, with crosses, stars, checkerboards, and patterns resembling the Greek fret occurring often. And the plant material can be decorated by interweaving other materials, such as strips of animal hide, feathers, insect wings, teeth, and shells. Finally, in North America, for each native basket there was a symbolic meaning or story, fully known only to the basketmaker.

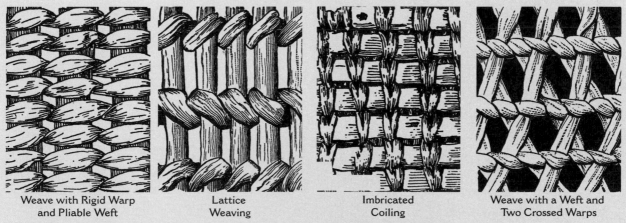

Weave with Rigid Warp and Pliable Weft

Lattice Weaving

Imbricated Coiling

Weave with a Weft and Two Crossed Warps

Otis Tufton Mason, "American Indian Basketry," Dover Publications, Inc. New York, 1988, p. 68, 71, 73, 101.

▲ **18–26** A coiled Pima basket tray from Arizona with a maze pattern, 10 in. (24.8 cm) in diameter.
Coiled Akimel O'odham (Pima) basketry tray with maze design. Arizona. Diam. 24.8 cm. Courtesy, National Museum of the American Indian, Smithsonian Institution 11/0415 (CDT00077). Photo by David Heald

It was one of the earliest of the crafts that they developed. Their first pots, in fact, were made by pressing baskets into damp clay, and, by baking clay-covered or clay-lined baskets, fireproof cooking containers were made. Clay-covered basketry was even used to make huts for dwellings and grain storage.

Every tribe and pueblo had its own basketry tradition. But most outstanding of all, perhaps, was the basketry of the Pima (fig. 18–26) in southern Arizona. In every case, basketmaking (as well as much of the other labor) was done by the women of the society.

Colorado. In appearance, it is similar to jade, but more opaque and more lustrous.

Turquoise with high copper content can be a bright sky blue, which is the most highly prized; that with high iron content can be grayish green, less prized. Softer than jade, it is much easier to form into jewelry, amulets, or decorative inlay.

Basketry   The decorative art that reached its highest level of attainment in the hands of the native peoples was basketry.

Textiles   The textile expressions of pre-Columbian North America are many and varied. They include the fringed "raven's-tail" robes of the Northwest Coast cultures, and the later Chilkat blankets or "dancing robes" of the same people. The painted cloths of the Anasazi are notable. From Carolina, there were blankets woven of opossum hair. From Ohio and Illinois, there were the plaited reed mats of the Ottowas and the rush matting of the Chippewas.

The most famous today are the textile products of the Navajo in northeast Arizona, the largest of the present-day American tribes. Outstanding textiles can be seen in the tapestry-woven Navajo blanket, adapted from the Spanish serape, and in the Navajo rug (fig. 18–27). These reached a peak of achievement in the nineteenth century, and fine examples are still produced today.

▶ **18–27** Navajo wool rug with a tapestry weave. New Mexico, late 19th century, 4 ft. (1.2 m) long.
© The Trustees of The British Museum

Summary: Pre-Columbian American Design

We have seen that Central and South America were home to a variety of cultures and North America to a variety of tribes, each with distinct traits and accomplishments. All these, however, share some history and character.

Looking for Character

With rare exceptions, such as the ill-fated Minoans on Crete, the civilizations we have seen so far had no abrupt end, but slowly evolved and changed as they aged. The breaks between the pre-Columbian civilizations and the European-based ones that replaced them caused relatively little of pre-Columbian life and thought to be assimilated into the world familiar to us today. Even when these native American societies were flourishing, they were somewhat isolated from one another and totally isolated (it is generally assumed) from other continents. Independent of outside influences and diversions, these people developed deeply felt connections to the metaphysical world that was for them ever-present and all-pervasive. These connections affected all that they designed.

Looking for Quality

On the scale of urban centers and architectural groupings, we see quality in generously scaled concepts of open space and the relationships of buildings to their surroundings; Teotihuacán and Monte Albán are southern examples, Mesa Verde a northern one. In individual buildings and interiors, particularly those with overt ceremonial use such as pyramids, altars, and kivas, we see quality in the careful accommodation of ritual. But for many of these peoples, no physical place or object was wholly secular; in all that they designed—stone walls, jade figures, tents, pots, baskets, rugs—there was a respect for materials infused with invisible spirits, though we cannot know all that their designers intended to express.

Making Comparisons

Having emphasized the metaphysical significance of pre-Columbian design, it may be interesting to compare it with other deeply religious design, such as Gothic and Islamic design. Both of those sought a dematerialization of physical structure in order to emphasize the otherworldly, while pre-Columbian design sought to express the spirit residing in the material world. It is more interested in tactile reality and in the true nature of stone, clay, turquoise, or reed. Pre-Columbian art is supreme in its respect for its materials.

Comparisons of a very different sort will be implicit in the next chapter, as we see people of a different background dealing with the same American geography, resources, and climate and yet producing design of completely new character.

Early America

Sixteenth to Eighteenth Centuries

19

"I called the New World into existence to redress the balance of the Old."

— George Canning (1770–1827), British statesman

The first permanent European settlement in what would become the United States was Saint Augustine, Florida, established in 1565 by the Spanish, and the first permanent English settlement was established at Jamestown, Virginia in 1607. They would be joined in the next two centuries by settlers from France, Germany, Holland, Sweden, and Finland. "Early American" has become the most commonly used term for the collective culture of their settlements, even though there were a great many inhabitants of other groups who were here earlier.

Determinants of Early American Design

The most obvious determinant of the society, customs, and design inclinations of the earliest colonists was their national origin. For all aspects of their culture the colonists looked back toward the lands from which they had come, but the influence of their various national heritages on the design of the

New World was tempered by the conditions of their new home (fig. 19–1).

Geography and Natural Resources

The earliest colonies were along the Atlantic coast, from present-day Florida to Maine. For the newcomers from long-settled Europe, America must have been terrifying but liberating: great mountains, rivers, and plains, mostly virgin and vast, and largely unoccupied. The land exacted hardship in its taming, but it offered a wealth of hardwoods, softwoods, dirt for adobe, reeds for thatch, clay for brick and tile, and stone. Some stone and brick were also brought from Holland to New York (originally New Amsterdam) as ships' ballast. Raw material for glassmaking, including wood to fuel the furnaces, was readily available. Oyster shells were available in some places for making lime, but the resultant plaster was of poor quality. The discovery of gold and silver was one of the objectives of colonization, and the silversmith became the foremost artisan in many colonial settlements. Iron and copper were also found, and from them, the alloys of pewter, brass, and bronze were made. Attention to agriculture was a prime necessity, and the untamed land proved abundantly fertile. Early in colonial history it was discovered that the

◀ **19–1** Detail of a painted floor from the Humphreys house, Dorchester, Massachusetts, simulating a woven carpet, 1634. Courtesy of Historic New England

429

farming of tobacco, adopted from the Native Americans, fostered a highly profitable trade with Europe.

Religion

The search for religious freedom was another objective of many colonists. Major contributions to Early American design were made by religious groups with independent customs and cultures, though all of them were Christian. The Mennonites (also called Amish) from Germany settled in Pennsylvania and were noted for their colorful quilts, samplers, rugs, and furniture. The Moravians from Czechoslovakia settled in Pennsylvania and North Carolina, where they produced ceramics and furniture. The Shakers from England first settled in New York, and their religious philosophy created interiors and furniture of admirable restraint. Pennsylvania had been founded in 1692 by William Penn as a colony for the Quakers (The Religious Society of Friends), who began building simple meetinghouses. Perhaps most influential of all were the Puritans from England who wanted to free the Protestant church from what it considered nonreligious activities. By 1640 there were thirty-five Puritan churches in New England. The Puritan belief in frugality, discipline, self-reliance, and industry led to design that was appropriately serious and severe. On the whole, Early American religious beliefs did not encourage fancy or frivolity.

History

Dissatisfaction with Europe had caused most of the colonization of America. And continued dissatisfaction with some aspects of the ties with Europe led to the American Revolution and the War of Independence (1776–83), during which the colonies declared themselves the United States of America.

The young nation did not long stay confined to the eastern seaboard. In 1803 Thomas Jefferson arranged the Louisiana Purchase, an acquisition of land from France that nearly doubled the size of American territory. It began a progress westward toward the Pacific that was a national obsession into the nineteenth century. As older settled areas enjoyed increased civility and more refined design, there remained for more than a century an American frontier.

Colonial design ambitions were at first to be as European as possible; colonial design realities, however, were tempered by the new conditions, which demanded and offered new solutions. And with unification, the sense of European superiority began to fade, replaced by pride in America and its own design achievements.

Early American Architecture and Interiors

If the native tribes had loved the country and felt communion with its spirit, the new Americans both loved and feared it; for them it was a resource to use but also a challenge to overcome. They were determined not to adapt to nature but to adapt nature to their own desires, which were rational, practical, and firmly based on the experiences and hopes of their ancestors. The design of the new Americans had as its chief goal the conquest and transformation of their new surroundings.

Even though unified in this aggressive attitude toward nature and eventually unified politically, early Americans necessarily designed in different ways. Design in the urbanized east was different from design on the western frontier. The most plentiful building material in the northern colonies was wood; in Pennsylvania it was stone, and in the South brick and adobe. The North moved toward an industrialized economy with a large middle class, the South toward an agrarian one with wealth concentrated in large plantation holdings. Climates with snow suggested steep roofs; climates with hot sun suggested shady verandas.

Even more dramatic changes came with passing time as the country grew and prospered. Some scholars divide the design of early American into three periods: Colonial, Georgian, and Federal. Some experts divide this design history in accordance with a succession of stylistic influences, coming chiefly from England: Jacobean in the seventeenth century, William and Mary in the first quarter of the eighteenth century, Queen Anne in the second quarter, Chippendale in the third; and then at last the emergence of the country's own Federal style. For our purposes, we shall simply make a single division between the Colonial period—before the Declaration of Independence in 1776—and the Federal period that came after it. American designers of the first period were dominated by England. American designers of the second, while still influenced by England (and France, because of its help in the war for independence) developed confidence in their own taste, choosing eclectically whatever they wanted from Europe and combining it with elements of their own invention.

Period and Date	Political Events	Design Achievements	Architects, Designers, and Craftsmen
Early Colonial, before c. 1720	Jamestown Colony, 1607; Plymouth Colony, 1620; Massachusetts Bay Colony, 1630; English take New York from Dutch, 1644	Wren Building, Williamsburg, 1695–1702; Governor's Palace, Santa Fe, 1610; Capitol, Williamsburg, 1701–5; Governor's Palace, Williamsburg, 1706–20	John Coney, 1655–1722; Caspar Wistar, 1696–1752
Late Colonial or Georgian, c. 1720–87	American Revolution, 1775–83; Declaration of Independence, 1776; first Shaker colony founded, 1776	Westover, 1730–34; Faneuil Hall, Boston, 1740–42; Redwood Library, Newport, 1747; King's Chapel, Boston, 1749; Parlange, Louisiana, 1750; St. Michael's, Charleston, 1751; first California mission, 1769; first Monticello, 1769–82; Mt. Vernon, 1757–87, Virginia State Capitol, 1785	Peter Harrison, 1716–75; William Savery, c. 1721–87; John Goddard, 1723–85; "Baron" Stiegel, 1729–85; John Townsend, 1732–1809; Paul Revere, 1735–1818; John Frederick Amelung, 1741–98; Thomas Jefferson, 1743–1826; Samuel McIntire, 1757–1811
Federal, after 1787	Federal Constitutional Convention, 1787; Constitution ratified, 1788; first meeting of U.S. Congress, 1789	White House, 1792–1801; U.S. Capitol, 1792–1830; Massachusetts State House, 1795–97; second Monticello, 1796–1809	William Thornton, 1761–1828; James Hoban, 1762–1831; Charles Bulfinch, 1763–1844; Benjamin Henry Latrobe, 1766–1820; Duncan Phyfe, 1768–1854

The Colonial Period (1565–1776)

Written records by colonists, including Captain John Smith, the leader at Jamestown in 1608 and 1609, indicate that the first English settlers built huts or tents of clay, mud, bark, and tree limbs, roofing them with thatch. The first church in the colony was a tent made of rotten sailcloth. It is thought that the Swedish, who came from a land of small wooden houses and settled in Deaware in 1638, introduced the log cabin to America. And so the first century of European settlement in North America was characterized by such unpretentious architecture and interiors, with little thought of design beyond the most utilitarian needs. In these log houses of early Colonial times, all rooms were multipurpose rooms; it would have been unusual to see a room without a bed in it. The earliest seventeenth-century houses consisted of a single all-purpose room with a large fireplace that served for both cooking and heating.

Construction in most of the northern colonies was of wood. The earliest wood joinery was simple, using solid woods and mortise-and-tenon joints (see table 2–1). Sometimes puddled mud filled the spaces between the vertical wood structural members called **studs**. Thin wedge-shaped planks long enough to span several studs, called **clapboards**, were overlapped for exterior sheathing, fastened to the studs with hand-forged nails with large flat heads. An alternative to clapboard was a wall faced with wood shingles; more popular with the Dutch settlers than with the English, these shingles were much larger, rougher, and far less uniform than today's mill-cut shingles. The earliest Colonial roofing was **thatch**, or straw matting, though thatch was short-lived, leaked in heavy rains, and was a fire hazard when dry. By the last quarter of the seventeenth century, the shingled roof had become standard.

Even when the construction was of mud brick, which in the earliest days was disappointingly porous, exteriors were often faced with clapboard. Brick manufacture became more skillful, however, and in the eighteenth century became the standard for the middle and southern colonies. Brick offered

TABLE 19–1　Brick Bonds

There are two chief ways of laying a brick. When it is laid with its long face visible, it is called a stretcher. When laid with its short face visible, it is called a header. These can be combined in different ways to produce different patterns called bonds. A pattern using only stretchers is called common bond. Alternating rows of stretchers and headers constitutes English bond. Stretchers and headers alternating in every row produces Flemish bond. And a variation of English bond, with stretchers of alternate rows not aligned, so that a diaper pattern of crossing diagonal joints occurs, is Dutch cross bond.

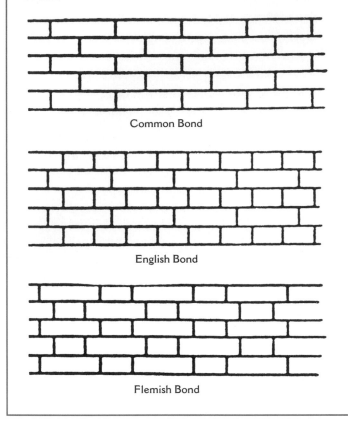

Common Bond

English Bond

Flemish Bond

Dutch Cross Bond

a variety of decorative effects: Bricks could be made in a range of colors, from pale yellow to red to dark brown, they could be glazed or not, and they could be laid in a variety of bonds (table 19–1).

When plaster became available but was still expensive, only the inside surfaces of the exterior walls of the house were sealed with it. In the two-room house that succeeded the one-room cabin, the interior walls remained sheathed in wood planking, at first oak and, after 1700, pine (fig. 19–2). Three plastered walls and one wooden wall therefore became a characteristic feature of the rooms of the two-room house.

The wood wall was of vertically placed planks. Cut from the first-growth trees of the virgin American forests, these were of great width, sometimes more than 3 feet (1 m) wide. To compensate for shrinkage of the planks, a **tongue** was cut along one edge of each plank to fit into **a groove** of the ad-

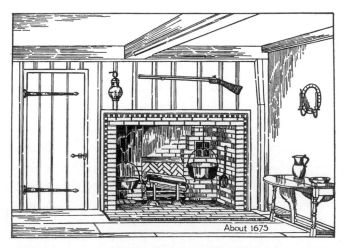

▲ 19–2 A Colonial American interior, c. 1675. The fireplace wall is faced with vertical pine planking, and the exposed structure includes a corner post and a summer beam supporting the low ceiling.
Gilbert Werlé/New York School of Interior Design

joining plank. Simple ornamental moldings were sometimes added to cover the joints. All the woodwork was left in a natural finish, and because pine becomes red with age, the walls were warm in color and rather dark. For expediency in building, the rooms had low ceilings, seldom more than 7 feet (2.1 m) high.

Windows were first of the casement type, the double-hung sliding sash not appearing until after 1700, and window panes (rectangular or diamond-shaped) were separated by either lead or wood bars. When glass was not available or was too costly, the panes—as we saw in Gothic England—were filled with **isinglass** (mica) or oiled paper. Some windows had no filling at all, being closed only with blinds or shutters.

The flooring of the ground floor was at first simply earth, but pine, oak, and chestnut planks of varying widths were soon adopted, and stone was used in some cases. Each of the two rooms in the simplest architecture had a fireplace centered in the wood wall, the two fireplaces sharing one central chimney. When the room was large, the ceiling span was cut in half by a **summer beam** (from the French *somme*, meaning "burden"), one end of it resting on the masonry chimney, the other on a post in the outside wall. Under the pitched roof there was often an attic reached by a steep stair.

Horton House, Southold, NY The Benjamin Horton House was built in 1649 in Southold, on the North Fork of Long Island, but was moved to nearby Cutchogue a dozen years later. It is thought to be the oldest dwelling still standing in New York State. Our first impression of the exterior (fig. 19–3) is of a vast expanse of clapboard with a few tiny windows. This suggests either that the occupants liked very dark rooms (unlikely) or that large window areas were beyond the owner's budget. At some point a one-story addition had been added to the back of the house, but this has not been preserved. While this addition was technically a lean-to, or an addition with its own roof, it was also common in early New England to incorporate such additional space under the main roof. In this manner, such a house would have a short pitch in front, like the Horton House, but a long pitch sweeping close to the ground in back, where the additions were incorporated. This house form was called a saltbox because of the container it resembled. The Horton roof is shingled, although the shingles we see today are not the originals.

The front door and brick chimney of the Horton House are slightly off center to provide each of the two main floors with one large room and one small room. On the ground

▲ **19–3** The Horton House, built in Southold, New York, in 1649. Its restored exterior reproduces the original clapboard siding and small three-section casement windows.
Stanley P. Mixon/Historic American Buildings Survey, Division of Prints & Photographs, Library of Congress

▲ **19–4** The Horton House parlor. A summer beam supports the low ceiling. Furniture includes a gate-leg table and rush-seated chairs.
Stanley P. Mixon/Historic American Buildings Survey, Division of Prints & Photographs, Library of Congress

floor the larger room is the parlor (fig. 19–4) and the smaller a keeping room for cooking, dining, and other family activities. The two rooms on the second floor, reached by a winding stairway, are both bedrooms, and the stairway continues to a single open space in the attic.

The parlor is a room roughly 20 feet (6 m) square with a sturdy corner post and a summer beam supporting its center. The outside walls are plastered between their studs, and the ceiling is plastered between its joists. (In other houses, the plaster would cover the studs and joists.) The floor is of wood planks in random widths, and, as was typical, there was no rug on the floor, such an item being considered much too fine to walk on. The item called a "rug" was at this time a bedcover, and the item called a "carpet" was a table cover (see fig. 19–24). Near one of the small casement windows is a spinning wheel. There being no closets in seventeenth-century American houses, chests and cupboards were needed. Around a gate-leg table are rush-seated chairs of slat-back and banister-back designs (see fig. 19–15) with turned legs, but this furniture is probably of a slightly later date than the house.

Mid–seventeenth-century building types in addition to houses and their various outbuildings were schools, trading posts, taverns, inns, and buildings for defense and for assembly. Buildings for defense against unfriendly Native American tribes were forts, which might be built of heavy logs, and blockhouses, which were often square in plan with pyramidal roofs. Buildings for assembly included the meetinghouse, the architectural focus of almost every New England village. It served as a church on Sunday and as a community center every other day. It was almost always a plain building, for Gothic drama and ornament would have been offensive to the straight-laced Puritans. In Virginia, however, where the Anglican church was established, and in Florida, where the Spanish settlers had Roman Catholic traditions, churches were built for religious use only and ornament was welcome.

Back in England, James I (reigned 1603–1625), for whom the **Jacobean** style was named, oversaw the chief architectural monument of his reign: Inigo Jones's Banqueting House in London (see fig. 16–9), which introduced the elements of classical design in a manner heavily influenced by Palladio. But such developments were not felt immediately in the faraway colonies. The first buildings in America that could be called **Palladian** would not be built for another century: Drayton Hall (built 1738–42) in Charleston, South Carolina, with its two-story columned portico, and Peter Harrison's Redwood Library (built 1749–50) in Newport, Rhode Island.

In the eighteenth century, houses grew larger and their plans more complex. The four-room, single-chimney house was developed, with a fireplace in the interior corner of each room; then the plan with rooms accessed from a central hallway and with a chimney on each side; then the larger house with rooms devoted to single purposes: parlors, dining rooms, kitchens, bedrooms. Movable sashes were now used for windows (see Tools & Techniques: Windows and Window Glass, page 459), and their rectangular panes replaced earlier diamond-shaped ones. Wall paneling was frequent, sometimes with plaster above.

As in England, the Jacobean style was followed by the more ornate **William and Mary** style, though—again—it came later to America. Similarly, **Queen Anne**, bringing a new simplicity of design, was a reigning style in America only after Anne had ceased her reign in England in 1714. The elaborate turnings and ornament of the earlier styles began to be seen as fussy and old-fashioned, and the shapely curves of the Queen Anne style were seen as beautiful and fresh. The new style's emphasis on form and outline rather than on decorative detail, carving, and gilt must have seemed pleasantly sympathetic to the limited size and grandeur of the American house.

Georgian is another term that needs to be acknowledged, even though we shall not use it here to denote a period of American design. Historically, it refers to the time when England was ruled by kings named George—that is, from 1714, when George I took the throne, until 1830, when George IV died. (George V and George VI did not reign until the twentieth century.) Stylistically, it is usually applied to design with a classical aspect. By 1670, in fact, brick houses were being built in Virginia and other southern states with evidences of classical trim in their interiors. Such details came later to the New England colonies. In the last years of the eighteenth century, the interior wood walls changed from vertical boards to rectangular panels with some pretension to architectural forms. Rooms in all but the most modest houses had by this time been given specific uses: bedrooms, kitchens, dining rooms, even sewing and reading rooms. American architecture and interiors began to display surprising sophistication and elegance. Indeed, it is difficult to believe that the Horton house of 1649 and the Georgian

Governor's Palace in Williamsburg, Virginia, of 1706–20, originated in the same country only half a century apart. In that half century the growth in Early American wealth, comfort, and design sophistication was remarkable.

That growth would continue: By the first years of the eighteenth century, the economic condition of the new country had improved and the struggle to tame the wilderness had been largely finished. The population of the North American colonies more than doubled between 1730 and 1760, and their prosperity grew as well. A new group of immigrants was attracted, many of them from England and Scotland, including skilled craftsmen, carpenters, and cabinetmakers. They would contribute greatly to the increasingly luxurious interiors of the colonies.

The Governor's Palace, Williamsburg, VA   Williamsburg was laid out as the capital of Virginia in 1699 and remained the capital until 1779. It is the site of a number of notable early buildings, many restored in the early 1930s through the funding of John D. Rockefeller, Jr., with the firm of Perry, Shaw, & Hepburn as restoration architects. The town's main thoroughfare, Duke of Gloucester Street, was, at 98 feet (30 m), the widest in the colonies. One end terminated at the Wren Building of the College of William and Mary, built between 1695 and 1702, perhaps to plans by Sir Christopher Wren (who never came to America). The other end terminated at the Capitol building, built 1699–1705. This layout, emphasizing college and government, was a democratic departure from European precedent, which would usually have given such places of honor to palace and church. Only a cross street leads to the Governor's Palace, built 1706–20.

The Governor's Palace (fig. 19–5) was a name first given derisively to the governor's house because of its extravagant cost and sumptuousness. It was begun just one year after the Capitol was finished, but it was already much more Georgian in character than the Capitol, where twin semicylindrical towers recalled medieval precedents. Its design is at least partly the work of Alexander Spotswood (1676–1740), the colonial governor of Virginia between 1706 and 1720.

The Palace is of a house type called a double pile because it has two rows of rooms—in this case, a row on either side of a central hall. Inside the Palace's classically regular exterior, the entrance hall has walnut paneling and flooring of black and white marble. This hall and the other rooms of the original palace have marble fireplaces. Extending from the back of the building is a wing added between 1749 and 1751

▲ **19–5** Governor's Palace, Williamsburg, Virginia, built 1706–20. We see it as it was restored in the 1930s.
© Robert Harding World Imagery/CORBIS All Rights Reserved

using plans by Richard Taliaferro. It holds a large ballroom and a smaller supper room, both with lofty coved ceilings, crystal chandeliers, and lavish details, though some of those visible now have had to be based on conjecture, both the Palace and the Capitol having been devastated by fire. One might expect these public rooms, meant for entertaining the colonial aristocracy, to be elaborately finished, but fine finishes and furnishings extended also to a typical private bedroom upstairs (fig. 19–6). On the fireplace mantel, between fluted pilasters, is a set of porcelain *garniture de cheminée*, probably imported from China (see "Porcelain" in Chapter 11). The bed hangings are in cotton *toile de Jouy*, a fabric popular in France (see fig. 15–40) and probably brought from there later in the century. Even in this fine room, however, there is a touch of Colonial period

thrift: The rug is a bed round, not rectangular but U-shaped so that costly fabric is not wasted under the bed.

In its day, the Governor's Palace must have been the most elaborate residence in the colonies, but it was not alone in its luxury. Other fine Colonial period houses in Virginia alone included the Lee family's Stratford Hall of 1725–30 on the Potomac River, Westover of 1730–34 on the James River (some of whose ornament we shall see in fig. 19–13), and Carter's Grove of 1750–53 in James City County. President Washington would begin construction on Mount Vernon in 1757, and President Jefferson would begin the first stage of Monticello in 1769, but neither house would be finished until the Federal period. In all these examples, academic versions of classical architecture were applied to important features, such as the mantels of fireplaces in important rooms (fig. 19–7).

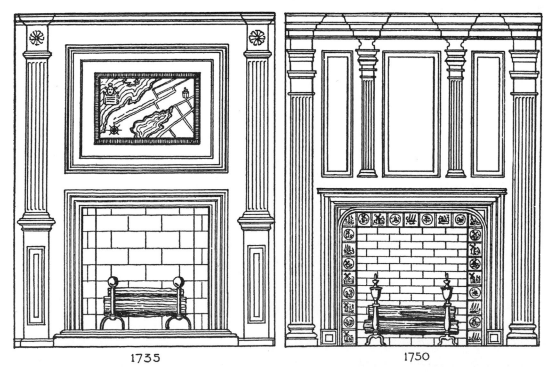

1735

1750

◀19-7 Two eighteenth-century American mantel treatments showing the early use of architectural elements such as pilasters and moldings.
Gilbert Werlé/New York School of Interior Design

The Federal Period (1776–1800)

The American Revolution absorbed all the colonists' attention and resources, halting the development of design just when rapid style changes were occurring in England. It was not until several years after peace was restored that American design began again to reflect the changes in foreign fashion.

The newly formed United States welcomed the **Adam** style, and the influence of Hepplewhite and Sheraton continued. Grateful for France's aid in their own revolution, Americans warmly sympathized with France during her struggle toward democracy, and President Jefferson's Louisiana Purchase in 1803 made U.S. citizens of many French settlers. There was a consequent fashion for French styles. They did not displace the prevailing English forms, however, but they were frequently fused with them.

Near the end of the eighteenth century, a dramatically different style of architecture and urban design was introduced to America—the **Neoclassical**. It would greatly affect interior design, and in America, the manifestation of this style would be called the Classical Revival style. It would become prevalent in official buildings of the eighteenth and early nineteenth centuries.

It began with Thomas Jefferson, then American ambassador to the court of Louis XVI at Versailles and not yet president, who in 1785 designed a new Virginia State Capitol for Richmond (fig. 19–8), the capital having recently been moved there from Williamsburg. With the help of French architect Charles-Louis Clérisseau, who guided him on a tour of European classical architecture (as he had earlier guided English architect Robert Adam), Jefferson based the design directly on an ancient Roman monument he had seen on his travels through France, the Maison Carrée at Nîmes. It was

the first pure example, not only in America but in the world, of the classical revival. We have seen Neoclassical design in the Petit Trianon at Versailles (see fig. 15–16) and in the Banqueting House in London (see fig. 16–9), but this was something far more radical. Jefferson was not merely using moldings, pilasters, and chair legs to refer to classical architecture; he was instead building a Roman temple to serve a modern function. The Virginia State Capitol began a movement that would dominate the first half of the following century.

In 1789, eight years after the end of the Revolutionary War, Congress voted to build a capital city for the young nation, strategically placed between the northern and southern

▲ **19–8** The Virginia State Capitol, Richmond, designed by Thomas Jefferson in Roman style in 1785.
Virginia Tourism Corporation

states, and President Washington appointed Pierre-Charles L'Enfant as its designer. L'Enfant (1754–1825) had been born in Paris into a family of artists who had served the French court, and he grew up well acquainted with André Le Nôtre's vast gardens at Versailles, with their long vistas and radiating avenues. L'Enfant had come to America to fight in its war for independence and had stayed on. Remembering Versailles, he devised the city's present plan of broad radial avenues with circular "rotaries" where the avenues intersected with an already existing rectangular street grid. We seldom think of city plans as having period styles, but L'Enfant's was clearly a Neoclassical one. Within it he provided sites for two important buildings, the President's house (the White House), which was begun in 1792, and the U.S. Capitol, begun in 1793. Their interiors would be completed in the nineteenth century.

Monticello, Albemarle County, VA

Monticello, Jefferson's own house on a Virginia hilltop near Charlottesville, was, like his Virginia State Capitol, a demonstration of his disdain for the Georgian style and his enthusiasm for a more correct classicism. It also reflected his taste for—and knowledge of—the latest artistic developments in Europe and the principles outlined by Palladio, which he knew from a 1715 English translation of Palladio's 1570 *Four Books of Architecture.*

The first version of Monticello was begun in 1769, when Jefferson was twenty-five, and there was scarcely a time from then until his death in 1826 when some construction or alteration was not taking place there. The first phase of building, however, was generally completed by 1782. This initial scheme was for a central block with two-story porticoes on both the entrance and garden fronts; half-octagonal bays were added to the ends of the building in 1777.

When the second phase began in 1796, Jefferson had returned from his years in France full of new ideas. His addition obliterated all but the central three rooms of the original house, enlarged it from a total of eight rooms to twenty-one, gave it the more reposeful appearance of a single story, and added a dome above the parlor on the garden front. The design of this second Monticello, familiar to us because of its appearance on our U.S. nickel, has an interior as distinctive as its exterior.

Spatially, the major public rooms (entrance hall, parlor, dining room, and tearoom) and Jefferson's own ground-floor bedroom were all given generous ceiling heights. The room

shapes were inventive combinations of squares, octagons, and half octagons. Jefferson, like Palladio before him, had great enthusiasm for fundamental geometry. (His later farmhouse, Poplar Forest, would be America's first octagonal building, and his rotunda for the University of Virginia would be based—as was the Roman Pantheon—on a sphere within a cylinder.) The house presented not only a vocabulary of geometry, but also a vocabulary of classical orders, as interpreted by Palladio and other authors represented in Jefferson's library. The Doric order was used in the dining room, the Ionic in the entrance hall, and the Corinthian in the parlor and the dome room on the third floor. Access to the upper-floor bedrooms and the dome room was by a pair of narrow, steep stairs, perhaps because Jefferson thought grand stairs wasteful, perhaps because he wanted to continue the illusion of a single story. The house's furnishings were less academic and much more eclectic. The entrance hall, for example, was filled with a collection of Native American artifacts and was known in Jefferson's day as the Indian Room. Other furnishings, some of them quite elegant, had been collected by Jefferson on his travels, and still others were probably made at Jefferson's direction by the Monticello slaves.

Finishes were as fine as Jefferson could afford. Wallpapers were imported from France. The curtains and bed hangings in Jefferson's bedroom are crimson damask with linings of pale green velvet and gold fringe. The parlor floor has a geometric parquet pattern of cherry and beech; added in 1804, it was one of the first parquet floors in America (fig. 19–9).

Evident throughout were Jefferson's own idiosyncratic inventions. His own quarters featured an alcove bed that opened on both sides, one to his bedroom and the other to his adjacent study (fig. 19–10), allowing him to rise at any hour and work on his inventions. These clever and practical inventions included double-acting doors between entrance hall and parlor (when one was opened, the other—connected by a chain beneath the floor—would open automatically); triple-sash windows (when the lower two were raised, a door-height opening gave access to the veranda); a double-faced clock readable from both the entrance portico and the entrance hall, its cannonball weights marking the day of the week as they descended the hall wall; pivoting service doors into the dining room, with shelves on one side; and dumbwaiters built into the sides of the dining room fireplace to bring wine bottles from the service areas on the floor below, a level that, because of Jefferson's change of grade, is

▼ **19–9** Monticello's parlor. The mantel clock is French. At left, under the large pier mirror, is Jefferson's daughter's piano.
Robert C. Lautman/Thomas Jefferson Foundation, Inc.

▼ **19–9** Monticello's parlor. The mantel clock is French. At left, under the large pier mirror, is Jefferson's daughter's piano.
Robert C. Lautman/Thomas Jefferson Foundation, Inc.

invisible from inside the house. The reason for the pivoting shelves, the dumbwaiters, and the service level was to offer a comfortable life with minimal interruption from servants.

Jefferson invented furniture as well: a folding music stand to be shared by a quartet, a Windsor chair, serving tables, clocks, and silverware. Monticello remains one of America's most interesting and accomplished houses, designed by one of its most interesting and accomplished citizens.

The Spanish Missions (1769–1823)

Away from the urban centers of the East Coast, and stylistically removed from either the Colonial or the Federal period styles, a different sort of design was being practiced. The heritage of the settlers in the American West was Spanish,

◄ **19–10** Jefferson's alcove bed opens to both his bedroom and his study. Above it is a closet reached by a narrow stair.
Monticello/Thomas Jefferson Foundation, Inc.

rather than English. Only two years after the first English settlement at Jamestown in 1607, Spanish explorers had pushed northward from Mexico across the Rio Grande and founded an outpost at Santa Fe, New Mexico, in what had been lands of the Pueblo tribe. The oldest survivor among the Spanish buildings in Sana Fe is the Governor's Palace, begun in 1610 and built of bricks made from **adobe** (sun-dried earth and straw), a material that the Pueblos had been using for centuries. In the eighteenth century the Spanish built a number of churches and missions in Mexico, New Mexico, Texas (notably the Alamo in San Antonio), Arizona, and—perhaps most memorably of all—California.

Father Junipero Serra (1713–84), a Franciscan missionary who arrived in America from Spain in 1749, was responsible for beginning the remarkable chain of twenty-one Spanish missions that dot the California coast. The first and most southern of these was Mission San Diego de Alcalá in San Diego, established in 1769, and the last and most northern was Mission San Francisco de Solano in Sonoma, established in 1823. Representative of these is Mission San Francisco de Asis in San Francisco, more familiarly known as Mission Dolores (fig. 19–11), that name derived from a nearby stream.

The first crude building on the site was begun five days before the signing of the Declaration of Independence in 1776 on the far side of the continent. The present Mission Dolores was begun in 1782 and finished in 1791. It has walls of adobe 4 feet (1.2 m) thick, and its roof construction was joined with rawhide thongs and wood pegs rather than nails. Despite this, it has endured earthquakes that have leveled more modern buildings. A striking feature of the interior, 114 feet (35 m) long, is the series of redwood roof beams painted by Ohlone tribe craftsmen in chevrons of red, bluish gray, and ochre. The Native Americans also painted a **reredos** (an ornamental screen behind an altar) on the apse wall, arched over by a false stone arch, but the painting was covered in 1796 by a wooden *reredos* in high relief brought to the mission from San Blas, Mexico. Mission Dolores was carefully restored by architect Willis Polk in 1920.

Early American Ornament

Except for work on some Spanish missions, the design of the North American tribes impinged not at all upon the design of the colonists. In rare cases, as at Jefferson's Monticello, native artifacts might be collected and admired, but not until years later would they be considered a design source. Instead, the

▲ **19–11** Mission Dolores, San Francisco, 1782–91. The roof beams were decorated by Native American painters.
© Richard Cummins/CORBIS All Rights Reserved

colonists turned to Europe for their ornament, and they did so with great appetite. Perhaps because so much of the earliest building in America for European settlers had to be done with limited resources and was consequently plainly finished, settlers aimed to add ornament as soon as they could afford it.

Motifs

In some of the earliest Colonial period building, we saw brick bonds being used ornamentally (see table 19–1), their patterns accentuated by the glazing of some bricks (headers, for example) and not others. Brickwork often reached its most virtuoso level in the chimneys of the early houses. For example, in the Horton house (see fig. 19–3), the chimney is not a simple rectangle but rather elaborately pilastered.

Early America was an insecure place, the colonists threatened by uprisings of natives and the British governors threatened with uprisings of colonists. Many ornamental displays—some as plain as a gun or hunting knife hanging on a wall—were meant as warnings of the owner's power to retaliate. Just as Louis XIV's Salon de la Guerre (see fig. 15–8) had been ornamented with displays of battle scenes and prisoners, the walls of the entrance hall of the Governor's Palace at Williamsburg was arrayed in 1770 with a whole armory of clustered sabers, pistols, and flags, and attached to the ceiling was a circle of 64 flintlock rifles, their bayonets all pointing toward a gilded central medallion. With the Revolutionary War, the popularity of militaristic motifs grew even stronger.

In 1782, the last year of the fighting, the eagle was officially adopted as a national symbol; it had already been popular as an ornament, as on the so-called Constitution mirror (see center left in fig. 19–16), but now it became ubiquitous. One sits atop the *girandole* over the mantel of the Otis House in fig. 19–14. It also appeared on clocks, on picture frames, and on pediments over important gates and doors. A ring of thirteen stars, representing the original colonies, became popular as well.

In the Federal period that followed the war, ornamental motifs were absorbed into American design from three chief sources. From England, still considered the homeland for many Americans despite the recent hostilities, came a parade of changing fashions. The one of greatest influence was the Neoclassical work of Robert Adam. From France, whose Revolution had been inspired by America's War of Independence, came motifs associated with rebellion and freedom: the torch, the *fasces* (see table 15–1), and the female figure of Liberty. From the example of Thomas Jefferson came all the ornament of ancient Rome—scrolls, festoons, egg-and-dart, and more—for the design of the Roman Republic had come to be seen as a fitting model for the design of the American Republic.

An additional design source came in 1784, with the voyage of the *Empress of China* from New York to Canton. In opening trade to the Far East, America began to import teas, silk, porcelain, and other goods expressing Chinese design and ornament, and with them in hand, Americans turned to adaptations of Chinese style or *chinoiserie* (such as the wallpaper in fig. 19–26).

Pattern Books

The American appetite for European design trends was enormous, but Europe was far away and travel was slow and arduous. Design ideas, including ideas about ornament, were chiefly transmitted by books, specifically pattern books, which published designs and details that builders and craftsmen could copy. They ranged from small inexpensive handbooks with practical tips for carpenters to large deluxe folios of exemplary buildings and their ornamental details, sometimes even touching on architectural theory and principles of composition. The first pattern book writer published in America in 1758 was London carpenter Abraham Swan. His 1745 *The British Architect* featured Palladian exteriors with Rococo interiors, and many of Swan's interior details were imitated in American buildings. His designs for chimneypieces appeared, for example, in two fine houses in Fairfax County, Virginia: William Buckland's Gunston Hall, built before 1760, and George Washington's Mount Vernon, finished in 1787.

Thomas Chippendale, who made his fame as a great English furniture designer and tastemaker, published a book titled *The Gentleman and Cabinet-Maker's Director*. Its first edition, published in 1754, contained 161 engraved plates showing furniture designs in the Rococo, Gothic, and Chinese styles, as well as some simpler domestic furniture, and by the end of the decade the book's influence was felt in America. Largely because of the book's popularity, Chinese porcelain, lacquerware, and *chinoiserie* wallpaper began to be imported from England, as well as English chintz imitating calicoes from India. A second edition in 1792 introduced designs in the new Neoclassical style.

The first pattern book actually written in America was the 1797 *Country Builder's Assistant* by Connecticut architect Asher Benjamin (1773–1845), who had begun his career as a carver of Ionic capitals and whose second and better-known book would be the *American Builder's Companion* of 1806. Benjamin's own design in the 1797 William Coleman House, in Greenfield, Massachusetts, features one of the country's first elliptical stairs, which he had copied from a pattern book published in London.

Chimneypieces, Ceilings, and Moldings

Guided by the publication of books on ornament and style, Early American period builders ornamented their houses, public buildings, and churches (as the religion allowed) with flair. Room paneling at first, though made of wood, was often designed in imitation of stonework and sometimes painted the color of stone. Proportions of moldings were naturally heavy.

Lighter proportions of the later Palladian style were popularized in writings of English architect and furniture designer William Kent (see figs. 16–10 and 16–24), bringing new shapeliness to chimneypieces, door frames, and window frames. Moldings became smaller. Although most of them were fashioned in America, some moldings were shipped from London.

In the Federal period, the influence of England's Robert Adam was important and, later, that of France's Percier and Fontaine. Thomas Jefferson, more scholarly than most in his choice of sources, based the frieze of a mantel design at Monticello (fig. 19–12) on a drawing in *Les edifices antiques de Rome* by French architect Antoine Desgodets (1653–1728), published in 1682 and reprinted in 1779. To complement it, Jefferson chose a life-size marble statue of the reclining Ariadne, mythical daughter of King Minos of Crete.

Studying the details of one Colonial period interior and one Federal period interior can illustrate the quality and finesse of Early American ornament. The colonial-era plantation house of Westover (begun in 1730) was built by the successful tobacco planter William Byrd II, the grandson of a London goldsmith, born in the colonies but educated in England. The house, on the banks of the James River just 25 miles (40 km) from Williamsburg, was the social and administrative center of Byrd's vast plantation, and its original front door faced the river, its main means of access. The house's central block, like the Governor's Palace a double-pile, was perfectly symmetrical on the exterior, but not quite symmetrical on the interior, its central hall shifted slightly off axis to give larger rooms on one side, smaller on the other. This hall (fig. 19–13) is notable for its simply paneled walls, its plain wood floor, its graceful stair with finely turned banisters (see table 19–2), and most of all for its Rococo plaster ceiling ornament, probably shipped from London in precast form. There is a tall-case clock, popular in the 1700s, on the stair landing and a Chippendale style settee below.

During the Federal period, the Harrison Gray Otis House in Boston (built 1795–6) by architect Charles Bulfinch

◀ **19–12** Mantel of entrance hall, Monticello. Thomas Jefferson based its ornament on a French pattern book of ancient Roman design.
Langdon Clay

(1763–1844) represents the aesthetic principles of the time. In its drawing room (fig. 19–14) we see delicate plaster reliefs on both the mantelpiece and the ceiling, but in this case they are geometric and Neoclassical, rather than curvaceous and Rococo as at Westover. These reliefs are supplemented by a wallpapered border along the cornice and above the paneled dado, or wainscot. The medallions in the carpet, on the chair backs, on the circular firescreen, and in the corners of the ceiling relief, might all have been taken from a Robert Adam ceiling in England (such as seen in fig. 16–1), and the window drapery seems to have come—by way of some pattern book—from a Directoire design in France (see fig. 15–18).

Early American Furniture

With a growing number of new households needing to be furnished and importation of furniture from England and Europe slow and expensive, American craftsmen turned to the ample supply of native American woods and (with woodworking skills learned from English, Dutch, and other

▲ **19–14** Parlor of Charles Bulfinch's Harrison Gray Otis house, Boston, 1795–6, with delicate moldings on the mantel and wainscot.

TABLE 19–2 Wood Turning

Turning is done by rotating a wood dowel on a lath while cutting into it with a chisel. The process is often used for decorating the legs of chairs and tables, the stretchers between the legs, the back posts of chairs (see fig. 19–21), and the balusters of stairs (see fig. 19–13). Turning can be done in many ways, producing a variety of forms. Shown here are simple turnings made in repeated single forms or in combinations of forms.

Turning can also be used for making goblets, bowls, and circular boxes, and can be applied to ivory and bone as well as to wood.

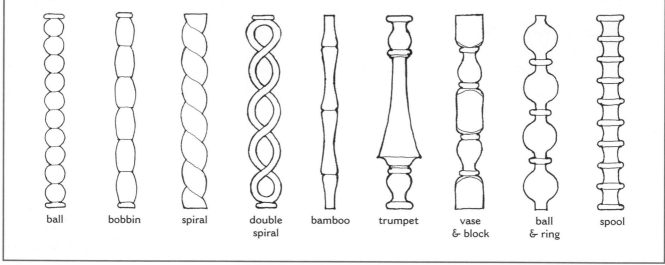

| ball | bobbin | spiral | double spiral | bamboo | trumpet | vase & block | ball & ring | spool |

apprenticeships) began to make the first American furniture. Not only every city but every community had its local joiners, turners, carvers, chairmakers, and cabinetmakers. By 1690 the Handicrafts Guild of Boston had registered more than forty upholsterers and more than sixty furniture makers in Boston alone.

In the seventeenth century, oak and pine were the most plentiful and popular furniture woods, although hickory and ash were also used. Furniture types included chairs, chests, stools, and benches (fig. 19–15). A long bench with arms was called a **settle**; it could have a hinged seat with storage beneath. Furniture making techniques included joining solid pieces of wood with such devices as the mortice-and-tenon (see table 2–1). Pegged construction was also used, in which wood members are joined not with nails but with small wood spikes or dowels. And furniture could be carved or ebonized, imitating ebony with black paint. American cabinetmakers, particularly in New England, copied the imported lacquered furniture coming from the Far East. Some of this furniture was painted to imitate tortoiseshell, and some was decorated with metallic paint.

In the first quarter of the eighteenth century, walnut and maple were also much used. In the second quarter of the

eighteenth century, cherry and gumwood came into use. Veneers and marquetry (see chapter 15 Tools & Techniques: Parquetry and Marquetry) also began to appear, although they were never as popular in America as in England and France. With the introduction of the William and Mary style (see chair on the left in fig. 19–24), which had been popular in England a quarter century earlier, the technique of **turning** (table 19–2) was used more often than before to shape chair and table legs.

In the third quarter of the eighteenth century, along with a fashion for the Chippendale style came a fashion for mahogany. In addition, larger, richer houses accommodated a variety of new furniture types and even the old types were treated to newly elaborate carving and gleaming brass hardware.

In the last quarter of the eighteenth century, satinwood and Virginia walnut added to the vocabulary of furniture woods, though mahogany was still the most preferred. And, as lighter alternatives to the Chippendale style, the Neoclassical styles of Adam, Hepplewhite, and Sheraton (fig. 19–16) began to appear. Rather than ornate carving, the most fashionable furniture used other techniques, such as veneering, inlay, and *reeding* (decorating surfaces with parallel convex

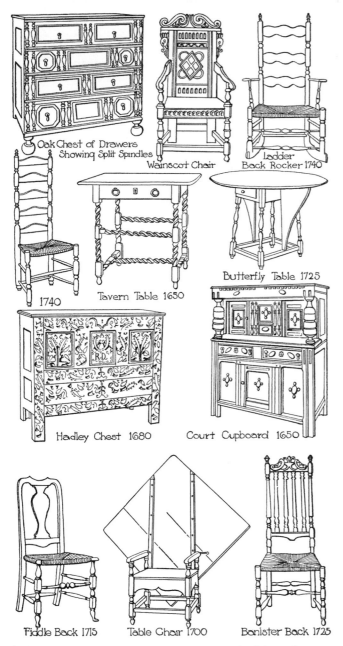

▲ **19–15** Types of seventeenth-century and early eighteenth-century American furniture.
Gilbert Werlé/New York School of Interior Design

▲ **19–16** Federal period furniture.
Gilbert Werlé/New York School of Interior Design

moldings of equal width). In addition, there was more attention than ever to the legs of furniture and to the variety of styles of feet accomplished by skilled carving (table 19–3).

Furniture Designers

In addition to the influences from English designers, there were original designers in America working in Boston, Newport, New York, Philadelphia, Charleston, and elsewhere to produce fine furniture of their own design. But before these talented individuals made their mark, there were some religious sects, such as the Shakers, who made significant contributions to interior design as they sought to express— and live by—their religious beliefs.

The Shakers Contributions to American furniture design and decorative arts were made by a number of religious groups who established their own communities and customs, and the protestant Christian sect called the Shakers became one such group. Although the Mennonites and the Amish also created their own aesthetic for their interiors and furniture, the Shakers created interiors and furniture of such clean, simple lines that their design influence is still felt today.

The Shakers originated in England as a Quaker sect in 1747, and in 1776 they founded a colony at Watervliet, New York, near Albany. Later colonies were founded at New Lebanon, New York, where a meeting house was built in 1785, and in Connecticut, Massachusetts, and other states from Maine to Kentucky. Partly due to its members' vows of celibacy, the Shakers are now virtually extinct.

TABLE 19–3 Furniture Feet

Furniture legs are often, but not always, given feet to distribute the weight of the chair, table, or case piece over a slightly larger area or simply to give the leg a graceful termination. They may take many decorative shapes. Shown here, left to right, are feet called spade, arrow, ball, bun, turnip, pad, slipper, drake, Spanish, and claw-and-ball.

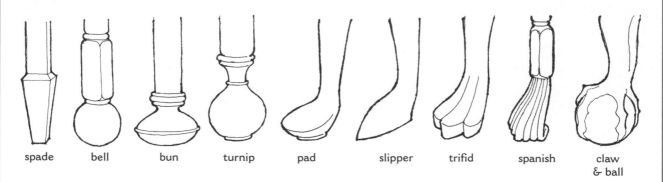

spade   bell   bun   turnip   pad   slipper   trifid   spanish   claw & ball

The Shaker aesthetic, which has been compared with the Japanese, is admirably spare, its asceticism arising from a disapproval of worldly extravagance. The sect's laws ordered that "odd or fanciful styles of architecture may not be used [and] beadings, mouldings and cornices may not be made." Similarly, Shaker historian Edward Deming Andrews quotes Shaker founder Ann Lee as having asked a Massachusetts hostess, "Never put on silver spoons for me nor tablecloths, but let your tables be clean enough to eat on without cloths."

Like Shaker tables, Shaker floors were usually bare and polished. Interior walls were smooth plaster with an eye-level wooden rail with pegs from which chairs, clocks, and other household items could be hung tidily off the floor (fig. 19–17). The walls were left white or painted only in approved colors, such as Meetinghouse Blue, Trustee Brown, and Ministry Green. Green was also specified for bedframes, blue for blankets, and white, blue, or green for window curtains, but not "checked, striped, or flowered." Shaker furniture makers disdained veneers as "sinful deception," using solid pieces of well-cured maple, pine, and cherry. In both the Shaker room and its furniture, beauty of form and an elegant lightness of parts amply compensated for the lack of ornamentation.

John Goddard In Newport, Rhode Island, two families produced more than a dozen skilled furniture makers and some of America's most extraordinary pieces of furniture. Among them, the best known are John Goddard and John Townsend. John Goddard (1723–85) was the son of Daniel

▲ **19–17** An interior from the Shaker colony at New Lebanon, New York, founded in 1787. A ladder-back chair and a straw bonnet hang from the pegboard. Below, two oval bentwood boxes on a blanket chest of painted pine.

The Metropolitan Museum of Art, Purchase, Emily C. Chadbourne Bequest, 1972. (1972.187.1-3). Photography by Paul Warchol. Photograph © 1995 The Metropolitan Museum of Art

Goddard, a carpenter and shipwright, who joined Newport's Quaker community. Both John and his brother James were apprenticed to Job Townsend, a prominent furniture maker, and both married Townsend daughters. John Goddard opened his own shop in Newport in 1748. He worked chiefly in the Queen Anne style, to which he added elements from Chippendale, Hepplewhite, and Sheraton, as well as ideas of his own. He designed slant-lid desks, secretaries, bookcases, clock cases, and even coffins. After his death, his business was continued by his sons Stephen and Thomas and by his grandson.

John Townsend   After an apprenticeship to his father, John Townsend (1732–1809) opened his own shop in Newport when he was twenty-one. He produced chests, kneehole desks, slant-lid desks, tall-case clocks, and high chests of drawers. He is most admired today for his blockfront case-goods with carved cockleshell ornament, called **block-and-shell** pieces (fig. 19–18). The term **blockfront** refers to a furniture front divided into three vertical panels, the center one slightly concave, the outer ones slightly convex. Such pieces were also called *tub front* or *swell'd front* pieces. They were popular in New England but rarely seen farther south.

Samuel McIntyre   With a father, grandfather, and two of uncles working as housebuilders, and two brothers both carpenters, it was natural that Samuel McIntyre (1757–1811) would be encouraged to follow the family tradition. He did,

▼ **19–18** A mahogany block-and-shell chest of drawers made in Newport in 1765 by John Townsend, 35 in. (88 cm) tall.

Woodwork–Furniture. American, Rhode Island, Newport. XVIII Century, 1765. Chest of Drawers. Maker: John Townsend (1732–1809). Mahogany, tulip, poplar, pine. H. 34½ in. W. 36¾ in. Depth 19 in. The Metropolitan Museum of Art. Rogers Fund, 1927. (27.57.1)

but he exceeded it. Studying drawing, art, and architecture, he became both an expert carver and a skilled architect, rivaling his contemporary Charles Bulfinch, whose buildings he admired and sketched. In fact, for Bulfinch's 1795–99 house for Salem merchant Elias Hasket Derby, McIntyre designed and carved chimney pieces, doorways, other interior details, and some furniture. In addition to designing the furniture wholly attributed to him (fig. 19–19), McIntyre also provided carvings for furniture that was designed by others.

McIntyre was able to harmonize all aspects of a house—exterior, interior, ornament, and furniture—and many think his masterpiece was the Gardner-Pingree house in Salem, Massachusetts, finished in 1805. In it McIntyre's work reflects the influence of Robert Adam and contains some very refined carving on mantels and doors.

Duncan Phyfe Duncan Phyfe (1768–1854) is Early America's best known furniture designer. Born Duncan Fife in Scotland, he came to America in 1783 or 1784 and settled in Albany, shortly after England had recognized the independence of the United States. About 1792 he moved to New York, opened his own cabinetmaking shop, and changed the spelling of his name to *Phyfe,* perhaps to seem fashionably French. His customers included the Astors of New York and the du Ponts of Delaware, and an agent in Savannah shipped his furniture throughout the South, much of it to Charleston.

The furniture was at first in the Chippendale style, but soon shifted to follow Sheraton (fig. 19–20), and certain favorite Phyfe motifs were taken from Adam, such as the lyre shape that he used for chair slats, table bases, and decorative carvings. Using fine mahogany from the Caribbean, his design was elegant (if not always highly original) and his craftsmanship was admirable. Phyfe was a savvy businessman who eagerly adapted the many new furniture styles coming from Europe.

Seating

Furniture in the Early American period expressed the expected types of chairs, tables, and other furniture, although there were some new types of furniture that were uniquely

▲ **19–19** Hepplewhite-style shield-back chair by Samuel McIntyre, Salem, Massachusetts, c. 1800. A scalloped row of brass nailheads embellishes the seat upholstery.

Hepplewhite side chair (one of a pair), ca. 1790, attributed to Samuel McIntyre. Mahogany; violet armure upholstery (replaced). Height: 38½ in. (97.79 cm). Los Angeles County Museum of Art, Mr. and Mrs. Allan C. Balch Fund. Photograph © 2001 Museum Associates/LACMA.

▲ **19–20** A mahogany window seat designed by Duncan Phyfe in the style of Sheraton, c. 1800.

Window seat, mahogany. Attributed to Duncan Phyfe. From the Hawley family. 1810–1815. © Museum of the City of New York. Gift of Miss Adelaide Milton de Groot. 36.352.17.

American. The earliest colonial seating was on backless stools or on long benches called **forms**. During the first half of the seventeenth century, these were gradually supplemented and replaced by chairs (or "back-stools"). These seventeenth-century chairs were of three chief types: the turned chair, the wainscot chair, and the slat-back chair.

Earliest in popularity were the **turned** chairs (see table 19–2), and they can be divided into two types: the Carver chair and the Brewster chair, both named for early New England governors. The Brewster type (fig. 19–21) has high back posts ending in finials and turnings in the back posts and spindles and also on the legs; the slightly simpler Carver type has turnings only above the seat. Both had seats of woven rush.

The **wainscot chair** (or *joined chair* or *great chair*) was more expensive and rarer than the turned chair. Its tall back was usually paneled like wainscoting, although at times it was elaborately carved (see top center, fig. 19–15). It was usually made of oak, but sometimes of walnut. Its seat, rather than rush, was a flat piece of wood, and comfort was added with a cushion.

By the end of the seventeenth century, turners had begun to produce more comfortable **slat-back** chairs, and these continued to be made in many parts of America throughout the nineteenth century and, in the Appalachian Mountains, even into the twentieth. They are also called **ladder-back** chairs (see top right, fig. 19–15, and fig. 19–22). Most of them have three or more identical horizontal slats with slightly curved profiles, but the most beautiful were made with subtle differences in slat shape. Like the turned chair, the slat-back had a rush seat.

▼ **19–21** A turned Brewster armchair of hickory and ash, made in New England c. 1650.
Woodwork-Furniture-American. XVII Century, ca. 1650. Brewster-type armchair. Hickory and ash. H. 44¾; W. 32½; D. 15¾ inches. Massachusetts. The Metropolitan Museum of Art, Gift of Mrs. J. Insley Blair, 1951. (51.12.2)

▼ **19–22** A rush-seated ladder-back or slat-back armchair. In this example, each slat has been given its own variation in shape and size.
Arm chair, American, 18th century. Maple and ash, H: 44 in. Wadsworth Atheneum, Hartford, Connecticut. Wallace Nutting Collection, Gift of J. Pierpont Morgan. Photo by E. Irving Blomstrann.

The eighteenth century saw the development of the slat-back and the introduction of the banister-back chair, the Boston chair, the American Windsor, and the fiddle back chair. The **banister-back** chair (see lower right, fig. 19–15, and the chair in the Horton parlor, fig. 19–4) had a back of four or five flat vertical slats (typically four on side chairs and five on armchairs) that were given the silhouette of turned banisters. They had real turnings (see table 19–2), however, on their legs, stretchers, and rush seats.

The **fiddle back** chair (see lower left in fig. 19–15, and see fig. 19–29) was an agreeable model. Its back slat, shaped like a fiddle or vase, was taken from a Queen Anne chair, but its other members were from the tradition of turned chairs. Its front stretcher is reminiscent of the William and Mary style, and its seat of rush resembles the slat-back. Resilient caning was added to rush and upholstery as a seat material. Cherry, pine, and maple were used as furniture woods. These were sometimes stained to look like the more highly prized walnut. Mahogany from the Caribbean began to be imported and used, and on the island of Bermuda a native aromatic cedar was used.

The light, strong, comfortable **Windsor** chair was imported from England shortly after it appeared there in the 1720s and soon replaced the slat-back as America's most popular chair. By the 1740s they were being made in Philadelphia and were for a while called Philadelphia chairs. American variations of the Windsor chair (fig. 19–23) included the low-back, which would be the basis of the nineteenth-century "captain's chair," the high-back or fan back with a straight top (on the left, fig. 19–23), and the loop-back or sack-back or roundtop with its top in a looping curve. The **comb-back** (in the middle, fig. 19–23) had a comblike projection above the central part of the back. There were also Windsors with writing arms, Windsor cradles, Windsor high chairs, and Windsor settees. After the American Revolution, their popularity increased, and they were made not only in Philadelphia but also in New York, Connecticut, and Rhode Island. They were most commonly painted green in the early century and consequently called **green chairs**, but near the end of the century statesman, scientist, and writer Benjamin Franklin is said to have bought some in white, and Thomas Jefferson, some in black and gold.

In sum, over the course of the eighteenth century, chairs became both more numerous and more comfortable. The easy chair (see right in fig. 19–24) was in use by 1710 and did provide easier seating than any previous American chairs. One type of easy chair was an American version of the French *bergère*, in the form of a large upholstered **wing** chair (as in fig. 19–24), so-named for the side pieces, or "cheeks," which shielded the face from the hot fire or drafts. The wing chair and the easy chair were large in scale and fully upholstered except for the turned legs and stretchers, and the upholstery was usually of fine fabric. The upholstered seat cushions were removable and called **squabs**. These types of chairs would remain prized possessions for the next 200 years, and they were prominently placed in the best room of the house.

Beds

The earliest beds in colonial North America were simple frames with wooden slats or ropes between them to support mattresses filled with straw or feathers. The most frequently used types of Early American beds are shown in figure 19–25.

Fan Back 1770 Comb Back 1770 Loop Back 1770

◀ **19–23** Early American Windsor chairs.
Gilbert Werlé/New York School of Interior Design

▲ **19–24** In the John Wentworth House, Portsmouth, New Hampshire, 1695–1700, we see details of a William and Mary armchair with vase and block turnings at left and an upholstered easy chair at right. Between them, an oval table is covered with a carpet.

The Metropolitan Museum of Art, Sage Fund, 1926. (26.290). Photograph © 1995 The Metropolitan Museum of Art.

Curtains around the bed provided privacy and protection from drafts; these were at first attached to the (usually low) ceiling, but later to a framework over the bed supported on the four extended corner posts. **Trundle** beds for children, which we noted having been used in Gothic interiors, were very low beds slipped under adult beds during the day and pulled out at night. Daybeds (chairs with long extended seats) appeared at the end of the seventeenth century.

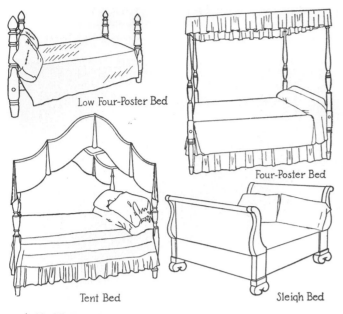

▲ 19-25 Early American beds.
Gilbert Werlé/New York School of Interior Design

Tables

The largest seventeenth-century table was the demountable **trestle** table, its design also inherited from Gothic times; its top, resting on wooden supports (often X-shaped) called *trestles,* was as long as 8 feet (2.5 m) or more. The **tavern** table was a smaller rectangular table on four turned legs connected by stretchers, with one or more drawers in the **apron** under the top (see center, fig. 19–15). By the eighteenth century, folding tables had become popular in both the **gateleg** type, usually with an oval top, which we saw in the Horton House parlor (see fig. 19–4) and the **butterfly** type (see center right, fig. 19–15); small versions of such folding tables were used for card games. A special type of table is the table chair (see lower center, fig. 19–15) that could be used as either chair or table. **Pier** tables were made to be set against a wall.

Afternoon tea drinking and card playing became fashionable for colonists with sufficient leisure, and so therefore did tea tables and card tables. Tea tables (fig. 19–26), some with tray tops or tops edged with raised molding, were made to be set before a seating group. **Tilt-top** tables (also fig. 19–26) had tops that could be tilted or revolved and were easily put aside when not in use; they frequently stood on a central support resting on a tripod base. Card tables often folded for storage, the drop-leaf table being popular in the Northern states and the handkerchief table (its hinge on a diagonal between opposite corners of its square top) in the Southern states.

▲ 19-26 In a room of the Powel House, Philadelphia, 1765-66, a tilt-top mahogany tea table with Chippendale-inspired chairs.
The Powel Room. Room from the second floor of the residence of Samuel Powel (1738–1793), 244 South Third Street, Philadelphia. Furnished as a parlor with furniture made in Philadelphia in Rococo style. Chinese wallpaper is of the period but not original to room. Cross-stitch wool carpet (1980.1) was made in England in 1764. View toward window and closed doorway.
The Metropolitan Museum of Art, Rogers Fund, 1918. (18.87.1–4)
Photograph © 1995 The Metropolitan Museum of Art.

Candlestands were made beginning in the seventeenth century, and in the eighteenth century they began to take a distinctive form, supported (like tilt-top tables) on a single turned post that rested on a tripod base of three cabriole legs.

Casegoods

American houses of the early seventeenth century had no closets, as we have noted, so casegoods provided the only storage. Among the earliest types made in the colonies were small boxes for Bibles and valuable family papers, and larger blanket chests for bedcovers. Both these had many variants in size and design, an interesting cousin of the Bible box being the *lap desk*, a box with a slanting lid for writing that was held on the lap. Two specific types of blanket chest were very popular. Both originated in the Connecticut River Valley. One was the **Hadley** chest, plain in form but richly carved and painted (see middle left, fig. 19–15). The front surface was paneled, and the central panel bore the initials of the owner; such chests were often used as "hope chests" or "dower chests," and the initials were then those of a young girl who would be given the chest's contents when she married. Another type of blanket chest was the **Connecticut** chest (fig. 19–27), with three panels across the top carved in patterns of tulips and sunflowers. Between the panels were applied half spindles of maple stained to look like ebony. There were drawers below.

Larger and more elaborate, intended for large and elaborate rooms, were the **court cupboard** and the **press cupboard**. They were fashionable throughout the seventeenth century. Both were divided into upper and lower sections with a variety of doors and drawers. Often the top sections had recessed corners with large turned corner posts supporting a cornicelike top (see middle right, fig. 19–15). The court cupboard was a furniture type brought from England, seldom more than 4 feet (1.2 m) high, and its name was probably derived from the French *court*, meaning "short." Its bottom section often had an open shelf or shelves. The press cupboard, also called a *wainscot cupboard* or simply a *press*, was similar but had doors or drawers in both its upper and lower sections. The **scrutoire** or **escritoire** was a writing desk with a slanted front that folded down to form a writing surface; it might or might not have a bookcase above it. Although the names are of French origin, these terms had been used in England.

The sideboard, thought to have been invented in England by Robert Adam, became an important part of American dining rooms, replacing earlier side tables or serving tables. American examples were usually Heppelwhite (see upper right, fig. 19–16) or Sheraton in style, or sometimes a combination of both. In the southern states the sideboard was slightly higher and narrower and was called a huntboard.

Among the very finest examples of Early American furniture are the tall chests made in Philadelphia from c. 1755 to c. 1790: the highboy (see fig. 19–16), the secretary, and the corner cupboard. One Philadelphia **highboy** (fig. 19–28),

▼ **19–27** An oak Connecticut-type blanket chest with a pine top and applied half-spindles of ebonized maple, 1680–1700. Courtesy of The Brooklyn Museum of Art, Gift of George D. Pratt 15.480

▲ **19–28** The "Pompadour" mahogany highboy from Philadelphia, c. 1765. It is topped with a double-scroll pediment, a central bust, and a pair of urn finials.
Woodwork-Furniture. American, Pennsylvania, Philadelphia. 18th Century, 1762–90. High Chest of Drawers. Chippendale style, with "Pompadour" finial bust. Mahogany and mahogany veneer, with yellow pine, tulip poplar and northern white cedar. H. 91¾ in. (233 cm.) W. 42⅝ in. (108.3 cm.) Depth 22½ in. (57.2 cm). The Metropolitan Museum of Art, John Stewart Kennedy Fund. 1918. (18.11.4)

attributed at one time to American furniture maker William Savery, shows figured wood carefully chosen and naturalistic carving carefully placed. It has been called the "Pompadour" chest because the bust between the pediment scrolls is thought to resemble Louis XV's mistress.

The **secretary** was a highboy that incorporated a fold-down writing surface. In the eighteenth century, a tall chest with six or more drawers in graduated sizes was called a **high daddy**. There were also slant-top desks with storage below but without the upper section of the secretary. The corner cupboard, which became popular in the eighteenth century, was shaped to fit in the corner of the room and had open shelves in its top section for the display of household goods and doors below.

The **kas** was an American version of an *armoire*, or wardrobe, made in the Netherlands, where it was called a *kast*. A favorite of Dutch settlers in the Hudson and Delaware river valleys, it was tall, large, fitted with paneled double doors and a pair of drawers beneath, was topped with a cornice, and sat on ball feet. Its typical decorative treatment was boldly scaled *grisaille* paintings of festoons and fruit, probably in imitation of relief carvings on the Dutch originals

(fig. 19–29), though many *kasten* were left plain or painted with grained or ebonized surfaces.

Clocks

Clocks as objects, both decorative and functional, were just becoming available for residential use when the colonies were being settled, and the largest of them were fully qualified to be called furniture. Clocks date back to the New Kingdom of Ancient Egypt, when the Egyptians used water clocks, which measured the passage of time by a controlled rate of water escaping from a hole in a vessel. Hourglasses and sundials also date back to ancient times. Famous clocks were installed in Canterbury Cathedral in the thirteenth century and in Strasbourg Cathedral in the fourteenth, but it was not until the development of the little device of the coiled spring (the "movement") at the beginning of the sixteenth century that clocks became small, light, and inexpensive enough for general production. By the middle of the seventeenth century, clocks were being shipped from England to America in great numbers. The very earliest of these had only an hour hand on their faces, as the imprecise movements of the time piece made minute hands pointless. By the early eighteenth

▶ **19–29** Prominent in this bedroom from the 1762 Hardenbergh House, Ulster County, New York, is the grisaille-painted *kas* at the far right. There are also a table with turned legs, some *fiddle-back* chairs, and a canopied bed. On top of the kas is *a garniture de cheminée.*
Courtesy, Winterthur Museum

century, accuracy had improved and some two-handed clocks were being made in America.

The great prize among Early American clocks, however, was the tall-case clock, one of which we saw on the stair landing at Westover (see fig. 19–13). It appeared around the beginning of the eighteenth century when longer pendulums were added to clock movements, necessitating longer cases to protect them. These new clocks stood on the floor rather than on tables, mantels, chests, or shelves. The cases were classically divided into three parts: the *bonnet* at top housed the clock movement and dial; the *shaft* housed the swinging pendulum, and the shaft and *base* together accommodated the drop of the weights over a period of (usually) eight days. (Tall-case clocks did not come to be called *grandfather clocks* until the last quarter of the nineteenth century.)

The most prominent names in Federal period clock making were from Massachusetts: Daniel Burnap (active 1780–1800) of Andover, Massachusetts, who was noted for his engraved faces, and the Willards. Members of the Willard family (active for more than a century beginning in 1743) made the small case clocks, an even smaller clock that was covered with a bell of glass and called a **lighthouse**, and a variety of mantel clocks. Around 1800, Simon Willard (1753–1848) introduced the **banjo clock**, a small wall-hung clock that was encased in a banjolike shape. A variation on the banjo clock was the lyre clock, a popular instrument referenced in Sheraton furniture. Eli Terry (1772–1853) of Connecticut would bring mass production and low prices to American clockmaking; his first clocks had wooden movements, his later ones brass. Terry would take as his partner Seth Thomas (1785–1859), who would open his own factory

in 1812 and greatly enlarge the American clock industry. Examples of clocks by the Willards, Terry, Thomas are seen in figure 19–30.

Early American Decorative Arts

Early American life seems to have been heavily accessorized. Among the myriad items devised to make life more comfortable or interesting were tea caddies, saltcellars, cellarets (wine storage boxes that fit beneath sideboards), pipe racks, and knife boxes. Small decorative objects carved of ivory or bone were called scrimshaw, a term of unknown origin. Many other decorative and useful objects made of carved or turned wood were classified as treen, perhaps referring to their origins in trees.

Ceramics

Although, as we have seen, Native Americans had an established pottery tradition, the colonists brought their tastes and techniques from Europe. Records show that both glazed and unglazed pottery was being made at Jamestown, Virginia, shortly after 1610. It was probably redware, made from common red or reddish brown clay. Where brickmaking was established (in Virginia and New England by 1650, in Pennsylvania by 1685), the brick kilns were also used for making earthenware and roofing tiles. Also by 1685, more hard-bodied stoneware was being made by Daniel Cox from London at his pottery near Burlington, New Jersey.

Early pottery decoration in America included the use of slip and **graffito**, the scratching of patterns through the slip to reveal a different color beneath. Abraham Miller of Philadelphia is credited with producing America's first silver **lusterware**, a pottery with an iridescent metallic sheen in the glaze. He also experimented with making hard-paste porcelain (see Tools & Techniques: Porcelain in Chapter 11), but he never produced any commercially. The only established porcelain maker in Early America was the Bonnin & Morris factory in Philadelphia; it began producing blue-decorated wares in 1770 (fig. 19–31), but it could not compete with the lower prices of foreign imports, and the factory was closed in 1772.

Gottfried Aust (1722–88), a German-born master potter, was an important figure in America's Moravian communities, first in Bethlehem, Pennsylvania, and later in Salem, North Carolina. His work was chiefly earthenware decorated in floral or geometric patterns with colored slips. The large number of

Early wooden wall clock by Eli Terry

Willard Banjo Clock

Sheraton Type Shelf Clock made by both Terry and Thomas

Shelf clock of Willard Type

Late type of shelf clock by Seth Thomas

▲ **19–30** Early American wall and shelf clocks.
Gilbert Werlé/New York School of Interior Design

▲ **19–31** Shell-shaped sweetmeat stand of soft-paste porcelain with cobalt blue decoration, made by Bonnin & Morris, Philadelphia, 1770–72, 5 in. (13 cm) high.
Sweetmeat Dish, 1770–1772 Philadelphia Pennsylvania. Gousse Bonnin, George Anthony Morris, American China Manufactory, Soft-paste porcelain, under glaze. 5¼ x 7¼ in (13.3 x 18.4 x 18.4 cm), Brooklyn Museum, 45.174. Musium Collection Fund.

▲ **19–32** Engraved lead-glass wine glass made by "Baron" Stiegel on the occasion of the marriage of his daughter to William Old in 1773, 7 in. (17 cm) high.
Goblet, 1773–1774, American. Flint Glass Manufactory of Henry William Stiegel, Manheim, Pennsylvania. Engraved by Lazarus Isaacs. Colorless, opaque white glass; blown; copper-wheel engraved. H: 17.2 cm, D (bowl): 8.4 cm, D (foot): 9.1 cm. Corning Museum of Glass, Corning, New York. Gift in part of Roland C. and Sarah Katheryn Luther, Roland C. Luther III, Edwin C. Luther III, and Ann Luther Dexter, descendants of H.W. Stiegel. 87.4.55a.

apprentices trained by Aust constituted a "school" of potters, using his style, in the Piedmont area of North Carolina.

In 1785 Captain John Norton moved his family from Connecticut to Bennington, Vermont, where he planned to farm. Finding a great need for simple ceramics in his own and neighboring households, he founded a pottery at Bennington in 1793. He made earthenware and, later, stoneware, and his company would become larger and much better known in the nineteenth century; it still exists.

Glass

Glassmakers were among the settlers at Jamestown in 1608 and were therefore some of the first craftsmen in colonial America. As there was plentiful need for window glass and utensils such as bottles and drinking vessels, and as there was a plentiful supply of wood fuel, the practice of glassmaking flourished. Most early American glassmaking was anonymous, but a few makers are well known today.

Caspar Wistar   Caspar Wistar (1696–1752) emigrated from Germany to Philadelphia when he was twenty-one. His first trade was making brass buttons, but he opened a glass factory, which he called Wistarburgh, in 1739 in the southern part of New Jersey. He was the first financially successful glass manufacturer in the colonies, but his products were mostly utilitarian: window glass, bottles, and equipment for scientific experiments. Some tableware was produced, rather crude

but delicately colored in tints of green and blue. Just after the Revolution, some brothers named Stanger who had worked for Wistar opened a new glass factory in the same area, and Wistar and Stanger products are sometimes jointly known as Jersey glass.

Henry William Stiegel   A generation later, Henry William Stiegel (1729–85), like Wistar, moved from Germany to Philadelphia at age 21 and opened a glasshouse in 1763. "Baron" Stiegel's first products were bottles and window glass, but he gradually added more artistic products. In 1769, he opened the American Flint Glass Manufactory at Manheim to produce tableware in lead glass (the first in America) and colored glass in opaque white, emerald green, amethyst, brown, and sapphire blue. Stiegel added etching and enameling as decoration, employing the first glass engraver known to work in America, Lazarus Isaac, who came to Philadelphia from London in 1773. Stiegel products included wine glasses (fig. 19–32), tumblers, mugs, decanters, cruets, cream pitchers, and candlesticks. Attribution of specific pieces to Stiegel's glasshouses seems less certain today than it once did, and most experts now use the term *Stiegel type* for any type of glass that Stiegel produced. Imitations of Stiegel ware were made in the Pittsburgh area and in the Ohio River Valley; these were known as *Midwestern glass*.

A glassworks in New Bremen, near Baltimore, Maryland, was founded in 1784 by John Frederick (originally Johann Friedrich) Amelung (1741–98) of Bremen, Germany, who staffed it with almost seventy craftsmen brought from Germany along with their equipment. His glasshouses produced window glass, utilitarian household objects, and some far-from-utilitarian, wheel-engraved presentation pieces made as gifts for President George Washington and other important figures.

Mirrors

Mirrors, or *looking glasses*, were rare in the American colonies before 1700, but they became popular as soon as they were made available as a way to multiply the dim light from candles and lamps. Early mirrors came in a range of qualities. The poorest were made of crown glass, cut from the crown of a great bubble of blown glass, annealed in a furnace, and cut into panes. The most distorted of these panes, called the bull's-eye, was the center one, scarred by the blower's pontil rod it was also used in windows, where light transmission was considered more important than clear vision (see Tools & Techniques: Windows and Window Glass). Crown glass mirrors were often silvered on the back with paint. The finest mirrors, made of plate glass poured on a slab of polished marble or a sheet of metal, were silvered on the back with mercury or tinfoil.

The first to reach America were wall and dresser mirrors in the Queen Anne style, with plain walnut or lacquered frames, and with the characteristic cresting of broken curves. The glass was usually beveled around the edges and was usually (for economy) in two parts until about 1750, when single large pieces of glass began to be used.

Simple Adam or Hepplewhite mirror types came in rectangular, oval, and shield shaped frames and were ornamented with **paterae** (round or oval-shaped ornamental disks), classical figures, husk garlands, drops, and arabesques, or even eagles as seen at center left in figure 19–16. These were hung on walls or made for table and bureau tops, in which case they might stand on small boxes of drawers.

The **girandole**, dating from 1760 but popular only after the Revolution, was a combination mirror and lighting fixture, always made with candle brackets. (The term was also used in the eighteenth century for chandeliers and candelabra without mirrors and in the nineteenth century for a

Tools & Techniques | WINDOWS AND WINDOW GLASS

In early houses in the Massachusetts settlements of Salem and Plymouth, windows were few and small (not much more than a foot square). Window glass, called **flat glass**, was still expensive in England; heavy taxes made it even more expensive in America. Even so, windows with very thin (about ⅟₁₆ in. or 0.16 cm) English glass were common in the colonies by the mid-seventeenth century for all but the poorest houses. This glass was not always clear, mineral impurities often tinting it purple or amber.

Early windows were generally of the **casement** kind, hinged at the sides and swinging open like a door, with small diamond-shaped panes held (like Gothic stained glass) in lead **cames** (slender, grooved rods). Some windows did not open, however, especially those in bedrooms, because it was thought that night air was unhealthy.

What became common in England around 1700 and in America shortly after were the vertically sliding **sash windows**, with wooden glazing **mullions** (small members holding the rectangular glass panes or lights) and with operating mechanisms of cords, counterweights, and pulleys. These were called **double-hung** because they had upper and lower sashes that could bypass one another to create an opening. In the early eighteenth century, sash windows were used in at least three buildings at Williamsburg: the College of William and Mary, the Capitol, and the Governor's Palace. These earliest American sash windows had many small panes, the size increasing throughout the eighteenth century from twelve-over-twelve (a sash of twelve panes above another of twelve panes) to nine-over-six and eventually to six-over-six.

banjo clock with a rounded base.) The mirror was generally round with either a concave or convex surface. The frame was heavy, richly carved or ornamented, gilded, and often crowned with an eagle. The girandole was prominently placed in the dining room or best parlor, as in the Harrison Gray Otis House in Boston (see fig. 19–14).

Metalwork

Early American fireplace accessories such as andirons, fire tongs, and fire shovels were made of iron, as were cooking pots and caldrons, locks, hinges, candlesticks, and lamps. The earliest known blacksmith among the colonists was James Read, at work in Jamestown in 1607. Iron hardware, such as that shown in figure 19–33, would have been used in such houses as the 1649 Horton House (see fig. 19–4). The first successful iron-producing furnace was built at Saugus, Massachusetts, in 1664, and operated for almost twenty years. By the eighteenth century there were foundries in most colonies. Benjamin Franklin invented an iron stove made of cast-iron plates in 1742, its iron hearth extending into the room; the "Franklin stove" had an air box in which a room's cold air was heated and from which it was then recirculated. It was much more efficient at heating than an open fire and was deservedly popular, being cast in many decorative shapes. In 1756 "Baron" Stiegel of Pennsylvania, who would become famous as a glassmaker, was making iron stoves of his own design.

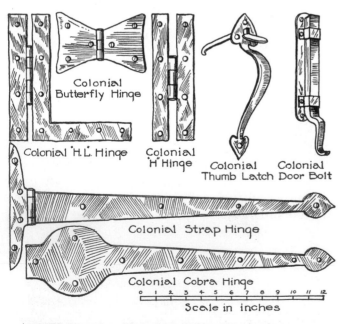

▲ **19–33** Examples of Colonial period iron door hardware.
Gilbert Werlé/New York School of Interior Design

Colonial tinsmiths coated iron with tin to make a variety of kitchen and household objects, and tin-faced ironware was also imported from England. The first American tinsmith may have been Shem Drowne (c. 1683–c. 1750) of Boston, who made candlesticks, trays, and lamps; he also made the copper weather vane in the shape of a grasshopper that is still in place above Boston's Faneuil Hall. Piercing was a method of decorating tinware that was particularly popular in New England, while the fashion in seventeenth-century Pennsylvania was wrigglework, made by rocking a chisel back and forth along the surface of the metal to make a zig-zag groove, a technique also used for pewter and silver.

The most generally popular treatment of tin, however, was to lacquer or "japan" it. *Japanned* tinware and tin-plated ironware were made from the early eighteenth century in both England and France, where they were called *Pontypool wares,* named for the town where many of them were made, and in France, where they were known as *tôle* (iron). In America tinware and tin-plated ironware were also called **tole.** Both types of ware were used for picture frames, lamps, trays, teapots, water jugs, buckets, tea caddies, bread baskets, and many other items. The object was first coated with a brownish black asphaltum varnish, which was dried in an oven. The result was a shiny black surface that was then decorated with gilt or colored paint, sometimes applied through a stencil, sometimes hand-painted.

Brass, made of copper and zinc, was used in colonial America for drawer pulls, cabinet knobs, and hinges, along with some implements such as warming pans, skillets, basins, and ewers. Joseph Jenks (died 1679) of Lynn, Massachusetts, is the earliest recorded American brassworker, but he and those who followed had to depend largely on melting down old brass for reuse because England restricted American brass-making (until the Revolution) in order to boost the market for English brass. The brass of the eighteenth century, with relatively more zinc and less copper than today's brass, was paler and more yellow. Two brasslike alloys used in the colonies, made—like brass—of copper and zinc, but in different proportions, were **latten**, made in thin sheets and often used for making spoons, and **Prince's metal**, which was thought to resemble gold and was used for ornamental castings.

Pewter, an alloy of tin with copper and lead, was probably made in the colonies before silver (fig. 19–34). It had been used by the Romans, the ancient Chinese, the French and the English in the Middle Ages, and in many other times

▲ 19–34 American silver and pewter wares.
Gilbert Werlé/New York School of Interior Design

Silver Porringer 1700
Silver Caster 1725
Silver Teapot
Silver Beaker 1650
Silver Tankard 1750
Silver Punch Bowl by Paul Revere
Silver Sauce Pan by Revere
Silver Teapot by Paul Revere
Pewter Plate
Pewter Caster
Pewter Porringer
Pewter Beaker
Pewter Teapot
Pewter Lamp
Pewter Sugar-bowl
Pewter Jug or Flagon
Pewter Whale-oil Lamp

was important in the colonies, and pewter wares included coffeepots, teapots, lamps, candlesticks, plates, cans, flatware (table utensils such as knives and forks), and *porringers*, small, shallow bowls for eating cereals or berries. Pewter tankards were commonplace in colonial America (see fig. 19–34).

All these objects were also made in **silver**. Silverware was first owned in quantity by the wealthy plantation owners of the South. Early America's two most famous silversmiths were John Coney and Paul Revere, both of Boston.

John Coney   John Coney (1655–1722) of Boston was the brother-in-law of Jeremiah Dummer and became an engraver as well as a silversmith and goldsmith, producing the plates with which the colonies' first paper money was printed. He was an excellent craftsman. His designs closely followed English models, and he was the first to introduce some English forms to America, such as the chocolate pot and the *monteith*, a bowl with a scalloped rim from which wine glasses could be suspended in water to cool them.

Paul Revere   Like Coney, Paul Revere (1735–1818) was an engraver as well as a silversmith, and also worked in Boston. At age 19 he took over the business of his father, a silversmith with the same name who had been an apprentice under Coney. The younger Revere's most famous design is a silver punch bowl (fig. 19–35) that he made for a group called the Sons of Liberty (to which Revere himself belonged); its simple, graceful shape was derived from a porcelain bowl imported from China and has been widely copied in a variety of sizes). Revere was also noted for his silver coffeepots, teapots, tankards, and pitchers. He also established a small iron foundry where he made church bells and a mill for making sheets of copper. His copper was used in 1802 to cover the dome of Charles Bulfinch's five-year-old Massachusetts State House in

and places. The tin content of pewter can vary between 60 and 90 percent, the lower percentage giving a dull finish and a soft, easily dented surface, the higher percentage giving a bright luster. It was much in use in America in the seventeenth and eighteenth centuries, but because of its low value (compared to silver) much pewter was melted down to make ammunition for the Revolution. After the Revolution, pewter was largely replaced by nickel, silver, silverplate, and china. In its day, however, pewter

▲ 19–35 The much-imitated Sons of Liberty silver bowl by Paul Revere, 1768, 11 in. (28 cm) high.
View: side inscribed "To the memory of the glorious Ninety-Two". Sons of Liberty Bowl. 1768. Paul Revere American, 1735–1818. Silver. Height 14.0 cm (5½ in.). uneven. Gift by Subscription and Francis Bartlett Fund. Courtesy, Museum of Fine Arts, Boston. Reproduced with permission. © 2000 Museum of Fine Arts, Boston. All Rights Reserved.

Boston, and the Revere Copper Company is still in business today. His fame as a metalsmith, however, has been both amplified and overshadowed by his fame as a Revolutionary hero who warned his fellow citizens of approaching British troops, as immortalized in Henry Wadsworth Longfellow's 1860 poem: "Listen, my children, and you shall hear / Of the midnight ride of Paul Revere. . . ."

Textiles

Silks, damasks, and velvets had been brought from Europe in the sea chests of the first settlers, and cargoes of cotton were shipped from the West Indies to Boston and Salem beginning in 1638. The first textiles made in America, however, were necessarily plain and simple.

In 1640 the General Court of Massachusetts ordered the domestic manufacture of wool and linen cloth, and the earliest recorded production came the following year. In 1643 twenty families from Yorkshire, a wool-producing county of England, settled at Rowley, near Ipswich, Massachusetts, and established the first professional textile mill in America; it would operate continuously until the nineteenth century, producing woolen broadcloth and, later, cotton and linen goods.

England began to watch its colonies carefully as potential competitors, and during the Commonwealth period (1649–59) wool produced in England was ordered to be kept there for English use. Other restrictive legislation followed, worsening in the eighteenth century. By then, textiles were being made in every part of the colonies, silk was being raised in Georgia and Carolina, cotton was being printed in Philadelphia, woolens being made in Hartford, and linen in Boston. In 1792 Massachusetts-born Eli Whitney invented the cotton gin, simplifying the separation of cotton fiber from seed and revolutionizing early nineteenth century textile manufacturing.

Bed and Window Coverings
The earliest and simplest colonial fabrics for both bed and window coverings were of homespun wool. The most readily available dyes were red, brown, and indigo blue, but yellow and green homespun were also made. Linen was also available to the early colonists, and a popular blend of wool and linen was used, called **linsey-woolsey**; coarse and loose, this fabric was often brightly colored.

Bed rugs were placed on beds for warmth and made like hooked rugs but on a heavier backing, canvas rather than linen, and their loops of wool were left uncut. Quilts, coverlets, and all kinds of bedcovers were also made, as seen in Williamsburg (see fig. 19–6) and Monticello (see fig. 19–10); some were woven on small hand looms, some pieced together in patchwork, some appliquéd.

Upholstery
The development of upholstery began in the seventeenth and eighteen centuries. Leather was sometimes used, but fabric was used more often (see fig. 19–14, 19–24, and 19–36). The stuffing beneath the upholstery was often of horsehair taken from the manes and tails of horses, then washed and dried to make it more pliable. Hair from cows' tails was also used.

A thick wool upholstery material of the seventeenth and eighteenth centuries called **moreen** was made with a wool **warp** and fillers of wool, linen, or cotton. Its name may have come from the fact that some of it, stamped while wet with a hot iron in wavy patterns, imitated the appearance of **moiré**. It was usually dyed in strong colors: crimson, green, blue, or yellow. Other popular upholstery materials were **serge** and horsehair. Serge was a flat fabric of wool or wool blend with a fine pattern of diagonal ribs, similar to today's cotton denim. Horsehair was a smooth, sturdy, shiny fabric, usually black, that was made with cotton, linen, or occasionally silk as the warp and with real horsehair as the weft. (In the early twentieth century the horsehair would be replaced with rayon.) Near the end of the eighteenth century, cotton prints made in England or France were popular imports for upholstery use.

We know from printed records and upholsterers' bills that slipcovers, sometimes referred to as "cases," were also made for many Early American chairs, but no example survives.

Carpets, Rugs, and Floorcloths
The first American objects called rugs and carpets, surprisingly, were not laid on the floor but were used as table covers and bedcovers and draped over chests, cupboards, mantels, shelves, and even windowsills as both decoration and protection.

Hooked rugs, which *were* used on the floor, had been popular in the northern countries of Europe and were probably introduced to the colonies by Scottish, Scandinavian, and Dutch settlers. They were made by using a small hook to pull narrow strips of cloth through a coarsely woven linen

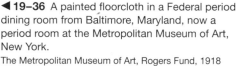 **19–36** A painted floorcloth in a Federal period dining room from Baltimore, Maryland, now a period room at the Metropolitan Museum of Art, New York.

The Metropolitan Museum of Art, Rogers Fund, 1918 (18.101.1-4). Photograph © 1981 The Metropolitan Museum of Art.

backing that had been stretched on a frame. Sometimes the exposed loops of cloth were cut; sometimes not. Geometric patterns were made, as well as representations of ships, animals, and flowers.

Braided rugs were also made for floors. Strips of cloth in various colors were plaited together, and the resultant braids were sewn together spirally, making round or oval rugs. A few rows of such braiding might be added to the outside of a hooked rug as a finishing touch. The hooked or braided rug on a painted floor was a standard for the average American room until the middle of the nineteenth century. These rugs are still seen today, staples of rooms in Colonial Revival style.

We saw an example of a bed round, a rug surrounding a bed in a U-shape, in the Williamsburg Governor's Palace (see fig. 19–6).

Floorcloths of painted canvas, mentioned in the chapter on English design, came to be much used in America

(fig. 19–36). In addition to serving as substitutes for fine carpets for covering large floor areas, they were also used in smaller sizes under dining tables or sideboards to protect the carpets beneath them from spilled food; these smaller versions were called **crumb cloths**. Floorcloths were also sometimes used as summer substitutes for more heavily textured carpets and were even used under carpets to provide a smooth surface and to stop drafts that might come through cracks in the flooring. Floorcloths of all sizes were often painted in striking geometric patterns, some of them imitating mosaics and marble tiles.

Stenciling and Wallpaper

Before the production of printed wallpapers in America, the technique of **stenciling** was much in use. Printed wallpaper began to replace stenciling in the early eighteenth century, when papers were imported from both England and France.

Stenciling is the reproduction of a design using masking shapes called *stencils* to guide the position of the paint. The stenciling process is as old as some prehistoric cave paintings that used human hands as outlines (see fig. 1–4). (In the prehistoric cave painting technique, painting around (rather than through) an object is called negative stenciling.) Stenciling was much in use by the Chinese and Japanese for decorating textiles, and it was used in Europe in the Middle Ages for making playing cards. It has also been used for making banners and sheet music. Its use on walls and floors is particularly identified with Colonial America. In the nineteenth century it would become popular for the decoration of furniture.

Stencils are most often thin sheets of stiff, moisture-proof material such as oiled cardboard (plastic is often used today) with holes cut in the shape of the desired pattern. Paint, ink, or dye can be brushed or rubbed (or, today, sprayed) through the holes.

A famous Early American stencil artist was the itinerant Moses Eaton (1753–1833) based in New Hampshire, whose kit of stencils, brushes, and wood blocks we see here; it was later used by his son of the same name (1796–1886). Eaton's stencils were made of oiled card, and his paint was dry pigment mixed with sour milk.

Early Americans used stenciling for floor treatment in cases where carpets or floorcloths were not possible, painting right onto the wooden boards in patterns resembling carpet (see fig. 19–1). When an overall background color was wanted under the stenciled motifs, yellow ochre was a frequent choice. Sometimes floors were painted to resemble marble rather than carpet, the marble veins imitated by painting lightly with feathers rather than brushes. Spatter effects, made by running a stick along a wet brush so that dots of paint are scattered about, were popular in New England. Repetitive patterns were used over large wall surfaces, borders were stenciled along the tops of walls, along stairways (fig. 19–37). Large display pieces were stenciled on overmantels, where a painting might normally hang in a more luxurious home.

Much American wall stenciling was done at home by amateurs, and there was also a custom of stenciling on velvet as an artistic pastime for ladies.

The first American wallpaper manufacturer is thought to have been Plunket Fleeson of Philadelphia, who opened his factory in 1739 (Fleeson was also an upholsterer). By the middle of the century, printed papers were being advertised in the newspapers of many American cities as a low-cost method of decoration. One wallpaper manufacturer, William Payntell, offered a stock of 4,000 patterns, some of them with flock textures, like those we saw used in England. Patterns were widely varied—geometric, scenic, floral, or combinations of these. Many of them were in the popular Chinese style (see fig. 19–26) or imitations of imports from France.

▼ **19–37** Stenciled border from a stairway wall in the Elisha Smith House, Stillwater, Rhode Island, c. 1696.
Janet Waring, "Early American Wall Stencils: Their Origin, History and Use," New York. Photo by William R. Scott, 1937.
Courtesy of Dover Publications, Inc.

Summary: Early American Design

Throughout all the previous chapters, we have seen the design of one time and place influencing that of a later time or a different place. In Early America, settled by people strongly tied to—yet displaced from—their European backgrounds, such influence was unusually strong. Early American history is a sometimes poignant record of reactions to earlier influences. At first, the people of the colonies yearned to reproduce their pasts but often lacked the resources to do so. In time, they became increasingly adept at imitation but quickly moved beyond it, rejecting European models in favor of more practical solutions and sometimes seeking to be fiercely independent of them.

Looking for Character

In the two and a half centuries studied here, the American colonists, however eager they were for political independence, were equally eager that their interiors, furniture, and decorative arts should have a character as close as possible to those of their European background. In this, they sometimes succeeded so well that it is difficult to tell if a chair or mirror was made in America or in Europe.

In early America, design character intentionally independent of European fashion is found in those communities whose religious beliefs held them apart from European custom. Most admirably, the Shakers demonstrated such independence. The honesty, simplicity, and directness of their design was truly American in spirit. A widespread admiration for such design has contributed to what would later be considered an expression of our true American character. Such independent character is found in the most important design leaders of our early history: Thomas Jefferson, with his Virginia State Capitol and Monticello, did not simply follow existing standards; he set new ones, and our design legacy is the richer for such innovative spirits.

Looking for Quality

In the seventeenth century, the colonists necessarily "made do" with design that was functional but rarely lavish. It is remarkable that by the eighteenth century, they had progressed enough to produce an object such as—to choose only one example—the John Townsend block-and-shell chest (see fig. 19–18). Although founded on utility and expediency, American design matured quickly and at its finest came to be the equal in quality of the best design anywhere.

Making Comparisons

An obvious comparison is to look at the design of the European colonists alongside the design of the native tribes, since both were dealing with so many of the same conditions but arriving at such different results. Because of their heritages, these two groups experienced different relationships to the land, different preferences in population density, different community and family structures, and different understandings about both the physical and metaphysical worlds. Naturally, they designed different houses, furniture, vessels, and textiles.

We may also compare the relatively plain and sturdy design in the English colonies with the relatively ornate and delicate design of the Spanish and French colonies. We might expect greater perfection of execution and polish from the colonies of the industrial north than from those of the agrarian south, but we would be surprised to find that the prosperity of the southern plantation and its supply of slave labor produced some of the finest design of all.

In looking at how Americans adopted and adapted European styles, it is interesting to notice what they did *not* choose to adopt. With a few exceptions (such as Chippendale chair backs and ceiling plasterwork), Americans made no use of the sweeping lyricism of the French Rococo. Neither did they express much interest in the weighty gilded richness of the English Baroque. Even at their most prosperous and light-hearted, Early Americans seemed to be aware of the hardships of the first years on their new continent and mindful, too, of the restraints of their religious beliefs. They were finally able to create for themselves beautiful and comfortable—even elegant—surroundings, but they almost always (at least through the end of the eighteenth century) stopped short of any excess.

For the Early Americans themselves, the comparison that dominated their consciousness was that between themselves and their European counterparts. The Old World was the measure of the New, and the remarkable progress just mentioned was surely spurred in part by a sense of competitiveness with the world the Americans had left behind. We can remain impressed with how well their design compared with—and how often it surpassed—that of their backgrounds.

20

The Nineteenth Century

"We cannot get rid of the body of tradition, murder it how we may."
— Edwin Lutyens (1869–1944), English architect and designer

The nineteenth century, in design as well as in other fields, was a time of conflicting ideas. Two opposing forces were expressed in different forms: progress toward the future versus a retreat to the past; the charm of the handmade versus the efficiency of the machine-made; beauty versus usefulness; a love of both natural materials and ornate surfaces (fig. 20–1).

Throughout the nineteenth century we shall see the conflict raging, sometimes with one winner, and sometimes with another.

Determinants of Nineteenth-Century Design

The determinants of nineteenth-century design are less the story of geography, politics, and religion, as has been the case previously, and more the story of the new age of British expansion, increased communication, and technological invention. It is the beginning of design globalization made possible by these factors.

◀ **20–1** Detail, oak and onyx fireplace surround of H. H. Richardson's New York State Court of Appeals, Albany, 1876–81. A clock and calendar are set into the carved oak.
Cervin Robinson

History

The history of earlier periods has been the history of the many successions of rulers, their conquests, and their influences, but in the nineteenth century, one country was dominant: England. Although a tiny country, its empire came to control a quarter of the world's population and a third of its land area. Meanwhile, earlier powerful empires—Spanish, Portuguese, Ottoman, and Mughal—weakened or disappeared. And, as it turned out, one ruler was dominant. In mighty England there was one monarch whose reign was virtually synchronous with the entire century. It was Queen Victoria, born in 1819, and ruler of the British Empire from 1830 to 1901.

Naturally, the nineteenth century has been called the Victorian era. Regrettably, the term Victorian connotes stuffy behavior and overstuffed interiors. These certainly existed, but they were far from being the whole story of the nineteenth century and its design. Far from the staid image that Victoria represents, it was a century of variety, vigor, and surprises.

Communications

The great innovation in written communication was lithography, a printing process based on the principle that grease and water do not mix. It was invented in 1798 by a German printer and first used for printing music scores. Color lithography and other new printing methods would follow for the

▲ **20–2** Thomas Hope's drawing of his gallery displaying the sculpture of John Flaxman. The figures are reflected in mirrored walls largely covered with curtains of blue, orange, and black satin.
Dover Publications, Inc.

▼ **20–3** An "Eastlake" walnut *méridienne*, probably made in Grand Rapids, Michigan c. 1890.
From the Collections of Henry Ford Museum & Greenfield Village

dissemination of design ideas in books and in the more recent print media of magazines. In addition, the Parisian painter Jacques-Mandé Daguerre produced the first *daguerrotype* (an image of his own studio) in 1837, and by the 1850s modern photography was in widespread use, also very useful, of course, for conveying design ideas.

In the tradition of earlier eighteenth-century style books was *Household Furniture and Interior Decoration*, 1807, by the English architect and collector Thomas Hope (1769–1831), its engravings showing interiors he designed for himself in a Robert Adam house in London (fig. 20–2). The rooms were highly eclectic, primarily Neoclassical, but with elements of Egyptian, "Hindu," and other exotic styles. The book also showed Hope's furniture designs (see figs. 20–39 and 20–40), and its title is said to have introduced the phrase "interior decoration." Influenced by Hope, George Smith wrote his *Collection of Designs for Household Furniture and Interior Decoration* in 1808.

Charles L. Eastlake's *Hints on House-hold Taste in Furniture, Upholstery, and Other Details*, 1868, had particular impact on the design of its time. Eastlake's own design, with which his book was illustrated, was a simplified and functional version of Gothic that he thought could be inexpensively manufactured. His ideas were taken up in America with more zeal than care, and what was called the Eastlake style flourished in America from c. 1875 to c. 1890 in architecture, interiors, and furniture design. It was an ornate version of the Queen Anne Revival style, busy with brackets, spindles, bobbins, turnings, and knobs (fig. 20–3).

Technology

The history of the nineteenth century is the history of invention—the steam engine, the railroad, the cotton gin, the automobile, the telephone, the phonograph, the motion picture camera, electric lights, and synthetic fibers. The first telegram was sent from Paris to Lille in 1794, and Alexander Graham Bell patented the telephone in England and the United States in 1876. The steamship *Savannah* crossed the Atlantic in 1818. For overland travel, cast-iron rails were made in 1767, though at first used only for horse-drawn cars. In the first decades of the nineteenth century, locomotives with names like "Rocket" and "Puffing Billy" were designed. In England, the 34-mile-long Liverpool-to-Manchester line went into service in 1830.

With improved communication and transportation, new designs were no longer limited to a local audience but were on their way to becoming international. The new technology spread quickly and widely, affecting not only the way interior-related products were made but also the functions for which interiors were designed. New methods of mass production were widely used for building materials and furniture. To an unprecedented degree, technology formed design. Sometimes design changes were the result of a resentful and suspicious reaction against the new, proving yet again that technology served as a major catalyst for design ideas.

Nineteenth-Century Architecture and Interior Design

The nineteenth century, spurred by many technological changes and the rapid communication of design ideas, was a time of many short-lived styles jostling for attention and favor. Most of them can be roughly divided into those that continued the established interest in classical Greek and Roman design and those that sought to revive the design of more exotic times and places. Then there were also some more independent new movements, some new building equipment, and some wholly new building forms.

Empire Style

The emperor for whom the **Empire** style was named was Napoleon Bonaparte, who led the French army into victory over much of Europe, then became first consul in 1799, and finally crowned himself emperor in 1804. His First Empire lasted until 1814, when he was forced to resign and was exiled. Although Napoleon's chief skills were military, not artistic, he was well aware of art's value as propaganda. He authorized the building of new quarters for the Académie des Beaux-Arts and the Ecole des Beaux-Arts in Paris, a new arcaded rue de Rivoli, and the Arc de Triomphe. He began to refurbish the palaces of deposed French royalty, many of which had been stripped of their contents, in a style appropriate for his new government. This policy revived the practice of interior design and the crafts that supplied it, and in bringing new life to the interiors of Fontainebleau, the Tuileries, and the Elysée Palace, there came a new decorative style.

Percier and Fontaine The chief practitioners who defined the Empire style were Charles Percier (1764–1838) and Pierre-François-Léonard Fontaine (1762–1853). The two had met as apprentices in a Paris studio and traveled to Rome, where they made drawings that were later published in 1798 and 1809. Among their interior commissions was Malmaison, the house of Josephine Bonaparte, Napoleon's wife (fig. 20–4). This work launched their career. In 1804, Napoleon named Percier and Fontaine *architects du Louvre et des Tuileries*.

▼ **20–4** The music room of Empress Josephine at the Château de Malmaison, near Paris, 1800. Percier and Fontaine designed the interior, the furnishings, and even the musical instruments.
Giraudon/Art Resource, NY

Percier and Fontaine felt that the design of both ancient Greece and Rome, particularly as had been depicted on Greek vases, was appropriate for the new French state. Revivals of classical design were not new, of course, but that of Percier and Fontaine was more severe and more correct than any France had known before. They laid the ground rules of the new style in their 1801 publication *Recueil de décorations intérieures . . .* (Collection of Interior Decorations . . .), actually defining what we now call the Empire style three years before there was an empire. "One tries in vain," Percier and Fontaine wrote, "to find forms better than those we have inherited from Antiquity." Their Empire style was indeed based on antique models, as had been the Directoire style of 1795–99 (see Chapter 15). It shared with the Directoire a vocabulary of simple, often angular and sharp-edged furniture shapes, but to those shapes the style applied a new richness of ornament, always being careful to keep form and ornament distinct. Among the motifs were carved sphinxes, eagles, swans, bees, **caryatids**, **terms** (male busts on pedestals),

winged torches, and winged griffins. There were also monogram *N*s circled with laurel leaves.

The most characteristic element of the Empire style, however, was the backdrop for these pieces: the walls. They were crowned with entablatures (or at least cornices), articulated with columns or pilasters, and plastered and painted in a semigloss polish or—even more dramatic—draped. The most extraordinary wall treatments employed stretched, shirred, or loosely draped fabric filling the whole area from the top, at the **cornice**, to the bottom, at the **dado** or **baseboard**, which was caught up at intervals and held with tassels and gold-headed nails. Josephine's bedroom at Malmaison (fig. 20–5), again by Percier and Fontaine, was circular and designed to represent the interior of a Roman emperor's military tent. Its walls were draped in red silk, which appeared to be supported by tent posts; the ceiling was draped in cloth enriched with gold **appliqué** ornaments. Typical of many Empire bedrooms, Josephine's bed was placed with the long side against the wall, and it, too, was given a tentlike drapery.

▼ **20–5** Empress Josephine's tented bedroom at Malmaison, as decorated by Percier and Fontaine in 1810. The furniture is signed by French cabinetmakers Jacob-Desmalter and Biennais.
Giraudon/Art Resource, NY

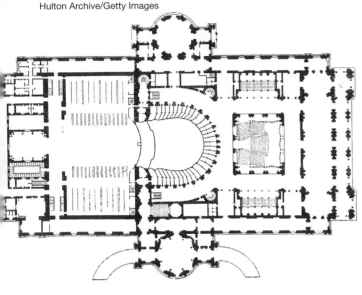

▲ 20–7 The grand staircase of the Paris Opéra designed by Charles Garnier, 1861–75, surrounded by marble columns and panels, bronze statues, and ornate stuccowork.
Stock Connection Distribution/Alamy Images

Empire doors had either square panels with center rosettes or rectangular panels with diamond shapes within them. Windows were hung with two or three sets of complex draperies with elaborate valances, fringes, tassels, **jabots**, and **swags**. The textiles were silk, wool, and cotton, all three often combined to cover one window. Marble mantels were severely classical with plain straight shelves. In palatial rooms, they were richly carved under the shelf and supported at the sides by caryatids or dwarf columns. In less grand rooms, the carving on the mantels was often omitted; the sides were simple pilasters, and interest was maintained by the color and graining of the marble. The mantelshelf was usually furnished with an ormolu clock, perhaps with Grecian figures and covered with a glass dome. Floors were often left bare and were patterned with black and white marble squares or wood parquet; they might also be partly covered with **Aubusson** rugs or carpets from the Far East.

Charles Garnier and the Second Empire Napoleon Bonaparte's nephew, Napoleon III, emperor of the Second Republic from 1852 to 1870, along with his wife Eugènie, would enjoy the glories of what is now known as the **Second Empire**. The Second Empire welcomed the continuation of Empire design but combined it with elements taken from the Renaissance and Baroque periods. It still worshipped the antique but with a more romantic, less clear-eyed devotion. In decorating her own rooms at the château of Compiègne, Empress Eugènie mixed Empire with Louis XVI and other styles.

It was under Napoleon III that Baron Georges-Eugène Haussmann began rebuilding the medieval street system of Paris into the wide radiating boulevards we know today. The monumental building of the new Louvre by Visconti and Lefuel was also begun in 1853. The Louvre employed such Second Empire characteristics as the **mansard** roof (a roof with two pitches, the lower one being steeper), plus pedimented dormers, as well as exterior and interior surfaces encrusted with French Renaissance detail.

A more important example of Second Empire style is the Paris Opéra House, designed by Charles Garnier (1825–98), begun in 1861. It lacked a mansard roof, but it amply demonstrated another important Second Empire trend: incorporating the work of painters, sculptors, and decorative artists into the interior design. The interior's sense of theatricality is by no means limited to its stage or even to its auditorium, which, as the floor plan (fig. 20–6) shows, is only a small part at the center of a complex of lobbies, foyers, vestibules, and grand stairways (fig. 20–7) that created a stage for the parade of French society. There, the dramas of the Second Empire played on, even as the performances ensued within.

Regency Style

When England's King George III became insane in 1811, his son began to rule as prince regent, becoming King George IV when his father died in 1820. The official Regency, therefore, lasted hardly a decade, but the **Regency** period in design is generally considered to have begun as early as 1780 and to have lasted until George IV's own death in 1830.

The chief chroniclers of the Regency style were Thomas Hope (see fig. 20–2) and George Smith, whose books were to have a strong influence on the period. Typical Regency rooms had plain plaster ceilings, but many also had curved coves joining ceiling and walls. Cornices and door and window frames were of straight classical molding, and a rather severe chimneypiece might be decorated only with a sculptured panel or a fluted frieze. Windows were often tall, reaching down to floor level. Marble busts of classical heroes and philosophers ornamented the rooms, often standing on short portions of column shafts.

John Nash One of the style's two leading architects was John Nash (1752–1835), a court-appointed architect who created the Royal Pavilion at Brighton for the Prince Regent. The Royal Pavilion (see figs. 20–18 and 20–19) exhibited the classical symmetry of the Regency style, but indulged in some fanciful and exotic details, and we shall see it later as an example of an Eastern style called Anglo–Indian.

Nash's work in a stricter and more recognizable Regency style is seen in a series of sedate stucco-faced blocks of row houses (called terraces in England) including a dozen such buildings at Regent's Park, London, built between 1812 and 1827. Other Nash designs in London include the Haymarket Theater and the conversion of Buckingham House into Buckingham Palace.

John Soane Nash's great rival was Sir John Soane (1753–1837). Soane's great work was the Bank of England building in London, which was finished in 1823 and has since been destroyed. Also notable was his own house in Lincoln's Inn Fields, London (fig. 20–8), which he left to the nation and which is now the Soane Museum, housing his fine collection of architectural drawings. In both buildings, the interiors are distinguished by Soane's virtuoso handling of spatial and lighting effects, combining shallow domes, vaults, lanterns, and hidden light sources.

Although among the finest accomplishments of Regency style, Soane's rooms are too idiosyncratic to be considered typical or to have been widely copied. They did, however, reinforce the trend away from the plaster ornament of Adam toward smooth plaster walls painted in rather strong dark colors, such as browns and deep reds.

Other Classicist Styles

The two great classicizing styles—Empire in France and Regency in England—in turn inspired other styles in other countries, such as Ireland, Germany, and Austria, as the Neoclassical ideals spread throughout Europe. In America, as we have seen, the Neoclassical flowered into the Federal style, which continued to flourish with Jefferson and others into the nineteenth century (see Chapter 19).

Neoclassicism in Ireland Neoclassical design in Ireland was led by James Gandon, a pupil of William Chambers who lived in Ireland from 1781, and by James Wyatt, who in 1790 began work on Castlecoole in County Fermanagh. The house was finished c. 1797 and furnished in the first quarter of the nineteenth century. Plasterwork was by Joseph Rose, Jr., who had worked for Robert Adam; chimneypieces were by

▲ **20–8** The breakfast room, Sir John Soane's house, London, 1812–13. Its complex lighting effects come from a series of skylights and mirrors.
Richard Bryant/Arcaid

▲ 20–9 James Wyatt's oval saloon at Castlecoole, County Fermanagh, Ireland, c. 1797, with brass-inlaid "Grecian" furniture designed by John Preston of Dublin in the 1810s and 1820s.
Patrick Prendergast/The National Trust Photographic Library, London, England

However, Germany's great Neoclassicist, and one of the outstanding architects of the nineteenth century, was Karl Friedrich Schinkel (1781–1841). In 1803 and 1824 he had gone to study Roman ruins, and he traveled to London in 1826 to see Sir Robert Smirke's British Museum, then under construction. An interior that displays his design style is the royal summer house at Schloss Charlottenburg, Originally called the Neue Pavillon (now the Schinkel-Pavillon), it contains a tent room draped in blue-and-white-striped linen twill, as well as a bedroom for Queen Louise (fig. 20–10) designed by Schinkel in 1809. The bedroom has pink wallpaper behind filmy drapes of white *mousseline*, a fine version of muslin, and the queen's bed uses motifs from the *Recueil...* of Percier and Fontaine.

The Biedermeier Style in Austria   The early and rigorously accurate examples of Neoclassicism mentioned above gave way, however, to a more casual style, the **Biedermeier**. In nineteenth century Austria, quiet family life and homely virtues came to be personified by a completely fictional and comic character called "Papa Biedermeier," pictured as stout, self-satisfied, and full of misinformation. The Biedermeier style, also popular in Germany and Scandinavia, disdained grandeur and the slavish copying of classical precedent. Its interiors, furniture, and decoration are sometimes charming, sometimes clumsy, sometimes both (see fig. 20–42). In interiors, furniture was not aligned against walls but clustered in functional groupings of sofas, chairs, and tables, for convenience and comfort over formality. The Biedermeier style could also be refreshingly simple. Walls were often painted a single color or papered in striped patterns, with painted or papered dadoes and cornices in complementary colors. Plants were a favorite element of the Biedermeier interior.

The Gustavian Style in Sweden   Named for Gustav III, who ruled Sweden from 1771 to 1792, the Gustavian style of the late eighteenth century first brought Neoclassical ideas to Scandinavia. Unlike some rulers for whom styles are named, Gustav was very interested in the visual arts and largely responsible for his namesake style. When he was still the crown prince, he commissioned a drawing-room interior from Jean Eric Rehn (1717–93), who had studied in Paris. Rehn also designed interiors for Gustav's brother and sister. With the Gustavian style as its base, Neoclassicism was firmly established in Sweden, its strictest representative being architect Carl Fredrik Sundvall (1754–1831), who decorated a large

London sculptor Richard Westmacott; and furniture was commissioned from John Preston, a leading Dublin upholsterer. Among the well-proportioned rooms, the oval saloon (fig. 20–9) is the most outstanding.

Neoclassicism in Germany   Frederick William II instituted a program of building in the Neoclassical style in 1786, employing architect Carl Gotthard Langhans to design interiors for the Winter Apartments at Schloss Charlottenburg, near Berlin. Begun in 1795, the apartments had unpainted paneling with restrained ornament. For the Potsdam Stadtschloss in 1803, the brothers Ludwig Friedrich Catel and Franz Ludwig Catel designed an Etruscan Room, painted with figures taken from Greek vases.

▲ **20–10** Schinkel's pearwood furniture and draped fabric for Queen Louise at Schloss Charlottenburg, Berlin, 1809.
© Fritz von der Schulenburg — The Interior Archive (Title: Empire/Charlottenburg)

▲ **20–11** The saloon at Rosendal Palace, Stockholm, 1823–27, designed by Fredrik Blom. The walls are hung with silk beneath a wallpaper frieze imported from France. The white cylinder in the corner is a stove.
Alex Starkey/Country Life Picture Library, London, England

manor house, Stiernsund in Närke, in 1800 with sculpture-filled niches and painted relief friezes. Fredrik Blom (1781–1853), who studied abroad, designed interiors for Rosendal Palace (fig. 20–11) and for the royal country house, Rosersberg.

Revivalist Styles

The group of styles that sought to revive the design of more exotic times and places corresponds to what is often called the **Victorian** style, meaning the style current in England—and to some extent in America—during the reign of Queen Victoria. Yet, so long did her reign last (from 1837 to 1901), and so varied was the design of those sixty-four years, that the term *Victorian* has only the most vague meaning. Revivalist styles did not, like the classicist styles, attempt to revive time-less principles of proportion and composition; they sought in-stead to revive old forms because of their novelty or charm or—in the case of the Gothic Revival—their association with religion.

Gothic Revival The Gothic style had never completely dis-appeared from Europe since its peak of accomplishment in the sixteenth century. Historians call Gothic design after 1750 Gothic Revival, with A. W. N. Pugin as its great scholar and advocate.

Pugin's most notable work was interiors for London's Houses of Parliament, which he designed between 1836 and

▲ **20–12** The House of Lords, Palace of Westminster, London, designed by A. W. N. Pugin with Charles Barry and John Gregory Crace, finished in 1847.
British Information Services

1852 in collaboration with the building's architect, Charles Barry, and with the help of John Gregory Crace (fig. 20–12). Crace was a member of the family that ran the decorating firm that, for most of its 131-year history from 1768 to 1899, was the most important in England. For the Houses of Parliament, Crace's contributions included wallpapers, carpets, decorative painting, and some furniture.

English Gothic Revivalists of the decades from 1860 to 1880 considered themselves Reformed. Rather than the rich ornament of Pugin and Crace, they developed an interior style of simply cut oak carvings in both paneling and furniture, and rather than paper their walls with bright patterns, they hung them with wool fabric in deep, muted colors such as rusts, ochres, and earthy greens. Wainscoting was popular, too, as were graining and stenciling. Among the Reformed Gothicists were the architects G. E. Street and Richard Norman Shaw and the designer William Morris. (Morris would soon discard the Reformed Gothic but keep its simplicity as he developed the Arts and Crafts style.)

Too young to have had a Gothic past of its own, the United States enthusiastically embraced the style. One notable example is Lyndhurst in Tarrytown, New York, designed by A. J. Davis from 1838 to 1842. Countless Gothic Revival churches were built throughout the United States, culminating (though not ending) in St. Patrick's Cathedral in New York (1858–88), designed by James Renwick.

Another American architect who drew upon Gothic Revival sources (among many others) was Frank Furness (1839–1912). In 1876, as chief designer for the firm Furness & Hewitt, he designed a remarkable series of gallery and circulation spaces for Philadelphia's Pennsylvania Academy of Fine Arts (fig. 20–13). In addition to Gothic Revival arches, the building incorporated a French mansard roof, a Greek frieze with triglyphlike blocks, Byzantine tilework, and paired columns that look like the giant pistons of industrial machinery.

Greek Revival   All Neoclassicism, including the Empire and Regency styles, is in part a revival of Greek design principles, but until c. 1790 the focus was on those principles as they had been revealed through Roman examples. The Greek Revival was a style apart, rejecting the Roman models and preferring the relative gravity, strength, and simplicity of their Greek antecedents. Although it was never heralded with the religious fervor of the Gothic Revival, the Greek Revival was considered the proper expression of civic virtues and therefore the correct style for the buildings and interiors of government. Beiges and pastels were considered appropriate interior colors, and marble, gilding, stenciling, and ornamental plasterwork were used.

The term **Néo-Grec** is not a synonym for the Greek Revival but denotes a phase of Second Empire design in France, based on the Neoclassical repertory of Greek and Roman forms. The Néo-Grec places special emphasis on the style of Pompeii and with more than a dash of Egyptian Revival.

Egyptian Revival   The earliest imitators of the distinctive style of the ancient Egyptians had been their Roman conquerors, and through Rome's imitations such features as the sphinx and the obelisk were accepted adjuncts to the classical and Neoclassical vocabularies.

The nineteenth-century Egyptian Revival owed its impetus to Napoleon, whose successful campaign in Egypt, waged in 1798, caused much excitement in France. Napoleon fueled his nation's interest by taking with him not only an army of soldiers but also an army of surveyors, scholars, and artists. One publication that resulted was the monumental *Description de l'Egypte*, published in twenty magnificently illustrated volumes (1809–28). Appropriately styled bookcases were also available to hold the folios of the *Description* (fig. 20–14).

▲ **20–13** Pennsylvania Academy of the Fine Arts, Philadelphia, designed by Frank Furness in a mixture of styles, 1876.
© Bob Krist/CORBIS All Rights Reserved

▲ **20–14** Wood carving on the corner of a bookcase made between 1813 and 1836 by French cabinetmaker Charles Morel after designs by Edme-François Jomard.
Carved corner of bookcase designed for 20-volume set of *Description de l'Egypte*. Bibliotheque de National, Paris. Photo from New York Public Library, General Research.

Many rushed to produce designs in the style. Percier and Fontaine had also offered Egyptian models for secretaries and clocks in their 1801 publication. Charles Percier designed a suite of furniture. France's Sèvres porcelain factory produced a *Vase égyptien* and in 1810–12 an entire Egyptian dinner service. Given by Louis XVIII to the first Duke of Wellington, the *Service égyptienne* is now at Apsley House in London. Even chimneypieces, andirons, clocks, candelabra, glassware, and silver appeared in Egyptian guise, and the fashion spread from France to Germany, England, and elsewhere.

Romanesque Revival   The Romanesque Revival, taken from its eleventh- and twelfth-century model, was a style of spare ornament, large masonry expanses, round-headed arches, and barrel vaults. In its interiors, this strong architecture was supplemented with natural wood wainscoting, stained glass, decorative tiles, and murals. The style is associated chiefly with the work of one architect, the American Henry Hobson Richardson (1838–86). Richardson may have been influenced by France's Emile Vaudreme, who had designed the church of St.-Pierre de Montrouge, built in 1864–70, as well as by original Romanesque examples, which he saw while attending the Ecôle des Beaux-Arts in Paris, from 1860 to 1865.

On his return to America, Richardson's first major work was Trinity Church (fig. 20–15) in Boston, 1872–77, which employed the round-headed arches of the Romanesque. However, it was more ornate than any Romanesque prece-

▼ **20–15** H. H. Richardson's Trinity Church, Boston, 1872–77, in a highly decorated version of Romanesque Revival.
Cervin Robinson

▲ 20–16 The library of the University Club, New York, by McKim, Mead & White, finished in 1900.
Museum of the City of New York, McKim, Mead & White Collection

▲ 20–17 The gold-encrusted Music Room of McKim, Mead and White's Villard Houses, New York, 1882–85. The paintings in the lunettes are by John La Farge.
Cervin Robinson

dent, with stained glass by artists Edward Burne-Jones and Henry Holiday. Richardson's work encouraged a proliferation of miniature Romanesque castles in residential construction throughout the American Northeast and Midwest. We have already seen (in fig. 20–1) a detail of Richardson's New York State Court of Appeals in Albany, 1876–81. Other well-known works by Richardson include the Marshall Field Warehouse (1887) in Chicago and, later, some residential architecture, which demonstrated the charms of simple forms, informal planning, and casually rambling masses with freely organized fenestration and wide, sprawling verandas.

Renaissance Revival   The name Renaissance Revival was used in the nineteenth century for buildings, interiors, furniture, ceramics, and enamels based mostly on Italian Renaissance models, its chief model being the Palazzo Farnese in Rome, although in practice it was fairly eclectic. The style was a particular favorite for club buildings, such as Charles Barry's Travellers Club (1829–32) and Reform Club (1837–41) in London. McKim, Mead & White, renowned architects of the nineteenth century, designed the Century Club (1891) and the University Club (1899) in New York (fig. 20–16) in the Renaissance Revival style.

McKim, Mead & White also turned to the Renaissance Revival for some residential work, such as the Villard Houses in New York, 1882–85, a complex of six town houses, of which the largest was for Henry Villard. The Music Room (fig. 20–17), the most splendid room of the complex, would become from 1998 through 2004 the site of the Le Cirque 2000 restaurant, designed by Adam Tihany.

Among other designers in the Renaissance Revival style were German emigrants Gustave and Christian Herter. Herter Brothers, as their firm was called, was in business from 1859 to 1906, offering both interior design services and interior components (see fig. 20–43). In 1878 they advertised their goods as "Furniture, Decoration, Gas Fixtures . . . recent importations of Fine French and English paper hangings. Rich Japanese silk brocades, Rare oriental embroideries, French moquette carpets" and a "stock of upholstery goods and curtain material." Their wealthy clients included J. Pierpont Morgan, William H. Vanderbilt, and John D. Spreckels of San Francisco (see fig. 20–20). They designed interiors for Detlef Lienau's 1869 Renaissance château for LeGrand Lockwood at Norwalk, Connecticut, and for New York's Union Club and St. Regis Hotel, and also they provided ornamental plasterwork and woodwork for all the major public rooms of the White House, Washington, DC.

▲ **20–18** Exterior view of the Royal Pavilion, Brighton, England, as redesigned by John Nash in 1815–22. The largest dome is over the Banqueting Room.

Eastern Styles

The nineteenth century saw a number of often overlapping styles that derived their character from the Far East and Near East.

The **Anglo-Indian** style is most closely associated with the Royal Pavilion in the seaside town of Brighton, England, designed by John Nash for the Prince Regent and built between 1815 and 1822 in the Regency period. There had originally been a farmhouse on the site, converted and enlarged by Henry Holland in 1786 as a Palladian villa for the Prince of Wales. Nash doubled the villa's size and transformed its appearance. The exterior (fig. 20–18) shows such Indian features as subtly curved domes, minarets, and stone trellises or **jales**. The interior includes the Banqueting Hall (fig. 20–19) beneath the largest dome; it features an enormous chandelier hanging from a cluster of bronze palm fronds. Other rooms are finished in black and gold or in **faux** bamboo, and a dining room and music room have ceilings imitating tents. Technically, Nash's work was up-to-the-minute, using cast-iron structure to support his complex forms and providing the royal bathroom with five different possibilities for bathing. In addition to his own work, Nash directed interior contributions by the firm of John Crace & Son, who had worked with Pugin and Barry on the Houses of Parliament

▼ **20–19** The Banqueting Hall of the Royal Pavilion, Brighton. Royal Pavilion Libraries and Museums, Brighton, England, U.K.

(fig. 20–12) and would later do decorative painting and gilding at Windsor Castle.

Closely related to the Anglo-Indian style of the Royal Pavilion, the Moorish style of the nineteenth century focused on the architecture and decoration of the Muslim inhabitants (the Moors) of northern Africa and southern Spain, more than that of the Muslims in India. Fascination with Moorish design had long existed. In 1856 the English architect Owen Jones, in his *Grammar of Ornament*, argued that the Moors were the inventors of fundamental principles of pattern and color use. Jones designed tiles in the Moorish style for the Minton ceramic factory and also Moorish ceiling tiles. The Moorish style was employed throughout the Western world in architecture for hotels, theaters, and synagogues. In interiors it has been thought especially appropriate for masculine retreats such as smoking rooms and billiard rooms. An example is the 1900 Turkish Room designed by Herter Brothers for the Spreckels mansion in San Francisco (fig. 20–20).

▼ **20–20** The Turkish Room in the John D. Spreckels House, San Francisco, designed by the Herter Brothers before 1900. San Francisco History Center, San Francisco Public Library

The Arts and Crafts Movement

The nineteenth-century revivals were sometimes applied with considerable purity, but more often they mingled with one another, producing stews flavored with every spice in the cabinet. Near the end of the century, however, came two styles that were relatively independent, original, and pure: the Arts and Crafts movement and Art Nouveau. Linking the two was the Aesthetic movement. And within these movements was design that would lay the foundations for the modernism that was to come.

The **Arts and Crafts** movement can be considered another revival, not of any specific visual expression, but of a way of working: in an age of increasing industrialization, it sought to bring back hand craftsmanship and to heighten the pleasure of the individual worker—a pleasure, it was thought, not possible in the factory. The movement's goal, said painter and designer Walter Crane (1845–1915), was to "turn our artists into craftsmen and our craftsmen into artists." Eventually, it developed a distinctive visual character of its own—simple, solid, and more at home in a country cottage than in an urban mansion. Natural oak and redwood were used; colors were light earth tones (greens, tans, rust); floors were covered with wood, decorative tile, linoleum, and small area rugs; and furniture was plain, sturdy, and relatively sparse.

The philosophical and aesthetic ideas behind the Arts and Crafts movement came from a group of English painters and designers called the Pre-Raphaelites, founded in 1848 by William Holman Hunt, John Everett Millais, and Dante Gabriel Rossetti. They shared a meticulously realistic technique, a resolve to be true to nature, and an admiration for Italian painting before the time of Raphael. Their ideas won the support of art critic John Ruskin and the admiration of the young designer William Morris (1834–96), who took from them a rather romantic view of the Middle Ages.

William Morris and Philip Webb William Morris was not an architect, but he was still a major proponent of the Arts and Crafts movement. In 1859, Morris's friend and architect Philip Webb (1831–1915) designed for Morris and his wife the first expression of what would come (after 1887) to be called Arts and Crafts: the Red House on the outskirts of London. Named for its red bricks and red tiles, the Red House was not historicist (although there were some simplified echoes of the Gothic), yet it did not seek to completely overthrow tradition. The Red House's forms and decorations were derived instead from practical considerations, from an honest use of new developments such as iron beams and sash windows, and from a shared love of fine craftsmanship (fig. 20–21).

The cooperative efforts of Webb, Morris, and their friends at Red House led to the formation in 1861 of a firm called Morris, Marshall, Faulkner, and Company, which produced stained glass, wall hangings, wallpapers, fabrics, fireplaces, paneling, and furniture for other clients. After 1875 it would be called Morris and Company. Morris went on to design residential interiors for his own country house, Kelmscott Manor, and for Standen in Sussex, also designed by Philip Webb (fig. 20–22). For St. James's Palace, London, Morris decorated the Armoury, the Tapestry Room, the Throne Room, and other interiors, and he designed a dining room for the South Kensington Museum, now the Victoria & Albert Museum.

▼ **20–21** Upper stair hall of Philip Webb's Red House for William Morris, London, 1859.
The National Trust Photographic Library

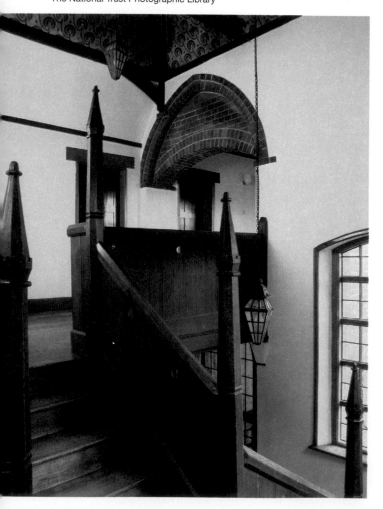

▲ **20–23** A fireplace inglenook with built-in seating in the living room of the Gamble House, Pasadena, California, by Greene and Greene.
Timothy Street-Porter

Morris turned to textile design in 1861, with the first of more than fifty patterns, and in 1879 he began to design tapestries. The greatest artistic achievements of Morris were probably his skillful flat patterns, often floral in inspiration, for carpets, fabrics (see fig. 20–60), wallpapers (see fig. 20–67),

and even some industrial materials like corticine, similar to linoleum (see fig. 20–64). His lasting message is expressed in his 1880 lecture called "The Beauty of Life": "[H]ave nothing in your house that you do not know to be useful, or believe to be beautiful."

Gustav Stickley and the Mission Style   In the United States the Arts and Crafts movement was taken up with enthusiasm, though it flowered later in America than it had in England. It seemed to flow naturally from the robust Romanesque Revival style of H. H. Richardson, and it suited the American taste for simplicity and strength. Arts and Crafts work was exhibited in both Philadelphia and Boston in the 1890s, and the Chicago Society of Arts and Crafts was founded in 1897. In Chicago, the style was employed by a number of silversmiths and metalworkers, and art potteries sprang up in Cincinnati and elsewhere. The chief figure among American Arts and Crafts, however, was Gustav Stickley (1858–1942), who had traveled to England in the 1890s. He called his version of the Arts and Crafts movement the Craftsman style, but it also came to be called Mission style. In 1901 he began publishing the *Craftsman*, a magazine devoted to Arts and Crafts; its first issue was dedicated to Morris, its second to Ruskin.

Greene and Greene   Related to these New York manifestations of the Arts and Crafts movement were the West Coast work of Bernard Maybeck, Irving Gill, and the Greene brothers, Charles Sumner Greene (1868–1957) and Henry Mather Greene (1870–1954). The West Coast work of Greene & Greene came from the sudden growth in population and prosperity there. On their way west to settle in Pasadena, California, the Greene brothers stopped at the 1893 World's Columbian Exposition in Chicago, where they were much impressed by a traditional Japanese pavilion called the *Ho-o-den*. This Japanese influence, together with Arts and Crafts and a respect for California's eighteenth-century Hispanic architecture, blended into a complex and personal style, at once rustic and impeccably detailed. Best known of their many wood-framed "bungalows" was the Gamble House, Pasadena, of 1907–09 (fig. 20–23).

The Aesthetic Movement

The Aesthetic Movement of the 1870s and 1880s in England, and somewhat later in the United States, was closely related to the Arts and Crafts movement and also included elements of japonisme, a French term for the nineteenth-century interest in Japanese design. But unlike the Arts and Crafts movement, which was concerned with morality, social issues, crafts guilds, and the evils of mechanization, the Aesthetic Movement concerned itself only with beauty.

The epitome of Aesthetic Movement interiors is a London dining room (fig. 20–24) designed by painter James McNeill Whistler in 1876 for the shipping and communications magnate F. R. Leyland. It was meant as a setting for one of Whistler's own paintings and for Leyland's collection of blue-and-white porcelain. Whistler covered the ceiling with gold leaf and with motifs resembling peacocks' feathers. He gilded the walnut shelves, and he painted the wooden window shutters with long-tailed gold peacocks. The dominant and unifying color of the room, however, is a deep blue-green against which the gold sparkles and the numerous blue-and-white porcelain vases gleam. Although popularly known as "the Peacock Room," Whistler himself called it "Harmony in Blue and Gold."

▼ **20–24** The Peacock Room, London, decorated by James McNeill Whistler in 1876. His painting, *The Princess*, is over the fireplace. The pendant lights were by the room's previous designer, Thomas Jeckyll.
James McNeill Whistler, "Harmony in Blue and Gold." The Peacock Room, northeast corner, from a house owned by Frederick Leyland, London. 1876–77. Oil paint and metal leaf on canvas, leather, and wood, 13'11⅞" × 33'2" × 19'11½" (4.26 × 10.11 × 6.83 m). Courtesy of the Freer Gallery of Art, Smithsonian Institution, Washington, D.C. Gift of Charles Lang Freer, F1904.61

Art Nouveau Style

By the last decade of the century, a new aesthetic movement was being born: the **Art Nouveau**. Unlike the revival styles, it had little apparent connection with the past, unless one sees it as a culmination of a century-long obsession with floral ornament. Unlike the Arts and Crafts and Aesthetic movements, it would extend beyond England and America to engage every country in Europe, but like the Aesthetic Movement, its concerns were purely visual.

The Art Nouveau style was characterized by sinuous curves and asymmetry, both based on plant forms. It also exhibited a concern for creating complete stylistic ensembles, and, in some cases, an integration of ornament with structure. An early appearance of the style was in graphic design and furniture by English architect Arthur Heygate Mackmurdo (1851–1942) in 1883, and the following year it appeared in architectural ornament by the American architect Louis Sullivan.

Louis Sullivan   Although Louis Sullivan (1856–1924) was a pioneer of Art Nouveau ornament, he applied that ornament (fig. 20–25) to building compositions that were foursquare, direct, and thoroughly foreign from anything remotely floral. His buildings show the influence of H. H. Richardson's Romanesque Revival, and the relationship between Sullivan's form and ornament has attracted much attention. Historian Nikolaus Pevsner wrote in 1946 that "Sullivan was in fact just as much a revolutionary in his ornament as in his use of plain, smooth surfaces . . . [H]is theory of severe functionalism . . . cannot be understood without a careful look at his flowing ornament, nor his ornament without a vivid memory of the austerity of the main lines and blocks of his buildings." In his body of work, his contemporaries must have seen what they were accustomed to looking for, a great flourish of Art Nouveau exuberance. What Sullivan's true disciples (such as Frank Lloyd Wright) would see were the strong forms beneath the flourish.

▼ **20–25** A terra-cotta block, designed by Louis Sullivan for his 1884 Rubin Rubel House in Chicago, is a precocious example of Art Nouveau. 16 in. (41 cm) wide. Abercrombie

▲ **20–26** The skylit foyer of Victor Horta's 1894 van Eetvelde House, Brussels. Victor Horta, Van Eetvelde House. Brussels, Belgium. 1895. Salon. The Museum of Modern Art/Licensed by Scala-Art Resource, NY

Victor Horta Art Nouveau's first complete example in architecture did not come until a decade after Sullivan's terra-cotta ornamentation. It was the Hôtel Tassel of 1892–93, built in Brussels, and designed by Victor Horta (1861–1947). Its rooms were freely disposed around a central staircase with its iron structure exposed throughout and supplemented with a "capital" of nonstructural iron tendrils. Mosaic floor patterns and painted walls and ceilings repeated the organic theme. Horta would continue the style in other Brussels buildings, including the Hôtel Eetvelde of 1894. Built around a central skylit foyer (fig. 20–26), its iron structure is again exposed throughout and again supplemented with "capitals" of nonstructural iron tendrils. Horta also built the Hôtel Solvay in the same year; in this building the handrails are supported by similarly entwining ironwork (see fig. 20–33).

Emile Gallé and Hector Guimard In France the Art Nouveau style was accepted with enthusiasm, especially in the cities of Paris and Nancy. The leaders of Art Nouveau in Nancy were Emile Gallé (1846–1904), a glassmaker (see fig. 20–55), potter, and furniture designer (see 20–47), and, following Gallé's example, the ébéniste Louis Majorelle (1859–1926), who also produced ceramics as well as furniture (see fig. 20–30). Although Marjorelle's design was generally more abstract than Gallé's, he expressed the general inspiration for Art Nouveau in his statement "My garden is my library."

In Paris, the leader of the style was Hector Guimard (1867–1942). After study at the Ecole des Beaux-Arts, instead of the usual pilgrimage to Rome and Greece, Guimard traveled to England and Belgium, where he met Horta and studied his work. His Castel Béranger, a Paris apartment block, was finished in 1897, and soon after he was given the commission for entrance pavilions at all the Métro (subway) stations in Paris. There were 141 of these (of which 86 survive), and their recognizable forms are quite well known today. Guimard's style and name became known to every Parisian. Understandably, French Art Nouveau is sometimes called the *Style Métro*. Guimard also designed furniture (see fig. 20–46), which also reflects his curvilinear artistry.

The Secessionists   In Austria, a late branch of Art Nouveau was called the **Secession**. Founded in 1897, its organization was so-named because its members had "seceded" from their fellow artists and designers in protest against eclecticism and historicist revivals. The Secession was characterized by greater symmetry and straighter lines than mainstream Art Nouveau, following the model of Viennese architect Otto Wagner (1841–1918). Wagner's followers in the Secession movement included the architects Adolf Loos and Joseph Maria Olbrich, the architect and designer Josef Hoffmann (see Chapter 21). Related to the Vienna Secession were the Munich Secession, founded in 1892 and including furniture designer Richard Riemerschmid among its members, and the Berlin Secession, founded in 1898.

▼ **20–27** Antoní Gaudi's chapel for the Colonia Guell, begun in 1898 and finished in 1915.

The Art Nouveau style also appeared in Italy (where it was called *Stile Liberty* or *Stile floreale*), in Spain (*Modernisme* or *Arte joven*), in Scotland and England (Glasgow style), in the Netherlands (*Nieuwe kunst*), in Russia (*Stil' modern*), and in the United States (Tiffany style, after Louis Comfort Tiffany).

Beyond Art Nouveau

Two designers whose work was clearly influenced by Art Nouveau, yet who carried that style into highly personal and idiosyncratic directions were Spain's Antoní Gaudi and Scotland's Charles Rennie Mackintosh.

Antoní Gaudi   Antoní Gaudi y Cornet (1852–1926) of Barcelona was a pious man, influenced by his area's medieval history and the structural logic and craftsmanship of its buildings. He was interested, too, in the ideas of John Ruskin and Viollet-le-Duc. In 1883, the young Gaudi was appointed architect of Barcelona's cathedral of the Sagrada Familia, a monumental work that occupied much of his time until his death. He never did complete it, and it remains a continuing work in progress in present-day Barcelona, based in part on his architectural plans.

Important among Gaudi's other commissions were the chapel for the Colonia Güell (fig. 20–27), of 1898–1915, the Casa Battló of 1904–06 and the Casa Milá of 1906–10. This last, an apartment building with a rocky, undulating façade (giving it the local nickname of *la pedrera*, "the stone quarry") is a thorough demonstration of Gaudi's ability to combine structure, interior planes, plasterwork, tile work, balustrades, hardware, grilles, and furniture of his own design into a rhythmic whole. As Jean-Paul Bouillon has written, Gaudi's integrated design follows Viollet-le-Duc's principle that "decoration adheres to the building not like a garment, but the way skin and muscles adhere to man."

Charles Rennie Mackintosh   Charles Rennie Mackintosh (1862–1928) was a Scottish architect, designer, and painter. The first demonstration of his originality came in his 1895 competition-winning design for the Glasgow School of Art, which was built in sections between 1896 and 1909 (fig. 20–28). In 1900 he married Margaret Macdonald, who would be his constant collaborator. High-

▲ **20–28** The Library, Glasgow School of Art, 1895. The building, the room, its furniture, and its lighting fixtures were designed by Charles Rennie Mackintosh.

Arcaid/Alamy Images

lights of his career included residential designs such as Windyhill at Kilmacolm, 1899–1901, Hill House at Helensburgh, 1902–05, and the interiors of a number of tearooms in Glasgow. He spent his last years in London and the south of France, concentrating on watercolors of flowers and landscapes.

His building exteriors have little overt decoration but have carefully proportioned dispositions of window groups. His interiors, like those of Gaudi, are impressively comprehensive compositions that include structure, cabinetwork, furniture, lighting, carpets, and other details. In the case of the tearooms, design attention extended to window curtains, flower vases, and cutlery.

The character of Mackintosh's design could never be mistaken for that of Gaudi or any other designer working in this period. The Spaniard's sensuous curves, writhing and looping, are replaced by the Scotsman's precise rectilinearity,

repeated parallels, and staccato squares, many enlivened with an occasional curve and all presented with delicacy and grace. Mackintosh's linear version of the Art Nouveau would have much more influence on twentieth century designers than the Secessionist style would. Mackintosh's furniture (see fig. 20–48) was an extension of his interiors and displayed similar forms.

New Equipment

In the nineteenth century, there were three innovations that drastically changed life lived indoors: innovations in heating, lighting, and plumbing, all of which affected how interiors were designed.

Heating   The fireplace and the stove served as the sole means of heating interiors until the late 18th century, but inventors were hard at work in the latter half of the nineteenth century devising new methods. A few breakthrough developments made indoor heating possible: James Watts's 1769 steam engine, William Strutt's warm-air heating system using gravity, Joseph Bramah's system of hot water radiators, and Jacob Perkins's heating system using hot water and steam. Despite these developments, central heating systems were slow to come, with the first in America thought to have been in the Eastern Hotel in Boston, c. 1845.

Efforts to improve heating were accompanied by efforts to rid interiors of airborne toxins and to improve air circulation. Windows could be opened in most cases, but that created unpleasant drafts and chills in winter, thought to be causes of disease as well. Inventions to improve matters included air inlets that deflected fresh air toward the ceiling, ventilating fireplaces, vacuum systems, and fans driven by steam engines, this last being too costly to have much application. Catherine Beecher's 1869 book, *The American Woman's Home*, suggested placing vents near the ceilings of rooms to carry off the foul air; others suggested vents near the floor. The subject was obscured by fear and misinformation until late in the nineteenth century, when the air was literally cleared by the advent of inexpensive electric fans.

Lighting   Oil lamps had been lighting interiors for centuries, but oil lamps were updated at the end of the eighteenth century by a Swiss inventor named Aimé Argand. Argand's lamp, used throughout the nineteenth century, introduced air around the wick to produce a brighter flame and make less smoke than earlier lamps. Many experiments

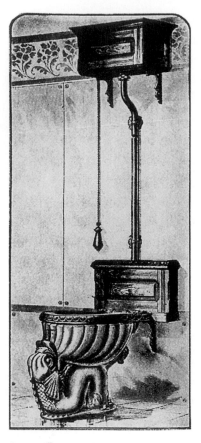

▲ 20–29 The "Dolphin" toilet as shown in an American advertisement from the 1880s.
After Giedion

followed, both in design and fuels, including gas and, after 1859, petroleum-based kerosene. As James Marston Fitch has written, "By the time of the Civil War, an entirely new concept had appeared in building design: that of a fixed, semiautomatic lighting system which *freed the building from its historic dependence upon natural daylight.*"

Arc-lighting, based on the luminosity of an electric current leaping between two conductors, was invented in Paris in the 1870s by Z. T. Gramme, but it was Thomas Alva Edison, in 1876, who demonstrated the practical use of electricity, with his carbon-filament electric lamp. Joseph Wilson Swan of London simultaneously made the same discovery, and his lamps were quickly placed in London's Savoy Theater, British Museum, and Royal Academy. Edison's version would be demonstrated to a large audience in the "City of Light" at the World's Columbian Exposition in Chicago in 1893. While the nineteenth century had begun with dark interiors, it ended with bright ones.

Plumbing   Two technical developments of the early 1800s contributed to sanitary progress: the recently developed steam engine, which could produce water pressure, and cast-iron pipes for carrying water and waste.

In most houses before midcentury, provisions for washing the body were simply a pail and a sponge, although some households enjoyed the use of elegant washstands, such as one designed by Percier and Fontaine (see fig. 20–37). Small metal hip baths, sometimes with showers above them, then became customary, and the white-enameled cast-iron bathtub appeared

c. 1870. The first toilet had been developed in England in 1788, and English inventor Thomas Crapper introduced the flush toilet in 1872, putting his name on his products. The earthenware washdown toilet, similar to those in use today, appeared in the United States c. 1890 (fig. 20–29), and were partitioned off in tiny cubicles ("water closets").

In the kitchen for much of the century, sink water still had to be drawn by a hand pump, but by the century's end many houses in America and Europe had hot and cold water piped to kitchen sinks, washbasins, and bathtubs. The nineteenth century was not inclined to revel in the new usefulness without giving it a proper appearance. All these new appliances were often encased in elaborate wood cabinetry (fig. 20–30), such as this elaborate Art Nouveau dressing table with sink, designed by Louis Majorelle.

New Building Types

The rise of the production of products and services, the increase in communications, and the sudden mobility of the masses all made new buildings necessary: the office tower, the railroad station, the department store, and the hotel.

Office Towers   When in 1854 Elisha Graves Otis, a Vermont inventor, devised a spring-operated safety catch that could prevent lifting platforms from falling, he introduced a device that would lead to something radical: vertical mobility. The modern elevator was born, and coupled with advances in steel construction, it made possible the birth of the skyscraper. Although early examples were built in New York, St. Louis, and Buffalo, Chicago claimed the most examples because the new technology was developed just as that city was rebuilding after the disastrous fire of 1871. Early Chicago office towers included the 10-story Rookery of 1886 by Burnham & Root, the 11-story Auditorium Building of 1889 by Adler & Sullivan, and the 15-story Monadnock Block of 1891, again by Burnham & Root.

Railroad Stations   The development of railroads required interior spaces where tickets could be bought and riders could wait. The 1830 Liverpool-to-Manchester line boasted the first two railroad stations, one at each end. The first of Paris's great railroad stations was the Gare du Nord, built to the design of Jacques-Ignace Hittorff in 1846, followed by François Duquesney's Gare de l'Est in 1852. In the

United States between 1881 and his death in 1886, H. H. Richardson designed a dozen urban and suburban railroad stations for the Boston and Albany line, no two stations alike.

Department Stores   In modern times, the gathering of many shops and stores under a single roof seems to have begun with the *passages* of Paris, shop-lined pedestrian ways connecting one street with another that were sometimes roofed with glazed vaults; in England similar structures were called *arcades*, in Germany *passagen*, and in Italy *gallerias*. Paris's Passage Feydeau, built in 1790, may have been the first of these, but by 1830 the city had almost twenty, with shops selling fruit, chocolate, shoes, gloves, sheet music, toys, and stationery. Perhaps the finest example is the Galleria

Vittorio Emanuele II in Milan, designed by Giuseppe Mengoni and opened in 1878 (fig. 20–31).

Paris was also the home of department stores in more conventional buildings. The Bon Marché store, designed by Louis-Charles Boileau with engineering by Gustave Eiffel, opened in 1852, followed by the Grand Magasin du Louvre (1855), Samaritaine (1867), and Printemps (1883). In London, what would become Harrod's opened in 1849 as a grocery store. In New York, Macy's started (on a small scale) in 1858 and Bloomingdale's in 1872.

Hotels   In 1809, Asher Benjamin designed a hotel for Boston called the Exchange Coffee House; it had seven floors and 200 rooms. The 1830s saw the opening of the Tremont House in Boston and the Astor House in New York, both designed by Isaiah Rogers; Brown's Hotel opened in London, and the Meurice and Bristol hotels in Paris.

▼ 20–30 Designed by Louis Majorelle, a dressing table with a sink in its marble top. The cabinetry is of mahogany and ebony with gilt bronze pulls.
Louis Majorelle (1859–1926). Woodwork-French-Nancy-XX, 1900–1910. Dressing Table-Sink. Honduras mahogany, Macassar ebony, gilt bronze, mirror glass, marble, ceramic. H.: 86⅜, W.: 45¼, D.: 25⅝ inches. The Metropolitan Museum of Art, Gift of The Sydney and Frances Lewis Foundation, 1979. (1979.4)

▼ 20–31 One of the new interiors for shopping was Giuseppe Mengoni's Galleria Vittorio Emmanuele, Milan, 1865–78.
Alinari/Art Resource, NY

▲ **20–32** The grand stairway of Henry Hardenbergh's Waldorf Hotel, New York, 1893.
Grand stairway, Waldorf Hotel, New York. From: Decorator and Finisher 22, No. 5 (August 1893): 174. Taken from The Wolfsonian-Florida International University, Miami, 2005. pg. 61, Fig. 17.

▲ **20–33** Bannister of the stairway of Victor Horta's Hôtel Solvay, Brussels, 1894.
© Hotel Slovay, Brussels/Bridgeman Art Library

The century's great innovator in hotel design, however, was Henry J. Hardenbergh (1847–1918). His designs included New York's Waldorf Hotel of 1893 (fig. 20–32) and the adjacent Astoria of 1896, which would be combined in 1897 as the Waldorf-Astoria, the world's first 1,000-room hotel. Hardenbergh's hotels of the first decade of the twentieth century included the Willard in Washington, DC, and the Plaza in New York. Hardenbergh set high standards for his time, not always met even in his own designs, such as one elevator for every 150 guests and one bathroom for every two rooms.

Nineteenth-Century Ornament

Nineteenth-century architecture and interiors included some of history's most florid design, such as that of the Renaissance Revival and Art Nouveau, and some of its most plain design, such as that of the Arts and Crafts movement. In some examples, ornament reigned supreme, for example in the Art Nouveau balustrade designed by Victor Horta for his 1894 Hôtel Solvay in Brussels (fig. 20–33). Here, any semblance to column-like balusters is swept away by a great flourish of swirling tendrils, some of them performing structural duties, some not.

In other examples, the interest in reviving past styles is expressed, though not always in strictly authentic terms. Even among classical examples, there were surprising innovations, such as in the classical orders Benjamin Henry Latrobe designed for the U.S. Capitol building (fig. 20–34). To express truly American forms, "Corinthian" capitals were composed of corncobs and tobacco plants instead of acanthus leaves.

However, of greater import to design history is that structure itself was used ornamentally in new ways.

Structure as Ornament

The nineteenth century was the first to celebrate the ornamental qualities of structure itself—particularly steel and glass structure—on an unprecedented scale and with unprecedented bravura.

A frank expression of the new possibilities came in the great exhibition hall of 1851: the Crystal Palace in Hyde Park, London. It was designed to house the first International Exhibition, featuring more than 100,000 exhibits of industrial arts, decorative arts, and sculpture (paintings being excluded). The Crystal Palace had a floor area four times that of St. Peter's in Rome, which demonstrated the tremendous spaces that the iron frame could span (fig. 20–35). Joseph Paxton, its designer, based it on a repetitive module of 4 feet (120 cm) square, the size of the largest pane of glass then manufactured. The modules were all factory-made and assembled on the building site, where erection took less than six months. Its principles of modularity and prefabrication would both become important aspects of twentieth-century design.

Color Theory

Michel Eugene Chevreul (1786–1889), the master dyer at the Gobelins tapestry factory, experimented with the effects of colored light, afterimages, and subjective reactions that altered appearances. The harmonies of adjacent colors and complementary colors were first noted by Chevreul, and his observations inspired both Impressionist and Pointillist painting. Hermann F. von Helmholtz (1821–94) and Wilhelm Ostwald (1853–1932) in Germany and Albert Munsell (1858–1918) in America carried the advance further, and Munsell's comprehensive theory would be published in 1905 as *A Color Notation*. By the end of the nineteenth century, the phenomenon of color had come to be scientifically understood.

Armed with new information about perceiving color, inventors made discoveries in re-creating and understanding it. The first breakthrough in synthetic color came in 1858, when William Henry Perkin, an 18-year-old English medical student, was in his lab and accidentally produced a blue-red dye. This Perkin's Violet, the first synthetic color, launched the science of color chemistry. The use of color had previously been based on the limitations of dyes and pigments and somewhat on personal taste. As the ability to reproduce colors in all materials improved, so too did the science of color theory.

▲ **20–35** Joseph Paxton's Crystal Palace, London, built to house the Great Exhibition, 1851.

The origin of **color** is visible light, a small part of the electromagnetic spectrum of radiant energy. Invisible parts of the spectrum include infrared rays, ultraviolet rays, x-rays, gamma rays, radio waves, and so on. Within the visible spectrum, each color has its characteristic **wavelength**, violet having the shortest and red having the longest.

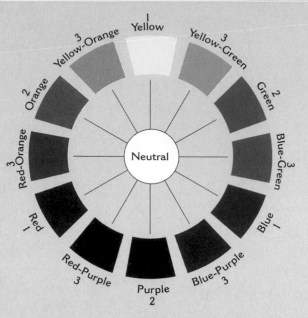

- Color has three chief characteristics: hue, intensity, and value. **Hue** is a function of wavelength, and different hues are denoted by names such as *yellow, green,* and *orange.* **Intensity** is a hue's degree of saturation, yellow having the least saturation because of its paleness, and blue the greatest saturation. **Value** is an attribute of lightness, determined by the amount of black or white added to a hue.
- A hue with black added is said to be a **shade** of the hue, and a hue with white added is said to be a **tint** of the hue.
- Hues *in light* are called **additive** because all hues of light added together produce white. Von Helmholtz found in 1867 that in the human eye there are three different cell types, each able to detect red, green, and blue wavelengths of light. This three-part division is also basic to the color of television, video, and computer monitors.
- Hues *in pigment* are called **subtractive**. All wavelengths of light are absorbed by a pigment except those of its distinguishing hue, which are reflected to the eye.
- The **primary colors** in pigment are red, blue, and yellow. The **secondary colors**, made by mixing two primary colors, are purple, green, and orange. Mixing a secondary and a primary produces a **tertiary color**, such as red-orange or yellow-green.
- Hues can be arranged on a **color wheel** (above) in the order of their wavelengths, with short-wavelength violet adjacent to long-wavelength red. Colors exactly opposite each other on the wheel, such as red and green, are said to be **complementary colors**. The color wheel can be divided into two halves, the **warm colors** of red, orange, and yellow, and the **cool colors** of green, blue, and violet. A pair of complementary colors, therefore, always contains one warm color and one cool one.

Nineteenth-Century Furniture

The furniture of the nineteenth century was as varied as the interior styles it was designed for. Furniture was specifically designed to fit each phase of all the style periods. In addition, from the midst of this design fervor emerged new types of furniture not seen before, which were more refined and stylistic than ever.

Empire and Regency Furniture

In seating, the Empire period in France brought the *rècamier,* a daybed that took its name from a painting, Jacques-Louis David's 1800 portrait *Mme. Rècamier* (fig. 20–36). Percier and Fontaine, the leaders of the Empire style, made many designs of furniture, among them, for example, the *athènienne,* a tripod-based stand for a washstand, designed in 1801 (fig. 20–37). They also popularized other new types of furniture, which included the *lit en bateau,* a bed with curved, upturned ends, resembling a boat; and the **mèridienne**, a daybed or sofa with scrolled arms and with one end higher than the other (see fig. 20–3). The **psyche** was a tall mirror that could be tilted inside its frame, which stood on the floor. The circular **pedestal table** was often placed in the center of a room. In a suite of furniture made for Napoleonís private apartments at Fontainebleau, we see yet another type: the *paumier,* a sofa that, like the *mèridienne,* has unequal arms, but unlike it, straight ones.

▼ **20–36** A *récamier* daybed in the painting that gave it its name, Jacques-Louis David's 1800 portrait, *Mme. Récamier.*
"Madame Recameir", Jacques Louis David. Reunion des Musees Nationaux/Art Resource, NY

▼ **20–38** The Blue Room of the White House as designed by Associated Artists in 1882–83. The circular settee in the center of the room is a *borne.*
Courtesy of the Library of Congress

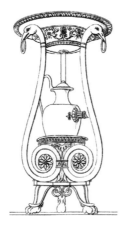

▲ **20–37** A washstand designed by Percier and Fontaine in 1801.
Rabatti-Domingie/AKG-Images

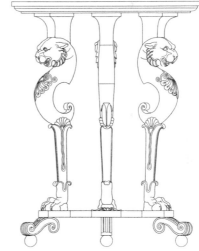

▲ **20–39** Tripod table from Thomas Hope's 1807 publication.
Dover Publications, Inc.

The most popular wood for Empire furniture was mahogany, but elm, yew, maple, and lemon were also used. Woods for veneers were imported from Africa, the West Indies, and the East Indies and included thuya, amboyna, amaranth, palisander, and rosewood. Marquetry and fluting were completely avoided, but ebony, silver, and other metals were sometimes used for inlay, and gilding was often applied. Beneath the impressive surfaces, however, much of the furniture was made with inferior woods.

During the Second Empire settees were developed, called *confidentes à deux places* and *indiscrets à trois places,* for two or three occupants to congregate. Later, the **borne** was designed, as a large circular upholstered settee with a central backrest. One can be seen in Tiffany's 1882–83 design of the White House's Blue Room (fig. 20–38). The borne was popular in grand drawing rooms and hotel lobbies.

During the English Regency period, Thomas Hope, in his 1807 publication, included a number of designs for furniture, among them his tripod table (fig. 20–39). The doubly curved cabriole leg and the straight leg of earlier English design were replaced by the singly curved sabre leg (fig. 20–40), recalling the Greek *klismos* (see fig. 4–26). Regency ornament included lyres, palmettes, Greek frets, and acanthus leaves (see fig. 20–2).

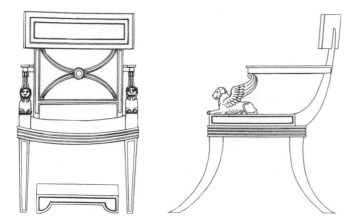

▲ **20–40** Front and side views of a Regency armchair designed by Thomas Hope. It was based on the Greek *klismos*, but with winged lions added to support the arms.
Dover Publications, Inc.

▲ **20–41** Small marble-topped mahogany center table or *guéridon* by Charles-Honoré Lannuier, c. 1810, now in the White House, 26 in. (66 cm) in diameter.
Small center table (gueridon), designed by Charles-Honore Lannuier (French-American, 1779–1819), ca. 1810. Mahogany, with mahogany, rosewood, satinwood, and possibly sycamore veneers, "vert antique," gilded brass, marble; secondary woods: yellow poplar, white pine, and mahogany. Height 23¾ in. (75.6 cm), diameter 26 in. (66 cm). The White House, Washington, D.C. Gift of Mr. and Mrs. C. Douglas Dillon (961.33.2.). Photograph by Bruce White.

In Regency furniture, mahogany continued its popularity, but was joined by lighter, more richly figured woods such as satinwood, rosewood, amboyna, zebrawood, and maple. Among the skillful Regency cabinetmakers was Charles Wyllys Elliott, who was working in London in the years 1783–1810. Satinwood was his favored wood, which he enhanced with delicate inlays.

In America, Duncan Phyfe continued to rein as the supreme furniture designer of his day (see Chapter 19), creating designs that mainly followed the English Regency styles. His only rival in America was the talented French **èbèniste** Charles-Honorè Lannuier (1779–1819), who arrived in America in 1803 and settled in New York. Lannuier, in contrast to Phyfe, produced finely crafted pieces in a delicate version of the Empire style (fig. 20–41). Lannuier's rich palette of materials included rosewood, ormolu, and white marble.

Other Classicist Furniture

Some of Germany's Neoclassical furniture can be seen in the room designed by Schinkel (see fig. 20–10). The beautiful pearwood furniture has Neoclassical details, such as the ribbon garlands and scrolled ends. Both it and Austria's Biedermeier furniture employed mostly light-colored woods such as pear, cherry, apple, birch, or maple, against which small ebony half columns or palmettes might be set as ornamentation, making a striking contrast. Perhaps the most skillful and certainly the most prolific of the Biedermeier designers was Joseph Danhauser (1780–1829) of Vienna, whose large factory from 1807 to 1829 produced furniture, clocks,

curtains, and lighting fixtures. One Danhauser customer was Archduke Charles of Austria, but his chief customers were the members of the middle class. Biedermeier was their style, and it was not a subtle one (fig. 20–42). It took the refined ornamental shapes of Empire furniture, such as volutes, lyres, and half columns, and enlarged them into structural members.

Revivalist Furniture

Renaissance Revival furniture had much success, particularly in the United States, where it was popularized by the Herter Brothers. Their furniture was beautifully crafted, as can be seen in their fall-front desk in ebonized maple, cherry, and cedar, with gilt-bronze fittings (fig. 20–43).

Three other noted designers worked in the Renaissance Revival style. Two had French backgrounds: A. Baudouine and Alexander Roux. They mixed motifs from the sixteenth,

▲ **20–42** A walnut and walnut-veneer side chair in Biedermeier style from the factory of Joseph Danhauser, 1815–20.
Josef Danhauser (Austrian, 1805–1845), side chair, 1815–1820, walnut and walnut veneer, modern upholstery. 237.5 × 123.2 × 121.9 cm. Gift of the Antiquarian Society through the Capital Campaign Fund, 1987.215.4. © 2000, The Art Institute of Chicago. All Rights Reserved.

▼ **20–43** A fall-front desk designed by Herter Brothers in ebonized maple, cherry, and cedar with gilt-bronze fittings.
The Metropolitan Museum of Art, Gift of Paul Martini,1969. (69.146.3). Photograph (c) 1982 The Metropolitan Museum of Art.

seventeenth, and eighteenth centuries and from Italy and France, although Baudouine's immense output (he employed 200 in his New York cabinetmaking shop) also included some simplified versions of Louis XV furniture. Also dabbling in an idiosyncratic version of Renaissance Revival furniture (fig. 20–44) was Sir Laurence Alma-Tadema (1836–1912), of Dutch birth but living in England, where he was best known for his stage sets and genre paintings with classical and ancient Egyptian themes. Rosewood was the most popular wood for Renaissance Revival furniture, and the style was considered particularly suitable for dining rooms. Upholstery was elaborate, and colors were rich: reds, browns, blues, and purples.

Arts and Crafts and Art Nouveau Furniture

In the much plainer Arts and Crafts style, Philip Webb adapted traditional rush-seated chairs from the English county of Sussex for a design that was manufactured by Morris (fig. 20–45).

▲ **20–44** An armchair designed by Sir Laurence Alma-Tadema in 1887. It is of mahogany with cedar and ebony veneer and with inlays of ebony, sandalwood, ivory, boxwood, and abalone. The upholstery is new, but based on original evidence.
Armchair. Mahogany. Veneered inlaid decoration. Designed by Alma-Tadema. Made by Norman Johnstone. English, c. 1884. Victoria & Albert Museum, London/Art Resource, NY.

In the Art Nouveau style there were furniture pieces with studied asymmetry and sweeping curves, such as the two-pedestal olive wood desk with ash panels by Hector Guimard (fig. 20–46), made c. 1899, and the delicate marquetry firescreen by Emile Gallé (fig. 20–47). Antoní Gaudi also designed furniture to fit his interiors; nothing else would have worked in his intricately formed rooms (see fig. 20–27).

Just as a Gaudi interior demanded Gaudi furniture, so too did a Charles Mackintosh interior call for more Mackintosh. His earliest furniture was sturdily made of dark-stained oak and, like his buildings and interiors, owed something to the Arts and Crafts movement. But Mackintosh's furniture was less florid and more dramatically attenuated (fig. 20–48). He later experimented with painting the furniture with white enamel. Then, insets of purple glass appeared, and upholstery of pink or purple silk was stenciled with stylized flowers. Some later furniture was ebonized and its design dominated by squares and ovals.

New Furniture Techniques

Primary among the new techniques that became available to nineteenth-century furniture makers were two advances in the use of wood: improvements in bending it and in laminating it. Both techniques yielded products lighter and more sparing of resources than construction with solid wood. Both techniques were also faster and cheaper. Although many other people contributed, each of these developments had a special hero: Michael Thonet in bending and John Henry Belter in lamination.

Thonet's Bentwood The English and American Windsor chairs in Chapters 16 and 18 were still being made in the nineteenth century, using spindles and curved back rails of bentwood, but it was Michael Thonet (1796–1871), a furniture maker in Germany's Rhine Valley, who began experimenting with bending

▲ 20–46 Hector Guimard's desk of olive wood with ash panels, c. 1899, 48 in. (121 cm) wide.
Hector Guimard. Desk. c 1899. (remodeled after 1909). Olive wood with ash panels, 28¾" × 47¾" (73 × 121 cm). Gift of Madame Hector Guimard, The Museum of Modern Art/Licensed by Scala-Art Resource, NY.

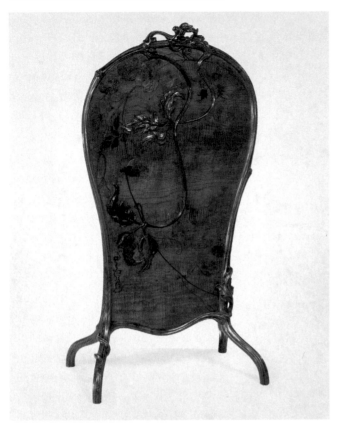

▼ **20–47** A firescreen of ash with marquetry and applied decoration in walnut, zebrawood, amboyna, and other woods. Designed by Emile Gallé before 1900.
Victoria & Albert Museum, London/Art Resource, NY

▼ **20–48** Charles Rennie Mackintosh's oak chair with an upholstered seat, designed for Miss Cranston's Argyle Street Tearooms, Glasgow, 1897.
High backed chair designed for Miss Cranston's Argyle Street Tea Rooms, Glasgow, 1897 (stained oak) by Mackintosh, Charles Rennie (1868–1928). Private Collection © The Fine Art Society, London/Bridgeman Art Library

and laminating wood, splicing narrow wood strips together while cooking them in glue. By 1841, Thonet had patented his process, and his medal-winning display at London's Great Exhibition of 1851 brought him international recognition. The company's first catalogue, issued in 1859, showed twenty-six items. They were all chairs with similar legs below the seats but with a variety of different backs. The Thonet rocker was introduced in 1860. An 1859 advertisement (fig. 20–49) shows other additions to the line, and by the 1880s hat stands, stools, bedsteads, mirror frames, and more had been added to the basic line.

Viewpoints | LE CORBUSIER ON A THONET CHAIR

The 1902 Thonet chair, originally called the Writing Desk Chair No. 9, was popularized beginning in 1922 by Le Corbusier, who used it in his Pavilion de l'Esprit Nouveau, Paris, in 1925. He went on to use it elsewhere in many other examples of his revolutionary modern architecture.

In 1925 he wrote, "We have introduced the humble Thonet chair of steamed wood, certainly the most common as well as the least costly of chairs. And we believe that this chair . . . possesses nobility."

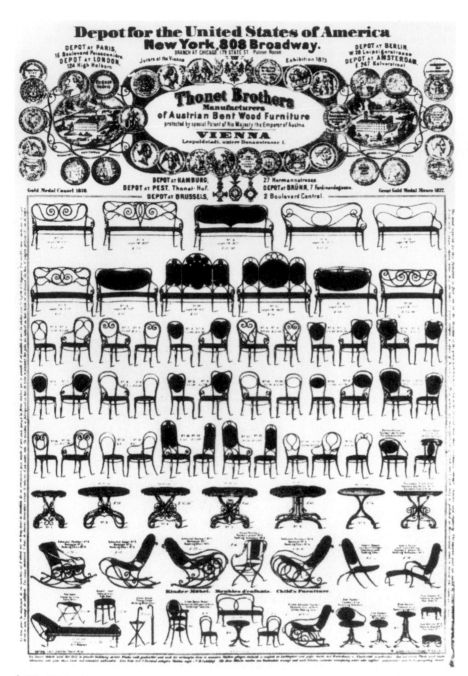

▲ **20—49** An 1874 advertisement for Thonet Brothers shows the variety of bentwood furniture designs then available.

Art Resource/The New York Public Library Photographic Services

and then bending them in steam; and, perhaps of most importance, giving three-dimensional curves to laminated wood. Some Belter chairbacks and bedframes were pierced with openwork decoration (fig. 20–50), but their real significance lay in Belter's ability to curve a plane both from top to bottom and from side to side. His techniques were precursors of the molded plywood chair shells that would be used by Charles and Ray Eames in the twentieth century—but with very different results.

Patent Furniture

Sometimes ingenious and sometimes farfetched is what has been called patent furniture, although some of it was never patented. These pieces collapsed or served multiple functions and were often meant as conveniences for travelers or those in small residences. Tables of all sizes were given extra leaves so they could be extended, armchairs were given attached footrests that could be raised, and dressing tables were given fold-down mirrors and compartments for concealing bidets and chamber pots. The folding chair was patented in 1855. The so-called **Morris chair** (fig. 20–51), manufactured by William Morris beginning c. 1866 (but probably not designed by him), was a lounge chair with removable cushions and a back that could be adjusted to different angles.

Growth in the complexities of business and the quantities of paperwork demanded new and more elaborate desks, perhaps the most elaborate being those developed by William S. Wooton of Indianapolis. In 1874 he patented a desk with over a hundred storage compartments and a drop-down writing surface, all hidden behind two massive hinged doors that could be closed and locked. When these doors were open, the occupant found himself in a nine-

Belter's Laminated Wood John Henry Belter (1804–63) came to America from Germany in 1833, and by 1854 he was operating a five-floor factory in New York. Belter's florid designs in the Renaissance Revival style were made possible by a series of inventions. His patents covered such things as sawing openwork patterns into curved chairbacks; laminating thin sheets of wood, their grains alternating directions,

▼ **20–50** A bedframe of carved laminated rosewood by John Henry Belter, c. 1856.
Courtesy of The Brooklyn Museum of Art; Gift of Mrs. Ernest Victor

▼ **20–51** An armchair with an adjustable reclining back, called a Morris chair, designed c. 1860, but probably not by William Morris.
Victoria & Albert Museum, London/Art Resource, NY

Open

Closed

▲ **20–52** The patented Wooton Desk, made between 1874 and 1882 of walnut-veneered pine with brass hardware, 81 in. (206 cm) high.
Courtesy, The Winterthur Library: Printed Book and Periodical Collection

teenth century version of an office cubicle (fig. 20–52). Among the purchasers of Wooton desks were oil magnate John D. Rockefeller, newspaper chief Joseph Pulitzer, and financier Jay Gould. The Wooton desk was shown to great acclaim at the 1876 Centennial exhibition in Philadelphia and remained popular until the typewriter, first produced in 1873, led to the standardization of stationery, which in turn led to the development of the filing cabinet.

Nineteenth-Century Decorative Arts

New techniques, materials, and design expressions were not limited to the field of furniture, of course. There were equally inventive developments in the decorative arts.

Ceramics

Nineteenth-century ceramics did not enjoy the dramatic manufacturing advances that revolutionized other decorative arts, such as textile production. Fine ceramics continued to be hand thrown (though many were molded) and hand painted. Stylistically, they reflected all the styles and influences noted in the other arts, playing supporting roles in the changing scenes of the Empire and Regency styles, the romantic revivals, the Arts and Crafts movement, and Art Nouveau design.

In England, Wedgwood's company would continue making pieces in the "Egyptian" style as that revival swelled, but production on both bone china and Jasperware was eventually halted in the nineteenth century. In France, porcelain production at the Sèvres factory virtually ceased after the Revolution of 1789, but revived again with new commissions in the Empire period, including an "Egyptian" dinner service for Napoleon himself. In Ireland, the Belleek Porcelain Factory was established in 1857 to produce utilitarian wares, but later it became known for decorative pieces. The Dublin Pottery was short-lived (1872–85) but noted for its Arts and Crafts pottery. Color printing on both bone china and earthenware, exhibited by several factories at London's Great Exhibition of 1851, was a step forward for Coalport and Minton, who won gold medals.

One development came at the Staffordshire pottery of Copelands, where they developed **Parian** porcelain in 1842, with such a surface sheen that it needed no glazing, leaving the sharpness of detail fully evident. Parian wares were also made in Sweden and in the United States. An example of

American Parian porcelain can be seen in the "Baseball" vase (fig. 20–53) that American ceramicists Ott & Brewer commissioned artist Isaac Broome to design for the 1876 Centennial Exhibition. Another important U.S. ceramic company was the Ceramic Art Co., founded in Trenton, New Jersey, in 1889, which would change its name to the Lenox China Co. in 1906.

The Gothic Revival invigorated the tile industry, with its great advocate A. W. N. Pugin designing tiles (fig. 20–54) for Minton in the 1830s and 1840s. English tiles were shown in the 1876 Centennial Exhibition in Philadelphia, fostering the founding of tile factories in Pennsylvania, Massachusetts, New Jersey, and Ohio.

▲ **20–53** The "Baseball" vase of Parian porcelain designed by Isaac Broome for Ott & Brewer, Trenton, NJ, 1875, 34 in. (86 cm) high.
Isaac Broome, designer. "Baseball Vase". Ott & Brewer Company, Trenton, NJ. Parian Porcelain. 32" H x 10½" W. New Jersey State Museum, The Brewer Collection, CH345.22

Glass

Technology transformed glassmaking in the nineteenth century. The efficiency of the production of cut glass was greatly increased by steam-powered cutting machines, and cutting became deeper and more intricate. Perhaps the most dramatic new technique, however, was in the production of **pressed glass**, in which ornamented surfaces are obtained by forcing molten glass into cast-iron molds. It was a far cheaper process than cut glass. The first pressed glass appeared in America in 1829 and in England soon thereafter.

Gallé Famous glass designer Emile Gallé (1846–1904) opened his workshop in France in 1874. He is well known for the variety of his decorative glass techniques: *clair de lune*, which used cobalt oxide to produce a distinctive sapphire blue color; *verreries parlantes*, on which he inscribed poetic phrases; his own version of eighteenth-century Chinese cased glass, with fused layers of colored glass; and *marqueterie de verre*, in which decorative glass pieces were inserted into larger glass bodies.

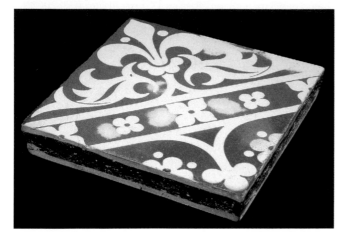

▲ 20–55 Two Art Nouveau overlay glass table lamps designed by Emile Gallé after 1890.
Galle triple-overlay glass table lamp. Christie's Images, London, UK/Bridgman Art Library

▼ 20–56 Tiffany's Dragonfly electric lamp with a shade of colored glass and copper foil, c. 1900. The bronze base is in the form of a twisted waterlily, 27 in. (69 cm) high.
Tiffany Studios, New York. Electric Lamp in Holden Dragonfly Shade and Twisted-Stem Waterlily Standard, ca 1910. Colored glass, copper foil, bronze; H:27 inches. Chrysler Museum of Art, Norfolk, Virginia. Gift of Walter P. Chrysler, Jr. 71.8123

His firm produced both inexpensive mass-produced pieces in the Art Nouveau style (fig. 20–55) and exquisite *piéces uniques*.

Tiffany　Louis Comfort Tiffany (1848–1933) was the son of the founder of Tiffany and Company. Tiffany was a notable artist in many media, particularly in glass and particularly in the Art Nouveau style. In 1879, he formed an interior design firm, Louis C. Tiffany and Associated Artists, in collaboration with Samuel Colman, whose specialty was color; Lockwood de Forest, knowledgeable about wood carvings and decorations; and Candace Wheeler, an educator, writer, and specialist in

textiles. Among other things, Associated Artists designed a 338-square-foot (31 m^2) colored-glass screen for the White House (now destroyed) that shielded the comings and goings of the president and his family from the more public entrance foyer. Tiffany left Associated Artists in 1883 to form Tiffany Glass and Decorating Company and shifted entirely to glass: stained-glass windows, glass mosaics, goblets, vases, and lamps.

It was in his glass that Tiffany captured the Art Nouveau spirit most purely. Sometimes Tiffany glass imitates nature directly, as in his Wisteria and Dragonfly lamps (fig. 20–56), but often the reference is more abstract. Not only the forms of his glass, but also its surfaces and colors expressed the flowing forms of nature. His most important and most characteristic technical development was the treatment of the hot glass with metallic oxides to create overlapping layers of iridescent colors; he called the products of this process **Favrile** glass (fig. 20–57). Fine, thin wares were within Tiffany's repertory, but he also developed an attractive, thicker, often milky glass that he called paperweight glass. He also used gold to create rich, corroded glassware that might have been made by the Romans and left buried for centuries.

Metalwork

In the French Empire and Restoration periods, exemplary gilt and bronze work was produced by Pierre-Philippe Thomire (1751–1843). Two important Empire silversmiths were at distinct poles of the Empire style. Jean Baptiste Claude Odiot (1763–1850) worked in a pure classical style, employing simple shapes and plain surfaces. A coffee urn commissioned from Odiot by Thomas Jefferson is now at Monticello. Martin-Guillaume Biennais (1764–1843) produced silverware for Napoleon and his family in a style ornate and densely decorated with sphinxes, swans, seahorses, and all the emblems of Napoleon and Josephine. He also produced silverware and furniture to the designs of Percier and Fontaine.

Second Empire metalworkers in France included Charles Christofle and Ferdinand Barbedienne. Charles Christofle (1805–63) turned his attention from jewelry to silver household wares in the 1830s, and in 1842 he obtained a monopoly on the making of electroplated wares in France. His firm, which also produced some bronze furniture, is still in business.

Ferdinand Barbedienne (1810–92) began his firm in 1838; it grew to employ 300 artisans. They made reproductions of antique sculpture by Michelangelo, Luca della Robbia, and others; busts of historical figures such as Voltaire and Benjamin Franklin; furniture; and a variety of decorative objects, many in metal. In the years 1850–54, Barbedienne furnished the interiors of the Hôtel de Ville, Paris, in the Renaissance Revival style. A gilt metal vase with champlevé enamel work (fig. 20–58) was exhibited in 1862.

In England, silverware design was influenced by architect Charles Heathcote Tatham, who suggested "massiveness" as the chief criterion for good silver, and his advice was followed widely. Regency silver is based on elegant classical models, but often with a burdensome amount of decoration. In the Gothic Revival style, A. W. N. Pugin and others produced designs for all kinds of ecclesiastical objects in silver and other metals.

The Western world's love affair with the design of China and Japan was evident at London's International Exhibition of 1862, where Japanese design was introduced to many who had been unaware of it, including metalwork designer Christopher Dresser (1834–1904). Dresser later traveled throughout Japan in 1877 collecting merchandise for Tiffany and Company. In the last decades of the century, Dresser produced some simple, elegant silver pieces showing the influences of Japanese and Arts and Crafts design (fig. 20–59). This austere work, as seen in the exposed rivets of the pitcher, shows his admiration both for Japanese simplicity and for undisguised industrial processes.

Gorham, an American silverware firm that is still operating, was founded in 1831 by Jabez Gorham (1792–1869). In the late nineteenth century it produced silver in a variety of revival styles and, during the 1890s, Art Nouveau. Gorham also supplied silver overlays for the Arts and Crafts ceramics of the Rookwood Pottery.

The earliest use of metal for ceiling surfaces came in the late 1860s when sheets of corrugated iron began to be used in warehouses, factories, and schools, metal being more fire-resistant and less expensive than wood or plaster. Lighter and more easily installed tiles of stamped tin were in widespread residential use by 1895. The tin tiles were available in hundreds of patterns, some imitating stucco or brick. Center medallions, borders, and beam covers were also made. There were even tin panels that could be applied as wainscoting or as whole wall surfaces. Tin surfacing materials, particularly the ceiling tile, remained popular until World War I brought a metal shortage.

Lustrous, silvery stainless steel became available in the middle of the nineteenth century and has been much used as an inexpensive substitute for silver in flatware, tableware, and other objects (see Chapter 21, page 550). Other substitutes include nickel silver, an alloy of copper, zinc, and nickel, sometimes called German silver. In the twentieth century nickel silver was often used for hotel and restaurant wares. Another lustrous substitute for silver, chromium was first produced at the end of the eighteenth century, and a process for plating it on base metal above a layer of nickel was devised in the middle of the nineteenth. It was not produced commercially until the 1920s.

Textiles

New machinery in the late eighteenth and early nineteenth centuries meant that complex multicolored patterns could be woven easily and quickly. Chintz and damask, satin and satin stripes, velvet and velour were all used extensively in the nineteenth century. The role of interior textiles was greater in the nineteenth century than it had ever been before or has been since. Fabric was often draped beneath mantelshelves,

▼ **20–57** An example of Tiffany's iridescent Favrile glass, c. 1900, 14 in. (35 cm) tall.
Vase, 1895-1920, U.S. Transparent iridescent gold and blue glasses, blown. H:35.1 cm, D (max) 16.5 cm. Corning Museum of Glass, Corning, New York. Gift of Mr. Edgar Kaufmann, Jr. 62.4.19.

▼ **20–58** Ferdinand Barbedienne's 1862 gilt metal vase, champlevé enameling.
Victoria & Albert Museum, London/Art Resource, NY

▲ **20–59** Christopher Dresser's 1879 design for a glass claret jug in silver mounts.
Victoria & Albert Museum, London/Art Resource, NY

and the fire openings themselves were sometimes curtained. Mirrors, chandeliers, tables, and lamps were all festooned with drapery. **Portieres**, often made of tapestry, were fabric hangings used over doorways or to separate rooms for alcoves. The most elaborate fabric treatments were reserved for windows.

Less elabarately, William Morris was a masterful designer of flat patterns for interior fabrics made for a variety of purposes, not just window treatments. He also designed carpets and wallpapers. Perhaps the most accomplished of his designs date from the last quarter of the century. They were produced in a variety of materials, our illustrated example being both a silk damask and a printed cotton (fig. 20–60). Despite this variety, Morris was very conscious of the nature of each material he used, trying, as he wrote in 1884, "to make woolen substances as woolen as possible, cotton as cottony as possible, and so on." Other Morris fabrics are visible in figures 20–22 and 20–45.

▲ **20–60** William Morris's "Kennet" fabric design of 1883 in two colorways and in two fabrics: left, as a silk damask in gold and gray; right, as a printed cotton in blue and yellow.
Left: William Morris, "Kennet" (1883). Silk damask. Accession No. T.11810. The Whitworth Art Gallery, The University of Manchester. Right: William Morris (1834–1896), Kennet, registered 1883, printed cotton. Birmingham Museums and Art Gallery, Birmingham, England, U.K.

Window Treatments Some window treatments were extremely simple, especially for people in modest circumstances. John Claudius Loudon's *An Encyclopedia of Cottage, Farm, and Villa Architecture* (1833) offered 2,000 illustrations on which to model middle-class residential interiors. One design was merely a piece of calico with small rings sewn along its top by which it was hung from a cord. Other treatments had fabric hanging by rings from exposed curtain rods, usually with finials at each end. But such simplicity was exceptional, and during the Victorian era, drapery became very ornate.

Sometimes two windows in the same wall were treated as a single unit, with the cornice board and valance spanning the wall area between them (fig. 20–61). In addition, between the glass curtains and the draperies might be added more curtains, more opaque than the glass curtains, which could be drawn over the whole window for privacy or light control. Or window shades might take that intermediate position. All these elements were generally trimmed with what is known collectively as *passementerie* (pronounced

▼ **20–61** An illustration from the October 1866 issue of *Godey's Lady's Book* shows a fancifully shaped cornice board extending over two windows and a mirror. Two alternate schemes for fabric valences and draperies are shown.
Courtesy of The Athenaeum of Philadelphia

"pahs-mahn-*tree*") from the French *passement,* a strip of lace. Types of passementeries (fig. 20–62) include braids, cords, ropes, fringes, and **gimp**, a braid or other trim that is applied in an ornate pattern rather than used simply as an edging. And each of these comes in many forms, from cotton ball fringe and silk tassel fringe to silk or wool loop fringe. There were also singular, less continuous ornaments, such as tassels, bows, and rosettes.

The coordination of the elements of window treatments—not only among themselves but also with the other parts of a room—was a major design undertaking. Sometimes the cornice board was covered with the same fabric used for the draperies and tiebacks; sometimes not. And care was given to making the silk threads of the passementerie match the colors of the fabric, which often required custom dyeing, a service still available today.

▲ **20–62** Examples of curtain trimmings or *passementerie.*
© Jacqui Hurst/CORBIS All Rights Reserved

Tools & Techniques | CURTAINS AND DRAPERY

Most windows were treated with two basic elements: a heading across the top and curtains below. Both these elements could have several parts.

The heading could be a combination of a cornice board and a valance. The **cornice board** (not to be confused with the cornice, the top portion of a classical entablature, which might be found above the window where the wall meets the ceiling) was a fixed projection at the top of the window treatment; it might be made of wood moldings or of fabric-covered wood. Beneath the cornice, the **valance** was a horizontal strip of gathered, shirred, or pleated fabric hung from the front edge of the cornice board and covering the tops of the curtains. If the bottom edge of either a cornice board or a valance were fringed or elaborately scalloped, it might be called a **lambrequin**. Sometimes the stiff cornice board

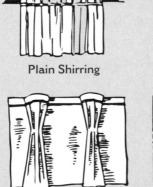

Plain Shirring

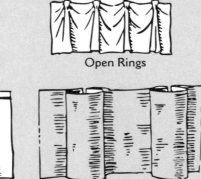

Open Rings

French Heading

Box Pleating

was eliminated and only the fabric valance used.

Below this heading, the curtains were usually of two types. Next to the window was the **glass curtain** or **casement curtain**, which was sheer and semitransparent. Inside were the **draperies** (never called "drapes" in professional usage), which were hung in a variety of arrangements. In most cases, the draperies met in the center at the top of the window and were held back to the sides three or four feet (90–120 cm) above the floor by fabric loops called **tiebacks**, or by tasseled ropes, or by looping the fabric over **curtain pins** projecting from the wall. These ornamental pins could be rosettes of metal, wood, or glass. If either the glass curtain or the drapery was closed at night and looped up during the day, its length was such that its hem reached the floor when looped up but "puddled" on the floor at night in a mass of folds.

Upholstery A new degree of seating comfort came with the nineteenth-century addition of springs to the traditional upholstery package of webbing and stuffing, which could be hay, hair, wool, feathers, down, or other materials (even inflated pig bladders were given a try). Coil springs were first developed in the eighteenth century to ease the bumpy ride of horse-drawn carriages, but their advantages for interior seating soon became apparent. In 1822 Viennese upholsterer Georg Junigl patented an upholstery improvement with "the assistance of iron springs." In 1826 London carriage maker Samuel Pratt patented a chair with spiral springs that, when used at sea, was supposed to prevent seasickness, and two years later he obtained a patent for a chair with springs for use on land. Pratt's springs were fastened directly to a wooden furniture frame, attached to the base of webbing, and used in loose cushions.

Iron springs were replaced later with spirals of steel wire that were either biconal (hourglass-shaped) or pyramidal; such springs are still in use. The new construction required greater depth, not only for the springs themselves, but also for extra padding on top to keep the springs from breaking through. This new depth led eventually to the development of all-upholstered seating in which most or all of the frame was covered.

Carpets In France, the establishment of the First Empire in 1804 revived both the privately owned carpet factory at Aubusson and the state-owned one at the Savonnerie with demands for replacing the palace carpets lost or damaged in the Revolution. The old designs were replaced in the style of Percier and Fontaine, and the new carpet patterns employed classical figures, floral bouquets, and classical military emblems, such as spears, trophies, and shields; the wreathed *N* also appeared. With Napoleon's fall in 1815, the Savonnerie was combined with the Gobelins workshops in 1825, and the design of its subsequent products was influenced by the traditional Gobelins tapestries. At Aubusson, the old practice of hand knotting was changed by the advent of machine weaving, which was adopted in the 1830s.

In England, three important centers of carpet making—Kidderminster, Axminster, and Wilton—continued to actively produce carpets with hand-knotting methods using the symmetrical or Turkish knot (see Tools & Techniques: Carpet Weaving in Chapter 9). A revival of hand knotting was attempted in Ireland, encouraged by the government to provide employment in the depressed area of Donegal. In Scotland, Richard Whytock of Edinburgh began in 1832 to use yarns preprinted in stripes of several colors as the warp (which formed the pile) of carpets he called Tapestry Brussels. Whereas an ordinary Brussels carpet had been limited to six colors, Whytock's Tapestry Brussels could have over a hundred colors (fig. 20–63). Another multicolor technique was developed in 1839 by James Templeton of Glasgow, who inserted wool **chenille** tufts into a jute or linen backing to produce what he called a Chenille Axminster. In 1841 he was commissioned to make such a carpet for St. George's Chapel at Windsor Castle. The chenille carpet was soft and therefore unsuitable for hard wear.

In America, there were a number of factories making Brussels-type rugs and carpets, in Philadelphia, Massachusetts, New York, and New Jersey. In 1844 a Brussels carpet with yellow stars on a scarlet background was woven in Germantown, Pennsylvania, for the floor of the U.S. Senate chamber. Among American innovators, Erastus Brigham Bigelow (1814–79), a Massachusetts inventor, developed several new kinds of carpet loom. One loom, invented in 1848, could weave carpet with either loop pile (Brussels type) or cut pile (Wilton), and it could produce them almost ten times as fast as a hand weaver. Over the next half of the century, various inventors in America and England worked to refine the carpet looms, and carpet production was forever changed.

However, hooked and braided rugs also continued to be widely used in America, and by the 1876 Philadelphia Centennial, there were new ideas. At the Centennial a variety of patterns for wood parquet flooring, sometimes called **wood carpeting**, were instantly recognized as a new floor treatment, even as the American craze for "Orientals" was somewhat dampened by new concerns about hygiene. In January 1884, according to Bishop and Coblentz, *Godey's Lady's Book* advised that wood floors were healthier than textile carpets, which could "harbor impregnating germs of disease and death." And there were new types of flooring just on the horizon that would become quite popular.

Wall and Floor Treatments

In the nineteenth century, inventors experimented with a variety of products for decorating the homes of the rising merchant class and other middle classes. The men who invented these materials aimed at producing goods that were more durable, less expensive, and easier and faster to produce. They did this by using the new machinery then available, rather than the traditional production of hand-skilled craftsmen.

Wall Treatments   In 1877, English inventor Frederick Walton invented an imitation leather material called **Lincrusta-Walton.** Set with linseed oil and gum, Lincrusta was made of wood pulp and paraffin wax. Intended for use on ceilings and walls, Lincrusta-Walton (from *linum*, meaning "flax," the source of both linen and linseed oil, and *crusta*,

meaning "relief") had a surface embossed in low r[...] painted brown and glazed, it could resemble em[...] leather, but when painted light colors, some patterns c[...] pass for decorative plasterwork. In fact, in a room with three different applications, Lincrusta could give the effect of a room with leather-covered walls, a plaster cornice, and a wood-paneled wainscot. It was widely used, appearing in the ocean liner *Titanic*, in the California State Capitol in Sacramento, and, in the 1880s, in the John D. Rockefeller mansion on New York's West 54th Street. A French company established a plant near Paris, supplying Hector Guimard (see fig. 20–46) with Lincrusta wainscoting for his own Art Nouveau design for the 1896 Castel Bèranger. An American company produced Lincrusta starting in 1883, and it is still made today.

Lincrusta found a competitor in Anaglypta, a lighter, more flexible, cheaper material made from paper and cotton pulp. It was patented in 1886 by Thomas J. Palmer, a showroom manager for Lincrusta-Walton. Anaglypta (from the Greek *ana* meaning "raised" and *glypta* meaning "cameo") was primarily a substitute for plaster ceilings and friezes, not—like Lincrusta—for a range of materials. It was immediately successful, counting Christopher Dresser (see fig. 20–59) among its designers, and is still on the market in England.

Another artificial substance that had great success beginning in the early nineteenth century was called composition or, more commonly, compo. Compo was a puttylike substance of linseed oil, glue, and resin that was pressed into decoratively shaped molds, the result then applied to ornamental woodwork on walls or to furniture. When painted, it was a convincing imitation of expensive wood carving. Robert

▼ **20–63** An English warp-printed Tapestry Brussels carpet, c. 1850, 7 ft. 4 in. (2.3 m) long. Victoria & Albert Museum, London/Art Resource, NY

been a compo proponent in England,
... ly made in America by Robert Well-
... beginning in 1800. The Decorators
... nded in Chicago in 1893, sold a 120-
... po ornaments, which they still sell

Floor Treatments

Floor Treatments The floorcloth of painted canvas, which we saw in England and America, did not wear well. Many experiments added materials—cement, coconut fiber, shredded sponges—to the paint to improve durability and resiliency. An early success was *Kamptulican*, cooked up by Englishman Elijah Galloway in 1844 from a mixture of rubber and cork pressed between cast-iron rollers. Architect Charles Barry specified it for the corridor floors of London's Houses of Parliament in the late 1840s. In 1871, Corticine, or cork carpet, was patented (fig. 20–64), and major designers like William Morris embraced the new material.

However, the big success among these experiments was **linoleum**. It was patented in 1863, again by Frederick Walton, who took its name from the Latin words *linum*, meaning "flax," and *oleum*, meaning "oil." It was made from linseed oil, gum, and cork pressed into a canvas backing, and its production was long and complicated. Walton later brought his process to America, and linoleum was made by the Armstrong Cork Company from 1909 until 1974, when more resilient petroleum-based vinyls had come to dominate the market. Linoleum was advertised "for every room in the house," but it was always most popular for kitchens and bathrooms, where it was valued for being easily cleaned. It is also biodegradable and recently has been back in production at very small companies.

Wallpaper

Wallpaper increased in popularity over the nineteenth century. It was less expensive than plasterwork and woodwork and required less artisanship to install. Sometimes papers covered the wall surface above a base of wood wainscoting, but, to economize, sometimes wallpapers were substituted for the wainscoting itself. When even greater economy was needed, the whole effect was accomplished with paper. Above a three-dimensional baseboard, there was a paper dado about 2 feet (60 cm) high, a "fill" paper covering most of the wall, and a paper frieze at the ceiling.

But wallpaper was a high quality artistic form in itself. In America, the taste for English papers, which had been available for most of the eighteenth century, was replaced by a taste for the stunning new French papers, of which Thomas Jefferson himself was an admiring customer. Prominent among the fashionable French paper manufacturers (after Rèveillon; see fig. 15–41) were Jean Zuber and Joseph Dufour.

Zuber and Dufour Jean Zuber (1773–1835) joined the Dolfuss firm (a maker of Indian-style textiles with a wallpaper department) in Alsace in 1791, and then changed its name to Jean Zuber et Compagnie in 1802. Zuber's specialty was the poetic landscape with courtly figures. Most of his landscape papers were based solely on imagination and on written accounts, such as "Hindustan" of 1807, "Italian Views" of 1818, and the 1834 "Views of America," a set of

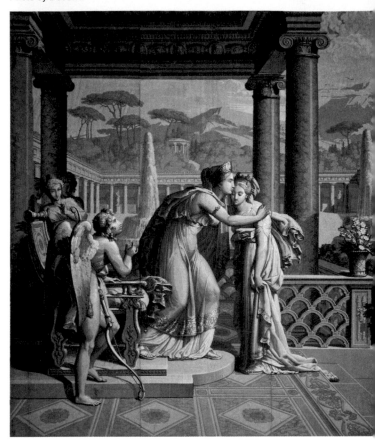

which would be hung in the White House during the Kennedy administration. Zuber's twenty-five-panel "Gardens of France" of 1821 may have been his finest work; certainly it was frequently reprinted. Zuber also produced paper friezes (fig. 20–65) to visually replace more expensive architectural moldings and fabric draperies.

Zuber's chief competitor was Joseph Dufour (1757–1827), who established his firm in 1804. Like Zuber, Dufour produced large scenic papers, such as Gabriel Charvet's "Sauvages de la Mer Pacifique" of 1804–5. Dufour's designer Christophe Xavier Mader painted **grisailles** (works in various tones of gray) based on mythology, such as the 1816 "Cupid and Psyche" (fig. 20–66). Later, military subjects became popular as well, such as Dufour's 1829 "French Campaigns in Italy" and Zuber's 1850 "War of American Independence." The rage for panoramic scenic papers was over by c. 1865, its decline probably reinforced

by the growth of machine printing, as such printing produced relatively small motifs and relatively short repeats. Floral motifs came to be the most popular of the century, stimulated by the botanical engravings of Joseph Redouté and others. Roses, peonies, poppies, lilacs, and more covered not only wallpapers, but also fabrics, porcelains, and (in the form of carvings, mother-of-pearl and gilt inlays, and applied papier-mâché) furniture.

Morris and Voysey   As the century progressed, however, these floral motifs became less realistic and more stylized. This trend was fueled by the Arts and Crafts movement in general and by William Morris in particular. Morris's early papers, such as "Trellis" (fig. 20–67), "Daisy," and "Fruit," issued beginning in 1864, were drawn from nature but with no desire to give the illusion of nature; their elements were simplified, balanced, spaced apart, and flattened.

▲ **20–67** William Morris's "Trellis" wallpaper design of 1864. The birds were painted by Philip Webb.
Dover Publications, Inc.

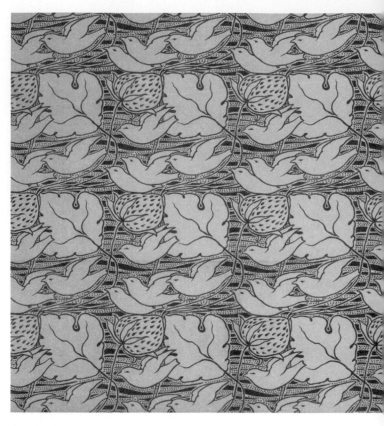

▲ **20–68** C. F. A. Voysey's highly stylized pattern for wallpaper and fabric, designed in 1897.
Victoria & Albert Museum, London/Art Resource, NY

At the end of the century, the wallpaper and fabric patterns of C. F. A. Voysey (1857–1941) would carry Morris's abstraction a step further, showing birds, animals, and plants "reduced to mere symbols" (fig. 20–68). Voysey was a prominent English architect and designer for the Arts and Crafts movement, and he worked well into the twentieth century.

Summary: Nineteenth-Century Design

The nineteenth century is the beginning of the modern world in which we live, and much of its history seems to have been one of struggles, rivalries, and competition. But the conflicting ideas and goals for design in the nineteenth century had, by the end of the century, largely been resolved. The winners were the machine-made over the handmade, invention over tradition, and the new over the old. Some revivals of past styles would continue into the twentieth century, but

in many ways the world had finally been made ready for design that matched the science and technology of the time. The nineteenth century had set the stage for the appearance of modernism.

Looking for Character

The nineteenth century is notable for presenting an ever-changing parade of styles, each with its own character. Some of those seem extremely curious to us today, but they were sincere efforts in their time. Developing technology brought the opportunity for—and, in some cases, the necessity for—new types of construction, but at the same time there were strong compulsions to repeat the look of the past. This combination of opposing forces led to anomalies, such as an Italian Renaissance palazzo façade stretched upward enclosing a brand-new 15-story office tower.

Looking for Quality

Just as it is impossible to assign a single character to the nineteenth century—other than expressing the advent of an ever-changing society—it is also impossible to look for the highest quality in a single style or phase. But, for all the century's struggles, changes, and contradictions, high quality did emerge at the hands of some designers of genius: Percier and Fontaine, Soane, Gaudi, and Sullivan were all extraordinarily gifted. And there were undisputed masterpieces in a variety of expressions: in the creative spirit of Garnier's Paris Opéra, in the clean lines of Mackintosh's buildings and furniture designs, and in the beauty of Morris's papers and textiles.

Making Comparisons

Because so much effort was spent in the nineteenth century to revive the spirit and design of other places and times, it is natural in every case to compare every revival to its original: How true was it to its source? But authenticity was not necessarily a nineteenth-century goal, so we might also ask in each case: How appropriate and adaptable was the revival to its own time?

But, in the end, comparing the whole body of revivals to the new directions that appeared near the end of the century, we can say that those new directions were more influential than any of the nineteenth-century revivals on the century that would follow.

The Twentieth Century

21

"Around 1910 an event of decisive importance occurred: the discovery of a new space conception in the arts."

— Sigfried Giedion (1888–1968), architectural historian, in his 1952 book, *Space, Time and Architecture*

The twentieth century brought an impressive wave of democratization and benefits for many (though far from all), including an unprecedented amount of good design, available not just to the nobility and the wealthy but to all classes and economic levels. This brought with it a heightened awareness of our need for the pragmatic benefits of design. In sum, if measured by the contributions and importance of design, this has been our richest century so far.

Determinants of Twentieth-Century Design

In some ways the twentieth century is the child of the nineteenth, with some design expressions—such as the restrained Arts and Crafts movement and the voluptuous Art Nouveau—continuing from one century into the next, yet in dramatic ways the twentieth century stands apart from all earlier times. The chair construction seen in figure 21–1 could not be mistaken for design in any other period. Design in the twentieth century was determined by political and social upheaval, by old and radically new ways of communicating design ideas, and by new technology and materials that brought new opportunities and forms.

◀ **21–1** Detail of the Red-Blue chair designed by Gerrit Rietveld in 1917. The whole chair is seen in fig. 21-13.
Gerrit Rietveld, "Red Blue Chair". KNA 1276. Stedelijk Museum Amsterdam

History

The positive progress of the human condition in the twentieth century was interrupted by two huge wars and a large number of smaller ones. The First World War (1914–18), unprecedented in scope, interrupted all aspects of life including design, but it was followed by a period of peace treaties, with the newly created League of Nations, and general optimism and confidence in the future. The year the war ended, French architect Le Corbusier and French painter Amédée Ozenfant published the *Purist Manifesto* praising the purity of form of the machine, and the following year the Bauhaus school was founded in Germany. The period between the world wars was a time of great innovation in design, in which modernism blossomed and matured.

The Second World War (1939–45) again brought shortages of materials, energy, and funds for design, and the postwar period brought the realization of many design ideas that had been held in abeyance. But the postwar conflict between the two chief powers that emerged from the war, the United States and the U.S.S.R., brought unease, as did growing awareness of wartime brutality and the immense challenge of reconstruction. "The Age of Anxiety" was the title of both a 1948 poem by W. H. Auden and a 1949 symphony by Leonard Bernstein. Modernism continued its progress, but in a context of new doubts and questions. The previous ideal of industrial efficiency combined with sleek beauty was challenged by occasional forays into roughness and irrationality.

Communications

Skill in the communication of images and design ideas grew enormously in the twentieth century. Those images and design ideas appeared in newspapers and magazines (in both advertising as well as the editorial pages). And they arose in the mail, in stores, in museums and galleries, on buses and subways, in designer showrooms, in film and television, and eventually on computers.

One positive influence of the media was to make interior design a matter of unprecedented popular concern. As an example of the change in mass consumption of design ideas, consider that in the eighteenth century, if a French king's mistress were said to prefer a particular chair, the lesser nobility might order copies of that chair for their own houses, the middle classes might eventually follow as best they could, but the lower classes would not only never own the chair but probably would not even know of its existence. In the twentieth century, design influences originated in any social class and were immediately conveyed to anyone interested, thereby encouraging instant fashion trends and fashion reversals. The section on "Design Media" will outline some of the media outlets for the dissemination of design ideas in the twentieth century.

Technology

The nineteenth century's efforts to deny the reality of industrialization could not succeed. Although nostalgia for preindustrial forms and materials persisted into the twentieth century and is with us still, design in the twentieth century learned to deal fully with—and benefit fully from—technology. There is hardly an aspect of daily life—communications, transportation, science, health, entertainment, or the production and distribution of goods and services—that was not transformed between 1900 and 2000. Technological improvements in lighting, heating, and acoustics culminated at the end of the century with yet another innovation, the computer, which affected not only many of the activities accommodated by interior design, but also the process of design itself. The section on "New Equipment" will cover the types of interior innovations that improved the quality of indoor living.

Twentieth-Century Architecture and Interiors

The central changes in living conditions in the twentieth century were the results of new technology. The central change in society, meanwhile, was progress toward democracy and equality, progress seen in design as well as in government. And the central artistic development of the century—a development that progressed hand in hand with technology and democracy—was modernism.

Modernism was not the century's only expression, but it was the one against which others were measured. It was not the only movement, but all others were judged by their relationships to it—as precursors to it in some cases, as reactions against it in others, as either participants in it or forces outside it. Many of modernism's enthusiasts saw it as more than a style. In its most extreme examples, modernism rejected all ornamentation, all allusions to earlier design, and all past styles. Modernism was seen as having grown naturally from function and therefore to have abolished the very concept of style. Today we can see that modernism was not as unified, logical, or objective as its advocates once thought. It is a style, after all, but one of rare importance and continuing vitality.

Forerunners

At the beginning of the century there were a number of architects and designers who, although never fully participating in modernism, were nevertheless influential.

Elsie de Wolfe   Elsie de Wolfe (1865–1950) turned to interior design as a profession in 1904. The following year Stanford White of McKim, Mead & White arranged for her to design the interiors of New York's new Colony Club, a club open only to women. Decorators (including de Wolfe) had done residential interiors before, but it was a breakthrough for a decorator to design a public interior, as this work was traditionally done by architects or antique dealers. De Wolfe's interiors for the club were painted in light colors. She furnished the rooms with light, movable chairs and tables and colorful chintzes. The club's tearoom (fig. 21–2) was treated as a conservatory with green painted trelliswork on the walls, a tile floor, and wicker furniture. The look was not yet modern, but it was fresh and pleasant.

▲ **21–3** The hall of Folly Farm, Berkshire, England, by Edwin Lutyens, 1908. Its woodwork is white against glossy black walls, and the open china cabinet is lacquered red.
Country Life Picture Library, London, England

De Wolfe is sometimes called the first professional designer, and she was also an **eclectic**, that is, she chose freely among elements of different styles. A shrewd and sensible designer, her three-word philosophy still garners respect: "Simplicity, Suitability, and Proportion."

Edwin Lutyens   The dominant English architect and designer for the first four decades of the twentieth century was Sir Edwin Landseer Lutyens (1869–1944). Lutyens (pronounced "Lutchens") was responsible for many large building projects. He worked at first in an Arts and Crafts manner, using vernacular elements such as casement windows with small leaded panes and steeply pitched tile roofs, all finely crafted. Gradually he moved towards greater classicism and formal symmetry.

It is in his residential work that Lutyen's skill and variety are most easily seen. His houses were a highly personal mixture of romanticism and classicism and a highly eclectic mixture of stylistic revivals. His Folly Farm, in Berkshire, 1908, employed an English Baroque style, reminiscent of design from two centuries earlier, but in its interiors (fig. 21–3) he used more classical elements, dramatically presented and strikingly colored.

Interestingly, the largest of all his projects was the government complex at New Delhi, India (1912–30), which was an example of Beaux Arts planning but one in which Lutyens introduced some motifs of the traditional architecture of India, such as the umbrella-shaped cupolas called *chattris*. The Viceroy's House, which terminated the main axis of the complex, was larger than Versailles.

Pioneers

Contemporary with de Wolfe and Lutyens were three key figures who had their roots in the century before but developed strong design characters of their own. Without their groundwork, modernism might never have established itself so securely.

Frank Lloyd Wright A singular genius from the American Midwest and an astonishingly prolific architect, Frank Lloyd Wright (1867–1959) designed over a thousand buildings, of which about 400 were built. All of them were of striking quality, for Wright was as skillful as he was prolific. Wright's career will intersect often with the story of design in the first six decades of the twentieth century.

Wright studied engineering in his native Wisconsin and apprenticed until 1893 in the Chicago office of Louis Sullivan, whose Art Nouveau ornament we saw in figure 20–25 and who was as noted for his functional forms as for his ornament. In 1901 Wright published a house design in the popular magazine *The Ladies' Home Journal* and called it "A Home in a Prairie Town." It proposed a low roof with wide eaves under which were long horizontal bands of casement windows, and its interior was to be of sand-finish plaster with strips of pine trim. Its intercon-

necting rooms included a double-height living room. It began what would be known as the Prairie Style, meant to be long and low like the Midwestern prairies, though in practice most of its examples were built in suburban areas outside Chicago.

It also began what would be known as the **open plan**, one of the century's greatest contributions to interior design. It was an idea that would be made more apparent in a slightly later and larger house, the 1902 Ward Willits House in Highland Park, Illinois (fig. 21–4). Around a central masonry block containing a cluster of fireplaces, space flows continuously, unimpeded by doorways, from entry to living room to dining room, modulated only by asymmetrically placed semitransparent wood screens. In another example, Wright's 1904 Larkin Building in Buffalo, New York, has private offices that overlooked a five-floor-high skylit atrium (see fig. 21–54). Here the spaces open to one another both vertically

▼ **21–4** The open plan of the ground floor, Frank Lloyd Wright's 1902 Ward Willits House, Highland Park, IL.
Georges Ed. Berthoud

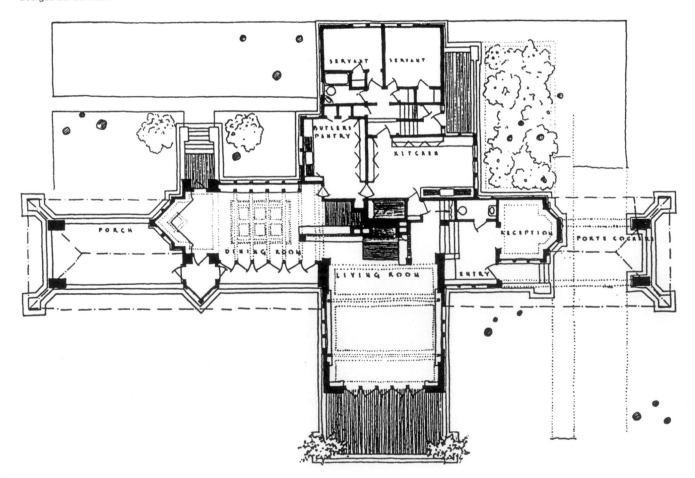

(from floor to skylight in the atrium) and horizontally (into and across the atrium from surrounding offices). Wright would continue to develop the open plan throughout his long career, using it in many other houses including his own two school/residential complexes, Taliesin in Spring Green, Wisconsin, built in 1911, and Taliesin West, near Phoenix, built in 1938.

Open planning was also apparent in the great 1936 country house called Fallingwater, near Pittsburgh, as were innumerable indoor-outdoor connections. The choice of Wright for the Kaufmann House had been urged by Kaufmann's son, Edgar, jr., who had been studying at Taliesin and who would later be a brilliant curator, historian, and connoisseur of modern design and decorative arts. The site was a dramatic one, featuring a waterfall in rocky terrain, and Wright increased the drama by cantilevering parts of the house directly over the stream. From a stone-faced core anchoring the house struc-

turally and visually to the landscape, three levels of great reinforced concrete trays project asymmetrically. Here Wright proved himself a virtuoso of modern composition and structural daring. Inside as outside, Fallingwater was a highly personal amalgam of elements that were natural and elements that could not have been achieved without technology. The masonry core, which partially encloses the kitchen, is as evident inside as out, and the expansive living room (fig. 21–5) and all major bedrooms have terraces within the concrete trays. Most of the furniture, as one would expect, was designed by Wright.

Wright's open planning would culminate in his final masterpiece, New York's Guggenheim Museum. Its central atrium is a more generous version of the one at the Larkin Building and is formed within a spiral gallery ramp for visitor movement. The views up, down, and across the great void are now infinite.

▼ **21–5** Living room of Fallingwater, the Kaufmann country house near Pittsburgh, designed by Frank Lloyd Wright in 1936.
Courtesy of Western Pennsylvania Conservancy

Peter Behrens German architect Peter Behrens (1868–1940) was a proponent of artistic involvement in many areas, and his design career was one of continuing simplification, moving from a classical vocabulary to a modern vocabulary that yet retained a classical basis. In addition to designing buildings and interiors, he was an educator and an artist producing paintings and woodcuts. As artistic advisor to the giant German electric company AEG, he created not only architecture and interiors, but also graphic design and a wide array of product designs. Apprentices in Behrens's Berlin office included three young men who would be largely responsible for the modern movement: Walter Gropius, Ludwig Mies van der Rohe, and Le Corbusier. Among Behrens's works are the 1909 AEG Turbine Factory in Berlin (fig. 21–6), a no-nonsense utilitarian structure of brick and steel that still echoes the form and bearing of a classical temple, and the 1912 German Embassy in St. Petersburg, Russia, on which the young Mies worked.

Josef Hoffmann Austrian architect and designer Josef Hoffmann (1870–1956) studied under Otto Wagner of the Vienna Secession, a more geometric development of the lyrical Art Nouveau movement. During a year in Rome, classical temples impressed him. He was also influenced by the contemporary Arts and Crafts scene in Britain. Returning to Vienna in 1896, Hoffmann joined both Wagner's office staff and the Secession group, just then being founded. In 1901 his sketches began to be published in the newly founded magazine *Das Interieur*, some of them showing his admiration for the work of Charles Rennie Mackintosh, who had contributed a room to the Secession exhibition of 1900. In that magazine, Hoffmann wrote "I believe a house should have the appearance of a homogenous whole—the outside should give evidence of the interior. . . ." In 1903 Hoffmann and Moser founded the Wiener Werkstätte (Viennese Workshop), a cooperative of architects, decorative artists, painters, and sculptors; it would be active until 1932. Two important early commissions followed, the Purkersdorf sanatorium and the Palais Stoclet.

The Purkersdorf sanatorium, built near Vienna in 1903–5, was Hoffmann's first major step away from Art Nouveau fluidity toward simpler cubic forms. The building is symmetrical, flat-roofed, and severely plain. The windows, for example, have no projecting cornices or sills to interrupt the wall plane. Colors are almost completely limited to black and white. It was also was the first large-

▼ **21–6** Peter Behrens's turbine factory for a major electric company, Berlin, 1909.
Behrens, Peter (1868–1940). "AEG Turbine Factory". 1909. Exterior. Berlin, Germany.
© ARS Artists Rights Society, NY/Erich Lessing/Art Resource, NY

scale opportunity for the Werkstätte artists to display the integration of all their skills, with all details of the interior furnishings supervised by Hoffmann in the Vienna workshops. In its unadorned surfaces and rationality of plan, it anticipated the sanatorium Alvar Aalto would design for Paimio, Finland, in 1929. Hoffmann's design is also a foretaste of the early work of Le Corbusier, whom he admired and supported.

The Palais Stoclet (fig. 21–7), a large private house for a wealthy art collector in Brussels, continued the cubic vocabulary of the sanatorium but was decoratively richer. Its design occupied Hoffmann and all members of the Werkstätte from 1905 to 1911. The house's exterior was of marble panels trimmed with bronze, and many interior walls and floors were marble as well, others with inlaid rosewood or, in the dining room, with mosaic murals by painter Gustav Klimt. Furniture, fabrics, carpets, hardware, lighting fixtures, art, and gardens were all designed as elements in the great ensemble.

In the same spirit of integrated design, Hoffmann himself designed furniture, porcelain, glassware, silverware (see fig. 21–75), fabrics, and all kinds of decorative objects. Many of these, even in the early years of the century, shunned the rich decorative effects of the Palais Stoclet and were severely geometric.

Bauhaus

In 1919, just after the First World War, an architect, Walter Gropius (1883–1969), was appointed director of two German art schools, which he combined to form the Staatliche Bauhaus (State-Controlled Building House) in Weimar, Germany. Despite its name, it did not at first teach architecture; that was a goal realized in subsequent years. It began by teaching a variety of applied arts, with each workshop (carpentry, weaving, metal work, etc.) headed by a pair of instructors—one of them an artist, the other a craftsman or technician. Its faculty members, some of whom began there as students, included painters Paul Klee and Wassily Kandinsky, architect and furniture designer Marcel Breuer, painter Josef Albers and his wife, weaver Anni Albers, painter/sculptor/photographer László Moholy-Nagy, and others well known today.

The Bauhaus was progressive politically as well as artistically, seeking a broad audience for its ideas and products. The "great work" of the Bauhaus, Gropius said, was to be the creation of a complete environment "by all and for all."

▲ **21–8** Bridge between two blocks of Walter Gropius's 1925 Bauhaus building, Dessau, Germany. The complex was restored in 1991.
Siftung Bauhaus Dessau.

In 1925, the city of Dessau invited the Bauhaus to move there from Weimar, and in 1926 Gropius designed the new school building himself. Gropius's Dessau Bauhaus was an asymmetrical composition of simple unadorned masses with some multistory glass walls, with a pattern of cantilevered balconies, a bridge over a city street (fig. 21–8), classrooms, offices, and student housing. With its white surfaces, large amounts of glass, asymmetrical massing, and lack of ornament, it defined modernism and offered a catalogue of its possibilities.

Gropius was succeeded as Bauhaus director by Hannes Meyer, who introduced architecture and city planning studies and emphasized technology over art. In 1930 Meyer was dismissed and replaced by architect Ludwig Mies van der Rohe (1886–1969), who would be one of the century's most influential designers.

Walter Gropius As a draftsman in Peter Behrens's office, Walter Gropius was notorious for his lack of drawing skills, a handicap that may have led to his interest in theory and teaching. Before his directorship of the Bauhaus, however, he

had designed two early monuments of modern design, both highly innovative. The first was his 1911 design for the Fagus factory at Alfeld, Germany, which was the first building wrapped almost completely in a glass skin. The second was his 1914 model factory for the Werkbund Exhibition in Cologne, the factory showing his knowledge of Frank Lloyd Wright. Curiously, his 1921 Sommerfeld house in Berlin, essentially a large log cabin, seemed to suggest second thoughts about the direction design should take. His Bauhaus complex was a clear return to the machine aesthetic, however, as were his two houses for a 1927 housing exhibition in Stuttgart, for which he experimented in prefabricated building techniques.

Marcel Breuer Many of the interiors and much of the furniture in Gropius's Dessau complex for the Bauhaus were designed by Marcel Breuer (1902–81). He had been a student in the Bauhaus carpentry workshop and became head of the

▼ **21–9** Wall-hung cabinetry and mirrors in the master bedroom of Marcel Breuer's Ventris apartment, London, 1936.
Marcel Breuer, "Ventris Flat". London. 1936. Master Bedroom. Exhibition: Marcel Breuer: Furniture and Interiors. July 25–September 15, 1981. Collection of Marcel Breuer Associates. The Museum of Modern Art/Licensed by Scala-Art Resource, NY.

workshop in 1924. In 1925 Breuer began experimenting with tubular steel as a furniture material (see fig. 21–55). In London, after leaving the Bauhaus, he designed more furniture, exhibitions, and residential work including a 1936 apartment and all its furnishings for modern art enthusiast Dorothea Ventris and her son Michael (fig. 21–9).

During the Second World War, Breuer was invited to teach at Harvard's Graduate School of Design where Gropius had gone and was now head of the architecture school. At Harvard, his students included I. M. Pei, Paul Rudolph, Ulrich Franzen, John Johansen, and Philip Johnson, and his continued partnership with Gropius produced engaging architecture that combined modern design with traditional New England building materials, such as wood and stone. Breuer continued this direction in work, such as the 1949 demonstration house, which he was invited to build in the garden of the Museum of Modern Art, New York (fig. 21–10) in order to illustrate for a wider audience the possibilities of the modern house.

Larger commissions that came later to Breuer included the 1958 UNESCO headquarters in Paris and the 1966 Whitney Museum in New York.

Ludwig Mies van der Rohe   Often known simply as "Mies," Ludwig Mies van der Rohe (1886–1969) was born in Aachen, Germany, to a family of stonemasons. Before his tenure at the Bauhaus, he had directed the 1927 Stuttgart housing exhibition to which Gropius had contributed two house designs; designers of other units at the exhibition included Le Corbusier from France, J. J. P. Oud from the Netherlands, Josef Frank from Austria, Peter Behrens, and Mies himself.

In 1930, Mies had just completed a landmark of modern architecture, the German Pavilion at the 1929 international exhibition in Barcelona (fig. 21–11), for which he also designed interiors and furniture. The Barcelona Pavilion, as it is generally called, was a building with only a ceremonial and public relations function. Its ornament was derived wholly

▼ **21–10** Living room of Marcel Breuer's demonstration house in the garden of the Museum of Modern Art, New York, 1949.
Ezra Stoller/Esto Photographics, Inc.

▲ **21–11** Mies's Barcelona Pavilion, 1929. The furniture is Mies's own. The sculpture in the pool is by Georg Kolbe.

Mies van der Rohe, Ludwig (1886–1969). "German pavillion for the International Art Exhibit, Barcelona, Spain". 1929. Sculpture by Georg Kolbe (1877–1947). © ARS, NY/Erich Lessing/Art Resource, NY.

from its rich materials: walls of onyx, green marble, and clear and green glass; floors of travertine; black glass lining the two pools; and upholstery of white leather. Even more remarkable was the pavilion's free-flowing plan, its floor-to-ceiling planes arranged independently of the structure of chrome-plated cruciform columns. The idea of an open plan, at the heart of so much twentieth-century design, was one Mies credited to the Prairie Style houses of Frank Lloyd Wright, but Mies developed it masterfully.

One visitor to the Barcelona Pavilion when it was new was Philip Johnson, a recent Harvard graduate (but not in architecture, which he would study later). He commissioned Mies's first American work, a New York apartment for himself. While limited in the disposition of walls, Mies devised another spare design of carefully chosen elements: blue raw

silk curtains, rosewood shelving on chrome supports, straw matting on the floor, and a Mies chair in white vellum at a desk topped in black leather.

In 1938, Mies went to Chicago as head of the architecture school at the Illinois Institute of Technology. But he practiced as well as taught, and outstanding among his early American work was the 1950 glass-and-steel Farnsworth House in the Chicago suburb of Plano, which clearly expressed its structure and continued Mies's exploration of the open plan. Other Miesian masterpieces are the Seagram Building in New York, 1958, and the National Gallery in Berlin, 1968. Mies was one of the most influential designers of his century, and we shall see examples of that influence in some of the work of Philip Johnson and in much of the work of Skidmore, Owings & Merrill.

Purism and De Stijl

The 1918 Purist Manifesto of architect Le Corbusier and painter Amedée Ozenfant expressed its authors' admiration for the beauty of machines (including ships, airplanes, and cars), their celebration of ordinary and mass-produced objects, and their preference for smooth contours and polished surfaces. The Purists called for geometry, simplicity, and purity of form in both painting and architecture, and advocated the use of a mathematical proportioning system called the **golden section**, which was based on the ratio of 1 to 1.618 . . . supposedly a source of harmony in such natural forms as spiral seashells and sunflowers.

Like Purism, **De Stijl** was a movement in both art and architecture. It was founded in the Netherlands, which, as the only European country remaining neutral in the First World War, emerged economically able to support new design and design theory. Based on a movement and the magazine *De Stijl* (*The Style*), first published in 1917, by 1920 the term *De Stijl* was being applied to a variety of artists and designers working with elementary forms, straight lines, and primary colors. Theo Van Doesburg was the leading theorist of the group, Piet Mondrian was its chief painter, J. J. P. Oud was an important architect and urban planner, and Gerrit Rietveld was its most brilliant architect, interior designer, and furniture designer.

Le Corbusier   Purism's chief architect and designer was Le Corbusier (1887–1965), who continued his theorizing in a 1923 book called *Vers une architecture,* usually translated as *Towards a New Architecture.* It contained a chapter on proportion titled "Regulating Lines" and, in a section on the beauty of airplanes, the famous aphorism, "The house is a machine for living in."

Le Corbusier was born in Switzerland. He worked in Paris in 1908 for Auguste Perret, studying Perret's revolutionary use of reinforced concrete (see fig. 21–50), returned to Switzerland, went to work in Peter Behren's office in Berlin, traveled widely, and experimented with low-cost concrete housing. In 1917 he moved permanently to Paris. An early success was his Pavillon de l'Ésprit Nouveau at the 1925 Exposition des Arts Décoratifs et Industriels Modernes, and others that soon followed were some remarkable private houses—flat-roofed, cubistic, and startlingly white—in and around Paris, the most celebrated of all being the 1931 Villa Savoye at Poissy (fig. 21–12).

▼ **21–12** In the living room of Le Corbusier's Villa Savoye, Poissy, France, 1931, a black cubic fireplace with square white chimney and a Le Corbusier/Perriand/Jeanneret chaise longue in ponyskin.
Arcaid/Alamy Images

Gerrit Rietveld Born in Utrecht, Gerrit Rietveld (1888–1964) worked there in his father's furniture workshop, setting up his own workshop at age 29. One of his first independent designs was the chair whose construction we saw in figure 21–1. First designed around 1917 in natural wood, he later painted it in 1923 in primary colors. Feeling that form should be emphasized with color, he renamed it the "Red-Blue" chair.

Rietveld's finest accomplishment, however, was a house he designed with its owner, Mrs. Truus Schröder-Schrader, in Utrecht, the Netherlands. Known as the Schröder House, it was completed in 1925 and stands as the chief built example of De Stijl principles. Its exterior is a composition of overlapping white and gray planes with touches of primary colors and black; inside, red, blue, and yellow surfaces predominate (fig. 21–13). The strikingly elementary vocabulary of forms and colors serves an equally striking functional program: The main floor's single room can become as many as six separate rooms by means of ingenious sliding and folding walls (fig. 21–14). Here Rietveld has devised an open plan of a different sort from that of Wright and Mies: It can be open, partly open, or completely compartmentalized.

▲ **21–13** Gerrit Rietveld's 1925 Schröder House, Utrecht, the Netherlands. Rietveld's Red-Blue chair is in the foreground; to its right is one of the sliding walls that can reconfigure the space.
James Linders Fotografie

Raised above the landscape on slender columns, the Villa Savoye seems, from the exterior, a simple rectangular solid; inside, however, its spaces are freely arranged. It demonstrates the "Five Points to a New Architecture" that Le Corbusier had formulated in 1927 to define his own style. There were to be columns for raising the building; a roof garden; a free plan, identical with the open plan advocated by Wright and Mies; the horizontal strip window; and the **free façade**, with windows placed as irregularly as desired because the exterior wall was not engaged with the supporting columns. We shall see the later work of Le Corbusier in the section entitled "Brutalism;" in that later work he would reject his Purist admiration for smooth, finished forms and seek a more rugged expression.

Art Deco

The design style named Art Deco came out of Paris's Exposition Internationale des Arts Décoratifs et Industriels Modernes of 1924 and 1925, but the name used at the time was *Style moderne*. The exposition was aimed at developing export markets for French decorative arts and luxury crafts and was meant to demonstrate a style that was simultaneously modern and in the French tradition.

Art Deco avoided the sinuous curves of the recently popular Art Nouveau. Plant forms were still a basis for decoration, but they were interpreted more geometrically, and the pale colors of Art Nouveau were replaced by stronger ones. Except for its rejection of Art Nouveau, however, Art Deco welcomed

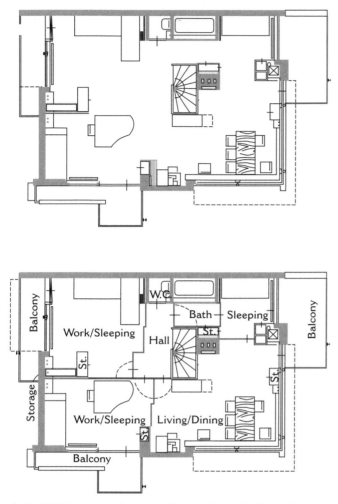

▲ **21–14** Plans show the second floor of Rietveld's Schröder house with sliding walls open and closed.

the influences of other styles and precedents, including the Louis XVI and Empire periods in France, the Wiener Werkstätte from Austria, and De Stijl from the Netherlands. This amalgam was often expressed with exotic materials and techniques: rare woods and veneers, ivory and mother-of-pearl inlays, marquetry, and lacquerwork. The exuberance and decorative extravagance of the Art Deco style seemed to make it particularly suitable for the interiors of ocean liners (such as the *Normandie* and the *Ile de France*) and movie theaters, the two fields in which it had the longest life.

Louis Süe and André Mare became leaders of the Art Deco, followed by the decorator Paul Follot, the silversmith Jean Puiforcat, the ironworker Edgar Brandt, the glassmaker René Lalique (who had previously worked in the Art Nouveau style), the painter and tapestry weaver Charles Dufresne, the

furniture and screen designer Jean Dunand, and the cabinet-maker and interior designer Jacques-Émile Ruhlmann.

Americans took up the Art Deco style with great enthusiasm; though Americans lacked some of the luxury materials and finishes available in France, they had the geometry of Native American art to add as a new ingredient. The American architectural masterpiece of Art Deco was New York's Chrysler Building by William Van Alen, and the great monument of Art Deco interiors was the Radio City Music Hall by Donald Deskey (see fig. 21–16). American Art Deco greatly influenced the "streamlined" look of locomotives and automobiles, a look employed as well in such stationary objects as home appliances, radios, and pencil sharpeners.

Jacques-Émile Ruhlmann　Considered the finest furniture designer of his time, Jacques-Émile Ruhlmann (1879–1933) continued the tradition of excellence of the great French *ébénistes* and emulated their marquetry and veneering techniques (see fig. 21–15). In 1907 Ruhlmann assumed the management of his father's company selling wallpapers, paintings, and mirrors, the Société Ruhlmann. In 1918 he formed a partnership with Pierre Laurent, the Établissement Ruhlmann et Laurent, and began concentrating on furniture design, some of which we will see in fig. 21–59. However, the company would also provide fabric, carpet, lighting, and upholstery, thus exemplifying the role of the interior designer as an *ensemblier* or "Master of Works." Ruhlmann's room designs for the 1925 Paris exposition were important ones, including pieces by Jean Puiforcat, Jean Dunand, Edgar Brandt, Pierre Legrain, and other designers and craftsmen. Ruhlmann designed the tearoom of the oceanliner Ile-de-France in 1926. He was an anomaly in twentieth-century design for his continuation of eighteenth-century French techniques, although he did also experiment with chromium-plated steel.

Donald Deskey　Born in Blue Earth, Minnesota, Donald Deskey (1894–1989) studied both architecture and painting before working in advertising. He traveled to Paris in the Art Deco–dominated year of 1925. Back in New York he designed modern window displays for Franklin Simon and Saks Fifth Avenue. In his interiors and furnishings, he enjoyed combining new materials like Bakelite, plastic laminate, and brushed aluminum with traditional woods and metals. He is best known for his 1931 interiors of the Radio City Music Hall in New York's Rockefeller Center. The Music Hall's great

▲ **21–15** Jacques–Émile Ruhlmann's 1916 *encoignure* (corner cabinet) of amboyna wood inlaid with ivory and ebony.
Christie's Images/CORBIS-NY

vaulted auditorium is seen in fig. 21–16, an exercise in primary geometry with its succession of vaulted forms circling the stage. Accompanying wallpaper design for the men's smoking lounge (see fig. 21–79) displays Deskey's expression of the Art Deco characteristics of vitality and geometry—in this case, angular geometry.

Jean-Michel Frank   Born in Paris, Jean-Michel Frank (1895–1941) took an inheritance and used it to live in Paris's fashionable circles. He hired designer Adolphe Chamaux to design his Paris apartment and then formed a design partnership with him, an early commission being an apartment for couturier Elsa Schiaparelli, which they designed all in white. In 1932 Frank opened a Paris shop where he sold his furniture to such notable designers as Syrie Maugham of England and Frances Elkins of California.

Frank's version of Art Deco was a rarefied and subtle one, often using pale neutral colors, walls lined with parchment or rare woods, and details emphasized in alabaster, rock crystal, or ivory. A high point of his career was the New York apartment (fig. 21–17) he designed in 1937 with architect Wallace Harrison for Mr. and Mrs. Nelson Rockefeller; the living room contained furniture by Frank, andirons and lamps by Giacometti, an overmantel panel by Matisse, and paintings by Picasso.

◄ **21–16** Auditorium of Donald Deskey's Radio City Music Hall, New York, 1931.
Peter Aaron/© Esto. All Rights Reserved/Esto Photographics, Inc.

▲ 21–17 Living room of the Nelson Rockefeller apartment, New York, designed by Jean-Michel Frank in 1937 and restored in 1978.

Ezra Stoller/© Esto. All Rights Reserved.

In the 1970s and 1980s his work was rediscovered by American designers led by Billy Baldwin (1903–83), a New York society decorator whose clients included Jacqueline Onassis, Greta Garbo, and Cole Porter.

Italian Rationalism

A development contemporary with Art Deco was the Rationalist movement (*Razionalismo*) in Italy between the two World Wars. It began with an aesthetic manifesto of 1926 written by a group of architecture students in Milan who called themselves Gruppo 7. The manifesto proclaimed a need for rational building types, denounced individualism, and sympathized with the new political era of fascism. Like contemporary work being done at the Bauhaus and else-

where, it reacted against nineteenth-century eclecticism and the Art Nouveau and proposed instead a sensible, simple, direct expression of function and construction. Italian Rationalists included the architect Adalberto Libera, the architectural partnerships of the BBPR studio and Figini and Pollini, and the architect and designer of interiors and furniture Giuseppe Terragni.

Giuseppe Terragni (1904–43) practiced in Como, Italy, beginning in 1927, and in 1928 showed his work at Mies's Weissenhof exhibition in Stuttgart. His first important built work was the Novocomum apartment block in Como, finished in 1928, but his most famous work was the Fascist party headquarters in Como, the Casa del Fascio (later renamed the Casa del Popolo), which he began to design in 1932 and which was completed in 1936. Square in plan with

▲ **21–18** The boardroom of Giuseppe Terragni's Casa del Fascio, Como, Italy, 1932–36. The board table and cantilevered steel-and-leather chairs are Terragni's own designs.
Centro Studi Giuseppe Terragni, Como, Italy

carefully proportioned openings and unornamented white surfaces, it must have projected a dazzling sense of newness in the old city. Its interior (fig. 21–18) was furnished with some of Terragni's inventive tubular steel furniture.

Terragni died at 39 after injuries in the war. His association with Fascism made him, for a time, an unsympathetic figure, obscuring his talent, but American architect Peter Eisenman did much to restore his reputation beginning in the 1970s. Italian architect Aldo Rossi, about the same time, declared a New Rationalism, one of its monuments being his San Cataldo cemetery complex in Modena, Italy, built in the mid-1970s and expanded in the mid-1980s.

Scandinavian Modern

The Scandinavian countries of Sweden, Denmark, and Norway and the neighboring country of Finland were not greatly receptive to Art Deco, but modernism found a firm footing there. However, the machine aesthetic was never as strong there as the craft aesthetic, nor synthetic materials as popular as natural ones. Those who found mainstream modernism to be "cold" found Scandinavian modernism "warm." It was exported to Western Europe and America in two great waves, so-called Swedish Modern in the 1930s and so-called

Danish Modern in the 1950s. Both were chiefly expressed in furniture design, but the influence originated from Finnish and Danish architects of international stature.

The Saarinens Eliel Saarinen (1873–1950) first practiced architecture in Helsinki, where his most prominent building was the Helsinki Railway Station, begun in 1904. He moved to the United States in 1923 and in 1932 became head of the Cranbrook Academy of Art.

Second only to the Bauhaus in its influence on twentieth-century design, Cranbrook opened in a suburb of Detroit in 1932, and Saarinen designed most of its campus. Like his Helsinki station, Saarinen's Cranbrook building designs were transitional between the traditional and modern styles without being overtly historicist. An example is the president's house (fig. 21–19) where the Saarinens lived. Notable among its faculty and graduates were interior designer Benjamin Baldwin (see fig. 21–25), sculptor and furniture designer Harry Bertoia, textile designer Jack Lenor Larson (see fig. 21–77), and—most notable of all—Charles Eames (1907–78) and his wife Ray Kaiser Eames (1912–88) (see figs. 21–64, 21–65, and 21–66).

Loja Saarinen (1879–1968), Eliel's wife, taught weaving at Cranbrook and wove many of the textiles for the president's house and other Cranbrook buildings. Some of her fabrics are visible in figure 21–19. She also experimented with fibre art, which includes materials not usually associated with textiles, such as film, wire, and paper.

Eero Saarinen (1910–61), the son of Eliel and Loja, carried their artistry into modern expressions. Also born in Finland, he studied sculpture in Paris. In America by 1930, he joined both his father's architecture firm and the Cranbrook faculty. He designed furniture for the Kingwood School for Girls, one of his father's campus buildings, and with Charles Eames he won two first prizes in the 1940–41 Museum of Modern Art competition for "Organic Design in Home Furnishings." Noted among his accomplishments are the 1948 stainless steel Gateway Arch in St. Louis; the 1962 Dulles International airport near Washington, DC; and the TWA terminal at JFK airport near New York (fig. 21–20). The TWA terminal expresses the spirit of flight in great sweeping wings of reinforced concrete.

Alvar Aalto   Almost as influential as Wright, Mies, and Le Corbusier in twentieth-century architecture and design was Alvar Aalto (1898–1976) of Finland, whose work displayed a more lyrical touch than theirs. His first important commission, the Paimio tuberculosis sanatorium, was completed in 1932. For Paimio, Aalto designed all the buildings and their interiors, hardware, lighting, glassware, porcelain, and furniture, including a chair of laminated wood (see fig. 21–60). With its carefully calculated exposure to light and air, Paimio was a potent symbol of the healthy world promised by new technology, but its furniture of wood, rather than steel, also suggested that technology could be humanized. Many other Aalto designs followed and became internationally celebrated, the key buildings including the municipal library in Viipuri (see fig. 21–49), 1933–35, the Villa Mairea in Noormarkku, 1938–39, and the Finnish pavilion for the 1939 New York World's Fair. For the Massachusetts Institute of Technology, Cambridge, where he also taught, he

▼ **21–19** The President's House, Cranbrook Academy of Art, by Eliel Saarinen with textiles by Loja Saarinen.
Marco Lorenzetti/Hedrich Blessing

▼ **21–20** The TWA terminal at John F. Kennedy airport near New York, designed by Eero Saarinen and completed in 1962.
Ezra Stoller/© Esto. All Rights Reserved.

▲ **21–21** The Kaufmann suite of conference rooms, New York, designed by Aalto for Edgar Kaufmann, jr., and finished in 1965.
Museum of Finnish Architecture

designed the 1948 Baker House dormitory, giving its river side a sinuous curve to provide more rooms with a view. Later came the Edgar Kaufmann, jr., suite of conference rooms at the Institute of International Education, New York, 1963–65 (fig. 21–21). Inserted into the rectangular envelope of a typical office building floor, Aalto managed, in both plan and ornament, to project his distinctive lyricism.

Modernism in America

The birth of modernism came from the work of three of its great masters: Frank Lloyd Wright, who contributed a new concept of open space; Mies van der Rohe, who continued Wright's spatial explorations and gave new attention to details and the expression of structure; and Le Corbusier, an artist of pure form and proportion. Modernism would flourish, taking many forms, in postwar America, as many of the Bauhaus faculty members migrated to the United States.

Richard Neutra   Richard Neutra (1892–1970) was born in Vienna, where he came to know the work of Otto Wagner and became friends with architect R. M. Schindler (1887–1953). The 1910 publication in Germany of Frank Lloyd Wright's work inspired him to come to America, which he finally did in 1923. In Chicago he met Louis Sullivan, and at Sullivan's funeral he met Frank Lloyd Wright, who invited him to work with him. Wright had little work at the time, however, and Neutra moved on to Los Angeles, where he briefly worked in partnership with Schindler. His breakthrough accomplishment was the Lovell "Health House" of concrete, metal panels, and glass, finished in 1929 in the Hollywood Hills.

Many other residential as well as commercial projects followed in what might be called a relaxed modernism, although Neutra was not relaxed—in fact, he was zealous—about the practical values of modernism, writing a 1954 book titled *Survival through Design*. For Edgar

▲ **21–22** The Kaufmann House in Palm Springs, CA, designed by Richard Neutra for Edgar Kaufmann, Sr., in 1946.
The Getty Research Institute for the History of Art and the Humanities

Kaufmann, Sr., the same client who hired Wright to build Fallingwater in the previous decade, Richard Neutra designed another house in 1946 in Palm Springs, California. Its desert site ringed by mountains is dramatic, and neighboring houses are cleverly screened. The house (fig. 21–22), though nec-essarily more complex in plan, reflects the vocabulary of Mies's 1929 Barcelona Pavilion without the earlier building's austerity, rigor, and authority. Yet, lacking rigor, the Kauf-mann House exudes an air of ease and grace, demonstrating the pleasures of modernist living.

Viewpoints | PHILIP JOHNSON ON MIES VAN DER ROHE

In 1947, to accompany an exhibition of Mies's work at the Museum of Modern Art, New York, Johnson wrote the first book devoted to Mies. In it he called the Farnsworth House "the first all glass House in the world." In com-menting on the spatial concept, which he admired (and later adapted for his own house (see fig. 21–23), he wrote:

"The independent walls and flowing spaces are devel-opments of motifs which Mies first evolved . . . in 1923 and on which he has been composing variations ever since. . . . The concept of flowing horizontal space, . . . carried on to its triumphant culmination in the Barcelona Pavilion, now expands: space eddies in all directions among interior planes of subaqueous weightlessness."

▲ **21–23** Philip Johnson's 1949 Glass House, New Canaan, CT, furnished with designs by Mies van der Rohe.
Steven Brooke Studios

Philip Johnson   An early and influential curator of New York's Museum of Modern Art and, as we have seen, an admirer of Mies's work, Philip Johnson (1906–2005) was also important in his promotion of the work of younger architects. Johnson is probably most famous for his Glass House, built in 1949 in New Canaan, Connecticut (fig. 21–23). It reflects a clear homage to Mies van der Rohe, who had designed a weekend house near Chicago for Dr. Edith Farnsworth, begun in 1945; its exterior walls were completely of glass. Mies's house was not finished until 1950, by which time Johnson, acknowledging his debt to Mies's idea, had completed his own version. Unlike Mies's version,

Beyond it, in our view, a row of wood-faced closets shields a sleeping area, and a low counter (its end just visible beyond the Elie Nadelman sculpture at right) holds kitchen equipment.

Later in 1958, Johnson had an opportunity to design an interior within a Mies building: He and William Pahlmann collaborated on the design for the Four Seasons restaurant on the plaza level of Mies's Seagram Building in New York (fig. 21–24). They incorporated Mies furniture, table settings by Garth Huxtable, a stage curtain by Picasso, and hanging sculptures by Richard Lippold. The overall effect of the high ceiling, wide spacing between tables, and rich materials was a sense of opulence not often achieved within the modern vocabulary.

Louis Kahn   Louis I. Kahn (1901–74) was born in Russia, taught at Yale and the University of Pennsylvania, and practiced in Philadelphia. Shortly after Johnson and Mies had completed their glass houses, Kahn produced a building of opposite character, presenting a solid masonry wall to the street. It was an addition to the Yale University Art Gallery and, finished in 1953, it was Kahn's first building to attract wide attention. Its galleries are visually dominated by their reinforced concrete ceiling in a triangulated trusslike pattern that also accommodates lighting and HVAC ducts.

Space, structure, and form were all important to Kahn (as they were, respectively, to Wright, Mies, and Le Corbusier), but he brought new considerations to architecture, such as a division between "served" and "servant" spaces and a search for "what a material wants to be." Some of his buildings were wrapped in not one but two closely spaced masonry envelopes. The openings between these envelopes provide new opportunities for environmental control and interior lighting effects and bring to his interiors a sense of mystery and spirituality. Kahn's most acclaimed buildings, perhaps, are the 1972 Kimbell Art Museum, Fort Worth, Texas, and the new capital complex for Bangladesh in Dhaka. It is interesting that for interiors of two of his works, the 1972 library and dining hall at Phillips Exeter Academy, Exeter, New Hampshire, and the 1974 Yale Center for British Art, New Haven, Connecticut (fig. 21–25), Kahn chose the minimalist sensibility of designer Benjamin Baldwin, one of the most talented of the Cranbrook graduates. The result is a quiet interior with clear hierarchies, a sense of order, and nothing unnecessary.

which is lifted above the ground on steel columns, Johnson's sits squarely and more prosaically on a brick podium. The debt to Mies continues inside, where Johnson used Mies's furniture almost exclusively (as ironically Dr. Farnsworth did not). A brick cylinder, which is the only floor-to-ceiling interruption of the interior, holds a fireplace and bathroom.

▼ **21–24** The 1958 Four Seasons restaurant by Philip Johnson and William Pahlmann in Mies's Seagram Building, New York.
Ezra Stoller/Esto Photographics, Inc.

▲ **21–25** A reading room in the 1977 Yale Center for British Art, New Haven, CT, with architecture by Louis Kahn and interior design by Benjamin Baldwin.
George Cserna/Yale Center for British Art/The Bridgeman Art Library International Ltd.

Skidmore, Owings & Merrill   Also strongly influenced by the work of Mies—particularly his attention to detail—is the large corporate firm of Skidmore, Owings & Merrill (SOM), founded in 1936 by Louis Skidmore, Nathaniel Owings, and John Merrill. It cannot be expected that a firm that would grow to have eight offices and hundreds of designers can bring to its work the intellectual rigor and exhaustive study of alternatives that Mies gave to his, but SOM, through the sheer size of its practice, has done more than any other entity to spread Mies's ideas.

SOM's chief interior designer for decades was Davis Allen (1916–83), who was hired in 1950 by Gordon Bunshaft, the chief architectural designer of SOM's New York office. An important early work by Allen, on which he was assisted by Ward Bennett and Richard McKenna, was for the 1961 interiors of Bunshaft's new headquarters building for Chase Manhattan Bank in New York. It included office space for 15,000 workers, but the highlight was a private office for bank chairman David Rockefeller, a 30-foot-square (9 m²) expanse of white walls, teak flooring, and spare furnishings (fig. 21–26). The office expressed authority without any of the traditional trappings; instead of gilt, tapestry, and lavish ornament, it offered space, serenity, and a few selections from Rockefeller's important and varied art collection.

Allen was not SOM's only designer. Charles Pfister of SOM is a designer whose work we shall see later. And Paul Vieyra and Raul de Armas of SOM designed the Palio restaurant in New York in 1986 (fig. 21–27). They used chair designs by Allen; graphics and tableware were by Massimo and Lella Vignelli; and the wrap-around mural was painted by Sandro Chia. The room's bar is wrapped with stainless steel

mesh and topped with granite, and the coffered ceiling and lower walls are of English oak. Here is another restaurant, like the Four Seasons, that is both modern and opulent, but in a less solemn tone.

Powell/Kleinschmidt In 1976 Donald D. Powell (1933–), after fifteen years at SOM, and Robert D. Kleinschmidt (1939–), after twelve years there, formed the Chicago firm Powell/Kleinschmidt. Powell lives in Mies's 860 Lake Shore Drive apartment tower, and Kleinschmidt in its twin, at 880, and both are dedicated to Miesian principles enriched by their own personal tastes in color and art. Their repeat clients, perhaps the best measure of a firm's success, have included Merrill Lynch, the Art Institute of Chicago, the developer Gerald Hines, the fabric companies Gretchen Bellinger and Cowtan & Tout, and the law firm Mayer, Brown & Platt.

Figure 21–28 shows a detail of Powell's own apartment as designed in 1985. The conventional three-bedroom plan was thoroughly revised to yield a much more open one-bedroom layout. Teak-paneled storage units acting as room dividers are raised slightly above the floor and stop well short of the ceiling, so that the openness is three-dimensional.

▲ 21–27 The bar of the Palio restaurant, New York, by SOM's Raul de Armas and Paul Vieyra, 1986. The chairs are designed by Davis Allen; the mural is by Sandro Chia.
Wolfgang Hoyt/Esto Photographics, Inc.

▲ 21–28 Foyer of Donald Powell apartment, Chicago, designed by Powell/Kleinschmidt in Mies van der Rohe's 860 Lake Shore Drive.
Chris Barrett/Hedrich–Blessing

Other materials are travertine flooring, wall coverings of steel mesh, and upholstery of leather and wool. Furniture is by Mies, and the bronze torso is by Rodin.

Minimalism The glass houses of Mies and Johnson led directly to a branch of modernism that had been inherent in Mies's work from the beginning and is still practiced: minimalism. For minimalists in all fields, the Miesian dictum "less is more" is law. Minimalists have included Benjamin Baldwin, Ward Bennett, and Massimo and Lella Vignelli. Benjamin Baldwin (1913–93), after education at Princeton and Cranbrook, worked for Eliel and Eero Saarinen and in partnerships with Harry Weese and William Machado. Baldwin later designed interiors for buildings by architects I. M. Pei, Edward Larrabee Barnes, and Louis Kahn (see fig. 21–25).

In 1946, shortly after the end of the war, Benjamin Baldwin and Ward Bennett , then working for SOM, designed interiors for the Terrace Plaza Hotel in Cincinnati; one of the hotel's dining rooms featured a long mural by Saul Steinberg, another a curved mural by Joan Miró (fig. 21–29).

Ward Bennett (1917–2003) studied under painter Hans Hoffman and sculptors Constantin Brancusi and Louise Nevelson; he was perhaps best known for his furniture design, but he also designed interiors, textiles, cutlery, and crystal. Here, we can see the principle of "less is more" at work: Miró's painting is allowed to be the star, and all else is kept subdued.

Massimo Vignelli (1931–) and Lella Vignelli (1934–) met when they were architecture students in Venice and opened their firm in New York in 1965, where they have designed interiors, exhibitions, furniture, products, graphics, and even clothing; a detail of their own offices, using their own furniture, is seen in figure 21–30, its palette of colors and materials characteristically limited.

The New York Five If glass houses and minimal interiors can be said to have continued the Miesian vein of twentieth-century design, the work of the New York Five can be said to have done the same for the Corbusian tradition. The name derives from a 1969 exhibition at the Museum of Modern Art, New York, that showed the work of five young New

▼ **21–29** A restaurant by Benjamin Baldwin and Ward Bennett of SOM for the Terrace Plaza Hotel, Cincinnati, 1946. The mural is by Joan Miró.
Ezra Stoller/Esto Photographics, Inc.

▼ **21–30** Vignelli Associates' own New York office, designed in 1986. The furniture is their own design.
Peter J. Paige

York architects: Peter Eisenman, John Hejduk, Richard Meier, Charles Gwathmey, and Michael Graves, the last of whom began in the style of Le Corbusier but moved on to a different type of design (see "Postmodernism and Pop" on page 539).

Eisenman (1932–) and Hejduk (1929–2000) are best known as theorists and teachers, Eisenman at the Institute for Architecture and Urban Studies, which he founded in 1967 and directed until 1982, Hejduk at the School of Architecture at Cooper Union, where he was dean from 1975 until his death. Eisenman's built work includes a number of experimental houses and the 1990 Wexner Center for the Visual Arts at Ohio State University, Columbus. Hejduk's first built work was his renovation of the Cooper Union architecture building in 1975, but since then several of his conceptual projects have been built in Berlin, Milan, Buenos Aires, and elsewhere.

Richard Meier (1934–) apprenticed in the offices of SOM and Marcel Breuer before opening his own firm in 1963. His subsequent work has continued Le Corbusier's experiments with white geometric forms. The 1967 Smith House in Rowayton, Connecticut (fig. 21–31), is a single coherent composition involving structural columns, walls, glass areas, and both built-in and movable furniture. Outstanding among his buildings have been the 1984 Museum für Kunsthandwerk in Frankfurt, Germany, and the sprawling Getty Center in Los Angeles, finished in 1998.

Charles Gwathmey (1938–) has worked for decades in partnership with Robert Siegel, and at times on his own. He came to public notice with a 1965–67 house and studio for his parents on Long Island, New York, in which he brought a playful angularity, including 45-degree angles, to the Corbusian geometry. But he finished the exteriors and interiors not in a Purist manner but in unpainted cedar siding (fig. 21–32). Important later works by the Gwathmey Siegel firm are the 1976 Thomas & Betts office building, Raritan, New Jersey, and the 1979 de Menil House, East Hampton, New York.

Reactions Against Modernism

No artistic movement as long-lived and widespread as modernism can avoid being questioned and reconsidered. Among those who sought to take modernism in new directions was one of its founders, Le Corbusier, who abandoned his Purist ideals for a more primitive expression.

▼ **21–31** Richard Meier's Smith House, Rowayton, CT, 1967.
© Ezra Stoller/Esto

▲ **21–32** Charles Gwathmey's 1966 house for his parents, Amagansett, Long Island, NY.
Architectural Association Photo Library

Brutalism The term brutalism is derived from the French phrase *beton brut,* meaning "raw concrete," and the first major building to which it was applied was Le Corbusier's Unité d'Habitation in Marseilles, France, begun in 1948 and finished six years later. The Unité was a large urban apartment block with its glass areas recessed behind rough concrete fins and with interior spaces accented with strong primary colors and faced with concrete, mahogany and varnished plywood. Soon after, Le Corbusier designed another work that admirers of his earlier work found even more shocking, the chapel of Notre-Dame-du-Haut in Ronchamp, France, completed in 1955 (fig. 21–33). Its convex ceiling in dark concrete floats mysteriously above a thick wall penetrated with deep, seemingly randomly placed frames for stained glass. The chapel is so rough in texture that it seemed, at the time, to be improperly finished. Its curved, tilted, and uneven forms seemed only casually assembled.

Marcel Breuer's 1966 Whitney Museum, New York, could be called brutalist in its massing, though not in its finely honed granite skin, and his later churches and office blocks were largely in exposed reinforced concrete. Brutalism was especially favored in postwar England, where it was practiced by the firms of Stirling & Gowan and Alison & Peter Smithson.

A more gentle form of brutalism, which might be called "decorative function," was popular in the 1960s and 1970s and even more recently. Designers, such as the firm of Hardy Holzman Pfeiffer, began to dramatize the building equipment as well as electrical conduit and water lines by exhibiting them boldly and painting them in bright colors. Their interior for Scholastic magazine's New York office (fig. 21–34) is an example. Kahn had exposed mechanical ducts in some of his interiors (as in fig. 21–25) but had done so discreetly, integrating them into walls and ceilings. By 1977, such decorative function appears in the Centre Georges Pompidou, Paris, by Renzo Piano and Richard Rogers, who placed all its structure, ducts, and elevators in full view on the building exterior in order to free its interior for art.

▼ **21–34** Custom carpeting in Hardy Holzman Pfeiffer's Scholastic Magazine offices, New York, 1994, is printed with company-related text. Above it are exposed wires, ducts, pipes, and structure.
Paul Warchol Photography, Inc.

▼ **21–33** The interior of Le Corbusier's 1951 chapel at Ronchamp, France. Most visible surfaces are concrete, some left as formed, others stuccoed. The openings in the wall at left frame stained-glass panels.
Ezra Stoller/© Esto. All Rights Reserved.

Robert Venturi and Denise Scott Brown Robert Venturi (1925–) and his wife Denise Scott Brown (1930–), of the Philadelphia-based firm Venturi Rauch & Scott Brown, provided a theoretical basis for alternatives to orthodox modernism in a book written by Venturi, *Complexity and Contradiction in Architecture* (1966). In it, Venturi advocated for an inclusiveness in design, of "both/and" rather than "either/or," and favored design with "messy vitality" rather than purity or clarity. It suggested replacing Mies's "less is more" with "less is a bore." A second book, the 1972 *Learning from Las Vegas* by Venturi, Scott Brown, and their associate Steven Izenour, stressed the symbolic possibilities of architecture, as in the Las Vegas casinos consisting of banal boxes fronted by elaborate signs. They suggested the ordinary rather than the ideal as a source for a proper twentieth-century style.

An example of "both/and" is seen in a Venturi Rauch & Scott Brown conference room ceiling for a Knoll furniture showroom in New York (fig. 21–35). It is both new (a suspended plastic ceiling lighted from above) and old (silkscreened with a pattern by eighteenth-century English designer Robert Adam).

An illustration of these designers' intent can also be seen in the series of chairs designed by Venturi for Knoll in 1984 (see fig. 21–70): while ordinary in form, each is painted to recall the character of a past style. The Venturis showed the way to postmodernism, but have never considered themselves fully part of that movement, being less overtly revivalist.

Postmodernism and Pop The term **postmodernism** was first used in the fields of music and literary criticism. In the 1970s it began to be applied to the work of architects and designers. An early practitioner was Charles W. Moore (1925–93), who had designed his own house interiors in New Haven in 1966 while serving as dean of Yale's architecture school, using a blend of modern and classical fragments (fig. 21–36). Another was Robert A. M. Stern (1939–), the current dean at Yale, whose 1974 Lang House in Washington, Connecticut, was striped with classical moldings. The most publicized example of postmodern design was Philip Johnson's 1983 AT&T (now Sony) Building in New York, topped with a giant broken pediment often referred to as a "Chippendale" top.

Michael Graves (1934–), during the 1960s was designing in the style of Le Corbusier's Purist white villas of the 1920s and 1930s, though some minor elements such as struts and stair railings were given primary colors. But his later work identifies him as the most consistent proponent of postmodernism. After his rejection of Purist models, Graves developed interior

▼ **21–35** Venturi & Scott Brown's 1980 conference room for Knoll's New York showroom. The luminous ceiling recalls an 18th-century plasterwork design by Robert Adam. The chair design is by Mies van der Rohe.
Venturi Scott Brown & Associates, Inc.

▲ **21–36** Charles Moore's 1966 "postmodern" remodeling of his own house in New Haven, CT.
B&B Italia U.S.A., Inc.

color schemes of grayed taupes and teals and forms referring to past architecture. All these, however, make no attempt at Neoclassical correctness but are instead cartoonlike emblems of classical forms. His buildings include the 1982 Public Services Building in Portland, Oregon, and the 1989 Swan and 1990 Dolphin hotels for Disney World, Orlando, Florida. Graves is most widely known now for his product designs, such as his teakettle and other objects for the Italian firm Alessi and, since 1999, his kitchen and tabletop wares for Target.

▲ 21–37 A 1968 hair salon in Great Neck, NY, designed by Alan Buchsbaum with oversize graphic elements.
Norman McGrath

▲ 21–38 Frank Gehry's cafeteria design for Condé Nast publications, New York, completed in 2000.
Michael Moran Photography, Inc.

Offshoots of postmodernism were called pop, supermannerism, and even psychedelic design. These were free of postmodernism's historical allusions, but alluded instead to the realms of advertising and popular culture. Large-scale graphic elements (called supergraphics) were often featured, and floor plans were spiky with elements angled at 45 degrees. Alan Buchsbaum (1935–87) worked with pop mannerisms in a series of shops, showrooms, and apartments, such as a 1968 hair salon (fig. 21–37). In it, the visual focus is on a series of oversize profiles of female faces edged with colored bands, references to femininity doubling as space dividers.

New Possibilities

In the last decades of the twentieth century design has taken many divergent paths. From the dogmatism of early modernism the twentieth-century eclectics demonstrated the shortcomings of absolute purity. New designers adhere to the principles of a single past master if they like, or they choose and combine elements from several sources. And, of course, they invent.

Frank Gehry When Frank Gehry (1929–) remodeled his own house in Santa Monica, California, beginning in 1978, he turned a simple bungalow into a mid-air collision of stud walls and chain-link fencing. This announced him as anti-Mies—if not antimodern and antineighborhood—because of his highly unconventional treatment of conventional materials. But, even though Philip Johnson labeled Gehry a deconstructionist, he is not a rebel of any recognizable stripe. Gehry has developed a personal and poetic style far removed from the straight lines and right angles of much twentieth-century design.

Celebrated Gehry works are the 1990 Vitra Design Museum in Germany, the 1997 Guggenheim Museum in Bilbao, Spain, and the 2003 Walt Disney Concert Hall, Los Angeles. All three are covered by eccentric roof forms, the last two by forms so eccentric that they could not have been built from Gehry's rough sketches and models without recently invented computer programs. They are inventive as well in their materials, particularly the titanium sheets that billow above the Guggenheim, a metal never before applied to a building at that scale.

Gehry's employee cafeteria in the Condé Nast building, New York (fig. 21–38), designed in 2000, shows how his thinking is applicable not only to freestanding buildings, such as museums and concert halls, but also to spaces within conventional office buildings. It also shows how that space can be expressed in materials less exotic than titanium.

Tadao Ando   Tokyo-based architect Tadao Ando (1941–) is both a modernist and a minimalist, but he pursues usually light minimalist goals with a heavy material, reinforced concrete. Unlike Le Corbusier, who in his late work exploited the weight and roughness of reinforced concrete, Ando has capitalized on its potential combination of gravity and polish, as did Breuer and Kahn in much of their work. Combining beautifully finished concrete with a Kahn-like awareness of the power of geometry, Ando has devised some of our most poetic interiors. Among these are the 1981 Koshino House in Ashiya, Japan, and the 1989 Church of the Light in a suburb of Osaka. In 1993, he designed Vitra House (fig. 21–39), a conference center adjoining Gehry's Vitra Design Museum in Germany. This last demonstrates Ando's meticulous concrete work, his control extending even to the precise placement of the ties that hold together the forms in which the concrete is poured, their positions visible as a pattern of dots on the surface. It also demonstrates Ando's characteristic attention to the way light enters his spaces and moves across his surfaces.

Norman Foster   Norman Foster (1935–), along with Richard Rogers, with whom he was a partner for the years 1963–65, and Renzo Piano, with whom Rogers was a partner in 1971–77, form a triumvirate that might be called the modernists' modernists. Their work stands squarely on the shoulders of the modern masters, particularly Mies, but they have introduced new levels of variety and lyricism.

Outstanding among Foster's works have been the 1975 Willis Faber & Dumas Office Building, Ipswich, England, within an amoeba-like exterior shape Aalto might have been proud of, and the 2006 Hearst headquarters in New York, its steel and glass skin triangulated not unlike the ceiling of Kahn's Yale Art

▲ **21–39** Tadao Ando's conference center adjoining the Vitra Design Museum, Weil am Rhein, Germany, 1993. The curved stair and wall beyond are of exposed reinforced concrete.
Richard Bryant/arcaid.co.uk/Courtesy Vitra Design Museum

▲ **21–40** The banking room of Norman Foster's 1986 Hong Kong & Shanghai Bank, Hong Kong, is entered through a glass floor from a plaza below.

Abercrombie

Gallery. However, figure 21–40 shows Foster's 1986 Hong Kong & Shanghai Bank in Hong Kong, still one of his most adventurous designs. From outside, we see bundles of floors hung from 2-story-high trusses spanning the width of the tower. A generous plaza is under the tower, connecting two busy streets, and from it, escalators rise through a glass floor into a ten-story banking hall lighted by exterior mirrors programmed to follow the sun.

Eclecticism

Eclecticism is name for a design approach that selects and combines desired elements from a variety of sources. Postmodernism might be said to be a form of eclecticism because it combines modern elements with classical references, but eclecticism is generally used to mean combinations without postmodernism's sardonic, sometimes witty, and sometimes disrespectful attitude toward the past. Prominent designers who have practiced eclecticism in the twentieth century have included Edwin Lutyens (see fig. 21–3), Frances Elkins, Dorothy Draper, William Pahlmann, John Dickinson, Albert Hadley, Andrée Putman, Charles Pfister, and decorator Billy Baldwin (see fig. 21–25). As Baldwin once said, "I am against the all-English house or the all-French house or the all-Spanish house."

Frances Elkins Frances Elkins (1888–1953), often worked in collaboration with her brother David Adler, a Chicago-based architect of "great houses" who had studied at the École des Beaux-Arts in Paris. Her taste was more progressive than Adler's, however, so the results of their joint work were often eclectic. In 1918, for her own use, she bought the Casa Amesti, a historic 1824 adobe house in Monterey, California. Within its existing walls of rough plaster and floors and ceilings of wood planks, Adler added some classical details such as cornices, door casings, and Georgian mantels. Elkins added English and French provincial furniture, a Neoclassical French dining table, *toile de Jouy* fabric, a low Art Deco table, and Chinese rugs, all somehow made compatible with a limited color palette of white, blue, and yellow. Elkins concentrated on residential work, but her commercial work included interiors for the 1946 Royal Hawaiian hotel in Honolulu.

Dorothy Draper Dorothy Draper became one of the best-known personalities in the design world, when she opened Dorothy Draper & Co. in 1925. Her first specialty was the

design of apartment house lobbies, and she soon moved into the field of hotel and restaurant design. Draper designed the hotel interiors for the Carlyle (1929) and Hampshire House (1937) in New York, the Mark Hopkins in San Francisco (1935), and the Mayflower in Washington, DC (1940).

Draper used a color palette of strong reds, greens, and pinks, and the ingredients of her designs were often over-scaled and bold: checkerboard floors of large black and white squares, wallpapers of wide pink and white stripes, black patent leather walls, white plaster swags and scrolls, and—her signature design detail—**chintz** with huge clusters of cabbage roses. The results were Baroque with a touch of Surrealism. The Greenbrier in White Sulphur Springs, West Virginia (fig. 21–41), done in 1947, shows her touch.

▼ **21–41** The Victorian Writing Room of the Greenbrier Hotel, White Sulphur Springs, WV, as designed by Dorothy Draper in 1947. The walls are painted a deep green.
Dorothy Draper & Co., Inc.

William Pahlmann A collaborator with Philip Johnson on the Four Seasons (see fig. 21–24), William Pahlmann (1900–1987) was also head of the decorating department at Lord & Taylor. One of his famous displays is the 1938 "Fantasy" exhibition (see fig. 21–46). Another store promotion, called the "Pahlmann Peruvian," attracted an estimated 1,000 visitors a day. This store display was the highly eclectic, with modern furnishings mixed with Peruvian imports, such as fringed handcrafted fabrics and Inca artifacts. Pahlmann was also eclectic in his color combinations. For example, the "Pahlmann Peruvian" display used "Cuzco blue," deep blue, lime, fuchsia, and "whitewash." In his 1955 book, *The Pahlmann Book of Interior Decorating*, he advocated palettes such as "pistachio green, grape, and white" and "sulphur yellow, olive green, and rosy red."

John Dickinson While he has been called eclectic, John Dickinson (1920–82) has also been called idiosyncratic. Like Elkins's Casa Amesti, his rooms achieved coherence through limited colors—in his case, usually black, white, brown, and tan. His best-known work was his own house, converted in 1979 from a former firehouse in San Francisco (fig. 21–42). The plaster walls and ceiling were scraped free of years of paint and then glazed. Beneath them was white wainscoting. A pair of white folding screens stood in the corner; an oval pine table doubled as desk and dining table; and nineteenth-century

▼ **21–42** Living room of John Dickinson's converted firehouse in San Francisco. Antiques mix with Dickinson's own plant- and animal-inspired pieces.
Fred Lyon Pictures

chairs were upholstered in beige Naugahyde. Typical Dickinson accessories included African sculpture, white ceramic phrenologists' heads, white ironstone bowls filled with white coral or bleached bones, and a display of brass fire hose nozzles. But he is perhaps best remembered for his furniture designs, including simple slipper chairs covered in canvas and plaster tables and lamps standing on animal feet.

Albert Hadley After studying at the Parsons School of Design, where he later taught, Albert Hadley (1920–) apprenticed at the New York decorating firm of McMillen Inc., and in 1963 formed a partnership with Mrs. Henry "Sister" Parish. Parish (1910–94) was already well established and known for her comfortable "English country house" style and for her determined eclecticism. "I have a horror," Parish once wrote, "of anything matching." After her death, Hadley opened his own firm. As seen in his sketch (fig. 21–43) for a library in a decorator showhouse, he is adept at unexpected combinations, with special penchants for bold colors, modern art, and elegant Neoclassical French chairs.

Andrée Putman Andrée Putman's (1925–) girlhood was spent partly in what had been a Romanesque monastery (see "Viewpoints" in Chapter 7), which may have given her a special affinity for past architecture and design as well as for spare construction. After years as a design journalist, Putman founded the Paris furniture company Ecart in 1978, which revived early modern furniture classics by Jean-Michel Frank (see fig. 21–17) and others. One of her earliest design commissions (and her first in the United States) was in 1984 for Morgans Hotel, New York, where she mixed new elements with older ones, such as overstuffed leather armchairs and back-and-white checked tile bathrooms. Her work established a trend for the "boutique" hotel, a trend carried further by Philippe Starck and others. In 1985 she designed interiors in Paris's Elysée Palace for French Minister of Culture Jack Lang (fig. 21–44), placing simple blond wood furnishings in ornately paneled eighteenth-century rooms. They are coordinated only through color, yet the two diverse styles do comment on one another, heightening the character of both.

▼ **21–43** Sketch by Albert Hadley of Parish-Hadley for a library at the second Kips Bay Designer Showhouse, New York, in 1974. Courtesy Albert Hadley

▶ **21–44** For the office of the French Minister of Culture. Andrée Putman inserted modern furniture into an eighteenth-century Paris salon.

Deidi Von Schaewen/Andrée Putman

▲ **21–45** The executive bar in the Shell headquarters, The Hague, 1986, by Charles Pfister with Pamela Babey.

Jaime Ardiles-Arce/Haags Gemeentemuseum, The Hague

Charles Pfister Charles Pfister (1939–1990) was SOM's chief designer for the 1971 "open office" interiors for Weyerhauser in Tacoma, with movable partitions taking the place of fixed walls. Pfister left SOM in 1981, when he formed his own practice in San Francisco. His design style is chiefly in the simplified modern vocabulary, but eclectic in its willingness to introduce elements from many different times and places.

In figure 21–45 we see an executive bar in 1986 offices for Shell Oil in a SOM building in The Hague, Netherlands, by Pfister assisted by Pamela Babey. Ceiling coffers are teak inset with sisal and edged in gold leaf, and the wall behind the bar is also covered in sisal. The chairs are a Ward Bennett design upholstered in Larsen silk; the three-legged side tables are by Cedric Hartman; and the secretary at right is an Italian antique. Teak shutters cover the windows at left. In other areas of the Shell installation, ingredients include Japanese screens, antique Delft tiles, textiles from Sumatra, stainless steel elevator doors, wallcoverings of Fortuny fabric, and furniture by Mies van der Rohe and Pfister himself.

Design Media

The twentieth century saw a great proliferation in the ways in which words and images describing design could be spread. This greatly aided the democratization of design and raised the general level of knowledge about design.

Books Books have long been one of the primary ways in which to distribute design ideas. In the early twentieth century two books were especially influential. *The Decoration of Houses* (1897), by Edith Wharton, the novelist, and Ogden Codman, Jr. (1863–1951), an architect and decorator, opened the century with a plea for decorum, sound proportions, classical repose, and the absence of clutter. This was in contrast to the "overstuffed" interiors of the Victorian era. Wharton and Codman argued that interior design should be considered a branch of architecture, an interior expression of the exterior building.

In 1913 Elsie de Wolfe (1865–1950), a friend and colleague of Codman's, published her own book, *The House in*

Good Taste, with the help of Ruby Ross Wood, who would later have her own successful decorating firm. *The House in Good Taste* advocated the same traditional design that Wharton and Codman had, but it did so with more practicality and less aloofness, showing rooms in narrow New York townhouses instead of expansive French chateaux and even suggesting that, in a small house, a dining room could double as a library.

Magazines and Other Media   During the twentieth century, magazines replaced books as the chief print source for new design information. The two chief American magazines for professional designers underwent a series of title changes, the succession of names indicating how the profession defined itself through the century. *The Upholsterer*, founded in 1888, changed its name in 1916 to *Upholsterer and Interior Decorator*, in 1935 to *Interior Decorator*, and in 1940 to *Interiors*. *The Decorator's Digest*, begun in 1932 as the organ of the American Institute of Interior Decorators, changed its name in 1937 to *Interior Design and Decoration* and in 1950 to *Interior Design.*

A different category of magazines, sometimes called "shelter" magazines, presented interior design to the lay public. Prominent among these were *House Beautiful*, founded in 1896, *House & Garden*, founded in 1901, and *Architectural Digest*, founded in 1925. Many others since then have joined that field, some recent arrivals being *Wallpaper* of 1996, *Nest* of 1998–2004, and *Dwell* of 2000.

In the twentieth century newspapers began to cover the field of interior design with some regularity. Perhaps the first newspaper column written by a professional designer was William Pahlmann's *A Matter of Taste*, which began in 1946 (see figs. 21–24 and 21–46). Radio commentary by a professional designer was pioneered by Dorothy Draper (see fig. 21–41), who began broadcasting *Lines about Living* in 1940. But interior design is chiefly a visual art, and it has made its strongest impressions on the screen—at first the movie screen, then the television screen, and now the computer screen.

Stores   The great rival for the importance of the exposition was the store. Municipal or national sponsorship was replaced by commercial sponsorship. The design department of a large-scale department store was something more than just a purveyor of goods and services; it was also an exhibitor—at times, even a setter—of design trends.

Many of the store-based design firms were remarkably well staffed. For example, William Pahlmann became head of the antiques and decorating department at Lord & Taylor in 1936, where he popularized the display of furniture in model room settings (fig. 21–46).

▼ **21–46** William Pahlmann's dining room for the 1938 "Fantasy" exhibition at Lord & Taylor's New York.
Downs Collection of Manuscripts and Printed Ephemera/Courtesy, Winterthur Museum

Following Pahlmann's example, designer Barbara D'Arcy began a series of adventurously designed model rooms at Bloomingdale's, New York, in 1957; they generated great interest, and stores all over the world tried to emulate them.

Museums and Exhibitions   Expositions and exhibitions sponsored by cities and countries played a major role in nineteenth-century design by showing the latest inventions and styles to crowds of visitors. In the twentieth century their role became less central as other ways of communicating grew, but they remained important, as in the case of the Glass House (fig. 21–47) designed by German architect Bruno Taut (1880–1938) for the 1914 Werkbund Exhibition in Cologne. On a thin steel skeleton, its skin capitalized on the translucency of many kinds and colors of glass (including glass blocks, which had been patented in 1886 by a French engineer but were still a novelty in 1914).

▼ **21–47**   Stair of Bruno Taut's Glass House for a 1914 exhibition in Cologne, Germany.
Avery Architectural and Fine Arts Library

The modern museum with an interest in applied design and decorative arts is at least as old as the Victoria & Albert Museum in London, which was conceived as a repository of the wares shown in the Great Exhibition of 1851. The V&A's closest American counterpart, the Cooper Union Museum for the Arts of Decoration (now the Cooper-Hewitt), was founded in New York in 1897. The Museum of Modern Art, founded in New York in 1929, had a larger mandate, and early on proved that its interests extended beyond painting and sculpture. Its 1932 exhibition *The International Style*, curated by Philip Johnson, Henry-Russell Hitchcock, and Alfred H. Barr, introduced the new modern architecture and interiors of Europe to America, and in 1936 there followed an exhibition of Mies van der Rohe's architecture.

Other museums took note, and there was a flurry of exhibitions that, like the flurry of books, showed the public the possibilities of design. One particularly inspired exhibition was the 1949 *Exhibition for Modern Living* at the Detroit Institute of the Arts. Curated by Alexander Girard, it featured model rooms by George Nelson (see fig. 21–73), Charles and Ray Eames, Alvar Aalto, Eero Saarinen, and others; its catalogue was written by Edgar Kaufmann, jr., with illustrations by Saul Steinberg.

New Equipment

Form followed function in many ways in the twentieth century. One was in the need to accommodate a variety of new technical developments and services. While these added comfort and convenience to interiors, they also added complexity to the design process.

Lighting   One of the most dramatic twentieth-century improvements to the quality of interiors came in the field of lighting. The quantity, quality, and control of interior lighting effects have improved radically since 1900. However, the **incandescent lamp**, developed in 1880, has remained the most popular type of lighting for residential uses; it generates light when an electric current is passed through a wire filament. Other lamp types include the **fluorescent**, which generates light when an electric current is passed through a gas or a metallic vapor, and the **halogen**, a type of incandescent light using a lamp filled with a halogen gas. For special effects there are fiber optics, which transmit light through thin strands of fiberglass, and lasers, which are devices that produce light amplification by stimulated emission of radiation, the stimulation caused by the movement of atoms generating electromagnetic waves in the visible spectrum of light.

To the lighting professional, the term bulb refers only to the glass container for other components, **lamp** refers to an entire light source (comprising, for example, bulb, filament, and electrical connection), and **luminaire** refers to a total lighting instrument, possibly including lamps, reflectors, lenses, wiring, and the structure housing such equipment. Working with the several types of lamp and the many types of luminaries and controls, the designer can achieve many different effects. The three broad categories of lighting effects are *general lighting* (also called *ambient lighting*), *local lighting* (called *task lighting* when it is focused on a work surface of some sort), and *sparkle*. For rooms in which the occupants spend large amounts of time, the designer usually provides lighting in all three categories.

The great twentieth-century innovator in lamps and luminaires was New York–based Edison Price (1918–97). Price pioneered the use of the **PAR floodlight** (named for its parabolic section) for even washes of light on walls, and he invented the Darklite recessed fixture, which, unlike its predecessors, does not appear as a bright spot on the ceiling. The bronze luminaire in Philip Johnson's 1949 Glass House (visible between two chairs in figure 21–23) is a collaboration by Johnson, Edison Price, and the American lighting consultant Richard Kelly; its conical bronze shade reflects a pool of light back to the floor.

Among the century's other outstanding luminaire designs is the 1U-VW "Pharmacy Lamp" (fig. 21–48) of nickel-plated brass and stainless steel by American designer Cedric Hartman (1929–). Track lighting was pioneered by George Nelson in his 1948 remodeling of a Herman Miller showroom in Chicago.

HVAC   There were many twentieth-century advances in the fields of heating, ventilating, and air conditioning, or **HVAC**. Coal and wood were replaced with natural gas, propane gas, and electricity. Convection heating, which distributes heat with the movement of air within a room, was joined mid-century by radiant heating from copper (and now plastic) tubing. Although in 1900 ventilation was thought desirable only to rid interiors of smoke and odors, by 2000 ventilation had become a necessary building component to rid interiors of harmful airborne substances, including carcinogens, toxins, positive ions, ozone, and particulates. And air condi-

tioning, once considered an industrial necessity for improving temperature, humidity, and cleanliness, is now a standard in building design. The first residential air-conditioning unit was marketed by Frigidaire in 1929 (it was 49 inches (1.24 m) wide and weighed 200 pounds), but in 1939 the technology (called "dew point control") was applied to an entire skyscraper.

Acoustics   In 1898, the physicist Wallace Clement Sabine formulated the "Sabine law," showing that a room's reverberation time multiplied by its total absorptivity is proportional to its volume. Sabine was asked to advise on McKim, Mead & White's new Symphony Hall in Boston, and he prescribed that the auditorium shape be like a shoebox and that many of its surfaces be faced with sound-absorbing materials. The science of acoustics was launched.

▼ **21–48** Cedric Hartman's 1U-VW luminaire, sometimes called the "Pharmacy lamp." Designed in 1966.
Vera Mertz-Mercer, Courtesy Cedric Hartman, Inc.

Glass consists chiefly of silica, obtained from sand or sandstone. As made today, it also contains an alkali, such as potassium oxide, to lower its melting point and lime as a stabilizer. This allows glass to take many forms.

It can be curved or prismatic, with ribs that refract light. It can be used for windows with two glass layers, called **double glazing**, enclosing a thin inner layer of dehydrated air or inert gas in the space between the glass panes to reduce heat transmission. It can be **tempered**, or treated by heat, so that it has greater strength and so that, if it does break, it will shatter into numerous small, harmless pieces. It can be **laminated**, or bound to a layer of plastic for special visual effects, for safety, for reducing sound transmission, for thermal insulation, or for the blocking of infrared radiation. It can also be sandwiched with wire mesh to produce **wire glass**, mandated by some fire codes for such locations as fire stair doors because the wire prevents the glass from shattering into dangerously large sheets. It can be made in the form of a **glass block** (see fig. 21–47) with varying degrees of transparency. It can be made sensitive to an electric current so that flipping a switch can change it from transparent to opaque. It can be phosphorescent, absorbing light during the day and glowing at night. And it can be decoratively etched (see Fig. 21–62), sandblasted, mirrored, tinted, or painted for different appearances.

Today, auditoriums and theaters are seldom designed without a professional acoustical engineer, but for other spaces where sound quality is important, interior designers need to make their own decisions dealing with the reduction of unwanted sounds. One strategy is using dead air space, or unventilated air within a hollow wall; another is replacing unwanted sounds with less objectionable ones by using **white noise** machines that emit barely audible noise. In the design itself, professionals aim to create spaces and shapes that affect the reverberation time (RT) of sound. For example, the undulating ceiling of a lecture room in Alvar Aalto's 1935 Viipuri Public Library (fig. 21–49) covers the ceiling beams and is shaped to help reflect the speaker's voice to the back of the room.

New Materials

In the twentieth century the importance of natural materials remained, of course, but it was overwhelmed by the importance of man-made ones, such as steel, new types of glass, reinforced concrete, plastics, plaster substitutes, and wood substitutes.

Steel and Glass   In the twentieth century steel and glass—as little steel and as much glass as possible—became a dominant type of building construction. It created a new lightness and transparency in buildings, making an enormous impact on the light, views, and privacy of interiors. Taut's little exhibition building (see fig. 21–47) was an early example, and a later example is Philip Johnson's Glass House (see fig. 21–23). Both of these exterior walls are almost completely glass rather than solid wall, and such design obviously brought profound changes in interior layout and furniture placement.

In furniture design, the first steel-based, glass-topped table was designed by Marcel Breuer around 1926, and so it became possible to have steel and glass furniture inside steel and glass buildings.

Other metal improvements were stainless steel, a steel alloy with 10 to 20 percent chromium, which can be given a high polish. Chromium came to used as plating over steel and other metals to create chrome. Both have been frequently used in furniture design, beginning with Breuer's 1925 chairs. Stainless steel has also found uses as interior surfacing, beginning with column covers for New York's Empire State Building in 1932.

Aluminum   Aluminum was discovered in 1886 through an electrolytic process, and within a couple of years, Alcoa (then, the Aluminum Company of America) was founded in Pittsburgh. Compared with other metals, aluminum is surprisingly light in relationship to its strength. It is also ductile, resistant to corrosion, and capable of taking a brilliant polish. Its surface can be **anodized** to prevent it from oxidizing and becoming cloudy, and the anodized coating can be given a wide range of colors. In the twentieth century, it found a place in architecture chiefly as a material for building exterior skins, and in interiors as a material for decorative screens,

▼ 21–49 Lecture room interior, Alvar Aalto's Viipuri Library, 1933–35.
Alvar Aalto/Viipuri Library/Museum of Finnish Architecture

▲ 21–50 Concrete stair in the lobby of Auguste and Gustave Perret's Museum of Public Works, Paris, 1937–39.
Cite' de L'architecture et du Partrimoine

wall panels, and light diffusers. In 1933, Marcel Breuer created an aluminum chaise longue, and in the following year, an armchair, side chair, office chair, and stool—all designs that would have been excessively heavy in any other metal.

A later example of aluminum versatility was Eero Saarinen's Tulip Chair, designed in 1956 for Knoll (see fig. 21–69). Saarinen had hoped the chair could be produced as a single piece of plastic, but plastic at mid-century was not strong enough for the job. Only by casting the pedestal base in aluminum could it be made structurally feasible without being unattractively thick. Other designers who have successfully employed aluminum in furniture have included George Nelson, as in his 1964 Action Office system (see fig. 21–68).

In New York's Four Seasons restaurant, there are rippling "draperies" of aluminum chains (see fig. 21–24), designed for Johnson and Pahlmann by Marie Nichols. Donald Deskey, in his new Radio City Music Hall (see fig. 21–16) designed wallpaper with thin sheets of aluminum foil pressed into it (see fig. 21–79). And, Russel Wright, whose pottery dinnerware we see in figure 21–74, also experimented with dinnerware in spun aluminum.

Reinforced Concrete Concrete, a favorite building material of the Romans (see Tools & Techniques: Concrete Construction in Chapter 5), has great strength under compression (being pushed) but little under tension (being pulled). But tensile strength can be added with steel reinforcing bars, and French inventor Joseph Monier patented a composite **reinforced concrete** with steel bars for construction around 1860.

Early masters in the use of the material, for both structure and interior finishes, were the French architects Auguste Perret (1874–1954) and his younger brother Gustave (1876–1952). An ambitious and accomplished project is the 1939 Museum of Public Works on the Place d'Iena in Paris (now the headquarters of the Economic Council). In the museum's lobby (fig. 21–50), columns increasing in diameter as they rise show the fluting-like lines of the wood forms in which they were poured (although they have been bush-hammered for texture), and the sweeping stair between them, one of the most graceful in modern architecture, is equally frank about its construction.

Similar to reinforced concrete is **ferrocement**, which uses wire mesh in place of reinforcing rods and can therefore be thinner and lighter. It was used for the inner face of the window wall in Le Corbusier's 1951 church of Notre-Dame-du-Haut at Ronchamp, France (see fig. 21–33).

Modern concrete, with or without reinforcing, can be remarkably strong and/or lightweight. It can be made to be translucent, to absorb carbon dioxide, or to display photographic images on its surface. At the end of the twentieth century, Japanese architect Tadao Ando produced his own virtuoso concrete work (see fig. 21–39).

Plastics   Plastics are substances that can be formed under heat or pressure and are both organic (containing compounds of the element carbon) and synthetic (created not in nature but in the laboratory). The plastics celluloid, styrene, melamine, vinyl chloride, and **polyester** had all been invented before 1850 but it was not until the twentieth century that these new materials were put to widespread use.

In 1907 Leo Baekeland, a Belgian chemist working in the United States, found an efficient way to mold a plastic called phenol-formaldehyde; in 1909 he patented his product as Bakelite. Bakelite was immensely popular and used for radios and telephones but also for many interior objects such as handles, light fixtures, and electrical plugs. Another popular plastic, **vinyl**, was patented by chemist Waldo Semon of the B. F. Goodrich Company in 1933; it was used for shower curtains, floor tiles and baseboards, and for protective coatings on more vulnerable materials.

Plastics have also been used in furniture design, not only for table tops, but also for seating. Beginning in 1939, Elsie de Wolfe made popular a lightweight side chair, manufactured by Grosfeld House, with a backsplat of Lucite, a product that DuPont had recently developed. And in 1957 the Laverne Company began producing an "Invisible" group of see-through plastic furniture. An influential chair designed by Charles and Ray Eames is of **fiberglass** (see fig. 21–65), which is a plastic reinforced with glass fibers for greater strength.

In 1979 the volume of plastics production exceeded the volume of steel production and the "Steel Age" was succeeded by the "Plastics Age." Especially useful in interiors today are the finishing materials called plastic laminates. These are composed of layers of paper bonded together with an outer layer of thin plastic, the result being a thin, lightweight sheet with a durable surface. In practice, these laminate sheets are applied to stronger backings such as plywood or one of the wood composition boards described below. The surfaces of plastic laminates can be given a wide variety of appearances: They can have matte or glossy finishes, be in any color or pattern, and, if wanted, even imitate other materials, such as wood grain.

Plaster Subsitutes   As the twentieth century began, interior walls and partitions were still often made of wet plaster applied to wood lath (see Tools & Techniques: Plasterwork in Chapter 16). Over the course of the century, this technique was largely replaced by a quicker and less expensive method—the use of a plaster substitute called **drywall**, marketed under a variety of other names: plasterboard, wallboard, gypsum board, gyp board, gypsum wallboard (GWB), and Sheetrock (this last name capitalized because it is a trade name). Drywall can imitate planes of real plaster; it cannot, of course, imitate plaster reliefs. In George Ranalli's 1981 Calendar School (fig. 21–51), it forms an extensive and apparently seamless sculptural element more quickly achieved and lighter in weight than would have been possible with wet plaster.

A variant somewhere between real plaster and drywall in both cost and appearance is veneer plaster. Sheets of drywall are again the foundation, but the tape over the joints is made of glass fiber, and the entire surface is coated with up to ⅛ inch (3 mm) of actual plaster.

Wood Products and Substitutes   Throughout history we have seen the appearance of wood altered by inlays, marquetry, carving, painting, and stenciling, but, beginning in the twentieth century, the treatment and very composition of wood were altered to give wood new characteristics and new forms.

Laminated wood products are made from thin sheets of actual wood. On a large scale, the most useful of these, produced commercially since 1910, is **plywood**, composed of stacked veneers that are glued together with the wood grain of one layer at a right angle to the grain of the next layer. This alternation of grain direction gives plywood its surprising strength. There are generally an odd number of layers—the more, the stronger—so that the top and bottom surfaces have parallel grains, and the material's strength is somewhat greater in that direction. Plywood is most often sold in sheets

▲ 21–51 An apparently seamless drywall composition in George Ranalli's 1981 renovation of the Calendar School in Newport, RI.
George Cserna/Courtesy George Renalli

that are 4 by 8 foot (1.2 × 2.4 m), and it comes in softwood or hardwood and in a great range of thicknesses and surface finishes.

An early example of wood substitutes came during the First World War, when a fibrous board called Homasote came on the market. Made entirely of recycled newspapers, Homasote has good insulating and acoustic properties and is used today for wall panels, carpet underlayment, roof decking, and tackboards. Soft and easily dented, Homasote and other types of recycled newspaper board are generally covered with fabric when used as wall surfaces.

A wood substitute similar to Homasote is a soft, low-density board called soundboard or building board. Generally ½ or ¾ inch (12 or 18 mm) thick, it has little strength, but its loose composition of wood fibers has good sound absorbing qualities, and it is often used as ceiling surfaces or as an acoustic element within walls and partitions.

Oriented-strand board (OSB), also known as flake board or wafer board, is made by bonding wood strands with a waterproof binder under heat and pressure. It is usually ¼ inch (6 mm) thick and can be used for carpet underlayment or wall paneling. Denser and generally more expensive than oriented-strand board is particleboard (also called chipboard). It is also composed of particles of wood waste bonded together under heat and pressure and is available in thicknesses

Tools & Techniques | DRYWALL CONSTRUCTION

The basic element of drywall, which can be attached directly to wood or steel studs without the use of lath, is a thin panel of processed *gypsum* (hydrous calcium sulfate, the substance that is the chief ingredient of plaster of Paris) between exterior surfaces of heavy paper. Such panels are most often ½ inch or ⅝ inch (12 or 15 mm) thick, but other thicknesses are also made. The most common panel length is 8 feet (2.5 m), but longer ones are available up to 12 feet (3.7 m). Panel widths are always 4 feet (1.2 m).

The edges of one face of the long sides of these panels are slightly tapered to a smaller thickness. When the panels are joined, therefore, these tapers meet to form a slight indentation within which a strip of reinforcing tape and a plasterlike substance called **drywall compound** (or taping compound) can be used to cover the joint. Another layer of drywall compound is usually used over the entire

surface to fill any dents or low spots, and a third coat is added for greater smoothness. If a textured surface is wanted, that can be applied in a fourth coat. Between each coat the surface should be allowed to dry for a day and then sanded.

Ceiling boards are given slightly greater stiffness than wall boards to prevent sagging. Panels can be faced with metal foil as a vapor block or **prefinished** with a vinyl face. Panels called **Type X** have greater fire resistance; panels called **greenboard** are resistant to moisture and have good sound absorbing qualities. Panels called **blueboard** have greater density in their gypsum core and are considered preferable for veneer plaster work. A whole family of specialized accessories—drywall screws, drywall nails, metal edge trims, metal corner beads, and more—is used in drywall construction.

of ⅛ to 1⅛ inch (3 to 28 mm). It is often used as a base for flooring and for plastic laminate countertops. Denser still is fiberboard, also called medium-density fiberboard (or MDF). Its surfaces are generally denser than its core, and this lack of uniformity can make the finishing of exposed edges difficult. It is available in thicknesses of 5/16 to 1⅜ inches (7.5 to 34 mm) and is used for cabinets, trim, and wall paneling; when treated with a protective finish, it can serve as countertops.

In 1924 William Mason ground and pressed discarded wood chips into Masonite, an early example of what is called hardboard, or high-density fiberboard (HDF). As its name suggests, HDF is denser than MDF, and it can be tempered in a curing process that adds further density and strength. Hardboard is available with two smooth sides or with one smooth and one rough side, and it is available in thicknesses of 1/16 to ½ inch (1.5 to 12 mm). It is used in cabinets, drawers, as countertops, wall panels, subflooring, or as flooring, when cut into tiles and given a protective coating. Both MDF and HDF present surfaces that can take paint well, but some of the softer composition boards do not.

Veneering, another wood technique, took on new importance beginning in the 1950s when improved glues, stains, and sealers became available. Veneers in use today are sometimes as thin as 2/100 of an inch (.005 cm), so that they make highly efficient use of woods that have become rare or expensive. Moreover, a composition of veneer bonded to plywood, particleboard, or MDF, is more stable than a solid piece of wood, which is subject to warping.

Paint Paint is one of the interior designer's most effective tools. Some interior schemes, such as a hotel's public room by Dorothy Draper (see fig. 21–41) or residential spaces by Edwin Lutyens (see fig. 21–3) and John Dickinson (see fig. 21–42), owe much of their character to the simple element of wall color.

Paint is made of two chief components: **pigments** that provide color and opacity, and binders that provide adhesion. Paints are identified by their color, of course, but also by their binders, which can be oil, water, varnish, glue, or synthetic resins.

It was only in the last third of the nineteenth century that commercially prepared paint began to be marketed, and that first prepared paint had an oil binder, which was considered superior for more than a century. The alternative, which became widely available after the Second World War, has a synthetic binder called latex, of which there are several types. Latex paints are water-soluble, meaning that they can be easily cleaned up with water. Latex paints dry more quickly than oil paints and often need only one coat rather than the several coats required when using oil paints.

In addition to names based on the type of binders or color, paint is classified by its luster. Ranging from least lustrous to most lustrous, the classifications are **flat**, **eggshell**, **satin**, **semi-gloss**, and **gloss**. Generally, the most lustrous paint surface will be the most easily washable, but it will also be the most likely to show irregularities and imperfections beneath it.

At the end of the twentieth century, the term oil paint was still in general use, but real oil paint was not. What has been substituted for an oil binder is an oil-modified synthetic resin binder called an alkyd. Alkyd paints, like the earlier oil paints, are not water soluble and must be thinned or removed with solvents. The choice between latex and alkyd paint will depend on the surface to be covered and the effect wanted.

Twentieth-Century Ornament

The above heading may seem as much an oxymoron as "an honest thief" or "a cheerful pessimist," for the twentieth century prided itself on its production of beautiful but unornamented form. In 1908, Viennese architect Adolf Loos wrote a famous essay "Ornament and Crime," a diatribe on the art of ornament. Yet few today think that ornament is criminal or that it has disappeared; it has simply taken a different guise and is more likely now than in the past to be inherent rather than applied. By "inherent" we mean that functional elements such as a building's structure, its exterior skin, window-shading devices, heating grilles, or hardware on its cabinetry can be seen as ornamental.

Alvar Aalto was particularly adept at creating ornament integral to functional elements. The undulating ceiling of Aalto's Viipuri lecture hall (see fig. 21–49), while arising from acoustic needs, is ornamental; his ornamentally curved wood strips on the wall of his Kaufmann conference room (see fig. 21–21) may also function acoustically by breaking up sound waves, while the pattern of pendant luminaries in the same room provide both light and ornament.

A more recent example is the pierced copper sheeting that covers the façade of Herzog & de Meuron's 2005

Twentieth-Century Furniture

Furniture design in the twentieth century was as varied and inventive as architecture and interior design, and generally followed the same sequence of styles. Sometimes, the leading furniture designers were the period architects; sometimes they were new. This survey will emphasize styles and designers rather than furniture types.

Pioneers in Furniture

An early twentieth century furniture designer was Italian Carlo Bugatti (1856–1940), whose son and grandson would become famous as designers of luxury automobiles. His designs were curious and idiosyncratic. They are surfaced with parchment (the smooth inner surface of sheepskin), gilded and embedded with plaques of beaten copper (fig. 21–53). Called the "Cobra" furniture, they were shown in Bugatti's "Snail" room at the 1902 exposition in Turin. Bugatti's curvaceous forms seem to presage some of the Art Deco furniture, which originated almost two decades later (see below).

In America, as Frank Lloyd Wright began designing his open-plan architecture, he also began designing furniture for it, much of it rigorously geometric. An example is the furniture for his 1904 Larkin Building in Buffalo, New York. In

▲ **21–52** In the 2005 de Young Museum, San Francisco, by Herzog & de Meuron, randomly punctured copper mesh panels cast shadows in a stairwell.
© Corporation of the Fine Arts Museums; Herzog & de Meuron, Primary Designers; Fong & Chan Architects, Principal Architects; Photography: Mark Darley

de Young Museum in San Francisco. From the inside, through a glass wall (fig. 21–52), the effect is deliberately ornamental, yet it is the material itself that provides the effect, not something applied to it. The patterns of piercings were derived from pixilated photographs of trees surrounding the museum's site, and a computerized engineering system allowed each of the building's 7,000 panels to be individually patterned and shaped.

▼ **21–53** The Cobra desk and chair of gilt and inlaid parchment designed by Carlo Bugatti for the 1902 Exposizione in Turin.
Carlo Bugatti, "Cobra Chair" 77.4. Brooklyn Museum of Art/Central Photo Archive

▲ **21–54** Looking from a private office into the central atrium of Frank Lloyd Wright's 1904 Larkin Building in Buffalo, NY. The steel desks and chairs are Wright's designs.
Buffalo and Erie County Historical Society

the private office shared by three of the company's partners (fig. 21–54), the chairs are of oak seats on painted steel frames, forerunners of the innovative tubular steel furniture by Marcel Breuer (see fig. 21–55). Wright's chair bases are of cast iron. The arms are joined in a continuous curve around the back, and the center support of the backrest continues to form the back leg. The desks are also of steel. Some of Wright's later furniture is seen in the living room of Falling-water (see fig. 21–5). Wright would not be the only master of modern architecture to design furniture; they all would.

Bauhaus Marcel Breuer's architecture and interior design was shown in figures 21–9 and 21–10, but it was his furniture that was truly innovative. After becoming head of the Bauhaus school's carpentry workshop in 1924, he began experimenting with tubular steel as a furniture material, reportedly inspired by the handles of his bicycle. An early result was the 1925 Wassily chair (fig. 21–55), named for painter Wassily Kandinsky, for whose Bauhaus studio it was designed.

▼ **21–55** Marcel Breuer's tubular steel and leather Wassily chair, designed in 1925.
Courtesy Marcel Breuer & Associates Architects

It was a cubist composition of chrome-plated steel tubing wrapped with leather straps that formed the seat, back, and armrests. It conveyed the modernist sense of materials appropriate to their use: tubular metal for the structural frame, more flexible leather for those parts in contact with the sitter.

The same year, Breuer designed a set of nesting side tables (fig. 21–56), their enameled wood tops held between tubing. Turning one of the tables on its side produced a cantilevered structure, which Breuer then employed in a chair design that would be one of the century's most popular and most imitated. The Cesca chair (fig. 21–57), which Breuer named for his daughter Francesca, used the cantilever principle in a way that gave the chair seat a bit of springy resiliency. The chair's seat and back were made of wood framed caning, the combination of steel and caning being an early example of Breuer's taste for combining the machine-made with the natural. It was designed in two versions, with and without arms.

Mies van der Rohe's celebrated furniture designs can be seen in his 1929 Barcelona Pavilion (see fig. 21–11). The same chair and stool, with their X-shaped chromium-plated steel bases, are seen in Philip Johnson's Glass House (see fig. 21–23). They are joined by a Mies daybed with a leather pad on a rosewood frame with chrome-plated legs. Also in the Glass House, at the dining table in the left foreground, is a cantilevered chair of flat steel bars that Mies designed for his 1930 Tugendhat House, and that house's dining chair, also cantilevered but with a frame of tubular steel, was used as a desk chair in Johnson's apartment of the same year and in Venturi and Scott Brown's Knoll showroom of 1979 (see fig. 21–35).

Purism and De Stijl   Around 1925, at the time of the design of the first of his Purist white houses, Le Corbusier began working with a young avant-garde designer named Charlotte Perriand, who would serve as his close collaborator. The chaise longue seen in the Villa Savoye living room (see fig. 21–12) was designed in 1928 by Le Corbusier, Perriand, and Pierre Jeanneret, a distant relative of Le Corbusier. The next year a rotating stool on four tubular steel legs was designed by the same threesome. After leaving Le Corbusier's office, Perriand was a successful designer on her own; her wood shelving design of 1953 is seen in figure 21–58. A more elaborate version of the design, with built-in lighting added, was used in Perriand's London interiors for Air France in 1958.

▼ **21–56** Breuer's 1925 nesting tables with tubular steel frames in graduated sizes.
Courtesy Marcel Breuer & Associates Architects

▲ **21–57** Breuer's 1927 cantilevered Cesca chair, a prototype for many that would follow.
Courtesy Marcel Breuer & Associates Architects

In Gerrit Rietveld's furniture there is the expression of De Stijl, as seen in the elementary forms, straight lines, and primary colors. His chair (see fig. 21–1) expressed all three in 1925. In the Schröder House (see fig. 21–13), it is possible to see how Rietveld meant the chair to fit into his vision of interior design.

Art Deco Furniture

Like Art Deco architecture and interiors, some Art Deco furniture was not wholly serious, but some was exquisitely made of fine materials. One beautiful example is a suite of desk, chair, and filing cabinet by Jacques-Émile Ruhlmann (fig. 21–59), all made of amboyna wood, ivory, and sharkskin—in this case, actually the skin of the ray-fish, a material much favored by Ruhlmann. In addition, there are silvered bronze mounts. The suite is an example of the lavish decorative finish that would be swept from fashion by the plainer expressions of modernism.

Modern Furniture

There were many varieties of modern furniture and many companies formed to make such furniture available to a wider audience than was ever before possible.

Scandinavian Modern   Finnish architect Alvar Aalto experimented with slicing, laminating, and bending techniques to

produce furniture forms as clear and as lyrical as his buildings. One of the simplest and most popular designs of the twentieth century was his three-legged stacking stool that furnished the lecture room of his 1935 Viipuri Library (see fig. 21–49), and three years earlier his chair design for the Paimio sanatorium (fig. 21–60) was a scroll of bent plywood within a base of laminated wood. The stackable chairs and stools that furnish the Kaufmann conference room (see fig. 21–21) were designed by Aalto about 1947; on laminated frames, their seats are upholstered and their backs made of stretched and cross-woven webbing.

In neighboring Denmark, the father figure in the field of furniture design was Kaare Klint (1888–1954). He was a fairly conservative designer, best remembered today for his 1933 "Safari" chair, but in 1924 he founded the school of furniture design at Copenhagen's Royal Academy School of Architecture. His influential teaching there was based on his respect for the natural character of materials and his study of the solid construction and fine proportions of eighteenth-century English furniture.

Another Danish designer, Hans Wegner (born 1914) adopted this design philosophy of well-made wood furniture but used it with new, often sensuous forms. Wegner's notable designs include the 1944 "Chinese" armchair (fig. 21–61) based on a seventeenth-century Chinese design with horseshoe back and a plain center splat (see fig. 11–11), the Peacock chair of 1947 with radiating back spokes like a Windsor, and a 1949 teak and cane armchair called simply "The Chair."

Two other Danish designers, instead, abandoned the wood tradition and embraced new materials and techniques. The first was Arne Jacobsen (1902–71), an architect and designer of interiors, furniture, textiles, and ceramics. His "Ant" stacking chair of 1952 for the Fritz Hansen Company sat on three metal legs. For the SAS Royal hotel in Copenhagen, 1958–60, he designed the building, the interiors, furniture, lighting fixtures, and tableware; two of those furniture pieces were the "Egg" and "Swan" chairs. The "Swan" chairs can be seen in a 2004 London office for Cisco Systems by HOK (fig. 21–62).

A Danish designer a generation younger than Jacobsen was Poul Kjærholm (1929–80), who was a successor to Klint as head of the Royal Academy furniture school and who combined chrome with wicker and leather, producing elegant variations (fig. 21–63), based on the earlier metal furniture designs of Marcel Breuer and Mies van der Rohe.

▼ **21–60** Alvar Aalto's Paimio chair, 1932, of bent plywood on a laminated wood frame.
Designmuseum, Helsinki, Finland

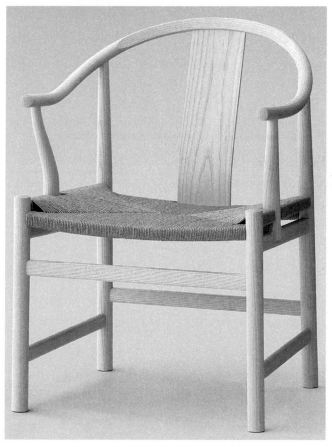

▲ **21–61** Hans Wegner's 1944 "Chinese" armchair of ash with a woven cord seat, inspired by a seventeenth-century Chinese design.
PP Møbler ApS, Allerod, Denmark

▲ **21–62** Arne Jacobsen's 1958 Swan chairs in a 2004 London conference room enclosed by etched glass panels. The interior design is by HOK.
Peter Cook/View Pictures Limited

▼ **21–63** The PK1 tubular stainless steel and wicker chair designed by Poul Kjærholm, 1955.
Hanne Kjærholm

Charles and Ray Eames Charles Eames and his wife Ray Kaiser Eames met at Cranbrook, where they were students under Eliel Saarinen and friends of his son Eero. Charles Eames and Eero Saarinen won the Museum of Modern Art's 1940 "Organic Design in Home Furnishings" competition for their winning designs of a modular storage unit and a molded plywood chair. As the catalog stated, the chair employed "a manufacturing method never previously applied to furniture . . . to make a light structural shell consisting of layers of plastic glue and wood veneer molded in three-dimensional forms." The competition brought them international recognition, and the chair is still reproduced today.

The Eameses' experiments with molding plywood shells for seating culminated in the 1946 LCW lounge chair made from five pieces of shaped wood (fig. 21–64); in 1999 *Time* magazine would call it "the chair of the century." Lighter versions were made with only the seat and back of wood, fastened to a thin metal frame. They applied molding techniques to fiberglass as well, one result being the 1948 one-piece molded fiberglass LAR chair, on a triangulated base of multiple metal rods (later called the "Eiffel Tower" base). We

▼ **21–64** Chair by Charles and Ray Eames of molded and bent birch plywood, manufactured by Evans Products Co. in 1946 and later by Herman Miller.
Victoria & Albert Museum, London/Art Resource, NY

see one (fig. 21–65) on the patio of the Eameses' Pacific Palisades house, sitting on Japanese *tatami* mats and surrounded by several of their small side tables on bases of crossed rods.

Other notable Eames furniture designs include the Eames Tandem Sling Seating (fig. 21–66), designed for Eero Saarinen's 1962 Dulles airport. It was produced by Herman Miller and became a familiar sight in airports around the world. With its black naugahyde seats and attached tables cantilevered from polished aluminum supports, the design brought a much-needed touch of elegance to many airport waiting rooms.

Herman Miller When the Second World War ended, European and American designers were fired with enthusiasm for producing modern interiors, but furniture and furnishings designed in the modern spirit were needed. These were first supplied to the American market by two companies, Herman Miller and Knoll. Their stories were important parts of the establishment of modern design in the United States.

▲ **21–65** On the patio of the house of Charles and Ray Eames, a 1948 fiberglass shell chair on a base of metal rods and some 1950 side tables on similar bases. Beneath them are Japanese *tatami* mats.
© 2006 Eames Office LLC (www.eamesoffice.com)

▼ **21–66** Tandem Sling Seating, designed by Charles and Ray Eames in 1962 for Eero Saarinen's Dulles Airport.
Herman Miller, Inc.

▲ **21–67** George Nelson's 1947 modular cabinets for Herman Miller. When the vanity lid is raised, a mirror is revealed and a light comes on.
Herman Miller, Inc.

The Michigan Star furniture company, founded in 1905, was purchased in 1923 by an employee, D. J. De Pree, who renamed it for his father-in-law and backer, Herman Miller. In 1930 De Pree hired designer Gilbert Rohde to direct the company's design, which had been previously in a highly decorative Renaissance Revival style. Rohde produced a series of sleek new designs, for both residential and office use, modern but with an Art Deco slant.

George Nelson (1908–86) took Rohde's place in 1944. Nelson had studied architecture, won the Rome Prize, and, while in Italy, had written for American publication on the European modernists. As design director, Nelson provided modern design undiluted by Art Deco. His early pieces include modular storage units (fig. 21–67), which he designed for residential use. He also designed a slat bench in 1946, which could do multiple duty as a platform for cabinets, as a coffee table, or as seating.

But it was in 1964 that Nelson, using research into office work habits that had been done for Herman Miller by Robert Propst, designed a radically different group of office furniture called Action Office (fig. 21–68). Its elements included a tall storage element that could double as a space divider, an

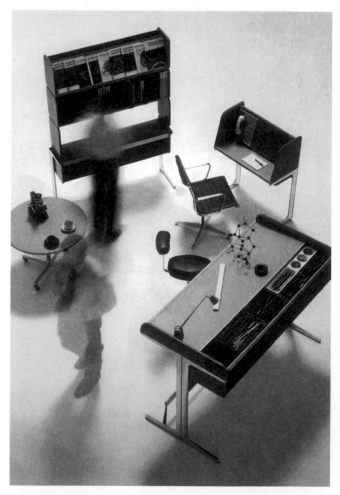

▲ **21–68** George Nelson's 1964 Action Office for Herman Miller, a radical departure from the traditional mahogany desk.
James Bayne/Herman Miller, Inc.

acoustically insulated communications center for telephone and Dictaphone use, and a tall desk with a plastic laminate work surface and a roll-down canvas or wood tambour cover, all cantilevered from polished aluminum legs. Action Office revolutionized office furniture design. Gone were the gentlemen's studies of the early 1900s; in their place was sleek, adaptable functionality.

At least as important as his design, however, was Nelson's insistence that Herman Miller hire other important and talented designers to work for them. Among them were Charles and Ray Eames, Isamu Noguchi, and Alexander Girard. Since the days of Nelson and the Eameses, Herman Miller has maintained its prominence with such products as Bruce Burdick's 1980 Burdick System and Bill Stumpf and Don Chardwick's 1994 Aeron chair.

Knoll Hans Knoll, son of a German furniture manufacturer, came to New York in 1938 and established his own company, HG Knoll. At first it was a one-person operation, selling designs manufactured by others. In 1943 Florence Schust, trained as an architect at Cranbrook, joined the firm and married Hans Knoll, forming Knoll Associates. Florence Schust Knoll headed the Knoll Planning Unit for interior design work until her retirement in 1965.

Early successes in Knoll's furniture design included architect Eero Saarinen's "Tulip" chair of 1956 (fig. 21–69), which displayed structural bravura. Also notable were sculptor Harry Bertoia's wire mesh chairs of 1950 and 1952. In 1960, Knoll began selling the furniture designs of Mies van der Rohe, including Mies's 1929 chair for the German Pavilion in Barcelona

(see fig. 21–11), and in 1968 it added those of Marcel Breuer, eventually selling more than a quarter million of Breuer's 1927 cantilevered Cesca chairs (see fig. 21–57). To complement the furniture, Knoll introduced textile designs by a number of talents, Anni Albers among them (see fig. 21–76).

In 1984 Knoll commissioned Robert Venturi for designs. Venturi demonstrated his concept of ordinary but symbolic design in a series of bent plywood chairs that were simple in form and construction but painted to suggest Queen Anne, Chippendale, Empire, and other past styles (fig. 21–70). Other recent Knoll designers have included the Vignellis, Charles Pfister, Richard Meier, and Frank Gehry.

▼ **21–69** Eero Saarinen's 1957 Tulip chair for Knoll has a molded plastic shell balanced on an aluminum base.
Knoll, Inc.

◄ **21–70** Two of Robert Venturi's 1984 plywood chairs for Knoll, the one at left named Art Deco, the one at right Sheraton.
Knoll, Inc.

New Possibilities in Furniture

Among those who reacted against the purity and order of orthodox modernism, the most interesting furniture designers were Italian. In Italy in the early 1970s, modernism's underlying optimism was dampened by terrorism and an oil-related economic crisis, and its concept of functional beauty began to be questioned. In Italy, the "Anti-Design" movement was formed from new groups of design rebels, with one called Memphis.

The Memphis design cooperative was founded by Ettore Sottsass, Jr., in 1981 and made its sensational début at that year's Milan Furniture Fair. Allegedly named for both the Egyptian city and the Tennessee city, it was seen by Sottsass as "quoting from suburbia," perhaps alluding to its imitation of the kitsch taste of the Italian middle class (fig. 21–71). Despite its high prices, the Memphis style was briefly taken up by a sophisticated following, its most publicized interior being fashion designer Karl Lagerfeld's apartment in Monte Carlo, which he furnished completely with Memphis furniture.

Japanese furniture designers have been adept at mainstream modernism, but some of them have also taken a wry, ironic view of Western models. Shiro Kuramata, for example, who was invited to design pieces for Memphis in the early 1980s, has experimented with sometimes outlandish materials. His 1986 armchair titled "How High the Moon" (fig. 21–72) is built of expanded steel mesh, and his 1988 chair titled "Miss Blanche" is of paper flowers embedded in clear acrylic resin.

Systems and Built-ins   An idea basic to all office furniture systems, and important to interior design and furniture design throughout the century, was **modularity**, as shown by George Nelson (see fig. 21–67 and 21–68). In 1925 Le Corbusier developed his Casiers Standard group of storage cabinets for the Pavillon de l'Ésprit Nouveau; their dimensions were based on a module of 15 inches (37.5 cm). Marcel Breuer built a similar system of units based on a module of 13 inches (33 cm), which appeared at the Weissenhof Siedlung housing exhibition.

In 1968 Propst and Nelson followed with Action Office 2. It abandoned the freestanding desk altogether in favor of a system of movable screens from which could be hung work surfaces and a variety of storage units. Everyone seemed to get involved in "systems furniture." Among the many examples that followed were Knoll's 1973 Stephens system designed by Charles Pfister, Olivetti's 1973 Synthesis 45 system by Ettore Sottsass, Jr. (designed before his Memphis phase), Herman Miller's 1985 Ethospace system by Bill Stumpf, and Tecno's 1985 Nomos system by Norman Foster.

▼ **21–71** From the Memphis collection, the Carlton bookcase of plastic laminate on wood, designed by Ettore Sottsass, Jr., in 1981, 76 in. (193 cm) high. Though called a bookcase, its form is distinctly inappropriate for books.
Ettore Sottsass (designed by), Italian, b. 1917, Carlton room divider, plastic laminate on wood, 1981, 194.3 × 190 × 40 cm. Photograph © 1997, the Art Institute of Chicago, All Rights Reserved.

▼ **21–72** Japanese designer Shiro Kurumata's How High the Moon armchair of steel mesh, 1986.
Hans Hansen, Courtesy Vitra Design Museum

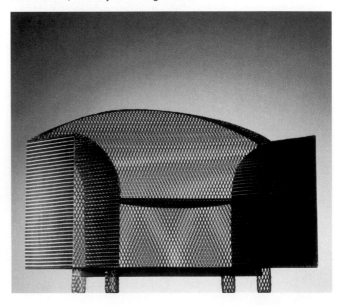

▲ 21–73 A model room, consisting almost entirely of built-in furniture and equipment, designed by George Nelson for Alexander Girard's 1949 *An Exhibition for Modern Living* in Detroit.
Elmer L. Astleford / Vitra Design Museum

The modern desire for the spacious rather than the cluttered and for the spare rather than the ornate led to a movement that sought the disappearance of as much furniture as possible. Instead, everything was built-in. Storage was built-in, seating was built-in, lighting and HVAC and electronic equipment were built-in. It began with the 1949 exhibition at the Detroit Institute of the Arts with a model room (fig. 21–73) of built-in features, again by George Nelson. The exhibit showed very little movable furniture: just two chairs and a small tray table by Nelson. Everything else, including cushioned benches in the foreground and rear, was built-in.

Twentieth-Century Decorative Arts

The decorative arts in the twentieth century underwent a huge change in the philosophies behind their design, in the materials used, and in the new technologies available to designers.

Ceramics and Glass

The English potteries at Minton and Doulton continued their production of Art Nouveau ceramics into the twentieth century, and the English ceramic designer and painter Clarice

Cliff, who ran a pottery in Staffordshire, produced pieces with angular geometric patterns sympathetic to Art Deco. The greatest successes of the century, however, were in modest, simply designed earthenware, such as the hugely popular American Modern pottery designed by Russel Wright for Steubenville in 1939 (fig. 21–74).

Lenox China, founded by Walter Scott Lenox in 1889, has become a household name, but its reputation was not made until 1917 when President Woodrow Wilson ordered a 1,700-piece Lenox dinner set for the White House. Other presidential orders followed, and by the end of the century Lenox's ivory-colored porcelain had come to dominate the fine dinnerware market.

In American glass, dominance came to be held by the Corning Glass Works, which had blown the first electric light bulb for Thomas Edison in 1880. In the first decade of the twentieth century, Corning developed a heat-resistant glassware called Pyrex, useful in both factories and kitchens. Pyrex was a modernist breakthrough.

Metalwork

Metals familiar from previous chapters—gold, silver, brass, copper, iron—continued to be used in the twentieth century.

An early master of silver design at the beginning of the century was Josef Hoffmann. As in his design for the 1911 Palais Stoclet (see fig. 21–7), Hoffmann's silver pieces (flatware, vases, milk pitchers, tea services, samovars, candelabra, lamp bases, and more) were also executed in simple geometry, most often in grids of squares (fig. 21–75). Such work earned him the German nickname *quadratl-Hoffmann* ("little square Hoffmann").

Another noted early twentieth-century silversmith was Denmark's Georg Jensen (1866–1935), who opened his Copenhagen shop in 1904. A shortage of silver in the Second World War led Jensen to produce flatware in stainless steel, which has remained popular ever since. Jensen disliked the historicist reproductions that flooded the market and sought to make a commercial success of modern designs. Some of the firm's designs were wholly abstract, and others were inspired by nature, such as the 1915 *Acorn* pattern and the 1919 *Blossom.*

▼ **21–74** Russel Wright's 1939 American Modern pottery for Steubenville.
© Indianapolis Museum of Art, USA/Gift of Marcus and Marie Chandler in memory of Ralph Chandler/The Bridgeman Art Library, NY

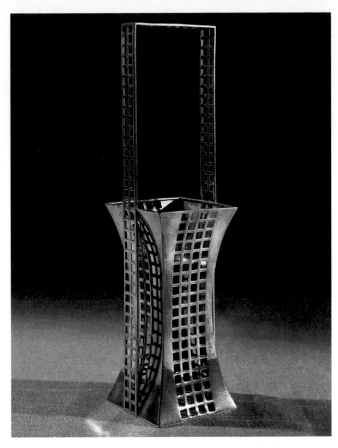

▲ **21–75** A silver flower basket designed by Josef Hoffmann in 1904–1906.
Erich Lessing/Art Resource, NY

▲ **21–76** Anni Albers's 1927 silk and cotton wall hanging, woven while she was at the Bauhaus. 58 in. (1.45 m) high.
Albers, Anni (1899–1994), "Wall Hanging". 1927. Cotton and silk, 58¼ × 47¾" (147.9 × 121.3 cm). Gift of the designer in memory of Greta Daniel. (246.1965). The Museum of Modern Art, New York, NY, U.S.A. Digital Image © The Museum of Modern Art/Licensed by SCALA/Art Resource, NY. The Museum of Modern Art/Licensed by Scala-Art Resource, NY. © 2007 ARS, Artists Rights Society, NY

Textiles

New textile technology in the twentieth century included the replacement of copper-roller printing (see "Toile de Jouy" in Chapter 16) with screen-printing, a process in which ink is forced through a screen from which the desired design has been cut out. As technology improved, however, there was a growing nostalgia for preindustrial methods such as handweaving. Similarly, the development of synthetic fibers brought a new appreciation for natural ones. Present practice encompasses both types: natural fibers and hand-woven goods for a small artistic market (including many textiles for interior design use) and more industrial goods with synthetic fibers for the mass market. Modern fabrics are also expected at times to be stain resistant, mildew resistant, moth repellant, fungus repellant, antibacterial, or antistatic, and a number of chemical substances and processes have been invented to impart such qualities.

Early in the century, Josef Hoffmann, whose family had founded a spinning mill, designed fabrics; like his metalwork, they were chiefly geometrical. A number of other twentieth century designers took their turns designing textiles, among them Ray Eames and Alexander Girard, both producing patterns for Herman Miller. Boris Kroll established his textile company in 1930 and opened a New York showroom in 1934.

Weaver and educator Anni Albers (1899–1994) was the wife of painter Josef Albers and taught first at the Bauhaus in Germany and then at Black Mountain College in North Carolina; she was adept at both handweaving and machine production, and was the first to experiment with adding cellophane to her natural fibers. Her abstract designs, such as her two-ply silk wall hanging in figure 21–76, shared the focus on geometry of her husband's paintings. She later designed textiles for the Knoll and Sunar furniture companies and wrote two influential books, the 1959 *On Designing* and the 1965 *On Weaving*.

There are four elements used in making traditional upholstery: the frame, the coiled support within the frame, the padding or cushioning, and the cover. The frame obviously developed from a long tradition of wood chair making, and the webbing used for support was adapted from horse harnesses. The idea of quilted padding dates from medieval times when it was used as lining for suits of armor.

Coiled metal springs of steel wire are now used for supporting the seating. The spiraled springs can either be fastened directly to a wooden furniture frame or attached to a base of webbing and used in a loose cushion. Even within a wood frame, a base of webbing can give extra resilience. Loose cushions are often used on top of this structure.

All the elements of upholstery can vary in quality. Frames of kiln-dried lumber are superior to those of air-dried lumber. A large number of springs is preferable to a small number, and each spring should be tied many times to its base. **Hand-tied** construction is therefore preferable, though today some upholstery is not tied but assembled in steel box units. Horsehair or cattle hair is superior, and if hair is combined with cotton padding, a larger percentage of hair is considered better. If feathers and down (very soft feathers from young birds, with their quill shafts removed) are used in cushions, **goose down**, which is curly and springy, is considered finer than **duck down**, which lies flat, an exception being **eiderdown**, which is taken from a large sea duck called an eider and is considered quite luxurious.

Tufting (a closely spaced pattern of stitching) was developed to keep all materials in place and became fashionable in Victorian upholstery. By the early twentieth century tufting was done mechanically. Tufting is used on such modern pieces as the 1930 Mies daybed and the 1956 Eames lounge chair and ottoman. Rolled edges were developed to help maintain cushion shape.

Among twentieth-century contributions to traditional upholstery are polyurethane foam, latex rubber cushioning (patented in 1929), stretch fabric, Naugahyde and other imitation leathers, metal and plastic frames, and tools such as the staple gun.

Jack Lenor Larsen (1927–) trained at Cranbrook and then opened a New York studio in 1952. His innovations included the first printed-velvet upholstery fabric in 1959 and the first stretch upholstery fabric in 1961. Larsen's 1970 "Magnum," designed with Win Anderson, mixed cotton with vinyl, nylon, polyester, and sparkling squares of mylar for the stage curtain of Symphony Hall in Phoenix. For the Sears Tower in Chicago, Laresen created quilted hangings in the public banking floor of SOM's 1974 building (fig. 21–77). The hangings not only add interest and color but also absorb sound.

More recently, handsome and experimental fabric designs have come from Gretchen Bellinger. Her 1993 "Golden Apples" (fig. 21–78) is a modern version of "Six Persimmons" by the thirteenth-century Chinese master Mu-Qi. Barbara Beckmann Studios produces strikingly patterned fabrics, some of them hand-painted.

Window Treatments   Just as the nineteenth century had witnessed a great proliferation of window treatments, the twentieth century experienced a retreat from such overabundance. While fabric window treatments are still in wide use today, though now simplified, much of the other interior fabric was swept away with the advent of modernism.

Some of the multiple tiers of curtains have been replaced by simpler hangings and by roller shades (which now can be rolled down from the top of the window or up from the bottom). **Venetian blinds** became popular; they are made up of a series of wooden, metal, or plastic slats strung together on tapes; the slats can be raised or lowered, or they can be angled up and down for light control or privacy. Other types of window treatments include vertical blinds, wood shutters, Japanese *shoji* screens, and other devices.

Fabric shades are raised not on spring rollers but on loops of cord hanging from the top of the window. They are of two chief types: the **Roman shade** that, when raised, folds like an accordion into horizontal pleats, and the **Austrian shade** that is gathered into swags, its lower edge a series of scallops between the cords. The window coverings in the Four Seasons restaurant (see fig. 21–24) are draped like Austrian shades, though they are made of aluminum chains, not fabric.

▼ 21–77 Quilted silk banners by Jack Lenor Larsen in the banking floor of SOM's 109-story Sears Tower, Chicago, finished in 1974.
Cowtan & Tout

▲ 21–78 "Golden Apples," a screen-print silk fabric introduced by Gretchen Bellinger in 1993, has a thirteenth-century Chinese precedent.
Gretchen Bellinger, Inc.

Upholstery Upholstery in the twentieth century gained in wider use and in techniques for making the upholstered furniture more comfortable and more durable.

Mattresses improved dramatically. They came to be constructed in three principal ways: stuffed, coiled, or made with foam. The fabric envelope filled with feathers or down was no longer in use, although such construction was still used for coverlets, or duvets, on top of the bed. A stuffed mattress is typically made of a pad of cotton or polyester wrapped with polyester foam; such construction can soon lose its resiliency and become lumpy. Foam construction is a fabric-covered slab of molded polyurethane; it is non-allergenic, lightweight, and resistant to insects and mildew, but it is relatively slow to recover its shape. The superior mattress type, also used for chairs and sofas, is the coiled construction, spirals of steel wire that are either biconal (hourglass-shaped) or pyramidal.

There are four chief ways of manufacturing carpets today: **Axminster**, **Wilton**, **velvet**, and **tufted**.

- **Axminster**. In 1874 two Americans, Alexander Smith and Halcyon Skinner, developed a power loom that could set individual tufts that had been dyed as wanted, thus allowing a great diversity of pattern. This is what is usually meant now by the name Axminster, and it usually has a surface of cut pile.
- **Wilton**. The name Wilton, like the name Axminster, is now applied to any carpet made with the Wilton method, which is to pull one color of yarn at a time to the surface and bury the others in the body of the carpet, thus creating a sturdy backing. Wilton pile can be either cut or looped.
- **Velvet**. Velvet carpet is similar in appearance to Wilton, but without the yarn buried in the backing. It is therefore less durable. It is often made in a single color, and patterns are added by having the pile, which can be either cut or looped, in different heights for a "sculptured" effect.
- **Tufted**. Tufted construction sews the ends of looped pile to a prepared fabric backing and secures it there with a coating of latex or some other adhesive. For extra strength, a second backing is sometimes laminated to the first. Tufting is a fast method of carpet making and, although originally limited to solid colors, it can now produce any desired pattern. **Berber** carpets are similar, with a smooth surface of tightly packed loops.

Carpets

The chief carpet type in use today is the **broadloom**, meaning simply a carpet woven on a broad loom, such as one 12 or 15 feet wide, allowing for fewer seams than narrower widths or tiles. Either broadloom or tiles can, of course, be made in many colors and designs. Any pattern or image can be scanned and transferred to carpet, as in Hardy Holzman Pfieffer's 1994 New York office for Scholastic Magazine (see fig. 21–34), where the magazine's corporate credo lines the corridors.

Modern carpets are also distinguished by the materials from which they are made. There are some natural fibers that are popularly used today. **Jute** is a glossy fiber made from East Indian plants of the linden family; it is used for making burlap sacking as well as carpeting. **Sisal** is a tough, durable material made from the leaves of the West Indian *agave* plant, but the term is sometimes used for similar materials such as jute or seagrass. There is also "wool sisal" made of wool, which is naturally soft but has the appearance of sisal.

The twentieth century's great development in carpet material, as in drapery and upholstery material, was the introduction of synthetic fibers, those that originate not in nature but in the laboratory. Many of the synthetics are identified by their manufacturers with trade-marked names, but almost all come from **rayon** (made from cellulose and, because of its sheen, sometimes called "artificial silk," marketed under trade names such as Durafil and Tricel), **nylon** (made from natural gas and petroleum, with trade names such as Antron and Quiana), **acrylic** (hard-wearing but soft, light but warm, with trade names such as Chemstrand and Orlon), olefin (a petroleum product resistant to dirt, mildew, and moths with trade names such as Herculon and Marvess), and **polyester** (another petroleum product, dirt-resistant and strong, with trade names such as Dacron and Trevira).

Wallpaper

Many of the designers discussed earlier were involved in wallpaper design. Peter Behrens designed wallpapers influenced by the earlier ones of William Morris (see fig. 20–67). Josef Hoffmann designed them in his distinctive square-obsessed geometrical style. Frank Lloyd Wright designed a collection of geometric fabrics and wallpapers under the title "Taliesin" for Schumacher in 1955. Le Corbusier made sixty-three wallpaper designs, each one a single solid color and referred to them as "a layer of oil paint on rolls." His idea was that applying color in paper form rather than paint would give a greater consistency of quality and color.

One paper of particular interest was designed by Donald Deskey for his 1931 Radio City Music Hall. Titled "Nicotine" (fig. 21–79), it was meant for the men's smoking lounge. Innovatively printed on aluminum foil, its design showed, among tobacco leaves, a number of supposedly masculine interests such as gardening, sailing, cards, and dice. Other Art Deco wallpapers were designed by Jacques-Émile Ruhlmann.

▲ **21–79** Donald Deskey's aluminum foil wallpaper for his own 1931 Radio City Music Hall, New York.
Angelo Hornak Photograph Library

Recent technical innovations include washable vinyls, reflective mylar, the application of woven threads or fibers to the paper surface ("grass cloth"), three-dimensional effects produced with foam, and nonflammable papers.

Summary: Twentieth-Century Design

Many of this book's previous chapters have shown us design that was different in appearance from that of prior eras. So has this final chapter, but with the twentieth century, more than the appearance of design has changed. The relationship of design to technology has been strengthened, and the relationship of design to its audience has been radically altered.

Looking for Character

We have seen design of many different characters here, yet inherent in them all has been a single mainstream of development: modernism. Within modernism, of course, we have seen many branches, and against the force of modernism we have seen some interesting but short-lived reactions. Still, it has been the dominant shaper of the century's design.

Edgar Kaufmann, jr., in his book *What Is Modern Interior Design?* (1953), wrote that "The two trends—toward nature and toward technology— . . . were never entirely divorced in practice. . . . The best designers of our epoch almost without exception have produced works which demon-

strate clearly man's growing interest in integration with the natural world which accompanies his increasing control over it through science."

Looking for Quality

In earlier times, we have found quality in Egyptian faience, Gothic stained glass, Italian frescoes, French marquetry, and other examples of highly skilled artistry and opulent materials. A few echoes of this view of quality were seen in some Art Deco designs of Ruhlmann and others. But in the twentieth century quality was less likely to be dependent on expensive amounts of time and materials and more likely to be associated with abstract qualities: consistency of horizontal or vertical emphasis, a free flow of space, a perfection of proportion, or a practical functional solution. Quality materials in the twentieth century might still be natural but were more often synthetic.

Not only has our sense of quality been transferred from material opulence to more abstract qualities, but the audience for quality has been broadened enormously. In furniture such as the Eameses' fiberglass shells, in buildings such as Breuer's demonstration house in the museum garden, and in public presentations such as Kaufmann's *Good Design* exhibitions—in all these and more, we have seen design reaching for the widest possible understanding and use. Modern design is not aimed at the royal or the rich; it is aimed at everyone. Quality in design has become associated with practicality, problem solving, and—a criterion not often seen in earlier times—affordability.

Making Comparisons

Interior design of the twentieth century offered more than good looks. We have come to depend on interior design's provision for function and the solution of problems, following modern design's mantra that "form follows function." In offices and factories, form in design assures efficiency; in hotels and restaurants, it attracts customers; in shops and stores, it promotes sales; in health care facilities, it saves lives; in residential buildings, it reflects personal tastes and habits and provides a sense of order.

In the context of cities plagued with crowding, traffic, noise, pollution, and even guns and bombs, we increasingly go inside for our solace, safety, and well-being. Today we need good interior design more than ever before. Today more people want good interior design than ever before, and today more people have it.

Glossary

A

Aalto, Alvar (1898–1976) Important Finnish architect and furniture designer.

Abacus In architecture, the slab that forms the uppermost portion of the capital of a column.

Abstract design Patterns or motifs that do not represent forms from nature.

AC Abbreviation for *alternating current*.

A/C Abbreviation for *air conditioning*.

Acacia A light brown hardwood from Australia and Africa. In ancient times it was used by the Eastern nations for religious and sacred buildings; today it is used for furniture and for architectural and ecclesiastical woodwork.

Acajou French term for *mahogany*.

Acanthus A large leaf conventionalized by the Greeks for ornamental use, as in the capital of the Corinthian column.

Accent lighting Lighting directed to emphasize a specific object or area. See also *ambient lighting* and *task lighting*.

Access floor In office buildings, a finished floor raised above the structural floor, allowing access through the panels of the finished floor to power cables and other equipment.

Aceitillo West Indian hardwood with fine grain, somewhat resembling satinwood in color and appearance. Used for furniture.

Acetate Fibers, yarn, or fabric made from cellulose acetate. The fabric has something of the look and feel of silk. Sometimes called diacetate to distinguish it from the more completely acetated *triacetate*.

Acoustical ceilings Ceilings treated with acoustical tiles or other material for the absorption of sound.

Acoustical tiles Sound-absorbent tiles.

Acoustics The sound characteristics of a particular place; the study of such characteristics.

Acroterion A block at the apex or at one of the low points of a pediment, often with carved ornament. The plural is acroteria. Also spelled acroterium.

Acrylic A synthetic plastic that resembles glass. In the United States and Germany it has been marketed under the name Plexiglass, and in England under the name Perspex.

Acrylic fabric Fabric from acrylic fibers, characterized by wrinkle resistance and a soft *hand*. Sometimes blended with wool and other natural fibers for improved performance. Brand names include Dynel and Orlon.

Acrylic paint A quick-drying synthetic medium.

ACT Acronym for Association for Contract Textiles.

ADA Acronym for the Americans with Disabilities Act, mandating accessible design. See *universal design*.

Adam, Robert (1728–92) and James Adam (1730–94) English designers in the Neoclassical style. Known for architecture, interior architecture, and furniture.

Adire Indigo resist-dyed cloth, specifically that of the Yoruba people of Nigeria.

Adobe A mud brick dried in the sun but not fired; a building made of such brick.

Aedicule A miniature shrine or temple generally consisting of a pediment and entablature supported on a pair of columns or pilasters; a door or window frame resembling such a structure.

Aedicule with ears As above, with the ends of the entablature projecting slightly beyond the columns or pilasters.

Aeolic An architectural order, a variant of the Ionic.

Aerial perspective In interior design and architecture, a drawing giving the illusion of viewing from above. Also called a "bird's-eye view."

Affleck, Thomas (active 1763–95) Philadelphia cabinetmaker in the Chippendale style.

AFMA Acronym for American Furniture Manufacturers Association.

African silk A type of wild silk made from the cocoons of moths feeding on fig trees.

Agate ware A type of pottery resembling agate or quartz. Made in England during the eighteenth century by Wedgwood and other potters.

Aggregate Granular material such as gravel, pebbles, or small stone chips that can be bonded together in a matrix to form a material such as concrete.

AIA Acronym for the American Institute of Architects.

Air conditioning The treatment of air to control its temperature, humidity, and cleanliness. Abbreviated as *A/C*.

Airwood See *harewood*.

Aisle A passage between sections of seats, as in a theater or church.

Ajouré French term for a design in ceramics, metal, wood, or other material, in which the design has been produced by piercing holes.

Alabaster A fine-grained, slightly translucent stone with a smooth, milk-white surface. Used for ornaments and statuary.

Alabastron A type of Greek vase.

Alae In a Roman house, alcoves at the sides of the atrium. The singular is *ala*.

Alberti, Leone Battista (1404–72) Early Italian Renaissance architect, scholar, and author.

Alkyd A synthetic binder for paint.

Allen, Davis (1916–99) American designer of interiors and furniture.

Alloy A mixture of two or more metals; for example, brass is an alloy of copper and zinc.

Almery See *ambry*.

Altar A place for worship, ritual, or sacrifice, often raised.

Altarpiece Painting, carving, or decorated screen above a church altar.

Alternating current An electric current that (most commonly in the United States) alternates directions at the rate of 60 Hertz (60 times per second). In Europe, the more common rate is 50 Hertz. Abbreviated as *AC*.

Alumina See *China clay*.

Amaranth A dark purplish wood imported from South Africa. It is usually fine-grained and figured and is much used in contemporary furniture.

Amberina glass A late nineteenth-century glass with colors from amber to deep red.

Ambient lighting General illumination. See also *task lighting* and *accent lighting*.

Ambo In medieval Italian churches, a raised stand for reading the Gospel. It was later replaced by the pulpit.

Amboyna A rich brown wood, highly marked, with yellow and red streaks. Much used for modern cabinetwork and veneering. It is of East Indian origin.

Ambry In residential interiors, a cabinet for food storage; in ecclesiastical interiors, a cabinet for the storage of altar cloths and altar vessels. In the second sense, it is also called an *almery*.

Ambulatory In a medieval church, a walkway around a choir or chancel.

American silk A type of wild silk made in the area of Oaxaca, Mexico, from the cocoons of moths feeding on ailanthus trees.

Amorini Italian term for childlike figures, such as cupids or cherubs. Used for ornamental purposes, especially during the Italian Renaissance. Young male figures are called *putti*.

Amphora A Greek vase form. A large, two-handled earthenware vessel with a narrow neck and usually an ovoid body, used for the storage of grain and other products.

Andiron Metal upright attached to a horizontal support for logs in a fireplace. Small andirons are sometimes called *fire dogs*. French terms are *feu* and *chenet*.

Angel bed In eighteenth-century England, a bed with a fabric canopy attached above the head to the wall or ceiling. Similar to the French *lit á la duchesse*.

Anigré A light, fine-grained wood.

Aniline dyes Dyes derived from coal tar, often brilliant in color.

Annealing The process of slowly cooling a heated metal to make it more easily workable.

Anodizing The process of treating metal (such as aluminum) with a smooth, durable finish by means of an electrochemical process.

ANSI Acronym for the American National Standards Institute.

Anta A type of projecting pier similar to a pilaster placed behind a column at the end of a sidewall of a Greek temple, the base and capital of the pier differing from those of the column; also used in Egyptian architecture. The plural is *antae*.

Antefix An upright conventionalized spreading leaf or fanlike ornament used at the ends of tile rows on the roofs of classical temples.

Anthemion A conventionalized honeysuckle or palm leaf ornament or pattern seen in Greek decoration.

Antimacassar Knit, crocheted, or embroidered cover placed over an upholstered chair back to protect it from the Macassar oil hairdressing commonly used during the mid-nineteenth century. Also called a *tidy*.

Antique A work of art that, according to U.S. law, must be at least 100 years old.

Antiquity A work of art or craft of the Classical era or older; ancient times.

Apple A light-colored, fine-grained wood used for furniture. It is suitable for staining or natural finish.

Appliqué French term for an applied motif, a wall bracket or sconce. In fabric, a pattern that is cut out and sewn or pasted on the surface of another material.

Apron A board placed at right angles to the underside of a shelf, sill, seat, or tabletop.

Apse The semicircular or angular extension at the east end of a basilica or Christian church.

Aquatint A method of engraving on copper by using a resinous solution of nitric acid.

Arabesque A scroll and leaf pattern with stems rising from a root or other motif and branching in spiral forms. It is usually designed for a vertical panel, and the sides resemble each other. See also *rinceau*.

Aranda, Count of Buenaventura Spanish Renaissance art patron and founder, in 1727, of the Alcora ceramic factory.

Arbor vitae An evergreen tree of the genus *Thuya*, native to North America and eastern Asia. An excellent building and furniture wood.

Arc light A high-intensity light created by a discharge of electricity (an arc) between two electrodes.

Arca Spanish term for chest.

Arcade A series of adjoining arches with their supporting columns or piers. The arcade usually forms a part of the architectural treatment of a corridor or passageway.

Arcaded panel A panel whose field is ornamented by two dwarf piers or columns supporting an arch form. Particularly used in early English Renaissance woodwork.

Arch A structural feature spanning an opening, supported at the two lower ends, and composed of several wedge-shaped parts.

Archaic Primitive or antiquated. In reference to Greek art, it denotes the period of development from 1000 to 480 B.C.

Archiepiscopal cross A cross with two transverse arms, the lower one longer. Also called a *patriarchal cross*. See Table 6-2.

Architect's table A combination drawing table and desk, with an adjustable lid that lifts to make a slanting surface.

Architrave The lowest part of the three principal divisions of a classical *entablature*, corresponding to the lintel; usually molded. It is directly supported by the *columns* and supports the *frieze*. The term is also used to define similar moldings used as door or window trim.

Archivolt Ornamentation on the face of an arch.

Arcuate or Arcuated Arched or archlike in form, distinct from *trabeated construction*.

Arfe or Arphe In the fifteenth and sixteenth centuries, a family of famous German silversmiths whose work influenced the *Plateresco* architectural ornament of the Spanish Renaissance.

Argand lamp Lamp invented by a Swiss named Argand in 1783. It had a round wick with provision for the introduction of air inside the wick as well as around the outside.

Armarium   A Roman cupboard for the display of family treasures.

Armoire   French term for a clothes wardrobe (Gothic period and more recently). Also called a *garde-robe*.

Armure   A kind of cloth with a *rep* background. The raised satin pattern, which is not reversible, is made of warp threads floated over the surface. The pattern usually consists of small, isolated, conventional motifs arranged to form an allover design. A good upholstery material.

Arras   Originally, a tapestry manufactured in Arras, France, during the fourteenth and fifteenth centuries. The fame of such tapestries was so great that the name of the town is sometimes used as a synonym for handwoven tapestries of Gothic design. There was also a notable porcelain factory in Arras in the late eighteenth century.

Arrazzi   Italian name for the town of Arras, France. In Italy, the word *Arrazzi* is sometimes used as a synonym for a Gothic tapestries.

Arris   In architecture, the sharp edge formed by the meeting of two surfaces coming together at an angle. An example is the angle formed by the two sides of a brick. More specifically, the sharp edges occurring between two adjoining concave flutings of the shaft of a column.

Art Deco   Style popular in Europe and America from the 1910s to the 1930s, inspired by Cubism.

Artesonado   Spanish term for Moorish woodwork or joinery, usually made of Spanish cedar, which is soft and fine-grained, somewhat like red pine.

Artifact   An article of great antiquity made by humans, especially prehistoric stone, bone, metal, or clay objects.

Artificial leather   A substitute for leather that is made by coating a cotton fabric with a nitrocellulose preparation. This surface is then stamped to simulate the surface of real leather. Many varieties are made, which are generally known by trade names. Widely used at present for cheap grades of upholstery.

Art Moderne   See *Art Deco*.

Art Nouveau   Style popular in Europe and America from the 1890s to the 1910s, characterized by sinuous curves derived from plant forms.

Arts and Crafts   Artistic movement of the late nineteenth and early twentieth centuries, valuing craftsmanship above industrial techniques.

Aryballos   A type of Greek vase for oils and perfumes.

Asbestos   A naturally occurring mineral fiber (a silicate of calcium and magnesium) once widely used for insulation and fireproofing, but later considered a hazard because the fibers were found to cause respiratory disease.

Ash   A blond wood with a handsome figure and pleasing texture, which, because of its hardness, is not extensively used for interior work, though it can be used to produce very rich effects. It is well adapted to dark stained effects.

Ash, Gilbert (1717–85)   American furniture maker working in New York. His son Thomas Ash (d. 1815) was known as a maker of American Windsor chairs.

Ashbee, Charles Robert (1863–1942)   Architect, designer, and influential writer of the Arts and Crafts movement.

Ashlar   Masonry constructed of flat-surfaced stones with straight squared joints.

ASHRAE   Acronym for American Society of Heating, Refrigerating, and Air Conditioning Engineers.

ASID   Acronym for the American Society of Interior Designers.

ASME   Acronym for the American Society of Mechanical Engineers.

ASTM   Acronym for the American Society for Testing and Materials.

Astragal   In architecture, a small *torus* molding. Often used to denote a molding that covers the joint between adjacent doors or windows.

Astral lamp   An oil lamp with swinging tubular arms, generally furnished with an *Argand* burner. Used in the early nineteenth century.

Asymmetrical knot   One of the two basic types of knot with which Islamic carpets are woven. See Tools & Techniques: Characteristics of Islamic Carpets in Chapter 9. Also called a *Persian knot*, a *Senna knot*, or an open knot.

Atrium   Originally, the principal central room or courtyard of a Roman house, with a central opening in the roof. Later, the forecourt of an Early Christian basilica. Now, an open space within a building or building complex.

Attic   In classical architecture, a low wall above a cornice or entablature, usually ornamentally treated with statuary or inscriptions; from, or relating to, the area around the city of Athens, Greece.

Aubusson   A tapestry-woven carpet without pile, named for the tapestry works in Aubusson, France.

Audubon, John J. (1785–1851)   American ornithologist and painter. Made illustrations for *Birds of America*.

Auricular style   Decorative style popular in seventeenth-century Dutch silverware and elsewhere, consisting of repeated shallow waves as might be found in a seashell or in the human ear (hence its name). The Dutch term is *kwabornament*, and the German term is *Knorpelwerk*. It is also sometimes called *lobate* style.

Austrian shade   A shade or curtain shirred in vertical panels. As it is raised by a series of parallel cords, the material is gathered. See also *Roman shade*.

Automatic sprinkler system   A system that, upon detection of smoke or excess heat, automatically disperses water or other fire-extinguishing material. See also *dry pipe automatic sprinkler system*.

Auvera, Johann Wolfgang van der (1708–56)   German Rococo sculptor and furniture maker.

Avisse, Jean (1723–c. 1800)   French furniture maker in the Rococo and Neoclassical styles, appointed *Maître Ébéniste* in 1745.

Avodire   A blond wood with strong, dark brown vertical streakings. It has a fine texture and is much used for modern furniture, for veneering purposes.

Axial   Descriptive of a room, building, or layout that is symmetrical about an axis.

Axminster   A pile carpet with a stiff jute back; the weave permits a great variety of colors and designs.

Axonometric drawing   A measured drawing in which three sides of an object are made visible. See also *isometric drawing*.

Azulejos   Spanish term for wall tiles produced in Spain and Portugal, painted with scenes of sports, bullfights, or social and amorous groups.

B

Baize   Coarse woolen cloth used for surfacing desks and writing tables.

Baldachino   Italian term for a canopy resting on columns, usually built over an altar. Also called a *ciborium*.

Baldwin, Benjamin (1913–93)   American interior designer.

Baldwin, William ("Billy") (1903–84)   American interior designer.

Ball foot   A loosely used term for any furniture foot or leg terminating in a ball. See Table 19–3.

Ball-and-claw foot   A furniture foot cut to imitate a talon or claw grasping a ball. Of Chinese origin, the motif was greatly used in English eighteenth-century furniture. See Table 19–3.

Ballast   A voltage-control device used with fluorescent and other electric-discharge types of lighting.

Ballin, Claude (c. 1615–78)   Goldsmith and silversmith to Louis XIV. His nephew, Claude Ballin II, followed him in the same trade.

Baluster   An upright support that is made in a variety of turned forms. In general, it curves strongly outward at some point between the base and the top; commonly an elongated vase or urn shape. Used for the support of hand railings and for furniture legs or ornament. See *spindle* and *split spindle*.

Balustrade   The railing along the open edge of a stair, including the *balusters*, the handrail, and the *newel post*.

Bambino   Italian term for a child or baby, or the representation of such in any art medium.

Bamboo   A woody, perennial plant that grows in tropical regions. The wood is used for furniture, ornaments, building purposes, pipes, paper-making, and food.

Bamboo-turned   Wood turnings in mahogany and other woods that imitate natural bamboo forms. See Table 19–2.

Banding   In cabinetwork, a strip of veneer used as a border for tabletops, drawer fronts, and so forth. In porcelain and other ceramic ware, a synonym for *edging*.

Bandy-legged   Literally, bow-legged. A lay term, used in old furniture inventories, for a chair or table with *cabriole* legs.

Banister   Same as *baluster*.

Banister-back chair   A late seventeenth-century American chair with back uprights consisting of split turned spindles or flat bars.

Banjo clock   A wall-hung clock in a banjo-shaped case.

Banker   A term of medieval origin for a piece of fabric draped over benches or chair backs.

Banquette   French term for bench, now used for a long, bench-like seat, usually upholstered.

Baptistery   A separate building or part of a church used primarily for the rite of baptism.

Barbotine   French term for *slip*.

Bargello stitch   See *flame-stitch*.

Barkcloth   See *tapa*.

Barley sugar turning   An old name for a *spiral leg* on a seventeenth-century English chair. Also called a *barley twist*.

Barn doors   Flaps that can be adjusted to direct the beam of a spotlight.

Barocco   Italian term for *Baroque*.

Baroque   A style of architecture, art, and decoration that originated in Italy during the late sixteenth century and spread to other parts of Europe. It is characterized by large-scale, bold detail, and sweeping curves. It was followed by the *Rococo* style and overlapped the latter.

Barragán, Luis (1902–88)   Mexican architect noted for simple forms and strong colors.

Barrel vault   See *vault*.

Barrier-free design   See *universal design*.

Bas-relief   French term for a low relief.

Basalt   Dark green or brown igneous rock, sometimes having columnar strata. Egyptian statues were frequently carved in this material. Most often used now for paving.

Basaltes ware   Black vitreous pottery, made to imitate basalt. Specifically, a very hard black stoneware invented by *Josiah Wedgwood* in England in the 1760s.

Base   Any block or molding at the bottom of an architectural or decorative composition, particularly a series of moldings at the bottom of the shaft of a classical column.

Base molding   A molding used on the lowest portion of any object or surface.

Baseboard   In carpentry, a board placed at the base of a wall and resting on the floor; usually treated with moldings. Sometimes called a base screed.

Basilica   In Roman times, an oblong, three-aisled building used as a hall of justice. The central aisle, or nave, was higher than the side aisles and was usually pierced with windows placed above the roof of the side aisles. This plan formed the basis for later Christian churches.

Basket weave   A textile weave in which the warp and weft are usually of large threads of similar size and in which the weft crosses the top of alternate warp threads.

Basse-taille   A decorative process of applying translucent enamel over reliefs of gold or silver. Similar to *champlevé*.

Batik   Javanese process of resist dyeing on cotton by using wax in a design. After dyeing the cloth, the wax is removed to leave undyed patterns. The method is practiced by modern designers on silk and rayon and is imitated in machine printing.

Batiste   A fine, lightweight fabric, but with more body than *gauze* or *voile*.

Batter   The slope of a wall away from the vertical.

Battersea enamels   Enamel work from a short-lived (1753–56) enamel factory in Battersea, England. The name, however, is often given to similar products from other factories.

Bauhaus   German school of art, crafts, and architecture from 1919 to 1933; Modernist style associated with the school's teaching.

Bay   In architecture, the space between columns or isolated supports of a building.

Bay window   A large projecting window that is polygonal in shape. If it is curved or semicircular, it is usually called a bow window.

Baywood   An alternate name for Honduras mahogany, which is lighter in color and softer than the Cuban or Spanish mahogany. Its fine marking makes the wood useful in veneered work.

Bead   A molding ornament that resembles a string of beads. Sometimes called pearl or beading.

Bead-and-reel   A half-round molding with alternating spherical and ovoid shapes.

Beaker Tall drinking vessel with slightly flaring sides.

Beam A long piece of timber or metal used to support a roof or ceiling, usually supported at each end by a wall, post, or girder.

Beaux-Arts The *École Supérieure des Beaux-Arts*, France's official school of art and architecture, founded in 1795; the traditional style based on the school's teaching.

Bedrug A rug used as a bed cover.

Bedstead A frame into which a mattress and linens can be fit.

Beech A pale straight-grained wood much used for flooring and furniture. It resembles maple and birch and can be similarly used.

Behrens, Peter (1868–1940) German architect and industrial designer.

Bell turning For furniture legs and pedestal supports, a type of turning shaped approximately like a conventional bell. Common in the *William and Mary* style.

Belladine A raw silk from the Levant, used for tassels and fringes. Also spelled *bellandine*.

Bellini, Mario (born 1935) Italian industrial designer and furniture designer.

Belter, John Henry (1804–63) New York cabinetmaker, designer of elaborate rosewood and carved laminated forms.

Bema In church interiors, a chancel or speaker's platform.

Benday A shading process made of small dots, sometimes used in printing fabrics. Named for the American printer Benjamin Day.

Beneman, Guillaume German-born cabinetmaker who settled in Paris, becoming one of the most important French craftsmen before the French Revolution. Appointed *Maître Ébéniste* in 1785. He worked for Marie-Antoinette at St. Cloud and also produced some designs of *Charles Percier*. His name is sometimes spelled *Benneman*.

Bengaline A plain-weave, warp-faced fabric of silk, cotton, or artificial fiber, more often used in clothing than in interior design.

Benjamin, Asher (1773–1845) American architect and author of architectural handbooks.

Bennett, Ward (1917–2003) American interior designer and furniture designer.

Bennington pottery Pottery originating in Bennington, Vermont.

Bentwood Artificially bent wood. Furniture or other objects made with such wood.

Bérain, Jean (1638–1710) French designer at the court of Louis XIV, responsible for much of the ornament, notably engraved *arabesque* and *cartouche* forms.

Bergère French term for an all-upholstered low armchair, usually with an exposed wood frame and a soft seat cushion. (From the Louis XV and XVI periods, but still produced today.)

Berlage, Hendrikus Petrus (1856–1934) Dutch architect and designer of glassware and furniture, a teacher of Ludwig Mies van der Rohe.

Bernini, Giovanni Lorenzo (1598–1680) A leading architect, sculptor, and painter of the Baroque period of the Italian Renaissance. Designer of the *baldachino* and the colonnade of St. Peter's.

Betty lamp A small oil lamp used in colonial America, designed to be hung from a hook.

Bevel The edge of any flat surface that has been cut at a slant to the main area.

Bianco-sopra-bianco Italian term meaning white-on-white, used to describe a tile-painting technique developed by Bristol potters.

Bib or **bibb** or **bibcock** A faucet with a downward-bent nozzle.

Bibelot French term for a small art object for personal use or as decoration.

Bibliotheca The library in a Roman house.

Bibliothèque French term for a large bookcase.

Bibvalve A bib with a handle that screws to close the flow of water or other liquid.

Bid An offer to perform specified work at a specified cost.

Biedermeier Style popular with the middle classes of central and Eastern Europe and Scandinavia from the 1810s through the 1830s.

Bifold doors A configuration of one or more pairs of doors, in which one folds against the next.

Bilston enamel Enamel ware made in the English town of Bilston.

Birch A fine-grained wood, strong and hard, usually a light brown in color. It requires no filler, takes paint and stain well, and can have a natural finish or be stained to imitate walnut, mahogany, and other more expensive woods. It is much used for doors and trim as well as for flooring, where it competes successfully with oak.

Bird's-eye Wood with fine circular markings caused by fiber distortions in the growth of the annual rings of the tree. It is most frequently found in sugar maple.

Bird's-eye view See *aerial perspective*.

Biscuit Pottery that has been fired once and has no glaze or a very thin glaze. Sometimes called bisque. Sometimes a distinction is made in which unglazed porcelain is called biscuit ware, but unglazed pottery of lesser quality is called terra cotta.

Black walnut In spite of its extensive use at a period when design was at its lowest level, it is one of the most beautiful woods grown in the United States. It has a rich color, takes a high polish, and shows a very handsome figure. It is fine-grained enough to allow intricate carving, though its open pores call for the use of a filler in finishing. It is among the more rare and expensive woods because of wasteful cutting at the end of the nineteenth century.

Blackamoor A statue of a Negro used for decorative purposes during the Italian Renaissance and revived in the Victorian period.

Black-figure vase Ancient Greek vase with black figures painted on a red pottery ground.

Blanc-de-Chine European name for white porcelain figurines and objects imported from Te-hua, Fukien, China, from the seventeenth century onward.

Bleach The process of removing the original color or of whitening a fabric by exposure to air and sunlight or by the chloride process.

Blind nailing The nailing of boards through their edges so that the nail heads are covered by adjoining boards.

Block foot A cube-shaped foot for a furniture leg, used by Chippendale in eighteenth-century England. Also called a *cube foot* or a *Marlborough foot*. When a block foot is slightly tapered, growing smaller towards the floor, it is called a *spade foot* or a *therm foot*.

Block print Fabric printed by hand, using carved wooden blocks. Can be distinguished from modern printing with metal rollers or screens by the marks of the joining of the pattern printed by different blocks. Screen printing has now been substituted almost entirely for hand blocking in the United States.

Block-and-shell A piece of *block-front* furniture with each panel topped by a shell carving.

Block-front A treatment of case furniture in which the front surface is articulated by a central panel sunk between two slightly raised surfaces of equal width. Often seen in English and American eighteenth-century furniture.

Block-printing A process of producing a colored pattern or picture on paper or textile by wooden blocks, each one producing a portion of the pattern in a single flat color.

Blue-and-white ware White ceramics decorated in cobalt blue.

Blue resist A type of fabric using a *resist dyeing* technique and blue dye. Popular in eighteenth-century England and the United States.

Boardman, Thomas D. (1784–1873) Hartford pewterer.

Bobbin A device on which threads are wound for use in weaving.

Bobbinet See *net*.

Bobêche French term for a candle socket.

BOCA Code A U.S. building code issued by the Building Officials and Code Administrators.

Body The clay or other material of which a piece of pottery or porcelain is manufactured, as distinguished from the glaze or finish later applied.

Bohemian glass See *cased glass*.

Bois de lit French term for a *bedstead*.

Boiserie French term for carved woodwork.

Bois naturel French term for unpainted wood.

Bokhara Textile center of Central Asia since the fifth century. Carpets of the style woven there.

Bolection moldings A series of moldings that project sharply beyond the plane of the woodwork or wall to which they are applied.

Bolection panel A panel that projects beyond its surrounding panels.

Bombé French term for a swelling curve; when the curve is applied to the front of a piece of furniture, it swells outward toward the center, at which point it recedes again.

Bonader Wall hangings of subject matter relating to peasant life, painted on paper or canvas. Made in Sweden or by Swedes in America and used to decorate homes on feast days.

Bone china Type of ceramic containing bone ash.

Bonheur-du-jour French term for a small desk with cabinet top.

Bonnet top In cabinetwork, a top with a broken arch or pediment, or a curved or scroll top with a central finial motif in the shape of a flame, urn, or other form.

Bonnetière French term for a hat cabinet.

Border pattern A continuous running motif used in the design of bands, borders, and panel frames.

Borne A large circular upholstered settee popular in the last half of the nineteenth century.

Borromini, Francesco (1599–1667) The most imaginative architect of the Roman Baroque style. He influenced most of Bavarian Baroque style as well as the design of St. Paul's Cathedral, London.

Boss The projecting ornament placed at the intersection of beams or moldings. It is often a carved head of an angel, flower, or foliage motif.

Boston rocker General term formerly applied to any chair with curved supports. Synonymous with rocking-chair.

Boteh The pear-shaped decorative motif repeated in the *Paisley* pattern.

Botta, Mario (born 1943) Swiss architect and furniture designer.

Botticelli, Sandro (1444–1510) Italian Renaissance poetical painter of Classical mythology and allegorical subjects.

Bottonée cross A Greek cross with each arm terminated in a cloverlike trefoil form. See Table 6-2. Also called a *cloverleaf cross*.

Boucher, François (1703–70) French decorative painter under Louis XV.

Bouclé Plain or twill weave in wool, rayon, cotton, silk, or linen. Distinctive by its small regularly spaced loops and flat irregular surfaces produced by the use of specially twisted yarns.

Bouillotte French term for a small table with gallery edge (Louis XVI). Also, a foot-warmer.

Bouillotte lamp Late eighteenth-century lamp in the form of a candlestick, often with three or four arms, often made of brass, and usually terminating at the top in a handle or finial by which it can be picked up.

Bouillotte shade A shallow shade for a lamp or candle, sometimes made of *tôle*.

Boulard, Jean Baptiste (1725–89) Both *ébéniste* and sculptor, appointed *Maître Ébéniste* in 1754. His most important work was a magnificent bed for Louis XVI at Fontainebleau.

Boulle, André-Charles (1642–1732) Important French cabinetmaker, he was the first great *Maître Ébéniste* and in 1672 was appointed head cabinetmaker to Louis XIV. After his death, his workshop was continued by his two sons, André-Charles and Charles-Joseph.

Boulle work Marquetry patterns in tortoise shell and German silver or brass, introduced by André-Charles Boulle, and used as furniture enrichment in the seventeenth century.

Bourette A silk of inferior strength, made from short, rough, uneven filaments.

Box-plaiting Pressed folds in a fabric, sewed in place in series, as in a drapery.

Boxwood A light-colored, fine-grained wood used for *marquetry*.

Bracket A flat-topped underprop that projects from a wall or pier and forms a support for a beam or other architectural member above it.

Bracket foot A low furniture support that has a straight corner edge and curved inner edges. It was used in eighteenth-century English and American furniture. In the French bracket foot, the outer corners are curved. It is a stunted *cabriole* form.

Brad Small headless nail.

Bradshaw, George and William (active 1736–50) English cabinetmakers and upholsterers.

Braid   A strip composed of intertwining several strands of silk, cotton, or other materials. Used as a binding or trimming.

Braided rug   A rug made by braiding together narrow lengths of fabric. The braids are wound and stitched in round or oval shapes.

Bramante, Donato d'Agnolo (1444–1514)   Italian Renaissance painter and architect of St. Peter's in Rome.

Brass   An alloy consisting primarily of copper and zinc.

Brasses   General term referring to cabinet hardware such as drawer-pulls and escutcheons.

Brazier   One who works in brass; also a pan with feet, for holding embers, used as a stove for heating rooms until the nineteenth century.

Breakfast table   A small drop-leaf table, similar to a *Pembroke table* but with a storage compartment underneath for china and silver. Popular in England from the middle of the eighteenth century.

Breakfront   Cabinet piece, the front of which has one or more projecting portions.

Breuer, Marcel (1902–81)   Important Hungarian-born architect and furniture designer, an instructor at the Bauhaus who later had a practice based in New York.

Brewster chair   A chair named for Elder Brewster, one of the first settlers of New England. It has a rush seat and turned spindles.

Bric-à-brac   A miscellaneous collection of small articles or curios. Pronounced "breek-ah-brah."

Brighton Pavilion chair   A six- or eight-legged bamboo chair with carved sides and back.

Bristol glass   Glass popular in England in the second half of the eighteenth century, characterized by its deep colors, including a rich cobalt called Bristol Blue.

Broadcloth   Twill, plain, or rib weave, of wool and spun rayon, and of cotton and rayon or silk. The cotton or spun rayon fabric has fine crosswise ribs.

Broad glass   See *flat glass*.

Broadloom   A term of the carpet trade, referring to carpets manufactured in wide strips (9, 12, and 15 feet and wider).

Brocade   A kind of weave; also, a finished silk cloth that, although made on a loom, resembles embroidery. The background may be of one color or may have a warp stripe, and its weave may be taffeta, twill, satin, or damask. A floral or conventional pattern in slight relief is usually multicolored and is produced by the filler thread. It is woven with the *Jacquard* attachment, and the threads that do not appear on the surface are carried across the width of the back. The finest old handmade brocades all included threads of real gold or silver. Excellent for draperies and upholstery, particularly in period rooms.

Brocadillo   An imitation brocade.

Brocatelle   A heavy silk fabric resembling a damask, except that the pattern appears to be embossed. The pattern (usually large and definite) is a satin weave against a twill background. Made with two sets of warps and two sets of fillers, it is not reversible, as the linen backing produced by one set of filler threads shows plainly. Its uses are similar to those of brocade.

Broché   A silk fabric similar to brocade. The small floral designs, which are quite separate from the background pattern, are made with swivel shuttles to resemble embroidery. The filler threads not in use are carried only across the width of the small design and not across the entire back as in brocade. Pronounced "bro-shay."

Broken pediment   A triangular pediment that is interrupted at the crest or peak.

Bronze   An alloy of copper and tin.

Bronze-doré   French term for gilded bronze.

Brunelleschi, Filippo (1377–1446)   Considered the earliest Italian Renaissance architect. Designed the dome of the Cathedral and the Hospital of the Innocents, both in Florence. Sometimes spelled *Brunellesco*.

Brussels carpet   A carpet with a looped woolen pile and a cotton back, first made in Brussels c. 1710 and made by machine in America after the middle of the nineteenth century.

Buckram   A strong jute cloth of plain weave, finished with glue sizing. It is used as a stiffening for valences, for interlining draperies, etc.

Buffet   French term for a cabinet used for holding dining table accessories; also a table from which food is served.

Bulbous form   In cabinetry, a stout turning resembling a large melon; used for furniture supports during the early Renaissance in England, France, and Italy.

Bulfinch, Charles (1763–1844)   American architect who designed the state capitols of Massachusetts, Maine, and Connecticut and put Dr. Thornton's plan for the Capitol at Washington into execution.

Bull's-eye   See *oeil-de-boeuf*.

Bun foot   A furniture support that resembles a slightly flattened ball or sphere. Common in Dutch and English furniture.

Bundle   The unit in which wallpaper is delivered. In the trade in the United States, a roll is 36 square feet of paper, but paper is delivered in bundles of 1, 2, or 3 rolls.

Bureau   French term for a desk or writing table.

Bureau-à-cylindre   French term for a roll-top desk. Also called a *bureau-à-rideau*.

Bureau-à-pente   French term for a folding, slant-lid desk. Sometimes called a *bureau-en-pente*.

Bureau plat   French term for a flat writing table, often leather-topped, and often with small drawers in the *frieze*.

Burette, Charles Marin   French cabinetmaker who flourished toward the end of the Empire period.

Burl   A curly-grained wood surface or veneer cut from irregular growths of the tree, such as the roots or crotches. Very common in walnut.

Burlap   Plain weave of cotton, jute, or hemp. Heavy, coarse, and loosely woven, in a variety of weights, and used for sacks, the backs of floor coverings, inside upholstery, and elsewhere.

Burnap, Daniel (active 1780–1800)   American clockmaker known for engraved faces.

Bürolandschaft   German term for *office landscape*.

Butt joint   In cabinetry, a type of joint in which the squared end of a plank meets the side or end of another plank head to head or at right angles.

Butt-wood veneer   Veneer that is cut from the part of the tree where the large roots join the trunk. It has fine curly and mottled markings.

Butterfly table   A popular name for a small drop-leaf table used in the American colonies; the raised leaf was supported by a board bracket cut to resemble a butterfly wing.

Butternut   A wood that resembles black walnut in all respects except color, and may be similarly used, where a lighter effect is desired. It works easily, is hard and durable, and has a handsome figure, formed by the annual rings. It is sometimes used for flooring and ceilings, sometimes for interior finish and furniture. The trees grow throughout the United States. It is also called *white walnut*.

Buttress   An exterior support built against a wall. Particularly seen in Gothic architecture, where it was introduced as extra masonry to resist the heavy thrust of the arched stone roof of the building.

By-passing door   One of two or more doors that slide to stack in front of one another, less accurately called a *sliding door*.

Byzantine   Style of art and architecture produced in the Eastern Roman or Byzantine Empire, A.D. 330–1453.

C

CAAD   Acronym for computer-aided architectural design. Also see *CAD* and *CADD*.

Cabinet-sécretaire   French term for a desk with cabinet above.

Cabinet-vitrine   French term for a cabinet with glass doors.

Cabled fluting   Term for the fluting of a column shaft when the lower parts of the flutes are filled with solid cylindrical elements.

Cabriole   A term used to designate a furniture leg or support that is designed in the form of a conventionalized animal's leg with knee, ankle, and foot; used particularly in France and England during the eighteenth century.

Cabriole chair   A chair with an upholstered back of oval or cartouche shape.

Cabriole seat   An upholstered chair seat of rounded shape.

Cabriolet   French term for a chair with a concave back.

Cachepot   French term for a pot of china or porcelain used as a container.

CAD   Acronym for computer-aided design.

CADD   Acronym for computer-aided design and drafting.

Caen stone   Limestone of a yellowish color, with rippled markings, found near Caen, in Normandy. Often used in French architecture and decoration.

Caffieri, Jacques (1678–1755), and his son Philippe (1714–74)   French cabinetmakers and sculptors under Louis XIV and XV.

Caffoy   A wool plush fabric used in the early eighteenth century, an inexpensive version of cut velvet.

Cage cup   A glass cup with a cagelike outer layer that is almost completely free of the inner body. In Roman times, such a cup was called a *diatretum*.

Calendering   A fabric finishing process producing a flat, smooth, glossy surface by passing the fabric between heated cylinders.

Calico   A term formerly used for a plain woven printed cotton cloth, similar to *percale*. Its name is taken from Calicut, India, where it was first made. Sometimes spelled *callicoa*.

Calligraphy   In general, beautiful penmanship; specifically, the brushstroke work done by the Chinese for reproduction of the written characters of the Chinese language.

Camber   A slight upward bend or convexity; a slight rise or arch in the middle.

Cambric   Plain weave linen or cotton. True linen cambric is very sheer. It is named for the original fabric made in Cambrai, France. Now, coarser fabrics are called cambric and used for linings, etc.

Came   A strip of lead in a leaded glass window.

Camel back   Chair back of late Chippendale or Hepplewhite style, the top rail of which was in the form of a serpentine curve.

Cameo   A striated stone or shell carved in relief.

Camlet   A fine, smooth-surfaced blend of wool and silk or wool and linen made in imitation of an earlier fabric from Asia that had contained camel's hair or Angora goat hair. Other spellings include *camlette, camblet*, and *Camelot*.

Canabas, Joseph (1712–97)   French cabinetmaker appointed *Maître Ébéniste* in 1766. Particularly noted for mechanical contrivances, such as folding tables for armies or to be carried aboard ships. His real name was Joseph Gegenbach.

Canapé   French term for a sofa or settee.

Canapé-à-corbeille   French term for a kidney-shaped sofa.

Candelabrum   A branched candlestick or lamp stand. The plural is *candelabra*.

Canephorus   In furniture or decoration, an ornament representing a maiden with a basket of offerings on her head. The plural is *canephora*. See also *caryatid*.

Canopic vase   A vase used by the ancient Egyptians to hold the organs of a dead person.

Canopy   A draped covering suspended over a piece of furniture, as over a bed or a seat of honor.

Canterbury   An ornamental stand having compartments and divisions for papers, portfolios, envelopes, and so forth. It was used beside a piano to hold music or by a dining table to hold plates. It was popular in England from 1790 to 1890.

Cantilever   A beam with one or both ends projecting beyond the supporting wall or columns. Used structurally for the support of projecting balconies, eaves, and other extensions.

Canton china   Original blue-and-white china imported from the Far East from the seventeenth century until the Sino-Japanese War in 1938. A traditional staple in Chinese ceramic history.

Canton enamels   Enamels with pink and gold decoration, similar to that of *famille rose* porcelain.

Cantonnière   French term for a *valance*.

Canvas   A heavy cotton cloth in plain weave. It may be bleached or unbleached, starched, dyed, or printed. Used for awnings, couch covers, and whenever a coarse, heavy material is required.

Capital   In architecture, the decorative crowning motif of the shaft of a column or pilaster, usually composed of moldings and ornament. The most characteristic feature of each Classical architectural order.

Captain's chair   Nineteenth-century chair based on a low-back Windsor. Also called a *firehouse Windsor*.

Caquetoire or caqueteuse   Early Renaissance French term for a "conversation chair," a small, light chair in which to sit and talk.

Carcase   The structural body of a piece of wooden furniture that is covered with veneer. Sometimes called the core.

Carding   A process for cleaning fibers before spinning them into yarn.

Carlin, Martin (died 1785)   French cabinetmaker appointed *Maître Ébéniste* in 1766. He made charming, delicate furniture during the Neoclassical period, using rosewood and *Sèvres* porcelain.

Carolean   See *Restoration style*.

Carpet   Today, fiber-based floor covering. In the sixteenth and seventeenth centuries, a table covering.

Carpet pad   A cushion used under a carpet.

Carpet tile   Modular units of carpet, usually square, and usually 18 to 24 inches in size.

Carrel   Originally, a niche in a monastery wall where a monk might sit and read; today, a private reading desk in a library.

Carrère and Hastings   Important American architecture firm in the late nineteenth and early twentieth centuries. Among its work is the New York Public Library, finished in 1911.

Carriage   A heavy board notched to support stair treads.

Cartibulum   In a Roman house, a ceremonial marriage table.

Carton pierre   A *gesso*-like composition material easily formed to imitate wood carving. It was introduced by *Robert Adam*.

Cartoon   The term used to designate a drawing or design made for reproduction in another medium, as the original design for a rug, tapestry, or painted mural decoration.

Cartouche   A conventionalized shield or ovoid form used as an ornament, often enclosed with wreaths, garlands, or scroll-like forms.

Carved rug   A rug with the pile cut to different levels to produce a pattern.

Carver chair   A type of Early American chair named for the governor of the Massachusetts Bay Colony. It is a simplified version of the *Brewster chair*.

Caryatid   In architecture, a column carved in human female form. The male equivalent is called a *term*, and the female equivalent at furniture scale is a *canephorus*.

Cased glass   Glass of one color coated with a thin layer of glass of another color. The outer layer is often cut away in decorative patterns to reveal the inner one. Also called *Bohemian glass* or *verre double* or *cup-overlay*.

Casegoods   Any furniture used to contain objects, such as a desk, a bookcase, a hutch, or a cabinet. Also called case furniture.

Casement cloth   A lightweight cloth originally made of wool and silk in plain weave. Now made of cotton, linen, mohair, silk, wool, rayon, or a combination. Although usually neutral in tone, this material may be had in colors and is popular for draw curtains.

Casement window   A window hinged at the side to swing in or out.

Cashmere   A soft wool textile made from Indian goat hair. The same breed of goat is now raised in the United States.

Cassapanca   Italian term for a long wooden seat with wooden back and arms, and with its lower portion used as a chest with hinged lid.

Cassone   Italian term for a chest or box with hinged lid. The plural is *cassoni*.

Cast   The reproduction of a sculpture in metal or plaster using a mold.

Cast glass   Glass that is formed in a mold rather than blown.

Caster   A small wheel fastened to supporting legs of heavy furniture to facilitate moving. First used in the early nineteenth century. Sometimes spelled *castor*.

Catacombs   Underground chambers in Rome used by the early Christians as hiding places and for religious worship.

Catenary arch   An arch form that is in the shape that a chain takes when its ends are supported a distance apart.

Cathedral   A large, important church; specifically, a church that is the seat of a bishop. The actual throne within the church is called the *cathedra* or bishop's throne.

Cavetto   A molding of concave form approximating a quarter-circle.

Cedar   A name applied to several woods that are fine-grained and fragrant. The North American cedar is a juniper; the West Indian is of the mahogany family. The wood is used for chests and for lining clothes closets. Persian cedar, or *nanmu*, is an eastern hardwood used for building.

Celadon   A pale grayish green; Korean or Chinese ceramics of that color.

Cella   The interior chamber of a Classical temple, in which usually stood the cult statue.

Cellaret   A portable chest, case, or cabinet for storing bottles, decanters, and glasses.

Cellini, Benvenuto (1500–71)   Italian Renaissance goldsmith and sculptor.

Cellulose   An insoluble starchlike substance taken from plants to form the base of many synthetic materials.

Celtic cross   A cross with a small circle at the intersection of its vertical and horizontal arms. See Table 6-2.

Cement   A powder composed of alumina, silica, lime, iron oxide, and magnesia burned together and then pulverized. It is a key ingredient in (but never properly a synonym for) *concrete*.

Cenotaph   A funerary monument not containing the body of the dead.

Centering   Temporary wooden framework used in the construction of vaults or domes. When the structure is finished and self-supporting, the centering is removed or "struck."

Ceramics   The art of molding, modeling, and baking in clay. The products of this art.

Cerceau, Jacques du   Sixteenth-century French architect and furniture designer under Henry IV.

Certosina   Italian term for an inlay of light wood, ivory, or other materials upon a dark background.

Chacmool   An Aztec sacrificial stone in the shape of a reclining figure.

Chair rail   The topmost molding of a *dado*, sometimes known as the *dado cap*. It is placed on a wall at the height of a chair back to protect the wall from being scraped.

Chair table   A chair with a hinged back that may be dropped to a horizontal position as a tabletop.

Chaise   French term for chair, usually applied to a side chair.

Chaise-à-capucine   French term for a low slipper chair.

Chaise-brisée   French term for a chaise-longue in two parts (with foot rest).

Chaise-longue   French term, literally "long chair," or chair for reclining. Also called a *duchesse*.

Chaitya In India, a Buddhist or Hindu temple, generally in the form of a basilica. Its characteristic horseshoe-shaped window is called a chaitya window.

Chalice A cup or goblet used for church sacraments.

Châlit French term for a bedstead.

Challis A soft woven fabric.

Chambers, Sir William (1726–96) English architect and first treasurer of the Royal Academy. Author of *Treatise on the Decorative Part of Civil Architecture*. Adhered to Palladian tradition during the Greek revival. After traveling in the Orient, shares honors with Chippendale in adapting Chinese forms to furniture.

Chambray A class of yarn-dyed, plain weave cotton or synthetic fabrics with a colored warp and white filling, often used for clothing. The name derives from the French town of Cambrai.

Chamfer See *bevel*.

Champlevé A type of enamel in which the pattern is grooved in a metal base and the grooves are filled with colored enamels. Pronounced "zhahm-play-vay."

Chancel The eastern end of a cruciform church, including the altar and the choir.

Chandelier French term for a hanging lighting fixture.

Charger A large dish.

Char-pai In India, a rope bed.

Charles X French Neoclassical style during the reign of Charles X, 1824–30.

Chase An enclosure that houses mechanical equipment, ducts, or pipes.

Chashitsu In Japan, a small pavilion or room used for the tea ceremony.

Chasing The tooling of a metal surface to smooth it or to raise a decorative pattern on it.

Chattri In Hindu architecture, umbrella-shaped forms atop slabs that are supported on posts. Also spelled *chatri*. The singular is *chattra*.

Chauffeuse French term for a small, low-seated fireside chair (from the French *chauffer*, meaning "to warm"). Sometimes spelled *chaffeuse*. The English term is *nursing chair*.

Check A small crack that sometimes appears in lumber unevenly or imperfectly dried, perpendicular to the annual rings, and radiating away from the heart of the trunk.

Checkerboard A pattern consisting of alternating light and dark squares.

Cheesecloth Unsized cotton gauze, sometimes used in cheesemaking.

Chelsea foot Popular in the Chelsea section of London in the 1930s, an upholstered leg on a sofa, chair, or ottoman.

Chêne French term for oak.

Chenets French term for andirons.

Chenille A type of woven yarn that has a pile protruding all around at right angles to the body thread. The yarn may be of silk, wool, mercerized cotton, or rayon and is used for various types of fabrics.

Cherry A durable hardwood of a reddish-brown color, which is produced only in small quantities, the trees being usually too small for lumbering. It is often used to imitate mahogany, which it greatly resembles, and is used for marquetry and inlay. In Japan it is called *sakura*.

Chest A piece of furniture used as a box or container.

Chesterfield Named for the Earl of Chesterfield, an overstuffed sofa, usually with its arms and back on a continuous level.

Chest-on-chest A chest of drawers consisting of two parts, one mounted on top of the other.

Chestnut A softwood, sometimes white and sometimes brown, which resembles plain oak, but has a coarser grain. Where a quartered effect is not desired, it can take the place of oak and is generally much less expensive. Because of its strongly marked rings and coarse grain, it is unsuitable for fine detail. In Japan it is called *kuri*.

Cheval glass Literally meaning "horse mirror" because the frame holding it was known as a "horse." It is a large full-length mirror, usually standing on the floor, often pivoting around a horizontal axis. See also *pier glass*.

Cheveret In late eighteenth-century England, a small lady's writing table, similar to the French *bonheur-de-jour*.

Chevet French term meaning the head of a bed, a bedside, or a bolster. It also refers to the east end of a church, or chancel, including the *apse*, the *choir*, and the *ambulatory*.

Chevron An ornamental motif composed of V-shapes pointing in alternating directions. Also called a *zigzag* or a *dancette*.

Chiaroscuro Literally meaning "clear-obscure," an Italian term referring to a strong contrast of light and dark areas in painting.

Chi-ch'ih-mu See *jichimu*.

Ch'ien Lung porcelain Chinese porcelain from the reign of the Ch'ing dynasty emperor Ch'ien Lung (1736–95).

Chiffon A descriptive term used to indicate the light weight and soft finish of a fabric, as in "chiffon velvet"; also, a sheer, gauze-like silk fabric.

Chiffonière French term meaning a chest of drawers. Often anglicized as *chiffonier*.

China The first European name for *porcelain* imported from the East.

China clay A fine white clay and an essential ingredient of true *porcelain*. Also called *kaolin* or *alumina*.

China silk Sheer plain weave fabric that is nearly transparent and is dyed in various colors.

Chinastone A fusible crystalline mineral that is an essential ingredient of true *porcelain*. In its raw form it is known in China as *tzu-shih*, and in its prepared form of small white blocks as *baidunzi* or *pai-tun-tzü*, anglicized as *petuntse*.

Ch'in dynasty Chinese dynasty, 256–206 B.C.

Ch'ing dynasty The last Chinese dynasty, 1644–1912, sometimes called the *Manchu dynasty*. Also spelled *Qing*, but pronounced "ching."

Chinoiserie French term meaning an object or decorative motif in the Chinese manner.

Chintz A fine cotton cloth usually having a printed design. Chintz originated in India in the seventeenth century and its name means spotted. Practically all modern chintz is produced with the *calendering* or glazing process, which makes it more resistant to dirt. In washing glazed chintz, the glaze is lost and cannot easily be renewed. The shiny surface and stiff texture produced by glazing also add to its charm. Chintz may be printed by blocks, copper plates, screens, or rollers, or it may be plain, in various colors. It is widely used for draperies, slipcovers, lamp shades, and upholstery.

Chip carving   Wood carving in which patterns are made with triangular and diamond-shaped depressions in the surface. An ancient technique, chip carving can be made using the simplest knife blades and chisels.

Chippendale, Thomas (1718–79)   Prominent English cabinet-maker and furniture designer. Published *Gentleman and Cabinet-Maker's Director* in 1754.

Chippendale, Thomas III (1749–1822)   Son of the above. Carried on his father's business with Thomas Haig, but became bankrupt in 1804. Worked mostly in the Regency style.

Chiton   A tunic worn by ancient Greeks, frequently shown in Classical ornament.

Choir   The section of a church where singing is done, part of the *chancel*.

Chosŏn   Period of Korean history better known as the *Yi*.

Chou dynasty   Chinese dynasty, 1045–256 B.C. Pronounced "Joe."

Chroma   A term used to designate the degree of intensity, brilliance, luminosity, or saturation of a spectrum color. Yellow, near the center of the spectrum, is the most brilliant but has the least saturation and palest chroma. Red has a medium chroma; and blue, the darkest chroma, with the greatest saturation. Sometimes the term *chromatic value* is used.

Chryselephantine   Compositions of gold and ivory, used for statuary and decorative objects since ancient Greek times.

Churriguera, José (1665–1725)   The most outstanding member of a Spanish Renaissance family of architects, who were mainly responsible for the Baroque and Rococo styles in Spain, later known as the *Churrigueresco*. Also a powerful influence in Latin America.

Churrigueresco   The seventeenth-century Spanish style introduced by the architect Churriguera. It is characterized by elaborate ornamentation and curved lines.

Ciborium   See *baldachino*.

Cimabue, Giovanni (1240?–1302?)   Florentine painter and a forerunner of the Italian Renaissance. Designed mosaics and frescoes. Pronounced "chee-mah-bway."

Cinquecento   Italian term for the sixteenth century in Italy (literally, "the 500s"). The first fifty years was considered the high period of Renaissance production.

Cinquefoil   French term literally meaning "five leaves." A pattern resembling a five-leaved clover. See also *trefoil* and *quatrefoil*.

Circassian walnut   A brown wood with a very curly grain, one of the handsomest finishing woods, which comes from the region near the Black Sea. It is used largely for furniture and paneling, and is very expensive.

Circulation   The traffic pattern in a room or building; the space devoted to the traffic pattern, such as hallways and corridors.

Cire-perdue   French term meaning "lost wax." An early method of making bronze castings, in which it was necessary to destroy the sculptor's original wax model as well as the mold, thereby allowing only one casting to be made. Pronounced "seer-pehr-dew."

Ciseleur   French term meaning a craftsman who ornaments bronze and other metals by chiselling.

Clapboard wall   A wall of planks laid horizontally, each one slightly overlapping the one below.

Classic   A term applying to a work of art of the first class or rank, or an established standard and acknowledged excellence; also used as a synonym for classical.

Classical   A term referring to the arts of Greece and Rome or any work based on such forms, often capitalized when used in this sense: Classical.

Clavated   Club-shaped. Applied to turnings used as furniture legs and stretchers, especially as seen in early Spanish furniture.

Clavichord   Seventeenth-century stringed instrument, ancestor of the piano.

Claw-and-ball foot   See *ball-and-claw foot*.

Clerestory   A story above an adjoining roof. Clerestory windows in the nave wall of a church are those above the roof of the side aisles. In general, a window placed near the top of a wall. Also spelled *clearstory*.

Cloche   Dome of glass fitted over a wood base to protect artificial flowers and waxworks from dust.

Cloison   French term for partition, applied to the divisions between sections of *cloisonné* or to divisions of stained-glass window tracery. Pronounced "klwa-zon."

Cloisonné   A type of enamel in which the various colors are separated and held by delicate metal partition filaments. From the French term *cloison*. Pronounced "klwa-zon-nay."

Cloister   A covered passageway around an interior courtyard; also the courtyard itself. A feature of medieval architecture.

Close chair   A latrine in the shape of a chair, with a chamber pot beneath a hinged seat. Sometimes called a *close stool*.

Cloven foot   Furniture foot resembling the cleft rear hoof of a deer.

Cloverleaf Cross   See *Bottonée Cross*.

Club foot   A foot used with the English cabriole furniture leg in the early years of the eighteenth century. The foot flares into a flat pad form that is round in shape. See also *bun foot* and *pad foot*.

Clustered columns   The system of placing several columns in close proximity or overlapping their shafts to form a support. Commonly seen in the European architectural styles of the Middle Ages.

CMG   Acronym for the Color Marketing Group, an organization that forecasts popular colors.

Cobb, John   See *Vile*.

Cobbler's bench   Shoemaker's bench with seat, last holder, bin, and compartments for pegs and tools.

Cochois, Jean-Baptiste   French cabinetmaker appointed *Maître Ébéniste* in 1770. Inventor of dual-purpose and changeabout furniture, such as a chiffonière that became a night table.

Cockfight chair   Chair for reading and writing or viewing sports events, used by straddling the seat and facing the back. The back had a small shelf. Popular in England from the Queen Anne to Chippendale periods. Similar to the French *fumeuse*.

Cocobolo   A dark brown wood with a violet cast. It takes a highly polished finish and has been used for modern furniture.

Coffer   An ornamental sunken panel in a ceiling, vault, or the lower surface of an arch, beam, or other architectural feature.

Coffre   French term meaning a chest.

Coiffeuse   French term meaning a dressing table.

Coin   See *encoignure*.

Coir   Fiber produced from coconut husks and used for doormats or roughly textured rugs.

Cold cutting   The process of forming glass objects by chipping at them with flint or quartz tools.

Collage   Composition made up of pieces of paper, photos, wallpaper, and the like glued together to a background surface to form a pattern or picture. Term sometimes used interchangeably with *montage*.

Colonial Revival style   Revival of the Colonial style, popular in the United States from the 1870s through the 1920s.

Colonial style   Strictly speaking, the style of the American colonies from their settlement to their independence. In practice, the term often includes aspects of American design after 1776.

Colonnade   A row of columns usually supporting an entablature and forming a part of the architectural treatment of a corridor or passageway.

Colonnette   A small column.

Color temperature   A figure, expressed in degrees Kelvin, of the warmth of the color of a particular light source.

Colorway   A color combination in which a fabric is available.

Colossal order   In architecture, an order rising to the height of two or more floors.

Colossus   A stature of a human (or god) that is much larger than life-size.

Columbo, Joe (1930–71)   Italian designer of furniture and lighting.

Column   An elongated cylindrical structural support, usually having a *base* and a *capital*. May be isolated or attached to a wall.

Comb back   A type of *Windsor chair*, with a central group of spindles that extend above the back and are crowned with an additional rail.

Commode   French term for a low chest of drawers, similar to—but generally wider than—a *chiffonière*.

Complementary colors   Pairs of colors opposite each other on the color wheel—for example, red and green or yellow and purple.

Compluvium   In a Roman house, the roof opening above the *atrium*.

Composite order   In architecture, a variant of the Corinthian order. The capital resembles the combination of an Ionic volute placed above rows of Corinthian acanthus leaves.

Composition   A term in design used to indicate a grouping of separate parts that produce the appearance of a coordinated whole and are aesthetically related to one another by position, line, and form.

Composition ornament   An ornament made of putty, plaster, or other material, that is cast in a mold and applied to a surface to form a relief pattern. Called *gesso* in Italy and *yeseria* in Spain.

Compotier   French term for a container for stewed fruit, jellies, jams, and the like.

Concrete   A mixture of sand and aggregate held together by *cement*. Concrete is *not* synonymous with cement, and the terms should not be used interchangeably.

Coney, John (1655–1722)   Important Boston silversmith, goldsmith, and engraver.

Confidante   French term for three seats attached as a single unit. The two outer seats are generally smaller and are separated from the center seat by arms. Hepplewhite illustrated such a piece in 1788. Sometimes seen as a *confident* or as a *canapé-à-confident*.

Confortable   French name used for an all-upholstered chair.

Connecticut chest   A type of Early American chest with double drawers, standing on four short legs; usually decorated with split spindles painted black. Also see *Hadley chest*.

Console   A wall table; an architectural element projecting from a wall to support a pier or cornice.

Console-desserte   French term for a serving table.

Continuous filament yarn   Yarn made from a group of extremely long parallel filaments. Yarns of this type include rayon, nylon, acetate, polyester, and other man-made materials, whereas most natural fabrics are made from spun yarn.

Conventionalization   The reproduction of forms in nature with such changes as to make them more suitable to the particular mediums or materials in which they are reproduced. Simplifying or exaggerating natural forms in reproduction.

Conversation chair   See *voyeuse*.

Conversation piece   Picture of a family group. See *genre*.

Cool color   Blue and the hues that are near blue, such as green, blue-green, blue-violet, and violet.

Coping   The uppermost part of a wall, or a protective course of stone that covers the top of a wall.

Copolymer finish   Nonblended mixture of enamel-like paints.

Corbeille   Also spelled *corbeil*. A sculpture representing a basket of flowers and fruits.

Corbel   A shoulder or bracket set in a wall to carry a beam; one of a series of such shoulders or brackets, each projecting slightly farther than the one below; any stone, brick, or timber-work projecting as a shoulder to carry a load.

Corbel arch   An arch formed by *corbels*.

Corduroy   A cotton or rayon cut pile fabric with ridges or cords in the pile that run lengthwise. Extensively used for upholstery, especially in modern treatments. Probably derived from the French term *cord du Roi*, meaning "king's cord."

Core   The area of a multifloor building, usually centrally located, that contains elevators, fire stairs, mechanical shafts, toilets, and other facilities of common use throughout the building.

Core forming   Glassmaking technique in which ropes of soft glass are wound around a core of earth or dung.

Corinthian order   The most elaborate, slender, and graceful of the Classical orders of architecture. The capital is enriched with two rows of acanthus leaves.

Corner block   In carpentry, the block of wood used to form a junction between the sides and head strip of door and window trim. In cabinetmaking, any block similarly used.

Corner cupboard   A triangular cupboard that fits into the corner of a room.

Cornice   The projecting, crowning portion of a classical *entablature*, uppermost of the entablature's three parts; or a crown molding.

Cornucopia   Decorative motif resembling a horn, its larger end overflowing with flowers, fruit, and so forth.

Coromandel   A hard, dark-brown wood with black stripes that grows in India and China and is much used for furniture. Also called *coromandel ebony* or *calamander*.

Coromandel lacquer   Chinese export lacquer ware, named for the site of the British East India Company's trading post.

Coromandel screen   A folding screen surfaced with Coromandel lacquer.

Cosmati   Members of the Cosmatus family of Rome, or those working in their style. The marble work practiced by them.

Couch   Layman's term for a *sofa*.

Coupe   French term for a high-footed cup.

Court cupboard   A low cupboard on short legs, after the French *court* for "short."

Cove   A concave surface often used to connect a wall and a ceiling; a cove-molding similar to the *cavetto*.

Cove lighting   Lighting, usually of a ceiling surface, from a source hidden by a recess or ledge.

Crapaud   French term for a low, upholstered armchair.

Crash   A group of cotton, jute, and linen fabrics having coarse, uneven yarns and rough texture. Used for draperies and upholstery, and often hand blocked or printed.

Crazing   Crackling in the glaze of ceramic ware.

Creamware   See *Queen's ware*.

Crédence   French Gothic term for a sideboard.

Credenza   A low furniture element with a work surface on top and files or storage compartments below. In office design, often placed behind a desk.

Crémaillère   French term for a swinging crane on a hearth.

Crêpe   A descriptive term applied to a large group of fabrics that have a crinkled or puckered surface, which may be produced by highly twisting the yarn in weaving or by a chemical process. The materials are made of cotton, wool, silk, or a combination of fibers, woven in any basic weave.

Crêpe de Chine   A type of crêpe in which the yarn is made of raw silk.

Crepidoma   The base of a Greek temple, usually three steps high, the highest step being called the *stylobate*.

Cressent, Charles (1685–1758)   Important French cabinetmaker in the Régence and early Rococo styles, appointed *Maître-Ébéniste* in 1715. Ébéniste to the Duc d'Orleans.

Cresson, Louis (1706–61) and his brother Michel (1709–c. 73)   French cabinetmakers. There were others as well with the same last name practicing in eighteenth-century France.

Crest rail   The top rail of a chair back, sometimes elaborately shaped and carved.

Cretonne   A heavy cotton cloth with printed pattern similar to *chintz*, though the designs are usually larger and less detailed. The background may be plain or a *rep* weave. The name comes from the Normandy village of Creton, where it was first produced. Cretonne is usually unglazed. It is useful for draperies and upholstery.

Crewel embroidery   A kind of embroidery with a pattern of varicolored wools worked on unbleached cotton or linen. The spreading design covers only part of the background, and usually includes a winding stem with various floral forms. It was used extensively during the English Jacobean period for upholstery as well as for draperies. The designs were often inspired by the East Indian *tree of life* motif.

Criaerd, Mathieu (1689–76)   French cabinetmaker of Flemish origin, appointed *Maître-Ébéniste* in 1738.

Crocket   Ornament used on the sides of pinnacles, usually leaf or bud shaped; commonly seen in Gothic art.

Crocking   The transfer of color from a dyed or painted fabric to another material by rubbing.

Cross   In general, a decorative device with a vertical bar traversed by a horizontal one; more specifically, such a device that invokes the Christian faith. See Table 6-2 for specific types of crosses.

Cross grain   Wood grain not parallel to the long dimension of the wood.

Cross section   A section cut at right angles to the long dimension of a building, room, or object. Also called a *transverse section*.

Cross-banding   A narrow band of wood veneer forming the frame or border of a panel; the grain of the wood is at right angles to the line of the frame.

Crosshatching   In a drawing, shading obtained by superimposing overlapping rows of closely spaced parallel lines.

Crossing   In church architecture, the intersection of nave and transept.

Crotch veneer   A thin sheet of wood cut from the intersection of the main trunk and branch of a tree, showing the irregular effect of the grain in that part of the tree.

Crown molding   The topmost molding, particularly the *fillets* and *cymas* placed above the *fascia* in a Classical *cornice*; or any molding at the top of a wall or structure.

Crumb cloth   A *floorcloth* for use under a dining table or sideboard.

Crusie   Scottish term for a shallow oil lamp made of iron.

Crypt   A subterranean chamber or burial area.

Cryptoporticus   In Roman architecture, a subterranean passage or a gallery formed by walls with a series of openings rather than by a *colonnade*.

Crystal   A clear and transparent quartz, resembling ice; an imitation of this material made in glass.

CSA   Acronym for the Canadian Standards Association, the Canadian equivalent of the United States's Underwriter's Laboratories, or *UL*.

Cube foot   See *block foot*.

Cubiculum   A bedroom in a Roman house.

Cucci, Domenico (c. 1635–c. 1704)   French cabinetmaker under Louis XIV, born in Todi, Italy.

Cuneiform   Literally, wedge-shaped. A system of writing on clay tablets used in Sumeria, Babylonia, and Assyria in which the characters were wedge-shaped.

Cupola   A small dome.

Cup-overlay   See *cased glass*.

Curing   The hardening process for freshly poured concrete.

Curule chair   A seventeenth-century chair design based on the Roman *sella curulis*. Its curved legs and curved seat meet at the center of the front, and its back is also curved.

Cusp or cusping   Pointed termination of a trefoil, quatrefoil, or cinquefoil in Gothic architecture.

Cusped arch   In Gothic and Islamic architecture, an arch composed of many small arches joining in pointed forms.

Cutting   A small fabric sample, usually about 3 inches square, smaller than a *memo*. A less professional term, taken from the fashion industry, is "swatch."

Cyclopean masonry Masonry using very large blocks, considered so heavy that only a monster such as the legendary Cyclops could lift them.

Cyma curve An S-shaped curve. In the cyma recta the curve starts and ends horizontally. In the *cyma reversa* the curve starts and ends vertically.

Cymatium See *crown molding*.

Cypress A wood with a light brown color, though it varies considerably according to its origin. It is a very handsome wood for interior use, quite inexpensive, adapted to all types of finish, and remarkably free from warping and twisting. This last property recommends it for kitchen use, or wherever heat and moisture are present. Cypress is too soft for flooring, though occasionally so employed, and too weak for structural timber; but for finish, few woods can equal it. It may be given a natural finish, or may be painted or stained to give almost any effect that may be desired, including imitations of many of the expensive hardwoods. A special treatment, to which cypress alone seems adapted, is so-called *sugi* finish, an imitation of Japanese driftwood. It is produced by charring the surface with a gasoline torch and rubbing off the charcoal with a wire brush. The spring wood burns away and the harder summer wood remains, leaving the grain in strong relief.

D

da Vignola, Giacomo Barozzi (1507–73) Italian Renaissance architect who wrote the *Treatise on the Five Orders* and revived the standardized proportions of *Vitruvius*.

da Vinci, Leonardo (1452–1519) Great Florentine painter, sculptor, architect, scientist, engineer, writer, and musician. One of the most imaginative and inventive figures of the Italian Renaissance.

Dado The lower portion of a wall, when treated differently from the surface above it. In the Classical styles the dado usually has a base, shaft, and cap molding (see *chair rail*), and is often paneled or ornamented. A low *wainscot*.

Dado cap The crowning or cap molding of a dado; sometimes called a *chair rail*.

Daguerreotype First photographic process invented in 1839 by Louis Daguerre in France. Involved the action of light on a plate sensitized by a solution of iodine and silver salts. Produced a faint image, which had to be viewed at an angle to be clearly seen.

Dais A low platform raised above the level of the floor and located at one side or at the end of a room. In medieval times, used for dining; in modern times, for speaking to a group.

Damascening or **Damascene work** A type of metal inlay. The design is incised by means of carvings or acid applications on a metal base, and the depressions are filled in with wires of different metals cut to fit. Usually the background is a base metal such as steel and the inlays are of more precious metal, such as silver or gold.

Damask A kind of *Jacquard* weave; also a fabric with a woven pattern similar to *brocade*, but flatter. In damask any combination of two of the three basic weaves may be used for the pattern and the background, provided that the weave of the pattern differs from that of the background. The pattern is made visible by the effect of light striking the portions of the fabric in the different weaves. Usually both *warp* and *filler* are of the same weight, quality, and color, though it may be woven in two colors. The pattern effect is usually reversible. Originally made of silk, damasks are now made of linen, cotton, wool, and any of the synthetic fibers, or of combinations of any two. The name originated with the beautifully patterned silks woven in Damascus during the twelfth century and brought to Europe by Marco Polo. Damask is widely used for draperies and upholstery.

Dancette See *chevron*.

Danforth, Samuel (active early nineteenth century) A pewterer working in Hartford, Connecticut.

Dante chair An X-shaped chair of the Italian Renaissance. Its legs cross and become the arm supports of the opposite side of the chair.

Daum French family of glassmakers, best known for work in the *Art Nouveau* style.

Davenport A *sofa*. The term was also used in England at the end of the eighteenth century for a small writing desk.

DC Abbreviation for direct current.

Dead seat or dead back In upholstered furniture, a seat or back made without springs.

Deal Generic term for any member of the pine family when it is cut up into planks. Also applied to furniture made of such planks. English and Early American use. Also used in England to designate standard merchandising dimensions of both pine and fir lumber. A misnomer for pine wood itself.

Decalcomania A process of decoration in which printed designs on thin paper are transferred to other materials, such as wood trays, ceramic plates, or glass vases. An item used in the process is called a *decal*.

Decorated style The term given to English Gothic architecture c. 1270–1370, characterized by elaborate, florid window tracery.

Découpage Decoration or picture-making by pasting down printed images, scraps of cloth, and other materials.

Dedicated circuit An electrical circuit independent of the main circuit, meant to be used solely by computers or other specified equipment.

Delanois, Louis (1731–92) French cabinetmaker appointed *Maître Ébéniste* in 1761. A protégé of Mme. Du Barry, he made a large amount of furniture for Versailles.

Delftware English term for the tin-glazed pottery and tiles made in Delft and in other Dutch cities. It was most often blue and white, but other colors were also sometimes used. In France, the term used is *faïence du Delft*, in Germany *Delfter Fayence*, and in Holland itself *Delfts blauw*.

Della Robbia family: Luca, Andrea, Giovanni, Girolamo (1400–1566) Italian Renaissance sculptors and originators of Della Robbia *faïence*.

Delorme, Philibert (1515–70) French court architect under Francis I, Henry II, and Charles IX.

Demijohn A narrow-necked glass or ceramic vessel encased in wickerwork.

Demilune French term meaning semicircular.

Demotic An abridged form of hieroglyphics, used by the Egyptians for ordinary correspondence conducted by the public scribes.

Denier   A measure of density in yarn.

Denim   A kind of heavy cotton cloth, of a twill weave. Usually a small woven pattern is introduced, or warp and filler may be in contrasting colored threads. Originally called *toile de Nîmes*. Used for upholstery and draperies and, in modern times, for clothing.

Dentil   A small square projecting block in a cornice, part of a series as in a molding.

Derbyshire chair   A popular name for a type of Jacobean chair of provincial origin.

Deskey, Donald (1894–1989)   American interior designer in the Art Deco style, best known for his interiors for the Radio City Music Hall, New York.

Desornamentado   The name applied to the severe style of architecture and decoration developed by the architect Herrera under the patronage of Phillip II of Spain. The word means "without ornament."

Desserte   French term for a serving table or sideboard.

De stijl   Dutch modernist design movement founded c. 1917.

DeWolfe, Elsie (1865–1950)   American interior designer, sometimes considered the first professional interior designer of modern times.

DFA   Acronym for Decorative Fabrics Association.

Dhurrie   A flat cotton carpet from India.

Diaeta   In a Roman house, a daytime resting area.

Diameter   The longest line that can be drawn through the center of a circle and touching the perimeter in two places; the length of such a line.

Diaper pattern   An allover or repeating pattern without definite limits, particularly such a pattern employing diamond shapes or a diagonal grid.

Diaphanie   In the nineteenth century, transparent designs applied to window glass in imitation of stained glass. See also *vitromania*.

Diatretum   See *cage cup*.

Diffrient, Niels (born 1928)   American industrial designer and furniture designer.

Diffuser   A device through which the light from a fixture is modified or redistributed.

Dimity   A sheer cotton fabric.

Dimmer   A device that, by controlling voltage, adjusts the intensity of light from a light source.

Dinanderie   Fifteenth-century metal alloy, the ancestor of pewter, being a combination of copper, tin, and lead. Used particularly in application to ornamental figures made in Dinant, Belgium.

Diorite   A type of dark-colored, hard stone much used in Egyptian sculpture.

Dip-dyeing   The process of dyeing textiles after they are woven by dipping whole pieces into the dye. Dip-dyeing is also known as *piece-dyeing*. See also *yarn-dyeing* and *stock-dyeing*.

Diphros   A Greek stool without arms or back, sometimes with folding legs. The plural is *diphroi*.

Dip-overlay   See *flashed glass*.

Dipteral   In Classical architecture, having two rows of columns along each side.

Diptych   A painting or relief on two adjacent panels.

Direct current   An electric current that flows in one direction only. Less commonly used than *alternating current*.

Directoire style   The Neoclassical style of the French Directory, 1799–1804.

Discharge printing   Textile printing technique involving the removal of color by bleaching agents.

Disk sander   A sanding machine with a circular rotating disk of sandpaper or other abrasive, used for smoothing floors and other surfaces.

Disk-turning   Flat circular turning used as furniture ornament.

Distant colors   Colors that produce the feeling of space and appear to recede, particularly light tones of blue and purple.

Distemper   Opaque watercolor pigments.

Distyle   Having two columns.

Dome   A hemispherical vaulted roof similar to an inverted cup.

Domino wallpaper   Wallpaper imitating marble graining, similar to that produced by the Dominotiers in France in the latter half of the sixteenth century.

Domus   A Roman town house.

Donjon   The massive tower that was used as a stronghold in medieval castles. Usually located in the interior of a courtyard. Also called a *keep*.

Doric order   The oldest and simplest Greek order of architecture, also used by the Romans.

Dormer window   A projecting upright window that breaks the surface of a sloping roof.

Dorser   A term of medieval origin meaning a fabric hanging between a wall and a piece of furniture.

Dos-à-dos   French term for a chair with two attached seats arranged so that they face in opposite directions. Also called a *tete-à-tete*.

Dosseret   A block, usually tapered, placed above a column capital to help receive the thrust of arches or vaults. Also called an impost block, a super-abacus, or a super-capital.

Dotted Swiss   See *Swiss*.

Double-hung sash   Window sash divided into two sliding sections, one lowering from the top and the other rising from the bottom.

Doublet   A pair, or the duplication of an outline in a surface pattern, usually in a reverse form.

Douglas fir   A western wood that resembles white pine in its physical properties, but has, in addition, a very handsome curly grain that makes it more suitable for natural or stained finish. It is strong and durable, works easily, and is adaptable to almost every type of use. It is, moreover, fairly inexpensive, being produced in great abundance, probably more than any other single species. There are several other species of fir, but they are of relatively little importance. It is used extensively for large plywood or laminated sheets.

Dou-gong   In Chinese architecture, the system of wooden brackets that supports the roof.

Dovetail   In carpentry, a wedge-shaped projection on the end of a piece of wood used to interlock with alternating similar grooves or projections on another piece of wood. See Table 2–1.

Dowel   In carpentry, a headless pin of metal or wood (or sometimes ivory) used to hold two pieces of wood together.

Downlight   A lighting fixture that directs light downward. It can be recessed in a ceiling plane or surface mounted.

Drape   The ability of a fabric to hang gracefully.

Draperies   Fabric hangings over or beside a door or window. The term "drapes" is not considered professional usage.

Draps de raz   Synonym for *arras*.

Draw curtain   A curtain that may be drawn along a rail or other support by means of a traverse arrangement of cords and pulleys.

Drawnwork   A pattern made by drawing threads from both the warp and weft of a fabric.

Dressed sizes   The finished dimensions of sawn lumber, smaller than *nominal* dimensions.

Dresser   A cabinet with drawers or shelves.

Dressoir   A dining room cupboard for the display of fine *plate*; a *buffet*.

Dreyfuss, Henry (1904–72)   American industrial designer.

Drier   A chemical preparation added to paint that causes it to dry quickly.

Dromos   A monumental approach to an Egyptian temple; a Greek racecourse.

Drop-in seat   An upholstered or caned seat that can be lifted from the chair frame for reupholstering or repair, in use since the early eighteenth century.

Drop-leaf table   A table with sections of the top that are hinged and can be lowered.

Drop-lid   A top or front of a desk hinged at the bottom and arranged to fall back, forming a surface for writing.

Drugget   An inexpensive fabric or *floorcloth* used under a dining table to protect a more valuable floorcovering beneath it. Sometimes called a *crumb cloth*.

Drum   Circular supporting wall for a dome. Also the cylindrical stones used to build up a column shaft. Any feature in cabinet-making resembling this shape.

Drum table   A drum-shaped table, usually with a three-footed base, and often with a leather top.

Drummer, Jeremiah (1645–1718)   Massachusetts silversmith.

Dry pipe automatic sprinkler system   A type of sprinkler system in which the pipes are normally filled with air or nitrogen, rather than water. Only when a fire is detected is the gas emitted and replaced with water.

Dry-point   An etching made from a metal plate upon which a picture has been scratched with a sharp-pointed metal tool.

Drywall   Common name for gypsum board or similar wall-surfacing material.

Dubois, René   Cabinetmaker to Louis XV and Louis XVI, appointed *Maître Ébéniste* in 1755.

Duchesse   A *chaise-longue*.

Duchesse-brisée   French term for a *chaise-longue* with separate footpiece.

Duck   A closely woven cotton fabric, sometimes called awning stripe or awning duck, of plain or ribbed weave. The stripe may be woven in, or painted or printed on one side only. Often given protective finishes against fire, water, and mildew. Similar to canvas.

Dumb-waiter   In eighteenth- and nineteenth-century England, a tiered table of circular surfaces cantilevered from a central sup-port. In modern usage, a small elevator for carrying material (not people) from one level to another.

D'Urso, Joseph Paul (born 1943)   American interior designer and furniture designer in a minimalist style.

Dust ruffle   Fabric ruffle extending to the floor from the bottom of a mattress cover, presumably keeping dust from gathering under the bed.

Dynasty   A succession of rulers, usually connected by family ties.

E

Eames, Charles (1907–78)   American furniture designer, product designer, exhibition designer, and filmmaker.

Eames, Ray Kaiser (1915–88)   Painter and designer, wife and partner of Charles Eames.

Early English style   Term given to English Gothic architecture c. 1170–1240, characterized by lancet windows. The style was followed by the *decorated* and then by the *perpendicular* styles.

Earthenware   Pottery of coarse clay.

Eastlake, Charles L., Jr. (1836–1906)   English architect and furniture designer. Advocate of Gothic revival. Wrote *Hints on Household Taste* in 1868.

Ébéniste   French term used to designate a high-grade cabinet-maker. See also *Maître Ébéniste* and *Menuisier*.

Ebony   A handsome dark heartwood of a tropical tree. Black ebony or gabon comes from Africa, is hard and heavy, takes a high polish, and is used for furniture and inlay. Macassar ebony is a coffee-brown wood with black streaks, and is used for modern furniture. Coromandel and striped ebony are names that are also applied to macassar ebony. Ebony is sometimes red or green.

Echinus   An ovoid shaped molding forming part of a Classical *capital*. It springs from the *shaft* of the column, just under the *abacus*.

Eclecticism   The borrowing and combining of art forms of various past periods, adapting them to contemporary conditions.

Ecran   French term for screen.

Ecran-à-cheval   French term for a frame with sliding panel used as fire screen.

Edging   A narrow decorative band around the rim of a piece of porcelain or other object. Also called *banding* or, in French, *filage*.

Edo   Old Japanese name for Tokyo.

Egas, Enrique de (died 1534)   Plateresco architect of the Spanish Renaissance, designed Holy Cross Hospital in Toledo (which is now destroyed).

Egg-and-dart   An ornament used as a molding decoration, consisting of ovoid forms separated by dartlike points. See also *bead-and-reel*.

Eggshell finish   A *semi-flat* paint finish, more lustrous than a *flat* finish, but less lustrous than *semi-gloss*.

Egyptian faïence   A glasslike ceramic made in ancient Egypt, characterized by its turquoise color.

Electric-discharge lamp   A type of lamp that produces light by sending an electric current through a vapor. Specific lamps of this type are sometimes named according to the vapor used, such as mercury-vapor lamp.

Electroplating   An electrical process of coating base metals with a very thin surfacing of a more valuable metal.

Elers, David, and John Philip Elers (fl. 1686–1722)   Two brothers of German descent active as potters in Staffordshire, England, in the last decade of the seventeenth century.

Elevation   In drafting, the vertical projection of any object. The delineation of an object or surface from in front, in which the dimensions are at specified scale, and not foreshortened as seen by the eye. Specifically, a drawing of a wall to scale to show its length, height, and various subdivisions and ornament.

Elgin marbles   The sculptures of the pediments and friezes of the Parthenon, named after Lord Elgin, who was responsible for having them removed to the British Museum in London.

Elliptical arch   An arch in the form of half an ellipse. See Table 7-1.

Elm   A strong and tough wood, with a less interesting figure than most other hardwoods. When treated with stain and polish, however, it makes a fine appearance. Because of its durability, it is used in large quantities for furniture, and its use for interior work might well be more extensive.

Embossing   A process of stamping, hammering, or molding a material so that a design protrudes beyond the surface.

Embroidery   The art of decorating a fabric with thread and needle. Its origin is a source of conjecture, but the form known today was developed in Italy during the sixteenth century. Handwork embroidery is little done today, and consequently most embroideries used in interior design antedate machine production.

Empire style   French Neoclassical style from the time of Napoleon's emperorship, 1804–15.

Empire style, Second   See *Second Empire style*.

Enamel   A colored glaze that is used to decorate metal and ceramic surfaces, becoming hard and permanent after firing; a substance that, in intense heat, vitrifies and adheres to a metal backing; a paint that imitates such a surface. Enamel ware refers to objects whose surfaces are treated with this material.

Encaustic painting   A method of painting with pigments mixed with hot wax. The wax mixture may be heated and applied with a spatula or brush, or it may be applied to the surface first, and the designs drawn with a stylus.

Encaustic tile   A ceramic tile first popular in medieval times, then again in England beginning in the 1830s and in America beginning in the 1870s. It is inlaid with a clay of another color before firing.

Encoignure or coin   French term for a *corner cupboard*.

Encrier   French term for an inkwell.

Endive   Decorative motif similar to a cluster of acanthus leaves, used in the Louis XIV period and by Thomas Chippendale.

Enfilade   A series of doors and/or windows aligned along a shared axis.

Engaged column   A column attached to a wall.

English bond   A brick pattern. See Table 19–10.

Engraving   The process whereby a design is incised with a sharp instrument upon a copper or steel plate; also, the impression so printed.

Enroulements découpés   See *strapwork*.

Entablature   The surfaces and moldings of a Classical order of architecture, consising of the *architrave*, *frieze*, and *cornice*, and forming the upper portion of the order. The portion of the order supported by the column.

Entasis   The slight curve on the shaft of a column. In the Roman orders the entasis reduces the diameter of the shaft at the capital to five-sixths the dimension of the diameter at the base. The curve is limited to the upper two-thirds of the shaft.

Entresol   French term for a *mezzanine* floor.

Epergne   An ornamental stand for the center of a dining table, with branching arms holding several containers that can be used for flowers, candles, or food. It is sometimes written with an accent (*épergne*), but because it seems to be of English origin rather than French it is more properly written without the accent.

Escabelle   An early French Renaissance stool or chair supported on trestles.

Escritoire   French term for a desk with drawers and compartments, one of the drawers having a hinged front that folds down to form part of a writing surface; such a drawer. See also *scrutoire*.

Escutcheon   A shield with a heraldic device. In hardware, it refers to a shaped plate for a keyhole or to a metal door fitting to which a handle or knob is attached. Also seen as *scutcheon*.

Espagnolette   In furniture design, a female bust carved on the post supporting a cabinet or table top. Used in the Louis XIV, Louis XV, and Régence styles.

Ester   A chemical compound used in the production of modern textiles.

Estrado   Raised platform or dais at one end of main living room in seventeenth-century Spanish houses.

Étagère   French term for a unit of hanging or standing open shelves.

Etchings   Prints from a copper plate upon which a drawing or design has been made by a metal tool and bitten into the plate by its immersion in acid.

Etruscan   Pertaining to the civilization that occupied Italy before the Romans; or, more rarely, another name for the *Tuscan order*.

Etui   French term for a container or box.

Eucalyptus   A pale reddish-yellow figured wood, much used in modern decoration and also in ship building. It is also called oriental wood or oriental walnut.

Evalde, Maurice   French (originally German) cabinetmaker, appointed *Maître Ébéniste* in 1765. He worked for Marie Antoinette and made a famous jewel cabinet for her.

Éventail   French term for a fan.

Évidence   Sixteenth-century French term for a *dressoir* or *buffet*.

Exedra   A public room in Roman or Pompeian dwellings; a semicircular niche or apse, often with raised seats.

Export wares   Products made for sale abroad, particularly Chinese and Japanese products meant for sale in Europe and America.

Extrados   The exterior curve of an arch.

F

Façade   A building face, often the most prominent or most richly ornamented.

Faïence   French term for a type of pottery made originally at Faenza, Italy. It is a glazed biscuit ware, and the name is now popularly applied to many such decorated wares. See also *Egyptian faïence*.

Faille   A kind of fabric with a slightly heavier weft than warp, producing a flat-ribbed effect. It is often all silk and lusterless. Used for trimmings and draperies.

Famille noire, verte, jaune, rose, and so forth   French names that designate particular types of Chinese pottery having a colored background. Translated, the words mean "black family," "green family," "yellow family," and "rose family."

Fan vaulting   Vaulting in the form of inverted half-cones with concave sides and ribs of equal length.

Fasces   A Roman ornament consisting of a bundle of rods enclosing an axe, for the Romans a symbol of power.

Fascia   In architecture, a molding whose section consists of a vertical flat surface, particularly the projecting crown molding of a *cornice*.

Fauces   In a Roman house, a narrow passage from the street to the *atrium*.

Fauteuil   French term for an upholstered armchair with open arms.

Fauteuil à châssis   French term for an armchair constructed with a simply built wooden frame inside a more elaborately carved frame. The inner frame can be removed for reupholstering.

Fauteuil de bureau   French term for a desk chair.

Fauteuil en gondole   French term for an armchair with a deeply rounded back.

Faux   French term for the imitation in one material of another; *faux-marbre*, for example, is the imitation of marble with paint or plaster, and *faux-satine* is the imitation of satin in some other fabric. Pronounced "foe."

Favrile glass   Name given to much of the glass produced by Louis Comfort Tiffany, some of it iridescent.

Federal style   American period of architecture and design, from the establishment of the federal government in 1789 to c. 1830. The leading designer of the period was Duncan Phyfe.

Felt   A material that is made by matting together and interlocking, under heat and pressure, woolen fibers, mohair, cowhair, or mixed fibers.

Fender   Metal guard placed in front of a fireplace to keep burning logs from rolling out.

Fenestration   The arrangement of windows in a building.

Feng shui   Literally meaning "wind and water," the Chinese art of propitious placement of buildings, building elements, furniture, and burial sites. Pronounced "fung shway."

Fenton, Christopher (1806–60)   Manufacturer of Bennington pottery.

Ferrocement   Construction with sand, cement, and wire mesh, often used for thin shells.

Ferroconcrete   Construction with steel-reinforced concrete.

Ferronerie velvet   Antique Venetian velvet made with patterns imitating delicate wrought iron forms.

Festoon   See *swag*.

Fiberglass   Fine filaments of glass woven as a textile fiber. It has great strength, yet is soft and pliable, and resists heat, chemicals, and soil. It is used for curtains and insulation.

Fiddleback chair   An American Colonial rush-seated chair of the Queen Anne type, with the back splat silhouetted in a form approximating a fiddle or vase shape.

FIDER   Acronym for the Foundation for Interior Design Education Research, the body that accredits schools of interior design in the United States and Canada.

Filage   French term for *edging*.

Filet lace   A lace produced by embroidering a pattern on a fine net, usually in thread similar to that of the net. See *lace*.

Filigree   Ornamental openwork in a delicate pattern. Usually refers to the pattern made by fine gold or silver wires or plates formed in minute lacelike tracery.

Filler   Threads that run crosswise through fabric from one *selvage* to another. Synonymous with *weft*.

Fillet   In architecture, a molding whose section consists of a small vertical flat surface, usually used at the start or finish of a curved molding.

Finial   An ornament used as a terminating motif. A finial is usually in the form of a knob, pineapple, or foliage.

Fir   See *Douglas fir*.

Firebacks   Metal linings, often ornamented and usually of cast iron, placed in a fireplace behind the fire to reflect heat and protect the masonry.

Firedogs   Small *andirons*.

Firehouse Windsor   See *captain's chair*.

Fireside figures   Wooden silhouettes painted to resemble royal personages, guards, pages, etc. Used as fire screens and fireplace adornment in Europe during the sixteenth and seventeenth centuries.

Firing   The term used in pottery manufacture to describe the heating of the clay in the kilns to harden it.

First style painting   First in a succession of four styles used in Roman wall painting. Employed in the second century B.C., the first style was noted for its imitation of marble and is also called the *incrustation style*.

Five-color ware   Type of Chinese porcelain popular in the Ming dynasty.

Fixed fee   A method of payment for design services in which the fee is agreed upon before the work is done.

Flamboyant   French term meaning flamelike, used to designate the late Gothic style in France, because the window tracery was designed in curved lines resembling conventional flamelike forms.

Flame-stitch   A fabric pattern of repeated jagged lines in different colors, resembling flames. Also called *bargello stitch* and *Florentine stitch*.

Flannel   Wool or cotton twilled fabric of coarse soft yarns, napped. The ends of the fibers are loosened by revolving cylinders covered with bristles. It is not a pile fabric. Used for interlinings.

Flap table   See *drop-leaf table*.

Flashed glass   Clear glass coated with a film of colored glass.

Flat glass   Glass made in flat sheets, such as common window glass. Also called *broad glass*.

Flat paint   The dullest, least lustrous type of paint or enamel finish.

Flemish bond   A brick pattern in which *headers* and *stretchers* alternate in each course, with headers placed over stretchers in a cross pattern. See Table 19-1.

Flemish foot   Furniture foot used in Flanders, England, and France during the seventeenth century.

Flemish scroll An S- or C-curved ornamental form, possibly of Spanish origin, but associated with Dutch and Flemish furniture design and used in England during the Restoration and William and Mary periods.

Fleur-de-lis The conventionalized iris flower used by the former kings of France as a decorative motif symbolizing royalty.

Fleury, Adrien French cabinetmaker who worked between 1740 and 1775.

Fleury cross Greek cross with each arm ending in a form like a *fleur-de-lis*. See Table 6-2.

Flocking or **flock printing** The application of very short fibers (flocks) to the surface of a fabric or paper to produce a textured effect. The flocks are held on with adhesive and may be applied electrostatically in order to keep them erect. They may also be shot onto the surface or mixed with the adhesive. Flock wallpapers are sometimes made by scattering powdered wool over a pattern printed in varnish on paper sheets.

Flood or **floodlight** A lamp that casts a broad beam of light.

Floor load The weight of elements supported by a floor, more commonly called a *live load*, and usually expressed (in the United States) in pounds per square foot.

Floorcloth An eighteenth- and early nineteenth-century floor covering made of canvas or heavy linen, sized and decoratively painted. Used frequently in entrance halls and dining rooms (like a *drugget*) to protect more expensive floor coverings underneath. In America, sometimes called an *oilcloth*. The German equivalent is called a *wachstuch-tapete*.

Florentine arch A semicircular arch that springs directly from a Renaissance column capital or pier and is trimmed with an architrave molding. Usually seen in series.

Florentine stitch See *flame-stitch*.

Fluid plan Type of planning in modern architecture, in which one room opens into another with little division between them, and the whole may be thrown open into one large area, if desired. Also called free plan or *open plan*.

Fluorescent lighting Lighting by means of electric-discharge lamps in which an arc of electricity passes through mercury vapor and phosphors, lining the tube, convert the resultant ultraviolet energy into light.

Flush In architecture, a term referring to any surface that is on the same plane or level as the surface adjoining it.

Flute A concave semicircular channel in a column capital.

Flutes or **flutings** Parallel concave grooves that are used to ornament a surface. In Classical architecture they are commonly seen on shafts of columns and run in a vertical direction. Spiral flutings are frequently used on furniture supports. Short flutings are used as a *frieze* ornament.

Flying buttress In Gothic architecture, an arch springing from the wall of a building to an exterior stone pier, intended as a counterthrust weight to resist the thrust of the arched roof.

Flying façade See *roof comb*.

Folwell, John (active last quarter of the eighteenth century) Cabinetmaker of the Philadelphia-Chippendale school, maker of the furniture for the Continental Congress. Called "the Chippendale of America."

Fontaine, Pierre-François-Léonard (1762–1853) French architect and designer, whose association with *Percier* made them the leaders of the Empire style.

Footcandle A measurement of light, 1 footcandle being the amount of light on 1 square foot of surface 1 foot away from a candle. One footcandle equals 1 *lumen* per square foot.

Foreshortening In drawing or painting, a diminishing perspective applied to an object or figure.

Form A stool or long bench without a back.

Fornasetti, Piero (1913–88) Italian decorative artist.

Fortuny, Mariano (1871–1949) Innovative fabric designer in silks and stenciled cottons. Born in Spain, he worked in Venice.

Forty-wink chair Obsolete name for a *wing chair*.

Forum In a Roman city, the area of general assembly.

Foulard A lightweight twill fabric; a small-scale repeat pattern.

Fourth style painting Last in a succession of styles in Roman wall painting. Popular in the second half of the first century A.D., it is also called the *intricate style*.

Fox edge A stuffed fabric tube used as edging on upholstered furniture.

Fractur painting Decorative birth certificates, marriage certificates, and the like made by Pennsylvania Germans during the eighteenth and nineteenth centuries.

Francis I style French Neoclassical style during the reign of King Francis I, 1515–47.

Frank, Jean-Michel (1895–1981) French interior designer and furniture designer.

Free-blown glass Glass blown into the air rather than into a mold.

French burl A term applied to a walnut that comes from Persia. It has small warts or knots that form on the side of the tree when young, giving the lumber an interesting curly grain. It is much used for cabinetwork.

French heading A term used in curtain making to designate the gathering of a drapery or valence into folds at regular intervals near the top. The folds are sewed together in place so that they will have a regular appearance.

French shawl See *swag*.

Fresco Method of painting on wet lime plaster with tempera or other lime-proof colors. The plaster absorbs the pigment, and when dry, the painting becomes hard and durable and a part of the plaster.

Fresquera Spanish term for an open-work hanging chest used for storing food.

Fret A Greek geometric band or border motif, consisting of interlacing or interlocking lines; also known as the *meander* or *key* pattern.

Frieze In architecture, the central part of the Classical entablature, below the *cornice* and above the *architrave*; or a horizontal painted or sculptured panel; or a horizontal member beneath a tabletop.

Frieze rail See *picture rail*.

Frigger Glassmaker's term for any small object made from leftover materials.

Fringe Trimming for draperies and upholstery. Threads on cords are grouped together in various ways and left loose at one end.

Frisé A pile fabric with uncut loops. The better quality is made with two sets of fillers to provide greater durability. Patterns are produced by cutting some of the loops, by using yarns of different colors, or by printing the surface. As it is used chiefly for upholstery, it is made of wool, mohair, or heavy cotton. The name is a French term meaning curled. Pronounced "free-zay."

Frit A granular material obtained from heating the ingredients of glass, then shattering the results in cold water. Frit is a basic component of *enamel* and of some *glazes*.

Fritware White ceramic ware made of frit, crushed quartz, and white clay, popular as an imitation of porcelain.

Fulcrum The headboard of a Roman *lectus* or couch.

Full-tone A color of which the hue is near its full chromatic value.

Fumeuse French term for a smoking chair, similar to a *cockfight chair*.

Furness, Frank (1839–1912) American architect working in and around Philadelphia.

Furring Building out from a surface by means of wood strips, metal channels, or other devices. A column or wall so built is said to be "furred out."

Fustian Twill-weave cotton fabric with a pile like that of *velvet*.

Fusuma-e Japanese paintings on sliding screens.

G

Gabardine Hard-finished twill fabric, with a steep diagonal effect to the twill, which is firm and durable.

Gabon Black ebony.

Gaboon Soft African wood, light brown in color, used for plywood, interior work, and sometimes for furniture.

Gabriel, Jacques-Ange (1698–1782) French architect of the Petit Trianon and Place de la Concorde under Louis XV.

Gadroon Elongated ovoid forms placed in a parallel series and projecting beyond the surface they enrich. Sometimes spelled *godroon* and derived from the French *gadron*.

Gaine An ornament or support in the form of a square post tapering toward the lower portion. It is usually crowned with a head or bust and has ornamental human or animal feet.

Gallé, Émile (1846–1904) French glassmaker and furniture designer in the Art Nouveau style.

Gallery A miniature railing placed along the edge of a shelf or tabletop, specifically the gallery-top table.

Galloon or galon A narrow close-woven braid used for trimming draperies and upholstery. A heavy *guimpe*.

Gambard, Aubertin French cabinetmaker in the services of the court at Versailles between 1771 and 1779, made *Maître Ébéniste* in 1779.

Garde-robe In architecture, a privy in a medieval castle; in furniture, an *armoire*.

Gargoyle A projecting stone waterspout grotesquely carved in fantastic animal or bird form. Used in Gothic architecture.

Garnier, Jean-Louis-Charles (1825–98) French architect best known for his Paris Opera House and for the Casino at Monte Carlo.

Garniture French term for any motif used for enrichment.

Garniture de cheminée A set of ornamental objects for the mantel or chimneypiece, sometimes consisting of three or five porcelain vases, sometimes of a central clock and flanking candlesticks.

Gate-leg table A *drop-leaf* table with rounded ends, its leaves supported by wing legs ("gates"). It originated in the Jacobean era and was popular in colonial America.

Gaudí i Cornet, Antoní (1852–1926) Spanish architect and furniture designer, working in a highly idiosyncratic version of the Art Nouveau style.

Gaudreau, Antoine Robert (1680–1751) Cabinetmaker who worked for the French court from 1726, on the Tuileries, and on the Bibliothèque Nationale. His name is sometimes spelled *Gaudreaux*.

Gauffrage Decorative embossing of leather.

Gauge A measure of thickness in sheet metal or metal tubing; the distance between rows of tufts in a tufted carpet; the diameter of a wire or screw; the exposed length of a roofing tile or shingle; a *screed*.

Gauze Thin, transparent fabrics made of leno or plain weave or a combination of the two. Formerly made of silk, it is now made of cotton, linen, wool, mohair, synthetic fibers, or combinations. Especially useful for *glass curtains*.

Gazebo Turret on a roof of a small garden shelter usually built of latticework; the shelter itself.

Gehry, Frank O. (born 1929) American architect and furniture designer.

Genie A creature of ancient folklore fashioned like a man but having supernatural powers; an imaginary form resembling this creature, used as an ornamental motif.

Genre French term for art that depicts the activities of the common people; also, a category of subject matter, such as landscape, still life, portrait, and so forth.

Georgian style English Neoclassical style during the period that begins with the crowning of King George I and ends with the Regency, 1714–1811.

Gesso A prepared plaster of chalk and white lead that may be cast to make repeating ornamental forms in relief to be applied to wood panels, plaster surfaces. It is also used as a base coat for decorative painting on picture frames, small wooden objects.

Ghiordes knot See *symmetrical knot*.

Gibbons, Grinling (1648–1720) English woodcarver and sculptor.

Gibbs, James (1682–1754) English architect and furniture designer. Published architectural designs in book form. Follower of *Wren*.

Gilbert, Cass (1859–1934) American eclectic architect, best known for his Woolworth Building, New York, 1913.

Gilding Surface decoration in gold by any of several techniques, although the term is sometimes used for surface decoration in other metals.

Gillow, Richard and Robert (active 1740–1811) English cabinetmakers in Lancaster (and later in London) who shipped much furniture to the British colonies in the West Indies. Robert Gillow (1701–73) was the father of Richard; another of his sons, Robert, was also a cabinetmaker.

Gimp See *guimpe*.

Gimson, Ernest (1864–1919) English designer of the Arts and Crafts style.

Gingham A lightweight, yarn-dyed cotton material, usually woven in checks or stripes. Useful for trimmings, draperies, and bedspreads.

Girandole French term for a type of branching chandelier; a wall mirror to which candle brackets are attached; or a wall sconce for candles.

Girard, Alexander (1907–93) American architect, interior designer, and textile designer.

Girardon, François (1628–1715) French sculptor whose work is at the Grand Trianon, Versailles, and the Louvre.

Girder A heavy beam used over wide spans and often supporting smaller beams or joists.

Glass cameos A type of *flashed glass* imitating carved onyx.

Glass curtain Curtains hung next to the glass of a window, usually sheer and translucent, often partially covered with heavier draperies.

Glaze In painting, a transparent layer of color that modifies but does not completely obscure the layer beneath; in pottery, a durable, glossy finishing layer.

Gloss paint Paint or enamel with the most lustrous finish.

Gobelins Important French decorative arts factory during the late seventeenth and eighteenth centuries, best known for its fine tapestries.

Goddard, John (1723–85) Prominent member of a family of cabinetmakers in Newport, Rhode Island.

Göggingen A German ceramics factory, active 1748–54.

Gold size An adhesive substance painted on a surface to which gold leaf is to be applied.

Golden section A proportion based on the division of a rectangle into two parts, with the ratio of the whole to the larger part being the same as the ratio of the larger to the smaller. It is the basis for many proportioning systems, including Le Corbusier's *Modulor*.

Gondola-back chair A chair of the Louis XV style with a rounded back that continued to form the arms.

Goodhue, Bertram Grosvenor (1869–1924) American architect. His buildings include the Byzantine-style St. Bartholomew's Church, New York, 1919, and the Nebraska State Capitol, Lincoln, 1922.

Goodison, Benjamin (died 1767) English cabinetmaker of the early Georgian period, supplier of furniture to royalty between 1727 and 1767.

Gooseneck lamp Light fixture on a flexible stem.

Göppingen A German ceramics factory active 1741–78.

Gopuram The monumental gateway to a Hindu temple; a lofty tower form that developed from such a gateway.

Gostelowe, Jonathan A Philadelphia cabinetmaker who produced furniture in the Chippendale style during the last half of the eighteenth century.

Gothic The style of art and architecture prevalent in northern Europe from the twelfth to the sixteenth century.

Gouache An opaque watercolor pigment, or any picture painted in this medium.

Goujon, Jean (1510–66) French architect and sculptor who worked on the Louvre.

Gouthière, Pierre (1740–1806) French *ciseleur* and metal sculptor, who made *ormolu* mounts, ornaments, and lighting fixtures.

Governor Winthrop desk An early American desk with an upper cabinet, three or four drawers below, and a hinged panel that opens to form a writing surface. It is named for the first governor of Massachusetts, John Winthrop, but it was probably not in use until after Winthrop died.

Go-with A supplementary fabric that complements the chief fabric in a decorative scheme.

Goya y Lucientes, Francisco de (1764–1828) Aragonese realistic artist and tapestry designer. Portrayed scathing and macabre scenes of Spanish life.

Graffito ware Ware of heavy pottery decorated with a roughly scratched design.

Grain The direction of fibers in wood or stone; in fabric, the direction parallel to the *selvages*.

Graining A painted imitation of the fiber lines of wood.

Grandfather clock Lay term for a *long-case clock*.

Granite Granular crystalline rock of quartz, feldspar, and mica. The hardest and most durable building stone.

Graves, Michael (born 1934) American architect and tableware designer in the postmodern style.

Gray, Eileen (1878–1976) Architect, interior designer, and furniture designer. Born in Ireland; worked mainly in Paris.

Great hall The large, two-storied central hall of a medieval castle, used principally for dining and entertaining.

Greatbach, Daniel (active 1839–60) Designer of Bennington pottery.

Greek cross A cross formed of two bars of equal length meeting at right angles. See Table 6-2.

Greek key ornament See *fret*.

Green chair An eighteenth-century American Windsor chair, often painted green.

Greene, Charles Sumner (1858–1957) and Henry Mather Greene (1870–1954) American architects, brothers and partners in a practice that produced notable buildings and furniture designs in an elegant, personal version of the *Arts and Crafts* style.

Greenough, Horatio (1805–52) American sculptor who first remarked that the design should be based on the function of the object and the possibilities of the material from which it is made.

Grenadine *Leno* weave fabric, similar to *marquisette*, but finer. Plain or with woven dots or figures.

Grendey, Giles (1693–1780) London cabinetmaker of the Georgian period, and exporter of furniture on a considerable scale. His furniture was of a simple, domestic type, much of it *japanned*.

Grès French term for stoneware.

Grisaille Decorative painting or glass work in monochrome gray and white.

Groin vault See *vault*.

Gropius, Walter (1883–1969) German architect and founder (in 1919) of the *Bauhaus*.

Grosgrain Ribbed or *rep* silk produced by weaving heavier *filler* threads so that they are covered with close, fine *warps*. Used for ribbons and draperies.

Grospoint See *needlepoint*.

Gross floor area Total floor area of a space or building, measured from the inside faces of its exterior walls and including circulation, interior wall thicknesses, interior columns, elevators, and mechanical shafts. See also *net floor area*.

Grosso, Niccolò (flourished c. 1500)   Italian Renaissance iron-smith.

Grotesques   In ornament, fanciful hybrid human forms, animals, and plants. In art, a combination of fanciful vegetation and fantastic human and animal forms, popular in ancient Rome and again in the Renaissance.

Grout   A mortar with a soupy consistency, used for setting tiles.

Guadamacileria   Spanish term for decorated leather produced by the Moors in Cordova, Spain, and elsewhere.

Guaranteed maximum cost   Also called an *upset price*. A cost limit that may be agreed upon in combination with another payment plan, such as an hourly fee.

Guas, Juan and Enrique (fifteenth century)   *Plateresco* architects of the Spanish Renaissance, perhaps of French origin.

Guéridon   In traditional usage, a small ornamental table, pedestal, or candlestand, a *torchère*. In modern usage, a serving table in a restaurant.

Guerite   A chair with a hooded top.

Guillemart, François (died 1724)   French cabinetmaker, active under Louis XIV and the Regency, appointed *Maître Ébéniste* in 1706. Built two commodes for the king's room at Marly.

Guilloche   In ornament, a band or border running pattern having the appearance of overlapping or interlacing circular forms.

Guimard, Hector (1867–1942)   French architect and furniture designer in the *Art Nouveau* style. His best-known works are his entrances to the Métro stations in Paris.

Guimpe   Narrow fabric, with a wire or heavy cord running through it, used for trimming furniture, draperies, etc., as an edging. Often used to cover upholstery nails. Also spelled *guimp* or *gimp*.

Guinoche   See *guilloche*.

Gul   A geometric emblem used in Islamic carpet patterns.

Gum   See *Red gum*.

Guttae   Conelike ornaments beneath the *mutules* of a Greek Doric order.

Gwathmey, Charles (born 1938)   American architect, partner with Robert Siegel in the firm of Gwathmey-Siegel.

Gypsum   A soft mineral consisting of hydrous calcium sulfate, it is used in *plaster of Paris*, *gypsum board*, and *gypsum plaster*. It is also used to retard the curing of Portland cement.

Gypsum board   A wallboard with a gypsum core and paper facings, much used for the faces of interior partitions. A trade name is Sheetrock, and common names are *plasterboard* and *drywall*.

Gypsum plaster   Often the base coat in plaster, a substance of gypsum, water, and aggregate.

H

Hadley, Albert (born 1920)   Important American interior designer, once a partner of *"Sister" Parish*.

Hadley chest   A type of Early American New England–made chest that stood on four feet, usually had one drawer, and was decorated with crude incised carving. Also called a *Connecticut chest*.

Haig, Thomas   English cabinetmaker, partner of Thomas Chippendale.

Hair cloth   A kind of cloth with cotton, worsted, or linen warp and horsehair filler. It is woven plain, striped, or with small patterns and is manufactured in narrow widths. As it is very durable, it is used for upholstery. It was popular during the mid-nineteenth century in England and America.

Half joint   A joint between two wood members in which the end of one is cut in half to provide a fit. See Table 2-1.

Half-timber   A type of house construction in which heavy wooden posts and beams form the skeleton of the structure. The area between them is filled in with brick, stone, or plaster.

Halfpenny, William (died 1755)   English architect, influential in popularizing the Chinese taste in architecture and decoration.

Halftone   A color that in tonal value is approximately halfway between white and black; a photoengraving process in which the image is rendered in a pattern of tiny dots.

Hallett, William (1707–81)   Popular English cabinetmaker under George II.

Hallmark   The mark or marks that designate that a piece of metalwork has received an official approval of quality, particularly the approval issued by Goldsmith's Hall, London.

Hall tree   A floor-standing coat rack, often placed in a front hall.

Halogen lighting   See *tungsten-halogen lighting*.

Hammer-beam truss   A form of roof support used during the early English Renaissance. It consists of a *Tudor arch* form in wood, each end of which rests on a large wooden bracket.

Hampton, Mark (1940–98)   American interior designer.

Han dynasty   Chinese dynasty, 206 B.C.–A.D. 220.

Hand   The tactile property of a fabric.

Handkerchief table   A folding table popular in the seventeenth century. Folded, its top was triangular and it was stored in a corner; unfolded, its top was square.

Hands of Fatima   Hand-shaped decorative motifs woven into Islamic prayer rugs.

Hard paste   Name used to identify hard-bodied or true *porcelain*, made of *kaolin*, or China clay. See also *soft paste*.

Hardouin-Mansart   See *Mansart*.

Harewood   Its common name is English sycamore. It has a fine cross-fiddle figure and is much used for cabinetwork, particularly after it has been dyed a silver gray. Also called silverwood or airwood.

Harland, Thomas (1735–1805)   Organizer of the clockmaking industry in Norwich, Connecticut.

Hassock   A heavy cushion or thick mat used as a footstool.

Hausmalerei   Pottery made in Germany by independent artists and amateurs, who decorated partially fired pieces and returned them to the kiln for glazing and further firing.

Haut-relief   See *relief*.

Header   The end of a brick; a brick laid at right angles to the face of a wall. See also *stretcher*. See Table 19-1.

Heddle   In weaving, the bar of a loom that separates groups of *warp* threads to allow passage of the *weft*. Looms are sometimes classified as single-heddle or double-heddle types.

Heisey glass   Glass manufactured in the late nineteenth century by the A. H. Heisey Company in Ohio.

Hellenistic   Period of Greek art under Alexander (third century B.C.) when the center of culture moved to Alexandria from Athens. The period, which was characterized by extreme realism and theatricalism, lasted until Greece became a Roman colony.

Hemlock A wood seldom used for finish, particularly in the eastern United States. The western hemlock, however, is a far better wood than the eastern variety and can be used for finish wherever strength, lightness, and ease of working are desirable. It greatly resembles white pine and may be used in a similar manner.

Hepplewhite, George (died 1786) Famous English cabinetmaker. His *Cabinet-Maker and Upholsterer's Guide* was published in 1788 and revised the following year. He produced satinwood and inlaid furniture in the classical style. No authentic pieces of his are known to remain.

Herati A floral motif on Islamic carpets.

Herrera, Juan de Spanish Renaissance architect of the Escorial (1575–1584) and protagonist of the *Desornamentado* style.

Herringbone A *zigzag* pattern.

Herter brothers American furniture designers and manufacturers prominent in the last half of the nineteenth century.

Hertz A measure of frequency, meaning cycles per second. Sometimes spelled *herz*.

Heurtat, Nicolas (born 1720) Parisian furniture maker, appointed *Maître Ébéniste* in 1755.

Hex sign A good luck symbol often placed on the exterior of buildings by the Pennsylvania Germans. It is usually in the shape of a circle, enclosing a six-pointed star or other motif.

Hexastyle A building or building element with six columns.

Hickory An American tree of the walnut family. Its wood is hard, tough, and heavy and is not used for decorative purposes.

Hicks, David (1929–98) English interior designer.

Hicks, Sheila (born 1934) American textile designer.

HID Acronym for high-intensity discharge.

Hieratic An abridged form of hieroglyphics, used by the Egyptians, and reserved for religious writings.

Hieroglyphics A system of writing used by the Egyptians, consisting of a combination of picture-writing and phonetic indications.

High-intensity discharge lamp A type of lamp that includes the mercury, metal halide, and high-pressure sodium lamps.

Highboy A tall chest of drawers supported by legs and usually crowned with cornice moldings or a pediment.

High daddy Eighteenth-century American term for a tall chest with six or more drawers in graduated sizes.

High relief See *relief*.

Hiking Distortion of a fabric due to swelling and shrinking as humidity changes.

Hispano-Mauresque The term used to designate Spanish art productions that show an influence of both Moorish and Renaissance origin. Sometimes spelled Hispano-Moresque.

Hitchcock, Lambert (1795–1852) Connecticut furniture designer, noted for his Hitchcock chairs, wood chairs with rush seats, usually painted black and stenciled with gold fruit and flower decoration.

Hoadley, Silas (1786–1870) Clockmaker and partner of Eli Terry.

Ho-no-ki Japanese name for magnolia wood.

Hoban, James (1762–1831) American architect who designed the state capitol in Columbia, South Carolina, and the White House in Washington.

Hoffmann, Josef (1870–1956) Austrian architect and designer, a pioneer of the modern style.

Holland, Henry (1740–1806) English interior designer and architect.

Holly A light-colored, fine-grained wood used for *marquetry*.

Hom Assyrian tree-of-life pattern.

Homespun A term applied generally to handloomed, woolen textiles. It is also a trade name given to imitations made on power looms. Useful for curtains and upholstery in informal settings.

Honeycomb work See also *muqarnas, stalactite work*.

Honeysuckle A decorative motif of Greek origin resembling a conventionalized fanlike arrangement of petals.

Hongmu A Chinese furniture wood.

Hooked rug A pile-surfaced rug made by pushing threads or strips of cloth through a canvas backing. By varying the colors of the pile, any pattern can be made.

Hope, Thomas (1770–1831) English cabinetmaker, designer of furniture in Regency style.

Horseshoe arch An arch whose total curve is greater than a semicircle. Used in Moorish and Spanish architecture.

Horta, Victor (1861–1947) Belgian architect, interior designer, and furniture designer in the Art Nouveau style.

Hortus The rear garden of a Roman house.

Hotelling A type of office design in which workspaces are temporarily assigned.

Hsia dynasty Ancient Chinese dynasty, once thought to have been legendary, now thought to have actually existed prior to 1766 B.C.

Huanghuali Chinese term for a fragrant rosewood used for furniture.

Huche French term for a hutch or chest.

Hue A color itself, as red or blue. Many tones of the same hue are possible. A tint is a hue with white added, and a shade is a hue with black added.

Huet, Christophe (died 1759) French decorative painter at the court of Louis XV.

Huet, Jean-Baptiste (1745–1811) French designer of *toiles de Jouy* for Oberkampf and wallpaper for Reveillon.

Huffelé, Lambert (died 1766) French cabinetmaker appointed *Maître Ébéniste* in 1745. He was a collaborator of André Charles Boulle, the son of the famous *ébéniste* of Louis XIV.

Humanism Intellectual trend of the Renaissance, away from the study of theology and toward the study of human activities.

Hunt table A crescent-shaped table, sometimes with drop leaves.

Hutch A chest, the most common piece of furniture in the Gothic household.

HVAC Acronym for heating, ventilating, and air conditioning.

Hydria A Greek water jar with three handles.

Hypostyle hall A large room with its roof carried on many columns.

Hz Abbreviation for *hertz*.

I

Icon   Portrait or image. In the Greek and Russian church, an image of a saint or sacred personage. Sometimes spelled *ikon*.

Iconostasis   In Byzantine churches, a screen, decorated with *icons*, that divides the *bema* from the *naos*.

Idealism   The tendency in art to express universal or spiritual concepts.

IDEC   Acronym for the Interior Design Educators Council.

IIDA   Acronym of the International Interior Design Association.

Ikat   A flat-weave textile, often patterned with resist dyeing techniques.

Ikebana   The Japanese art of flower arranging.

Illumination   Hand decoration of manuscripts in color and gold and silver. Practiced to a great extent by monks in the monasteries in the Middle Ages.

Imari ware   Japanese porcelain, often gilded and enameled.

Imperial carpet   See *three-ply carpet*.

Impluvium   In the *atrium* of a Roman house, the basin set into the floor that catches the rain falling through the *compluvium*.

Impost   A feature or structural member upon which an arch rests. The level of the top of such a member is called the impost line, and a transitional sculptural block, usually tapered, at this level is called an impost block. In most arches, the impost line coincides with the spring line; an exception is a *stilted arch*.

Impost capital   In Byzantine architecture, a column capital shaped like the base of an upside-down pyramid, similar to an *impost block*.

In antis   Between antae. See *anta*.

Incandescent lamp   Popular category of lamp in which a filament (most commonly, tungsten) is heated by an electric current until it becomes incandescent. See also *fluorescent lighting* and *tungsten-halogen lamp*.

Ince, William (active 1758–1810)   English cabinetmaker, follower of Chippendale, and partner of John Mayhew, with whom he published *The Universal System of Household Furniture* (1759–1763).

Incised   Cut into; said of a pattern or carving produced by cutting into a stone, wood, or other hard surface. The reverse of a relief carving, the pattern of which projects from the surface or background. Incised engraving is called *intaglio*.

Incrustation style   See *first style painting*.

India print   A printed cotton cloth made in India or Persia, with clear colors and designs characteristic of each country. The many colors are printed on a white or natural ground. Useful for draperies, bedspreads, wall hangings, and so forth.

Indian head   Permanent-finish cotton, smooth and lightweight. Colors are vat-dyed and guaranteed fast. Shrinkage is reduced to a minimum. Originally the trade name for a cotton *crash* made since 1831 by the Nashua Manufacturing Company.

Indienne   French interpretation of the Indian printed cottons that were being imported into France in the late seventeenth century and during the eighteenth century. French designers produced them to supply the demand for this type of fabric at a lower cost than that of the imported originals.

Indirect lighting   Lighting in which all or most of the light is directed toward a ceiling or other surface from which it is reflected toward the viewer.

Indiscret   French term for a settee formed of three linked armchairs in a spiral arrangement, popular during the Second Empire.

Infrared light   Light with wavelengths longer than those of visible light and with lower temperature than visible light. See also *ultraviolet light*.

Ingrain   A flat-woven wool or wool-and-cotton carpet with a *Jacquard* design; usually reversible. See *two-ply carpet*.

Inlay   Ornament or a pattern that is produced by inserting cut forms of one material into holes of similar shape previously cut in another material. The contrast of materials or colors produces the effect as well as the design of the cutting. Strictly speaking, *marquetry* is not inlay work, as both pattern and field are cut at the same time from a thin veneer. The inlaying of precious metals into base metals is called *damascening*.

Insula   A Roman apartment building.

Intaglio   Incised or countersunk decoration, as opposed to relievo decoration, which is in *relief*.

Intarsia   An Italian type of wood *inlay* often used for the carvings of choir stalls.

Intrados   The interior curve or *soffit* of an arch.

Intricate style   See *fourth style painting*.

Ionic order   One of the Classical orders of architecture. The characteristic feature of the capital of the column is the spiral-shaped *volute* or scroll. The standard proportion of the Roman column is nine diameters high.

Irisé   See *rainbow paper*.

Ironstone   A hard, opaque English stoneware imitating porcelain.

Isinglass   A translucent glass substitute made from mica or from animal gelatins.

Isometric drawing   A type of axonometric drawing in which the horizontal lines of the subject are represented by lines drawn at 30 and 60 degrees from the horizontal.

Isozaki, Arata (born 1931)   Japanese architect and designer.

Itten, Johannes   German-Swiss design educator and color theorist, an instructor at the Bauhaus.

Iznik ware   The most famous of Islamic ceramics and ceramic tiles, made from the end of the fifteenth century in blue-and-white patterns and later with red, green, and turquoise added.

J

Jabot   Fabric at the sides of a swagged valance. Also called *tails*.

Jacarandá   Brazilian *rosewood*.

Jacob, Georges (1739–1814)   One of the most famous cabinetmakers of France, active during Louis XVI, Directoire, and Empire periods. Appointed *Maître Ébéniste* in 1784.

Jacob-Desmalter, François Honoré (1770–1841?)   The son of Georges Jacob, very active as a cabinetmaker, in business with his older brother during the Empire period. Made furniture for Percier and Fontaine.

Jacobean style   The period in English history from 1603 to 1649, covering the reigns of James I and Charles I; the art, architecture, and ornament of that period. First phase of the Early Renaissance in England.

Jacobsen, Arne (1902–71) Danish modern architect, furniture designer, and product designer.

Jacquard, Joseph-Marie (1752–1834) Inventor of the Jacquard attachment for producing colored woven patterns in machine-made textiles.

Jacquard loom A mechanical loom type introduced by Joseph-Marie Jacquard in 1801.

Jacquemart and Benard French wallpaper manufacturers, successors to *Reveillon*, 1791–1840.

Jade An imprecise term for various hard stones used in decorative carving. Two types are nephrite (a calcium-magnesium silicate) and jadeite (a sodium-aluminum silicate).

Jali In Indian architecture, a perforated screen or lattice. Sometimes spelled jalee.

Jalousie A slatted window blind.

Jamb The vertical side of a door or window frame.

Japanning A process, much used in the eighteenth century, by which furniture and metalwork were enameled with colored shellac and the decoration raised and painted with gold and colors.

Jardinière French term for a plant container. Pronounced "zhar-deen-yare."

Jardinière velvet A silk velvet with a multicolored pattern resembling a flower grouping set against a light background. The weaving is most intricate, as there may be several heights of velvet and uncut loops set against a damask or satin background. Originally made in Genoa.

Jaspé A streaked or mottled effect in a fabric, produced by uneven dyeing of the warp threads. The name is derived from its resemblance to the mineral jasper. Pronounced "zhas-pay."

Jasper An opaque variety of quartz that may be bright red, yellow, or brown.

Jasper ware A name given by Wedgwood to a type of hard biscuit ware that he introduced in the late eighteenth century.

Jefferson, Thomas (1743–1826) President of the United States and father of the Classical Revival in the United States. Designed Monticello (his own house) and the University of Virginia.

Jensen, Georg (1866–1935) Danish sculptor, ceramicist, and metalsmith.

Jichimu Chinese furniture wood.

Johnson, Philip (1906–2005) American architect.

Johnson, Thomas (1714–c. 78) English author of books of eccentric and fanciful designs for carvings.

Joinery The craft of assembling woodwork by means of mortise and tenon, dovetail, tongue and groove, dowels, and so forth.

Joist A horizontal timber used to support a floor or ceiling.

Jones, Inigo (1572–1653) English Renaissance architect, responsible for the introduction into England of the Palladian style.

Jones, Owen (1809–74) English architect, designer, and writer. Author of *The Grammar of Ornament*, first published in 1856, and *Examples of Chinese Ornament* (later called *The Grammar of Chinese Ornament*) in 1867.

Joubert, Gilles (1689–1775) French cabinetmaker renowned for small furniture, such as tables and secretaries, ornamented with wood inlay. Date of appointment as *Maître Ébéniste* not def-initely established, but probably around 1749. Employed at court from 1748.

Judaica Objects related to Jewish religion or life.

Jugendstil In German, literally, "youth style." The German version of *Art Nouveau*.

Juhl, Finn (1912–1989) Danish architect and furniture designer.

Junction box In electrical wiring, a box protecting a junction of cables.

Jute A subtropical plant fiber used for carpet backing or for coarsely textured rugs.

Juvarra, Felipe (originally Filippo) Eighteenth-century architect, pupil of Bernini. Worked in Turin, and was called to Spain to design the Royal Palace.

K

KD Abbreviation for knockdown, a term applied to furniture that is shipped in pieces that must later be assembled. See also *package furniture*.

Kachina North American Indian doll-fetish.

Kahn, Louis I (1901–74) American architect.

Kakemono A Chinese or Japanese painting, mounted on brocade and hung on the wall without a frame. A print imitating such an art work is called a kakemono-e.

Kakiyemon, Sakaida (1596–1666) A Japanese painter and pottery artist who developed the use of colored enamel designs on Japanese porcelain. The name is also applied to decorations inspired by his works. His name is also spelled Kakiemon.

K'ang A Chinese platform for sitting or sleeping.

K'ang Hsi porcelain Chinese porcelain made during the reign of the *Ch'ing dynasty* emperor K'ang Hsi (1662–1722). Wares include *blue and white*, *famille verte*, and *famille jaune*.

Kantharos A Greek drinking cup.

Kaolin A white clay used in the manufacture of true *porcelain*, sometimes called *China clay*.

Kapok A filling material used for stuffing upholstery and pillows.

Kas Dutch term for a cupboard or wardrobe.

Kauffman, Angelica (1741–1807) Swiss decorative painter of furniture and interiors who worked in England. She was married to Antonio Pietro Zucchi.

Kaufmann, Edgar, jr Scholar of the history of architecture and decorative arts; curator of the *Good Design* exhibitions at the Museum of Modern Art, New York, in the 1950s.

Keep See *donjon*.

Kent, William (1685–1748) English architect, collaborated with his patron the Earl of Burlington in the design of Chiswick House. He was also a painter, landscape gardener, and furniture designer.

Kente Ceremonial cloth woven in strips by the people of Ghana. Once used as clothing only by kings and important chiefs, it is now in common use on special occasions; once made only of silk, it is now sometimes made of synthetic fibers.

Kettle base Synonym for *bombé*.

Kettle stand A stand or small table to hold a hot-water kettle for making tea or coffee. Popular in England in the eighteenth century.

Key ornament See *fret*.

Keyaki A Japanese wood, also known as *zelkowa*.

Keystone   The wedge-shaped central stone at the top of an arch.

Khaki   A heavy cotton twill fabric of an earthy color. The name is derived from a Hindu word meaning dust.

Kibotos   In ancient Greece, a wooden storage chest.

Kidderminster carpets   Carpets of the two-ply or ingrain type, made at the Kidderminster factory near Birmingham, England, beginning in the early eighteenth century. Popularly called *Scotch carpets*.

Kierstead, Cornelius (active during the seventeenth century) Dutch silversmith who worked in New York and New Haven and was noted for his tankard designs.

Kilim   Sometimes spelled khilim, khelim, or kelim. A double-faced rug without nap or pile, usually with hard-twisted wool filling and with a decorative geometric pattern.

King-size bed   A large double bed, generally 72 inches to 78 inches wide and 76 to 84 inches long.

Kingwood   A dark brown wood with black and golden yellow streakings. It comes from Sumatra and Brazil and is a fine cabinetwood.

Kiri   A Japanese wood, also known as paulownia.

Kiva   A ceremonial chamber in Native American structures of the American Southwest.

Kjaerholm, Poul (1929–1980)   Danish furniture designer.

Klee, Paul (1879–1940)   Swiss painter and instructor at the *Bauhaus*.

Kline   A Greek bed. The plural is *klini*.

Klinium   A sofa (*lectus*) in the Roman dining room (*triclinium*). Also called a *lectus tricliniaris*.

Klismos   A Greek type of chair having a concave curved back rail and curved legs.

Kneehole desk   Desk with a solid lower portion but with an opening for the knees of the person seated at it.

Knee-kicker   A tool used in fastening carpet to a tackless strip.

Knock-down furniture or **KD furniture**   Furniture sold as a kit of parts that the buyer must assemble. The English term is *package furniture*.

Knole sofa   A sofa, similar to one made in 1610–20 for the country house called Knole in Kent. It has arms that can be lowered to convert it into a daybed.

Knoll Associates   American furniture company founded in 1938.

Knorpelwerk   German term for *auricular style*.

Knot-work   Decorative motif typical of Celtic art, incorporating ribbonlike elements elaborately interlaced.

Knotted rug   An Oriental rug weave in which the surface or pile is formed by the ends of threads knotted around the warps, the weft threads serving merely as a binder.

Kondo   In Japan, the chief room of a Buddhist monastery.

Korina   A wood resembling *primavera*, and having a light yellow color. Used for wall veneers.

Koryo   One of the great periods of Korean history, beginning in the tenth century and ending in 1392. Along with the *Yi*, it constituted Korea's "golden age."

Kraak porcelain   Chinese blue and white porcelain made for export to the Netherlands.

Krater   A wide-mouthed, two-handled bowl used by the Greeks for mixing wine and water.

Kuft work   In India, the name for *damascening*.

Kuramata, Shiro (1934–90)   Japanese furniture designer and interior designer.

Kuri   Japanese term for chestnut wood.

Kuwa   The Japanese term for the wood known in the West as white mulberry.

Kwabornament   Dutch term for *auricular style*.

Kylin   A chimerical beast often used in Chinese decoration.

Kylix   A flat-shaped Greek drinking cup on a slender center foot.

L

Lac   A resinous fluid secreted by an insect, an ingredient of *shellac*.

Lacca contrafatta   Italian term for imitation lacquer work popular in the eighteenth century.

Lace   An openwork textile produced by needle, pin, or bobbin by the process of sewing, knitting, knotting (tatting), or crocheting. Real lace is a handmade product, but in the late eighteenth century, machines were invented to imitate the hand productions. Probably first made in Greece, lace enjoyed a great revival in Renaissance Italy, particularly in Venice. Among the principal types are the following:
- *Brussels*, of several varieties
- *filet*, embroidered on a net
- *Irish*, principally of the crocheted type, although the *Limerick* variety is made on a net and the *Carrickmacross* variety is cut work
- *Nottingham*, a general term used for machine-made productions, particularly inexpensive lace curtains made in one piece
- *reticella*, a combination of drawn and cut work
- *Valenciennes, Cluny, Duchesse*, and *Chantilly*, elaborate bobbin-made patterns in which the ornament and fabric are identical

Lacquer   Specifically, a hard varnish obtained from the sap of the lacquer tree (an Asiatic sumac), the base of Chinese and Japanese lacquer; more generally, any varnish or shellac dissolved in alcohol.

Ladder back   A chair having a ladder effect produced by the use of a series of horizontal back rails in place of a splat.

Ladychapel   The most revered and elaborately decorated chapel at the east end of a cathedral, dedicated to the Virgin.

LaFarge, John (1835–1910)   American stained-glass artist.

Lake   A type of pigment, the result of combining a dye and a *mordant*.

Lalique, René (1860–1945)   French glass artist and jeweler in the Art Nouveau style.

Lambrequin   French term for a valance board for draperies.

Lamé   Fabric woven with metallic yarn or bonded with a metallic layer.

Lamp   The part of a lighting fixture that is the actual light source. The lighting professional's term for what is commonly called a light bulb or tube.

Lampas   A patterned textile with a compound weave having two *warps* and two or more *fillers*. The distinguishing feature is that the pattern is always a *twill* or plain weave, the background in *satin* or plain weave, or both, and may be in two or more colors. Philippe de la Salle made it famous, and it was much woven in the eighteenth and nineteenth centuries, so that the pattern is usually classical in inspiration. It is similar to a two-colored *damask*, but heavier. Silk lampas was much used for upholstery in the eighteenth century. Some fabrics commonly called *brocade* are more properly called lampas.

Lancet Tall, narrow window topped by a pointed arch.

Lang-yao See *sang de boeuf*.

Langley, Batty (1696–1751) English architect, designer, and author of practical guides for designers, carpenters, gardeners, and others.

Langlois, Peter (active c. 1763–1770) English cabinetmaker, probably an immigrant Frenchman, who worked in a metal technique based on that of Boulle, using brass and tortoiseshell.

Lannuier, Charles-Honoré (1779–1819) French cabinetmaker who produced Directoire- and Empire-styled furniture in New York; a contemporary and competitor of Duncan Phyfe.

Lantern In architecture, a small structure placed at the crowning point of a dome, turret, or roof, with openings for light to come through. Frequently its purpose is decorative only.

Lapautre, Jean (1618–1682) Royal French architect under Louis XIV.

Laqué French term for *lacquered*.

Lararium In a Roman house, a shrine for household gods.

Larsen, Jack Lenor (born 1927) American textile designer.

LaSalle, Philippe de (1720–1803) French designer, manufacturer of textiles, and inventor of devices for weaving, under Louis XVI. Most famous for his *lampases* and realistic floral patterns.

Lath The base for constructing an interior partition, supporting plaster, Gypsum board, or some other finish material, and most commonly made of either wood strips or expanded metal.

Latin cross A cross form with the vertical arm longer than the horizontal one. See Table 6-2.

Latrobe, Benjamin Henry (1764–1820) American architect who designed the Bank of Pennsylvania and who introduced the Greek revival to the United States.

Latten An alloy of copper and zinc similar to brass, but with a small amount of tin added. It was used in the American colonies, often for making spoons.

Latz, Jean-Pierre (c. 1691–1754) French cabinetmaker from the period of Louis XV.

Laurel A dark, reddish-brown wood with a pronounced wavy grain. It takes a high polish.

Lavabo French term for a washstand or washbowl, often with a fountain or water supply; the support for such an object.

Lavoro di basso rilievo Italian term for work in *low relief*.

Lawn See *batiste*.

Leading Lead strips that hold glass panes in a window construction.

Lebrun, Charles (1619–1690) French architect, director of fine arts under Louis XIV, and, after 1663, head of the *Gobelins* works. He was responsible for the interior design of many rooms at Versailles, including the Galerie des Glaces, and for the design of many pieces of royal furniture. Sometimes spelled *Le Brun*.

Le Corbusier (1887–1965) Important Swiss-born French modernist architect and furniture designer.

Lectern A pedestal support for a large book or Bible.

Lectus A Roman couch.

Lectus tricliniaris See *klinium*.

LED Acronym for light-emitting diode, producer of lighted signage often used on appliances and electronic equipment.

Lekythos A long narrow-necked flask used by the Greeks for pouring oil.

Lelarge, Jean Baptiste (1743–1802) Appointed *Maître Ébéniste* in 1786. There were three members of the same family with the same name. This one worked at Fontainebleau and made *bergères* and *fauteuils*.

Leleu, François (1729–1807) Appointed *Maître Ébéniste* in 1764. Famous for marquetry. Worked under Oeben at Versailles. Also worked for Mme. Du Barry.

L'Enfant, Pierre Charles (1754–1825) French architect and engineer who arrived in America at the end of the eighteenth century. He planned the city of Washington, DC.

Leno Type of weave in which pairs of *warp* yarns are wound around each other between picks of *filler* yarns, resulting in a loosely woven net effect. Various versions of this weave are used for *glass curtain* fabrics and others.

Lenôtre, André (1613–1700) French architect famous for his garden designs at Versailles and Vaux-le-Vicomte.

Lescot, Pierre (1510–78) French architect under Henry II; worked on the Louvre.

Letto Italian term for a bed.

Levasseur, Étienne (1721–98) Appointed *Maître Ébéniste* in 1767. Made furniture for the Petit Trianon. Very celebrated.

Liebes, Dorothy (1899–1972) American textile designer, noted for strong colors.

Lierne In a Gothic church, a short rib connecting two main ribs of a vault.

Light bulb Lay term for a *lamp*.

Lighthouse clock A small late eighteenth-century clock covered by a glass bell.

Lignereux, Martin Eloy (1750–1809) French designer associated with Jacob-Desmalter c. 1798 in the furniture business, chiefly during the Louis XVI period. Previously he had directed the design, making, and sale of various decorative accessories. Firm believed to have been discontinued in 1800.

Lime A white powder made from limestone and used in mortar; whitewash.

Limoges French center for the production of *porcelain* and *enamel*.

Lincrusta or **Lincrusta-Walton** A thick, embossed, leatherlike wall covering made of linseed oil, developed in England in 1877 by Frederick Walton, the inventor of *linoleum*.

Linenfold A carved Gothic panel enrichment that resembles folded linen or a scroll of linen.

Lingam Phallus-shaped symbol of the Hindu god Siva (pronounced "shee-vah").

Linnell, John and William William (c. 1703–63) established an English cabinetmaking and upholstering firm c. 1730. His son John (1729–96) joined the firm and continued it after his father's death. They worked in Rococo, Chinese, and Classical styles, and designed furniture for some interiors by Robert Adam.

Linoleum A durable floor covering made of linseed oil and flax, invented in England in 1864 by Frederick Walton. The name derives from two Latin words—*linum*, meaning flax, and *oleum*, meaning oil.

Linoleum cut   A print made from blocks of linoleum that have been cut into grooves to form a picture or pattern.

Linsey-woolsey   Early American textile, a blending of wool and linen.

Lintel   A horizontal beam, supported at each end, that spans an opening.

List   See *selvage*.

Lit   French term for a bed, pronounced "lee." Some of many variations include:
- *Lit à la duchesse* A bed with a canopy suspended from the wall or ceiling; more rarely, a bed with a canopy supported by four bedposts
- *Lit à la Française* A bed placed with its long side against a wall with a canopy above
- *Lit à la Polonaise* A bed with pointed crown canopy
- *Lit à travers* A bed with its long side against a wall, but without a canopy
- *Lit canapé* A sofa bed
- *Lit d'ange* A bed with a small canopy cantilevered from the back bedposts
- *Lit de repos* A daybed

Lite or **light**   A pane of glass.

Live load   The load on a structure, not including the weight of the structure itself, but consisting of things added to it, such as interior constructions, furniture, stored material, and occupants.

Load bearing   Providing structural support to the parts of the building above.

Lobate   See *auricular* style.

Lock, Matthias (active 1740–69)   Early English Rococo designer, a disciple of Chippendale and later of the Adam brothers.

Loewy, Raymond (1893–1986)   American industrial designer.

Loggia   Italian term for a room or area with an open arcade or colonnade on one side.

Long-case clock   Clock with a tall, narrow case designed to hold long pendulum weights. Since the late nineteenth century, more commonly called a *grandfather clock*.

Loos, Adolf (1870–1933)   Austrian architect and designer, an early modernist.

Lost wax process   Called *cire-perdue* in France, the method of casting glass or metal with a wax model that is destroyed in the process.

Louis XIV   French Baroque style identified with the reign of King Louis XIV, 1643–1715.

Louis XV   French Rococo style identified with the reign of King Louis XV, 1715–74.

Louis XVI   French Neoclassical style identified with reign of King Louis XVI, 1774–93.

Louis-Philippe   French Neoclassical style identified with the reign of King Louis-Philippe, 1830–48. It led to the *Second Empire style*.

Louver   One of a series of slats placed at an angle to protect an opening from sun or rain.

Loveseat   A *sofa* or *settee* large enough for only two people.

Low relief   See *relief*.

Low-voltage lighting   Lighting using less than standard voltage.

Lozenge   In ornament, a diamond-shaped motif.

Lumen   A unit measuring the flow of light energy.

Luminaire   A complete lighting fixture, including the *lamp*.

Lunette   In ornament, a form resembling a crescent or half moon.

Luster   A thin metallic (most often, copper or silver) glaze used on pottery to produce a rich, iridescent color. Used in Persian ceramics, Spanish and Italian faïence, and English and American ware. Also spelled *lustre*.

Lustre   French term for a table light or wall sconce in crystal.

Lutyens, Sir Edwin (1869–1944)   Important and highly eclectic English architect.

M

Macassar   A seaport city in the Dutch East Indies exporting a type of ebony to which its name is given, macassar ebony. See also *antimacassar*.

Machicolate   Literally, to furnish with a projecting gallery. In medieval castle architecture, machicolations were openings in the vault of a portal or passage or in the floor of a projecting gallery, for use in hurling missiles down on an enemy.

Mackintosh, Charles Rennie (1868–1928)   Brilliant Scottish architect who developed a highly personal version of *Art Nouveau*. His most notable building, designed early in his career, was the Glasgow School of Art.

Mackmurdo, Arthur H. (1851–1942)   English architect and designer inspired by John Ruskin and William Morris.

Macret, Pierre (1727–96)   Appointed *Maître Ébéniste* in 1758. Made furniture for Versailles.

Madrassa   Islamic religious school.

Mahal or **mahall**   Indian term for a palace.

Mahogany   A wood with a beautiful reddish color and handsome grain that has long made it a favorite for furniture. It is imported from South America and the West Indies, the various islands of which produce several distinct species. The best of these is found in Santo Domingo, and is sometimes known as Spanish mahogany. White mahogany or *primavera* has a creamy color and comes from Mexico. Mahogany is easily worked, takes a high polish, and warps and shrinks but little. Honduras mahogany is known as *baywood*. In addition, mahogany for various purposes comes from Cuba, Africa, Nicaragua, Costa Rica, and the Philippines.

Maître-Ébéniste   French term for a master cabinetmaker, a position of honor in the furniture makers' guild. Unlike the *menuisier*, the *ébéniste* worked with veneers, and the term comes from the French word for ebony, a wood frequently used for veneer.

Majolica   Italian and Spanish pottery coated with a tin enamel and painted with bright colors. See *faïence*. Also spelled *maiolica*.

Majorelle, Louis (1859–1926)   French furniture designer and manufacturer. His factory at Nancy produced pieces in *Art Nouveau* style.

Malachite   A bright green stone, found chiefly in Russia.

Mallet-Stevens, Robert (1886–1945)   French architect and designer.

Maltese cross   A cross in which the four similar arms are wedge-shaped with their points meeting. See Table 6-2.

Mameluke rugs   Cut-pile rugs or carpets made in Egypt.

Manchette   French term for a padded arm cushion on a chair or sofa.

Manchu dynasty   See *Ch'ing dynasty*.

Mandala A Hindu or Buddhist symbol of the universe, often a circle enclosing a square.

Mandapa In a Hindu temple complex, a large open hall.

Mandorla Literally meaning "almond," an Italian term for an almond-shaped halo surrounding religious figures in some paintings and reliefs. Also called a *vesica piscis*.

Mannerism Italian art style c. 1520–90 that disregarded some Classical rules in favor of exaggeration, energy, and distortion.

Mansard roof Hipped roof with two pitches, the lower one steeper than the upper, named for François Mansart, who popularized it.

Mansart, François (1598–1666) French Classical architect. His works include the Orléans wing of the Château of Blois and the Church of the Val-de-Grâce, Paris.

Mansart, Jules Hardouin (1646–1708) Royal architect of Louis XIV. His most notable works include the Dome of the Invalides and parts of the Palace of Versailles, including the Hall of Mirrors. He was a great-nephew of François Mansart. His name is also seen as Jules Hardouin-Mansart.

Mantel The projecting shelf above a fireplace.

Manwaring, Robert (active 1765) English designer and author, known only through his publications of the *Carpenter's Complete Guide to the Whole System of Gothic Railing* and *The Cabinet and Chair-Maker's Real Friend and Companion*, 1765. His designs have originality, though the books' perspective is bad and the engraving is crude.

Maple A wood similar to birch, though usually lighter in color. It is adapted for the same uses, including flooring. Straight-grained maple is one of the handsomest woods for interior finish, while the curly or *bird's-eye* varieties are used for veneered furniture. It is very hard and strong.

Maquette Miniature or model room, usually furnished to show the appearance of a proposed scheme of decoration.

Maratti, Carlo (1625–1713) Italian artist, known for a decorative frame composed of twisted ribbons and bands of acanthus leaves.

Marbling A painted imitation of the veining of marble.

Mare, André French designer, partner of Louis *Süe*.

Marlborough foot A *block foot*.

Marlborough leg A heavy, straight-grooved furniture leg, with a *block foot*. Much used for English and American mahogany furniture in the mid-eighteenth century.

Marot, Daniel (1661–1720?) French designer of ornament, paneling, and furniture under Louis XIV. After the revocation of the Edict of Nantes, he emigrated to Holland and established the French Baroque style there; later, he introduced it to England.

Marquetry A flush pattern produced by inserting contrasting materials in a veneered surface. Rare, grained, and colored woods are the most common materials for marquetry, but thin layers of tortoise-shell, ivory, mother-of-pearl, and metals are also occasionally seen.

Marquise French term for a small sofa or wide armchair.

Marquisette A sheer cloth having the appearance of gauze and woven in a *leno* weave. The cotton, silk, rayon, nylon, glass, or wool thread is usually hard-twisted to give it greater serviceability. An excellent *glass curtain* material.

Martin brothers (Guillaume, Étienne-Simon, Julian, and Robert) Eighteenth-century French cabinetmakers during the reign of Louis XV. The four brothers introduced Chinese lacquer as a finish on French furniture. The finish and the furniture so treated are called *vernis Martin*.

Martines, Antonio An eighteenth-century Spanish silversmith whose work was influenced by Pompeian discoveries.

Masjid Arabic or Persian term for a *mosque*.

Masonry Natural or artificial stone (such as brick) used for building construction; the art of building with such material.

Massok Indian term for a plain, hand-loomed, heavily ribbed cotton *rep* fabric.

Mastaba An Arabic word meaning bench. Applied to the early mound-shaped tombs of Egypt, and later to those built underground.

Matelassé A fabric with two sets of *warps* and *wefts*. Its embossed pattern gives the effect of quilting. Imitations are stitched or *embossed*.

Mathsson, Bruno (1907–88) Swedish interior designer and furniture designer.

Mayhew, John See *William Ince*.

McCobb, Paul (1917–69) American furniture and product designer.

McComb, John (1763–1853) American architect, designer of the New York City Hall in association with Joseph Mangin, a French engineer.

McIntyre, Samuel (1757–1811) Colonial American architect, master carpenter, and woodcarver, who designed many of the houses built in Salem, Massachusetts, in the Classical tradition.

Meander See *fret*.

Medallion In ornament, a circular or oval frame having within it an ornamental motif.

Medium The substance, material, or agency through which an artist expresses ideas; in painting, the vehicle or liquid with which color pigment is mixed or thinned, such as water, oil, wax, and so forth.

Megaron In the architecture of Crete and Mycenae, an oblong (or, more rarely, square) hall with a columned porch.

Meier, Richard (born 1934) American architect and furniture designer.

Memo A fabric sample, usually about 10 inches square, larger than a *cutting*.

Memory The ability of a fabric to recover its original state after being stretched.

Menagère French term for a dresser with open shelves for crockery.

Mendelsohn, Erich (1887–1953) German expressionist architect.

Mendl, Lady See *Elsie DeWolfe*.

Mensa In a Roman house, a low dining table; a slab that forms the top of an altar.

Menuisier A French joiner working with chairs and other furniture made from solid wood. See also *ébéniste*.

Mercerized materials Fabrics that have a lustrous surface produced by subjecting the material to a chemical process. The cloth is treated in a cold, caustic alkali bath while held in a state of tension. By this treatment the yarn is changed from a flat, ribbonlike shape to a rounded form, making the cloth more lustrous, more durable, and more susceptible to dye. Mercerized cotton has a silky appearance. The process is called after its originator, John Mercer, an English calico printer.

Mercury switch or **mercury-contact switch**   An on/off switch for interior wiring in which the electric contact is by means of a tube of mercury and the switching is therefore silent.

Mercury vapor lamp   An electric-discharge lamp producing light by passing an electric arc through mercury vapor.

Méridienne   French Empire term for a sofa or daybed with one arm higher than the other.

Merino   Spanish sheep, the ancestor of nearly all the wool-growing sheep in the world; the wool from such sheep.

Mesquita   Spanish term for a mosque.

Metal cloth   A fabric the surface of which has a metallic appearance. It is made by weaving cotton warp threads with tinsel filling yarns. The latter are made by winding strips of metallic substance around a cotton yarn. Creases cannot be removed from this material. Useful for trimmings.

Metal halide lamp   An electric-discharge lamp producing light with metal halides.

Metope   The space between the triglyphs of a Doric entablature, often featuring a sculptured relief.

Meubles   French term for furniture. The singular form, for one piece of furniture, is meuble. The term *mobilier* is also used.

Mezzanine   A low-ceilinged story between two high ones, especially one placed above the ground floor. In French, an *entresol*.

Mezzotint   A type of copper-plate engraving that produces an even gradation of tones, as in a photograph.

Michelangelo Buonarotti (1475–1564)   Major Italian Renaissance painter, sculptor, architect, and poet. Called the father of the Baroque.

Micron   A unit of length used in measuring textile fiber thickness. It is equal to one-millionth of a meter or 0.000039 inch.

Mies van der Rohe, Ludwig (1886–1969)   Important German architect and furniture designer, the last head of the Bauhaus and later director of the school of architecture at the Illinois Institute of Technology, Chicago.

Mihrab   A prayer niche in a Mohammedan mosque located so that the worshiper faces in the direction of Mecca. Sometimes spelled *mehrab*.

Millefleurs   French term literally meaning "a thousand flowers." A term particularly used to designate a fifteenth-century Gothic tapestry pattern showing numerous small leaves, plants, and flowers.

Minaret   Tower attached to a Mohammedan mosque, with one or more balconies from which Muslims are summoned to prayer. A large tower or lighthouse is called a minar.

Minbar   The pulpit in a mosque. Sometimes spelled *mimbar*.

Ming dynasty   Chinese dynasty, 1368–1644.

Miniature   A small painting in illuminated manuscripts, also any very small painting or undersized object.

Minstrel gallery   The small balcony above the main entrance to the great hall of a medieval castle where the entertainers performed during the feasts.

Minton   English ceramics factory founded in 1796.

Mirador   In Spanish architecture, a bay window or other element used as a lookout.

Miroir   French term for mirror.

Miter   In carpentry, a corner junction of two strips of wood or other material, the end of each piece being cut at a similar angle, as in the corner of a picture frame or door trim. See Table 2–1.

Mixing table   Small sideboard or butler's cabinet, with compartments at the end for bottles.

Mobilier   French term for furniture. The term *meubles* is also used.

Mock-up   A rough model, usually built full size.

Modacrylic   Type of synthetic textile fiber.

Modillion   The projecting bracket used to support the Corinthian cornice. Also frequently used as an independent decorative motif in architectural and furniture design.

Module   A measuring unit for an architectural order. The full diameter or half diameter of the lower portion of the shaft of the column.

Modulor   A proportioning system developed and advocated by the modern architect *Le Corbusier*.

Mohair   A yarn and cloth made from the fleece of the Angora goat. The fiber is wiry and strong, making a very durable textile. It is now woven in combination with cotton and linen into many types of plain, twill, and pile fabrics. Widely used for upholstery.

Moiré   A finish on silk or cotton cloth that gives a watermarked appearance. Woven as a *rep*, the marks are produced by engraved rollers, heat, and pressure applied to the cloth after it has been folded between selvages. The crushing of the ribs produces a symmetrical pattern along the fold. The pattern is not permanent, as cleaning and pressing tend to remove it. When made of synthetic fibers moiré holds the marks better than when made of all silk. Pronounced "mwa-ray."

Monk's cloth   A heavy cotton fabric of coarse weave. Groups of *warp* and *weft* threads are interlaced in a plain or basket weave. Used for hangings and upholstery in informal rooms. Sometimes called friar's cloth.

Monochrome or **monotone**   Decoration in a single color or different tints of one color. See also *grisaille*.

Monolithic   Literally, one stone. A structural mass of one solid piece, such as a concrete wall.

Monostyle   Having a single column.

Montage   A composition made by fitting together parts of various drawings or photographs and attaching them to a background.

Montigny, Philippe Claude (1734–1800)   French cabinetmaker appointed *Maître Ébéniste* in 1766. Repaired much of the furniture made by Boulle. That furniture which he made was inspired by the work of Boulle, but he copied his predecessor with taste.

Monument   In interior electrical work, a small, monument-shaped outlet box attached to the floor. Sometimes called a *tombstone*.

Moon gate   A circular opening in a wall large enough for human passage. Characteristic of Chinese architecture.

Moquette   An uncut pile fabric similar to *frisé*. It is woven on a *Jacquard loom* and has small, set patterns of different colors.

When used for upholstery, it is made of mohair, wool, or heavy cotton. A coarse type is used for floor coverings.

Mordant   A substance, such as a metallic salt, used to give permanence to dyes.

Moreen   Wool upholstery fabric of the seventeenth and eighteenth centuries, often with a wool warp and a filler of wool, linen, or cotton.

Moríne   An earlier spelling of *moreen*.

Morris, William (1834–1896)   Important English designer, founder and leader of the English Arts and Crafts movement.

Morris chair   Reclining upholstered chair designed by William Morris.

Morse, Samuel F. B. (1791–1872)   American painter and lecturer on fine arts as well as the inventor of the wireless telegraph.

Mortar   Binding material between bricks or stones, usually made from lime, sand, and water.

Mortise   A hole cut in a piece of wood and intended to receive a *tenon* projecting from another piece of wood. See Table 2-1.

Mosaic   Small squares of colored stone or glass (*tesserae*) set in cement and arranged in a picture or pattern. A popular and beautiful form of mural decoration used extensively in Early Christian and Byzantine art.

Mosque   Mohammedan place of worship.

Mother of pearl   Irridescent material that lines some seashells and is used in decorative trim or inlay work. Sometimes hyphenated: *mother-of-pearl*.

Mounts   Ornamental or utilitarian metal work such as handles, drawer pulls, and *escutcheons*, used on cabinetwork.

Mozarabic   The arts in the Moorish parts of Spain in which Christian elements were in evidence.

Mudejar   A transitional style of art in the Christian parts of Spain in which Moorish and Italian Renaissance details were seen in the same design.

Mullion   A vertical or horizontal bar that acts as a division piece between windows or glass panels.

Multifoil   A pattern having many-lobed forms; an arch having more than five foils or arcuate divisions. Sometimes called a scalloped arch.

Munsell color system   Color system devised by Albert F. Munsell, in which all colors are identified by three qualities: hue, value, and chroma.

Muntin   A narrow bar that divides a window into individual glass panes. It is more slender than a mullion.

Muqarnas   In Islamic architecture and ornament, collections of small *corbels* that form a transition from one plane to another. Also called *honeycomb work* and *stalactite work*.

Murphy bed   A bed that can be folded away into a closet.

Murrhine   Fragile opalescent glassware made by the Romans and used for ornamental and useful purposes.

Muslin   A plain-woven, white cotton fabric, bleached or unbleached. Used for sheeting and other household purposes. Originally woven in the Mesopotamian city of Mosul.

Mutule   A projecting block above the *triglyph* of a Doric *frieze*.

Myrtle   A blond wood with fine markings. It is much used in cabinetwork for inlay and veneer.

N

Nacré   French term for *mother of pearl*.

NAHB   Acronym for the National Association of Home Builders.

Nail claw   Tool used for removing nails.

Nanmu   A wood used in China for building and decoration. It is aromatic and turns a deep rich brown with age. It is also called *Persian cedar*.

Naos   The main interior space of an ancient Greek or Roman temple, later becoming synonymous with *nave*.

Narthex   A porch on the west end of a church, originally an accommodation for the unbaptized who were not allowed to enter the church. Sometimes called an *antechurch*.

Nash, John (1752–1837)   One of the foremost English architects of the Regency period.

Naturalism   The close imitation or representation in art of natural objects. Opposed to *conventionalization*.

Nave   The main or central part of a cruciform church, usually flanked by *aisles* and terminated by an *apse*.

NCIDQ   Acronym for the National Council for Interior Design Qualification, the body that prepares and administers a uniform examination for the profession of interior design.

Near colors   Colors that have an approaching tendency, therefore making a room appear smaller than it is actually. Dark tones, particularly those derived from red and yellow, are near colors.

NEC   Acronym for the National Electrical Code.

Needlepoint   An old-fashioned cross-stitch done on net, heavy canvas, or coarse linen. The threads are wool. The effect achieved is that of a coarse tapestry. Petit point and gros point are two variations of this embroidery. *Petit point* is very fine, made on a single net, and has about 20 stitches to a lineal inch. *Gros point* is coarse, made on a double net, and has about 12 stitches to the lineal inch.

Nelson, George (1908–1986)   American architect and designer of furniture, exhibitions, graphics, and products, also known for his theoretical writings about design.

Neoclassicism   The revival of the forms and ornament of Classical civilization, primarily that of Greece and Rome. The prevailing style in Europe and America from the middle of the eighteenth century to the middle of the nineteenth.

Néo-Grec   A branch of *Second Empire style* that focused on ornamental motifs with Greek, Roman, Egyptian, and Etruscan origins.

Net   Open weave fabric. There are various types, as follows:
- *bobbinet*, machine-made net with hexagonal meshes
- *cable net*, coarse mesh
- *dotted Swiss*, a net with small dots
- *filet net*, square mesh, used as base for embroidery (the handmade variety having knots at corners of meshes, the machine-made variety having no knots)
- *maline*, net with a diamond mesh
- *mosquito net*, coarser than others, of cotton
- *novelty net*, made in a variety of effects
- *point d'esprit*, a cotton net with small dots over its surface in a snowflake effect

Net floor area   The occupied area of a room or building, not including partition thicknesses, mechanical shafts, and vertical transportation. Compare *gross floor area*.

Neutral colors   Colors that result from the mixture of several spectral hues. Pigments that have an admixture of white or black. Tints and shades. Hues that are at low chromatic values.

Newel post   A heavy post at the termination of the handrail of a stairway.

Niche   A recessed or hollow space in a wall, intended to hold a statue or ornament.

Niello   A decorative inlay, black in color, in a metal surface.

Ninon   Often called triple voile. Sheer rayon used for *glass curtains*, made in various weaves.

Noguchi, Isamu (1904–1988)   American sculptor and furniture and *luminaire* designer.

Nominal dimensions   The dimensions of sawn lumber before it is dried and planed. The finished or dressed sizes of lumber are generally ½ inch less in width and ⅜ inch less in thickness than the nominal dimensions.

Non-bearing wall   A wall or partition supporting only its own weight. Also called a non-load-bearing wall.

NOPA   Acronym for the National Office Products Association.

Norman   Term used for Romanesque architecture in the lands ruled by the Normans (such as England after 1066).

Nosing   The leading edge of a stair tread, usually rounded.

Nøstetangen   Norwegian glass factory founded in 1741.

Nottingham   A machine-made lace curtain material first made in Nottingham, England; a ceramics factory in the same town.

Nove   Ceramics factory near Venice founded in the late eighteenth century.

Novelty weave   General name for a variety of modern fabrics, having unusual textural effects produced by using *warp* and *filler* of different size, color, or fibers, nubby yarns, or the introduction of tinsel, metallic threads, or even cellophane. Rayon and cotton are especially adaptable.

Noyer   French term for walnut.

NRC   Acronym for noise reduction coefficient, a measure obtained by averaging the sound absorbing coefficients of an acoustical material at four different frequencies (250, 500, 1000, and 2000 Hz.)

Numdah   A wool-embroidered felt rug made in Kashmir.

Nursing chair   English term for a *chauffeuse*.

Nylon   Generic term for a proteinlike chemical that may be formed into bristles, fibers, sheets, and so forth. Has extreme toughness, elasticity, and strength. Its fibers are used in almost all types of textiles where silk and rayon were previously used.

O

Oak   The most important of all woods for interior use. It may be sawed, either plain or quartered, the latter being generally preferred for fine work because of the striking pattern produced by the medullary rays. Plain oak is less expensive, because there is less waste in its production, and it is used for the less important features or where durability rather than beauty is the chief consideration. Oaks are divided into over fifty species, but the differences in the wood are not great. They are all hard, durable, and very similar in grain. The wood lends itself well to carving of all kinds and is also well adapted to panelling. Because of its open grain, oak should be treated with a filler before applying stain or varnish. English and French oak have finer graining than the American variety.

OBD   Acronym for the Organization of Black Designers.

Oberkampf, Christophe-Philippe (1738–1815)   French textile designer, creator of *toile de Jouy*, and founder of the Jouy manufactory.

Objects of vertu   Literally, objects of excellence. The term is used in the antiques trade for small decorative objects made of precious metals and precious stones.

Objet d'art   French term for any small art object.

Obverse   The side of any medal, coin, or medallion, upon which is the principal design. Opposite to *reverse*.

Occhio di bue   Italian for *oeil-de-boeuf*.

Octastyle   A building or building element with eight columns.

Oculus   A round window or roof opening; more rarely, a circular ornament or *rondel*.

Odeum   In Roman architecture, a small roofed theater. It was based on a Greek model called an odeion. The term *theatrum tectum* is also sometimes used.

Oeben, Jean François (died 1765)   French cabinetmaker of the Louis XV period. Appointed *Maître-Ébéniste* in 1754. Worked for Mme. Pompadour and trained Riesener. His younger brother, Simon François Oeben, was also an ébéniste, and their sister married cabinetmaker Martin Carlin.

Oecus   In a Roman *domus*, a large room for entertaining guests.

Oeil-de-boeuf   French for "bull's eye," a round or oval window.

Oeil-de-perdrix   French for "partridge's eye," a type of porcelain decoration consisting of dots ringed with smaller dots.

Office landscape   Type of office layout in which private offices are replaced by freely disposed workstations, their arrangement based on patterns of communication among workers. It was pioneered by the German Quickborner team. The German term is *Bürolandschaft*.

Off-white   A color that is a pure white with a very slight admixture of a definite hue.

Ogee or ogive   A molding or an arch form composed of two opposing curves whose convex sides meet in a point. A *cyma* curve.

Oilcloth   A fabric having a cotton base that has been coated with a preparation of linseed oil and pigments. Its finish may be smooth, shiny, dull, or pebbled. Used for table and shelf coverings and other household purposes. In America, the term is also sometimes used as a synonym for *floorcloth*.

Oiled silk   A thin silk that has been waterproofed by a process of soaking the silk in boiled linseed oil and drying it. It was originally used for surgical purposes, but has also been used as a drapery fabric, particularly for kitchen and bathroom curtains.

Oinochöe   The Greek name for a wine pitcher.

Olbrich, Josef (1867–1908)   Austrian architect and designer, an important figure in the Vienna Secession movement.

Olive   A light yellow wood with greenish-yellow figures. It takes a high polish and is popular for inlay purposes.

Ombré   A pattern consisting of stripes in gradations of a single color; a type of wallpaper more commonly known as *rainbow paper*. The word is derived from the French word for shadow.

Onion dome   A bulbous dome shaped like an onion, popular in Islamic architecture and seen in The Netherlands, Russia, and India.

On-the-glaze   A pattern produced by colors applied to the pottery after the glaze has been added to the *biscuit*.

Onyx   A beautifully banded, slightly translucent quartz.

Open plan   A building plan with minimal built limitations between areas; in office design, a plan featuring work stations without doors or full-height partitions enclosing them.

Oppenordt, Gilles-Marie (1672–1742)   Of Dutch origin, a French interior designer and ornamentalist of the *Régence* period.

Optical balance   An approach to symmetry obtained by making the two halves of a composition similar in general appearance but not identical in detail.

Order of architecture   A term used to designate a Classical column and entablature. The pedestal and attic are sometimes included. There are three Greek orders, the Doric, Ionic, and Corinthian, and five Roman orders, the Tuscan, Doric, Ionic, Corinthian, and Composite.

Organdy   A lightweight, crisp fabric of muslin construction woven of very fine cotton threads. It may be white, piece-dyed, or printed, and is used for trimmings and glass curtains.

Organzine   A raw silk yarn. A textile made with such yarn.

Oriel window   A large projecting window that is supported by a *corbeled* brick or stone construction.

Ormolu   Gilded bronze, brass, or copper, often used for mounts on furniture, particularly that of the Louis XIV period. From the French *or moulu*, meaning "ground gold."

Orrefors   Swedish glass factory founded in 1898.

Orthogonal   A drawing or construction in which chief elements are parallel or perpendicular to one another.

OSHA   Acronym for the Occupational Safety and Health Administration.

Ostvald color system   Color system devised by Wilhelm Ostvald, in which all colors are identified by hue, value, and level of saturation.

Ottoman   A large footstool designed to be used with an easy chair; a plain, heavy, ribbed fabric.

Ovolo   In architecture, a convex molding with a section approximating a quarter circle.

P

Package furniture   English term for *knockdown furniture*. See *KD*.

Pad foot   A *club foot* that rests on a small disk, often used as a termination for a cabriole leg in an early eighteenth-century chair. See Table 19-3.

Pagoda   In China and Japan, a tower, usually having several stories, built in connection with a temple or monastery. The word is of European origin, the Chinese equivalent being *ta*, and the Japanese equivalent being *shoro* (or sometimes *tahoto*).

Pahlmann, William C. (1900–87)   A leading American interior designer of his time.

Paisley   Printed or woven design in imitation of the original Scotch shawl patterns made in the town of Paisley.

Palampore   Hand-painted or resist-dyed cotton, chintz, and calico, made before the invention of block printing for fabrics. Original *tree of life* prints were so made in India.

Palazzo   Italian term for a palace or important town house.

Palette   A small rounded board on which a painter mixes colors; the range of colors in use.

Palisander   A brown wood with a violet cast. It comes from Brazil and the East Indies and is much used for modern furniture.

Palissy, Bernard (1510–1589)   Early French Renaissance potter.

Palladian window   A three-part window, with two rectangular sections flanking a central arched section. Although named for Andrea Palladio, who used them frequently, they were used also by Bramante and Sansovino, and described by Serlio. When the tripartite form is used for unglazed arcades, it is called a Palladian motif.

Palladio, Andrea (1518–1580)   Italian Renaissance architect and author of a book on antique architecture. Noted designer of villas and churches.

Palmette   A conventionalized ornamental motif derived from a fanlike branch of the palm tree.

Panel   A surface usually enclosed by a frame. Sometimes a surface of limited dimensions without a frame. In a sunk panel the frame is above or in front of the panel area. In a *bolection* panel, the panel area is above or in front of the frame.

Panel-hung system   A furniture system in which elements such as files and work surfaces are hung from vertical panels.

Panier   French term for a basket or scrap basket.

Panné   A term applied to pile fabrics having a shiny or lustrous surface. This appearance is produced by having the pile pressed back.

Papelera   Spanish term for a small cabinet intended to hold papers and writing materials.

Papier-mâché   French term for pulped paper, molded while wet into various ornamental forms or useful shapes.

Papier-peint   French term for patterned wallpaper, used in the late seventeenth century to distinguish such paper from the plain type previously used.

Papillon, Jean (1661–1723)   French wallpaper designer and maker.

PAR lamp   Acronym for parabolic aluminized reflector, a type of *lamp*.

Parcel   Partly, as in the term "parcel gilt," meaning partly gilded.

Pargework   Ornamental plaster or stucco work applied to a flat surface in relief. The term is most often used when the work represents the wooden structural members that may lie above or beyond it. Sometimes called *pargetry*.

Parian ware   Term used in England and America for unglazed *porcelain* or *biscuit*.

Paris enamel   *Basse-taille* work made in France beginning in the fourteenth century.

Parish, Mrs. Henry II (1910–94)   Known familiarly as "Sister" Parish, a leading American interior designer and partner with *Albert Hadley* in the firm Parish-Hadley.

Parquet   Flooring made of strips of wood laid in a pattern. The pattern of such a floor is sometimes known as *parquetry*.

Parsons, Frank Alvah   Design educator, head from 1910 to 1940 of the Chase School, founded in 1896 and renamed in his honor in 1940.

Parsons table   Straight-legged table first designed at the Paris branch of the Parsons School of Design.

Parti   French term for a design scheme or concept.

Pashmina   A fine, soft wool gathered from the goats of Kashmir in northern India.

Pastel   A crayon made of a color or colors ground and mixed with gum and water, and used for art work. Any work made with this crayon. Pastel colors are commonly associated with light shades.

Pâte de verre   An ornamental colored glass made in France in the late nineteenth century.

Patera   A round or oval-shaped ornamental disk, often enriched by a rosette or other ornament. The plural is *paterae*.

Paternoster   Literally, "our father." The term is sometimes used for a *bead and reel* molding; also, a passenger lift on a continuously moving belt, as sometimes used in a parking garage.

Pâte-sur-pâte   In ceramics, a French term for low relief decoration built up by successive layers of *slip*.

Patina   Incrustation that forms on bronze and other materials through chemical action. Also the gloss on woodwork and the mellowing or softening in color that develops with age.

Patio   An inner court, open to the sky.

Patriarchal cross   See *archiepiscopal cross*.

Pearwood   A pinkish-brown, finely grained wood that is frequently used for inlay and fine cabinetwork.

Pedestal   A supporting base or block for a statue, vase, or order of architecture. It usually is treated with moldings at the top and a base block at the bottom. Without moldings it is called a *plinth*.

Pediment   Originally the triangular space following the roof line at each exterior end of a Greek temple, accentuated by the moldings of the entablature. Later the same treatment was used as an ornamental feature and varied in shape, having segmental, scroll, and broken forms.

Peintures-vivantes   High reliefs of religious groups, modeled and colored in lifelike reality, framed in fanciful architectural detail, and lighted by natural and artificial means that made them seem alive. Used extensively in Italy and Spain.

Pelike   A Greek storage vessel.

Pelmet   See *valance*.

Pembroke table   A small four-legged drop-leaf table with one or more small drawers under the fixed part of the top. It was popular in England after the middle of the eighteenth century. Also called a *sofa table* and similar to a *breakfast table*.

Pencil and pearl   Rather rare synonym for a *bead and reel* ornament.

Pendant   As an adjective, hanging; as a noun, a lighting fixture, ornament, or other object that hangs.

Pendentive   The triangular concave masonry surface that transmits the weight of a circular dome to four isolated corner supports. Shaped like a portion of the inside of a hemisphere, it originated in Byzantine architecture. See also *squinch*, another method of supporting a dome.

Penne d'oiseau   French term literally meaning "bird's feather" and referring to a featherlike ornamental carving on wooden furniture.

Pentastyle   Having five columns.

Pentes   A fifteenth-century term for a *valance* or *lambrequin*.

Percale   Plain closely woven fabric of muslin in dull finish, which may be bleached, dyed, or printed. Similar to *calico*.

Percier, Charles (1764–1838)   French architect and designer who, with *P. F. L. Fontaine*, established the *Empire style* in France.

Pergolesi, Michelangelo (died 1801)   Italian-born decorative painter, architect, and furniture designer who worked in England under Robert Adam.

Peristyle   A continuous row of columns surrounding a building or a court.

Perpendicular style   Term for late Gothic architecture in England (c. 1350–1530), in which window tracery is dominated by vertical elements.

Perriand, Charlotte (1903–99)   French interior designer and furniture designer, a collaborator of *Le Corbusier*.

Perroquet   French term for a chair with legs crossed in the form of an X.

Persane   Term used to describe the French eighteenth-century printed cottons that had designs inspired by Persian originals.

Perse   French term for *chintz*.

Persiana   Venetian blind used in Spain.

Persian cedar   See *nanmu*.

Persian knot   See *asymmetrical knot*.

Pesce, Gaetano (born 1939)   Italian-born industrial and furniture designer.

Petit point   Embroidery done in a cross-stitch on a fine single net. Also see *needlepoint*.

Petite-commode   French term for a small table with three drawers.

Petuntse   The prepared form of *Chinastone*, an essential ingredient of true *porcelain*.

Pewter   An alloy of tin and lead that has a dull gray appearance and is used for tableware and ornaments. Originally it was intended as a substitute for silver. More rarely, an alloy of tin and some other metal.

Pfister, Charles (1940–90)   American interior designer and furniture designer.

Phyfe, Duncan (1768–1854)   The most famous of American cabinetmakers, born in Scotland, settled in Albany, then moved to New York, where he headed a hugely successful furniture workshop, producing designs based on late eighteenth-century English and Empire styles.

Picoté   A type of pattern design consisting of small floral or other motifs surrounded by numerous minute dots to soften their silhouette. Credited to Christophe-Philippe Oberkampf.

Picture rail   A wall molding close to the ceiling, from which pictures can be hung. Also called a picture molding or a *frieze rail*.

Piece-dyeing   A term used in textile manufacturing to indicate that the fiber of a cloth has been dyed after the completion of the weaving. Compare *yarn-dyeing*.

Piecrust table   A small table having a top with its edge carved or molded in scallops. Common in eighteenth-century English furniture.

Pied de biche   See *cloven foot*.

Pier   A heavy vertical masonry support for a superstructure. This type of support lacks the detail and proportions of a column or pilaster.

Pier glass   Originally, a glass or mirror designed to stand on the floor against a wall surface, also called a *cheval glass*; later, a mirror designed to be placed between windows, over a chimney-piece, or over a console table.

Pier table   A table, such as a console, meant to be used against a wall under a mirror.

Pietà   Literally meaning "pity," an Italian term for an art work representing the dead Christ in the arms of his mother.

Pietra dura   Italian term for an inlaid design composed of hard, semiprecious stones.

Pigment colors   Colors made from natural or synthetic materials and used to produce the various hues in common paints. Opposed to the spectral colors produced by the decomposition of light.

Pilaster   A flat-faced vertical projection from a wall, rectangular in plan but with the general proportions, capital, and base of a column.

Pile   In textile and carpet construction, the upright ends or loops (if uncut) of thread that are woven at right angles to the *warp* and *weft*. The nap generally has the appearance of velvet.

Pile fabrics   Fabrics with raised loops or tufts (cut loops) that form the visible surface. Various types of pile fabrics are velvet, velours, frisé, moquette, plush, and terry cloth.

Pillar   A popular term used to designate a pier or column. Also an isolated structure used for commemorative purposes.

Pillar rug   A rug designed to be wrapped around a pillar or column.

Pillement, Jean (1727–1808)   French decorative painter and textile designer, noted for his *chinoiseries*.

Pilling   Small tangles of fibers on the surface of a fabric.

Pinch pleat   Three pleats pinched and sewn together at the top, left to fall open below.

Pine (white)   Known sometimes as soft pine, this was once the most important of softwoods, and is still used in large quantities, though its price is now rather high. It works easily and is used for both structural and finishing purposes, though it is nearly always painted, its texture being of little interest.

Pine (yellow)   Called hard pine, it has several species varying greatly in strength and other properties. In general it is stronger and harder than white pine. It makes good and cheap flooring, trim, doors, and furniture. For interior finish, its natural yellow color is not very pleasant, but by the use of dark stains, effects are obtained that are little inferior to dark oak. Yellow pine grows in Georgia and the Carolinas, and the tree's needles are longer than those of white pine.

Pinnacle   Small pyramidal or coneshaped turret used in architecture to crown roofs and buttresses. In the decorative arts, any form resembling the architectural feature.

Pinturicchio, Bernardino (1454–1513)   Decorative painter of the Italian Renaissance.

Piping   A method of applying and holding in place upholstery or padding to a curved surface by means of ribs resembling pipes.

Piqué   A heavy cotton fabric with raised cords running lengthwise. Used for trimmings, bedspreads, and curtains. Decorative work, popular in early eighteenth-century France, in which thin strips of gold or silver were inlaid into tortoiseshell or other materials.

Piranesi, Giovanni Battista (1720–1778)   Italian architect and engraver.

Pitch   The slope of a roof surface, often expressed as a ratio of height to width (for example, 1 in 12, or 3 in 5); a distillate of tar; a quality of sound related to frequency; in carpet, the number of yarn ends in a 27-inch width.

Placage   French term for *veneering*.

Plain weave   A basic weave in which *warp* and *weft* are of the same size, and alternate over and under each other.

Plain-sawing   The cutting of a plank of wood from the outside edge of a tree trunk. The grain appears in V-shapes, unlike *quarter-sawing* in which the plank is cut through or near the center of the trunk and causes the grain to appear in parallel lines.

Plan   The horizontal projection of any object. The delineation of an object or surface from above. The shape or internal arrangement of an object as indicated by a section cut parallel to the ground. Specifically, a drawing showing the arrangement and horizontal dimensions of the rooms of a building.

Plaque   French term for a plate or panel usually made of metal, glass, or pottery, treated with a surface enrichment, and used for decorative purposes.

Plaster   A pastelike substance that sets to form a hard finished material, most frequently composed of Portland cement, lime, sand, and water, but sometimes also containing gypsum, hair, or fibers.

Plasterboard   See *gypsum board*.

Plaster of Paris   Calcined gypsum, a quick-setting type of plaster used primarily for casting ornament.

Plate   A collective term for objects made of silver or gold.

Plate glass   A type of *flat glass* cast onto metal tables, first developed in France in the late seventeenth century.

Plateresco   The name given to the period of Spanish art during the first half of the sixteenth century. The word is derived from *platero*, meaning silversmith, because the style of ornament often imitated the fine detail of the silversmith's work.

Platner, Warren (1919–2006)   American architect, interior designer, and furniture designer.

Plenum   The space between a finished ceiling and the structural ceiling above, available for use for air supply, air return, etc.

Pliant   French term for a folding stool with legs crossed in the shape of an X. Sometimes spelled *ployant*.

Plinth   Square member at the base of a column or pedestal. In carpentry, the plinth-block is the small block of wood used at the bottom of door trim against which the baseboard butts. See also *pedestal*.

Plique-à-jour   A type of enameling in which translucent glass pastes are held in a metal network without backing, giving a small-scaled stained glass effect.

Plissé   A method of printing on plain weave rayon or cotton that produces a permanent crinkled surface in stripes or patterns.

Ployant   See *pliant*.

Plush   A fabric with a long pile. Made like velvet, its nap is sometimes pressed down to form a surface resembling fur. It may be made of silk, wool, cotton, or any synthetic fiber. Extensively used for upholstery.

Plywood   Wood composition made of thin sheets of veneer glued together.

P.O.   Abbreviation for *purchase order*.

Poché   In a plan or section, the shaded areas that represent solids; to produce such areas.

Pocket door   A door that slides into a recess, sometimes less accurately called a *sliding door*.

Podium   A pedestal; also the enclosing platform of the arena of an amphitheater.

Point d'Hongrie   Needlepoint having a design vaguely resembling an irregular series of chevron forms or V shapes usually made with silk and used for chair upholstery.

Pole screen   Adjustable panel mounted on a vertical pole.

Polychrome   An ornament or pattern in several colors.

Polyester   An *ester* formed by polymerization, used in modern textiles.

Polymerization   A chemical process in which small molecules combine to form larger ones.

Polyvinyl chloride   Synthetic material made from the derivatives of petroleum, used for floor covering in both sheets and tiles. Abbreviated both as *PVC* and as *vinyl*.

Pomegranate   Decorative motif or ornament used in many periods; symbol of fertility.

Pongee   A fabric of plain weave made from wild silk in the natural tan color. It is very durable and has an interesting texture. Used for draw curtains. The name is derived from a corruption of two Chinese words that signify "natural color."

Ponti, Gio (1891–1979)   Italian architect, designer, ceramicist, and magazine editor.

Pontil   An iron rod used in glass manufacturing to carry hot materials. A pontil mark is the permanent mark left by the pontil after the material has cooled.

Poplin   A fabric similar to a lightweight *rep*. It is made with a heavy filler, producing a light corded effect across the material. Cotton, silk, wool, synthetic, or combination fibers may be used in its weaving. A trimming and drapery fabric.

Porcelain   A hard, vitreous, nonporous pottery. Opposed to earthenware, which, if unglazed, is absorptive. True porcelain is made of *kaolin* or *China clay* and *petuntse* or *Chinastone*.

Porcelaneous ware   Pottery with the appearance of porcelain. Also spelled *porcellaneous*.

Porphyry   Rock composed of crystals of white or red feldspar in a red ground mass. A valuable stone for architectural or ornamental use.

Porringer   A small, shallow one-handled bowl.

Portico   A colonnaded porch or walkway. Also see *stoa*.

Portière   A curtain hung over a doorway.

Portland cement   A powder chiefly composed of hydraulic calcium silicates, the cementitious ingredient of most structural concrete.

Portland vase   Roman vase now in the British Museum, of blue-black glass with superimposed opaque white figures, having a cameo effect. It was copied in dark slate-blue *jasper* ware by *Josiah Wedgwood*.

Posset pot   English term for a small vessel to hold a posset, a mixture of milk and ale or milk and wine.

Postmodern design   Design in reaction against modernism.

Pottery   Sometimes used as a synonym for *earthenware*; sometimes used as a more inclusive term covering all types of fired wares such as earthenware, *stoneware*, *porcelaneous ware*, and *porcelain*; a factory in which such wares are made.

Poudreuse   French term for a toilet table or vanity, so called because it once held wig powders.

Powdered ornament   Ornament in which identical discrete elements, such as stars, flowers, or the *fleur-de-lis* are scattered over a field.

Practice legislation   Laws that limit the practice of interior design (or some other profession) to those legally certified. See also *title legislation*.

Pre-Raphaelite Brotherhood   In the second half of the nineteenth century, a group of artists who, with John Ruskin, revolted against the mechanization and eclecticism in the arts of the Victorian era and against the decline in craftsmanship. They started a movement looking back to Italian primitives, to nature, and to hand production in the crafts. Members were William Morris, Dante Gabriel Rossetti, William Holman Hunt, John Everett Millais, Sir Edward Burne-Jones, and others.

Preclassic   The classification given to the arts and cultures of the Western peoples who preceded the civilizations of ancient Greece and Rome: Egypt, Babylon, Assyria, Chaldea, Persia, Crete, and so forth.

Press or press cupboard   In seventeenth-century England and America, a two-tiered cupboard with hinged doors and drawers.

Pressed glass   Glass that is ornamented in relief by pressing into a mold.

Prie-dieu   A piece of furniture designed for kneeling in prayer. In the Middle Ages, the name was given to a small desk with a projecting shelf on which to kneel. In the seventeenth century and later it was given to a chair with a padded back, the user kneeling on the seat.

Primary colors   The three pigment colors, red, yellow, and blue, that cannot be produced by any mixture of other pigments. Combinations of any two of the primaries are known as *secondaries*. The combination of any secondary with a primary is known as a *tertiary*. The *spectral* primaries are those seen in the rainbow.

Primavera   See *mahogany*.

Priming coat   A mixture used by painters for a first or preparatory coat.

Primitive   Early, simple, naïve. The term applied to the early artists of any school or period when they have not yet mastered the later and more highly developed principles.

Prince of Wales feathers   A decorative motif of three ostrich feathers tied together, a symbol of the Prince of Wales and popular in late eighteenth-century English design.

Prince's metal   A brasslike alloy of copper and zinc thought to resemble gold. It was used in the American colonies and in seventeenth-century England, where it was also called "Prince Rupert's metal."

Pronaos   In ancient Greek architecture, the vestibule leading to the *naos* of a temple.

Propylaeum   In ancient Greek architecture, the gateway to a sacred precinct.

Proscenium   In a theater of ancient Greece or Rome, the platform on which the drama was enacted; in a modern theater, the arch (often curtained) between the auditorium and the stage.

Psyche   An upholstered sofa dating from about 1840, designed with Greek curves; French Empire term for a full-length mirror in a frame, later called a *cheval glass*.

Psykter   A Greek vessel for cooling wine.

Pugin, Augustus Welby Northmore (1812–52)   Victorian Gothic Revival architect and author.

Pure design   The theory that all art and design is based on a set of universal, fundamental, and abstract principles that create the ideal of beauty.

Putman, Andrée (born 1925)   French interior designer.

Putto   Italian term for a young boy. A favorite subject in Italian painting and sculpture. The plural is *putti*.

PVC   Acronym for *polyvinyl chloride*.

Pylon   Monumental obelisk or the heavy mass of masonry at the entrance of an Egyptian temple.

Q

Qing dynasty   See *Ch'ing dynasty*.

Quarter-round   A convex molding in the shape of a quarter circle. An *ovolo* molding.

Quarter-sawing   To saw wood planks toward or through the center of the tree trunk. Also see *plain sawing*. See Table 2-1.

Quaternary color   An intermediate hue in the pigment color wheel, formed by a mixture of a *tertiary* color with either its adjoining *primary* or *secondary* color.

Quatrefoil   A four-lobed ornamentation.

Quattrocento   Italian term for the fifteenth century (literally, "the 400s").

Queen Anne style   The style prevalent in England during the reign of Queen Anne (1702–1714), characterized by cabriole legs, shell ornaments, swan's-neck pediments, and other gracefully curved details.

Queen-size bed   A bed with a mattress width of 60 inches (152 cm).

Queen's ware   A thinly glazed stoneware produced by Wedgwood. Also called *creamware*.

Quickborner team   German management consultants from the Hamburg suburb of Quickborn, early developers of *office landscaping*.

Quilted fabric   A double fabric with padding between the layers, held in place by stitches that usually follow a definite pattern.

Quimper pottery   Faïence ware from a French factory founded at the end of the seventeenth century. Pronounced "kim-pair."

Quincunx   A building plan in which four subsidiary elements are arranged symmetrically about a central element, frequently used for Byzantine churches.

Quirk   An incised groove in a molding.

Quirked cyma   A *cyma curve* molding with a flat vertical band added top and bottom.

Quoin   A prominent brick or stone at the corner of a building.

R

Rabbet   In carpentry, a joint in which a recess in one piece of wood receives another piece of wood.

Rafraîchissoir   From the Louis XV period, a small table on casters, with drawers and shelves below, and with receptacles in the (usually marble) top for holding wine bottles. Also called a *servante*.

Rafter   A beam supporting a roof and usually following the pitch of the roof.

Rag carpet   A woven carpet using strips of fabric as the weft.

Rag rug   A braided carpet of fabric strips.

Rail   In paneling, any horizontal strip forming a portion of the frame, the vertical strips being called *stiles*; in a chair, the top member of the back.

Rainbow paper   A wallpaper with a design of softly blended colors. Also called *ombré* or *irisé*.

Raku   Japanese ceramics with a crackled glaze.

Randolph, Benjamin (active last half of the eighteenth century to 1790)   American cabinetmaker, a leader in the Philadelphia-Chippendale school.

Raphael (Raffaello Sanzio) (1483–1520)   Important Italian Renaissance painter and architect. Painter of frescoes in the Vatican Palace.

Ratiné   Name of yarn and of fabric in plain or twill weave. Owes its coarse, spongy, nubby texture to the knotlike irregularities of the yarn used in the warp.

Rato   A Portuguese *faïence* factory founded in 1767.

Ravrio, Antoine André (1759–1814)   Brilliant French *ciseleur* in the Empire period.

Raw silk   Silk as it is reeled from the cocoon, before the gum has been removed.

Rayon   A trade name for a synthetic fiber having a cellulose base. Originally highly lustrous, it can now be handled as a lusterless thread. It is more lustrous, stiffer, and less expensive than silk. In combination with silk, wool, or cotton its possibilities are limitless. Textiles of rayon are known by various trade names.

Rayonnant   The style of mid–thirteenth-century French Gothic architecture, characterized by window tracery in the form of radiating rays or spokes.

Récamier   A daybed with scrolled head and a shorter scrolled foot, named for the Paris society hostess Mme. Julie Récamier (1777–1849), who was painted reclining on such a daybed.

Red cedar   A wood little used for decorative purposes, though great quantities are used for making shingles and lead pencils. Its chief use as a finish wood is for the lining of clothes closets and chests. The small use made of cedar for finish is doubtless the result of its great variation in color, ranging from a decided red to almost white. Both colors are often found in a single piece, the heartwood being red and the sapwood white. Its odor is also too pungent for constant association.

Red-figure vase   Ancient Greek vase with red figures showing through a black-painted background.

Red gum   A handsome, fine-grained wood of a reddish-brown color. Sap gum is the sapwood of the same tree, and is much lighter in color. Red gum is much used for veneered doors, as well as for general interior finish, though its use has only become general in recent years. It may be used as a base for white enamel, or may be stained to imitate a variety of other woods, including walnut, mahogany, and maple, while selected specimens may even be found to imitate the striking figure of Circassian walnut. The figure of red gum varies in different trees, and it must be selected according to the use intended. In addition to various stained finishes, it may be given a natural finish by the use of wax, producing a handsome satiny effect that wears remarkably well.

Redwood   A wood of a very handsome and uniformly red color. It takes stain and paint readily, and can be obtained in very wide boards because of the great size of the trees. It is used for open beams and trim.

Reeding   A long, semicylindrical, stemlike ornamental form or a grouping of such used to enrich moldings.

Refectory   A dining hall, especially in ecclesiastical or collegiate buildings.

Régence   French style during the regency of Philippe, duc d'Orleans, 1715–23. It was a transitional style between French Baroque and Rococo.

Regency style   English style during the regency of George Augustus Frederick, Prince of Wales, 1811–20 (later King George IV). It was a late phase of English Neoclassicism.

Regulateur   A tall clock case.

Reich, Lilly (1885–1947)   German designer of interiors, furniture, and textiles, known for her collaboration with *Ludwig Mies van der Rohe*.

Reinforced concrete   Concrete strengthened with iron reinforcing rods.

Relief   A type of decoration in which the design is made prominent by raising it from the surface or background of the material. High relief designates that the design is raised greatly; low relief (or *bas-relief*) that the design is only slightly raised from the background.

Reliquary   A small receptacle designed to hold a sacred relic; usually made of ornamented precious metals enriched with jewels or enamel decoration.

Renaissance   Specifically, the period c. 1400–1530, when there was a rebirth of interest in intellectual and artistic activity based on Classical models; generally, any such rebirth.

Rep   A plain-weave fabric made with a heavier *filler* thread than *warp* thread (or vice versa), giving a corded effect, as in poplin or corduroy. A warp rep is made with heavier filler threads, producing a ribbing across the material. A filler rep uses coarser warps, and the ribbed effect is vertical. Rep is unpatterned and reversible, and may be made of cotton, wool, silk, or synthetic fibers. Used for drapery and upholstery purposes. Sometimes spelled *repp*.

Repeat   On fabric, the distance at which a decorative motif reoccurs.

Repoussé   Relief work on metal materials, the design being pushed out by hammering the material on the reverse side; *embossed*.

Reredos   A screen or wall-facing set behind a church altar, usually decorated with sculpture or carving. Also called a *retable*.

Resilient flooring   Floor covering, such as carpet or some kinds of tile, that is resilient.

Resist dyeing   A technique for producing a pattern or design on fabric. The sections to remain uncolored are coated with wax or other dye-resistant material before the fabric is dipped into the dye.

Restauration style   French style during the reigns of Louis XVIII (1814–15 and, following Napoleon's "100 Days," 1815–24) and Charles X (1824–30).

Restoration style   English style during the period (1660–88) of the Stuarts' restoration to the throne following the Commonwealth. It replaced austerity with exuberance.

Retable   See *reredos*.

Reticella   Cutwork lace, similar to network or filet. See *lace*.

Réveillon, Jean Baptiste (died 1811)   French wallpaper designer and maker from 1752 to 1789.

Revere, Paul (1735–1818)   Boston silversmith, copperplate engraver, caricaturist, and bell-founder.

Reverse   The side of a coin or medal on which is placed the less important impression or design. The more important face is called the *obverse*.

Revetment   A retaining wall; a facing of fine material over less attractive material.

Rez-de-chaussée   French term for a building's ground floor.

R.F.P.   Abbreviation for Request for Proposal.

Rib   A projecting band on a ceiling, vault, or other surface.

Ribband back   Chair back designed with a pattern of interlacing ribbons, similar to *strapwork*. Characteristic of the *Chippendale* style. Sometimes called ribbon back.

Ribbed vault   See *vault*.

Richardson, Henry Hobson (1838–86)   American architect; leader in the Romanesque Revival style.

Riemerschmidt, Richard (1868–1957)   German furniture and product designer.

Riesener, Jean-Henri (1734–1806)   French cabinetmaker appointed *Maître Ébéniste* in 1768. Worked for Marie Antoinette. First worked under Oeben, and became his successor.

Rietveld, Gerrit (1888–1964)   Dutch architect and furniture designer of the *De Stijl* movement.

Rinceau   French term for a scroll and leaf ornament, sometimes combined with cartouches or grotesque forms and applied to friezes, panels, or other architectural forms. It is usually a symmetrical horizontal composition. Similar to an *arabesque*. The plural is *rinceaux*. In eighteenth-century England, it was spelled *rainceau*.

Riser   The vertical surface between stair treads.

Rising stretchers   *X-shaped stretchers* or *saltires* that curve upward as they approach their intersection. Used in Italian Renaissance furniture.

Risom, Jens (born 1916)   Danish-born interior designer and furniture designer.

Rittenhouse, David (1732–96)   Philadelphia clockmaker.

Robsjohn-Gibbings, Terence Harold (1909–73)   British-American interior designer and furniture designer.

Rocaille   Literally, a French term for an artificial grotto encrusted with elaborately shaped shells and rock formations. More generally, the term is used as a synonym for *Rococo*.

Rococo   A style in architecture and decoration. It is characterized by lightness and delicacy of line and structure, by asymmetry, and by the abundant use of foliage, curves, and scroll forms of decoration. The name is derived from the French words *rocaille* and *coquille* (rock and shell), prominent motifs in this decoration.

Rodrigue, Ventura (1717–85)   Spanish architect who became a leading exponent of Neoclassic style.

Roentgen, David (1743–1807) French cabinetmaker of German origin, appointed *Maître Ébéniste* in 1780. Worked for Marie Antoinette. Sometimes spelled *Röntgen*.

Rogers, Richard (born 1933) British architect.

Rognon French term meaning kidney, applied to desks or tables with a kidney shape.

Rohde, Gilbert (1894–1944) American industrial designer and furniture designer.

Roll In the United States, a wallpaper trade and sales unit that designates 36 square feet of paper. Several rolls are usually included in a bundle or bolt or stick.

Roller blind Nineteenth-century term for window shade.

Rollwork See *strapwork*.

Roman shade A shade or curtain made in flat panels. As the panels are lifted, the material is pleated. See also *Austrian shade*.

Romanesque The style of architecture prevalent in Europe between 800 and 1150 and in England after 1066 (where it is called *Norman*). It is characterized by round-headed arches and vaults.

Romayne work Carved medallion heads in roundels, used as plaster ornaments, paneling details, furniture ornaments, or drawer pulls, characteristic of the English Jacobean and later periods. It is sometimes spelled *Romagne*.

Rondel Round outline or object in a surface pattern; a small circular panel or window. Also spelled *roundel*. Also see *tondo* and *oculus*.

Rood A cross or crucifix.

Rood screen In church interiors, an open screen separating the body of the church from the choir or chancel.

Roof comb In Mayan architecture, the ornamental continuation of the façade to a height far above the roof. Also called a *flying façade*.

Rookwood pottery American ceramics workshop founded in Cincinnati in 1880.

Rope bed Any bed with rope laced to the frame for holding the mattress.

Rose window A circular window with *mullions* of *tracery* radiating from a center in wheel form, the spaces between being filled with richly colored glass. Originally introduced in Gothic cathedrals, the form was later applied to wood paneling and furniture design.

Rosenthal German ceramics manufacturer.

Rosette An ornamental motif formed by a series of leaves arranged around a central point. The leaves are usually arranged to form a circle, ellipse, or square.

Rosewood A fine, reddish-brown wood with black streakings. There are many varieties, of which the most popular is Brazilian rosewood, called *jacarandá*. It takes a high polish and is much used for fine cabinetwork and for musical instruments.

Rossi, Aldo (1931–97) Italian architect and theorist.

Rotunda A building or room cylindrical in shape, usually topped with a dome. In Italy the spelling is *rotonda*.

Roundabout chair A type of chair designed to fit into a corner, having a low back on two adjoining sides of a square seat.

Roundel See *rondel*.

Roviro, Hipolito Spanish architect of the *Churrigueresco* style. He designed the Palace of the Marquis de Dos Aguas at Valencia (1740–45).

Ruhlmann, Émile-Jacques (1869–1933) French interior designer and furniture designer in the *Art Deco* style.

Running dog Decorative motif of repeated scroll forms. Sometimes called a *Vitruvian scroll*.

Ruskin, John (1819–1900) Influential English writer and art critic.

Rustication In stonework, a type of beveling on the edges of each block to make the joints between stones more conspicuous.

R-value The measure of a material's resistance to heat flow.

S

Saarinen, Eero (1910–61) American architect and furniture designer, at times a collaborator with Charles Eames. Son of Eliel Saarinen.

Saarinen, Eliel (1873–1950). Finnish architect who moved to the United States and became president of the Cranbrook Academy.

Sabot foot See *spade foot*.

Sacristy In a church, a small room for the storage of books, vestments, altar vessels, and the like.

Saddle See *threshold*.

Sailcloth Very heavy and durable fabric, similar to canvas. Lightweight sailcloth is often used for couch covers, summer furniture, and so forth.

Sakura Japanese term for cherrywood.

Saladino, John (born 1939) American interior designer.

Saltire An *X-shaped stretcher* of Italian origin between the legs of chairs, stools, or tables. Some saltires are *rising stretchers*.

Salver A plate or tray for serving food.

Salviati Important Venetian glass factory founded in 1866.

Sambin, Hugues (c. 1515–c. 1600) French architect and furniture designer under Catherine de' Medici.

Sampler A piece of needlework intended to show examples of a beginner's skill. Specifically, a small piece of linen embroidered with alphabets and naïve patterns, made by children in the early nineteenth century in Europe and in North and South America.

Sanderson, Robert (active 1638–93) Boston silversmith.

Sandwich glass American pressed glass with lacy decoration, some (but not all) of it made in Sandwich, Massachusetts.

Sang de boeuf Literally, blood of the bull. A deep red glaze for pottery. The Chinese equivalent is called *lang-yao*.

Sanguine drawing A drawing in red crayon or chalk.

Sansovino, Jacopo (1486–1570) Venetian architect and sculptor of the sixteenth century.

Sardonyx A type of *onyx* with alternating bands of milky white and reddish brown.

Sash The operable part of a window.

Sash bar See *muntin*.

Sash curtain A lightweight curtain that is hung on or nearest the sash of a window. Also called a *glass curtain*.

Sateen A fabric, imitative of satin, with a lustrous surface and dull back. It is made with floating weft threads and is, therefore, smooth from side to side. It is usually made of cotton, the better quality being mercerized. Sometimes spelled satine.

Satin A basic weave; also, a fabric having a glossy surface and dull back. The whole face of the fabric seems to be made of warp threads, appearing smooth and glossy. No two adjacent *warp* threads are crossed by the same *weft* thread, and the skip may vary from eight to twelve *fillers*. Because of the length of the warp floats, it is not an extremely durable material for heavy usage. It may be made of all silk, but is stronger when linen or cotton wefts are used. Used extensively for upholstery and draperies. There are several different types, as follows:

- antique satin, a type with a dull, uneven texture, heavy and rich looking
- charmeuse, with *organzine* warp and spun silk weft
- hammered satin, treated to give the effect of hammered metal
- ribbed satin, *bengaline* and *faille* woven with satin face ribs, giving a lustrous, broken surface; may have a *moiré* finish.

Satinwood   A light blond wood with a satiny finish and a handsome figure, used for finishing only in the finest work. It is largely used for furniture, and particularly for *inlay* and *parquetry*. Satinwood is cut from various species of trees that grow in India, Florida, and the West Indies.

Satsuma ware   Japanese ceramics from Satsuma province dating to the late sixteenth century. One type, made for Japanese use, was very simple earthenware; another type, made for export, was highly decorated tin-glazed ware.

Sausage turning   Furniture turning resembling a string of sausages.

Savery, William (c. 1721–c. 28)   American cabinetmaker, prominent in the Philadelphia-Chippendale school, and particularly noted for *highboys*.

Savonarola chair   See *X-chair*.

Savonnerie carpet   Knotted-pile carpet from the Savonnerie factory founded by Louis XIII in 1627.

Scagliola   Italian term for a composition of plaster and small chips of marble or other stone. It is durable and takes a high polish. Used extensively in eighteenth-century English interiors and still in some use today.

Scallop shell   In ornament, a semicircular shell with ridges radiating from a point at the bottom. This motif was especially common in furniture design during the Queen Anne and Georgian periods in England and the United States. It was also extensively used in the early Spanish Renaissance.

Scarpa, Carlo (1906–78)   Italian architect, interior designer, and furniture designer.

Scenic paper   Wallpaper depicting a landscape.

Sconce   Ornamental wall bracket to hold candles or electric bulbs.

Scotch carpet   Common name for a *Kidderminster carpet*.

Scotia   A concave molding approximating a curve produced by two tangential curves of different radii.

Scott Brown, Denise   See *Robert Venturi*.

Scratch carving   Shallow or deep scratching to form a design, used in woodwork and pottery products.

Screed   A form that limits the boundaries of a concrete pour; a tool used to smooth the surface of such a pour.

Scribe   In carpentry, to fit one material to another, as the side of a wooden strip to an uneven surface of plaster or adjoining wood surface. A scribe-molding is a small strip of wood that can be easily cut or bent to fit an uneven surface or cover up an irregular joint or crack.

Scrim   A sheer fabric made like a *marquisette*, but with coarser cotton, wet-twisted thread. Sometimes a cheaper variety is not wet-twisted, which causes it to thicken when laundered. Used for curtains and needlework.

Scritoire or scriptoire   See *scrutoire*.

Scroll   A spiral line used for ornamental purposes, as in the *arabesque* and *rinceau*. A parchment roll used as an ornament.

Scroll pediment   A broken pediment with each half shaped in the form of a reverse curve, and ending in an ornamental scroll. Usually a finial of some sort is placed in the center between the two halves of the pediment.

Scrutoire   French term for a desk that has a blank top panel that can fold down to form a horizontal writing surface. Not exactly the same as an *escritoire*, in which only a drawer front folds down.

Scutcheon   See *escutcheon*.

Seaweed marquetry   An inlay of various woods in an *arabesque* design of small leaf and seaweed forms. Much used during the William and Mary period.

Secession   Austrian art movement founded in 1897 and based in Vienna, related to the *Art Nouveau* movement.

Second Empire style   French neoclassical style from the period of Louis-Napoleon Bonaparte's reign as Emperor Napoleon III, 1852–70. See also *Néo-Grec*.

Second style painting   Second in a succession of four styles used in Roman wall painting. Employed in the first century B.C., the second style was noted for its representation of buildings and colonnades and is also called the architectural style.

Secondary colors   Orange, purple, and green, each of which is produced by the combination of two primary colors.

Sécretaire   French term for a desk.

Sécretaire-à-abattant   French term for a drop-lid desk.

Section   A term used to express the representation of a building, molding, or other object cut into two parts, usually by a vertical slice. The purpose of a sectional representation is better to show a silhouette shape or interior construction, showing vertical dimensions or heights. A section cut horizontally is commonly called a *plan*.

Sedan chair   Enclosed chair, carried by four men, used for transportation in the eighteenth century.

Seddon, George (1727–1801)   English cabinetmaker, furniture designer, and upholsterer, active about 1760–75. From 1793 to 1800, his firm was known as Seddon Sons and Shackleton, Seddon having taken his sons, George and Thomas, into partnership in 1785 and 1788, and his son-in-law, Thomas Shackleton, in 1793. Made much satinwood furniture.

Sedia   Italian term for chair.

Segmental arch   An arch shaped as a part of a circle less than a semicircle.

Sella   In ancient Rome, a folding stool.

Selvage   Sometimes called list and probably originating in the term *self-edge*. In fabric, it is a narrow woven edge parallel to the warp. Names of fabric manufacturers or names of patterns are sometimes printed at intervals on the selvage. Also called *selvedge*.

Semainier   French term for a tall bedroom chest with seven drawers, intended to hold personal linens for each day of the week.

Semigloss   Paint or enamel finish less lustrous than *gloss*, but more lustrous than *eggshell*.

Senna knot   See *asymmetrical knot*.

Serge   Silk, wool, cotton, or rayon in twill weave, with a clear and hard finish and a pattern of small diagonal ribs.

Serigraph   See *silk-screen*.

Serlio, Sebastiano (1475–1554)   Italian renaissance architect and theorist, author of the treatise *L'Architettura*, published between 1537 and 1575.

Serpentine curve   An undulating curve used for the fronts of chests, desks, cupboards, and similar pieces. The curve is formed by two tangential *cymas*.

Servante   See *rafraîchissoir*.

Settee   A small sofa, sized to seat two. The distinction is sometimes made that a sofa is completely upholstered, but a settee is not.

Settle   An all-wood settee with solid panels at the ends.

Severe style   See *desornamentado*.

Sèvres   Porcelain ware from the factory at Sèvres, France, founded in 1756.

Sfumato   From the Italian term for "smoky," a blurred effect in painting or decoration.

Sgabello   Italian term for a small wooden Renaissance chair, usually having a carved splat back, an octagonal seat, and carved trestle supports.

Sgraffito   Italian term for a method of surface decoration using a pattern that is first scratched on the surface and then colored or revealing a colored ground beneath.

Shade   Something that serves to intercept light; a color or pigment that contains a percentage of black.

Shadow prints   Also called warp prints. Fabrics with a pattern printed on the warp only; the filler is a plain thread. When woven, the design is blurred and indistinct.

Shaft   Central portion of a column or pilaster between the capital and the base.

Shaker furniture   A type of furniture made in the late eighteenth and early nineteenth centuries by the Shakers, a religious sect in New York State and later in New England. The designs were plain and functional; built-ins were characteristic.

Shalloon   A twilled worsted fabric.

Shang dynasty   Early Chinese dynasty, 1766–1045 B.C.

Shantung   A heavy grade of *pongee*. It is usually made of wild silk, cotton, or a combination of both.

Shearer, Thomas   English furniture designer and author of *Designs for Household Furniture*, published in 1788. The designs are almost entirely limited to case furniture.

Shed   In textile manufacture, an opening formed by the *warp* threads being lifted by a heddle; through this opening the shuttle holding the *weft* thread passes.

Sheer   General name for diaphanous or translucent fabrics.

Sheffield plate   Triple-plated silver on copper. The plating process was invented by Thomas Boulsover at Sheffield, England, in 1743 and later refined by Matthew Boulton.

Shellac   Natural resin derived from insects and dissolved in alcohol. It is used as a primer or sealer and can also be molded.

Sheraton, Thomas (1751–1806)   Noted English furniture designer and author of the *Cabinet-Maker's and Upholsterer's Drawing Book* (1791–94). No authenticated pieces of his are in existence.

Shiki   A heavy silk or rayon *rep* made with irregular sized filling threads.

Shirring   Gathering a textile in small folds on a thread, cord, or rod.

Shoro   See *pagoda*.

Shuttle   In weaving, the boat-shaped container for filling yarns that carries them through the *warp*.

Sick building syndrome   The phenomenon of a building's physical characteristics causing the sickness of its occupants.

Siegel, Robert   See *Gwathmey*.

Sikhara   The tower over the shrine of an Indian temple.

Silhouette   A profile or outline drawing, model, or cut-out, usually in one color. The outline of any object.

Silk   Lustrous fabric woven from the filaments reeled from the cocoons of silk worms.

Silk chiffon   Lightweight, sheer, plain silk fabric.

Silk shantung   See *shantung*.

Silk-screen   Printmaking by the process of squeezing paint through silk, sections of which have been masked to produce the desired pattern. Also called *serigraphy*.

Sill   In carpentry, a horizontal board or strip forming the bottom or foundation member of a structure, especially the board at the bottom of a window that serves as a finishing member for the trim and casing. A door sill is sometimes called a *saddle*.

Silla   Korean dynasty from the first to tenth centuries A.D.

Siloe, Diego de (c. 1495–1563)   Early Spanish Renaissance architect. He designed the cathedral at Granada and the "golden staircase" of Burgos cathedral.

Silverwood   See *harewood*.

Singeries   Designs showing monkeys at play, popular in France during the Louis XV period. Literally, "monkey tricks."

Single bed   Bed with a mattress width of 34 inches (86 cm).

Sisal   Fiber made from the spiky leaves of a subtropical bush. Made into rugs or carpet, it is attractively textured and hardwearing, but easily stained and difficult to clean.

Size   Gelatinous solution used for stiffening textiles, glazing paper, and in other manufacturing processes. It is also often used as a first coat in painting.

Skeleton construction   Building construction of posts and beams assembled before the walls are erected. In steel construction the walls are nonbearing, being supported by the steel work, and are merely screens against the weather.

Skirt   In cabinetry, the wooden strip that lies just below a shelf, window sill, or table top. Also called *apron* or *frieze*.

Skyphos   A Greek drinking cup.

Slash cutting   In the milling of lumber, the process of making radial cuts rather than parallel slices.

Slat   A thin, flat, narrow strip of metal or wood, as in a window blind.

Slat-back chair   A type of Early American chair with wide horizontal ladder *rails* between the back uprights.

Sleeping chair   An adjustable chair with a back that can be lowered level with the seat.

Sleigh bed   A bed, resembling a sleigh, with headboard and footboard of equal height.

Sliding door   A door that slides on a track. Specific types include the *pocket door* and the *by-passing door*.

Slip   In pottery, clay and water of a creamlike consistency used as a bath for pottery, to produce a glaze or color effect. A molding process using slip is called slip-casting.

Slipper chair   Any short-legged chair with its seat close to the floor.

Slipper foot   A furniture foot with a protruding and pointed toe. See Table 19-3.

Slip seat   A chair seat that can be easily taken out of the chair frame for cleaning or recovering

Slub   The irregularites and nubs in a fabric, specifically a silk.

Slurry   Thin mixture of water with a soluble material such as clay or cement.

Smoke chamber   In fireplace design, a transitional chamber between the fireplace throat and the chimney flue.

Smoke detector   A fire protection device that sounds an alarm when it detects smoke.

Snake foot   In cabinetwork, a foot carved to resemble a snake's head.

Snakewood   A yellow-brown or red-brown wood with dark spots and markings. It is popular for *inlay* work.

Soane, Sir John (1750–1837)   English architect of the *Regency style*.

Socle   Plain, square and unmolded base or pedestal for a statue, or superstructure.

Sofa   A long seat, able to accommodate at least two people. The origin is probably the Arabic word *suffa*. It is similar to a settee, but more completely upholstered. A common term, seldom used by professionals, is *couch*.

Sofa table   See *Pembroke table*.

Soffit   The ceiling or underside of any architectural member.

Soft paste   Base of ceramics made before the introduction of *kaolin*, products of which lack the whiteness and extreme hardness of true *porcelain*.

Soho tapestries   Tapestries made in any of several tapestry workshops in the Soho district of London in the late seventeenth and early eighteenth centuries.

Solar   A medieval term for an upper chamber in a castle. Usually the private room of the owner.

Solium   In ancient Rome, a seat of honor, sometimes carved in stone.

Sottsass, Ettore, Jr. (born 1917)   Italian industrial designer and furniture designer, leader of the Memphis group.

Sound masking   See *white sound*.

Spade foot   A square, tapering foot used in furniture design. It is separated from the rest of the leg by a slight projection. Also called a *sabot* or *thimble* or *therm foot*. See Table 19-3.

Spandrel   The approximately triangular panel or wall space between two adjoining arches and a horizontal line above them. On the face of a multistory building, the panel between the top of one window and the bottom of the window above.

Spanish foot   Foot in the shape of an inward curving scroll. Used in eighteenth-century English and American furniture. See Table 19-3.

Spanish knot   A knot used in carpet weaving in Spain and other places. See figure 14-32.

Specifications   Written information supplementing construction drawings.

Spectral colors   The colors produced by a beam of white light as it is refracted through a prism. Although they are unlimited in number, they are usually designated as violet, indigo, blue, green, yellow, orange, and red. Commonly seen in the rainbow.

Spindle   A long slender rod often ornamented with turned moldings or baluster forms. See also *split spindle*.

Spinet   Keyboard instrument, ancestor of the piano, in which the sound was produced by the action of quills upon strings.

Spiral leg   A furniture support carved in a twist, with a winding and descending groove or fluting. Also called a *barley sugar turning* or a *barley twist*. See Table 19-2.

Splat   A plain, shaped, or carved vertical strip of wood, particularly that used to form the center of a chairback. Sometimes spelled splad.

Splay   A line or surface that is spread out or at a slant. A *bevel* or *chamfer*.

Spline   In cabinetry, a small strip of wood inserted between and projecting into two adjoining pieces of wood to form a stronger joint between them.

Split spindle   A long, slender turned and molded wooden rod that is cut in two lengthwise so that each half has one flat and one rounded side. Used as an applied ornament in seventeenth-century English and American furniture.

Spode, Josiah (1733–97) and his son of the same name (1755–1827)   Staffordshire potters, noted for transfer-printed *earthenware*, *stoneware*, and *bone china*.

Sponge painting   Painting technique used in early America, in which paint is irregularly applied by dabbing the surface with a sponge.

Spot or spotlight   A lamp with a narrowly focused beam spread.

Sprig   A small ceramic ornament in relief, made in a mold and attached with slip to a pot before firing.

Spring-line   In architecture, the theoretical horizontal line in arch construction at which the upward curve of the arch proper starts.

Sprinkler system   See *automatic sprinkler system*.

Spruce   A variety of pine closely related to fir. Important ornamental tree with a soft, light, straight-grained wood used for interior and exterior construction and for sounding boards of musical instruments.

Spun silk   Silk yarn made from waste fibers from damaged or pierced cocoons and weaving mill waste. Heavier and less lustrous than reeled silk.

Spun yarn   Yarn assembled from a collection of short fibers. Spun yarn includes cotton, wool, silk, linen, and most natural staples. Another general category of yarn is *continuous filament*.

Squab   A removable chair cushion.

Squinch   Arched corbelling at the corner of a square room to support a dome above. Another method of supporting a dome is the *pendentive*.

Stalactite work   Small vertical polygonal or curved niches rising and projecting in rows above one another so that they resemble stalactite formations. See also *muqarnas* and *honeycomb work*.

Stamnos   Greek vessel for the storage of wine, water, or spices.

Starck, Philippe (born 1940)   French interior designer, furniture designer, and product designer.

Statuary bronze   Bronze that has been surfaced with an acid application causing its color to become a dark brown. A finish often given to bronze statues.

Steamboat Gothic   A richly ornamented type of Gothic Revival based on the appearance of steamboats and seen on nineteenth-century buildings of the Mississippi River valley.

Steinzeug   German term for *stoneware*.

Stela   A stone slab or pillar used commemoratively, as a gravestone, or to mark a site. The plural is *stelae*.

Stencil   The method of decorating or printing a design by brushing ink or dye through a cut-out pattern.

Sterling   A term used in connection with silverware, indicating that the silver is 92.2 percent pure.

Stern, Robert A. M. (born 1939)   American architect and author.

Stickback   Chair with a back of thin spindles, such as a *Windsor* chair.

Stickley, Gustav (1857–1942)   American cabinetmaker in the Arts and Crafts style and founder of the periodical *The Craftsman*.

Stiegel, Henry William (1729–85)   Pre-Revolutionary American glassmaker, founder of a factory at Manheim, Pennsylvania. Familiarly known as "Baron" Steigel.

Stile   The vertical strips of the frame of a panel. The horizontal strips are called *rails*.

Still life   Paintings or decorative renderings of inanimate, motionless objects.

Stilted arch   An arch "on stilts," in which the *spring line* is raised above the *impost line*.

Stippling   Process of applying paint or ink to a surface in dot form, by means of a coarse brush or spray.

Stoa   In Greek architecture, a *colonnade* or *portico* enclosing an open area used for a public meeting space.

Stock millwork   Milled lumber available in stock shapes and sizes, often in nominal dimensions.

Stock-dyeing   A term used in textile manufacturing to indicate that a fiber is dyed before being spun into a thread. See also *piece-dyeing* and *yarn-dyeing*.

Stoneware   A heavy, opaque, nonporous and nonabsorbent pottery made from a silicious paste.

Strap hinge   A surface-mounted hinge with long plates of metal on either side of the hinge; one plate can be attached to the fixed surface, the other to the movable surface.

Strapwork   A term applied to carved wooden *arabesque* and *rinceau* patterns of interlaced flat bands that appear as if cut from a sheet of leather. Sometimes the realistic effect is heightened by the representation of nailheads, as if the straps were being held to a background. Popular in England in the Elizabethan and Jacobean periods. It is sometimes called *rollwork*, and similar ornaments in France are called *enroulements découpés*. Also similar are the *ribband backs* (or *ribbon backs*) of *Chippendale* chairs.

Stretcher   A brace or support that horizontally connects the legs of pieces of furniture. In brickwork, the long face of a brick laid horizontally. See Table 19-1.

Strié   A fabric with an uneven, streaked effect produced by using warp threads of varying tones. A two-toned effect may be given to *taffeta*, *satin*, or corded upholstery materials by this process. Pronounced "stree-ay." Similar to *Jaspé*.

String course   In architecture, a molding or projecting horizontal motif running along the face of a building.

Stucco   A material, usually textured, used as a coating for exterior walls. It is most commonly made from Portland cement, lime, sand, and water, although some modern versions may also contain epoxy or other man-made materials as binders.

Stud   A small post, most commonly a nominal dimension of 2 by 4 inches, and of any height, used to form the wall construction in wooden structures. The studs support the joists and receive the *lath* or sheet material used for the finish.

Student lamp   Nineteenth-century oil lamp with the oil reservoir higher than the burner, usually made of brass.

Stumpwork or stump embroidery   A type of embroidered picture worked in silk or wool threads over padding, giving a relief effect.

Stupa   An Indian sacred mound, precursor of the *pagoda*.

Stylobate   The stone blocks or steps that form the lowest architectural feature of a Greek temple and upon which the columns stand.

Süe, Louis (1875–1968)   French architect and interior designer working in the Art Deco style in partnership with André Mare.

Sugi finish   A Japanese method for finishing woodwork. The surface is charred and then rubbed with a wire brush.

Sui dynasty   Chinese dynasty, A.D. 581–618, constituting, with the *T'ang dynasty* that followed, the "Golden Age" of Chinese art.

Sullivan, Louis H (1856–1924)   American architect; early promoter of functional design in architectural structures.

Summer beam   A large timber laid horizontally and used as a bearing beam. In Early American dwellings it was usually supported at one end by the masonry of the chimney and at the other end by a post, and it extended across the middle of the room. The name is derived from *sommier*, a French term meaning saddle or support.

Summer bed   Two single beds placed together under a single canopy.

Summers, Gerald (born 1902)   English furniture designer.

Sung dynasty   Chinese dynasty, A.D. 960–1279.

Superimposed order   The placing of one order of architecture above another in an arcaded or colonnaded building; usually Doric on the first story, Ionic on the second, and Corinthian on the third. Found in the Greek *stoas*, in Roman architecture, and later in the Renaissance.

Suzani   A variety of cotton grown in Turkestan; an embroidered wall hanging.

Swag   Cloth draped in a looped garland effect, or an imitation of such an effect in another material. At the end of the nineteenth century, it was called a *French shawl*.

Swan, Abraham   Early eighteenth-century English cabinetmaker known for his mantels, door and window trim, and staircases.

Swansea   English pottery of the Staffordshire type.

Swastika   A cross composed of four equal L-shaped arms placed at right angles. A sacred symbol of ancient origin. Sometimes spelled *svastika*. Also called a fylfot, a filfot, or a gammadion, and with similarities to the Greek *meander*.

Swatch   See *cutting*.

Swatow wares   Chinese export porcelain of the *Ming* dynasty, erroneously supposed to have been shipped from the port of Swatow.

Swiss   A very fine, sheer cotton fabric that was first made in Switzerland. It may be plain, embroidered, or patterned in dots or figures that are chemically applied. It launders well, but has a tendency to shrink. Often used for *glass curtains*.

Sycamore   A wood that ranges from white to light brown in color. It is heavy, tough, and strong, and handsome in appearance. It is extensively used for finishing work.

Symmetrical balance   Having the two halves of a design or composition exactly alike in mass and detail.

Symmetrical Knot   One of the two basic knots with which Islamic carpets are woven. Also called a *Turkish knot* or a *Ghiordes knot*. See Tools & Techniques: Characteristics of Islamic Carpets in Chapter 9.

Synthetic fibers   These are made from various chemical compounds and are used as yarns in modern textile weaving. They are known by trade names given to them by individual manufacturers. Combinations of natural and synthetic yarns are often used. Among the leading types are those known as rayon, bemberg, celanese, dacron, fortisan, lurex, nylon, and orlon.

T

Ta   See *pagoda*.

Taber test   A test to measure a fabric's resistance to abrasion. Similar to a *Wyzenbeek test*.

Tabernae   Small shops opening to the street along the front of a Roman *domus*.

Tabernacle mirror   A mirror in an architectural frame with a panel of painted glass above the mirror. Also called a *Sheraton mirror*.

Table-à-écran   French term for a table with sliding screen.

Table-à-écrire   French term for a writing table, a small version of a *bureau plat*.

Table-à-jeu   French term for a game table.

Table-à-l'anglaise   French term for a dining room extension table. (Louis XVI and later.)

Table-à-l'architect   French term for a table with hinged top.

Table-de-chevet   French term for a night table.

Table-jardinière   French term for a table with top pierced for plant containers.

Table rug   A rug used as a table cover.

Tablinum   In a Roman house, a reception room with one side open to the *atrium*.

Tabonuco   A light-colored, beautifully grained West Indian hardwood used for furniture.

Tabouret   French term for a stool.

Tackless strip   Wood strip with embedded tacks used for laying carpet.

Taffeta   The basic plain weave. Also, a fabric woven in that manner. The fabric is usually made of a silk fiber with warp and weft thread of equal size. It is often weighted with metallic salts. Useful for trimmings and draperies.

Tahoto   See *pagoda*.

Tails   See *jabot*.

Talavera de la Reina   A group of Spanish earthenware factories.

Talbert, Bruce (1838–81)   English furniture designer.

Tambour   French term meaning drum-shaped.

T'ang dynasty   Chinese dynasty, A.D. 618–906, constituting, with the *Sui dynasty* that preceded it, the "Golden Age" of Chinese art.

Tapa   Cloth made in the Pacific islands from the bark of certain trees, particularly the paper mulberry.

Tapestry   Originally a hand-woven fabric with a ribbed surface like *rep*. The design is woven during manufacture, becoming an essential part of the fabric structure. Machine-made tapestry is produced by several sets of *warp* and *filling* yarns woven with the *Jacquard* attachment, which brings the warp threads of the pattern to the surface. Machine-made tapestry can be distinguished from hand woven by its smooth back and the limited numbers of colors used in the pattern.

Tapestry knot   A type of knot used in weaving tapestries. See Tools & Techniques: Tapestry Weaving in Chapter 8.

Tarlatan   A thin, open cotton fabric of plain weave that is almost as coarse as a fine *cheesecloth*. It is *sized*, wiry, and transparent, and made in white and colors. It cannot be laundered.

Task lighting   Lighting specifically designed to aid work. See also *accent lighting* and *ambient lighting*.

Tatami   A traditional Japanese floor mat made of woven reeds, approximately 1 meter by 2 meters.

Tatlin, Vladimir (1885–1953)   Russian constructivist architect and designer.

Tavern table   Plain wooden table without leaves.

Tazza   Italian term for a large ornamental cup or footed salver.

Teak   A wood that is yellow to brown in color, often with fine black streaks. It is more durable than oak and is used for shipbuilding as well as for furniture.

Tempera   A paint composed of pigments that are soluble in water. Sometimes glue or eggwhite is also added to the solvent.

Templum   In Byzantine churches, a stone screen dividing the *bema* and the *naos*, a precursor of the *iconostasis*.

Tenon   In carpentry, a projection at the end of a piece of wood intended to fit into a hole (a *mortise*) of corresponding shape on another piece of wood. See Table 2-1.

Term   A tapered pedestal, smaller at its base, supporting a bust or sculptured figure; or a male *caryatid* standing on such a base.

Terne   An alloy of lead and tin, sometimes used for roofing.

Terra cotta   A hard-baked pottery extensively used in the decorative arts and as a building material, usually made of a red-brown clay, but sometimes colored with paint or baked glaze; the color typical of such material.

Terra sigillata   Roman ceramic ware made from fine red clay.

Terrazzo   A concrete made of small pieces of crushed marble and cement. Used for surfacing floors and walls.

Terre-cuite   French term for *terra cotta*.

Terry, Eli (active eighteenth and early nineteenth century)   American clockmaker.

Terry cloth   Heavy, loosely woven, uncut pile fabric, as used in bath towels.

Tertiary color   A color that is formed by the combination of a *primary color* and a *secondary color*.

Tesselated   Imbedded with *tesserae*.

Tessera   A small cube of stone, marble, or glass used in making a mosaic. The plural is *tesserae*.

Tester   Canopy framework over a four-poster bed. Pronounced "tees-ter."

Tete-á-tete   A *confidante*. Also called *dos-à-dos*.

Tetrastyle   Having four columns.

Thatch   Roof covering made of plant material such as straw, reeds, rushes, or palm leaves.

Theatrical gauze   A loosely woven open cotton or linen fabric. Because of its transparency and shimmering texture, theatrical gauze is used for window draperies.

Theatrum tectum   See *odeum*.

Therm foot   See *spade foot*.

Thermae   The public baths of ancient Rome.

Thimble foot   See *spade foot*.

Third style painting   Third in a succession of four styles used in Roman wall painting. Employed between c. 20 B.C. and c. A.D. 50, the third style was also called the ornate style.

Tholos   In Greek and Mycenaean architecture, a round, domed building or tomb. The plural is *tholoi*.

Thomas, Seth (1785–1859)   American clockmaker, active in Thomaston, Connecticut, and founder of the Seth Thomas clock factory.

Thomire, Pierre Philippe (1751–1843)   Brilliant French *ciseleur* in the Empire period.

Thonet   Furniture company founded in Austria in 1849 by Michael Thonet. Its first specialty was furniture using bentwood, but it later also produced furniture with metal frames.

Thornton, Dr. William (1759–1828)   First architect of the U. S. Capitol.

Three-color ware   Type of Chinese porcelain popular in the Ming dynasty.

Three-ply carpet   Flat-pile carpet using three layers of interwoven fabric, first developed in 1824 and also called an *Imperial*.

Threshold   Molding or strip fastened to the floor beneath or before a door.

Thronos   A Greek chair of honor.

Through cutting   In the milling of lumber, the process of cutting a log with parallel slices.

Thrown silk   Type of silk in which long filaments are thrown or twisted together, the more twists per inch producing the stronger product.

Thrust   In architecture, the outward force exerted by an arch or vault that must be counterbalanced by abutments.

Thuya   A dark, red-brown wood from North Africa. It takes a high polish and is used in contemporary cabinetwork. It is also called citron burl, and *Arbor vitae* is of the same genus. The wood was known to the Chinese and Greeks. Used for table tops, turnery, and veneering.

Ticking   Closely woven cotton in twill or satin weave. It usually has woven stripes, but they may be printed. Damask ticking is also made in mixed fibers and used for mattress covers, pillows, and upholstery.

Tidy   See *antimacassar*.

Tie-beam   In architecture, a horizontal beam that connects the rafters of a roof and prevents them from spreading. Used in truss construction to counteract the outward thrust of the slanting members.

Tie-dyeing   Fabric patterning process in which, before dyeing, small areas of fabric are gathered and tied to prevent the penetration of the dye. The process has been popular in India, Indonesia, and other places.

Tielimu   Chinese furniture wood.

Tiffany, Louis Comfort (1848–1933)   Prominent American glass artist in the *Art Nouveau* style, and son of the founder of Tiffany & Company. As an interior designer, he collaborated with Stanford White, Carrère and Hastings, and other architects.

Tilliard, Jean-Baptiste (1685–1766)   French chair maker of the Louis XV period.

Tilt-top   A tabletop that is attached to a hinge on a pedestal support so that the top may be swung to a vertical position when not in use.

Tin glaze   A ceramic glaze of lead to which tin oxide has been added, making it white and opaque.

Tinsel pictures   Decorative objects made from cutout tinsel, paper, and pictures, mounted and pasted together.

Tint   A color made from a pigment that is mixed with white.

Title legislation   Laws that limit the use of the term "interior designer" to those professionals who are legally certified. See also *practice legislation*.

Toiles de Jouy   Famous printed fabrics produced at Jouy, near Paris, by Philippe Oberkampf, from 1760 to 1815. Modern reproductions continue the typical design of landscapes and figure groups in monotones of brick red, blue, or other colors on a white or cream-colored background. Effectively used for draperies, bedspreads, and wall hangings.

Toiles d'Indy   Printed cotton and linen of floral or pictorial design, which began to be imported into France during the latter years of the seventeenth century from India and Persia.

Tokonoma   In a Japanese house, a niche that customarily holds a scroll or other art work and a flower arrangement.

Tôle   French term for painted sheet metal or tin; the useful or decorative objects made of such material.

Tombstone   See *monument*.

Tonal value   One of the characteristics of a color. The relative strength of a color in contrast to white or black.

Tondo   A painting or relief in circular form. See also *rondel*.

Tongue-and-groove   A type of wood joint in which a long, narrow, straight projection, known as the tongue, fits into a corresponding groove in the adjacent piece.

Tope   See *stupa*.

Torchère   Originally a French design from the Louis XV period and later, being a small table for holding a candle or candelabrum, also called a *guéridon*. The term is now used for a standing floor lamp with a shade that directs the (electric) light upward toward the ceiling.

Torus   In architecture, a convex semicircular molding.

Townsend, John (1732–1809)   One of a famous family of cabinetmakers in Newport, Rhode Island, most noted for his *block-and-shell* pieces.

Trabeated construction   Construction in which the supporting members are the post and lintel, as distinct from arched construction.

Tracery   The stone *mullions* in a Gothic window.

Tracery pattern   A pattern in woodwork, textile, or other material imitating stone tracery.

Tram   A type of *thrown silk*.

Transept   In church architecture, that portion of the building that crosses the *nave* at right angles, near the *apse* or east end of the building.

Transitional   A style that shows evidence of two chronologically consecutive styles, possessing elements of both styles in its design.

Transom   The upper panel of a window or a window placed above a doorway.

Trapeza   A Greek table; the plural is *trapezai*.

Travertine   A type of limestone with irregular open cells.

Tray-table   A small table, popular in the eighteenth century, with a low *gallery* around three (or all four) sides of the top surface.

Tread   The horizontal surface of a stair.

Trecento   Italian term for the fourteenth century (literally, "the 300s").

Tree-of-life pattern   A pattern resembling a tree or vine, showing branches, leaves, flowers, and small animals. Originating in ancient Assyria, it was borrowed by the Persians, East Indians, and early English Renaissance designers, and was a feature of *palampores*. Also called *hom*.

Trefoil   A three-lobed ornamentation resembling a clover.

Trencher   A large wooden platter upon which food is served.

Trestle table   A table supported on X-shaped trestles or sawbucks.

Triacetate   Man-made fiber or fabric of cellulose *acetate*, similar to acetate, but more completely acetylated and able to withstand higher temperatures. Its heat tolerance allows it to be permanently pleated.

Tric-trac table   French term for a backgammon table.

Triclinium   The dining room in a Roman house.

Tricoteuse   French term for a small sewing table.

Trifid foot   A furniture foot resembling the English 3-lobed spoon called a trifid. See Table 19-3.

Triforium   In a Gothic church, an arcaded walkway along the *nave* and above the level of the *arcade*.

Triglyphs   Blocks with vertical channels that are spaced at intervals between *metopes* in the *frieze* of the Doric entablature.

Triptych   Any threefold picture, usually of religious character, often an altarpiece.

Troffer   Long, linear lighting fixture, usually recessed with its visible surface flush with the ceiling.

Trompe l'oeil   Literally, "fool the eye," a French term for illusionistic painting or carving.

True silk   Silk made from a specific species of silkworm, the *Bombyx mori*.

Trumeau   French term for the decorative treatment of the space over a mantel, door, or window, usually consisting of a mirror or painting or both. Specifically, the overmantel panel treatment of the Louis XV and VXI periods.

Trumpet leg   A conical leg turned with flared end and shaped in the form of a trumpet. See Table 19-2.

Trundle bed   A term of Gothic origin for a child's or servant's bed on wheels, which was rolled under a full-sized bed when not in use. Sometimes called a truckle bed.

Truss   A support used for a wide span of roof or ceiling, consisting of beams or posts assembled together, often in a triangular manner, for greater rigidity and strength.

Tudor arch   A flat, pointed arch characteristic of English Gothic and early Renaissance architecture and decoration. See Table 6-2.

Tudor rose   Decorative motif seen in English Renaissance work consisting of a conventionalized rose with five petals, with another smaller rose inside it. It was the royal emblem of England, symbolizing the marriage of Henry VII of Lancaster (red rose) to Elizabeth of York (white rose).

Tudor style   English style from the time of the reigns of the Tudor kings, 1485–1603. A phase of the Early Renaissance in England.

Tulipière   Vase for holding tulips, often of *Delftware*.

Tulipwood   A light yellow wood with red streaks. It comes from Brazil and is much used for ornamental *inlay*.

Tungsten-halogen lamp   A type of incandescent lighting that has a tungsten filament inside a lamp filled with gas including halogen. The lamp is small, compared with others of equal power, but its surface can reach dangerously high temperatures. Other names for such lamps are *halogen*, quartz, and quartziodine.

Turkey-work   A handmade textile imitating Oriental pile rugs, produced by pulling worsted yarns through a coarse cloth of open texture, then knotting and cutting them.

Turkish knot   See *symmetrical knot*.

Turning   In carpentry, a type of ornamentation produced by rotating wood on a lathe and shaping it into various forms with cutting tools. See Table 19-2.

Turnip foot   A furniture foot resembling a ball foot but with a flattened bottom. See Table 19-3.

Turpentine   A resinous fluid used as a solvent and drying constituent in paint mixing.

Turret   A small tower superimposed on a larger structure.

Tuscan order   A simplified Roman variant of the Doric order of architecture. It is plain and sturdy, and the standard proportion of its column is 7 diameters high. It has an undecorated *frieze* and a *cornice* without *mutules*. Sometimes called the *Etruscan* order.

Tussah silk   Wild silk, from cocoons of worms that have fed on oak or other leaves. Light brown in color. Used for *pongee*, *shantung*, and *shiki*.

Tweed   Originally a woolen homespun material made in Scotland. Now the term is applied to a large group of woolen goods made from *worsted* yarns; they may be woven in plain, twill, or herringbone twill weaves.

Twill   A basic weave; also, the fabric woven in that manner. The *weft* thread is carried over one *warp* and under two. Sliding along one to the left on each row, still going over one and under two warp threads, a diagonal ribbed effect is achieved. A *herringbone* pattern is a variation of this weave, with which squares and zigzags can also be made.

Twin bed   A bed with a mattress width of 39 inches (99 cm).

Two-ply carpet   An *ingrain* carpet.

Tyg   A mug with several handles or with two closely spaced handles, popular in sixteenth- and seventeenth-century England.

Tympanum   In architecture, the interior triangular surface of a *pediment* bounded by the sloping sides and the lower molding.

T'zu-chou   A Chinese *stoneware*.

Tzu-tan   Chinese furniture wood.

U

UBC   Acronym for the Uniform Building Code, a code much used on the West Coast of the United States and as a model for many local codes.

UL Acronym for Underwriter's Laboratories, an independent testing agency. If an electrical device is tested and approved by the agency, it is said to be "UL approved." The Canadian counterpart is the Canadian Standards Association, or CSA.

Ultraviolet light Light with wavelengths shorter than those of visible light. See also *infrared light*.

Underglaze A term used to define a pigment or pattern that is applied to pottery before the final glazing is applied.

Unicorn An imaginary animal with a single horn often featured in the arts of the Middle Ages. The symbol of chastity.

Universal design Design that accommodates all, including those with physical disabilities.

UPS Acronym for uninterrupted power supply, used for computer equipment, emergency lighting, and so forth.

Upset price See *guaranteed maximum cost*.

Usable square footage The area within a building that can actually be used by its occupants (not generally including such shared facilities as lobbies, corridors, and toilets).

Utrecht velvet A velvet with a pattern created by flattening some areas of the pile. The term velours d'Utrecht is also sometimes seen, usually referring to a wool velvet.

V

Vaisselier French term for a dining room cabinet and shelves.

Valance A horizontal feature used as the heading of overdraperies and made of textile, wood, metal, or other material; fabric in vertical folds falling from a pole or cornice over a door or window.

Valdevira, Pedro (died 1565) Spanish Renaissance architect. The cathedral of Jaen, the style of which had an important influence in Latin America, was begun under him.

Value of a color The relative amount of white or black in a color.

Van Briggle, Artus (1869–1904) American potter in the *Art Nouveau* style.

Vanbrugh, Sir John (1664–1726) English architect, furniture designer, and scenic designer. His best-known works are Blenheim Castle and Castle Howard.

Van de Velde, Henri (1863–1957) Belgian architect and designer in the *Art Nouveau* style.

Vandergoten, Jacobo (died 1725) Brussels tapestry maker called to Madrid by Philip V. Directed Spain's royal manufactory of tapestries and rugs.

Van Dyck, Peter (active during the seventeenth century) Dutch silversmith in New York.

van Risamburgh, Bernard II (c. 1696–c. 1766) One of a family of French cabinetmakers, van Risamburgh was a *Maître-Ébéniste* in service to Louis XV. His work is best known by the initials with which his furniture was stamped, "B.V.R.B."

Vargueño Spanish term for a cabinet and desk with a drop-lid.

Varnish A coating, usually made of shellac and alcohol, that gives wood a glossy protective finish.

Vault A roof constructed on the arch principle. A *barrel vault* is semicylindrical in shape. A *groin vault* is made by the intersection of two barrel vaults at right angles. In a *ribbed vault* the framework of arched ribs supports light masonry.

Veduta Italian term literally meaning "view" and applied to a painting or drawing of a scenic view. The painter of such a scene is called a *vedutiste*.

Veilleuse French term for a *chaise longue* of the Louis XV period.

Velarium A fabric covering for an amphitheater.

Velour-de-Gênes Silk velvet. Made in Genoa and usually having a small allover pattern.

Velours A general term for any fabric resembling velvet. It is the French word for velvet, but has been so misused that it no longer has a definite meaning.

Velours d'Utrecht See *Utrecht velvet*.

Velvet A fabric having a thick, short *pile* on the surface and a plain back. A true velvet is woven with two sets of *warps*, one for the back and one for the pile, which is made by looping the warp thread over a wire, which later cuts the loops. Cheaper velvets and some chiffon velvets are woven face to face and have two backs using two warps and two fillers. The pile is made by slicing apart the two pieces of fabric. Velvet may be plain, striped, or patterned. It may be made of all cotton, linen, mohair, synthetic fibers, or silk, though it is seldom woven with all silk threads. The finer quality may be used for draperies, and the heavier for upholstery. There are several variations, as follows:

- *brocaded*, a velvet with its pattern made by removing part of the pile by heat and chemicals
- *ciselé*, a velvet with its pattern made by contrasting areas of cut and uncut loops
- *embossed*, its pattern imprinted by rollers
- *façonné*, with a small pattern, similar to brocaded velvet
- *moquette*, uncut velvet with a large *Jacquard* pattern
- *nacré*, velvet with a pile of one color and a backing of another, giving an iridescent effect
- *panné*, having its pile pressed down in one direction by rollers under steam pressure
- *plush*, with deep and thinly woven pile, often with a crushed effect
- *upholstery velvet*, the heaviest type, with a stiff back and very thick pile

Velvet carpet A type of carpet closely resembling a *Wilton*, but without the wool backing and consequently without the wearing qualities of the Wilton.

Velveteen A fabric sometimes called cotton velvet. It is not woven with a *pile*, but like a heavy *sateen*, with the *weft* threads floated loosely over the *warp*. It must then be sheared to produce a fine close pile. It is ordinarily made of cotton and is suitable for upholstery.

Veneer A thin sheet of finishing wood or other material that is applied to a body of coarser material.

Venetian blinds Window shades made of small horizontal slats of wood or other material strung together on tapes. The slats may be turned up or down to exclude or let in sunlight and to control views.

Venetian carpet A reversible flat-pile carpet commonly woven of wool and jute.

Venetian enamel From the late fifteenth and sixteenth centuries, wares of enameled copper, mostly in deep blue and white, with repeated flower motifs in white or gold.

Venetian furniture Extravagantly curved and ornamented furniture of Baroque and Rococo influence, produced in Italy during the late Renaissance.

Venetian glass   Glass made, since the tenth century, on the island of Murano near Venice.

Venini, Paolo (1895–1959)   Venetian glassmaker of the twentieth century.

Venturi, Robert (born 1925)   American architect, designer, theorist, and author, in practice with his wife, architect and urbanist Denise Scott Brown.

Verdure Tapestry   A tapestry design showing trees and flowers.

Vermeil   French term for gilded silver (or, less frequently, gilded bronze or copper).

Vermiculation   The carving of masonry blocks in imitation of worm tracks. Such blocks are said to be vermicular.

Vernis Martin   French term used as a term to describe the lacquer work done by a cabinetmaker named Martin and his brothers during the eighteenth century in France in imitation of Far Eastern lacquer.

Verre de fongére   French equivalent of *waldglás*.

Verre doublé   French equivalent of *cased glass*.

Verre églomisé   Glass decorated on the back by gilding or painting.

Verrerie   French term for a glass manufactory.

Verrier   French term for a glassware cabinet.

Vertical circulation   Stairs, ramps, elevators, or escalators that connect different levels.

Vesica piscis   See *mandorla*.

Vestibule   An entrance hall or foyer.

Victorian style   Strictly, the style prevailing in England during the reign of Queen Victoria, 1837–1901. In practice, the term extends almost a decade later in time and includes work in the United States during the same period.

Vignelli Associates   American multidiscipline design firm headed by Italian-born Massimo (born 1931) and Lella Vignelli.

Vignette   Ornamental motif, pattern, or portrait isolated in a large field.

Vignola   See *da Vignola*.

Vile, William (born 1767)   Partner of John Cobb from about 1750. Responsible for the finest Rococo furniture made for the crown in the early years of George III's reign.

Villa   In ancient Rome, a country estate, including both house and grounds; in later times, a country house or a small detached house.

Villapando, Francisco Corral de (died 1561)   Spanish Renaissance architect who designed the silver choir screen of the Cathedral of Toledo.

Vinette   In Gothic ornament, a motif resembling vines and tendrils.

Vinyl   Common term for *polyvinyl chloride*.

Vinyl fabrics   Textiles fused or coated with *vinyl*. In the coated types the vinyl is opaque, and the surface is printed or embossed.

Viollet-le-duc, Eugène-Emanuel (1814–79)   French architect, author, and theorist, a key figure in the revival of Gothic forms.

Vis-à-vis   French term for two seats facing in opposite directions, attached in the center.

Vitrification   The process of becoming glass or glass-like, usually as a result of intense heat.

Vitrine   French term for a curio cabinet with glass front (particularly Louis XVI). The term is still in use for showcases in museums or shops.

Vitromania   Nineteenth-century practice of decorating plain window glass so that it resembles stained glass. See also *diaphanie*.

Vitruvian scroll   See *running dog*.

Vitruvius Pollio, Marcus (flourished 46–30 B.C.)   Roman architect and architectural theorist.

VOC   Acronym for a volatile organic compound, a material that can emit harmful vapors.

Voile   A light, transparent fabric of plain weave used for *glass curtains*. Hard-twisted thread is used to make it durable. It is usually piece-dyed, striped, or figured, and can be made of cotton, wool, silk, or any synthetic fiber.

Volute   A spiral, scroll-like form, as in the Ionic and Corinthian capitals; a similar shape at the end of a stair railing.

Voussoir   In architecture, a wedge-shaped block used in the construction of a true arch. The central voussoir is called the *keystone*.

Voyeuse   French term for a chair with a padded back rail. The occupant sat facing the back, arms resting on the pad. The equivalent English term is *conversation chair*.

Voysey, C. F. A. (1857–1941)   English domestic architect and designer of furniture, wallpaper, and textiles. His style was inspired by the work of Arthur H. Mackmurdo and influenced that of Charles Rennie Mackintosh.

Vyse   A spiral stair wrapped around a central column.

W

Wachstuch-tapete   German term for a *floorcloth*.

Wag-on-wall   A weight-driven clock with exposed weights and pendulum, intended to hang on the wall.

Wagner, Otto (1841–1918)   Austrian architect and designer of the *Secession* movement.

Wainscot   A wooden lining for interior walls, usually paneled; any treatment resembling same. In classical interiors, the wainscot is usually divided into three parts—a base, a panel (corresponding to the shaft of a column), and a cap molding, this last part being also called a *chair rail*. A wainscot is also called a *dado*. The word is probably derived from the Dutch *wagenschot*, which refers to a fine quality of quartered oak.

Wainscot chair   An early seventeenth-century wooden chair used in England and America. Its back is paneled like a wainscot.

Wainscot cupboard   A *press cupboard*.

Waldglás   A rustic glass, usually with a green or brown tint, that was popular in Germany in medieval times. It is also known as forest glass.

Walnut   A light brown wood taken from trees that grow throughout Europe, Asia, and Africa. Much used for cabinetwork. There are English, French, and Italian varieties. The American walnut has a coarser grain than the European varieties and is often called English walnut or black walnut. The hickory tree has a similar wood and leaf, and is often called a walnut in the United States. See also *butternut* and *black walnut*.

Warm colors   Red and the hues that approach red, orange, and yellow.

Warp   In weaving, the threads that run lengthwise on a loom.

Waterford   Famous Irish glass factory in operation 1784–1851.

Waterleaf   A conventionalized leaf pattern of classical origin used to enrich a *cyma reversa* molding.

Wattle and daub   Construction made of interwoven poles or sticks (wattle) on which is plastered a layer of clay, dung, or mud (daub).

Wave pattern   A continuous pattern conventionally imitating a series of breaking wave crests.

Weald glass   English equivalent of *waldgläs*.

Webbing   Strips of woven burlap used as a support for springs in upholstery.

Wedgwood, Josiah (1730–1795)   Staffordshire potter who established the Wedgwood works.

Weft   In weaving, the threads that run crosswise from selvage to *selvage* and are woven in and out of the *warp* threads by means of a shuttle or bobbin. These are also called the *woof*, but are now more commonly called the *filler* threads.

Weisweiler, Adam (c. 1750–c. 1810)   Louis XVI ébéniste, appointed *Maître Ébéniste* in 1778.

Welting   Strips of material sewn between upholstery seams to give a finished appearance.

What-not   A set of ornamental shelves used to hold *bric-à-brac* and china.

Whieldon, Thomas (1719–86)   A potter at Fenton, Staffordshire, England. The "Whieldon ware" named for him was a speckled earthenware also called "Tortoiseshell." Whieldon employed *Josiah Spode* as an apprentice and was an early partner of *Josiah Wedgwood*.

Whistler, James Abbott McNeill (1834–1903)   American painter, etcher, and decorator.

White lead   A heavy white substance that does not dissolve in water and is used as a base in paints when mixed with linseed oil.

White sound   A low, barely discernible background noise deliberately created to soften the effects of more potentially disturbing noise.

White, Stanford (1853–1906)   American architect, partner in the firm McKim, Mead, & White.

Whitewash   A thin water-base paint containing lime and chalk, also called whiting.

Whitewood   A trade name for poplar and cottonwood. There are several species, but all are characterized by a uniform grain of little interest, so that the wood is used mainly for shelving, interior parts of furniture, and cores in veneered work. It is soft and works easily, but is durable in ordinary use, excellent for painted surfaces.

Wicker   Construction of interwoven pliant twigs, such as willow, often used in furniture.

Wiener Werkstätte   Literally, "Vienna Workshop," a school and design center founded in Vienna in 1903. Its designers included *Josef Hoffmann* and Koloman Moser.

Wild silk   Roughly textured silk obtained from silkworms that feed on oak, cherry, and other leaves, rather than on cultivated mulberry leaves.

Willard family: Simon, Benjamin, Aaron, and Ephraim (active 1743–1848)   Famous family of Massachusetts clockmakers. Simon is credited with introducing the *banjo clock* to America from England.

William and Mary   The baroque style prevailing in England and America during the reigns of King William, 1689–1702, and Queen Mary, 1689–94.

Willow pattern   Scenic pattern for porcelain and ceramic ware, Chinese in character though it originated in England. Very popular in the eighteenth century.

Wilton carpet   A carpet with cut woolen pile and a cotton back.

Windsor chair   Domestic wooden chair popular in eighteenth- and nineteenth-century England and America, its back composed of parallel vertical spindles. Also called a *stickback*.

Wing chair   A tall upholstered chair with wings or ears projecting on either side of the back.

Winslow, Edward (1669–1753)   Boston silversmith.

Wire glass   Glass with a layer of wire imbedded in it to protect against shattering. Also called wired glass.

Wood carpet   An inexpensive alternative to *parquet*, consisting of thin pieces of wood glued to a fabric or paper backing that is nailed or glued to the floor.

Woodcut   A design engraved upon a block of wood in such a way that all the wood is cut away to a slight depth except the lines forming the design. For use in printing papers and textiles.

Woof   See *filler*.

Wormley, Edward (1907–96)   Prolific American furniture designer.

Worsted   Yarn spun from combed wool. Fabric made with such yarn.

Wren, Sir Christopher (1632–1723)   English inventor, astronomer, and—after 1666—architect. He designed St. Paul's Cathedral and many other churches in London.

Wright, Frank Lloyd (1869–1959)   Eminent architect and author, follower of Louis Sullivan in promoting functional and organic design in architecture and the industrial arts.

Wyzenbeek test   Test of a fabric's reistance to abrasion by rubbing it with rollers covered in wire mesh. The number of cycles the fabric can withstand before breakdown is considered a measure of durability.

X

X-shaped chair   A chair, sometimes a folding chair, with legs in the shape of an X when viewed from the sides. Types of X-shaped chairs include the *curule chair*, the *Dante chair*, and the *Savonarola* chair.

X-shaped stretchers   Crossed *stretchers* between chair legs. See also *saltire*.

Xenon arc lamp   A lamp used in testing the degradation of fabric under ultraviolet light.

Xystus   In Greek architecture, an *ambulatory* or *portico*.

Y

Yarn   A strand of textile fibers; the basic material from which thread, twine, or cloth is made. There are two basic categories of yarn: *spun yarn* and *continuous filament yarn*.

Yarn-dyeing   A process of dyeing the yarns before they are woven into a textile. See also *piece-dyeing* and *stock-dyeing*.

Yesería   Spanish term for small lacelike patterns of plaster relief that were colored and used extensively on the walls of Moorish rooms.

Yew   A close-grained hardwood of a deep reddish-brown. It is a European evergreen and thrives especially in England. Frequently used in cabinetwork where an elastic quality is desirable.

Yi   Korean dynasty from 1392 to 1910, also called the *Chosŏn* period.

Yoke   A cross-bar in the form of two S-curves used for the top rail of chair backs, similar in profile to an ox-yoke. Typical of English Georgian furniture. A chair with such a feature is called a yokeback chair.

Yorkshire chair   A popular name for a type of Jacobean chair of provincial origin. Similar to a *Derbyshire chair*.

Yüan dynasty   Mongol dynasty of China, A.D. 1260–1368. Its most famous emperor was Kublai Khan.

Z

Zarf   A footed holder for a handleless cup.

Zebrawood   A light golden-yellow wood with dark brown stripes. It is used for ornamental cabinetwork.

Zelkowa   A Japanese wood, also known as *keyaki*.

Zigzag   See *chevron*.

Zitan   Chinese furniture wood.

Zucchi, Antonio Pietro (1726–1795)   Venetian painter who did decorative paintings for interiors and for some of the furniture of Robert Adam. He was married to the painter Angelica Kauffman.

Zwiebelmuster   A German phrase for "onion pattern," a pattern popular in Meissen porcelain and in wallcoverings and fabrics.

Zwischengoldglas   A glass vessel ornamented with gold, the gold then protected by another layer of glass. The technique was used in ancient Rome and again, from the eighteenth century, in Germany.

Bibliography

General Bibliography

In addition to the books listed specifically for each subject, there are a few books so general as to be applicable to the entire history of interior design or to the entire field of design. These include the following:

Abercrombie, Stanley. *A Philosophy of Interior Design*. New York: Harper & Row, 1990.

Arnheim, Rudolf. *Art and Visual Perception: A Psychology of the Creative Eye*, 60th anniv. ed. (first published 1954). Berkeley: University of California Press, 2004.

Bachelard, Gaston. *The Poetics of Space*. Boston: Beacon, 1969. English translation of *La poètique de l'espace*, 1958. Reprinted with a new foreword by John R. Stilgoe. Boston: Beacon Press, 1994.

Banham, Joanna, ed. *Encyclopedia of Interior Design*, 2 vols. London: Fitzroy Dearborn, 1997.

Blakemore, Robbie G. *History of Interior Design & Furniture*. New York: Van Nostrand Reinhold, 1997.

Bowers, Helen. *Interior Materials & Surfaces: The Complete Guide*. Buffalo, NY: Firefly Books, 2005.

Byars, Mel. *The Design Encyclopedia*. New York: Museum of Modern Art, 2004.

Caplan, Ralph. *By Design*. New York: St. Martin's Press, 1982.

Davidson, Paul, et al. *Antique Collector's Directory of Period Detail*. London: Aurum Press, 2000. Stylistic characteristics from Baroque to Modern.

Dubos, Rene. *So Human an Animal*. New York: Scribner's, 1968. Especially the chapter "Our Buildings Shape Us."

Edwards, Clive. *Encyclopedia of Furniture Materials: Trades and Techniques*. Brookfield, VT: Ashgate, 2000.

Ferebee, Ann. *A History of Design from the Victorian Era to the Present*. New York: Van Nostrand Reinhold, 1970.

Fleming, John, and Hugh Honour. *Dictionary of the Decorative Arts*. New York: Harper & Row, 1977.

Frank, Isabelle, ed. *The Theory of Decorative Art*. New Haven, CT: Yale University Press, 2000. An anthology of essays on the decorative arts written between 1750 and 1940, including pieces by Ruskin, Pugin, Gropius, Wright, and Le Corbusier.

Gloag, John. *A Complete Dictionary of Furniture*, revised and updated by Clive Edwards. Woodstock, NY: Overlook Press, 1991.

Gombrich, E. H. *The Sense of Order: A Study in the Psychology of Decorative Art*. Ithaca, NY: Cornell University Press, 1984.

Gura, Judith. *The Abrams Guide to Period Styles for Interiors*. New York: Abrams, 2005. Comprehensive and attractive survey of Western styles from the seventeenth century to the present.

Hall, E. T. *The Hidden Dimension*. Garden City, NY: Doubleday, 1966.

Harwood, Buie, Bridget May, and Curt Sherman. *Architecture and Interior Design through the 18th Century*. Upper Saddle River, NJ: Prentice Hall, 2002.

Hauser, Arnold. *The Social History of Art*, 4 vols. New York: Knopf, 1952.

Honour, Hugh. *Cabinet Makers and Furniture Designers*. London: Spring Books, 1969. Reprinted 1972 by the Hamlyn Publishing Group, London. In the order of their births, from Jacques Androuet de Cerceau to Charles Eames, profiles of fifty outstanding furniture craftsmen.

Kepes, Gyorgy, ed. *Arts of the Environment*. New York: Braziller, 1972.

———. *The Man-Made Object*. New York: Braziller, 1966.

Kubler, George. *The Shape of Time*. New Haven, CT: Yale University Press, 1962; reprinted 1971. A historian's view of the continuity of history.

Lethaby, W. R. *Form in Civilization*. London: Oxford University Press, 1957. Especially the section "Housing and Furnishing."

Lucie-Smith, Edward. *Furniture: A Concise History*. London: Thames & Hudson, 1979. Especially the first chapter, "Meanings of Furniture."

McCorquodale, Charles. *History of the Interior*. New York: Vendome, 1983.

Morley, John. *The History of Furniture*. New York: Bulfinch Press/Little, Brown, 1999.

Muller, H. J. *The Uses of the Past*, New York: Oxford University Press, 1957.

Pile, John F. *Design: Purpose, Form, and Meaning*. Amherst: University of Massachusetts Press, 1979. Paperback edition, New York: W. W. Norton, 1982.

———. *A History of Interior Design*. New York: Wiley, 2000.

———. *Interior Design*, 2nd rev. ed. New York: Abrams, 2003.

Praz, Mario. *The House of Life*. New York: Oxford University Press, 1964. English translation of *La casa della vita*, 1958, an autobiography in the form of a description of the author's house in Rome and its contents.

———. *An Illustrated History of Interior Decoration from Pompeii to Art Nouveau*. London: Thames & Hudson, 1982. English translation of *La filosofia dell'arredamento*, 1964. Especially valuable for Praz's 55-page introduction.

Rasmussen, Steen Eiler. *Experiencing Architecture*. Cambridge, MA: MIT Press, 1962. Includes many wise observations on the nature of interior space.

Rompilla, Ethyl. New York School of Interior Design. *Color for Interior Design*. New York: Abrams, 2005.

Trench, Lucy, ed. *Materials and Techniques in the Decorative Arts: An Illustrated Dictionary*. Chicago: University of Chicago Press, 2000.

Zevi, Bruno. *Architecture as Space*. New York: Horizon, 1957.

1   Design Before History (Before 3400 B.C.)

Chauvet, Jean-Marie, et al. *Dawn of Art: The Chauvet Cave*. New York: Abrams, 1996.

Fagan, Brian M. *World Prehistory: A Brief Introduction*. New York: Harper Collins, 1993.

Gibson, Michael F. "Reading the Mind before It Could Read," *New York Times*, April 21, 2002.

Gowlett, John A. J. *Ascent to Civilization: The Archaeology of Early Man*. New York: Knopf, 1984.

Haviland, William A. *Cultural Anthropology*, 7th ed. Fort Worth, TX: Harcourt Brace Jovanovich College Publishers, 1973.

Huyghe, René, ed. *The Larousse Encyclopedia of Prehistoric and Ancient Art*. New York: Prometheus, 1962. Especially see André Leroi-Gourhan, "The Beginnings of Art."

Lewis-Williams, David. *The Mind in the Cave: Consciousness and the Origins of Art*. New York: Thames & Hudson, 2002.

Mellaart, James. *Çatal Hüyük: A Neolithic Town in Anatolia*. London: Thames & Hudson, 1967.

———. "A Neolithic City in Turkey," *Scientific American*, April 1964, reprinted in *Prehistoric Times: Readings from Scientific American*. San Francisco: W. H. Freeman, 1983.

2   Egypt (4500 B.C.–A.D. 30)

Egyptian Architecture and Interiors

Aldred, Cyril. *The Egyptians*. London: Thames & Hudson, 1961, 1984.

Badawy, Alexander. *Architecture in Ancient Egypt and the Near East*. Cambridge, MA: MIT Press, 1966.

Bagnall, Roger S. *Egypt in Late Antiquity*. Princeton, NJ: Princeton University Press, 1995. Egypt under Roman rule, with information about the Coptic language, Coptic Christianity, and Coptic art.

Bowman, Alan K. *Egypt after the Pharaohs, 332 B.C.–A.D. 642*. Berkeley: University of California Press, 1986. Paperback edition, London: British Museum Press, 1996.

Breasted, J. H. *A History of Egypt from the Earliest Times to the Persian Conquest*, 3 vols. New York: Scribner, 1909. The work by James Henry Breasted (1865–1935) is the Great Pyramid of Egyptian scholarship, looking a bit old but still immense and awesome. Both Breasted and Flinders Petrie have a number of books about Egypt to their credit in addition to those listed here.

Budge, E. A. Wallis. *The Dwellers on the Nile*. London: Religious Tract Society, 1926. New York: Dover, 1977.

de Cenival, Jean-Louis. *Egypt*. Lausanne: Office du Livre, 1964. Part of the series Architecture of the World, this book has excellent photography by the editor of the series, Henri Stierlin, and an introduction by modern architect Marcel Breuer, in which he discusses the influence of Egyptian architecture on his own work.

Description de l'Egypt. Köln: Taschen, 1994. Despite the French title, the brief introduction is also in English. In any case, this is primarily a picture book, reproducing the thousands of drawings from the expedition to Egypt ordered by Napoleon in 1798. The drawings, displaying exemplary draftsmanship, were first published in 1802.

Edwards, I. E. S. *The Pyramids of Egypt*. Baltimore, MD: Penguin, 1947, rev. 1964. A standard text.

Erman, Adolf. *Life in Ancient Egypt*. 1894. Reprinted, New York: Dover, 1971.

Hodges, Henry. *Technology in the Ancient World*. 1970. New York: Barnes & Noble, 1992.

Hornung, Erik, and Betsy M. Bryan, eds. *The Quest for Immortality: Treasures of Ancient Egypt*. New York: Prestel, 2002.

Huyghe, René, ed. *Larousse Encyclopedia of Prehistoric and Ancient Art*. London: Paul Hamlyn, 1962.

James, T. G. H. *Ancient Egypt: The Land and Its Legacy*. Austin: University of Texas Press, 1988.

———. *Egyptian Painting and Drawing in the British Museum*. Cambridge, MA: Harvard University Press, 1986.

Lucas, Alfred. *Ancient Egyptian Materials and Industries*. London: 1926. J. R. Harris, 4th rev. ed. London: Edward Arnold, 1962.

Malek, Jaromir. *Egyptian Art*. London: Phaidon, 1999.

Montet, Pierre. *Eternal Egypt*. New York: New American Library, 1964.

Morkot, Robert G. *The Egyptians: An Introduction*. London and New York: Routledge, 2005.

Orgogozo, Chantal. *The Discovery of Egypt: Artists, Travelers, and Scientists*. New York: Abbeville, 1993.

Petrie, W. M. Flinders. *Decorative Patterns of the Ancient World*. 1930. New York: Crescent, 1990.

———. *Egyptian Decorative Art*. London, 1895. New York: Benjamin Blom, 1972.

Reeves, Nicholas. *The Complete Tutankhamun: The King, The Tomb, The Royal Treasure*. New York: Thames & Hudson, 1990.

Robins, Gay. *The Art of Ancient Egypt*. London: British Museum Press, 1997.

Roehrig, Catharine H., ed. *Hatshepsut: From Queen to Pharaoh*. New Haven, CT: Yale University Press, 2005.

Russmann, Edna R. *Eternal Egypt: Masterworks of Ancient Art from the British Museum*. Berkeley: University of California Press, 2001.

Siliotti, Alberto. *Egypt: Splendors of an Ancient Civilization*. New York: Thames & Hudson, 1996. Oversize volume with impressive color illustrations.

Smith, W. Stevenson. *The Art and Architecture of Ancient Egypt*. Pelican History of Art series. Harmondsworth, Middlesex, England: Penguin, 1958. Reprinted, New Haven, CT: Yale University Press, 1981.

Stafford-Deitsch, Jeremy. *The Monuments of Ancient Egypt*. Bloomington and Indianapolis: Indiana University Press, 2001.

Tiradritti, Francesco, ed. *Egyptian Treasures from the Egyptian Museum in Cairo*. New York: Abrams, 1999.

Wilkinson, Richard H. *The Complete Temples of Ancient Egypt*. New York: Thames & Hudson, 2001.

Wilkinson, Toby. *The Thames & Hudson Dictionary of Ancient Egypt*. New York: Thames & Hudson, 2005.

Wilson, John A. *The Culture of Ancient Egypt*. Chicago: University of Chicago Press, 1951.

Ziegler, Christiane, ed. *The Pharaohs*. New York: Rizzoli, 2002.

Egyptian Furniture

Baker, Hollis S. *Furniture in the Ancient World*. New York: Macmillan, 1966. Baker is the son of the founder of the Baker Furniture Company of Grand Rapids, MI, and is himself the founder of the Baker Museum of Furniture in that city.

Killen, Geoffrey. *Egyptian Woodworking and Furniture*. Princes Risborough, Buckinghamshire, England: Shire, 1994.

———. "The Style and Development of Ancient Egyptian Furniture," *The Magazine Antiques*, Part 1, April 1997; Part 2, September 1997.

Richter, Gisela. *Ancient Furniture*. Oxford: Oxford University Press, 1926. Also see other books by Richter in the bibliography for Greece.

Wanscher, Ole. *The Art of Furniture*. Oxford: Reinhold, 1966. Includes measured drawings of a few pieces.

Egyptian Decorative Arts: Faience and Glass

Cooney, J. D. *Catalogue of Egyptian Antiquities in the British Museum, IV: Glass*. London: British Museum Press, 1976.

Friedman, Florence Dunn. *Gifts of the Nile: Ancient Egyptian Faience*. New York: Thames & Hudson, 1998.

Goldstein, S. M. *Pre-Roman and Early Roman Glass in the Corning Museum of Glass*. New York: Corning Museum of Glass, 1979.

Kaczmarczyk, A., and R. E. M. Hedges. *Ancient Egyptian Faience*. Warminster, Wiltshire, England: Arris and Phillips, 1983.

Nicholson, Paul T. *Egyptian Faience and Glass*. Princes Risborough, Buckinghamshire, England: Shire, 1986.

Riefstahl, E. *Ancient Egyptian Glass and Glazes in the Brooklyn Museum*. Brooklyn, NY: Brooklyn Museum, 1968.

Egyptian Decorative Arts: Textiles

Hall, Rosalind. *Egyptian Textiles*. Princes Risborough, Buckinghamshire, England: Shire, 1986.

Riefstahl, E. *Patterned Textiles in Pharaonic Egypt*. Brooklyn, NY: Brooklyn Museum, 1945.

Roth, H. L. *Ancient Egyptian and Greek Looms*, 2nd ed. Halifax, N.S.: F. King and Sons, 1951.

Thomas, Thelma K. *Textiles from Medieval Egypt, A.D. 300–1300*. Pittsburgh, PA: Carnegie, 1990.

3   The Ancient Near East (2800–331 B.C.)

Amiet, Pierre. *Art of the Ancient Near East*. New York: Abrams, 1980. Wide-ranging text with over a thousand illustrations.

Burney, Charles. *The Ancient Near East*. Ithaca, NY: Cornell University Press, 1964.

Caubet, Annie, and Patrick Pouyssegur. *The Ancient Near East*. Paris: Terrail, 1998.

Collon, Dominique. *Ancient Near Eastern Art*. Berkeley: University of California Press, 1995.

Du Ry, Carel J. *Art of the Ancient Near and Middle East*. New York: Abrams, 1969.

———. *The Birth of Civilization in the Near East*. New York: Doubleday, 1959.

Frankfort, Henri. *Art and Architecture of the Ancient Orient*, 3rd rev. ed. Baltimore, MD: Penguin Books, 1963. A standard text.

Ghirshman, Roman. *The Art of Ancient Iran*. New York: Golden Press, 1964. Part of the series The Arts of Mankind, edited by André Malraux and Georges Salles. Excellent photographs of Persepolis.

Kuhrt, Amélie, and Susan Sherwin-White, eds. *Hellenism in the East*. London: Duckworth, 1989.

Lloyd, Seton. *The Art of the Ancient Near East*. New York: Praeger, 1961.

Mahboubian, Houshang. *Art of Ancient Iran: Copper and Bronze*. London: Philip Wilson, 1997.

Millar, Fergus. *The Roman Near East, 31 B.C.–A.D. 337*. Cambridge, MA: Harvard University Press, 1995.

Nissen, Hans J. *The Early History of the Ancient Near East, 9000–2000 B.C.* Chicago: University of Chicago Press, 1988.

Postgate, J. N. *Early Mesopotamia: Society and Economy at the Dawn of History*. New York and London: Routledge, 1997.

Pritchard, James B., ed. *The Ancient Near East, Vol. I: An Anthology of Texts and Pictures*. Princeton, NJ: Princeton University Press, 1958.

———. *The Ancient Near East, Vol. II: A New Anthology of Texts and Pictures*. Princeton, NJ: Princeton University Press, 1973.

Roebuck, Carl. *The World of Ancient Times*. New York: Scribner, 1966.

Saggs, H. W. F. *Babylonians*. Norman: University of Oklahoma Press, 1995.

Note: Some of these titles are also applicable to the next chapter, on Greece.

4   Greece (2000–146 B.C.)

The Beginnings of the Classical World

In addition to the following, the University of Pennsylvania Museum of Archaeology and Anthropology has published a series of scholarly texts based on its Minoan collection. For a Classical Greek source, the *Oresteia*, the trilogy of plays—consisting of the *Agamemnon*, *Choephori*, and *Eumenides*—by the Greek dramatist Aeschylus has as its principal figure Agamemnon, King of Mycenae, and much of its action takes place in Mycenae. Among popular fiction, two novels by Mary Renault, *The King Must Die* (1958) and *The Bull from the Sea* (1961), have settings in Minoan Crete.

Boardman, John. *Pre-Classical: From Crete to Archaic Greece*. Harmondsworth, Middlesex, England: Penguin, 1967.

Branigan, Keith. *The Foundations of Ancient Crete: A Survey of Crete in the Early Bronze Age*. New York: Praeger, 1970.

Castleden, Rodney. *Minoans: Life in Bronze Age Crete*. London: Routledge, 1990.

Chadwick, John. *The Minoans*. New York: Praeger, 1971.

———. *The Mycenaean World*. New York: Cambridge University Press, 1976.

Farnoux, Alexandre. *Knossos: Searching for the Legendary Palace of King Minos*. New York: Abrams, 1996. Colorful little paperback in the Discoveries series.

Graham, J. W. *The Palaces of Crete*. Princeton, NJ: Princeton University Press, 1962.

Hampe, Roland. *The Birth of Greek Art: From the Mycenaean to the Archaic Period*. New York: Oxford University Press, 1981.

Higgins, Reynold. *The Archaeology of Minoan Crete*. New York: Henry Z. Walck, 1973.

————. *Minoan and Mycenaean Art*. New York: Praeger, 1967.

Hood, Sinclair. *The Arts in Prehistoric Greece*. Pelican History of Art series. Harmondsworth, Middlesex, England: Penguin, 1978.

————. *The Home of the Heroes*. New York: McGraw-Hill, 1967.

————. *The Minoans: Crete in the Bronze Age*. New York: Praeger, 1971.

Matz, Friedrich. *The Art of Crete and Early Greece: The Prelude to Greek Art*. Art of the World series. New York: Greystone Press, 1962.

Mellersh, H. E. L. *The Destruction of Knossos: The Rise and Fall of Minoan Crete*. 1970. Reprinted, New York: Barnes & Noble, 1993.

Willetts, R. F. *The Civilization of Ancient Crete*. 1976. New York: Barnes & Noble, 1995.

————. *Everyday Life in Ancient Crete*. New York: G. P. Putnam, 1969.

————. "The Minoans," in Arthur Cotterell, ed. *The Penguin Encyclopedia of Ancient Civilizations*. Harmondsworth, Middlesex, England: Penguin, 1980.

Greek Architecture and Interiors

Ashmole, Bernard. *Architect and Sculptor in Classical Greece*. New York: New York University Press, 1972.

Boardman, John. *Greek Art*, 4th ed. New York: Thames & Hudson, 1996.

————, ed. *The Oxford History of Classical Art*. New York: Oxford University Press, 1993.

Boardman, John, Jasper Griffin, and Oswyn Murray, eds. *The Oxford History of the Classical World*. New York: Oxford University Press, 1986.

Bowra, C. M. *The Greek Experience*. London: Weidenfield and Nicolson, 1957.

Carpenter, Rhys. *The Esthetic Basis of Greek Art*, 2nd ed. Bloomington: Indiana University Press, 1959 Interesting reflections on the character of Greek art.

Chamoux, François. *The Civilization of Greece*, trans. W. S. Maguinness. New York: Simon & Schuster, 1965.

Dinsmoor, William Bell. *The Architecture of Ancient Greece*. London: B. T. Batsford, 1950. 3rd rev. ed. New York: Biblo and Tannen, 1973. A standard text.

Durando, Furio. *Ancient Greece: The Dawn of the Western World*. New York: Stewart, Tabori & Chang, 1997.

Fullerton, Mark D. *Greek Art*. New York: Cambridge University Press, 2000.

Grant, Michael. *The Rise of the Greeks*. New York: Scribner, 1988.

Holloway, R. Ross. *A View of Greek Art*. Providence, RI: Brown University Press, 1973.

Kitto, H. D. F. *The Greeks*. Harmondsworth, Middlesex, England: Penguin, 1951. rev. ed. 1985.

Lawrence, A. W. *Greek Architecture*. Pelican History of Art series. Harmondsworth, Middlesex, England: Penguin, 1957. rev. ed. 1973.

Martin, Roland. *Living Architecture: Greece*. New York: Grosset & Dunlap, 1967. Reprinted in Benedikt Taschen Verlag's Architecture of the World series.

Mertens, Joan R., et al. *The Metropolitan Museum of Art: Greece and Rome*. New York: Metropolitan Museum of Art, 1987. Over a hundred objects from the museum's collection.

Nevett, Lisa C. *House and Society in the Ancient Greek World*. New York: Cambridge University Press, 1999.

Pollitt, J. J. *Art and Experience in Classical Greece*. New York: Cambridge University Press, 1972.

Richter, Gisela M. A. *A Handbook of Greek Art: A Survey of the Visual Arts of Ancient Greece*. Oxford: Phaidon, 1959. Reprinted, New York: Da Capo, 1987.

Rider, Bertha Carr. *Ancient Greek Houses*. Chicago: Argonaut, 1964. Reprinted, New York: Benjamin Blom, 1967.

Schefold, Karl. *The Art of Classical Greece*. Art of the World series. New York: Greystone Press, 1967.

Scranton, Robert L. *Greek Architecture*. New York: Braziller, 1962.

————. "Interior Design of Greek Temples," *American Journal of Archaeology, I*. 1946.

Scully, Vincent. *The Earth, the Temple, and the Gods: Greek Sacred Architecture*. New Haven, CT: Yale University Press. Rev. ed. New York: Praeger, 1969. Speculations, some of them controversial, of an eminent architectural historian.

Spivey, Nigel. *Greek Art*. London: Phaidon, 1997.

Tzonis, Alexander, and Liane Lefaivre. *Classical Architecture: The Poetics of Order*. Cambridge, MA: MIT Press, 1986. Excellent survey of the principles of classical composition, available in paperback.

Wycherley, R. E. *The Stones of Athens*. Princeton, NJ: Princeton University Press, 1978.

Note: Some of these titles are also applicable to the next chapter, on Rome.

Greek Architecture and Interiors: The Acropolis and the Parthenon

Virtually every book on Greek art mentions the Parthenon. Those with a specific focus on the building include the following:

Boardman, J. *The Parthenon and Its Sculptures*. London: Thames & Hudson, 1985. Well illustrated.

Bruno, Vincent J., ed. *The Parthenon*. New York: W. W. Norton, 1974. Essays on the history, the aesthetic refinements, and the sculpture of the Parthenon. Included is an eyewitness account of the building's bombardment in the seventeenth century. Glossary and excellent bibliography, arranged by topics.

Cook, B. F. *The Elgin Marbles*. London: British Museum Press, 1984.

Hambridge, Jay. *The Parthenon and Other Greek Temples: Their Dynamic Symmetry*. New Haven, CT: Yale University Press, 1924. An idiosyncratic view of the principles of proportion on which the Parthenon might have been based. Hambridge wrote a number of books on the system of proportion he called *dynamic symmetry*.

Haynes, D. E. L. *The Parthenon Frieze*. London: Batchworth Press, 1973. A portfolio of detail photographs.

Hitchens, Christopher. *The Elgin Marbles: Should They Be Returned to Greece?* London: Chatto and Windus, 1987. Also published by Hill & Wang, New York, 1987 under the title *Imperial Spoils: The Curious Case of the Elgin Marbles*.

Jenkins. Ian. *The Parthenon Frieze*. Austin: University of Texas Press, 1994.

Rhodes, Robin Francis. *Architecture and Meaning on the Athenian Acropolis*. New York: Cambridge University Press, 1995.

Greek Furniture

Baker, Hollis S. *Furniture in the Ancient World*. New York: Macmillan, 1966.

Richter, Gisela M. A. *Ancient Furniture*. Oxford: Oxford University Press, 1926.

———. *The Furniture of the Greeks, Etruscans, and Romans*. London: Phaidon, 1966.

Robsjohn-Gibbings, T. H., and Carlton W. Pullin. *Furniture of Classical Greece*. New York: Knopf, 1963. An appreciation and re-creation of Greek furniture by Robsjohn-Gibbings, a modern author and designer (1909–73).

Greek Decorative Arts: The Greek Vase

Like the Parthenon, Greek vases are mentioned in almost every book on Greek art. Among more specialized texts are the following:

Arias, Paolo Enrico. *A History of Greek Vase Painting*. New York: Thames & Hudson, 1962.

Beazley, J. D. *Attic Black Figure Vase Painters*. Oxford: Oxford University Press, 1956. This and the following book are standard scholarly references, as are the 1974 and 1975 books by Boardman.

———. *Attic Red Figure Vase Painters*. Oxford: Oxford University Press, 1942.

Boardman, John. *Athenian Black Figure Vases*. New York: Oxford University Press, 1974.

———. *Athenian Red Figure Vases*. New York: Oxford University Press, 1975.

———. *The History of Greek Vases*. New York: Thames & Hudson, 2001.

Folsom, Robert S. *Attic Black-Figured Pottery*. Park Ridge, NJ: Noyes Press, 1975.

———. *Handbook of Greek Pottery: A Guide for Amateurs*. Greenwich, CT: New York Graphic Society, 1967.

Herford, Mary A. B. *A Handbook of Greek Vase Painting*. Sparks, NV: Falcon Hill Press, 1995. Reprint of the 1919 original published in Manchester and London.

Morris, Sarah P. *The Black and White Style*. New Haven, CT: Yale University Press, 1984.

Rasmussen, Tom, and Nigel Spivey, eds. *Looking at Greek Vases*. New York: Cambridge University Press, 1991.

Schreiber, Toby. *Athenian Vase Construction: A Potter's Analysis*. Malibu, CA: J. Paul Getty Museum, 1999. How they were made.

Shapiro, H. A. *Myth into Art: Poet and Painter in Classical Greece*. London and New York: Routledge, 1994.

Shapiro, H. A., Carlos A. Picún, and Gerry D. Scott, III, eds. *Greek Vases in the San Antonio Museum of Art*. San Antonio, TX: San Antonio Museum of Art, 1995.

Williams, Dyfri. *Greek Vases*. Cambridge, MA: Harvard University Press, 1985. A highly readable summary available in paperback.

5 Rome (753 B.C.–A.D. 550)

The Etruscan Heritage

Boëthius, Axel. *Etruscan and Early Roman Architecture*. Harmondsworth, Middlesex, England: Penguin, 1978.

Haynes, Sybille. *Etruscan Civilization: A Cultural History*. Los Angeles: Getty Trust, 2001. Reprinted in paperback, 2005.

Sprenger, Maja, and Gilda Bartolini. *Etruscan Art*. World of Art series. New York: Abrams, 1983.

Steingräber, Stephan, ed. *Etruscan Painting: Catalogue Raisonné of Etruscan Wall Painting*. New York: Harcourt Brace Jovanovich, 1985.

Roman Architecture and Interiors

D'Arms, John H. *Romans on the Bay of Naples*. Cambridge, MA: Harvard University Press, 1970.

Deiss, Joseph J. *Herculaneum: Italy's Buried Treasure*. New York: Harper & Row, 1985.

Etienne, Robert. *Pompeii: The Day a City Died*, trans. Caroline Palmer. In the paperback Discoveries series. New York: Abrams, 1992.

Feder, Theodore H. *Great Treasures of Pompeii and Herculaneum*. New York: Abbeville, 1978.

Grant, Michael. *Cities of Vesuvius: Pompeii and Herculaneum*. New York: Penguin, 1971.

Hibbert, Christopher. *Rome: The Biography of a City*. New York: W. W. Norton, 1985.

MacDonald, William L. *The Architecture of the Roman Empire, I: An Introductory Study*. New Haven, CT: Yale University Press, 1965.

Packer, James E., and Kevin Lee Sarring. *The Forum of Trajan in Rome: A Study of the Monuments*, 3 vols. Berkeley: University of California Press, 1997.

Richardson, L., Jr. *Pompeii: An Architectural History*. Baltimore, MD: Johns Hopkins University Press, 1988.

Ward-Perkins, J. B. *Roman Imperial Architecture*. Harmondsworth, Middlesex, England: Penguin, 1981.

Wheeler, Mortimer. *Roman Art and Architecture*. World of Art series. New York: Thames & Hudson, 1985.

Roman Architecture and Interiors: The Pantheon

MacDonald, William L. *The Pantheon: Design, Meaning, and Progeny*. Cambridge, MA: Harvard University Press, 1976.

Mark, Robert, and Paul Hutchinson. "On the Structure of the Roman Pantheon," *Art Bulletin*, vol. LXVIII, no. 3, March 1986, pp. 24–34.

Roman Architecture and Interiors: Baths

Yegül, Fikret. *Baths and Bathing in Classical Antiquity*. New York and Cambridge, MA: Architectural History Foundation and MIT Press, 1992.

Roman Architecture and Interiors: Houses

Barton, Ian M., ed. *Roman Domestic Buildings*. Exeter, Devon, England: University of Exeter Press, 1996.

Clarke, John R. *The Houses of Roman Italy, 100 B.C.–A.D. 250: Ritual, Space, and Decoration*. Berkeley: University of California Press, 1991.

McKay, A. G. *Houses, Villas and Palaces in the Roman World*, ed. H. H. Scullard. Aspects of Greek and Roman Life series. Ithaca, NY: Cornell University Press, 1975.

Roman Architecture and Interiors: The Domus Aurea

Boëthius, Axel. *The Golden House of Nero*. Ann Arbor: University of Michigan Press, 1960.

Roman Architecture and Interiors: Hadrian's Villa

MacDonald, William L., and John A. Pinto. *Hadrian's Villa and Its Legacy*. New Haven, CT: Yale University Press, 1995.

Roman Ornament: Wall Treatments

Amery, Colin, and Brian Curran, Jr. *The Lost World of Pompeii*. Los Angeles: J. Paul Getty Museum and the World Monuments Fund, 2002. Includes descriptions of the four styles of Roman frescoes.

Davey, Norman, and Roger Ling. *Wall-Painting in Roman Britain*. Gloucester, Gloucestershire, England: Alan Sutton, 1982. Descriptions of restoration work based on assembling fragments.

Mazzoleni, Donatella. *Domus: Wall Painting in the Roman House*. Los Angeles: Getty, 2005. Well illustrated.

Roman Furniture

Liversidge, Joan. *Furniture in Roman Britain*. London: Tiranti, 1955.

Roman Decorative Arts: Glass

Battie, David, and Simon Cottle, eds. *Sotheby's Concise Encyclopedia of Glass*. London: Conran Octopus, 1991. Especially see the chapter "Roman Glass" by Martine Newby.

Fleming, Stuart J. *Roman Glass: Reflections on Everyday Life*. Philadelphia: University of Pennsylvania Museum of Archaeology and Anthropology, 1997.

Harden, Donald Benjamin, et al. *Glass of the Caesars*. Milan: Olivetti, 1987.

Hodges, Henry. *Technology in the Ancient World*. New York: Barnes & Noble, 1992.

Price, J. "Glass," in M. Henig, ed. *Handbook of Roman Art*. Ithaca, NY: Cornell University Press, 1983.

Stern, E. Marianne. *Roman, Byzantine, and Early Medieval Glass*. Ostfildern-Ruit, Germany: Hatje Cantz, 2001. Distributed in the United States by Distributed Art Publishers, New York.

Tait, Hugh, ed. *Glass: 5,000 Years*. New York: Abrams, 1991.

Whitehouse, David. *Glass of the Roman Empire*. Ithaca, NY: Corning Museum, 1988.

Roman Decorative Arts: Mosaics

Blanchard-Lemèe, Michèle, et al. *Mosaics of Roman Africa: Floor Mosaics from Tunisia*. New York: Braziller, 1996.

Dunbabin, Katherine M. *Mosaics of the Greek and Roman World*. New York: Cambridge University Press, 1999.

Ling, Roger. *Ancient Mosaics*. Princeton, NJ: Princeton University Press, 1998.

6 Early Christian and Byzantine Design (A.D. 1–800 and 330–1453)

Early Christian and Byzantine Architecture and Interiors

Beckwith, John. *Early Christian and Byzantine Art*. Harmondsworth, Middlesex, England: Pelican, 1970. An authoritative survey.

Eco, Umberto. *Art and Beauty in the Middle Ages*. New Haven, CT: Yale University Press, 1986.

Huyghe, René, ed. *Larousse Encyclopedia of Byzantine and Medieval Art*. New York: Prometheus, 1968. Translated from the French original, Paris: Librairie Larousse, 1958.

Kazhdan, Alexander P., ed. *The Oxford Dictionary of Byzantium*, 3 vols. New York: Oxford University Press, 1991. Reference books with many relevant entries.

Kitzinger, Ernst. *Byzantine Art in the Making*, 2nd ed. Cambridge, MA: Harvard University Press, 1980.

Krautheimer, Richard. *Early Christian and Byzantine Architecture*. Penguin, 1965; New Haven, CT: Yale University Press, 1986. A standard authority. The 1986 revision was prepared with the collaboration of Slobodan Ćurčić.

Lancaster, Osbert. *Sailing to Byzantium*. Boston: Gambit, 1969. Observations by a well-informed modern traveler.

Lowden, John. *Early Christian and Byzantine Art*. Art and Ideas series. London: Phaidon, 1997.

Lowrie, Walter. *Art in the Early Church*. New York: Pantheon, 1947.

MacDonald, William. *Early Christian and Byzantine Architecture*. Great Ages of World Architecture series. New York: Braziller, 1970.

Maguire, Henry. *Art and Eloquence in Byzantium*. Princeton, NJ: Princeton University Press, 1981.

Mâle, Emile. *Art and Artists of the Middle Ages*, trans. Sylvia Stallings Lowe. Redding Ridge, CT: Black Swan, 1986.

Martindale, Andrew. *The Rise of the Artist in the Middle Ages and Early Renaissance*. London: Thames & Hudson, 1972.

Morey, Charles Rufus. *Early Christian Art*. Princeton, NJ: Princeton University Press, 1953. Covers the period before the eighth century.

Rice, David Talbot. *Byzantine Art*, rev. ed. Baltimore, MD: Penguin, 1954.

Rodly, L. *Byzantine Art and Architecture: An Introduction*. Cambridge: Cambridge University Press, 1994.

Runciman, Steven. *Byzantine Civilization*. London: Edward Arnold, 1933; New York: Barnes & Noble, 1994.

———. *Byzantine Style and Civilization*. Harmondsworth, Middlesex, England: Pelican, 1975.

Saalman, Howard. *Medieval Architecture: European Architecture 600–1200*. Great Ages of World Architecture series. New York: Braziller, 1967.

Shaver-Crandall, Annie. *The Middle Ages*. Cambridge Introduction to Art series. New York: Cambridge University Press, 1982.

Snyder, James. *Medieval Art: Painting, Sculpture, Architecture, Fourth–Fourteenth-Century*. New York: Abrams, 1989.

Stewart, Cecil. *Early Byzantine and Romanesque Architecture*. New York: David McKay, 1954.

Stoddard, Whitney S. *Art and Architecture in Medieval France*. New York: Harper & Row, 1972.

Volbach, W. F. and M. Hirmer. *Early Christian Art*. New York: Abrams, 1961.

Webb, G. *Architecture in Britain: The Middle Ages*. Harmondsworth, Middlesex, England: Pelican, 1956.

Early Christian and Byzantine Architecture and Interiors: Hagia Sophia, Constantinople

Balfour, John Patrick Douglas, and Lord Kinross. *Hagia Sophia: A History of Constantinople*. Newsweek's Wonders of Man series. New York: Newsweek Book Division, 1972.

Kähler, Heinz, ed. *Hagia Sophia*. New York: Praeger, 1967.

MacDonald, William. "The Structure of St. Sophia," *Architectural Forum*, May 1963, pp. 131–38, 210.

Mainstone, Roland J. *Hagia Sophia: Architecture, Structure and Liturgy of Justinian's Great Church*. New York: Thames & Hudson, 1988.

Mark, Robert, and Ahmet S. Cakmak, eds. *Hagia Sophia from the Age of Justinian to the Present*, New York: Cambridge University Press, 1992.

Nelson, Robert S. *Hagia Sophia, 1850–1950: Holy Wisdom Modern Monument*. Chicago: The University of Chicago, 2004. The ancient building's significance in modern times.

Swift, E. H. *Hagia Sophia*. New York: Columbia University Press, 1940.

Early Christian and Byzantine Architecture and Interiors: San Vitale, Ravenna

von Simson, Otto G. *Sacred Fortress: Byzantine Art and Statecraft in Ravenna*. Chicago: University of Chicago Press, 1948. Concentrates on three churches: San Vitale, Sant' Apollinare in Classe, and Sant' Apollinare Nuovo.

Early Christian and Byzantine Architecture and Interiors: St. Mark's, Venice

Demus, Otto. *The Church of San Marco in Venice*. Washington, DC: Dumbarton Oaks, 1960.

———. *The Mosaic Decoration of San Marco Venice*, ed. Herbert L. Kessler. Chicago: University of Chicago Press, 1988.

The Treasury of San Marco Venice. Milan: Olivetti, with the Metropolitan Museum of Art, New York: 1984. Exhibition catalog.

Unrau, John. *Ruskin and St Marks*. New York: Thames & Hudson, 1984.

Early Christian and Byzantine Ornament

von Heideloff, Karl Alexander. *Medieval Ornament*. Mineola, NY: Dover, 1995. Reprint of a work first published in the nineteenth century.

Early Christian and Byzantine Decorative Art

Buckton, David, ed. *Byzantium: Treasures of Byzantine Art and Culture*. London: British Museum Press, 1994. Exhibition catalog.

Dark, Ken. *Byzantine Pottery*. Stroud, Gloucestershire, England: Tempus, 2001.

Evans, Helen C., ed. *Byzantium: Faith and Power (1261–1557)*. New Haven, CT: Yale University Press, 2004. Catalog of an exhibition at the Metropolitan Museum of Art, New York, 2004.

Temple, Richard, ed. *Early Christian and Byzantine Art*. London: Element Books and the Temple Gallery, 1990. Good illustrations of textiles, metalwork, frescoes, tile, and ceramics.

Early Christian and Byzantine Decorative Art: Mosaics

Demus, Otto. *Byzantine Mosaic Decoration*. London: Routledge, Kegan Paul, 1953. Many plates.

Gary, Dorothy Hales, and Robert Payne. *The Splendors of Byzantium*. New York: Viking, 1967. Minimal text, but many full-page plates of Byzantine mosaics.

Jolly, Penny Howell. *Made in God's Image: Eve and Adam in the Genesis Mosaics at San Marco, Venice*. Berkeley: University of California Press, 1997.

Mango, Cyril. "The Mosaics of Hagia Sophia," in *Hagia Sophia*, ed. Heinz Kähler, New York: Praeger, 1967.

"Mosaic," in *The Dictionary of Art*, ed. Jane Shoaf Turner. New York: Grove/Macmillan, 1996, vol. 22.

7 Romanesque and Norman Design (c. 800–c. 1200)

Romanesque Architecture and Interiors

Beckwith, John. *Early Medieval Art: Carolingian, Ottonian, Romanesque*. New York: Thames & Hudson, 1964; rev. ed. 1969.

Conant, Kenneth J. *Carolingian and Romanesque Architecture, 800–1200*. Harmondsworth, Middlesex, England: Penguin, 1959; rev. ed. 1966.

Davis-Weyer, Caecilia. *Early Medieval Art, 300–1150.* Sources and Documents in the History of Art series. Englewood Cliffs, NJ: Prentice Hall, 1971.

Focillon, Henri. *The Art of the West, Volume I: Romanesque.* Ithaca, NY: Cornell University Press, 1963. Focillon's Volume II is *Gothic.*

Henderson, George. *Early Medieval.* In the Style and Civilization series. Harmondsworth, Middlesex, England: Penguin, 1972.

Kidson, Peter. *The Medieval World.* In the Landmarks of the World's Art series. New York: McGraw-Hill, 1967. This book divides its subject into three chapters: Pre-Romanesque, Romanesque, and Gothic. Well illustrated, with illustrations well tied to the text.

Martindale, Andrew. *The Rise of the Artist in the Middle Ages and Early Renaissance.* London: Thames & Hudson, 1972.

Nebolsine, George. *Journey into Romanesque.* New York: G. P. Putnam, 1969. A traveler's guide to Romanesque monuments in Europe, but with good general information about the style.

Romanesque Architecture and Interiors: Ste.-Madeleine, Vézelay, France

Mouilleron, Véronique Rouchon. *Vézelay: The Great Romanesque Church.* New York: Abrams, 1999. Fine photography by Daniel Faure of the church's stone carvings.

Romanesque Ornament

Pajares-Ayuela, Paloma. *Cosmatesque Ornament.* New York: W. W. Norton, 2001.

Romanesque Furniture

Mercer, Eric. *Furniture, 700–1700.* Social History of the Decorative Arts series, ed. Hugh Honour. New York: Meredith, 1969.

Romanesque Decorative Arts

Demus, Otto. *The Mosaics of Norman Sicily.* London: Routledge, Kegan Paul, 1949.

Wilson, David M. *The Bayeux Tapestry.* New York: Thames & Hudson, 2004.

8 The Gothic (1132–c. 1500)

Gothic Architecture and Interiors

Adams, Henry. *Mont-Saint-Michel and Chartres.* Boston: Houghton Mifflin, 1913. Famous study that contrasts the Romanesque Mont-Saint-Michel with the Gothic Chartres, the unity of the thirteenth century with the diversity of the twentieth century, and the symbol of the Virgin with the symbol of the dynamo.

Anderson, William. *The Rise of the Gothic.* Salem, NH: Salem House, 1985.

Bony, Jean. *French Cathedrals.* Boston: Houghton Mifflin, 1951. Well illustrated with photographs by Martin Hürlimann.

Branner, Robert. *Gothic Architecture.* Great Ages of World Architecture series. New York: Braziller, 1964.

Erlande-Brandenburg, Alain. *Gothic Art.* New York: Abrams, 1989. English translation of a book first published in France in 1983. Richly illustrated.

———. *Notre-Dame de Paris.* New York: Abrams, 1998. Photography by Caroline Rose.

Frisch, Teresa G. *Gothic Art, 1140–c. 1450.* Sources and Documents in the History of Art series. Englewood Cliffs, NJ: Prentice Hall, 1971.

Gimpel, Jean. *The Cathedral Builders,* trans. Teresa Waugh. Salisbury, Wiltshire, England: Michael Russell, 1983; New York: Harper Collins, 1984. First published in France as *Les Bâtisseurs de Cathédrales,* 1961. Includes an eloquent account of the differing views of St. Bernard and Abbot Suger.

Grodecki, Louis. *Gothic Architecture.* History of World Architecture series. Milan: Electa Editrice, 1978; New York: Rizzoli, 1985.

Henderson, George. *Gothic.* Style and Civilization series. Harmondsworth, Middlesex, England: Penguin, 1967.

Icher, François. *Building the Great Cathedrals.* New York: Abrams, 1998. A simple presentation of practical information about how the cathedrals were commissioned, funded, designed, and built.

Macaulay, David. *Cathedral: The Story of Its Construction.* Boston: Houghton Mifflin, 1973. Informative picture story of how the building was accomplished.

Mâle, Emile. *The Gothic Image: Religious Art in France of the Thirteenth Century.* New York: Harper & Row, 1958.

Martindale, Andrew. *Gothic Art.* New York: Thames & Hudson, 1985.

Panofsky, Erwin, ed. and trans. *Abbot Suger on the Abbey Church of St. Denis and Its Art Treasures.* Princeton, NJ: Princeton University Press, 1946. English translation of Abbot Suger's own account of the rebuilding of St.-Denis in the new Gothic style.

Scott, Robert A. *The Gothic Enterprise: A Guide to Understanding the Medieval Cathedral.* Berkeley: University of California Press, 2003.

Simson, Otto Georg von. *The Gothic Cathedral: The Origins of Gothic Architecture and the Medieval Concept of Order.* New York: Pantheon, 1956.

Wilson, Christopher. *The Gothic Cathedral: The Architecture of the Great Church, 1130–1530.* London: Thames & Hudson, 1990. Winner of the Alice Davis Hitchcock Medallion of the Society of Architectural Historians of Great Britain for its "outstanding contribution to architectural history."

Worringer, Wilhelm. *Form in Gothic.* London: Tiranti, 1957. First published as *Formprobleme der Gotik.* See especially Chapter XVIII, "The Interior Structure of the Cathedral."

Gothic Architecture and Interiors: Chartres Cathedral

Branner, Robert, ed. *Chartres Cathedral.* New York: W. W. Norton, 1969. An interesting collection of old and new descriptions of the building.

Burckhardt, Titus. *Chartres and the Birth of the Cathedral.* Bloomington, IN: World Wisdom Books, 1996. First published in German in 1962.

Favier, Jean. *The World of Chartres.* New York: Abrams, 1990. First published in Paris in 1998 as *L'Univers de Chartres.* Photography by Jean Bernard.

Jantzen, Hans. *High Gothic: The Classic Cathedrals of Chartres, Reims, and Amiens.* Princeton, NJ: Princeton University Press, 1984. First published in Hamburg, 1957.

Gothic Architecture and Interiors: Amiens Cathedral

Murray, Stephen. *Notre-Dame: Cathedral of Amiens.* New York: Cambridge University Press, 1996.

Gothic Architecture and Interiors: Ca d'Oro, Venice

Goy, Richard J. *The House of Gold.* New York: Cambridge University Press, 1992.

Gothic Ornament: Stained Glass

Armitage, E. Liddall. *Stained Glass.* Newton, MA: Charles T. Branford, 1959. A history of stained glass followed by technical information about producing it.

Arnold, Hugh. *Stained Glass of the Middle Ages in England and France.* London: A. and C. Black, 1956.

Brown, Sarah, and David O'Connor. *Glass-Painters.* Toronto: University of Toronto Press, 1991. Part of the Medieval Craftsmen series, which also includes small books on painters, embroiderers, masons, and sculptors.

Cowen, Painton. *Rose Windows.* San Francisco: Chronicle, 1979. Color plates and geometric diagrams of window patterns.

———. *The Rose Window: Splendor and Symbol.* New York: Thames & Hudson, 2005. With more than 300 color illustrations.

Grodecki, Louis, and Catherine Brisac. *Gothic Stained Glass, 1200–1300.* Ithaca, NY: Cornell University Press, 1985. Originally published as *Le Vitrail gothique au XIIIe siècle.*

Gothic Decorative Arts: Tapestries

Ackerman, Phyllis. *Tapestry: The Mirror of Civilization.* 1933. New York: AMS Press, 1970.

Jarry, Madeleine. *World Tapestry.* New York: G. P. Putnam, 1968.

Phillips, Barty. *Tapestry.* London: Phaidon, 1994.

"Tapestry," in *The Dictionary of Art,* ed. Jane Shoaf Turner. New York: Grove/Macmillan, 1996, vol. 30.

Thomson, Francis Paul. *Tapestry: Mirror of History.* New York: Crown, 1980.

9 Islamic Design (A.D. 622 to the Present)

Islamic Architecture and Interiors

Aslanapa, Oktay. *Turkish Art and Architecture.* New York: Praeger, 1971.

Barry, Michael. *Figurative Art in Medieval Islam.* Paris: Flammarion, 2004. Distributed in the United States by Rizzoli.

Blair, Sheila S., and Jonathan M. Bloom. *The Art and Architecture of Islam, 1250–1800.* New Haven, CT: Yale University Press, 1994. Part of the Pelican History of Art series, following the book by Ettinghausen and Grabar.

Bloom, Jonathan, and Sheila Blair. *Islamic Arts.* Art and Ideas series. London: Phaidon, 1997.

Brend, Barbara. *Islamic Art.* Cambridge, MA: Harvard University Press, 1991.

Ettinghausen, Richard, et al. *The Arts of Islam: Masterpieces from the Metropolitan Museum of Art.* New York: Abrams, 1982. Published in conjunction with the exhibition "The Arts of Islam" at the Museum für Islamische Kunst, Berlin, 1981.

Ettinghausen, Richard, and Oleg Grabar. *The Art and Architecture of Islam, 650–1250.* Pelican History of Art series. New Haven, CT: Yale University Press, 1987. See also Balir and Bloom, above.

Frishman, Martin, and Hasan-Uddin Khan, eds. *The Mosque: History, Architectural Development, and Regional Diversity.* New York: Thames & Hudson, 1994.

Goodwin, Godfrey. *History of Ottoman Architecture.* London: Thames & Hudson, 1971.

Grabar, Oleg. *The Formation of Islamic Art.* New Haven, CT: Yale University Press, 1973.

Hattstein, Markus, and Peter Delius, eds. *Islam: Art and Architecture.* Königswinter: Konemann, an imprint of Tandem Verlag GmbH, 2004.

Hillenbrand, Robert. *Islamic Art and Architecture.* World of Art series, New York: Thames & Hudson, 1999.

Hoag, John D. *Western Islamic Architecture.* Great Ages of World Architecture series. New York: Braziller, 1963.

Irwin, Robert. *Islamic Art in Context: Art, Architecture, and the Literary World.* Perspective series. New York: Abrams, 1997. Includes interesting sections on artisan guilds, calligraphy, and Islamic art in Spain, Sicily, India, and China.

"Islamic Art," various authors, in *The Dictionary of Art,* ed. Jane Turner. New York: Grove/Macmillan, 1996, vol. 16, pp. 94–561.

Michell George, ed. *Architecture of the Islamic World: Its History and Social Meaning.* London: Thames & Hudson, 1978. See especially Chapter 5, "The Elements of Decoration: Surface, Pattern, and Light" by Dalu Jones.

Nuseibeh, Saïd, and Oleg Grabar. *The Dome of the Rock.* New York: Rizzoli, 1996.

Papadopoulos, Alexandre. *Islam and Muslim Art.* New York: Abrams, 1979.

Rice, David Talbot. *Islamic Art,* rev. ed. World of Art series. New York: Thames & Hudson, 1975.

Scarce, Jennifer. *Domestic Life in the Middle East.* Edinburgh: National Museums of Scotland, 1996. Interesting details of urban households in Turkey, Iran, and Egypt between the sixteenth and nineteenth centuries.

Seherr-Thoss, Sonia P. *Design and Color in Islamic Architecture: Afghanistan, Iran, Turkey.* Washington, DC: Smithsonian Institution Press, 1968. With photography by Hans C. Seherr-Thoss.

Smithsonian Institution. *7,000 Years of Iranian Art.* Washington, DC: Smithsonian Institution Press, 1964. Exhibition catalog, obviously not limited to Islamic art.

Tabbaa, Yasser. *The Transformation of Islamic Art during the Sunni Revival*. Seattle: University of Washington Press, 2001.

Vogt-Göknil, Ulya. *Living Architecture: Ottoman*. London: Oldbourne, 1966.

Islamic Ornament

Grabar, Oleg. *The Mediation of Ornament*. Princeton, NJ: Princeton University Press, 1992. Based on the author's 1989 Mellon Lectures in the Fine Arts, the book uses Islamic ornament as a basis for studying the role of ornament in general.

Islamic Ornament: Tile

Barry, Michael. *Design and Color in Islamic Architecture: Eight Centuries of the Tile-Maker's Art*. New York: Vendome, 1996. Features photography by Roland and Sabrina Michaud.

Pickett, Douglas. *Early Persian Tilework*. Madison, NJ: Fairleigh Dickinson University Press, 1997.

Islamic Decorative Arts

Jereb, James F. *Arts and Crafts of Morocco*. San Francisco: Chronicle, 1996.

Paccard, André. *Traditional Islamic Craft in Moroccan Architecture*, 2 vols. Saint-Jorioz, France: Editions Ateliers 74, 1980. Richly illustrated study by a French architect working in Morocco.

Palace of Gold and Light: Treasures from the Topkapi, Istanbul. Washington, DC: Palace Arts Foundation, Inc., 2000.

Wulff, H. E. *The Traditional Crafts of Persia*. Cambridge, MA: MIT Press, 1966. The emphasis is on the techniques and technology underlying the crafts, and there is an extensive glossary of technical terms.

Islamic Decorative Arts: Ceramics

Atasoy, Nurhan, and Julian Raby. *Iznik, the Pottery of Ottoman Turkey*. London: Alexandria Press, 1989.

Moonan, Wendy. "Iznik Wares, Even Rarer Than Ming," *New York Times*, May 29, 1998.

Watson, Oliver. *Ceramics from Islamic Lands*. New York: Thames & Hudson, 2006.

Islamic Decorative Arts: Metalwork

Barrett, Douglas. *Islamic Metalwork in the British Museum*. London: British Museum Press, 1949.

Islamic Decorative Arts: Textiles

Baker, Patricia L. *Islamic Textiles*. London: British Museum Press, 1995.

Raby, Julian, and Alison Effeny, eds. *İpek: The Crescent and the Rose: Imperial Ottoman Silks and Velvets*. London: Azimuth Editions, 2001.

Islamic Decorative Arts: Carpets

Coen, Luciano, and Louise Duncan. *The Oriental Rug*. New York: Harper & Row, 1978.

Eiland, Murray L., Jr., and Murray Eiland, III. *Oriental Carpets: A Complete Guide*, 4th ed. Boston: Little, Brown, 1998. An updated version by the original author and his son of the classic reference first published in 1973.

Ford, P. R. J. *Oriental Carpet Design: A Guide to Traditional Motifs, Patterns, and Symbols*. New York: Thames & Hudson, 1981.

Petsopoulos, Yanni. *Kilims: Masterpieces from Turkey*. New York: Rizzoli, 1991.

Pickering, Brooke, W. Russell Pickering, and Ralph S. Yohe. *Moroccan Carpets*. London: Hali Publications Limited, in association with Laurence King, 1998.

Sakhai, Essie. *Oriental Carpets: A Buyer's Guide*. Wakefield, RI: Moyer Bell, 1995. Small but well-illustrated paperback guide by a prominent London dealer.

———. *The Story of Carpets*. Wakefield, RI: Moyer Bell, 1997.

Stone, Peter F. *The Oriental Rug Lexicon*. Seattle: University of Washington Press, 1997. Over 3,000 carpet-related terms defined, some with illustrations.

Summers, Janice. *Oriental Rugs: The Illustrated World Buyers' Guide*. New York: Crown, 1994.

von Bode, Wilhelm. *Antique Rugs from the Near East*. Ithaca, NY: Cornell University Press, 1984.

Wearden, Jennifer. "Carpet," in *The Dictionary of Art*, ed. Jane Turner. New York: Grove/Macmillan, 1996, vol. 5, pp. 828–42.

Wright, Richard E., and John T. Wertime. *Caucasian Carpets and Covers: The Weaving Culture*. London: Hali Publications Limited, in association with Laurence King, 1995.

10 India (2500 B.C. to the Nineteenth Century)

Indian Architecture and Interiors

Berinstain, Valérie. *India and the Mughal Dynasty*. Discoveries series. New York: Abrams, 1998. Colorful little paperback.

Brand, Michael. *The Vision of Kings: Art and Experience in India*. New York: Thames & Hudson, 1996.

Chandra, Pramod. *On the Study of Indian Art*. Cambridge, MA: Harvard University Press, 1983. A survey of scholarly treatments of Indian art.

Coomaraswamy, Ananda K. *The Dance of Siva: Essays on Indian Art and Culture*. London: Simpkin, Marshall, Hamilton, Kent, 1924; reprinted, New York: Dover, 1985. See especially "Hindu View of Art: Theory of Beauty."

———. *History of Indian and Indonesian Art*. New York: Weyhe, 1927; reprinted, New York: Dover, 1965.

Fisher, Robert E. *Buddhist Art and Architecture*. New York: Thames & Hudson, 1993.

Gascoigne, Bamber. *The Great Moghuls*. New York: Dorset, 1971.

Goetz, Hermann. *The Art of India*. Art of the World series. New York: Greystone Press, 1964.

Harle, J. C. *The Art and Architecture of the Indian Subcontinent*. Pelican History of Art series. Harmondsworth, Middlesex, England: Penguin, 1986. A standard authority. In addition to what is now India, the book covers Pakistan, Nepal, Afghanistan, Bangladesh, and Sri Lanka.

Herdeg, Klaus. *Formal Structure in Indian Architecture*. Ithaca, NY: Center for Housing and Environmental Studies, Cornell University, 1967. A portfolio of measured drawings.

Huntington, Susan L., and John C. Huntington. *The Art of Ancient India: Buddhist, Hindu, Jain*. New York: Weatherhill, 1985.

Koch, Ebba. *Mughal Architecture*. Munich: Prestel-Verlag, 1991.

McArthur, Meher. *The Arts of Asia: Materials, Techniques, Styles*. New York: Thames & Hudson, 2005.

Michell, George. *The Hindu Temple*. London: Paul Elek, 1977.

——. *Princely Rajasthan*. New York: Vendome, 2004.

——. *The Royal Palaces of India*. New York: Thames & Hudson, 1994.

Mukerjee, Radhakamal. *The Flowering of Indian Art*. New York: Asia Publishing House, 1964.

Nicholson, Louise. *The Red Fort, Delhi*. London: Tauris Parke, 1989.

O'Flaherty, Wendy Doniger, et al. *Elephanta: The Cave of Shiva*. Princeton, NJ: Princeton University Press, 1983.

Rewal, Raj, et al. *Architecture in India*. Milan and Paris: Electa France, 1985.

Rowland, Benjamin. *Art and Architecture of India: Buddhist, Hindu, Jain*. Pelican History of Art series. Harmondsworth, Middlesex, England: Penguin, 1953. Rowland's book was replaced by Harle's 1986 book in the series. It lacks Harle's coverage of Mughal architecture, but it is more inclusive geographically, covering Southeast Asia as well as the areas covered by Harle.

Stierlin, Henri, ed. *India*. Architecture of the World series. Lausanne: Office du Livre, 1969.

——, ed. *Islamic India*. Architecture of the World series. Lausanne: Office du Livre, 1969.

Tadgell, Christopher. *The History of Architecture in India*. London: Phaidon, 1990.

Tillotson, G. H. R. *Mughal India*. New York: Viking Penguin, 1991. A travel guide, but with good descriptions and illustrations.

——. *The Tradition of Indian Architecture*. New Haven, CT: Yale University Press, 1989. Focuses on influences on building since 1850.

Volwahsen, Andreas. *Living Architecture: Indian*. New York: Grosset & Dunlap, 1969.

Watson, Francis. *A Concise History of India*. New York: Thames & Hudson, 1979.

Welch, Stuart Cary. *India: Art and Culture, 1300–1900*. New York: Holt, Rinehart & Winston with the Metropolitan Museum of Art, 1985. Catalog for the exhibition *India!* at the Metropolitan Museum of Art, 1985–86.

Zimmer, Heinrich. *The Art of Indian Asia*. New York: Pantheon, 1955. Two volumes, compiled and edited by Joseph Campbell.

Indian Architecture and Interiors: The Taj Mahal

Moynihan, Elizabeth B., ed. *The Moonlight Garden: New Discoveries at the Taj Mahal*. Seattle: University of Washington Press and Washington, DC: Arthur M. Sackler Gallery, Smithsonian Institution, 2000.

Pal, Pratapaditya, et al. *Romance of the Taj Mahal*. New York: Thames & Hudson, with the Los Angeles County Museum of Art, 1989.

Rai, Raghu, and Usha Rai. *Taj Mahal*. New York: Vendome, 1986. Oversize photo album, but with some text.

Indian Furniture

Jaffer, Amin. *Luxury Goods from India: The Art of the Indian Cabinet-Maker*. London: Victoria & Albert Publications, 2001, distributed in the United States by Abrams, 2002.

——. *Furniture from British India and Ceylon*. Salem, MA: Peabody Essex Museum, 2001.

Indian Decorative Arts

Aditi: The Living Arts of India. Washington, DC: Smithsonian Institution Press, 1985.

Aryan, Subhashini. *Crafts of Himachal Pradesh*. Middletown, NJ: Grantha, 1993.

Birdwood, George C. M. *The Arts of India*, especially the chapter "Art Furniture and Household Decoration," 1880; reprinted, Jersey, U.K.: Channel Islands, 1986.

Coomaraswamy, Ananda K. *The Arts and Crafts of India and Ceylon*. New York: Noonday, a division of Farrar, Straus, 1964.

Cooper, Ilay, and John Gillow. *Arts and Crafts of India*. New York: Thames & Hudson, 1996.

Cunningham, Michael, Stanislaw J. Czuma, Anne E. Wardwell, and J. Keith Wilson. *Masterworks of Ancient Art*. The Cleveland Museum of Art, in association with Thames & Hudson, New York. Cover design from China and Central Asia, India and Southeast Asia, Japan, and Korea.

Jain, Jyotindra, and Aarti Aggarwala. *National Handicrafts and Handlooms Museum*. Ahmedabad, India: Mapin, 1989.

Jaitly, Jaya. *Crafts of Kashmir, Jammu, and Ladakh*. New York: Abbeville, 1990.

Krishna, Nanditha. *Arts and Crafts of Tamilnadu*. Middletown, NJ: Grantha, 1992.

Mode, Heinz, and Subodh Chandra. *Indian Folk Art*. New York: Alpine Fine Arts Collection, 1985.

Sen, Prabhas. *Crafts of West Bengal*. Middletown, NJ: Grantha, 1994.

Swarup, Shanti. *The Arts and Crafts of India and Pakistan*. Bombay: Taraporevala, 1957.

Watt, G., and P. Brown. *Arts and Crafts of India—A Descriptive Study*. New Delhi: Cosmo, 1979. First published in 1904.

Indian Decorative Arts: Textiles

Ashton, Sir Leigh, ed. *The Art of India and Pakistan*. New York: Coward-McCann, 1948. See especially the chapter "Textiles and the Minor Arts" by John Irwin.

Askari, Nasreen, and Rosemary Crill. *Colours of the Indus: Costume and Textiles of Pakistan*. London: Merrell Holberton, with the Victoria & Albert Museum, 1997.

Benedict, Rosalind Candlin. "Paisley," *Interior Design*, February 1988, pp. 272–77.

Gillow, John, and Nicholas Barnard. *Traditional Indian Textiles*. London: Thames & Hudson, 1991.

Guy, John. *Woven Cargoes: Indian Textiles in the East*. New York: Thames & Hudson, 1998.

Irwin, John, and Margaret Hall. *Indian Painted and Printed Fabrics*, vol. I: *Historic Textiles of India at the Calico Museum*. Ahmedabad, India: S. R. Bastikar on behalf of the Calico Museum of Textiles, 1971.

Irwin, John, and Katharine B. Brett. *Origins of Chintz*. London: Her Majesty's Stationery Office, 1970. Includes a catalog of Indo-European cottons in the Victoria & Albert Museum, London.

Kokyo Hatanka, et al. *Textile Arts of India*. San Francisco: Chronicle, 1996. See especially the chapter "History of Indian Textiles" by Zahid Sardar.

Paine, Sheila. *Embroidery from India and Pakistan*. Seattle: University of Washington Press, 2001.

Pathak, Anamika. *Pashmina*, 2nd impression. New Delhi: Roli & Janssen BV.

Rossbach, Ed. *Art of the Paisley*. New York: Van Nostrand Reinhold, 1980.

Skelton, Robert. *Rajasthani Temple Hangings of the Krishna Cult*. New York: American Federation of the Arts, 1973.

Wheeler, Monroe, ed. *Textiles and Ornaments of India*. New York: Museum of Modern Art, 1956.

Indian Decorative Arts: Carpets

Gans-Ruedin, Erwin. *Indian Carpets*. New York: Rizzoli, 1984.

Walker, Daniel. "The Fine-Weave Carpets of India," *The Magazine Antiques*, December 1997, pp. 824–31.

———. *Flowers Underfoot: Indian Carpets of the Mughal Era*. New York: Metropolitan Museum of Art, distributed by Abrams, 1997.

11 China (4000 B.C.–A.D. 1912)

Chinese Architecture and Interiors

Bussagli, Mario. *Oriental Architecture*. New York: Abrams, 1973.

Liu, Laurence G. *Chinese Architecture*. New York: Rizzoli, 1989.

Sickman, Lawrence, and Alexander Soper. *The Art and Architecture of China*, 3rd ed. Harmondsworth, Middlesex, England: Penguin, 1968.

Chinese Architecture and Interiors: The Forbidden City

Béguin, Gilles, and Dominique Morel. *The Forbidden City: Center of Imperial China*. New York: Abrams, 1997. Part of the colorful, inexpensive Discoveries series.

Zhuoyun, Yu. *Palaces of the Forbidden City*. New York: Viking, 1982.

Chinese Architecture and Interiors: Houses

Berliner, Nancy. *Yin Yu Tang: The Architecture and Daily Life of a Chinese House*. Boston: Tuttle, 2003.

Knapp, Ronald G. *China's Vernacular Architecture: House Form and Culture*. Honolulu: University of Hawaii Press, 1989.

———. *The Chinese House: Craft, Symbol, and the Folk Tradition*. Images of Asia series. New York: Oxford University Press, 1990.

Chinese Furniture

Berliner, Nancy. *Beyond the Screen: Chinese Furniture of the 16th and 17th Centuries*. Boston: Museum of Fine Arts, 1996.

———. "Furniture of the Ming Dynasty," *The Magazine Antiques*, August 1996, pp. 178–87.

Berliner, Nancy, and Sarah Handler. *Friends of the House: Furniture from China's Towns and Villages*. Salem, MA: Peabody Essex Museum, 1996.

Beurdeley, Michel. *Chinese Furniture*. New York: Kodansha, 1979. Excellent source.

Buckley, Chris. *Tibetan Furniture*. Warren, CT: Floating World Editions, 2005. Furniture from the mountainous region of Tibet, now controlled by China but an autonomous country before 1951.

Cescinsky, Herbert. *Chinese Furniture*. London: Benn Bros., 1922.

Clunas, Craig. *Chinese Furniture*. London: Bamboo, 1988. Chinese furniture in the collection of the Victoria & Albert Museum, London.

Ecke, Gustav. *Chinese Domestic Furniture in Photographs and Measured Drawings*. Beijing: Editions Henri Vetch, 1944; reprinted, New York: Towse, 1962; reprinted, Mineola, NY: Dover, 1986.

Ellsworth, Robert Hatfield. *Chinese Furniture*. New York: Random House, 1971.

Handler, Sarah. *Ming Furniture in the Light of Chinese Architecture*. Berkeley, CA: Ten Speed Press, 2005. Excellent survey, well illustrated.

Kates, George N. *Chinese Household Furniture*. New York: Harper & Brothers, 1948; reprinted, Mineola, NY: Dover, 1962.

Tian Jiaqing. *Classic Chinese Furniture of the Qing Dynasty*. London: Philip Wilson, 1996.

Wang Shixiang. *Classic Chinese Furniture of the Ming and Early Qing Dynasties*. London: Han-Shan Tang, 1986.

———. *Connoisseur of Chinese Furniture*, 2 vols. Hong Kong: Joint; distributed by Art Media Resource, 1990.

———. "Development of Furniture Design and Construction from the Song to the Ming," *Orientations*, January 1991.

Chinese Decorative Arts

Avril, Ellen B. *Chinese Art in the Cincinnati Art Museum*. Cincinnati, OH: Cincinnati Art Museum; distributed by University of Washington Press, Seattle, 1997.

Burling, Judith, and Arthur Hart Burling. *Chinese Art*. New York: Viking, 1953.

Clunas, Craig. *Art in China*. Oxford and New York: Oxford University Press, 1997. Part of the excellent Oxford History of Art series, available in paperback.

Eberhard, Wolfram. *A History of China*. Berkeley: University of California Press, 1960; 4th ed., 1977.

Hutt, Julia. *Understanding Far Eastern Art*. New York: E. P. Dutton, 1987.

Lee, Sherman E. *History of Far Eastern Art*, 4th ed. New York: Abrams, 1982.

Moore, Janet Gaylord. *The Eastern Gate: An Invitation to the Arts of China and Japan*. Cleveland, OH, and New York: William Collins, 1979.

Munsterberg, Hugo. *Art of the Far East*. New York: Abrams, 1968.

———. *A Short History of Chinese Art*. Philosophical Library, 1949; reprinted, New York: Greenwood, 1969.

Siu, Anita. "Splendors of Imperial China," *The Magazine Antiques*, March 1996, pp. 428–37.

Smith, Bradley, and Wan-go Weng. *China: A History in Art*. New York: Doubleday, 1978.

Stuart, Jan. "Beyond Paper: Chinese Calligraphy on Objects," *The Magazine Antiques*, October 1995, pp. 502–13.

Thorp, Robert L. *Son of Heaven: Imperial Arts of China*. Seattle: Son of Heaven Press, 1988.

Tregear, Mary. *Chinese Art*. New York: Oxford University Press, 1980.

Tregear, Mary, and Shelagh Vainker. *Art Treasures in China*. New York: Abrams, 1994.

Watson, William. *The Arts of China to A.D. 900*. Pelican History of Art series. New Haven, CT: Yale University Press, 1995.

———. *Style in the Arts of China*. Harmondsworth, Middlesex, England: Penguin, 1974.

Wilkinson, Jane, and Nick Pearce. *Harmony and Contrast: A Journey through East Asian Art*. Edinburgh: National Museums of Scotland, 1996. Brief illustrated essays on lacquer, silk, porcelain, and other media.

Willetts, William. *Chinese Art*. Harmondsworth, Middlesex, England: Penguin, 1958.

———. *Foundations of Chinese Art*. New York: McGraw-Hill, 1965.

Chinese Decorative Arts: Ceramics

Atterbury, Paul, ed. *The History of Porcelain*. New York: William Morrow, 1982. Particularly see the chapters "The Origins of Porcelain" by Richard Gray and "Qing Dynasty Porcelain for the Domestic Market" by Gordon Lang.

Beilly, Roslyn. "Chinese Porcelain," *Interior Design*, June 1988, p. 148.

Beurdeley, Cécile, and Michel Beurdeley. *A Connoisseur's Guide to Chinese Ceramics*. New York: Harper & Row, 1974.

Beurdeley, Michel, and Guy Raindre. *Qing Porcelain: Famille Verte, Famille Rose*. New York: Rizzoli, 1987.

Curtis, Julia B. *Chinese Porcelains of the Seventeenth Century*. New York: China Institute; distributed by the University of Washington Press, Seattle, 1995.

Cushion, John P. *Pottery and Porcelain*. London: The Connoisseur, 1972; New York: Hearst Books, 1972.

Donnelly, P. J. *Blanc de Chine: The Porcelain of Têhua in Fukien*. London: Faber and Faber, 1969.

Garner, Sir Harry. *Oriental Blue and White*. London: Faber and Faber, 1954; 3rd ed., 1970.

He Li. *Chinese Ceramics: A New Comprehensive Survey from the Asian Art Museum of San Francisco*. New York: Rizzoli, 1996. Illustrated with more than 700 color plates.

Hobson, R. L. *Chinese Pottery and Porcelain*. New York: Dover, 1976. Reprint of a classic work first published in two volumes in 1915.

———. *The Wares of the Ming Dynasty*. Rutland, VT: Charles E. Tuttle, 1962.

Hobson, R. L., and A. L. Hetherington. *The Art of the Chinese Potter: An Illustrated Survey*. New York: Knopf; London: Benn, 1923; reprinted, New York: Dover, 1982.

Itoh, Ikutaro, and Yutaka Mino. *The Radiance of Jade and the Clarity of Water: Korean Ceramics from the Ataka Collection*. New York: Hudson Hills Press, in association with The Art Institute of Chicago, 1991.

Jorg, Christiaan J. A. *Chinese Ceramics in the Collection of the Rijksmuseum, Amsterdam: The Ming and Qing Dynasties*. London: Philip Wilson, 1997.

Kerr, Rose. *Song Dynasty Ceramics*. London: Victoria & Albert Publications, 2004.

Laufer, Berthold. *Chinese Pottery of the Han Dynasty*. 1909; reprinted, Rutland, VT: Charles E. Tuttle, 1962.

Macintosh, Duncan. *Chinese Blue and White Porcelain*, 3rd ed. Woodbridge, Suffolk, England: Antique Collectors' Club, 1994.

McFadden, David Revere, "Early Porcelain in Europe," in *Porcelain: Traditions and New Visions*, ed. Jan Axel and Karen McCready. New York: Watson-Guptill, 1981.

Medley, Margaret. *The Chinese Potter: A Practical History of Chinese Ceramics*. New York: Scribner, 1976.

Mudge, Jean McClure. *Chinese Export Porcelain for the American Trade, 1785–1835*. Newark, DE: University of Delaware Press, 1981.

Rotondo-McCord, Lisa. *Five Thousand Years of Chinese Ceramics*. New Orleans: New Orleans Museum of Art, 2005.

Chinese Decorative Arts: Metalwork—Bronzes

Ackerman, Phyllis. *Ritual Bronzes of Ancient China*. New York: Dryden, 1945.

d'Argencé, René-Yvon Lefebvre. *Ancient Chinese Bronzes in the Avery Brundage Collection*. Berkeley, CA: Diablo Press for the de Young Museum Society, 1966.

Li, Xueqin. *The Wonder of Chinese Bronzes*. Beijing: Foreign Languages Press, 1980.

Chinese Decorative Arts: Metalwork—Enamel and Cloisonné

Bates, Kenneth F. *The Enamelist: A Comprehensive Study of Advanced Enameling Techniques*. Cleveland, OH: World, 1967.

Brinker, Helmut, and Albert Lutz. *Chinese Cloisonné: The Pierre Uldry Collection*. New York: Asia Society, 1989. First published in Zurich in 1985.

Chu, Arthur, and Grace Chu. *Oriental Cloisonné and Other Enamels*. New York: Crown, 1975.

Cosgrove, Maynard G. *The Enamels of China and Japan: Champlevé and Cloisonné*. New York: Dodd, Mead, 1974.

Garner, Sir Harry. *Chinese and Japanese Cloisonné Enamels*. London: Faber and Faber, 1962; rev. ed., 1970.

National Palace Museum. *Masterpieces of Chinese Enamel Ware*. Taipei: National Palace Museum, 1971.

Chinese Decorative Arts: Lacquer and Shellac

Scott, Rosemary. "China," in *Lacquer, An International History and Illustrated Survey*. New York: Abrams, 1984.

White, Julia M. *Masterpieces of Chinese Lacquer from the Mike Hardy Collection*. Honolulu, HI: Honolulu Academy of Arts, 2005.

Chinese Decorative Arts: Textiles

Anquetil, Jacques. *Silk*. New York: Flammarion, 1996.

Corrigan, Gina. *Miao Textiles from China*. Seattle: University of Washington Press, 2001.

Hanyu, Gao. *Chinese Textile Designs*, trans. Rosemary Scott and Susan Whitfield. New York: Viking, 1992.

Hawley, Walter A. *Oriental Rugs: Antique and Modern*. New York: Tudor, 1937; reprinted, New York: Dover, 1970.

Rothstein, Natalie. "Silk," in *The Dictionary of Art*. New York: Grove/Macmillan, 1996, vol. 28, pp. 715–23.

Scott, Philippa. *The Book of Silk*. New York: Thames & Hudson, 1993.

12 Japan (A.D. 593–1867)

Japanese Architecture and Interiors

Blaser, Werner. *Japanese Temples and Tea-Houses*, trans. D. Q. Stephenson. New York: Dodge, 1957.

———. *Structure and Form in Japan*. New York: Wittenborn, 1963.

Bussagli, Mario. *Oriental Architecture*, vol. 2. Milan: Electa, 1981, New York: Rizzoli, 1989.

Drexler, Arthur. *Architecture of Japan*. New York: Museum of Modern Art, 1955.

Harada, Jiro. *The Lesson of Japanese Architecture*. 1936. Boston: Charles T. Branford, 1954.

Inoue, Mitsuo. *Space in Japanese Architecture*. Tokyo and New York: Weatherhill, 1985.

Isozaki, Arata. *Japan-ness in Architecture*. Cambridge, MA: MIT Press, 2006. A noted contemporary architect examines the essence of Japanese spirit in buildings from the seventh century to today.

Masuda, Tomoya. *Japan*. Architecture of the World series, ed. Henri Stierlin. Lausanne: Benedikt Taschen, n.d.

Morse, Edward S. *Japanese Homes and Their Surroundings*. Rutland, VT: Charles E. Tuttle, 1972. 9th ed., 1980.

Nishi, Kazuo, and Kazuo Hozumi. *What Is Japanese Architecture?* Tokyo and New York: Kodansha, 1985.

Ooka, Minoru. *Temples of Nara and Their Art*. Heibonsha Survey of Japanese Art series. Tokyo and New York: Weatherhill, 1973.

Paine, Robert Treat, and Alexander Soper. *The Art and Architecture of Japan*. Harmondsworth, Middlesex, England: Penguin, 1955, 1975. A standard authority.

Soper, Alexander Coburn, III. *The Evolution of Buddhist Architecture in Japan*. Princeton, NJ: Princeton University Press, 1942.

Stierlin, Henri, ed. *Architecture of the World: Japan*. Lausanne: Benedikt Taschen, n.d. Features excellent photography by Yukio Futagawa.

Suzuki, Kakichi. *Early Buddhist Architecture in Japan*. Japanese Arts Library Series, ed. John Rosenfield. Tokyo and New York: Kodansha, 1980.

Japanese Architecture and Interiors: A Country Villa

Fujioka, Michio. *Kyoto Country Retreats: The Shugakuin and Katsura Palaces*. Tokyo and New York: Kodansha, 1983.

Isozaki, Arata. *Katsura Villa: The Ambiguity of Its Space*. New York: Rizzoli, 1987. Isozaki discusses the views of three earlier admirers of the villa—Bruno Taut, Horiguchi Sutemi, and Kenzo Tange—and then gives his own interpretation. Color photography by Yasuhiro Ishimoto.

Naito, Akira, *Katsura: A Princely Retreat*. Tokyo and New York: Kodansha, 1977. Color photographs by Tajeshi Nishikawa.

Ponciroli, Virginia, ed. *Katsura Imperial Villa*. Milan: Electa, 2004. Distributed in the United States by Phaidon. Repeats Gropius's introduction to Tange's book and adds essays by Bruno Taut, Kenzo Tange, Francesco Dal Co, and others. Many color photographs by Yoshiharu Matsumura.

Tange, Kenzo. *Katsura: Tradition and Creation in Japanese Architecture*. New Haven, CT: Yale University Press, 1960. Includes an introduction by modern architect Walter Gropius and black-and-white photography by Yasuhiro Ishimoto.

Japanese Furniture

Clarke, Rosy. *Japanese Antique Furniture: A Guide to Evaluating and Restoring*. Tokyo and New York: Weatherhill, 1983.

Heinekin, Ty, and Kiyoko Heinekin. *Tansu: Traditional Japanese Cabinetry*. Tokyo and New York: Weatherhill, 1981.

Impey, Oliver. *The Art of the Japanese Folding Screen*. Tokyo and New York: Ashmolean Museum, Oxford, in association with Weatherhill, 1997.

Koizumi, Kazuko. *Traditional Japanese Furniture*. Tokyo and New York: Kodansha, 1986.

Japanese Decorative Arts

Addiss, Stephen. *How to Look at Japanese Art*. New York: Abrams, 1996.

Boger, H. Batterson. *The Traditional Arts of Japan*. Garden City, NY: Doubleday, 1964. Very comprehensive coverage, including folk art, floral art, fans, the lacquered medicine cases called *inro*, and the small buckles called *netsuke*.

Dresser, Christopher. *Traditional Arts and Crafts of Japan*. New York: Dover, 1994. Originally published in London by Longmans, Green in 1882 as *Japan: Its Architecture, Art, and Art Manufacturers*.

Dunn, Michael. *Inspired Design: Japan's Traditional Arts*. Milan: 5 Continents Editions, 2005.

Kakudo, Yoshik. *The Art of Japan: Masterworks in the Asian Art Museum of San Francisco*. San Francisco: Asian Art Museum and Chronicle, 1991.

Lee, Sherman E. *A History of Far Eastern Art*, 4th ed. New York: Abrams, 1982.

———. *Japanese Decorative Style*. New York: Harper & Row, 1972.

Saint-Gilles, Amaury. *Mingei: Japan's Enduring Folk Art*. Rutland, VT: Charles E. Tuttle, 1989.

Stanley-Baker, Joan. *Japanese Art*. New York: Thames & Hudson, 1992.

Japanese Decorative Arts: Ceramics

Yakimono: 4000 Years of Japanese Ceramics. Honolulu, HI: Honolulu Academy of Arts, 2005.

Japanese Decorative Arts: Ceramics—Tea Ceremony Wares

Fujioka, Ryochi. *Tea Ceremony Utensils*. Tokyo and New York: Weatherhill/Shibundo, 1973.

Munsterberg, Hugo. *Zen and Oriental Art*. Rutland, VT, and Tokyo: Charles E. Tuttle, 1993.

Japanese Decorative Arts: Textiles

Ito, Toshiko. *Tsujigahana: The Flower of Japanese Textile Art*. Tokyo and New York: Kodansha, 1985.

Yang, Sunny, and Rochelle M. Narasin. *Textile Art of Japan*. Tokyo: Shufunotomo, 1989.

13 Italy: Renaissance to Neoclassical (Fifteenth to Eighteenth Centuries)

History and Patronage

Chambers, D. S. *Patrons and Artists in the Italian Renaissance*. Columbia: University of South Carolina Press, 1971.

Hibbert, Christopher. *The House of Medici: Its Rise and Fall*. New York: William Morrow, 1975.

Hollingsworth, Mary. *Patronage in Sixteenth Century Italy*. London: John Murray, 1996. Relationships between patrons and artists.

Massinelli, Anna Maria, and Filippo Tuena. *Treasures of the Medici*. New York: Vendome, 1992.

Italian Architecture and Interiors

Ackerman, James S. "On Early Renaissance Color Theory and Practice," in *Distance Points*. Cambridge, MA: MIT Press, 1991.

———. *The Villa: Form and Ideology in Country Houses*. Princeton, NJ: Princeton University Press, 1990.

Barasch, Moshe. *Light and Color in the Italian Renaissance Theory of Art*. New York: New York University Press, 1978.

Burckhardt, Jacob. *The Architecture of the Italian Renaissance*, trans. James Palmes, ed. Peter Murray. Chicago: University of Chicago Press, 1985. First published in German in 1867.

———. *The Civilization of the Renaissance in Italy*. Oxford: Oxford University Press, 1944; London: Phaidon, 1960. First published in German in 1860.

Burke, Peter. *The Italian Renaissance: Culture and Society in Italy*, rev. ed. Princeton, NJ: Princeton University Press, 1987.

Chastel, André. *The Flowering of the Italian Renaissance*. New York: Odyssey, 1965. Part of the excellent Arts of Mankind series, ed. André Malraux.

———. *Italian Art*, trans. Peter and Linda Murray. New York: Thomas Yoseloff, 1963. Published in France in 1956 as *L'art italien*.

———. *Studios and Styles of the Italian Renaissance*. Arts of Mankind series. New York: Odyssey. Includes an extensive glossary/index with brief identifications of sites, artists, and terms.

Coffin, David R. *The Villa in the Life of Renaissance Rome*. Princeton, NJ: Princeton University Press, 1979.

Durant, Will. *The Renaissance: A History of Civilization in Italy from 1304 to 1576 A.D.* New York: Simon & Schuster, 1953. Story of Civilization series, vol. 5. Durant takes a bewilderingly sour view of Italian Renaissance architecture, but there is interesting reading on other subjects.

Gombrich, E. H. *Norm and Form*. London: Phaidon, 1966. See especially the two essays, "The Renaissance Conception of Artistic Progress and Its Consequences" and "Norm and Form: The Stylistic Categories of Art History and Their Origins in the Renaissance."

Hartt, Frederick. *History of Italian Renaissance Art: Painting, Sculpture, Architecture*. Englewood Cliffs, NJ: Prentice Hall, 1979; 4th ed., New York: Abrams, 1994.

———. *Renaissance and Baroque*. Ithaca, NY: Cornell University Press, 1964.

Hersey, George Leonard. *Pythagorean Palaces: Magic and Architecture in the Italian Renaissance*. Ithaca, NY: Cornell University Press, 1976.

Hopkins, Andrew. *Italian Architecture from Michelangelo to Borromini*. New York: Thames & Hudson, 2002.

Jestaz, Bertrand. *Architecture of the Renaissance from Brunelleschi to Palladio*. New York: Abrams, 1996. Colorful little paperback in Abrams's Discoveries series.

Letts, Rosa Maria. *The Renaissance*. New York: Cambridge University Press, 1981. Cambridge Introduction to the Arts series.

Markschies, Alexander, ed. *Icons of Renaissance Architecture*. New York: Prestel, 2003. Includes brief descriptions of the Palazzo Medici-Riccardi, Palazzo Farnese, the Villa Capra, and Saint Peter's.

Masson, Georgina. *Italian Villas and Palaces*. London: Thames & Hudson, 1951, 1959.

Murray, Peter. *The Architecture of the Italian Renaissance*. New York: Schocken, 1963.

Onians, John. *The Bearers of Meaning: The Classical Orders of Antiquity, the Middle Ages, and the Renaissance*. Princeton, NJ: Princeton University Press, 1988.

Panofsky, Erwin. *Renaissance and Renascences in Western Art*. Stockholm: Almqvist and Wiskell, 1960.

Paoletti, John T., and Gary M. Radke. *Art in Renaissance Italy*. Upper Saddle River, NJ: Prentice Hall, 1997.

Payne, Alina A. *The Architectural Treatise in the Italian Renaissance*. New York: Cambridge University Press, 1999.

Pedretti, Carlo. *Leonardo, Architect*. New York: Rizzoli, 1985.

Shearman, John. *Only Connect . . . , Art and the Spectator in the Italian Renaissance*. Princeton, NJ: Princeton University Press, 1992; The A. W. Mellon Lectures in the Fine Arts, 1988.

Symonds, John Addington. *The Renaissance in Italy: The Fine Arts*. London: Smith, Elder, 1899.

Thornton, Peter. *The Italian Renaissance Interior, 1400–1600*. London: Weidenfeld and Nicolson, 1991. The single most informative text on the subject. Well illustrated.

Weiss, Roberto. *The Renaissance Discovery of Classical Antiquity*. Oxford: Basil Blackwell, 1973.

Welch, Evelyn. *Art and Society in Italy 1350–1500*. New York: Oxford University Press, 1997.

Wharton, Edith. *Italian Villas and Their Gardens*. New York: Da Capo Press, 1976. First published in 1904 and written by the famous American novelist.

Wittkower, Rudolph. *Architectural Principles in the Age of Humanism*. London: Tiranti, 1952. The theories behind the architecture and design.

———. *Art and Architecture in Italy, 1600–1750*. Baltimore, MD: Penguin, 1958. 6th rev. ed., 3 vols., eds. Joseph Conners and Jennifer Montagu. New Haven, CT: Yale University Press, 1999.

———. *Gothic vs. Classic: Architectural Projects in Seventeenth Century Italy*. New York: Braziller, 1974.

Wohl, Hellmut. *The Aesthetics of Italian Renaissance Art*. New York: Cambridge University Press, 1999.

Wölfflin, Heinrich. *Classic Art: An Introduction to the Italian Renaissance*. London: Phaidon, 1994. First published in English as *The Art of the Italian Renaissance: A Handbook for Students and Travelers*. New York: Schocken, 1963. Chapters on Leonardo, Michelangelo, Raphael, and others.

Early Renaissance Style

Baldassarri, Stefano Ugo, and Arielle Saiber, eds. *Images of Quattrocento Florence*. New Haven, CT: Yale University Press, 2000. Original documents give firsthand accounts of fifteenth-century Florence.

Levey, Michael. *Early Renaissance*. Harmondsworth, Middlesex, England: Penguin, 1967. Part of the Style and Civilization series.

Stokes, Adrian. *The Quattrocento*. New York: Schocken, 1968. First published in England in 1932.

Early Renaissance Style: Palazzo Davanzati, Florence

Rosenburg, L. C. *The Davanzati Palace: Florence, Italy*. New York: Architectural Book Publishing, 1922. Brief text with photographs and measured drawings.

Early Renaissance Style: Old Sacristy, San Lorenzo, Florence

Battisti, Eugenio. *Brunelleschi*. New York: Rizzoli, 1981.

Klotz, Henrich. *Filippo Brunelleschi: The Early Works and the Medieval Tradition*. New York: Rizzoli, 1990.

Saalman, Howard. *Filippo Brunelleschi: The Buildings*. University Park: Pennsylvania State University Press, 1993.

High Renaissance Style and Mannerism

Hauser, Arnold. *Mannerism: The Crisis of the Renaissance and the Origin of Modern Art*. New York: Knopf, 1965. In two volumes, one of text and one of plates.

Murray, Linda. *The High Renaissance and Mannerism: Italy, the North, and Spain, 1500–1600*. London: Thames & Hudson, 1995. First published in 1967 in two volumes, *The High Renaissance* and *The Late Renaissance and Mannerism*; now part of the World of Art series.

Rowland, Ingrid D. *The Culture of the High Renaissance: Ancients and Moderns in Sixteenth-Century Rome*. New York: Cambridge University Press, 1998.

High Renaissance Style and Mannerism: Palazzo Medici-Riccardi, Florence

Cardini, Franco. *The Chapel of the Magi in Palazzo Medici*. Florence: Mandragora, 2001.

High Renaissance Style and Mannerism: Vatican Loggie, Rome

Davidson, Bernice F. *Raphael's Bible: A Study of the Vatican Logge*. University Park: Pennsylvania State University Press, 1985.

Hersey, George Leonard. *High Renaissance Art in St. Peter's and the Vatican*. Chicago: University of Chicago Press, 1993.

Jones, Roger, and Nicholas Penny. *Raphael*. New Haven, CT: Yale University Press, 1983.

Penny, Nicholas, "Raphael," in *The Dictionary of Art*, ed. Jane Turner. New York: Grove/Macmillan, 1996, vol. 25, pp. 896–910.

Ponente, Nello. *Who Was Raphael?* Geneva: Skira, 1967. A much better book than the title suggests.

Pope-Hennessy, John. *Raphael*. New York: New York University Press, 1970.

High Renaissance Style and Mannerism: Medici Chapel and Laurentian Library, San Lorenzo, Florence

Ackerman, James S. *The Architecture of Michelangelo*. London: A. Zwemmer, 1961; Harmondsworth, Middlesex, England: Penguin, 1971. Despite its age, still the standard authority.

Argan, Giulio Carlo, and Bruno Contardi. *Michelangelo: Architect*. New York: Abrams, 1993.

Goldscheider, Ludwig. *Michelangelo: Paintings, Sculptures, Architecture*. London: Phaidon, 1953.

Murray, Linda. *Michelangelo*. New York: Oxford University Press, 1980.

Rolland, Romain. *Michelangelo*. New York: Crowell-Collier, 1962. Readable biography; no illustrations.

Wallace, William E. *Michelangelo at San Lorenzo: The Genius as Entrepreneur*. New York: Cambridge University Press, 1994. Unusual account that considers Michelangelo's relations with his clients as well as the results of his work.

High Renaissance Style and Mannerism: Villa Capra, near Vicenza

Ackerman, James S. *Palladio*. Balitimore, MD: Penguin, 1966. Still the standard text.

Boucher, Bruce. *Andrea Palladio: The Architect in His Time*. New York: Abbeville, 1998.

Holberton, Paul. *Palladio's Villas: Life in the Renaissance Countryside*. London: John Murray, 1990.

Palladio, Andrea. *The Four Books on Architecture*. Cambridge, MA: MIT Press, 1997. Palladio's Renaissance treatise in a new translation by Robert Tavernor and Richard Schofield.

Puppi, Lionello. *Andrea Palladio: The Complete Works*. Milan: Electa, 1973; New York: Rizzoli.

Scully, Vincent. *The Villas of Palladio*. Boston: Little, Brown, 1986. Black and white photographs by Philip Trager. Introduction by Michael Graves.

Smart, Alastair. *The Renaissance and Mannerism in Italy*. New York: Harcourt Brace Jovanovich, 1971.

Streitz, Robert. *La Rotonde et Sa Gèomètrie (The Geometry of the Rotonda)*. Lausanne and Paris: Bibliothëque des Arts, 1973. Text in French, Italian, and English.

Tavernor, Robert. *Palladio and Palladianism*. New York: Thames & Hudson, 1991.

Wittkower, Rudolf. *Palladio and Palladianism*. New York: Braziller, 1974.

Wundram, Manfred, Thomas Papre, and Paolo Marton. *Palladio 1508–1580: Architect between the Renaissance and Baroque*. Köln: Benedikt Taschen, n.d.

Baroque Style

Bazin, Germain. *Baroque and Rococo Art*. New York: Praeger, 1964.

Blunt, Anthony. *Guide to Baroque Rome*. New York: Harper & Row, 1982. Guide to hundreds of churches, palaces, and villas, as well as some fountains, with an extensive bibliography.

Busch, Harald. *Baroque Europe*. New York: Macmillan, 1962.

Charpentrat, Pierre. *Baroque: Italy and Central Europe*. Köln: Benedikt Taschen, n.d. Part of the Architecture of the World series, ed. Henri Stierlin.

Hersey, George Leonard. *Architecture and Geometry in the Age of the Baroque*. Chicago: University of Chicago Press, 2000.

Lees-Milne, James. *Baroque in Italy*. London: Batsford, 1959.

Martin, John Rupert. *Baroque*. New York: Harper & Row, 1977.

Millon, Henry, ed. *The Triumph of the Baroque: Architecture in Europe, 1600–1750*. New York: Rizzoli, 2000. See especially Paolo Portoghesi, "Birth of the Baroque in Rome," pp. 33–56.

Minor, Vernon Hyde. *Baroque and Rococo Art and Culture*. New York: Abrams, 1999.

Sewter, A. C. *Baroque and Rococo*. New York: Harcourt Brace Jovanovich, 1972.

Smith, Gil R. *Architectural Diplomacy: Rome and Paris in the Late Baroque*. New York: The Architectural History Foundation, with MIT Press, Cambridge, MA, 1993.

Tapié, Victor-Lucien. *The Age of Grandeur: Baroque Art and Architecture*. New York: Praeger, 1961. Published in France in 1957 as *Baroque et Classicisme*.

Walker, Stefanie, and Frederick Hammond, eds. *Life and the Arts in the Baroque Palaces of Rome: Ambiente Barocco*. New Haven, CT: Yale University Press, 1999.

Baroque Style: St. Peter's, Rome

Bergere, Thea, and Richard Bergere. *The Story of St. Peter's*. New York: Dodd, Mead, 1966.

Brushci, Arnaldo. *Bramante*. London: Thames & Hudson, 1973, 1977.

Chastel, André. *The Sistine Chapel: Michelangelo Rediscovered*. London: Muller, Blond, and White, 1986.

———. *The Vatican Frescoes of Michelangelo*. New York: Abbeville, 1980.

Hersey, George Leonard. *High Renaissance Art in St. Peter's and the Vatican*. Chicago: University of Chicago Press, 1993

Lees-Milne, James. *Saint Peter's: The Story of Saint Peter's Basilica in Rome*. Boston: Little, Brown, 1967.

Marder, T. A. *Bernini and the Art of Architecture*. New York: Abbeville, 1998.

———. *Bernini's Scala Regia at the Vatican Palace*. New York: Cambridge University Press, 1997.

Pietrangeli, Carlo, et al. *The Sistine Chapel: The Art, the History, the Restoration*. New York: Harmony, 1986.

Rococo and Neoclassical Styles

Kimball, Fiske. *The Creation of the Rococo*. Philadelphia: Philadelphia Museum of Art, 1943; New York: W. W. Norton, 1964.

Piranesi Architetto. Rome: Edizione dell'Elefante, 1992. Catalog of an exhibition at the American Academy in Rome, with text in Italian and English.

Robison, Andrew. *Piranesi: Early Architectural Fantasies, A Catalogue Raisonné of the Etchings*. Washington and Chicago: The National Gallery of Art and the University of Chicago Press, 1986.

Schonberger, Arno. *The Rococo Age: Art and Civilization of the 18th Century*. New York: McGraw-Hill, 1960.

Wilton-Ely, John. *Piranesi as Architect and Designer*. New York and New Haven, CT: Pierpont Morgan Library and Yale University Press, 1993.

Wittkower, Rudolf. "Piranesi as Architect," in *Piranesi*, ed. O. Parks. Northampton, MA: Smith College Museum, 1961.

Italian Ornament

Miller, Elizabeth. *16th-Century Italian Ornament Prints in the Victoria and Albert Museum*. London: Victoria & Albert Publications, 1999.

Italian Ornament: Frescoes

Borsook, E. *The Mural Painters of Tuscany*. Oxford: Oxford University Press, 1960, 1980.

Meiss, Millard. *The Great Age of Fresco: Discoveries, Recoveries, and Survivals*. New York: Braziller, in association with the Metropolitan Museum of Art, 1970.

Italian Ornament: Intarsia Work

Clough, C. "Art as Power in the Decoration of the Study of an Italian Renaissance Prince: The Case of Federico da Montefeltro," *Artibus et historiae*, 31 (1995), pp. 19–50.

Italian Furniture

Hunter, George Leland. *Italian Furniture and Interiors*. New York: Helburn, 1918.

Odom, W. M. *A History of Italian Furniture*. Garden City, NY: Doubleday, 1918.

Schottmüller, Frida. *Furniture and Interior Decoration of the Italian Renaissance*. New York: Brentano's, 1921. An introductory text and a fine collection of photographs.

Italian Decorative Arts

Griguat, Paul L. *Decorative Arts of the Italian Renaissance, 1400–1600*. Detroit, MI: Detroit Institute of Arts, 1958.

Hess, Catherine, ed. *The Arts of Fire: Islamic Influences on Glass and Ceramics of the Italian Renaissance*. Los Angeles: J. Paul Getty Museum, 2004.

Hills, Paul. *Venetian Colour: Marble, Mosaic, Painting, and Glass, 1250–1550*. New Haven, CT: Yale University Press, 1999.

Holman, Beth L. *Disegno: Italian Renaissance Designs for the Decorative Arts*. New York: Cooper-Hewitt National Design Museum, Smithsonian Institution, 1997. Exhibition catalog.

Thornton, Peter. *Form and Decoration: Innovation in the Decorative Arts, 1470–1870*, New York: Abrams, 1998. Six of sixteen chapters are devoted to Italy; the rest to other parts of Europe.

Italian Decorative Arts: Ceramics—Majolica

Coutts, Howard. *The Art of Ceramics: European Ceramic Design, 1500–1830*. New Haven, CT: Yale University Press, 2001.

Karmason, Marilyn G., with Joan B. Stacke. *Majolica: A Complete History and Illustrated Survey*. New York: Abrams, 1989. Also covers Etruscan, English, and Early American wares.

Ladis, Andrew. *Italian Renaissance Majolica from Southern Collections*. Athens, GA: Georgia Museum of Art, 1989.

Rackham, Bernard. *Italian Majolica*, 2nd ed. London: Faber and Faber, 1963. Rackham also wrote 1933 and 1940 guidebooks to the Italian Majolica collection of the Victoria & Albert Museum, London.

Vydrova, Jilina. *Italian Majolica*. London: Peter Nevill, 1960.

Italian Decorative Arts: Glass and Mirrors

Perrot, Paul N., et al. *Three Centuries of Venetian Glass*. Corning, NY: Corning Museum of Glass, 1958.

Tait, Hugh, ed. *Glass: 5,000 Years*. New York: Abrams and the Trustees of the British Museum, 1991.

Turner, Guy. *"Allume Catina* and the Aesthetics of Venetian *Cristallo,"* *Journal of Design History*. Oxford: Oxford University Press, 1999, vol. 12, no. 2, pp. 111–22.

Italian Decorative Arts: Textiles

Paine, Sheila. *Embroidery from India and Pakistan*. Seattle: University of Washington Press, 2001.

Italian Decorative Arts: Textiles—Tapestries

Adelson, Candace J. *"Italy: Tapestry,"* in *The Dictionary of Art*, ed. Jane Turner. New York: Grove/Macmillan, 1996, vol. 16, pp. 755–58.

Brown, Clifford M., and Guy Delmarcel. *Tapestries for the Courts of Federico II, Ercole, and Ferrante Gonzaga, 1522–63*. Seattle: University of Washington Press, 1996.

Campbell, Thomas P. *Tapestry in the Renaissance: Art and Magnificence*. New Haven, CT: Yale University Press, with the Metropolitan Museum of Art, New York, 2002. See Especially "Patronage and Production in Italy, 1380–1510," pp. 85–130.

Fermor, Sharon. *The Raphael Tapestry Cartoons*. London: Scala Books, in association with the Victoria & Albert Museum, 1996.

Italian Decorative Arts: Textiles—Silks

Anquetil, Jacques. *Silk*. Paris: Flammarion, 1995. See especially "Renaissance Italy," pp. 29–52.

Levey, Santina M. "Italy: Silk," in *The Dictionary of Art*, ed. Jane Turner. New York: Macmillan, 1996, vol. 16, pp. 752–54.

Scott, Philippa. *The Book of Silk*. New York: Thames & Hudson, 1993. See especially "Silk Weaving Comes to Europe," pp. 149–68.

Thornton, Peter. *Baroque and Rococo Silks*. London: Faber and Faber, 1965.

14 Spain: Hispano-Moorish to Neoclassical (Eighth to Eighteenth Centuries)

Spanish Architecture and Interiors

Barral i Altet, Xavier, ed. *Art and Architecture of Spain*. New York: Bulfinch/Little, Brown, 1998.

Barrucand, Marianne, and Achim Bednorz. *Moorish Architecture in Andalusia*. Köln: Benedikt Taschen, 1992.

Bowe, Patrick. *Houses and Gardens of Portugal*. New York: Rizzoli, 1998.

Brotherston, Jody. "Spanish and American Encounters in Interior Architecture," in *Spain's Hopes and Realities: Architecture, History and Politics*, ed. Jody Brotherston. Ruston, LA: Louisiana Tech University, 1993. Proceedings of an international symposium.

———. *Sorolla's House: The Interiors and Gardens*. Shreveport, LA: Graphic Industries, 2005. The Madrid house of painter Joaquìn Sorolla y Bastida (1863–1923) and its furnishings, many of them antique.

Brown, Jonathan, and J. H. Elliott. *A Palace for a King: The Buen Retiro and the Court of Philip IV*. New Haven, CT: Yale University Press, 1980. Revised and expanded edition, 2004.

Byne, Arthur. *Majorcan Houses and Gardens*. New York: Helburn, 1928. Arthur Byne was an American architect and antiques dealer who lived in Spain for more than a decade. His clients for Spanish antiques included William Randolph Hearst and his architect Julia Morgan. Byne wrote a dozen books (some coauthored with his wife) on Spanish buildings, interiors, furniture, and decorative details. They are distinguished by valuable documentary photographs and measured drawings.

———. *Provincial Houses in Spain*. New York: Helburn, 1925.

Byne, Arthur, and Mildred Stapley Byne. *Spanish Architecture of the Sixteenth Century*. New York: G. P. Putnam, 1917.

Clute, Eugene, ed. *Masterpieces of Spanish Architecture*. New York: Pencil Points Press, 1925.

Espinosa de los Monteros, Patricia. *Houses and Palaces of Andalusia*. New York: Rizzoli, 1998.

Ferro, Maria Inês. *Queluz: The Palace and Gardens*. London: Scala, 1997. An eighteenth-century Portuguese royal palace in French Rococo style.

Harvey, John. *The Cathedrals of Spain*. London: B. T. Batsford, 1957.

Hernández Ferrero, Juan A. *The Royal Palaces of Spain*. New York: Abbeville, 1997.

Hernandez Nuñez, Juan Carlos, and Alfredo J. Morales. *The Royal Palace of Seville*. London: Scala, in association with Aldeasa S.A., 1999.

Kubler, George. *Portuguese Plain Architecture: Between Spices and Diamonds, 1521–1706*. Middletown, CT: Wesleyan University Press, 1972.

Kubler, George, and Martin Soria. *Art and Architecture in Spain and Portugal and Their American Dominions, 1500 to 1800*. Baltimore, MD: Penguin, 1959.

Levenson, Jay A., ed. *The Age of the Baroque in Portugal*. New Haven, CT: Yale University Press, 1993. Catalog of an exhibition at the National Gallery of Art, Washington, DC, in 1993 and 1994.

Luis Filipe, Marques da Gama. *Palacio Nacional de Mafra*. Lisbon and Mafra: ELO-Publicidade, Artes Graficas, 1985. A guide in four languages to the eighteenth-century Portuguese palace.

Mack, Gerstle, and Thomas Gibson. *Architectural Details of Northern and Central Spain*. New York: Helburn, 1930. This and the following book have photographs and measured drawings of Spanish patios, doorways, ironwork, and other features.

———. *Architectural Details of Southern Spain*. New York: Helburn, 1928.

Neves, José Cassiano. *The Palace and Gardens of Fronteira*. Quetzal Editores. Distributed in the United States by Antique Collector's Club, Wappingers Falls, NY, 1995. A seventeenth-century Portuguese palace.

Orso, Steven N. *Philip IV and the Decoration of the Alcázar of Madrid*. Princeton, NJ: Princeton University Press, 1986.

Rodrìguez G. de Ceballos, Alfonso. *The Cathedral of Santiago de Compostela*. London: Scala, in association with Aldeasa S.A., 2000.

Vlieghe, Hans. *Flemish Art and Architecture, 1585–1700*. New Haven, CT: Yale University Press, 1998. Pelican History of Art series. Presents the design of Flanders under Spanish rule.

Hispano-Moorish Style: The Alhambra, Granada

Grabar, Oleg. *The Alhambra*. Cambridge, MA: Harvard University Press, 1978.

Jacobs, Michael. *Alhambra*. New York: Rizzoli, 2000.

Jones, Owen. *The Grammar of Ornament*. New York: Van Nostrand Reinhold, 1982; Mineola, NY: Dover, 1987. Modern reprints of the 1856 original. See especially Chapter X, "Moresque Ornament from the Alhambra."

Gothic Styles: The Cathedral of Seville

Montiel, Luis, and Alfredo J. Morales. *The Cathedral of Seville*. London: Scala, in association with Aldeasa S.A., 1999.

Renaissance Styles: El Escorial, Near Madrid

Cable, Mary, and the editors of the Newsweek Book Division. *El Escorial*. New York: Newsweek, 1971.

Collazos, Oscar. *Royal Palaces in the National Heritage of Spain*. Madrid: Patrimonio Nacional and Lunwerg Editores, 1988. El Escorial and six other palaces.

El Escorial, Eighth Marvel of the World. Madrid: Patrimonio Nacional, 1967.

Kubler, George. *Building the Escorial*. Princeton, NJ: Princeton University Press, 1982.

———. "Palladio and the Escorial," in *Studies in Ancient American and European Art: The Collected Essays of George Kubler*. New Haven, CT: Yale University Press, 1985. First published in Italian in 1963.

Wilkinson, Catherine. "Planning a Style for the Escorial: An Architectural Treatise for Philip of Spain," *Journal of the Society of Architectural Historians*, XLIV, no. 1, March 1985, pp. 37–47.

Spanish Ornament

Byne, Arthur, and Mildred Stapley Byne. *Decorated Wooden Ceilings in Spain*. New York: Hispanic Society of America, 1920; New York and London: G. P. Putnam, 1920.

Spanish Furniture

Burr, Grace Hardendorff. *Hispanic Furniture from the Fifteenth through the Eighteenth Century*, 2nd ed. New York: Archive, 1964.

Byne, Arthur, and Mildred Stapley Byne. *Spanish Interiors and Furniture*, 3 vols. New York: Helburn, 1921–25; reprinted, Mineola, NY: Dover, 1969.

Doménech (Galissá), Rafael, and Luis Pérez Bueno. *Antique Spanish Furniture*. Barcelona: c. 1921; new edition with English translation by Grace Hardendorff Burr, New York: Bonanza, 1965. The authors were the first two directors of what is now the National Museum of Decorative Arts in Madrid.

Eberlein, Harold Donaldson. *Spanish Interiors, Furniture, and Details*. New York: Architectural Book Publishing, 1925.

Feduchi, L. *El Meuble Espanol*. Barcelona: Ediciones Poligrafa, 1969. An excellent survey, with text in English and three other languages.

Katz, Sali. *Hispanic Furniture*. Stamford, CT: Architectural Book Publishing, 1986.

Spanish Decorative Arts

Ainaud de Lasarte, Juan. *Art Treasures in Spain*. New York: McGraw-Hill, 1969.

The Art of Medieval Spain, A.D. 500–1200. New York: Metropolitan Museum of Art, 1993. Distributed by Abrams, New York. Catalog of a 1993–94 exhibition.

Cerici-Pellicer, Alexandre. *Treasures of Spain from Charles V to Goya*. Treasures of the World series. Geneva: Skira, 1965.

Dodds, Jeffilyn, ed. *Al-Andalus: The Art of Islamic Spain*. New York: Metropolitan Museum of Art, 1992. Distributed by Abrams, New York. Catalog of a 1992 exhibition seen first at the Alhambra and then at the Metropolitan.

Hagen, Oskar. *Patterns and Principles of Spanish Art*. Madison I: University of Wisconsin Press, 1948.

O'Neill, John P. *The Art of Medieval Spain*, A.D. 500–1200. New York: Metropolitan Museum of Art, 1993. Distributed by Abrams, New York.

Pita Andrade, J. M. *Treasures of Spain from Altamira to the Catholic Kings*. Geneva: Skira, 1967. Distributed in the United States by World Publishing, Cleveland, OH.

Tarradell, M. *Iberian Art*. New York: Rizzoli, 1978. Artifacts in pre-Roman Spain.

Spanish Decorative Arts: Tile

Berendsen, Anne, et al. *Tiles: A General History*. New York: The Viking Press, 1967. See especially "The Tiles of Spain and Portugal," pp. 65–74.

Castel-Branco Pereira, João. *Portuguese Tiles from the National Museum of Azulejo, Lisbon*. London: Zwemmer, 1995.

Frothingham, Alice Wilson. *Tile Panels of Spain*. New York: Hispanic Society of America, 1969.

Graves, Alun. *Tiles and Tilework of Europe*. London: Victoria & Albert Publications, 2002. A general history, well illustrated.

Herbert, Tony, and Kathryn Huggins. *The Decorative Tile in Architecture and Interiors*. London: Phaidon, 1995. Discusses tiles of the Alhambra, but also much, much more.

Spanish Decorative Arts: Metalwork

Byne, Arthur. *Rejería of the Spanish Renaissance*. New York: Hispanic Society of America, 1914.

Spanish Decorative Arts: Leatherwork

Waterer, John William. *Spanish Leather: A History of Its Use from 800 to 1800*. London: Faber and Faber, 1971.

Spanish Decorative Arts: Textiles

Galea-Blanc, Clothilde, "The Carpet in Spain and Portugal," in *Great Carpets of the World*, ed. Valérie Bérinstai, et al. New York: Vendome, 1996.

Ortiz, Antonio Dominguez, et al. *Resplendence of the Spanish Monarchy: Renaissance Tapestries and Armor from the Patrimonio Nacional*. New York: Metropolitan Museum of Art, 1991.

Stone, Patricia. *Portuguese Needlework Rugs*. McLean, VA: EPM Publications, 1981.

15 France: Renaissance to Neoclassical (Sixteenth to Eighteenth Centuries)

French Architecture and Interiors

Berger, Robert W. *The Palace of the Sun: The Louvre of Louis XIV*. University Park, PA: University of Pennsylvania Press, 1993.

Blunt, Anthony. *Art and Architecture in France, 1500–1700*. Baltimore, MD: Penguin, 1954. Pelican History of Art series.

Cloulas, Ivan. *Treasures of the French Renaissance: Architecture, Sculpture, Paintings, Drawings*. New York: Abrams, 1998.

de Montclos, Jean-Marie Pérouse. *Fontainebleau*. London: Scala, 1998.

———. *Vaux-le-Vicomte*. London: Scala, 1997.

Frégnac, Claude, and Wayne Andrews. *The Great Houses of Paris*. New York: Vendome, 1979.

Gebelin, François. *The Châteaux of France*, trans. H. Eaton Hart. New York: G. P. Putnam, 1964. Descriptions of châteaux from the Middle Ages to the nineteenth century. Included is an argument for Leonardo da Vinci's influence on the design of Chambord.

Huyghe, Renè. *Art Treasures of the Louvre*. New York: Abrams, 1960. Largely a survey of the collections, but with a brief history of the building by Milton S. Fox.

Polidori, Robert, and Jean-Marie Pèrouse de Montclos. *Châteaux of the Loire Valley*. Köln: Konemann, 1997. Chambord and sixty-one other châteaux.

Thornton, Peter. *Seventeenth-Century Interior Decoration in England, France, and Holland*. New Haven, CT: Yale University Press, 1978.

Von Kalnein, Wend. *Architecture in France in the Eighteenth Century*. Pelican History of Art series. New Haven, CT: Yale University Press, 1995. First published in 1972.

Wheeler, Daniel, and the editors of Réalités-Hachette. *The Châteaux of France*. New York: Vendome, 1979.

Whitehead, John. *The French Interior in the Eighteenth Century*. London: Laurence King, 1992; New York: E. P. Dutton, 1993.

French Architecture and Interiors: Renaissance and Baroque (Louis XIV) Styles—Versailles

Berger, Robert W. *A Royal Passion: Louis XIV as Patron of Architecture*. New York: Cambridge University Press, 1994.

———. *Versailles: The Château of Louis XIV*. University Park: Pennsylvania State University Press, 1985.

Constans, Claire, and Xavier Salmon, eds. *Splendors of Versailles*. Jackson: Mississippi Commission for International Cultural Exchange, 1998. Exhibition catalog.

Mitford, Nancy. *The Sun King: Louis XIV at Versailles*. New York: Harper & Row, 1966. Illustrated biography with much information about the palace and its interiors.

Van der Kemp, Gérald. *Versailles*. New York: Park Lane, 1978.

Walton, Guy. *Louis XIV's Versailles*. Chicago: University of Chicago Press, 1986.

French Architecture and Interiors: Régence and Rococo (Louis XV) Styles

Kimball, Fiske. *Creation of the Rococo*. Philadelphia: Philadelphia Museum of Art, 1943; reprinted, New York: Dover, 1980. A standard work on the subject.

Park, William. *The Idea of Rococo*. Newark: University of Delaware Press, 1992. A survey not limited to France.

Scott, Katie. *The Rococo Interior: Decoration and Social Spaces in Early Eighteenth-Century Paris*. New Haven, CT: Yale University Press, 1995.

French Architecture and Interiors: Neoclassical (Louis XVI) and Directoire Styles—The Petit Trianon

Arnott, J., and H. Wilson. *The Petit Trianon*. London: Batsford, 1908; New York: Architectural Book Publishing, 1914. Oversized portfolio with measured drawings and photographs of the building, its interiors, its furniture, and details of its metalwork.

Ducamp, Emmanuel, ed. *Views and Plans of the Petit Trianon at Versailles*. Paris: Alain de Gourcuff Éditeur, 1998.

French Ornament

Lambell, Ronald. *French Period Houses and Their Details*. Oxford: Butterworth, 1992. Photos and line drawings of balustrades, moldings, fireplaces, door handles, and other details from fifteen *hôtels particuliers*. Paperback.

Myers, Mary L. *French Architectural and Ornament Drawings of the Eighteenth Century*. New York: Metropolitan Museum of Art; distributed by Abrams, 1991.

French Ornament: Parquetry and Marquetry

Chastang, Yannick. *Paintings in Wood: French Marquetry Furniture*. London: The Wallace Collection, 2001.

Ramond, Pierre. *Marquetry*. Newtown, CT: Taunton Press, 1989.

French Furniture

Chadenet, Sylvie. *French Furniture from Louis XIII to Art Deco*. Boston: Little, Brown, 2001.

Costantino, Ruth T. *How to Know French Antiques*. New York: Clarkson N. Potter, 1961. Chapters on furniture, painting and drawing, sculpture, textiles, ceramics, glass, clocks, and more. See in the appendix the illustrated "Chronology of Chair Legs."

Hughes, Peter. *French Eighteenth Century Clocks and Barometers in the Wallace Collection*. London: Trustees of the Wallace Collection, 1994.

Leben, Ulrich. *Molitor: Ébéniste from the Ancien Régime to the Bourbon Restoration*. London: Philip Wilson, 1992.

Pradère, Alexandre. *French Furniture Makers: The Art of the Ébéniste from Louis XIV to the Revolution*, trans. Perran Wood. Malibu, CA: J. Paul Getty Museum, 1989.

Ricci, Seymour de. *Louis XIV and Regency Furniture and Decoration*. New York: William Helburn, 1929.

Souchal, Geneviève. *French Eighteenth-Century Furniture*, trans. Simon Watson Taylor. New York: G. P. Putnam, 1961.

Verlet, Pierre. *French Furniture of the Eighteenth Century*, trans. Penelope Hunter-Stiebel. Charlottesville: University Press of Virginia, 1991. First published in Paris in 1955.

Watson, F. J. B. *Louis XVI Furniture*. London: Alec Tiranti, 1960; New York: Philosophical Library, 1960.

French Decorative Arts

Cliff, Stafford. *The French Archive of Design and Decoration*. New York: Abrams, 1999.

French Decorative Arts: Ceramics

Amico, Leonard. *Bernard Palissy: In Search of Earthly Paradise*. New York and Paris: Flammarion, 1996.

French Decorative Arts: Tapestries

Campbell, Thomas P. *Tapestry in the Renaissance: Art and Magnificence*. New Haven, CT: Yale University Press, with the Metropolitan Museum of Art, New York, 2002.

French Decorative Arts: Carpets

Verlet, Pierre. *Savonnerie: The James A. de Rothschild Collection at Waddesdon Manor*. Fribourg, Switzerland: Office du Livre, 1982; published for the National Trust, London.

French Decorative Arts: Other Textiles— Toile De Jouy

Riffel, Mélanie, and Sophie Rouart. *Toile de Jouy: Printed Textiles in the Classic French Style*. New York: Thames & Hudson, 2003.

Straeten, Judith. *Toiles de Jouy*. Salt Lake City, UT: Gibbs Smith, 2002.

French Decorative Arts: Wallpaper

Hoskins, Lesley, ed. *The Papered Wall: History, Pattern, Technique*. New York: Abrams, 1994. See especially Chapter 4, "Luxury Perfected: The Ascendancy of French Wallpaper, 1770–1870"; Chapter 5, "Arabesques and Allegories: French Decorative Panels"; and Chapter 6, "Wide Horizons: French Scenic Papers."

Teynac, Françoise, Pierre Nolot, and Jean-Denis Vivien. *Wallpaper: A History*. New York: Rizzoli, 1982. Especially the chapter on Jean-Baptiste Réveillon.

16 England: Renaissance to Neoclassical (Fifteenth to Eighteenth Centuries)

English Architecture and Interiors

Aslet, Clive, and Alan Powers. *The National Trust Book of the English House*. Harmondsworth, Middlesex, England: Viking, 1985.

Beard, Geoffrey. *Craftsmen and Interior Decoration in England 1660–1820*. Edinburgh: John Bartholomew, 1981; London: Bloomsbury Books, an imprint of Godfrey Cave, 1986.

———. *The National Trust Book of the English House Interior*. London and New York: Viking Penguin, 1990.

Betjeman, John. *A Pictorial History of English Architecture*. New York: Macmillan, 1970.

Brooke, Iris. *Four Walls Adorned: Interior Decoration, 1485–1820*. London: Methuen, 1952. A readable account of English residential décor in the Tudor, Stuart, and Georgian periods, with an emphasis not on the great houses but on the modest ones.

Cliffe, J. T. *The World of the Country House in Seventeenth-Century England*. New Haven, CT: Yale University Press, 1999.

Colvin, Howard. *Essays in English Architectural History*. New Haven, CT: Yale University Press, 1999. Includes essays on Wilton House, the Great Fire of London, and Lord Burlington.

Cooper, Nicholas. *Houses of the Gentry, 1480–1680*. New Haven, CT: Yale University Press, 2000.

Cornforth, John. *English Interiors, 1790–1848*. London: Barrie and Jenkins, 1978.

Cruickshank, Dan. *A Guide to the Georgian Buildings of Britain & Ireland*. New York: Rizzoli, 1986.

Dutton, Ralph. *The English Interior, 1500 to 1900*. London and New York: Batsford, 1948.

Foss, Arthur. *Country House Treasures of Britain*. New York: G. P. Putnam, 1980.

Fowler, John, and John Cornworth. *English Decoration in the Eighteenth Century*. London: Barrie and Jenkins, 1974.

Girouard, Mark. *A Country House Companion*. New Haven, CT: Yale University Press, 1987.

Gore, Alan, and Ann Gore. *English Interiors: An Illustrated History*. New York: Thames & Hudson, 1991. Also published by Phaidon, London, in 1991 as *The History of English Interiors*.

Jackson-Stops, Gervase. *The English Country House: A Grand Tour*. Boston: Little, Brown; Washington, DC: National Gallery of Art, 1985. Photography by James Pipkin. A survey of country house interiors arranged by room type—saloons, dining rooms, withdrawing rooms, libraries, chapels and so on.

Jackson-Stops, Gervase, et al., eds. *The Fashioning and Functioning of the British Country House*. Washington, DC: National Gallery of Art, 1989.

Jenkins, Simon. *England's Thousand Best Houses*. New York: Viking Studio, 2004.

Pearce, David. *The Great Houses of London*. New York: Rizzoli, 1986.

Sitwell, Sacheverell, ed. *Great Houses of Europe*. London and New York: Spring, Books, 1961. Photography by Edwin Smith. Includes essays on Wilton House and Blenheim Castle, both written by John Summerson, and one on Hardwick Hall by Robin Fedden.

Summerson, John. *Architecture in Britain, 1530 to 1830*. Harmondsworth, Middlesex, England: Penguin, 1953.

Sykes, Christopher Simon. *Private Palaces: Life in the Great London Houses*. New York: Viking, 1986.

Tinniswood, Adrian. *Historic Houses of Britain*. New York: Abrams, 1992. Includes descriptions of Hardwick Hall and Knole.

Von Einsiedel, Andreas, and Nadia Mackenzie, with text by Margaret Willes. *Historic Interiors of England, Wales, and Northern Ireland*. New York: Abrams, 1999. Portfolio of color photographs of country house interiors.

Watkin, David. *English Architecture: A Concise History*. New York: Oxford University Press, 1979.

English Architecture and Interiors: Early Renaissance Styles

Mowl, Timothy. *Elizabethan and Jacobean Style*. London: Phaidon, 1993.

Wells-Cole, Anthony. *Art and Decoration in Elizabethan and Jacobean England: The Influence of Continental Prints, 1558–1625*. New Haven, CT: Yale University Press, 1997.

English Architecture and Interiors: Early Renaissance Styles—Hardwick Hall, Derbyshire

Girouard, Mark. *Robert Smythson and the Elizabethan Country House*. New Haven, CT: Yale University Press, 1983.

See also Santina Levey's book under "Textiles."

English Architecture and Interiors: High Renaissance Styles—The Banqueting House, London, and Wilton House, Wiltshire

Harris, John, and Gordon Higgott. *Inigo Jones: Complete Architectural Drawings*. New York: The Drawing Center, 1989. Includes some of Jones's original studies for the Banqueting House.

Leapman, Michael. *Inigo: The Life of Inigo Jones: Architect of the English Renaissance*. London: Review Books, 2003. A biography reprinted in paperback in 2004.

Summerson, John. *Inigo Jones*. New Haven, CT: Yale University Press, 1966. Reprinted in paperback in 2000.

Thurley, Simon. *Whitehall Palace: An Architectural History of the Royal Apartments, 1240–1690*. New Haven, CT: Yale University Press, 2000.

English Architecture and Interiors: Baroque Styles—Sir Christopher Wren And St. Paul's Cathedral, London

Beard, Geoffrey. *The Work of Christopher Wren*. London: Bloomsbury Books, 1982.

Downes, Kerry. *The Architecture of Wren*. New York: Universe Books, 1982.

———. *Sir Christopher Wren: The Design of St. Paul's Cathedral*. London: Trefoil Publications and the American Institute of Architects Press, 1988; reprinted 1990.

Keene, Derek, Arthur Burns, and Andrew Saint, eds. *St. Paul's: The Cathedral Church of London, 604–2004*. New Haven, CT: Yale University Press, 2004. A definitive history.

Whinney, Margaret. *Wren*. New York: Thames & Hudson, 1998.

English Architecture and Interiors: Baroque Styles—Blenheim Palace, Oxfordshire

Fowler, Marian. *Blenheim: Biography of a Palace*. New York: Viking Penguin, 1989.

Lees-Milne, James. *English Country Houses: Baroque, 1685–1715*. London: Country Life, 1970.

English Architecture and Interiors: Neoclassical Style

Irwin, David. *Neoclassicism*. Art and Ideas series. London: Phaidon, 1997.

Middleton, Robin, and David Watkin. *Neoclassical and 19th Century Architecture*. New York: Rizzoli, 1987. A two-volume work, the first volume is *The Enlightenment in France and England;* the second, *The Diffusion and Development of Classicism and the Gothic Revival*.

Stillman, Damie. *English Neo-Classical Architecture*. London: Zwemmer, 1988.

Summerson, John. *Georgian London: An Architectural Study.* Harmondsworth, Middlesex, England: Penguin, 1962; New York: Praeger, 1970.

English Architecture and Interiors: Neoclassical Style—Chiswick House, London

Wittkower, Rudolf. *Palladio and English Palladianism.* New York: Thames & Hudson, 1983.

English Architecture and Interiors: Neoclassical Style—Robert and James Adam and Syon House, London

Adam, Robert, and James Adam. *The Works in Architecture,* 2 vols. London, 1773–79; vol. 3, 1822.

Beard, Geoffrey. *The Work of Robert Adam.* New York: Arco, 1978.

Fleming, John. *Robert Adam and His Circle.* London: John Murray, 1962.

Harris, Eileen. *The Genius of Robert Adam: His Interiors.* New Haven, CT: Yale University Press, 2001. Handsomely illustrated, including a nineteen-page section on Syon House.

Parissien, Steven. *Adam Style.* Washington, DC: The Preservation Press, National Trust for Historic Preservation, 1992.

Tait, A. A. *Robert Adam, The Creative Mind: From the Sketch to the Finished Drawing.* London: The Soane Gallery, 1996. Exhibition catalog.

———. *Robert Adam: Drawings & Imagination.* New York: Cambridge University Press, 1993.

Yarwood, Doreen. *Robert Adam.* New York: Scribner, 1970.

English Ornament: Woodwork— Grinling Gibbons

Beard, Geoffrey. *The Work of Grinling Gibbons.* Chicago: University of Chicago Press, 1989.

Esterly, David. *Grinling Gibbons and the Art of Carving.* New York: Abrams, 1998.

Oughton, Frederick. *Grinling Gibbons and the English Woodcarving Tradition.* London: Stobart & Son, 1979.

English Furniture

Beard, Geoffrey, and Christopher Gilbert, eds. *Dictionary of English Furniture Makers, 1660–1840.* Leeds, Yorkshire, England: W. S. Maney, 1986.

———. *The National Trust Book of English Furniture.* Harmondsworth, Middlesex, England: Viking, 1985.

Cotton, Bernard D. *The English Regional Chair.* Woodbridge, Suffolk, England: Antique Collectors' Club, 1990.

English Chairs. London: His Majesty's Stationery Office for the Victoria & Albert Museum, 1951.

Fastnedge, Ralph. *English Furniture Styles, 1550–1830.* Harmondsworth, Middlesex, England: Penguin, 1955. Reprinted 1961.

Gilbert, Christopher. *English Vernacular Furniture, 1750–1900.* New Haven, CT: Yale University Press, 1991.

Hayward, Charles H. *English Period Furniture.* New York: Van Nostrand Reinhold, 1982. Interestingly divides English furniture history into "Age of the Carpenter, Age of the Cabinet Maker, and Age of the Designer."

Hayward, Helena, and Pat Kirkham. *William and John Linnell: Eighteenth-Century London Furniture Makers,* 2 vols. New York: Rizzoli, 1980.

Heal, Sir Ambrose. *The London Furniture Makers from the Restoration to the Victorian Era, 1660–1840.* London: Batsford, 1953. With a chapter by Robert Wemyss Symonds on "The Problem of Identification."

Hughes, Therle. *Old English Furniture.* New York: Praeger, 1963. A survey by furniture types: chests, chairs, tables, and so on.

Kinmonth, Claudia. *Irish Country Furniture, 1700–1950.* New Haven, CT: Yale University Press, 1993.

Lennox-Boyd, Edward, ed. *Masterpieces of English Furniture: The Gerstenfeld Collection.* London: Christie's Books, 1998.

Strange, Thomas Archer. *English Furniture: Decoration, Woodwork, and Allied Arts.* London: Studio Editions, 1986.

Symonds, Robert Wemyss. *English Furniture from Charles II to George II.* New York: International Studio, 1929. Symonds was a prolific writer or English furniture in the 1940s and 1950s.

———. *Masterpieces of English Furniture and Clocks.* London: Batsford, 1940.

Synge, Lanto. *Mallett's Great English Furniture.* Boston: Little, Brown, a Bulfinch Press Book, 1991. Examples from the wares of the well-known London antique dealer.

White, Elizabeth, ed. *Pictorial Dictionary of British 18th Century Furniture Design.* Wappingers Falls, NY: Antique Collectors' Club, 1990.

Wills, Geoffrey. *English Furniture, 1550–1760.* Garden City, NY: Doubleday, 1971.

English Furniture: Furniture Woods

MacQuoid, Percy. *A History of English Furniture.* London: Studio Editions, 1988; reprinted 1991. A one-volume reprint of MacQuoid's earlier four-volume work: *The Age of Oak, The Age of Walnut, The Age of Mahogany*, and *The Age of Satinwood*, first published between 1904 and 1908.

Rogers, John C. *English Furniture.* London: Country Life, 1950. Revised and enlarged by Margaret Jourdain. First published by Country Life in 1923. A historical survey by wood types: "The Period of Oak . . . Walnut . . . Mahogany Furniture."

English Furniture: Furniture Designers— William Kent

Nuttall, Nicholas. "Kent, William," in *Encyclopedia of Interior Design,* ed. Joanna Banham. London and Chicago: Fitzroy Dearborn, 1997.

Sicca, Cinzia Maria, "Kent, William," in *The Dictionary of Art*, ed. Jane Turner. New York: Grove/Macmillan, 1996, vol. 17, pp. 900–906.

English Furniture: Furniture Designers— Thomas Chippendale

Chippendale, Thomas. *The Gentleman and Cabinet-Maker's Director*. New York: Dover, 1966. Modern reprint of Chippendale's 3rd edition (London, 1762). First edition published 1754.

Gilbert, Christopher. *The Life and Work of Thomas Chippendale*. New York: Tabard Press; London: Cassell, 1978.

Hardy, Paul. "Thomas Chippendale," in *Encyclopedia of Interior Design*, ed. Joanna Banham. London and Chicago: Fitzroy Dearborn, 1997.

Harris, Nathaniel. *Chippendale*. Secaucus, NJ: Chartwell, 1989.

English Furniture: Furniture Designers— Robert Adam

Harris, Eileen. *The Furniture of Robert Adam*. London: Tiranti, 1963. Reprinted, London: Academy Editions; New York: St. Martin's Press, 1973.

Stillman, Damie. *Decorative Work of Robert Adam*. London: Tiranti, 1966. Reprinted, London: Academy Editions; New York: St. Martin's Press, 1973.

Tomlin, Maurice. *Catalogue of Adam Period Furniture*. London: Victoria & Albert Museum, 1982. Concentrates on furniture in the museum and at Osterley Park, the house designed by Adam between 1761 and 1780.

English Furniture: Furniture Designers— George Hepplewhite

Hinckley, F. Lewis. *Hepplewhite, Sheraton & Regency Furniture*. New York: Washington Mews, 1987.

English Furniture: Furniture Designers— Thomas Sheraton

Beilly, Roslyn. "Sheraton Furniture," *Interior Design*, August, 1989, p. 110.

Fastnedge, Ralph. *Sheraton Furniture*. New York: Thomas Yoseloff, 1962.

Sheraton, Thomas. *The Cabinet-Maker and Upholsterer's Drawing-Book*. New York: Dover, 1972. Reprint of Sheraton's book first published between 1791 and 1793.

English Decorative Arts

Cliff, Stafford. *The English Archive of Design and Decoration*. New York: Abrams, 1998. Excellent source of a variety of visual information.

Jackson, Anna. *The V&A Guide to Period Styles: 400 Years of British Art and Design*. London: Victoria & Albert Museum, 2002. Covers British decorative arts from 1500 to 1900.

Jackson-Stops, Gervase, ed. *The Treasure Houses of Britain: Five Hundred Years of Private Patronage and Art Collecting*. Washington, DC: National Gallery of Art; New Haven, CT: Yale University Press, 1985. Exhibition catalog of almost six hundred examples of art and decorative arts from British houses.

English Decorative Arts: Ceramics

Cushion, John, and Margaret Cushion. *A Collector's History of British Porcelain*. Woodbridge, Suffolk: Antique Collectors' Club, 1992. Excellent history from the middle of the eighteenth century to the present.

Poole, Julia E. *English Pottery*. New York: Cambridge University Press, 1995. Examples from the collection of the Fitzwilliam Museum at the University of Cambridge.

English Decorative Arts: Ceramics— Wedgwood

Dawson, Aileen. *British Museum Masterpieces of Wedgwood*. London: British Museum Press, 1984.

Herman, Michael. *Wedgwood Jasper Ware: A Shape Book and Collector's Guide*. Atglen, PA: Schiffer, 2003.

Kelly, Alison. *Decorative Wedgwood in Architecture and Furniture*. New York: Born-Hawes, 1965.

Reilly, Robin. *Wedgwood*, 2 vols. New York: Stockton; London: Macmillan, 1989.

English Decorative Arts: Glass

Mortimer, Martin. *The English Glass Chandelier*. Wappingers Falls, NY: Antique Collectors' Club, 2000.

Truman, Charles. *English Glassware to 1900*. London: Her Majesty's Stationery office for the Victoria & Albert Museum, 1984. A brief history.

English Decorative Arts: Metalwork

Alcorn, Ellenor M. *English Silver in the Museum of Fine Arts, Boston, vol. 2: Silver from 1697*. Boston: Museum of Fine Arts, 2000.

Rowe, Robert. *Adam Silver, 1765–1795*. New York: Taplinger, 1965.

English Decorative Arts: Textiles

Beard, Geoffrey. *Upholsterers and Interior Furnishing in England, 1530–1840*. New Haven, CT: Yale University Press, 1997. Published for the Bard Graduate Center for Studies in the Decorative Arts.

Levey, Santina M. *Elizabethan Treasures: The Hardwick Hall Textiles*. London: National Trust, distributed in the United States by Abrams, 1998.

English Decorative Arts: Wallpaper

Banham, Joanna, "Print Rooms," in *Encyclopedia of Interior Design*, ed. Joanna Banham. London and Chicago: Fitzroy Dearborn, 1997.

17 Africa (Prehistory to the Present)

Bacquart, Jean-Baptiste. *The Tribal Arts of Africa*. New York: Thames & Hudson, 1998.

Bargna, Ivan. *African Art*. Milan: Editoriale Jaca Book SpA, 2000. Distributed in the United States by Antique Collectors' Club, Wappingers Falls, NY.

Bocola, Sandro, ed. *African Seats*. Munich and New York: Prestel, 1995.

Denyer, Susan. *African Traditional Architecture*. New York: Africana, a division of Holme & Meier, 1978.

Gillow, John. *Printed and Dyed Textiles from Africa*. Seattle: University of Washington Press, 2001.

Koloss, Hans-Joachim, ed. *Africa: Art and Culture*. Munich and New York: Prestel, n.d.

Laude, Jean. *The Arts of Black Africa*. Berkeley: University of California Press, 1973.

Morris, James, and Suzanne Preston Blier. *Butabu: Adobe Architecture of West Africa*. New York: Princeton Architectural Press, 2004.

Ross, Doran H. *Gold of the Akan from the Glassell Collection*. Houston: Museum of Fine Arts, 2002.

Spring, Chris, and Julie Hudson. *Silk in Africa*. Seattle: University of Washington Press, 2002.

Wenzel, Marian. *House Decoration in Nubia*. London: Duckworth, 1972.

Willett, Frank. *African Art*. New York: Thames & Hudson, 1993.

18 Pre-Columbian America (Before the Sixteenth Century)

Townsend, Richard F., ed. *The Ancient Americas: Art from Sacred Landscapes*. Chicago: Art Institute of Chicago, 1992. Includes an extensive bibliography.

Central and South America

Bruhns, Karen Olsen. *Ancient South America*. New York: Cambridge University Press, 1994.

Coe, Michael D., and Rex Koontz. *Mexico: From the Olmecs to the Aztecs*, 5th ed. New York: Thames & Hudson, 2002. A text first published in 1962, covering several Mexican civilizations but excluding the Mayas.

Covarrubias, Miguel. *Indian Art of Mexico and Central America*. New York: Knopf, 1957; reprinted, 1971. Illustrated by the author, a noted illustrator and caricaturist.

Disselhoff, H. D., and S. Linné. *The Art of Ancient America: Civilizations of Central and South America*. Art of the World series. New York: Crown, 1960.

Emmerich, André. *Art before Columbus*. New York: Simon & Schuster, 1963. Photographs by Lee Boltin. An appreciative view of early Mexican cultures by a prominent New York gallery owner. The Emmerich Gallery has also published the catalogs *Abstract Art before Columbus* (1957), *The Art of Ancient Peru* (1969), and *Sweat of the Sun and Tears of the Moon: Gold and Silver in Pre-Columbian Art* (1984).

Hardoy, Jorge Ferrari. *Pre-Columbian Cities*. New York: Walker, 1973. The author is an architect who worked in Le Corbusier's Paris studio and for whom the Hardoy (or "sling" or "butterfly") chair is named.

Krichman, Michael, and Eva Ungar Grudin. *Ancient American Art: An Aesthetic View*. Boston: Triad Press, 1981. Catalog for an exhibition at the Rose Art Museum, Brandeis University.

Kubler, George. *The Art and Architecture of Ancient America: The Mexican, Maya, and Andean Peoples*. Harmondsworth, Middlesex, England: Penguin, 1962; reissued by Yale University Press, 1993. An authoritative account, beautifully written.

"Mesoamerica, Pre-Columbian," in *Dictionary of Art*. New York: Grove/Macmillan, 1996, vol. 21, pp. 177–266.

Miller, Mary Ellen. *The Art of Mesoamerica from Olmec to Aztec*. New York: Thames & Hudson, 1986. Revised in 1996 in the World of Art series.

Pasztory, Esther. *Pre-Columbian Art*. New York: Cambridge University Press, 1998.

Paz, Octavio. *Essays on Mexican Art*. New York: Harcourt Brace, 1987. Begins with three essays on Pre-Columbian art.

Stierlin, Henri. *Ancient Mexico*. Living Architecture series. New York: Grosset & Dunlap, 1968. Illustrated with striking photographs by the author.

"South America, Pre-Columbian," in *Dictionary of Art*. New York: Grove/Macmillan, 1996, vol. 29, pp. 123–224.

Von Hagen, Victor Wolfgang. *The Ancient Sun Kingdoms of the Americas: Aztec, Maya, Inca*. Cleveland, OH, and New York: World, 1957.

Central and South America: The Olmecs

Benson, Elizabeth P., and Beatriz de la Fuente. *Olmec Art of Ancient Mexico*. New York: Abrams, 1996.

Clark, John E., and Mary Pye, eds. *Olmec Art and Archaeology in Mesoamerica*. New Haven, CT: Yale University Press, 2000.

Coe, Michael D., et al. *The Olmec World: Ritual and Rulership*. Princeton, NJ: Art Museum, Princeton University, 1996. Catalog for an exhibition at Princeton and at the Museum of Fine Arts, Houston.

Diehl, Richard A. *The Olmecs: America's First Civilization*. New York: Thames & Hudson, 2004.

Central and South America: Teotihuacán

Berrin, Kathleen, and Esther Pasztory, eds. *Teotihuacán: Art from the City of the Gods*. New York: Thames & Hudson, 1993.

Central and South America: The Mayas

Andrews, George F. *Maya Cities: Placemaking and Urbanization*. Civilization of the American Indian series. Norman: University of Oklahoma Press, 1975.

Fields, Virginia M., and Dorie Reents-Budet. *Lords of Creation: The Origins of Sacred Maya Kingship*. London: Scala, with the Los Angeles County Museum of Art, 2005.

Gallenkamp, Charles. *Maya: The Riddle and Rediscovery of a Lost Civilization*. New York: David McKay, 1959; revised and reprinted by Viking, 1985.

Gallenkamp, Charles, and Regina Elise Johnson. *Maya: Treasures of an Ancient Civilization*. New York: Abrams, 1985. Catalog of an exhibition organized by the Albuquerque Museum.

Miller, Mary Ellen. *Maya Art and Architecture*. New York: Thames & Hudson, 1999. Part of the World of Art series.

Miller, Mary Ellen, and Karl Taube. *The Gods and Symbols of Ancient Mexico and the Maya: An Illustrated Dictionary of Mesoamerican Religion*. New York: Thames & Hudson, 1997.

Morley, Sylvanus G., and George W. Brainerd, rev. Robert J. Sharer. *The Ancient Maya*, 4th ed. Palo Alto, CA: Stanford University Press, 1983.

Ranney, Edward. *Stonework of the Maya*. Albuquerque: University of New Mexico Press, 1974. Photography by the author.

Schele, Linda, and Mary Ellen Miller. *The Blood of Kings: Dynasty and Ritual in Maya Art*. New York: Braziller, 1986. Catalog for an exhibition first seen at the Kimbell Art Museum, Fort Worth, TX.

Schevill, Margot Blum, ed. *The Maya Textile Tradition*. New York: Abrams, 1997.

Schmidt, Peter, Mercedes de la Garcia, and Enrique Nalda, eds. *Maya*. New York: Rizzoli, 1998.

Central and South America: The Moche

Pillsbury, Joanne. *Moche Art and Archaeology in Ancient Peru*. New Haven, CT: Yale University Press, 2002.

Central and South America: The Incas

Berrin, Kathleen, ed. *The Spirit of Ancient Peru*. New York and San Francisco: Thames & Hudson and the Fine Arts Museums of San Francisco, 1997. Exhibition catalog.

Gasparini, Graziano, and Luise Margolies. *Inca Architecture*. Bloomington: Indiana University Press, 1980.

Minelli, Laura Laurencich, ed. *The Inca World: The Development of Pre-Columbian Peru, A.D. 1000–1534*. Norman: University of Oklahoma Press, 2000. First published in Milan in 1992.

Morris, Craig, and Adriana von Hagen. *The Inca Empire and Its Andean Origins*. New York: Abbeville, 1983. Publication sponsored by the American Museum of Natural History.

Peternosto, César. *The Stone and the Thread: Andean Roots of Abstract Art*. Austin: University of Texas Press, 1996.

Central and South America: The Incas—Machu Picchu

Brukoff, Barry. *Machu Picchu*. Boston: Little, Brown, 2001. Photographs by San Francisco interior designer Barry Brukoff, with an introduction by Isabel Allende and poems (in Spanish and English) by Pablo Neruda.

Central and South America: The Incas—Textiles

Meisch, Lynn A. *Traditional Textiles of the Andes: Life and Cloth in the Highlands*. New York and San Francisco: Thames & Hudson and the Fine Arts Museums of San Francisco, 1997. Exhibition catalog.

Reid, James W. *Textile Masterpieces of Ancient Peru*. New York: Dover, 1986.

Rowe, Ann Pollard, and John Cohen. *Hidden Threads of Peru: Oíero Textiles*. London: Merrell, 2002.

Stone-Miller, Rebecca, et al. *To Weave for the Sun: Ancient Andean Textiles in the Museum of Fine Arts, Boston*. New York: Thames & Hudson, 1992.

North American Architecture and Interiors

Nabokov, Peter, and Robert Easton. *Native American Architecture*. New York: Oxford University Press, 1989.

Scully, Vincent. *Pueblo: Mountain, Village, Dance*. New York: Viking, 1975.

North American Decorative Arts

Averill, Lloyd J., and Daphne K. Morris. *Northwest Coast Native and Native-Style Art*. Seattle: University of Washington Press, 1996.

Berlo, Janet Catherine, and Ruth B. Phillips. *Native North American Art*. New York: Oxford University Press, 1998.

Covarrubias, Miguel. *The Eagle, the Jaguar, and the Serpent: Indian Art of the Americas—North America: Alaska, Canada, the United States*. New York: Knopf, 1954; reprinted, 1967. Illustrated by the author.

Dockstader, Frederick J. *Indian Art in America: The Arts and Crafts of the North American Indian*. Greenwich, CT: New York Graphic Society, 1966.

———. *Indian Art of the Americas*. New York: Museum of the American Indian, 1973.

Douglas, Frederic H., and René D'Harnoncourt. *Indian Art of the United States*. New York: Museum of Modern Art, 1941; reprinted, 1970. This catalog of an exhibition at the Museum of Modern Art is the first comprehensive treatment of native North American art history.

Feder, Norman. *Two Hundred Years of North American Indian Art*. New York: Praeger, 1971, published in association with the Whitney Museum of American Art.

Feest, Christian F. *Native Arts of North America*. New York: Oxford University Press, 1980.

———, ed. *Studies in American Indian Art*. Seattle: University of Washington Press, 2002.

Friedman, Martin, et al. *American Indian Art: Form and Tradition*. New York: E. P. Dutton, 1972. Exhibition catalog.

Grimes, John R., Christian F. Feest, and Mary Lou Curran. *Uncommon Legacies: Native American Art from the Peabody Essex Museum*. Seattle: University of Washington Press in association with American Federation of Arts, New York, 2002.

"Native North American Art," in *Dictionary of Art*. New York: Grove/Macmillan, 1996, vol. 22, pp. 541–679.

Penney, David W. *Art of the American Indian Frontier.* Seattle: University of Washington Press, 1992.

———. *Native Arts of North America.* Paris: Terrail, 1998.

North American Decorative Arts: Ceramics

Berlant, Tony, et al. *Mimbres Pottery: Ancient Art of the American Southwest.* New York: Hudson Hills Press, 1983. Catalog of an exhibition organized by the American Federation of Arts.

Bernstein, Bruce, and J. J. Brody. *Voices in Clay: Pueblo Pottery from the Edna M. Kelly Collection.* Seattle: University of Washington Press, 2002.

Brody, J. J., Catherine J. Scott, and Steven A. LeBlanc. *Mimbres Pottery: Ancient Art of the American Southwest.* New York: Hudson Hills Press, 1983.

Dillingham, Rick. *Acoma and Laguna Pottery.* Santa Fe, NM: School of American Research Press, 1992.

Harlow, Francis H. *Historic Pueblo Indian Pottery.* Santa Fe, NM: Museum of New Mexico Press, 1970.

North American Decorative Arts: Basketry

James, George Wharton. *Indian Basketry.* Pasadena, CA: privately printed, 1902; reprinted, New York: Dover, 1972.

Mason, Otis Tufton. *Aboriginal Indian Basketry.* Mineola, NY: Dover, 1988. Reprint of a book first published in 1902 by the Smithsonian Institution.

Tanner, Clara Lee. *Apache Indian Baskets.* Tucson: University of Arizona Press, 1982.

———. *Indian Baskets of the Southwest.* Tucson: University of Arizona Press, 1983.

Whiteford, Andrew Hunter. *Southwestern Indian Baskets: Their History and Their Makers.* Santa Fe, NM: School of American Research Press, 1988.

North American Decorative Arts: Textiles

Amsden, Charles Avery. *Navajo Weaving: Its Technic and History.* Mineola, NY: Dover, 1991. Reprint of a 1934 original.

Dockstader, Frederick J. *Weaving Arts of the North American Indian.* New York: Thomas Y. Crowell, 1978.

19 Early America (Sixteenth to Eighteenth Centuries)

Early American Architecture and Interiors

Brownell, Charles E., Calder Loth, William M. S. Rasmussen, and Richard Guy Wilson. *The Making of Virginia Architecture.* Richmond: Virginia Museum of Fine Arts, 1992.

Chamberlain, Samuel, and Narcissa G. Chamberlain. *New England Rooms, 1639–1863.* Stamford, CT: Architectural Book Publishing, 1993.

Davidson, Marshall B. *The American Heritage History of Notable American Houses.* New York: American Heritage division of McGraw-Hill, 1971.

Fitch, James Marston. *American Building: The Historical Forces That Shaped It.* Boston: Houghton Mifflin, 1947; rev. ed., 1966.

Gowans, Alan. *Images of American Living: Four Centuries of Architecture and Furniture as Cultural Expression.* Philadelphia: J. B. Lippincott, 1964.

Howard, Hugh. *Colonial Houses: The Historic Homes of Williamsburg.* New York: Abrams, 2004. Thirteen houses, but not including the Governor's Palace.

Lane, Mills. *Architecture of the Old South: Georgia.* Savannah, GA: The Beehive Press, 1986. All Lane's books are beautifully produced with fine black and white illustrations.

———. *Architecture of the Old South: Louisiana.* New York: Abbeville, 1990.

———. *Architecture of the Old South: Maryland.* New York: Abbeville, 1991.

———. *Architecture of the Old South: Mississippi and Alabama.* New York: Abbeville, 1989.

———. *Architecture of the Old South: North Carolina.* Savannah, GA: The Beehive Press, 1985.

———. *Architecture of the Old South: South Carolina.* Savannah, GA: The Beehive Press, 1984.

———. *Architecture of the Old South: Virginia.* Savannah, GA: The Beehive Press, 1987.

Monkman, Betty C. *The White House: Its Historic Furnishings and First Families.* New York: Abbeville, 2000.

Morgan, William. *The Abrams Guide to American House Styles.* New York: Abrams, 2004.

Peterson, Harold L. *American Interiors from Colonial Times to the Late Victorians.* New York: Scribner, 1979. Interiors seen in paintings, drawings, needlework, advertisements, and so on.

Pierson, William H., Jr. *American Buildings and Their Architects: The Colonial and Neo-Classical Styles.* Garden City, NY: Doubleday, 1970.

Ryan, William, and Desmond Guinness. *The White House: An Architectural History.* New York: McGraw-Hill, 1980.

Seale, William. *The White House: The History of an American Idea.* Washington, DC: American Institute of Architects Press, 1992.

Early American Architecture and Interiors: Monticello, Albemarle County, Virginia

Adams, William Howard. *Jefferson's Monticello.* New York: Abbeville, 1983.

Guinness, Desmond, and Julius Trousdale Sadler, Jr. *Mr. Jefferson, Architect.* New York: Viking, 1973. Covers both phases of Monticello plus the University of Virginia and much more.

Kimball, Fiske. *Thomas Jefferson, Architect.* Cambridge, MA: Riverside Press, 1916; reprinted, New York: Da Capo, 1968. A pioneering study.

Lautman, Robert C. *Thomas Jefferson's Monticello: A Photographic Portrait.* New York: Monacelli, in association with the Thomas Jefferson Memorial Foundation, 1997.

McLaughlin, Jack. *Jefferson and Monticello: The Biography of a Builder.* New York: Henry Holt, 1988.

Early American Architecture and Interiors: The Spanish Missions

Levick, Melba. *The Missions of California.* San Francisco: Chronicle Books, 2004.

Neuerburg, Norman. *The Decoration of the California Missions.* Santa Barbara, CA: Bellerophon, 1996.

Treib, Marc. *Sanctuaries of Spanish New Mexico.* Berkeley: University of California Press, 1993.

Early American Furniture

Bishop, Robert. *Centuries and Styles of the American Chair, 1640–1970.* New York: E. P. Dutton, 1972.

Evans, Nancy Goyne. *American Windsor Chairs.* New York: Hudson Hills Press, in association with the Henry Francis du Pont Winterthur Museum, 1996. An authoritative study.

Fitzgerald, Oscar P. *Four Centuries of American Furniture.* Englewood Cliffs, NJ: Prentice Hall, 1982, originally titled *Three Centuries of American Furniture.* An enlarged edition was published by Wallace-Homestead, Radnor, PA, in 1995.

Forman, Benno M. *American Seating Furniture, 1630–1730.* New York: W. W. Norton, 1988. A Winterthur book.

Greene, Jeffrey P. *American Furniture of the Eighteenth Century: History, Technique, Structure.* Newtown, CT: Taunton, 1996.

Heckscher, Morrison. *American Furniture in the Metropolitan Museum of Art, Late Colonial Period: The Queen Anne and Chippendale Styles.* New York: Metropolitan Museum of Art and Random House, 1985.

Hurst, Ronald L., and Jonathan Prown. *Southern Furniture, 1680–1830: The Colonial Williamsburg Collection.* New York: Abrams, 1997.

Kenny, Peter M., et al. *Honoré Lannuier, Cabinetmaker from Paris.* New York: Metropolitan Museum of Art, Exhibition Catalog.

Lyon, Irving W. *The Colonial Furniture of New England.* New York: E. P. Dutton, 1977.

Madigan, Mary Jean, and Susan Colgan, eds. *Early American Furniture from Settlement to City.* New York: *Art and Antiques* Magazine, 1983. Excellent essays include "Country Chippendale" by Marvin D. Schwartz and "The Kast and the Schrank" by Joseph T. Butler.

Margon, Lester. *Masterpieces of American Furniture, 1620–1840.* New York: Architectural Book Publishing, 1965; reprinted, 1972.

Montgomery, Charles F. *American Furniture: The Federal Period (1788–1825).* New York: Viking, 1966.

Ormsbee, Thomas Hamilton. *Early American Furniture Makers.* New York: Thomas Y. Crowell, 1930; republished, Detroit: Gale Research, 1976.

———. *The Windsor Chair.* Deerfield Books, distributed by Hearthside, New York, 1962. Despite the general title, the subject is American Windsors.

Richards, Nancy E., and Nancy Goyne Evans. *New England Furniture at Winterthur.* Winterthur, DE: Winterthur Museum, 1997.

Steinbaum, Bernice. *The Rocker: An American Design Tradition.* New York: Rizzoli, 1992.

Venable, Charles L. *American Furniture in the Bybee Collection.* Austin: University of Texas Press, in association with the Dallas Museum of Art, 1989.

Ward, Gerald W. R., ed. *American Furniture with Related Decorative Arts, 1660–1830.* New York: Hudson Hills, 1991. Pieces from the Milwaukee Art Museum and the Layton Art Collection.

———, ed. *Perspectives on American Furniture.* New York: W. W. Norton, 1988. A collection of scholarly essays published for the Henry Francis du Pont Winterthur Museum.

Warren, David B., Michael K. Brown, Elizabeth Ann Coleman, and Emily Ballew Neff. *American Decorative Arts and Paintings in the Bayou Bend Collection.* Houston: The Museum of Fine Arts, in association with Princeton University Press, 1998. The book's largest section (162 pp.) is on furniture.

Early American Furniture: The Shakers

Becksvoort, Christian. *The Shaker Legacy: Perspectives on an Enduring Furniture Style.* Newtown, CT: Taunton, 1998.

Kindred Spirits: The Eloquence of Function in American Shaker and Japanese Arts of Daily Life. San Diego, CA: Mingei International, 1995. Distributed by the University of Washington Press, Seattle. Catalog of a fascinating exhibition comparing Japanese and Shaker pottery, baskets, chests, and so forth.

Kirk, John T. *The Shaker World: Art, Life, Belief.* New York: Abrams, 1997.

Meader, Robert F. W. *Illustrated Guide to Shaker Furniture.* New York: Dover, 1972.

Nicoletta, Julie. *The Architecture of the Shakers.* Woodstock, VT: Countryman Press, 1995.

Rieman, Timothy D., and Jean M. Burks. *The Encyclopedia of Shaker Furniture.* Atglen, PA: Schiffer, 2003. Thorough coverage of the subject, with more than a thousand illustrations.

Shea, John G. *The American Shakers and Their Furniture.* New York: Van Nostrand Reinhold, 1971. Includes measured drawings of many pieces.

Sprigg, June, and Paul Rocheleau. *Shaker Built: The Form and Function of Shaker Architecture.* New York: Monacelli, 1994.

Sprigg, June, and David Larkin. *Shaker: Life, Work, and Art.* New York: Stewart, Tabori, and Chang, 1987.

Early American Furniture: Duncan Phyfe

Cornelius, Charles Over. *Furniture Masterpieces of Duncan Phyfe.* New York: Doubleday, Page & Co. for the Metropolitan Museum of Art, 1922. Reprinted by Dover, Mineola, NY, in 1970.

McClelland, Nancy. *Duncan Phyfe and the English Regency, 1795–1830.* First published in a limited edition in 1939. Republished in 1980 by Dover, Mineola, NY. Many illustrations.

Early American Decorative Arts

Drepperd, Carl W. *Primer of American Antiques.* Garden City, NY: Doubleday, 1944. Seventy-two brief chapters, each on a different aspect of American decorative arts: weather vanes, firebacks, pressed glass, mirrors, rugs, pewter, scrimshaw, buttons, samplers, and so on. Still a useful book.

Dreppard, Carl W., and Lurelle Van Arsdale Guild. *New Geography of American Antiques.* Garden City, NY: Doubleday, 1948.

Hume, Ivor Noël. *A Guide to Artifacts of Colonial America.* New York: Knopf, 1970.

Quimby, Ian M. G., ed. *The Craftsman in Early America.* New York: W. W. Norton, for the Henry Francis du Pont Winterthur Museum, 1984.

Early American Decorative Arts: Ceramics

Levin, Elaine. *The History of American Ceramics.* New York: Abrams, 1988. Covers a wide variety of ceramics from 1607 to the present.

Myers, Susan H. "The Business of Potting, 1780–1840," in *The Craftsman in Early America*, ed. Ian M. G. Quimby. New York: W. W. Norton, 1984.

Watkins, Lura Woodside. *Early New England Potters and Their Wares.* Cambridge, MA: Harvard University Press, 1950.

Early American Decorative Arts: Glass

McKearin, George S., and Helen McKearin. *American Glass.* New York: Crown, 1941.

Revi, Albert Christian. *American Engraved Glass.* Nashville and New York: Thomas Nelson, 1965. The products of hundreds of American glass manufacturers, arranged geographically.

Schwind, Arlene Palmer. "The Glassmakers of Early America," in *The Craftsman in Early America*, ed. Ian M. G. Quimby. New York: W. W. Norton, 1984.

Early American Decorative Arts: Metalwork

McLanathan, Richard B. K., ed. *Colonial Silversmiths: Masters & Apprentices.* Boston: Museum of Fine Arts, 1956. Exhibition catalog. Includes pieces by Coney, Revere, and Revere's father.

Phillips, John Marshall. *American Silver.* Mineola, NY: Dover, 2001. Originally published in 1949 by Chanticleer, New York.

Ward, Barbara McLean. "Boston Goldsmiths," in *The Craftsman in Early America*, ed. Ian M. G. Quimby. New York: W. W. Norton, 1984.

Early American Decorative Arts: Textiles

Cooke, Edward S., Jr., ed. *Upholstery in America and Europe from the Seventeenth Century to World War I.* New York: W. W. Norton, 1987.

Cummings, Abbott Lowell. *Bed Hangings: A Treatise on Fabrics and Styles in the Curtaining of Beds, 1650–1850.* Boston: Society for the Preservation of New England Antiquities, 1994. Includes an essay by Nina Fletcher Little.

Hughes, Robert, and Julie Silber. *Amish: The Art of the Quilt.* New York: Knopf, 1990.

Montgomery, Florence M. *Textiles in America, 1650–1870.* New York: W. W. Norton, 1984.

Peck, Amelia. *American Quilts and Coverlets in the Metropolitan Museum of Art.* New York: Metropolitan Museum of Art and Dutton Studio, 1990.

Early American Decorative Arts: Stenciling and Wallpaper

Katzenbach, Lois, and William Katzenbach. *The Practical Book of American Wallpaper.* Philadelphia and New York: Lippincott, 1951. Includes a dozen samples of actual papers. Covers mostly twentieth century papers, but includes a documentary design from Colonial Williamsburg.

Little, Nina Fletcher. *American Decorative Wall Painting, 1700–1850.* First published in 1952. Enlarged edition published, New York: E. P. Dutton, 1989.

Lynn, Catherine. *Wallpaper in America from the Seventeenth Century to World War I.* New York: W. W. Norton, 1980.

Waring, Janet. *Early American Wall Stencils.* New York: W. R. Scott, 1943. First published in 1937 in a limited edition as *Early American Stencils on Walls and Furniture.*

20 The Nineteenth Century

Determinants of Nineteenth-Century Design: Communications

Eastlake, Charles L. *Hints on Household Taste.* London: Longmans, Green, 1868; reprinted, Mineola, NY: Dover, 1986.

Hope, Thomas. *Household Furniture and Interior Decoration.* London: Longman, Hurst, Rees, and Orme, 1807; reprinted, New York: Dover, 1971. A later Dover reprint changed the title to *Regency Furniture and Interior Decoration.*

Nineteenth-Century Architecture and Design

Art and Design in Europe and America 1800–1900 at the Victoria & Albert Museum. London: The Herbert Press, 1987.

Dixon, Roger, and Stefan Muthesius. *Victorian Architecture.* London: Thames & Hudson, 1978. Includes a dictionary of over 300 Victorian architects.

MacKenzie, John M. *The Victorian Vision: Inventing New Britain.* London: Victoria & Albert Publications, 2001. Distributed in the United States by Abrams, New York.

Maynard, W. Barksdale. *Architecture in the United States, 1800–1850.* New Haven, CT: Yale University Press, 2002.

Pevsner, Nikolaus. *Pioneers of Modern Design: From William Morris to Walter Gropius.* Harmondsworth, Middlesex, England: Penguin, 1974. First published in 1936 as *Pioneers of the Modern Movement.*

Winkler, Gail Caskey, and Roger W. Moss. *Victorian Interior Decoration: American Interiors, 1830–1900.* New York: Henry Holt, 1986.

Nineteenth-Century Architecture and Design: Empire Style

Kahane, Martine, and Thierry Beauvert. *The Paris Opéra.* New York: Vendome, 1987. Minimal text, but fine photography by Jacques Moatti.

Mead, Christopher Curtis. *Charles Garnier's Paris Opera: Architectural Empathy and the Renaissance of French Classicism.* New York and Cambridge, MA: The Architectural History Foundation and MIT Press, 1991.

Percier, Charles, and Pierre-François-Léonard Fontaine. *Recueil de decorations intérieures, comprenant tout ce qui a Rapport à ameublement.* Paris: 1801, 1812. Translated as *Empire Stylebook of Interior Design.* Mineola, NY: Dover, 1991.

Nineteenth-Century Architecture and Design: Regency Style

Morley, John. *Regency Design 1790–1840: Gardens, Buildings, Interiors, Furniture.* New York: Abrams, 1993.

Parissien, Steven. *Regency Style.* Washington, DC: Preservation Press, 1992.

Watkin, David. *The Royal Interiors of Regency England.* New York: Vendome, 1984. Focuses on seven residences: Windsor Castle, Hampton Court, St. James's Palace, Kensington Palace, Buckingham House, Frogmore House, and Carlton House.

Nineteenth-Century Architecture and Design: Regency Style—John Nash

Davis, Terence. *John Nash: The Prince Regent's Architect.* South Brunswick, NJ: A. S. Barnes, 1967.

Mansbridge, Michael. *John Nash: A Complete Catalog.* New York: Rizzoli, 1991; reprinted, London: Phaidon, 2004.

Summerson, John. *The Life and Work of John Nash, Architect.* Cambridge, MA: MIT Press, 1980. Summerson's revised version of his own pioneering *John Nash: Architect to King George the Fourth,* published in 1935.

Nineteenth-Century Architecture and Design: Regency Style—John Soane

Darley, Gillian. *John Soane, An Accidental Romantic.* New Haven, CT: Yale University Press, 1999.

Dean, Ptolemy. *Sir John Soane and the Country Estate.* Brookfield, VT: Ashgate, 1999.

du Prey, Pierre de la Ruffinière. *John Soane: The Making of an Architect.* Chicago: University of Chicago Press, 1982.

Richardson, Margaret, and Mary Anne Stevens, eds. *John Soane, Architect: Master of Space and Light.* London: Royal Academy of Arts, 1999.

Schumann-Bacia, Eva. *John Soane and the Bank of England.* New York: Princeton Architectural Press, 1991.

Stroud, Dorothy. *Sir John Soane, Architect.* London: Faber and Faber, 1984.

Thornton, Peter, and Helen Dorey. *Sir John Soane: The Architect as Collector.* New York: Abrams, 1992.

Watkin, David. *Sir John Soane: Enlightenment Thought and the Royal Academy Lectures.* New York: Cambridge University Press, 1995. Complete edition of Soane's lectures, with fifty of his lecture illustrations.

Nineteenth-Century Architecture and Design: Other Classicist Styles

Honour, Hugh. *Neoclassicism.* Harmondsworth, Middlesex, England: Penguin, 1968.

Praz, Mario, *On Neoclassicism.* London: Thames & Hudson, 1969.

Nineteenth-Century Architecture and Design: Other Classicist Styles— Neoclassicism in Germany

Schinkel, Karl Friedrich. *Sammlung Architektonischer Entwürfe (Collection of Architectural Drawings).* Berlin, 1866; reprinted, New York: Princeton Architectural Press, 1989.

Snodin, Michael. *Karl Friedrich Schinkel: A Universal Man.* New Haven, CT: Yale University Press in association with the Victoria & Albert Museum, London, 1991.

Zukowsky, John, ed. *Karl Friedrich Schinkel, 1781–1841: The Drama of Architecture.* Chicago: Art Institute of Chicago, 1994.

Nineteenth-Century Architecture and Design: Other Classicist Styles— The Biedermeier Style in Austria

Chase, Linda, Karl Kemp, and Lois Lammerhuber. *The World of Biedermeier.* New York: Thames & Hudson, 2001. Lavishly illustrated.

See also under "Nineteenth-Century Furniture: Other Classicist Furniture."

Nineteenth-Century Architecture and Design: Other Classicist Styles—The Gustavian Style in Sweden

Groth, Håkan. *Neoclassicism in the North: Swedish Furniture and Interiors, 1770–1850.* London: Thames & Hudson; New York: Rizzoli, 1990.

Nineteenth-Century Architecture and Design: Revivalist Styles—Gothic Revival

Aldrich, Megan. *Gothic Revival.* London: Phaidon, 1994.

Brooks, Chris. *The Gothic Revival.* London: Phaidon, 1999. Part of the series Art & Ideas.

Germann, Georg. *Gothic Revival in Europe and Britain: Sources, Influences and Ideas.* Cambridge, MA: MIT Press, 1973. Reprinted in paperback 1978.

Lewis, Michael J. *The Gothic Revival.* New York: Thames & Hudson, 2002.

Port, M. H. *The Houses of Parliament.* New Haven, CT: Yale University Press, 1976.

Riding, Jacqueline, and Christine Riding, eds. *The Houses of Parliament: History, Art, Architecture.* London: Merrell, 2000.

Stanton, Phoebe B. *The Gothic Revival & American Church Architecture: An Episode in Taste 1840–1856.* Baltimore, MD: Johns Hopkins University Press, 1968. Reprinted in paperback, 1997.

Nineteenth-Century Architecture and Design: Revivalist Styles—Greek Revival

Cooper, Wendy A. *Classical Taste in America, 1800–1840.* New York: Abbeville, 1993.

Crook, J. Mordaunt. *The Greek Revival*. London: John Murray. 1972.

Kennedy, Roger G. *Greek Revival America*. New York: Stewart, Tabori & Chang, 1989. A National Trust for Historic Preservation book.

Tsigakou, Fani-Maria. *The Rediscovery of Greece: Travellers and Painters of the Romantic Era*. New Rochelle, NY: Caratzas Brothers, 1981.

Nineteenth-Century Architecture and Design: Revivalist Styles—Egyptian Revival

Curl, James Stevens. *The Egyptian Revival: An Introductory Study of a Recurring Theme in the History of Taste*. London: George Allen and Unwin, 1982.

Egyptomania: Egypt in Western Art, 1730–1930. Ottawa: National Gallery of Canada, 1994. Exhibition catalog.

Nineteenth-Century Architecture and Design: Revivalist Styles—Renaissance Revival

Roth, Leland M. *McKim, Mead & White, Architects*. New York: Harper & Row, 1983.

Shopsin, William C., and Mosette Glaser Broderick. *The Villard Houses*. New York: Viking, 1980.

White, Samuel G. *The Houses of McKim, Mead & White*. New York: Rizzoli, 1998.

White, Samuel G., and Elizabeth White. *McKim, Mead & White: The Masterworks*. New York: Rizzoli, 2003.

Nineteenth-Century Architecture and Design: Eastern Styles

Crinson, Mark. *Empire Building: Orientalism and Victorian Architecture*. New York: Routledge, 1996.

Head, Raymond. *The Indian Style*. Chicago: University of Chicago Press, 1986. Traces the influence of India on European design from the seventeeth century to the present.

Jacobson, Dawn. *Chinoiserie*. London: Phaidon, 1993.

Lambourne, Lionel. *Japonisme: Cultural Crossings between Japan and the West*. London: Phaidon, 2005.

Morley, John. *The Making of the Royal Pavilion, Brighton: Designs and Drawings*. Boston: David R. Godine, 1984.

Sweetman, John. *The Oriental Obsession: Islamic Inspiration in British and American Art and Architecture, 1500–1920*. New York: Cambridge University Press, 1988.

Wichmann, Siegfried. *Japonisme: The Japanese Influence on Western Art since 1858*. New York: Thames & Hudson, 1999.

Nineteenth-Century Architecture and Design: The Arts and Crafts Movement

Anscombe, Isabelle. *Arts and Crafts Style*. New York: Rizzoli, 1991.

Cumming, Elizabeth. *The Arts and Crafts Movement*. London: Thames & Hudson, 1991.

Kaplan, Wendy. *"The Art That Is Life": The Arts and Crafts Movement in America, 1875–1920*. Boston: Museum of Fine Arts, 1987. Catalog of an exhibition in Boston, Los Angeles, Detroit, and New York.

Nineteenth-Century Architecture and Design: The Arts and Crafts Movement— William Morris and Philip Webb

Kirk, Sheila. *Philip Webb, Pioneer of Arts & Crafts Architecture*. New York: Wiley, 2005.

MacCarthy, Fiona. *William Morris: A Life for Our Time*. New York: Knopf, 1995. An extensive biography with some illustrations.

Waggoner, Diane, ed. *The Beauty of Life: William Morris and the Art of Design*. New York: Thames & Hudson, 2003.

See also under "Nineteenth-Century Decorative Arts."

Nineteenth-Century Architecture and Design: The Arts and Crafts Movement— Greene & Greene

Bosley, Edward R. *Greene & Greene*. London: Phaidon, 2000.

Makinson, Randell L. *Greene & Greene: Architecture as a Fine Art*. Salt Lake City, UT: Peregrine Smith, 1977.

———. *Greene & Greene: The Passion and the Legacy*. Salt Lake City, UT: Gibbs Smith, 1998.

Smith, Bruce, and Alexander Vertikoff. *Greene & Greene Masterworks*. San Francisco: Chronicle, 1998.

Nineteenth-Century Architecture and Design: The Aesthetic Movement

Lambourne, Lionel. *The Aesthetic Movement*. London: Phaidon, 1996.

Merrill, Linda. *The Peacock Room: A Cultural Biography*. New Haven, CT, and Washington, D.C.: Yale University Press and the Freer Gallery of Art, 1998.

Spencer, Robin. *The Aesthetic Movement: Theory and Practice*. London and New York: Studio Vista/Dutton, 1972.

Nineteenth-Century Architecture and Design: Art Nouveau Style

Bouillon, Jean-Paul. *Art Nouveau, 1870–1914*. Geneva and New York: Skira/Rizzoli, 1985.

Escritt, Stephen. *Art Nouveau*. Art and Ideas series. London: Phaidon, 2000.

Selz, Peter, and Mildred Constantine, eds. *Art Nouveau: Art and Design at the Turn of the Century*. New York: The Museum of Modern Art, 1959. Catalog of an exhibition that opened at the Museum of Modern Art in 1960. A revised edition appeared in 1975.

Nineteenth-Century Architecture and Design: Art Nouveau Style—Louis Sullivan

Elia, Mario Manieri. *Louis Henry Sullivan*. New York: Princeton Architectural Press, 1996.

Sullivan, Louis Henry. *A System of Architectural Ornament According with a Philosophy of Man's Power*. Washington, DC: American Institute of Architects, 1924.

Nineteenth-Century Architecture and Design: Art Nouveau Style—Victor Horta

Aubry, Françoise, and Jos Vandenbreeden, eds. *Horta: Art Nouveau to Modernism*. Ghent: Ludion Press, 1996.

Borsi, Franco, and Paolo Portoghesi. *Horta*. New York: Rizzoli, 1991.

Dernie, David, and Alastair Carew-Cox. *Victor Horta*. London: Academy Editions, 1995.

Nineteenth-Century Architecture and Design: Art Nouveau Style—Emile Gallé and Hector Guimard

Vigne, Georges. *Hector Guimard: Architect Designer, 1867–1942*. New York: Delano Greenridge Editions, 2003.

Rheims, Maurice. *Hector Guimard*. New York: Abrams, 1988. With photography by Felipe Ferré.

For Gallé, see under "Glass."

Nineteenth-Century Architecture and Design: Art Nouveau Style—The Secessionists

Graf, Otto Antonia. *Masterdrawings of Otto Wagner*. New York: The Drawing Center, 1987. Exhibition catalog.

Haiko, Peter, and Bernd Krimmel. *Joseph Maria Olbrich: Architecture*. New York: Rizzoli, 1988.

Mallgrave, Harry Francis, ed. *Otto Wagner: Reflections on the Raiment of Modernity*. Chicago: University of Chicago Press, 1993.

Sketches, Projects and Executed Buildings by Otto Wagner. Portfolios first published in 1889, 1897, 1906, and 1922. Collected and reprinted by Rizzoli, New York, in 1987.

Nineteenth-Century Architecture and Design: Beyond Art Nouveau—Antoní Gaudi

Crippa, Maria Antonietta. *Antoni Gaudí, 1852–1926: From Nature to Architecture*. Köln: Taschen, 2003.

Descharnes, Robert, and Clovis Prévost. *Gaudi the Visionary*. New York: Viking, 1971; revised edition, 1982.

Sweeney, James Johnson, and José Luís Sert. *Antoni Gaudi*. New York: Praeger, 1960.

Nineteenth-Century Architecture and Design: Beyond Art Nouveau—Charles Rennie Mackintosh

Buchanan, William, et al. *Mackintosh's Masterwork*. San Francisco: Chronicle Books, 1989. Focuses on the Glasgow School of Art.

Cooper, Jackie, ed. *Mackintosh Architecture: The Complete Buildings and Selected Projects*. New York: St. Martin's Press, 1977, 1984.

Crawford, Alan. *Charles Rennie Mackintosh*. New York: Thames & Hudson, 1995.

Fiell, Charlotte, and Peter Fiell. *Charles Rennie Mackintosh*. Köln: Taschen, 1995.

Kaplan, Wendy. *Charles Rennie Mackintosh*. New York: Abbeville, 1996. Exhibition catalog.

Macleod, Robert. *Charles Rennie Mackintosh, Architect and Artist*. New York: Dutton, 1983.

Steele, James. *Charles Rennie Mackintosh: Synthesis in Form*. London: Academy Editions, 1994.

Nineteenth-Century Architecture and Design: New Equipment

Fitch, James Marston. *Architecture and the Esthetics of Plenty*. New York: Columbia University Press, 1961. Includes a good description of Catherine Beecher's writings.

Giedion, Sigfried. *Mechanization Takes Command*. New York: Oxford University Press, 1948. Still an impressive survey.

Quimby, Ian M. G., and Polly Anne Earl. *Technological Innovation and the Decorative Arts*. Charlottesville: University Press of Virginia, 1974, 1984. Papers from a 1973 Winterthur conference, with subjects including wallpaper, textiles, pressed glass, and John Henry Belter.

Nineteenth-Century Architecture and Design: New Building Types

Donzel, Catherine, Alexis Gregory, and Marc Walter. *Grand American Hotels*. New York: Vendome, 1989.

Hendrickson, Robert. *The Grand Emporiums: The Illustrated History of America's Great Department Stores*. New York: Stein and Day, 1979.

Landau, Sarah Bradford, and Carl W. Condit. *Rise of the New York Skyscraper, 1865–1912*. New Haven, CT: Yale University Press, 1996.

Meeks, Carrol L. V. *The Railroad Station: An Architectural History*. New Haven, CT: Yale University Press, 1956.

Morrison, Kathryn A. *English Shops and Shopping*. New Haven, CT: Yale University Press, 2003.

Stern, Robert A. M., Thomas Mellins, and David Fishman. *New York 1880: Architecture and Urbanism in the Gilded Age*. New York: Monacelli, 1999.

Watkin, David, et al. *Grand Hotel: The Golden Age of Palace Hotels*. New York: Vendome, 1984. Covers European hotels only.

Zukowsky, John, ed. *Chicago Architecture, 1872–1922: Birth of a Metropolis*. Munich and Chicago: Prestel-Verlag and the Art Institute of Chicago, 1987.

Nineteenth-Century Ornament: Color Theory

Birren, Faber. *Color for Interiors, Historic and Modern*. New York: Whitney Library of Design, 1963. A prolific writer about color, Birren was a follower of color theorist Wilhelm Ostwald.

Kuehni, Rolf G. *Color: An Introduction to Practice and Principles*. New York: Wiley, 1997.

Miller, Mary C. *Color for Interior Architecture*. New York: Wiley, 1997.

Pile, John F. *Color in Interior Design*. New York: McGraw-Hill, 1997.

Rompilla, Ethyl, and the New York School of Interior Design. *Color for Interior Design*. New York: Abrams, 2005. Excellent text, well illustrated.

Nineteenth-Century Furniture

Cook, Clarence. *The House Beautiful: Essays on Beds and Tables, Stools and Candlesticks.* New York: Scribner, 1881; reprinted, Mineola, NY: Dover, 1995.

Hanks, David A. *Innovative Furniture in America from 1800 to the Present.* New York: Horizon Press, 1981.

Symonds, R. W., and B. B. Whineray. *Victorian Furniture.* London: Country Life, 1962. Republished by Studio Editions, London, 1987.

Tracy, Berry, et al. *Nineteenth-Century America: Furniture and Other Decorative Arts.* New York: Metropolitan Museum of Art, 1970.

Nineteenth-Century Furniture: Empire and Regency Furniture

Grandjean, Serge. *Empire Furniture, 1800 to 1825.* London: Faber and Faber; New York: Taplinger, 1966.

Nineteenth-Century Furniture: Other Classicist Furniture

Himmelheber, Georg. *Biedermeier Furniture.* London: Faber and Faber, 1974.

Pressler, Rudolf, and Robin Straub, *Biedermeier Furniture.* Atglen, PA: Schiffer, 1996.

Nineteenth-Century Furniture: Revivalist Furniture

Howe, Katherine S., et al. *Herter Brothers: Furniture and Interiors for a Gilded Age.* New York: Abrams, in association with the Museum of Fine Arts, Houston, 1994.

Nineteenth-Century Furniture: Arts and Crafts Furniture

Bavaro, Joseph J., and Thomas L. Mossman. *The Furniture of Gustav Stickley: History, Techniques, Projects.* New York: Van Nostrand Reinhold, 1982.

Cathers, David. *Gustav Stickley.* London: Phaidon, 2003.

Clark, Michael, and Jill Thomas-Clark. *The Stickley Brothers.* Salt Lake City, UT: Gibbs Smith, 2002.

Nineteenth-Century Furniture: Art Nouveau Furniture

Alison, Filippo. *Charles Rennie Mackintosh as a Designer of Chairs.* Woodbury, NY: Barron's, 1977.

Bilcliffe, Roger. *Charles Rennie Mackintosh: The Complete Furniture, Furniture Drawings, and Interior Design.* New York: E. P. Dutton, 1986.

Dalisi, Riccardo. *Gaudi: Furniture and Objects.* Woodbury, NY: Barron's, 1980.

New Furniture Techniques: Thonet's Bentwood

Ostergard, Derek E. *Bent Wood and Metal Furniture: 1850–1946.* New York: The American Federation of Arts, 1987.

von Vegesack, Alexander. *Thonet: Classic Furniture in Bent Wood and Tubular Steel.* New York: Rizzoli, 1997.

Wilk, Christopher. *Thonet: 150 Years of Furniture.* Woodbury, NY: Barron's, 1980.

New Furniture Techniques: Belter's Laminated Wood

Schwartz, Marvin D., Edward J. Stanek, and Douglas K. True. *The Furniture of John Henry Belter and the Rococo Revival.* New York: E. P. Dutton, 1981.

Nineteenth-Century Decorative Arts

Jervis, Simon. *High Victorian Art.* Woodbridge, Suffolk, England: Boydell Press, 1983.

Naylor, Gillian, ed. *William Morris by Himself: Designs and Writings.* Boston: Little, Brown, 1988.

Newton, Charles. *Victorian Designs for the Home.* London: Victoria & Albert Publications, 1999.

Wainwright, Clive. *The Romantic Interior: The British Collector at Home, 1750–1850.* New Haven, CT: Yale University Press, 1989.

Wilhide, Elizabeth. *William Morris: Decoration and Design.* New York: Abrams, 1991.

Nineteenth-Century Decorative Arts: Glass: Gallé

Duncan, Alastair, and Georges de Bartha. *Glass by Gallé.* New York: Abrams, 1984.

Nineteenth-Century Decorative Arts: Glass: Tiffany

Baal-Teshuva, Jacob. *Louis Comfort Tiffany.* New York: Taschen, 2001.

Duncan, Alastair. *Louis C. Tiffany: The Garden Museum Collection.* Easthampton, MA: Antique Collectors' Club, 2004.

Eidelberg, Martin, and Nancy A. McClelland. *Behind the Scenes of Tiffany Glassmaking.* New York: St. Martin's Press in association with Christie's Fine Arts Auctioneers. Based on the notebooks of Leslie Hayden Nash, who helped Tiffany develop "Favrile" glass.

Eidelberg, Martin, and Alice Cooney Frelinghuysen. *The Lamps of Louis Comfort Tiffany.* New York: Vendome, 2005.

Johnson, Marilynn A. *Louis Comfort Tiffany: Artist for the Ages.* London: Scala, 2005.

Loring, John. *Louis Comfort Tiffany at Tiffany & Co.* New York: Abrams, 2002.

Nineteenth-Century Decorative Arts: Window Treatments

Dornsife, Samuel J. "Design Sources for Nineteenth-Century Window Hangings," in *Winterthur Portfolio 10,* ed. Ian M. G. Quimby, Charlottesville: University Press of Virginia, 1975.

Nineteenth-Century Decorative Arts: Upholstery

Cooke, Edward S., Jr., and Andrew Passeri, "Spring Seats of the Nineteenth and Early-Twentieth Centuries," in *Upholstery in America and Europe from the Seventeenth Century to World War I*, ed. Edward S. Cooke, Jr. New York: W. W. Norton, 1987.

Edwards, Clive D., "Upholstery," in *Encyclopedia of Interior Design*, ed. Joanna Banham. London and Chicago: Fitzroy Dearborn, 1997.

Nineteenth-Century Decorative Arts: Wall and Floor Treatments

Bradbury, Bruce, "Lincrusta-Walton," p. 250ff, and "Anaglypta and Other Embossed Wallcoverings," p. 255ff, in *The Old-House Journal New Compendium*, ed. Patricia Poore and Clem Labine. Garden City, NY: Doubleday, 1983.

Kaldewei, Gerhard, ed. *Linoleum: History, Design, Architecture, 1882–2000*. Ostfildern-Ruit, Germany: Hatje Cantz, 2000.

Simpson, Pamela H. *Cheap, Quick, and Easy: Imitative Architectural Materials, 1870–1930*. Knoxville: University of Tennessee Press, 1999.

Nineteenth-Century Decorative Arts: Wallpaper

Cuadrado, John A. "Nineteeth-Century French Wallpaper," *Architectural Digest*, vol. 52, no. 10, October 1995, pp. 162ff.

Hoskins, Lesley. *The Papered Wall: History, Pattern, Technique*. London: Thames & Hudson, and New York: Abrams, 1994.

21 The Twentieth Century

Abercrombie, Stanley. *A Century of Interior Design, 1900–2000: The Design, the Designers, the Products, and the Profession*. New York: Rizzoli, 2003.

Blake, Peter. *The Master Builders*. New York: Knopf, 1964. Still the most readable account of the work of Frank Lloyd Wright, Le Corbusier, and Ludwig Mies van der Rohe.

Calloway, Stephen. *Twentieth-Century Decoration*. New York: Rizzoli, 1988.

Julier, Guy. *The Thames and Hudson Encyclopedia of 20th-Century Design and Designers*. New York: Thames & Hudson, 1993.

Kaufmann, Edgar, Jr. *What Is Modern Interior Design?* New York: Museum of Modern Art, 1953. Still an excellent overview.

McDermott, Catherine. *Design Museum Book of 20th-Century Design*. Woodstock, NY: Overlook Press for the Design Museum, London, 1998.

Massey, Anne. *Interior Design of the 20th Century*. New York: Thames & Hudson, 1990. Revised and expanded edition, 2001.

Pile, John. *Dictionary of 20th-Century Design*. New York: Facts on File, 1990.

Raizman, David. *History of Modern Design*. Upper Saddle River, NJ: Prentice Hall, 2004.

Woodham, Jonathan M. *Twentieth-Century Design*. New York: Oxford University Press, 1999.

Twentieth-Century Architecture and Interiors: Forerunners—Elsie de Wolfe

Campbell, Nina, and Caroline Seebohm. *Elsie de Wolfe: A Decorative Life*. New York: Clarkson Potter, 1992.

Smith, Jane S. *Elsie de Wolfe: A Life in the High Style*. New York: Atheneum, 1982.

Sparke, Penny. *Elsie de Wolfe: The Birth of Modern Interior Decoration*. New York: Acanthus Press, 2006.

Twentieth-Century Architecture and Interiors: Forerunners—Edwin Lutyens

O'Neill, Daniel. *Lutyens Country Houses*. New York: Watson-Guptill, 1980.

Richardson, Margaret. *Sketches by Edwin Lutyens*. London: Academy Editions, 1994.

Wilhide, Elizabeth. *Sir Edwin Lutyens: Designing in the English Tradition*. New York: Abrams, 2000.

Twentieth-Century Architecture and Interiors: Pioneers—Frank Lloyd Wright

De Long, David, ed. *Frank Lloyd Wright: Designs for an American Landscape, 1922–1932*. New York: Abrams, 1996.

Hanks, David A. *The Decorative Designs of Frank Lloyd Wright*. New York: E. P. Dutton, 1979.

Quinan, Jack. *Frank Lloyd Wright's Larkin Building: Myth and Fact*. New York: Architectural History Foundation; Cambridge, MA: MIT Press, 1987.

Twentieth-Century Architecture and Interiors: Pioneers—Peter Behrens

Anderson, Stanford. *Peter Behrens and a New Architecture for the Twentieth Century*. Cambridge, MA: MIT Press, 2000.

Windsor, Alan. *Peter Behrens: Architect and Designer, 1868–1940*. New York: Watson-Guptill, 1981.

Twentieth-Century Architecture and Interiors: Pioneers—Josef Hoffmann

Sekler, Eduard F. *Josef Hoffmann: The Architectural Work*. First published in Germany in 1982. Published in English by Princeton Architectural Press, Princeton, NJ, 1985. The authoritative study of Hoffmann's buildings.

See also under "Twentieth-Century Decorative Arts: Metalwork."

Twentieth-Century Architecture and Interiors: Bauhaus

Wingler, Hans. *The Bauhaus*. Cambridge, MA: MIT Press, 1969.

Twentieth-Century Architecture and Interiors: Bauhaus—Walter Gropius

Isaacs, Reginald. *Gropius: An Illustrated Biography of the Creator of the Bauhaus*. Boston: Little, Brown, 1991.

Nerdinger, Winfried. *Walter Gropius.* Berlin: Bauhaus-Archiv, and Cambridge, MA: Busch-Reisinger Museum, Harvard University, 1985. Contains a complete catalog of projects.

Twentieth-Century Architecture and Interiors: Bauhaus—Marcel Breuer

Blake, Peter, ed. *Marcel Breuer: Sun and Shadow: The Philosophy of an Architect.* New York: Dodd, Mead, 1955. Still the most appealing treatment of his early work.

Driller, Joachim. *Breuer Houses.* London: Phaidon, 2000.

Gatje, Robert. *Marcel Breuer: A Memoir.* New York: Monacelli, 2000. Foreword by I. M. Pei.

Von Vegesack, Alexander, and Mathias Remmele, eds. *Marcel Breuer: Design and Architecture.* Weil am Rhein, Germany: Vitra Design Museum, 2003.

See also under "Pioneers in Furniture: Bauhaus."

Twentieth-Century Architecture and Interiors: Bauhaus—Ludwig Mies van der Rohe

Johnson, Philip. *Mies van der Rohe.* New York: Museum of Modern Art, 1947. A pioneering study.

Lambert, Phyllis, ed. *Mies in America.* New York: Abrams, for the Canadian Centre for Architecture, Montréal, and the Whitney Museum of American Art, New York, 2001.

Riley, Terence, and Barry Bergdoll, eds. *Mies in Berlin.* New York: Museum of Modern Art, distributed by Abrams, 2001. Exhibition catalog.

Schulze, Franz. *Mies van der Rohe: A Critical Biography.* Chicago: University of Chicago Press, 1985.

See also under "Pioneers in Furniture: Bauhaus."

Twentieth-Century Architecture and Interiors: Purism and De Stijl—Le Corbusier

Le Corbusier 1910–60. Zürich: Editions Girsberger, 1960. Still a useful one-volume survey.

Marcus, George B. *Le Corbusier: Inside the Machine for Living.* New York: Monacelli, 2000.

See also under "Pioneers in Furniture: Purism and de Stijl."

Twentieth-Century Architecture and Interiors: Purism and De Stijl—Gerrit Rietveld

Küper, Maijke, and Ida van Zijl. *Gerrit Th. Rietveld: The Complete Works.* Utrecht: Centraal Museum, distributed in the United States by Princeton Architectural Press, New York.

Overy, Paul. *De Stijl.* New York: Thames & Hudson, 1991.

Overy, Paul, et al. *The Rietveld Schröder House.* Cambridge, MA: MIT Press, 1988.

See also under "Pioneers in Furniture: Purism and De Stijl."

Twentieth-Century Architecture and Interiors: Art Deco—Jacques-Émile Ruhlmann

See under "Twentieth-Century Furniture: Art Deco."

Twentieth-Century Architecture and Interiors: Art Deco—Donald Deskey

Hanks, David A., and Jennifer Toher. *Donald Deskey: Decorative Designs and Interiors.* New York: E. P. Dutton, 1987.

Twentieth-Century Architecture and Interiors: Art Deco—Jean-Michel Frank

Bandot, François. *Jean-Michel Frank.* Paris: Assouline, 2004.

Twentieth-Century Architecture and Interiors: Italian Rationalism

Eisenman, Peter. *Giuseppe Terragni: Transformations, Decompositions, Critiques.* New York: Monacelli, 2003.

Terragni, Attilio, Daniel Liebeskind, and Paolo Rosselli. *The Terragni Atlas: Built Architecture.* Geneva: Skira, 2004.

Twentieth-Century Architecture and Interiors: Scandinavian Modern—The Saarinens

Clark, Robert Judson, David G. De Long, et al. *Design in America: The Cranbrook Vision, 1925–1950.* Detroit, MI: Detroit Institute of the Arts; New York: Metropolitan Museum of Art, 1983.

Hausen, Marika, et al. *Eliel Saarinen: Projects 1896–1923.* Cambridge, MA: MIT Press, 1990.

Román, Antonio. *Eero Saarinen: An Architecture of Multiplicity.* New York: Princeton Architectural Press, 2003.

Wittkopp, Gregory, and Diana Balmori. *Saarinen House and Garden: A Total Work of Art.* New York: Abrams, 1995.

Twentieth-Century Architecture and Interiors: Scandinavian Modern—Alvar Aalto

Weston, Richard. *Alvar Aalto.* London, Phaidon, 1995.

See also under "Modern Furniture: Scandinavian Modern."

Twentieth-Century Architecture and Interiors: Modernism in America—Richard Neutra

Hines, Thomas. *Richard Neutra and the Search for Modern Architecture: A Biography and History.* Berkeley: University of California Press, 1994.

Mac Lamprecht, Barbara. *Richard Neutra: The Complete Works.* Köln: Taschen, 2000.

Twentieth-Century Architecture and Interiors: Modernism in America—Philip Johnson

Jenkins, Stover, and David Mohney. *The Houses of Philip Johnson*. New York: Abbeville, 2001. With excellent photography by Steven Brooke.

Whitney, David, and Jeffrey Kipnis. *Philip Johnson: The Glass House*. New York: Pantheon, 1993.

Twentieth-Century Architecture and Interiors: Modernism in America—Louis Kahn

Brownlee, David B., and De Long, David G. *Louis I. Kahn: In the Realm of Architecture*. New York: Rizzoli, 1991.

Twentieth-Century Architecture and Interiors: Modernism in America—Skidmore, Owings & Merrill

Slavin, Maeve. *Davis Allen: Forty Years of Interior Design at Skidmore, Owings & Merrill*. New York: Rizzoli, 1990. Focuses on the firm's longtime chief interior designer.

Twentieth-Century Architecture and Interiors: Modernism in America—Powell/Kleinschmidt

Blaser, Werner. *Powell/Kleinschmidt Interior Architecture*. Basel: Birkhäuser, 2001.

Twentieth-Century Architecture and Interiors: Modernism in America—Minimalism

Baldwin, Benjamin. *An Autobiography in Design*. New York: W. W. Norton, 1995.

Vignelli, Massimo, et al. *Design: Vignelli*. New York: Rizzoli, 1990.

Twentieth-Century Architecture and Interiors: Modernism in America—The New York Five

Collins, Brad. *Gwathmey Siegel Buildings and Projects, 1965–2000*. New York: Rizzoli Universe, 2000.

Eisenman, Peter, et al. *Five Architects: Eisenman, Graves, Gwathmey, Hejduk, Meier*. New York: Oxford University Press, 1975. Introduction by Colin Rowe.

Frampton, Kenneth. *Richard Meier*. Milan: Mondadori Electa, 2003. Text in English.

Twentieth-Century Architecture and Interiors: Reactions Against Modernism

Ghirardo, Diane. *Architecture after Modernism*. New York: Thames & Hudson, 1996.

Twentieth-Century Architecture and Interiors: Reactions Against Modernism—Brutalism

Banham, Reyner. *The New Brutalism*. London: Architectural Press, 1966. An eyewitness account.

Le Corbusier. *The Chapel at Ronchamp*. New York: Praeger, 1957. The master's voice.

Stoller, Ezra. *The Chapel at Ronchamp*. New York: Princeton Architectural Press, 1999. A portfolio of fine photography by Stoller.

———. *Whitney Museum of American Art*. New York: Princeton Architectural Press, 2000. Another portfolio of fine photography by Stoller.

Twentieth-Century Architecture and Interiors: Reactions Against Modernism—Robert Venturi and Denise Scott Brown

Brownlee, David B., David G. De Long, and Kathryn B. Hiesinger. *Out of the Ordinary: Robert Venturi, Denise Scott Brown and Associates*. New Haven, CT: Yale University Press in association with the Philadelphia Museum of Art, 2001.

Twentieth-Century Architecture and Interiors: Reactions against Modernism—Postmodernism and Pop

Collins, Michael, and Andreas Papadakis. *Post-Modern Design*. New York: Rizzoli, 1989. Focuses on furniture and decorative objects.

Klotz, Heinrich. *The History of Postmodern Architecture*. Cambridge, MA: MIT Press, 1988.

Schwartz, Frederic, ed. *Alan Buchsbaum, Architect and Designer: The Mechanics of Taste*. New York: Monacelli, 1996.

Twentieth-Century Architecture and Interiors: New Possibilities—Frank Gehry

Dal Co, Francesco, and Kurt W. Forster. *Frank Gehry: The Complete Works*. New York: Monacelli, 1998.

Ragheb, J. Fiona, ed. *Frank Gehry, Architect*. New York: Guggenheim Museum, distributed by Abrams, 2001.

Twentieth-Century Architecture and Interiors: New Possibilities—Tadao Ando

Ando, Tadao. *Light and Water*. New York: Monacelli, 2003. Introduction by Kenneth Frampton and book design by Massimo Vignelli.

Jodidio, Philip. *Tadao Ando: Complete Works*. Köln: Taschen, 2004.

Pare, Richard. *Tadao Ando: The Colours of Light*. London: Phaidon, 1996.

Twentieth-Century Architecture and Interiors: New Possibilities—Norman Foster

Jenkins, David, ed. *On Foster . . . Foster On.* New York: Prestel, 2000. Essays by and about Foster, with an accompanying CD-ROM.

Pawley, Martin. *Norman Foster: A Global Architecture.* New York: Rizzoli Universe, 1999.

Twentieth-Century Architecture and Interiors: Eclecticism—Frances Elkins

Salny, Stephen M. *Frances Elkins: Interior Design.* New York: W. W. Norton, 2005. With a foreword by Albert Hadley.

Twentieth-Century Architecture and Interiors: Eclecticism—Dorothy Draper

Varney, Carleton. *The Draper Touch: The High Life and High Style of Dorothy Draper.* New York: Prentice Hall, 1988.

Twentieth-Century Architecture and Interiors: Eclecticism—William Pahlmann

Pahlmann, William. *The Pahlmann Book of Interiors.* New York: Studio, 1968,

Twentieth-Century Architecture and Interiors: Eclecticism—Albert Hadley

Hampton, Mark, et al. *Albert Hadley: Drawings and the Design Process.* New York: Elements Media for the New York School of Interior Design, 2005.

Lewis, Adam. *Albert Hadley: The Story of America's Preeminent Interior Designer.* New York: Rizzoli, 2005.

Parish, "Sister," Albert Hadley, and Christopher Petkanas. *Parish Hadley: Sixty Years of American Design.* Boston: Little, Brown, 1995.

Twentieth-Century Architecture and Interiors: Eclecticism—Andrée Putman

Rousseau, François Olivier. *Andrée Putman: A Designer Apart.* New York: Rizzoli, 1990.

Tasma-Anargyros, Sophie. *Andrée Putman.* Woodstock, NY: Overlook Press, 1997.

Twentieth-Century Architecture and Interiors: Design Media—Books

de Wolfe, Elsie. *The House in Good Taste.* First published in 1913. Reprinted by Rizzoli, New York, in 2005 with a new introduction by Albert Hadley.

Metcalf, Pauline C., ed. *Ogden Codman and The Decoration of Houses.* Boston: Boston Athenæum and David R. Godine, 1988.

Wharton, Edith, and Ogden Codman, Jr. *The Decoration of Houses.* First published in 1897 and reprinted in 1901. Reprinted by W. W. Norton, New York, in 1978 with new notes by John Barrington Bayley and William A. Coles.

Twentieth-Century Architecture and Interiors: Design Media—Museums and Exhibitions

Kantor, Sybil Gordon. *Alfred H. Barr, Jr., and the Intellectual Origins of the Museum of Modern Art.* Cambridge, MA: MIT Press, 2003.

Schwartz, Frederic J. *The Werkbund: Design Theory and Mass Culture before the First World War.* New Haven, CT: Yale University Press, 1996.

Twentieth-Century Architecture and Interiors: New Equipment—Lighting

Brandi, Ulrike, and Christoph Geissmer-Brandi. *Lightbook: The Practice of Lighting Design.* Basel: Birkhäuser, 2001.

Turner, Janet. *Lighting: An Introduction to Light, Lighting, and Light Use.* London: B. T. Batsford, 1994.

Twentieth-Century Architecture and Interiors: New Equipment—Acoustics

Cavanaugh, William J., and Joseph A. Wilkes. *Architectural Acoustics: Principles and Practice.* New York: Wiley, 1999.

Egan, M. David. *Architectural Acoustics.* New York: McGraw-Hill, 1988.

Twentieth-Century Architecture and Interiors: New Materials

Beylerian, George, Andrew Dent, and Anita Moryadas. *Material ConneXion: The Global Resource of New and Innovative Materials for Architects, Artists, and Designers.* New York: Wiley, 2005. Comprehensive sourcebook of recently developed materials, arranged in categories of their composition.

Twentieth-Century Architecture and Interiors: New Materials—Reinforced Concrete

Britton, Karla. *Auguste Perret.* London: Phaidon, 2001.

Twentieth-Century Architecture and Interiors: New Materials—Plastics

Bijker, Wiebe E. *Of Bicycles, Bakelites, and Bulbs: Toward a Theory of Sociotechnical Change.* Cambridge, MA: MIT Press, 1997. Essays on the development and cultural effects of the safety bicycle, Bakelite, and the fluorescent lamp.

Fenichell, Stephen. *Plastic: The Making of a Synthetic Century.* New York: Harper Collins, 1996.

Sparke, Penny, ed. *The Plastics Age: From Bakelite to Beanbags and Beyond.* Woodstock, NY: Overlook Press, 1993.

Twentieth-Century Ornament

Ketchum, Diana, et al. *The de Young in the 21st Century: A Museum by Herzog and de Meuron.* New York: Thames & Hudson, 2005.

Loos, Adolf. *Ornament and Crime: Selected Essays.* Riverside, CA: Ariadne Press, 1997.

Schezen, Roberto, Kenneth Frampton, and Joseph Rosa. *Adolf Loos: Architecture 1903–1932.* New York: Monacelli, 1996.

Woodham, Joanthan M. *Twentieth-Century Ornament.* New York: Rizzoli, 1990.

Twentieth-Century Furniture

Edwards, Clive D. *Twentieth-Century Furniture: Materials, Manufacture and Markets.* Manchester, England: Manchester University Press, 1994.

Fiell, Charlotte, and Peter Fiell. *Modern Furniture Classics Since 1945.* Washington, DC: American Institute of Architects Press, 1991.

Twentieth-Century Furniture: Pioneers—Bauhaus

Blaser, Werner. *Mies van der Rohe Furniture and Interiors.* Woodbury, NY: Barron's, 1982.

Wilk, Christopher. *Marcel Breuer: Furniture and Interiors.* New York: Museum of Modern Art, 1981.

Twentieth-Century Furniture: Pioneers—Purism and De Stijl

Baroni, Daniele. *The Furniture of Gerrit Thomas Rietveld.* Woodbury, NY: Barron's, 1978.

De Fusco, Renato. *Le Corbusier, Designer: Furniture, 1929.* Woodbury, NY: Barron's, 1977.

McLeod, Mary, ed. *Charlotte Perriand: An Art of Living.* New York: Abrams, in association with the Architectural League of New York, 2003.

Perriand, Charlotte. *Charlotte Perriand: A Life of Creation, An Autobiography.* New York: Monacelli, 2003.

Twentieth-Century Furniture: Art Deco

Bréon, Emmanuel. *Jacques-Émile Ruhlmann: The Designer's Archives.* Paris: Flammarion, 2004. Two volumes: one on furniture, the other on interior design.

Camard, Florence. *Ruhlmann, Master of Art Deco.* New York: Thames & Hudson and Abrams, 1984.

Duncan, Alastair. *Art Deco Furniture.* New York: Thames & Hudson, 1992.

Twentieth-Century Furniture: Modern—Scandinavian

Hiort, Esbjørn. *Finn Juhl: Furniture, Architecture, Applied Art.* Copenhagen: Danish Architectural Press, 1990.

Kjaerholm, Poul, Michael Juul Holm, and Michael Sheridan. *Poul Kjaerholm.* Humlebæk, Denmark: Louisiana Museum of Modern Art, 2006.

Oda, Noritsugu. *Danish Chairs.* San Francisco: Chronicle, 1999.

Pallasmaa, Juhani, ed. *Alvar Aalto Furniture.* Cambridge, MA: MIT Press, 1985.

Polster, Bernd. *Design Directory Scandinavia.* New York: Rizzoli, 1999.

Twentieth-Century Furniture: Modern—Charles and Ray Eames

Albrecht, Donald, et al. *The Work of Charles and Ray Eames: A Legacy of Invention.* New York: Abrams, in association with the Library of Congress and the Vitra Design Museum, 1997.

Kirkham, Pat. *Charles and Ray Eames: Designers of the Twentieth Century.* Cambridge, MA: MIT Press, 1995.

Neuhart, John, Marilyn Neuhart, and Ray Eames. *Eames Design.* New York: Abrams, 1989.

Twentieth-Century Furniture: Modern—Herman Miller

Abercrombie, Stanley. *George Nelson: The Design of Modern Design.* Cambridge, MA: MIT Press, 1995.

Caplan, Ralph. *The Design of Herman Miller.* New York: Whitney Library of Design, 1976.

Piña, Leslie. *Alexander Girard Designs for Herman Miller.* Atglen, PA: Schiffer, 1998.

Twentieth-Century Furniture: Modern—Knoll

Larrabee, Eric, and Massimo Vignelli. *Knoll Design.* New York: Abrams, 1981.

Twentieth-Century Furniture: New Possibilities

Aikawa, Michiko, ed. *Shiro Kuramata.* Hara, Japan: Hara Museum of Contemporary Art, 1997. Exhibition catalog, with text in Japanese and English.

Labaco, Ronald T. *Ettore Sottsass: Architect and Designer.* New York: Merrell, 2006.

Muschamp, Herbert, and Andrea Branzi. *Ettore Sottsass: The Architecture and Design of Sottsass Associates.* New York: Rizzoli Universe, 1999.

Twentieth-Century Decorative Arts: Ceramics and Glass

Albrecht, Donald, Robert Schonfeld, and Lindsay Stamm Shapiro. *Russel Wright: Creating American Lifestyle.* New York: Abrams for the Cooper-Hewitt National Design Museum, Smithsonian Institution, 2001. Exhibition catalog.

Slater, Greg, and Jonathan Brough. *Comprehensively Clarice Cliff.* New York: Thames & Hudson, 2005.

Twentieth-Century Decorative Arts: Metalwork

Huey, Michael, ed. *Viennese Silver, Modern Design, 1780–1915.* Oostfildern-Ruit, Germany: Hatje Cantz for the Neue Gallery, New York, 2003.

Noever, Peter, ed. *Josef Hoffmann: Designs.* Munich: Prestel, 1992.

Twentieth-Century Decorative Arts: Textiles

Albers, Anni. *Anni Albers: Selected Writings on Design.* Lebanon, NH: University Press of New England, 2001.

Albers, Anni, Nicholas Fox Weber, and Pandora Tabatabai Asbaghi. *Anni Albers.* New York: Solomon Guggenheim Foundation, 2003.

Larsen, Jack Lenor. *Jack Lenor Larsen: A Weaver's Memoir.* New York: Abrams, 1998.

McFadden, David Revere, et al. *Jack Lenor Larsen: Creator and Collector.* New York: Merrell, 2004.

Völker, Angela. *Textiles of the Wiener Werkstätte.* New York: Rizzoli, 1994.

Weltge, Sigrid Wortmann. *Women's Work: Textile Art from the Bauhaus.* San Francisco: Chronicle Books, 1993.

Map Appendix

Map 1. Prehistoric Europe. As the Ice Age glaciers receded, Paleolithic, Neolithic, Bronze Age, and Iron Age settlements increased from south to north. (See Chapter 1.)

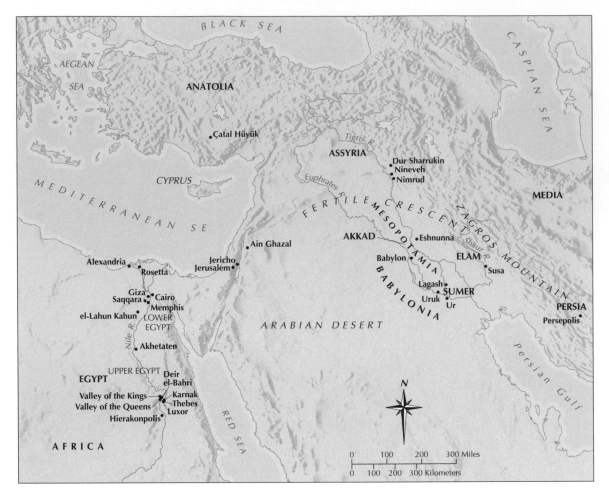

Map 2. Ancient Egypt and the Ancient Near East. Upper (southern) Egypt and Lower (northern) Egypt were united about 3100 B.C. Ancient Mesopotamia (modern Iraq) was the Fertile Crescent between the Tigris and Euphrates Rivers. (See Chapters 2 and 3.)

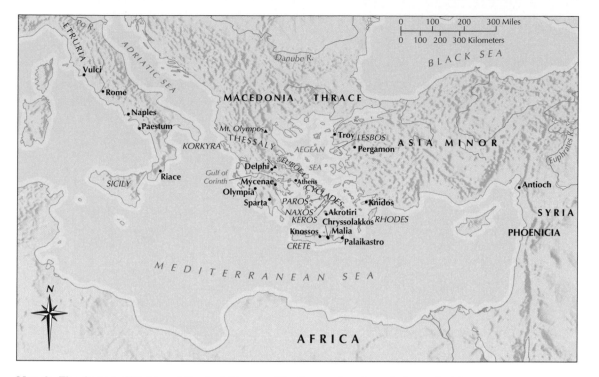

Map 3. The Aegean World and Ancient Greece. The three main cultures in the ancient Aegean were the Cycladic in the Cyclades; the Minoan on Crete; and the Mycenaean on the mainland. During the Hellenistic period, Greek influence extended beyond mainland Greece to Macedonia, Egypt, and Asia Minor. (See Chapter 4.)

Map 4. The Roman Republic and Empire. After defeating the Etruscans in 509 B.C., Rome became a republic, which reached its greatest area by the time of Julius Caesar's death in 44 B.C. The Roman Empire began in 27 B.C. and extended its borders from Mesopotamia to Scotland under Trajan in 106 A.D. It was split into the Eastern and Western Empires in the fourth century (See Chapter 5.)

Map 5. The Early Jewish, Christian, and Byzantine World. The eastern Mediterranean lands of Canaan and Judaea were centers of Jewish settlement. Rome was a major center of early Christianity. Byzantine culture took root in Constantinople and flourished throughout this Eastern Roman, or Byzantine, Empire and extended into northern areas such as Russia and the Ukraine. (See Chapter 6.)

Map 6. Europe in the Romanesque Era. On this map, modern names have been used for medieval regions in northern and western Europe to make sites easier to locate. The term *Romanesque* is used for all the arts in Europe between the ninth and thirteenth centuries. (See Chapter 7.)

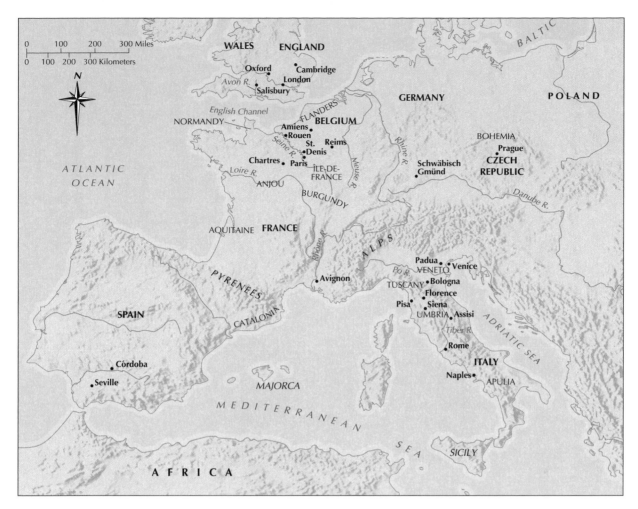

Map 7. Europe in the Gothic Era. The Gothic style began in northern France in 1132 and spread throughout Europe during the next three centuries. (See Chapter 8.)

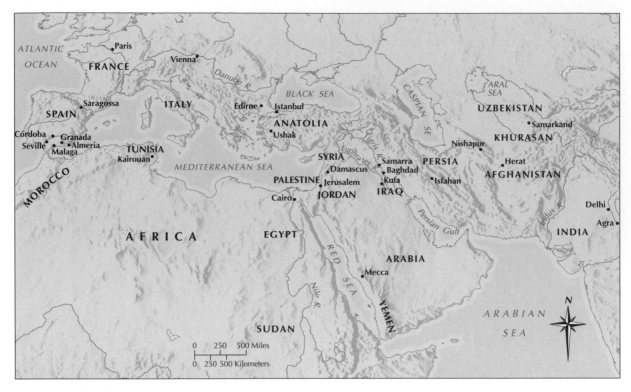

Map 8. The Islamic World. Within 200 years of its founding in the early seventh century, the Islamic world expanded from Mecca to India in the east, to Spain in the northwest, and to Africa in the south. (See Chapters 9 and 14.)

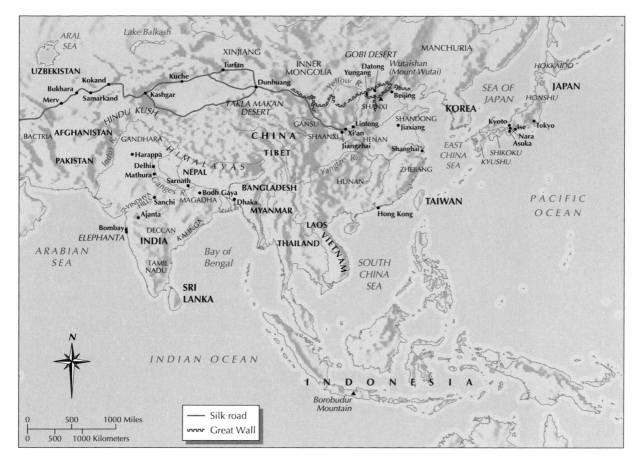

Map 9. Early Asia. In India the Vindhya Hills are a natural feature dividing North and South India. In China the heart of the country is crossed by three rivers—the Yellow, Yangtze, and Xi. In Japan melting glaciers at the end of the Ice Age 15,000 years ago raised the sea level and formed the four main islands of Japan: Hokkaido, Honshu, Shikoku, and Kyushu. (See Chapters 10, 11, and 12.)

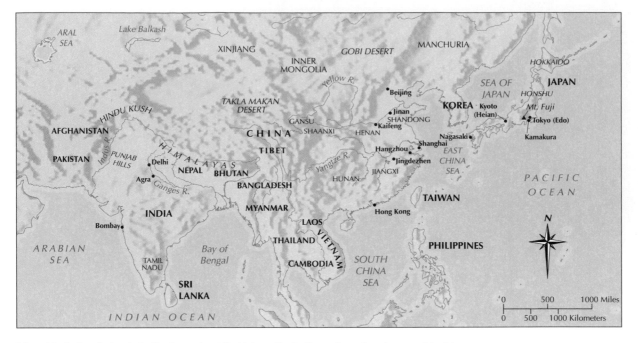

Map 10. Later Asia. In India, throughout its history, the Indian subcontinent was subject to continual invasion that caused the borders of its kingdoms to contract and expand until the establishment of modern-day India in the twentieth century. In China a mountain range called the Qin Ling Mountains, in the Shaanxi province, divides the country into northern and southern regions with distinctively different climates and cultures. In Japan ideas and artistic influences from the Asian continent flowed to Japan before and after the island nation's self-imposed isolation from the seventeenth century to the nineteenth century. (See Chapters 10, 11, and 12.)

Map 11. Fifteenth-Century Europe. The Early Renaissance was born in Florence, Italy, in the early fifteenth century, then spread throughout Italy and all of Europe. (See Chapters 13, 14, 15, and 16.)

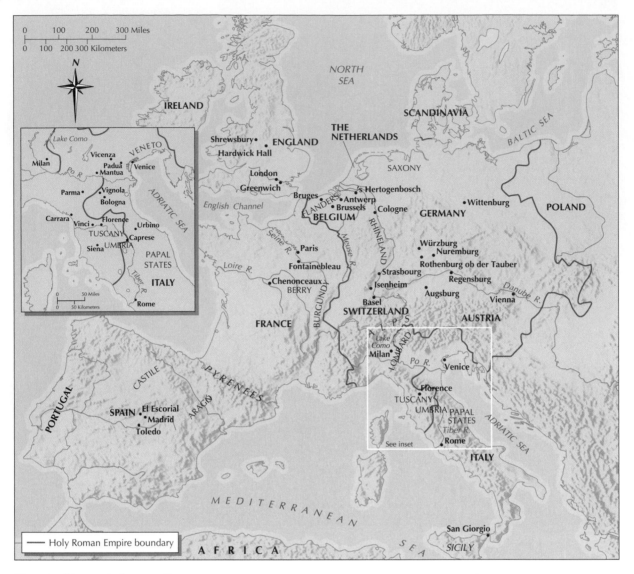

Map 12. Sixteenth-Century Europe. The sixteenth century in Europe was a period of dramatic political, intellectual, religious, and artistic change, which became known as the High Renaissance. (See Chapters 13, 14, 15, and 16.)

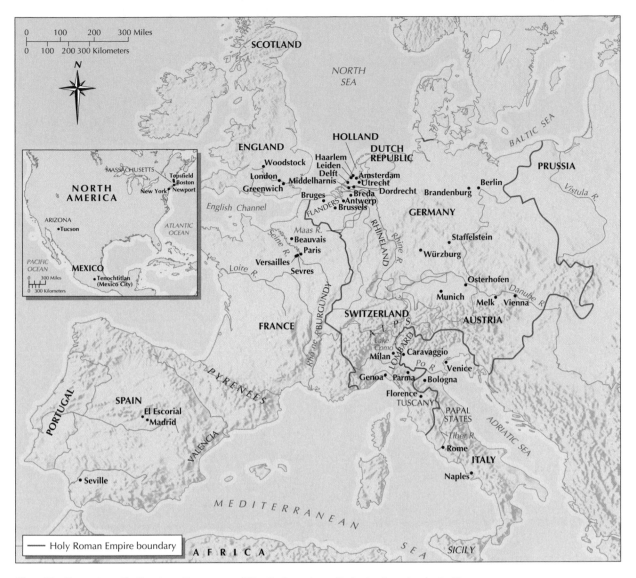

Map 13. Seventeenth-Century Europe and North America. Protestantism dominated in northern Europe, while Roman Catholicism remained strong after the Counter-Reformation in southern Europe. (See Chapters 13, 14, 15, 16, and 19.)

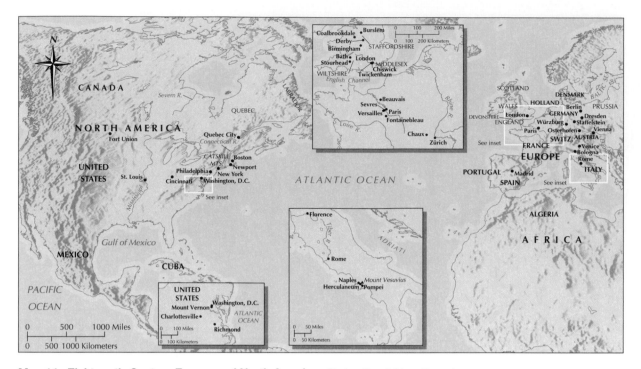

Map 14. Eighteenth-Century Europe and North America. During the eighteenth century, a variety of major artistic styles—Régence and Rococo, Neoclassical, Federal, and Georgian—flourished in Europe and North America. (See Chapters 13, 14, 15, 16, and 19.)

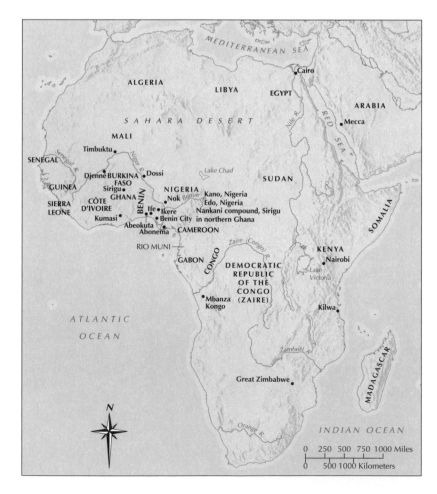

Map 15. Africa. Nearly 5,000 miles from north to south, Africa is the second-largest continent on earth. Africa has been the home to some of the earliest and most advanced cultures of the ancient world and is still home to many diverse countries and cultures. (See Chapter 17.)

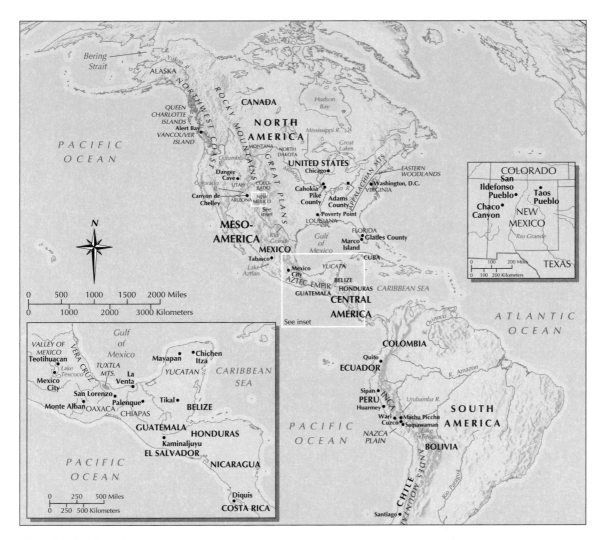

Map 16. The Americas. Between 15,000 and 17,000 years ago, nomadic people moved across North America, then southward through Central America and into South America, until they reached its southern tip, about 12,500 years ago. Diverse peoples spread throughout the Americas, each shaping a distinct culture in the area it settled. In North America, many areas of the continent were settled, but the most notable architecture and design innovations that still remain are those found in the West. (See Chapter 18.)

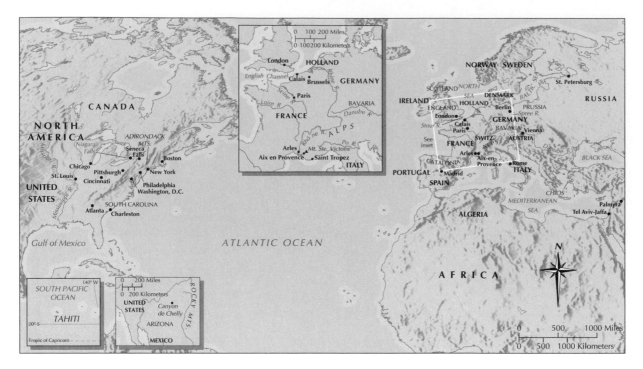

Map 17. Nineteenth-Century Europe and North America. In the nineteenth century Europe took the lead in industrialization, and France and England became the cultural beacons of the Western world. The world was changing, and design changed with it. (See Chapter 20.)

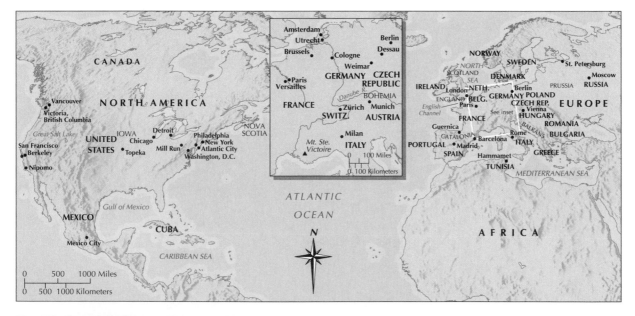

Map 18. Twentieth-Century Europe and North America. Through the end of World War II, western Europe was home to many forms of modernism. In the United States new design expressions reacted against modernism, but by the end of the century, modernism's dominance remained, tempered with various forms of eclecticism. (See Chapter 21.)

Index